Leadership

Enhancing the Lessons of Experience

Tenth Edition

Richard L. Hughes

Robert C. Ginnett

Gordon J. Curphy

LEADERSHIP

Published by McGraw Hill LLC, 1325 Avenue of the Americas, New York, NY 10121. Copyright ©2022 by McGraw Hill LLC. All rights reserved. Printed in the United States of America. No part of this publication may be reproduced or distributed in any form or by any means, or stored in a database or retrieval system, without the prior written consent of McGraw Hill LLC, including, but not limited to, in any network or other electronic storage or transmission, or broadcast for distance learning.

Some ancillaries, including electronic and print components, may not be available to customers outside the United States.

This book is printed on acid-free paper.

1 2 3 4 5 6 7 8 9 LCR 24 23 22 21

ISBN 978-1-265-10788-8
MHID 1-265-10788-2

Cover Image: *Construction: Ariel Skelley/Blend Images LLC; Backpackers: Brand X Pictures/Superstock: Surgeons: Chris Ryan/age fotostock*

All credits appearing on page or at the end of the book are considered to be an extension of the copyright page.

The Internet addresses listed in the text were accurate at the time of publication. The inclusion of a website does not indicate an endorsement by the authors or McGraw Hill LLC, and McGraw Hill LLC does not guarantee the accuracy of the information presented at these sites.

mheducation.com/highered

About the Authors

Rich Hughes has served on the faculties of both the Center for Creative Leadership (CCL), the U.S. Air Force Academy, and Denver Seminary. CCL is an international organization devoted to behavioral science research and leadership education. Rich worked there with senior executives from all sectors in the areas of strategic leadership and organizational culture change. At the Air Force Academy he served for a decade as head of its Department of Behavioral Sciences and Leadership. Rich later served at the Academy as its Transformation Chair. In that capacity he worked with senior leaders across the Academy to help guide organizational transformation of the Academy in ways to ensure it is meeting its mission of producing leaders of character. He is a clinical psychologist and a graduate of the U.S. Air Force Academy. He has an MA from the University of Texas and a PhD from the University of Wyoming.

Robert Ginnett is an independent consultant specializing in the leadership of high-performance teams and organizations. He has worked with hundreds of for-profit organizations as well as NASA, the Defense and Central Intelligence Agencies, the National Security Agency, and the U.S. Army, Navy, and Air Force. Prior to working independently, Robert was a senior fellow at the Center for Creative Leadership and a tenured professor at the U.S. Air Force Academy, where he also served as the director of leadership and counseling. Additionally, he served in numerous line and staff positions in the military, including leadership of an 875-man combat force and covert operations teams in the Vietnam War. He spent over 10 years working as a researcher for the National Aeronautics and Space Administration, focusing his early work in aviation crew resource management, and later at the Kennedy Space Center in the post-*Challenger* period. Robert is an organizational psychologist whose education includes an MBA, an MA, an MPhil, and a PhD from Yale University. He now enjoys doing pro bono work with local fire and police departments and teaching leadership courses at the Gettysburg National Military Park.

Gordy Curphy is a managing partner at Curphy Leadership Solutions and has been running his own consulting business since 2002. As a leadership consultant Gordy has worked with numerous *Fortune* 500 firms to deliver more than 2,500 executive assessments, 150 executive coaching programs, 200 team engagements, and 150 leadership training programs. He has also played a critical role in helping organizations formulate winning strategies, drive major change initiatives, and improve business results. Gordy has published numerous books and articles and presented extensively on such topics as business, community, school, military, and team leadership; the role of personality and intelligence in leadership; building high-performing teams; leading virtual teams; teams at the top; managerial incompetence; followership; on-boarding; succession planning; and employee engagement. Prior to starting his own firm Gordy spent a year as the vice president of institutional leadership at the Blandin Foundation, eight years as a vice president and general manager at Personnel Decisions International, and six years as a professor at the U.S. Air Force Academy. He has a BS from the U.S. Air Force Academy and a PhD in industrial and organizational psychology from the University of Minnesota.

Foreword

The first edition of this popular, widely used textbook was published in 1993, and the authors have continually upgraded it with each new edition including this one.

In a sense, no new foreword is needed; many principles of leadership are timeless. For example, references to Shakespeare and Machiavelli need no updating. However, the authors have refreshed examples and anecdotes, and they have kept up with the contemporary research and writing of leadership experts. Unfortunately, many of the reasons why leaders fail have also proved timeless. Flawed strategies, indecisiveness, arrogance, the naked pursuit of power, inept followers, the inability to build teams, and societal changes have resulted in corrupt governments, lost wars, failed businesses, repressive regimes around the globe, and sexual discrimination and/or harassment. These occurrences remind us that leadership can be used for selfless or selfish reasons, and it is up to those in charge to decide why they choose to lead.

Such examples keep this book fresh and relevant; but the earlier foreword, reprinted here, still captures the tone, spirit, and achievements of these authors' work.

Often the only difference between chaos and a smoothly functioning operation is leadership; this book is about that difference.

The authors are psychologists; therefore, the book has a distinctly psychological tone. You, as a reader, are going to be asked to think about leadership the way psychologists do. There is much here about psychological tests and surveys, about studies done in psychological laboratories, and about psychological analyses of good (and poor) leadership. You will often run across common psychological concepts in these pages, such as personality, values, attitudes, perceptions, and self-esteem, plus some not-so-common "jargon-y" phrases like double-loop learning, expectancy theory, and perceived inequity. This is not the same kind of book that would be written by coaches, sales managers, economists, political scientists, or generals.

Be not dismayed. Because these authors are also teachers with a good eye and ear for what students find interesting, they write clearly and cleanly, and they have also included a host of entertaining, stimulating snapshots of leadership: quotes, anecdotal highlights, and personal glimpses from a wide range of intriguing people, each offered as an illustration of some scholarly point.

Also, because the authors are, or have been at one time or another, together or singly, not only psychologists and teachers but also children, students, Boy Scouts, parents, professors (at the U.S. Air Force Academy), Air Force officers, pilots, church members, athletes, administrators, insatiable readers, and convivial raconteurs, their stories and examples are drawn from a wide range of personal sources, and their anecdotes ring true.

As psychologists and scholars, they have reviewed here a wide range of psychological studies, other scientific inquiries, personal reflections of leaders, and philosophic writings on the topic of leadership. In distilling this material, they have drawn many practical conclusions useful for current and potential leaders. There are suggestions here for goal setting, for running meetings, for negotiating, for managing conflict within groups, and for handling your own personal stress, to mention just a few.

All leaders, no matter what their age and station, can find some useful tips here, ranging over subjects such as body language, keeping a journal, and how to relax under tension.

In several ways the authors have tried to help you, the reader, feel what it would be like "to be in charge." For example, they have posed quandaries such as the following: You are in a leadership position with a budget provided by an outside funding source. You believe strongly in, say, Topic A, and have taken a strong, visible public stance on that topic. The head of your funding source takes you aside and says, "We disagree with your stance on Topic A. Please tone down your public statements, or we will have to take another look at your budget for next year."

What would you do? Quit? Speak up and lose your budget? Tone down your public statements and feel dishonest? There's no easy answer, and it's not an unusual situation for a leader to be in. Sooner or later, all leaders have to confront just how much outside interference they will tolerate in order to be able to carry out programs they believe in.

The authors emphasize the value of experience in leadership development, a conclusion I thoroughly agree with. Virtually every leader who makes it to the top of whatever pyramid he or she happens to be climbing does so by building on earlier experiences. The successful leaders are those who learn from these earlier experiences, by reflecting on and analyzing them to help solve larger future challenges. In this vein, let me make a suggestion. Actually, let me assign you some homework. (I know, I know, this is a peculiar approach in a book foreword; but stay with me—I have a point.)

Your Assignment: To gain some useful leadership experience, persuade eight people to do some notable activity together for at least two hours that they would not otherwise do without your intervention. Your only restriction is that you cannot tell them why you are doing this.

It can be any eight people: friends, family, teammates, club members, neighbors, students, working colleagues. It can be any activity, except that it should be something more substantial than watching television, eating, going to a movie, or just sitting around talking. It could be a roller-skating party, an organized debate, a songfest, a long hike, a visit to a museum, or volunteer work such as picking up litter or visiting a nursing home. If you will take it upon yourself to make something happen in the world that would not have otherwise happened without you, you will be engaging in an act of leadership with all of its attendant barriers, burdens, and pleasures, and you will quickly learn the relevance of many of the topics that the authors discuss in this book. If you try the eight-person-two-hour experience first and read this book later, you will have a much better understanding of how complicated an act of leadership can be. You will learn about the difficulties of developing a vision ("Now that we are together, what are we going to do?"), of motivating others, of setting agendas and timetables, of securing resources, of the need for follow-through. You may even learn about "loneliness at the top." However, if you are successful, you will also experience the thrill that comes from successful leadership. One person *can* make a difference by enriching the lives of others, if only for a few hours. And for all of the frustrations and complexities of leadership, the tingling satisfaction that comes from success can become almost addictive. The capacity for making things happen can become its own motivation. With an early success, even if it is only with eight people for two hours, you may well be on your way to a leadership future.

The authors believe that leadership development involves reflecting on one's own experiences. Reading this book in the context of your own leadership experience can aid in that process. Their book is comprehensive, scholarly, stimulating, entertaining, and relevant for anyone who wishes to better understand the dynamics of leadership, and to improve her or his own personal performance.

David P. Campbell
Psychologist/Author

Preface

With each new edition, we have found ourselves both pleasantly surprised (as in "You mean there'll be another one?") and also momentarily uncertain just what new material on leadership we might add—all the while knowing that in this dynamic field, there is *always* new material to add. Illustrations from history and current leadership practice seem inexhaustible, and there is always new research that deepens both our conceptual understanding and appreciation of evolving trends in the field.

We continue in this tenth edition with the general approach we have followed for a number of preceding editions. The book's overall structure remains essentially the same, following our conceptualization of leadership as a process involving an interaction among leaders, followers, and situations. So once again **Part One** of our text looks at the nature of the leadership process itself as well as how a person *becomes* a better leader. **Part Two** is titled *Focus on the Leader*, with **Parts Three** and **Four** logically following as *Focus on the Followers* and *Focus on the Situation*. And also continuing the format of previous editions, there is a specific "skills chapter" in each of those parts addressing essential leadership competencies appropriate to each of those four broad areas.

As you would expect, this new edition brings research updates to virtually every chapter as well as updates to our *Highlights, Profiles in Leadership*, and *Mini-Case* features. Generally speaking, we have tried to make "one-for-one" trades on these features so as new material was added, less relevant or interesting material was eliminated. As a result, our new set of Highlights includes topics such as these (among others):

- Growth versus fixed mindsets
- The ethics of dropping atom bombs on Hiroshima and Nagasaki
- Lawrence Kohlberg's theory of moral development
- Moral challenges of leadership
- The dangers of hubris
- The relationship between humility and charisma
- Helicopter parenting and its impact on a person's leadership potential
- The accelerating rate of change in the world
- The Space Shuttle *Challenger* disaster
- The impact of the COVID-19 pandemic

Similarly, our *Profiles in Leadership* introduce new subjects as diverse as Harry Truman, Fred Rogers, U.S. Secretary of State Michael Pompeo, and 20th-century German theologian Dietrich Bonhoeffer (who was part of the plot to assassinate Adolf Hitler). New *Mini-Cases* include the examination of Army Lieutenant General Laura Yeager, the first woman to command a combat division in the U.S. Army; Carlsson Systems Ltd. (CSL); and the nuclear disaster at the Chernobyl power plant in the former Soviet Union.

The greatest *structural* change to the book (i.e., to the table of contents) pertains to a new approach to the subject matter covered in the ninth edition's Chapters 9 and 10. The subject matter per se remains essentially the same, but we believe it is treated more appropriately in three rather than just two chapters. Therefore, in this tenth edition **Chapter 9** is titled "Follower Motivation," **Chapter 10** is titled "Follower Satisfaction and Engagement," and **Chapter 11** is titled "Follower Performance, Effectiveness, and Potential." You will also see other changes to the content of certain chapters, including a *Highlight* on punishment in **Chapter 4**, "Power and Influence"; the subject matter seems more appropriate in that chapter than in the final chapter of the book, where it previously had been presented as a leadership skill. We also moved coverage of the Vroom and Yetton model of decision-making from the chapter on contingency theories of leadership to a skills chapter (**Chapter 8**). And there is also updated material on high-performing teams and geographically dispersed teams in **Chapter 12** ("Groups, Teams, and Their Leadership").

As always, we are indebted to the superb editorial staff at McGraw-Hill Education including Michael Ablass-meir, Director; Laura Hurst Spell, Associate Portfolio Manager; Melissa Leick, Senior Content Project Manager; Emily Windelborn, Assessment Content Project Manager; Alyson Platt, Copy Editor; Beth Blech, Designer; Sarah Blasco, Product Developer; Vinoth Prabhakaran, Vendor Customer Service Representative; and Lisa Granger, Marketing Manager.

We are also indebted to the experienced and insightful perspectives of the following scholars who provided helpful feedback to guide changes to the tenth and previous editions:

Douglas Lee Akins, North Central Texas College; Barbara Altman, Texas A&M; Lynn Becker, University of Central Florida; Audrey Blume, Wilmington University; Barry Boyd, Texas A&M University; Patricia Ann Castelli, Lawrence Technological University; Elizabeth Cooper, University of Rhode Island; Marian M. Extejt, Bridgewater State University; Cherly Furdge, North Central Texas College; Diane D. Galbraith, Slippery Rock University; Melissa K. Gibson, Edinboro University; Dr. Gerry Herbison, The American College of Financial Services; Cecil Douglas Johnson, Georgia Gwinnett College; Barbara Limbach, Chadron State College; Michael Monahan, Frostburg State University; Kevin O'Neill, State University of New York at Plattsburgh; Michelle Roach; Susan Pope, University of Akron; Dr. Eric Terry, Miami Dade College; Debra Touchton, Stetson University; Richard S. Voss, Troy University; and Belinda Johnson, White Morehouse College.

Finally, there is one small set of changes to this edition we want to mention. They are not remarkable in either their volume or particular insight; in truth, they represent literally last-minute changes. That is because it was only in our final stage of prepublication work that—like the rest of the world—we found ourselves in the midst of the coronavirus pandemic. And as we progressed through weeks and months of "sheltering at home," we found ourselves becoming increasingly mindful of questions like "How are our leaders responding to this crisis?" and "How might this change life—and leadership—in the future?" As this edition goes to press, we do not yet pretend to know the answers to these questions. But we do believe the enormity of the issues deserves at least some acknowledgment and thoughtful reflection in this text—however superficially we may do so now. Therefore, here and there as it was even *possible* in the process, we've added a Highlight or end-of-chapter questions and activities regarding the pandemic—and for that we appreciate the publisher's considerable flexibility.

And precisely because of the timing of these events, and somewhat in the same spirit and consciousness of the impact the pandemic is having on all our lives, we want to dedicate this edition to the first responders and medical personnel who so bravely, tirelessly, and selflessly are risking their lives to help us all.

Richard L. Hughes

Robert C. Ginnett

Gordon J. Curphy

You're in the driver's seat.

Want to build your own course? No problem. Prefer to use our turnkey, prebuilt course? Easy. Want to make changes throughout the semester? Sure. And you'll save time with Connect's auto-grading too.

65%

Less Time Grading

Laptop: McGraw-Hill; Woman/dog: George Doyle/Getty Images

They'll thank you for it.

Adaptive study resources like SmartBook® 2.0 help your students be better prepared in less time. You can transform your class time from dull definitions to dynamic debates. Find out more about the powerful personalized learning experience available in SmartBook 2.0 at **www.mheducation.com/highered/connect/smartbook**

Make it simple, make it affordable.

Connect makes it easy with seamless integration using any of the major Learning Management Systems—Blackboard®, Canvas, and D2L, among others—to let you organize your course in one convenient location. Give your students access to digital materials at a discount with our inclusive access program. Ask your McGraw-Hill representative for more information.

Padlock: Jobalou/Getty Images

Solutions for your challenges.

A product isn't a solution. Real solutions are affordable, reliable, and come with training and ongoing support when you need it and how you want it. Our Customer Experience Group can also help you troubleshoot tech problems—although Connect's 99% uptime means you might not need to call them. See for yourself at **status.mheducation.com**

Checkmark: Jobalou/Getty Images

FOR STUDENTS

Effective, efficient studying.

Connect helps you be more productive with your study time and get better grades using tools like SmartBook 2.0, which highlights key concepts and creates a personalized study plan. Connect sets you up for success, so you walk into class with confidence and walk out with better grades.

Study anytime, anywhere.

Download the free ReadAnywhere app and access your online eBook or SmartBook 2.0 assignments when it's convenient, even if you're offline. And since the app automatically syncs with your eBook and SmartBook 2.0 assignments in Connect, all of your work is available every time you open it. Find out more at **www.mheducation.com/readanywhere**

> *"I really liked this app—it made it easy to study when you don't have your textbook in front of you."*
>
> - Jordan Cunningham, Eastern Washington University

No surprises.

The Connect Calendar and Reports tools keep you on track with the work you need to get done and your assignment scores. Life gets busy; Connect tools help you keep learning through it all.

Calendar: owattaphotos/Getty Images

Learning for everyone.

McGraw-Hill works directly with Accessibility Services Departments and faculty to meet the learning needs of all students. Please contact your Accessibility Services office and ask them to email accessibility@mheducation.com, or visit **www.mheducation.com/about/accessibility** for more information.

Top: Jenner Images/Getty Images, Left: Hero Images/Getty Images, Right: Hero Images/Getty Images

Brief Contents

Contents

Part 1

Leadership Is a Process, Not a Position

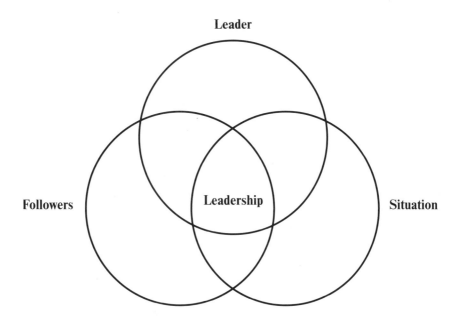

If any single idea is central to this book, it is that leadership is a process, not a position. The entire first part of this book explores that idea. One is not a leader—except perhaps in name only—merely because one holds a title or position. Leadership involves something happening as a result of the interaction between a leader and followers.

In **Chapter 1** we define leadership and explore its relationship to concepts such as management and followership, and we also introduce the interactional framework. The interactional framework is based on the idea that leadership involves complex interactions between the leader, the followers, and the situations they are in. That framework provides the organizing principle for the rest of the book. **Chapter 2** looks at how we can become better leaders by profiting more fully from our experiences, which is not to say that either the study or the practice of leadership is simple. Part 1 concludes with a chapter focusing on basic leadership skills. There also will be a corresponding skills chapter at the conclusion of each of the other three parts in this book.

CHAPTER 1

What Do We Mean by Leadership?

Introduction

According to a poll by the Center for Public Leadership at Harvard Kennedy School, 70 percent of Americans believe our country is in desperate need of better leaders and faces national decline unless something changes.[1] And a 2013 Harris Poll showed that the percentage of people expressing even *some* confidence in governmental, corporate, and financial leadership has plummeted from about 90 percent to 60 percent since 1996.[2] Yet we also sometimes see stories of extraordinary leadership by otherwise ordinary people.

In the spring of 1972, an airplane flew across the Andes mountains carrying its crew and 40 passengers. Most of the passengers were members of an amateur Uruguayan rugby team en route to a game in Chile. The plane never arrived. It crashed in snow-covered mountains, breaking into several pieces on impact. The main part of the fuselage slid like a toboggan down a steep valley, coming to rest in waist-deep snow. Although a number of people died immediately or within a day of the impact, the picture for the 28 survivors was not much better. The fuselage offered little protection from the extreme cold, food supplies were scant, and a number of passengers had serious injuries from the crash. Over the next few days, several surviving passengers became psychotic and several others died from their injuries. The passengers who were relatively uninjured set out to do what they could to improve their chances of survival.

Several worked on "weatherproofing" the wreckage; others found ways to get water; and those with medical training took care of the injured. Although shaken by the crash, the survivors initially were confident they would be found. These feelings gradually gave way to despair as search and rescue teams failed to find the wreckage. With the passing of several weeks and no sign of rescue in sight, the remaining passengers decided to mount expeditions to determine the best way to escape. The most physically fit were chosen to go on the expeditions because the thin mountain air and the deep snow made the trips difficult. The results of the trips were both frustrating and demoralizing: The expedition members determined they were in the middle of the Andes mountains, and walking out to find help was believed to be impossible. Just when the survivors thought nothing worse could possibly happen, an avalanche hit the wreckage and killed several more of them.

The remaining survivors concluded they would not be rescued, and their only hope was for someone to leave the wreckage and find help. Three of the fittest passengers were chosen for the final expedition, and everyone else's work was directed toward improving the expedition's chances of success. The three expedition members were given more food and were exempted from routine survival activities; the rest spent most of their energies securing supplies for the trip. Two months after the plane crash, the expedition members set out on their final attempt to find help. After hiking for 10 days through some of the most rugged terrain in the world, the expedition stumbled across a group of Chilean peasants tending cattle. One of the expedition members stated, "I come from a plane that fell in the mountains. I am Uruguayan . . ." Eventually 14 other survivors were rescued.

When the full account of their survival became known, it was not without controversy. It had required extreme and unsettling measures: The survivors had lived only by eating the flesh of their deceased comrades. Nonetheless, their story is one of the most moving survival dramas of all time, magnificently told by Piers Paul Read in *Alive*.[3] It is a story of tragedy and courage, and it is a story of leadership.

> *Lives of great men all remind us We can make our lives sublime And, departing, leave behind us Footprints on the sands of time.*
>
> **Henry Wadsworth Longfellow, American poet**

Perhaps a story of survival in the Andes is so far removed from everyday experience that it does not seem to hold any relevant lessons about leadership for you personally. But consider some of the basic issues the Andes survivors faced: tension between individual and group goals, dealing with the different needs and personalities of group members, and keeping hope alive in the face of adversity. These issues are not so different from those facing many groups we're a part of. We can also look at the Andes experience for examples of the emergence of informal leaders in groups. Before the flight, a young man named Parrado was awkward and shy, a "second-stringer" both athletically and socially. Nonetheless, this unlikely hero became the best loved and most respected among the survivors for his courage, optimism, fairness, and emotional support. Persuasiveness in group decision-making also was an important part of leadership among the Andes survivors. During the difficult discussions preceding the agonizing decision to survive on the flesh of their deceased comrades, one of the rugby players made his reasoning clear: "I know that if my dead body could help you stay alive, then I would want you to use it. In fact, if I do die and you don't eat me, then I'll come back from wherever I am and give you a good kick in the ass."[4]

What Is Leadership?

> *The halls of fame are open wide and they are always full. Some go in by the door called "push" and some by the door called "pull."*
>
> **Stanley Baldwin, British prime minister in the 1930s**

The Andes story and the experiences of many other leaders we'll introduce to you in a series of profiles sprinkled throughout the chapters provide numerous examples of leadership. But just what *is* leadership? People who do research on leadership disagree more than you might think about what leadership really is. Most of this disagreement stems from the fact that **leadership** is a complex phenomenon involving the leader, the followers, and the situation. Some leadership researchers have focused on the personality, physical traits, or behaviors of the leader; others have studied the relationships between leaders and followers; still others have studied how aspects of the situation affect how leaders act. Some have extended the latter viewpoint so far as to suggest there is no such thing as leadership; they argue that organizational successes and failures are often falsely attributed to the leader, but the situation may have a much greater impact on how the organization functions than does any individual, including the leader.[5]

> *Remember the difference between a boss and a leader: a boss says, "Go!"–a leader says, "Let's go!"*
>
> **E. M. Kelly**

Perhaps the best way for you to begin to understand the complexities of leadership is to see some of the ways leadership has been defined. Leadership researchers have defined leadership in many different ways:

- The process by which an agent induces a subordinate to behave in a desired manner.[6]
- Directing and coordinating the work of group members.[7]
- An interpersonal relation in which others comply because they want to, not because they have to.[8]

- The process of influencing an organized group toward accomplishing its goals.[9]
- Actions that focus resources to create desirable opportunities.[10]
- Creating conditions for a team to be effective.[11]
- The ability to engage employees, the ability to build teams, and the ability to achieve results; the first two represent the how and the latter the what of leadership.[12]
- A complex form of social problem solving.[13]

As you can see, definitions of leadership differ in many ways, and these differences have resulted in various researchers exploring disparate aspects of leadership. For example, if we were to apply these definitions to the Andes survival scenario described earlier, some researchers would focus on the behaviors Parrado used to keep up the morale of the survivors. Researchers who define leadership as influencing an organized group toward accomplishing its goals would examine how Parrado managed to convince the group to stage and support the final expedition. One's definition of leadership might also influence just *who* is considered an appropriate leader for study. Thus each group of researchers might focus on a different aspect of leadership, and each would tell a different story regarding the leader, the followers, and the situation.

Although having many leadership definitions may seem confusing, it is important to understand that there is no single correct definition. The various definitions can help us appreciate the multitude of factors that affect leadership, as well as different perspectives from which to view it. For example, in the first definition just listed, the word *subordinate* seems to confine leadership to downward influence in hierarchical relationships; it seems to exclude informal leadership. The second definition emphasizes the directing and coordinating aspects of leadership, and thereby may deemphasize emotional aspects of leadership. The emphasis placed in the third definition on subordinates' "wanting to" comply with a leader's wishes seems to exclude any kind of coercion as a leadership tool. Further, it becomes problematic to identify ways in which a leader's actions are really leadership if subordinates voluntarily comply when a leader with considerable potential coercive power merely asks others to do something without explicitly threatening them. Similarly, a key reason behind using the phrase *desirable opportunities* in one of the definitions was precisely to distinguish between leadership and tyranny. And partly because there are many different definitions of leadership, there is also a wide range of individuals we consider leaders. In addition to the stories about leaders and leadership that we sprinkle throughout this book, we highlight several in each chapter in a series of Profiles in Leadership. The first of these is **Profiles in Leadership 1.1**, which highlights Sheikh Zayed, the founder of the United Arab Emirates.

> *"Future generations will be living in a world that is very different from that to which we are accustomed. It is essential that we prepare ourselves and our children for that new world."*
>
> **Sheikh Zayed bin Sultan Al Nahyan**

Sheikh Zayed bin Sultan Al Nahyan

PROFILES IN LEADERSHIP 1.1

Sheikh Zayed founded the United Arab Emirates (UAE) in 1971 and led it through arguably the world's greatest national transformation of the past 100 years. When he was born in 1918 the area was a desert dominated by warring Arab tribes, and its economy was based largely on fishing and pearl-diving. But consider the UAE today:

- The city of Dubai is one of the safest cities in the world, its airport is the busiest international airport in the world, and a new skyscraper is built every day.
- One of those buildings, the Burj Khalifa, is the tallest building in the world, and the Dubai Mall is the largest shopping center in the world.
- Women hold leadership roles throughout society including in business, government, and the military. Religious openness is evident in the major cities with Muslim mosques, Christian churches, Hindu temples, and even Jewish synagogues found throughout the major cities. It is the first country in the Arab region to enact a comprehensive law combating human trafficking.

So how did Zayed launch this amazing transformation? The story begins with the early life of the man himself. As a boy and young man, he traveled extensively throughout the region living alongside Bedouin tribesmen, learning about their way of life in the desert. That same thirst for learning prompted him to conduct extensive research into the ancient history of the region, leading to his discovery that 15,000 years ago the Arabian Peninsula was originally covered by thick forests and only later transformed into a desert. But those ancient forests–transformed through eons into oil–still lay under the desert sand. He committed himself to returning the region to greenness.

One element of that quest became the planting of trees, and now more than a million trees are growing within the UAE. He established experimental agricultural stations across the country. He initiated projects of water distribution, conservation, and desalination. And he believed that the real resource of any nation is its people, and committed his considerable wealth, energy, and talents to make education for all citizens–men and women–a top national priority. The list of his transformations goes on: health care, wildlife conservation, and job rights, to name just a few.

This was a man who transformed a desert into a modern, thriving region still affirming the moderate Islamic values that his entire life embodied.

Mindful of the Profiles in Leadership running throughout the book, you might wonder (as we do) about just what kind of leaders *ought* to be profiled in these pages. Should we use illustrations featuring leaders who rose to the top in their respective organizations? Should we use illustrations featuring leaders who contributed significantly to enhancing the effectiveness of their organizations?

We suspect you answered yes to both questions. But there's the rub. You see, leaders who rise to the top in their organizations are not always the same as those who help make their organizations more effective. As it turns out, **successful managers** (that is, those promoted quickly through the ranks) spend relatively more time than others in organizational socializing and politicking; and they spend relatively less time than the latter on traditional management responsibilities like planning and decision-making. Truly **effective managers**, however, make real contributions to their organization's performance.[14] This distinction is a critical one, even if quite thorny to untangle in leadership research.

A recent 10-year study of what separated the "best of the best" executives from all the rest in their organizations offers some valuable insights even for people at the very beginning of their careers (and this study was studying real effectiveness, not just success-at-schmoozing, as described in the preceding paragraph). These "best of the best" executives demonstrated expertise and across their careers excelled across all facets of their organization's functions–they knew the *whole* business, not just a piece of it. And they also knew and cared about the people they worked with. These top-performing leaders formed deep and trusting relationships with others, including superiors, peers, and direct reports. They're the kind of people others want working for them, and the kind others want to work for. By the way, relational failure with colleagues proved to be the quickest route to failure among the second-best executives.[15]

All considered, we find that defining leadership as "the process of influencing an organized group toward accomplishing its goals" is fairly comprehensive and helpful. Several implications of this definition are worth further examination.

Leadership Is Both a Science and an Art

Saying leadership is both a science and an art emphasizes the subject of leadership as a field of scholarly inquiry, as well as certain aspects of the practice of leadership. The scope of the science of leadership is reflected in the number of studies—approximately 8,000—cited in an authoritative reference work, *Bass & Stogdill's Handbook of Leadership: Theory, Research, and Managerial Applications.*[16] A review of leadership theory and research over the past 25 years notes the expanding breadth and complexity of scholarly thought about leadership in the preceding quarter century. For example, leadership involves dozens of different theoretical domains and a wide variety of methods for studying it.[17] And using an innovative methodology of "mapping" research trends over time, a 2019 review of the leadership research between 1990 and 2017 identified 200 demonstrably "landmark" studies that indicate significant areas of study in the evolution of the field.[18]

However, being an expert on leadership research is neither necessary nor sufficient for being a good leader. Some managers may be effective leaders without ever having taken a course or training program in leadership, and some scholars in the field of leadership may be relatively poor leaders themselves. What's more, new academic models of leadership consider the "locus" of leadership (where leadership emanates from) as not just coming from an *individual* leader (whether holding a formal position or not, as we'll explore later in this chapter) but also as emanating alternatively from groups or even from an entire organization.[19]

> *Any fool can keep a rule. God gave him a brain to know when to break the rule.*
> **General Willard W. Scott**

Nonetheless, knowing something about leadership research is relevant to leadership effectiveness. Scholarship may not be a prerequisite for leadership effectiveness, but understanding some of the major research findings can help individuals better analyze situations using a variety of perspectives. That, in turn, can tell leaders how to be more effective—presuming, of course, that they *believe* evidence from research is a valid basis for informing one's own leadership practice.[20]

Even so, because skills in analyzing and responding to situations vary greatly across leaders, leadership will always remain partly an art as well as a science. **Highlight 1.1** raises the question of whether leadership should be considered a true science or not.

Is the Study of Leadership a "Real" Science?

HIGHLIGHT 1.1

In this chapter we posit that leadership is both a science and an art. Most people, we think, accept the idea that some element of leadership is an art in the sense that it can't be completely prescribed or routinized into a set of rules to follow, that there is an inherent personal element to leadership. Perhaps even because of that, many people are skeptical about the idea that the study of leadership can be a "real" science like physics and chemistry. Even when acknowledging that thousands of empirical studies of leadership have been published, many still resist the idea that it is in any way analogous to the "hard" sciences.

It might interest you to know, then, that a lively debate is ongoing today among leadership scholars about whether leadership ought to model itself after physics. And the debate is about more than "physics envy." The debate is reminiscent of the early 20th century, when some of the great minds in psychology proposed that psychological theory should be based on formal and explicit mathematical models rather than armchair speculation. Today's debate about the field of leadership looks at the phenomena from a systems perspective and revolves around the extent to which there may be fundamental similarities between leadership and thermodynamics.

So are you willing to consider the possibility that the dynamics governing molecular bonding can also explain how human beings organize themselves to accomplish a shared objective?

Source: R. B. Kaiser, "Beyond Physics Envy? An Introduction to the Special Issue," *Consulting Psychology Journal: Practice & Research* 66 (2014), pp. 259-60.

Leadership Is Both Rational and Emotional

A democracy cannot follow a leader unless he is dramatized. A man to be a hero must not content himself with heroic virtues and anonymous action. He must talk and explain as he acts—drama.

William Allen White, American writer and editor, *Emporia Gazette*

Leadership involves both the rational and emotional sides of human experience. Leadership includes actions and influences based on reason and logic as well as those based on inspiration and passion. We do not want to cultivate merely intellectualized leaders who respond with only logical predictability. Because people differ in their thoughts and feelings, hopes and dreams, needs and fears, goals and ambitions, and strengths and weaknesses, leadership situations can be complex. People are both rational and emotional, so leaders can use rational techniques and emotional appeals to influence followers, but they must also weigh the rational and emotional consequences of their actions.

A full appreciation of leadership involves looking at both of these sides of human nature. Good leadership is more than just calculation and planning, or following a checklist, even though rational analysis can enhance good leadership. Good leadership also involves touching others' feelings; emotions play an important role in leadership, too. Just one example of this is the civil rights movement of the 1960s, which was based on emotions as well as on principles. Dr. Martin Luther King Jr. inspired many people to action; he touched people's hearts as well as their minds.

Aroused feelings, however, can be used either positively or negatively, constructively or destructively. Some leaders have been able to inspire others to deeds of great purpose and courage. By contrast, as images of Adolf Hitler's mass rallies or present-day angry mobs attest, group frenzy can readily become group mindlessness. As another example, emotional appeals by the Reverend Jim Jones resulted in approximately 800 of his followers volitionally committing suicide.

The mere presence of a group (even without heightened emotional levels) can also cause people to act differently than when they are alone. For example, in airline cockpit crews, there are clear lines of authority from the captain down to the first officer (second in command) and so on. So strong are the norms surrounding the authority of the captain that some first officers will not take control of the airplane from the captain even in the event of impending disaster. Foushee reported a study wherein airline captains in simulator training intentionally feigned incapacitation so that the response of the rest of the crew could be observed.[21] The feigned incapacitations occurred at a predetermined point during the plane's final approach in landing, and the simulation involved conditions of poor weather and visibility. Approximately 25 percent of the first officers in these simulated flights allowed the plane to crash. For some reason, the first officers did not take control even when it was clear the captain was allowing the aircraft to deviate from the parameters of a safe approach. This example demonstrates how group dynamics can influence the behavior of group members even when emotional levels are *not* high. (Believe it or not, airline crews are so well trained that this is *not* an emotional situation.) In sum, it should be apparent that leadership involves followers' feelings and nonrational behavior as well as rational behavior. Leaders need to consider *both* the rational and the emotional consequences of their actions.

In fact, some scholars have suggested that the very idea of leadership may be rooted in our emotional needs. Belief in the potency of leadership, however—what has been called the **romance of leadership**—may be a cultural myth that has utility primarily insofar as it affects how people create meaning about causal events in complex social systems. Such a myth, for example, may be operating in the tendency of many people in the business world to automatically attribute a company's success or failure to its leadership. Rather than being a casual factor in a company's success, however, it might be the case that "leadership" is merely a romanticized notion—an obsession people want to and need to believe in.[22] Related to this may be a tendency to attribute a leader's success primarily if not entirely to that person's unique *individual* qualities. That idea is further explored in **Profiles in Leadership 1.2**.

Bill Gates's Head Start

PROFILES IN LEADERSHIP 1.2

Belief in an individual's potential to overcome great odds and achieve success through talent, strength, and perseverance is common in America, but usually there is more than meets the eye in such success stories. Malcolm Gladwell's best seller *Outliers* presents a fascinating exploration of how situational factors contribute to success in addition to the kinds of individual qualities we often assume are all-important. Have you ever thought, for example, that Bill Gates was able to create Microsoft because he's just brilliant and visionary?

Well, let's take for granted he *is* brilliant and visionary—there's plenty of evidence of that. The point here, however, is that's not always enough (and maybe it's *never* enough). Here are some of the things that placed Bill Gates, with all his intelligence and vision, at the right time in the right place:

- Gates was born to a wealthy family in Seattle that placed him in a private school for seventh grade. In 1968, his second year there, the school started a computer club—even before most *colleges* had computer clubs.

- In the 1960s, virtually everyone who was learning about computers used computer cards, a tedious and mind-numbing process. The computer at Gates's school, however, was linked to a mainframe in downtown Seattle. Thus in 1968, Bill Gates was practicing computer programming via time-sharing as an eighth grader; few others in the world then had such opportunity, whatever their age.

- Even at a wealthy private school like the one Gates attended, however, funds ran out to cover the high costs of buying time on a mainframe computer. Fortunately, at about the same time, a group called the Computer Center Corporation was formed at the University of Washington to lease computer time. One of its founders, coincidentally a parent at Gates's own school, thought the school's computer club could get time on the computer in exchange for testing the company's new software programs. Gates then started a regular schedule of taking the bus after school to the company's offices, where he programmed long into the evening. During one seven-month period, Gates and his fellow computer club members averaged eight hours a day, seven days a week, of computer time.

- When Gates was a high school senior, another extraordinary opportunity presented itself. A major national company (TRW) needed programmers with specialized experience—exactly, as it turned out, the kind of experience the kids at Gates's school had been getting. Gates

successfully lobbied his teachers to let him spend a spring doing this work in another part of the state for independent study credit.

- By the time Gates dropped out of Harvard after his sophomore year, he had accumulated more than *10,000 hours* of programming experience. It was, he's said, a better exposure to software development than anyone else at a young age could have had—and all because of a lucky series of events.

It appears that Gates's success is at least partly an example of the right person being in the right place at just the right time.

Source: Malcolm Gladwell, *Outliers: The Story of Success* (New York: Little, Brown and Company, 2008).

Leadership and Management

If you want some ham, you gotta go into the smokehouse.

Huey Long, governor of Louisiana, 1928–1932

In trying to answer the question "What is leadership?" it is natural to look at the relationship between leadership and management. To many people, the word **management** suggests words like *efficiency, planning, paperwork, procedures, regulations, control,* and *consistency.* Leadership is often more associated with words like *risk taking, dynamic, creativity, change,* and *vision.* Some people say leadership is fundamentally a value-choosing, and thus a value-laden, activity, whereas management is not. Leaders are thought to *do the right things,* whereas managers are thought to *do things right.*[23, 24] Here are some other distinctions between managers and leaders:[25]

- Managers administer; leaders innovate.
- Managers maintain; leaders develop.
- Managers control; leaders inspire.
- Managers have a short-term view; leaders, a long-term view.
- Managers ask how and when; leaders ask what and why.
- Managers imitate; leaders originate.
- Managers accept the status quo; leaders challenge it.

While acknowledging this general distinction between leadership and management is essentially accurate and even useful, however, it has had unintended negative effects: "Some leaders now see their job as just coming up with big and vague ideas, and they treat implementing them, or even engaging in conversation and planning about the details of them, as mere 'management' work that is beneath their station and stature."[26]

Zaleznik goes so far as to say these differences reflect fundamentally different personality types: Leaders and managers are basically different kinds of people.[27] He says some people are managers *by nature*; other people are leaders *by nature*. One is not better than the other; they are just different. Their differences, in fact, can be useful because organizations typically need both functions performed well. For example, consider again the U.S. civil rights movement in the 1960s. Dr. Martin Luther King Jr. gave life and direction to the civil rights movement in America. He gave dignity and hope of freer participation in national life to people who before had little reason to expect it. He inspired the world with his vision and eloquence, and he changed the way we live together. America is a different nation today because of him. Was Dr. Martin Luther King Jr. a leader? Of course. Was he a manager? Somehow that does not seem to fit, and the civil rights movement might have failed if it had not been for the managerial talents of his supporting staff. Leadership and management complement each other, and both are vital to organizational success.

With regard to the issue of leadership versus management, the authors of this book take a middle-of-the-road position. We think of leadership and management as closely related but distinguishable functions. Our view of the relationship is depicted in **Figure 1.1**, which shows leadership and management as two overlapping functions. Although some functions performed by leaders and managers may be unique, there is also an area of overlap. In reading **Highlight 1.2**, do you see more good management in the response to the 1906 San Francisco earthquake, more good leadership, or both? And in **Profiles in Leadership 1.3** you can read about leaders from two different eras in American history.

FIGURE 1.1 Leadership and Management Overlap

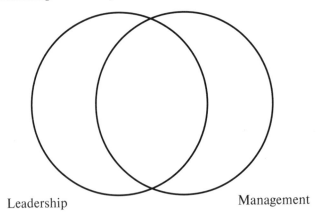

Leadership   Management

The Response of Leadership to a Natural Disaster

HIGHLIGHT 1.2

After terrible natural disasters occur, it is common for observers to comment about the adequacy or inadequacy of government responses-tothem. It may be instructive to compare the response of government agencies to a natural

disaster that occurred more than a century ago: the San Francisco earthquake and fire of 1906.

While the precipitant disaster was the earthquake itself, much destruction resulted from the consequent fire, one disaster aggravating the impact of the others. Poles throughout the city fell, taking the high-tension wires they were carrying with them. Gas pipes broke; chimneys fell, dropping hot coals into thousands of gallons of gas spilled by broken fuel tanks; stoves and heaters in homes toppled over; and in moments fires erupted across the city. Because the earthquake's first tremors also broke water pipes throughout the city, fire hydrants everywhere suddenly went dry, making fighting the fires virtually impossible. In objective terms, the disaster is estimated to have killed as many as 3,000 people, rendered more than 200,000 homeless, and by some measures caused $195 billion in property loss as measured by today's dollars.

How did authorities respond to the crisis when there were far fewer agencies with presumed response plans to combat disasters, and when high-tech communication methods were unheard of? Consider these two examples:

- The ranking officer assigned to a U.S. Army post in San Francisco was away when the earthquake struck, so it was up to his deputy to help organize the army's and federal government's response. The deputy immediately cabled Washington, D.C., requesting tents, rations, and medicine. Secretary of War William Howard Taft, who would become the next U.S. president, responded by immediately dispatching 200,000 rations from Washington state. In a matter of days, every tent in the U.S. Army had been sent to San Francisco, and

the longest hospital train in history was dispatched from Virginia.

- Perhaps the most impressive example of leadership initiative in the face of the 1906 disaster was that of the U.S. Post Office. It recovered its ability to function in short order without losing a single item that was being handled when the earthquake struck. And because the earthquake had effectively destroyed the city's telegraphic connection (telegrams inside the city were temporarily being delivered by the post office), a critical question arose: How could people struck by the disaster communicate with their families elsewhere? The city postmaster immediately announced that all citizens of San Francisco could use the post office to inform their families and loved ones of their condition and needs. He further stipulated that for outgoing private letters it would not matter whether the envelopes bore stamps. This was what was needed: Circumstances demanded that people be able to communicate with friends and family whether or not they could find or pay for stamps.

This should remind us that modern leadership is not necessarily better leadership, and that leadership in government is not always bureaucratic and can be both humane and innovative.

A Tale of Two Leaders

PROFILES IN LEADERSHIP 1.3

In 2015, the musical *Hamilton* opened on Broadway. It would go on to win a Pulitzer Prize and 11 Tony awards. It tells the story of Alexander Hamilton, a founding father whose singularly

important role in our history has been largely forgotten.

If you are like most people—at least before *Hamilton* opened on Broadway—you probably knew very little about Alexander Hamilton's life. So consider just a few noteworthy pieces of his life story:

- He was born out of wedlock to a mixed-race couple in the West Indies in 1755. He served an apprenticeship in St. Croix with a trading company where his experience with seafaring traders and smugglers provided insight key to his later establishment of the U.S. Coast Guard and customs service.
- He attended college in the American colonies, and at the age of 22, served as George Washington's private secretary and as his unofficial chief-of-staff during the Revolutionary War. He was the main architect of the new American government following the Constitutional Convention of 1787.

Rather impressive accomplishments for someone you had not heard much about before the musical became popular. But Lin-Manuel Miranda became fascinated with the character when he read Ron Chernow's excellent biography of Hamilton. It inspired him to write the musical (both the script and the music) and to star in the title role.

And just as many Americans have become newly acquainted with Alexander Hamilton the leader, many have come to appreciate Lin-Manuel Miranda the leader as well. Among his accomplishments was his selection as one of

Time magazine's 100 most influential people of 2016. In reflecting on the award and his own legacy, he told *Time* magazine, "We have this amount of time. It's the tiniest grain of sand of time we're allowed on this earth, and what do we leave behind? I think that question has gnawed at me as long as I've been conscious. That's something that Hamilton outright states in our show, and I think that's something I share with him."

Largely as a result of *Hamilton*'s success, Miranda is now estimated to earn $105,000 a week in royalties. But his now unquestioned success does not—in his own mind, at least—make *Hamilton* the turning point in his life. He still lives in the same predominantly Latino neighborhood of Washington Heights where he grew up and which inspired his first Broadway musical. In recalling that milestone, he recalls, "I think honestly the biggest leap [in my life] was the first production of *In The Heights*, because I went from being a substitute teacher to a Broadway composer. I'll never make a leap that big again in my life."

Sources: R. Chernow, *Alexander Hamilton* (New York: Penguin, 2004); J. McGregor, "How Hamilton's Lin-Manuel Miranda Makes Us Think about Legacy," *The Washington Post*, May 4, 2016; and "Miranda's Life as a Rich Man," *The Week*, November 15, 2019, p. 10.

Leadership Myths

Few things pose a greater obstacle to leadership development than certain unsubstantiated and self-limiting beliefs about leadership. Therefore, before we begin examining leadership and leadership development in more detail, we consider what they are not. Here we examine several beliefs (we call them myths) that stand in the way of fully understanding and developing leadership.

Myth: Good Leadership Is All Common Sense

At face value, this myth says one needs only common sense to be a good leader. It also implies, however, that most if not all of the studies of leadership reported in scholarly journals and books only confirm what anyone with common sense already knows.

The problem, of course, is with the ambiguous term *common sense*. It implies a common body of practical knowledge about life that virtually any reasonable person with moderate experience has acquired. A simple experiment, however, may convince you that common sense may be less common than you think. Ask a few friends or acquaintances whether the old folk wisdom "Absence makes the heart grow fonder" is true or false. Most will say it is true. After that, ask a different group whether the old folk wisdom "Out of sight, out of mind" is true or false. Most of that group will answer true as well, even though the two proverbs are contradictory.

> *If you miss seven balls out of ten, you're batting three hundred and that's good enough for the Hall of Fame. You can't score if you keep the bat on your shoulder.*
>
> **Walter B. Wriston, chairman of Citicorp, 1970–1984**

A similar thing sometimes happens when people hear about the results of studies concerning human behavior. On hearing the results, people may say, "Who needed a study to learn that? I knew it all the time." However, several experiments showed that events were much more surprising when subjects had to guess the outcome of an experiment than when subjects were told the outcome.[28, 29] What seems obvious after you know the results and what you (or anyone else) would have predicted beforehand are not the same thing. Hindsight is always 20/20.

The point might become clearer with a specific example. Read the following paragraph:

> After World War II, the U.S. Army spent enormous sums of money on studies only to reach conclusions that, many believed, should have been apparent at the outset. One, for example, was that southern soldiers were better able to stand the climate in the hot South Sea islands than northern soldiers were.

This sounds reasonable, but there is a problem: The statement here is exactly contrary to the actual findings. Southerners were no better than northerners in adapting to tropical climates.[30] Common sense can often play tricks on us.

Put a little differently, one challenge of understanding leadership may be to know when common sense applies and when it does not. Do leaders need to act confidently? Of course. But they also need to be humble enough to recognize that others' views are useful, too. Do leaders need to persevere when times get tough? Yes. But they also need to recognize when times change and a new direction is called for. If leadership were nothing more than common sense, there should be few, if any, problems in the workplace. However, we venture to guess you have noticed more than a few problems between leaders and followers. Effective leadership must be something more than just common sense.

Myth: Leaders Are Born, Not Made

Some people believe that being a leader is either in one's genes or not; others believe that life experiences mold the individual and that no one is born a leader. Which view is right? In a sense, both and neither. Both views are right in that innate factors as well as formative experiences influence many sorts of behavior, including leadership. Yet both views are wrong to the extent they imply leadership is *either* innate *or* acquired; what matters more is how these factors *interact*. It does not seem useful, we believe, to think of the world as comprising two mutually exclusive types of people, leaders and nonleaders. It is more useful to address how each person can make the most of leadership opportunities he or she faces.

> *Never reveal all of yourself to other people; hold back something in reserve so that people are never quite sure if they really know you.*
>
> **Michael Korda, author, editor**

It may be easier to see the pointlessness of asking whether leaders are born or made by looking at an alternative question of far less popular interest: Are *college professors* born or made? Conceptually the issues are the same, and here too the answer is that every college professor is both born *and* made. It seems clear enough that college professors are partly "born" because (among other factors) there is a genetic component to intelligence, and intelligence surely plays some part in becoming a college professor (well, at least a *minor* part!). But every college professor is also partly "made." One obvious way is that college professors must have advanced education in specialized fields; even with the right genes one could not become a college professor without certain requisite experiences. Becoming a college professor depends partly on what one is born with and partly on how that inheritance is shaped through experience. The same is true of leadership.

More specifically, research indicates that many cognitive abilities and personality traits are at least partly innate.[31] Thus natural talents or characteristics may offer certain advantages or disadvantages to a leader. Consider physical characteristics: A man's above-average height may increase others' tendency to think of him as a leader; it may also boost his own self-confidence. But it doesn't make him a leader. The same holds true for psychological characteristics that seem related to leadership. The stability of certain characteristics over long periods (for example, at school reunions people seem to have kept the same personalities we remember them as having years earlier) may reinforce the impression that our basic natures are fixed, but different environments nonetheless may nurture or suppress different leadership qualities.

Myth: The Only School You Learn Leadership from Is the School of Hard Knocks

Progress always involves risks. You can't steal second base and keep your foot on first.

Frederick B. Wilcox

Some people skeptically question whether leadership can develop through formal study, believing instead it can be acquired only through actual experience. It is a mistake, however, to think of formal study and learning from experience as mutually exclusive or antagonistic. In fact, they complement each other. Rather than ask whether leadership develops from formal study or from real-life experience, it is better to ask what kind of study will help students learn to discern critical lessons about leadership from their own experience. Approaching the issue in such a way recognizes the vital role of experience in leadership development, but it also admits that certain kinds of study and training can improve a person's ability to discern important lessons about leadership from experience. It can, in other words, accelerate the process of learning from experience.

We argue that one advantage of formally studying leadership is that formal study provides students with a variety of ways of examining a particular leadership situation. By studying the different ways researchers have defined and examined leadership, students can use these definitions and theories to better understand what is going on in any leadership situation. For example, earlier in this chapter we used different leadership definitions as a framework for describing or analyzing the situation facing Parrado and the survivors of the plane crash, and each definition focused on a different aspect of leadership. These frameworks can similarly be applied to better understand the experiences one has as both a leader and a follower. We think it is difficult for leaders, particularly novice leaders, to examine leadership situations from multiple perspectives; but we also believe developing this skill can help you become a better leader. Being able to analyze your experiences from multiple perspectives may be the greatest single contribution a formal course in leadership can give you. Maybe you can reflect on your own leadership over a cup of coffee in Starbucks as you read about the origins of that company in **Profiles in Leadership 1.4**.

Harry Truman Takes Charge

PROFILES IN LEADERSHIP 1.4

The first four months of Harry Truman's presidency might be the most important four months in American history in politically shaping today's world.

Truman assumed the presidency upon the death of Franklin Delano Roosevelt (FDR) in 1945, and Roosevelt was not an easy act to follow. FDR had served in the office longer than anyone before (or since) and was widely regarded as one of the greatest and most popular presidents in history. Truman, on the other hand, was described as the "prototypical ordinary man." He had no college degree and never had enough money to own a home. His only slightly tongue-in-cheek self-description is revealing: "My choice early in life was either to be a piano player in a whorehouse or a politician. And to tell the truth, there's hardly any difference."

He would recall the day of FDR's death–in 1945, during what would be the last year of WWII–as the day "the whole weight of the moon and the stars fell on me." When told by First Lady Eleanor Roosevelt of her husband's death, he immediately asked if there was anything he could do to help her. She answered, "Is there anything *we* can do for *you*? For you are the one in trouble now." He could not have known on that first day all that he would be facing, because there was much, even as vice president, that he had not been made privy to. Late on his first day as president, the Secretary of War told him about a project underway to develop a weapon of incomprehensible destructive power. It was called the Manhattan Project, and the weapon was the atom bomb. Only four months later, Truman would have to decide whether to use it to end the war. During the first four months of his presidency, he also oversaw the collapse of the Nazi empire, fire-bombings of Japanese cities that killed hundreds of thousands of people, and the creation of the United Nations. He is now regarded as among the greatest of American presidents of all time.

Source: A. J. Baime, *The Accidental President: Harry S. Truman and the Fourth Months That Changed the World* (Boston: Mariner Books, 2017).

The Interactional Framework for Analyzing Leadership

Perhaps the first researcher to formally recognize the importance of the leader, follower, and situation in the leadership process was Fred Fiedler.[32] Fiedler used these three components to develop his contingency model of leadership, a theory of leadership discussed in more detail in **Chapter 15**. Although we recognize Fiedler's contributions, we owe perhaps even more to Hollander's transactional approach to leadership.[33] We call our approach the **interactional framework**.

Several aspects of this derivative of Hollander's approach are worthy of additional comment. First, as shown in **Figure 1.2**, the framework depicts leadership as a function of three elements–the **leader**, the **followers**, and the **situation**. Second, a particular leadership scenario can be examined using each level of analysis separately. Although this is a useful way to understand the leadership process, we can understand the process even better if we also examine the **interactions** among the three elements, or lenses, represented by the overlapping areas in the figure. For example, we can better understand the leadership process if we not only look at the leaders and the followers but also examine how leaders and followers affect each other in the leadership process. Similarly, we can examine the leader and the situation separately, but we can gain a better under-standing of the leadership process by looking at how the situation can constrain or facilitate a leader's actions and how the leader can change different aspects of the situation to be more effective. Thus a final important aspect of the framework is that leadership is the result of a complex set of interactions among the leader, the followers, and the situation. These complex interactions may be why broad generalizations about leadership are problematic: Many factors influence the leadership process (see **Highlight 1.3**).

An example of one such complex interaction between leaders and followers is evident in what have been called in-groups and out-groups. Sometimes there is a high degree of mutual influence and attraction between the leader and a few subordinates. These subordinates belong to the **in-group** and can be distinguished by their high degree of loyalty, commitment, and trust felt toward the leader. Other subordinates belong to the **out-group**. Leaders have considerably more influence with in-group followers than with out-group followers. However, this greater degree of influence has a price. If leaders rely primarily on their formal authority to influence their followers (especially if they punish them), then leaders risk losing the high levels of loyalty and commitment followers feel toward them.[34]

The Leader

This element examines primarily what the leader brings *as an individual* to the leadership equation. This can include unique personal history, interests, character traits, and motivation.

Leaders are *not* all alike, but they tend to share many characteristics. Research has shown that leaders differ from their followers, and effective leaders differ from ineffective leaders, on various personality traits, cognitive abilities, skills, and values.[35, 36, 37, 38, 39, 40] Another way personality can affect leadership is through temperament, by which we mean whether a leader is generally calm or is instead prone to emotional outbursts. Leaders who have calm dispositions and do not attack or belittle others for bringing bad news are

FIGURE 1.2   An Interactional Framework for Analyzing Leadership

Source: Adapted from E. P. Hollander, *Leadership Dynamics: A Practical Guide to Effective Relationships* (New York: Free Press, 1978).

more likely to get complete and timely information from subordinates than are bosses who have explosive tempers and a reputation for killing the messenger.

Another important aspect of the leader is how he or she achieved leader status. Leaders who are appointed by superiors may have less credibility with subordinates and get less loyalty from them than leaders who are elected or emerge by consensus from the ranks of followers. Often emergent or elected officials are better able to influence a group toward goal achievement because of the power conferred on them by their followers. However, both elected and emergent leaders need to be sensitive to their constituencies if they wish to remain in power.

More generally, a leader's experience or history in a particular organization is usually important to her or his effectiveness. For example, leaders promoted from within an organization, by virtue of being familiar with its culture and policies, may be ready to "hit the ground running." In addition, leaders selected from within an organization are typically better known by others in the organization than are leaders selected from the outside. That is likely to affect, for better or worse, the latitude others in the organization are willing to give the leader; if the leader is widely respected for a history of accomplishment, she may be given more latitude than a newcomer whose track record is less well known. On the other hand, many people tend to give new leaders a fair chance to succeed, and newcomers to an organization often take time to learn the organization's informal rules, norms, and "ropes" before they make any radical or potentially controversial decisions.

A leader's legitimacy also may be affected by the extent to which followers participated in the leader's selection. When followers have had a say in the selection or election of a leader, they tend to have a heightened sense of psychological identification with her, but they also may have higher expectations and make more demands on her.[41] We also might wonder what kind of support a leader has from his own boss. If followers sense their boss has a lot of influence with the higher-ups, subordinates may be reluctant to take their complaints to higher levels. On the other hand, if the boss has little influence with higher-ups, subordinates may be more likely to make complaints at these levels.

I must follow the people. Am I not their leader?

Benjamin Disraeli, 19th-century British prime minister

The foregoing examples highlight the sorts of insights we can gain about leadership by focusing on the individual leader as a level of analysis. Even if we were to examine the individual leader completely, however, our understanding of the leadership process would be incomplete.

The Followers

The crowd will follow a leader who marches twenty steps in advance; but if he is a thousand steps in front of them, they do not see and do not follow him.

Georg Brandes, Danish scholar

Followers are a critical part of the leadership equation, but their role has not always been appreciated, at least in empirical research (but read **Highlight 1.3** to see how the role of followers has been recognized in literature). For a long time, in fact, "the common view of leadership was that leaders actively led and subordinates, later called followers, passively and obediently followed."[42] Over time, especially in the last century, social change shaped people's views of followers, and leadership theories gradually recognized the active and important role that followers play in the leadership process.[43] Today it seems natural to accept the important role followers play.

The *First* Band of Brothers

HIGHLIGHT 1.3

Perhaps you have seen or heard of the award-winning series *Band of Brothers* that followed a company of the famous 101st Airborne division during World War II, based on a book of the same title by Stephen Ambrose. You may not be aware that an earlier band of brothers was made famous by William Shakespeare in his play *Henry V.*

In one of the most famous speeches by any of Shakespeare's characters, the young Henry V tried to unify his followers when their daring expedition to conquer France was failing. French soldiers followed Henry's army along the rivers, daring them to cross over and engage the French in battle. Just before the battle of Agincourt, Henry's rousing words rallied his vastly outnumbered, weary, and tattered troops to victory. Few words of oratory have ever better bonded a leader with his followers than Henry's call for unity among "we few, we happy few, we band of brothers."

Hundreds of years later, Henry's speech is still a powerful illustration of a leader who empha-sized the importance of his followers. Modern leadership concepts like vision, charisma, relationship orientation, and empowerment are readily evident in Henry's interactions with his followers. Here are the closing lines of Henry's famous speech:

From this day to the ending of the world,
But we in it shall be remembered—
We few, we happy few, we band of brothers;
For he today that sheds his blood with me
Shall be my brother; be he ne'er so vile,
This day shall gentle his condition;
And gentlemen in England now-a-bed
Shall think themselves accurs'd they were not here,
And hold their manhoods cheap whiles any speaks
That fought with us upon Saint Crispin's day.

Shakespeare's insights into the complexities of leadership should remind us that while modern research helps enlighten our understanding, it does not represent the only, and certainly not the most moving, perspective on leadership to which we should pay attention.

Source: S. E. Ambrose, *Band of Brothers* (New York: Simon & Schuster, 2001).

All men have some weak points, and the more vigorous and brilliant a person may be, the more strongly these weak points stand out. It is highly desirable, even essential, therefore, for the more influential members of a general's staff not to be too much like the general.

Major General Hugo Baron von Freytag-Loringhoven, anti-Hitler conspirator

One aspect of our text's definition of leadership is particularly worth noting in this regard: Leadership is a social influence process shared among *all* members of a group. Leadership is not restricted to the influence exerted by someone in a particular position or role; followers are part of the leadership process, too. In recent years both practitioners and scholars have emphasized the relatedness of leadership and **followership**. As Burns observed, the idea of "one-man leadership" is a contradiction in terms.[44]

Obvious as this point may seem, it is also clear that early leadership researchers paid relatively little attention to the roles followers play in the leadership process.[45, 46] However, we know that the followers' expectations, personality traits, maturity levels, levels of competence, and motivation affect the leadership process, too. **Highlight 1.4** describes a systematic approach to classifying different kinds of followers that has had a major impact on research.[47, 48, 49, 50]

Followership Styles

HIGHLIGHT 1.4

The concept of different styles of leadership is reasonably familiar, but the idea of different styles of followership is relatively new. The very word *follower* has a negative connotation to many, evoking ideas of people who behave like sheep and need to be told what to do. Robert Kelley, however, believes that followers, rather than representing the antithesis of leadership, are best viewed as collaborators with leaders in the work of organizations.

Kelley believes that different types of followers can be described in terms of two broad dimensions. One of them ranges from **independent, critical thinking** at one end to **dependent, uncritical thinking** on the other end. According to Kelley, the best followers think for themselves and offer constructive advice or even creative solutions. The worst followers need to be told what to do. Kelley's other dimension ranges from whether people are **active followers** or **passive followers** in the extent to which they are engaged in work. According to Kelley, the best followers are self-starters who take initiative for themselves, whereas the worst followers are passive, may even dodge responsibility, and need constant supervision.

Using these two dimensions, Kelley has suggested five basic styles of followership:

1. *Alienated followers* habitually point out all the negative aspects of the organization to others. While alienated followers may see themselves as mavericks who have a healthy skepticism of the organization, leaders often see them as cynical, negative, and adversarial.

2. *Conformist followers* are the "yes people" of organizations. While very active at doing the organization's work, they can be dangerous if their orders contradict societal standards of behavior or organizational policy. Often this style is the result of either the demanding and authoritarian style of the leader or the overly rigid structure of the organization.

3. *Pragmatist followers* are rarely committed to their group's work goals, but they have learned not to make waves. Because they do not like to stick out, pragmatists tend to be mediocre performers who can clog the arteries of many organizations. Because it can be difficult to discern just where they stand on issues, they present an ambiguous image with both positive and negative characteristics. In organizational settings, pragmatists may become experts in mastering the bureaucratic rules that can be used to protect them.

4. *Passive followers* display none of the characteristics of the exemplary follower (discussed next). They rely on the leader to do all the thinking. Furthermore, their work lacks enthusiasm. Lacking initiative and a sense of responsibility, passive followers require constant direction. Leaders may see them as lazy, incompetent, or even stupid. Sometimes, however, passive followers adopt this style to help them cope with a leader who expects followers to behave that way.

5. *Exemplary followers* present a consistent picture to both leaders and coworkers of being independent, innovative, and willing to stand up to superiors. They apply their talents for the benefit of the organization even when confronted with bureaucratic stumbling blocks or passive or pragmatist coworkers. Effective leaders appreciate the value of exemplary followers. When one of the authors was serving in a follower role in a staff position, he was introduced by his

leader to a conference as "my favorite subordinate because he's a loyal 'No-Man'."

Exemplary followers–high on both critical dimensions of followership–are essential to organizational success.

Leaders, therefore, would be well advised to select people who have these characteristics and, perhaps even more important, *create the conditions that encourage these behaviors.*

Source: R. Kelley, *The Power of Followership* (New York: Doubleday Currency, 1992).

The nature of followers' motivation to do their work is also important. Workers who share a leader's goals and values, and who feel intrinsically rewarded for performing a job well, might be more likely to work extra hours on a time-critical project than those whose motivation is solely monetary.

Even the number of followers reporting to a leader can have significant implications. For example, a store manager with three clerks working for him can spend more time with each of them (or on other things) than can a manager responsible for eight clerks and a separate delivery service; chairing a task force with 5 members is a different leadership activity than chairing a task force with 18 members. Still other relevant variables include followers' trust in the leader and their degree of confidence that he or she is interested in their well-being. Another aspect of followers' relations to a leader is described in **Profiles in Leadership 1.5**.

Paul Revere

PROFILES IN LEADERSHIP 1.5

A fabled story of American history is that of Paul Revere's ride through the countryside surrounding Boston, warning towns that the British were coming, so that local militia could be ready to meet them. As a result, when the British did march toward Lexington on the following day, they faced unexpectedly fierce resistance. At Concord the British were beaten by a ragtag group of locals, and so began the American Revolutionary War.

It has been taken for granted by generations of Americans that the success of Paul Revere's ride lay in his heroism *and* in the self-evident importance of the news itself. A little-known fact, however, is that Paul Revere was not the only rider that night. A fellow revolutionary by the name of William Dawes had the same mission: to ride simultaneously through a separate set of towns surrounding Boston to warn them that the British were coming. He did so, car-

rying the news through just as many towns as Revere did. But his ride was not successful; those local militia leaders weren't aroused and did not rise up to confront the British. If they had been, Dawes would be as famous today as Paul Revere.

Why was Revere's ride successful when Dawes's ride was not? Paul Revere started a word-of-mouth epidemic, and Dawes did not, *because of differing kinds of relationships the two men had with others.* It wasn't, after all, the nature of the news itself that proved ultimately important so much as the nature of the men who carried it. Paul Revere was a gregarious and social person—what Malcolm Gladwell calls a *connector.* Gladwell writes that Revere was "a fisherman and a hunter, a cardplayer and a theater-lover, a frequenter of pubs and a successful businessman. He was active in the local Masonic Lodge and was a member of several select social clubs." He was a man with a knack for always being at the center of things. So when he began his ride that night, it was Revere's nature to stop and share the news with anyone he saw on the road, and he would have known who the key players were in each town to notify.

Dawes was not by nature so gregarious as Revere, and he did not have Revere's extended social network. It's likely he *wouldn't* have known whom to share the news with in each town and whose doors to knock on. Dawes did notify some people, but not enough to create the kind of impact that Revere did. Another way of saying this is simply to note that the people Dawes notified didn't know *him* the way that Revere was known by those *he* notified.

It isn't just the information or the ideas you have as a leader that make a difference. It's also whom you know, and how many you know—and what they know about you.

Source: M. Gladwell, *The Tipping Point* (New York: Little, Brown and Company, 2002).

Never try to teach a pig to sing; it wastes your time and it annoys the pig.

Paul Dickson, baseball writer

I don't like it when you people force me to do things.

Orion Farrell, age 6

In the context of the interactional framework, the question "What is leadership?" cannot be separated from the question "What is followership?" There is no simple line dividing them; they merge. The relationship between leadership and followership can be represented by borrowing a concept from topographical mathematics: the Möbius strip. You are probably familiar with the curious properties of the Möbius strip: When a strip of paper is twisted and connected in the manner depicted in **Figure 1.3**, it has only one side. You can prove this to yourself by putting a pencil to any point on the strip and tracing continuously. Your pencil will cover the entire strip (that is, both "sides"), eventually returning to the point at which you started. To demonstrate the relevance of this curiosity to leadership, cut a strip of paper. On one side write *leadership*, and on the other side write *followership*. Then twist the strip and connect the two ends in the manner of the figure. You will have created a leadership/followership Möbius strip wherein the two concepts merge, just as leadership and followership can become indistinguishable in organizations.[51]

He who would eat the fruit must climb the tree.

Scottish proverb

This does not mean leadership and followership are the same thing. When top-level executives were asked to list qualities they most look for and admire in leaders and followers, the lists were similar but not identical.[52]

FIGURE 1.3 The Leadership/Followership Möbius Strip

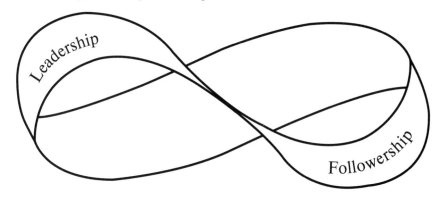

Ideal leaders were characterized as honest, competent, forward-looking, and inspiring; ideal followers were described as honest, competent, independent, and cooperative. The differences could become critical in certain situations, as when a forward-looking and inspiring subordinate perceives a significant conflict between his own goals or ethics and those of his superiors. Such a situation could become a crisis for the individual and the organization, demanding a choice between leading and following.

> *If you act like an ass, don't get insulted if people ride you.*
>
> **Yiddish proverb**

As the complexity of the leadership process has become better understood, the importance placed on the leader–follower relationship itself has undergone dynamic change.[53, 54] One reason for this is an increasing pressure on all kinds of organizations to function with reduced resources. Reduced resources and company downsizing have reduced the number of managers and increased their span of control, which in turn leaves followers to pick up many of the functions traditionally performed by leaders. Another reason is a trend toward greater power sharing and decentralized authority in organizations, which create greater interdependence among organizational subunits and increase the need for collaboration among them. Furthermore, the nature of problems faced by many organizations is becoming so complex and the changes are becoming so rapid that more and more people are required to solve them.

These trends suggest several different ways in which followers can take on new leadership roles and responsibilities in the future. For one thing, followers can become much more proactive in their stance toward organizational problems. When facing the discrepancy between the way things are in an organization and the way they could or should be, followers can play an active and constructive role collaborating with leaders in solving problems. In general, making organizations better is a task that needs to be "owned" by followers as well as by leaders. With these changing roles for followers, it should not be surprising to find that qualities of good followership are statistically correlated with qualities typically associated with good leadership. One recent study found positive correlations between the followership qualities of active engagement and independent thinking and the leadership qualities of dominance, sociability, achievement orientation, and steadiness.[55]

In addition to helping solve organizational problems, followers can contribute to the leadership process by becoming skilled at "influencing upward." Because followers are often at the levels where many organizational problems occur, they can give leaders relevant information so that good solutions are implemented. Although it is true that some leaders need to become better listeners, it is also true that many followers need training in expressing ideas to superiors clearly and positively. Still another way followers can assume a greater share of the leadership challenge in the future is by staying flexible and open to opportunities. The future portends more change, not less, and followers who face change with positive anticipation and an openness to self-development will be particularly valued and rewarded.[56]

Among other things, this openness to change and self-development likely will include openness to reconsidering how we use the words *leader* and *followers*. Even when followers' importance in the leadership process was finally receiving the attention it deserved, early attention tended to focus on followership as a *role* (that is, a part that is played), often if not always designated by a term like *subordinate*. In contrast—to carry the theatrical analogy a bit further—the role of leader virtually always remained the "lead" role.

Recently, however, an alternative approach to understanding followership has been advanced. In contrast to the aforementioned **role approach** to understanding followership, the **constructionist approach** views leadership as combined acts of leading and following by different individuals, whatever their formal titles or positions in an organization may be.[57] In other words, leadership emerges from the intertwined acts of individuals in complex social interactions that may include times when "followers may be leading" and "leaders may be following." From the perspective of the constructionist approach, leadership is co-created through acts of leading and following, *whoever may be performing those acts.*

Thus, to an ever-increasing degree, leadership must be understood in terms of both leader variables and follower variables, as well as the interactions among them. But even that is not enough—we must also understand the particular situations in which leaders and followers find themselves.

The Situation

You've got to give loyalty down, if you want loyalty up.

Donald T. Regan, former CEO and White House chief of staff

The situation is the third critical part of the leadership equation. Even if we knew all we could know about a given leader and a given set of followers, leadership often makes sense only in the context of how the leader and followers interact in a particular situation.

This view of leadership as a complex interaction among leader, follower, and situational variables was not always taken for granted. To the contrary, most early research on leadership was based on the assumption that leadership is a general personal trait expressed independently of the situation in which the leadership is manifested. This view, commonly known as the **heroic theory**, has been largely discredited but for a long time represented the dominant way of conceptualizing leadership.[58]

In the 1950s and 1960s a different approach to conceptualizing leadership dominated research and scholarship. It involved the search for effective leader *behaviors* rather than the search for universal *traits* of leadership. That approach proved too narrow because it neglected important contextual, or situational, factors in which presumably effective or ineffective behaviors occur. Over time, the complexities of interactions among leader, follower, and situational variables increasingly have been the focus of leadership research.[59] (See **Chapters 6**, **7**, and **14** for more detailed discussions of leader attributes, leader behaviors, and formal theories of leadership that examine complex interdependencies between leader, follower, and situational variables.) Adding the situation to the mix of variables that make up leadership is complicated. The situation may be the most ambiguous aspect of the leadership framework; it can refer to anything from the specific task a group is engaged in to broad situational contexts such as the remote predicament of the Andes survivors. One facet of the complexity of the situation's role in leadership is examined in **Highlight 1.5**.

Decision-Making in a Complex World

HIGHLIGHT 1.5

Decision-making is a good example of how leaders need to behave differently in various situations. Until late in the 20th century, decision-making in government and business was largely based on an implicit assumption that the world was orderly and predictable enough for virtually all decision-making to involve a series of specifiable steps: assessing the facts of a situation, categorizing those facts, and then responding based on established practice. To put that more simply, decision-making required managers to *sense, categorize*, and *respond*.

The Situation	The Leader's Job
Simple: predictable and orderly; right answers exist.	Ensure that proper processes are in place, follow best practices, and communicate in clear and direct ways.
Complex: flux, unpredictability, ambiguity, many competing ideas, lots of unknowns.	Create environments and experiments that allow patterns to emerge; increase levels of interaction and communication; use methods that generate new ideas and ways of thinking among everyone.

That process is still effective in simple contexts characterized by stability and clear cause-and-effect relationships. Not all situations in the world, however, are so simple, and new approaches to decision-making are needed for situations that have the elements of what we might call complex systems: large numbers of interacting elements, nonlinear interactions among those elements by which small changes can produce huge effects, and interdependence among the elements so that the whole is more than the sum of its parts. The challenges of dealing with the threat of terrorism represent one example of the way complexity affects deci-sion-making, but it's impacting how we think about decision-making in business as well as government. To describe this change succinctly, the decision-making process in complex contexts must change from sense, categorize, and respond to probe, sense, and respond.

In other words, making good decisions is about both *what* decisions one makes and understanding the role of the situation in affecting *how* one makes decisions.

Source: D. F. Snowden and M. E. Boone, "A Leader's Framework for Decision Making," *Harvard Business Review*, November 2007, pp. 69–76.

Illustrating the Interactional Framework: Women in Leadership Roles

Not long ago, if people were asked to name a leader they admired, most of the names on the resulting list could be characterized as "old white guys." Today the names on that same list would be considerably more heterogeneous. That change—which we certainly consider progress—represents a useful illustration of the power of using the interactional framework to understand the complexities of the leadership process.

A specific example is women in leadership roles, and in this section we examine the extent to which women have been taking on new leadership roles, whether there are differences in the effectiveness of men and women in leadership roles, and what explanations have been offered for differences between men and women in being selected for and succeeding in positions of leadership. This is an area of considerable academic research and popular polemics, as evident in many articles in the popular press that claim a distinct advantage for women in leadership roles.[60]

It is clear that women are taking on leadership roles in greater numbers than ever before. Yet the percentage of women in leadership positions has stayed relatively stable. For example, a report released in 2010 by the U.S. Government Accountability Office indicated that women represent an estimated 40 percent of managers in the U.S. workforce in 2007 compared with 39 percent in 2000.[61] The percentage of women in top executive positions is considerably less encouraging. A review of the 2019 S&P 500 list by the nonprofit organization

Catalyst shows that only 6 percent of CEOs in the United States were women.[62] Problems clearly still exist that constrain the opportunity for capable women to rise to the highest leadership roles in organizations. Many studies have considered this problem, a few of which we examine here.

One study reported that a higher percentage of women executives now receive on-the-job mentoring than men. The same study, however, found that the mentors of those women executives had less organizational influence and clout than did the mentors of their male counterparts. While such mentoring can still provide invaluable psychosocial support for personal and professional development, it does not seem sufficient to ensure promotion to higher level jobs (we explore mentoring in greater detail in **Chapter 2**).[63] Another study examined differences in the networking patterns of men and women. Compared to men, women's trust in each other tends to decrease when work situations become more professionally risky. Such a pattern of behavior could potentially become a kind of self-imposed promotion disadvantage by women on themselves.[64]

In a classic study of sex roles, Schein demonstrated how bias in sex-role stereotypes created problems for women moving up through managerial roles.[65, 66] Schein asked male and female middle managers to complete a survey in which they rated various items on a five-point scale in terms of how characteristic they were of men in general, women in general, or successful managers. Schein found a high correlation between the ways both male and female respondents perceived "males" and "managers," but no correlation between the ways the respondents perceived "females" and "managers." It was as though being a manager was defined by attributes thought of as masculine.

Furthermore, it does not appear that the situation has changed much over the past two decades. In 1990, management students in the United States, Germany, and Great Britain, for example, still perceived successful middle managers in terms of characteristics more commonly ascribed to men than to women.[67] A 2011 meta-analysis of studies of gender stereotyping continued to find strong evidence of a tendency for leadership to be viewed as culturally masculine. It involved sophisticated statistical analyses of the results of 40 separate studies similar to Schein's paradigm of *think manager–think male*; of 22 other studies that looked at gender stereotyping in an *agency-communion* paradigm; and of a third group of 7 studies that looked at stereotyping through the lens of occupational stereotyping. The study concluded that a strong masculine stereotype of leadership continues to exist in the workplace and that it will continue to challenge women for some time to come.[68]

Even more recently, a 2016 review of research noted the persistent tendency of gender stereotypes that women are seen as more communal (kind and nurturing) but less agentic (ambitious and dominant) than men. Since leadership is believed to require agency, women are seen as less well suited to the requirements of leadership than men. Furthermore, because women may outwardly display their emotions more than men, people infer that women are more apt to allow their decisions and actions to be "controlled" by their emotions; that is, they are seen as less rational and objective than men.[69] One area where views *do* seem to have changed over time involves women's perceptions of their own roles. In contrast to the earlier studies, women today see as much similarity between "female" and "manager" as between "male" and "manager."[70] To women, at least, being a woman and being a manager are not contradictory.

Believing that one can be both a woman and a manager or leader does not, however, necessarily insulate a woman from feeling unfairly scrutinized and judged by others. Through the impact of **stereotype threat**, the person's awareness of being judged by stereotypes can nonetheless have a deleterious impact on performance (see **Highlight 1.6**).

Stereotype Threat

HIGHLIGHT 1.6

One of the most important concepts in social psychology is a phenomenon known as stereotype threat, which refers to situations in which people feel themselves at risk of being judged by others holding negative stereotypes about them.

Numerous studies, for example, demonstrate how the performance of African American students on certain tests is affected by the ways a test is described to the students. When a test was described as a measure of intellectual ability, African American students typically score lower than other students. When the *same test* was described as nondiagnostic of ability, however, there were no differences between the groups; the Black students did just as well as other students. The stereotype some people hold of the intellectual inferiority of Black students can actually depress Black student performance *when that stereotype is salient* (for example, when a test is described as a measure of intellectual ability). When the stereotype is not salient, however (when the same test was described as not indicative of intellectual ability), the Black students performed much better on it.

Or consider this example: Some white college males were told that a golfing task measured "natural athletic ability" whereas other white male students were given the same task but told nothing about it. Those that were told it measured natural athletic ability performed significantly worse on it than the white males who were told nothing about it. It seems the idea that the task measured natural athletic ability created a threatening situation related to the widespread stereotype in this society that, compared to Blacks, at least, white males have less natural athletic ability.

In a similar manner, stereotype threat can adversely impact the behavior and performance of women in leadership roles. For example, the gender stereotypes that "women take care" and "men take charge" would be most likely to become salient to women—and thus adversely impact their behavior—in situations rife with stereotypical displays of masculinity and competitiveness.

You can get a deeper and more comprehensive understanding of stereotype threat in Claude Steele's wonderful book *Whistling Vivaldi*.

Source: C. M. Steele, *Whistling Vivaldi: How Stereotypes Affect Us and What We Can Do* (New York: Norton, 2010).

In another study of the role of women in management, *Breaking the Glass Ceiling*,[71] researchers documented the lives and careers of 78 of the highest-level women in corporate America. A few years later the researchers followed up with a small sample of those women to discuss any changes that had taken place in their leadership paths. The researchers were struck by the fact that the women were much like the senior men they had worked with in other studies. Qualitatively, they had the same fears: They wanted the best for themselves and for their families. They wanted their companies to succeed. And not surprisingly, they still had a drive to succeed. In some cases (also true for the men), they were beginning to ask questions about life balance—was all the sacrifice and hard work worth it? Were 60-hour workweeks worth the cost to family and self?

More quantitatively, however, the researchers expected to find significant differences between the women who had broken the glass ceiling and the men who were already in leadership positions. After all, the popular literature and some social scientific literature had conditioned them to expect that there is a feminine versus a masculine style of leadership, the feminine style being an outgrowth of a consensus/team-oriented leadership approach. Women, in this view, are depicted as leaders who, when compared to men, are better listeners, more empathic, less analytical, more people oriented, and less aggressive in pursuit of goals.

In examining women in leadership positions, the researchers collected behavioral data, including ratings by both self and others, assessment center data, and their scores on the California Psychological Inventory. Contrary to the stereotypes and popular views, however, there were no statistically significant differences between men's and women's leadership styles. Women and men were equally analytical, people oriented, forceful, goal oriented, empathic, and skilled at listening. There were other differences between the men and women, however, beyond the question of leadership styles. The researchers did find (and these results must be interpreted cautiously because of the relatively small numbers involved) that women had significantly lower well-being scores, their commitment to the organizations they worked for was more guarded than that of their male counterparts, and the women were much more likely to be willing to take career risks associated with going to new or unfamiliar areas of the company where women had not been before.

Continued work with women in corporate leadership positions has both reinforced and clarified these findings. For example, the lower scores for women in general well-being may reflect the inadequacy of their support system for dealing with day-to-day issues of living. This is tied to the reality for many women that, in addition to having roles in their companies, they remain chief caregivers for their families. Further, there may be additional pressures of being visibly identified as proof that the organization has women at the top.

Other types of differences—particularly those around "people issues"—are still not evident. In fact, the hypothesis is that such supposed differences may hinder the opportunities for leadership development of women in the future. For example, turning around a business that is in trouble or starting a new business are two of the most exciting opportunities a developing leader has to test her leadership abilities. If we apply the "women are different" hypothesis, the type of leadership skills needed for successful completion of either of these assignments may leave women off the list of candidates. However, if we accept the hypothesis that women and men are more alike as leaders than they are different, women will be found in equal numbers on the candidate list.

That such exciting opportunities for leadership development may pose a double-edged sword for women, however, is suggested by a variant of the glass ceiling: the **glass cliff**. The glass cliff refers to the intriguing finding that female candidates for an executive position are *more* likely to be hired than equally qualified male candidates when an organization's performance is declining. At first that may seem like good news for women, but the picture is not quite so positive. When an organization's performance is declining, there is inherently an increased risk of failure. The increased likelihood of women being selected in those situations may actually reflect a greater willingness to put women in precarious positions.[72] It could also, of course, represent an increased willingness to take some chances when nothing else seems to be working. In any case, a recent review of the past decade's study of the glass cliff confirmed that it is a "robust and pervasive phenomenon and a significant feature of the organizational landscape for women who achieve high office."[73]

Research on women leaders from medium-sized, nontraditional organizations has shown that successful leaders don't all come from the same mold. Such women tended to be successful by drawing on their shared experience as women, rather than by adhering to the "rules of conduct" by which men in larger and more traditional organizations have been successful. Survey research by Judith Rosener identified several differences in how men and women described their leadership experiences.[74] Men tended to describe themselves in somewhat transactional terms, viewing leadership as an exchange with subordinates for services rendered. They influenced others primarily through their organizational position and authority. The women, by contrast, tended to describe themselves in transformational terms. They helped subordinates develop commitment to broader goals than their own self-interest, and they described their influence more in terms of personal characteristics like charisma and interpersonal skill than mere organizational position.

According to Rosener, such women leaders encouraged participation and shared power and information, but went far beyond what is commonly thought of as participative management. She called it **interactive leadership**. Their leadership self-descriptions reflected an approach based on enhancing others' self-worth and believing that the best performance results when people are excited about their work and feel good about themselves.

How did this interactive leadership style develop? Rosener concluded it was due to these women's socialization experiences and career paths. As we have indicated, the social role expected of women has emphasized that they be cooperative, supportive, understanding, gentle, and service oriented. As they entered the business world, they still found themselves in roles emphasizing these same behaviors. They found themselves in staff, rather than line, positions, and in roles lacking formal authority over others so that they had to accomplish their work without reliance on formal power. What they had to do, in other words, was employ their socially acceptable behavioral repertoire to survive organizationally.

Neither shall you allege the example of the many as an excuse for doing wrong.

Exodus 23.2

What came easily to women turned out to be a survival tactic. Although leaders often begin their careers doing what comes naturally and what fits within the constraints of the job, they also develop their skills and styles over time. The women's use of interactive leadership has its roots in socialization, and the women interviewees believe that it benefits their organizations. Through the course of their careers, they have gained conviction that their style is effective. In fact, for some it was their own success that caused them to formulate their philosophies about what motivates people, how to make good decisions, and what it takes to maximize business performance. Some claim there is even a "female advantage" in leadership stemming from their more collaborative style. Nearly a half-century of research on the subject, however, does not support such a broad generalization.[75, 76] Many factors interact with gender in affecting ratings of leadership effectiveness, including context (for example, whether it is a business or educational situation) and raters (whether a leader is rating herself or himself, or others are rating the leader).

Rosener has called for organizations to expand their definitions of effective leadership—to create a *wider* band of acceptable behavior so that both men and women will be freer to lead in ways that take advantage of their true talents. We discuss stereotype-based "bands of acceptable behavior" further in **Highlight 1.7**.

The Narrow Band of Acceptable Behavior

HIGHLIGHT 1.7

One of the most important factors that seems to impede the advance of women and other minorities into leadership roles is bias. A bias that might be labeled "the narrow band of acceptable behavior" is depicted below.

The characteristics and behaviors in the top right-hand circle are those associated with traditional masculine behavior, and the characteristics and behaviors in the top left-hand circle are those associated with traditional feminine behavior. The narrow band of overlap between the two circles can be thought of as a "hoop" women executives need to pass through.

The concept of a narrow band of acceptable behavior is not limited to women. It may be applied to any individual's deviation from organizationally defined standards (bottom circles). The more a person looks like, acts like, dresses like, and talks like other leaders in the organization, the wider the band of acceptable behavior (the greater the overlap of the two circles). The less one looks like, acts like, dresses like, and talks like other leaders in the organization (some aspects of which, such as gender and race, are beyond a person's control), the narrower the band of acceptable behavior. One implication of this view is that an individual who differs in obvious ways from the prototypical image of a leader (as with gender) has less "wiggle room" available; it's as though there are already one or two strikes against that person. It's like walking a tightrope.

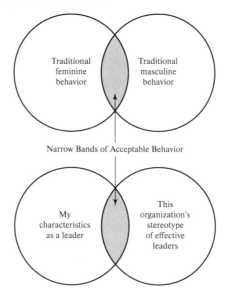

Source: Adapted from A. M. Morrison, R. P. White, and E. Van Velsor, *Breaking the Glass Ceiling* (Reading, MA: Addison-Wesley, 1987).

Aside from questions of possible gender differences in leadership style or leadership effectiveness, there does seem to be a rise in the number of women in leadership positions. This shift is due to several factors.[77]

The first of these is that *women themselves have changed*. That's evident in the ways women's aspirations and attitudes have become more similar to those of men over time. This is illustrated in findings about the career aspirations of female university students;[78] in women's self-reports of traits such as assertiveness, dominance, and masculinity;[79, 80] and in the value that women place on characteristics of work such as freedom, challenge, leadership, prestige, and power.[81] The second factor is that *leadership roles have changed*, particularly with regard to a trend toward less stereotypically masculine characterizations of leadership. Third, *organizational practices have changed*. A large part of this can be attributed to legislation prohibiting gender-based discrimination at work, as well as changes in organizational norms that put a higher priority on results than on an "old boy" network. Finally, the *culture has changed*. This is evident, for example, in the symbolic message often intended by appointment of women to important leadership positions, one representing a departure from past practices and signaling commitment to progressive change.

It also may be evident in evidence-based arguments that women in leadership roles help an organization's bottom line. "Research points to the same conclusion: gender diversity in leadership is good for business (as is diversity in general, for that matter). It's better for financial performance. It inspires more innovation. Yes, it has societal benefit, but it also provides a company with competitive advantage and is considered a key enabler of growth. A recent Credit Suisse report, for example, found that companies where women made up at least 15 percent of senior managers had more than 50 percent higher profitability than those where female representation was less than 10 percent."[82]

Even with these factors contributing to the rise of women in leadership positions, however, those at the top still represent a formidable challenge, as evident in **Highlight 1.8**.

Why Are Women Still Not Reaching the Top?

HIGHLIGHT 1.8

In the business world, women still lag behind men in selection to top positions. Rob Kaiser and Wanda Wallace suggest the explanation may be a bit like the imaginary family scenario described here. Say Dad proposes that the whole family take a vacation to Disney World:

> Mom does all the research and planning: which resort to stay in, when to go to what park, which meal reservations to make, which rides to go on in what order and when to get the fast passes, what clothes to pack from shorts and swimsuits to sweatshirts and parkas, and all the little things it takes to make the vacation a success. In getting it all arranged, Mom got a little stressed out and short-tempered—she may have even hollered at the kids. But everyone had a blast. And they all agreed: Dad had a great idea to go to Disney.

Perhaps you are wondering what this scenario has to do with women executives making it to the top in the workplace? Kaiser and Wallace see a similar pattern playing out both in the preceding scenario and in the careers of many women executives with whom they work.

High-potential women may be rewarded early in their careers for minding the details and getting results. They may show strong command of the technical aspects of their jobs with a nose-to-the-grindstone focus on accomplishing objectives. Almost by default this may lead to perceptions that their strength is not *strategic* in nature. They write,

> We believe that the main reason women are not making it to the top is not because they are too feminine or because they are not sufficiently masculine. It is because they come on a bit too strong and get themselves boxed in carving out a niche by executing someone else's agenda. They get stuck in the technical expert, implementer role and are seen as not strategic enough to lead the entire enterprise.

Source: R. Kaiser and W. T. Wallace, "Changing the Narrative on Why Women Aren't Reaching the Top," *Talent Quarterly* 3 (2014), pp. 15-20.

There Is No Simple Recipe for Effective Leadership

To fill the gaps between leadership research and practice, this book critically reviews major findings about the nature of leadership and provides practical advice for improving leadership. As our first step in that journey, **Chapter 2** describes how leadership develops through experience. The remainder of the book uses the leader–follower–situation interaction model as a framework for organizing and discussing various theories and research findings related to leadership. In this study, it will become clear that although there is no simple recipe for effective leadership, there *are* many different paths to effective leadership.

Little things affect little minds.

Benjamin Disraeli, British prime minister, 1874-1880

As noted previously, it is important to understand how the three domains of leadership interact—how the leader, the followers, and the situation are all part of the leadership process. Understanding their interaction is necessary before you can draw valid conclusions from the leadership you observe around you. When you

The historic milestone of Yeager becoming the first woman to command an American combat division came nearly a quarter century *after* a government-financed study determined that "the integration of women into the armed forces did not degrade readiness, cohesion, and morale, despite dire warnings that all three would suffer." And there have been many other milestones *between* that report and now, including that of three women in 2015 who graduated from U.S. Army Ranger School facing identical standards for evaluation as the men in the school (of 19 who entered the grueling Ranger training). Today, at least a dozen women have graduated from Ranger training.

To this day, the integration of women into combat roles continues to be the official policy of the U.S. Department of Defense, but that doesn't mean it is easy. Among other things, the military services face an uphill battle to recruit women who are interested and able to serve in combat roles. And not entirely surprisingly, the various services are approaching the challenge in their own unique ways because of their own unique service identities. The Navy and Air Force, for example, face somewhat different situations than the Army and Marine Corps since their service members (Navy and USAF) tend to be further removed from direct combat. Nonetheless, women pilots now fly fighters in combat operations.

1. Do you think there may have been inappropriate political influences contributing to Yeager's selection to command the 40th Infantry Division?

2. Do you think her "command style" is fundamentally any different from the men who have commanded the division in the past?

3. Do you believe women have served effectively in combat situations at any time throughout history?

4. Do you think others in the division might experience any particular challenges because their commander is a woman?

Sources: J. Bacon, "Meet Brig. Gen. Laura Yeager, First Woman to Lead Army Infantry Division," *USA Today*, June 9, 2019; and "Laura Yeager, General," *The Economist*, July 6, 2019, pp. 20–21, www.economist.com/united-states/2019/07/06/laura-yeager-general.

Endnotes

1. S. A. Rosenthal, *National Leadership Index 2011: A National Study of Confidence in Leadership* (Cambridge, MA: Center for Public Leadership, Harvard Kennedy School, Harvard University, 2012).

2. Harris Poll, Archival Data, 2013. Retrieved from http://www.harrisinteractive.com/Insights/HarrisVault.aspx.

3. P. P. Read, *Alive* (New York: J. B. Lippincott, 1974).

4. Ibid., p. 77.

5. J. R. Meindl and S. B. Ehrlich, "The Romance of Leadership and the Evaluation of Organizational Performance," *Academy of Management Journal* 30 (1987), pp. 90–109.

6. W. G. Bennis, "Leadership Theory and Administrative Behavior: The Problem of Authority," *Administrative Science Quarterly* 4 (1959), pp. 259–60.

7. F. Fiedler, *A Theory of Leadership Effectiveness* (New York: McGraw-Hill, 1967).

8. R. K. Merton, *Social Theory and Social Structure* (New York: Free Press, 1957).

9. C. F. Roach and O. Behling, "Functionalism: Basis for an Alternate Approach to the Study of Leadership," in *Leaders and Managers: International Perspectives on Managerial Behavior and Leadership*, eds. J. G. Hunt, D. M. Hosking, C. A. Schriesheim, and R. Stewar (Elmsford, NY: Pergamon, 1984).

10. D. P. Campbell, *Campbell Leadership Index Manual* (Minneapolis: National Computer Systems, 1991).

11. R. C. Ginnett, "Team Effectiveness Leadership Model: Identifying Leverage Points for Change," *Proceedings of the 1996 National Leadership Institute Conference* (College Park, MD: National Leadership Institute, 1996).

12. R. Hogan, G. Curphy, R. B. Kaiser, and T. Chamorro-Premuzic, "Leadership in Organizations," in *The Sage Handbook of Industrial, Work, and Organizational Psychology.* Vol. 2: *Organizational Psychology*, eds. N. Anderson, D. S. Ones, H. K. Sinangil, and C. Viswesvaran (London: Sage, in press).

13. M. D. Mumford, S. J. Zaccaro, F. D. Harding, T. O. Jacobs, and E. A. Fleishman, "Leadership Skills for a Changing World," *Leadership Quarterly* 11, no. 1 (2000), pp. 11–35.

14. F. Luthans, "Successful vs. Effective Real Managers," *The Academy of Management Executive* 2 (1988), pp. 127–32.

15. R. Carucci, "A 10-Year Study Reveals What Great Executives Know and Do," *Harvard Business Review*, January 2016, pp. 2–5.

16. B. M. Bass, *Bass and Stogdill's Handbook of Leadership*, 3rd ed. (New York: Free Press, 1990).

17. J. E. Dinh, R. G. Lord, W. L. Gardner, J. D. Meuser, R. C. Liden, and J. Hu, "Leadership Theory and Research in the New Millennium: Current Theoretical Trends and Changing Perspectives," *Leadership Quarterly* 25 (2014), pp. 36–62.

18. M. B. Eberly, M. D. Johnson, M. Hernandez, and B. J. Avolio. "An Integrative Process Model of Leadership: Examining Loci, Mechanisms, and Event Cycles," *The American Psychologist* 68, no. 6 (2013), pp. 427–43.

19. H. C. Foushee, "Dyads and Triads at 35,000 Feet: Factors Affecting Group Process and Aircrew Performance," *American Psychologist* 39 (1984), pp. 885–93.

20. J. R. Meindl, S. B. Ehrlich, and J. M. Dukerich, "The Romance of Leadership," *Administrative Science Quarterly* 30 (1985), pp. 78–102.

21. W. G. Bennis and B. Nanus, *Leaders: The Strategies for Taking Charge* (New York: Harper & Row, 1985).

22. J. R. Meindl, S. B. Ehrlich, and J. M. Dukerich, "The Romance of Leadership," *Administrative Science Quarterly* 30 (1985), pp. 78–102.

23. W. G. Bennis and B. Nanus, *Leaders: The Strategies for Taking Charge* (New York: Harper & Row, 1985).

24. A. Zaleznik, "The Leadership Gap," *Washington Quarterly* 6, no. 1 (1983), pp. 32–39.

25. W. G. Bennis, *On Becoming a Leader* (Reading, MA: Addison-Wesley, 1989).

26. B. Sutton, "Management vs. Leadership: A Dangerous but Accurate Distinction," LinkedIn, December 16, 2013, www.linkedin.com/today/post/article/20131216160520-15893932-management-vs-leadership-a-dangerous-but-accurate-distinction?trk=tod-home.

27. Zaleznik, "The Leadership Gap."

28. P. Slovic and B. Fischoff, "On the Psychology of Experimental Surprises," *Journal of Experimental Social Psychology* 22 (1977), pp. 544–51.

29. G. Wood, "The Knew-It-All-Along Effect," *Journal of Experimental Psychology: Human Perception and Performance* 4 (1979), pp. 345–53.

30. P. E. Lazarsfeld, "The American Soldier: An Expository Review," *Public Opinion Quarterly* 13 (1949), pp. 377–404.

31. For example, A. Tellegen, D. T. Lykken, T. J. Bouchard, K. J. Wilcox, N. L. Segal, and S. Rich, "Personality Similarity in Twins Reared Apart and Together," *Journal of Personality and Social Psychology* 54 (1988), pp. 1031–39.

32. Fiedler, *A Theory of Leadership Effectiveness.*

33. E. P. Hollander, *Leadership Dynamics: A Practical Guide to Effective Relationships* (New York: Free Press, 1978).

34. G. B. Graen and J. F. Cashman, "A Role-Making Model of Leadership in Formal Organizations: A Developmental Approach," in *Leadership Frontiers*, eds. J. G. Hunt and L. L. Larson (Kent, OH: Kent State University Press, 1975).

35. R. M. Stogdill, "Personal Factors Associated with Leadership: A Review of the Literature," *Journal of Psychology* 25 (1948), pp. 35–71.

36. R. M. Stogdill, *Handbook of Leadership* (New York: Free Press, 1974).

37. R. T. Hogan, G. J. Curphy, and J. Hogan, "What We Know about Personality: Leadership and Effectiveness," *American Psychologist* 49 (1994), pp. 493–504.

38. R. G. Lord, C. L. DeVader, and G. M. Allinger, "A Meta-Analysis of the Relationship between Personality Traits and Leadership Perceptions: An Application of Validity Generalization Procedures," *Journal of Applied Psychology* 71 (1986), pp. 402–10.

39. R. M. Kanter, *The Change Masters* (New York: Simon & Schuster, 1983).

40. E. D. Baltzell, *Puritan Boston and Quaker Philadelphia* (New York: Free Press, 1980).

41. E. P. Hollander and L. R. Offermann, "Power and Leadership in Organizations," *American Psychologist* 45 (1990), pp. 179–89.

42. S. D. Baker, "Followership: The Theoretical Foundation of a Contemporary Construct," *Journal of Leadership & Organizational Studies* 14, no. 1 (2007), p. 51.

43. Baker, "Followership."

44. J. M. Burns, *Leadership* (New York: Harper & Row, 1978).

45. B. M. Bass, *Bass and Stogdill's Handbook of Leadership*, 3rd ed. (New York: Free Press, 1990).

46. Stogdill, *Handbook of Leadership.*

47. C. D. Sutton and R. W. Woodman, "Pygmalion Goes to Work: The Effects of Supervisor Expectations in the Retail Setting," *Journal of Applied Psychology* 74 (1989), pp. 943–50.

48. L. I. Moore, "The FMI: Dimensions of Follower Maturity," *Group and Organizational Studies* 1 (1976), pp. 203–22.

49. T. A. Scandura, G. B. Graen, and M. A. Novak, "When Managers Decide Not to Decide Autocratically: An Investigation of Leader-Member Exchange and Decision Influence," *Journal of Applied Psychology* 52 (1986), pp. 135–47.

50. C. A. Sales, E. Levanoni, and D. H. Saleh, "Satisfaction and Stress as a Function of Job Orientation, Style of Supervision, and the Nature of the Task," *Engineering Management International* 2 (1984), pp. 145–53.

51. Adapted from K. Macrorie, *Twenty Teachers* (Oxford: Oxford University Press, 1984).

52. J. M. Kouzes and B. Z. Posner, *The Leadership Challenge: How to Get Extraordinary Things Done in Organizations* (San Francisco: Jossey-Bass, 1987).

53. R. Lippitt, "The Changing Leader–Follower Relationships of the 1980s," *Journal of Applied Behavioral Science* 18 (1982), pp. 395–403.

54. P. Block, *Stewardship* (San Francisco: Berrett-Koehler, 1992).

55. G. F. Tanoff and C. B. Barlow, "Leadership and Followership: Same Animal, Different Spots?" *Consulting Psychology Journal: Practice and Research*, Summer 2002, pp. 157–65.

56. P. M. Senge, *The Fifth Discipline: The Art and Practice of the Learning Organization* (New York: Doubleday/Currency, 1990).

57. M. Uhl-Bien, R. E. Riggio, K. B. Lowe, and M. K.Carsten, "Followership Theory: A Review and Research Agenda," *Leadership Quarterly* 25 (2014), pp.83–104.

58. V. Vroom and A. G. Jago, "The Role of the Situation in Leadership," *American Psychologist* 62, no. 1 (2007), pp. 17–24.

59. Vroom and Jago, "The Role of the Situation in Leadership."

60. For example, M. Conlin, "The New Gender Gap: From Kindergarten to Grad School, Boys Are Becoming the Second Sex," *Business Week*, May 26, 2003.

61. GAO, *Women in Management: Female Managers' Representation, Characteristics, and Pay*, GAO-10-1064T (Washington, DC: September 28, 2010).

62. Catalyst, *Women CEOs of the S&P 500* (February 11, 2020), www.catalyst.org/research/women-ceos-of-the-sp-500.

63. H. Ibarra, N. M. Carter, and C. Silva, "Why Men Still Get More Promotions Than Women," *Harvard Business Review*, September 2010, pp. 80–85.

64. D. Bevelander and M. J. Page, "Ms. Trust: Gender, Networks and Trust—Implications for Management and Education," *Academy of Management Learning & Education* 10, no. 4 (2011), pp. 623–42.

65. V. Schein, "The Relationship between Sex Role Stereotypes and Requisite Management Characteristics," *Journal of Applied Psychology* 57 (1973), pp. 95–100.

66. V. Schein, "Relationships between Sex Role Stereotypes and Requisite Management Characteristics among Female Managers, *Journal of Applied Psychology* 60 (1975), pp. 340–44.

67. V. Schein and R. Mueller, "Sex Role Stereotyping and Requisite Management Characteristics: A Cross Cultural Look," *Journal of Organizational Behavior* 13 (1992), pp. 439–47.

68. A. M. Koenig, A. H. Eagly, A. A. Mitchell, and T. Ristikari, "Are Leader Stereotypes Masculine? A Meta-analysis of Three Research Paradigms," *Psychological Bulletin* 137, no. 4 (2011), pp. 616–42.

69. V. L. Brescoll, "Leadingwith Their Hearts? How Gender Stereotypes of Emotion Lead to Biased Evaluationsof Female Leaders," *Leadership Quarterly* 27, no. 3 (2016), pp. 415–28.

70. O. C. Brenner, J. Tomkiewicz, and V. E. Schein, "The Relationship between Sex Role Stereotypes and Requisite Management Characteristics Revisited," *Academy of Management Journal* 32 (1989), pp. 662–69.

71. A. M. Morrison, R. P. White, and E. Van Velsor, *Breaking the Glass Ceiling* (Reading, MA: Addison-Wesley, 1987).

72. S. A. Haslam and M. K. Ryan, "The Road tothe Glass Cliff: Differences in the Perceived Suitability of Men and Women for Leadership Positions in Succeeding and Failing Organizations," *The Leadership Quarterly* 19 (2008), pp. 530–46.

73. M. K. Ryan, S. A. Haslam, T. Morgenroth, F. Rink, J. Stoker, and K. Peters, "Getting on Top of the Glass Cliff: Reviewing a Decade of Evidence, Explanations, and Impact," *Leadership Quarterly* 27 (2016), pp. 446–55.

74. J. B. Rosener, "Ways Women Lead," *Harvard Business Review* 68 (1990), pp. 119–25.

75. R. Williams, "Why Women May Be Better Leaders Than Men," *Psychology Today*, December 2012. Retrieved from www.psychologytoday.com/blog/wired-success/201212/why-women-may-be-better-leaders-men

76. S. C. Paustian-Underdahl, L. S. Walker, and D. J. Woehr, "Gender and Perceptions of Leadership Effectiveness: A Meta-Analysis of Contextual Moderators," *Journal of Applied Psychology* 99, no. 6 (2014), pp. 1129–45.

77. A. H. Eagly and L. L. Carli, "The Female Leadership Advantage: An Evaluation of the Evidence," *Leadership Quarterly* 14 (2003), pp. 807–34.

78. A. W. Astin, S. A. Parrrott, W. S. Korn, and L. J. Sax, *The American Freshman: Thirty Year Trends* (Los Angeles: Higher Education Research Institute, University of California, 1997).

79. J. M. Twenge, "Changes in Masculine and Feminine Traits over Time: A Meta-analysis," *Sex Roles* 36 (1997), pp. 305–25.

80. J. M. Twenge, "Changes in Women's Assertiveness in Response to Status and Roles: A Cross-Temporal Meta-analysis, 1931–1993," *Journal of Personality and Social Psychology* 81 (2001), pp. 133–45.

81. A. M. Konrad, J. E. Ritchie, Jr., P. Lieb, and E. Corrigall, "Sex Differences and Similarities in Job Attribute Preferences: A Meta-analysis," *Psychological Bulletin* 126 (2000), pp. 593–641.

82. J. Ames, C. Coplen, and R. Mallory, "Women Leaders: How We Got Here," Stuart Spencer (online), 2019, www.spencerstuart.com/research-and-insight/women-leaders-how-we-got-here.

CHAPTER 2

Leader Development

Introduction

In **Chapter 1** we discussed the importance of using multiple perspectives to analyze various leadership situations. It's also true that there are multiple paths by which one's own leadership is developed. That's what this chapter is about: how to become a better leader.

As an overview, we begin this chapter by presenting a general model that describes how we learn from experience. Next we describe how perceptions can affect a leader's interpretation of, and actions in response to, a particular leadership situation and why reflection is important to leadership development. The chapter also examines several specific mechanisms often used to help leaders become *better* leaders.

Perhaps a word here might be useful about titling this chapter *leader development*. We have done so deliberately to distinguish the phrase from *leadership development*. Although the two may seem synonymous to the reader, they have come to be treated by scholars and practitioners in the field as having distinct meanings. That wasn't always the case. Until a decade or so ago, scholars and practitioners, too, considered them essentially synonymous. Gradually, however, it became useful to use *leader development* when referring to methods intended to facilitate growth in an *individual's* perspectives or skills. For example, training designed to develop skill in giving feedback to another person would be considered leader development. Over the past decade, though, the term *leadership* has taken on a somewhat richer meaning transcending a focus on individual-level characteristics and skills even when the focus is on developing such qualities in *many* individuals. Paralleling a gradual shift in understanding that leadership is a process in which many people in an organization share in complex and interdependent ways (as we discussed in **Chapter 1**), the term *leadership development* has come to designate a focus on developing shared properties of whole groups or social systems such as the degree of trust among all the members of a team or department, or on enhancing the reward systems in an organization to better encourage collaborative behavior.[1] Although such things are addressed frequently throughout this text, the focus of this chapter is on processes and methods designed to foster individual-level growth—hence, the choice of chapter title.

And one more thing before we get into those substantive parts of the chapter: It might be useful to start with a fundamental question about the value of an academic course in leadership. Before the authors wrote this textbook, we and other colleagues taught an undergraduate course in leadership required of all cadets at the U.S. Air Force Academy. Undergraduate courses in leadership are fairly common now, but they weren't in the 1980s. For many decades the U.S. Air Force Academy and the U.S. Military Academy were among the few undergraduate schools offering such courses.

Because undergraduate leadership courses were somewhat uncommon then, the idea of an academic course in leadership was a novel idea to many faculty members from other departments. Some were openly skeptical that leadership was an appropriate course for an academic department to offer. It was a common experience for us to be asked, "Do you really think you can *teach* leadership?" Usually this was asked in a tone of voice that made it clear the questioner took it for granted that leadership couldn't be taught. Colleagues teaching leadership courses at other institutions have found themselves in similar situations.

Over time, we formulated our own response to this question, and it still reflects a core belief we continue to hold. Not coincidentally, that belief has been hinted at in the subtitle to every edition of our text: *Enhancing the Lessons of Experience*. Let us describe how that idea represents the answer to those skeptical questioners, and also how reflecting on their questions shaped our thinking about one important objective of an academic course in leadership.

Just to be clear, we *don't* disagree completely with the premise of those skeptical questioners. We don't believe that merely taking a one-semester college course in leadership will make one a better leader. However, we believe strongly that it can lay a valuable foundation to becoming a better leader over time.

Here's our reasoning. If you accept that leadership can be learned (rather than just "being born" in a person), and if you also believe that the most powerful lessons about leadership come from your own experience, then the matter boils down to the process of how you learn from experience. If one important factor in learning from experience pertains to how complex or multifaceted your conceptual lenses are for construing experience, then it's no big stretch to claim that becoming familiar with the complex variables that affect leadership gives you a greater variety of ways to make sense of the leadership situations you confront in your own life. In that way, completing a college course in leadership may not make you a better leader directly and immediately, but actively mastering the concepts in the course can nonetheless *accelerate the rate at which you learn from the natural experiences you have* during and subsequent to your course.

> *Leadership, like swimming, cannot be learned by reading about it.*
>
> **Henry Mintzberg, scholar**

For efficiency, organizations that value developing their leaders usually create intentional pathways for doing so. In other words, leader development in most large organizations is not left to osmosis. There typically are structured and planned approaches to developing internal leaders or leaders-to-be. Formal training is the most common approach to developing leaders, even when research consistently shows that it's not the most effective method. It should not be surprising, then, that organizational members are often not satisfied with the opportunities generally provided within their organizations for developing as leaders. A recent study of more than 4,500 leaders from over 900 organizations found that only half were satisfied with their developmental opportunities.[2]

Findings like that do not prove that leader development opportunities are inherently inadequate or poorly designed. It must be remembered, for example, that developmental opportunities by their nature typically are not free despite whatever long-term advantages might accrue from them for both the individual and the organization. It would seem desirable, then, to ensure that developmental opportunities are provided based on our best understanding of leader development processes. Morgan McCall has summarized some of the key things we've learned about leader development over the past several decades in these seven general points:[3]

1. To the extent that leadership is learned at all, it is learned from experience. In fact, about 70 percent of variance in a person's effectiveness in a leadership role is due to the results of her experience; only 30 percent is due to heredity.

2. Certain experiences have greater developmental impact than others in shaping a person's effectiveness as a leader.

3. What makes such experiences valuable are the challenges they present to the person.

4. Different types of experience teach different leadership lessons.

5. Some of the most useful experiences for learning leadership come in the jobs we're assigned to, and they can be designed to better enhance their developmental richness.

6. Obstacles exist to getting all the developmental experiences we may desire, but we can still get many of them through our own diligence and with some organizational support.

7. Learning to be a better leader is a lifelong pursuit with many twists and turns.

> *Leadership and learning are indispensable to each other.*
>
> **John F. Kennedy, U.S. president, 1961–1963**

The Action–Observation–Reflection Model

Consider for a moment what a young person might learn from spending a year working in two very different environments: as a staff assistant in the U.S. Congress or as a carpenter on a house construction crew. Each activity offers a rich store of leadership lessons. Working in Congress, for example, would provide opportunities to observe political leaders both onstage in the public eye and backstage in more private moments. It would provide opportunities to see members of Congress interacting with different constituencies, to see them in political defeat and political victory, and to see a range of leadership styles. A young person could also learn a lot by working on a building crew as it turned plans and materials into the reality of a finished house: watching the coordination with subcontractors, watching skilled craftspeople train younger ones, watching the leader's reactions to problems and delays, watching the leader set standards and ensure quality work. At the same time, a person could work in either environment and *not* grow much if he or she were not disposed to. Making the most of experience is key to developing your leadership ability. In other words, leadership development depends not just on the kinds of experiences you have but also on how you use them to foster growth. A study of successful executives found that a key quality that characterized them was an "extraordinary tenacity in extracting something worthwhile from their experience and in seeking experiences rich in opportunities for growth."[4]

But how do you do that? Is someone really more likely to get the lessons of experience by looking for them? Why is it not enough just to be there? Experiential learning theorists, such as Kolb, believe people learn more from their experiences when they spend time thinking about them.[5] These ideas are extended to leadership in the **action–observation–reflection (A-O-R) model**, depicted in **Figure 2.1**, which shows that leadership development is enhanced when the experience involves three different processes: action, observation, and reflection. If a person acts but does not observe the consequences of her actions or reflect on their significance and meaning, then it makes little sense to say she has learned from an experience. Because some people neither observe the consequences of their actions nor reflect on how they could change their actions to become better leaders, leadership development through experience may be better understood as the growth resulting from repeated movements through all three phases rather than merely in terms of some objective dimension like time (such as how long one has been on the job). We believe the most productive way to develop as a leader is to travel along the **spiral of experience** depicted in **Figure 2.1**.

Perhaps an example from Colin Powell's life will clarify how the spiral of experience pertains to leadership development. Powell held positions at the highest levels of U.S. military and civilian leadership as Chairman of the Joint Chiefs of Staff and U.S. Secretary of State, but in 1963 he was a 26-year-old officer who had just returned to the United States from a combat tour in Vietnam. His next assignment would be to attend a month-long advanced airborne Ranger course. Near the end of the course, he was to parachute with other troops from a helicopter. As the senior officer on the helicopter, Powell had responsibility for ensuring it went well. Early in the flight he shouted for everyone to make sure their static lines were secure—these are the cables that automatically pull the parachutes open when people jump. Nearing the jump site, he yelled for the men to check their hookups one more time. Here are his words describing what happened next:

> Then, like a fussy old woman, I started checking each line myself, pushing my way through the crowded bodies, running my hand along the cable and up to each man's chute. To my alarm, one hook belonging to a sergeant was loose. I shoved the dangling line in his face, and he gasped. . . . This man would have stepped out of the door of the helo and dropped like a rock.[6]

What did Powell learn from this experience?

> Moments of stress, confusion, and fatigue are exactly when mistakes happen. And when everyone else's mind is dulled or distracted the leader must be doubly vigilant. "Always check small things" was becoming another one of my rules.[7]

Let us examine this incident in light of the A-O-R model. *Action* refers to Powell's multiple calls for the parachutists to check their lines. We might speculate from his self-description ("like a fussy old woman") that Powell might have felt slightly uncomfortable with such repeated emphasis on checking the lines, even though he persisted in the behavior. Perhaps you, too, sometimes have acted in a certain manner (or were forced to by your parents), despite feeling a little embarrassed about it, and then, if it was successful, felt more comfortable the next time acting the same way. That seems to be what happened with Powell here. The *observation* phase refers to Powell's shocked realization of the potentially fatal accident that would have occurred had he *not* double-checked the static lines. And the *reflection* phase refers to the lesson Powell drew from the experience: "Always check the small things." Even though this was not a totally new insight, its importance was

FIGURE 2.1   The Spiral of Experience

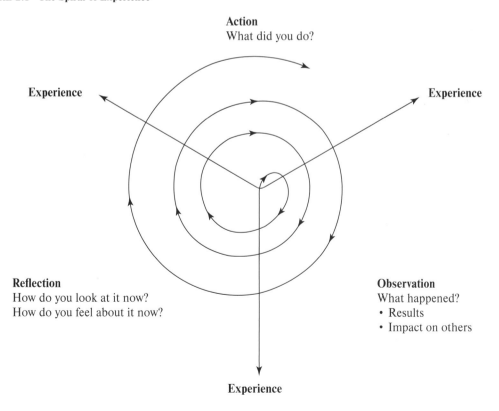

strongly reinforced by this experience. In a real sense Powell was "spiraling" through a lesson he'd learned from other experiences too, but embracing it even more this time, making it part of his style.

We also should note that Powell himself described his learning in a manner consistent with our interactional framework. He emphasized the situational importance of the leader's attention to detail, especially during moments of stress, confusion, and fatigue, when mistakes may be most likely to happen. Finally, it's worth noting that throughout Powell's autobiography he discusses many lessons he learned from experience. A key to his success was his ability to keep learning throughout his career.

The Key Role of Perception in the Spiral of Experience

Experience is not just a matter of what events happen to you; it also depends on how you perceive those events. Perception affects all three phases of the action–observation–reflection model and thus plays an important role in what anyone will extract from a leadership course or from any leadership situation. Human beings are not passive recorders of experiences that happen to them; rather, people actively shape and construct their experiences. To better understand how perception affects experience, we will examine its role in each part of the A-O-R model. We begin with the part that seems to correspond most directly with perception—the observation phase. In **Highlight 2.1** you might discover something about your observational skills and how lucky you think you are.

On Being Observant and Lucky and Learning from Experience

HIGHLIGHT 2.1

It's often said that some people have all the luck. Do you think that's true—are some people luckier than others? Richard Wiseman, a professor at the University of Hertfordshire, has written a book about just that question, and his findings are relevant to the role observation plays in our spiral of experience.

In one of his experiments, Wiseman placed advertisements in national newspapers asking for people to contact him who felt either consistently lucky or consistently unlucky. In one experiment, he gave both self-described lucky and unlucky people a newspaper to read and asked them to look it over and tell him how many photographs were inside. Halfway through the paper he'd put a half-page message with two-inch lettering saying, "Tell the experimenter you have seen this and win $250."

The advertisement was staring everyone in the face, but the unlucky people tended to miss it whereas the lucky people tended to notice it. One reason may be related to the fact that Wiseman claims unlucky people are somewhat more anxious than lucky people, and that might disrupt their ability to notice things that are unexpected.

How observant are *you,* and might developing your own observation skills help you learn from experience more effectively?

Source: R. Wiseman, *The Luck Factor* (New York: Miramax Books, 2003).

Perception and Observation

Observation and perception both deal with attending to events around us. Both seem to take place spontaneously and effortlessly, so it is easy to regard them as passive processes. Our usual mental images of the perceptual process reflect this implicit view. For example, it is a common misconception that the eye operates essentially like the film in a continuously running camera. The fallacy of this passive view of perception is that it assumes we attend to all aspects of a situation equally. However, we do not see everything that happens in a particular leadership situation, nor do we hear everything. Instead we are selective in what we attend to and what we, in turn, perceive. A phenomenon that demonstrates this selectivity is called **perceptual set**. Perceptual sets can influence any of our senses, and they are the tendency or bias to perceive one thing and not another. Many factors can trigger a perceptual set, such as feelings, needs, prior experience, and expectations. Its role in distorting what we hear proved a costly lesson when a sympathetic airline pilot told his depressed copilot, "Cheer up!" The copilot thought the pilot had said, "Gear up," and raised the wheels while the plane was still on the ground.[8] Try your own ability to overcome perceptual set with the following exercise. Read through this narrative passage several times:

> FINISHED FILES ARE THE RESULT OF YEARS OF SCIENTIFIC STUDY COMBINED WITH THE EXPERIENCE OF MANY YEARS.

Make sure you have read it to yourself several times *before going any further*. Now go back to the text and count the number of times the letter *F* appears.

How many did you count? Three? Four? Five? Six? Most people do not get the correct answer (six) the first time. The most frequent count is three; perhaps that was how many you saw. If you did not find six, go back and try again. The most common error in this seemingly trivial task is overlooking the three times the word *of* appears. People easily overlook it because the word *of* has a *V* sound, not an *F* sound. Most people unconsciously make the task an auditory search task and listen for the sound of *F* rather than look for the shape of *F*; hence, they find three *F*s rather than six. Listening for the sound constitutes a counterproductive perceptual set for this task, and having read the passage several times before counting the *F*s only exaggerates this tendency. Another reason people overlook the word *of* in this passage is that the first task was to *read* the passage several times. Because most of us are accomplished readers, we tend to ignore small words like *of*–they disappear from our perceptual set. Then, when we are asked to count the number of *F*s, we have already defined the passage as a reading task, so the word *of* is really not there for us to count.

> It's not what we don't know that hurts, it's what we know that ain't so.
>
> **Will Rogers**

There are strong parallels between this example of a perceptual set and the perceptual sets that come into play when we are enrolled in a leadership course or observe a leadership situation. For example, your instructor for this class may dress unstylishly, and you may be prejudiced in thinking that poor dressers generally do not make good leaders. Because of your biases, you may discount or not attend to some things your instructor has to say about leadership. This would be unfortunate because your instructor's taste in clothes has little to do with his or her ability to teach (which is, after all, a kind of leadership).

A similar phenomenon takes place when one expects to find mostly negative things about another person (such as a problem employee). Such an expectation becomes a perceptual set to look for the negative and look past the positive things in the process. Stereotypes about gender, race, and the like represent powerful impediments to learning because they function as filters that distort one's observations. For example, if you do not believe women or minorities are as successful as white males in influencing others, you may be biased to identify or remember only instances when a woman or minority leader failed, and discount or forget instances when women or minority members succeeded as leaders. Unfortunately we all have similar biases, although we are usually unaware of them. Often we become aware of our perceptual sets only when we spend time reflecting about the content of a leadership training program or a particular leadership situation. **Highlight 2.2** describes yet another way our "observations" may be less objective than we think—and a way you can try to improve them. And **Highlight 2.3** encourages you to practice observing using various kinds of "lenses."

Can You Become a Better Leader by Learning to Draw Your Hand?

HIGHLIGHT 2.2

The title of this Highlight may seem preposterous at first, but please withhold judgment for a moment and read on.

In developing their craft, visual artists must learn to see the world as it is; truly seeing the world in its complexity, however, is more difficult than it seems. After all, seeing the world around us feels so effortless that we generally assume that "what we see is what there is." In fact, however, the fact that we "know" what things look like—from hands to horses to bowls of fruit and so on—actually poses obstacles for most of us to accurately drawing or painting them.

Nancy Adler, an artist as well as a leadership expert, sees parallels between "learning to see" in the physical world and learning to see —that is, to accurately observe—the organizational world. She says that the discipline of learning to draw the contours of any object you are looking at (for example, your own hand) "forces you to see what is actually there, rather than allowing you to impose a caricature of what you imagine the object to look like. As you attempt to depict your hand, for example, contour drawing compels you to see your particular hand, as opposed to some semblance of what hands in general look like."

And she relates this to learning to see leadership more accurately too: "In the context of leadership . . . drawing gives us back the capacity to perceive uniqueness—for example, the dynamics of a specific company at a particular moment in time, rather than a composite of how most comparable companies act in similar situations. This type of close attention is particularly powerful for highly experienced leaders. It gives them back the ability to combine their experience-based expectations with a capacity to see the novelty in the situations currently confronting them."

Source: N. J. Adler, "Finding Beauty in a Fractured World: Art Inspires Leaders—Leaders Change the World," *Academy of Management Review* 40, no. 3 (2015), pp. 480–94.

Observing through Various "Lenses"

Highlight 2.3

There are various kinds of lenses that aid eyesight. Here are some ways that your observational skills can be enhanced by becoming mindful of ways to use different "lenses" to assist your ability to see the world.

Binoculars

Binoculars help you see things that are so far away you can't see them as well as you'd like.

Observing "with binoculars" involves looking at things far removed from you—a kind of environmental scanning for what might be worth looking at more closely with other kinds of glasses. It involves stepping back from the situation and choosing a vantage point to better observe the overall scene; looking "with binoculars" establishes context.

Bifocals

Bifocals provide two different views of any situation. With actual bifocals (if you need them!), you can clearly see things both far away as well as very close to your face. One of the authors, for example, uses bifocals when he's both reading and watching TV at more-or-less the same time. Observing "with bifocals" encourages you to overcome bias by always looking for alternate or contrasting perspectives by which to view a scene.

Magnifying Glasses

Magnifying glasses let you examine small details of something that otherwise seem nearly invisible. It lets you see aspects of a situation that might be so small as to seem negligible or not meaningful. Observing "with a magnifying glass" helps you focus on items of critical importance. It is a way of looking that helps you clearly attend to what is most significant.

Rose-Colored Glasses

The idea of looking through rose-colored glasses typically suggests that one is viewing a situation in an unrealistically favorable light. But "observing through rose-colored glasses" as an intentional act of seeing opportunities and not being being distracted or deceived by obvious flaws can prove very helpful. It can help you see "the right idea" behind a flawed action. It is a way of looking that learns from mistakes and failure.

Blindfolds

Blindfolds, of course, *prevent* us from seeing and thus "observing with a blindfold" (or with eyes closed) is fundamentally different from the other ways of observing noted above. You can think of it as seeing with the mind's eye, maybe essentially similar to the reflection stage of our A-O-R model. It reminds you to be mindful of *what* has been seen—or not; and of *how* it had been seen—or not. It can help you summon what has already been seen or noticed in order to reflect on why something was missed or misunderstood. It's the way of thinking that can actually reinforce the other ways of looking.

Source: J. Gilmore, "Observational Skills: Eye-openers for Observation," *Strategy & Leadership* 45 (2017), pp. 20–26.

Perception and Reflection

Success is a lousy teacher. It seduces smart people into thinking they can't lose.

Bill Gates

Perceptual sets influence what we attend to and what we observe. In addition, perception also influences the next phase of the spiral of experience—reflection—because reflection is how we interpret our observations. Perception is inherently an interpretive, or a meaning-making, activity. An important aspect of this is a process called **attribution**.

Attributions are the explanations we develop for the characteristics, behaviors, or actions to which we attend. For example, if you see Julie fail in an attempt to get others to form a study group, you are likely to attribute the cause of the failure to dispositional factors within Julie. In other words, you are likely to attribute the failure to form a study group to Julie's intelligence, personality, physical appearance, or some other factor even though factors beyond her control could have played a major part. This tendency to overestimate the dispositional causes of behavior and underestimate the environmental causes when others fail is called the

fundamental attribution error.[9] People prefer to explain others' behavior on the basis of personal attributions even when obvious situational factors may fully account for the behavior.

> *Common sense is the collection of prejudices acquired by age 18.*
>
> **Albert Einstein**

By contrast, if *you* attempted to get others to form a study group and failed, you would be more likely to blame factors in the situation for the failure (there was not enough time, or the others were not interested, or they would not be good to study with). This reflects a **self-serving bias**[10]—the tendency to make external attributions (blame the situation) for one's own failures yet make internal attributions (take credit) for one's successes. A third factor that affects the attribution process is called the **actor/observer difference**.[11] This refers to the fact that people who are observing an action are much more likely than the actor to make the fundamental attribution error. Consider, for example, a student who gets a bad score on an exam. The person sitting next to her (an observer) would tend to attribute the bad score to *internal* characteristics (not very bright, weak in this subject) whereas the student herself would be more likely to attribute the bad score to *external* factors (the professor graded unfairly). Putting these factors together, each of us tends to see our own success as due to our intelligence, personality, or physical abilities, but others' success as more attributable to situational factors or to luck.

We note in concluding this section that reflection also involves higher functions like evaluation and judgment, not just perception and attribution. We next address these broader aspects of reflection, which are crucial to learning from experience.

Perception and Action

We have seen how perception influences both the observation and reflection phases in the spiral of experience. It also affects the actions we take. For example, Mitchell and his associates have examined how perceptions and biases affect supervisors' actions in response to poorly performing subordinates.[12, 13, 14] In general, these researchers found that supervisors were biased toward making dispositional attributions about a subordinate's substandard performance and, as a result of these attributions, often recommended that punishment be used to remedy performance deficits.

Another perceptual variable that can affect our actions is the **self-fulfilling prophecy**, which occurs when our expectations or predictions play a causal role in bringing about the events we predict. It is not difficult to see how certain large-scale social phenomena may be affected this way. For example, economists' predictions of an economic downturn may, via the consequent decreased investor confidence, precipitate an economic crisis. But the self-fulfilling prophecy occurs at the interpersonal level, too. A person's expectations about another may influence how he acts toward her, and in reaction to his behavior she may act in a way that confirms his expectations.[15] An illustrative interaction sequence is shown in **Figure 2.2**.

Some of the best evidence to support the effects of self-fulfilling prophecies on leadership training was collected by Eden and Shani in the context of military boot camp.[16] They conducted a field experiment in which they told leadership instructors their students had unknown, regular, or high command potential. However, the students' actual command potential was never assessed, and unknown to the instructors, the students were actually randomly assigned to the unknown, regular, or high-command potential conditions. Nevertheless, students in the high-potential condition had significantly better objective test scores and attitudes than the students in the unknown- or regular-potential conditions, even though instructors simultaneously taught all three types of students. Somehow the students picked up on their instructors' expectations and responded accordingly. Thus merely having expectations (positive or negative) about others can subtly influence our actions, and these actions can, in turn, affect the way others behave.

FIGURE 2.2   The Role of Expectations in Social Interaction

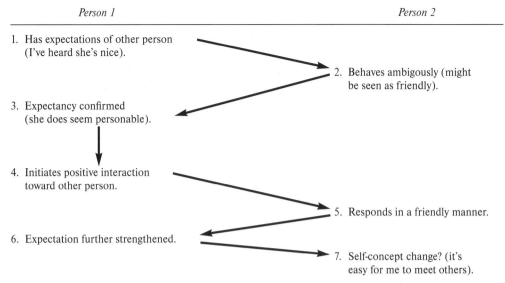

Source: Adopted from Edward E. Jones, "Interpreting Interpersonal Behavior: The Effects of Expectancies," *Science* 234, no. 3 (October 1986), p. 43.

Reflection and Leadership Development

Perhaps the most important yet most neglected component of the action–observation–reflection model is reflection. Reflection is important because it can provide leaders with a variety of insights into how to frame problems differently, look at situations from multiple perspectives, or better understand subordinates. However, most managers spend relatively little time on this activity, even though the time spent reflecting about leadership can be fruitful. The importance of reflection in developing executive competence continues to be a major element of advancing scholarly thought and practice.[17] Something else that is helpful in leadership development is mindset—an idea explored further in **Highlight 2.4**.

Having a Helpful Mindset

HIGHLIGHT 2.4

Consider these two statements and see whether you agree or disagree with each one:

- *Your intelligence is something very basic about you that you can't change very much.*
- *You can do things differently, but the important parts of who you are can't really be changed.*

People who agree with these statements may have what is called a "fixed" mindset, whereas people who disagree with them may have what is called a "growth" mindset. What difference do these two different mindsets actually make in life? Quite a bit, it turns out. Psychologist Carol Dweck provides considerable evidence that mindset has a big impact on one's success in almost any endeavor. So just how do these mindsets differ from each other?

First, beliefs about the very nature of success and failure depend upon which mindset one has. For people with a fixed mindset, success is all about proving that you're smart or talented. As Dweck wrote, "People who believe in fixed traits feel an urgency to succeed, and when they do, they may feel more than pride. They may feel a sense of superiority since success means that their fixed traits are better than other people's." For people with a growth mindset, on the other hand, success depends upon *developing* oneself—on getting better. For people with a fixed mindset, failing at something is "proof" that *you're* a failure—that you don't have the right stuff. For people with a growth mindset, however, failing at something just indicates they need to work harder to master it—and so they do. Mindset even affects the kinds of people we prefer as mates. People with a fixed mindset think the ideal mate would be one who puts them on a pedestal and make them feel perfect; people with a growth mindset think the ideal mate would be one who sees their faults and helps them improve, who challenges them to be better.

These differences have been validated in numerous studies. In one experiment, Dweck offered four-year-olds a chance to re-do an easy jigsaw puzzle or to next tackle a harder one. The four-year-olds with the fixed mindset chose to do the easy one again while those with the growth mindset chose the harder one. In another study, seventh graders were questioned about how they would respond to getting a poor test grade in a new course. Those with a growth mindset answered that they would study harder next time, but those with a fixed mindset said they would study *less*. If you believe abilities are fixed, then why waste time trying to change something you believe you can't change? But it's not just studies like these that demonstrate the importance of mindset: the life stories of successful individuals from astronauts to athletes demonstrate how a growth mindset is a critical component of success.

In an analogous way, a growth mindset is critical to being a person who can *develop others*—including their leadership skills. And remember that mindset itself is something you can change. Anyone can change their mindset, and thus their behavior, including your own and the people with whom you work.

Source: C. Dweck, *Mindset: The New Psychology of Success* (New York: Ballantine Books, 2006).

One reason the reflection component is often neglected is because of the implicit or taken-for-granted beliefs about leadership that many people have. By their unrecognized and untested nature, implicit beliefs can inadvertently insulate a person from seeing things in new ways and from potential learning. Leadership development can be enhanced by raising such implicit beliefs to conscious awareness and thereby more to thoughtful reflection. One approach, for example, used a variety of art prints to stimulate personal and group reflection on ideal forms of leadership. The prints were used to evoke *metaphors* of leadership, and ultimately five fundamental archetypes of leadership were identified:

- **Teacher–Mentor**, who cares about developing others and works beside them as a role model.
- **Father–Judge**, who provides oversight, control, moral guidance, and caring protectiveness.
- **Warrior–Knight**, who takes risks and action in a crisis.
- **Revolutionary–Crusader**, who challenges the status quo and guides adaptation.
- **Visionary–Alchemist**, who imagines possibilities that can benefit all members and brings them into reality.

The process by which these archetypes were identified demonstrated the value of helping developing leaders articulate their tacit knowledge of leadership, see similarities and differences between their own views and others, and better understand the complexities of leadership.[18] That the process of forming implicit beliefs about leadership can begin very early in life.

Being ignorant is not so much a shame as being unwilling to learn.

Benjamin Franklin

One reason a person may neglect opportunities for reflection is the idea that leadership development may not even be possible (for example, as with a fixed mindset described in **Highlight 2.4**). Another reason the reflection component is often neglected may be time pressure at work. Leaders are usually busy working in pressure-filled situations and often do not have time to ponder all the possible consequences of their actions or reflect on how they could have accomplished a particular action better. Sometimes it takes an out-of-the-ordinary experience to focus your attention on developmental challenges. Some leaders may not be aware of the value of reflection in leadership development, and others may be so overconfident in their own expertise and experience that they fall victim to their self-imposed blinders and fail to see situations from alternative possible perspectives.[19] Intentional reflection might even prompt you to see potential benefits in experience not initially considered relevant to leadership in organizational settings. We hope this section clarifies the value of reflection and, in so doing, complements the emphasis, throughout the remainder of the book, on looking at leadership from different perspectives.

Single- and Double-Loop Learning

It is difficult for leaders to fundamentally change their leadership style without engaging in some kind of reflection. Along these lines, Argyris described an intensive effort with a group of successful chief executive officers who became even better leaders through increased self-awareness.[20] His model for conceptualizing this growth is applicable to any level of leader and is worth considering in more detail.

Argyris said that most people interact with others and the environment on the basis of a belief system geared to manipulate or control others, and to minimize one's own emotionality and the negative feelings elicited from others. This belief system also tends to create defensive interpersonal relationships and limits risk taking. People "programmed" with this view of life (as most of us are, according to Argyris) produce group and organizational dynamics characterized by avoidance of conflict, mistrust, conformity, intergroup rivalry, misperceptions of and miscommunications with others, ineffective problem solving, and poor decision-making.

Most important for our purposes here, this belief system generates a certain kind of learning that Argyris called **single-loop learning**. Single-loop learning describes a kind of learning between the individual and the environment in which learners seek relatively little feedback that may significantly confront their fundamental ideas or actions. There is relatively little public testing of ideas against valid information. Consequently, an actor's belief system becomes self-sealing and self-fulfilling, and little time is spent reflecting about the beliefs. Argyris used the term *single-loop learning* because it operates somewhat like a thermostat: Individuals learn only about subjects within the comfort zone of their belief systems. They might, for example, learn how well they are achieving a designated goal. They are far less likely, however, to question the validity of the goal or the values implicit in the situation, just as a thermostat does not question its temperature setting. That kind of self-confrontation would involve double-loop learning.

Double-loop learning involves a willingness to confront your own views and an invitation to others to do so, too. It springs from an appreciation that openness to information and power sharing with others can lead to better recognition and definition of problems, improved communication, and increased decision-making effectiveness. Mastering double-loop learning can be thought of as learning how to learn. With considerable collective work, including the difficult task of working through personal blind spots, Argyris's group of leaders did move to this stage. In other words, through reflection they learned how to change their leadership styles by questioning their assumptions about others, their roles in the organization, and their underlying assumptions about the importance of their own goals and those of the organization.

What makes double-loop learning so difficult? By their very nature, leadership experiences are often ambiguous; they typically involve multiple stakeholders having multiple perspectives and interests; and emotional stakes can be high. Such ambiguity, complexity, and emotionality can make it difficult for a leader to determine causal relationships between his or her behavior and specific outcomes, or whether different behavior would have led to different outcomes. Learning about leadership from your raw experience is *not* easy, not even for those deeply committed to doing so. A recent study sheds further light on how it can be enhanced.

It turns out that although *unaided* learning from experience is difficult for all the reasons just noted, it can be enhanced through a practice of systematic reflection or **after event reviews (AERs)**.[21] These AERs involved reflection and facilitated discussion on personal leadership experiences such as what the potential impact of alternative leadership behaviors might have been and how individuals believe they might behave differently in the future. The study found that individuals who participated in these AERs improved the effectiveness of their leadership over time whereas little or no development occurred *from the same experiences* among those who did not participate in the AER process.

Making the Most of Your Leadership Experiences: Learning to Learn from Experience

This section builds on the ideas previously introduced in this chapter by giving leadership practitioners a few suggestions to enhance learning from experience. For decades, researchers have been studying the role of learning from experience as an important developmental behavior for people in executive positions. Although this research has contributed a great deal to *what* people need to learn to be successful (see **Highlight 2.5** for a comparison of lessons men and women managers learn from experience), less is known about the process of learning or *how* we learn to be successful. But often it involves simply throwing oneself into a situation and being willing to take advantage of opportunities that present themselves, as **Profiles in Leadership 2.1** portrays.

What Do Men and Women Managers Learn from Experience?

HIGHLIGHT 2.5

For a quarter century or so, significant numbers of women have been represented in the management ranks of companies. During that period companies have promoted large pools of high-potential women, but relatively few of them have achieved truly top-level positions. Several factors probably account for this, but one possibility is that men and women learn differently from their work experiences. Researchers have studied how male and female executives describe the important lessons they've learned from their career experiences, and there are some interesting differences between the genders as well as significant overlap.

Most Frequent Lessons for . . .		
Men and Women	**Men Only**	**Women Only**
Directing and motivating employees	Technical/professional skills	Personal limits and blind spots
Self-confidence	All about the business	Taking charge of your career
Basic management values	Coping with ambiguous situations	Recognizing and seizing opportunities
How to work with executives	Shouldering full responsibility	Coping with situations beyond your control
Understanding other people's perspective	Persevering through adversity	Knowing what excites you
Dealing with people over whom you have no authority		
Handling political situations		

Why would there be any learning differences between the genders? One hypothesis is that men and women managers tend to have different career patterns. For example, there is some evidence that women receive fewer truly challenging developmental opportunities. Do you believe there is any difference at your school between the opportunities provided to male and female students?

Source: E. Van Velsor and M. W. Hughes, *Gender Differences in the Development of Managers: How Women Managers Learn from Experience*, Technical Report No. 145 (Greensboro, NC: Center for Creative Leadership, 1990).

What would a man be wise; let him drink of the river
That bears on its bosom the record of time;
A message to him every wave can deliver
To teach him to creep till he knows how to climb.

John Boyle O'Reilly, poet

Bunker and Webb asked successful executives to list adjectives describing how they felt while working through powerful learning events and potent developmental experiences.[22] Their typical responses were a combination of both positive and negative feelings:

Negatives	Positives
Pained	Challenged
Fearful	Successful
Frustrated	Proud
Stressed	Capable
Anxious	Growing

Negatives	Positives
Overwhelmed	Exhilarated
Uncertain	Talented
Angry	Resourceful
Hurt	Learning

This pattern strongly supports the long-hypothesized notion of a meaningful link between stress and learning.[23] The learning events and developmental experiences that punctuate our lives are usually—perhaps always—stressful.[24, 25, 26, 27]

Teach a highly educated person that it is not a disgrace to fail and that he must analyze every failure to find its cause. He must learn how to fail intelligently, for failing is one of the greatest arts in the world.

Charles F. Kettering, inventor, automotive pioneer, and corporate leader

Bunker and Webb note that executives try to be successful without experiencing stress. They are most comfortable when they can draw on a proven repertoire of operating skills to tackle a challenge they have conquered in the past. Combined with the organizational pressure to have "proven performers" in important positions, there is a tremendous initial pressure to "continue to do what we've always done." In stressful situations, this tendency may become even more powerful. What results is one of the great challenges of adult development: The times when people most need to break out of the mold created by past learning patterns are the times when they are most unwilling to do so. Being able to *go against the grain* of one's personal historical success requires an unwavering commitment to learning and a relentless willingness to let go of the fear of failure and the unknown.

ZAP!!! POW!!! The Marvel(ous) Legacy of Stan Lee

PROFILES IN LEADERSHIP 2.1

Stan Lee is credited with being the genius behind Marvel comics and a godfather of superheroes. He created some of the most popular and successful characters in comic book and (later) movie history including Spider Man, the Hulk, the Fantastic Four, Iron Man, the X-Men, and many more. So how do you even get into a career like that, let alone become the genius behind so many superheroes?

When he was 17 and looking for a job in New York City, Lee learned from his cousin's husband of a possibility with a company called Timely Publications. The company was looking for an assistant, and Lee learned that the opening was in the comic book department. The job sounded like it might be fun so he accepted the offer. He became your basic gofer there ("go for this, go for that"). At that time, there were only two employees besides the publisher and Lee. When those two were fired, there was no one left to run the department. The publisher asked Lee, "Can you do it?" Seventy years later in life, Lee remembered the moment. "I was 17. When you're 17, what do you know? I said, 'Sure, I can do it'." Lee became interim editor of that comic book series, rose to editor-in-chief of the company's entire comic book division, and ultimately became president and chairman of Marvel Comics.

Talk about making the most of an opportunity!

To be successful, learning must continue throughout life, beyond the completion of one's formal education. The end of extrinsically applied education should be the start of an education that is motivated intrinsically. At that point the goal of studying is no longer to make the grade, earn a diploma, and find a good job. Rather, it is to understand what is happening around one, to develop a personally meaningful sense of what one's experience is about.[28]

> *Anyone who stops learning is old, whether at 20 or 80. Anyone who keeps learning stays young. The greatest thing in life is to keep your mind young.*
>
> **Henry Ford, founder of the Ford Motor Company**

This applies to the specific challenge of *becoming* and *remaining* an effective leader, too. People who lead in modern organizations need to be engaged in a never-ending learning process.[29] Ron Riggio of the Kravis Leadership Institute characterized this challenge well in observing that organizational leaders are practitioners of leadership at the same time they must continue to be students of leadership:

> The practice of leadership, just like the practice of medicine, or law, or any other profession, is a continual learning process. The complexity of these professions means that one can always improve and learn how to do it

better. The wise leader accepts this and goes through the sometimes painful process of personal leader development.[30]

So just what does it take to be a good student of leadership? Kevin Wilde has had decades of experience in developing executive leaders, and he believes it can be summed up in the concept of *coachability*. He says that a person's coachability, or ability to learn from experience, can be captured in terms of a few key practices, such as:

- Valuing and signaling to others an interest in feedback and an intent to improve.
- Seeking feedback proactively and regularly.
- Reflecting on that feedback and responding constructively to it.
- Acting on valued feedback, and sustaining improvement over time.[31]

Do such practices actually work? In one study, derailed leaders showed significantly lower interest than others in seeking and acting upon feedback, suggesting they have blind spots about their abilities and impact on others.[32] And in a study of over 5,100 leaders, the most coachable leaders among them were four times as likely to be rated in the top 20 percent of overall leadership capabilities.[33]

Read **Profiles in Leadership 2.2** and form your own impression of how wisely or well Steve Jobs learned from his own experience, his business success notwithstanding.

Steve Jobs

PROFILES IN LEADERSHIP 2.2

Steve Jobs was one of the most famous and successful business leaders in the world, even if also known as having a temperamental, aggressive, and demanding style with others. At the age of 20, with partner Steve Wozniak, he helped launch the personal computer revolution with Apple Computer and ultimately through its premier PC, the Macintosh. After leaving Apple, he founded another company, NeXT Computer, and in 1986 he bought a computer animation company called Pixar. The company's first film, *Toy Story*, made history by being the first entirely computer-animated feature film. After returning to Apple, Jobs created even further revolutions in consumer technology products with the iPod, iPhone, and iPad.

In 2005, Jobs delivered the commencement address at Stanford University. In that address, he talked about one of the most difficult and yet most valuable experiences of his life: getting fired from Apple, the company that he had helped found. He and Wozniak started Apple, he said, in 1970 in his parents' garage. In 10 years, it had grown into a $2 billion company. He could not believe it, amid that success, when he was fired by Apple's board of directors. "How can you get fired from a company you started? What had been the focus of my entire adult life was gone, and it was devastating." Yet now, reflecting on the opportunities that he was able to take advantage of because he left Apple, Jobs said to the graduating class, "I didn't see it then, but it turned out that getting fired from Apple was the best thing that ever could have happened to me."

Jobs believed that leadership meant creating an environment where excellence is expected and innovation flourishes. But he also had a dark side that punctuated and colored his success and genius as a business leader. Walter Isaacson pulled no punches in depicting both sides of Jobs's character in his gripping 2011 biography.

For example, Jobs had a mercurial personality and might change his mood in minutes, crying or throwing tantrums, for example, over things that others might take more in stride. His tyrannical interpersonal style caused him to be banished off the night shift at Atari. He tended to categorize his own staff as either "gods" or "s___heads," yet even the "gods" knew they might fall off that pedestal at any moment. He perfected the art of silence and staring in order to intimidate others and could behave in incredibly mean and demeaning ways toward others. He was a consummate con man who seemed able to convince anyone of anything. He took to heart Picasso's observation that "Good artists borrow, great artists steal": He shamelessly stole ideas from other companies and others within his own company. He simply believed that the laws and rules of conduct that governed others did not apply to him. He created his own idiosyncratic perceptions of reality that, to everyone else, had no basis in fact. Jobs, nonetheless, was absolutely convinced his view alone was correct despite all evidence to the contrary. Others even gave this "flying in the face of reality" characteristic a name—his "reality distortion field."

So what do you think: Was Steve Jobs as successful as he was because of these dark-side qualities, or might he have been even more successful without them?

Source: W. Isaacson, *Steve Jobs* (New York: Simon & Schuster, 2011).

Leader Development in College

Good flutists learn from experience; unfortunately, so do bad flutists.

Anonymous

Virtually everyone using this text is taking a college course in leadership for academic credit. But one academic course in leadership is only part of what at some schools is an entire curriculum of leadership studies. Riggio, Ciulla, and Sorenson, representing three different institutions, have described the rise and key elements of leadership studies programs in liberal arts colleges, and note that there are now nearly 1,000 recognized leadership development programs in institutions of higher education.[34] Few, of them, though, are curriculum-based programs that offer academic credit in the form of, for example, an academic minor. As such programs continue to increase in number, several features should guide their design.

I took a great deal o' pains with his education, sir; let him run the streets when he was very young, and shift for his-self. It's the only way to make a boy sharp, sir.

Charles Dickens, *Pickwick Papers*

An educated man can experience more in a day than an uneducated man in a lifetime.

Seneca, Roman statesman, 1st century A.D.

At liberal arts institutions, leadership studies programs should be multidisciplinary. As you will notice in this text, the field of leadership encompasses a broad range of disciplines including psychology, organizational behavior, history, education, management, and political science, to name just a few. Also, leadership studies need to be academically authorized courses of study (obvious as this may seem, one challenge to it was evident in the anecdote shared in the introduction to this chapter). Another important feature is that leadership programs need to deliberately cultivate values represented in the broader field, especially those that are particularly salient at each local institution. These values could include social responsibility and the expectation to become engaged in one's community; in such cases **service learning** is a common part of the programs. In other programs, global awareness is another guiding value. Finally, consistent with requirements across higher education, leadership studies programs should focus on expected developmental outcomes, with associated assessment and evaluation to determine program effectiveness.[35]

All rising to a great place is by a winding stair.

Francis Bacon, philosopher

Tell me and I'll forget; show me and I may remember; involve me and I'll understand.

Chinese proverb

Some key curricular components of college-based leadership studies programs include coursework examining foundational theories and concepts in leadership (the kind this textbook is intended to support). In addition, coursework in ethics is vital to leadership studies. As just mentioned, service learning and other experiential learning opportunities should be provided and integrated with the classroom elements of the program. An understanding of group dynamics is critical to effective leadership, and its development requires student experiences interacting with others; leadership studies inherently require a social dimension of experience. Finally, as implied by the interdisciplinary nature of leadership studies, a variety of faculty from many different departments and disciplines should be involved in the program.[36]

How few there are who have the courage to own their own faults, or resolution enough to mend them!

Benjamin Franklin

Within leadership studies programs, various leader development methods may be used beyond service learning. Some courses or program elements might involve **individualized feedback** to students in the form of personality, intelligence, values, or interest test scores or leadership behavior ratings. **Case studies** describe leadership situations and are used as a vehicle for leadership discussions. **Role playing** is also a popular methodology. In role playing, participants are assigned parts to play (such as a supervisor and an unmotivated subordinate) in a job-related scenario. Role playing has the advantage of letting trainees actually practice relevant skills and thus has greater transferability to the workplace than do didactic lectures or abstract discussions about leadership. **Simulations** and **games** are other methods of leader development. These are relatively structured activities designed to mirror some of the challenges or decisions commonly faced in the work environment. A newer approach puts participants in relatively unfamiliar territory (such as outdoors rather than offices) and presents them physical, emotionally arousing, and often team-oriented challenges.

All these sorts of methods likely contribute to development in a variety of ways, including providing opportunities for self-discovery, practice, and generalization of behaviors to multiple contexts and groups. As methodologies they share a capability to move learning from the purely cognitive domain to affective, social, and behavioral ones as well. Recent research suggests that development as a leader may most authentically and enduringly occur when the context and design of the experiences afford learners the opportunity to deeply *personalize* their lessons of experience. This might be, for example, through structured and psychologically safe opportunities to reflect on development experiences that students might have found personally disturbing or confusing.[37]

Leader Development in Organizational Settings

The title of this section does not imply that colleges and universities are not organizations; obviously they are. Nonetheless, college-based leadership studies differ in some significant ways from the leader development programs one finds in the corporate sector or in the military. Most obvious, perhaps, is the fact that the essential purpose of college-based programs is to prepare students for their ultimate productive service as citizens, including in their own vocations. Our focus in this section is on methods of leader development provided in organizations not just for the individual's personal development but also (and maybe primarily) for the organization's benefit. Although all of the relatively short-term development methods just mentioned are used routinely in organizational programs, some of the most potent work-based leader development methods are longer term in nature.

The matter of longer-term development methods, in fact, raises an important issue concerning the matter of what exactly "causes" improvement from developmental experiences (for example, training) even when they appear to be successful. Consider, for example, a scenario in which a manager attends a one-week training program focused on leadership development (disregard for this purpose the particular components of the training). And assume that we observe real improvement in the manager's effectiveness a month later—what, do you think, "caused" the change? It may be tempting to assume that it was due to the training program, and it might well have played some part. But it is also possible (maybe likely) that something else was happening too: that the manager was *practicing new behaviors* during the intervening month. Thus it may be that formal leadership development experiences are sometimes useful but maybe not sufficient for development to occur. In fact, it is usually difficult to make changes to one's interpersonal behavior in the workplace, and making such changes usually requires extended practice over time. It even has been suggested that the truly important place where development occurs is not in any particular developmental event itself (for example, a week of training). In fact, "it is highly unlikely that anyone would be able to develop fully as a leader merely through participation in a series of programs, workshops, or seminars. The actual development takes place in the so-called white space between such leader development events."[38] This view corresponds well, we think, with the A-O-R model that is at the heart of this chapter.

Even if practice in the "white space" between formal developmental events is a necessary element of leader development, most organizations believe that formal leader development efforts are still necessary. In light of the considerable amount of money spent on leadership development—some have estimated it to be a $50 billion industry—it is reasonable to ask, "Is it worth it?" Until recently, there has been little basis for answering that question beyond the obvious fact that countless people must have *believed* it was worth it or else the money wouldn't have been spent. But critical voices have questioned certain assumptions on which much of the leadership development effort in organizations seems to be based. One recent critique, for example, highlights these three questionable assumptions:

- Successful organizations are created by leaders who possess "the right stuff." Thus, if organizations can find and develop enough leaders with the "right stuff," then organizational success will follow.

- Leadership potential (having the "right stuff") is best assessed by gauging individual attributes. Thus, the winning formula for organizational success is fundamentally based on a constellation of individual traits and characteristics.

- Leadership effectiveness can be assessed and developed in environments independent of the context in which a leader works.[39]

Beyond such questionable assumptions sometimes conceptually underlying leadership development, the actual *design* of leadership initiatives often has been—at least now in retrospect—inadequate.[40] In fact, leadership development has only recently been subjected to the same kind of rigorous analysis that other business decisions, especially capital investments, routinely face. That kind of analysis is used to determine **return on investment**, or ROI. The logic is rather straightforward. To illustrate a simple case, suppose that a leadership development program for one manager cost the company $2,000. The company would have a positive ROI, or a positive return on that investment, if after the training the increase in that manager's productivity was greater than $2,000. Such enhanced productivity might result from improved decision-making, more motivated and better-managed direct reports, and more. What matters is that the person who went through the development program has demonstrably improved leader behavior. And while there seems to be widespread uncertainty about the value of organizational investment in leadership training, a recent meta-analysis of 335 independent samples suggested that "leadership training is substantially more effective than previously thought."[41] In fact, other research indicates that, on average, the ROI for investments in leadership development is both positive and substantial.[42]

There are numerous leadership training programs aimed particularly toward leaders and supervisors in industry or public service. In many ways these programs have strong parallels to the content and techniques used in university-level courses on leadership. However, they tend to be more focused than a university course that typically lasts an entire semester. The content of industry programs also depends on the organizational level of the recipients; programs for first-level supervisors focus on developing supervisory skills such as training, monitoring, giving feedback, and conducting performance reviews with subordinates. Generally these programs use lectures, case studies, and role-playing exercises to improve leadership skills. The programs for mid-level managers often focus on improving interpersonal, oral communication, and written communication skills, as well as giving tips on time management, planning, and goal setting. These programs rely more heavily on individualized feedback, case studies, presentations, role-playing, simulations, and **in-basket exercises** to help leaders develop. With in-basket exercises, participants are given a limited amount of time to prioritize and respond to a number of notes, letters, and phone messages from a fictitious manager's in-basket. This technique is particularly useful in assessing and improving a manager's planning and time management skills. In leaderless group discussions, facilitators and observers rate participants on the degree of persuasiveness, leadership, followership, or conflict each member manifests in a group that has no appointed leader. These ratings are used to give managers feedback about their interpersonal and oral communication skills.

In reviewing the general field of leadership development and training, Conger offered this assessment: "Leadership programs can work, and work well, if they use a multi-tiered approach. Effective training depends on the combined use of four different teaching methods which I call personal growth, skill building, feedback, and conceptual awareness."[43] Some programs seek to stimulate leadership development by means of emotionally intense personal growth experiences such as river rafting, wilderness survival, and so forth. Conger's skill-building facet of leadership development is the focus of four different chapters in this book. Some approaches to leadership development emphasize individualized feedback about each person's strengths and weaknesses, typically based on standardized assessment methods. Feedback-based approaches can help identify "blind spots" an individual may be unaware of, as well as help prioritize which aspects of leadership development represent the highest priorities for development focus. Still other sorts of programs develop leadership by emphasizing its conceptual or intellectual components. An example of this approach would be an emphasis on theory and the use of case studies, common in many MBA programs. There are merits in each of these approaches, but Conger was on solid ground when he emphasized the value of combining elements of each. **Highlight 2.6** can give you a more detailed look at leadership development in a company highly regarded for its work in this area.

Leadership Development in the Private Sector: 3M

HIGHLIGHT 2.6

3M is a science and product company that generates approximately $30 billion in annual revenues and consists of 85,000 employees located in more than 70 countries. Headquartered in St. Paul, Minnesota, 3M has a portfolio of 65,000 products that includes adhesives, abrasives, nanotechnology, electronics and software, lighting management, microreplication, and nonwoven materials and some 40 other technological platforms. Many of these products, such as Post-it Notes, are highly recognizable. 3M has always put a premium on innovation, and to date its 8,000 research scientists have generated more than 3,100 U.S. patents. Because of the success of its products, 3M has consistently been ranked as one of the top 10 Most Admired Companies by *Fortune* magazine.

In 2006, the company noticed that the costs for getting new products to the market were rising at an alarming rate. 3M did not want to focus exclusively on reducing costs, however, as this could negatively impact the development of new products. Company managers believed that the key to improving both efficiency and innovation was employee engagement, which it defined as "an individual's sense of purpose and focused energy, evident to others in the display of personal initiative, effort, and persistence directed towards organizational goals." 3M management felt that the more people who were engaged with their work, the more likely they would be to offer and execute ideas to improve innovation and reduce costs.

3M had been measuring employee satisfaction and attitudes toward work since the early 1950s and redesigned these companywide surveys as part of the focus on employee engagement. The data were collected in such a way that individual first-line supervisors, mid-level managers, country managers, regional executives, and functional managers could see the average engagement levels of their respective employees. At the same time, the leadership development function at 3M supplemented its offerings in order to educate leaders on what employee engagement is, how it can be a competitive advantage, and what they can do to improve it.

3M's leadership development function has been recognized as one of the best in the world and makes extensive use of leaders teaching leaders (that is, the CEO and executive leadership team all spend time teaching leadership courses to fellow 3M leaders). The function's action learning programs are offered to some of the best and brightest in the company and consist of tempo-rary teams that are tasked with developing ideas and business plans to generate an additional $25 million in sales or significant revenue and cost improvements within a geographic region. The function also offers traditional classroom training and hundreds of e-learning modules for leaders in first-line, mid-level, and executive-level leadership positions. Social media, do-it-yourself YouTube-type videos, blogs, wikis, and the like are also used extensively to teach leaders how to promote employee engagement. As a result of these leadership development efforts, overall employee engagement has improved dramatically to a rating of 4.8/5.0, new products are being released, revenues are growing, and costs are being managed more effectively.

3M's CEO Inge Thulin, himself a product of this well-established company widely known for its innovation and leadership development, has brought an even greater focus on people development. Within a week of his appointment as CEO, he announced a new vision for the company and six major business strategies, one of which was aimed directly at raising the bar even higher for "building high-performing and diverse global talent" at 3M. Certainly, many companies *think* leadership effectiveness at all levels is critical to driving an aggressive growth strategy: Thulin, however, has operationalized this, making development of all talent, including leaders, a core business strategy.

Sources: K. B. Paul and C. J. Johnson, "Engagement at 3M: A Case Study," in *The Executive Guide to Integrated Talent Management*, eds. K. Oakes and P. Galagan (Alexandria, VA: American Society for Training and Development Press, 2011); "World's Most Admired Companies," *Fortune*, March 29, 2012, http://money.cnn.com/magazines/fortune/most-admired/2012/full_list; and 3M, www.3M.com.

In a related vein, others have emphasized that leader development in the 21st century must occur in more lifelike situations and contexts.[44] Toward that end, they have advocated creating better practice fields for leadership development analogous to the practice fields on which skills in competitive sports are honed, or practice sessions analogous to those in music training in which those skills are sharpened. Increasingly leadership development is occurring in the context of work itself.[45]

Leadership programs for senior executives and CEOs tend to focus on strategic planning, developing and communicating a vision, public relations, and interpersonal skills. Many times the entire senior leadership of a company will go through a leadership program at the same time. One goal of such a group might be to learn how to develop a strategic plan for their organization. To improve public relations skills, some programs have CEOs undergo simulated, unannounced interviews with television reporters and receive feedback on how they could have done better.

In the following sections we discuss research surrounding four popular and increasingly common methods of leader development: action learning, development planning, coaching, and mentoring. Some less well-established approaches to leadership development are described in **Highlight 2.7**.

Innovative Approaches to Leader Development

HIGHLIGHT 2.7

This chapter highlights a number of well-established methods of leader development, such as coaching and mentoring, but many other innovative or nontraditional approaches are also worth noting. We've listed a few of them here, grouped into three broad categories: arts-based approaches, technology-based approaches, and adventure-based approaches.

ARTS-BASED APPROACHES

Some arts-based approaches may be described as "projective" because they involve some form of artistic creation or interpretation that allows participants to reveal inner thoughts and feelings (the name *projective* was originally associated with the Rorschach Inkblot test, a projective psychological test). For example, visual images (such as photographs or artwork) can provide a stimulus for a person to elaborate on in describing some leadership theme (the best team I've ever been on, what it feels like to work in this company, or the like). It's striking how rich and candid a person's reflections typically are when made in response to something tangible like an evocative image. Another projective technique would be to use simple building materials (like Legos) and instruct participants to create some depiction (perhaps of their organizational structure or strategy). Critical skills such as demonstrating empathy can be learned with dramatic and theatrical training (especially valuable for medical personnel). And films,

which often have high emotional impact, can be used to facilitate rich discussions of various leadership issues.

The theater arts, too, play a part (pun intended) in leadership development. Although learning how to be perceived by others as authentic may sound inherently contradictory, being perceived as authentic is nonetheless important for leaders, and training leaders in specific ways to behave to enhance such perceptions is a growing part of leadership development methodologies.

TECHNOLOGY-BASED APPROACHES

Video games and virtual reality simulations also open new doors for leadership development because they share several distinctly advantageous characteristics for training and development. For one thing, they require speedy thought and action. Actions that might take weeks or longer to unfold in real life can be compressed into hours or minutes, and thus the pace of leadership can be heightened. These venues also encourage risk taking, and leadership roles in gaming or virtual reality contexts are often temporary, involving frequent swapping of roles. Even the U.S. Air Force has developed virtual reality simulations for leadership development in situations that are complex, ambiguous, and highly interdependent.

Adventure-Based Approaches

Organizations such as the National Outdoor Leadership School and Outward Bound use the unfamiliarity and inherent challenges of outdoor wilderness experience as a laboratory for leadership development. Learning to work effectively with diverse strangers while navigating difficult terrain, forging rivers, setting up tents, and fixing meals in foul-weather conditions creates countless opportunities to learn about oneself and how to work with others in novel and often stressful situations. It's not just the wilderness, though, that can provide a challenging environment for leadership development. Urban environments can, too. The New York City Fire Department (FDNY) offers a program called the Firefighter for a Day Team Challenge, and the FDNY has partnered with the Wharton Business School in adapting the program for executive education. The program immerses participants in realistic firefighting scenarios such as a terrorist bus-bombing incident. The philosophy underlying most adventure-based approaches is that deeper levels of personal and interpersonal insight can occur when the context of learning is unfamiliar and one's customary repertoire of "office" survival skills and roles are inadequate and maybe even irrelevant.

Sources: S. S. Taylor and D. Ladkin, "Understanding Arts-Based Methods in Managerial Development," *Academy of Management Learning & Education* 8, no. 1 (2009), pp. 55–69; B. Reeves, T. W. Malone, and T. O'Driscoll, "Leadership's Online Labs," *Harvard Business Review*, May 2008, pp. 59–66; R. L. Hughes and A. Stricker, "Outside-in and Inside-out Approaches to Transformation," in *Crosscutting Issues in International Transformation: Interactions and Innovations among People, Organizations, Processes, and Technology*, eds. D. Neal, H. Friman, R. Doughty, and L. Wells (Washington, DC: Center for Technology and National Security Policy, National Defense University, 2009); J. Kanengieter and A. Rajagopal-Durbin, "Wilderness Leadership—On the Job," *Harvard Business Review*, April 2012, pp. 127–31; G. Peifer, "Soapbox: Learn to Take the Heat," *Training*; and A. E. Weischer, J. Weibler, and M. Petersen, "'To Thine Self Be True': The Effects of Enactment and Life Storytelling on Perceived Leader Authenticity," *The Leadership Quarterly* 24 (2013), pp. 477–95.

Action Learning

Perhaps the best way to appreciate the nature of **action learning** is to contrast it with more traditional **training programs**. The latter term refers to leadership development activities that typically involve personnel attending a class, often for several days or even a week. In such classes, many of the kinds of developmental activities already mentioned might be included such as exercises, instrument-based feedback, and various presentations on different aspects of leadership. The key point is that attendance at a training program inherently involves time away from immediate job responsibilities. And although the various exercises presumably address many common leadership issues such as communication, conflict, feedback, and planning, the inevitably artificial nature of such activities makes transfer back to the actual work situation more difficult.

Action learning, by contrast, refers to the use of actual work issues and challenges as the developmental activity itself. The basic philosophy of action learning is that for adults in particular, the best learning is *learning by doing*. Further, action learning often is conducted in teams of work colleagues who are addressing real company challenges; the members of action learning teams are placed into problem-solving roles and are expected to reach team decisions concerning the challenge or problem, and formally present their analysis and recommendations to others (often senior executives in their own company). Importantly, action learning also involves built-in opportunities for feedback and reflection for the participants about the perceived quality of their analysis and recommendations as well as, ideally, about aspects of their respective individual strengths and weaknesses as leaders working on the collaborative project together.

In the past 15 years or so, action learning has gone from being a relatively rare development vehicle to being found in many companies' internal portfolios of leader development opportunities. Unfortunately, however, its demonstrated effectiveness for leader development, as distinguished from its use in generating fresh ideas for thorny company problems, has not kept pace with its increasing popularity and widespread use.

When you're in a new job where you're stretched, your focus should be on learning, not getting an A.

Mary Dee Hicks, consultant

There are many reasons for this—not the least of which is that the links between a particular action learning project and its leadership challenges may be tenuous. Too often personnel are assigned to action learning teams assuming that they'll inevitably learn critical leadership lessons along the way; it usually doesn't happen so easily. If it were easy and automatic, we should expect more "leadership learning" from the experience of one's primary job and not need action learning at all. Furthermore, the time-critical, high-visibility, and all-too-real elements that can make action learning problems so engaging and popular also often require a work pace that does not allow for the kind of reflection we know is an important part of leader development. A final reason action learning projects may not achieve their desired leader development outcomes is that teams at work often fall prey to the same kinds of problems that you probably have experienced in team-based projects in your own academic coursework. It's one thing to *call* something a project requiring teamwork; it's quite another thing for the work on that project to truly *reflect* good teamwork. In poorly designed and supported action learning projects, the work might be dominated by one person or by just one perspective within the organization. Action learning holds great promise but has not yet delivered uniform results.[46]

Development Planning

How many times have you resolved to change a habit, only to discover two months later that you are still exhibiting the same behaviors? This is often the fate of well-intentioned New Year's resolutions. Most people do not even make such resolutions because the failure rate is so high. Given this track record, you might wonder if it is possible to change one's behavior, particularly if an existing pattern has been reinforced over time and is exhibited almost automatically. Fortunately, however, it *is* possible to change behavior, even long-standing habits. For example, many people permanently quit smoking or drinking without any type of formal program. Others may change after they gain insight into how their behavior affects others. Some will need support to maintain a behavioral change over time, whereas others seem destined never to change.[47, 48, 49]

Managers seem to fall into the same categories: Some managers change once they gain insight, others change with social and organizational support, and others may not ever change. But do people just fall into one of these groups by accident? Is there any way to stack the odds in favor of driving behavioral change? Research suggests several strategies that leaders can use to accelerate the development of their own leadership skills.[50, 51, 52, 53, 54, 55] These include five critical behavioral change questions, and leaders must provide positive answers to all five questions if they want to maximize the odds of enduring behavior change taking place.

Question 1: Do leaders know which of their behaviors need to change? Leaders are capable of exhibiting hundreds of different behaviors, but do they precisely know which behaviors they need to start, stop, or keep doing to build effective teams or achieve better results? The insight component of the development pipeline is concerned with giving leaders accurate feedback on their strengths and development needs, and 360-degree feedback (360-degree feedback involves receiving feedback from a "circle" of people who have different perspectives on your behavior such as a boss, peers or coworkers, and yourself). can provide useful information in this regard. Other sources of information about development needs can come from the results of an assessment center, a performance appraisal, or direct feedback from others.

Question 2: Is the leader motivated to change these behaviors? The next step in developing one's own leadership skills is working on development goals that matter. No leader has all of the knowledge and skills necessary to be successful; as a result, most leaders have multiple development needs. Leaders need to determine which new skills will have the highest personal and organizational payoffs and build development plans that address these needs. The development plan should be focused on only one or two needs; plans addressing more than this tend to be overwhelming and unachievable. If leaders have more than two development needs, they should first work to acquire one or two skills before moving on to the next set of development needs.

Question 3: Do leaders have plans in place for changing targeted behaviors? For leaders, this means creating a written **development plan** that capitalizes on available books, seminars, college courses, e-learning modules, and so forth to acquire the knowledge underlying a particular development need. For example, you can either learn how to delegate through the school of hard knocks or take a seminar to learn the best delegation skills. As we will see, knowledge alone is not enough to develop a new skill, but relevant books and courses can accelerate the learning process.[56] In addition, it is important not to underestimate the power of a written development plan. Leaders (and followers) who have a written plan seem more likely to keep development on their radar screens and take the actions necessary to acquire new skills.

> *The more you crash, the more you learn.*
> **David B. Peterson, Personnel Decisions International**

Question 4: Do leaders have opportunities to practice new skills? Taking courses and reading books are good ways for leaders to acquire foundational knowledge, but new skills will be acquired only when they are practiced on the job. Just as surgeons can read about and watch a surgery but will perfect a surgical technique only through repeated practice, so too will leaders acquire needed skills only if they practice them on the job. Therefore, good development plans use on-the-job experiences to hone needed leadership skills. These on-the-job activities are so important to development that 70 to 80 percent of the action steps in a development plan should be job related.

> *The only thing more painful than learning from experience is not learning from experience.*
> **Archibald MacLeish, Librarian of Congress**

Question 5: Are leaders held accountable for changing targeted behaviors? The last step in acquiring new skills is accountability, and there are several ways to make this happen with a development plan. One way to build in accountability is to have different people provide ongoing feedback on the action steps taken to develop a skill. For example, leaders could ask for feedback from a peer or direct report on their listening skills immediately after staff meetings. Another way to build accountability is to periodically review progress on development plans with the boss. This way the boss can look for opportunities to help the leader further practice developing skills and determine when it is time to add new development needs to the plan.

Development planning is more than a plan—it is really a process. Good development plans are continually being revised as new skills are learned or new opportunities to develop skills become available. Leaders who take the time to write out and execute best-practice development plans usually report the most improvement in later 360-degree feedback ratings. Development planning provides a methodology for leaders to improve their behavior, and much of this development can occur as they go about their daily work activities.

Coaching

Development plans tend to be self-focused; leaders and followers use them as a road map for changing their own behaviors. When trying to change the behavior of followers, however, leaders can often do more than review followers' development plans or provide ongoing feedback. The next step in followers' development often involves coaching. Coaching is a key leadership skill that can help leaders improve the bench strength of the group, which in turn should help the group accomplish its goals. Because of its role in development, coaching can also help to retain high-quality followers.[57] Because of these outcomes, coaching is a popular topic these days, but it is also frequently misunderstood.

> *The best executive is one who has enough sense to pick good men to do what he wants done, and the self-restraint to keep from meddling while they do it.*

Theodore Roosevelt, U.S. president, 1901–1909

Coaching is the "process of equipping people with the tools, knowledge, and opportunities they need to develop and become more successful."[58] In general, there are two types of coaching: informal and formal. **Informal coaching** takes place whenever a leader helps followers to change their behaviors. According to Peterson and Hicks, the best informal coaching generally consists of five steps:[59] forging a partnership, inspiring commitment, growing skills, promoting persistence, and shaping the environment (see **Table 2.1**).

TABLE 2.1   The Five Steps of Informal Coaching

Forge a partnership: Coaching works only if there is a trusting relationship between the leader and his or her followers. In this step leaders also determine what drives their followers and where they want to go with their careers.

Inspire commitment: In this step leaders help followers determine which skills or behaviors will have the biggest payoff if developed. Usually this step involves reviewing the results of performance appraisals, 360-degree feedback, values, personality assessment reports, and so on.

Grow skills: Leaders work with followers to build development plans that capitalize on on-the-job experiences and create coaching plans to support their followers' development.

Promote persistence: Leaders meet periodically with followers to provide feedback, help followers keep development on their radar screens, and provide followers with new tasks or projects to develop needed skills.

Shape the environment: Leaders need to periodically review how they are role-modeling development and what they are doing to foster development in the workplace. Because most people want to be successful, doing this step well will help attract and retain followers to the work group.

Source: D. B. Peterson and M. D. Hicks, *Leader as Coach: Strategies for Coaching and Developing Others* (Minneapolis, MN: Personnel Decisions International, 1996).

Several points about informal coaching are worth additional comment. First, the five-step process identified by Peterson and Hicks can be used by leadership practitioners to diagnose why behavioral change is *not* occurring and what can be done about it. For example, followers may not be developing new skills because they do not trust their leader, the skills have not been clearly identified or are not important to them, or they do not have a plan to acquire these skills. Second, informal coaching can and does occur anywhere in the organization. Senior executives can use this model to develop their staffs, peers can use it to help each other, and so forth. Third, this process is just as effective for high-performing followers as it is for low-performing followers. Leadership practitioners have a tendency to forget to coach their solid or top followers, yet these individuals are often making the greatest contributions to team or organizational success. Moreover, research has shown that the top performers in a job often produce 20–50 percent more than the average performer, depending on the complexity of the job.[60] So if leaders would focus on moving their solid performers into the highest-performing ranks and making their top performers even better, chances are their teams might be substantially more effective than if they focused only on coaching those doing most poorly. It would also behoove coaches to be mindful of the kinds of coaching that coachees themselves regard as most helpful (see **Figure 2.3**).

Fourth, both "remote" coaching of people and coaching of individuals from other cultures can be particularly difficult.[61, 62] It is more difficult for leaders to build trusting relationships with followers when they are physically separated by great distances. The same may be true with followers from other cultures. For example, cultures vary in the extent to which members are receptive to feedback. The importance of "saving face" in certain cultures makes it correspondingly more challenging when coaching individuals from such cultures to give feedback (especially negative feedback) in ways that do not seem like an attack on the coachee.[63]

Most people are familiar with the idea of a personal fitness trainer—a person who helps design a fitness program tailored to a specific individual's needs and goals. **Formal coaching** programs provide a similar kind of service for executives and managers in leadership positions. Approximately 65 percent of the Global 1,000 companies use some form of formal coaching.[64] Formal coaching programs are individualized by their nature, but several common features deserve mention. There is a one-on-one relationship between the manager and the coach (that is, an internal or external consultant) that lasts from six months to more than a year. The process usually begins with the manager's completion of extensive tests of personality, intelligence, interests, and value; 360-degree feedback instruments; and interviews by the coach of other individuals in the manager's world of work. As the result of the assessment phase of this process, both the manager and the coach have a clear picture of development needs. The coach and the manager then meet regularly (roughly monthly) to review the results of the feedback instruments and work on building skills and practicing target behaviors. Role plays and video recordings are used extensively during these sessions, and coaches provide immediate feedback to clients practicing new behaviors in realistic work situations. Another valuable outcome of coaching programs can involve clarification of managers' values, identification of discrepancies between their espoused values and their actual behaviors, and development of strategies to better align their behaviors with their values.

> *No man is so foolish but he may sometimes give another good counsel, and no man so wise that he may not easily err if he takes no other counsel than his own. He that is taught only by himself has a fool for a master.*
>
> **Ben Jonson, English playwright and poet**
>
> *Parents are the first leadership trainers in life.*
>
> **Bruce Avolio, leadership researcher**

FIGURE 2.3   What Were the Most Useful Factors in the Coaching You Received?

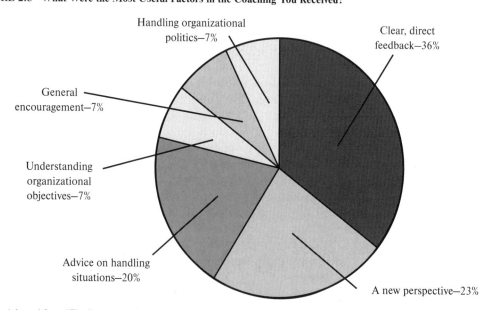

Source: Adapted from "The Business Leader as Development Coach," *PDI Portfolio*, Winter 1996, p. 6.

A formal coaching program can cost more than \$100,000, and it is reasonable to ask if this money is well spent. A solid body of research shows that well-designed and well-executed coaching programs do in fact change behavior if, as **Highlight 2.8** points out, certain conditions are met.[65, 66, 67, 68] **Figure 2.4** shows that coaching may be more effective at changing behavior than more traditional learning and training approaches.

Some Critical Lessons Learned from Formal Coaching

HIGHLIGHT 2.8

1. **The person being coached must want to change.** It is difficult to get someone to change their behavior unless they want to change. Coaches need to ensure that coachees clearly understand the benefits of changing their behavior and the consequences if they do not change. Often it is much easier to get people to change when coaches link the new behaviors to coachees' values and career goals.

2. **Assessments are important.** Formal assessments involving personality, values, mental abilities, and multirater feedback are essential to understanding what behaviors coachees need to change, what is driving these needed changes, and how easy or difficult it will be to change targeted behaviors.

3. **Some behaviors cannot be changed.** Some behaviors are so ingrained or unethical that the best option may be termination. For example, one of the authors was asked to coach a married vice president who got two of his executive assistants pregnant in less than a year. Given that the coach was not an expert in birth control, the coach turned down the engagement.

4. **Practice is critical.** Good coaches not only discuss what needs to change but also make coachees practice targeted behaviors.

Often the initial practice takes place during coaching sessions, where the coach may play the role of another party and give the coachee feedback and suggestions for improvement. These practices are then extended to work, where the coachee must use these newly acquired behaviors in real-world situations.

5. **There is no substitute for accountability.** Superiors must be kept in the loop about coachees' progress and must hold them accountable for on-the-job changes. If coaches are working with individuals whose future is at dire risk due to deficient performance, then superiors must be willing to let coachees go if they do not make needed changes. Although fear and threats are not the best way to get people to change, some derailment candidates are in so much denial about their problems that it is only by fear of losing their high-status jobs that they are motivated to change.

As you read through this list of coaching "best practices," how might you distinguish good coaching from giving advice?

Sources: S. Berglas, "The Very Real Dangers of Executive Coaching," *Harvard Business Review*, June 2002, pp. 86–93; and G. J. Curphy, "What Role Should I/O Psychologists Play in Executive Education?" in *Models of Executive Education*, R. T. Hogan (chair), presentation at the 17th Annual Conference of the Society for Industrial and Organizational Psychology, Toronto, Canada, April 2002.

Mentoring

In an organization, you also can gain valuable perspectives and insights through close association with an experienced person willing to take you under her or his wing. Such an individual is often called a **mentor**, after the character in Greek mythology whom Odysseus trusted to run his household and see to his son's education when Odysseus went off to fight the Trojans. Now, 3,000 years later, Mentor's name is used to describe the process by which an older and more experienced person helps to socialize and encourage younger organizational colleagues.[69]

Mentoring is a personal relationship in which a more experienced mentor (usually someone two to four levels higher in an organization) acts as a guide, role model, and sponsor of a less experienced protégé. Mentors provide protégés with knowledge, advice, challenge, counsel, and support about career opportunities, organizational strategy and policy, office politics, and so forth. Although mentoring has a strong developmental component, it is not the same as coaching. One key difference is that mentoring may not target specific development needs. Protégés often meet with their mentors to get a different perspective on the organization or for advice on potential committee and task force assignments or promotion opportunities. Another difference is that this guidance is not coming from the protégé's immediate supervisor, but rather from someone several leadership levels higher in the organization. Protégés often do receive informal coaching from their bosses but may be more apt to seek career guidance and personal advice from their mentors. Another difference is that the mentor may not even be part of the organization. A mentor may have retired from the organization or may have been someone for whom the protégé worked a number of years earlier.

As in coaching, there are both formal and informal mentoring programs. *Informal mentoring* occurs when a protégé and mentor build a long-term relationship based on friendship, similar interests, and mutual respect.

FIGURE 2.4   The Power of Coaching

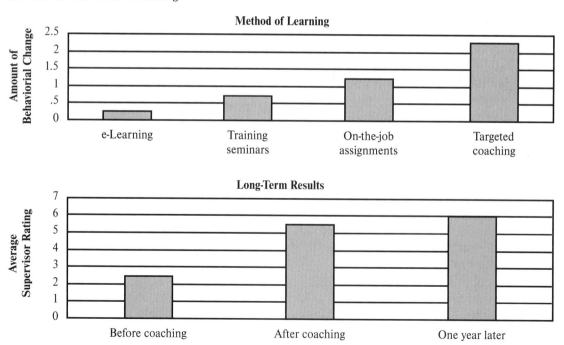

Source: D. B. Peterson, *Individual Coaching Services: Coaching That Makes a Difference* (Minneapolis, MN: Personnel Decisions International, 1999).

These relationships often begin with the protégé working in some part of the mentor's organization or on a high-visibility project for the mentor. *Formal mentoring* programs occur when the organization assigns a relatively inexperienced but high-potential leader to one of the top executives in the company. The protégé and mentor get together on a regular basis so that the protégé can gain exposure and learn more about how decisions are made at the top of the organization. Often organizations implement formal mentoring programs to accelerate the development of female or minority protégés.[70, 71, 72]

Mentoring is quite prevalent in many organizations today. Researchers reported that 74 percent of the noncommissioned officers and officers in the U.S. Army had mentors and 67 percent of all U.S. Navy admirals had mentors sometime in their careers. Moreover, many admirals reported having an average of 3.5 mentors by the time they retired.[73, 74, 75] Other researchers have reported positive relationships between mentoring, personal learning, career satisfaction, pay, promotions, and retention.[76, 77, 78, 79, 80] But some of this research also found that formal mentoring programs were better than no mentoring programs but less effective than informal mentoring for protégé compensation and promotion.[81, 82, 83] The reason for these diminished results may be that most formal mentoring programs have a difficult time replicating the strong emotional bonds found in informal programs. In addition, most formal mentoring programs last only a year, whereas many informal mentoring relationships can last a lifetime.

It also seems likely that these diminished results are due to increasingly sloppy use over time of the term *mentoring*, extending it to developmental relationships qualitatively far removed from the concept's original and core meaning. Alderfer pointed out that a true mentoring relationship "consists of senior people helping junior colleagues develop the younger person's sense of personal authority based on the junior person's Dream of themselves in a mature adult role. It is decidedly not imposing (or subtly promoting) an organization's or a mentor's version of what that person should become."[84] As such, being a mentor is different from being either a coach or a sponsor to another person (a sponsor is a person holding a senior organizational position who sees to it that selected high-potential junior employees receive especially valuable developmental assignments and/or promotions).

Building Your Own Leadership Self-Image

This chapter has explored various aspects of how leadership develops, but we must acknowledge that not everyone *wants* to be a leader or believes he or she can be. John Gardner has argued that many of our best and brightest young people actually have been immunized against, and dissuaded from, seeking leadership opportunities and responsibilities.[85] Other young people, even if they want to be leaders, may not believe they have what it takes. Both groups, we believe, are selling themselves short. Remember that you are a "work in progress," who even yet may not be ready to take full advantage of the leadership opportunities available to you (not that you shouldn't try). Even biologically, if you are a typical-age college student, your brains are still maturing. Advances in neuroscience technology provide insights into how adolescent decision-making and information processing differ from mature decision-making because of continuing structural brain development processes, which thus impact (among other things) capabilities for benefiting fully from leadership development opportunities.[86]

Nurture, of course, also plays a role in one's readiness for leadership development. Some parents' styles of raising their children prepare them to learn from experience better than others. Take, for example, overparenting or "helicopter parenting." It reflects a parental style of hovering over offspring, ensuring that the children experience little distress. Such parents typically have good intentions and believe that their behavior enhances their children's chances of success. However, such hovering behavior is developmentally inappropriate and unhelpful for the child's maturation into adulthood. With regard to readiness for leadership development, overparenting has been linked negatively to a young person's likelihood of emerging as a leader in group situations.[87]

For those who may be tempted to avoid the responsibilities of leadership, we encourage an openness of mind about the importance and pervasiveness of leadership. We hope this book offers ways of thinking about leadership that make it at once more immediate, more relevant, and more interesting than it may have seemed before. We hope this book helps develop your *motivation* to lead, as well as some ideas about developing your leadership skills.[88] For others, we encourage flexibility in self-image. As we noted earlier, developing one's identity as a leader is a lifelong "work-in-progress." It is a dynamic process the trajectory of which arcs with each person's ongoing opportunities and self-perceived changes in leadership skills.[89] Do not stay out of the leadership arena based on some self-defeating generalization such as "I am not the leader type." Experiment and take a few risks with different leadership roles. This will help you appreciate new facets of yourself as well as broaden your leadership self-image. It would be wise, in fact, to build your leadership self-image through carefully selected developmental experiences that don't necessarily have the words "leadership development" emblazoned across them.

Summary

This chapter reviewed several major points regarding how leadership can be developed through both formal education and experience. One way to get more out of your leadership courses and experiences is through the application of the action–observation–reflection model. This model provides a framework for better understanding of leadership situations. In addition, being aware of the role perception plays in leadership development is important because it affects what you observe, how you interpret your observations, and what actions you take as a leader. Finally, remember that both education and experience can contribute to your development as a leader by enhancing your ability to reflect on and analyze leadership situations. Exposure to formal leadership education programs can help you develop multiple perspectives to analyze leadership situations, and the people you work with and the task itself can also provide you with insights on how to be a better leader. However, what you gain from any leadership program or experience is a function of what you make of it. Successful leaders are those who have "an extraordinary tenacity in extracting something worthwhile from their experience and in seeking experiences rich in opportunities for growth."[90] If you want to become a better leader, you must seek challenges and try to get all you can from any leadership situation or opportunity.

The chapter also examined several specific ways of changing behavior and developing leadership. For most people, behavior change efforts are most successful if some formal system or process of behavioral change is put into place; these systems include action learning, development planning, informal and formal coaching programs, and mentorships. Action learning involves using real work experience as the context for leadership development (as contrasted, for example, with off-site training). Development planning is the process of pinpointing development needs, creating development plans, implementing plans, and reflecting on and revising plans regularly. Good development plans focus on one or two development needs, capitalize on on-the-job experiences, and specify sources of feedback. Organizations with formal development systems are likely to realize greater behavioral changes from more managers than organizations having no system or only an informal one.

Leaders can create development plans for themselves, and they can also help their followers with behavioral change through coaching or mentoring programs. Informal coaching programs often consist of a series of steps designed to create permanent behavioral changes in followers, and both leaders and followers play active roles in informal coaching programs. Formal coaching typically involves a formal assessment process and a series of one-on-one coaching sessions over a 6- to 12-month period. These sessions target specific development needs and capitalize on practice and feedback to acquire needed skills. Mentoring programs have many of the same objectives as coaching programs but take place between an individual (the protégé) and a leader several levels higher in the organization (the mentor).

Key Terms

action–observation–reflection (A-O-R) model

spiral of experience

perceptual set

attribution

fundamental attribution error

self-serving bias

actor/observer difference

self-fulfilling prophecy

Teacher–Mentor

Father–Judge

Warrior–Knight

Revolutionary–Crusader

Visionary–Alchemist

single-loop learning

double-loop learning

after event reviews (AERs)

service learning

individualized feedback

case studies

role playing

simulations

games

return on investment

in-basket exercises

action learning

training programs

development plan

development planning

coaching

informal coaching

formal coaching

mentor

mentoring

Questions

1. Not all effective leaders seem to be reflective by nature. How do you reconcile that with the concept of the spiral of experience and its role in leadership development?

2. Explain how you can use knowledge about each of the following to enrich the benefits of your own present leadership experiences:

    a. The action–observation–reflection model

    b. The people you interact and work with

    c. The activities you are involved in

3. Using the role of teacher as a specific instance of leadership, discuss how a teacher's perceptual set, expectations of students, and attributions may affect student motivation and performance. Do you think some teachers could become more effective by becoming more aware of these processes? Would that be true for leaders in general?

4. If you were to design the perfect leadership development experience for yourself, how would you do so and what would it include? How would you know whether it was effective?

5. Do you think people have a need for growth and development?

6. One important aspect of learning from experience is observing the consequences of one's actions. Sometimes, however, the most significant consequences of a leader's actions do not occur for several years (for example, the ultimate impact of certain personnel decisions or a strategic decision to change a product line). Is there any way individuals can learn from the consequences of those actions in a way to modify their behavior? If consequences are so delayed, is there a danger they might draw the wrong lessons from their experiences?

7. What would a development plan for student leaders look like? How could you capitalize on school experiences as part of a development plan?

8. What would a leadership coaching or mentoring program for students look like? How could you tell whether the program worked?

Activities

1. Divide yourselves into groups, and in each group contrast what attributions you might make about the leadership style of two different individuals. All you know about them is the following:

	Person A	**Person B**
Favorite TV Show	*60 Minutes*	*Survivor*
Car	Ford Mustang	Volkswagen Beetle
Favorite Sport	American football	Mountain biking
Political Leaning	Conservative Republican	Liberal Democrat
Favorite Music	Country and western	New age

2. Read the development planning material in **Chapter 13** of this book. Complete a GAPS analysis and create a development plan for yourself. Share your development plan with someone else in your class. Check with your partner in two to four weeks to review progress on your plans.

Minicase

Developing Leaders at UPS

UPS is the nation's fourth-largest employer with 357,000 employees worldwide and operations in more than 200 countries. UPS is consistently recognized as one of the "top companies to work for" and was recently recognized by *Fortune* as one of the 50 best companies for minorities. A major reason for UPS's success is the company's commitment to its employees. UPS understands the importance of providing both education and experience for its next generation of leaders—spending $300 million annually on education programs for employees and encouraging promotion from within. All employees are offered equal opportunities to build the skills and knowledge they need to succeed. A perfect example of this is Jovita Carranza.

Jovita Carranza joined UPS in 1976 as a part-time clerk in Los Angeles. Carranza demonstrated a strong work ethic and a commitment to UPS, and UPS rewarded her with opportunities—opportunities Carranza was not shy about taking advantage of. By 1985 Carranza was the workforce planning manager in metropolitan Los Angeles. By 1987 she was district human resources manager based in central Texas. By 1990 she had accepted a move to district human resources manager in Illinois. She received her first operations assignment, as division manager for hub, package, and feeder operations, in Illinois in 1991. Two years later, she said yes to becoming district operations manager in Miami. In 1996 she accepted the same role in Wisconsin. By 1999 Carranza's progressive successes led UPS to promote her to president of the Americas Region.

The $1.1 billion air hub she oversaw sprawled across the equivalent of more than 80 football fields. It could handle 304,000 packages an hour, its computers process nearly 1 million transactions per minute, and it served as the lynchpin for the $33 billion business that became the world's largest package delivery company.

Carranza attributes much of her success to her eagerness to take on new challenges: "The one error that people make early on in their careers is that they're very selective about opportunities so they avoid some, prefer others," she says. "I always accepted all opportunities that presented themselves because from each one you can learn something, and they serve as a platform for future endeavors."

It has also been important, she says, to surround herself with capable, skilled employees who are loyal to the company and committed to results. After nearly 30 years with UPS, Carranza says teamwork, interaction, and staff development are the achievements of which she is proudest: "Because that takes focus, determination, and sincerity to perpetuate the UPS culture and enhance it through people."

Carranza's corporate achievements, determination, drive, innovation, and leadership in business earned her the distinction of being named *Hispanic Business Magazine*'s Woman of the Year. She credits her parents, both of Mexican descent, with teaching her "the importance of being committed, of working hard, and doing so with a positive outlook"—principles she says continue to guide her personal and professional life. These principles mirror those of the company whose corporate ladder she has climbed nonstop, an organization she says values diversity and encourages quality, integrity, commitment, fairness, loyalty, and social responsibility.

Among Carranza's words of wisdom: "Sit back and listen and observe," she says. "You learn more by not speaking. Intelligent people learn from their own experiences; with wisdom, you learn from other people's mistakes. I'm very methodical about that."

1. What are the major skills Jovita Carranza has demonstrated in her career at UPS that have made her a successful leader?

2. Consider the spiral of experience that Carranza has traveled. How has her experience affected her ability as a leader?

3. Do you think Carranza would have been equally successful had she worked in any other organization?

Sources: www.antiessays.com/free-essays/01-29-2015-Mini-Case-Developing-Leaders-At-723934.html.

Endnotes

1. D. V. Day, "Leadership Development: A Review in Context," *The Leadership Quarterly* 11, no. 4 (2000), pp. 581–613.

2. P. Bernthal and R. Wellins, "Trends in Leader Development and Succession," *Human Resource Planning* 29, no. 2 (2006), pp. 31–40.

3. M. McCall, "Recasting Leadership Development," *Industrial and Organizational Psychology* 3 (2010), pp. 3–19.

4. M. W. McCall Jr., M. M. Lombardo, and A. M. Morrison, *The Lessons of Experience: How Successful Executives Develop on the Job* (Lexington, MA: Lexington Books, 1988), p. 122.

5. D. Kolb, *Experiential Learning: Experience as the Source of Learning and Development* (Englewood Cliffs, NJ: Prentice Hall, 1983).

6. C. Powell, with Joe Pirsico, *My American Journey* (New York: Random House, 1995), p. 109.

7. Powell, *My American Journey.*

8. J. Reason and K. Mycielska, *Absent-Minded? The Psychology of Mental Lapses and Everyday Errors* (Englewood Cliffs, NJ: Prentice Hall, 1982), p. 183.

9. L. Ross, "The Intuitive Psychologist and His Shortcomings: Distortions in the Attribution Process," in *Advances in Experimental Social Psychology* 10, ed. L. Berkowitz (New York: Academic Press, 1977), pp. 173–220.

10. D. T. Millerand M. Ross, "Self-Serving Biases in the Attribution of Causality: Fact or Fiction?" *Psychological Bulletin* 82 (1975), pp. 213–25.

11. E. E. Jones and R. E. Nisbett, "The Actor and the Observer: Divergent Perceptions of the Causes of Behavior," in *Attribution: Perceiving the Causes of Behavior*, eds. E. E. Jones, D. E. Kanouse, H. H. Kelley, R. E. Nisbett, S. Valins, and B. Weiner (Morristown, NJ: General Learning Press, 1972).

12. S. G. Green and T. R. Mitchell, "Attributional Processes of Leaders in Leader–Member Interactions," *Organizational Behavior and Human Performances* 23 (1979), pp. 429–58.

13. T. R. Mitchell, S. G. Green, and R. E. Wood, "An Attributional Model of Leadership and the Poor Performing Subordinate: Development and Validation," in *Research in Organizational Behavior*, eds. B. M. Staw and L. L. Cummings (Greenwich, CN: JAI, 1981), pp. 197–234.

14. T. R. Mitchell and R. E. Wood, "Supervisors Responses to Subordinate Poor Performance: A Test of an Attributional Model," *Organizational Behavior and Human Performance* 25 (1980), pp. 123–38.

15. E. E. Jones, "Interpreting Interpersonal Behavior: The Effects of Expectancies," *Science* 234, no. 3 (October 1986), pp. 41–46.

16. D. Eden and A. B. Shani, "Pygmalion Goes to Boot Camp: Expectancy, Leadership, and Trainee Performance," *Journal of Applied Psychology* 67 (1982), pp. 194–99.

17. K. D. Roglio and G. Light, "Executive MBA Programs: The Development of the Reflective Executive," *Academy of Management Learning & Education* 8, no. 2 (2009), pp. 156–73.

18. J. L. Lindsey, "Fine Art Metaphors Reveal Leader Archetypes," *Journal of Leadership & Organizational Studies* 18 (2011), pp. 56–63.

19. S. Finkelstein, "Don't Be Blinded By Your Own Expertise," *Harvard Business Review* 97, no. 3 (2019), p. 5.

20. C. Argyris, *Increasing Leadership Effectiveness* (New York: John Wiley, 1976).

21. S. S. DeRue, J. D. Nahrgang, J. R. Hollenbeck, and K. Workman, "A Quasi-Experimental Study of After-Event Reviews and Leadership Development," *Journal of Applied Psychology* 97, no. 5 (2012), pp. 997–1015.

22. K. A. Bunker and A. Webb, *Learning How to Learn from Experience: Impact of Stress and Coping*, Report No. 154 (Greensboro, NC: Center for Creative Leadership, 1992).

23. I. L. Janis, *Stress and Frustration* (New York: Harcourt Brace Jovanovich, 1971).

24. R. J. Grey and G. G. Gordon, "Risk-Taking Managers: Who Gets the Top Jobs?" *Management Review* 67 (1978), pp. 8–13.

25. D. C. Hambrick, "Environment, Strategy and Power within Top Management Teams," *Administrative Science Quarterly* 26 (1981), pp. 253–75.

26. G. Jennings, *The Mobile Manager* (New York: McGraw-Hill, 1971).

27. E. Schein, *Career Dynamics: Matching Individual and Organizational Needs* (Reading, MA: Addison-Wesley, 1978).

28. M. Csikszentmihalyi, *Flow: The Psychology of Optimal Experience* (New York: Harper & Row, 1990), p. 142.

29. R. T. Hogan and R. Warrenfelz, "Educating the Modern Manager," *Academy of Management Learning and Education* 2, no. 1 (2003), pp. 74–84.

30. R. E. Riggio, "Leadership Development: The Current State and Future Expectations," *Consulting Psychology Journal: Practice and Research* 60, no. 4 (2008), pp. 383–92.

31. K. Wilde, "Do They Really Want to Learn? The Science & Practice of Coachability," http://www.thecoachableleader.com.

32. R. Kaplan and R. Kaiser, "Developing Versatile Leadership," *MIT Sloan Management Review* 44 (2003).

33. G. Calvin, *Talent Is Overrated* (New York: Portfolio/Penguin, 2008).

34. R. E. Riggio, J. B. Ciulla, and G. J. Sorenson, "Leadership Education at the Undergraduate Level: A Liberal Arts Approach to Leadership Development," in *The Future of Leadership Development*, eds. S. E. Murphy and R. E. Riggio (Mahwah, NJ: Lawrence Erlbaum Associates), pp. 223–36.

35. Riggio et al., "Leadership Education at the Undergraduate Level."

36. Riggio et al., "Leadership Education at the Undergraduate Level."

37. G. P. Insed, J. D. Wood, and J. L. Petriglieri, "Up Close and Personal: Building Foundations for Leaders' Development through the Personalization of Management Learning," *Academy of Management Learning & Education* 10, no. 3 (2011), pp. 430–50.

38. D. V. Day, J. W. Fleenor, L. E. Atwater, R. E. Sturm, and R. A. McKee, "Advances in Leader and Leadership Development: A Review of 25 Years of Research and Theory," *The Leadership Quarterly* 25 (2014), pp. 63–82.

39. H. Cohen, "An Inconvenient Truth about Leadership Development," *Organizational Dynamics* 49, no. 1 (2019), pp. 8–15.

40. C. Feser, N. Nielsen, and M. Rennie, "What's Missing in Leadership Development?" *The McKinsey Quarterly* 3 (2017).

41. C. N. Lacerenza, D. L. Reyes, S. L. Marlow, D. L. Joseph, and E. Salas, "Leadership Training Design, Delivery, and Implementation: A Meta-analysis," *Journal of Applied Psychology* 102, no. 12 (2017), pp. 1686–718.

42. B. J. Avolio, J. B. Avey and D. Quisenberry, "Estimating Return on Leadership Development Investment," *The Leadership Quarterly* 21 (2010), pp. 633–44.

43. J. Conger, "Can We Really Train Leadership?" *Strategy, Management, Competition*, Winter 1996, pp. 52–65.

44. M. Nevins and S. Stumpf, "21st-Century Leadership: Redefining Management Education," *Strategy, Management, Competition*, 3rd quarter (1999), pp. 41–51.

45. G. Hernez-Broome and R. L. Hughes, "Leadership Development: Past, Present and Future," *Human Resource Planning* 27, no. 1 (2004), pp. 24–32.

46. J. A. Conger and G. Toegel, "Action Learning and Multirater Feedback: Pathways to Leadership Development?" in *The Future of Leadership Development*, eds. S. E. Murphy and R. E. Riggio, pp. 107–25 (Mahwah, NJ: Lawrence Erlbaum Associates, 2003).

47. W. R. Miller and S. Rollnick, *Motivational Interviewing: Preparing People to Change Addictive Behavior* (New York: Guilford Press, 1991).

48. J. Polivy and C. P. Herman, "If at First You Don't Succeed: False Hopes of Self-Change," *American Psychologist* 57, no. 9 (2002), pp. 677–89.

49. M. D. Peterson and M. D. Hicks, *Development FIRST: Strategies for Self-Development* (Minneapolis, MN: Personnel Decisions International, 1995).

50. J. F. Hazucha, S. A. Hezlett, and R. J. Schneider, "The Impact of 360-Degree Feedback on Management Skills Development," *Human Resource Management* 32 (1993), pp. 325–51.

51. C. D. McCauley, M. N. Ruderman, P. J. Ohlott, and J. E. Morrow, "Assessing the Developmental Components of Managerial Jobs," *Journal of Applied Psychology* 79, no. 4 (1994), pp. 544–60.

52. D. B. Peterson and M. D. Hicks, *Leader as Coach: Strategies for Coaching and Developing Others* (Minneapolis, MN: Personnel Decisions International, 1996).

53. K. Behar, D. Arvidson, W. Omilusik, B. Ellsworth, and B. Morrow, *Developing Husky Oil Leaders: A Strategic Investment* (Calgary, Canada: Husky Energy, 2000).

54. D. B. Peterson, *The Science and Art of Self-Development.* Paper presented at the Arabian States Human Resource Management Society Annual Conference, Bahrain, October 2001.

55. G. J. Curphy, "Good Leadership Is Hard to Find," *JobDig*, August 21–28 (2006), pp. 23–24.

56. W. Arthur Jr., W. Bennett Jr., P. S. Edens, and S. T. Bell. "Effectiveness of Training in Organizations: A Meta-analysis of Design and Evaluation Features," *Journal of Applied Psychology* 88, no. 2 (2003), pp. 234–45.

57. K. M. Wasylyshyn, B. Gronsky, and J. W. Hass, "Tigers, Stripes, and Behavior Change: Survey Results of a Commissioned Coaching Program," *Consulting Psychology Journal* 58, no. 2 (2006), pp. 65–81.

58. Peterson and Hicks, *Leader as Coach.*

59. Peterson and Hicks, *Leader as Coach.*

60. J. E. Hunter, F. L. Schmidt, and M. K. Judiesch, "Individual Differences in Output Variability as a Function of Job Complexity," *Journal of Applied Psychology* 74 (1990), pp. 28–42.

61. G. J. Curphy, *The Accelerated Coaching Program Training Manual* (North Oaks, MN: Curphy Consulting Corporation, 2003).

62. D. B. Peterson and M. D. Hicks, *Professional Coaching: State of the Art, State of the Practice* (Minneapolis, MN: Personnel Decisions International, 1998).

63. C. W. Coultas, W. L. Bedwell, C. S. Burke, and E. Salas, "Values Sensitive Coaching: The Delta Approach to Coaching Culturally Diverse Executives," *Consulting Psychology Journal: Practice and Research* 63, no. 3 (2011), pp. 149–61.

64. Peterson and Hicks, *Professional Coaching.*

65. K. M. Wasylyshyn et al., "Tigers, Stripes, and Behavior Change."

66. W. J. G. Evers, A. Brouwers, and W. Tomic. "A Quasi-Experimental Study on Management Coaching Effectiveness," *Consulting Psychology Journal* 58, no. 3 (2006), pp. 174–82.

67. D. B. Peterson and J. Millier, "The Alchemy of Coaching: You're Good, Jennifer, But You Could Be Really Good," *Consulting Psychology Journal* 57 no. 1 (2005), pp. 14–40.

68. S. V. Bowles and J. J. Picano, "Dimensions of Coaching Related to Productivity and Quality of Life," *Consulting Psychology Journal* 58, no. 4 (2006), pp. 232–39.

69. J. A. Wilson and N. S. Elman, "Organizational Benefits of Mentoring," *Academy of Management Executive* 4 (1990), pp. 88–93.

70. B. R. Ragins, J. L. Cotton, and J. S. Miller, "Marginal Mentoring: The Effects of Types of Mentor, Quality of Relationship, and Program Design of Work and Career Attitudes," *Academy of Management Journal* 43, no. 6 (2000), pp. 1177–94.

71. D. A. Thomas, "The Truth about Mentoring Minorities: Race Matters," *Harvard Business Review*, April (2001), pp. 98–111.

72. Menttium, *Menttium 100: Cross-Company Mentoring for High Potential Women* (Minneapolis, MN: The Menttium Corporation, 2007).

73. A. G. Steinberg and D. M. Foley, "Mentoring in the Army: From Buzzword to Practice," *Military Psychology* 11, no. 4 (1999), pp. 365–80.

74. R. Lall, "Mentoring Experiences of Retired Navy Admirals," paper presented at Personnel Decisions International, Denver, CO, May 6, 1999.

75. S. C. De Janasz, S. E. Sullivan, and V. Whiting, "Mentor Networks and Career Success: Lessons for Turbulent Times," *Academy of Management Executive* 17, no. 3 (2003), pp. 78–88.

76. Menttium, *Menttium 100.*

77. T. D. Allen, L. T. Eby, M. L. Poteet, E. Lentz, and L. Lima, "Career Benefits Associated with Mentoring for Protégés: A Meta-analysis," *Journal of Applied Psychology* 89, no. 1 (2004), pp. 127–36.

78. T. D. Allen, L. T. Eby, and E. Lentz. "The Relationship between Formal Mentoring Program Characteristics and Perceived Program Effectiveness," *Personnel Psychology* 59 (2006), pp. 125–53.

79. L. T. Eby, M. Butts, A. Lockwood, and S. A. Simon, "Protégés' Negative Mentoring Experiences: Construct Development and Nomological Validation," *Personnel Psychology* 57, no. 2 (2004), pp. 411–48.

80. M. Abrahams, "Making Mentoring Pay," *Harvard Business Review*, June 2006, p. 21.

81. B. R. Ragins et al., "Marginal Mentoring."

82. T. D Allen, L. T. Eby, and E. Lentz, "Mentorship Behaviors and Mentorship Quality Associated with Formal Mentoring Programs: Closing the Gap between Research and Practice," *Journal of Applied Psychology* 91, no. 3 (2006), pp. 567–78.

83. Allen, Eby, and Lentz, "The Relationship between Formal Mentoring Program Characteristics."

84. C. P. Alderfer, "Clarifying the Meaning of Mentor-Protege Relationships," *Consulting Psychology Journal: Practice and Leadership* 66 (2014), pp. 6–19.

85. J. W. Gardner, "The Antileadership Vaccine," essay in the Carnegie Corporation of New York annual report, 1965.

86. P. Riddell, "Reward and Threat in the Adolescent Brain: Implications for Leadership Development," *Leadership & Organization Development Journal* 38, no. 4 (2017), pp. 530–48.

87. Z. Liu, R. Riggio, D. Day, C. Zheng, S. Dai, and Y. Bian, "Leader Development Begins at Home: Over parenting Harms Adolescent Leader Emergence," *Journal of Applied Psychology* 104 (2019), pp. 1226–42.

88. D. Waldman, G. Galvin, and F. Walumbwa, "The Development of Motivation to Lead and Leader Role Identity," *Journal of Leadership & Organizational Studies* 20 (2013), pp. 156–68.

89. D. Miscenko, H. Guenter, and D. Day, "Am I a Leader? Examining Leader Development Over Time," *The Leadership Quarterly* 28 (2017), pp. 605–20.

90. McCall Jr., Lombardo, and Morrison, *The Lessons of Experience.*

CHAPTER 3

Skills for Developing Yourself as a Leader

Introduction

Any person can improve his or her leadership effectiveness in part because leadership involves skills, and skills can be practiced and developed. Another advantage of looking at leadership skills is that most people are less defensive about deficits in skills (which can be improved) than they are about suggested deficits in, say, personality. At the end of each of the four parts of this book, we present a chapter about leadership skills that seem particularly relevant to various facets of our interactional framework. Because these skills chapters are quite different in purpose than the other chapters in the text, their format is correspondingly different. Specifically, they do not include the same closing sections found in the other chapters.

Not surprisingly, this first segment deals with some of the most fundamental, immediate, and yet in other ways most enduring challenges you will face as a leader. Key among these challenges is continuing to learn as a leader what you need to know now to be successful, and how to keep learning and developing throughout your life and career. The skills in this chapter will help in that effort. By the way, it might be useful to say more here about development planning, the last skill addressed in this chapter. Generally speaking, development planning would be considered an advanced leadership skill because it typically involves a leader developing her or his subordinates or followers. It is included with other skills in this introductory section so that you might think about how to apply some of the ideas about development planning *to yourself*.

These are the leadership skills covered in this chapter:

- Your First 90 Days as a Leader
- Learning from Experience
- Building Technical Competence
- Building Effective Relationships with Superiors
- Building Effective Relationships with Peers
- Development Planning

Your First 90 Days as a Leader

People often find moving into a new leadership position to be a highly stressful work experience. Often these promotions involve relocations, working for new organizations and bosses, leading new teams, and being responsible for products or services that may be outside their immediate areas of expertise. Whether the move is from individual contributor to first-line supervisor or into senior executive positions, the stresses and strains of the first 90 days are both real and acute. Although the first three months give leaders unique opportunities to make smooth transitions, paint compelling pictures of the future, and drive organizational change, far too many new leaders stumble during this critical time period. This is unfortunate—these early activities often are instrumental to a leader's future success or failure. Many of these early mistakes are avoidable, and what follows is a road map for helping people make successful transitions into new leadership positions. It is important to note that the onboarding road map developed by Roellig and Curphy is focused on external hires—those outside an organization who have been brought in to leadership positions.[1] (See **Figure 3.1**.) Some of the steps in the onboarding road map can be ignored or need to be modified for individuals who have been promoted from within.

Before You Start: Do Your Homework

In all likelihood, people wanting to move into a leadership role with another organization have already done a considerable amount of preparation for the interview process. Candidates should have read as much as they can about the organization by reviewing its website, annual reports, press releases, and marketing literature. They should also use Facebook, LinkedIn, Plaxo, and other social networking sites to set up informational interviews with people inside the organization. These informational interviews will help candidates learn more about the organization's history and culture and provide additional insight about the vacant position. Sometime during the interview process candidates should also seek answers to the following questions:

- Why is the organization looking for an outside hire for the position?
- What can make the function or team to be led more effective?
- What is currently working in the function or team to be led?
- What is currently not working in the function or team to be led?
- What about the function or team is keeping interviewers awake at night?

Once candidates have landed new positions, they should seek additional information about their new jobs as well as set up some of the activities that need to take place during their first two weeks at work. New hires

FIGURE 3.1 New Leader Onboarding Road Map

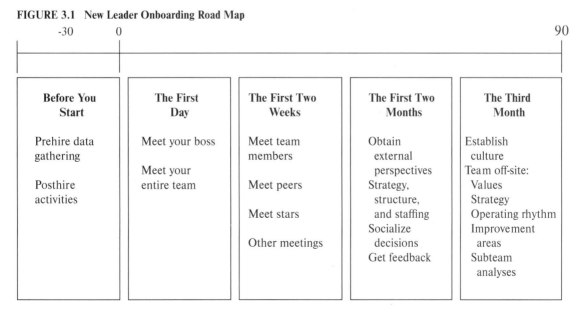

should check with their bosses to see if they can get copies of the results or metrics pertaining to the group to be led, any presentations predecessors made about the group or department, budget information, contact information for their direct reports, and so forth. They should also ask their new bosses what they need to do to set up access cards and e-mail, office, and cell phone accounts, as being able to get into the facility and having functional computers and phones at the start is crucial to a smooth beginning. Prior to arrival, a new hire should also set up one-hour meetings with the boss and with the entire team on the first day and follow-up two- to three-hour one-on-one meetings with each team member during the first two weeks on the job.

The First Day: You Get Only One Chance to Make a First Impression

New leaders have two critical tasks the first day on the job: to meet their new boss and their new team. The first meeting should happen in the boss's office and be about an hour long. Here are some key topics to discuss in this meeting:

- Identifying the team's key objectives, metrics, and important projects.
- Understanding the boss's view of team strengths and weaknesses.
- Working through meeting schedules and communication styles. (How, when, and on what does the boss want to be kept informed?)
- Sharing plans for the day and the next several weeks.

New hires should end the discussion by arranging a follow-up meeting with their bosses to review progress and to ask whether weekly or monthly one-on-one meetings would be helpful.

New leaders should also meet with their entire teams the first day on the job. Depending on the size of the team, this meeting could be held in a small conference room or it could be in a large auditorium with webcasts or conference calls to remote sites. It usually takes new leaders about an hour to share their backgrounds, the attributes and values they feel are important to success, expectations for themselves and employees, work habits and preferred ways of interacting, family and recreational activities, and what they plan on doing over the next few weeks. After sharing this information, new leaders should ask team members whether they have any questions but should not expect many takers. Because team members do not know new leaders well, these initial meetings tend to have more one-way communication than interactive dialogue.

The First Two Weeks: Lay the Foundation

New leaders should spend the first two weeks meeting with many people both inside and outside the team. The key objectives for these meetings are to (1) learn as much as possible, (2) develop relationships, and (3) determine future allies. New leaders need to be particularly mindful about what they say or write in these meetings because they have no idea in whom they can confide. They also need to be aware of the fact that some of the people they are meeting with, for whatever reason, are not happy about their arrival and may not want them to succeed.

During the first two weeks, new leaders will want to have one-on-one meetings with key team members. If the team has fewer than 15 people, new leaders should meet individually with everyone on the team; if the team is larger, new leaders should meet one-on-one with direct reports during the first two weeks and have small group or individual meetings with everyone else on the team sometime during the first 90 days. The one-on-one meetings usually last from two to three hours, and some of the critical questions to ask include these:

- *What is the team member working on?* New leaders should ask about major projects and where people are spending their time because this will help identify the critical issues facing the team.

- *What are the team member's objectives?* This is an important question that needs to be asked after the previous question. Often team members spend their time and energy working on projects that are completely unrelated to their work objectives, and new leaders need to understand what these gaps are and why they are occurring.

- *Who are the "stars" a level or two down in the organization?* This question may be omitted if new leaders are in charge of groups consisting of fewer than 15 people. But if groups are significantly larger, it is important for new leaders to know who their top performers are. In all likelihood direct reports will name many of the same people as stars, and these high-performing individuals can play critical roles during the first 90 days of a new leader's tenure.

- *What are the people issues on the team?* This can be a difficult question to ask—new leaders don't want team members to think they are asking them to disparage others. However, it is important for new leaders to find out who is displaying inappropriate behavior or is difficult to work with. Once properly identified, new team leaders will need to address these people issues within the first 60 days in order to make clear who is in charge and to show what type of behavior will and will not be tolerated on the team.

- *What can the team do better?* Team members' answers to this question can help new leaders develop ideas for improving team performance. These answers also indicate whether team members are capable of thinking about, accepting, and driving change.

- *What advice do team members have for the new leader, and what can the new leader do to help team members?* New team leaders should close their meetings with these two questions and pay particular attention to what they can do to help their direct reports be successful. New leaders should avoid making any immediate promises but commit to closing the loop on those requests they will or will not fulfill sometime during the next two months.

Although new leaders should start building rapport during these one-on-one meetings, they should minimize their personal interactions with direct reports during their first two months on the job. Business lunches and team get-togethers are fine, but meeting with families and spouses during the first 60 days can make later structure and staffing decisions more difficult. New leaders need to make personnel decisions with team performance, not personal friendships, in mind.

During the first two weeks on the job, new leaders should also schedule one-on-one meetings with all their peers. These meetings should last about an hour and take place in peers' offices; this will give new leaders opportunities to build rapport by observing office décor, diplomas, family pictures, awards, and so on. New leaders should discuss the following issues with peers:

- Their peers' objectives, challenges, team structure, and the like
- Their perspectives on what the new leader's team does well and could do better
- Their perspectives on the new leader's team members
- How to best communicate with the boss
- How issues get raised and decisions made on their boss's team

New leaders should make it clear that they want and appreciate their peers' help. Scheduling regular meetings with their peers will build relationships and help new leaders stay ahead of potential conflicts or work issues. Unlike more personal meetings with direct reports, it is perfectly acceptable to socialize with peers and their families during the first 60 days. And because the boss will likely ask peers how the new leader is doing, meeting with peers on a regular basis becomes even more important.

If the team being led is fairly large, new leaders should also meet with their stars during the first two weeks on the job. Stars will be full of ideas for improving team performance, and these individuals are likely candidates for direct report positions should the new leader decide to change the structure of the team. If chosen for promotion, stars are likely to be loyal and well respected by others because they were widely recognized as being among the top performers on the team.

During the first two weeks, new leaders should also try to meet with individuals who were once part of the team but have taken positions in other parts of the organization. These individuals can offer unique insights into the history of the team and team members, and this source of information should not be overlooked. The two other pieces of information new leaders should gather during the first two weeks are what the organization sees as the critical roles on the team and if there were any internal candidates for the team leader position. This information can be gathered from the boss, peers, former team members, the human resources representative, or the like. New leaders need this information to ensure they have the best talent filling key roles and to see if anyone on the team may be hoping they fail.

The First Two Months: Strategy, Structure, and Staffing

After their initial round of meetings with the boss, peers, and direct reports, new leaders need to spend the next six weeks gathering more information, determining the direction, and finalizing the appropriate structure and staffing for the team. Some of the tasks to be performed during this time include gathering benchmarking information from other organizations, meeting with key external customers and suppliers, and if appropriate, meeting with the former team leader. This additional information, when combined with the information gleaned from bosses, peers, direct reports, and stars, should help new team leaders determine the proper direction for their teams. This direction, or vision, may be more or less the same as what is already in place, or it may represent a significant change in direction. In either case, new leaders need to be able to articulate where the team has been and where it needs to go over the next one to three years, what it needs to accomplish, what changes will be needed to make this happen, and their expectations for team members. Depending on the new leader's vision, some of these changes may involve changing the team's structure and membership. In making these changes, new leaders need to remember that team strategy (vision and goals) should drive team structure, which in turn should drive team staffing decisions. Leaders who alter the strategy–structure–staffing sequence risk building dysfunctional, underperforming teams.

Although the first 90 days on the job provide a unique window for driving change, new leaders need to "socialize" their strategy, structure, and staffing ideas with their bosses and peers before making any personnel decisions. Gathering input and working through potential disruptions with these two groups before moving ahead should improve buy-in and support for any change decisions. Once the proposed changes have been agreed to, new leaders need to have one-on-one meetings with all team members affected by any strategy, structure, and staffing decisions. During these meetings, new leaders need to describe their vision and rationale for the changes and clarify roles and expectations for affected team members.

Although gathering additional information, developing the team's vision, and socializing key changes with affected parties take a considerable amount of time, new leaders must remember to stay focused on team performance. Team leaders may have less leeway to make needed changes if team performance drops precipitously during their first 60 days because dealing with day-to-day team issues will take up so much time that there will be little time left to drive change. Although it will be hard to obtain, new leaders should also seek feedback from others during their first two months with the organization. Possible sources for feedback include peers and recruiters. Recruiters have vested interests in seeing their placed candidates succeed and often tap their contacts within organizations to give new leaders feedback.

The Third Month: Communicate and Drive Change

At this point in a new leader's tenure, he or she has developed a vision of the future and can articulate how the team will win; identified the what, why, and how of any needed changes; and defined a clear set of expectations for team members. The two major events for the third month are meeting with the entire team and meeting off-site with direct reports (if the team is large). The purpose of the first team meeting is for the new leader to share what he or she learned from whom during the information gathering process, his or her vision of the future, the new team structure and staffing model, his or her expectations for team members, and the rationale for any team changes. New leaders need to tie their changes to the attributes and values they shared during their first day on the job. Change is not about a new leader's PowerPoint presentation or the posters put up, but instead involves the tangible actions taken. And the actions team members pay the most attention to are the hiring, firing, promotion, restructuring, and staffing decisions made by new team leaders. One of the fastest ways to change the culture and norms of a team is to change the people in it.

If the group being led is large, new leaders will want to have a separate second meeting with direct reports. This meeting may last one to two days and should be held off-site to minimize interruptions. The key issues to work through off-site include these:

- *Get agreement on the critical attributes and values of team members.* Although new leaders will have clear ideas about the values and attributes they are looking for in team members, they cannot be sure direct reports have fully bought into this set of attributes. New leaders should set aside time during the off-site meeting to finalize and clearly define the positive and negative behaviors for all the attributes and values they want to see in team members.
- *Create a team scorecard.* New leaders will paint a vision and some overall objectives for the future, but direct report teams need to formulate a set of concrete, specific goals with timelines and benchmarks for measuring success.
- *Establish an operating rhythm.* Once the direction and goals have been clarified, teams will need to work on their meeting cadence and rules of engagement. New leaders and direct report teams need to determine how often they will meet, when they will meet, the purpose and content of the meetings, meeting roles and rules (sending substitutes to meetings, showing up to meetings on time, taking calls during meetings, and the like). This new meeting schedule should be published in a one-year calendar and sent to everyone in the group.
- *Establish task forces to work on key change initiatives.* In all likelihood a number of issues will need to be addressed by the team. Some of these issues can be discussed and resolved during the off-site meeting, whereas task forces might be a better venue for resolving other issues. The task forces should be staffed by stars, which will both improve the odds that good recommendations are made and allow new leaders to see the stars in action.

After finalizing team structure and staffing, creating a team scorecard, and establishing a new operating rhythm, new leaders should be well on their way to success. As stated at the beginning of this section, the first 90 days give new leaders a unique opportunity to put in place many of the components needed to drive long-term change in their teams. Thus they need to use this time wisely.

Learning from Experience

Leadership practitioners can enhance the learning value of their experiences by (1) creating opportunities to get feedback; (2) taking a 10 percent stretch; (3) learning from others; (4) keeping a journal of daily leadership events; and (5) having a developmental plan.

Creating Opportunities to Get Feedback

It may be difficult for leaders to get relevant feedback, particularly if they occupy powerful positions in an organization. Yet leaders often need feedback more than subordinates do. Leaders may not learn much from their leadership experiences if they get no feedback about how they are doing. Therefore, they may need to create opportunities to get feedback, especially from those working for them.

Leaders should not assume they have invited feedback merely by saying they have an open-door policy. A mistake some bosses make is presuming that others perceive them as open to discussing things just because they say they are open to such discussion. How truly open a door might be is in the eye of the beholder. In that sense, the key to constructive dialogue (that is, feedback) is not just expressing a policy but also being perceived as approachable and sincere in the offer.

Some of the most helpful information for developing your own leadership can come from asking for feedback from others about their perceptions of your behavior and its impact on your group's overall effectiveness. Leaders who take psychological tests and use periodic surveys or questionnaires will have greater access to feedback than leaders who fail to systematically solicit feedback from their followers. Unless leaders ask for feedback, they may not get it.

Taking a 10 Percent Stretch

Learning always involves stretching. Learning involves taking risks and reaching beyond your comfort zone. This is true of a toddler's first unsteady steps, a student's first serious confrontation with divergent worlds of thought, and leadership development. The phrase *10 percent stretch* conveys the idea of voluntary but determined efforts to improve leadership skills. It is analogous to physical exercise, though in this context stretching implies extending your behavior, not your muscles, just a bit beyond the comfort zone. Examples could include making a point of conversing informally with everyone in the office at least once each day, seeking an opportunity to be chair of a committee, or being quieter than usual at meetings (or more assertive, as the case may be). There is much to be gained from a commitment to such ongoing "exercise" for personal and leadership development.

Several positive outcomes are associated with leaders who regularly practice the 10 percent stretch. First, their apprehension about doing something new or different gradually decreases. Second, leaders will broaden their repertoire of leadership skills. Third, because of this increased repertoire, their effectiveness will likely increase. And finally, leaders regularly taking a 10 percent stretch will model something valuable to others. Few things send a better message to others about the importance of their own development than the example of how sincerely a leader takes his or her own development.

A final aspect of the 10 percent stretch is worth mentioning. One reason the phrase is so appealing is that it sounds like a measurable yet manageable change. Many people will not offer serious objection to trying a 10 percent change in some behavior, whereas they might well be resistant (and unsuccessful) if they construe a developmental goal as requiring fundamental change in their personality or interpersonal style. Despite its nonthreatening connotation, though, an actual 10 percent change in behavior can make an enormous difference in effectiveness. In many kinds of endeavors the difference between average performers and exceptional performers is 10 percent. In baseball, for example, many players hit .275, but only the best hit over .300—a difference of about 10 percent.

Learning from Others

Leaders learn from others, first of all, by recognizing that they *can* learn from others and, importantly, from *any* others. That may seem self-evident, but in fact people often limit what and whom they pay attention to, and thus what they may learn from. For example, athletes may pay a lot of attention to how coaches handle leadership situations. However, they may fail to realize they could also learn a lot by watching the director of the school play and the band conductor. Leaders should not limit their learning by narrowly defining the sorts of people they pay attention to.

Similarly, leaders also can learn by asking questions and paying attention to everyday situations. An especially important time to ask questions is when leaders are new to a group or activity and have some responsibility for it. When possible, leaders should talk to the person who previously had the position to benefit from his or her insights, experience, and assessment of the situation. In addition, observant leaders can extract meaningful leadership lessons from everyday situations. Something as plain and ordinary as a high school car wash or the activities at a fast-food restaurant may offer an interesting leadership lesson. Leaders can learn a lot by actively observing how others react to and handle different challenges and situations, even common ones.

Keeping a Journal

Another way leaders can mine experiences for their richness and preserve their learning is by keeping a journal.[2] Journals are similar to diaries, but they are not just accounts of a day's events. A journal should include entries that address some aspect of leaders or leadership. Journal entries may include comments about insightful or interesting quotes, anecdotes, newspaper articles, or even humorous cartoons about leadership. They may also include reflections on personal events, such as interactions with bosses, coaches, teachers, students, employees, players, teammates, roommates, and so on. Such entries can emphasize a good (or bad) way somebody handled something, a problem in the making, the differences between people in their reactions to situations, or people in the news, a book, or a film. Leaders should also use their journals to "think on paper" about leadership readings from textbooks or formal leadership programs or to describe examples from their own experience of a concept presented in a reading.

There are at least three good reasons for keeping a journal. First, the process of writing increases the likelihood that leaders will be able to look at an event from a different perspective or feel differently about it. Putting an experience into words can be a step toward taking a more objective look at it. Second, leaders can (and should) reread earlier entries. Earlier entries provide an interesting and valuable autobiography of a leader's evolving thinking about leadership and about particular events in his or her life. Third, journal entries provide a repository of ideas that leaders may later want to use more formally for papers, pep talks, or speeches. As shown in **Highlight 3.1**, good journal entries give leaders a wealth of examples that they can use in speeches, presentations, and so on.

Sample Journal Entries

HIGHLIGHT 3.1

I went skiing this weekend and saw the perfect example of a leader adapting her leadership style to her followers and situation. While putting on my skis, I saw a ski instructor teaching little kids to ski. She did it using the game "red light, green light." The kids loved it and seemed to be doing very well. Later that same day, as I was going to the lodge for lunch, she was teaching adults, and she did more demonstrating than talking. But when she talked she was always sure to encourage them so that they did not feel intimidated when some little kid whizzed by. She would say to the adults that it's easier for children, or that smaller skis are easier. She made the children laugh and learn, and made the adults less self-conscious to help them learn, too. . . .

Today may not exactly be a topic on leadership, but I thought it would be interesting to discuss. I attended the football game this afternoon and could not help but notice our cheerleaders. I was just thinking of their name in general, and found them to be a good example (of leadership). Everyone gets rowdy at a football game, but without the direction of the cheerleaders there would be mayhem. They do a good job of getting the crowd organized and the adrenaline pumping (though of course the game is most important in that, too!). It's just amazing to see them generate so much interest that all of the crowd gets into the cheering. We even chant their stupid-sounding cheers! You might not know any of them personally, but their enthusiasm invites you to try to be even louder than them. I must give the cheerleaders a round of applause. . . .

I've been thinking about how I used to view/ understand leadership, trying to find out how my present attitudes were developed. It's hard to remember past freshman year, even harder to go past high school. Overall, I think my father has been the single most important influence on my leadership development—long before I even realized it. Dad is a strong "Type A" person. He drives himself hard and demands a great deal from everyone around him, especially his family and especially his only son and oldest child. He was always pushing me to study, practice whatever sport I was involved in at the time, get ahead of everybody else in every way possible.

Having a Developmental Plan

Leadership development almost certainly occurs in ways and on paths that are not completely anticipated or controlled. That is no reason, however, for leaders to avoid actively directing some aspects of their own development. A systematic plan outlining self-improvement goals and strategies will help leaders take advantage of opportunities they otherwise might overlook. This important skill is addressed in greater detail in the last part of this chapter.

A leader's first step in exercising control over his or her personal development is to identify some actual goals. But what if a leader is uncertain about what he or she needs to improve? As described earlier, leaders should systematically collect information from a number of different sources. One place a leader can get information about where to improve is through a review of current job performance, if that is applicable. Ideally, leaders will have had feedback sessions with their own superiors, which should help them identify areas of relative strength and weakness. Leaders should treat this feedback as a helpful perspective on their developmental needs. Leaders also should look at their interactions with peers as a source of ideas about what they might work on. Leaders should especially take notice if the same kind of problem comes up in their interactions with different individuals in separate situations. Leaders need to look at their own role in such instances as objectively as they can; there might be clues about what behavioral changes might facilitate better working relationships with others. Still another way to identify developmental objectives is to look ahead to what new skills are needed to function effectively at a higher level in the organization, or in a different role than the leader now has. Finally, leaders can use formal psychological tests and questionnaires to determine what their relative strengths and weaknesses as a leader may be.

Building Effective Relationships with Superiors

As defined here, superiors are individuals with relatively more power and authority than the other members of the group. Thus superiors could be teachers, band directors, coaches, team captains, heads of committees, or first-line supervisors. Needless to say, there are a number of advantages to having a good working relationship with superiors. First, superiors and followers sharing the same values, approaches, and attitudes will experience less conflict, provide higher levels of mutual support, and be more satisfied with superior–follower relationships than superiors and followers having poor working relationships.[25, 26] Relatedly, individuals having good superior–follower relationships are often in the superior's in-group and thus are more likely to have a say in decisions, be delegated interesting tasks, and have the superior's support for career advancement.[27] Second, followers are often less satisfied with their supervisors and receive lower performance appraisal ratings when superior–follower relationships are poor.[28, 29]

Although the advantages of having a good working relationship with superiors seem clear, you might think that followers have little, if any, say in the quality of the relationship. In other words, you might believe that followers' relationships with their superiors are a matter of luck: Either the follower has a good superior or a bad one, or the superior just happens to like or dislike the follower, and there is little the follower can do about it. However, the quality of a working relationship is not determined solely by the superior, and effective subordinates do not limit themselves to a passive stance toward superiors. Effective subordinates have learned how to take active steps to strengthen the relationship and enhance the support they provide their superior and the organization.[30, 31]

Wherever a person is positioned in an organization, an important aspect of that person's work is to help his superior be successful, just as an important part of the superior's work is to help followers be successful. This does not mean followers should become apple polishers, play politics, or distort information to make superiors look good. However, followers should think of their own and their superior's success as interdependent. Followers are players on their superior's team and should be evaluated on the basis of the team's success, not just their own. If the team succeeds, both the coach and the team members should benefit; if the team fails, the blame should fall on both the coach and the team members. Because team, club, or organizational outcomes depend to some extent on good superior–follower relationships, understanding how superiors view the world and adapting to superiors' styles are two things followers can do to increase the likelihood their actions will have positive results for themselves, their superiors, and their organizations.[32]

Understanding the Superior's World

Followers can do a number of things to better understand their superior's world. First, they should try to get a handle on their superior's personal and organizational objectives. Loyalty and support are a two-way street, and just as a superior can help subordinates attain their personal goals most readily by knowing what they are, so can subordinates support their superior if they understand the superior's goals and objectives. Knowing a superior's values, preferences, and personality can help followers understand why superiors act as they do and can show followers how they might strengthen relationships with superiors.

Second, followers need to realize that superiors are not supermen or superwomen; superiors do not have all the answers, and they have both strengths and weaknesses. Subordinates can make a great contribution to the overall success of a team by recognizing and complementing a superior's weaknesses and understanding his or her constraints and limitations. For example, a highly successful management consultant might spend over 200 days a year conducting executive development workshops, providing organizational feedback to clients, or giving speeches at various public events. This same consultant, however, might not be skilled in designing and making effective visual aids for presentations, or she might dislike having to make her own travel and accommodation arrangements. A follower could make both the consultant and the consulting firm more successful through his own good organization and planning, attention to detail, computer graphics skills, and understanding that the consultant is most effective when she has at least a one-day break between engagements. A similar process can take place in other contexts, such as when subordinates help orient and educate a newly assigned superior whose expertise and prior experience may have been in a different field or activity.

In an even more general sense, subordinates can enhance superior–follower relationships by keeping superiors informed about various activities in the work group or new developments or opportunities in the field. Few superiors like surprises, and any news should come from the person with responsibility for a particular area—especially if the news is potentially bad or concerns unfavorable developments. Followers wishing to develop good superior–follower relationships should never put their superior in the embarrassing situation of having someone else know more about her terrain than she does (her own boss, for instance). As Kelley maintained, the best followers think critically and play an active role in their organizations, which means followers should keep their superiors informed about critical information and pertinent opinions concerning organizational issues.[33]

Adapting to the Superior's Style

Research has shown that some executives fail to get promoted (that is, are derailed) because they are unable or unwilling to adapt to superiors with leadership styles different from their own.[34] Followers need to keep in mind that it is their responsibility to adapt to their superior's style, not vice versa. For example, followers might prefer to interact with superiors face-to-face, but if their superior appreciates written memos, then written memos it should be. Similarly, a follower might be accustomed to informal interactions with superiors, but a new superior might prefer a more businesslike and formal style. Followers need to be flexible in adapting to their superiors' decision-making styles, problem-solving strategies, modes of communication, styles of interaction, and so on.

One way followers can better adapt to a superior's style is to clarify expectations about their role on the team, committee, or work group. Young workers often do not appreciate the difference between a job description and their own role in a job. A job description is a formalized statement of tasks and activities; a role describes the personal signature an incumbent gives to a job. For example, the job description of a high school athletic coach might specify such responsibilities as selecting and training a team or making decisions about lineups. Two different coaches, however, might accomplish those basic responsibilities in quite different ways. One might emphasize player development in the broadest sense, getting to know her players personally and using sports as a vehicle for their individual growth; another might see his role as simply to produce the most winning team possible. Therefore, just because followers know what their job is does not mean their role is clear.

Although some superiors take the initiative to explicitly spell out the roles they expect subordinates to play, most do not. Usually it is the subordinate's task to discern his or her role. One way followers can do this is to make a list of major responsibilities and use it to guide a discussion with the superior about different ways the tasks might be accomplished and the relative priorities of the tasks. Followers will also find it helpful to talk to others who have worked with a particular superior.

Finally, followers interested in developing effective relationships with superiors need to be honest and dependable. Whatever other qualities or talents a subordinate might have, a lack of integrity is a fatal flaw. No one—superior, peer, or subordinate—wants to work with someone who is untrustworthy. After integrity, superiors value dependability. Superiors value workers who have reliable work habits, accomplish assigned tasks at the right time in the right order, and do what they promise.[35]

Building Effective Relationships with Peers

The phrase *influence without authority*[36] captures a key element of the work life of increasing numbers of individuals. More and more people are finding that their jobs require them to influence others despite having no formal authority over them. No man is an island, it is said, and perhaps no worker in today's organizations can survive alone. Virtually everyone needs a coworker's assistance or resources at one time or another. Along these lines, some researchers have maintained that a fundamental requirement of leadership effectiveness is the ability to build strong alliances with others, and groups of peers generally wield more influence (and can get more things done) than individuals working separately.[37] Similarly, investing the time and effort to develop effective relationships with peers not only has immediate dividends but also can have long-term benefits if a peer ends up in a position of power in the future. Many times leaders are selected from among the members of a group, committee, club, or team; and having previously spent time developing a friendly rather than an antagonistic relationship with other work group members, leaders will lay the groundwork for building effective relationships with superiors and becoming a member of superiors' in-groups. Given the benefits of strong relationships with peers, the following are a few ideas about how to establish and maintain good peer relationships.

Recognizing Common Interests and Goals

Although Chapters 4, **5**, **6**, **7**, and **8** describe a variety of ways people vary, one of the best ways to establish effective working relationships with peers is to acknowledge shared interests, values, goals, and expectations.[38] To acknowledge shared aspirations and interests, however, one must know what peers' goals, values, and interests actually are. Establishing informal communication links is one of the best ways to discover common interests and values. To do so, one needs to be open and honest in communicating one's own needs, values, and goals, as well as being willing to acknowledge others' needs, aspirations, and interests. Little can destroy a relationship with peers more quickly than a person who is overly willing to share his own problems and beliefs but unwilling to listen to others' ideas about the same issues. Moreover, although some people believe that participating in social gatherings, parties, committee meetings, lunches, company sport teams, or community activities can be a waste of time, peers with considerable referent power often see such activities as opportunities to establish and improve relationships with others. Thus an effective way to establish relationships with other members of a team, committee, or organization is to meet with them in contexts outside normal working relationships.

Understanding Peers' Tasks, Problems, and Rewards

Few things reinforce respect between coworkers better than understanding the nature of each other's work. Building a cooperative relationship with others depends, therefore, on knowing the sorts of tasks others perform in the organization. It also depends on understanding their problems and rewards. With the former, one of the best ways to establish strong relationships is by lending a hand whenever peers face personal or organizational problems. With the latter, it is especially important to remember that people tend to repeat behaviors that are rewarded and are less likely to repeat behaviors that go unrewarded. A person's counterproductive or negative behaviors may be due less to his personal characteristics ("He is just uncooperative") than to the way his rewards are structured. For example, a teacher may be less likely to share successful classroom exercises with others if teachers are awarded merit pay on the basis of classroom effectiveness. To secure cooperation from others, it helps to know which situational factors reinforce both positive and negative behaviors in others.[39] By better understanding the situation facing others, people can determine whether their own positive feedback (or lack thereof) is contributing to, or hindering the establishment of, effective relationships with peers. People should not underestimate the power of their own sincere encouragement, thanks, and compliments in positively influencing the behavior of their colleagues.

Practicing a Theory Y Attitude

Another way to build effective working relationships with peers is to view them from a Theory Y perspective (see **Chapter 5** for more about Theory Y and a contrasting approach called Theory X). When a person assumes that others are competent, trustworthy, willing to cooperate if they can, and proud of their work, peers will view that person in the same light. Even if one practices a Theory Y attitude, however, it may still be difficult to get along with a few coworkers. In such cases it is easy to become preoccupied with the qualities one dislikes. This should be resisted as much as possible. A vicious cycle can develop in which people become enemies, putting more and more energy into criticizing each other or making the other person look bad than into doing constructive work on the task at hand. The costs of severely strained relationships can extend beyond the individuals involved. Cliques can develop among other coworkers, which can impair the larger group's effectiveness. The point here is not to overlook interpersonal problems, but rather not to let the problems get out of hand.

Practicing Theory Y does *not* mean looking at the world through rose-colored glasses, but it *does* mean recognizing someone else's strengths as well as weaknesses. Nevertheless, sometimes peers will be assigned to work on a task together when they don't get along with each other, and the advice "Practice a Theory Y attitude" may seem too idealistic. At such times it is important to decide whether to focus energy first on improving the relationship (before addressing the task) or to focus it solely on the task (essentially ignoring the problem in the relationship).

Cohen and Bradford have suggested several guidelines for resolving this problem.[40] It is best to work on the task if there is little animosity between the parties, if success can be achieved despite existing animosities, if group norms inhibit openness, if success on the task will improve the feelings between the parties, if the other person handles directness poorly, or if you handle directness poorly. Conversely, it is best to work on the relationship if there is great animosity between the parties, if negative feelings make task success unlikely, if group norms favor openness, if feelings between the parties are not likely to improve even with success on the task, if the other person handles directness well, *and* if you handle directness well.

Development Planning

Development planning is the systematic process of building knowledge and experience or changing behavior. Two people who have done a considerable amount of cutting-edge research in the development planning process are Peterson and Hicks.[41, 42, 43] These two researchers believe development planning consists of five interrelated phases. The first phase of development planning is identifying development needs. Here leaders identify career goals, assess their abilities in light of career goals, seek feedback about how their behaviors are affecting others, and review the organizational standards pertaining to their career goals. Once this information has been gathered, the second phase consists of analyzing these data to identify and prioritize development needs. The prioritized development needs in turn are used to create a focused and achievable development plan, the third phase of this process. The fourth phase in development planning is periodically reviewing the plan, reflecting on learning, and modifying or updating the plan as appropriate. As you might expect, the action–observation–reflection (AOR) model, described in **Chapter 2**, is a key component during this phase of the development planning process. The last phase in development planning is transferring learning to new environments. Just because a leader can successfully delegate activities to a three-person team may not mean he will effectively delegate tasks or use his staff efficiently when he is leading 25 people. In that case the leader will need to build and expand on the delegation skills he learned when leading a smaller team. These five phases are well grounded in research—several studies have shown that approximately 75 percent of the leadership practitioners adopting these phases were successful in either changing their behaviors permanently or developing new skills. Because these five phases are so important to the development planning process, the remainder of this section describes each phase in more detail.[44, 45, 46]

> *Change before you have to.*
>
> **Jack Welch, former General Electric CEO**

Conducting a GAPS Analysis

The first phase in the development planning process is to conduct a GAPS (goals, abilities, perceptions, standards) analysis. A GAPS analysis helps leadership practitioners to gather and categorize all pertinent development planning information. A sample GAPS analysis for an engineer working in a manufacturing company can be found in **Figure 3.2**. This individual wants to get promoted to a first-line supervisor position within the next year, and all of the information pertinent to this promotion can be found in her GAPS analysis. The specific steps for conducting a GAPS analysis are as follows:

- *Step 1: Goals.* The first step in a GAPS analysis is to clearly identify what you want to do or where you want to go with your career over the next year or so. This does not necessarily mean moving up or getting promoted to the next level. An alternative career objective might be to master one's current job—you may have just gotten promoted, and advancing to the next level is not important at the moment. Other career objectives might include taking on more responsibilities in your current position, taking a lateral assignment in another part of the company, taking an overseas assignment, or even cutting back on job responsibilities to gain more work–life balance. This last career objective may be appropriate for leaders who are starting a family or taking care of loved ones who are suffering from poor health. The two most important aspects of this step in the GAPS analysis are that leadership practitioners will have a lot more energy to work on development needs that are aligned with career goals, and in many cases advancing to the next level may not be a viable or particularly energizing career goal. This latter point may be especially true in organizations that have been recently downsized. Management positions often bear the brunt of downsizing initiatives, resulting in fewer available positions for those wishing to advance.

- *Step 2: Abilities.* People bring a number of strengths and development needs to their career goals. Over the years you may have developed specialized knowledge or a number of skills that have helped you succeed in your current and previous jobs. Similarly, you may also have received feedback over the years that there are certain skills you need to develop or behaviors you need to change. Good leaders know themselves—over the years they know which strengths they need to leverage and which skills they need to develop.

- *Step 3: Perceptions.* The perceptions component of the GAPS model concerns how your abilities, skills, and behaviors affect others. What are others saying about your various attributes? What are their reactions to both your strengths and your development needs? A great way of obtaining this information is by asking others for feedback or through performance reviews or 360-degree feedback instruments.

- *Step 4: Standards.* The last step in a GAPS analysis concerns the standards your boss or the organization has for your career objectives. For example, your boss may say you need to develop better public speaking, delegation, or coaching skills before you can get promoted. Similarly, the organization may have policies stating that people in certain overseas positions must be proficient in the country's native language, or it may have educational or experience requirements for various jobs.

FIGURE 3.2   A Sample GAPS Analysis

Step 1: Goals Where do you want to go?	Step 2: Abilities What can you do now?
Career objectives: Career strategies:	What strengths do you have for your career objectives? What development needs will you have to overcome?
Step 4: Standards What does your boss or the organization expect?	Step 3: Perceptions How do others see you?
Expectations:	360-degree and performance review results, and feedback from others: • *Boss* • *Peers* • *Direct reports*

Sources: Adapted from D. B. Peterson and M. D. Hicks, *Leader as Coach* (Minneapolis, MN: Personnel Decisions International, 1996); and G. J. Curphy, *Career and Development Planning Workshop: Planning for Individual Development* (Minneapolis MN: Personnel Decisions International, 1998).

When completing a GAPS analysis you may discover that you do not have all the information you need. If you do not, then you need to get it before you complete the next step of the development planning process. Only you can decide on your career objectives; but you can solicit advice from others on whether these objectives are realistic given your abilities, the perceptions of others, and organizational standards. You may find that your one-year objectives are unrealistic given your development needs, organizational standards, or job opportunities. In this case, you may need to either reassess your career goals or consider taking a number of smaller career steps that will ultimately help you achieve your goals. If you are lacking information about the other quadrants, you can ask your boss or others whose opinions you value about your abilities, perceptions, or organizational standards. Getting as much up-to-date and pertinent information for your GAPS analysis will help ensure that your development plan is focusing on high-priority objectives.

Identifying and Prioritizing Development Needs: Gaps of GAPS

As shown in **Figure 3.3,** the goals and standards quadrants are future oriented; these quadrants ask where you want to go and what your boss or your organization expects of people in these positions. The abilities and perceptions quadrants are focused on the present: What strengths and development needs do you currently have, and how are these attributes affecting others? Given what you currently have and where you want to go, what are the gaps in your GAPS? In other words, after looking at all the information in your GAPS analysis, what are your biggest development needs, and how should these development needs be prioritized? You need to review the information from the GAPS model, look for underlying themes and patterns, and determine what behaviors, knowledge, experiences, or skills will be the most important to change or develop if you are to accomplish your career goals.

Bridging the Gaps: Building a Development Plan

A gaps-of-the-GAPS analysis helps leadership practitioners identify high-priority development needs, but it does not spell out what leaders need to do to meet these needs. A good development plan is like a road map: It clearly describes the final destination, lays out the steps or interim checkpoints, builds in regular feedback to keep people on track, identifies where additional resources are needed, and builds in reflection time so that people can periodically review progress and determine whether an alternative route is needed. The specific steps for creating a high-impact development plan are as follows:

- *Step 1: Career and development objectives.* Your career objective comes directly from the goals quadrant of the GAPS analysis; it is where you want to be or what you want to be doing in your career a year or so in the future. The development objective comes from your gaps-of-the-GAPS analysis; it should be a high-priority development need pertaining to your career objective. People should be working on no more than two or three development needs at any one time.

- *Step 2: Criteria for success.* What would it look like if you developed a particular skill, acquired technical expertise, or changed the behavior outlined in your development objective? This can be a difficult step in development planning, particularly with "softer" skills such as listening, managing conflict, or building relationships with others.

- *Step 3: Action steps.* The focus in the development plan should be on the specific, on-the-job action steps leadership practitioners will take to meet their development needs. However, sometimes it is difficult for leaders to think of appropriate on-the-job action steps. Three excellent resources that provide on-the-job action steps for a variety of development needs are two books, *The Successful Manager's Handbook*[47] and *For Your Improvement,*[48] and the development planning and coaching software *DevelopMentor.*[49] These three resources can be likened to restaurant menus in that they provide leadership practitioners with a wide variety of action steps to work on just about any development need.

FIGURE 3.3 A Gaps-of-the-GAPS Analysis

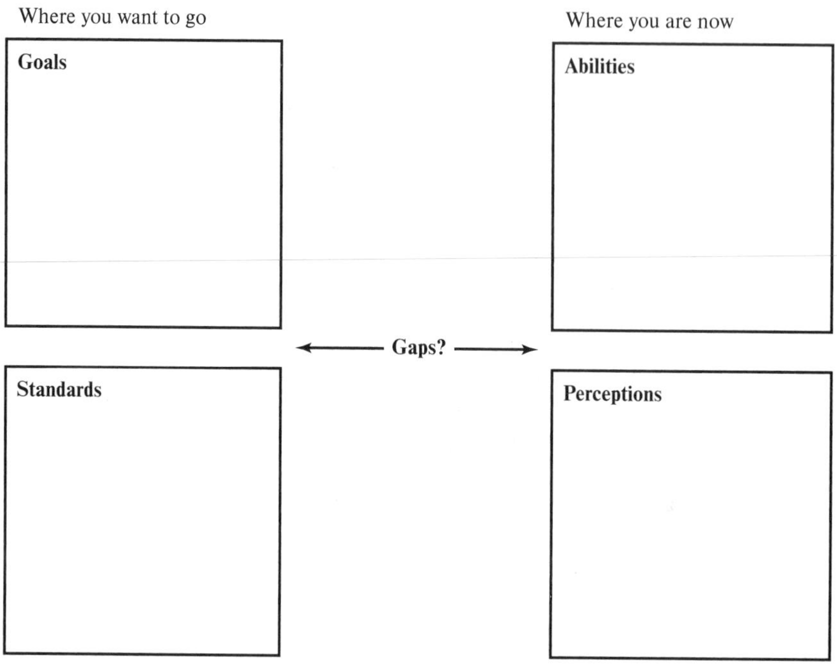

Where you want to go   Where you are now

Goals	Abilities

←——— Gaps? ———→

Standards	Perceptions

Developmental Objectives
Current position: _____
                     _____
                     _____
                     _____
                     _____
                     _____
                     _____

Next proposed position: _____
                         _____
                         _____
                         _____
                         _____
                         _____

Sources: Adapted from D. B. Peterson and M. D. Hicks, *Leader as Coach* (Minneapolis, MN: Personnel Decisions International, 1996); and G. J. Curphy, *The Leadership Development Process Manual* (Minneapolis, MN: Personnel Decisions International, 1998).

- *Step 4: Whom to involve and when to reassess dates.* This step in a development plan involves feedback—whom do you need to get it from, and how often do you need to get it? This step in the development plan is important because it helps keep you on track. Are your efforts being noticed? Do people see any improvement? Are there things you need to do differently? Do you need to refocus your efforts?

- *Step 5: Stretch assignments.* When people reflect on when they have learned the most, they often talk about situations where they felt they were in over their heads. These situations stretched their knowledge and skills and often are seen as extremely beneficial to learning. If you know of a potential assignment, such as a task force, a project management team, or a rotational assignment, that would emphasize the knowledge and skills you need to develop and accelerate your learning, you should include it in your development plan.

- *Step 6: Resources.* Often people find it useful to read a book, attend a course, or watch a recorded program to gain foundational knowledge about a particular development need. These methods generally describe the how-to steps for a particular skill or behavior.

- *Step 7: Reflect with a partner.* In accordance with the AOR model described in **Chapter 2**, you should periodically review your learning and progress with a partner. The identity of the partner is not particularly important as long as you trust his or her opinion and the partner is familiar with your work situation and development plan.

Reflecting on Learning: Modifying Development Plans

Just as the development plan is a road map, this phase of development planning helps leaders to see whether the final destination is still the right one, if an alternative route might be better, and whether there is a need for more resources or equipment. Reflecting on your learning with a partner is also a form of public commitment, and people who make public commitments are much more likely to fulfill them. All things considered, in most cases it is probably best to periodically review your progress with your boss. Your boss should not be left in the dark with respect to your development, and periodically reviewing progress with your boss will help ensure there are no surprises at your performance appraisal.

Transferring Learning to New Environments

The last phase in development planning concerns ongoing development. Your development plan should be a "live" document: It should be changed, modified, or updated as you learn from your experiences, receive feedback, acquire new skills, and meet targeted development needs. There are basically three ways to transfer learning to new environments. The first way is to continually update your development plan. Another way to enhance your learning is to practice your newly acquired skills in a new environment. A final way to hone and refine your skills is to coach others in the development of your newly acquired skills. Moving from the student role to that of a master is an excellent way to reinforce your learning.

Endnotes

1. M. Roellig and G. J. Curphy, *How to Hit the Ground Running: A Guide to Successful Executive On-Boarding* (Springfield, MA: Author, 2010).

2. M. Csikszentmihalyi, *Flow: The Psychology of Optimal Experience* (New York: Harper & Row, 1990).

3. G. Yukl, *Leadership in Organizations*, 2nd ed. (Englewood Cliffs, NJ: Prentice Hall, 1989).

4. G. J. Curphy, "Leadership Transitions and Succession Planning," in *Developing and Implementing Succession Planning Programs*, ed. J. Locke (chair). Symposium conducted at the 19th Annual Conference for the Society of Industrial and Organizational Psychology, Chicago, April 2004.

5. F. L. Schmidt and J. E. Hunter, "Development of a Causal Model of Job Performance," *Current Directions in Psychological Science* 1, no. 3 (1992), pp. 89–92.

6. W. C. Borman, L. A. White, E. D. Pulakos, and S. A. Oppler, "Models Evaluating the Effects of Rated Ability, Knowledge, Proficiency, Temperament, Awards, and Problem Behavior on Supervisor Ratings," *Journal of Applied Psychology* 76 (1991), pp. 863–72.

7. J. Hogan, "The View from Below," in *The Future of Leadership Selection*, ed. R. T. Hogan (chair). Symposium conducted at the 13th Biennial Psychology in the Department of Defense Conference, United States Air Force Academy, Colorado Springs, CO, 1992.

8. D. E. Bugental, "A Study of Attempted and Successful Social Influence in Small Groups as a Function of Goal-Relevant Skills," *Dissertation Abstracts* 25 (1964), p. 660.

9. G. F. Farris, *Colleagues' Roles and Innovation in Scientific Teams*, Working Paper No. 552–71 (Cambridge, MA: Alfred P. Sloan School of Management, MIT, 1971).

10. D. Duchon, S. G. Green, and T. D. Taber, "Vertical Dyad Linkage: A Longitudinal Assessment of Antecedents, Measures, and Consequences," *Journal of Applied Psychology* 71 (1986), pp. 56–60.

11. H. D. Dewhirst, V. Metts, and R. T. Ladd, "Exploring the Delegation Decision: Managerial Responses to Multiple Contingencies," paper presented at the Academy of Management Convention, New Orleans, LA, 1987.

12. C. R. Leana, "Power Relinquishment vs. Power Sharing: Theoretical Clarification and Empirical Comparison of Delegation and Participation," *Journal of Applied Psychology* 72 (1987), pp. 228–33.

13. A. Lowin and J. R. Craig, "The Influence of Level of Performance on Managerial Style: An Experimental Object-Lesson in the Ambiguity of Correlational Data," *Organizational Behavior and Human Performance* 3 (1968), pp. 68–106.

14. B. Rosen and T. H. Jerdee, "Influence of Subordinate Characteristics on Trust and Use of Participative Decision Strategies in a Management Simulation," *Journal of Applied Psychology* 59 (1977), pp. 9–14.

15. P. M. Blau, "The Hierarchy of Authority in Organizations," *American Journal of Sociology* 73 (1968), pp. 453–67.

16. A. Howard, "College Experiences and Managerial Performance," *Journal of Applied Psychology* 71 (1986), pp. 530–52.

17. A. Howard and D. W. Bray, "Predictors of Managerial Success over Long Periods of Time," in *Measures of Leadership*, eds. M. B. Clark and K. E. Clark (West Orange, NJ: Leadership Library of America, 1989).

18. K. N. Wexley and G. P. Latham, *Developing and Training Human Resources in Organizations* (Glenview, IL: Scott Foresman, 1981).

19. P. M. Podsakoff, W. D. Todor, and R. S. Schuler, "Leadership Expertise as a Moderator of the Effects of Instrumental and Supportive Leader Behaviors," *Journal of Management* 9 (1983), pp. 173–85.

20. T. G. Walker, "Leader Selection and Behavior in Small Political Groups," *Small Group Behavior* 7 (1976), pp. 363–68.

21. B. M. Bass, *Leadership and Performance beyond Expectations* (New York: Free Press, 1985).

22. D. D. Penner, D. M. Malone, T. M. Coughlin, and J. A. Herz, *Satisfaction with U.S. Army Leadership*, Leadership Monograph Series, No. 2 (U.S. Army War College, 1973).

23. B. J. Avolio and B. M. Bass, "Transformational Leadership, Charisma, and Beyond," in *Emerging Leadership Vista*, eds. J. G. Hunt, B. R. Baliga, and C. A. Schriesheim (Lexington, MA: D. C. Heath, 1988).

24. G. J. Curphy, "An Empirical Examination of Bass' 1985 Theory of Transformational and Transactional Leadership," PhD dissertation, University of Minnesota, 1991.

25. D. Duchon et al., "Vertical Dyad Linkage."

26. D. A. Porter, "Student Course Critiques: A Case Study in Total Quality in the Classroom," in *Proceedings of the 13th Biennial Psychology in Department of Defense Conference* (Colorado Springs, CO: U.S. Air Force Academy, 1992), pp. 26–30.

27. Yukl, *Leadership in Organizations*, 2nd ed.

28. E. D. Pulakos and K. N. Wexley, "The Relationship among Perceptual Similarity, Sex, and Performance Ratings in Manager-Subordinate Dyads," *Academy of Management Journal* 26 (1983), pp. 129–39.

29. H. M. Weiss, "Subordinate Imitation of Supervisor Behavior: The Role of Modeling in Organizational Socialization," *Organizational Behavior and Human Performance* 19 (1977), pp. 89–105.

30. J. J. Gabarro and J. P. Kotter, "Managing Your Boss," *Harvard Business Review* 58, no. 1 (1980), pp. 92–100.

31. R. E. Kelley, "In Praise of Followers," *Harvard Business Review* 66, no. 6 (1988), pp. 142–48.

32. Gabarro and Kotter, "Managing Your Boss."

33. Kelley, "In Praise of Followers."

34. M. W. McCall Jr. and M. M. Lombardo, "Off the Track: Why and How Successful Executives Get Derailed," Technical Report No. 21 (Greensboro, NC: Center for Creative Leadership, 1983).

35. J. M. Kouzes and B. Z. Posner, *The Leadership Challenge: How to Get Extraordinary Things Done in Organizations* (San Francisco: Jossey-Bass, 1987).

36. A. R. Cohen and D. L. Bradford, *Influence without Authority* (New York: John Wiley, 1990).

37. G. J. Curphy, A. Baldrica, M. Benson, and R. T. Hogan, *Managerial Incompetence*, unpublished manuscript, 2007.

38. Cohen and Bradford, *Influence without Authority*.

39. Cohen and Bradford, *Influence without Authority*.

40. Cohen and Bradford, *Influence without Authority*.

41. D. B. Peterson and M. D. Hicks, *Professional Coaching: State of the Art, State of the Practice* (Minneapolis, MN: Personnel Decisions International, 1998).

42. D. B. Peterson and M. D. Hicks, "Coaching across Borders: It's Probably a Long Distance Call," *Development Matters*, no. 9 (1997), pp. 1–4.

43. D. B. Peterson and M. D. Hicks, *Leader as Coach: Strategies for Coaching and Developing Others* (Minneapolis, MN: Personnel Decisions International, 1996).

44. J. F. Hazucha, S. A. Hezlett, and R. J. Schneider, "The Impact of 360-Degree Feedback on Management Skills Development," *Human Resource Management* 32 (1993), pp. 325–51.

45. D. B. Peterson, "Skill Learning and Behavioral Change in an Individually Tailored Management Coaching and Training Program," unpublished doctoral dissertation, University of Minnesota, 1993.

46. S. A. Hezlett and B. A. Koonce, "Now That I've Been Assessed, What Do I Do? Facilitating Development after Individual Assessments," paper presented at the IPMA Assessment Council Conference on Public Personnel Assessment, New Orleans, LA, June 1995.

47. B. L. Davis, L. W. Hellervik, and J. L. Sheard, *The Successful Manager's Handbook*, 3rd ed. (Minneapolis, MN: Personnel Decisions International, 1989).

48. M. M. Lombardo and R. W. Eichinger, *For Your Improvement: A Development and Coaching Guide* (Minneapolis, MN: Lominger, 1996).

49. Personnel Decisions International, *Develop Mentor: Assessment, Development, and Coaching Software* (Minneapolis, MN: Personnel Decisions International, 1995).

Part 2

Focus on the Leader

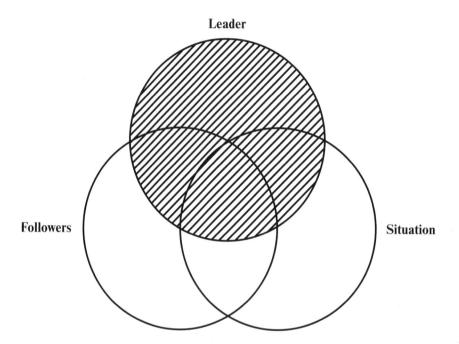

Part 2 focuses on the leader. The effectiveness of leadership, good or bad, is typically attributed to the leader much more than to the other elements of the framework. Sometimes the leader is the only element of leadership we even think of. One great leader's views were clear enough about the relative importance of leaders and followers:

> Men are nothing; it is the man who is everything. . . . It was not the Roman army that conquered Gaul, but Caesar; it was not the Carthaginian army that made Rome tremble in her gates, but Hannibal; it was not the Macedonian army that reached the Indus, but Alexander.

Napoleon

Because the leader plays such an important role in the leadership process, the next three chapters of this book review research related to the characteristics of leaders and what makes leaders effective. Part 2 begins with this chapter about power and influence because those concepts provide the most fundamental way to understand the process of leadership. **Chapter 5** looks at the closely related issues of leadership values, ethics, and character. In **Chapter 6** we consider what aspects of personality are related to leadership, and in **Chapter 7** we examine how all these variables are manifested in effective or ineffective leader behavior.

CHAPTER 4

Power and Influence

Introduction

We begin **Part 2** by examining the phenomenon of power. Some of history's earliest characterizations of leaders concerned their use of power. Shakespeare's plays were concerned with the acquisition and failing of power,[1] and Machiavelli's *The Prince* has been described as the "classic handbook on power politics."[2] Current scholars have also emphasized the need to conceptualize leadership as a power phenomenon.[3, 4] Power may be the single most important concept in all the social sciences,[5] though scholars today disagree over precisely how to define power or influence. But it's not just scholars who have different ideas about power. The concept of power is so pervasive and complex that each of us probably thinks about it a little differently.

What comes to *your* mind when you think about power? Do you think of a person wielding enormous authority over others? Do you think of high office? Do you think of making others do things against their will? Is power ethically neutral, or is it inherently dangerous, as Lord Acton said? ("Power tends to corrupt and absolute power corrupts absolutely.") Do you think a leader's real power is always obvious to others? What sorts of things might enhance or detract from a leader's power? What are the pros and cons of different ways of trying to influence people? These are the kinds of issues we explore in this chapter.

Some Important Distinctions

Power has been defined as the capacity to produce effects on others[6] or the potential to influence others.[7] Although we usually think of power as belonging to the leader, it is actually a function of the leader, the followers, and the situation. Leaders have the potential to influence their followers' behaviors and attitudes. However, followers also can affect the leader's behavior and attitudes. Even the situation itself can affect a leader's capacity to influence followers (and vice versa). For example, leaders who can reward and punish followers may have a greater capacity to influence followers than leaders who cannot use rewards or punishments. Similarly, follower or situational characteristics may diminish a leader's potential to influence followers, such as when the latter belong to a strong, active union.

The fact that power is not merely a function of leaders is reflected in the continuing research on the use of power in organizations. In addition to ongoing research examining the negotiation of power dynamics within and across organizations,[8] other research has examined power relationships between shareholders and governance boards[9] and power related to gender (a topic we examine in more detail later in this chapter) in entrepreneurial relationships.[10]

Several other aspects of power are worth noting. Leaders do not need to actually exercise power to bring about its effects. (See **Profiles in Leadership 4.1**.) Thus merely having the capacity to exert influence can often bring about intended effects, even though the leader may not take any action to influence his or her followers. For example, some months after the end of his term, President Dwight Eisenhower was asked if leaving the White House had affected his golf game. "Yes," he replied, "a lot more people beat me now." Alternatively, power represents an inference or attribution made on the basis of an agent's observable acts of influence.[11] From this perspective, power is never directly observed but rather attributed to others on the basis and frequency of influence tactics they use and on their outcomes.

Michael Dell

PROFILES IN LEADERSHIP 4.1

The problem of having power you didn't know you had and might not even want.

It's hard to imagine anyone not recognizing the name Michael Dell. As founder of the computer company Dell, Inc., he created one of the most profitable computer companies in the world, with annual sales of up to $50 billion. Michael Dell has also become one of the wealthiest people in the world with a 25th place listing on the *Forbes* rich Americans list in 2013 and an estimated worth of $15.9 billion. In July 2007, *USA Today* published its ranking of the 25 most influential business leaders in the last 25 years. Number 17 on this list was Michael Dell.

With just $1,000 in his pocket, Dell started PC's Limited in 1984. From his university dorm room Dell started building and selling personal computers from stock computer parts. In 1988 PC's Limited changed its name to Dell Computer Corporation and had an initial public offering (IPO) that valued the company at roughly $80 million. By 1992 Dell Computer Corporation was listed on the *Fortune* 500 list of the largest companies in the world, making Dell the youngest CEO ever to head a *Fortune* 500 company.

One of this book's authors worked with Michael Dell in the early 1990s (and wishes he had bought stock). He was chatting with Michael and describing the problems that can happen in large organizations when the leader has a lot of personal or referent power. Michael said, "Oh, I'm learning about that. We've even got a name for that problem. We call them, 'Michael saids'."

Here's an example of a "Michael said." One afternoon, Michael was walking around the plant and stopped to ask one of the assembly employees how things were going and what could be done to make things better. The assembler said that things were great but that occasionally there was some confusion with a particular electronic component (let's call it a resistor). Sometimes the resistors were red and sometimes they were green, and the red ones looked like another component. The assembler suggested that this problem could be eliminated if this particular resistor came only in green. Michael said that seemed like a reasonable solution and passed that information along to the people who bought resistors from the suppliers.

Six months later, Michael was having a meeting in his office when someone knocked on the door. It was a frazzled person who said he was terribly sorry to interrupt but there was a crisis down in manufacturing and production was about to stop. "Why?" asked Michael. The messenger said that the supplier of green resistors had a problem and the only resistors they could get were red and they couldn't use the red resistors. "Why not?" asked Michael. The messenger looked sheepishly at his feet and passed along the bad news. They couldn't use the red ones because "Michael said we could only use green resistors."

While referent and expert power may be good to use, as Dell and others have found out, there can be a potential downside of which you might not even be aware.

Many people use the terms *power, influence*, and *influence tactics* synonymously,[12] but it is useful to distinguish among them. **Influence** can be defined as the change in a target agent's attitudes, values, beliefs, or behaviors as the result of influence tactics. **Influence tactics** refer to one person's actual behaviors designed to change another person's attitudes, beliefs, values, or behaviors. Although these concepts are typically examined from the leader's perspective (such as how a leader influences followers), we should remember that followers can also wield power and influence over leaders as well as over each other. Leadership practitioners can improve their effectiveness by reflecting on the types of power they and their followers have and the types of influence tactics that they may use or that may be used on them.

The true leader must submerge himself in the fountain of the people.

V. I. Lenin, Leader of the 1917 Bolshevik Revolution

Whereas power is the *capacity* to cause change, influence is the degree of actual change in a target person's attitudes, values, beliefs, or behaviors. Influence can be measured by the behaviors or attitudes manifested by followers as the result of a leader's *influence tactics*. For example, a leader may ask a follower to accomplish a particular task, and whether or not the task is accomplished is partly a function of the leader's request. (The follower's ability and skill as well as access to the necessary equipment and resources are also important factors.) Such things as subordinates' satisfaction or motivation, group cohesiveness and climate, or unit performance measures can be used to assess the effectiveness of leaders' influence attempts. The degree to which leaders can change the level of satisfaction, motivation, or cohesiveness among followers is a function of the amount of power available to both leaders and followers. On one hand, leaders with relatively high amounts of power can cause fairly substantial changes in subordinates' attitudes and behaviors; for example, a new and respected leader who uses rewards and punishments judiciously may cause a dramatic change in followers' perceptions about organizational climate and the amount of time followers spend on work-related behaviors. On the other hand, the amount of power followers have in work situations can also vary dramatically, and in some situations particular followers may exert relatively more influence over the rest of the group than the leader does. For example, a follower with a high level of knowledge and experience may have more influence on the attitudes, opinions, and behaviors of the rest of the followers than a brand-new leader. Thus the amount of change in the attitudes or behaviors of the targets of influence is a function of the agent's capacity to exert influence and the targets' capacity to resist this influence.

Leaders and followers typically use a variety of tactics to influence each other's attitudes or behaviors (see **Highlight 4.1** for a description of some nonverbal power cues common to humans). Influence tactics are the overt behaviors exhibited by one person to influence another. They range from emotional appeals, to the exchange of favors, to threats. The particular tactic used in a leadership situation is probably a function of the power possessed by both parties. Individuals with a relatively large amount of power may successfully employ a wider variety of influence tactics than individuals with little power. For example, a well-respected leader could make an emotional appeal, a rational appeal, a personal appeal, a legitimate request, or a threat to try to modify a follower's behavior. The follower in this situation may be able to use only ingratiation or personal appeals to change the leader's attitude or behavior.

Gestures of Power and Dominance

HIGHLIGHT 4.1

We can often get clues about relative power just by paying attention to behaviors between two people. There are a number of nonverbal cues we might want to pay attention to. The phrase **pecking order** refers to the status differential between members of a group. It reminds us that many aspects of human social organization have roots, or at least parallels, in the behavior of other species. The animal kingdom presents diverse and fascinating examples of stylized behaviors by which one member of a species shows its relative dominance or submissiveness to another. There is adaptive significance to such behavioral mechanisms because they tend to minimize actual physical struggle and maintain a stable social order. For example, lower-ranking baboons step aside to let a higher-status male pass; they become nervous if he stares at them. The highest-status male can choose where he wants to sleep and whom he wants to mate with. Baboons "know their place." As with humans, rank has its privileges.

Our own stylized power rituals are usually so ingrained that we aren't conscious of them. Yet there is a "dance" of power relations among humans just as among other animals. The following are some of the ways power is expressed nonverbally in humans:

Staring: In American society, it is disrespectful for a person of lower status to stare at a superior, though superiors are not bound by a similar restriction. Children, for example, are taught not to stare at parents. And it's an interesting comment on the power relationship between sexes that women are more likely to avert their gaze from men than vice versa.

Pointing: Children are also taught that it's not nice to point. However, adults rarely correct each other for pointing because, more than mere etiquette, pointing seems to be a behavior that is acceptable for high-status figures or those attempting to assert dominance. An angry boss may point an index finger accusingly at an employee; few employees who wanted to keep their jobs would respond in kind. The same restrictions apply to frowning.

Touching: Invading another person's space by touching the person without invitation is acceptable when one is of superior status but not when one is of subordinate status. It's acceptable, for example, for bosses or teachers to put a hand on an employee's or a student's shoulder, respectively, but not vice versa. The disparity also applies to socioeconomic status; someone with higher socioeconomic status is more likely to touch a person of lower socioeconomic status than vice versa.

Interrupting: Virtually all of us have interrupted others, and we have all been interrupted ourselves. Again, however, the issue is who interrupted whom. Higher-power or status persons interrupt; lower-power or status persons are interrupted. A vast difference in the frequency of this behavior also exists between the sexes in American society. Men interrupt much more frequently than women do.

Source: D. A. Karp and W. C. Yoels, *Symbols, Selves, and Society* (New York: Lippincott, 1979).

At the same time, because the formal leader is not always the person who possesses the most power in a leadership situation, followers often can use a wider variety of influence tactics than the leader to modify the attitudes and behaviors of others. This would be the case if a new leader were brought into an organization in which one of his or her subordinates was extremely well liked and respected. In this situation, the subordinate may be able to make personal appeals, emotional appeals, or even threats to change the attitudes or behaviors of the leader, whereas the new leader may be limited to making only legitimate requests to change the attitudes and behaviors of the followers. And finally, as if figuring out relative status isn't enough of a problem, when working globally, the various rules and customs of cultures often clash. Michelle Obama discovered this in 2009 when attending a social function at Buckingham Palace for the G20 conference. While posing for pictures, Obama reached out and patted Queen Elizabeth on the back, a nonverbal message that was unheard of and apparently seen as inappropriate to many. For further insights into the complexity of exercising power when working globally across cultures, see **Highlight 4.5**, later in this chapter.

Power and Leadership

And when we think we lead, we are most led.

Lord Byron, British poet

We began this chapter by noting how an understanding of power has long been seen as an integral part of leadership. Several perspectives and theories have been developed to explain the acquisition and exercise of power. In this section we first examine various *sources* of power. Then we look at how individuals vary in their personal *need* for power.

Sources of Leader Power

Where does a leader's power come from? Do leaders *have* it, or do followers *give* it to them? As we will see, the answer may be both . . . and more.

Something as seemingly trivial as the arrangement of furniture in an office can affect perceptions of another person's power. One vivid example comes from John Ehrlichman's book *Witness to Power*.[13] Ehrlichman described his first visit to J. Edgar Hoover's office at the Department of Justice. The legendary director of the FBI had long been one of the most powerful men in Washington, D.C., and as Ehrlichman's impressions reveal, Hoover used every opportunity to reinforce that image. Ehrlichman was first led through double doors into a room replete with plaques, citations, trophies, medals, and certificates jamming every wall. He was then led through a second similarly decorated room into a third trophy room, and finally to a large but bare desk backed by several flags and still no J. Edgar Hoover. The guide opened a door behind the desk, and Ehrlichman went into a smaller office, which Hoover dominated from an impressive chair and desk that stood on a dais about six inches high. Erhlichman was instructed to take a seat on a lower couch, and Hoover peered down on Ehrlichman from his own loftier and intimidating place.

On a more mundane level, many people have experienced a time when they were called in to talk to a boss and left standing while the boss sat behind the desk. Probably few people in that situation misunderstand the power message there. In addition to the factors just described, other aspects of office arrangements also can affect a leader's or follower's power. One factor is the shape of the table used for meetings. Individuals sitting at the ends of rectangular tables often wield more power, whereas circular tables facilitate communication and minimize status differentials. However, specific seating arrangements even at circular tables can affect participants' interactions; often individuals belonging to the same cliques and coalitions will sit next to each other. By sitting next to each other, members of the same coalition may exert more power as a collective group than they would sitting apart from each other. Also, having a private or more open office may not only *reflect* but also *affect* power differentials between people. Individuals with private offices can dictate to a greater degree when they want to interact with others by opening or closing their doors or by giving instructions about interruptions. Individuals with more open offices have much less power to control access to them. By being aware of dynamics like these, leaders can somewhat influence others' perceptions of their power relationship.

Prominently displaying symbols like diplomas, awards, and titles also can increase one's power. This was shown in an experiment in a college setting where a guest lecturer to several different classes was introduced in a different way to each. To one group he was introduced as a student; to other groups he was introduced as a lecturer, senior lecturer, or professor, respectively. After the presentation, when he was no longer in the room, the class estimated his height. Interestingly, the same man was perceived by different groups as increasingly taller with each increase in academic status. The "professor" was remembered as being several inches taller than the "student."[14]

This finding demonstrates the generalized impact a seemingly minor matter like one's title can have on others. Another study points out more dramatically how dangerous it can be when followers are overly responsive to the *appearances* of title and authority. This study took place in a medical setting and arose from concern among medical staff that nurses were responding mechanically to doctors' orders. A researcher made telephone calls to nurses' stations in numerous different medical wards. In each, he identified himself as a hospital physician and directed the nurse answering the phone to administer a particular medication to a patient in that ward. Many nurses complied with the request even though it was against hospital policy to transmit prescriptions by phone. Many did so despite never even having talked to the particular "physician" before the call. In fact, 95 percent of the nurses complied with the request made by the most easily falsifiable symbol of authority, a bare title.[15] (See also **Highlight 4.2**.)

The Milgram Studies

HIGHLIGHT 4.2

One intriguing way to understand power, influence, and influence tactics is to read a synopsis of Stanley Milgram's classic work on obedience and to think about how this work relates to the concepts and theories discussed in this chapter. Milgram's research explored how far people will go when directed by an authority figure to do something that might injure another person. More specifically, Milgram wanted to know what happens when the dictates of authority and the dictates of one's conscience seem incompatible.

The participants were men from the communities surrounding Yale University. They were led to believe they were helping in a study concerning the effect of punishment on learning; the study's legitimacy was enhanced by the study being conducted on the Yale campus. Two subjects at a time participated in the study—one as a teacher and the other as a learner. The roles apparently were assigned randomly. The teacher's task was to help the learner memorize a set of word pairs by providing electric shocks whenever the learner (who would be in an adjacent room) made a mistake.

A stern experimenter described procedures and showed participants the equipment for administering punishment. This "shock generator" looked ominous, with rows of switches, lights, and warnings labeled in 15-volt increments all the way to 450 volts. Various points along the array were marked with increasingly dire warnings such as *extreme intensity* and *danger: severe*. The switch at the highest level of shock was simply marked *XXX*. Every time the learner made a mistake, the teacher was ordered by the experimenter to administer the next higher level of electric shock.

In actuality, there was only one true subject in the experiment—the teacher. The learner was really a confederate of the experimenter. The supposed random assignment of participants to teacher and learner conditions had been rigged in advance. The real purpose of the experiment was to assess how much electric shock the teachers would administer to the learners in the face of the latter's increasingly adamant protestations to stop. This included numerous realistic cries of agony and complaints of a heart condition—all standardized, predetermined, tape-recorded messages delivered via the intercom from the learner's room to the teacher's room. If the subject (that is, the teacher) refused to deliver any further shocks, the experimenter prodded him with comments such as "The

experiment requires that you go on" and "You have no other choice; you must go on."

Before Milgram conducted his experiment, he asked mental health professionals what proportion of the subjects would administer apparently dangerous levels of shock. The consensus was that only a negligible percentage would do so—perhaps 1 or 2 percent of the population. Milgram's actual results were dramatically inconsistent with what any experts had predicted. Fully 70 percent of the subjects carried through with their orders, albeit sometimes with great personal anguish, and delivered the maximum shock possible—450 volts!

Source: S. Milgram, "Behavioral Study of Obedience," *Journal of Abnormal and Social Psychology* 67 (1963), pp. 371–78.

He who has great power should use it lightly.

Seneca, Roman philosopher

Even choice of clothing can affect one's power and influence. Uniforms and other specialized clothing have long been associated with authority and status, including their use by the military, police, hospital staffs, clergy, and so on. In one experiment, people walking along a city sidewalk were stopped by someone dressed either in regular clothes or in the uniform of a security guard and told this: "You see that guy over there by the meter? He's overparked but doesn't have any change. Give him a dime!" Whereas fewer than half complied when the requestor was dressed in regular clothes, over 90 percent did when he was in uniform.[16]

This same rationale is given for having personnel in certain occupations (such as airline crew members) wear uniforms. Besides identifying them to others, the uniforms increase the likelihood that in emergency situations their instructions will be followed. Similarly, even the presence of something as trivial as tattoos can affect the amount of power wielded in a group. One of the authors of this text had a friend named Del who was a manager in an international book publishing company. Del was a former merchant marine whose forearms were adorned with tattoos. Del would often take off his suit coat and roll up his sleeves when meetings were not going his way, and he often exerted considerably more influence by merely exposing his tattoos to the rest of the group.

A final situational factor that can affect one's potential to influence others is the presence or absence of a crisis. Leaders usually can exert more power during a crisis than during periods of relative calm. Perhaps this is because during a crisis leaders are willing to draw on bases of power they normally forgo. For example, a leader who has developed close interpersonal relationships with followers generally uses her referent power to influence them. During crises or emergency situations, however, leaders may be more apt to draw on their legitimate and coercive bases of power to influence subordinates. That was precisely the finding in a study of bank managers' actions; the bank managers were more apt to use legitimate and coercive power during crises than during noncrisis situations.[17] This same phenomenon is observable in many dramatizations. In the television series *Blue Bloods*, for example, Police Commissioner Frank Reagan (played by Tom Selleck) normally uses his referent and expert power to influence subordinates. During emergencies, however, he will often rely on his legitimate and, occasionally, his coercive power. Another factor may be that during crises followers are more willing to accept greater direction, control, and structure from leaders, whatever power base may be involved.

A Taxonomy of Social Power

French and Raven identified five sources, or bases, of power by which an individual can potentially influence others.[18] As shown in **Figure 4.1**, these five sources include one that is primarily a function of the leader; one that is a function of the relationship between the leader and followers; one that is primarily a function of the leader and the situation; one that is primarily a function of the situation; and finally, one that involves aspects of all three elements. Understanding these bases of power can give leadership practitioners greater insight about the predictable effects—positive or negative—of various sorts of influence attempts. Following is a more detailed discussion of French and Raven's five bases of social power.[19]

Expert Power

Expert power is the power of knowledge. Some people can influence others through their relative expertise in particular areas. A surgeon may wield considerable influence in a hospital because others depend on her knowledge, skill, and judgment, even though she may have no formal authority over them. A mechanic may be influential among his peers because he is widely recognized as the best in the city. A longtime employee may be influential because her corporate memory provides a useful historical perspective to newer personnel. Legislators who are experts in the intricacies of parliamentary procedure, athletes who have played in championship games, and soldiers who have been in combat are valued for the lessons learned and the wisdom they can share with others.

FIGURE 4.1   Sources of Leader Power in the Leader–Followers–Situation Framework

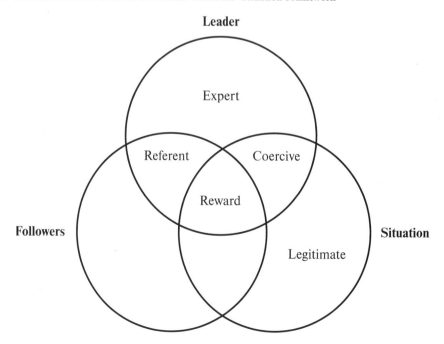

Because expert power is a function of the amount of knowledge one possesses relative to the rest of the members of the group, it is possible for followers to have considerably more expert power than leaders in certain situations. For example, new leaders often know less about the jobs and tasks performed in a particular work unit than the followers do, and in this case the followers can potentially wield considerable influence when decisions are made regarding work procedures, new equipment, or the hiring of additional workers. Probably the best advice for leaders in this situation is to ask a lot of questions and perhaps seek additional training to help fill this knowledge gap. So long as different followers have considerably greater amounts of expert power, it will be difficult for a leader to influence the work unit on the basis of expert power alone.

Referent Power

One way to counteract the problems stemming from a lack of expertise is to build strong interpersonal ties with subordinates. **Referent power** refers to the potential influence one has due to the strength of the relationship between the leader and the followers. When people admire a leader and see her as a role model, we say she has referent power. For example, students may respond positively to advice or requests from teachers who are well liked and respected, while the same students might be unresponsive to less popular teachers. This relative degree of responsiveness is primarily a function of the strength of the relationship between the students and the different teachers. We knew one young lieutenant who had enormous referent power with the military security guards working for him due to his selfless concern for them, evident in such habits as bringing them hot chocolate and homemade cookies on their late-night shifts. The guards, sometimes taken for granted by other superiors, understood and valued the extra effort and sacrifice this young supervisor put forth for them. When Buddy Ryan was fired as head coach of the Philadelphia Eagles football team, many of the players expressed fierce loyalty to him. One said, "We'd do things for Buddy that we wouldn't do for another coach. I'd sell my body for Buddy."[20] That is referent power.

> *Power in an organization is the capacity generated by relationships.*
>
> **Margaret A. Wheatley, futurist**

Another way to look at referent power is in terms of the role friendships play in making things happen. It is frequently said, for example, that many people get jobs based on whom they know, not what they know. This is true. But we think the best perspective on this issue was offered by David Campbell, who said, "It's not who you know that counts. It's what who you know *knows about you* that counts!" (personal communication).

Referent power often takes time to develop, but it can be lost quickly—just ask Tiger Woods. Furthermore, it can have a downside in that a desire to *maintain* referent power may limit a leader's actions in particular situations. For example, a leader who has developed a strong relationship with a follower may be reluctant to discipline the follower for poor work or chronic tardiness because such actions could disrupt the nature of the relationship between the leader and the follower. Thus referent power is a two-way street; the stronger the relationship, the more influence leaders and followers exert over each other. Moreover, just as it is possible for leaders to develop strong relationships with followers and, in turn, acquire more referent power, it is also possible for followers to develop strong relationships with other followers and acquire more referent power. Followers with relatively more referent power than their peers are often the spokespersons for their work units and generally have more latitude to deviate from work unit norms. Followers with little referent power have little opportunity to deviate from group norms. For example, in an episode of the television show *The Simpsons*, Homer Simpson was fired for wearing a pink shirt to work (everybody else at the Springfield nuclear power plant had always worn white shirts). Homer was fired partly because he "was not popular enough to be different."

Legitimate Power

Legitimate power depends on a person's organizational role. It can be thought of as one's formal or official authority. Some people make things happen because they have the power or authority to do so. The boss assigns projects; the coach decides who plays; the colonel orders compliance with uniform standards; the teacher assigns homework and awards grades. Individuals with legitimate power exert influence through requests or demands deemed appropriate by virtue of their role and position. In other words, legitimate power means a leader has authority because she or he has been assigned a particular role in an organization. Note that the leader has this authority only while occupying that position and operating within the proper bounds of that role.

Legitimate authority and leadership are not the same thing. Holding a position and being a leader are not synonymous, despite the relatively common practice of calling position holders in bureaucracies the leaders. The head of an organization may be a true leader, but he or she also may not be. Effective leaders often intuitively realize they need more than legitimate power to be successful. Before he became president, Dwight Eisenhower commanded all Allied troops in Europe during World War II. In a meeting with his staff before the Normandy invasion, Eisenhower pulled a string across a table to make a point about leadership. He was demonstrating that just as you can pull a string, not push it, officers must lead soldiers and not push them from the rear.

It is also possible for followers to use their legitimate power to influence leaders. In these cases, followers can actively resist a leader's influence attempt by doing only work specifically prescribed in job descriptions, bureaucratic rules, or union policies. For example, many organizations have job descriptions that limit both the time spent at work and the types of tasks and activities performed. Similarly, bureaucratic rules and union policies can be invoked by followers to resist a leader's influence attempts. Often the leader will need to change the nature of his or her request or find another way to resolve the problem if these rules and policies are invoked by followers. If this is the case, the followers will have successfully used legitimate power to influence their leader.

Reward Power

Reward power involves the potential to influence others due to one's control over desired resources. This can include the power to give raises, bonuses, and promotions; to grant tenure; to select people for special assignments or desirable activities; to distribute desired resources like computers, offices, parking places, or travel money; to intercede positively on another's behalf; to recognize with awards and praise; and so on. Many corporations use rewards extensively to motivate employees. At McDonald's, for example, great status is accorded the All-American Hamburger Maker—the cook who makes the fastest, highest-quality hamburgers in the country. At individual fast-food restaurants, managers may reward salespeople who handle the most customers during rush periods. Tupperware holds rallies for its salespeople. Almost everyone wins something, ranging from pins and badges to lucrative prizes for top performers.[21] Schools pick teachers of the year, and professional athletes are rewarded by selection to all-star teams for their superior performance.

The potential to influence others through the ability to administer rewards is a joint function of the leader, the followers, and the situation. Leaders vary considerably in the types and frequency with which they give rewards, but the position they fill also helps determine the frequency and types of rewards administered. For example, employees of the month at Kentucky Fried Chicken are not given new cars; the managers of these franchises do not have the resources to offer such awards. Similarly, leaders in other organizations are limited to some extent in the types of awards they can administer and the frequency with which they can do so. Nevertheless, leaders can enhance their reward power by spending some time reflecting on the followers and the situation. Often a number of alternative or innovative rewards can be created, and these rewards, along with ample doses of praise, can help a leader overcome the constraints his or her position puts on reward power.

> *Unreviewable power is the most likely to self-indulge itself and the least likely to engage in dispassionate self-analysis.*
>
> **Warren E. Burger, U.S. Supreme Court chief justice, 1969–1986**

Although using reward power can be an effective way to change the attitudes and behaviors of others, in several situations it can be problematic. For example, the perception that a company's monetary bonus policy is handled equitably may be as important in motivating good work (or avoiding morale problems) as the amounts of the bonuses. Moreover, a superior may mistakenly assume that a particular reward is valued when it is not. This would be the case if a particular subordinate were publicly recognized for her good work when she actually disliked public recognition. Leadership practitioners can avoid the latter problem by developing good relationships with subordinates and administering rewards that they, not the leader, value. Another potential problem with reward power is that it may produce compliance but not other desirable outcomes like commitment.[22] In other words, subordinates may perform only at the level necessary to receive a reward and may not be willing to put forth the extra effort needed to make the organization better. An overemphasis on rewards as payoff for performance may also lead to resentment and feelings by workers of being manipulated, especially if it occurs in the context of relatively cold and distant superior–subordinate relationships. Extrinsic rewards like praise, compensation, promotion, privileges, and time off may not have the same effects on behavior as intrinsic rewards such as feelings of accomplishment, personal growth, and development. There is evidence that under some conditions extrinsic rewards can decrease intrinsic motivation toward a task and make the desired behavior less likely to persist when extrinsic rewards are not available.[23,24] Overemphasis on extrinsic rewards may instill an essentially contractual or economic relationship between superiors and subordinates, diluting important aspects of the relationship like mutual loyalty or shared commitment to higher ideals.[25] These cautions about reward power should not cloud its real usefulness and effectiveness. As noted previously, top organizations make extensive use of both tangible and symbolic rewards in motivating their workers. Furthermore, all leaders can use some of the most important rewards—sincere praise and thanks to others for their loyalty and work. The bottom line is that leaders can enhance their ability to influence others based on reward power if they determine what rewards are available, determine what rewards are valued by their subordinates, and establish clear policies for the equitable and consistent administration of rewards for good performance.

Finally, because reward power is partly determined by one's position in the organization, some people may believe followers have little, if any, reward power. This may not be the case. If followers control scarce resources, they may use the administration of these resources to get leaders to act as they want. Moreover, followers may reward their leader by putting out a high level of effort when they feel their leader is doing a good job, and they may put forth less effort when they feel their leader is doing a poor job. By modifying their level of effort, followers may in turn modify a leader's attitudes and behaviors. And when followers compliment their leader (such as for running a constructive meeting), it is no less an example of reward power than when a leader compliments a follower. Thus leadership practitioners should be aware that followers can also use reward power to influence leaders.

> *You do not lead by hitting people over the head—that's assault, not leadership.*
>
> **Dwight D. Eisenhower, U.S. president, 1953–1961**

Coercive Power

Coercive power, the opposite of reward power, is the potential to influence others through the administration of negative sanctions or the removal of positive events. In other words, it is the ability to control others through the fear of punishment or the loss of valued outcomes. Like reward power, coercive power is partly a function of the leader, but the situation often limits or enhances the coercive actions a leader can take (see **Highlight 4.3**). Examples of coercive power include police giving tickets for speeding, the army court-martialing AWOL soldiers, a teacher detaining disruptive students after school, employers firing lazy workers, and parents reprimanding children.[26] Even presidents resort to their coercive powers. Historian Arthur Schlesinger Jr., for example, described Lyndon Johnson as having a "devastating instinct for the weaknesses of others." Lyndon Johnson was familiar and comfortable with the use of coercion; he once told a White House staff member, "Just you remember this. There's only two kinds at the White House. There's elephants and there's ants. And I'm the only elephant."[27]

Leadership Lessons from the Stanford Prison Experiment

HIGHLIGHT 4.3

Almost nowhere is power as unequally distributed as in a prison. The administration and guards have both freedom and control while the prisoners have neither, at least officially. But there are important leadership lessons to be learned here as well.

A short review of the history of leadership might be helpful. If your grandparents happened to study leadership anytime from 1900 until about 1950, they would have read case studies of famous leaders. This "great man" theory of leadership hoped to unearth the traits that differentiated great leaders from lesser leaders. For the most part, this quest to identify underlying innate leadership abilities stopped in the late 1940s when Ralph Stogdill published his findings that there was no clear set of traits responsible for great leaders.

From the 1950s to the 1980s, we decided that because leadership could not be comprehended by focusing solely on the leader, we should look at the relationship between the leader and the followers. As you will learn in **Part 3** of this book, as the maturity and skills of the followers change, so should the behavior of the leader.

In the mid-1980s we started to consider the leadership implications of research done about 25 years earlier. We began to acknowledge that even if it were possible to know everything about

a leader and everything about her or his followers, another variable powerfully affected leadership and performance: the situation (the focus of **Part 4**).

Two troubling studies clearly demonstrated this situational impact. The first, conducted by Stanley Milgram, was described in **Highlight 4.2**. The lesson learned was that reasonable, normal people, when put in a situation where authority told them to behave in a nefarious manner, for the most part did just that.

Ten years after Milgram's research, Phillip Zimbardo at Stanford University recruited students to serve as either "prisoners" or "guards" in a "prison" that was simulated in the basement of a campus building. Neither the guards nor the prisoners were given any instructions about how to behave. The experiment was to have lasted for approximately two weeks but was canceled after only six days because the "guards" were abusing their fellow student "prisoners" both physically and emotionally. It's not that the student guards were bad people; rather, they were put in a power situation that overcame their own beliefs and values.

Fortunately an occasional noble hero rises to stand on higher moral ground. But as leaders, we cannot rely on that. For the masses, the situation is a powerful determinant of behavior. Incidentally, the Stanford Prison Experiment has its own website at www.prisonexp.org

should you care to learn more about it, and the experiment is described in more detail in **Chapter 12**.

Knowing what Milgram and Zimbardo demonstrated, it is at least possible to comprehend how someone like Pfc. Lynndie England, who according to her family would not even shoot a deer, could have become caught up in clearly inappropriate behavior in her role as a U.S. Army guard in the notorious Abu Ghraib prison debacle in Iraq. This is not to excuse her behavior but to help us understand it. And if we should not excuse the behavior of an undertrained soldier, we should be even less willing to excuse the leadership that put her and others in this situation without clear behavioral guidelines. After all, we've known about these studies for over 50 years!

Whether under the direction of authority as in the Milgram study, or under role assignments as in the Zimbardo study, the Abu Ghraib case showed a leadership vacuum that should not be tolerated.

And what about the business world? Leaders cannot claim they want and expect teamwork and collaboration from their subordinates if they place them in a situation that fosters competition and enmity. Neither can leaders claim that they want creativity from their subordinates if they have created a situation where the slightest deviation from rigid rules brings punishment. And perhaps most important, leaders cannot expect egalitarian behaviors if people are put in highly differentiated power situations. People in organizations are smart. They are less likely to give you the behaviors you espouse in your speeches and more likely to give you the behavior demanded by the situation in which you place them. The leader's job is to create the conditions for the team to be successful, and the situation is one of the most important variables. What to consider in the situation is discussed in more detail in **Chapter 13**.

Nearly all men can stand adversity, but if you want to test a man's character, give him power.

Abraham Lincoln, U.S. president, 1961–1965

Coercive power, like reward power, can be used appropriately or inappropriately (see **Highlight 4.4**).

Punishment

HIGHLIGHT 4.4

In an ideal world, perhaps everyone would be dependable, achievement-oriented, and committed to their organization's goals. However, leaders sometimes must deal with followers who are openly hostile or insubordinate, create conflicts among coworkers, do not work up to standards, or openly violate important rules or policies. In such cases, leaders may need to administer punishment to change the followers' behavior.

Of all the different aspects of leadership, few are as controversial as punishment. Some of the primary reasons for this controversy stem from myths surrounding the use of punishment, as well as lack of knowledge of the effects of punishment on followers' motivation, satisfaction, and performance. This section is designed to shed light on the punishment controversy by (1) addressing several myths about the use of punishment, (2) reviewing an important research finding concerning the relationships between punishment and various organizational variables, and (3) giving leadership practitioners advice on how to properly administer punishment.

Defining Punishment

We should begin by repeating the definition of punishment stated earlier in the book. Punishment is the administration of an aversive event or the withdrawal of a positive event or stimulus, which in turn, decreases the likelihood that a particular behavior will be repeated. Examples of punishment might include verbal reprimands, being moved to a less prestigious office, having pay docked, being fired, being made to run several laps around an athletic field, or losing eligibility for a sport entirely. We should note that, according to this definition, only those aversive events administered on a contingent basis are considered to be forms of punishment; aversive events administered on a noncontingent basis may constitute harsh and abusive treatment but are not punishment.

Additionally, punishment appears to be in the eye of the beholder; aversive events that effectively change the direction, intensity, or persistence of one follower's behavior may have no effect on another's. It is even possible that some followers may find the administration of a noxious event or the removal of a positive event to be reinforcing. For example, it is not uncommon for some children to misbehave if that increases the attention they receive from parents, even if the latter's behavior outwardly may seem punishing. (To the children, some parental attention of any kind may be preferable to no attention.) Similarly, some followers may see the verbal reprimands and notoriety they receive by being insubordinate or violating company policies as forms of attention. Because these followers enjoy being the center of attention, they may find this notoriety rewarding, and they may be even more likely to be insubordinate in the future.

Myths Surrounding the Use of Punishment

Three of these myths were reviewed by Arvey and Ivancevich and include beliefs that the use of punishment results in undesirable emotional side effects on the part of the recipient, is unethical and inhumane, and rarely works anyway (that is, it seldom eliminates the undesirable behavior).

B. F. Skinner's work in behavioral psychology lent support to the idea that punishment is ineffective and causes undesirable side effects. He based his conclusions on the unnatural behaviors manifested by rats and pigeons punished in various conditioning experiments. Despite the dangers of generalizing from the behavior of rats to humans, many people accepted Skinner's contention that punishment is a futile and typically counterproductive tool for controlling human behavior. This was so despite the fact that considerable research regarding the emotional effects of punishment on humans did not support Skinner's claim.

With respect to the myth that punishment is unethical or inhumane, it has been suggested that there is an ethical distinction between "future-oriented" and "past-oriented" punishment. Future-oriented punishment, intended to help improve behavior, may be effective in diminishing or eliminating undesirable behavior. Past-oriented punishment, or what we commonly think of as retribution, on the other hand, is simply a payback for past misdeeds. This sort of punishment may be more ethically questionable, especially when it is intended only as payback and not, say, as deterrent to others. Moreover, when considering the ethics of administering punishment, we must also consider the ethics of failing to administer punishment. The costs of failing to punish a potentially harmful behavior, such as unsafe workplace practices, may far outweigh those associated with the punishment itself.

A third myth concerns the efficacy of punishment. Skinner and others claimed that punishment did not result in permanent behavior change but instead only temporarily suppressed behavior. However, judicious administration of sanctions, combined with advice about how to avoid punishment in the future, may successfully eliminate undesirable behaviors on a more permanent basis. Furthermore, it may be a moot point to argue (as Skinner did) that punishment only temporarily suppresses behavior; so long as sanctions for misdeeds remain in place, their impact on behavior should continue. In that regard, the "temporary" effects of punishment on behavior are no different from the "temporary" effects of reinforcement on behavior.

Punishment, Satisfaction, and Performance

It appears that properly administered punishment does not cause undesirable emotional side effects, is not unethical, and may effectively suppress undesirable behavior. However, we also should ask what effect punishment has on followers' satisfaction and performance. Most people probably would predict that leaders who use punishment frequently will have less satisfied and lower-performing followers. Interestingly, this does not appear to be the case—at least when punishment is used appropriately. Let us look more closely at this issue.

Several researchers have looked at whether leaders who administer punishment on a contingent basis also administered rewards on a contingent basis. Generally, researchers have found that there is a moderate positive relationship between leaders' contingent reward behaviors and contingent punishment behaviors. There also are consistently strong negative correlations between leaders' contingent reward and noncontingent punishment behaviors. Thus, leaders meting out rewards on a contingent basis are also more likely to administer punishment only when followers behave inappropriately or are not performing up to standards.

Several other authors have found that contingent punishment either is unrelated to followers' satisfaction with their supervisor or has a low positive relationship with it. In other words, leaders who follow certain rules in administering punishment need not have dissatisfied subordinates. In fact, judicious and appropriate use of punishment by leaders may result in somewhat higher overall satisfaction of followers. These findings make sense when the entire work

unit is considered; failing to use punishment when it seems called for in most followers' eyes may lead to perceptions of inequity, which may in turn reduce group cohesiveness and satisfaction.

Overall, the evidence about punishment's impact on performance appears mixed. Some authors report a strong positive relationship between punishment and performance, whereas others found either no relationship between punishment and performance or a negative one.

Despite such mixed findings, several points about the relationship between punishment and performance findings are worth noting. First, the levels of punishment as well as the manner in which it was administered across studies could have differed dramatically, and these factors could have affected the results.

Second, one of the studies reporting less favorable punishment–performance results made an important point about the opportunities to punish. It examined the relationships between Little League coaches' behaviors and their teams' win–loss records. They found that coaches who punished more often had less successful teams. These coaches also, however, had less talented players and, therefore, had many more opportunities to use punishment. Coaches of successful teams had little if any reason to use punishment.

Third, many behaviors that are punished may not have a direct link to job performance. For example, being insubordinate, violating company dress codes, and arriving late to meetings are all punishable behaviors that may not be directly linked to solving work-related problems or producing goods or services.

In summary, the research evidence shows that punishment can lead to positive organizational outcomes if administered properly. When administered on a contingent basis, it may help increase job satisfaction, may decrease role ambiguity and absenteeism rates, and, depending on the behaviors being punished, may improve performance. However, administering intense levels of punishment in a noncontingent or capricious manner can have a devastating effect on the work unit. Group cohesiveness may suffer, followers are likely to become more dissatisfied and less apt to come to work, and they may perform at a lower level in the long term. Thus learning how to properly administer punishment may be the key to maximizing the benefits associated with its use.

Administering Punishment

Administering punishment properly depends on effective two-way communication between the leader and follower. Leaders need to provide a clear rationale for punishment and indicate the consequences for unacceptable behavior in the future. Finally, leaders need to provide followers with guidance about how to improve. This guidance may entail role-modeling proper behaviors for followers, suggesting that followers take training courses, or giving followers accurate feedback about their behavior at work.

Overall, it may be the manner in which punishment is administered, rather than the level of punishment, that has the greatest effect on followers' satisfaction and performance. Leaders need to realize that they may be biased toward administering punishment to rectify followers' substandard performance, and the best way to get around this bias is to collect as much information as possible before deciding whether to punish. By collecting the facts, leaders will be better able to focus on the act, not the person;

be able to administer a punishment consistent with company policy; provide the rationale for the punishment; and give guidance to followers on how to improve.

A final caution that leaders need to be aware of concerns the reinforcing or rewarding nature of punishment. Behaviors that are rewarded are likely to be repeated. When leaders administer punishment and subsequently see improvement in a follower's behavior, the leaders will be rewarded and be more apt to use punishment in the future. Over time, this may lead to an over-reliance on punishment and an underemphasis on the other motivational strategies as means of correcting performance problems.

Again, by collecting as much information as possible and by carefully considering the applicability of goal setting, job characteristics theory, and so on, to the problem, leaders may be able to successfully avoid having only one tool in their motivational toolkit.

Sources: R. D. Arvey and J. M. Ivancevich, "Punishment in Organizations: A Review, Propositions, and Research Suggestions," *Academy of Management Review* 5 (1980), pp. 123–32; G. J. Curphy, F. W. Gibson, B. W. Asiu, C. P. McCown, and C. Brown, "A Field Study of the Causal Relationships between Organizational Performance, Punishment, and Justice," working paper, 1992; R. D. Arvey, G. A. Davis, and S. M. Nelson, "Use of Discipline in an Organization: A Field Study," *Journal of Applied Psychology* 69 (1984), pp. 448–60; and P. M. Podsakoff and W. D. Todor, "Relationships between Leader Reward and Punishment Behavior and Group Process and Productivity," *Journal of Management* 11 (1985), pp. 55–73.

It is carried to its extreme in repressive totalitarian societies. One of the most tragic instances of coercive power was the cult led by Jim Jones, which unbelievably self-exterminated in an incident known as the Jonestown massacre.[28] Virtually all of the 912 people who died there drank, at Jones's direction, from large vats of a flavored drink containing cyanide. The submissiveness and suicidal obedience of Jones's followers during the massacre were due largely to the long history of rule by fear that Jones had practiced. For example, teenagers caught holding hands were beaten, and adults judged slacking in their work were forced to box for hours in marathon public matches against as many as three or four bigger and stronger opponents. Jim Jones ruled by fear, and his followers became self-destructively compliant.

Perhaps the preceding example is so extreme that we can dismiss its relevance to our own lives and leadership activities. Yet abuses of power, especially abuses of coercive power, continue to make the news, whether we are seeing reports of U.S. military abuse in Iraq or Taliban abuse in Afghanistan. However, such examples provide a dramatic reminder that reliance on coercive power has inherent limitations and drawbacks. But this is not to say disciplinary sanctions are never necessary; sometimes they are. Informal coercion, as opposed to the threat of formal punishment, can also change the attitudes and behaviors of others. Informal coercion is usually expressed implicitly, and often nonverbally, rather than explicitly. It may be the pressure employees feel to donate to the boss's favorite charity, or it may be his or her glare when they bring up an unpopular idea. One of the most common forms of coercion is simply a superior's temperamental outbursts. The intimidation caused by a leader's poorly controlled anger is usually, in its long-term effects, a dysfunctional style of behavior for leaders.

It is also possible for followers to use coercive power to influence their leader's behavior. For example, a leader may be hesitant to take disciplinary action against a large, emotionally unstable follower. Followers can threaten leaders with physical assaults, industrial sabotage, or work slowdowns and strikes, and these threats can modify a leader's behavior. Followers are more likely to use coercive power to change their leader's behavior if they have a relatively high amount of referent power with their fellow coworkers. This may be particularly true for threats of work slowdowns or strikes.

Concluding Thoughts about French and Raven's Power Taxonomy

Can we reach any conclusions about what base of power is best for a leader to use? As you might have anticipated, we must say that's an unanswerable question without knowing more facts about a particular situation. For example, consider the single factor of whether a group is facing a crisis. This might affect the leader's exercise of power simply because leaders usually can exert more power during crises than during periods of relative calm. Furthermore, during crises followers may be more eager to receive direction and control from leaders.

Can we make any generalizations about using various sources of power? Actually, considerable research has examined French and Raven's ideas, and generally the findings indicate that leaders who rely primarily on referent and expert power have subordinates who are more motivated and satisfied, are absent less, and perform better.[29] However, Yukl[30] and Podsakoff and Schriesheim[31] have criticized these findings, and much of their criticism centers on the instrument used to assess a leader's bases of power. Hinkin and Schriesheim developed an instrument that overcomes many of the criticisms,[32] and future research should more clearly delineate the relationship between the five bases of power and various leadership effectiveness criteria.

Four generalizations about power and influence seem warranted. First, effective leaders typically take advantage of *all* their sources of power. Effective leaders understand the relative advantages and disadvantages of different sources of power, and they selectively emphasize one or another depending on their objectives in a given situation. Second, whereas leaders in well-functioning organizations have strong influence over their subordinates, *they are also open to being influenced by them*. High degrees of reciprocal influence between leaders and followers characterize the most effective organizations.[33] Third, leaders vary in the extent to which they share power with subordinates. Some leaders seem to view their power as a fixed resource that, when shared with others (like cutting a pie into pieces), reduces their own portion. They see power in zero-sum terms. Other leaders see power as an expandable pie. They see the possibility of increasing a subordinate's power without reducing their own. Needless to say, which view a leader subscribes to can have a major impact on the leader's support for power-sharing activities like delegation and participative management. A leader's support for power-sharing activities (or in today's popular language, *empowerment*) is also affected by the practice of holding leaders responsible for subordinates' decisions and actions as well as their own. It is, after all, the coach or manager who often gets fired when the team loses.[34, 35] Fourth, effective leaders generally work to increase their various power bases (whether expert, referent, reward, or legitimate) or become more willing to use their coercive power.

Cultural Differences and Power

HIGHLIGHT 4.5

Dutch sociologist Geert Hofstede and his colleagues have quantified the business culture in more than 100 countries on six parameters: individualism, masculinity, uncertainty avoidance, long-term orientation, indulgence, and of importance in this chapter, power distance. They define **power distance** as the degree to which the less powerful members of a society accept and expect that power is distributed unequally. The fundamental issue here is how a society handles inequalities among people. People in societies exhibiting a large degree of power distance accept a hierarchical order in which everybody has a place and that needs no further justification. In societies with low power distance, people strive to equalize the distribution of power and demand justification for inequalities of power. A few examples will help demonstrate the Power Distance Index.

At the low end of the Power Distance Index is a country like Austria. Austria scores very low on this dimension (score of 11), which means that the following characteristics typify the Austrian style: being independent, hierarchy for convenience only, equal rights, superiors accessible, coaching leader, management facilitates and empowers. Power is decentralized and managers count on the experience of their team members. Employees expect to be consulted. Control is disliked. Communication is direct and participative.

In contrast are countries with high scores on the Power Distance Index. It is important to note here that although low scores can usually be generalized as above, high scores tend to be more culturally specific and can be influenced not only by tradition but also by geography. Again, a few examples will help.

Saudi Arabia scores high on this dimension (score of 95), which means that people accept a hierarchical order in which everybody has a place and that needs no further justification. Hierarchy in an organization is seen as reflecting inherent inequalities, centralization is popular, subordinates expect to be told what to do, and the ideal boss is a benevolent autocrat.

Russia, scoring 93, is a nation where power holders are very distant in society. This is underlined by the fact that the largest country in the world is extremely centralized. Roughly two-thirds of all foreign investments go into Moscow, where 80 percent of all financial potential is concentrated. The huge discrepancy between the less and the more powerful people leads to a great importance of status symbols. Behavior has to reflect and represent the status roles in all areas of business interactions, whether in visits, negotiations, or cooperation; the approach should be top-down and provide clear mandates for any task.

Although we are focusing on the power distance factor here, Hofstede points out that it is important to consider the potential interaction with other cultural indices. The United States provides a useful example of these interactions. The fairly low score on power distance (40) in combination with one of the most individualist (91) cultures in the world plays out in the following ways:

- The American premise of "liberty and justice for all." This is evidenced by an explicit emphasis on equal rights in all aspects of American society and government.
- Within American organizations, hierarchy is established for convenience, superiors are accessible, and managers rely on individual employees and teams for their expertise.

- Both managers and employees expect to be consulted, and information is shared frequently. At the same time, communication is informal, direct, and participative to a degree.

- The society is loosely knit; the expectation is that people look after themselves and their immediate families only and should not rely (too much) on authorities for support.

- There is also a high degree of geographic mobility in the United States.

- Americans are the best joiners in the world; however, it is often difficult, especially among men, to develop deep friendships.

- Americans are accustomed to doing business or interacting with people they don't know well. Consequently, Americans are not shy about approaching their prospective counterparts in order to obtain or seek information. In the business world, employees are expected to be self-reliant and display initiative. Also, within the exchange-based world of work, we see that hiring, promotion, and assignment decisions are based on merit or evidence of what one has done or can do.

Finally, Hofstede points out that his indices are most useful when used to compare two cultures. To the degree the cultures are similar, work across and between the two countries will be easier with little need for specific consideration of the differences. But when the differences are great, leaders are well advised to consider the differences and adjust their behaviors to be most effective.

One of your authors failed to recognize this power difference when conducting a workshop with both American and Russian participants. (Partially in his defense, this event occurred prior to the publication of Hofstede's first book.) In setting the stage for the workshop, he presented a tentative agenda and asked the participants what they would like to add, delete, or change. This seemed perfectly reasonable to the American participants, but the Russians completely disapproved and rejected this effort. As it turns out, your author misjudged two critical factors. First, he considered himself a "facilitator" for the workshop, whereas the Russians, who saw him standing in front of the room and addressing the participants, considered him the "leader." This error contributed to the second problem, related directly to Hofstede's power difference. In the United States, it is reasonable and even expected that the agenda will be developed informally and in a participative manner including the facilitator and all participants. Not so much in Russia. The Russian leader is expected to provide clear mandates for the task at hand. Not only did it take a while to discover this error had been made, but it took even longer to recover from it. Though not of dramatic international consequences, this was certainly a failure to recognize the leadership impact of inattention to cross-cultural power expectations. One can only imagine how these differences influence our perceptions of leadership effectiveness between the United States and Russia.

Sources: G. Hofstede, *Culture's Consequences: Comparing Values, Behaviors, Institutions, and Organizations across Nations*, 2nd ed. (Thousand Oaks, CA: Sage Publications, 2001); and G. Hofstede, G. J. Hofstede, and M. Minkov, *Cultures and Organizations: Software of the Mind*, revised and expanded 3rd ed. (New York: McGraw-Hill, 2010).

Leader Motives

Thus far we have been looking at how different *sources* of power can affect others, but that's only one perspective. Another way of looking at the relationship between power and leadership involves focusing on the individual leader's personality. We will look most closely at the role personality plays in leadership in an upcoming chapter, but it will be nonetheless useful now to briefly examine how all people (including leaders) vary in their personal motivation to have or wield power.

People vary in their motivation to influence or control others. McClelland called this the **need for power**,[36] and individuals with a high need for power derive psychological satisfaction from influencing others. They seek positions where they can influence others, and they are often involved concurrently in influencing people in many different organizations or decision-making bodies. In such activities they readily offer ideas, suggestions, and opinions, and also seek information they can use in influencing others. They are often astute at building trusting relationships and assessing power networks, though they can also be quite outspoken and forceful. They value the tangible signs of their authority and status as well as the more intangible indications of others' deference to them. Two different ways of expressing the need for power have been identified: **personalized power** and **socialized power**. Individuals who have a high need for personalized power are relatively selfish, impulsive, uninhibited, and lacking in self-control. These individuals exercise power for their own needs, not for the good of the group or the organization. Socialized power, by contrast, implies a more emotionally mature expression of the motive. Socialized power is exercised in the service of higher goals to others or organizations and often involves self-sacrifice toward those ends. It often involves an empowering, rather than an autocratic, style of management and leadership.

Although the need for power has been measured using questionnaires and more traditional personality inventories, McClelland and his associates have used the Thematic Apperception Test (TAT) to assess the need for power. TAT is a **projective personality test** consisting of pictures such as a woman staring out a window or a boy holding a violin. Subjects are asked to make up a story about each picture, and the stories are then interpreted in terms of the strengths of various needs imputed to the characters, one of which is the need for power. Because the pictures are somewhat ambiguous, the sorts of needs projected onto the characters are presumed to reflect needs (perhaps at an unconscious level) of the storyteller. Stories concerned with influencing or controlling others would receive high scores for the need for power.

The need for power is positively related to various leadership effectiveness criteria. For example, McClelland and Boyatzis found the need for power to be positively related to success for nontechnical managers at AT&T,[37] and Stahl found that the need for power was positively related to managers' performance ratings and promotion rates.[38] In addition, Fodor reported that small groups of ROTC students were more likely to successfully solve a subarctic survival situation if their leader had a strong need for power.[39] Although these findings appear promising, several cautions should be kept in mind. First, McClelland and Boyatzis also reported that the need for power was unrelated to the success of technical managers at AT&T.[40] Apparently the level of knowledge (that is, expert power) played a more important role in the success of the technical managers versus that of the nontechnical managers. Second, McClelland concluded that although some need for power was necessary for leadership potential, successful leaders also have the ability to inhibit their manifestation of this need.[41] Leaders who are relatively uninhibited in their need for power will act like dictators; such individuals use power impulsively, to manipulate or control others, or to achieve at another's expense. Leaders with a high need for power but low activity inhibition may be successful in the short term, but their followers, as well as the remainder of the organization, may pay high costs for this success. Some of these costs may include perceptions by fellow members of the organization that they are untrustworthy, uncooperative, overly competitive, and looking out primarily for themselves. Finally, some followers have a high need for power, too. This can lead to tension between leader and follower when a follower with a high need for power is directed to do something.

Individuals vary in their motivation to manage, just as in their need for power. Miner described the **motivation to manage** in terms of six composites:[42]

- Maintaining good relationships with authority figures
- Wanting to compete for recognition and advancement

- Being active and assertive
- Wanting to exercise influence over subordinates
- Being visibly different from followers
- Being willing to do routine administrative tasks

Like McClelland, Miner also used a projective test to measure a person's motivation to manage. Miner's Sentence Completion Scale (MSCS) consists of a series of incomplete sentences dealing with the six components just described (such as "My relationship with my boss . . . "). Respondents are asked to complete the sentences, which are scored according to established criteria. The overall composite MSCS score (though not component scores) has consistently been found to predict leadership success in hierarchical or bureaucratic organizations.[43] Thus individuals who maintained respect for authority figures, wanted to be recognized, acted assertively, actively influenced subordinates, maintained "psychological distance" between themselves and their followers, and readily took on routine administrative tasks were more apt to be successful in bureaucratic organizations. However, Miner claimed that different qualities were needed in flatter, nonbureaucratic organizations, and his review of the MSCS supports this view.[44]

Findings concerning both the need for power and the motivation to manage have several implications for leadership practitioners. First, not all individuals like being leaders. One reason may be that some have a relatively low need for power or motivation to manage. Because these scores are relatively stable and fairly difficult to change, leaders who do not enjoy their role may want to seek positions where they have fewer supervisory responsibilities.

Second, a high need for power or motivation to manage does not guarantee leadership success. The situation can play a crucial role in determining whether the need for power or the motivation to manage is related to leadership success. For example, McClelland and Boyatzis found the need for power to be related to leadership success for nontechnical managers only,[45] and Miner found that motivation to manage was related to leadership success only in hierarchical or bureaucratic organizations.[46]

Third, to be successful in the long term, leaders may require both a high need for socialized power and a high level of activity inhibition. Leaders who impulsively exercise power merely to satisfy their own selfish needs will probably be ineffective in the long term. Finally, it is important to remember that followers, as well as leaders, differ in the need for power, activity inhibition, and motivation to manage. Certain followers may have stronger needs or motives in this area. Leaders may need to behave differently toward these followers than they might toward followers having a low need for power or motivation to manage.

Three recent studies offer a fitting conclusion to this section about power and the individual's motives and a transition to our next topic. Magee and Galinsky not only have presented a comprehensive review of the nature of power in hierarchical settings but also have noted that the acquisition and application of power induce transformation of individual psychological processes, with the result being manifested by actions to further increase power![47] This is not the first time this phenomenon has been observed (recall Lord Acton's words about power and corruption). That power actually transforms individual psychological processes as an underlying cause of this phenomenon is fascinating.

But just having power, by either situation or individual transformation, does not guarantee success. Treadway and colleagues have presented research showing that although past work performance is a source of personal reputation and can increase an individual's power, this increase does not necessarily translate into influence over others.[48] Many people fail to achieve this increased influence due to their lack of political skills for influence, and the application of influence is our next topic.

Finally, in research that will lead us later in this book to look more closely at groups and teams, Karriker and her colleagues found a positive relationship between distributed or shared leadership and overall performance in teams.[49] As they note in their title, when it comes to power, it's good to share.

Influence Tactics

Whereas power is the capacity or potential to influence others, influence tactics are the actual behaviors used by an agent to change the attitudes, opinions, or behaviors of a target person. Kipnis and his associates accomplished much of the early work on the types of influence tactics one person uses to influence another.[50] Various instruments have been developed to study influence tactics, but the Influence Behavior Questionnaire (IBQ),[51] seems to be the most promising. Here is a detailed discussion of the different influence tactics assessed by the IBQ.

Types of Influence Tactics

> *A leader is like a shepherd. He stays behind the flock, letting the most nimble go out ahead, whereupon the others follow, not realising that all along they are being directed from behind.*
>
> **Nelson Mandela, South African president, 1994–1999**

The IBQ is designed to assess nine types of influence tactics, and its scales give us a convenient overview of various methods of influencing others. **Rational persuasion** occurs when an agent uses logical arguments or factual evidence to influence others. An example of rational persuasion would be when a politician's adviser explains how demographic changes in the politician's district make it important for the politician to spend relatively more time in the district seeing constituents than she has in the recent past. Agents make **inspirational appeals** when they make a request or proposal designed to arouse enthusiasm or emotions in targets. An example here might be a minister's impassioned plea to members of a congregation about the good works that could be accomplished if a proposed addition to the church were built. **Consultation** occurs when agents ask targets to participate in planning an activity. An example of consultation would be if a minister established a committee of church members to help plan the layout and use of a new church addition. In this case the consultative work might not only lead to a better building plan but also *strengthen member commitment* to the idea of a new addition. **Ingratiation** occurs when an agent attempts to get you in a good mood before making a request. A familiar example here would be a salesperson's good-natured or flattering banter with you before you make a decision about purchasing a product. Agents use **personal appeals** when they ask another to do a favor out of friendship. A sentence that opens with, "Bill, we've known each other a long time and I've never asked anything of you before" represents the beginning of a personal appeal, whereas influencing a target through the exchange of favors is labeled **exchange**. If two politicians agree to vote for each other's pet legislation despite minor misgivings about each other's bills, that is exchange. **Coalition tactics** differ from consultation in that they are used when agents seek the aid or support of others to influence the target. A dramatic example of coalition tactics occurs when several significant people in an alcoholic's life (such as spouse, children, employer, or neighbor) agree to confront the alcoholic in unison about the many dimensions of his or her problem. Threats or persistent reminders used to influence targets are known as **pressure tactics**. A judge who gives a convicted prisoner a suspended sentence but tells him to consider the suspension a "sword hanging over his head" if he breaks the law again is using pressure tactics. Finally, **legitimizing tactics** occur when agents make requests based on their position or authority. A principal may ask a teacher to be on the school's curriculum committee, and the teacher may accede to the request despite reservations because it is the principal's prerogative to appoint any teacher to that role. In practice, of course, actual tactics often combine these approaches. Rarely, for example, is an effective appeal purely inspirational without any rational elements.

Don't threaten. I know it's done by some of our people, but I don't go for it. If people are running scared, they're not going to make the right decisions. They'll make decisions to please the boss rather than recommend what has to be done.

Charles Pilliod, American business executive and diplomat

Influence Tactics and Power

As alluded to throughout this chapter, a strong relationship exists between the relative power of agents and targets and the types of influence tactics used. Because leaders with high amounts of referent power have built close relationships with followers, they may be more able to use a wide variety of influence tactics to modify the attitudes and behaviors of their followers. For example, leaders with referent power could use inspirational appeals, consultations, ingratiation, personal appeals, exchanges, and even coalition tactics to increase the amount of time a particular follower spends doing work-related activities. Note, however, that leaders with high referent power generally do not use legitimizing or pressure tactics to influence followers because, by threatening followers, leaders risk some loss of referent power. Leaders who have only coercive or legitimate power may be able to use only coalition, legitimizing, or pressure tactics to influence followers. In fact, influence tactics can be so effective, Cialdini refers to them as "Weapons of Influence."[52]

Other factors also can affect the choice of influence tactics.[53] People typically use hard tactics (that is, legitimizing or pressure tactics) when an influencer has the upper hand, when they anticipate resistance, or when the other person's behavior violates important norms. People typically use soft tactics (such as ingratiation) when they are at a disadvantage (see **Highlight 4.6** comparing football and judo for an example of using a disadvantage to your advantage), when they expect resistance, or when they will personally benefit if the attempt is successful. People tend to use rational tactics (the exchange and rational appeals) when parties are relatively equal in power, when resistance is not anticipated, and when the benefits are organizational as well as personal. Studies have shown that influence attempts based on factual, logical analyses are the most frequently reported method by which middle managers exert lateral influence[54] and upward influence.[55] Other important components of successful influence of one's superiors include thoroughly preparing beforehand, involving others for support (coalition tactics), and persisting through a combination of approaches.[56]

Power and Influence (or Football and Judo)

HIGHLIGHT 4.6

While great leaders use both power and influence effectively (see **Highlight 4.9** for perhaps the quintessential example of using both techniques effectively), it can also be instructive to compare and contrast the two at their most obvious polarities. At least for one of your authors, football and judo are cases in point.

Football, and by that I mean what is known in Europe as "American football," is a game about power. Of course, influence can also be used and often is quite effectively. But overwhelm-ingly, football is a game about size, strength, and speed. If one combines those three concepts and then searches for a single word to describe them, I would submit that "power" might work. If you have ever been around professional football players, you will discover this for yourself. They are a powerful group of men. Quite a while back, my brother-in-law was a professional football player. He played as an offensive end in college but was converted to a linebacker as a pro. I remember back in college that I thought he was about the largest human being I had ever known; if he was in a room with normal-sized, non-football-playing people, he readily stood out, and above, everyone else. As a result of these experiences, the first time I attended a game in which he was playing as a pro, I expected to be able to pick him out easily. But on the field with other powerful pro football players, he was indistinguishable except for his jersey number.

This notion of the importance of power to the game of football was summed up once by one of my coaches who repeatedly informed us that "a good big man is always better than a good small man."

Contrast this with judo, or its cousin, jujitsu (see Robert Cialdini's excellent book entitled *Influence: Science and Practice* for more details on using jujitsu as "a weapon"). Again, your author's experience is cited as but one example. After a not-so-great experience as an undersized high school football player, I tended to blame my lack of power (size, strength, and speed) for my results. That notion changed later in life. Having been selected to be part of a covert operations group during the Vietnam War, I was sent to a number of preparatory courses, and one of these was a course in judo. I remember quite vividly my first day in the *dojo*, as we stood around in our ill-fitting *gis*. I had the sense that most of us were engaged in the same mental activity; we were sizing up our classmates hoping to avoid the most "powerful" of our peers. In this search for the most powerful among us, there was one small person meekly sitting over against the wall who received no consideration as a threat and for whom I almost felt sorry. He appeared more timid than the rest of us and was not even prone to make eye contact with anyone. Clearly possessing the smallest and "least powerful" body in the room, he just sat quietly, thumbing through some sort of notebook.

As the minute hand moved to the top of the clock, we all kept an eye on the door, watching for our instructor to enter the room at any moment. We didn't even notice when the small fellow put down his notebook and stood quietly against the wall. Then he spoke, saying that his name was Tze Lang Chen, and he would be our *sensei*. Really? This was the instructor? I was sure he was going to be crushed, especially by some of our larger classmates. Let me assure you, that notion was rapidly and completely dispelled.

In judo, the power of your opponent is a weapon to be used against him. In fact, the word *judo* means "the gentle way," which is somewhat antithetical to the football word *power*. According to our *sensei* Tze Lang Chen, the founder of judo, Jigoro Kano, was quoted as saying that "resisting a more powerful opponent will result in your defeat, while adjusting to and evading your opponent's attack will cause him to lose his balance, his power will be reduced, and you will defeat him. This can apply whatever the relative values of power, thus making it possible for weaker opponents to beat significantly stronger ones." I believe a paraphrase of the profound statement might well be "the bigger they are, the harder they fall."

We quickly learned that the more we resisted the force of our *sensei*, the sooner we would find ourselves flat on our backs looking up at this rather small man hovering over us. Such is the nature of power versus influence. Power can be used to force movement whereas influence may be hardly felt at all.

Source: R. B. Cialdini, *Influence: Science and Practice*, 5th ed. (Boston: Pearson Education, 2009).

Findings about who uses different tactics, and when, provide interesting insights into the influence process. It is clear that one's influence tactic of choice depends on many factors, including intended outcomes and one's power relative to the target person. Although it may not be surprising that people select influence tactics as a function of their power relationship with another person, it is striking that this relationship holds true so universally across different social domains—for business executives, for parents and children, and for spouses. There is a strong tendency for people to resort to hard tactics whenever they have an advantage in clout if other tactics fail to get results.[57] As the bank robber Willie Sutton once said, "You can get more with a kind word and a gun than you can get with just a kind word." This sentiment is apparently familiar to bank managers, too. The latter reported greater satisfaction in handling subordinates' poor performance when they were relatively more punishing.[58] **Highlight 4.7** offers thoughts on how men and women managers sometimes use different influence techniques.

Gender Differences in Managing Upward: How Male and Female Managers Get Their Way

HIGHLIGHT 4.7

Both male and female managers in a *Fortune* 100 company were interviewed and completed surveys about how they influence upward—that is, how they influence their own bosses. The results generally supported the idea that female managers' influence attempts showed greater concern for others, whereas male managers' influence attempts showed greater concern for self. Female managers were more likely to act with the organization's broad interests in mind, consider how others felt about the influence attempt, involve others in planning, and focus on both the task and interpersonal aspects of the situation. Male managers, by contrast, were more likely to act out of self-interest, show less consideration for how others might feel about the influence attempt, work alone in developing their strategy, and focus primarily on the task.

One of the most surprising findings of the study was that, contrary to prediction, female managers were less likely than male managers to compromise or negotiate during their influence attempts. The female managers were actually more likely to persist in trying to persuade their superiors, even to the point of open opposition. At first this may seem inconsistent with the idea that the female managers' influence style involved greater concern for their relatedness to others. However, it seems consistent with the higher value placed by the women managers on involvement. Perhaps female managers demonstrate more commitment to their issues, and greater self-confidence that they are doing the "right thing," precisely because they have already interacted more with others in the organization and know they have others' support.

Although male and female managers emphasized different influence techniques, neither group overall was more effective than the other. Nonetheless, there may be significant implications of the various techniques for a manager's career advancement. At increasingly higher management levels in an organization, effectiveness may be defined primarily by its fit with the organization's own norms and values. Managers whose style most closely matches that of their superior may have an advantage in evaluations and promotion decisions. This may be a significant factor for women, given the highly skewed representation of men in the most senior executive ranks.

Source: K. E. Lauterbach and B. J. Weiner, "Dynamics of Upward Influence: How Male and Female Managers Get Their Way," *The Leadership Quarterly* 7, no. 1 (1996), pp. 87–107.

It is not power that corrupts, but fear. Fear of losing power corrupts those who wield it and fear of the scourge of power corrupts those who are subject to it.

Aung San Suu Kyi, Burmese politician and diplomat

All forms of tampering with human beings, getting at them, shaping them against their will to your own pattern, all thought control and conditioning, is, therefore, a denial of that in men which makes them men and their values ultimate.

A. A. Berle Jr., writer about corporations

Although hard tactics can be effective, relying on them can change the way we see others. This was demonstrated in an experiment wherein leaders' perceptions and evaluations of subordinates were assessed after they exercised different sorts of authority over the subordinates.[59] Several hundred business students acted as managers of small work groups assembling model cars. Some of the students were told to act in an authoritarian manner, exercising complete control over the group's work; others were told to act as democratic leaders, letting group members participate fully in decisions about the work. As expected, authoritarian leaders used more hard tactics, whereas democratic leaders influenced subordinates more through rational methods. More interesting was the finding that subordinates were evaluated by the two types of leaders in dramatically different ways even though the subordinates of both types did equally good work. Authoritarian leaders judged their subordinates as less motivated, less skilled, and less suited for promotion. Apparently, bosses who use hard tactics to control others' behavior tend not to attribute any resultant good performance to the subordinates themselves. Ironically, the act of using hard tactics leads to negative attributions about others, which, in turn, tend to corroborate the use of hard tactics in the first place.

Finally, we should remember that using influence tactics can be thought of as a social skill. Choosing the right tactic may not always be enough to ensure good results; the behavior must be *skillfully executed*. We are not encouraging deviousness or a manipulative attitude toward others (although that has certainly been done by some, as illustrated in **Highlight 4.8** and discussed more in **Chapter 5**, on ethics). Instead, we are merely recognizing the obvious fact that clumsy influence attempts often come across as phony and may be counterproductive. See **Highlight 4.9** for a perspective of a political leader who used power appropriately but was arguably the quintessential master of using influence effectively.

The Clout of Influence and the Big Con

HIGHLIGHT 4.8

The confidence game, or "con game" is certainly nothing new, although some people might argue it has been taken to new heights by the likes of Bernie Madoff. The term *confidence man* was first used by the New York press during the trial of William Thompson in 1849. What remains unchanged over the years is that the con game is not about violence or power but much more about the illicit use of influence. It is about the nefarious manipulation of trust.

Amy Reading has written a detailed history of "the big con" while wrapping it around a fascinating story of one of the largest swindles in U.S. history. Reading describes the preparations and staging necessary to win over the "mark"

as if it were a form of theater. The mark in her historical account is one J. Frank Norfleet, a man who by his own description is as straight as they come. "I don't drink, chew tobacco, smoke, cuss, or tell lies," he would say. And he trusted others, which led to his involvement in the big con.

While not intending to glamorize the swindlers, or "grifters" as they are often called, their use of psychological influence is quite remarkable and instructive. Perhaps most telling are psychological traps one and two in the series of three.

In the prelude to the first psychological moment, Norfleet has graciously refused a $100 reward for returning a wallet he found in the hotel lobby—a wallet planted, of course, by the grifters. The swindlers then announced they had to go conclude a business deal involving the use of what we would today refer to as "insider trading." Since Norfleet had refused the reward, would he mind if they took that same money and "invest it along with their own." Twenty minutes later, the swindlers return and proudly offer Norfleet the $800 return on his declined $100 reward money.

Perhaps no aspect of the big con is more so than the second psychological moment. This is also the most telling difference between street crime, where the engine is power, and the confidence game, where the engine is influence.

The big con succeeds not because it *forces* the mark to hand over his valuables. It succeeds because it *influences* the mark to believe that he not only is acting in his own self-interest but also is helping others, even if it is acknowledged to be with a wink and a smile. Those interested in how this plays out, both in a theatrical sense and in the big con, would find Reading's book informative.

Source: A. Reading, *The Mark Inside: A Perfect Swindle, a Cunning Revenge, and a Small History of the Big Con* (New York: Alfred A. Knopf, 2012).

Nelson Mandela: The Master of Political Influence

HIGHLIGHT 4.9

Invictus is both the title of the cited poem that provided inspiration to Nelson Mandela during his 27-year imprisonment for fighting apartheid and also became the title of the 2009 Clint Eastwood movie. This film takes us from Mandela's 1994 election through South Africa's World Cup journey the following year. The poem becomes the central inspirational gift from Mandela (played by Morgan Freeman) to Springbok rugby team captain François Pienaar (played by Matt Damon).

Invictus

Out of the night that covers me,

Black as the pit from pole to pole,

I thank whatever gods may be

For my unconquerable soul.

In the fell clutch of circumstance

I have not winced nor cried aloud.

Under the bludgeonings of chance

My head is bloody, but unbowed.

Beyond this place of wrath and tears

Looms but the Horror of the shade,

And yet the menace of the years

Finds and shall find me unafraid.

It matters not how strait the gate,

How charged with punishments the scroll,

I am the master of my fate:

I am the captain of my soul.

—William Ernest Henley

Rugby was more than just a game in South Africa; it was a preoccupation. Mandela had won the election as the African National Congress's (ANC) first Black president. With that position came power, but Mandela knew that his political victory was tenuous. Even though the ANC dominated Parliament, whites still controlled the economy. And it was the country's history of white-dominated apartheid that had resulted in the national rugby team's exclusion from international sports competitions.

Against the advice of his supporters among the ANC, Mandela fought to retain the Springbok name and their beloved green and gold jerseys. Mandela recognized that this was a reminder of decades of oppression to the now-black majority, but he also knew that white extremist Afrikaners posed a continuing threat. Their ongoing resistance to a Black-dominated government could plunge the fragile government into anarchy and insurrection. Power would not work—but influence might.

The movie, based on John Carlin's book *Playing the Enemy: Nelson Mandela and the Game That Made a Nation*, takes us through a moving scene in which Mandela exhibits his dramatic ability to influence the struggling rugby team. Taking the team to visit Robben Island, where he had been imprisoned for 17 years, Mandela recites "Invictus" as Pienaar and the team imagines the struggles of Mandela and his fellow prisoners. The underdog Springboks rallied to win the Rugby World Cup, hosted by South Africa in 1995. But, as noted by Arlene Getz, "[I]t was South Africa's good fortune that Mandela opted for reconciliation over retribution." It was also South Africa's good fortune that Nelson Mandela was a master of influence.

Sources: J. Carlin, *Playing the Enemy: Nelson Mandela and the Game that Made a Nation,* (New York: Penguin Press, 2008); and A. Getz, "The Real Story of 'Invictus'," *Newsweek,* December 9, 2009, www.newsweek.com/2009/12/09/sports-politics-and-mandela.html.

A Concluding Thought about Influence Tactics

In our discussion here, an implicit lesson for leaders is the value of being conscious of what influence tactics one uses and what effects are typically associated with each tactic. Knowledge of such effects can help a leader make better decisions about her or his manner of influencing others. It might also be helpful for leaders to think carefully about why they believe a particular influence tactic will be effective. Research indicates that some reasons for selecting among various possible influence tactics lead to successful outcomes more frequently than others. Specifically, thinking an act would improve an employee's self-esteem or morale was frequently associated with successful influence attempts. On the other hand, choosing an influence tactic because it followed company policy and choosing one because it was a way to put a subordinate in his place were frequently mentioned as reasons for unsuccessful influence attempts.[60] In a nutshell, these results suggest that leaders should pay attention not only to the actual influence tactics they use—to *how* they are influencing others—but also to *why* they believe such methods are called for. It is perhaps obvious that influence efforts intended to build others up more frequently lead to positive outcomes than do influence efforts intended to put others down.

Summary

This chapter defined *power* as the capacity or potential to exert influence, *influence tactics* as the behaviors used by one person to modify the attitudes and behaviors of another, and *influence* as the degree of change in a person's attitudes, values, or behaviors as the result of another's influence tactic. Because power, influence, and influence tactics play such important roles in the leadership process, this chapter provided ideas to help leaders improve their effectiveness. By reflecting on their different bases of power, leaders may better understand how they can affect followers and even expand their power. The five bases of power also offer clues to why subordinates can influence leaders and successfully resist leaders' influence attempts.

Leaders also may gain insight into why they may not enjoy certain aspects of their responsibilities by reflecting on their own need for power or motivation to manage; they may also better understand why some leaders exercise power selfishly by considering McClelland's concepts of personalized power and activity inhibition. Leaders can improve their effectiveness by finding ways to enhance the value of their personal contribution to their team while not permitting in-group and out-group rivalries to develop in the work unit.

Although power is an extremely important concept, having power is relatively meaningless unless a leader is willing to exercise it. The exercise of power occurs primarily through the influence tactics leaders and followers use to modify each other's attitudes and behaviors. The types of influence tactics used seem to depend on the amount of different types of power possessed, the degree of resistance expected, and the rationale behind the different influence tactics. Because influence tactics designed to build up others are generally more successful than those that tear others down, leadership practitioners should always consider why they are using a particular influence attempt before they actually use it. By carefully considering the rationale behind the tactic, leaders may be able to avoid using pressure and legitimizing tactics and find better ways to influence followers. Being able to use influence tactics that modify followers' attitudes and behaviors in the desired direction while they build up followers' self-esteem and self-confidence is a skill all leaders should strive to master.

Key Terms

power	coercive power	inspirational appeals
influence	power distance	consultation
influence tactics	need for power	ingratiation
pecking order	personalized power	personal appeals
expert power	socialized power	exchange
referent power	projective personality test	coalition tactics
legitimate power	motivation to manage	pressure tactics
reward power	rational persuasion	legitimizing tactics

Questions

1. The following questions pertain to the Milgram studies (**Highlight 4.2**):

    a. What bases of power were available to the experimenter, and what bases of power were available to the subjects?

    b. Do you think subjects with a low need for power would act differently from subjects with a high need for power? What about subjects with differing levels of the motivation to manage?

    c. What situational factors contributed to the experimenter's power?

    d. What influence tactics did the experimenter use to change the behavior of the subjects, and how were these tactics related to the experimenter's power base?

e. What actually was influenced? In other words, if influence is the change in another's attitudes, values, or behaviors as the result of an influence tactic, then what changes occurred in the subjects as the result of the experimenter's influence tactics?

f. Many people have criticized the Milgram study on ethical grounds. Assuming that some socially useful information was gained from the studies, do you believe this experiment could or should be replicated today?

2. Some definitions of leadership exclude reliance on formal authority or coercion (that is, certain actions by a person in authority may work but should not be considered leadership). What are the pros and cons of such a view?

3. Does power, as Lord Acton suggested, tend to corrupt the power holder? If so, what are some of the ways it happens? Is it also possible subordinates are corrupted by a superior's power? How? Is it possible that superiors can be corrupted by a subordinate's power?

4. Some people say it dilutes a leader's authority if subordinates are allowed to give feedback to the leader concerning their perceptions of the leader's performance. Do you agree?

5. Is *leadership* just another word for *influence*? Can you think of some examples of influence that you would *not* consider leadership?

Activity

During the COVID-19 pandemic, the USS *Theodore Roosevelt*, a modern nuclear-powered aircraft carrier with a crew of 5,000, reported that sailors were experiencing symptoms of the virus. Tests confirmed that at least 150 sailors had contracted the illness. In the days following, a battle of leadership power emerged. The commander of the vessel, Captain Brett Crozier, wrote a letter sounding the alarm and requesting that the ill sailors be taken ashore. For that letter, the acting Secretary of the Navy, Thomas Modly, relieved Captain Crozier of his command. Captain Crozier said he was acting solely in the interest of his crew, as evidenced by the outpouring of support as he departed the ship. When Modly himself spoke to the crew on the carrier after firing Crozier, he cited the letter as evidence of Crozier's poor judgment, naivety, or stupidity. That speech led to Modly's resignation just a few days later. In small groups, determine which source(s) of power were used by each man and discuss its effectiveness. What could each have done that might have led to a better outcome?

Minicase

The Prime Minister's Powerful Better Half

Ho Ching's power has been recognized by many. As chief executive officer of Temasek Holdings, she ranked number 18 on a list of Asia's most powerful businesspeople and number 24 on the *Forbes* list of the world's most powerful women. How did a shy, Stanford-educated electrical engineer end up with this kind of power? Ho was a government scholar who started off in civil service and ended up working for the Defense Ministry in Singapore. There she met and married Lee Hsien Loong, Singapore's current prime minister and the son of Lee Kwan Yew—one of modern Singapore's founding fathers. Ho's experience, education, and connections led to her appointment as chief executive of Temasek, where she oversees a portfolio worth over $50 billion and influences many of Singapore's leading companies.

Temasek Holdings was established in 1974 in an attempt by the Singapore government to drive industrialization. Through Temasek Holdings the Singapore government took stakes in a wide range of companies, including the city-state's best-known companies: Singapore Airlines, Singapore Telecommunications, DBS Bank, Neptune Orient Lines, and Keppel Corp. The company's website describes Temasek's "humble roots during a turbulent and uncertain time" and its commitment "to building a vibrant future [for Singapore] through successful enterprise." Ho's appointment to Temasek in May 2002 caused some controversy; as her prime minister husband has a supervisory role over the firm. Ho denies any conflict of interest:

> The issue of conflict does not arise because there are no vested interests. Our goal is to do what makes sense for Singapore, I don't always agree with him (Mr. Lee) and he doesn't always agree with me. We have a healthy debate on issues.

In her role as CEO, Ho is pushing for a more open policy and an aggressive drive into the Asian market. Under Ho's leadership Temasek has decided to publicly disclose its annual report with details of its performance—details that have formerly remained private and been known only to Temasek executives.

Ho is concentrating on broadening Temasek's focus beyond Singapore, most recently opening an office in India. At a conference of top Indian companies, Ho appealed to investors to look to India for opportunities for Asian growth:

> Since the Asian financial crisis in 1997, the word *Asia* had lost a bit of its sparkle. But that sparkle is beginning to return. In the 1960s and 1970s, the Asia economic miracle referred to East Asia, specifically Japan. The 1970s and 1980s saw the emergence of the four Asian Tigers of Korea, Taiwan, Hong Kong, and Singapore.
>
> Now is India's turn to stir, standing at an inflexion point, after 10 years of market liberalisation and corporate restructuring. Since 1997, Singapore's trade with India grew by 50 percent, or a respectable CAGR of about 7.5 percent. Confidence is brimming in India, and Indian companies began to reach out boldly to the world over the last five years.
>
> All these waves of development have shown that Asia, with a combined population of 3 billion, has been resilient. If Asia continues to work hard and work smart, honing her competitive strengths and leveraging on her complementary capabilities across borders, the outlook in the next decade or two looks very promising indeed.

1. We have described *power* as the capacity to cause change and *influence* as the degree of actual change in a target's behaviors. Ho Ching's power as a leader has been recognized by many, but would you describe Ho Ching as an influential leader? Why?

2. Based on the excerpt from Ho Ching's speech, what type of tactics does she use to influence the behavior of others?

3. Ho Ching has been named one of the most powerful leaders in Asia. What are her major sources of power?

Sources: www.fastcompany.com/online/13/womenofpr.html; www.forbes.com/finance/lists/11/2004/LIR.jhtml?passListId=11&passYear=2004&passListType=Person&uniqueId=OO5O&datatype=Person; www.businessweek.com/magazine/content/02_36/b3798161.htm; www.laksamana.net/vnews.cfm?ncat=31&news_id=5292; S. D. Gupta, "Temasek Roars as India Shines," *Rediff*, April 3, 2004, http://in.rediff.com/money/2004/apr/03spec.htm; www.theaustralian.news.com.au/common/story_page/0%2C5744%2C10427548%255E2703%2C00.html; and http://in.news.yahoo.com/040812/137/2fgoc.html.

Endnotes

1. N. Hill, "Self-Esteem: The Key to Effective Leadership," *Administrative Management* 40, no. 9 (1985), pp. 71–76.

2. D. Donno, "Introduction," in *The Prince and Selected Discourses: Machiavelli*, ed. and trans. D. Dunno (New York: Bantam, 1966).

3. J. W. Gardner, *On Leadership* (New York: Free Press, 1990); and J. W. Gardner, *The Tasks of Leadership*, Leadership Paper No. 2 (Washington, DC: Independent Sector, 1986).

4. T. R. Hinkin and C. A. Schriesheim, "Development and Application of New Scales to Measure the French and Raven (1959) Bases of Social Power," *Journal of Applied Psychology* 74 (1989), pp. 561–67.

5. J. M. Burns, *Leadership* (New York: Harper & Row, 1978).

6. R. J. House, "Power in Organizations: A Social Psychological Perspective," unpublished manuscript, University of Toronto, 1984.

7. B. M. Bass, *Bass and Stogdill's Handbook of Leadership*, 3rd ed. (New York: Free Press, 1990).

8. N. Levina and W. Orlikowski, "Understanding Shifting Power Relations within and across Organizations," *Academy of Management Journal* 52, no. 4 (2009), pp. 672–703.

9. J. Nelson, "Corporate Governance Practices, CEO Characteristics, and Firm Performance," *Journal of Corporate Finance* 11 (2005), pp. 197–228.

10. D. E. Winkel and B. R. Ragins, "Navigating the Emotional Battlefield: Gender, Power, and Emotion in Entrepreneurial Relationships," *Academy of Management Proceedings* (2008), pp. 1–6.

11. C. A. Schriesheim and T. R. Hinkin, "Influence Tactics Used by Subordinates: A Theoretical and Empirical Analysis and Refinement of the Kipnis, Schmidt, and Wilkinson Subscales," *Journal of Applied Psychology* 75 (1990), pp. 246–57.

12. Bass, *Bass and Stogdill's Handbook of Leadership*.

13. J. Ehrlichman, *Witness to Power* (New York: Simon & Schuster, 1982).

14. P. R. Wilson, "The Perceptual Distortion of Height as a Function of Ascribed Academic Status," *Journal of Social Psychology* 74 (1968), pp. 97–102.

15. R. B. Cialdini, *Influence* (New York: William Morrow, 1984).

16. L. Bickman, "The Social Power of a Uniform," *Journal of Applied Social Psychology* 4 (1974), pp. 47–61.

17. M. Mulder, R. D. de Jong, L. Koppelar, and J. Verhage, "Power, Situation, and Leaders' Effectiveness: An Organizational Study," *Journal of Applied Psychology* 71 (1986), pp. 566–70.

18. J. French and B. H. Raven, "The Bases of Social Power," in *Studies of Social Power*, ed. D. Cartwright (Ann Arbor, MI: Institute for Social Research, 1959).

19. French and Raven, "The Bases of Social Power."

20. Brown, Jerome. *Associated Press*, January 9, 1991.

21. T. J. Peters and R. H. Waterman, *In Search of Excellence* (New York: Harper & Row, 1982).

22. G. A. Yukl, *Leadership in Organizations*, 2nd ed. (Englewood Cliffs, NJ: Prentice Hall, 1989).

23. E. L. Deci, "Effects of Contingent and Noncontingent Rewards and Controls on Intrinsic Motivation," *Organizational Behavior and Human Performance* 22 (1972), pp. 113–20.

24. E. M. Ryan, V. Mims, and R. Koestner, "Relation of Reward Contingency and Interpersonal Context to Intrinsic Motivation: A Review and Test Using Cognitive Evaluation Theory," *Journal of Personality and Social Psychology* 45 (1983), pp. 736–50.

25. M. M. Wakin, "Ethics of Leadership," in *Military Leadership*, eds. J. H. Buck and L. J. Korb (Beverly Hills, CA: Sage, 1981).

26. S. B. Klein, *Learning*, 2nd ed. (New York: McGraw-Hill, 1991).

27. F. Barnes, "Mistakes New Presidents Make," *Reader's Digest*, January 1989, p. 43.

28. F. Conway and J. Siegelman, *Snapping* (New York: Delta, 1979).

29. G. A. Yukl, *Leadership in Organizations*, 1st ed. (Englewood Cliffs, NJ: Prentice Hall, 1981).

30. Yukl, *Leadership in Organizations*, 1st ed.

31. P. M. Podsakoff and C. A. Schriesheim, "Field Studies of French and Raven's Bases of Power: Critique, Reanalysis, and Suggestions for Future Research," *Psychological Bulletin* 97 (1985), pp. 387–411.

32. Hinkin and Schriesheim, "Development and Application of New Scales."

33. Yukl, *Leadership in Organizations*, 2nd ed.

34. E. P. Hollander and L. R. Offermann, "Power and Leadership in Organizations," *American Psychologist* 45 (1990), pp. 179–89.

35. J. Pfeffer, "The Ambiguity of Leadership," in *Leadership: Where Else Can We Go?* eds. M. W. McCall Jr. and M. M. Lombardo (Durham, NC: Duke University Press, 1977).

36. D. C. McClelland, *Power: The Inner Experience* (New York: Irvington, 1975).

37. D. C. McClelland and R. E. Boyatzis, "Leadership Motive Pattern and Long-Term Success in Management," *Journal of Applied Psychology* 67 (1982), pp. 737–43.

38. M. J. Stahl, "Achievement, Power, and Managerial Motivation: Selecting Managerial Talent with the Job Choice Exercise," *Personnel Psychology* 36 (1983), pp. 775–89.

39. E. Fodor, "Motive Pattern as an Influence on Leadership in Small Groups," paper presented at the meeting of the American Psychological Association, New York, August 1987.

40. McClelland and Boyatzis, "Leadership Motive Pattern."

41. D. C. McClelland, *Human Motivation* (Glenview, IL: Scott Foresman, 1985).

42. J. B. Miner, "Student Attitudes toward Bureaucratic Role Prescriptions and the Prospects for Managerial Shortages," *Personnel Psychology* 27 (1974), pp. 605–13.

43. J. B. Miner, "Twenty Years of Research on Role Motivation Theory of Managerial Effectiveness," *Personnel Psychology* 31 (1978), pp. 739–60.

44. Miner, "Twenty Years of Research."

45. McClelland and Boyatzis, "Leadership Motive Pattern and Long-Term Success in Management."

46. Miner, "Twenty Years of Research."

47. J. C. Magee and A. D. Galinsky, "Social Hierarchy: The Self-Reinforcing Nature of Power and Status," *Academy of Management Annals* 2, no. 1 (2008), pp. 351–98.

48. D. C. Treadway, J. W. Breland, J. Cho, J. Yang, and A. B. Duke, "Performance Is Not Enough: Political Skill in the Longitudinal Performance–Power Relationship," *Academy of Management Proceedings* (2009), pp. 1–6.

49. J. H. Karriker, L. T. Madden, and L. A. Katell, "Team Composition, Distributed Leadership, and Performance: It's Good to Share," *Journal of Leadership & Organizational Studies* 24, no. 4 (2017), pp. 507–18.

50. D. Kipnis and S. M. Schmidt, *Profiles of Organizational Strategies* (San Diego, CA: University Associates, 1982).

51. G. A. Yukl, R. Lepsinger, and T. Lucia, "Preliminary Report on the Development and Validation of the Influence Behavior Questionnaire," in *Impact of Leadership*, eds. K. E. Clark, M. B. Clark, and D. P. Campbell (Greensboro, NC: Center for Creative Leadership, 1992).

52. R. B. Cialdini, *Influence: Science and Practice*, 5th ed. (Boston: Pearson Education, 2009).

53. D. Kipnis and S. M. Schmidt, "The Language of Persuasion," *Psychology Today* 19, no. 4 (1985), pp. 40–46.

54. B. Keys, T. Case, T. Miller, K. E. Curran, and C. Jones, "Lateral Influence Tactics in Organizations," *International Journal of Management* 4 (1987), pp. 425–37.

55. T. Case, L. Dosier, G. Murkison, and B. Keys, "How Managers Influence Superiors: A Study of Upward Influence Tactics," *Leadership and Organization Development Journal* 9, no. 4 (1988), pp. 4, 25–31.

56. Case, Dosier, Murkison, and Keys, "How Managers Influence Superiors."

57. Kipnis and Schmidt, "The Language of Persuasion."

58. S. G. Green, G. T. Fairhurst, and B. K. Snavely, "Chains of Poor Performance and Supervisory Control," *Organizational Behavior and Human Decision Processes* 38 (1986), pp. 7–27.

59. D. Kipnis, "Technology, Power, and Control," *Research in the Sociology of Organizations* 3 (1984a), pp. 125–56.

60. L. Dosier, T. Case, and B. Keys, "How Managers Influence Subordinates: An Empirical Study of Downward Influence Tactics," *Leadership and Organization Development Journal* 9, no. 5 (1988), pp. 22–31.

CHAPTER 5

Values, Ethics, and Character

Introduction

In **Chapter 4** we examined many facets of power and its use in leadership. Leaders can use power for good or ill, and a leader's personal values and ethical code may be among the most important determinants of how that leader exercises the various sources of power available. That this aspect of leadership needs closer scrutiny seems evident enough in the face of the past decade's wave of scandals involving political, business, and even religious leaders who collectively rocked trust in both our leaders and our institutions. Even in purely economic terms, in 2010 the Association of Certified Fraud Examiners estimated that businesses around the world lose $2.9 billion every year to fraudulent activity.[1] Further, in the 2016 presidential election one party's nominee consistently referred to his opponent as "Crooked Hillary" while his own character and ethics were themselves questioned throughout the election—and continue to be. In the face of this distressing situation, it is not surprising that scholarly and popular literature have turned greater attention to the question of ethical leadership.[2]

Leadership and "Doing the Right Things"

In **Chapter 1** we referred to a distinction between leaders and managers that says leaders do the right things whereas managers do things right. But what are the "right things"? Are they the morally right things? The ethically right things? The right things for the company to be successful? And who says what the right things are?

Leaders face dilemmas that require choices between competing sets of values and priorities, and the best leaders recognize and face them with a commitment to doing what is right, not just what is expedient. Of course, the phrase *doing what is right* sounds deceptively simple. Sometimes it takes great moral courage to do what is right, even when the right action seems clear. At other times, though, leaders face complex challenges that lack simple black-and-white answers. Whichever the case, leaders set a moral example to others that becomes the model for an entire group or organization, for good or bad. Leaders who themselves do not honor truth do not inspire it in others. Leaders concerned mostly with their own advancement do not inspire selflessness in others. Leaders should internalize a strong set of **ethics**—principles of right conduct or a system of moral values.

> *Leadership cannot just go along to get along. . . . Leadership must meet the moral challenge of the day.*
>
> **Jesse Jackson, American civil rights activist**

Both Gardner and Burns have stressed the centrality and importance of the moral dimension of leadership.[3, 4] Gardner said leaders ultimately must be judged on the basis of a framework of values, not just in terms of their effectiveness. He put the question of a leader's relations with his or her followers or constituents on the moral plane, arguing (with the philosopher Immanuel Kant) that leaders should always treat others as ends in themselves, not as objects or mere means to the leader's ends (which does not necessarily imply that leaders need to be gentle in interpersonal demeanor or "democratic" in style). Burns took an even more extreme view regarding the moral dimension of leadership, maintaining that leaders who do not behave ethically do not demonstrate true leadership.

Whatever "true leadership" means, most people would agree that at a minimum it is characterized by a high degree of trust between leader and followers. Bennis and Goldsmith described four qualities of leadership that engender trust: vision, empathy, consistency, and integrity.[5] First, we tend to trust leaders who create a compelling *vision*: who pull people together on the basis of shared beliefs and a common sense of organizational purpose and belonging. Second, we tend to trust leaders who demonstrate *empathy* with us—who show they understand the world as we see and experience it. Third, we trust leaders who are *consistent*. This does not mean that we only trust leaders whose positions never change, but that changes are understood as a process of evolution in light of relevant new evidence. Fourth, we tend to trust leaders whose *integrity* is strong, who demonstrate their commitment to higher principles through their actions.

Another important factor affecting the degree of trust between leaders and followers involves fundamental assumptions people make about human nature. Several decades ago Douglas McGregor explained different styles of managerial behavior on the basis of people's implicit attitudes about human nature, and his work remains quite influential today.[6] McGregor identified two contrasting sets of assumptions people make about human nature, calling these **Theory X** and **Theory Y**.

In the simplest sense, Theory X reflects a more pessimistic view of others. Managers with this orientation rely heavily on coercive, external control methods to motivate workers, such as pay, disciplinary techniques, punishments, and threats. They assume people are not naturally industrious or motivated to work. Hence it is the manager's job to minimize the harmful effects of workers' natural laziness and irresponsibility by closely overseeing their work and creating external incentives to do well and disincentives to avoid slacking off. Theory Y, by contrast, reflects a view that most people are intrinsically motivated by their work. Rather than needing to be coaxed or coerced to work productively, such people value a sense of achievement, personal growth, pride in contributing to their organization, and respect for a job well done. Peter Jackson, director of the *Lord of the Rings* film trilogy, seems to exemplify a Theory Y view of human nature. When asked, "How do you stand up to executives?" Jackson answered, "Well, I just find that most people appreciate honesty. I find that if you try not to have any pretensions and you tell the truth, you talk to them and you treat them as collaborators, I find that studio people are usually very supportive."

> *There is nothing so fast as the speed of trust.*
>
> **Stephen Covey, American author and educator**

But are there practical advantages to holding a Theory X or Theory Y view? Evidently there are. There is evidence that success more frequently comes to leaders who share a positive view of human nature. Hall and Donnell reported findings of five separate studies involving over 12,000 managers that explored the relationship between managerial achievement and attitudes toward subordinates.[7] Overall, they found that managers who strongly subscribed to Theory X beliefs were far more likely to be in their lower-achieving group.

The dilemma, of course, is that for the most part both Theory X and Theory Y leaders would say they have the right beliefs and are doing the right things. This begs the question of what people generally mean by "right," which in turn raises an array of issues involving ethics, values, moral reasoning, and the influence they have on our behavior.

Values

Values are "constructs representing generalized behaviors or states of affairs that are considered by the individual to be important."[8] When Patrick Henry said, "Give me liberty, or give me death," he was expressing the value he placed on political freedom. The opportunity to continually study and learn may be the fundamental value or "state of affairs" leading a person to pursue a career in academia. Someone who values personal integrity may be forced to resign from an unethical company. Values are learned through the socialization process, and they become internalized and for most people represent integral components of the self.[9] Thus values play a central role in one's overall psychological makeup and can affect behavior in a variety of situations. In work settings, values can affect decisions about joining an organization, organizational commitment, relationships with coworkers, and decisions about leaving an organization.[10] It is important for leaders to realize that individuals in the same work unit can have considerably different values, especially because we cannot see values directly. We can only make inferences about people's values based on their behavior. An interesting perspective on the importance of the consistency between one's behavior and their values can be seen in **Highlight 5.1**.

On the Danger of Making Small Compromises to Your Values

HIGHLIGHT 5.1

What do you think? Is it easier to stick to your values 100 percent of the time or 98 percent of the time? That is a question Professor Clay Christensen (an expert in business innovation) posed to his students at Harvard in an end-of-semester lecture requested by them. The students wanted to know whether and how the business principles he taught in class applied to their personal lives.

One of the personal stories Christensen shared in the lecture occurred when he played on the Oxford University basketball team. It was a good team, and it had been a very successful year. They were going to play in the British equivalent of the NCAA tournament, and they made it to the final four. When Christensen saw the tourney schedule, however, he was chagrined: Their championship game would be played on a Sunday. Christensen told his students that because of deep religious convictions, he'd made a firm commitment never to play on a Sunday. At the time, his coach and teammates were incredulous; after all, it would be an exception, "just this once." What difference would it really make? Christensen stood by his principles, though, and did not play in the championship game.

The point he was making to his Harvard students was that, as counterintuitive as it might seem, it *is* easier to stick to your values 100 percent of the time than it is to stick to them 98 percent of the time. Christensen explained that, tempting as it might be to make an exception "just this once" because of extenuating circumstances, "you've got to define for yourself what you stand for and draw the line in a safe place."

Source: C. M. Christensen, "How Will You Measure Your Life? Don't Reserve Your Best Business Thinking for Your Career," *Harvard Business Review*, July/August 2010: 46–51.

Table 5.1 lists some of the major values that may be considered important by individuals in an organization. The instrumental values found in the table refer to modes of behavior, and the terminal values refer to desired end states.[11] For example, some individuals value equality, freedom, and a comfortable life above all else; others may believe that family security and salvation are important goals. In terms of instrumental values, such individuals may think it is important always to act in an ambitious, capable, and honest manner, whereas others may think it is important only to be ambitious and capable. The point to keep in mind here is not just that different people often have different values. It is that their different values sometimes lead them to *behave* very differently. Consider, for example, whether someone decides to share with others (for example, the boss) a challenging but potentially constructive opinion about the organization. Whether the person speaks up or not depends, in part, on her values. If "sense of duty" were more important to the person than "getting ahead," then she would be more likely to speak up than if the reverse were true.[12]

TABLE 5.1   People Vary in the Relative Importance They Place on Values

Terminal Values	Instrumental Values
An exciting life	Being courageous
A sense of accomplishment	Being helpful
Family security	Being honest
Inner harmony	Being imaginative
Social recognition	Being logical
Friendship	Being responsible

Source: Adapted from M. Rokeach, *The Nature of Human Values* (New York: Free Press, 1973).

> *Glass, china, and reputation are easily crack'd, and never well mended.*
> **Benjamin Franklin**

Various researchers have said that the pervasive influence of broad forces like major historical events and trends, technological changes, and economic conditions tends to create common value systems among people growing up at a particular time that distinguish them from people who grow up at different times.[13, 14, 15] They attribute much of the misunderstanding that may exist between older leaders and younger followers to the fact that their basic value systems were formulated during different social and cultural conditions, and these analyses offer a helpful perspective for understanding how differences in values can add tension to the interaction between some leaders and followers.

Zemke is another researcher who has looked at differences in values across generations and how those value differences affect their approaches to work and leadership.[16] Following is his delineation of four generations of workers, each molded by distinctive experiences during critical developmental periods:

The Veterans (1922–1943): Veterans came of age during the Great Depression and World War II, and they represent a wealth of lore and wisdom. They've been a stabilizing force in organizations for decades, even if they are prone to digressions about "the good old days."

The Baby Boomers (1942–1960): These were the postwar babies who came of age during violent social protests, experimentation with new lifestyles, and pervasive questioning of establishment values. But they're graying now, and they don't like to think of themselves as "the problem" in the workplace even though they sometimes are. Boomers still have passion about bringing participation, spirit, heart, and humanity to the workplace and office. They're also concerned about creating a level playing field for all, but they hold far too many meetings for the typical Gen Xer. As the Boomers enter their retirement years, they take with them a work ethic characterized by ambition, an achievement orientation, and organizational loyalty.[17]

The Gen Xers (1961–1981): Gen Xers grew up during the era of the Watergate scandal, the energy crisis, higher divorce rates, MTV, and corporate downsizing; many were latchkey kids. As a group they tend to be technologically savvy, independent, and skeptical of institutions and hierarchy. They are entrepreneurial and they embrace change. Having seen so many of their parents work long and loyally for one company only to lose their jobs to downsizing, Xers don't believe much in job security; to an Xer, job security comes from having the kinds of skills that make you attractive to an organization. Hence they tend to be more committed to their vocation than to any specific organization. In fact, the free-agency concept born in professional sports also applies to Xers, who are disposed to stay with an organization until a better offer comes along. Among the challenges they present at work is how to meet their need for feedback despite their dislike of close supervision. Xers also seek balance in their lives more than preceding generations; they work to live rather than live to work.

Millennials (1982–2005): This is *your* generation, so any generalizations we make here are particularly risky! In general, however, Millennials share an optimism born, perhaps, from having been raised by parents devoted to the task of bringing their generation to adulthood; they are the children of soccer moms and Little League dads. They doubt the wisdom of traditional racial and sexual categorizing—perhaps not unexpected from a generation rich with opportunities like having Internet pen pals in Asia with whom they can interact any time of the day or night. As they move into the workplace, Millennials are seeking teamwork, security, and work–life balance.[18] As "digital natives," Millennials bring to the workplace sharing habits born of extensive experience with social media; their comfort level with transparency of action may well have a profound long-term effect on the workplace.[19] Of more concern, many college professors perceive Millennials to lack drive and a sense of accountability yet still expect positive evaluations despite marginal effort.[20]

Some research has looked at how the values of Gen Xers impact the leadership process at work. One clear finding from this research involved the distinctively different view of authority held by Xers than previous generations. "While past generations might have at least acknowledged positional authority, this new generation has little respect for and less interest in leaders who are unable to demonstrate that they can personally produce. In other words, this generation doesn't define leading as sitting in meetings and making profound vision statements, but instead as eliminating obstacles and giving employees what they need to work well and comfortably."[21] Gen Xers expect managers to "earn their stripes" and not be rewarded with leadership responsibilities merely because of seniority. Often that attitude is interpreted as an indication of disrespect toward elders in general and bosses in particular. It may be more accurate, however, to characterize the attitude as one of skepticism rather than disrespect.

> *Question authority, but raise your hand first.*
>
> **Bob Thaves, cartoonist**

Lest we overemphasize the significance of intergenerational differences, however, consider the results of a scientific sampling of over 1,000 people living in the United States that found *little* evidence of a generation gap in basic values. Indeed, the director of one of the largest polling organizations in the world called the results some of the most powerful he had seen in 30 years of public opinion research. They showed, he said, that even though young people have different tastes, they do *not* have a different set of values than their elders.[22] Considering the weight of scholarly research on value differences across generations, it has been said that the idea of a generational gap in values may be more popular culture than good social science.[23] That is consistent with results from a study that found "overwhelming consistency" in the ways managers from different generations evaluated the importance of various leadership practices as well as proficiency in them. The study concluded that Boomers, Xers, and Millennials in the managerial workforce are much more similar in their views of organizational leadership than they are different.[24] The story of a leader whose work impacted the values and moral development of individuals is presented in **Profiles in Leadership 5.1.**

Fred Rogers

PROFILES IN LEADERSHIP 5.1

The film *A Beautiful Day in the Neighborhood* was released in 2019 and won rave reviews from fans and critics alike. It is a fitting epitaph for the man who, for over 30 years, wrote, directed, and starred in the children's television show, *Mr. Rogers' Neighborhood*. His declaration to young viewers of each show that "I like you just the way you are" illustrates how his priority was not merely their entertainment, but rather their emotional and moral development.

That the show dealt with children's emotional well-being and moral development may not be not surprising in light of the fact that Rogers himself had graduated from seminary, did graduate study in child development, and became a Presbyterian minister. But his interest in children's moral development was no mere academic matter. His own strength of convictions on children's developmental needs drove his never-relenting press for the show to tackle challenging social and moral issues like war, divorce, death, and racism—almost unique in television then, let alone children's programming.

But what was he like as a real person, unfiltered by the Mr. Rogers persona he played in the show? His wife Joanne said, "Just don't make Fred into a saint ... If you make him out to be a saint, people might not know how hard he worked." One of Fred's friends of many decades described him as more like an artist—disciplined, focused, and a perfectionist. While people commonly and rightfully perceive him as a moral example, he was more than that; he was also a *creator*.

Source: J. Laskas, "The Making of Mr. Rogers," *The Week*, December 13, 2019, pp. 40–41.

Moral Reasoning and Character-Based Leadership

Until now our discussion has focused primarily on the content of people's values—that is, on *what* people claim to value. Related to this are matters concerning *how people think and act concerning matters of right and wrong*, to matters of moral reasoning and character. We look first at moral reasoning and then turn our attention to the somewhat broader question of leader character. That distinction may be clearer by considering the results of some recent research dealing with the impact of a person's beliefs about whether behaving honestly requires relatively greater or lesser effort. A recent study has shown that the more people associate honesty with effort, the more likely they are to behave dishonestly.[25] A theory of how moral reasoning develops in progressive stages over time is described in **Highlight 5.2**.

Values play a key role in the moral reasoning process because value differences among individuals often result in different judgments regarding ethical and unethical behavior. In addition, fundamental and dramatic changes occur during young adulthood in how people define what is morally right or wrong. Those individuals whose moral judgment develops most are those who "love to learn, seek new challenges, who enjoy intellectually stimulating environments, who are reflective, who make plans and set goals, who take risks, and who take responsibility for themselves in the larger social context of history and institutions, and who take responsibility for themselves and their environs."[26]

Kohlberg's Theory of Moral Development

HIGHLIGHT 5.2

Lawrence Kohlberg believes that moral development occurs as people progress through successive and qualitatively "higher" stages of moral reasoning. Like Piaget before him, Kohlberg assesses moral development based on how people resolve various ethical dilemmas, such as whether a man would be morally justified in stealing an overpriced drug to save his dying wife. One's stage of moral reasoning is based on the way one's answer is explained rather than by the particular answer given. Two individuals, for example, may each argue that the husband was morally wrong to steal the drug—even in those extenuating circumstances—yet offer qualitatively different reasons for why the action was wrong. Similarly, two individuals may each argue that the husband was morally justified in stealing the drug, yet offer different reasons for why it was justifiable. The focus is on the reasoning *process* rather than on the decision per se.

Kohlberg believes there are six stages of moral development that fall under three broader levels. Those three basic levels are called the *preconventional* level, the *conventional* level, and the *postconventional* level. In the preconventional level, a person's criteria for moral behavior are based primarily on self-interest such as avoiding punishment or being rewarded. In the conventional level, the criteria for moral behavior are based primarily on gaining others' approval and *behaving* conventionally as defined by societal norms. In the postconventional level, criteria are based on universal, abstract principles that may even transcend the laws and norms of a particular society.

Here are brief descriptions of Kohlberg's six stages of moral development within the framework of those three levels noted above:

Preconventional Level

Stage 1: "Bad" behavior is that which is punished.

Stage 2: "Good" behavior is that which is concretely rewarded.

Conventional Level

Stage 3: "Good" behavior is that which is approved by others; "bad" behavior is that which is disapproved by others.

Stage 4: "Good" behavior conforms to standards set by societal institutions; transgressions lead to feelings of guilt or dishonor.

Postconventional Level

Stage 5: "Good" behavior conforms to community standards set through democratic participation; concern with maintaining self-respect and the respect of equals.

Stage 6: "Good" behavior is a matter of individual conscience based on responsibly chosen commitments to ethical principles.

Source: Adapted from L. Kohlberg, *The Psychology of Moral Development,* Vol. 2 (San Francisco: Harper & Row, 1984).

Of course, not everyone fully develops their moral judgment. For example, research suggests that whereas most people believe they behave ethically, there is considerable reason to believe that they are significantly more biased than they think and that their actions fall short of their self-perceptions of ethical purity. Several unconscious biases affect our moral judgments, and paradoxically, the more strongly one believes that she is an ethical manager, the more one may fall victim to these biases.[27] That is probably one reason why in business and government many organizations are developing practical programs to develop moral decision-making competence among their leaders.[28]

We take it for granted that the effectiveness of any such programs to develop moral decision-making depends a lot on the quality of our understanding of the process itself, and recent research suggests that the psychological processes involved are more complicated than you might imagine. Perhaps this should not be surprising given that philosophers long have disagreed over the essential nature of moral judgment. Philosophers such as Plato and Kant believed mature moral judgment to be an essentially rational process whereas other philosophers, such as David Hume and Adam Smith, believed that emotions are at the heart of moral judgment (no pun intended!). Joshua Greene, a Harvard psychologist, finds research support for both views. He has proposed a **dual-process theory** of moral judgment wherein moral judgments dealing primarily with "rights" and "duties" are made by automatic emotional responses whereas moral judgments made on a more utilitarian basis are made more cognitively. Greene's methodology is fascinating and includes brain-imaging studies while people are pondering dilemmas similar to those featured in **Highlight 5.3**.[29, 30]

Studying Moral Judgment: The Trolley Problem

HIGHLIGHT 5.3

The trolley problem, originally posed by philosopher Philippa Foot, involves two different dilemmas, a "switch" dilemma and a "footbridge" dilemma.

In the *switch* dilemma a runaway trolley is racing toward five people who will be killed if the train does not change course. You can save these five people by diverting the train onto another set of tracks. That alternative set of tracks has only one person on it, but if you divert the train onto those tracks that person will be killed. Is it morally permissible to switch the train onto the other track and thus save five lives at the cost of one? According to Greene's research, most people say yes.

In the *footbridge* dilemma the trolley is again heading for five people. You happen to be standing next to a large man on a footbridge spanning the tracks, and if you push the man off the footbridge and into the path of the trolley you can save the other five people. Is it morally permissible to push the man into the path of the trolley? According to Greene, most people say no.

These results pose a challenge for moral philosophers: Why does it seem right to most people to sacrifice one person to save five others in the first situation but not in the second? Greene's answer to that puzzle is his dual-process theory mentioned in the text.

Although moral dilemmas like the trolley problem are useful for scholarly and heuristic purposes, the scenarios may seem far from our everyday experience. A far more common yet still challenging **ethical dilemma** involves choosing between two "rights." Rushworth Kidder has identified four ethical dilemmas that are so common to our experience that they serve as models or paradigms:[31]

- **Truth versus loyalty**, such as honestly answering a question when doing so could compromise a real or implied promise of confidentiality to others.

- **Individual versus community**, such as whether you should protect the confidentiality of someone's medical condition when the condition itself may pose a threat to the larger community.

- **Short term versus long term**, such as how a parent chooses to balance spending time with children now as compared with investments in a career that may provide greater benefits for the family in the long run.

- **Justice versus mercy**, such as deciding whether to excuse a person's misbehavior because of extenuating circumstances or a conviction that he or she has "learned a lesson."

Kidder offers three principles for resolving ethical dilemmas such as these: ends-based thinking, rule-based thinking, and care-based thinking.

Ends-based thinking is often characterized as "do what's best for the greatest number of people." Also known as utilitarianism in philosophy, it is premised on the idea that right and wrong are best determined by considering the consequences or results of an action. Critics of this view argue that it's almost impossible to foresee all the consequences of one's personal behavior, let alone the consequences of collective action like policy decisions affecting society more broadly. Even if outcomes could be known, however, there are other problems with this approach. For example, would this view ethically justify the deaths of dozens of infants in medical research if the result might save thousands of others?

Rule-based thinking is consistent with Kantian philosophy and can be characterized colloquially as "following the highest principle or duty." This is determined not by any projection of what the results of an act may be but rather by determining the kinds of standards everyone should uphold all the time, whatever the situation. In Kant's words, "I ought never to act except in such a way that I can also will that my maxim should become a universal law." Lofty as the principle may sound, though, it could paradoxically *minimize* the role that human judgment plays in ethical decision-making by consigning all acts to a rigid and mindless commitment to rules absent consideration of the specific context of a decision ("If I let you do this, then I'd have to let *everyone* do it").

Care-based thinking describes what many people think of as the Golden Rule of conduct common in some form to many of the world's religions: "Do what you want others to do to you." In essence, this approach applies the criterion of reversibility in determining the rightness of actions. We are asked to contemplate proposed behavior as if we were the object rather than the agent, and to consult our feelings as a guide to determining the best course.

It's important to emphasize that Kidder does not suggest any one of these principles is always best. Rather, he proposes that it would be a wise practice when considering the rightness of an action to invoke them all and reach a decision only after applying each to the specific circumstances one is facing and weighing the collective analyses. In other words, one principle may provide wise guidance in one situation whereas a different one may seem most helpful in a different one. There can be such critical yet subtle differences across situations that all three principles should be applied tentatively before any final course of action is chosen.

Although most of the research and training applications pertaining to ethical behavior have focused on the essentially cognitive process of moral reasoning, it is important to recognize that the ability to make reasoned judgments about ethically laden situations does not guarantee a person will *act* ethically (witness the case of athlete Lance Armstrong, who after many years of public lies to the contrary finally admitted he had long taken performance-enhancing drugs to win his many Tour de France races; or consider the notorious and career-damaging "sexting" by New York politician Anthony Wiener).

Research has identified four particular biases that can have a pervasive and corrosive effect on our moral decision-making. One of these is **implicit prejudice**. Although most people purport to judge others by their merits, research shows that implicit prejudice often distorts their judgments. The insidious nature of implicit prejudice lies in the fact that people are by nature unconscious of it. When someone is queried, for example, about whether he or she harbors prejudice against, say, Eskimos, the individual answers based on his or her self-awareness of such attitudes. Some people are overtly racist or sexist, but offensive as such prejudice may be, it is at least something known to the person. In the case of implicit prejudice, however, judgments about some group are systematically biased *without their awareness*.

This has been documented in a fascinating series of experimental studies designed to detect unconscious bias.[32] These studies require people to rapidly classify words or images as "good" or "bad." Using a keyboard, individuals make split-second classifications of words like *love, joy, pain,* and *sorrow.* At the same time, they sort images of faces that are black or white, young or old, fat or thin (depending on the type of bias being examined). The critical results indicating implicit prejudice involve subtle shifts in reaction time in associating a particular image (such as a black face) with "good" words. People who consciously believe they have no prejudice or negative feelings about particular groups, say Black Americans or the elderly, are nonetheless systematically slower in associating "good" words with those faces than they are in associating white or young faces with them.

Another bias that affects moral decision-making is **in-group favoritism**. Most of us can readily point to numerous favors and acts of kindness we've shown toward others, and we understandably regard such acts as indicators of our own generosity and kindly spirit. If the whole pattern of one's generous acts were examined, however, ranging from things like job recommendations to help on a project, there is typically a clear pattern to those whom we've helped: Most of the time they're "like us." This may not seem surprising, but one needs to consider who's not being helped: people "not like us." In other words, when we may make an exception favoring a job applicant who is "like us," and fail to make such an exception for an identical candidate who is "not like us," we have effectively discriminated against the latter.[33]

Overclaiming credit is yet another way we may fool ourselves about the moral virtue of our own decision-making. In many ways we tend to overrate the quality of our own work and our contributions to the groups and teams to which we belong.[34] This has been widely documented, but one of the most telling studies was a 2007 poll of 2,000 executives and middle managers conducted by *BusinessWeek* magazine. One question in that poll asked respondents, "Are you one of the top 10 percent of performers in your company?" If people were objective in rating themselves, presumably 10 percent would have placed themselves in the top 10 percent. But that's not what the results showed. Overall, 90 percent of the respondents placed themselves in the top 10 percent of performers![35]

Finally, our ethical judgments are adversely impacted by **conflicts of interest**. Sometimes, of course, we may be conscious of a potential conflict of interest, as when you benefit from a recommendation to someone else (such as getting a sales commission for something that may not be in the consumer's best interest). Even then, though, we misjudge our own ability to discount the extent to which the conflict actually biases our perception of the situation in our own favor.[36]

One leader's decision that has been ethically scrutinized for the last 75 years is described in **Profiles in Leadership 5.2**.

Would You Have Dropped an Atom Bomb to End World War II?

PROFILES IN LEADERSHIP 5.2

In **Chapter 1**, we considered the challenges Harry Truman faced when he became president following the death of Franklin Delano Roo-sevelt. One of the most significant decisions Truman faced during his first months in office was whether or not to drop the newly developed atom bomb on Japan in hopes of ending the war.

It now has been 75 years since he authorized dropping the atom bomb on Hiroshima, and for that entire 75 years, there has been no clear resolution whether it needed to have been done or *should* have been done. Few decisions by any leader in world history have been so ethically scrutinized as Truman's decision to drop the bomb.

When Vice President Truman became president upon the death in office of Franklin Roosevelt, he was unaware of the "most ambitious industrial and scientific undertaking in human history." It was called the Manhattan Project, and its purpose was to develop a single bomb that could obliterate an entire city. Yet, when the Manhattan Project was briefed to President Truman, there was no evidence that the atom bomb would even work. The nation's highest ranking military officer, Chief-of-Staff Fleet Admiral Leahy believed it *wouldn't* work, calling the whole Manhattan Project "the biggest fool thing we have ever done."

On moral grounds, even some of the scientists working on the project believed the weapon should not be used until after its awesome power was demonstrated before an international audience on a remote Pacific island. And perhaps there could have been some other way to prompt the Japanese to admit defeat and sue for peace.

But Winston Churchill, the British prime minister and Truman's key ally in the war, believed that an invasion of Japan would cost one-and-a-half million American and British lives, a belief arising in part because of stories of atrocities committed by Japanese soldiers; there also were verified reports of Japanese soldiers' fanatical willingness to fight to the death, even when facing hopeless odds—a sobering consideration in estimating the casualties of an allied invasion of Japan.

Among the things Harry Truman is remembered for is a plaque on his presidential desk that said, "The buck stops here." And so the decision to drop the atom bomb was ultimately his and his alone. What might you have decided?

Source: A. J. Baime, *The Accidental President* (Houghton Mifflin Harcourt, 2017).

Other research strikes even more fundamentally at the idea that progress in understanding ethical behavior and increasing its likelihood or prevalence can adequately be based on a purely rational or reasoning-based approach.[37] The nature of human information processing at the cognitive and neurological levels inherently involves nonconscious processes of association and judgment. Earlier in this section we introduced the term *implicit prejudice*, but the word *implicit* should not itself be deemed undesirable. Some of the most impressive—and distinctly human—aspects of our thinking are inherently tacit or implicit. For example, one line of study suggests that in making moral judgments people often follow something more like scripts than any formal and rational process of ethical reasoning. Behavioral scripts from one's religious tradition (such as the Good Samaritan story) may be subconsciously triggered and lead to ethical behavior without explicit moral reasoning.[38] Some go so far as to say that "moral reasoning is rarely the direct cause of ethical judgment."[39] Although that kind of perspective initially may seem to represent a pessimistic outlook on the possibility of truly improving ethical conduct, the reality is not so gloomy. Advocates of this view recognize that constructive things can be done to enhance ethical decision-making. They also propose that a more complete answer lies not only in enhancing ethical and moral reasoning but also in approaches that enhance people's awareness of their ways of construing or constructing moral dimensions of any situation.

> *So near is a falsehood to truth that a wise man would do well not to trust himself on the narrow edge.*
>
> **Cicero, Roman politician**

As noted earlier, just because we profess certain values or moral codes does not ensure we will act that way when confronted with situations that engage them. That is one reason it is vital for leadership development programs to broaden and deepen one's sensitivity to the challenge and importance of ethical leadership. It should be no surprise that in general when people are confronted with situations they've never faced before, their behavior may be different than they might have predicted. Unexpected natural disasters or threatening engagements with ill-willed people easily come to mind as situations in which our own behavior can surprise us. But it's also true that we don't always behave as ethically as we think we would in morally demanding situations.

In studying how accurately people can forecast their own ethical behavior, social psychologist Ryan Brown found that although their predictions were generally consistent with their personal values, their actual behavior often was not. The general design of these experiments placed individuals in situations where they could choose to behave rather selflessly or somewhat more selfishly. A typical situation required the individual to choose between one of two sets of anagrams to complete (ostensibly as part of a study having a different purpose): either a short set of anagrams that would take only about 10 minutes to complete, or a longer set that would take about 45 minutes to complete. Whichever set the subject did *not* select presumably would be given to another soon-to-arrive experimental subject. As it turned out, 65 percent of the participants acted selfishly, selecting the easier task for themselves. Maybe you're saying to yourself, "Well, of course . . . you'd be crazy not to choose the easier one for yourself if given the chance to get the same credit for it." Perhaps, but only 35 percent predicted that they would make a selfish choice. It seems that when we are asked to *forecast* our behavior, we take our actual personal values into account. But the results of these studies also make a persuasive case that our personal values represent how we think we ought to act rather than how we often actually do act.[40]

These results should give us some pause when, in the face of unethical behavior by others, we feel confident that we would have acted differently facing the same situation. Such apparent overconfidence seems to be caused by the bias of idealizing our own behavior, and this bias, ironically, may leave us ill-prepared to make the most ethical choices when we actually confront ethically challenging situations. Being aware of this bias is a good first step in avoiding the same trap. **Highlight 5.4** offers some suggestions for this kind of self-awareness.[41]

Ask Yourself These Questions

HIGHLIGHT 5.4

An important foundation of behaving ethically at work is to become more self-conscious of one's own ethical standards and practices. The National Institute of Ethics uses the following questions in its self-evaluation to facilitate that kind of self-reflection:

- How do I decide ethical dilemmas?
- Do I have set ethical beliefs or standards?
- If so, do I live by these beliefs or standards?
- How often have I done something that I am ashamed of?

- How often have I done things that I am proud of?
- Do I admit my mistakes?
- What do I do to correct mistakes that I make?
- Do I often put the well-being of others ahead of mine?
- Do I follow the Golden Rule?
- Am I honest?
- Do people respect my integrity?
- What are the three best things that have ever happened to me?

- What is the most dishonest thing I have ever done?
- Did I ever rectify the situation?
- What is the most honest thing I have ever done?

All leaders should regularly ask themselves questions like these.

Source: N. Trautman, *Integrity Leadership*, Director, National Institute of Ethics, www.ethicsinstitute.com.

A related aspect of ethical conduct involves the mental gymnastics by which people can dissociate their moral thinking from their actions. As noted earlier, the ability to reason about hypothetical moral issues, after all, does not ensure that one will *act* morally; one's moral actions may not always be consistent with one's espoused values. Bandura, in particular, has pointed out several ways people with firm moral principles nonetheless may behave badly without feeling guilt or remorse over their behavior. We should look at each of these, especially since Bandura's analysis has been validated in a major study of moral disengagement at work—in other words, why employees do bad things.[42, 43, 44]

Moral justification involves reinterpreting otherwise immoral behavior in terms of a higher purpose. This is most dramatically revealed in the behavior of combatants in war. Moral reconstruction of killing is illustrated dramatically by the case of Sergeant York, one of the phenomenal fighters in the history of modern warfare. Because of his deep religious convictions, Sergeant York registered as a conscientious objector, but his numerous appeals were denied. At camp, his battalion commander quoted chapter and verse from the Bible to persuade him that under appropriate conditions it was Christian to fight and kill. A marathon mountainside prayer finally convinced him that he could serve both God and country by becoming a dedicated fighter.[45]

Another way to dissociate behavior from one's espoused moral principles is through **euphemistic labeling**. This involves using cosmetic words to defuse or disguise the offensiveness of otherwise morally repugnant or distasteful behavior. Terrorists, for example, may call themselves "freedom fighters," and firing someone may be referred to as "letting him or her go." **Advantageous comparison** lets one avoid self-contempt for one's behavior by comparing it to even more heinous behavior by others. ("If you think *we're* insensitive to subordinates' needs, you should see what it's like working for Acme.")

Through **displacement of responsibility** people may violate personal moral standards by attributing responsibility to others. Nazi concentration camp guards, for example, attempted to avoid moral responsibility for their behavior by claiming they were merely carrying out orders. A related mechanism is **diffusion of responsibility**, whereby reprehensible behavior becomes easier to engage in and live with if others are behaving the same way. When everyone is responsible, it seems, no one is responsible. This way of minimizing individual moral responsibility for collective action can be a negative effect of group decision-making. Through **disregard** or **distortion of consequences**, people minimize the harm caused by their behavior. This can be a problem in bureaucracies when decision makers are relatively insulated by their position from directly observing the consequences of their decisions. **Dehumanization** is still another way of avoiding the moral consequences of one's behavior. It is easier to treat others badly when they are dehumanized, as evidenced in epithets like "illegal aliens" or "Satan-worshippers." Finally, people sometimes try to justify immoral behavior by claiming it was caused by someone else's actions. This is known as **attribution of blame**.

How widespread are such methods of minimizing personal moral responsibility? When people behave badly, Bandura said, it is *not* typically because of a basic character flaw; rather, it is because they use methods like these to construe their behavior in a self-protective way.[46]

Perhaps, but there is a demonstrable crisis of confidence in leadership,[47] and even if character flaws per se among leaders are not the root cause, it is still telling that scholars have been giving increasing attention to that very concept of character. It's rather remarkable, in fact, that a term that until recently was virtually ignored in the scholarly literature is now described as "an indispensable component of sustainable leadership performance"[48] and "a central and defining feature of ethical leadership."[49] One reason may be belated recognition that the long-standing preoccupation with the narrower concept of moral judgment simply did not square with the fact that it explained only about 80 percent of the variance in ethical behavior. That has led Hannah and Avolio to recommend greater attention be paid to a concept they call **moral potency**.[50] It has three main components:

- **Moral ownership:** A felt sense of responsibility not only for the ethical nature of one's own behavior but also for one's commitment not to allow unethical things to happen within their broader sphere of influence including others and the organization.

- **Moral courage:** The fortitude to face risk and overcome fears associated with taking ethical action.

- **Moral efficacy:** Belief or confidence in one's capability to mobilize various personal, interpersonal, and other external resources to persist despite moral adversity.

Riggio and his associates have taken a complementary approach to studying leader character in their focus on the virtues of prudence, temperance, fortitude, and justice as hallmarks of an ethical leader. And although they freely admit that this approach is in some ways "just" a renewed call to recognize age-old wisdom, their development of an assessment instrument (the Leadership Virtues Questionnaire) should generate new ways of studying and deeper ways of understanding these ideas.[51]

Another advance in the challenging task of assessing seemingly hard-to-measure constructs was the analysis of alternative approaches to measuring managerial integrity by Kaiser and Hogan.[52] They suggest that the common method of measuring managerial integrity using coworker ratings of observed ethical behavior probably seriously underestimates the problem since it is relatively rare for managers to get caught in ethical lapses. As an alternative, they recommend assessing managerial integrity using what they call the *dubious reputation* approach. In essence, this approach asks subordinates (presumably the most likely group to see a manager's "dark side") to speculate on the likelihood that the manager *would be likely* to behave unethically, as distinguished from having directly observed such behavior.

> *It takes many good deeds to build a good reputation, and only one bad one to lose it.*
>
> **Benjamin Franklin, author, inventor, statesman**

Character-Based Approaches to Leadership

Can you be a good leader without being a good person? Does it make any sense to say, for example, that Adolf Hitler was an effective leader even if he was an evil person? In that sense, although some people might consider the phrase *ethical leadership* to be redundant, Avolio and his associates have defined ethical leadership as having two core components: the **moral person** and the **moral manager**.[53] The moral person is seen as a principled decision maker who cares about people and the broader society.[54] The actions of such people indicate they try to do the right things personally and professionally, and they can be characterized as honest, fair, and open. In addition, ethical leaders have clear ethical standards that they pursue in the face of pressure to do otherwise. More than being just moral people, ethical leaders are moral managers who "make ethics an explicit part of their leadership agenda by communicating an ethics and values message, by visibly and intentionally role modeling ethical behavior."[55] In recent years there has been a rekindling of interest in approaches to leadership that are inherently and explicitly based on the interdependence between effective leadership and certain value systems. This is in bold contrast to decades of tradition in the social sciences of being self-consciously "values-free" in pursuit of objectivity. Two prominent approaches in this movement are described in greater detail here.

Authentic Leadership

Authentic leadership is grounded in the principle found in the familiar adage "to thine own self be true." Authentic leaders exhibit a consistency among their values, their beliefs, and their actions.[56] The roots of authentic leadership are also in various expressions of the humanistic movement in psychology including Maslow's theory of self-actualization (see **Chapter 9**) and Carl Rogers's concept of the fully functioning person.[57] Central to both Maslow's and Rogers's theories is the idea that individuals can develop modes of understanding and interacting with their social environments so as to become more truly independent of others' expectations of them (individual, group, and cultural) and guided more by the dictates of universal truths and imperatives. Such individuals manifest congruence between how they feel on the inside and how they act, between what they say and what they do. They have realistic self-perceptions, free from the blind spots and misperceptions of self that are common to most people. At the same time, they are accepting of themselves, their nature, and that of others too.

Authentic leaders have strong ethical convictions that guide their behavior not so much to avoid doing "wrong" things as to always try to do the "right" things, including treating others with respect and dignity. They know where they stand on fundamental values and key issues. Authentic leaders behave as they do because of personal conviction rather than to attain status, rewards, or other advantages. As Avolio puts it, authentic leaders both are self-aware and self-consciously align their actions with their inner values.[58] He points out that such authenticity is not just something you either "have or don't have." Authenticity as a leader is something that you must always be striving to enhance. It requires regularly identifying with your best self, checking in with your core values concerning your leadership agendas and operating practices, and verifying that your actions are aligned with the highest ethical and moral principles you hold. In this way, practicing authentic leadership becomes taking actions that serve high moral principles concerning relationships, social responsibilities, and performance standards.[59]

> *The most important thing in acting is honesty. Once you've learned to fake that, you're in.*
>
> **Samuel Goldwyn, early film producer**

One way to understand authentic leadership is to contrast it with what might be called *inauthentic* leadership. If you think of a leader who "plays a role," or puts on different acts with different audiences to manage their impressions, that is being inauthentic. For example, two detectives playing the roles of "good cop" and "bad cop" when interviewing a suspect are being inauthentic (you may believe that it makes sense for them to do so, but it's inauthentic nonetheless). A boss who exaggerates his anger at an employee's mistake to "teach a lesson" is being inauthentic. A leader who denies that her feelings were affected by critical feedback from her direct reports is being inauthentic. It must be recognized, of course, that authenticity in and of itself does not ensure effective leadership. One might point out, after all, that Hitler and Osama bin Laden were pretty open about their true values; so the *nature* of a leader's character matters, too—not just whether one is "authentic" in one's presentation of self.

The study of authentic leadership has gained considerable momentum in the last decade because of beliefs that (1) enhancing self-awareness can help people in organizations find more meaning and connection at work; (2) promoting transparency and openness in relationships—even between leader and followers—builds trust and commitment; and (3) fostering more inclusive structures and practices in organizations can help build more positive ethical climates.[60] In contrast to stereotypical notions of the stoic "hero leader" who shows no weakness and shares no feelings, authentic leaders are willing to be viewed as vulnerable by their followers—a vital component of building a trusting leader–follower relationship. Equally important to building trust is a leader's willingness to be transparent—in essence, to say what she means and mean what she says. A major review of the scholarly literature on authentic leadership concluded by noting that the "assumption of authentic leadership theory that people in organizations can effectively lead, and follow, in a way that enables them to express their own unique identity and style, has created a sense of excitement among leadership scholars and practitioners."[61]

Some scholars, however, still view the excitement about authentic leadership with a bit of a jaundiced eye, as **Highlight 5.5** points out.

Will Humility and Authenticity Get You to the Top?

HIGHLIGHT 5.5

For the most part, the approaches to leadership presented in this chapter collectively call for leaders of the 21st century to be humble and authentic—servants, even, to others in their organizations. This stands in marked contrast to the style of leadership demonstrated by Donald Trump, who before he ran for president of the United States may have been best known for the saying, "You're fired!" But is the Trump style truly out of favor in the 21st century?

Stanford professor Jeffrey Pfeffer thinks not. Pfeffer finds, for example, that self-centered narcissists are more likely to get promoted than are their more humble counterparts. He also says the value of authenticity in the workplace is overrated. In fact, he says authenticity is hardly even possible. "Leaders don't need to be true to themselves; in fact, being authentic is the opposite of what they should do." Instead, he says, leaders need to do what the situation calls for, which involves playing a role and at least sometimes putting on an act. How helpful would it

be, for example, if a military commander in combat told the troops, "I don't know about you, but I'm scared as hell and not sure we're going to make it?"

It's far more important for leaders to understand what a particular situation requires and to act in an appropriate way, says Pfeffer. "Each of us plays a number of different roles in our lives, and people behave and think differently in each of those roles, so demanding authenticity doesn't make sense." In his book, Pfeffer cites sociological research that has shown how the attitudes of employees change depending on their situation at work—whether they are rank-and-file employees or managers, for example, or whether they are members of a union. Research has also shown that a person's personality can be affected and changed by his or her job and workplace conditions.

Source: J. Pfeffer, *Leadership BS: Fixing Workplaces and Careers One Truth at a Time* (New York: HarperBusiness, 2015).

Servant Leadership

Servant leadership has since 1970 described a quite different approach to leadership than that derived from a bureaucratic and mechanistic view of organizations wherein workers are thought of as mere cogs in a machine. In the latter, the leader's primary role may be understood as doing whatever it takes to ensure that things run smoothly, tasks are performed, and goals are met. This has commonly involved a hierarchical approach to leadership. From the contrasting perspective of servant leadership, the leader's role is literally to serve others.

The modern idea of servant leadership was developed and popularized by Robert Greenleaf after he read a short novel by Herman Hesse called *Journey to the East*.[62, 63] This is the mythical story of a group of people on a spiritual quest. Accompanying the party is a servant by the name of Leo, whose nurturing character sustained the group on its journey until one day he disappeared. The group fell apart and abandoned its quest when it realized that it was helpless without its servant. Finally, after many years of continued searching, the story's narrator found the religious order that had sponsored the original quest. It turned out that Leo, whom the narrator had only known as a servant, was actually the order's revered leader. To Greenleaf, this story meant that true leadership emerges when one's primary motivation is to help others.

The idea of servant leadership, of course, has been around for thousands of years. It stems at least in part from the teachings of Jesus, who instructed his disciples that servanthood is the essence of worthy leadership (such as through the example of *him* washing *their* feet). Ten characteristics are often associated with servant leaders. As you'll see, most of them also seem in line with the idea of authentic leadership just described:[64]

- *Listening:* While all leaders need to communicate effectively, the focus is often on communicating *to* others; but servant leadership puts the emphasis on *listening* effectively to others.
- *Empathy:* Servant leaders need to understand others' feelings and perspectives.
- *Healing:* Servant leaders help foster each person's emotional and spiritual health and wholeness.
- *Awareness:* Servant leaders understand their own values, feelings, strengths, and weaknesses.
- *Persuasion:* Rather than relying on positional authority, servant leaders influence others through their persuasiveness.
- *Conceptualization:* Servant leaders need to integrate present realities and future possibilities.
- *Foresight:* Servant leaders need to have a well-developed sense of intuition about how the past, present, and future are connected.
- *Stewardship:* Servant leaders are stewards who hold an organization's resources in trust for the greater good.
- *Commitment to others' growth:* The ultimate test of a servant leader's work is whether those served develop toward being more responsible, caring, and competent individuals.
- *Building community:* Such individual growth and development is most likely to happen when one is part of a supportive community. Unfortunately numerous factors like geographic mobility and the general impersonal nature of large organizations have eroded people's sense of community. Thus it is the servant leader's role to help create a sense of community among people, and effective servant leaders are able to inspire in others a "circle of service in which followers learn to serve each other, customers, and the broader community."[65] Such a community or "serving culture" is epitomized in the world-class hotel chain Ritz-Carlton, with its core value of "ladies and gentlemen serving ladies and gentlemen."[66, 67]

Not surprisingly, the concept of servant leadership has detractors as well as adherents. The most common criticism is that although the idea of servant leadership has a certain popular appeal in what we might call its "soft" form (for example, leaders should be more concerned about others' well-being and development, should create a more developmental climate in their organizations, and should seek what's good for the whole organization rather than just their own advancement), when taken more literally and extremely the concept seems to suggest that serving others is an end in itself rather than a means to other organizational goals and purposes. One form of leader that seems to be the complete antithesis of a servant leader is a narcissistic one, and **Highlight 5.6** examines that style of leadership.

Narcissistic Leadership

HIGHLIGHT 5.6

Some leaders suffer from hubris, or excessive self-confidence. As noted in **Highlight 1.9**, hubristic leadership is a relatively transient state, whereas narcissistic leaders create problems because of relatively permanent and enduring qualities of personality. And those problems can include unethical behavior.

In less extreme forms, narcissists may project an image of self-confidence, comfort in the spotlight, and readiness to act when others are hesitant—in other words, the type of person you might want as your leader. In more extreme forms, however, narcissism is classified as a personality disorder. Narcissism includes an array of personality characteristics that includes a grandiose sense of self-importance, fantasies of unlimited power, entitlement, weak self-control, an inability to tolerate criticism, lack of empa-thy, and interpersonal exploitativeness (American Psychological Association [APA], 1994).

Over the years, there have been plenty of warnings about the dangers that narcissistic leaders can pose to their organizations, but for a long time, there had been little empirical evidence to validate such warnings. A recent controlled study, however, demonstrated that "managers who scored high on a narcissism scale were likely to ignore input from others, censure critical viewpoints, demand that their decisions be accepted without question, and undermine others' authority . . . they also had a tendency to alienate others [and] falsify information to support their actions." In other words, the more narcissistic leaders were more likely to behave unethically.

Source: C. A. Blair, K. Helland, and B. Walton, "Leaders Behaving Badly: The Relationship between Narcissism and Unethical Leadership," *Leadership & Organization Development* 38, no. 2 (2017), pp. 333–46.

A scholarly review of the theory of servant leadership noted an almost irreconcilable conflict between the ideas of servant leadership and the inherent realities of organizational life: Servant leaders develop people, helping them to strive and flourish. Servant leaders want those they serve to become healthier, wiser, freer, and more autonomous. Servant leaders serve followers. But managers are hired to contribute to organizational goal attainment. It would seem that these goals can be attained only by having subordinates (not followers) solving tasks that lead to productivity and effectiveness.[68] Productivity and effectiveness, however, may not be inherently incompatible with servant leadership. For example, the results of one study suggest that servant leadership can impact profits by increasing trust in the organization, reducing customer turnover, and increasing employee satisfaction.[69] Nonetheless, even if the ideas of servant leadership and the realities of organizational life are not irreconcilable, they at least present clear challenges. For example, just how empathetically can and should a leader act? Showing genuine empathy toward others is emotionally exhausting; it is self-limiting (people may have only "so much" empathy—showing it toward one person may limit the amount shown to another); and it even may erode ethics by causing lapses in ethical judgment (for example, by making us more willing to overlook someone else's transgressions).[70] A recent comprehensive review of the servant leadership literature further underscores the practical challenges of effectively and comprehensively introducing a servant leadership approach into a functioning organization.[71]

The Roles of Ethics and Values in Organizational Leadership

Just as individuals possess a set of personal values, so too do organizations have dominant values. Many times these values are featured prominently in the company's annual report, website, and posters. These values represent the principles by which employees are to get work done and treat other employees, customers, and vendors. Whether these stated values represent true operating principles or so much "spin" for potential investors will depend on the degree of alignment between the organization's stated values and the collective values of top leadership.[72, 73] For example, many corporate value statements say little about making money, but this is the key organizational priority for most business leaders and, as such, is a major factor in many company decisions. There is often a significant gap between a company's stated values and the way the company operates. Knowing the values of top leadership can sometimes tell you more about how an organization operates than will the organization's stated values.

> *Subordinates cannot be left to speculate as to the values of the organization. Top leadership must give forth clear and explicit signals, lest any confusion or uncertainty exist over what is and is not permissible conduct. To do otherwise allows informal and potentially subversive "codes of conduct" to be transmitted with a wink and a nod, and encourages an inferior ethical system based on "going along to get along" or the notion that "everybody's doing it."*
>
> **Richard Thornburgh, former U.S. attorney general**

In any organization, the top leadership's collective values play a significant role in determining the dominant values throughout the organization, just as an individual leader's values play a significant role in determining team climate. Related to the notion of culture and climate is employee "fit." Research has shown that employees with values similar to the organization or team are more satisfied and likely to stay; those with dissimilar values are more likely to leave.[74, 75] Thus one reason leaders fail is due not to a lack of competence but rather to a misalignment between personal and organizational values. Although the advantages of alignment between personal and organizational values may seem self-evident, leaders with *dissimilar* values may be exactly what some organizations need to drive change and become more effective.

Finally, values are often a key factor in both intrapersonal and interpersonal conflict. Many of the most difficult decisions leaders make are choices between opposing values. A leader who valued both financial reward and helping others, for example, would probably struggle mightily when having to make a decision about cutting jobs to improve profitability. A leader who highly valued financial reward and did *not* strongly value helping others (or vice versa) would have much less trouble making the same decision. Likewise, some leaders would have difficulties making decisions if friendships get in the way of making an impact, or when taking risks to gain visibility runs counter to maintaining comfortable levels of stability in a team or organization. Values also play a key role in conflict between groups. The differences between Bill O'Reilly and Al Franken, Israelis and Palestinians, Shiite and Sunni Muslims in Iraq, Muslims and Hindus in Kashmir, and Christians and Muslims in Kosovo are all based at least partly on differences in values. Because values develop early and are difficult to change, it's usually extremely difficult to resolve conflicts between such groups.

In sum, it's vital for a leader to set a personal example of values-based leadership, and it is also important for leaders—especially senior ones—to make sure clear values guide *everyone's* behavior in the organization. That's likely to happen only if the leader sets an example of desired behavior. You might think of this as a necessary but not sufficient condition for principled behavior throughout the organization. If there is indifference or hypocrisy toward values at the highest levels, it is fairly unlikely that principled behavior will be considered important by others throughout the organization. Bill O'Brien, the former CEO of a major insurance company, likened an organization's poor ethical climate to a bad odor one gets used to:

> Organizations oriented to power, I realized, also have strong smells, and even if people are too inured to notice, that smell has implications. It affects performance, productivity, and innovation. The worst aspect of this environment is that it stunts the growth of personality and character of everyone who works there.[76]

Carried to an extreme, this can lead to the kinds of excesses all too frequently evident during the past decade:

> Who knew the swashbuckling economy of the '90s had produced so many buccaneers? You could laugh about the CEOs in handcuffs and the stock analysts who turned out to be fishier than storefront palm readers, but after a while the laughs became hard. Martha Stewart was dented and scuffed [and subsequently convicted]. Tyco was looted by its own executives. Enron and WorldCom turned out to be the twin towers of false promises. They fell. Their stockholders and employees went down with them. So did a large measure of faith in big corporations.[77]

Leading by Example: The Good, the Bad, and the Ugly

One of the most quoted principles of good leadership is "leadership by example." But what does it mean to exemplify ethical leadership and be an ethical role model? In one study, people from a range of organizations were interviewed about a person they knew who had been an ethical role model at work. Not all ethical role models exhibited exactly the same qualities, but four general categories of attitudes and behaviors seemed to characterize the group:[78]

- *Interpersonal behaviors:* They showed care, concern, and compassion for others. They were hardworking and helpful. They valued their relationships with others, working actively to maintain and sustain them. They tended to focus on the positive rather than the negative, and accepted others' failures.

- *Basic fairness:* A specific quality of their interpersonal behaviors was manifested in the fairness shown others. They were not only open to input from others but actively sought it. They tended to offer explanations of decisions. They treated others respectfully, never condescendingly, even amid disagreements.

- *Ethical actions and self-expectations:* They held themselves to high ethical standards and behaved consistently in both their public and private lives. They accepted responsibility for and were open about their own ethical failings. They were perceived as honest, trustworthy, humble, and having high integrity.

- *Articulating ethical standards:* They articulated a consistent ethical vision and were uncompromising toward it and the high ethical standards it implied. They held others ethically accountable and put ethical standards above personal and short-term company interests.

Arguably the most important example for anyone is his or her boss, and it raises difficult and complex challenges when a boss is a *bad* ethical role model. This becomes a challenge far greater than merely the hypocrisy inherent in being told, "Do as I say, not as I do."

It should go without saying that those in responsible positions have a particular responsibility to uphold ethical standards—but what if they *don't*? What should you do when your own boss does not behave ethically?

One approach to addressing these challenges is to reject the notion that organizational leadership is synonymous with formal position or hierarchical power in the organization, and to embrace instead the idea that *all* organizational members have a role in organizational leadership, including responsibility for ethical leadership in the organization. The term **upward ethical leadership** has been used to refer to "leadership behavior enacted by individuals who take action to maintain ethical standards in the face of questionable moral behaviors by higher-ups."[79]

> *A man who wants to lead the orchestra must turn his back on the crowd.*
>
> **Max Lucado, preacher and author**

However, there are almost always reasons that may constrain employee behavior in such situations, including fear of retribution by bosses. More generally, do employees feel they have a safe outlet for raising ethical concerns about misbehavior by superiors in the organization?

One variable that moderates an employee's likelihood of raising such concerns is the general quality of ethical climate in the organization. **Ethical climates** refer to those in which ethical standards and norms have been consistently, clearly, and pervasively communicated throughout the organization and embraced and enforced by organizational leaders in both word and example. **Unethical climates** are those in which questionable or outright unethical behavior exists with little action taken to correct such behavior, or (worse) where such misbehavior is even condoned.[80] It's likely that employees experience some degree of moral distress whenever a manager is perceived to behave unethically, but the distress is usually greater in unethical climates.

Even in ethical climates, however, some individuals may be more likely than others to address perceived ethical problems in an active and constructive manner. This inclination is likely to be enhanced among individuals who feel a sense of personal power. Employees tend to feel greater power, for example, if they believe they have attractive opportunities in the broader employment marketplace, if they're respected for their credibility and competence in the organization, and if others within the organization are somewhat dependent on them. Organizations can further enhance the likelihood that employees will address perceived ethical problems in an active and constructive manner by nurturing a culture that is not all "command and control," by fostering a sense of shared leadership more than hierarchy, and by valuing upward leadership.[81] In the end, though, the most powerful way organizations can enhance the likelihood that employees will address ethical problems in a constructive manner is by proactively creating an ethical climate throughout the organization, and that is not just a responsibility of informal ethical leaders throughout the organization but inescapably a responsibility of formal organizational leaders.

In fact, being in a formal leadership role imposes unique ethical responsibilities and challenges. Leaders more than followers (1) possess unique degrees of both legitimate and coercive power; (2) enjoy greater privileges; (3) have access to more information; (4) have greater authority and responsibility; (5) interact with a broader range of stakeholders who expect equitable treatment; and (6) must balance sometimes competing loyalties when making decisions.[82] With conditions like these, which sometimes also may represent seductive temptations to excuse one's own behavior, it is all the more important for leaders to take positive steps to create an ethical climate and hold themselves accountable to it. The dangers of *not* doing so are underscored in the downfall of Enron, described in **Highlight 5.7**.

It's important that people know what you stand for. It's equally important that they know what you won't stand for.

Mary H. Waldrip, author

The Cult of Enron

HIGHLIGHT 5.7

Enron has come to represent the epitome of greed, ethical lapse, and spectacular failure in the business world. Its senior executives CEO Kenneth Lay and Jeffrey Skilling were blamed and prosecuted for the company's collapse and callous indifference to the welfare of its employees. But the problems at Enron ran deeper than just the shoddy ethics and illegal actions of a few people at the top. A large part of the prob-

lem was the Enron culture itself that people *throughout* the company perpetuated.

A root of the problem may be that Enron's culture had many characteristics of a cult. Cults are characterized as having these four qualities:

- Charismatic leadership.
- A compelling and totalistic vision.
- A conversion process.
- A common culture.

Here are some of the ways that Enron's corporate culture was like a cult. You can see how corporations as well as religious cults can encourage counterproductive conformity and penalize dissent.

Charismatic Leadership

Enron's leaders created an aura of charisma around themselves through ever more dramatic forms of self-promotion. Skilling, for example, cultivated his image as the Enron version of Darth Vader, even referring to his traders as "Storm Troopers." The reputations of Skilling and other top executives at Enron were further reinforced by the ways in which they were lionized in respected business publications and by the opulent lifestyles they enjoyed.

Compelling and Totalistic Vision

Hyperbole was rampant at Enron, as in banners proclaiming its vision of being the "world's leading company." Such exalted self-images encourage members to feel a sense of privilege and destiny. Employees were bombarded with messages that they were the best and the brightest. Their commitment to organizational success had an almost evangelistic fervor, and workweeks of even 80 hours were considered normal.

Conversion and Indoctrination

From an employee's recruitment to Enron onward, communication was one-way: top-down. In the early stages this involved intense and emotionally draining rituals over several days wherein the recruit would hear powerful messages from the leaders. Group dynamics research has shown that such initiation rituals incline people to exaggerate the benefits of group membership in their minds. In Enron's case the purpose was to ingrain in employees a single-minded personal commitment to continued high rates of corporate growth.

Common Culture

Despite all the effort put into selecting new employees and imbuing them with a sense of privilege, a punitive internal culture was also nurtured through which all the psychic and material benefits of being in Enron could be withdrawn on a managerial whim. Enron was quick to fire any of these "best and brightest" who did not conform; they could be branded, almost overnight, as "losers" in others' eyes. This could happen for mere dissent with the corporate line as well as for failing to meet Enron's exceedingly high performance goals.

Source: D. Tourish and N. Vatcha, "Charismatic Leadership and Corporate Cultism at Enron: The Elimination of Dissent, the Promotion of Conformity, and Organizational Collapse," *Leadership* 1, no. 4 (2005), pp. 455–80.

Creating and Sustaining an Ethical Climate

So how do leaders do this? Several "fronts" of leadership action are needed to establish an ethical organizational climate:[83]

- *Formal ethics policies and procedures:* It's sometimes said that "you can't legislate morality," and the same may be said about legislating an ethical climate. Nonetheless, certain formal policies and procedures are probably necessary if not sufficient conditions for creating an ethical climate. These include formal statements of ethical standards and policies, along with reporting mechanisms, disciplinary procedures, and penalties for suspected ethical violations.

- *Core ideology:* A core ideology is basically an organization's heart and soul. It represents the organization's purpose, guiding principles, basic identity, and most important values. Starbucks is a good example. Starbucks's guiding principles include (1) respect and dignity for partners (employees); (2) embracing diversity; (3) applying the highest standards of excellence to the business; (4) developing "enthusiastically satisfied customers"; (5) contributing positively to local communities and to the environment more generally; and (6) maintaining profitability.[84]

- *Integrity:* The core ideology cannot be a mere set of boardroom plaques or other exhortations to behave well. The core ideology must be part of the fabric of every level and unit in the organization. Just as personal integrity describes an individual whose outward behavior and inward values are congruent and transparent, organizational integrity describes an organization whose pronouncements are congruent with its public and private actions at every level and in every office. And it is especially important that the highest level of executives in any organization is perceived as demonstrating high integrity.[85]

- *Structural reinforcement:* An organization's structure and systems can be designed to encourage higher ethical performance and discourage unethical performance. Performance evaluation systems that provide opportunities for anonymous feedback increase the likelihood that "dark side" behaviors would be reported, and thus discourage their enactment. Reward systems can promote honesty, fair treatment of customers, courtesy, and other desirable behaviors. If poorly designed, however, reward systems can also promote dishonesty. In an effort to increase the speed of repairs in its auto repair facilities, for example, Sears gave its mechanics a sales goal of $147 an hour. What that did, however, was to encourage the mechanics to overcharge for services and "repair" things that didn't need repairing.[86]

- *Process focus:* There also needs to be explicit concern with process, not just the achievement of tangible individual, team, and organizational goals. *How* those goals are achieved needs to be a focus of attention and emphasis, too. When senior leaders set exceptionally high goals and show that they expect goals to be achieved no matter what it takes, employees may be tempted to engage in unethical behavior. And when leaders turn a blind eye even to seemingly small organizational transgressions, it can lead one down a slippery slope of moral disengagement that enables larger transgressions later on.[87]

Another way to think about the essence of creating an ethical climate in organizations is to recognize that it is not simply the sum of the collective moralities of its members. Covey has developed and popularized an approach called **principle-centered leadership**,[88] which postulates a fundamental interdependence between the personal, the interpersonal, the managerial, and the organizational levels of leadership. The unique role of each level may be thought of like this:

Personal: The first imperative is to be a trustworthy person, and that depends on both one's character *and* competence. Only if one is trustworthy can one have trusting relationships with others.

Interpersonal: Relationships that lack trust are characterized by self-protective efforts to control and verify each other's behavior.

Managerial: Only in the context of trusting relationships will a manager risk empowering others to make full use of their talents and energies. But even with an empowering style, leading a high-performing group depends on skills such as team building, delegation, communication, negotiation, and self-management.

Organizational: An organization will be most creative and productive when its structure, systems (training, communication, reward, and so on), strategy, and vision are aligned and mutually supportive. Put differently, certain organizational alignments are more likely than others to nurture and reinforce ethical behavior.

Interestingly, the interdependence between these levels posited in principle-centered leadership is quite similar to recent conceptualizations of authentic leadership that also view it as a multilevel phenomenon. That is, authentic leadership can be thought of not only as a quality characterizing certain individual leaders but also as a quality of certain leader–follower dyads, groups or teams, and even organizations. Thus it makes just as much sense to talk about authentic organizations as it does to talk about authentic leaders.[89]

In concluding this chapter, we would be remiss not to explicitly address a question that has been implicit throughout it: *Why* should a company go to the trouble of creating and sustaining an ethical climate?[90] One answer—perhaps a sufficient one—is because it's the right thing to do. Sometimes, however, it's too easy merely to assume that because something is the right thing to do there must be some costs or disadvantages associated with it. As is apparent from this chapter, it's not easy to create and sustain an ethical environment in an organization; it takes conviction, diligence, and commitment. In some ways, such continuing focus and effort can be thought of as a cost. However, such focus and effort can pay dividends beyond an intrinsic sense of satisfaction.

Only mediocrities rise to the top in a system that won't tolerate wave making.

Laurence J. Peter, author of *The Peter Principle*

Johnson has identified a number of tangible positive outcomes for an organization that creates an ethical climate. One of these is greater collaboration within the organization: An ethical climate produces greater trust within an organization, and trust is a key element underlying collaboration. Another positive outcome can be improved social standing and improved market share for the organization. Eighty-four percent of Americans said that if price and quality were similar, they would switch allegiance to companies associated with worthy causes. Over $2 trillion is now invested in mutual funds focusing on companies demonstrating commitment to the environment, ethics, and social responsibility.[91, 92] There also is evidence that ethical companies often outperform their competitors.[93]

I do believe in the spiritual nature of human beings. To some it's a strange or outdated idea, but I believe there is such a thing as a human spirit. There is a spiritual dimension to man which should be nurtured.

Aung San Suu Kyi

Similar tangible advantages were identified by Harvard professors John Kotter and James Heskett among companies that aligned espoused values with organizational practices. Such companies increased revenues by an average of 682 percent versus 166 percent for companies that didn't.[94] Paying attention to ethics and values *can* be good business. Ultimately, though, it is probably not a "business decision" to choose ethical leadership but rather a moral one. Seven moral challenges of leadership are presented in **Highlight 5.8**.

Seven Moral Challenges of Leadership

HIGHLIGHT 5.8

Nicholas Emler describes seven moral challenges particular to leadership:

The Temptation of Personal Gain

It goes without saying that it is unwise to put significant opportunities for criminal gain in front of people we do not trust. It is also true that the higher one's level in an organizational hierarchy, the greater opportunity there is to manipulate one's position for criminal gain. Therefore, the greater temptations inherently present at higher organizational levels call for great resources of character in the incumbents.

The Attraction of Tyranny

There are numerous reasons we may be tempted to hurt others: some people are simply irritating or annoying; they may act in an insulting or disrespectful way; they may pose obstacles to our goals or plans; they may simply be bullies. When feeling such ways toward others, people in high enough positions of authority may enforce their will through intimidation or coercion.

Ensuring Justice

Research on justice tells us a lot about how the recipients of justice in organizational settings react—reactions to how they have been treated. We know relatively little, however, about *dispensing* justice in organizations. That is problematic in light of two other things we know: (1) in general, people value fairness even more than maximizing personal gain; and (2) there is an ever-present temptation of leaders to play favorites.

Pursuing a Moral Mandate

When people choose among candidates for positions of leadership, they do so based not only upon judgments of competency and moral integrity but also because of their judgments about moral *priorities*. Prospective leaders, therefore, need to articulate their values-driven visions for the enterprise as a whole—especially in organizations that confront multiple competing values.

Avoiding Mission Failure

At first, this may not seem like a moral challenge, but organizational failures attributable to leadership incompetence can be seen as a *moral failure* of leadership as well as merely a shortfall in competence. Leaders who willfully ignore advice or their own limitations of expertise may be morally culpable for potentially ruinous outcomes.

Avoiding Collateral Damage

There are countless examples where corporate decisions have resulted in consumer deaths, ranging from defective automobiles to drugs with unintended side effects. And in other spheres as well (e.g., military actions), collateral damage can be an inherent cost of achieving mission success. But the question always is "at what cost" is the outcome achieved? Emler says we "need an exceptional level of vigilance for consequences beyond the explicit goals of one's organization, together with a recognition of one's responsibility for these."

Doing Good

This challenge focuses on the very issue with which we began the chapter—*doing the right thing*, and Emler says it is the challenge least often met. It is also the most difficult challenge to define. At its essence is the idea that leadership provides opportunities to address injustice and other wrongs, as in an airline CEO's decision after a fatal airline crash to support the bereaved and injured with measures demonstrating empathy and humaneness far beyond the company's legal obligations.

Source: N. Emler, "Seven Moral Challenges of Leadership," *Consulting Psychology Journal* 71 (2019), pp. 32–46.

Summary

This chapter has reviewed evidence regarding the relationships among ethics, values, and leadership. Ethics is a branch of philosophy that deals with right conduct. Values are constructs that represent general sets of behaviors or states of affairs that individuals consider important, and they are a central part of a leader's psychological makeup. Values affect leadership through a cultural context within which various attributes and behaviors are regarded differentially—positively or negatively.

It's not just the content of one's beliefs about right and wrong that matters, though. *How* one makes moral or ethical judgments, or the manner by which one solves moral problems, is also important and is referred to as moral reasoning.

Ethical action, of course, involves more than just the cognitive process of moral reasoning. That's why people's behavior does not always conform to how they predict they'll act, or with their espoused values. Furthermore, the thorniest ethical dilemmas people face tend not to involve choices between what is right or wrong but between two different "rights." In such cases it is useful to apply several different principles for resolving moral dilemmas.

Recently many approaches to leadership have explicitly addressed the interdependencies between effective leadership and particular value systems. The concepts of authentic leadership and servant leadership are among these. There also has been increased interest in recent years in the kinds of practices that can be instituted within organizations to enhance the likelihood that they will have ethical climates.

Key Terms

ethics	implicit prejudice	moral potency
Theory X	in-group favoritism	moral ownership
Theory Y	overclaiming credit	moral courage
values	conflicts of interest	moral efficacy
dual-process theory	moral justification	moral person
ethical dilemmas	euphemistic labeling	moral manager
truth versus loyalty	advantageous comparison	authentic leadership
individual versus community	displacement of responsibility	servant leadership
short term versus long term	diffusion of responsibility	upward ethical leadership
justice versus mercy	disregard	ethical climate
ends-based thinking	distortion of consequences	unethical climate
rule-based thinking	dehumanization	principle-centered leadership
care-based thinking	attribution of blame	

Questions

1. Do you think it always must be "lonely at the top" (or that if it is not, you are doing something wrong)?
2. How do you believe one's basic philosophy of human nature affects one's approach to leadership?
3. Identify several values you think might be the basis of conflict or misunderstanding between leaders and followers.
4. Can a leader's public and private morality be distinguished? Should they be?
5. Can a bad person be a good leader?
6. During the early stages of the coronavirus pandemic, did you ever observe conflicting values being expressed by different public figures? Did you see public health officials, government office-holders, or other leaders expressing conflicting priorities or courses of action?
7. During the coronavirus pandemic, were you aware of the possibility that if a worst-case scenario did unfold, life-and-death decisions might have to be made concerning the allocation of limited life-saving equipment and procedures—basically, decisions about who would be allowed to receive treatment and who would not?

Activities

1. Each person should select his or her own 10 most important values from the following list, and then rank-order those 10 from most important (1) to least important (10). Then have an open discussion about how a person's approach to leadership might be influenced by having different value priorities. The values are achievement, activity (keeping busy), advancement, adventure, aesthetics (appreciation of beauty), affiliation, affluence, authority, autonomy, balance, challenge, change/variety, collaboration, community, competence, competition, courage, creativity, economic security, enjoyment, fame, family, friendship, happiness, helping others, humor, influence, integrity, justice, knowledge, location, love, loyalty, order, personal development, physical fitness, recognition, reflection, responsibility, self-respect, spirituality, status, and wisdom.

2. Explore how the experiences of different generations might have influenced the development of their values. Divide into several groups and assign each group the task of selecting representative popular music from a specific era. One group, for example, might have the 1950s, another the Vietnam War era, and another the 1990s. Using representative music from that era, highlight what seem to be dominant concerns, values, or views of life during that period.

Minicase

Balancing Priorities at Clif Bar

Gary Erickson is a man of integrity. In the spring of 2000 Erickson had an offer of more than $100 million from a major food corporation for his company Clif Bar Inc. He had founded Clif Bar Inc. in 1990 after a long bike ride. Erickson, an avid cyclist, had finished the 175-mile ride longing for an alternative to the tasteless energy bars he had brought along. "I couldn't make the last one go down, and that's when I had an epiphany—make a product that actually tasted good." He looked at the list of ingredients on the package and decided he could do better. He called on his experience in his family's bakery, and after a year in the kitchen, the Clif Bar—named for Erickson's father—was launched in 1992. Within five years sales had skyrocketed to $20 million. He considered the $100 million offer on the table and what it meant for his company and decided against the deal. He realized that the vision he had for the company would be compromised once he lost control, so he walked away from the $100 million deal.

He has stuck to his vision and values ever since. His commitment to environmental and social issues are evident in everything he does. On the environmental front, his company has a staff ecologist who is charged with reducing Clif Bar's ecological footprint on the planet. More than 70 percent of the ingredients in Clif Bars are organic. A change in packaging has saved the company (and the planet) 90,000 pounds of shrink-wrap a year. And the company funds a Sioux wind farm to offset the carbon dioxide emissions from its factories. On the social side, Erickson launched a project called the 2,080 program (2,080 is the total number of hours a full-time employee works in one year). Through the 2,080 program employees are encouraged to do volunteer work on company time. Recently Erickson agreed to support (with salaries and travel expenses) employees who wanted to volunteer in developing countries.

Erickson is also committed to his team. He thinks about things like, "What should our company be like for the people who come to work each day?" He sees work as a living situation and strives to make Clif Bar Inc.'s offices a fun place to be—there are plenty of bikes around; a gym and dance floor; personal trainers; massage and hair salon; a game room; an auditorium for meetings, movies, and music; dog days every day; and great parties.

As the company grows, however, maintaining such values may not be easy. According to Erickson. "We're at a point where we have to find a way to maintain this open culture while we may be getting bigger," says Shelley Martin, director of operations. "It's a balancing act."

1. Without knowing Gary Erickson's age, where would you guess he falls in the four generations of workers as delineated by Zemke?

2. Consider the key work values in **Table 5.1**. Recalling that leaders are motivated to act consistently with their values, what values appear to be most important to Gary Erickson?

Sources: "The Clif Bar & Company Story," Clif Bar & Company, www.clifbar.com/article/the-clif-bar-and-company-story; and Gabriela Rodrigues, "Leading by Example: The Founder of Clif Bar Grows a Sustainable Company by Green Actions and an Unconventional Office," *The Free Library*, 2014, www.thefreelibrary.com/Leading+by+example%3a+the+founder+of+Clif+Bar+grows+a+sustainable...-a0159285785.

Endnotes

1. C. Moore, J. R. Detert, L. K. Trevino, V. L. Baker, and D. M. Mayer, "Why Employees Do Bad Things: Moral Disengagement and Unethical Behavior," *Personnel Psychology* 65 (2012), pp. 1–48.

2. M. E. Brown and L. K. Trevino, "Ethical Leadership: A Review and Future Directions," *The Leadership Quarterly* 17 (2006), pp. 595–616.

3. J. W. Gardner, *On Leadership* (New York: Free Press, 1990).

4. J. M. Burns, *Leadership* (New York: Harper & Row, 1978).

5. W. Bennis and J. Goldsmith, *Learning to Lead* (Reading, MA: Perseus Books, 1997).

6. D. McGregor, *Leadership and Motivation* (Cambridge, MA: MIT Press, 1966).

7. J. Hall and S. M. Donnell, "Managerial Achievement: The Personal Side of Behavioral Theory," *Human Relations* 32 (1979): 77–101.

8. L. V. Gordon, *Measurement of Interpersonal Values* (Chicago: Science Research Associates, 1975): 2.

9. W. L. Gardner, B. Avolio, F. Luthans, D. May, and F. Walumbwa, "'Can You See the Real Me?' A Self-Based Model of Authentic Leader and Follower Development," *The Leadership Quarterly* 16 (2005): 343–72.

10. R. E. Boyatzis and F. R. Skelly, "The Impact of Changing Values on Organizational Life," in *Organizational Behavior Readings*, 5th ed., eds. D. A. Kolb, I. M. Rubin, and J. Osland (Englewood Cliffs, NJ: Prentice Hall, 1991): 1–16.

11. M. Rokeach, *The Nature of Human Values* (New York: Free Press, 1973).

12. W. A. Gentry, K. L. Cullen, J. J. Sosik, J. U.Chun, C. R. Leupold, and S. Tonidandel, "Integrity's Place among the Character Strengths of Middle Level Managers and Top-Level Executives," *The Leadership Quarterly* 24 (2013), pp. 395–404.

13. Boyatzis and Skelly, "The Impact of Changing Values on Organizational Life."

14. M. Maccoby, "Management: Leadership and the Work Ethic," *Modern Office Procedures* 28, no. 5 (1983), pp. 14, 16, 18.

15. M. Massey, *The People Puzzle: Understanding Yourself and Others* (Reston, VA: Reston, 1979).

16. R. Zemke, C. Raines, and B. Filipczak, *Generations at Work: Managing the Class of Veterans, Boomers, Xers, and Nexters in Your Workplace* (New York: AMA Publications, 2000).

17. C. S. Alexander and J. M. Sysko, "A Study of the Cognitive Determinants of Generation Y's Entitlement Mentality," *Academy of Educational Leadership Journal* 16 (2012), pp. 63–68.

18. N. Howe and W. Strauss, "The Next 20 Years: How Customer and Workforce Attitudes Will Evolve," *Harvard Business Review*, July/August (2007), pp. 41–51.

19. A. McAfee, "How Millennials' Sharing Habits Can Benefit Organizations," *Harvard Business Review*, November 2010, p. 24.

20. Alexander and Sysko, "A Study of the Cognitive Determinants of Generation Y's Entitlement Mentality."

21. J. J. Deal, K. Peterson, and H. Gailor-Loflin, *Emerging Leaders: An Annotated Bibliography* (Greensboro, NC: Center for Creative Leadership, 2001).

22. E. C. Ladd, "Generation Gap? What Generation Gap?" *The New York Times*, December 9, 1994, p. A 16.

23. F. Giancola, "The Generation Gap: More Myth Than Reality," endnote 22, *Resource Planning* 29, no. 4 (2006), pp. 32–37.

24. W. A. Gentry, T. L. Griggs, J. J. Deal, S. P. Mondore, and B. D. Cox, "A Comparison of Generational Differences in Endorsement of Leadership Practices with Actual Leadership Skill Level," *Consulting Psychology Journal: Practice and Research*, 63 (2011), pp. 39–49.

25. J. J. Lee, M. Ong, B. Parmar, and E. Amit, "Lay Theories of Effortful Honesty: Does the Honesty-Effort Association Justify Making a Dishonest Decision?" *Journal of Applied Psychology* 104 (2019), pp. 659–70.

26. J. Rest, "Research on Moral Judgment in College Students," in *Approaches to Moral Development: New Research and Emerging Themes*, ed. A. Garrod (New York: Teachers College Press, Columbia University, 1993), pp. 201–13.

27. M. R. Banaji, M. H. Bazerman, and D. Chugh, "How (Un) ethical Are You?" *Harvard Business Review* 81, no. 12 (2003), pp. 56–64.

28. S. Seiler, A. Fischer, and S. A. Voegtli, "Developing Moral Decision-Making Competence: A Quasi-Experimental Intervention Study for the Swiss Armed Forces," *Ethics & Behavior* 21, no. 6 (2011), pp. 452–70.

29. J. Greene, "From Neural 'Is' to Moral 'Ought': What Are the Moral Implications of Neuroscientific Moral Psychology?" *Nature Reviews/Neuroscience* 4 (2003), pp. 847–50.

30. J. Greene, "The Cognitive Neuroscience of Moral Judgment," in *The Cognitive Neurosciences*, 4th ed., ed. M. S. Gazzaniga (Cambridge, MA: MIT Press, 2009).

31. R. Kidder, *How Good People Make Tough Choices: Resolving the Dilemmas of Ethical Living* (New York: HarperCollins, 1995).

32. A. G. Greenwald, D. E. McGhee, and J. L. K. Schwartz, "Measuring Individual Differences in Implicit Cognition: The Implicit Association Test," *Journal of Personality and Social Psychology* 74 (1998), pp. 1464–80.

33. Banaji, Bazerman, and Chugh, "How (Un) ethical Are You?"

34. Banaji, Bazerman, and Chugh, "How (Un) ethical Are You?"

35. P. Coy, "Ten Years from Now," *BusinessWeek*, August 20 and 27, 2007, pp. 42–44.

36. Banaji, Bazerman, and Chugh, "How (Un) ethical Are You?"

37. S. Sohenshein, "The Role of Construction, Intuition, and Justification in Responding to Ethical Issues at Work: The Sensemaking–Intuition Model," *Academy of Management Review* 32, no. 4 (2007), pp. 1022–40.

38. Sohenshein, "The Role of Construction, Intuition, and Justification in Responding to Ethical Issues at Work."

39. J. Haidt, "The Emotional Dog and Its Rational Tail: A Social Intuitionist Approach to Moral Judgment," *Psychological Review* 108, no. 4 (2001), pp. 814–34.

40. C. D. Barnes and R. P. Brown, "A Value-Congruent Bias in the Forgiveness Forecasts of Religious People," *Psychology of Religion and Spirituality* 2, no. 1 (2010), pp. 17–29.

41. R. T. Marcy, W. Gentry, and R. McKinnon, "Thinking Straight: New Strategies Are Needed for Ethical Leadership," *Leadership in Action* 28, no. 3 (2008), pp. 3–7.

42. A. Bandura, *Social Foundations of Thought and Action* (Englewood Cliffs, NJ: Prentice Hall, 1986).

43. A. Bandura, "Mechanisms of Moral Disengagement," in *Origins of Terrorism: Psychologies, Ideologies, Theologies, States of Mind*, ed. W. Reich (Cambridge: Cambridge University Press., 1990), pp. 161–91.

44. C. Moore, J. R. Detert, L. K. Trevino, V. L. Baker, and D. M. Mayer, "Why Employees Do Bad Things: Moral Disengagement and Unethical Behavior," *Personnel Psychology* 65, no. 1 (2012), pp. 1–48.

45. Bandura, "Mechanisms of Moral Disengagement."

46. A. Bandura, "Self-Efficacy: Toward a Unifying Theory of Behavioral Change," *Psychological Review* 84, no. 2 (1977), pp. 191–215.

47. S. T. Hannah and B. J. Avolio, "Moral Potency: Building the Capacity for Character-Based Leadership," *Consulting Psychology Journal: Practice and Research* 62, no. 4 (2010), pp. 291–310.

48. S. T. Hannah and B. J. Avolio, "The Locus of Leader Character," *The Leadership Quarterly* 22 (2011), pp. 979–83.

49. T. A. Wright and J. C. Quick, "The Role of Character in Ethical Leadership Research," *The Leadership Quarterly* 22, no.5 (2011), pp. 975–78.

50. Hannah and Avolio, "Moral Potency."

51. R. E. Riggio, W. Zhu, C. Rheina, and J. A. Maroosis, "Virtue-Based Measurement of Ethical Leadership: The Leadership Virtues Questionnaire," *Consulting Psychology Journal: Practice and Research* 62, no. 4 (2010), pp. 235–50.

52. R. B. Kaiser and R. Hogan, "How To (and How Not To) Assess the Integrity of Managers," *Consulting Psychology Journal: Practice and Research* 62, no. 4 (2010), pp. 216–34.

53. F. O. Walumbwa, B. Avolio, W. Gardner, T. Wernsing, and S. Peterson, "Authentic Leadership: Development of a Theory-Based Measure," *Journal of Management* 34, no. 1 (2008), pp. 89–126.

54. M. E. Brown and L. Trevino, "Ethical Leadership: A Review and Future Directions," *Leadership Quarterly* 17 (2006), pp. 595–616.

55. Brown and Trevino, "Ethical Leadership," p. 597.

56. Walumbwa, Avolio, Gardner, Wernsing, and Peterson, "Authentic Leadership."

57. C. Rogers, *On Becoming a Person: A Therapist's View of Psychotherapy* (London: Constable, 1961).

58. B. J. Avolio and T. S. Wernsing, "Practicing Authentic Leadership," in *Positive Psychology: Exploring the Best in People (Vol. 4: Exploring Human Flourishing)*, ed. Shane Lopez (Santa Barbara, CA: Praeger, 2008).

59. Avolio and Wernsing, "Practicing Authentic Leadership," p. 161.

60. B. J. Avolio and W. L. Gardner, "Authentic Leadership Development: Getting to the Root of Positive Forms of Leadership," *The Leadership Quarterly* 16 (2005), pp. 315–38.

61. B. J. Avolio and R. Reichard, "The Rise of Authentic Followership," in *The Art of Followership: How Great Followers Create Great Leaders and Organizations*, eds. R. E. Riggio, I. Chaleff, and J. Lipman-Bluman (San Francisco: Jossey-Bass, 2008), pp. 325–37.

62. L. Spears, "Practicing Servant-Leadership," *Leader to Leader* 34 (Fall 2004), pp. 7–11.

63. R. K. Greenleaf, *Servant Leadership* (New York: Paulist Press, 1977).

64. Spears, "Practicing Servant-Leadership."

65. E. M. Hunter, M. J. Neubert, S. J. Perry, L. A. Witt, L. M. Penney, and E. Weinberger, "Servant Leaders Inspire Servant Followers: Antecedents and Outcomes for Employees and the Organization," *The Leadership Quarterly* 24 (2013), pp. 316–31.

66. R. C. Liden, S. J. Wayne, C. Liao, and J. D. Meuser, "Servant Leadership and Serving Culture: Influence on Individual and Unit Performance," *Academy of Management Journal* 57, no. 5 (2014), pp. 1434–52.

67. J. A. Michelli, *The New Gold Standard* (New York: McGraw-Hill, 2008).

68. J. A. Andersen, "When a Servant-Leader Comes Knocking . . ." *Leadership & Organization Development Journal* 30, no. 1 (2009), pp. 4–15.

69. D. Jones, "Does Servant Leadership Lead to Greater Customer Focus and Employee Satisfaction?" *Business Studies Journal* 4, no. 2 (2012), pp. 21–23.

70. A. Waytz, "The Limits of Empathy," *Harvard Business Review* 94, no. 1 (2016), pp. 68–73.

71. N. Eva, M. Robin, S. Sendjaya, D. van Dierendonck, and R. C. Liden, "Servant Leadership: A Systematic Review and Call for Future Research," *The Leadership Quarterly* 30, no. 1 (2019), pp. 111–32.

72. R. T. Hogan, J. Hogan, and B. W. Roberts, "Personality Measurement and Employment Decisions: Questions and Answers," *American Psychologist* 51, no. 5 (1996), pp. 469–77.

73. R. T. Hogan and G. J. Curphy, "Leadership Matters: Values and Dysfunctional Dispositions," Working Paper, 2004.

74. Hogan, Hogan, and Roberts, "Personality Measurement and Employment Decisions."

75. Hogan and Curphy, "Leadership Matters."

76. B. O'Brien, "Designing an Organization's Governing Ideas," in *The Fifth Discipline Fieldbook*, eds. P. Senge et al. (New York: Doubleday, 1994), p. 306.

77. R. Lacayo and A. Ripley, "Persons of the Year 2002: The Whistleblowers," *Time*, December 30, 2002.

78. G. Weaver, L. Trevfino, and B. Agle, "Somebody I Look Up To: Ethical Role Models in Organizations," *Organizational Dynamics* 34, no. 4 (2005), pp. 313–30.

79. M. Uhl-Bien and M. Carsten, "Being Ethical When the Boss Is Not," *Organizational Dynamics* 36, no. 2 (2007), pp. 187–201.

80. Uhl-Bien and Carsten, "Being Ethical When the Boss Is Not."

81. Uhl-Bien and Carsten, "Being Ethical When the Boss Is Not."

82. C. E. Johnson, *Meeting the Ethical Challenges of Leadership: Casting Light or Shadow*, 2nd ed. (Thousand Oaks, CA: Sage, 2005).

83. C. E. Johnson, "Best Practices in Ethical Leadership, 2007," in *The Practice of Leadership: Developing the Next Generation of Leaders*, eds. J. Conger and R. Riggio (San Francisco: Jossey-Bass, 2006), pp. 150–71.

84. Johnson, "Best Practices in Ethical Leadership, 2007."

85. W. A. Gentry, K. L. Cullen, J. J. Sosik, J. U.Chun, C. R. Leupold, and S. Tonidandel, "Integrity's Place among the Character Strengths of Middle Level Managers and Top-Level Executives," *The Leadership Quarterly* 24, no. 3 (2013), pp. 395–404.

86. M. H. Bazerman and A. E. Tenbrunsel, "Ethical Breakdowns," *Harvard Business Review* 89, no. 4 (2011), pp. 58–65.

87. D. T. Welsh, L. D. Ordonez, D. G. Snyder, and M.S. Christian, "The Slippery Slope: How Small Ethical Transgressions Pave the Way for Larger Future Transgressions," *Journal of Applied Psychology* 100, no. 1 (2015), pp. 114–27.

88. S. R. Covey, *Principle-Centered Leadership* (New York: Simon & Schuster, 1990).

89. F. J. Yammarino, S. D. Dionne, C. A. Schriesheim, and F. Dansereau, "Authentic Leadership and Positive Organizational Behavior: A Meso, Multi-Level Perspective," *The Leadership Quarterly* 19, no. 6 (2008), pp. 693–707.

90. Johnson, "Best Practices in Ethical Leadership, 2007."

91. Johnson, "Best Practices in Ethical Leadership, 2007."

92. P. Kottler and N. Lee, *Corporate Social Responsibility: Doing the Most Good for Your Company and Your Cause* (New York: John Wiley, 2005).

93. S. A. Waddock and S. B. Graves, "The Corporate Social Performance–Financial Performance Link," *Strategic Management Journal* 18, no. 4 (1997), pp. 303–19.

94. J. P. Kotter and J. L. Heskett, *Corporate Culture and Performance* (New York: Free Press, 1992).

CHAPTER 6
Leadership Attributes

Introduction

Watch your thoughts, for they become words. Watch your words, for they become actions. Watch your actions, for they become habits. Watch your habits, for they become character. Watch your character, for it becomes your destiny.

Anonymous

In **Chapter 1** leadership was defined as "the process of influencing an organized group toward accomplishing its goals." Given this definition, one question that leadership researchers have tried to answer over the past century is whether certain personal attributes or characteristics help or hinder the leadership process. In other words, does athletic ability, height, personality, intelligence, or creativity help a leader to build a team, get results, or influence a group? Put in the context of national U.S. presidential elections, are candidates who win the primaries and eventually go on to become president smarter, more creative, more ambitious, or more outgoing than their less successful counterparts? Do these leaders act in fundamentally different ways than their followers, and are these differences in behavior owing to differences in their innate intelligence, certain personality traits, or creative ability? If so, could these same characteristics be used to differentiate successful from unsuccessful leaders, executives from first-line supervisors, or leaders from individual contributors? Questions such as these led to what was perhaps the earliest theory of leadership, the **Great Man theory**.[1]

The roots of the Great Man theory can be traced back to the early 1900s, when many leadership researchers and the popular press maintained that leaders and followers were fundamentally different. This led to hundreds of research studies that looked at whether certain personality traits, physical attributes, intelligence, or personal values differentiated leaders from followers. Ralph Stogdill was the first leadership researcher to summarize the results of these studies, and he came to two major conclusions. First, leaders were not qualitatively different from followers; many followers were just as tall, smart, outgoing, and ambitious as the people who were leading them. Second, some characteristics, such as intelligence, initiative, stress tolerance, responsibility, friendliness, and dominance, were modestly related to leadership success. In other words, people who were smart, hardworking, conscientious, friendly, or willing to take charge were often more successful at building teams and influencing a group to accomplish its goals than people who were less smart, lazy, impulsive, grumpy, or not fond of giving orders.[2] Having "the right stuff" did not guarantee leadership success, but it improved the odds of successfully influencing a group toward the accomplishment of its goals.

Everyone is a star in their own movie. Unfortunately, the you that you know is not worth knowing about.

R. T. Hogan, American psychologist

Subsequent reviews involving hundreds of more sophisticated studies came to the same two conclusions.[3] Although these reviews provided ample evidence that people with the right stuff were more likely to be successful as leaders, many leadership researchers focused solely on the point that leaders were not fundamentally different from followers. However, given that most people in leadership positions also play follower roles (supervisors report to managers, managers report to directors, and so forth), this finding is hardly surprising. This erroneous interpretation of the findings, along with the rising popularity of behaviorism in the 1960s and 1970s, caused many leadership researchers to believe that personal characteristics could not be used to predict future leadership success and resulted in a shift in focus toward other leadership phenomena. Not until the publication of seminal articles published in the 1980s and 1990s did intelligence and personality regain popularity with leadership researchers.[4, 5, 6] Because of these articles and subsequent leadership research, we now know a lot about how intelligence and various personality traits help or hinder leaders in their efforts to build teams and get results.[7, 8, 9, 10] This research also provided insight into the role of various situational and follower characteristics in affecting how a leader's intelligence and personality play out in the workplace.

> *There is an optical illusion about every person we ever meet. In truth, they are all creatures of a given temperament, which will appear in a given character, whose boundaries they will never pass: but we look at them, they seem alive, and we presume there is impulse in them. In the moment, it seems like an impulse; in the year, in the lifetime, it turns out to be a certain uniform tune, which the revolving barrel of the music box must play.*
>
> **Ralph Waldo Emerson, American essayist and poet**

The purpose of this chapter is to summarize what we currently know about personality, intelligence, and leadership. In other words, what does the research say about the leadership effectiveness of people who are smart, outgoing, innovative, and calm versus those who are dumb, shy, practical, and excitable? Do smarter people always make better leaders? Are there situations where tense and moody leaders are more effective than calm leaders? This chapter answers many common questions regarding the roles of personality, emotional intelligence, intelligence, and creativity in leadership effectiveness. As an overview, the chapter defines these four key attributes, reviews some important research findings for these attributes, and discusses the implications of this research for leadership practitioners.

Personality Traits and Leadership

What Is Personality?

Despite its common usage, Robert Hogan noted that the term **personality** is fairly ambiguous and has at least two quite different meanings.[11] One meaning is essentially a summation of past behavior and refers to the impression a person makes on others. This view of personality emphasizes a person's **public reputation** and reflects not only a description but also an evaluation of the person in the eyes of others. From the standpoint of leadership, this view of personality addresses two distinct issues: "What kind of leader or person is this?" and "Is this somebody I would like to work for or be associated with?" In a practical sense, this view of personality comes into play whenever you describe the person you work for to a roommate or friend. For example, you might describe him or her as pushy, honest, outgoing, impulsive, decisive, friendly, and independent. Furthermore, whatever impression this leader made on you, chances are others would use many of the same terms of description. In that vein, many Democratic voters would describe former U.S. president Barack Obama as smart, self-confident, poised, and articulate; and many Republican voters would describe U.S. president Donald Trump as a passionate, outspoken, and straight-talking leader who is willing to challenge the status quo. (See **Profiles in Leadership 6.1.**)

Angela Merkel

PROFILES IN LEADERSHIP 6.1

Angela Merkel is commonly acknowledged as the most powerful female in the world. Assuming office in November 2005, she is the first female to have been elected as the chancellor of Germany, the first person from the former German Democratic Republic to lead a unified Germany, only the third female to serve on the G7 council, and she is widely regarded as the de facto leader of the EU.

Merkel grew up in a rural community in Eastern Germany and showed an aptitude for math and science at an early age. A member of the communist youth movement in Eastern Germany, she went on to earn both undergraduate and doctoral degrees in physics, specializing in quantum chemistry. She spent much of the 1970s and 1980s in academic positions doing cutting-edge chemical research and publishing her work in such periodicals as *Molecular Physics* and *International Journal of Quantum Chemistry*. Chancellor Merkel did not get involved in politics until the fall of the Berlin Wall in 1989.

In the 1990s she was appointed to several ministerial positions in the Helmut Kohl government and was a young protégé of Chancellor Kohl's. A quick study, she learned the intricacies of national politics and international diplomacy under Kohl's mentorship and used this knowledge to run for and win national elections in Germany in 2005. Merkel currently is party chair of the Christian Democratic Union and leads a coalition of parties representing both the left and right wings of German politics.

Since being elected chancellor, Merkel has dealt with four major crises. The first occurred in 2010 when Greece almost defaulted on its loans. This was an existential crisis for the European Union, for if Greece defaulted on its loan payments then the viability of the euro, a currency adopted by 19 countries, would be called into question. Merkel gained the consensus of fellow EU members for a path forward to resolve the problem and set clear expectations for the Greek government's austerity plans. The second crisis happened a few years later when Russia took over Crimea. Merkel worked with a group of allies to develop a set of agreed-upon actions and sanctions to impose on Russia for its invasion of a foreign country. Third, in 2015 Merkel decided to allow more than a million refugees from the Middle East, Africa, and Asia to settle in Germany. Fourth, she has been instrumental in the EU's response to Brexit, the United Kingdom's decision to leave the European Union.

Because of Merkel's insatiable need for data, her preference for consensus, and her slow but steady approach, the German economy is now the largest in Europe and she was named *Time* magazine's person of the year in 2015. The Germans have even coined the term *merkeling* to describe her approach to problem solving.

Although Merkel's popularity has waxed and waned over the years, she has announced that she is resigning from the Chancellorship when her term expires in 2021. Given Chancellor Merkel's background, what can you discern about her public reputation, personality traits, values, and intelligence?

Sources: "Angela Merkel," IMDB, www.imdb.com/name/nm1361767/bio; "Person of the Year 2015," *Time*, http://time.com/time-person-of-the-year-2015-angela-merkel; "Angela Merkel," Biography, www.biography.com/political-figure/angela-merkel; and "Angela Merkel's Leadership: Now What?" *The Economist*, May 13, 2010, www.economist.com/europe/2010/05/13/now-what.

The second meaning of personality is concerned with **identity**. Whereas public reputation can be defined as how *others* perceive a particular individual, identity is concerned with how people see or define *themselves*.

For example, one person may see herself as outgoing, easy to get along with, considerate, planful, and organized (identity) whereas others may see this same individual as quiet, hard to know, factual, disorganized, and spontaneous (reputation). Research shows that there can be considerable gaps between one's public reputation and identity, and an interesting question is whether public reputation is more important than identity or vice versa. How one views oneself may be interesting, but overwhelming research shows that public reputation is a much better predictor of leadership success and effectiveness than identity.[12, 13] Because public reputation plays such a critical role in determining who gets hired, promoted, or selected to be on teams, people spend a lot of time and effort managing their public reputations. (See **Highlight 6.1**.)

> *Men acquire a particular quality by constantly acting a particular way. You become a just man by performing just actions, temperate by performing temperate actions, and brave by performing brave actions.*

Aristotle, Greek philosopher

Identity, Public Reputation, and Authenticity

HIGHLIGHT 6.1

Chapter 5 described Authentic Leadership, which is concerned with behaving in accordance to one's personal values. Given that personality can be defined in terms of identity and public reputation, there is an interesting relationship between these concepts and Authentic Leadership. Identity is concerned with how a person describes him or herself, so Authentic Leadership can be defined as the extent to which someone aligns his or her behavior with their identity. If a person sees herself as intelligent, ambitious, leader-like, and easy-going, then acting in a manner aligned with these self-perceptions would be a path to becoming an Authentic Leader. The problem here, like the problem with identity in general, is that self-perceptions can be wildly different from public reputation. A person may believe she is attractive, interesting, and worthy of attention, but if others find her boring and dull, then she is not likely to garner much of a following. It turns out that many people who see themselves as leadership legends in their own minds are often seen as "charismatically challenged" in the eyes of others. Paying attention to and managing one's public reputation is much more important than aligning behaviors with identity when it comes to a person's ability to engage and develop employees, build teams, and achieve results.

Sources: R. T. Hogan and S. Sherman, "Personality and the Nature of Human Nature," *The Science of Personality*, July 29, 2019, www.hoganassessments.com/personality-theory-and-the-nature-of-human-nature; D. Lusk, R. Sherman, and R. T. Hogan, "The Nature of Human Nature," *Talent Quarterly*, June 2019; S. B. Kaufman, "Authenticity Under Fire," *Scientific American*, June 14, 2019, https://blogs.scientificamerican.com/beautiful-minds/authenticity-under-fire; and T. Chamorro-Premuzic, "How to Work for a Boss Who Lacks Self-Awareness," *Harvard Business Review*, April 3, 2018, https://hbr.org/2018/04/how-to-work-for-a-boss-who-lacks-self-awareness.

Although there are many different personality theories, most of the research addressing the relationship between personality and leadership success and effectiveness has been based on the trait approach, and that emphasis is most appropriate here. **Traits** refer to recurring regularities or trends in a person's behavior, and the **trait approach** to personality maintains that people behave as they do because of the strengths of the traits they possess.[14, 15, 16, 17] Traits cannot be seen but can be inferred from consistent patterns of behavior and reliably measured by personality inventories. For example, the personality trait of conscientiousness differentiates leaders who tend to be hardworking and rule abiding from those who tend to be lazy and are more prone to break rules. Leaders getting higher scores on the trait of conscientiousness on personality inventories would be more likely to come to work on time, do a thorough job in completing work assignments, and rarely leave work early. We would also infer that leaders getting lower scores on the trait of conscientiousness would be more likely to be late to appointments, make impulsive decisions, or fail to follow through with commitments and achieve results.

Personality traits are useful concepts for explaining why people act fairly consistently from one situation to the next. This cross-situational consistency in behavior may be thought of as analogous to the seasonal weather patterns in different cities.[18, 19] We know that it is extremely cold and dry in Minneapolis in January and hot and humid in Hong Kong in August. Therefore, we can do a pretty good job of predicting what the weather will generally be like in Minneapolis in January, even though our predictions for any particular day will not be perfect. Although the average January temperature in Minneapolis hovers around 20°F, the temperature ranges from −30°F to 30°F on any single day in January. Similarly, knowing how two people differ on a particular personality trait can help us predict more accurately how they will tend to act in a variety of situations.

Just as various climate factors can affect the temperature on any single day, so can external factors affect a leader's behavior in any given situation. The trait approach maintains that a leader's behavior reflects an interaction between his or her personality traits and various situational factors. Traits play a particularly important role in determining how people behave in unfamiliar, ambiguous, or what we might call **weak situations**. By contrast, situations that are governed by clearly specified rules, demands, or organizational policies—**strong situations**—often minimize the effects that traits have on behavior.[20, 21, 22, 23, 24, 25]

The strength of the relationship between personality traits and leadership effectiveness is often inversely related to the relative strength of the situation; that is, personality traits are more closely related to leadership effectiveness in weak or ambiguous situations. Given the accelerated pace of change in most organizations today, it is likely that leaders will face even more unfamiliar and ambiguous situations in the future. Therefore, personality traits may play an increasingly important role in a leader's behavior. If organizations can accurately identify the personality traits of leadership and the individuals who possess them, they should be able to do a better job of promoting the right people into leadership positions. And if the right people are in leadership positions, the odds of achieving organizational success should improve dramatically. The next section describes some research efforts to identify those personality traits that help leaders build teams and get results through others. (See **Highlight 6.2**.)

A great leader's courage to fulfill his vision comes from passion, not position.

John Maxwell, author

Assessing Public Reputation

HIGHLIGHT 6.2

It turns out we spend a lot of time discussing the public reputations of others. Many of our conversations about roommates, friends, classmates, coworkers, bosses, significant others, celebrities, politicians, and sports figures involve judgments about how curious, outgoing, planful, impulsive, tense, humorous, hardworking, law abiding, considerate, smart, trustworthy, or creative they may be. Knowing a person's reputation is a good predictor of future behavior, so getting this right is critically important. So how can one evaluate someone's public reputation? It turns out that there are three common ways to do this. The first is to simply ask mutual friends whose opinions you trust. If four or five people essentially say the same thing about the person in question then you will probably have good insight about what the individual is like, and research shows there is more agreement than disagreement among observers when it comes to public reputation.

Another way to gain insight into someone's reputation is to review his or her social media presence, whether on reality TV, YouTube, Facebook, LinkedIn, Twitter, or reviews posted through any of a number of apps. Over the past few years research has shown these electronic signatures can reliably predict scores on the five **OCEAN** personality traits (described in the next section). People get fired from Uber for being terrible passengers or drivers, and Internet videos can quickly ruin the reputation someone spent years cultivating (an example would be Travis Kalanick, the former CEO of Uber). Because college selection committees and recruiters review social media as part of a selection or hiring process, applicants are now taking considerably more care crafting their social media presence. An interesting question is whether body cameras or temporary messages from applications like Snapchat provide more accurate insights into an applicant's personality than Facebook or LinkedIn.

A third way to assess public reputation is by taking personality tests. Well-designed personality measures provide takers with feedback on how they are "hardwired to behave" and likely to be perceived by others, and one of the biggest reasons leaders participate in formal development or coaching programs is to gain **self-awareness**. The focus of self-awareness is not to help leaders figure out who they are (that is, their identity) but rather how others see them (their public reputation). Gaining self-awareness is vitally important because (1) leaders are like everyone else, self-deluding (in other words, there is often a big gap between their identities and public reputation); (2) direct reports, particularly those keen on getting promoted, will often not tell the whole truth and share only the information that makes them look good; and (3) authority dynamics may cause staff to be reluctant to provide leaders with constructive feedback. Once leaders gain insight into how they are perceived by others, they can then decide whether they

want to change their public reputation and, if so, identify the behaviors they need to change to make this happen.

Sources: I. S. Oh, G. Wang, and M. K. Mount, "Validity of Observer Ratings of the Five-Factor Model of Personality Traits: A Meta-Analysis," *Journal of Applied Psychology* 96, no. 4 (2011), pp. 762–73; R. T. Hogan and T. Chamorro-Premuzic, "Personality and Career Success," in *The APA Handbook for Personality and Social Psychology, Vol. 4: Personality Processes and Individual Differences*, eds. M. Miculincer and P. R. Shaver (Washington, DC: American Psychological Association, 2015); *Sticks & Stones: Gossip, Reputation, and How Whispered Words Kill Careers* (Tulsa, OK: Hogan Press, 2012); *Who Are You?* (Tulsa, OK: Hogan Press, 2013); M. Barney, "A Victor in the Science Wars," *Forbes*, December 16, 2011, www.forbes.com/sites/infosys/2011/12/16/business-leadership-bte-2; T. Chamorro-Premuzic, "How Different Are Your Online and Offline Personalities?" *The Guardian*, September 24, 2015, www.theguardian.com/media-network/2015/sep/24/online-offline-personality-digital-identity; R. T. Hogan, "How to Flunk Uber," unpublished white paper, 2014; J. Stein, "Snapchat Faces the Public," *Time*, March 13, 2017, pp. 26–32; L. Penny, "Every Time We Take Uber We're Spreading Its Social Poison," *The Guardian*, March 3, 2017, www.theguardian/commentisfree/2017/mar/03/uber-spreading-social-poison-travis-kalanick; "Road Rage: The Woes of Uber's Boss," *The Economist*, March 4, 2017, pp. 51–52; G. J. Curphy, "The Misguided Romance of Authentic Leadership," LinkedIn, August 11, 2014, https://linkedin.com/pulse/20140811130045-36824143-the-misguided-romance-of-authentic-leadership; M. J. Del Giudice, M. Yanovsky, and S. E. Finn, "Personality Assessment and Feedback Practices among Executive Coaches: In Search of a Paradigm," *Journal of Consulting Psychology: Practice and Research* 66, no. 3 (2014), pp. 155–72; R. I. Sutton, "Some Bosses Live in a Fool's Paradise," *Harvard Business Review*, June 3, 2010, https://hbr.org/2010/06/some-bosses-live-in-a-fools-pa; O. Staley, "The No. 1 Thing CEOs Want from Executive Coaching? Self-Awareness," *Quartz*, May 2, 2016, https://qz.com/670841/the-no-1-thing-ceos-want-from-executive-coaching-self-awareness; R. M. Sapolsky, "When Computers Assess Personality Better Than We Do," *The Wall Street Journal*, July 25–26, 2015, p. C2; D. Winsborough, "Should I Use Social Media as a Selection Tool? Winsborough," www.winsborough.co.nz/blog/should-i-use-social-media-as-a-selection-tool-0; "Staff and Nonsense: Why Companies Are so Bad at Hiring," *The Economist*, May 11, 2019, p. 55; Z. Ihsan and A. Furnham, "The New Technologies in Personality Assessment: A Review," *Journal of Consulting Psychology: Practice and Research*, 70, no. 2 (2019), pp. 147–66; and T. Eurich, "What Self-Awareness Really Is (and How to Cultivate It)," *Harvard Business Review*, January 4, 2018, https://hbr.org/2018/01/what-self-awareness-really-is-and-how-to-cultivate-it.

The Five-Factor or OCEAN Model of Personality

Although personality traits provide a useful approach to describing distinctive, cross-situational behavioral patterns, one potential problem is the sheer number of traitlike terms available to describe another's stereotypical behaviors. As early as 1936 researchers identified more than 18,000 trait-related adjectives in a standard English dictionary.[26] Despite this large number of adjectives, research has shown that most of the traitlike terms people use to describe others' behavioral patterns can be reliably categorized into five broad personality dimensions. Historically this five-dimensional model was first identified as early as 1915 and independently verified in 1934, but over the years a number of researchers using diverse samples and assessment instruments have noted similar results.[27, 28, 29] Given the robustness of these findings, a compelling body of evidence appears to support these five dimensions of personality. These dimensions are referred to in personality literature as the **five-factor model (FFM) or OCEAN model of personality**, and most modern personality researchers endorse some version of this model.[30, 31, 32, 33, 34, 35, 36, 37]

At its core, the FFM or OCEAN model of personality is a categorization scheme. Most, if not all, of the personality traits that you would use to describe someone else could be reliably categorized into one of the five OCEAN personality dimensions. A description of the model can be found in **Table 6.1**. The five major dimensions include openness to experience, conscientiousness, extraversion, agreeableness, and neuroticism. The first of these dimensions, openness to experience, is concerned with curiosity, innovative thinking, assimilating new information, and being open to new experiences. Leaders higher in **openness to experience** tend to be imaginative, broad minded, and curious and are more strategic, big-picture thinkers; they seek new experiences through travel, the arts, movies, sports, reading, going to new restaurants, or learning about new cultures. Individuals lower in openness to experience tend to be more practical, tactical, and have narrower interests; they like doing things using tried-and-true ways rather than experimenting with new methods. Note that openness to experience is not the same thing as intelligence—smart people are not necessarily intellectually curious.

TABLE 6.1   The Five-Factor or OCEAN Model of Personality

Factor	Behaviors/Items
Openness to experience	I like traveling to foreign countries. I enjoy going to school.
Conscientiousness	I enjoy putting together detailed plans. I rarely get into trouble.
Extraversion	I like having responsibility for others. I have a large group of friends.
Agreeableness	I am a sympathetic person. I get along well with others.
Neuroticism	I remain calm in pressure situations. I take personal criticism well.

> *Persistence. Nothing in the world can take the place of persistence. Talent will not; nothing is more common than unsuccessful men with talent. Genius will not; unrewarded genius is almost a proverb. Education will not; the world is full of educated derelicts. Persistence and determination alone are omnipotent. "Press on" has solved and always will solve the problems of the human race.*

> **Calvin Coolidge, U.S. president, 1923–1929**

A key research question is whether people who are curious and big-picture thinkers are more effective leaders than those who are more pragmatic. Research has shown that openness to experience is an important component of leadership effectiveness and seems particularly important at higher organizational levels or for success in overseas assignments.[38, 39, 40, 41, 42, 43, 44] People with higher openness to experience scores take a more strategic approach to solving problems, and this can help CEOs and other senior leaders keep abreast of market trends, competitive threats, new products, and regulatory changes. And because people with higher openness to experience scores also like new and novel experiences, they often enjoy the challenges associated with living and leading in foreign countries. Nonetheless, there are many leadership positions where curiosity, innovation, and big-picture thinking are relatively unimportant. For example, production supervisors on assembly lines, store managers at McDonald's, or platoon leaders for the U.S. Army do not need to be particularly strategic. These jobs put a premium on pragmatic decision-making rather than on developing elegant solutions, so being higher in openness to experience in these roles can harm leadership effectiveness.

Conscientiousness concerns those behaviors related to people's approach to work. Leaders who are higher in conscientiousness tend to be planful, organized, and earnest, take commitments seriously, and rarely get into trouble. Those who are lower in conscientiousness tend to be more spontaneous, creative, impulsive, rule bending, and less concerned with following through with commitments. The characters Bart and Lisa Simpson from the television show *The Simpsons* provide a nice illustration of low- and high-conscientiousness trait scores. Lisa is organized, hardworking, and reliable and never gets into trouble; Bart is disorganized, mischievous, and lazy and rarely keeps promises. There is a wide body of research showing that individuals with higher conscientiousness scores are more likely to be effective leaders than those with lower scores. [45, 46, 47, 48, 49, 50, 51, 52, 53, 54, 55, 56]

> *We are given to the cult of personality; when things go badly we look for some messiah to save us. If by chance we think we have found one, it will not be long before we destroy him.*
>
> **Constantine Karamanlis, former Greek statesman**

In many ways conscientiousness may be concerned more with management than with leadership. That is because people with higher scores are planful, organized, goal oriented, and prefer structure; but they are also risk averse, uncreative, somewhat boring, and dislike change. Although the situation will determine how important these tendencies are for building teams and getting results, research has shown that conscientiousness is a good predictor of leadership potential. Along these lines, conscientiousness seems to be a particularly good predictor of leadership success in jobs that put a premium on following procedures, managing budgets, coordinating work schedules, monitoring projects, and paying attention to details. People having higher scores on conscientiousness would probably do well in the production supervisor, store manager, and platoon leader jobs described earlier but may not be as effective if leading teams made up of sales representatives, graphic designers, or musicians.

> *Question: How do you tell an extraverted engineer from an introverted engineer?*
> *Answer: Extraverted engineers look at your shoes when they are talking to you.*
>
> **Anonymous**

Extraversion involves behaviors that are more likely to be exhibited in group settings and are generally concerned with getting ahead in life.[57, 58, 59] Such behavioral patterns often appear when someone is trying to influence or control others, and individuals higher in extraversion come across to others as outgoing, competitive, decisive, outspoken, opinionated, and self-confident. Individuals lower in extraversion generally prefer to work by themselves and have relatively little interest in influencing or competing with others. Because leaders' decisiveness, competitiveness, and self-confidence can affect their ability to successfully influence a group, build a team, and get results, it is not surprising that leaders often have higher extraversion scores than nonleaders.[60, 61, 62, 63, 64, 65] You can see differences in people's standing on extraversion every time a group of people gets together. Some people in a group are going to be outgoing and will try to get the group to do certain things; others are more comfortable going along with rather than arguing over group activities.

> *What we're dealing with is a new class of bastard: the bro gone pro, the free-wheeling post Randian douchebag whose insecure sense of entitlement is the foundation of his business model.*
>
> **Laurie Penny, talking about Travis Kalanick**

This strong need to assume leadership positions in groups is often associated with taking risks, making decisions, and upward mobility. A key question is whether these extraverted behaviors are exhibited to facilitate team performance or for self-aggrandizement. There is a subset of leaders who demonstrate self-confidence, decisiveness, and risk taking for the sole purpose of getting promoted. These ambitious, upwardly mobile individuals could not care less about team or group results and are able to convince team members to complete high-visibility (but often low-impact) projects that enable them to move up the corporate ladder. There is another subset of leaders who demonstrate extraverted behaviors in order to help their groups to perform at higher levels. Because both subsets of leaders make strong first impressions, it will take time before people are able to differentiate between these two subsets of leaders. Too much extraversion can also be problematic, as these leaders do not take others' inputs into consideration, think they are the only ones capable of making decisions, and make overly risky decisions. Many times those with the highest extraversion scores make poor decisions about their projects or fail to get the people on their projects to work together effectively. Although possessing too much extraversion can be problematic, in general people who are more decisive, self-confident, and outgoing seem to be more effective leaders, and thus extraversion is an important measure of leadership potential.[66, 67] (See **Highlight 6.3**.)

Another OCEAN personality dimension is **agreeableness**, which concerns how one gets along with, as opposed to gets ahead of, others.[68, 69, 70, 71, 72] Individuals high in agreeableness come across to others as charming, diplomatic, warm, empathetic, approachable, and optimistic; those lower in agreeableness are more apt to appear as insensitive, socially clueless, grumpy, cold, and pessimistic. Agreeableness essentially concerns one's need for approval. Some people work hard to be liked by others, are known as being "a good guy," and are quite popular. Others would rather stick to the facts, no matter how uncomfortable, and do not care whether they are liked. The latter is often associated with jobs requiring the evaluation of others, such as judges, referees, police officers, or quality assurance representatives. Their unbridled ambition and insatiable quest for power can make it hard to discern, but there are characters in *Game of Thrones* who exhibit low versus high agreeableness scores. Joffrey Baratheon, Ramsay Bolton, and Sandor Clegane (aka The Hound) are mean spirited and could not care less about what others think of them. At the high end of agreeableness, Lord Varys is extremely manipulative but goes out of his way not to make any enemies, and Samwell Tarly comes across as a truly considerate and likable person.

Although people with high agreeableness trait scores are well liked and tend to be better at building teams than those with lower scores, they can struggle with getting results through others. This is because persons with higher scores believe relationships trump performance and often have trouble making unpopular decisions or dealing with conflict and performance issues, which can negatively erode the effectiveness of their teams. Research has shown that, because of these difficulties, agreeableness has had mixed results in predicting leadership effectiveness.[73, 74, 75, 76, 77]

Neuroticism is concerned with how people react to stress, change, failure, or personal criticism. Leaders lower in neuroticism tend to be thick-skinned, calm, and optimistic, tend not to take mistakes or failures personally, and hide their emotions; those higher in neuroticism are passionate, intense, thin-skinned, moody, and anxious and lose their tempers when stressed or criticized. Followers often mimic a leader's emotions or behaviors under periods of high stress, so leaders who are calm under pressure and thick-skinned can often help a group stay on task and work through difficult issues. Unfortunately the opposite is also true.

> *On far too many occasions I have had to remind people that leadership is a verb, not a noun.*
>
> **James Michael, organizational consultant**

Differences in neuroticism can be difficult to observe in predictable, routine situations but become readily apparent during times of uncertainty or crises. Under stress, those lower in neuroticism stay cool, calm, and collected, whereas those higher on this trait become nervous, tense, and emotional. Emotional volatility certainly can affect a person's ability to build teams and get results, and research has shown that neuroticism is another good predictor of leadership potential.[78, 79, 80, 81, 82, 83, 84, 85, 86, 87] Although lower neuroticism scores are generally associated with leadership effectiveness, people with low scores can struggle to rally the troops when extra effort is needed to achieve results or drive change. This is because these individuals are so flat emotionally that they have a hard time exhibiting any passion or enthusiasm. Charismatic leaders, by contrast, often have higher neuroticism scores.[88]

Leadership Success versus Effectiveness

HIGHLIGHT 6.3

Chapter 1 described the distinction between *successful* leaders (those who are driven to get promoted) and *effective* leaders (those who focus on engaging employees, building teams, and achieving results). One might think that career success and leadership effectiveness go hand in hand, but the personalities of those making it to the top of organizations can look quite different from those needed to build winning teams that achieve superior results. Many of those making it to the top, particularly in large bureaucratic organizations, cultivate public reputations of being loyal soldiers, doing whatever is asked, not making mistakes, not questioning decisions, making no enemies, building extensive networks, and building relationships with organizational power players. They flatter their bosses, do whatever they need to position themselves for promotion, and tend to see their direct reports as people to be exploited. From a personality perspective, successful leaders have low-neuroticism, high-extraversion, and high-agreeableness scores.

Effective leaders are more likely to believe in the **just world hypothesis**, which states that if one simply works hard and achieves superior results then good things will happen. As such, effective leaders spend little time networking or lobbying for promotions and have reputations for surrounding themselves with the right people,

painting a compelling vision of the future, motivating others, overcoming obstacles, and getting things done. They tend to have low to moderate neuroticism, extraversion, and agreeableness and higher conscientious and openness to experience scores.

Although most organizations want effective leaders, more often than not they promote successful leaders. This is the case because successful leaders spend a lot of time engaged in strategic sucking up whereas effective leaders keep their heads down and focus on getting things done. Which of these two types of leaders get promoted at your university or in your organization? Which of these two paths do you plan to pursue as you start your work career?

Sources: F. Luthans, *Organizational Behavior: An Evidence Based Approach*, 12th ed. (New York: McGraw-Hill Irwin, 2011); G. J. Curphy, "Key Differences between Successful and Effective Leaders," LinkedIn, March 14, 2014, www.linkedin.com/pulse/20140314142437-36824143-key-differences-between-successful-and-effective-leaders; G. J. Curphy, "Does High-Potential Success Lead to Organizational Failure?" LinkedIn, August 25, 2014, www.linkedin.com/pulse/20140825110125-36824143-does-high-potential-success-lead-to-organizational-failure; G. J. Curphy, "Stupid High-Potential Tricks," LinkedIn, September 8, 2015, www.linkedin.com/pulse/stupid-high-potential-tricks-gordon-gordy-curphy-phd; R. T. Hogan, G. J. Curphy, R. B. Kaiser, and T. Chamorro-Premuzic, "Leadership in Organizations," in *The Sage Handbook of Industrial, Work, and Organizational Psychology, Vol. 2: Organizational Psychology*, eds. N. Anderson, D. Ones, H. K. Sinangil, and C. Viswesvaran (London: Sage, in press); and J. Pfeffer, *Power: Why Some People Have It and Others Don't* (New York: HarperCollins, 2010).

Implications of the Five-Factor or OCEAN Model

The trait approach and the FFM or OCEAN model of personality give leadership researchers and practitioners several useful tools and insights. Personality traits help researchers and practitioners explain leaders' and followers' tendencies to act in consistent ways over time. They tell us why some leaders appear to be dominant versus deferent, outspoken versus quiet, planful versus spontaneous, warm versus cold, and so forth. Note that the behavioral manifestations of personality traits are often exhibited automatically and without much conscious thought. People high in extraversion, for example, will often maneuver to influence or lead whatever groups or teams they are a part of without even thinking about it. Although personality traits predispose us to act in certain ways, we can nonetheless learn to modify our behaviors through experience, feedback, and reflection.

> *Ascending to the top of any organization is a political game. Building a winning organization is a leadership game.*
>
> **R. T. Hogan and Tim Judge, leadership researchers**

As shown in **Figure 6.1**, personality traits are a key component of behavior, fairly consistent over time, and difficult to change. Moreover, because personality traits tend to be stable over the years and the behavioral manifestations of traits occur somewhat automatically, it is important for leaders and leaders-to-be to have insight into their personalities. For example, consider a leader who is relatively high in the trait of neuroticism and is deciding whether to accept a high-stress/high-visibility job. On the basis of his personality trait scores, we might predict that this leader could be especially sensitive to criticism and could be moody and prone to emotional outbursts. If the leader understood that he may have issues dealing with stress and criticism, he could choose not to take the position, modify the situation to reduce the level of stress, or learn techniques for effectively dealing with these issues. A leader who lacked this self-insight would probably make poorer choices and have more difficulties coping with the demands of this position.[89]

The OCEAN model has proven useful in several other ways. Most personality researchers currently embrace some form of this model because it has provided a useful scheme for categorizing the findings of the personality–leadership performance research.[90, 91, 92, 93, 94] Because research has shown personality to be an effective measure of leadership potential, organizations now use the results of OCEAN personality assessments for hiring new leaders, for giving leaders developmental feedback about various personality traits, and as a key component when promoting leaders.[95, 96, 97, 98, 99]

FIGURE 6.1 The Building Blocks of Skills

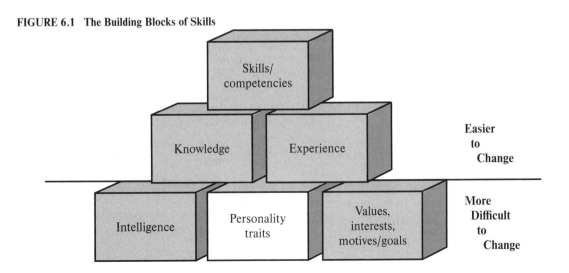

One advantage of the OCEAN model is that it is a useful method for profiling leaders. An example of a school principal's results on an OCEAN personality assessment can be found in **Figure 6.2**. According to this profile, this leader will generally come across to others as self-confident, goal-oriented, competitive, outgoing, eager to be the center of attention, but also distractible and a poor listener (high extraversion); optimistic, resilient, and calm under pressure (low neuroticism); reasonably warm and approachable (medium agreeableness); moderately planful, rule-abiding, and earnest (medium conscientiousness); and a pragmatic, tactical thinker (low openness to experience). Other leaders will have different behavioral tendencies, and knowing this type of information *before* someone is hired or promoted into a leadership position can help improve the odds of organizational success. (See **Highlight 6.4**.)

FIGURE 6.2 Example OCEAN Profile

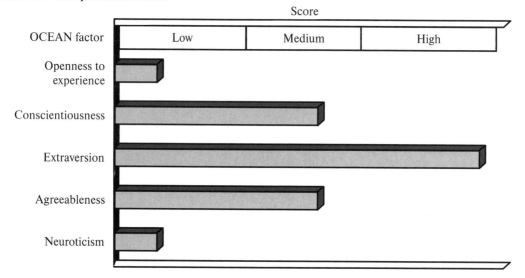

Personality and Life

HIGHLIGHT 6.4

Many organizations currently use personality testing as part of their process for hiring leaders or in leadership development programs. Despite their prevalence in both the private and public sector, there is still some controversy surrounding the use of personality testing in organizational settings. Some of the arguments against using personality testing are that (1) personality test scores are unrelated to job performance; (2) personality tests are biased or "unethical"; and (3) personality test results can be faked.

These are important questions: If personality test scores are biased, are unrelated to job performance, and can be faked, there would be little reason to use them in work settings. However, a comprehensive review of personality research reveals the following:

- Personality traits predict overall managerial effectiveness, promotion rates, and managerial-level attainment.

- Personality traits predict leader success and effectiveness.

- CEO personality traits predict company financial performance.

- Personality traits predict expatriate performance.

- Personality traits predict career success.

- Personality traits predict effort, persistence, creativity, and willingness to help others.

- Personality traits predict overall job performance across virtually all job types.

- Personality traits predict absenteeism and other counterproductive work behaviors.

- Personality traits predict job and career satisfaction.

- Personality traits predict mortality rates, divorce, alcohol and drug use, health behaviors, and occupational attainment.

- Personality test scores predict teamwork and team performance.

- Personality test scores yield similar results for protected groups. In other words, males, females, African Americans, Hispanics, and Asian Americans generally score the same on personality tests.

- Personality tests results can be faked to some extent, but the degree to which test scores are faked depends on the test setting and administration. Faking, however, does not seem to affect the overall relationships between personality test results and work outcomes and can be detected and corrected.

- Personality tests suffer less from adverse impact and faking than traditional selection techniques, such as résumés and job interviews.

These findings show that personality tests can help organizations hire leaders who have the potential to be effective and can help leaders hire followers who are more likely to be successful. The arguments against the use of personality testing simply do not stand up to the facts, and because of these findings there has been a renewed interest in personality among leadership researchers.

Sources: L. M. Hough and F. L. Oswald, "Personality Testing and Industrial–Organizational Psychology: Reflections, Progress, and Prospects," *Industrial and Organizational Psychology: Perspectives on Science and Practice* 1, no. 3 (2008), pp. 272–90; G. J. Curphy, *Hogan Assessment Systems Certification Workshop Training Manual* (Tulsa, OK: Hogan Assessment Systems, 2003); G. J. Curphy, "Comments on the State of Leadership Prediction," in *Predicting Leadership: The Good, the Bad, the Indifferent, and the Unnecessary*, J. P. Campbell and M. J. Benson (chairs), symposium conducted at the 22nd Annual Conference for the Society of Industrial and Organizational Psychology, New York, April 2007; R. T. Hogan and T. Chamorro-Premuzic, "Personality and Career Success," in *APA Handbook of Personality and Social Psychology*, vol. 3, eds. L. Cooper and R. Larsen (Washington, D.C.: American Psychological Association, 2012); D. S. Chiaburu, I. S. Oh, C. M. Berry, N. Li, and R. G. Gardner, "The Five-Factor Model of Personality Traits and Organizational Citizenship Behaviors: A Meta-Analysis," *Journal of Applied Psychology* 96, no. 6 (2011), pp. 1140–65; J. Antonakis, D. V. Day, and B. Schuns, "Leadership and Individual Differences: At the Cusp of a Renaissance," *The Leadership Quarterly* 23, no. 4, (2012), pp. 643–50; A. E. Colbert, T. A. Judge, D. Choi, and G. Wang, "Assessing the Trait Theory of Leadership Using Self and Observer Ratings of Personality: The Mediating Role of Contributions to Group Success," *The Leadership Quarterly* 23, no. 4, (2012), pp. 670–85; M. O'Connell, "The Five Biggest Myths about Pre-Employment Assessments," PSI, July 7, 2015, https://blog.psionline.com/talent/the-5-biggest-myths-about-pre-employment-assessments; D. Winsborough and T. Chamorro-Premuzic, "Great Teams Are about Personalities, Not Just Skills," *Harvard Business Review*, January 25, 2017, https://hbr.org/2017/01/great-teams-are-about-personalities-not-just-skills; I. D. Grow, S. N. Kaplan, D. F. Larcker, and A. A. Zakolyukina, "CEO Personality and Firm Policies," *Working Paper 22345* (Cambridge, MA: National Bureau of Economic Research, July 2016); R. I. Damian, M. Spengler, A. Sutu, and B. W. Roberts, "Sixteen Going on Sixty-Six: A Longitudinal Study of Personality Stability and Change across 50 Years," *Journal of Personality and Social Psychology* 117, no. 3 (2018), pp. 674–95; P. D. Harms and B. J. Brummel, "The Five Big Mistakes," *Talent Quarterly*, August 2019; A. Furnham, "Why do Personality Tests Fail at Selection?" Hogan Assessments, April 23, 2019, www.hoganassessments.com/why-do-personality-tests-fail-at-selection; A. Furnham, "Twelve Myths about Psychometric Tests That You Have Fallen For," Chartered Management Institute, November 30, 2017, www.managers.org.uk/insights/news/2017/november/twelve-myths-about-psychometric-tests-that-youve-fallen-for; and R. Sherman, "Five Marketing Trends in the New Era of Assessment and Why You Shouldn't Fall for Them," Hogan Assessments, October 14, 2019, www.hoganassessments.com/five-marketing-trends-in-the-new-era-of-assessment-and-why-you-shouldnt-fall-for-them.

People believe what they want to believe and disregard the rest.

Paul Simon and Art Garfunkel, musicians

Another advantage of the OCEAN model is that it appears universally applicable across cultures.[100, 101, 102, 103, 104, 105] People from Asian, Western European, Middle Eastern, Eastern European, and South American cultures seem to use the same five personality dimensions to categorize, profile, or describe others. Not only do people from different cultures describe others using the same five-factor framework—these dimensions all seem to predict job and leadership performance across cultures. For example, in a comprehensive review of the research, Salgado reported that all five of the OCEAN dimensions predicted blue-collar, professional, and managerial performance in various European countries.[106] But the strength of the personality–job performance relationship depends on the particular job. Some jobs, such as sales, put a premium on interpersonal skills and goal orientation (extraversion and agreeableness), whereas manufacturing jobs put more of a premium on planning and abiding by safety and productivity rules (conscientiousness). Researchers often get much stronger personality–job performance relationships when the personality traits being measured have some degree of job-relatedness.[107, 108, 109, 110] (See **Profiles in Leadership 6.2**.)

Robert "RT" Hogan

PROFILES IN LEADERSHIP 6.2

Robert Hogan has arguably been one of the most prominent and influential leadership researchers for the past 40 years. His papers and books are among the most widely cited in the behavioral sciences, and he is regularly asked to give keynote presentations to government, business, and academic audiences. His personality inventories are widely recognized as "best in class" and are used around the world to hire and develop everyone from truck drivers to CEOs. At this point well over 3 million individuals have taken one or more Hogan assessments, and the popularity of these instruments continues to grow.

Hogan grew up in East Los Angeles and was the first in his family to attend college. He attended the University of California, Los Angeles, and obtained an engineering degree on a Navy ROTC scholarship before spending the next seven years working on a destroyer in the U.S. Navy. It was in the Navy that Hogan became interested in leadership and psychology; he read all he could about Freud, Jung, and other promi-

nent psychologists while at sea. After leaving the Navy, Hogan became a parole officer for the Los Angeles Police Department. As a parole officer, Hogan realized that the process used to determine a juvenile's fate was based completely on the whim of his or her parole officer and that there was no standardized system or process for keeping these individuals out of trouble. Thinking there had to be a better way to do this, Hogan decided to attend the University of California, Berkeley, to obtain a PhD in personality psychology. While working on his graduate degree, Hogan conducted personality testing on police officers and devised selection systems to combat unfair hiring and promotion practices. After graduation he spent some time as a professor at Johns Hopkins University before becoming a professor at the University of Tulsa. Hogan eventually became chair of the psychology department at the University of Tulsa while starting his own company.

A true entrepreneur, RT started Hogan Assessment Systems; the company now has over 100 full-time employees and distributor partnerships around the globe. Hogan Assessment Systems has been a great way for RT to mentor and develop graduate students and to help junior faculty get published. He has also been able to leverage the data they have collected through their instruments to publish hundreds of articles and books about personality and leadership, many of which can be found in the most prestigious psychology journals. One of the authors of this textbook, Gordy Curphy, credits Hogan with having a bigger impact on his thinking about leadership and success as a leadership consultant than anyone else with whom he has worked.

Source: R. B. Kaiser, "Robert Hogan and the Revival of Personality Theory and Assessment," LinkedIn, December 21, 2015, www.linkedin.com/pulse/robert-hogan-proud-say-hes-been-my-mentor-12-years-jeremy-sutton.

An Alternative to Traits: Personality Types

Traits are not the only way to describe stereotypical behaviors. An alternative framework to describe the differences in people's day-to-day behavioral patterns is through **types**, or in terms of a **personality typology**. Whereas each personality factor in the OCEAN model (such as neuroticism) is conceptualized as a continuum along which people can vary, types are usually thought of as relatively *discrete categories*.

This distinction may become clearer with the example below. Let us take the trait of dominance and compare it with a hypothetical construct we will call a "dominant type." The upper line refers to the continuum of the trait defined at one end by submissiveness and at the other end by dominance. The trait scores of four different individuals—Jim, John, Joe, and Jack—are indicated on the scale. You can infer from their relative positions on the scale that John is more like Joe than he is like either Jim or Jack. Now look at the lower line. This refers to the typology of submissive and dominant types. The theory behind personality types suggests that John is more like Jim than Joe, and Joe is more like Jack than John.

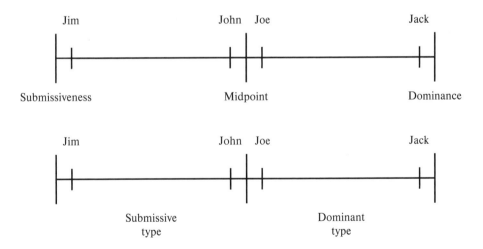

The most popular personality type assessment is the **Myers-Briggs Type Indicator (MBTI)**, and over 2 million people take the test every year.[111] According to Myers and Myers,[112] there are four basic preference dimensions in which people can differ. These four dimensions include extraversion–introversion (outgoing vs. quiet), sensing–intuition (detail vs. big picture oriented), thinking–feeling (rational vs. emotional-based decision-making), and judging–perceiving (planful vs. flexible approach to work). These four dimensions are bipolar, meaning that individuals generally prefer being either, say, extraverted or introverted. The results for each of the four bipolar dimensions are used to create 16 psychological types. For example, someone with high preferences for introversion, sensing, thinking, and judging would be categorized as an ISTJ type. Another with high preferences for extraversion, intuition, feeling, and perceiving would be an ENFP type. Preference advocates believe that individuals within any particular type are more similar to each other than they are to individuals in any of the other 15 types.[113, 114, 115]

Despite its popularity, leadership practitioners need to be aware of the MBTI's many limitations. First, the four preference dimensions omit critical aspects of personality, such as neuroticism.[116] Second, types can and do change over time. Some research indicates that at least one letter in the four-letter type may change in half the people taking the test in as little as five weeks.[117] Data also show major developmental changes in distribution of types with age.[118] It is difficult to see how the MBTI can be used to select leaders and followers if types change on a frequent basis. Third, the test suffers from the **Forer effect**, which occurs when people are provided with descriptive statements that are personally flattering but so vague that they could apply to virtually anyone. You can see the Forer effect at play in any astrological chart, and the MBTI 16 type descriptions are not all that different. Everyone may believe they are beautiful in their own way, but more often than not their public reputation (how others see them) does not match their personality type descriptions. Another serious problem is that the MBTI dimensions and types are unrelated to career success or leadership effectiveness, and there is no reputable research showing the MBTI predicts any of the outcomes listed in **Highlight 6.5**.[119, 120, 121, 122, 123, 124]

Positive Psychology and Strengths-Based Leadership

HIGHLIGHT 6.5

Much of traditional psychology has focused on the diagnosis and treatment of mental disorders. Positive psychology looks at the other end of the mental health continuum and asks what people can do to promote genius, talent, competence, and happiness. Rather than worrying about what is going wrong, what would happen if people thought only about what is going right? Would this approach result in more career success, higher incomes, and greater satisfaction with life? Some people, such as Norman Vincent Peale, Joel Osteen, and Tony Robbins have developed loyal followings and made millions of dollars by emphasizing the positive. This approach has proved so popular that it has spilled over to the leadership arena, and one way it has done so is known as **strengths-based leadership**.

The strengths-based leadership approach is predicated on three tenets, which are to (1) get clarity about what a person is good at, (2) find jobs or tasks that leverage each person's strengths, and (3) minimize the time spent improving weaknesses, as this negatively impacts overall effectiveness. The Strengths-Finder 2.0 assessment is a personality-like tool that helps leaders identify their top five strengths (that is, traits). The authors of this assessment believe the most effective leaders spend the majority of their time doing the activities in which they excel and surrounding themselves with followers whose strengths make up for their shortcomings.

Although this approach is intuitively appealing, as leaders need to do only what they are good at and can ignore or staff around their shortcomings, there are five problems with strengths-based leadership. First, what leaders believe to be their own strengths may not match up to their public reputations. A self-rated Strengths-Finder 2.0 assessment may indicate a particular leader is good at five things, but people who know the leader well could think there are five other things the leader is good at. Thus, the leader could spend all his or her time doing the wrong activities. Second, the strengths-based approach can become a convenient excuse for narcissism; people may think they are really good at X, Y, and Z and as a result believe they should only have to do X, Y, and Z. Although the job requires the person to do tasks A, B, and C, he or she may not do these activities because they do not fit with the person's "strengths." Third, simply ignoring weaknesses will not make them go away. If a leader is not very good at visioning, building teams, or inspiring others, then it can be hard to staff around these short-comings. Fourth, situations are in a constant state of flux; leaders get new bosses, are assigned new tasks or responsibilities, are promoted, move to different divisions or companies, and more. Strengths-oriented behaviors that are advantageous in some situations often turn out to be liabilities in others. Leaders get new bosses, are assigned new tasks or responsibilities, are promoted, move to different divisions or companies, and more. Fifth, there is ample research to show that overleveraging strengths can result in managerial incompetence. Leaders who are naturally charming can become manipulative, and those who are detail oriented can become micromanagers when leveraging their strengths. Many leaders prescribing to the strengths-based approach tend to overdo the approach and alienate their teams as a result. Leaders should have insight into their strengths, but the best leaders are those who understand the implications of overusing their strengths and who work on improving their weaknesses.

Because of these many problems, it should come as no surprise that scientific studies have not shown the strengths-based approach to predict any of the outcomes listed in **Highlight 6.4**.

Sources: M. E. P. Seligman and M. Csikszentmihalyi, "Positive Psychology: An Introduction," *American Psychologist* 55, no. 1 (2000), pp. 5–14; T. Rath and B. Conchie, *Strengths-Based Leadership: Great Leaders, Teams, and Why People Follow* (New York: Gallup, 2009); J. Asplund, S. J. Lopez, T. Hodges, and J. Harter, *The Clifton Strengths-Finder 2.0 Technical Report: Development and Validation* (New York: Gallup, 2009); R. B. Kaiser and D. V. Overfield, "Strengths, Strengths Overused, and Lopsided Leadership," *Consulting Psychology Journal* 63, no. 2 (2011), pp. 89–109; R. B. Kaiser and J. Hogan, "Personality, Leader Behavior, and Overdoing It," *Consulting Psychology Journal* 63, no. 4 (2011), pp. 219–42; H. Le, I. S. Oh, S. B. Robbins, R. Ilies, E. Holland, and P. Westrick, "Too Much of a Good Thing: Curvilinear Relationships between Personality Traits and Job Performance," *Journal of Applied Psychology* 96, no. 1 (2011), pp. 113–33; T. Chamorro-Premuzic, "Strengths-Based Coaching Can Actually Weaken You," *Harvard Business Review*, January 4, 2016, https://hbr.org/2016/01/strengths-based-coaching-can-actually-weaken-you; G. Karris, "The Danger of the Strengths-finder Test," March 24, 2016, https://stepoutoftherace.com/strengthsfinder-test-danger; "Too Much of a Good Thing: Leaders Need to Learn to Beware Their Strengths," *The Economist*, June 8, 2013, p. 72; M. Loftus, "When Virtue Becomes Vice," *Psychology Today*, October 2013, pp. 52–60; and G. J. Curphy, "Strengths, Jedi Mind Tricks, and Leadership Development," LinkedIn, January 23, 2016, www.linkedin.com/pulse/strengths-jedi-mind-tricks-leadership-development-curphy-phd.

Emotional Intelligence and Leadership

What Is Emotional Intelligence?

There is no single entity called EQ (emotional intelligence quotient) as people have defined it. One sympathetic interpretation of what journalists were saying is that there were a dozen unrelated things, which collectively might predict more than intelligence, things like warmth, optimism, and empathy. But there was nothing new about that. Instead, the story became this fabulous new variable that is going to outpredict intelligence. There is no rational basis for saying that.

John Mayer, EQ researcher

So far we have discussed the role personality traits play in a leader's day-to-day behavioral patterns, but we have not discussed the role emotions play in leadership success and effectiveness. To put it differently, do moods affect a person's ability to get promoted, build teams, or get results through others? Moods and emotions are continually at play at work, yet most people are hesitant to discuss moods with anybody other than close friends. It also appears that moods can be contagious, in that the moods of leaders often affect followers in both positive and negative ways. And charismatic or transformational leaders use emotions as the catalyst for achieving better-than-expected results (see **Chapter 15**). Given the importance and prevalence of emotions in the workplace, there should be a wealth of research regarding mood and leadership effectiveness, but this is not the case. Researchers have begun to seriously examine the role of emotions in leadership only over the past 25 years.

The relationship between leaders' emotions and their effects on teams and outcomes became popularized by researcher Daniel Goleman with the publication of the book *Emotional Intelligence.*[125] But what is emotional intelligence (EQ), and how is it the same as or different from personality traits or types or the three types of intelligence described later in this chapter? Unfortunately there appear to be at least four major definitions of **emotional intelligence**. The term *emotional intelligence* can be attributed to two psychologists, Peter Salovey and John Mayer, who studied why some bright people fail to be successful. Salovey and Mayer discovered that many of them run into trouble because of their lack of interpersonal sensitivity and skills, and defined emotional intelligence as a group of mental abilities that help people to recognize their own feelings and those of others.[126, 127] Reuven Bar-On believed that emotional intelligence was another way of measuring human effectiveness and defined it as a set of 15 abilities necessary to cope with daily situations and get along in the world.[128] Rick Aberman defined *emotional intelligence* as the degree to which thoughts, feelings, and actions were aligned. According to Aberman, leaders are more effective and "in the zone" when their thoughts, feelings, and actions are perfectly aligned.[129, 130] Goleman, who is also a science writer for the *New York Times,* substantially broadened these definitions and summarized some of this work in his books *Emotional Intelligence* and *Working with Emotional Intelligence.*[131, 132] Goleman argued that success in life is based more on one's self-motivation, persistence in the face of frustration, mood management, ability to adapt, and ability to empathize and get along with others than on one's IQ. EQ has proven to be an influential concept over the past 20 years, and *Time* magazine touted *Emotional Intelligence* as one of the top 25 most influential management books of all time.[133] **Table 6.2** compares the Salovey and Mayer, Bar-On, and Goleman models of emotional intelligence.

TABLE 6.2   **Ability and Mixed Models of Emotional Intelligence**

Ability Model	Mixed Models	
Mayer, Salovey, and Caruso	**Goleman et al.**	**Bar-On**
Perceiving emotions	Self-awareness	Intrapersonal
	Emotional awareness	Self-regard
	Accurate self-assessment	Emotional self-awareness
	Self-confidence	Assertiveness
		Independence
		Self-actualization
Managing emotions	Self-regulation	Adaptability
	Self-control	Reality testing
	Trustworthiness	Flexibility
	Conscientiousness	Problem-solving
	Adaptability	
	Innovation	

Ability Model	Mixed Models	
Using emotions	Motivation	Stress management
	Achievement	Stress tolerance
	Commitment	Impulse control
	Initiative	
	Optimism	
Understanding emotions	Empathy	Interpersonal
	Understanding others	Empathy
	Developing others	Social responsibility
	Service orientation	Interpersonal relationship
	Diversity	
	Political awareness	General mood
		Optimism
	Social skills	Happiness
	Influence	
	Communication	
	Conflict management	
	Leadership	
	Change catalyst	
	Building bonds	
	Collaboration/cooperation	
	Team capabilities	

Sources: R. Bar-On, *Emotional Quotient Inventory* (North Tonawanda, NY: Multi-Health Systems, 2001); D. Goleman, *Working with Emotional Intelligence* (New York: Bantam Doubleday Dell, 1998); D. R. Caruso, J. D. Mayer, and P. Salovey, "Emotional Intelligence and Emotional Leadership," in *Multiple Intelligences and Leadership*, ed. R. E. Riggio, S. E. Murphy, and F. J. Pirozzolo (Mahwah, NJ: Lawrence Erlbaum Associates, 2002), pp. 55–57; and Consortium for Research on Emotional Intelligence in Organizations (CREIO), www.eiconsortium.org.

Although these definitions can cause confusion for people interested in learning more about emotional intelligence, it appears that these four definitions of EQ can be broken down into two models: an ability model and a mixed model of emotional intelligence.[134, 135] The ability model focuses on how emotions affect how leaders think, decide, plan, and act. This model defines emotional intelligence as four separate but related abilities, which include (1) the ability to accurately perceive one's own and others' emotions; (2) the ability to generate emotions to facilitate thought and action; (3) the ability to accurately understand the causes of emotions and the meanings they convey; and (4) the ability to regulate one's emotions. According to Caruso, Mayer, and Salovey, some leaders might be good at perceiving emotions and leveraging them to get results through others but have difficulties regulating their own emotions. Or they could be good at understanding the causes of emotions but not as good at perceiving others' emotions. The ability model is not intended to be an all-encompassing model of leadership, but rather supplements the OCEAN model of personality.[136, 137] Just as leaders differ in neuroticism or agreeableness, so do they differ in their ability to perceive and regulate emotions. The ability model of EQ is helpful because it allows researchers to determine if EQ is in fact a separate ability and whether it can predict leadership effectiveness apart from the OCEAN personality model and cognitive abilities.

The Goleman and Bar-On definitions of EQ fall into the mixed-model category. These researchers believe emotional intelligence includes not only the abilities outlined in the previous paragraph but also a number of other attributes. As such, the mixed model provides a much broader, more comprehensive definition of emotional intelligence. A quick review of **Table 6.2** shows that the attributes of emotional intelligence are qualities that most leaders should have, and Goleman, Boyatzis, and McKee maintain that leaders need more or less all of these attributes to be emotionally intelligent.[138, 139, 140] Moreover, the mixed model of emotional intelligence has been much more popular with human resource professionals and in the corporate world than the ability model. But does the mixed model really tell us anything different from what we already know? More specifically, is the mixed model different from the OCEAN personality model? Research shows that the mixed model assesses the same characteristics as the OCEAN model and is no more predictive of job performance and other important job outcomes than OCEAN personality assessments.[141, 142, 143, 144, 145, 146, 147, 148] Goleman and Bar-On deserve credit for popularizing the notion that noncognitive abilities are important predictors of leadership success. But on the negative side, they also maintain that they have discovered something completely new and do not give enough credit to the 100 years of personality research that underlie many attributes in the mixed model. (See **Profiles in Leadership 6.3**.)

Scott Rudin

PROFILES IN LEADERSHIP 6.3

Few people know who Scott Rudin is, but many have seen his work. Rudin has been a Hollywood movie producer for over 35 years and has produced such movies as *The Girl with the Dragon Tattoo, There Will Be Blood, No Country for Old Men, Moonrise Kingdom, The Social Network, The Queen, Team America: World Police, Zoolander, The School of Rock, Notes on a Scandal, The Grand Budapest Hotel, ex Machina, Fences*, and many others, as well as popular theater productions (*The Book of Mormon*) and television shows (*Silicon Valley*). He is the first producer to have won Emmy, Grammy, Oscar, and Tony awards, among others. Collectively his films have generated over $4 billion in sales.

Rudin also has the reputation for being the most difficult boss to work for in Hollywood. It is estimated that he has fired more than 250 assistants over the past five years. His caustic rants, shrieking threats, impulsive firings, and revolving door for assistants are legendary. For example, he allegedly once fired an assistant for bringing in the wrong breakfast muffin and is attributed with the following quotes:

"Don't ever f–king think–I hired you from the neck down."

"This is a new level of stupid."

"You have three things to do: answer the phone, listen to me and die."

Rudin describes his own leadership style as a cross between Attila the Hun and Miss Jean Brodie, and it is rumored that the role of Miranda Priestly in *The Devil Wears Prada* was modeled loosely on him.

An extreme micromanager, Rudin is involved with every detail of the films he is producing. Because he is producing several films at any one time, it is not unusual for Rudin to make over 400 calls in a single day. Rudin's assistants start their days at 6:00 a.m. with a 30-page annotated list of phone calls that are to be set up that day. During the day assistants will also do anything from picking up dry cleaning to answering phones, scheduling appointments, arranging travel, buying birthday presents, dropping off kids, and so on—you name it, the assistant does it. So why do assistants put up with Rudin? The hours are long but the pay is good—most interns make $70,000 to $150,000 per year. More important, aides who survive get a chance to rub shoulders with A-list talent and learn the ins and outs of the movie business. Plus the opportunities for advancement for those who survive are good—many of Rudin's aides have themselves become movie producers.

Given this background, what personality traits help Rudin to produce successful movies? Does he have any overused strengths? How would you rate Rudin's emotional intelligence?

Sources: K. Kelly and M. Marr, "Boss-Zilla!" *The Wall Street Journal*, September 24–25, 2005, p. A1; E. Gould, "New York's Worst Bosses: Scott Rudin," *Gawker*, March

13, 2007, http://gawker.com/243908/new-yorks-worst-bosses-scott-rudin; M. Callahan, "The Man Known as Hollywood's Biggest A-Hole," *Page Six*, December 14, 2014, http://pagesix.com/2014/12/14/the-man-known-as-hollywoods-biggest-a-hole; and R. Gustini, "The Four Types of Scot Rudin Temper Tantrums," *The Atlantic*, December 2011, www.theatlantic.com/entertainment/archive/2011/12/four-types-scott-rudin-temper-tantrums/334726.

Can Emotional Intelligence Be Measured and Developed?

The publication of *Emotional Intelligence* has encouraged an industry of books, training programs, and assessments related to measurement and development of emotional intelligence. Mayer, Salovey, and Caruso's Emotional Intelligence Test (MSCEIT) is a measure of the ability model of emotional intelligence; it asks subjects to recognize the emotions depicted in pictures, what moods might be helpful in certain social situations, and so forth.[149, 150] Bar-On has self, self–other, youth, and organizational measures of emotional intelligence, such as the Bar-On Emotional Quotient–360 or EQi-S.[151]

The Emotional Competence Inventory (ECi), developed by Goleman, consists of 10 questionnaires. These questionnaires are completed by the individual and nine others; the responses are aggregated and given to the participant in a feedback report. Because these researchers have defined emotional intelligence differently and use a different process to assess EQ, it is not surprising that these instruments often provide leaders with conflicting results.[152] Nevertheless, the U.S. Air Force Recruiting Service has used an emotional intelligence assessment to screen potential recruiters and found that candidates scoring higher on the attributes of assertiveness, empathy, happiness, self-awareness, and problem-solving were much less likely to turn over prematurely in the position and had a 90 percent chance of meeting their recruiting quotas.[153]

One issue that most EQ researchers agree on is that emotional intelligence can be developed. Goleman and Aberman have developed one- to five-day training programs to help leaders improve their emotional intelligence; Bar-On has developed 15 e-learning modules that are available at EQUniversity.com. One big adopter of EQ training has been the sales staff at American Express Financial Advisors (AEFA). Leaders at AEFA discovered that the company had a well-respected set of investment and insurance products for customers, but many sales staff were struggling with how to respond to the emotions exhibited by clients during sales calls. Moreover, the best salespeople seem to be better able to "read" their clients' emotions and respond in a more empathetic manner. Since 1993 more than 5,500 sales staff and 850 sales managers at AEFA have attended a five-day training program to better recognize and respond to the emotions exhibited by clients. AEFA found that sales staff attending this program increased annual sales by an average of 18.1 percent, whereas those who did not attend training achieved only a 16.1 percent increase. These differences are not very big and do not provide strong support that the EQ training content adds value over and above five days of sales training.[154]

> The essential difference between emotion and reason is that emotion leads to action while reason leads to conclusions.
>
> **Donald Calne, neurologist**

Implications of Emotional Intelligence

Aberman maintained that people can be extremely ineffective when their thoughts, feelings, and actions are misaligned—for example, arguing with someone on a cell phone when driving on a highway.[155, 156] It seems likely that leaders who are thinking or feeling one thing and actually doing something else are probably less effective in their ability to influence groups toward the accomplishment of their goals. The EQ literature should also be credited with popularizing the idea that noncognitive abilities, such as stress tolerance, assertiveness, and empathy, can play important roles in leadership success. Today many organizations are using *both* cognitive and noncognitive measures as part of the process of hiring or promoting leaders. Finally, the EQ literature has also helped to bring emotion back to the workplace. Human emotions are important aspects of one-on-one interactions and teamwork,[157, 158, 159, 160, 161, 162, 163, 164, 165, 166, 167] but too many leadership practitioners and researchers have chosen to ignore the role they play. When recognized and leveraged properly, emotions can be the motivational fuel that helps individuals and groups to accomplish their goals. When ignored or discounted, emotions can significantly impede a leader's ability to build teams or influence a group. As discussed in the personality section of this chapter, leaders who can empathize and get along with others are often more successful than those who cannot.

Some of the more recent research in emotional intelligence indicates that it moderates employees' reactions to job insecurity and their ability to cope with stress when threatened with job loss. Employees with lower EQ reported more negative emotional reactions and used less effective coping strategies when dealing with downsizing, compared to those with higher EQ.[168] Along these lines, other researchers report relationships between leaders' moods and followers' moods, job performance, job satisfaction, and creativity.[169] And Boyatzis, Stubbs, and Taylor accurately point out that most MBA programs focus more on cognitive abilities and developing financial skills than on those abilities needed to successfully build teams and get results through others.[170]

> *What really matters for success, character, happiness and lifelong achievements is a definite set of emotional skills—your EQ—not just purely cognitive abilities that are measured by conventional IQ tests.*
>
> **Daniel Goleman, EQ researcher**

Given these results, is it possible to develop emotional intelligence? The answer to this question is yes, but the path taken to develop EQ would depend on whether the training program was based on an ability or mixed model of emotional intelligence. An ability-based EQ training program would focus on improving participants' ability to accurately perceive one's own and others' emotions, generate emotions to facilitate thought and action, accurately understand the causes of emotions and the meanings they convey, and regulate one's emotions. These programs make extensive use of videos, role plays, and other experiential exercises in order to help people better recognize, exhibit, and regulate emotion. Because the mixed model of EQ encompasses such a wide array of attributes, virtually any leadership development program could be considered an EQ training program.

Despite the positive contributions of emotional intelligence, the concept has several limitations. First, Goleman and his associates and Bar-On have not acknowledged the existence of personality, much less 100 years of personality–leadership effectiveness research. As shown in **Table 6.3**, Goleman's conceptualization of EQ looks similar to the OCEAN model found in **Table 6.1**. At least as conceptualized by these two authors, it is difficult to see how EQ is any different from personality and there is ample research that proves this point.[171, 172, 173] Second, if the EQ attributes are essentially personality traits, it is difficult to see how they will change as a result of a training intervention. Personality traits are difficult to change, and the likelihood of changing 20 to 40 years of day-to-day behavioral patterns as the result of some e-learning modules or a five-day training program seems highly suspect. As described in **Chapter 1**, people can change their behavior, but it takes considerable effort and coaching over the long term to make it happen. Finally, an important question to ask is whether EQ is really something new or is simply a repackaging of old ideas and findings. If EQ is defined as an ability model, such as the one put forth by Mayer, Salovey, and Caruso, then emotional intelligence probably is a unique ability and worthy of additional research (see **Figure 6.3**). A leader's skills in accurately perceiving, regulating, and leveraging emotions seem vitally important in building cohesive, goal-oriented teams, and measures like the MSCEIT could be used in conjunction with OCEAN measures to hire and develop better leaders. But if EQ is defined as a mixed model, then it is hard to see that Goleman and his associates and Bar-On are really telling us anything new. (See **Highlight 6.6**.)

TABLE 6.3   Comparison between the OCEAN Model and Goleman's Model of EQ

Goleman et al.	Likely OCEAN Correlates
Self-awareness	
Emotional awareness	Agreeableness
Accurate self-assessment	Neuroticism
Self-confidence	Extraversion
Self-regulation	
Self-control	Neuroticism, conscientiousness
Trustworthiness	Conscientiousness
Conscientiousness	Conscientiousness
Adaptability	Neuroticism, conscientiousness
Innovation	Openness to experience, conscientiousness
Motivation	
Achievement	Extraversion
Commitment	Extraversion
Initiative	Extraversion
Optimism	Neuroticism
Empathy	
Understanding others	Agreeableness
Developing others	Openness to experience
Service orientation	Agreeableness
Diversity	Agreeableness
Political awareness	Agreeableness
Social skills	
Influence	Extraversion, agreeableness
Communication	Extraversion
Conflict management	Agreeableness
Leadership	Extraversion
Change catalyst	Extraversion
Building bonds	Agreeableness
Collaboration/cooperation	Agreeableness
Team capabilities	Extraversion, agreeableness

FIGURE 6.3   Emotional Intelligence and the Building Blocks of Skills

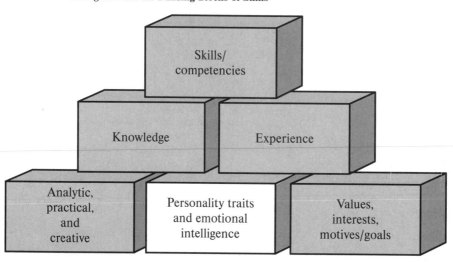

Neuroleadership: Fact or Fad?

HIGHLIGHT 6.6

When all is said and done, EQ deserves credit for bringing emotions back to the workplace, but in many ways it may be nothing more than a slick repackaging of personality traits and concepts. Because of these marketing campaigns, EQ is much like the MBTI and has become ubiquitous in organizational settings. Another leadership fad that is getting a lot of public attention is **neuroleadership**. There has been considerable research on brain chemistry, activity, structures, and processes over the past 25 years, and these findings have found their way into everyday life. For example, the websites Match.com and Chemistry.com purportedly use the latest brain research to find ideal dates for those looking for relationships, and Brain Gym supposedly helps users improve their cognitive skills. Neuroleadership attempts to apply cognitive science to such concepts as situational awareness, stress tolerance, focus, motivation, personality, values, judgment and decision-making, followership, and leadership, and it has become a major enterprise. Neuromania has

become so popular that there are now a number of consulting firms, such as the Neuroleadership Institute, that sell leadership development programs based on the latest research from cognitive science.

It is seductive to think that leadership or attractiveness may be nothing more than the ability to activate or suppress certain activities in the brain, yet there is no evidence showing this to be the case. Match.com, Brain Gym, and neuroleadership development programs take advantage of this wishful thinking by marketing offerings that far outstrip what we know about human brain functioning. Research shows that Brain Gym exercises cannot prevent the onset of Alzheimer's disease or memory loss or improve overall cognitive abilities or academic performance, but this is how the company markets its activities. Likewise, many neuroleadership development programs replace well-known psychological effects discovered in the 1970s with nonsensical references to neurotransmitters and scientific-sounding terms. In reality the content offered in these programs is no different from those offered by other firms. The brain is incredibly complex, leadership is similarly complex, and it will be a long time before our understanding of brain functioning can be used to select or develop leaders.

One area from cognitive science that may have relevance to leadership is **mindfulness**. Mindfulness can be defined as the ability to intentionally pay attention to the present moment while letting go of judgment, and organizations such as Amazon and Google have adopted mindfulness training to help leaders and employees better focus and cope with stress. Mindfulness training borrows heavily from the world of meditation and includes setting aside dedicated time to observe the present, letting go of judgments as they pop into the mind, and returning the mind back to the present whenever it wanders. Mindfulness does seem to help people reduce stress levels, become more aware of their surroundings, and stay focused. Whether this technique is really anything new or provides results superior to other situational awareness and stress management techniques has yet to be determined.

Sources: R. J. Richardson and A. J. Kaszniak, "Conceptual and Methodological Issues in Research on Mindfulness and Meditation," *American Psychologist* 70, no. 7 (2015), pp. 581–92; N. Lee, C. Senior, and M. Butler, "Leadership Research and Cognitive Neuroscience: The State of This Union," *The Leadership Quarterly* 23, no. 2 (2012), pp. 213–18; J. Schwartz, J. Thomson, and A. Kleiner, "The Neuroscience of Strategic Leadership," www.strategy-business.com/article/The-Neuroscience-of-Strategic-Leadership?gko=d196c; "Does Not Compute: Modeling Brains," *The Economist*, January 21, 2017, pp. 65–66; A. Beard, "If You Understand How the Brain Works, You Can Reach Anyone: A Conversation with Biological Anthropologist Helen Fisher," *Harvard Business Review*, March 2017, https://hbr.org/2017/03/the-new-science-of-team-chemistry#if-you-understand-how-the-brain-works-you-can-reach-anyone; B. Eichinger, "What's Next for Leadership/Talent Development?" Keynote address given at the Minnesota Professional Psychology and Work Meeting, Minneapolis, MN, February 16, 2016; M. Wall, "How Neuroscience Is Being Used to Spread Quackery in Business and Education," *The Conversation*, August 26, 2014, http://theconversation.com/how-neuroscience-is-being-used-to-spread-quackery-in-business-and-education-30342; K. Nowack and D. Radecki, "Introduction to the Special Issue: Neuro-Myth-conceptions in Consulting Psychology—Between a Rock and a Hard Place," *Journal of Consulting Psychology: Practice and Research* 70, no. 1 (2018), pp. 1–10; and R. J. Davidson and A. Huffington, "Don't Buy in to the Backlash—the Science on Meditation Is Clear," *Thrive Global*, June 25, 2018, https://thriveglobal.com/stories/don-t-buy-into-the-backlash-the-science-on-meditation-is-clear.

Intelligence and Leadership

Good brains don't necessarily translate into good judgment.

Peggy Noonan, writer

What Is Intelligence?

The first formal linkage between intelligence and leadership was established around 1115 BC in China, where the dynasties used standardized tests to determine which citizens would play key leadership roles in the institutions they had set up to run the country.[174] Using intelligence tests to identify potential leaders in the United States goes back to World War I, and to a large extent this use of intelligence testing continues today. Over 100 years of very comprehensive and systematic research provides overwhelming evidence to support the notion that general intelligence plays a substantial role in human affairs.[175, 176, 177, 178, 179, 180, 181, 182, 183, 184, 185, 186] Still, intelligence and intelligence testing are among the most controversial topics in the social sciences today. There is contentious debate over questions like how heredity and the environment affect intelligence, whether intelligence tests should be used in public schools, and whether ethnic groups differ in average intelligence test scores. For the most part, however, we will bypass such controversies here. Our focus will be on the relationship between intelligence and leadership.

> *Perhaps no concept in the history of psychology has had or continues to have as great an impact on everyday life in the Western world as that of general intelligence.*
>
> **Sandra Scarr, researcher**

We define **intelligence** as a person's all-around effectiveness in activities directed by thought.[187, 188, 189, 190, 191, 192, 193, 194, 195, 196] What does this definition of intelligence have to do with leadership? Research has shown that more intelligent leaders are faster learners; make better assumptions, deductions, and inferences; are better at creating a compelling vision and developing strategies to make their vision a reality; can develop better solutions to problems; can see more of the primary and secondary implications of their decisions; and are quicker on their feet than leaders who are less intelligent.[197, 198, 199, 200, 201, 202, 203, 204, 205, 206, 207, 208, 209, 210, 211, 212, 213, 214, 215, 216] To a large extent people get placed into leadership positions to solve problems, whether they are customer, financial, operational, interpersonal, performance, political, educational, or social in nature. Therefore, given the behaviors associated with higher intelligence, it is easy to see how a more intelligent leader will often be more successful than a less intelligent leader in influencing a group to accomplish its goals. Like personality traits, however, intelligence alone is not enough to guarantee leadership success. Plenty of smart people make poor leaders, and plenty of dumb people make poor leaders too. Nevertheless, many leadership activities seem to involve some degree of decision-making and problem-solving ability, which means a leader's intelligence can affect the odds of leadership effectiveness in many situations.

As shown in **Figure 6.4**, intelligence is relatively difficult to change. Like personality, it is also an unseen quality and can be inferred only by observing behavior. Moreover, intelligence does not affect behavior equally across all situations. Some activities, such as following simple routines, put less of a premium on intelligence than others.[217, 218] Nor does our definition of intelligence imply that intelligence is a fixed quantity. Although heredity plays a role, intelligence can be modified through education and experience.[219, 220, 221, 222] Finally, intelligence is also part of a person's public reputation. We often label others as being bright, smart, creative, slow, or dumb, and these attributes are closely associated with someone's level of intelligence.

> *The first method for estimating the intelligence of a ruler is to look at the men he has around him.*
>
> **Niccolò Machiavelli, Italian historian and writer**

FIGURE 6.4   The Building Blocks of Skills

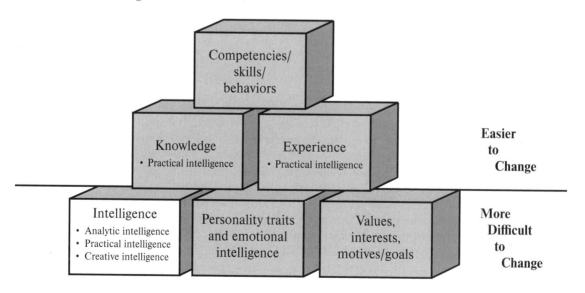

The Triarchic Theory of Intelligence

Intelligence and leadership effectiveness are related, but there is still an ____
intelligence. Many psychologists have tried to determine the structure of ____
ability, or does it involve a collection of related mental abilities?[223, 2]____
said that the *process* by which people do complex mental work is mu____
the number of mental abilities.[227, 228, 229] One of the most comprehe____
ligence developed and tested over the past 30 years is Sternberg's **tria**____
[233, 234] It also offers some of the most significant implications for lead____
what a leader *does* when solving complex mental problems, such as h____
sized when solving problems, what assumptions and errors are made, ____
there are three basic types of intelligence. **Analytic intelligence** is general problem-solving ____
assessed using standardized mental abilities tests. Analytic intelligence is important because leaders and fol
lowers who possess higher levels of this type of intelligence tend to be quick learners, do well in school, see
connections between issues, and have the ability to make accurate deductions, assumptions, and inferences
with relatively unfamiliar information.

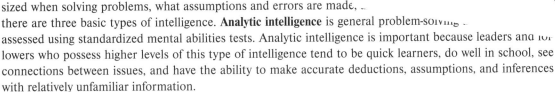

> *Everyone is ignorant, only on different subjects.*
>
> **Will Rogers, American humorist**

There is still much, however, that analytic intelligence does not explain. Many people do well on standardized
tests but not in life.[235, 236, 237, 238] And some people do relatively poorly on standardized intelligence tests
but develop ingenious solutions to practical problems. For example, Sternberg and his associates described
a situation in which students in a school for the mentally retarded did very poorly on standardized tests yet
consistently found ways to defeat the school's elaborate security system. In this situation the students possessed a relatively high level of **practical intelligence**, or "street smarts." People with street smarts know how
to adapt to, shape, or select new situations to get their needs met better than people lacking street smarts (for
example, think of a stereotypical computer nerd and an inner-city kid both lost in downtown New York City).
In other words, practical intelligence involves knowing how things get done and how to do them. For leaders,
practical intelligence is important because it involves knowing what to do and how to do it when confronted
with a particular leadership situation, such as dealing with a poorly performing subordinate, resolving a problem with a customer, or getting a team to work better together.[239, 240]

> *I am a stable genius. . . . I know more about the Middle East than the generals. . . . I know more about the Internet than
> anyone.*
>
> **Donald Trump, U.S. President**

Because of its potential importance to leadership effectiveness, several other aspects of practical intelligence
are worth noting. First, practical intelligence is much more concerned with knowledge and experience than
is analytic intelligence (see **Figure 6.4**). Leaders can build their practical intelligence by building their leadership knowledge and experience. Undergraduate and graduate courses, corporate education programs, and
leadership textbooks like this one can help you build your practical intelligence. Getting a variety of leadership experiences, and perhaps more important, reflecting on these experiences, will also help you build practical intelligence. But you should understand that it takes some time before you will become an "expert" at
leadership—research shows that it takes 10 years to truly master any particular topic.[241] (See **Highlights 6.7**.)

...rt People Can't Learn

...g able to learn and adapt is a critical leadership skill, but it turns out that many professionals are not good at it. Leaders get paid to solve problems and are generally good at this, but many are lousy at determining what role *they* played in causing these problems. Leaders are good at **single-loop learning**—reviewing data and facts and identifying the underlying root causes from the information gathered—but are not good at **double-loop learning**—determining what they as leaders need to do differently to avoid problems in the future. The primary reason why many leaders are not good at double-loop learning is because most have not experienced real failure. Many people in positions of authority have enviable track records of success, so when things go badly they erroneously believe that it cannot be their fault because they have always been successful. Something else must be causing the group's substandard performance, such as underachieving followers, market conditions, difficult customers, government regulations, or cutthroat competitors. Thus many leaders react to failure by laying the blame on circumstances or other people. Although external factors can and do affect group performance, a leader's actions or inactions can also be a major cause of team failure. Before leaders point at external factors they need to ask how their actions contributed to the problem. Unfortunately it appears that the more formal education one has, the less likely it is that one will engage in double-loop learning. Intelligence alone will not help people extract the maximum value from their experiences—reflection also plays a key role in learning and adaptation.

Source: Adapted from C. Argyris, "Teaching Smart People How to Learn," *Harvard Business Review*, May–June 1991, Reprint Number 91301.

There is no better way to get people angry than by making them look dumb in public. Smart people are very good at this.

Jim Earley, executive coach

Second, practical intelligence is *domain specific*. A leader who has a lot of knowledge and experience in leading a pharmaceutical research team may feel like a duck out of water when asked to lead a major fund-raising effort for a charitable institution. As another example, one of the authors worked with a highly successful retail company having over 100,000 employees. All the key leaders had over 20 years of retail operations and merchandising experience, but they also did poorly on standardized intelligence tests. The company had successfully expanded in the United States (which capitalized on their practical intelligence), but their attempt to expand to foreign markets was an abysmal failure. This failure was due in part to the leaders' inability to learn, appreciate, or understand the intricacies of other cultures (analytic intelligence), their lack of knowledge and experience in foreign markets (practical intelligence), and in turn their development of inappropriate strategies for running the business in other countries (a combination of analytic and practical intelligence). Thus practical intelligence is extremely useful for leading in familiar situations, but analytic intelligence may play a more important role when leaders face new or novel situations. (See **Highlight 6.8.**)

Clueless or Culpable?

HIGHLIGHT 6.8

Over the past few years there have been a number of high-visibility incidents where senior leaders claimed ignorance of organizational malfeasance. Some of the more noteworthy are described here:

Wells Fargo. John Stumpf had been the CEO and chairman of the board of Wells Fargo for nine years before he resigned in the fall of 2016. Named Morningstar's CEO of the year in 2015, Stumpf saw Wells Fargo's assets grow to $500 billion under his leadership and the company was the envy of the financial services industry. A key factor in the company's growth was its emphasis on cross-selling, which included an incentive program that rewarded bank employees for selling clients multiple products, such as credit cards, loans, or checking, savings, or retirement accounts (or punished them for failing to do so). There was so much pressure to cross-sell that bankers set up over 2 million fake customer accounts in order to meet sales goals. Employees who blew the whistle on these illegal practices were retaliated against, often by being fired and blacklisted from jobs at other financial services companies. When questioned about these tactics Stumpf, proclaimed that Wells Fargo did not have a problem, the company had a great culture, and the fake accounts were the result of a few bad apples. It turned out that 5,300 employees were in on the scam—hardly the work of a few bad apples. Warren Buffett, a key investor in Wells Fargo, said the company had a dumb incentive system, and when they found out it was dumb they didn't do anything to fix it. Four years later, Wells Fargo appears to not have learned anything, as they still have a massive backlog of human resource complaints and poor pay controls.

Petrobras. An energy company located in Brazil, Petrobras is the world's fourth-largest publicly traded company in market capitalization in Brazil. Investigations by Brazilian authorities uncovered $22 billion of questionable contracts, illicit payments, and kickbacks given to Petrobras officials, construction companies, and members of Brazil's Workers' Party. Dilma Rousseff was the minister of energy, chairman of the board for Petrobras, and a key leader of the Workers' Party when many of these events allegedly occurred. Rousseff claimed to have no knowledge of Petrobras's corruption and bribery but was ousted as president of Brazil when this scandal came to light.

Atlanta Public Schools. The intent of the *No Child Left Behind* law is to close chronic achievement gaps between ethnic groups in primary and secondary schools, and standardized academic testing has been instituted to determine progress in reducing these gaps. Federal and state funding and educator bonuses were tied to test results, and over several years the Atlanta Public School system received numerous educational awards, favorable press, and additional dollars for unprecedented improvements in student achievement. An investigation by the Georgia Bureau of Investigation found that these educational gains were largely fictitious, as 178 teachers and administrators in 44 out of 56 schools in the Atlanta Public School system had systematically changed students' answers before tests were scored. Beverly Hall, the school superintendent, claimed to have no knowledge of widespread cheating across the district.

Every sector is populated with those who are clueless or culpable, as government, police, military, media, corporations, public education, professional sports teams, philanthropic, and nongovernmental organization leaders regularly claim ignorance of malfeasance that occurs under their watch. Certainly top leaders can't be expected to know everything that happens in their organizations, but when independent investigations find systemic maltreatment of employees or citizens, dishonesty, corruption, bribery, cheating, stealing, cover-ups, or other bad behavior, one has to wonder why these individuals are still being paid. Top leaders have a profound effect on organizational culture, and if it is rotten then they have only themselves to blame. If cluelessness is the problem, then it raises questions about how organizations select and oversee the performance of their top leaders.

Sources: E. Glazer, "Wells Fargo CEO John Stumpf Steps Down," *The Wall Street Journal*, October 12, 2016, www.wsj.com/articles/wells-fargo-ceo-stumpf-to-retire-1476306019; Z. Faux, L. J. Keller, and J. Surane, "Wells Fargo CEO Stumpf Quits over Fallout from Fake Accounts," *Bloomberg*, October 12, 2016, www.bloomberg.com/news/articles/2016-10-12/wells-fargo-ceo-stumpf-steps-down-in-fallout-from-fake-accounts; G. J. Curphy, "Clueless or Culpable?" LinkedIn, June 1, 2015, www.linkedin.com/pulse/clueless-culpable-gordon-gordy-curphy-phd; and R. L. Ensign, "Well Fargo's List of Woes Grows," *The Wall Street Journal*, December 5, 2019, pp. A1 and A8.

Third, this example points out the importance of having both types of intelligence. Organizations today are looking for leaders and followers who have the necessary knowledge and skills to succeed (practical intelligence) and the ability to learn (analytic intelligence).[242, 243, 244, 245, 246, 247] Fourth, high levels of practical intelligence may compensate for lower levels of analytic intelligence. Leaders with lower analytic abilities may still be able to solve complex work problems or make good decisions if they have plenty of job-relevant knowledge or experience. But leaders with more analytic intelligence, all things being equal, may develop their street smarts more quickly than leaders with less analytic intelligence. Analytic intelligence may play a lesser role once a domain of knowledge is mastered, but a more important role in encountering new situations.

> *I try to buy stock in companies so wonderful that an idiot can run them. Because sooner or later one will.*
>
> **Warren Buffett, investor**

The third component of the triarchic theory of intelligence is **creative intelligence**, which is the ability to produce work that is both novel and useful.[248, 249, 250, 251, 252, 253, 254, 255, 256] Using *both* criteria (novel and useful) as components of creative intelligence helps to eliminate outlandish solutions to a potential problem by ensuring that adopted solutions can be realistically implemented or have some type of practical payoff. Several examples might help to clarify the novel and practical components of creative intelligence. The inventor of Velcro got his idea while picking countless thistles out of his socks; he realized that the same principle that produced his frustration might be translated into a useful fastener. The inventor of 3M's Post-it Notes was frustrated because bookmarks in his church hymnal were continually sliding out of place, and he saw a solution in a low-tack adhesive discovered by a fellow 3M scientist. The scientists who designed the *Spirit* and *Opportunity* missions to Mars were given a budget that was considerably smaller than those of previous missions to Mars. Yet the scientists were challenged to develop two spacecraft that had more capabilities than the *Pathfinder* and the *Viking Lander*. Their efforts with *Spirit* and *Opportunity* were a resounding success, due in part to some of the novel solutions used both to land the spacecrafts (an inflatable balloon system) and to explore the surrounding area (both were mobile rovers).

Two interesting questions surrounding creativity concern the role of intelligence and the assessment of creative ability. Research shows that analytic intelligence correlates at about the 0.5 level with creative intelligence.[257] Thus the best research available indicates that analytic intelligence and creativity are related, but the relationship is imperfect. Some level of analytic intelligence seems necessary for creativity, but having a high level of analytic intelligence is no guarantee that a leader will be creative. And like practical intelligence, creativity seems to be specific to certain fields and subfields.[258, 259, 260, 261, 262, 263, 264, 265]

> *The fastest way to succeed is to double the failure rate.*
>
> **Thomas Watson Sr., former chairman and CEO of IBM**

Assessing creativity is no simple matter. Tests of creativity, or **divergent thinking**, differ from tests that assess **convergent thinking**. Tests of convergent thinking usually have a single best answer; good examples here are most intelligence and aptitude tests. Conversely, tests of creativity or divergent thinking have many possible answers.[266] Although Sternberg and his associates showed that it is possible to reliably judge the relative creativity of different responses, judging creativity is more difficult than scoring convergent tests.[267, 268, 269] For example, there are no set answers or standards for determining whether a movie, a marketing ad, or a new manufacturing process is truly creative. Another difficulty in assessing creativity is that it may wax and wane over time; many of the most creative people seem to have occasional dry spells or writer's block. This is different from analytic intelligence, where performance on mental abilities tests remains fairly constant over time (see **Profiles in Leadership 6.4**).

Despite being difficult to measure and domain specific, given the rapid pace of globalization, automation, big data, artificial intelligence, the Internet of Things, and digital disruption, it may not be surprising that a survey of 1,500 senior leaders revealed that creativity was the most important leadership quality, even more important than integrity or global thinking.[270] Certainly the technology, telecommunications, consumer products, medical, entertainment, advertising, and transportation industries place huge premiums on innovation, but even more mundane industries such as grocery stores and waste disposal are continually looking for new ways to cut costs or deliver better services. There is also some research showing that evil genius may in fact exist; cheating is correlated with creativity, and existential threats such as wars spur creativity. Governments allocate a tremendous amount of resources to invade, or to stop from being invaded by, other countries, and unfortunately people are continually thinking of novel ways to kill each other. The only good news is that some of these innovations (for example, satellites, drones, composite materials, GPS) find their way into beneficial civilian uses.[271, 272]

Ruth Bader Ginsburg

PROFILES IN LEADERSHIP 6.4

Until her death in September, 2020, Ruth Bader Ginsburg was an Associate Justice on the Supreme Court of the United States (SCOTUS) since 1993. While in this position she was recognized as one of *Time* and *Forbes* magazines' 100 Most Influential People and has been nominated into the National Women's Hall of Fame. A champion of liberal causes, Ginsburg was a leading advocate of gender equality and women's rights. She was also a justice who believed in building on legal precedence rather than on promoting her own vision of constitutional law.

Born in Brooklyn, New York, Justice Ginsburg did not have an easy childhood. Her only sister died when she was very young, and her mother died the day before she graduated from high school. Her mother's lack of opportunity left a lasting impression on Ginsburg. Encouraged by her mother to do well in school, Ginsburg graduated at only 15 years old. After graduation, she went to work to help pay for her brother's education and eventually went on to obtain an undergraduate degree at Cornell. She was the highest-ranked female in her class and attended Harvard Law School—one of only nine females of the 500 accepted by Harvard Law School that year. Over dinner the dean asked Ginsburg and her fellow female cohorts, "Why are you at Harvard Law School taking the place of a man?" Ginsburg's husband got a job in New York City a year later, and she transferred to and subsequently graduated from Columbia Law School, where she tied for the top graduate in her class.

As a female attorney in the 1950s, Ginsburg had a difficult time finding employment after law school. She was demoted for getting pregnant while working for the Social Security Administration, and she eventually landed an academic position at Rutgers University, where she received less pay "because her husband had a full-time job." She became the first female tenured professor at Columbia Law School and was one of only 20 female legal professors in the United States at the time. Ginsburg spent time in Sweden doing research on international law and noted that women were treated much more equitably in that country. She subsequently coauthored the first law casebook on sex discrimination and cofounded the Women's Rights Project with the American Civil Liberties Union. She argued six and won five gender discrimination cases before the SCOTUS, and her legal arguments were usually built around the Equal Protection Clause of the U.S. Constitution.

Ginsburg and her husband were early advocates of shared earning and parenting, and together they raised two children and have four grandchildren. Her husband passed away in 2010, and Ginsburg herself had a number of health issues in recent years. She nevertheless remained a fitness buff; Ginsburg could do 20 pushups at age 80 and worked out with a personal trainer two times a week.

How would you rate Justice Ginsburg on each of the five OCEAN traits? How would she fare on measures of emotional, analytic, practical, and creative intelligence?

Sources: R. B. Ginsburg, M. Harnett, and W. W. Williams, *My Own Words* (New York: Simon & Schuster, 2016); B. A. Macaluso, "15 Things You Should Know about Ruth Bader Ginsburg," *Mental Floss*, December 25, 2018, www.mentalfloss.com/article/76804/15-things-you-should-know-about-ruth-bader-ginsburg; P. Galanes, "Ruth Bader Ginsburg and Gloria Steinem on the Unending Fight for Women's Rights," *New York Times*, November 14, 2015, www.nytimes.com/2015/11/15/fashion/ruth-bader-ginsburg-and-gloria-steinem-on-the-unending-fight-for-womens-rights.html; "Ruth Bader Ginsburg," National Women's Hall of Fame, www.womenofthehall.org/inductee/ruth-bader-ginsburg; "The 100 Most Powerful Women," *Forbes*, August 19, 2009, www.forbes.com/lists/2009/11/power-women-09_Ruth-Bader-Ginsburg_D8D7.html; N. Gibbs, "How We Pick the Time 100," *Time*, April 21, 2016, https://time.com/4300131/how-editors-pick-the-time-100; and P. Ryan, "'RBG': How Ruth Bader Ginsburg Became a Legit Pop-Culture Icon," *USA Today*, May 1, 2018, www.usatoday.com/story/life/movies/2018/05/01/rbg-documentary-shows-how-ruth-bader-ginsburg-became-pop-icon/562930002.

Implications of the Triarchic Theory of Intelligence

Some 200 separate studies have examined the relationship between intelligence test scores and leadership effectiveness or emergence, and these studies have been the topic of major reviews.[273, 274, 275, 276, 277, 278, 279, 280, 281, 282, 283, 284, 285, 286, 287, 288, 289, 290, 291, 292] These reviews provide overwhelming support for the idea that leadership effectiveness or emergence is positively correlated with analytic intelligence. Nonetheless, the correlation between analytic intelligence and leadership success is not as strong as previously assumed. It now appears that personality can at times be more predictive of leadership emergence and effectiveness than analytic intelligence.[293, 294, 295, 296, 297] Leadership situations that are relatively routine or unchanging, or that require specific in-depth product or process knowledge, may place more importance on personality and practical intelligence than analytic intelligence. Having a high level of analytic intelligence seems more important for solving ambiguous, complex problems, such as those encountered by executives at the top levels of an organization. Here leaders must be able to detect themes and patterns in seemingly unrelated information; make accurate assumptions about market conditions; or make wise merger, acquisition, or divestiture decisions. Further evidence that higher levels of analytic intelligence are associated with top leaders can be found in **Figure 6.5**. (See **Highlight 6.9**.)

The next time you are afraid to share your ideas, remember someone once said in a meeting, "Let's make a film with a tornado full of sharks."

Adam Grant, researcher

FIGURE 6.5   Average Intelligence Test Scores by Management Level

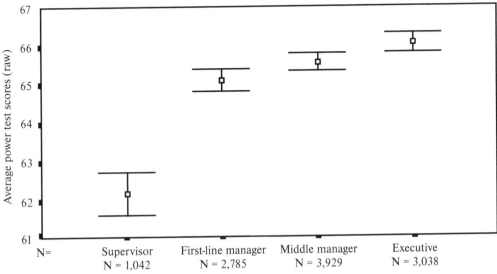

Source: N. Kuncel, "Personality and Cognitive Differences among Management Levels," unpublished manuscript (Minneapolis: Personnel Decisions International, 1996).

The Competent Hot Potato

HIGHLIGHT 6.9

What should leaders do when a follower is smart, competent, and creative (that is, has a high level of practical, analytic, and creative intelligence) but has difficulties getting along with other team members? Clearly creative followers with high levels of analytic intelligence and domain knowledge can help their teams make better decisions, but the cost of this knowledge is often strained relationships or high levels of turnover among teammates. Research shows that when given a choice, team members would prefer to work with a lovable but incompetent fool than with an irritable but competent jerk. On the one hand, team performance is likely to suffer if everyone on the team is happy but incompetent. On the other hand, performance is also likely to suffer when a toxic follower is part of a team. It appears that many managers resolve this dilemma by having

competent jerks on their teams during the initial phases of projects—when ideas about project direction, possibilities, and solutions are being determined. Once these decisions are made, many managers then arrange to have the competent jerks leave their teams. The good news is that the team gets to capitalize on the competent jerks' expertise during the decision-making phase of the project but doesn't have to suffer their dysfunctional behavior during the execution phase. The bad news is that a common way to get rid of competent jerks is to promote them. Many managers would rather see a toxic follower become a toxic leader than confront difficult performance issues. Subsequent bosses often repeat the "hot potato" process, helping toxic leaders move into roles with ever-increasing responsibilities.

Certainly competent jerks are no fun to manage, but what happens when smart, competent, and likable followers raise legitimate questions about a company's goals, strategies, products, or services? It turns out that this may be the fastest way for employees to lower their IQs, as many leaders say they want their people to challenge the way things get done, but more often than not those who do are labeled as ignorant troublemakers "who just don't get it." After a few ill-fated attempts to raise alarms, employees become disengaged and team performance begins to suffer. Leaders should be ruthless when it comes to hiring smart, competent team members, but they also need to understand these individuals have high expectations and leaders need to be on their A games if they want to effectively lead teams full of A players.

Sources: J. Sandberg, "Sometimes Colleagues Are Just Too Bad to Not Get Promoted," *The Wall Street Journal*, August 17, 2005, p. A5; J. Casciaro and M. S. Lobo, "Competent Jerks, Lovable Fools, and the Formation of Social Networks," *Harvard Business Review*, June 2006, pp. 92–100; J. Stricker, "Is it Smart to Play Dumb on the Job?" *Star Tribune*, June 2, 2013, pp. E1, E12; and G. J. Curphy, "The Fastest Way to Lower Your IQ," LinkedIn, April 5, 2015, www.linkedin.com/pulse/fastest-way-lower-your-iq-gordon-gordy-curphy-phd.

> *You'll get hired for your intelligence, but fired for your personality.*
>
> **Dianne Nilsen, business executive**

Although a high level of analytic intelligence is usually an asset to a leader, research also suggests that in some situations analytic intelligence may have a *curvilinear* relationship with leadership effectiveness.[298, 299, 300, 301] When differences in analytic intelligence between leader and followers are too great, communication can be impaired; a leader's intelligence can become an impediment to being understood by subordinates. An alternative explanation for the curvilinear relationship between analytic intelligence and leadership effectiveness may have to do with how stress affects leader–subordinate interactions. Fiedler and his associates found that smart but inexperienced leaders were less effective in stressful situations than less intelligent, experienced leaders.[302, 303, 304] An example of this finding was clearly demonstrated in the movie *Platoon*. In one frantic scene, an American platoon is ambushed by the Viet Cong. An inexperienced, college-educated lieutenant calls for artillery support from friendly units. He calls in the wrong coordinates, however, and as a result artillery shells are dropped on his own platoon's position rather than on the enemy's position. The situation comes under control only after an experienced sergeant sizes up the situation and tells the artillery units to cease firing. This example points out the importance of practical intelligence in stressful situations. Leaders revert to well-practiced behaviors under periods of high stress and change, and leaders with high levels of practical intelligence have a relatively broad set of coping and problem-solving behaviors to draw upon in these situations. Because of the levels of stress and change associated with many leadership positions today, systematically improving practical leadership skills through education and experience is important for leaders and leaders-to-be.

> *Silicon Valley doesn't have better ideas and isn't smarter than the rest of the world, but it has the edge in filtering ideas and executing them.*
>
> **Sergey Brin, Google co-founder**

With respect to creative intelligence, perhaps the most important point leaders should remember is that their primary role is not so much to be creative themselves as to *build an environment where others can be creative*. This is not to say that leaders should be uncreative, but rather that most innovations have roots in ideas developed by people closest to a problem or opportunity (that is, the workers). Leaders can boost the creativity throughout their groups or organizations in many ways, but particularly through selecting creative employees and providing opportunities for others to develop their creativity, and through broader interventions like making sure the motivation and incentives for others are conducive to creativity and providing at least some guidance or vision about what the creative product or output should look like.[305, 306, 307, 308, 309, 310, 311, 312, 313, 314, 315, 316, 317]

Leaders can do several things to improve the group and organizational factors affecting creativity. Leaders should hire followers who are diverse in terms of education, experience, and expertise, as this will be beneficial to idea generation. However, they should also be aware that diverse teams are better at developing breakthrough ideas but not as good at translating them into marketable or usable products and services.[318] Crowdsourcing is also an option; reaching across an entire organization can help leaders tap a much larger and more diverse audience to provide solutions to difficult problems. Leaders also need to be mindful of the effect various sorts of incentives or rewards can have on creativity; certain types of motivation to work are more conducive to creativity than others. Research has shown that people tend to generate more creative solutions when they are told to focus on their intrinsic motivation for doing so (the pleasure of solving the task itself) rather than on the extrinsic motivation (public recognition or pay).[319, 320] When they need to foster creativity, leaders may find it more effective to select followers who truly enjoy working on the task at hand rather than relying on rewards to foster creativity.

Creativity can be hindered if people believe their ideas will be evaluated. Experiments by Amabile and Zhou showed that students who were told their projects were to be judged by experts produced less creative projects than students who were not told their projects would be judged.[321, 322] A similar phenomenon can occur in groups. When a group knows its work must ultimately be evaluated, there is a pronounced tendency for members to be evaluative and judgmental too early in the solution-generating process. This tends to reduce the number of creative solutions generated, perhaps because of a generally shared belief in the value of critical thinking (and in some groups the norm seems to be the more criticism, the better) and of subjecting ideas to intense scrutiny and evaluation. When members of a group judge ideas as soon as they are offered, two dysfunctional things can happen. People in the group may censor themselves (not share all their ideas with the group) because even mild rejection or criticism has a significant dampening effect, or they may prematurely reject others' ideas through focus on an idea's flaws rather than its possibilities.[323] Given these findings, leaders may want to hold off on evaluating new ideas until they are all on the table, and should encourage their followers to do the same.

Making the simple complicated is commonplace; making the complicated simple, awesomely simple, that's creativity.

Charles Mingus, jazz bassist and composer

Finally, leaders who need to develop new products and services should try to minimize turnover in their teams and give them clear goals. Teams with unclear goals may successfully develop new or novel products, but these products may have low marketability or usefulness. An example illustrates this point. In the 1980s Texas Instruments (TI) decided to delve into the personal computer business. TI had a reputation for technical excellence, and one of the best managers in the company was asked to head up the project. The manager did not have a clear sense of what customers wanted or what a personal computer should be able to do. This lack of clarity had some dramatic effects. As more and more engineers were added to the project, more innovative hardware ideas were added to the computer design. These additions caused the project to take much longer and cost a lot more than planned, but the TI personal computer ended up winning a number of major engineering awards. Unfortunately it was also a business disaster because the product failed to meet customer needs. The TI project serves as a good example of a concept called **creeping elegance**. Leaders without a clear vision of what a final project should look like may end up with something that fails to meet customer needs. Leaders need to provide enough room for creativity to flourish, but enough direction for effort to be focused.[324, 325, 326] **Table 6.4** describes several factors leaders should keep in mind when trying to foster creativity.

TABLE 6.4   Creativity Killers: How to Squelch the Creativity of Direct Reports

The following is a list of things leaders can do if they wish to stifle the creativity of their followers:

Hire clones: Homogeneous teams develop fewer and less innovative ideas. Diverse teams generate diverse ideas.

Take away all discretion and autonomy: People like to have some sense of control over their work. Micromanaging staff will help to either create yea-sayers or cause people to mentally disengage from work.

Create fragmented work schedules: People need large chunks of uninterrupted time to work on novel solutions. Repeated interruptions or scheduling "novel solution generation time" in 15-minute increments around other meetings will disrupt people's ability to be innovative.

Provide insufficient resources: People need proper data, equipment, and money to be creative. Cut these off, and watch creativity go down the tubes.

Focus on short-term goals: Asking a person to be creative at a specific moment is like asking a comedian to be funny the first time you meet him or her. People can be creative and funny if given enough time, but focusing on only short-term outcomes will dampen creativity.

Create tight time lines and rigid processes: The tighter the deadlines and less flexible the processes, the more chance that innovation will be reduced.

Discourage collaboration and coordination: The best ideas often come from teams having members with different work experiences and functional backgrounds. By discouraging cross-functional collaboration, leaders can help guarantee that team members will offer up only tried-and-true solutions to problems.

Keep people happy: If you keep workers happy enough, they will have little motivation to change the status quo.

Sources: T. M. Amabile and M. Khaire, "Creativity and the Role of the Leader," *Harvard Business Review*, October 2008, pp. 100–10; T. M. Amabile and J. Zhou, in S. F. Dingfelder, "Creativity on the Clock," *Monitor on Psychology*, November 2003, pp. 56–58; and T. Chamorro-Premuzic, "Does Diversity Actually Increase Creativity?" *Harvard Business Review*, June 28, 2017, https://hbr.org/2017/06/does-diversity-actually-increase-creativity.

One industry that places a premium on creativity is the motion-picture industry. Because creativity is so important to the commercial success of a movie, it is relatively easy for a movie to succumb to creeping elegance. But how do movie directors successfully avoid creeping elegance when dealing with highly creative people having huge egos? Part of the answer may lie in the approach of two of Hollywood's most successful directors. Steven Spielberg and Ron Howard have said that before they shoot a scene they first have a clear picture of it in their own minds. If they don't have a clear picture, they sit down with the relevant parties and work it out. This shows the importance of having a clear vision when managing creativity. (See **Highlight 6.10**.)

A Creative Solution to a Big Problem: The Ocean Cleanup Project

HIGHLIGHT 6.10

One of the biggest environmental problems facing the planet is ocean trash. You do not have to go far from any harbor before seeing floating bottles and cans, pallets, plastic bags, and other sorts of trash. A 2014 survey estimated that there were over 5.25 trillion floating pieces of plastic in the sea, which may be a gross underestimate, as even more may have sunk to the ocean floor. There are vast tracts of ocean trash; the Pacific Trash Vortex is estimated to be the size of Texas.

Passing and enforcing international laws banning the dumping of trash has proved problematic, and the distances between pieces of trash make collection problematic. Yet a young Dutch entrepreneur may have invented a cost-effective way for collecting ocean trash. Boyan Slat was 16 when he noticed vast amounts of trash during an ocean dive. He wanted to do something about the problem and came up with an idea of using a floating boom in the shape of an arc to collect trash. The arc would be oriented in such a way so that as waves hit the line of booms trash would be forced toward the center of the arc, which would concentrate the trash

and make it easier to collect. Because the booms would be floating on the surface, fish and migratory animals could swim under or otherwise easily avoid the trash-collection device.

After his 2012 TEDx talk went viral, Slat started a crowdsourcing campaign and raised enough money for a proof-of-concept prototype with a 40-meter arc. The prototype passed with flying colors, and work has now begun to clean up the 1,000 rivers that contribute 80 percent of the ocean's plastic pollution. The Interceptor is the first scalable solution to gather river trash without interfering with navigation, and it is capable of capturing 100,000 to 200,000 pounds of trash per day. Four Interceptors have been deployed to rivers in Asia and Latin America, and the first in North America should come online in the near future.

Sources: A. Anderson, "Garbage in, Garbage out," *The Economist*, June 23, 2016, p. 153; Boyan Slat TEDx Talk, www.youtube.com/watch?v=ROW9F-c0kIQ; and "The Ocean Cleanup Unveils Plan to Address the Main Source of Ocean Plastic Pollution: Rivers," *The Ocean Cleanup*, October 26, 2019, https://theoceancleanup.com/updates/the-ocean-cleanup-unveils-plan-to-address-the-main-source-of-ocean-plastic-pollution-rivers.

Intelligence and Stress: Cognitive Resources Theory

In the preceding section we noted that intelligence may be a more important quality for leaders in some situations than in others. You may be surprised to learn, however, that research suggests there are times when intelligence may be a disadvantage. A key variable affecting this paradoxical finding seems to be whether the leader is in a stressful situation. Recent research suggests that stress plays a key role in determining how a leader's intelligence influences his or her effectiveness. Although it is not surprising that stress affects behavior in various ways, Fiedler and Garcia developed the **cognitive resources theory (CRT)** to explain the interesting relationships between leader intelligence and experience levels, and group performance in stressful versus nonstressful conditions.[327, 328]

CRT consists of several key concepts, one of which is intelligence. Fiedler and Garcia defined *intelligence* as we have earlier—it is one's all-around effectiveness in activities directed by thought and is typically measured using standardized intelligence tests (in other words, analytic intelligence). Another key concept is experience, which represents the habitual behavior patterns, overlearned knowledge, and skills acquired for effectively dealing with task-related problems (that is, practical intelligence). Although experience is often gained under stressful and unpleasant conditions, experience also provides a "crash plan" to revert back to when under stress.[329, 330, 331, 332, 333] As Fiedler observed, people often act differently when stressed, and the crash plan describes this change in behavior patterns. For most CRT studies, experience has been defined as time in the job or organization. A third key concept in CRT is stress. *Stress* is often defined as the result of conflicts with superiors or the apprehension associated with performance evaluation.[334, 335] This interpersonal stress is believed to be emotionally disturbing and can divert attention from problem-solving activities. In other words, people can get so concerned about how their performance is being evaluated that they may fail to perform at an optimal level. In sum, cognitive resources theory provides a conceptual scheme for explaining how leader behavior changes under stress to impact group performance.

Cognitive resources theory makes two major predictions with respect to intelligence, experience, stress, and group performance. First, because experienced leaders have a greater repertoire of behaviors to fall back on, leaders with greater experience but lower intelligence are hypothesized to have higher-performing groups under conditions of high stress. Experienced leaders have "been there before" and know better what to do and how to get it done when faced with high-stress situations. Leaders' experience levels can interfere with performance under low-stress conditions, however.

That leads to a second hypothesis. Because experience leads to habitual behavior patterns, leaders with high levels of experience tend to misapply old solutions to problems when creative solutions are called for. Experienced leaders rely too much on the tried and true when facing new problems, even under relatively low stress. Thus leaders with higher levels of intelligence but less experience are not constrained by previously acquired behavior patterns and should have higher-performing groups under low-stress conditions. In other words, experience is helpful when one is under stress but can hinder performance in the absence of stress.

These two major predictions of CRT can be readily seen in everyday life. For the most part, it is not the most intelligent but the most experienced members of sporting teams, marching bands, acting troupes, or volunteer organizations who are selected to be leaders. These leaders are often chosen because other members recognize their ability to perform well under the high levels of stress associated with sporting events and public performances. In addition, research with combat troops, firefighters, senior executives, and students has provided strong support for the two major tenets of CRT.[336, 337, 338, 339, 340]

Despite this initial empirical support, one problem with CRT concerns the apparent dichotomy between intelligence and experience. Fiedler and Garcia's initial investigations of CRT did not examine the possibility that leaders could be *both* intelligent and experienced. Subsequent research by Gibson showed not only that many leaders were both intelligent and experienced, but also that these leaders would fall back on their experience in stressful situations and use their intelligence to solve group problems in less stressful situations.[341]

Another issue with CRT concerns the leader's ability to tolerate stress. As Schonpflug and Zaccaro correctly pointed out, some leaders are better able than others to tolerate high levels of stress.[342, 343] Some leaders have personalities characterized by low neuroticism scores, and they may do well in high-stress situations even when they lack experience because of their inherent ability to handle stress. Further research on this issue seems warranted.

In general, solid evidence appears to support the major tenets of CRT. Because of this research, CRT has several important implications for leaders. First, the best leaders may be smart *and* experienced. Although intelligence tests are good indicators of raw mental horsepower, it is just as important for leaders to broaden their leadership knowledge and experience if they want to succeed in high-stress situations. The ability to switch between using one's analytic versus practical intelligence is precisely why military units practice under high-stress situations, and research has shown it is possible to train leaders to improve decision-making under combat conditions.[344] This latter point may be important today, when the additional stress of globalization, technology, and organizational change may cause the performance of leaders to be scrutinized even more closely than in the past. In fact, this additional scrutiny may cause leaders who were previously successful to perform poorly.

Second, leaders may not be aware of the degree to which they are causing stress in their followers. If followers perceive that their performance is being watched closely, they are likely to revert to their crash plans in order to perform. If a situation calls for new and novel solutions to problems, however, such leader behavior may be counterproductive. A key point here is that leaders may be unaware of their impact on followers. For example, they may want to review their followers' work more closely in order to be helpful, but followers may not perceive it this way.

Reality is the leading cause of stress for those in touch with it.

Jane Wagner, writer

Third, the level of stress inherent in the position needs to be understood before selecting leaders. Those filling high-stress leadership positions can either look for experienced leaders or reduce the stress in the situation so that more intelligent leaders can succeed. Another alternative could be to hire more intelligent leaders and put them through stress management training or work simulations so that the effects of stress are minimized.[345, 346] It is also possible that experienced leaders may get bored if placed into low-stress positions.[347] (See **Highlight 6.11**.)

Intelligence and Judgment

HIGHLIGHT 6.11

Some popular business writers, such as Daniel Goleman and Angela Duckworth, believe emotional intelligence or work ethic are the key characteristics that separate successful from unsuccessful people. Both minimize the role intelligence plays in success at work and life. However, there is overwhelming research that shows being smarter has many advantages. For instance, it improves the odds that the person will be perceived as a leader of a group and that the group will be successful at accomplishing its goals, have a wide choice of career options, be more successful in his or her career, and be better paid and accumulate more wealth. Intelligence matters, and it matter quite a bit.

At the organizational level, Robert Hogan argues that the term *intelligent* applies mostly to decisions. Decisions that successfully solve problems or improve organizational performance are deemed "intelligent"; those that do not are usually described as "dumb." Decision-making is critically important in business, politics, and warfare, where money and people's lives are on the line. According to Hogan, an organization's success can be measured by the collective decisions it makes. Generally speaking, armies that win or companies that outperform their rivals make many more intelligent decisions than those that fail.

Good judgment occurs when leaders choose the right means to solve a problem and change course when information indicates to do so. Bad judgment occurs when people impose the wrong solution onto a problem and then stick with their solution even when it is obviously not working. Good judgment may not be that easy, as approximately 25 percent of the users of social media post things they later regret, the divorce rate in the United States is 50 percent, and the tattoo removal industry has grown over 400 percent over the past 10 years. It is estimated that about half of all business decisions turn out to be wrong; the key to success seems to be to recognize when the decision is not working out and quickly devise new solutions. Unfortunately, many organizational failures can be attributed to leaders letting their egos get the best of them and not changing course despite overwhelming evidence to the contrary.

Sources: R. T. Hogan, *Intelligence and Good Judgment*, unpublished manuscript (Tulsa, OK: Hogan Assessment Systems, 2009); P. Ingrassia, "How Detroit Drove into a Ditch," *The Wall Street Journal*, October 25–26, 2008, pp. W1–2; T. E. Ricks, *Fiasco: The American Military Adventure in Iraq* (New York: Penguin Press, 2006); T. Chamorro-Premuzic, "Book Smart vs. Street Smart-The Psychology of Good versus Bad Judgment," *HR Examiner: The New Architecture of Work*, November 10, 2015; Hogan Assessment Systems, "Why Smart People Make Dumb Decisions," white paper, November 2015, www.hoganassessments.com/wp-content/uploads/2016/12/Why-Smart-People-Make-Bad-Decisions.pdf; and G. J. Curphy, "IQ, EQ, and Personality, Oh My!" LinkedIn, March 23, 2015, www.linkedin.com/pulse/iq-eq-personality-oh-my-gordon-gordy-curphy-phd.

Summary

This chapter has examined the relationships of personality, emotional intelligence, and intelligence with leadership emergence and effectiveness. In general, all of these attributes can help a leader to influence a group toward the accomplishment of its goals, but by themselves they are no guarantee of leadership success. Often the situation will dictate which personality traits, components of intelligence, or emotional intelligence attributes will positively affect a leader's ability to build a team or get results through others.

Although the term *personality* has many different meanings, we use it to describe one's typical or characteristic patterns of behavior. There are several different theories to describe why people act in characteristic ways, but the trait approach to personality has been the most thoroughly researched and, as such, plays a key role in the chapter. The adoption of the OCEAN model of personality has helped to clarify personality–leadership relationships, and researchers have noted that leadership success is positively correlated with the OCEAN personality dimensions of openness to experience, conscientiousness, extraversion, agreeableness, and neuroticism.

Emotional intelligence is generally concerned with accurately understanding and responding to one's own and others' emotions. Leaders who can better align their thoughts and feelings with their actions may be more effective than leaders who think and feel one way about something but then do something different about it. Although emotional intelligence has helped to point out the role that emotions and noncognitive abilities play in leadership success, much of the concept seems to be nothing more than another label for personality. If this is the case, then emotional intelligence may be a leadership fad that will fade over time.

One theory for understanding intelligence divides it into three related components: analytic intelligence, practical intelligence, and creative intelligence. All three components are interrelated. Most research shows that leaders possess higher levels of analytic intelligence than the general population, and that more intelligent leaders often make better leaders. Analytic intelligence appears to confer upon leaders two primary benefits. First, leaders who are smarter seem to be better problem solvers. Second, and perhaps more important, smarter leaders seem to profit more from experience.

The roles of practical and creative intelligence in leadership are receiving increasing attention. Practical intelligence, or one's relevant job knowledge or experience, is proving to be extremely important for leaders. Leaders with higher levels of practical intelligence seem to be better at solving problems under stress. Moreover, practical intelligence seems to be the easiest of the three components to change. Creative intelligence involves developing new and useful products and processes, and creativity is extremely important to the success of many businesses today. It is important that leaders learn how to successfully stimulate and manage creativity, even more than being creative themselves.

Key Terms

Great Man theory

personality

public reputation

identity

traits

trait approach

weak situations

strong situations

self-awareness

five-factor model (FFM) or
OCEAN model of personality

openness to experience

conscientiousness

extraversion

agreeableness

neuroticism

just world hypothesis

types

personality typology

Myers-Briggs Type Indicator
(MBTI)

Forer effect

strengths-based leadership

emotional intelligence

neuroleadership

mindfulness

intelligence

triarchic theory of intelligence

analytic intelligence

practical intelligence

single-loop learning

double-loop learning

creative intelligence

divergent thinking

convergent thinking

creeping elegance

cognitive resources theory
(CRT)

Questions

1. What OCEAN personality traits, intelligence components, or EQ components do you think helped political leaders successfully navigate the run-up, lockdown, and economic restart phases of the coronavirus pandemic?

2. How would you rank-order the importance of analytic intelligence, practical intelligence, creative intelligence, or emotional intelligence for politicians? Would this ranking be the same for college professors or store managers at a Walmart or Aldi store?

3. Think of all the ineffective leaders you have ever worked or played for. What attributes did they have (or, perhaps more importantly, lack) that caused them to be ineffective?

4. Individuals may well be attracted to, selected for, or successful in leadership roles early in their lives and careers based on their analytic intelligence. But what happens over time and with experience? Do you think *wisdom*, for example, is just another word for intelligence, or is it something else?

5. What role would downsizing play in an organization's overall level of practical intelligence?

6. We usually think of creativity as a characteristic of individuals, but might some organizations be more creative than others? What factors do you think might affect an organization's level of creativity?

7. Can better leaders more accurately perceive and leverage emotions? How could you determine if this was so?

Activities

1. Your instructor has access to a self-scored personality-type assessment as well as to an online OCEAN personality assessment. The online assessment takes about 10 minutes to complete and could be given as homework. Once the assessments are completed, you should review the feedback reports and discuss in class.

2. Kanye West, Donald Trump, and Jacinda Ardern are figures on the world stage. All three have made statements describing themselves, and they also have public reputations. After reviewing their accomplishments, activities, and communications, rate each of these individuals on the five OCEAN personality traits and the three components of intelligence. Then compare your notes with others in your class. How did they score on openness to experience, agreeableness, neuroticism, and practical intelligence? Did everyone review their public reputations the same way? Do these individuals possess a high level of self-awareness—do their public reputations match closely with their identities? Do music, religious, or political preferences affect how these individuals are perceived by the public?

Minicase

Lessons on Leadership from Ann Fudge

How do you rescue one of the largest advertising and media services firms in the world from a downward spiral? That is the question Martin Sorrell faced when his London-based WPP Group acquired Young & Rubicam (Y&R) in 2000. After many years on top, Y&R was starting to lose momentum—and clients. Kentucky Fried Chicken, United Airlines, and Burger King all decided to take their advertising dollars elsewhere. Sorrell needed to stop the exodus, but how? Sorrell decided a fresh face was needed and started a search for a dynamic new CEO to revitalize Y&R. He found such a leader in Ann Fudge.

Ann Fudge was formerly president of Kraft Foods. At Kraft she had been responsible for the success of the $5 billion division that included well-known brands such as Maxwell House, Grape Nuts, Shredded Wheat, and General Foods International Coffees. Fudge's reputation as a charismatic leader who listens was a major issue for Sorrell when he went looking for a new CEO for Y&R. Among the talents Fudge had to offer was an ability to interact effectively with all constituencies of a consumer business. Mattel chairman and CEO Bob Eckert was Fudge's boss when he was president and CEO of Kraft. Of Fudge, Eckert says, "She is equally comfortable with consumers at the ballpark, factory workers on a production line, and executives in the boardroom. She could engage all three constituents in the same day and be comfortable. She is very comfortable with herself, and she's not pretending to be someone else. That's what makes her such an effective leader."

Fudge's commitment to her work and to the people she works with is evident in the lessons she offers to other leaders:

1. Be yourself; do not feign behavior that you think will make you "successful."

2. Always remember it's the people, not you. A leader cannot be a leader if he or she has no followers. Be honest with people. Give them feedback. Put the right people in the right jobs. Surround yourself with the smartest people you can find—people who will offer differing perspectives and diversity of experience, age, gender, and race.

3. Touch your organization. It's easy to get stuck behind your desk. Fight the burden of paperwork and get out in the field. Don't be a remote leader. You cannot create a dynamic culture if people can't see, hear, and touch you. Let them know you as a person.

4. Steer the wheel with a strategic focus, yet maintain a wide peripheral vision. Know when to stop, speed up, slow down, brake quickly, swerve, or even gun it!

Fudge had a difficult decision to make when she was approached by Sorrell about the position at Y&R. She was in the midst of a two-year break—after 24 years working for corporate America, Fudge had decided to take some time for herself. She had left her position as president of Kraft Foods in 2001 based not on her dissatisfaction with her job, but on a desire to define herself by more than her career. "It was definitely not satisfaction, it was more about life," says Fudge about her sabbatical. During her two-year break she traveled, cycling around Sardinia and Corsica; she took up yoga; and she completed the activities in a book called *The Artist's Way at Work*—a manual for improving creativity and innovation on the job.

Fudge took on the challenge and has not looked back. In her tenure at Y&R she has worked hard to get Y&R back on top. She has traveled the globe to visit Y&R employees. She frequently puts in 15-hour days pushing her strategy to focus on clients, encouraging teamwork, and improving creativity. A major undertaking for Fudge is to bring together the various business entities under the Y&R umbrella to better meet client needs. She's also trying to institute a Six Sigma method for creativity—looking for ways to increase productivity so that employees have more time to be creative. Fudge's hard work is paying off. Y&R has added Microsoft and other major companies to its client list, and if Fudge has her way, the list will continue to grow until Y&R is back on top.

1. Where would Ann Fudge be placed in each of the five-factor model (FFM) categories?

2. Consider the three components of the triarchic theory of intelligence. How did these components come into play over Ann Fudge's career?

3. Ann Fudge decided to take a sabbatical to focus on her personal life. Based on her experience, what are the benefits of such a break? What might be some drawbacks?

Sources: Diane Brady, "Act Two: Ann Fudge's Two-Year Break from Work Changed Her Life. Will Those Lessons Help Her Fix Young & Rubicam?" *BusinessWeek*, March 29, 2004, p. 72, www.bloomberg.com/news/articles/2004-03-28/act-ii; "Ann Fudge Biography," http://biography.jrank.org/pages/2912/Fudge-Ann.html; and L. Sanders, "Ann Fudge Retires from Young & Rubicam Brands," *AdAge*, November 28, 2006, http://adage.com/article/news/ann-fudge-retires-young-rubicam-brands/113487.

Endnotes

1. R. M. Stogdill, *Handbook of Leadership* (New York: Free Press, 1974).

2. R. M. Stogdill, "Personal Factors Associated with Leadership: A Review of the Literature," *Journal of Psychology* 25 (1948), pp. 35–71.

3. R. D. Mann, "A Review of the Relationships between Personality and Performance in Small Groups," *Psychological Bulletin* 56 (1959), pp. 241–70.

4. R. G. Lord, C. L. DeVader, and G. M. Allinger, "A Meta-analysis of the Relationship between Personality Traits and Leadership Perceptions: An Application of Validity Generalization Procedures," *Journal of Applied Psychology* 71 (1986), pp. 402–10.

5. R. T. Hogan, G. J. Curphy, and J. Hogan, "What Do We Know about Personality: Leadership and Effectiveness?" *American Psychologist* 49 (1994), pp. 493–504.

6. R. T. Hogan, "Personality and Personality Measurement," in *Handbook of Industrial and Organizational Psychology*, vol. 2, eds. M. D. Dunnette and L. M. Hough (Palo Alto, CA: Consulting Psychologists Press, 1991), pp. 873–919.

7. T. Chamorro-Premuzic, *The Talent Delusion* (London: Pratkus, 2017).

8. G. Curphy, M. Hartgrove, A. Licata, and E. Paulson, "How HR Can Help Organizations Foster Teamwork," *Talent Q*, in press.

9. R. T. Hogan, G. J. Curphy, R. B. Kaiser, and T. Chamorro-Premuzic, "Leadership in Organizations," in *The Sage Handbook of Industrial, Work, and Organizational Psychology, Vol. 2: Organizational Psychology*, eds. N. Anderson, D. Ones, H. K. Sinangil, and C. Viswesvaran (London: Sage, in press).

10. P. R. Sackett, F. Lievens, C. H. Van Iddekinge, and N. R. Kuncel, "Individual Differences and their Measurement: A Review of 100 Years of Research," *Journal of Applied Psychology* 102, no. 3 (2017), pp. 254–73.

11. R. T. Hogan, "Personality and Personality Measurement."

12. R. T. Hogan, "Personality and Personality Measurement."

13. D. L. Nilsen, *Using Self and Observers' Ratings of Personality to Predict Leadership Performance*, unpublished doctoral dissertation, University of Minnesota, 1996.

14. R. T. Hogan, "Personality and Personality Measurement."

15. T. Chamorro-Premuzic, *The Talent Delusion* (London: Pratkus, 2017).

16. R. T. Hogan and T. Chamorro-Premuzic, "Personality and Career Success," in *The APA Handbook for Personality and Social Psychology, Vol. 4: Personality Processes and Individual Differences*, eds. M. Miculincer and P. R. Shaver (Washington, DC: American Psychological Association, 2015).

17. R. T. Hogan, *Personality and the Fate of Organizations* (Mahwah, NJ: Lawrence Erlbaum, 2007).

18. G. J. Curphy, *The Consequences of Managerial Incompetence*, presentation given at the Third Hogan Assessment Systems International Users Conference, Prague, Czech Republic, September 2004.

19. J. Antonakis, D. V. Day, and B. Schyns, "Leadership and Individual Differences: At the Cusp of a Renaissance," *The Leadership Quarterly* 23, no. 4 (2012), pp. 643–50.

20. G. J. Curphy, *Personality, Intelligence, and Leadership*, presentation given to the Pioneer Leadership Program at Denver University, Denver, CO, 1997.

21. G. J. Curphy, "Personality and Work: Some Food for Thought," in *Personality Applications in the Workplace: Thinking Outside the Dots*, R. T. Hogan (chair). Symposium presented at the 12th Annual Conference of the Society of Industrial and Organizational Psychology, St. Louis, MO, 1997.

22. G. J. Curphy, "New Directions in Personality," in *Personality and Organizational Behavior*, R. T. Hogan (chair). Symposium presented at the 104th Annual Meeting of the American Psychological Association, Toronto, Canada, 1996.

23. J. Hogan and B. Holland, "Using Theory to Evaluate Personality and Job-Performance Relations: A Socio-analytic Perspective," *Journal of Applied Psychology* 88, no. 1 (2003), pp. 100–12.

24. R. P. Tett and D. D. Burnett, "A Personality Trait-Based Interactionalist Model of Job Performance," *Journal of Applied Psychology* 88, no. 3 (2003), pp. 500–17.

25. "When Hiring Executives, Context Matters Most," *Harvard Business Review*, September–October 2017, pp. 20–22.

26. G. W. Allport and H. S. Odbert, "Trait-Names: A Psycho-lexical Study," *Psychological Monographs* 47 (1936), pp. 171–220.

27. R. T. Hogan, G. J. Curphy, and J. Hogan, "What Do We Know about Personality: Leadership and Effectiveness?" *American Psychologist* 49 (1994), pp. 493–504.

28. J. J. Deary, "A (Latent) Big-Five Personality Model in 1915? A Reanalysis of Webb's Data," *Journal of Applied Psychology* 71, no. 5 (1996), pp. 992–1005.

29. L. L. Thurstone, "The Factors of the Mind," *Psychological Review* 41 (1934), pp. 1–32.

30. R. T. Hogan et al., "What Do We Know about Personality."

31. M. R. Barrick and M. K. Mount, "The Big Five Personality Dimensions and Job Performance: A Meta-analysis." *Personal Psychology* 44 (1991), pp. 1–26.

32. P. T. Costa Jr. and R. R. McCrae, "Domains and Facets: Hierarchical Personality Assessment Using the Revised NEO Personality Inventory," *Journal of Personality Assessment* 64 (1995), pp. 21–50.

33. M. R. Barrick, "Answers to Lingering Questions about Personality Research," paper presented at the 14th Annual Conference of the Society of Industrial and Organizational Psychology, Atlanta, GA, 1999.

34. C. J. Thoresen, J. C. Bradley, P. D. Bliese, and J. D. Thoresen, "The Big Five Personality Traits and Individual Job Growth Trajectories in Maintenance and Transitional Job Stages," *Journal of Applied Psychology* 89, no. 5 (2004), pp. 835–53.

35. J. E. Bono and T. A. Judge, "Personality and Transformational and Transactional Leadership," *Journal of Applied Psychology* 89, no. 5 (2004), pp. 901–10.

36. L. E. Hough and F. L. Oswald, "Personality Testing and Industrial-Organizational Psychology: Reflections, Progress, and Prospects," *Industrial and Organizational Psychology: Perspectives on Science and Practice* 1, no. 3 (2008), pp. 272–90.

37. D. S. Ones, S. Dilchert, C. Viswesvaran, and T. A. Judge, "In Support of Personality Assessment in Organizational Settings," *Personnel Psychology* 60, no. 4 (2007), pp. 995–1028.

38. R. T. Hogan et al., "What Do We Know about Personality."

39. J. F. Salgado, "Predicting Job Performance Using FFM and Non-FFM Personality Measures," *Journal of Occupational and Organizational Psychology* 76, no. 3 (2003), pp. 323–46.

40. R. T. Hogan, "The Role of Big Five Personality Traits in Executive Selection," in *The Role of I/O Psychology in Executive Assessment and Development*, G. J. Curphy (chair). Paper presented at the 15th Annual Conference of the Society of Industrial and Organizational Psychology, New Orleans, LA, 2000.

41. G. J. Curphy and K. D. Osten, *Technical Manual for the Leadership Development Survey*, Technical Report No. 93-14 (Colorado Springs, CO: U.S. Air Force Academy, 1993).

42. R. T. Hogan, *Personality and the Fate of Organizations* (Mahwah, NJ: Lawrence Erlbaum Associates, 2007).

43. F. Lievens, M. H. Harris, E. Van Keer, and C. Bisqueret, "Predicting Cross-Cultural Training Performance: The Validity of Personality, Cognitive Ability, and Dimensions Measures by an Assessment Center and a Behavior Description Interview," *Journal of Applied Psychology* 88, no. 3 (2003), pp. 476–89.

44. R. Akhtar, C. Humphreys, A. Furnham, "Exploring the Relationships among Personality, Values, and Business Intelligence," *Journal of Consulting Psychology: Practice and Research* 67, no. 3, 2015, pp. 258–76.

45. R. T. Hogan et al., "What Do We Know about Personality."

46. C. J. Thoresen et al., "The Big Five Personality Traits and Individual Job Growth Trajectories in Maintenance and Transitional Job Stages."

47. J. E. Bono and T. A. Judge, "Personality and Transformational and Transactional Leadership."

48. L. E. Hough and F. L. Oswald, "Personality Testing and Industrial-Organizational Psychology."

49. D. S. Ones et al., "In Support of Personality Assessment in Organizational Settings."

50. J. F. Salgado, "Predicting Job Performance Using FFM and Non-FFM Personality Measures."

51. R. T. Hogan, "The Role of Big Five Personality Traits in Executive Selection."

52. G. J. Curphy and K. D. Osten, *Technical Manual for the Leadership Development Survey.*

53. R. T. Hogan, *Personality and the Fate of Organizations.*

54. F. Lievens et al., "Predicting Cross-Cultural Training Performance."

55. A. Duckworth, *Grit: The Power of Passion and Perseverance* (New York: Scribner, 2016).

56. M. P. Wilmot and D. A. Ones, "A Century of Research on Conscientiousness at Work," *PNAS*, http://www.gwern.net/docs/conscientiousness/2019-wilmot.pdf.

57. R. T. Hogan et al., "What Do We Know about Personality."

58. R. T. Hogan, *Personality and the Fate of Organizations.*

59. E. Bernstein, "The Case of the Introverted Entrepreneur," *The Wall Street Journal*, August 24, 2015, pp. R1–2.

60. R. T. Hogan et al., "What Do We Know about Personality."

61. L. E. Hough and F. L. Oswald, "Personality Testing and Industrial-Organizational Psychology."

62. D. S. Ones et al., "In Support of Personality Assessment in Organizational Settings."

63. R. T. Hogan, *Personality and the Fate of Organizations.*

64. T. A. Judge and J. D. Kanmeyer-Mueller, "On the Value of Aiming High: The Causes and Consequences of Ambition," *Journal of Applied Psychology* 97, no. 4 (2012), pp. 758–75.

65. T. A. Judge and A. Erez, "Interaction and Intersection: The Constellation of Emotional Stability and Extraversion in Predicting Performance," *Personnel Psychology* 60 (2007), pp. 573–96.

66. M. P. Wilmot, C. R. Wanberg, J. D. Kanmeyer-Mueller, and D. S. Ones, "Extraversion Advantages at Work: A Quantitative Review and Synthesis of the Meta-Analytic Evidence," *Journal of Applied Psychology* 104, no. 12 (2019), pp. 1447–70.

67. Hogan Assessments, "It's Time to Stop Vilifying Ambition," *The Science of Personality*, January 8, 2019, http://www.hoganassessments.com/its-time-to-stop-vilifying-ambition.

68. R. T. Hogan et al., "What Do We Know about Personality."

69. T. Chamorro-Premuzic, *The Talent Delusion* (London: Pratkus, 2017).

70. R. T. Hogan, "The Role of Big Five Personality Traits in Executive Selection."

71. R. T. Hogan, *Personality and the Fate of Organizations.*

72. S. Shellenbarger, "Why Likeability Matters More Than Ever at Work," *The Wall Street Journal*, March 26, 2014, p. D3.

73. R. T. Hogan et al., "What Do We Know about Personality."

74. L. E. Hough and F. L. Oswald, "Personality Testing and Industrial-Organizational Psychology."

75. D. S. Ones et al., "In Support of Personality Assessment in Organizational Settings."

76. R. T. Hogan, "The Role of Big Five Personality Traits in Executive Selection."

77. R. T. Hogan, *Personality and the Fate of Organizations.*

78. R. T. Hogan et al., "What Do We Know about Personality."

79. L. E. Hough and F. L. Oswald, "Personality Testing and Industrial-Organizational Psychology."

80. D. S. Ones et al., "In Support of Personality Assessment in Organizational Settings."

81. J. F. Salgado, "Predicting Job Performance Using FFM and Non-FFM Personality Measures."

82. R. T. Hogan, "The Role of Big Five Personality Traits in Executive Selection."

83. G. J. Curphy and K. D. Osten, *Technical Manual for the Leadership Development Survey.*

84. R. T. Hogan, *Personality and the Fate of Organizations.*

85. F. Lievens et al., "Predicting Cross-Cultural Training Performance."

86. T. A. Judge and J. D. Kanmeyer-Mueller, "On the Value of Aiming High."

87. T. A. Judge and A. Erez, "Interaction and Intersection."

88. J. E. Bono and T. A. Judge, "Personality and Transformational and Transactional Leadership."

89. R. T. Hogan, "Personality and Personality Measurement."

90. R. T. Hogan, "Personality and Personality Measurement."

91. L. E. Hough and F. L. Oswald, "Personality Testing and Industrial-Organizational Psychology."

92. D. S. Ones et al., "In Support of Personality Assessment in Organizational Settings."

93. J. F. Salgado, "Predicting Job Performance Using FFM and Non-FFM Personality Measures."

94. R. T. Hogan, *Personality and the Fate of Organizations.*

95. T. Chamorro-Premuzic, *The Talent Delusion.*

96. R. T. Hogan, G. J. Curphy, R. B. Kaiser, and T. Chamorro-Premuzic, "Leadership in Organizations," in *The Sage Handbook of Industrial, Work, and Organizational Psychology, Vol. 2: Organizational Psychology*, ed. N. Anderson, D. Ones, H. K. Sinangil, and C. Viswesvaran (London: Sage, in press).

97. R. T. Hogan and T. Chamorro-Premuzic, "Personality and Career Success," in *The APA Handbook for Personality and Social Psychology, Vol. 4: Personality Processes and Individual Differences*, eds. M. Miculincer and P. R. Shaver (Washington, DC: American Psychological Association, 2015).

98. R. T. Hogan, *Personality and the Fate of Organizations.*

99. T. A. Judge and J. D. Kanmeyer-Mueller, "On the Value of Aiming High."

100. R. T. Hogan, "Personality and Personality Measurement."

101. J. F. Salgado, "Predicting Job Performance Using FFM and Non-FFM Personality Measures."

102. F. Lievens et al., "Predicting Cross-Cultural Training Performance."

103. R. J. House, P. W. Dorfman, M. Javidan, P. J. Hanges, and M. F. Scully de Luque, *Strategic Leadership across Cultures: The GLOBE Study of CEO Leadership and Effectiveness in 24 Countries* (Thousand Oaks, CA: Sage, 2014).

104. G. J. Curphy, "Comments on the State of Leadership Prediction," in *Predicting Leadership: The Good, The Bad, the Indifferent, and the Unnecessary*, J. P. Campbell and M. J. Benson (chairs). Symposium conducted at the 22nd Annual Conference for the Society of Industrial and Organizational Psychology, New York, April 2007.

105. R. T. Hogan and J. Hogan, *The Leadership Potential Report* (Tulsa, OK: Hogan Assessment Systems, 2002).

106. J. F. Salgado, "Predicting Job Performance Using FFM and Non-FFM Personality Measures."

107. R. T. Hogan, "Personality and Personality Measurement."

108. L. E. Hough and F. L. Oswald, "Personality Testing and Industrial-Organizational Psychology."

109. D. S. Ones et al., "In Support of Personality Assessment in Organizational Settings."

110. A. Furnham, "Why Do Personality Tests Fail at Selection?" Hogan Assessments, April 23, 2019, http://www.hoganassessments.com/why-do-personality-tests-fail-at-selection.

111. N. L. Quenk, *In the Grip*, 2nd ed. (Mountain View, CA: CPP, 2000).

112. P. B. Myers and K. D. Myers, *The Myers-Briggs Type Indicator Step II (Form Q) Profile* (Palo Alto, CA: Consulting Psychologists Press, 2003).

113. N. L. Quenk, *In the Grip*.

114. P. B. Myers and K. D. Myers, *The Myers-Briggs Type Indicator Step II*.

115. N. L. Quenk and J. M. Kummerow, *The Myers-Briggs Type Indicator Step II (Form B) Profile* (Palo Alto, CA: Consulting Psychologists Press, 2001).

116. A. Grant, "Say Goodbye to the MBTI, the Fad That Won't Die," *Psychology Today*, September 18, 2013, http://www.psychologytoday.com/blog/give-and-take/201309/goodbye-mbti-the-fad-won-t-die.

117. I. B. Myers and B. H. McCaulley, *Manual: A Guide to the Development and Use of the Myers-Briggs Type Indicator* (Palo Alto, CA: Consulting Psychologists Press, 1985).

118. W. H. Cummings, "Age Group Differences and Estimated Frequencies of the MBTI Types: Proposed Changes," *Proceedings of the Psychology in the Department of Defense Thirteenth Symposium* (Colorado Springs, CO: United States Air Force Academy, April 1992).

119. J. Stromberg and E. Caswell, "Why the Myers-Briggs Test Is Totally Meaningless," *Vox*, October 8, 2015, http://www.vox.com/2014/7/15/5881947/myers-briggs-personality-test-meaningless.

120. M. Ahmed, "Is Myers-Briggs Up to the Job?" *Financial Times*, February 11, 2016, https://www.ft.com/content/8790ef0a-d040-11e5-831d-09f7778e7377.

121. A. Grant, "Say Goodbye to the MBTI."

122. A. Grant, "MBTI, If You Want Me Back, You Need to Change Too," LinkedIn, September 22, 2013, https://www.linkedin.com/pulse/20130922141533-69244073-mbti-if-you-want-me-back-you-need-to-change-too.

123. R. T. Hogan, "The Value of the Myers-Briggs Type Indicator," *The Science of Personality*, September 11, 2018, http://www.hoganassessments.com/the-value-of-the-myers-briggs-type-indicator.

124. C. I. Diaz, "The Mythical Land of Psychological Types and Its Impact on Education," June 27, 2018, http://www.learningscientists.org/blog/2018/6/27-1.

125. D. Goleman, *Emotional Intelligence* (New York: Bantam Doubleday Dell, 1995).

126. P. Salovey and J. D. Mayer, "Emotional Intelligence," *Imagination, Cognition, and Personality* 9 (1990), pp. 185–211.

127. J. D. Mayer, P. Salovey, and D. R. Caruso, "Emotional Intelligence: New Ability or Eclectic Traits?" *American Psychologist* 63, no. 6 (2008), pp. 503–17.

128. R. Bar-On, *The Emotional Quotient Inventory (EQ-i)* (Toronto, Canada: Multi-Health Systems, 1996).

129. R. Aberman, "Emotional Intelligence," paper presented at the Quarterly Meeting of the Minnesota Human Resource Planning Society, Minneapolis, MN, November 2000.

130. R. Aberman, "Emotional Intelligence and Work," presentation given to the Minnesota Professionals for Psychology Applied to Work, Minneapolis, MN, January 2007.

131. D. Goleman, *Emotional Intelligence*.

132. D. Goleman, *Working with Emotional Intelligence* (New York: Bantam Doubleday Dell, 1998).

133. A. Sachs, *Emotional Intelligence* (1995), by Daniel Goleman," *Time*, August 9, 2011, http://content.time.com/time/specials/packages/article/0,28804,2086680_2086683_2087663,00.html.

134. J. D. Mayer et al., "Emotional Intelligence."

135. D. R. Caruso, J. D. Mayer, and P. Salovey, "Emotional Intelligence and Emotional Leadership," in *Multiple Intelligences and Leadership*, eds. R. E. Riggio, S. E. Murphy, and F. J. Pirozzolo (Mahwah, NJ: Lawrence Erlbaum Associates, 2002), pp. 55–74.

136. J. D. Mayer et al., "Emotional Intelligence."

137. D. R. Caruso et al., "Emotional Intelligence and Emotional Leadership."

138. D. Goleman, *Working with Emotional Intelligence.*

139. D. Goleman, R. Boyatzis, and A. McKee, "Primal Leadership: The Hidden Driver of Great Performance," *Harvard Business Review*, December 2001, pp. 42–53.

140. D. Goleman, R. Boyatzis, and A. McKee, *Primal Leadership: Realizing the Power of Emotional Intelligence* (Boston: Harvard Business School Press, 2002).

141. J. D. Mayer et al., "Emotional Intelligence."

142. D. R. Caruso et al., "Emotional Intelligence and Emotional Leadership."

143. F. Cavazotte, V. Moreno, and M. Hickmann, "Effects of Leader Intelligence, Personality, and Emotional Intelligence on Transformational Leadership and Managerial Performance," *The Leadership Quarterly* 23, no. 3 (2012), pp. 443–55.

144. D. L. Van Rooy and C. Viswesvaran, "Emotional Intelligence: A Meta-analytic Investigation of Predictive Validity and Nomological Net," *Journal of Vocational Behavior* 65, pp. 71–95.

145. D. L. Joseph and D. A. Newman, "Emotional Intelligence: An Integrative Meta-Analysis and Cascading Model," *Journal of Applied Psychology* 95, no. 1, pp. 54–78.

146. D. Joseph, J. Jin, D. A. Newman, and E. H. O'Boyle, "Why Does Self-Reported Emotional Intelligence Predict Job Performance: A Meta-analytic Investigation of Mixed EI," *Journal of Applied Psychology* 100, no. 2 (2015), pp. 298–342.

147. R. Briner, "What Is the Evidence for ... Emotional Intelligence?" *HR*, November 18, 2015, http://www.hrmagazine.co.uk/article-details/whats-the-evidence-for-emotional-intelligence.

148. P. R. Sackett, F. Lievens, C. H. Van Iddekinge, and N. R. Kuncel, "Individual Differences and Their Measurement: A Review of 100 Years of Research," *Journal of Applied Psychology* 102, no. 3 (2017), pp. 254–73.

149. J. D. Mayer et al., "Emotional Intelligence."

150. J. D. Mayer, D. R. Caruso, and P. Salovey, "Selecting a Measure of Emotional Intelligence: The Case for Ability Testing," in *Handbook of Emotional Intelligence*, eds. R. Bar-On and J. D. A. Parker (New York: Jossey-Bass, 2000).

151. R. Bar-On, "The Bar-On Emotional Quotient Inventory (EQ-i): Rational, Description, and Summary of Psychometric Properties," in *Measuring Emotional Intelligence: Common Ground and Controversy*, ed. Glenn Geher (Hauppauge, NY: Nova Science Publishers, 2004), pp. 111–42.

152. T. Schwartz, "How Do You Feel?" *Fast Company*, June 2000, pp. 297–312.

153. T. Schwartz, "How Do You Feel?"

154. T. Schwartz, "How Do You Feel?"

155. R. Aberman, "Emotional Intelligence."

156. R. Aberman, "Emotional Intelligence and Work."

157. J. D. Mayer et al., "Emotional Intelligence."

158. D. Goleman, *Working with Emotional Intelligence.*

159. D. Goleman et al., *Primal Leadership.*

160. V. U. Druskat and S. B. Wolff, "Building the Emotional Intelligence of Groups," *Harvard Business Review*, March 2001, pp. 80–91.

161. T. Sy, S. Cote, and R. Saavedra, "The Contagious Leader: Impact of the Leader's Mood on the Mood of Group Members, Group Affective Tone, and Group Processes," *Journal of Applied Psychology* 90, no. 2 (2005), pp. 295–305.

162. C. Ting Fong, "The Effects of Emotional Ambivalence on Creativity," *Academy of Management Journal* 49, no. 5 (2006), pp. 1016–30.

163. F. Walter, M. S. Cole, and R. H. Humphrey, "Emotional Intelligence: Sine Qua Non of Leadership or Folderol?" *The Academy of Management Perspectives* 25, no. 1 (2011), pp. 45–59.

164. D. Ackley, "Emotional Intelligence: A Practical Review of Models, Measures, and Applications," *Journal of Consulting Psychology, Practice and Theory* 68, no. 4 (2016), pp. 269–86.

165. R. E. Boyatzis, "Commentary on Ackley (2016): Updates on the ESCI as the Behavioral Level of Emotional Intelligence," *Journal of Consulting Psychology, Practice and Theory* 68, no. 4 (2016), pp. 287–93.

166. A. Grant, "The Dark Side of Emotional Intelligence," *The Atlantic*, January 2, 2014, https://www.theatlantic.com/health/archive/2014/01/the-dark-side-of-emotional-intelligence/282720.

167. T. Chamorro-Premuzic and M. Sanger, "How to Boost Your (and Others') Emotional Intelligence," *Harvard Business Review*, January 2017, https://hbr.org/2017/01/how-to-boost-your-and-others-emotional-intelligence.

168. P. J. Jordan, N. M. Ashkanasy, and C. E. J. Hartel, "Emotional Intelligence as a Moderator of Emotional and Behavioral Reactions to Job Security," *Academy of Management Review* 27, no. 3 (2002), pp. 361–72.

169. C. S. Wong and K. S. Law, "The Effects of Leader and Follower Emotional Intelligence on Performance and Attitude: An Exploratory Study," *The Leadership Quarterly* 13, no. 3 (2002), pp. 243–74.

170. R. E. Boyatzis, E. C. Stubbs, and S. N. Taylor, "Learning Cognitive and Emotional Intelligence Competencies through Graduate Management Education," *Academy of Management Learning and Education* 1, no. 2 (2002), pp. 150–62.

171. T. Chamorro-Premuzic and M. Sanger, "How to Boost Your (and Others') Emotional Intelligence," *Harvard Business Review*, January 9, 2017, https://hbr.org/2017/01/how-to-boost-your-and-others-emotional-intelligence.

172. D. Joseph, J. Jin, D. A. Newman, and E. H. O'Boyle, "Why Does Self-Reported Emotional Intelligence Predict Job Performance: A Meta-analytic Investigation of Mixed EI," *Journal of Applied Psychology* 100, no. 2 (2015), pp. 298–342.

173. R. Briner, "What Is the Evidence for ... Emotional Intelligence?" *HR*, November 18, 2015, http://www.hrmagazine.co.uk/article-details/whats-the-evidence-for-emotional-intelligence.

174. P. H. Dubois, "A Test Dominated Society: China 1115 b.c.–1905," in *Testing Problems in Perspective*, ed. A. Anastasi (American Council on Education, 1964).

175. R. D. Arvey et al., "Mainstream Science on Intelligence," *The Wall Street Journal*, December 13, 1994.

176. R. E. Riggio, "Multiple Intelligences and Leadership: An Overview," in *Multiple Intelligences and Leadership*, eds. R. E. Riggio, S. E. Murphy, and F. J. Pirozzolo (Mahwah, NJ: Lawrence Erlbaum Associates, 2002), pp. 1–7.

177. F. L. Schmidt and J. E. Hunter, "Development of a Causal Model of Job Performance," *Current Directions in Psychological Science* 1, no. 3 (1992), pp. 89–92.

178. S. Scarr, "Protecting General Intelligence: Constructs and Consequences for Interventions," in *Intelligence: Measurement, Theory, and Public Policy*, ed. R. L. Linn (Chicago: University of Illinois Press, 1989).

179. R. J. Sternberg, "The Concept of Intelligence: Its Role in Lifelong Learning and Success," *American Psychologist* 52, no. 10 (1997), pp. 1030–37.

180. R. J. Sternberg, "Creativity as a Decision," *American Psychologist*, May 2002, p. 376.

181. F. Schmidt, H. Le, I. Oh, and J. Schaffer, "General Mental Ability, Job Performance, and Red Herrings: Responses to Osterman, Hauser, and Schmitt," *The Academy of Management Perspectives* 21, no. 4 (2007), pp. 64–76.

182. T. A. Judge, R. Ilies, and N. Dimotakis, "Are Health and Happiness the Product of Wisdom? The Relationship of General Mental Ability to Education and Occupational Attainment, Health, and Well-Being," *Journal of Applied Psychology* 95, no. 3 (2010), pp. 454–68.

183. T. A. Judge, R. L. Klinger, and L. S. Simon, "Time Is on My Side: Time General Mental Ability, Human Capital, and Extrinsic Career Success," *Journal of Applied Psychology* 95, no. 1 (2010), pp. 92–107.

184. S. Dilchert, D. A. Ones, R. D.Davis, and C. D. Rostow, "Cognitive Ability Predicts Objectively Measured Counter productive Work Behaviors," *Journal of Applied Psychology* 92, no. 3 (2007), pp. 616–27.

185. N. Kuncel and P. Sackett, "The Gate keeper Tests," *The Wall Street Journal*, Saturday–Sunday, March 10–11, 2018, pp. A1–2.

186. N. Mondragon, "Should You Hire for Culture Fit?" *Harvard Business Review*, August 20, 2019, https://blog.hrps.org/blogpost/Should-You-Hire-for-Culture-Fit.

187. R. D. Arvey et al., "Mainstream Science on Intelligence."

188. R. E. Riggio, "Multiple Intelligences and Leadership."

189. F. L. Schmidt and J. E. Hunter, "Development of a Causal Model of Job Performance."

190. S. Scarr, "Protecting General Intelligence."

191. R. J. Sternberg, "The Concept of Intelligence: Its Role in Lifelong Learning and Success," *American Psychologist* 52, no. 10 (1997), pp. 1030–37.

192. R. J. Sternberg, "Creativity as a Decision."

193. F. Schmidt et al., "General Mental Ability, Job Performance, and Red Herrings."

194. T. A. Judge et al., "Are Health and Happiness the Product of Wisdom?"

195. T. A. Judge et al., "Time Is on My Side."

196. L. J. Cronbach, *Essentials of Psychological Testing*, 4th ed. (San Francisco: Harper & Row, 1984).

197. R. D. Arvey et al., "Mainstream Science on Intelligence."

198. R. E. Riggio, "Multiple Intelligences and Leadership."

199. F. L. Schmidt and J. E. Hunter, "Development of a Causal Model of Job Performance."

200. S. Scarr, "Protecting General Intelligence."

201. R. J. Sternberg, "The Concept of Intelligence."

202. R. J. Sternberg, "Creativity as a Decision."

203. F. Schmidt et al. "General Mental Ability, Job Performance, and Red Herrings."

204. T. A. Judge et al., "Are Health and Happiness the Product of Wisdom?"

205. T. A. Judge et al., "Time Is on My Side."

206. L. J. Cronbach, *Essentials of Psychological Testing.*

207. R. J. Sternberg, "WICS: A Model of Leadership in Organizations," *Academy of Management: Learning and Education* 2, no. 4 (2003), pp. 386–401.

208. R. J. Sternberg, "A Model of Leadership: WICS," *American Psychologist* 62, no. 1 (2007), pp. 34–42.

209. J. F. Salgado, N. Anderson, S. Moscoso, C. Bertua, F. de Fruyt, and J. P. Rolland, "A Meta-analytic Study of General Mental Ability Validity for Different Occupations in the European Community," *Journal of Applied Psychology* 88, no. 6 (2003), pp. 1068–81.

210. C. A. Scherbaum, H. W. Goldsmith, K. P. Yusko, R. Ryan, and P. J. Hanges, "Intelligence 2.0: Reestablishing a Research Program on G in I-O Psychology," *Industrial and Organizational Psychology* 5, no. 2 (2012), pp. 128–48.

211. R. J. Herrnstein and C. Murray, *The Bell Curve: Intelligence and Class Structure in American Life* (New York: Free Press, 1994).

212. G. J. Curphy, "Concluding Remarks on Executive Assessment and Development," in *The Role of I/O Psychology in Executive Assessment and Development*, G. J. Curphy (chair). Symposium presented at the 15th Annual Conference of the Society for Industrial and Organizational Psychology, New Orleans, LA, 2000.

213. G. J. Curphy, "Early Leadership Talent Identification and Development," paper presented at the Conference for Executives of Saudi Aramco, Dhahran, Saudi Arabia, October 2001.

214. G. J. Curphy, "What Role Should I/O Psychologists Play in Executive Education?" in *Models of Executive Education*, R. T. Hogan (chair). Presentation given at the 17th Annual Society for Industrial and Organizational Psychology, Toronto, Canada, April 2002.

215. G. J. Curphy, "Leadership Transitions and Succession Planning," in *Developing and Implementing Succession Planning Programs*, J. Lock (chair). Symposium conducted at the 19th Annual Conference for the Society of Industrial and Organizational Psychology, Chicago, April 2004.

216. R. Hogan, P. Barrett, and J. Hogan, *Brief Technical Manual: Hogan Business Reasoning Inventory* (Tulsa, OK: Hogan Assessment Systems, 2009).

217. J. F. Salgado et al., "A Meta-analytic Study of General Mental Ability Validity for Different Occupations in the European Community."

218. R. T. Hogan and J. Hogan, *The Hogan Business Reasoning Inventory* (Tulsa, OK: Hogan Assessment Systems, 2007).

219. R. D. Arvey et al., "Mainstream Science on Intelligence."

220. R. J. Sternberg, "Creativity as a Decision."

221. R. J. Sternberg, "A Model of Leadership: WICS."

222. R. T. Hogan and J. Hogan, *The Hogan Business Reasoning Inventory.*

223. L. J. Cronbach, *Essentials of Psychological Testing.*

224. G. J. Curphy, "Early Leadership Talent Identification and Development."

225. B. Azar, "Searching for Intelligence Beyond G," *APA Monitor* 26, no. 1 (1995), p. 1.

226. H. Gardner, *Frames of Mind: The Theory of Multiple Intelligences* (New York: Basic Books, 1983).

227. R. J. Sternberg, "The Concept of Intelligence."

228. R. J. Sternberg, "Creativity as a Decision."

229. R. J. Sternberg, *Beyond IQ: A Triarchic Theory of Human Intelligence* (New York: Cambridge University Press, 1985).

230. R. J. Sternberg, "The Concept of Intelligence."

231. R. J. Sternberg, "Creativity as a Decision."

232. R. J. Sternberg, "WICS."

233. R. J. Sternberg, "A Model of Leadership."

234. R. J. Sternberg, *Beyond IQ.*

235. C. A. Scherbaum et al., "Intelligence 2.0."

236. G. J. Curphy, "Leadership Transitions and Succession Planning."

237. R. T. Hogan and J. Hogan, *The Hogan Business Reasoning Inventory.*

238. R. J. Sternberg, *Beyond IQ.*

239. G. J. Curphy, "Leadership Transitions and Succession Planning."

240. R. J. Sternberg, *Beyond IQ.*

241. R. J. Sternberg, *Handbook of Creativity* (New York: Cambridge University Press, 1999).

242. R. J. Sternberg, "The Concept of Intelligence."

243. R. J. Sternberg, "WICS."

244. R. J. Sternberg, "A Model of Leadership."

245. R. Hogan et al., *Brief Technical Manual.*

246. R. J. Sternberg, *Beyond IQ.*

247. R. J. Sternberg, "A Broad View of Intelligence: The Theory of Successful Intelligence," *Journal of Consulting Psychology* 55, no. 3 (2003), pp. 139–54.

248. R. J. Sternberg, "The Concept of Intelligence."

249. R. J. Sternberg, "Creativity as a Decision."

250. R. J. Sternberg, "A Model of Leadership."

251. R. J. Sternberg, *Beyond IQ.*

252. R. J. Sternberg, *Handbook of Creativity.*

253. R. J. Sternberg, "A Broad View of Intelligence."

254. L. M. Kersting, "What Exactly Is Creativity?" *Monitor on Psychology*, November 2003, pp. 40–41.

255. R. J. Sternberg and T. I. Lubart, "Investing in Creativity," *American Psychologist* 52, no. 10 (1997), pp. 1046–50.

256. R. J. Sternberg, E. L. Grigorenko, and J. L. Singer, *Creativity: From Potential to Realization* (Washington, DC: American Psychological Association Press, 2004).

257. R. J. Sternberg and T. I. Lubart, "Investing in Creativity."

258. R. J. Sternberg, "Creativity as a Decision."

259. L. J. Cronbach, *Essentials of Psychological Testing.*

260. R. J. Sternberg, "A Broad View of Intelligence."

261. R. J. Sternberg and T. I. Lubart, "Investing in Creativity."

262. R. J. Sternberg et al., *Creativity.*

263. J. C. Kaufman and J. Baer, "Hawking's Haiku, Madonna's Math: Why It Is Hard to Be Creative in Every Room," in *Creativity: From Potential to Realization*, eds. R. J. Sternberg, E. L. Grigorenko, and J. L. Singer (Washington, DC: American Psychological Association Press, 2004).

264. T. Lubart and J. H. Guigard, "The Generality-Specificity of Creativity: A Multivariate Approach," in *Creativity: From Potential to Realization*, eds. R. J. Sternberg, E. L. Grigorenko, and J. L. Singer (Washington, DC: American Psychological Association Press, 2004).

265. G. J. Feist, "The Evolved Fluid Specificity of Human Creative Talent," in *Creativity: From Potential to Realization*, eds. R. J. Sternberg, E. L. Grigorenko, and J. L. Singer (Washington, DC: American Psychological Association Press, 2004).

266. J. P. Guilford, *The Nature of Human Intelligence* (New York: McGraw-Hill, 1967).

267. R. J. Sternberg, "A Broad View of Intelligence."

268. R. J. Sternberg and T. I. Lubart, "Investing in Creativity."

269. R. J. Sternberg, "What Is the Common Thread of Creativity? Its Dialectical Relationship to Intelligence and Wisdom," *American Psychologist* 56, no. 4 (2001), pp. 360–62.

270. B. Schroeder, "1,500 CEO's Surveyed: What Is the Most Important Leadership Skill?" Linked In, July 18, 2016, https://www.linkedin.com/pulse/1500-ceos-surveyed-what-most-important-leadership-skill-schroeder.

271. R. A., "The War Dividend," *The Economist*, June 24, 2014, www.economist.com/free-exchange/2014/06/24/the-war-dividend.

272. "Creativity and Cheating: Mwahahaha..." *The Economist*, February 1, 2014, www.economist.com/science-and-technology/2014/02/01/mwahahaha.

273. R. M. Stogdill, *Handbook of Leadership* (New York: Free Press, 1974).

274. R. M. Stogdill, "Personal Factors Associated with Leadership: A Review of the Literature," *Journal of Psychology* 25 (1948), pp. 35–71.

275. T. Chamorro-Premuzic, *The Talent Delusion* (London: Pratkus, 2017).

276. R. D. Arvey et al., "Mainstream Science on Intelligence."

277. R. E. Riggio, "Multiple Intelligences and Leadership."

278. F. L. Schmidt and J. E. Hunter, "Development of a Causal Model of Job Performance."

279. S. Scarr, "Protecting General Intelligence."

280. R. J. Sternberg, "The Concept of Intelligence: Its Role in Lifelong Learning and Success," *American Psychologist* 52, no. 10 (1997), pp. 1030–37.

281. R. J. Sternberg, "Creativity as a Decision."

282. F. Schmidt et al., "General Mental Ability, Job Performance, and Red Herrings."

283. T. A. Judge et al., "Are Health and Happiness the Product of Wisdom?"

284. T. A. Judge et al., "Time Is on My Side."

285. L. J. Cronbach, *Essentials of Psychological Testing.*

286. R. J. Sternberg, "WICS."

287. R. J. Sternberg, "A Model of Leadership."

288. J. F. Salgado et al., "A Meta-analytic Study of General Mental Ability Validity for Different Occupations in the European Community."

289. C. A. Scherbaum et al., "Intelligence 2.0."

290. R. J. Herrnstein and C. Murray, *The Bell Curve.*

291. R. T. Hogan and J. Hogan, *The Hogan Business Reasoning Inventory.*

292. R. J. Sternberg, "A Broad View of Intelligence."

293. R. T. Hogan, G. J. Curphy, and J. Hogan, "What Do We Know about Personality: Leadership and Effectiveness?" *American Psychologist* 49 (1994), pp. 493–504.

294. J. E. Bono and T. A. Judge, "Personality and Transformational and Transactional Leadership," *Journal of Applied Psychology* 89, no. 5 (2004), pp. 901–10.

295. L. E. Hough and F. L. Oswald, "Personality Testing and Industrial-Organizational Psychology: Reflections, Progress, and Prospects," *Industrial and Organizational Psychology: Perspectives on Science and Practice Perspectives on Science and Practice* 1, no. 3 (2008), pp. 272–90

296. D. S. Ones et al., "In Support of Personality Assessment in Organizational Settings."

297. R. T. Hogan, *Personality and the Fate of Organizations.*

298. R. M. Stogdill, *Handbook of Leadership.*

299. E. E. Ghiselli, "Intelligence and Managerial Success," *Psychological Reports* 12 (1963), p. 89.

300. J. Antonakis, R. J. House, and D. K. Simonton, "Can Super Smart Leaders Suffer From too Much of a Good Thing? The Curvilinear Effect of Intelligence on Perceived Leadership Behavior," *Journal of Applied Psychology* 102, no. 7 (2017), pp. 1003–21.

301. D. Robson, *The Intelligence Trap: Why Smart People Make Dumb Mistakes* (New York: W.W. Norton & Company, 2019).

302. F. E. Fiedler, "The Effect and Meaning of Leadership Experience: A Review of Research and a Preliminary Model," in *Impact of Leadership*, eds. K. E. Clark, M. B. Clark, and D. P. Campbell (Greensboro, NC: Center for Creative Leadership, 1992).

303. F. E. Fiedler, "The Curious Role of Cognitive Resources in Leadership," in *Multiple Intelligences and Leadership*, eds. R. E. Riggio, S. E. Murphy, and F. J. Pirozzolo (Mahwah, NJ: Lawrence Erlbaum Associates, 2002), pp. 91–104.

304. F. W. Gibson, "A Taxonomy of Leader Abilities and Their Influence on Group Performance as a Function of Interpersonal Stress," in *Impact of Leadership*, eds. K. E. Clark, M. B. Clark, and D. P. Campbell (Greensboro, NC: Center for Creative Leadership, 1992).

305. M. A. Collins and T. M. Amabile, "Motivation and Creativity," in *Handbook of Creativity*, ed. R. J. Sterberg (New York: Cambridge University Press, 1999).

306. T. M. Amabile, E. A. Schatzel, G. B. Moneta, and S. J. Kramer, "Leader Behaviors and the Work Environment for Creativity: Perceived Leader Support," *The Leadership Quarterly* 15, no. 1 (2004), pp. 5–32.

307. R. Reiter-Palmon and R. Ilies, "Leadership and Creativity: Understanding Leadership from a Creative Problem Solving Perspective," *The Leadership Quarterly* 15, no. 1 (2004), pp. 55–77.

308. J. Zhou, "When the Presence of Creative Co-Workers Is Related to Creativity: Role of Supervisor Close Monitoring, Developmental Feedback, and Creative Personality," *Journal of Applied Psychology* 88, no. 3 (2003), pp. 413–22.

309. C. E. Shalley and L. L. Gilson, "What Leaders Need to Know: A Review of the Social and Contextual Factors That Can Foster or Hinder Creativity," *The Leadership Quarterly* 15, no. 1 (2004), pp. 33–53.

310. S. F. Dingfelder, "Creativity on the Clock," *Monitor on Psychology*, November 2003, p. 58.

311. M. Basadur, "Leading Others to Think Innovatively Together: Creative Leadership," *The Leadership Quarterly* 15, no. 1 (2004), pp. 103–21.

312. R. Florida and J. Goodnight, "Managing for Creativity," *Harvard Business Review*, July–August 2005, pp. 125–31.

313. R. Florida, R. Cushing, and G. Gates, "When Social Capital Stifles Innovation," *Harvard Business Review*, August 2002, p. 20.

314. M. D. Mumford, G. M. Scott, B. Gaddis, and J. M. Strange, "Leading Creative People: Orchestrating Expertise and Relationships," *The Leadership Quarterly* 13, no. 6 (2002), pp. 705–50.

315. R. J. Sternberg, "WICS."

316. X. Zhang and K. M. Bartol, "Linking Empowering Leadership and Employee Creativity: The Influence of Psychological Empowerment, Intrinsic Motivation, and Creative Process Engagement," *Academy of Management Journal* 53, no. 1 (2010), pp. 107–28.

317. T. M. Amabile and M. Khaire, "Creativity and the Role of the Leader," *Harvard Business Review*, October 2008, pp. 100–10.

318. T. Chamorro-Premuzic, "Does Diversity Actually Increase Creativity?" *Harvard Business Review*, June 28, 2017, https://hbr.org/2017/06/does-diversity-actually-increase-creativity.

319. M. A. Collins and T. M. Amabile, "Motivation and Creativity."

320. T. M. Amabile, "Beyond Talent: John Irving and the Passionate Craft of Creativity," *American Psychologist* 56, no. 4 (2001), pp. 333–36.

321. T. M. Amabile, "The Motivation to Be Creative," in *Frontiers in Creativity: Beyond the Basics*, ed. S. Isaksen (Buffalo, NY: Bearly, 1987).

322. J. Zhou, "Feedback Valence, Feedback Style, Task Autonomy, and Achievement Orientation: Interactive Effects on Creative Performance," *Journal of Applied Psychology* 83, no. 2 (1998), pp. 261–76.

323. G. M. Prince, "Creative Meetings through Power Sharing," *Harvard Business Review* 50, no. 4 (1972), pp. 47–54.

324. C. E. Shalley and L. L. Gilson, "What Leaders Need to Know."

325. R. Florida and J. Goodnight, "Managing for Creativity."

326. R. Florida et al., "When Social Capital Stifles Innovation."

327. F. E. Fiedler and J. E. Garcia, *New Approaches to Leadership: Cognitive Resources and Organizational Performance* (New York: John Wiley, 1987).

328. F. E. Fiedler, "Cognitive Resources and Leadership Performance," *Applied Psychology: An International Review* 44, no. 1 (1995), pp. 5–28.

329. F. E. Fiedler, "The Effect and Meaning of Leadership Experience."

330. F. E. Fiedler, "The Curious Role of Cognitive Resources in Leadership."

331. F. W. Gibson, "A Taxonomy of Leader Abilities and Their Influence on Group Performance as a Function of Interpersonal Stress."

332. F. E. Fiedler and J. E. Garcia, *New Approaches to Leadership*.

333. F. E. Fiedler, "Cognitive Resources and Leadership Performance."

334. F. W. Gibson, "A Taxonomy of Leader Abilities and Their Influence on Group Performance as a Function of Interpersonal Stress."

335. F. E. Fiedler, "Cognitive Resources and Leadership Performance."

336. F. E. Fiedler, "The Effect and Meaning of Leadership Experience."

337. F. E. Fiedler, "The Curious Role of Cognitive Resources in Leadership."

338. F. W. Gibson, "A Taxonomy of Leader Abilities and Their Influence on Group Performance as a Function of Interpersonal Stress."

339. F. E. Fiedler and J. E. Garcia, *New Approaches to Leadership*.

340. F. E. Fiedler, "Cognitive Resources and Leadership Performance."

341. F. W. Gibson, "A Taxonomy of Leader Abilities and Their Influence on Group Performance as a Function of Interpersonal Stress."

342. W. Schonpflug, "The Noncharismatic Leader-Vulnerable," *Applied Psychology: An International Review* 44, no. 1 (1995), pp. 39–42.

343. S. J. Zaccaro, "Leader Resources and the Nature of Organizational Problems," *Applied Psychology: An International Review* 44, no. 1 (1995), pp. 32–36.

344. A. B. Adler, P. D. Bliese, M. A. Pickering, J. Hammermeister, J. Williams, C. Harada, L. Csoka, B. Holliday, and C. Ohlson, "Mental Skills Training with Basic Combat Training Soldiers: A Group-Randomized Trial," *Journal of Applied Psychology* 100, no. 6 (2015), pp. 1752–64.

345. F. E. Fiedler, "The Curious Role of Cognitive Resources in Leadership."

346. F. W. Gibson, "A Taxonomy of Leader Abilities and Their Influence on Group Performance as a Function of Interpersonal Stress."

347. T. Chamorro-Premuzic, *The Talent Delusion.*

CHAPTER 7

Leadership Behavior

Introduction

Researcher:	Are all the captains you fly with pretty much the same?
Aircrew Member:	Oh, no. Some guys are the greatest guys in the world to fly with. I mean they may not have the greatest hands in the world, but that doesn't matter. When you fly with them, you feel like you can work together to get the job done. You really want to do a good job for them. Some other captains are just the opposite . . . you just can't stand to work with them. That doesn't mean you'll do anything that's unsafe or dangerous, but you won't go out of your way to keep him or her out of trouble either. So you'll just sit back and do what you have to and just hope he or she screws up.
Researcher:	How can you tell which kind of captain you're working with?
Aircrew Member:	Oh, you can tell.
Researcher:	How?
Aircrew Member:	I don't know how you tell, but it doesn't take very long. Just a couple of minutes and you'll know.

The truth of the matter is that you always know the right thing to do. The hard part is doing it.

Norman Schwartzkopf, former U.S. Army general

Throughout this book we have been talking about different ways to assess leaders. But when all is said and done, how can we tell good leaders from bad ones? This is a critically important question: If we can specifically identify what leaders do that makes them effective, then we can hire or train people to exhibit these behaviors. One way to differentiate leaders is to look at what they do on a day-to-day basis. Some leaders do a good job of making decisions, providing direction, creating plans, giving regular feedback, getting their followers the resources they need to be successful, and building cohesive teams. Other leaders have difficulty in making decisions, set vague or unclear goals, ignore followers' requests for equipment, and cannot build teams. Although a leader's values, personality, and intelligence are important, variables like these have only an indirect relationship with leadership effectiveness. Their effect presumably comes from the impact they have on leader behavior, which appears to have a more direct relationship with a leader's ability to engage followers, build teams, and get results through others. One advantage of looking at leaders in terms of behavior instead of, say, personality is that behavior is often easier to measure; leadership behaviors can be observed, whereas personality traits, values, or intelligence must be inferred from behavior or measured with tests. Another advantage of looking at leader behavior is that many people are less defensive about—and feel in more control of—specific behaviors than they are about their personalities or intelligence.

Nonetheless, leaders with certain traits, values, or attitudes may find it easier to effectively perform some leadership behaviors than others. For example, leaders with higher agreeableness scores (as defined in **Chapter 6**) may find it relatively easy to show concern and support for followers but may also find it difficult to discipline followers. Likewise, leaders with a low friendship value (**Chapter 5**) and who score low on the personality trait of extraversion (**Chapter 6**) will prefer working by themselves versus with others. Because behavior is under conscious control, we can always choose to change our behavior as leaders if we want to. However, the ease with which we exhibit or can change behavior will partly be a function of how we are hardwired, that is, our values, personality, and intelligence.

Followers and the situation are the other two major factors to keep in mind when evaluating leadership behavior. As described in **Chapter 6**, strong situational norms can play pervasive roles in leaders' behavior. Similarly, follower and situational factors can help determine whether a particular leadership behavior is "bad" or "good." Say a leader gave a group of followers extremely detailed instructions on how to get a task accomplished. If the followers were new to the organization or had never done the task before, this level of detail would probably help the leader get better results through others. But if the followers were experienced, this same leader behavior would likely have detrimental effects. The same would be true if the company were in a financial crisis versus having a successful year.

This chapter begins with a discussion of why it is important to study leadership behavior. We then review some of the early research on leader behavior and discuss several ways to categorize different leadership behaviors. The next section describes a model of community leadership, and we conclude the chapter by summarizing what is currently known about a common leadership behavior assessment technique: the 360-degree, or multirater, feedback questionnaire.

Studies of Leadership Behavior

Why Study Leadership Behavior?

Thus far we have reviewed research on a number of key variables affecting leadership behavior, but we have not directly examined what leaders actually do to successfully build a team or get results through others. For example, what behaviors did Jacinda Ardern exhibit as a student at the University of Waikato, as a researcher for the prime minister's office, and as the leader of the New Zealand Labour Party (see **Profiles in Leadership 7.1**)? What did former president Barack Obama specifically do to rescue the financial services and automotive industries, pass comprehensive health care legislation, deal with the oil spill in the Gulf of Mexico, and end the wars in Iraq and Afghanistan? What do Mark Zuckerberg, CEO of Facebook, and Satya Nadella, the CEO of Microsoft, do to keep their companies profitable? What exactly has Marine Le Pen done to lead the opposition in France or Greta Thunberg done to bring attention to the impending dangers of climate change? To answer questions such as these, it is appropriate to turn our attention to leader behavior itself; if we could identify how successful leaders act compared with unsuccessful leaders, we could design leadership talent management systems allowing organizations to hire, develop, and promote people who have the skills necessary for future success. Unfortunately, as we can see in the *Dilbert* comic strip, *The Office* television series, and the explosive growth of management consulting firms, many people in positions of authority either do not know how to build teams or get results through others, or do not realize how their behavior negatively affects the people who work for them.[1, 2, 3, 4, 5, 6, 7, 8, 9, 10]

Before we describe the different ways to categorize what leaders do to build teams or influence a group, let's review what we know about leadership skills and behaviors. As shown in **Figure 7.1**, leadership behaviors (which include skills and competencies) are a function of intelligence, personality traits, emotional intelligence, values, attitudes, interests, knowledge, and experience. The factors in the bottom layer of blocks are relatively difficult to change, and they predispose a leader to act in distinctive ways. As described in **Chapter 6**,

FIGURE 7.1 The Building Blocks of Skills

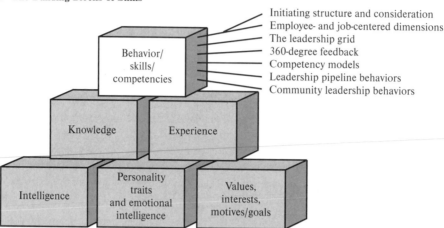

one's personality traits are pervasive and almost automatic, typically occurring without much conscious attention. The same could be said about how values, attitudes, and intelligence affect behaviors. Over time, however, leaders can learn and discern which behaviors are more appropriate and effective than others. It is always useful to remember the pivotal roles individual differences, followers, and situational variables can play in a leader's actions[11, 12, 13] (see **Profiles in Leadership 7.1** and **7.2**).

Jacinda Ardern

PROFILES IN LEADERSHIP 7.1

Jacinda Ardern is the Prime Minister of New Zealand and one of the youngest people ever elected to lead a country. Under her leadership, New Zealand passed a comprehensive ban of all semiautomatic weapons and has achieved increased global approval and importance ratings. She is commonly acknowledged as the most powerful woman in the Southern Hemisphere.

Jacinda Ardern grew up as a Mormon in rural New Zealand, where her father was a police officer and her mother worked as a school caterer. Because of its stance against gay rights, she left the Mormon church at around the time she graduated from the University of Waikato with a degree in communications and public rela-

tions. Her aunt recruited her into the Labour Party, where she helped on election campaigns and worked as a researcher for the Prime Minister. She then moved to New York City to spend time doing volunteer work in a soup kitchen before moving to London to work as a policy advisor for Prime Minister Tony Blair. In 2008, Ardern was elected president of the International Union of Socialist Youth and traveled to several countries as part of this role.

Returning to New Zealand that year, Ardern took a full-time position with the Labour Party, where she worked on campaigns and ran for election several times. Not all of her campaigns were successful, as she lost two elections to be an MP in 2011 and 2014. She finally became an MP in 2017 and later that year was voted to be the Deputy Head of the Labour Party. Just seven weeks before a national election and facing historically low polling numbers, Andrew

Little, the head of the Labour Party, resigned. Ardern became the Leader of the Opposition going into the election and ran a campaign of "relentless positivity." The Labour Party's popularity rose dramatically, gained a number of seats during the election, and was able to form a coalition with the Green Party to lead the country.

A progressive leader who participated in the global Women's March in 2017, Jacinda Ardern has focused on housing, child poverty, and social inequality. She made headlines by bringing her infant to a United Nations General Assembly meeting and speaking out against China's reeducation camps for Uyghurs and Myanmar's treatment of the Rohingas. She may be best known for getting New Zealand to pass a comprehensive semiautomatic weapons ban after a white nationalist killed 51 and wounded 49 Muslims during an attack on a Christchurch mosque. She got all three of New Zealand's major parties to support the new legislation, and it got passed one month after the shooting.

A two-time guest on *The Late Show with Stephen Colbert*, Ardern invited Colbert to visit New Zealand and picked him up at the Auckland airport upon his arrival. During interviews with Colbert and others, she has come across as thoughtful, humorous, approachable, and considerate. What behaviors did Jacinda Ardern exhibit that made her an effective or ineffective leader?

Sources: "The World's Youngest Female Leader Takes Over New Zealand," *The Economist*, www.economist.com/asia/2017/10/26/the-worlds-youngest-female-leader-takes-over-in-new-zealand; J. St. John, "How Jacinda Ardern Became New Zealand's Youngest Female Prime Minister," *Nation Builder*, https://nationbuilder.com/jacinda_ardern; "Australian Journalist Surprised by Jacinda Ardern's Accessibility," *Stuff*, October 21, 2017, www.stuff.co.nz/national/politics/98121814/australian-journalist-surprised-by-jacinda-arderns-accessibility; I. Tharoor, "New Zealand Shooting: The World Is Praising Jacinda Ardern's Response to Terrorist Attack," *Independent*, March 20, 2019, www.independent.co.uk/news/world/australasia/new-zealand-shooting-jacinda-ardern-video-reaction-world-praise-a8832186.html; "Prime Minister Jacinda Ardern Explains Why the UN Laughed at Trump," *The Late Show with Stephen Colbert*, www.youtube.com/watch?v=aYsZv9JXmio; and "Stephen Colbert: The Newest Zealander Visits PM Jacinda Ardern," *The Late Show with Stephen Colbert*, www.youtube.com/watch?v=DUPo62ouU84.

Captains Thomas Musgrave and George Dalgarno

PROFILES IN LEADERSHIP 7.2

Three hundred miles south of New Zealand are the Auckland Islands. They are isolated and forbidding, and 150 years ago they brought almost certain death to ships that got too close. The howling sub-Antarctic winds drove ships onto the shallow reefs and most sailors quickly drowned. Those who made it to shore died of exposure and starvation. The few who survived did so in dreadful conditions. In *Island of the Lost*, Joan Druett (2007) recounts the story of two parties that were shipwrecked in 1864 on opposite sides of the island; this is a story of leadership and teamwork.

The first, a party of five led by Captain Thomas Musgrave of England, behaved like Shackleton's crew stranded in the Weddell Sea. Encouraged by Musgrave, the men banded together in a common quest for survival. Over a period of 20 months, using material salvaged from their ship, they built a cabin, found food, rotated cooking duties, nursed one another, made tools, tanned seal hides for shoes, built a bellows and a furnace, made bolts and nails, and then built a boat that they used to sail to safety.

Meanwhile, 20 miles away, a Scottish ship led by Captain George Dalgarno went aground, and 19 men made it safely to shore. Delgarno became depressed and went "mad," and the rest of the crew fell into despair, anarchy, and then cannibalism. A sailor named Robert Holding tried to encourage the others to act together to build shelter and find food, but other members of the crew threatened to kill and eat him. After three months, only three men were alive and subsequently rescued.

Although these events happened almost 150 years ago, the story has strong parallels to modern leadership. How did the leadership behav-iors exhibited by Captains Musgrave and Dalgarno differ, and what impact did these behaviors have on their crews? Are there any parallels between these two captains and leaders in government, industry, or philanthropic organizations?

Sources: R. T. Hogan, *The Pragmatics of Leadership* (Tulsa, OK: Hogan Assessment Systems, 2007); G. J. Curphy and R. T. Hogan, *A Guide to Building High Performing Teams* (North Oaks, MN: Curphy Consulting Corporation, 2009); G. J. Curphy and R. T. Hogan, *The Rocket Model: Practical Advice for Building High Performing Teams* (Tulsa, OK: Hogan Press, 2012); and Joan Druett, *Island of the Lost: Shipwrecked on the Edge of the World* (Chapel Hills, NC: Algonquin Books, 2007).

We know what a person thinks not when he tells us what he thinks, but by his actions.

Isaac Bashevis Singer, writer

The Early Studies

If you were asked to study and identify the behaviors that best differentiated effective from ineffective leaders, how would you do it? You could ask leaders what they do, follow the leaders around to see how they actually behave, or administer questionnaires to ask them and those they work with how often the leaders exhibited certain behaviors. These three approaches have been used extensively in past and present leadership research.

Much of the initial leader behavior research was conducted at Ohio State University and the University of Michigan. Collectively, the Ohio State University studies developed a series of questionnaires to measure different leader behaviors in work settings. These researchers began by collecting over 1,800 questionnaire items that described different types of leadership behaviors. These items were collapsed into 150 statements, and these statements were then used to develop a questionnaire called the **Leader Behavior Description Questionnaire (LBDQ)**.[14, 15] To obtain information about a particular leader's behavior, subordinates were asked to rate the extent to which their leader performed behaviors like the following:

He lets subordinates know when they've done a good job.

He sets clear expectations about performance.

He shows concern for subordinates as individuals.

He makes subordinates feel at ease.

In analyzing the questionnaires from thousands of subordinates, the statistical pattern of responses to all the different items indicated that leaders could be described in terms of two independent dimensions of behavior called consideration and initiating structure.[16, 17] **Consideration** refers to how friendly and supportive a leader is toward subordinates. Leaders high in consideration engage in many different behaviors that show supportiveness and concern, such as speaking up for subordinates' interests, caring about their personal situations, and showing appreciation for their work. **Initiating structure** refers to how much a leader emphasizes meeting work goals and accomplishing tasks. Leaders high in initiating structure engage in many different task-related behaviors, such as assigning deadlines, establishing performance standards, and monitoring performance levels.

The LBDQ was not the only leadership questionnaire developed by the Ohio State researchers. They also developed, for example, the Supervisory Behavior Description Questionnaire (SBDQ), which measured the extent to which leaders in industrial settings exhibited consideration and initiating structure behaviors.[18] The Leadership Opinion Questionnaire (LOQ) asked leaders to indicate the extent to which they believed different consideration and initiating behaviors were important to leadership success.[19] The LBDQ-XII was developed to assess 10 other categories of leadership behaviors in addition to consideration and initiating structure.[20] Some of the additional leadership behaviors assessed by the LBDQ-XII included acting as a representative for the group, being able to tolerate uncertainty, emphasizing production, and reconciling conflicting organizational demands.

Rather than trying to describe the variety of behaviors leaders exhibit in work settings, the researchers at the University of Michigan sought to identify leader behaviors that contributed to effective group performance.[21] They concluded that four categories of leadership behaviors are related to effective group performance: leader support, interaction facilitation, goal emphasis, and work facilitation.[22]

Both goal emphasis and work facilitation are **job-centered dimensions** of behavior similar to the initiating structure behaviors described earlier. **Goal emphasis** behaviors are concerned with motivating subordinates to accomplish the task at hand, and **work facilitation** behaviors are concerned with clarifying roles, acquiring and allocating resources, and reconciling organizational conflicts. Leader support and interaction facilitation are **employee-centered dimensions** of behavior similar to the consideration dimension of the various Ohio State questionnaires (see **Table 7.1**). **Leader support** includes behaviors where the leader shows concern for subordinates; **interaction facilitation** includes those behaviors where leaders act to smooth over and minimize conflicts among followers. Like the researchers at Ohio State, those at the University of Michigan also developed a questionnaire, the Survey of Organizations, to assess the degree to which leaders exhibit these four dimensions of leadership behaviors.[23]

TABLE 7.1   Early Leadership Behavior Dimensions

Ohio State Dimensions	University of Michigan Dimensions
Initiating structure	Goal emphasis and work facilitation
Consideration	Leader support and interaction facilitation

Although the behaviors composing the task-oriented and people-oriented leadership dimensions were similar across the two research programs, there was a fundamental difference in assumptions underlying the work at the two institutions. Researchers at the University of Michigan considered job-centered and employee-centered behaviors to be at *opposite ends of a single continuum of leadership behavior*. Leaders could theoretically manifest either strong employee- or job-centered behaviors, but not both. By contrast, researchers at Ohio State believed that consideration and initiating structure were *independent continua*. Thus leaders could be high in both initiating structure and consideration, low in both dimensions, or high in one and low in the other.

The key assumption underlying both research programs was that certain behaviors could be identified that are universally associated with a leader's ability to successfully influence a group toward the accomplishment of its goals. Here are the kinds of questions in which researchers were interested:

- From the University of Michigan perspective, who tends to be more effective in helping a group to accomplish its goals—job- or employee-centered leaders?
- From the Ohio State perspective, are leaders who exhibit high levels of *both* task- and people-oriented behaviors more effective than those who exhibit *only* task or people behaviors?

- What role do situational factors play in leadership effectiveness? Are employee-centered leadership behaviors more important in nonprofit organizations or downsizing situations, whereas job-centered behaviors are more important in manufacturing organizations or start-up situations?

The answers to these questions have several practical implications. If leaders need to exhibit only job- or employee-centered behaviors, selection and training systems need to focus on only these behaviors. But if situational factors play a role, researchers need to identify which variables are the most important and train leaders in how to modify their behavior accordingly. As you might suspect, the answer to all these questions is "It depends." In general, researchers have reported that leaders exhibiting a high level of consideration or employee-centered behaviors have more satisfied subordinates. Leaders who set clear goals, explain what followers are to do and how to get tasks accomplished, and monitor results (that is, initiating structure or job-centered) often have higher-performing work units if the group faces relatively ambiguous or ill-defined tasks.[24, 25, 26] At the same time, however, leaders whose behavior is highly autocratic (an aspect of initiating structure) are more likely to have relatively dissatisfied subordinates.[27] Findings like these suggest that *no universal set of leader behaviors is always associated with leadership success.* Often the degree to which leaders need to exhibit task- or people-oriented behaviors depends on the situation, and this finding prompted the research underlying the contingency theories of leadership described in **Chapter 15**. If you review these theories, you will see strong links to the job- and employee-centered behaviors identified 50 years ago.

The Leadership Grid

The Ohio State and University of Michigan studies were good first steps in describing what leaders actually do. Other researchers have extended these findings into more user-friendly formats or developed different schemes for categorizing leadership behaviors. Like the earlier research, these alternative conceptualizations are generally concerned with identifying key leadership behaviors, determining whether these behaviors have positive relationships with leadership success, and helping people develop behaviors related to leadership success. One popular conceptualization of leadership is really an extension of the findings reported by the University of Michigan and Ohio State leadership researchers. The **Leadership Grid** profiles leader behavior on two dimensions: **concern for people** and **concern for production**.[28, 29] The word *concern* reflects how a leader's underlying assumptions about people at work and the importance of the bottom line affect leadership style. In that sense, then, the Leadership Grid deals with more than just behavior. Nonetheless, it is included in this chapter because it is such a direct descendant of earlier behavioral studies.

As **Figure 7.2** shows, leaders can get scores ranging from 1 to 9 on both concern for people and concern for production, depending on their responses to a leadership questionnaire. These two scores are then plotted on the Leadership Grid, and the two score combinations represent different leadership orientations. Each orientation reflects a unique set of assumptions for using power and authority to link people to production.[30] Amid the different leadership styles, the most effective leaders are claimed to have both high concern for people and high concern for production, and Leadership Grid training programs are designed to move leaders to a 9,9 leadership style. Whereas this objective seems intuitively appealing, where do you think the Supreme Leader of North Korea, Kim Jong-un, or Elon Musk, the CEO of Tesla, score on these two dimensions? Do both of them show a high concern for production and people? Are there differences between the two leaders, or are both 9,9 leaders?

> *No institution can possibly survive if it needs geniuses or supermen to manage it. It must be organized in such a way as to be able to get along under a leadership composed of average human beings.*
>
> **Peter Drucker, management expert**

Although the Leadership Grid can be useful for describing or categorizing different leaders, we should note that the evidence to support the assertion that 9,9 leaders are the most effective comes primarily from Blake, Mouton, and their associates. However, other research might shed some light on whether 9,9 leaders are really the most effective. A large-scale study involving 15,000 global leaders conducted by the consulting firm Development Dimensions International reported that 17 percent of senior executives demonstrated strong execution skills (concern for results) and only 10 percent demonstrated strong engagement skills (concern for people). Only a handful of leaders scored high on both dimensions, and this study indicates that 9,9 leaders may not be that prevalent, particularly in the senior ranks.[31] Robie, Kanter, Nilsen, and Hazucha studied 1,400 managers in the United States, Germany, Denmark, the United Kingdom, Italy, Spain, France, and Belgium to determine whether the same leadership behaviors were related to effectiveness across countries. They reported that leadership behaviors associated with problem solving and driving for results (initiating structure or 9,1 leadership) were consistently related to successfully building teams, influencing a group to accomplish its goals, and getting results, regardless of country.[32] Similar results about initiating structure and job performance were reported by Judge, Piccolo, and Ilies.[33] Using 800 managers in a U.S. high-tech firm, Goff reported that managers who spent more time building relationships (consideration or 1,9 leadership) also had more satisfied followers who were less likely to leave the organization.[34] Likewise, other researchers

FIGURE 7.2   The Leadership Grid

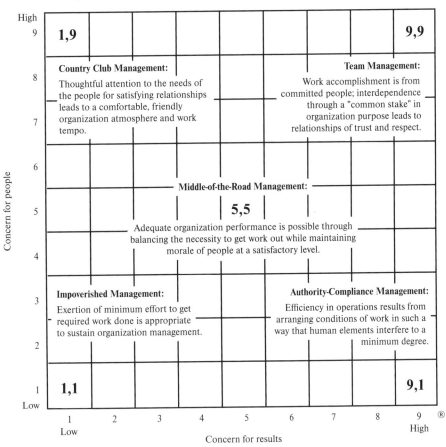

Source: Robert R. Blake and Anne Adams McCanse, *Leadership Dilemmas–Grid Solutions* (Houston, TX: Gulf Publishing, 1991), p. 29. Copyright 1991. Reprinted with permission of Grid International.

reported strong support for the notion that higher consideration behavior can reduce employee turnover.[35,] [36] At the opposite end of the spectrum, researchers have shown that authoritarian leaders (9,1 types) can negatively impact job performance, organizational commitment, and intentions to stay.[37] These results seem to indicate that the most effective leadership style might depend on the criteria used to judge effectiveness. The context and style of leaders' behavior are also factors that affect their ability to build teams and get results through others (see **Highlights 7.1** and **7.2**).

Behaviors versus Skills

HIGHLIGHT 7.1

Leadership behaviors differ somewhat from leadership skills. A **leadership behavior** concerns a specific action, such as "setting specific performance goals for team members." A **leadership skill** consists of three components, which include a well-defined body of knowledge, a set of related behaviors, and clear criteria of competent performance. Perhaps leadership skills may be better understood by using a basketball analogy. People differ considerably in their basketball skills; good basketball players know when to pass and when to shoot and are adept at making layups, shots from the field, and free throws. Knowing when to pass and when to shoot is an example of the knowledge compo-

nent, and layups and free throws are examples of the behavioral component of skills. In addition, shooting percentages can be used as one criterion for evaluating basketball skills.

Leadership skills, such as delegating, can be seen in much the same way. Good leaders know when and to whom a particular task should be delegated (knowledge); they effectively communicate their expectations concerning a delegated task (behavior); and they check to see whether the task was accomplished in a satisfactory manner (criteria). Thus a leadership skill is knowing when to act, acting in a manner appropriate to the situation, and acting in such a way that it helps the leader accomplish team goals.

Does Appearance Matter?

HIGHLIGHT 7.2

Do personal appearance and fitness levels play a role in getting promoted and being an effective leader? Research conducted at the Center for Creative Leadership (CCL) can shed some light on this question. CCL regularly conducts weeklong leadership development programs for senior executives that includes personality, mental ability, and physiological testing; public-speaking assessments; and the results of leadership behavior feedback surveys from bosses,

peers, and direct reports (that is, 360-degree feedback, which is described later in this chapter). This research looked at the relationship between body mass index (BMI), a measure of body fat, and leadership behavior feedback results for 757 executives between 2006 and 2010 and found that overweight executives tended to get lower leadership behavior ratings from others. In other words, fatter leaders tended to be seen as less effective in the eyes of their coworkers.

Workplace obesity is a taboo subject in most organizations, yet this research shows that personal appearance matters when it comes to hiring and promotion decisions. Very few *Fortune 500* CEOs are overweight, and the CCL researchers attribute this to the fact that people at the top need to be in good shape to handle the high workloads and travel schedules associated with these jobs. But is this really true, or does bias play a role in determining who gets to the top? It turns out appearance is a very big deal in the corporate world, and many business schools, consulting firms, and executive coaches offer programs in **executive presence**. Although there are many definitions, executive presence is, in general, concerned with a person's ability to radiate confidence, poise, and authority; in other words, these programs teach participants how to show up like a leader. Dress, grooming, weight, eye contact, speaking with confidence

and energy, avoiding tentative language, using the latest corporate buzzwords, and networking are some of the modules covered in executive presence programs.

Do people with high levels of executive presence have an advantage when it comes to engaging employees, building teams, or achieving results? Or is having a strong executive presence more important to managing one's career and getting promoted?

Sources: L. Kwoh, "Want to Be CEO? What's Your BMI?" *The Wall Street Journal*, January 16, 2013, pp. B1, B6; G. J. Curphy, "Executive Presence: When Confidence Trumps Competence," LinkedIn, December 8, 2014, www.linkedin.com/pulse/20141208135825-36824143-executive-presence-when-confidence-trumps-competence; and M. Forbes, "Are You 'Leadership Material'?" *Forbes*, July 10, 2014, www.forbes.com/sites/moiraforbes/2014/07/10/are-you-leadership-material.

Competency Models

So far in this section we have described several ways to categorize leaders or leadership behaviors, but what are the implications of this research for leadership practitioners? Believe it or not, you can see the practical application of this leadership behavior research in just about every Global 1000 company. **Competency models** describe the behaviors and skills managers need to exhibit if an organization is to be successful.[38, 39, 40, 41, 42, 43, 44, 45, 46, 47, 48, 49, 50] Just as leaders in different countries may need to exhibit behaviors uniquely appropriate to each setting to be successful, different businesses and industries within any country often emphasize different leadership behaviors. Therefore, it is not unusual to see different organizations having distinct competency models depending on the nature and size of each business, its business model, its level of globalization, and the role of technology or teams in the business.[51, 52, 53, 54, 55, 56] An example of a typical competency model for middle managers can be found in **Figure 7.3**.

Many of the best organizations now have competency models for different levels of management. For example, the behaviors and skills needed by department supervisors, store managers, district managers, regional vice presidents, and division presidents at the Home Depot vary considerably, and these differences are reflected in the competency models for each management group. These models help to clarify expectations of performance for people in different leadership positions and describe the skills necessary for promotion. They also help human resource professionals design selection, development, performance management, and succession planning programs so that organizations have a steady supply of leadership talent.[57, 58, 59, 60, 61, 62, 63, 64, 65, 66]

> *I have often said my job is rather simple; all I do is four things, which are easy to say, but hard to effectively execute: (1) pick the team; (2) set the team's direction; (3) recognize and reward those who help the team achieve superior results; and (4) have the strength and fortitude to make timely decisions, with good judgment, including deciding who says and who leaves the team.*
>
> **Mark Roellig, retired General Counsel**

FIGURE 7.3   An Example of a Leadership Competency Model

Competency

Analyzing problems and making decisions: Effectively analyzes issues and makes sound, logical business decisions in a timely manner.

Thinking strategically: Brings a broad perspective to bear on issues and problems (for example, considers information from different industries, markets, competitors); deliberately evaluates strategic "fit" of possible decisions and actions.

Financial and technical savvy: Demonstrates strong technical and financial knowledge when resolving customer, operational, and/or financial problems. Makes sound customer, operational, and financial trade-offs.

Planning and organizing: Establishes clear goals and action plans, and organizes resources to achieve business outcomes.

Managing execution: Directs and monitors performance, and intervenes as appropriate to ensure successful achievement of business objectives.

Inspiring aligned purpose: Successfully engages people in the mission, vision, values, and direction of the organization; fosters a high level of motivation.

Driving change: Challenges the status quo and looks for ways to improve team or organizational performance. Champions new initiatives and stimulates others to make changes.

Building the talent base: Understands the talent needed to support business objectives (for example, qualifications, capabilities); identifies, deploys, and develops highly talented team members.

Fostering teamwork: Creates an environment where employees work together effectively to achieve goals.

Creating open communications: Communicates clearly and creates an environment in which important issues are shared.

Building relationships: Develops and sustains effective working relationships with direct reports, peers, managers, and others; demonstrates that maintaining effective working relationships is a priority.

Customer focus: Maintains a clear focus on customer needs; demonstrates a strong desire to provide exemplary customer service; actively seeks ways to increase customer satisfaction.

Credibility: Earns others' trust and confidence; builds credibility with others through consistency between words and actions and follow-through on commitments.

Personal drive: Demonstrates urgency in meeting objectives and achieving results; pursues aggressive goals and persists to achieve them.

Adaptability: Confidently adapts and adjusts to changes and challenges; maintains a positive outlook and works constructively under pressure.

Learning approach: Proactively identifies opportunities and resources for improvement.

Source: G. J. Curphy, K. Louiselle, and S. Bridges, *Talent Assessment Overview: 360-Degree Feedback Report* (Eagan, MN: Advantis Research & Consulting, 2003).

According to Hogan and Warrenfelz, the skills and behaviors found in virtually every organizational competency model fall into one of four major categories. **Intrapersonal skills** are leadership competencies and behaviors having to do with adapting to stress, goal orientation, and adhering to rules. These skills and behaviors do not involve interacting with others, and they are among the most difficult to change. **Interpersonal skills** are those that involve direct interaction, such as communicating and building relationships with others. These skills are somewhat easier to develop. **Leadership skills** are skills and behaviors concerned with building teams and getting results through others, and these are more easily developed than the skills and behaviors associated with the first two categories. Finally, competencies concerned with analyzing issues, making decisions, financial savvy, and strategic thinking fall into the **business skills** category. These skills and competencies are often the focus of MBA programs and are among the easiest to learn of the four categories. The Hogan and Warrenfelz domain model of leadership competencies is important because it allows people to see connections between seemingly different organizational competency models and makes predictions about how easy or difficult it will be to change various leadership behaviors and skills.[67] (See **Highlights 7.3** and **7.4**.)

Why U.S. Military Veterans Have a Hard Time Getting Hired

HIGHLIGHT 7.3

The United States has an all-volunteer military, and only one out of 100 U.S. citizens join the U.S. Army, Air Force, Navy, Marines, or Coast Guard. The military provides extensive leadership training and experiences and consists of some of the best and brightest leaders in the United States—leaders who have proven themselves able to engage soldiers, build teams, and accomplish mission objectives under extremely adverse conditions. Despite the high caliber of talent military veterans bring to the table, most have a difficult time getting hired into corporate jobs. Boris Groysberg's research on talent management sheds some light on why companies are reluctant to hire veterans and what can be done to ease the transition of those hired.

One of the concepts promoted by Groysberg is the difference between **portable** and **nonportable skills**. Portable skills, like coding or PowerPoint expertise, can easily be transferred from one job to the next. Other skills, like running an artillery battery or loading a missile onto a fighter aircraft, do not readily transfer to other organiza-

tions. The knowledge and skills needed to do these latter activities are extremely important to the military but have little application in the corporate sector. One challenge military veterans face is the percentage of portable versus nonportable skills they have acquired while on active duty. Many have skill portfolios made up of a high percentage of nonportable skills, which makes it difficult for companies to see how these skills transfer to corporate job requirements.

Groysberg further divides skills into three buckets: produce, leadership, and management. Anyone in a position of authority needs relevant technical and functional expertise and depending on the position will need to know how call centers work, scrum teams create business apps, manufacturing lines create product, or which levers to pull to achieve financial results (that is, produce skills). They also need to know how to build a compelling vision, drive change, convey a sense of urgency, develop and engage employees, and build teams (leadership skills); and set goals, establish metrics, create processes, execute plans, and hold people accountable (management skills). It turns out that leadership and management skills are more portable than produce skills, and military veterans tend to be above average in these latter two areas. The problem is that military veterans never get considered for the jobs posted by recruiters and human resource managers because of their strict technical, functional, and business requirements.

There are several things veterans and corporations can do get the most out those with military experience. First, corporations need to take a hard look at the technical, functional, and business criteria they set in job postings. Some of these criteria have become so ridiculous that no one, not even current incumbents, would make the cut. Easing up on nonportable skills requirements would open the applicant pool and improve the odds for hiring veterans. If there is anything military veterans are good at it is adapting to rapidly changing situations, and in many cases it will take them only a few months to acquire enough produce knowledge and skills to be effective. Second, veterans can make it easier to get hired by writing résumés that focus more on portable versus nonportable skills. Those filled with military acronyms and highly technical military terms have no relevance to

the civilian world and lower the odds of getting hired. Likewise, those veterans obtaining degrees while on active duty must ensure they have relevance to the civilian world. Having a master's degree in military history or aviation science may help veterans garner military promotions but have little applicability to the private sector. Fourth, veterans need more help transitioning to corporate positions than other hires, so on-boarding is critically important to this group. On-boarding programs should include the standard HR fare and provide fundamental, nonportable knowledge and skills relevant to the position and programmatic boss, peer, employee, customer, and supplier relationship building activities so that veterans understand how to get things done and be successful in their new roles.

Sources: G. J. Curphy, "Why Veterans Have a Hard Time Getting Hired," LinkedIn, May 23, 2016, www.linkedin.com/pulse/why-veterans-have-hard-time-getting-hired-gordon-gordy-curphy-phd; G. J. Curphy, "Veteran Status and Interview Behavior," LinkedIn, June 1, 2016, www.linkedin.com/pulse/veteran-status-interview-behavior-gordon-gordy-curphy-phd; B. Groysberg, *Chasing Stars: The Myth of Talent and the Portability of Performance* (Princeton, NJ: Princeton University Press, 2010); and S. Young, "How Veterans Outscore their Counterparts on Leadership," Center for Creative Leadership, August 26, 2019, www.ccl.org/blog/veterans-outscore-civilian-leaders.

The Fatal Flaw in Leadership Competency Models

HIGHLIGHT 7.4

Model 1	Model 2	Model 3
Think strategically	Strategic perspective	Coaching
Analyze issues	Being a quick study	Decision-making
Use sound judgment	Decisiveness	Delegating
Apply technical expertise	Change management	Gaining commitment
Use financial acumen	Leading employees	Driving for results
Establish plans	Confronting problems	Change leadership

Model 1	Model 2	Model 3
Drive execution	Participative management	Establishing direction
Managing change	Building relationships	Executive disposition
Drive for results	Compassion and sensitivity	Selling the vision
Lead courageously	Putting people at ease	
Influence others	Respect for differences	
Coach and develop	Taking initiative	
Engage and inspire	Composure	
Foster collaboration	Work–life balance	
Build relationships	Self-awareness	
Manage conflict	Career management	
Foster communication		
Listen to others		
Inspire trust		
Demonstrate adaptability		

The vast majority of Global 1000 companies, federal and state government agencies, nongovernmental organizations, and philanthropic organizations use leadership competency models to describe the skills and behaviors leaders need to be successful and are the foundation for many recruiting, selection, on-boarding, development, succession planning, and performance management systems. Because these models largely determine who gets hired and promoted and who gets rewarded and trained, organizations tend to take the identification of leadership competencies very seriously. Human resources either buys off-the-shelf leadership competencies from consulting firms to adhere to "best practices" or builds their own models. The latter involves interviewing dozens of incumbents and superiors, running multiple focus groups, and getting final buy-in from senior leadership. Both approaches have a fatal flaw that causes successful leaders to get promoted over effective leaders.

The problem is that many consulting firms and HR departments fail to realize that leadership is a group phenomenon. Leadership does not happen without followers, and the primary role of a leader is to engage employees and build teams that beat the competition. Leadership competency models therefore need to define the skills and behaviors needed to build teams and get things done through others. As seen in the three leadership models listed above, none say anything about building teams. Instead, they encourage a **hub-and-spoke model of leadership**, which focuses on the behaviors leaders need to exhibit when dealing with followers on a one-on-one basis. Two of the three say something about results, but the behaviors in these competencies say more about the leader accomplishing personal goals than about getting work done through others or beating the competition. Many leadership competency models do a marvelous job identifying the skills needed to get promoted; whether they identify the skills needed to be effective (that is, to build teams that win) is questionable. Model 2 is a particularly good example of this.

To fix this problem, organizations need to take a hard look at their leadership competency models and see whether they promote hub-and-spoke leadership and describe the skills and behaviors needed to build teams and achieve results that beat the competition.

Sources: G. J. Curphy, "The Fatal Flaw in Leadership Competency Models," LinkedIn, September 1, 2014, www.linkedin.com/pulse/20140901121513-36824143-the-fatal-flaw-in-leadership-competency-models; R. B. Kaiser and G. J. Curphy, "Leadership Development: The Failure of an Industry and the Opportunity for Consulting Psychol-ogists," *Consulting Psychology Journal: Practice and Theory* 65, no. 4 (2013), pp. 294–302; and G. J. Curphy, M. Hartgrove, A. Licata, and E. Paulson, "Are Teams a Missed Opportunity for Human Resources?" *TalentQ,* in press.

Every significant human achievement has been the result of collective effort, and groups and teams are the building blocks of modern organizations. Yet the leadership development industry has focused on individuals to the detriment of teams, and we are all paying the price for this mistake.

Gordon Curphy, author

The Hogan and Warrenfelz model is also important because it points out what behaviors leaders need to exhibit to build teams and get results through others. Because organizational competency models are more alike than different, the behaviors needed to build teams and get results are fairly universal across organizations. Leaders wanting to build high-performing teams need to hire the right people, effectively cope with stress, set high goals, play by the rules, and hold people accountable. They also need to communicate and build relationships with others. Effective leaders also get followers involved in decisions, fairly distribute workloads, develop talent, keep abreast of events that could affect the team, and make sound financial and operational decisions. Thus competency models provide a sort of recipe for leaders wanting to build teams and get results in different organizations. Many of these leadership behaviors may be fairly universal across industries, but recent advances in automation, AI, machine learning, digitization, and the Internet of Things, along with increasing globalization, may cause organizations to put more emphasis on certain competencies over others.[68] Longitudinal research has shown that the relative importance of certain competencies has changed over time. For example, building relationships, administrative/organizational skills, and time management skills have grown considerably more important over the past 20 to 25 years.[69] There may also be some important differences by company and leadership level. Ancona, Malone, Orlikowski, and Senge aptly point out that most leaders don't possess all the skills listed in many competency models, but effective leaders are those who understand their strengths and have learned how to staff around the areas in which they are less skilled.[70]

Despite the widespread adoption of leadership competency models across for- and nonprofit organizations, there has been some backlash to this approach. As described on Highlight 7.4, most competency models promote a hub-and-spoke leadership style and say little about building teams or achieving collective results. Moreover, line and staff managers sometimes find leadership competency models to be overly complex, misaligned with organizational strategy, and of little practical use. Having a comprehensive and well-specified set of behaviors to define effective leadership is important for organizations, but they need to ensure these behaviors are easy to understand, promote effective teamwork, lead to the achievement of superior results, and are aligned with their long-term vision of the future.[71, 72]

The Leadership Pipeline

We started this chapter by exploring the notion that there was a universal set of behaviors associated with leadership effectiveness. Yet research shows that initiating structure, interactional facilitation, and 9,9 leadership can be important in some situations and relatively unimportant in others. Situational and follower factors play important roles in determining the relative effectiveness of different leadership behaviors, and researchers and human resource professionals have created competency models to describe the behaviors needed by leaders in particular jobs and companies. Leaders heading up virtual teams of people located around the globe or working in sales versus manufacturing organizations may need to exhibit different types of behaviors to be effective, and competency models are useful in capturing these differences. Although globalization, the industry, and the functional area affect the type of leadership behaviors needed, another factor that impacts leadership behavior is **organizational level**. For example, the behaviors first-line supervisors need to manifest to keep a group of call center employees motivated and on task differ from those a CEO needs to exhibit when meeting a group of investors or running company business strategy sessions. Although both types of leaders need to build teams and get results through others, the types of teams they lead and the results they need to obtain are so dramatically different that they exhibit very different types of behaviors.

The **Leadership Pipeline** is a useful model for explaining where leaders need to spend their time, what they should be focusing on and what they should be letting go, and the types of behaviors they need to exhibit as they move from first-line supervisor to functional manager to CEO.[73, 74, 75, 76, 77] This model also describes the lessons people should learn as they occupy a particular organizational level and the challenges they will likely face as they transition to the next level. As such, this model provides a type of road map for people wanting to occupy the top leadership positions in any organization. And because people at different organizational levels need to exhibit different behaviors, many companies have created competency models to describe the behaviors needed to be successful at different organizational levels. According to the Leadership Pipeline model, the most effective leaders are those who can accurately diagnose the organizational level of their job and then exhibit behaviors commensurate with this level. The pipeline also provides potential explanations for why some people fail to advance: These individuals may not be focusing on the right things or may be exhibiting leadership behaviors associated with lower organizational levels.

A depiction of the seven organizational levels and their competency requirements, time application, and work values can be found in **Table 7.2**. The items listed in the table correspond to a large for-profit organization; smaller for-profit or nonprofit organizations may not have all these levels. Nonetheless, the Leadership Pipeline provides a useful framework for thinking about how leadership competencies change as people are promoted through organizations (as illustrated in **Profiles in Leadership 7.3**).

TABLE 7.2   The Leadership Pipeline

Organizational Level	Competency Requirements	Time Applications	Work Values
Individual contributor	Technically proficient. Use company tools. Build relationships with team members.	Meet personal due dates. Arrive/depart on time.	Get results through personal proficiency. High-quality work. Accept company values.
First-line supervisor	Plan projects. Delegate work. Coach and provide feedback. Monitor performance.	Annual budget plan. Make time available for followers. Set priorities for team.	Get results through others. Success of followers. Success of the team.
Mid-level manager	Select, train, and manage first-line supervisors. Manage boundaries and deploy resources to teams.	Monitor performance of each team. Make time to coach first-line supervisors.	Appreciate managerial versus technical work. Develop first-line supervisors.

Organizational Level	Competency Requirements	Time Applications	Work Values
Functional leader	Manage the whole function. Communicate with and listen to everyone in the function. Make subfunction trade-offs. Interact with other functions.	Determine three-year vision for the function. Interact with business unit leader's team.	Clarify how the function supports the business. Value all subfunctions.
Business unit leader	Build cross-functional leadership team. Financial acumen. Balance future goals with short-term business needs.	Develop three-year vision for the business unit. Monitor financial results. Effectively manage time.	Value all staff functions. Value organizational culture and employee engagement.
Group manager	Manage business portfolio. Allocate capital to maximize business success. Develop business unit leaders.	Develop strategies for multiple business units. Monitor financial results for multiple businesses. Interact with CEO's team.	Value the success of all the business units. Interact with internal and external stakeholders.
CEO or enterprise leader	Analyze and critique strategy. Manage the entire company and multiple constituencies. Deliver predictable business results. Set company direction. Create company culture. Manage the board of directors.	Manage external stakeholders. Spend significant time reviewing financial results. Spend significant time doing strategic planning.	Value a limited set of key long-term objectives. Value advice from board of directors. Value inputs from a wide variety of stakeholders.

Source: R. Charan, S. Drotter, and J. Noel, *The Leadership Pipeline: How to Build the Leadership-Powered Company* (San Francisco: Jossey-Bass, 2001).

Indra Nooyi

PROFILES IN LEADERSHIP 7.3

PepsiCo is commonly acknowledged as having one of the best leadership talent management systems in the world. Pepsi's talent management systems make extensive use of competency models, 360-degree feedback tools, personality and intelligence assessments, in-basket simulations, and unit performance indexes. One of the people who has benefited from this in-depth assessment and development is Indra Nooyi. Nooyi recently retired as the CEO of PepsiCo and was ranked by *Forbes* as the 12th most powerful woman in the world and as the 2nd most powerful businesswoman in the world. Nooyi grew up in India and received an undergraduate degree from Madras Christian College and a postgraduate diploma in management from the Indian Institute in Management. She also has a degree from the Yale School of Management. While in college Nooyi fronted an all-female rock band, and she is refreshingly funny and candid when speaking in public. In May 2005 Nooyi started a controversy when she spoke to Columbia Business School graduates and said the United States "must be careful that when we extend our arm in either a business or a political sense, we take pains to ensure we are giving a hand ... not the finger."

Before emigrating to the United States in 1978, Nooyi was a product manager for Johnson & Johnson and the textile firm Mettur Beardsell in India. Her first job after graduating from Yale was to work as a consultant with the Boston Consulting Group. She then took senior leadership positions at Motorola and Asea Brown Boveri before moving to PepsiCo in 1994. While at Pepsi, Nooyi played a vital role in the spin-off of Tricon, which is now known as Yum! Brands Inc. (Taco Bell and Kentucky Fried Chicken are some of the franchises in Yum! Brands Inc.)

She also took the lead in Pepsi's acquisition of Tropicana and Quaker Oats in the late 1990s. Nooyi was promoted to CFO in 2001 and to the CEO position in 2006. When she was the CEO of PepsiCo, Nooyi headed up a company of 300,000 employees that generated over $60 billion in annual revenues through the worldwide sales of products such as Pepsi, Mountain Dew, Tropicana, Gatorade, Aquafina, Dole, Lipton, Doritos, Ruffles, Lays, Quaker Oats, Life cereal, and Rice-A-Roni. Under Nooyi, Pepsi developed new products and marketing programs through the liberal use of cross-cultural advisory teams and managed 22 brands that each generated over $1 billion in annual revenues.

Given Pepsi's global reach and emphasis on brand management, Nooyi's background seems well suited for a variety of leadership challenges. In 2006 a group of individuals in India claimed that both Coke and Pepsi products were tainted with pesticides. Later investigations disproved these allegations, but the surrounding publicity damaged Pepsi's brand in a large, developing market. Nooyi worked hard to restore the Indian public's confidence in the safety of PepsiCo's products and has more recently spent time developing healthier beverages and snacks.

Nooyi believes people need to do three things to advance their careers. The first is to be an outstanding performer in your current job. People who want to advance should not fixate on being promoted but should instead focus on doing their current job better than anyone else. The second is to have a "hip-pocket" skill, a skill that truly stands out and can be developed even further. Nooyi's hip pocket skill is the ability to simplify complex problems to help people formulate and execute solutions. The third is to demonstrate leadership courage. Great leaders stand up for what they believe in, and Nooyi has a history of standing up for nonwhites, females, and members of the LGBT community, some of which was in reaction to the election of Donald Trump. There is another aspect of Indra Nooyi that is different from other CEOs: each year she writes personal thank-you letters to the parents of her top 400 executives. She attributes her success to her mother's and father's sacrifices, and these letters are her way of thanking the parents who made similar sacrifices for PepsiCo's top leaders.

How do you think Indra Nooyi's career matches up to the Leadership Pipeline? What lessons do you think she learned as she traveled through the Leadership Pipeline that help her be an effective CEO for PepsiCo?

M. Ward, "PepsiCo CEO Shares Her 3-Step Path to Advancing Your Career," CNBC, December 28, 2016, http://www.cnbc.com/2016/12/28/pepsico-ceo-shares-her-3-step-path-to-advancing-your-career.html.

According to the Leadership Pipeline model, many people who fail to demonstrate the competencies, work values, and time applications commensurate with their positions will struggle with building teams and getting results through others. For example, functional leaders who have not given up acting like first-line supervisors and spend a lot of time coaching and monitoring the performance of the individual contributors not only have no time to build a vision and manage the function, but they also disempower the first-line supervisors and mid-level managers in their functions. So one key to having a successful career is exhibiting competencies appropriate for your current organizational level and then letting go of these competencies and learning new ones when moving up the organizational ladder. Charan, Drotter, and Noel maintain that transitioning from individual contributor to first-line supervisor and from functional to business unit leader are the two hardest transitions for people.[78] It is difficult for people who have spent all their time selling to customers or writing code to transition to managing the people who do this work and for people whose entire careers have been in sales or information technology to manage, value, and leverage the work done by other functions.[79]

Fifty percent of organizations with annual revenues over $500 million report having "no meaningful succession plans."

Personnel Decisions International

Five other implications of this model are worth mentioning. First, intelligence and certain personality traits have been found to improve the odds of getting promoted and successful transitioning to new leadership levels.[80] Second, it is critically important that organizations help people as they transition to new leadership levels. Organizations usually offer **on-boarding** programs to help external hires transition into new roles, which helps them learn about the organization's history, values, and unwritten rules; build relationships with critical stakeholders and influencers; gain an understanding of the key goals, processes, products, and services; build a high-performing team of direct reports; and figure out how to operate at this leadership level. Organizations often fail to do the same for internal candidates moving into bigger roles, and this can be a big (and easily avoidable) mistake. For example, the goals, relationships, allocation of time spent, and other leadership requirements needed to run a single Starbucks versus overseeing the operations of 10 Starbucks are very different, and internal on-boarding programs can help ease these transitions.[81, 82, 83]

Third, people who skip organizational levels often turn out to be ineffective leaders. For example, it is not unusual for organizations to offer jobs to consultants. A consultant may have been called in to fix a particularly difficult problem, such as implementing a new sales initiative or information technology program, and because the solution was so successful he or she is asked to join the company. The problem is that many of these job offers are for functional or business unit leader types of roles, and to a large extent consultants have spent their entire careers doing nothing but individual contributor–level work. Because consultants may have never formally led a team or managed multiple teams or functions, they continue to exhibit those behaviors they got rewarded for in the first place, which is individual contributor–level work. No matter how good these former consultants are at doing individual contributor work, these jobs they are put in are much too big for them to do all the sales calls, write all the computer code, or the like. If they do not adjust their leadership behaviors to fit the demands of the position, they quickly burn out and will be asked to pursue other options.

So if your career aspirations include leading a function, business unit, or company, you need to think through the sequence of positions that will give you the right experiences and teach you the right competencies needed to prepare you for your ultimate career goal.

Fourth, acquisitions often result in people being assigned to positions lower in the leadership pipeline. For example, CEOs from acquired companies may end up being assigned to mid-level manager roles in new companies. Although the number of people led and the budgets managed could be larger, they would need to reallocate their time and do the activities associated with this level in order to be effective. Many former CEOs and business unit leaders have strong entrepreneurial streaks and chafe at the prospect of being "demoted" to mid-level manager positions. Many only stay with the parent company for a year or two before leaving to start up new companies.[84]

Last, the importance of operating at the right leadership level cannot be overemphasized. Far too many leaders operate a level that is one or two lower than appropriate for their positions, and this has deleterious effects across their teams and the organizations they lead. If the CEO is acting like a functional leader, then he or she will spend all their time focusing on metrics, details, projects, processes, and projections within a particular function and do little external scanning, spend no time on strategic planning and solving the big problems facing the business, and not leverage other functions to get things done. This has a ripple effect across their teams and organizations, as the only way everyone else can add value is to do work that is at one or two lower levels. Operating at lower levels may be appropriate when facing a crisis, during turnarounds, or being short-staffed, but this should only last for short periods of time. Most leaders operating at too low a level do so out of preference—they either greatly enjoy it or erroneously believe they are the only ones capable of solving technical problems, dealing directly with customers, or resolving conflicts between lower-level employees. They believe they are adding value by engaging in these activities, when in reality, they are disempowering their staffs and causing followers to look for other employment opportunities.[85, 86]

Waffle House Taught Me Everything I Learned about Leadership

HIGHLIGHT 7.5

Waffle House is a $1 billion restaurant chain consisting of almost 2,000 restaurants located across 25 states. Each restaurant is a 24/7 operation, and restaurants are made up of managers, shift supervisors, and employees. The chain's reputation for staying open during natural disasters is one of the factors the Federal Emergency Management Agency uses to determine the level of damage from hurricanes, tornadoes, and snowstorms—if the Waffle Houses are closed, then things must be really bad.

Restaurant managers are responsible for everything that happens in their restaurants, including customer service, hiring and training staff, setting up staffing schedules, ordering supplies, managing costs, and the financial performance of their restaurants. Customers are expected to be warmly welcomed and served within eight minutes after placing orders. Managers are expected to pitch in where necessary, be it attending to customers, busing tables, cooking meals, or waiting tables. This expectation is not unique to restaurant managers, as the CEO and other senior staff wear aprons and do whatever is necessary when out in the field visiting restaurants. The pressures and challenges of running a quick-service restaurant are varied and intense, as customers are visiting at any time of day, some are intoxicated or belligerent, others make unreasonable demands, and employees may or may not show up for work. Hiring and training new employees and shift supervisors to run a 24/7 hour operation can take up a considerable amount of time, and during peak hours, the pace of restaurant operations can be frenetic. It is also not unusual for restaurant managers to get calls in the middle of the night to deal with emergencies.

Waffle House only promotes from within, so restaurant managers have to spend time as waiters, cooks, bussers, dishwashers, and shift supervisors before getting the opportunity to run their own restaurants. The starting salary for new restaurant managers is only $45,000, but if restaurants perform well, they can be making $117,000 in five years, which is good for someone who could be less than 30 years old and lack a college degree. Restaurant performance is based on sales, profitability, customer satisfaction ratings, operational metrics, and turnover. Unlike many fast-food chains, Waffle House puts a premium on retaining employees,

and restaurant managers are rewarded for achieving low turnover levels.

The leadership lessons that can be learned from Waffle Houses, Starbucks, McDonald's, Subways, Taco Bells, and similar fast-food restaurants are powerful and varied. Effective restaurant managers learn how to select the right employees, set clear expectations, develop skills, get staff working as cohesive teams, monitor and evaluate performance, retain staff, deal with problematic customers and employees, improve restaurant operations and costs, manage financials, and handle emergencies. According to the Leadership Pipeline, what is the leadership level of restaurant managers? What about the CEO when he or she dons an apron and washes dishes? What do you think would happen if restaurant managers were hired from the outside and did not spend time as cooks or shift supervisors?

Source: S. Walker, "If You Can Manage a Waffle House, You Can Manage Anything," *The Wall Street Journal*, Saturday–Sunday, November 2–3, 2019, p. B7.

Community Leadership

Never doubt that a group of thoughtful, committed citizens can change the world. Indeed, it is the only thing that ever has.

Margaret Mead, anthropologist

Although organizational competency models have played a pervasive role in selecting, developing, and promoting government and business leaders, they have not been used much in community leadership. **Community leadership** is the process of building a team of volunteers to accomplish some important community outcome and represents an alternative conceptualization of leadership behavior.[87, 88, 89] Examples of community leadership might include forming a group to raise funds for a new library, gathering volunteers for a blood or food drive, or organizing a campaign to change immigration or health care laws. Thus community leadership takes place whenever a group of volunteers gets together to make something happen (or not happen) in their community.

But leading a group of volunteers is very different from being a leader in a publicly traded company, the military, or a nongovernmental organization. For one thing, community leaders do not have any position power; they cannot discipline followers who do not adhere to organizational norms, get tasks accomplished, or show up to meetings. They also tend to have fewer resources and rewards than most other leaders. And because there is no formal selection or promotion process, anyone can be a community leader. But whether such leaders succeed in their community change efforts depends on three highly interrelated competencies (see **Figure 7.4**). Just as you need the three ingredients of oxygen, fuel, and an igniter to start a fire, so do you need the three competencies of framing, building social capital, and mobilization to successfully drive community change efforts.

FIGURE 7.4 **The Components of Community Leadership**

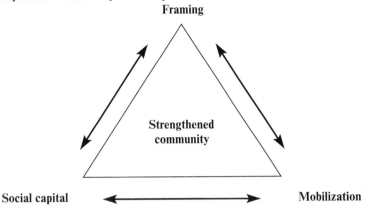

Source: J. Krile, G. Curphy, and D. Lund, *The Community Leadership Handbook: Framing Ideas, Building Relationships, and Mobilizing Resources* (St. Paul, MN: Fieldstone Alliance, 2006).

Framing is the leadership competency of helping a group or community recognize and define its opportunities and issues in ways that result in effective action. Framing helps the group or community decide *what* needs to be done, *why* it is important that it be done, and *how* it is to be done, and communicate that in clear and compelling ways. Any community could take on myriad potential projects, but many of these projects never get off the ground because the person "in charge" never framed the project in such a way that others could understand the outcome, how they would benefit by the outcome, and what they must do to achieve the outcome. (See **Profiles in Leadership 7.4**.)

Father Greg Boyle

PROFILES IN LEADERSHIP 7.4

Father Greg Boyle grew up in a family of eight children in the Los Angeles area. Working on his father's dairy farm while growing up, Father Greg opted to become a Jesuit after graduating from high school and was ordained as a minister in 1984. After graduating with degrees from Gonzaga University, Loyola Marymount University, and Wheaton College, he spent several years teaching high school, running a mission in Los Angeles, and serving as a chaplain for Folsom Prison and Islas Marias Penal Colony in Mexico. It was while Father Greg was a pastor at the Dolores Mission in Los Angeles that he started Jobs for the Future (JFF), a program designed to keep gang-involved youths out of trouble. JFF involved developing positive alternatives, establishing an elementary school and day care centers, and providing jobs for disadvantaged youth.

Partly as a result of the civil unrest in Los Angeles in 1992, Father Greg started the first of several Homeboy businesses. Homeboy Bakery was created to teach gang-involved youths life and work skills and how to work side-by-side with rival gang members. Other businesses started by Father Greg include Homeboy Silkscreen and Embroidery, Homeboy Maintenance, Homeboy Farmers Markets, Homeboy Diner, Homeboy Grocery, Homeboy/Homegirl Merchandise, and Homegirl Café and Catering. All of these businesses teach needed business, conflict resolution, and teamwork skills to gang members who are eager to leave the streets.

With Los Angeles County home to 34 percent of California's poor, a poverty rate of 16 percent, and a high school dropout rate between 35 and 45 percent for Latinos and African Americans, the county is an epicenter for gang activity. Homeboy Industries is known as the largest gang intervention, rehabilitation, and reentry program in the United States. Having run as a nonprofit company since 2001, it has expanded several times to keep up with the increasing demand for its services. Some of these services include tattoo removal; employment, education, legal, substance abuse, and mental health services; and solar panel installation certification training. The organization currently serves well over 1,000 people as either employees or participants in its many outreach programs. Although Homeboy Industries generates revenues, it does not generate enough cash to fund all of its programs and uses donations and speaking fees to cover any financial shortfalls.

Where do the concepts of framing, social capital, and mobilization come into play with the start-up of Homeboy Industries? What skills does Father Greg possess that help him build teams and achieve results? Do you think public money is better spent getting gang members to join Homeboy Industries or putting them in prison?

Sources: G. Boyle, *Tattoos on the Heart: The Power of Boundless Compassion* (New York: Free Press, 2010); Homeboy Industries, www.homeboyindustries.org; and T. Gross, "Interview with Greg Boyle," *Fresh Air*, May 21, 2010.

Nobody has ever met a hopeful kid who joined a gang.

Father Greg Boyle, Homeboy Industries

Building social capital is the leadership competency of developing and maintaining relationships that allow people to work together in the community across their differences. Just as financial capital allows individuals to make choices about what they can purchase, such as buying a new television, car, or house, social capital allows a community leader to make choices about which community change initiatives or projects are likely to be successful. If you have little money, your options are severely limited. Likewise, leaders lacking social capital will have a difficult time getting anything done in their communities because they will not be able to mobilize the resources necessary to turn their vision into reality. Social capital is the power of relationships shared between individuals, between an individual and a group, or between groups.

Engaging a critical mass to take action to achieve a specific outcome or set of outcomes is the leadership competency of **mobilization**. Community leaders will have achieved a critical mass when they have enough human and other resources to get what they want done. People, money, equipment, and facilities are often needed to pass bond issues or attract new businesses to a community. Mobilization is strategic, planned purposeful activity to achieve clearly defined outcomes. Almost anyone can get resources moving, but it takes leadership to get enough of the right resources moving toward the same target.

Pity the leader caught between unloving critics and uncritical lovers.

John Gardner, writer

How would the community leadership model come into play if you wanted to have a new student union built on your campus? First, you would need to frame the issue in such a way that other students understood what was in it for them and what they would need to do to make a new student union become a reality. Second, you would need to reach out and build relationships with all of the current and potential users of the new student union. You would need to identify the formal and informal leaders of the different user groups and meet with them to gain and maintain their trust. Third, you would need these different user groups to take action to get the new student union built. Some of these actions might include raising funds, making phone calls, canvasing students to sign petitions, mounting a publicity campaign, and meeting with university and state officials who are the key decision makers about the issue.

You need to do all three of the community leadership components well if you are to build teams of volunteers and successfully accomplish community outcomes. You might be able to succinctly frame the issue, but if you lack social capital or cannot get a critical mass mobilized, you will probably not get far in building the new student union. The same would be true if you had a broad and well-established network of students but did not frame the issue in such a way that followers could take action. It is likely that as many community change efforts fail as succeed, and the reasons for failure often have to do with inadequate framing, social capital, or mobilization. These three components are critical when it comes to building teams of volunteers and achieving community goals.

Assessing Leadership Behaviors: Multirater Feedback Instruments

One way to improve leader effectiveness is to give leaders feedback regarding the frequency and skill with which they perform various types of leadership behaviors. A $200 million industry has developed over the past three decades to meet this need. This is the **360-degree**, or **multirater, feedback** instrument industry, and it is difficult to overestimate its importance in management development both in the United States and overseas. Jack Welch, the former CEO of General Electric, has stated that these tools have been critical to GE's success.[90] Practically all of the Global 1,000 companies are using some type of multirater feedback instrument for managers and key individual contributors.[91, 92, 93, 94, 95, 96, 97, 98, 99, 100, 101, 102, 103, 104] Multirater feedback instruments have been translated into 16 different languages, and well over 5 million managers have now received feedback on their leadership skills and behaviors from these instruments.[105] Because of the pervasiveness of multirater feedback in both the public and private sectors, it will be useful to examine some issues surrounding these instruments.

Many managers and human resource professionals have erroneously assumed that a manager's self-appraisal is the most accurate source of information regarding leadership strengths and weaknesses. This view has changed, however, with the introduction of multirater feedback instruments. These tools show that direct reports, peers, and superiors can have very different perceptions of a leader's behavior, and these perspectives can paint a more accurate picture of the leader's strengths and development needs than self-appraisals alone (see **Figures 7.5** and **7.6**). A manager may think he or she gets along well with others, but if 360-degree feedback ratings from peers and direct reports indicate that the manager is difficult to work with, the manager should gain new insights on what to do to improve his or her leadership effectiveness. Prior to the introduction of 360-degree instruments, it was difficult for managers to get accurate information about how others perceived their on-the-job behaviors because the feedback they received from others in face-to-face meetings tended to be adulterated or watered down.[106, 107, 108, 109, 110, 111, 112, 113, 114, 115, 116, 117, 118, 119] Moreover, the higher one goes in an organization, the less likely one is to ask for feedback, which results in bigger discrepancies between self and other perceptions.[120, 121, 122, 123, 124] And, as described in **Chapter 6**, many of the most frequent behaviors exhibited by leaders are rooted in personality traits and occur almost automatically; as a result many leaders lack self-awareness and do not understand or appreciate their impact on others. It was difficult for managers to accurately determine their leadership strengths and development needs until the advent of 360-degree feedback instruments. Today most organizations use 360-degree tools as an integral part of the training, coaching, succession planning, and performance management components of a comprehensive leadership talent management system.[125, 126, 127, 128, 129, 130]

In general, three types of 360-degree feedback processes can be found in organizations today. The most prevalent are **competency-based 360-degree questionnaires**. Organizations using this approach identify the behaviors leaders need to exhibit to be effective at a particular organizational level; build questionnaires that reflect these behaviors; administer the questionnaires to target individuals, superiors, peers, and direct reports; and then generate feedback reports that reflect the consolidated rating results similar to those depicted in **Figure 7.6**. Another way to collect 360-degree information about leaders is to use a **leadership versatility approach**.[131, 132] In this case superiors, peers, and direct reports provide ratings on the extent to which target individuals demonstrate too much, just the right amount, or too little strategic, operations, enabling, or forcing leadership behavior for a particular position, and this approach is very good at identifying leaders who overuse their strengths. For example, a leader may have been promoted for her strong operational and forceful skills but her new role puts greater emphasis on strategic and enabling skills. She could be in danger of derailing if she does not learn how to adjust her behavior to fit with the requirements of the new role. A third approach is the **verbal 360-degree technique**. With this approach 10 to 15 superiors, peers, and direct reports are asked to share a target individual's strengths and areas of improvement as a leader in phone or face-to-face interviews. Verbal 360s provide very detailed and context-specific information on what leaders need to keep doing, do more of, and change in order to be more effective. Because of the time and expense involved, however, verbal 360s tend to be used more with senior leaders.

Given the pervasive role 360-degree feedback plays in many organizations today, it is not surprising that there has been an extensive amount of research on the construction, use, and impact of these tools. Much of this research has explored how to use competency models to build effective 360-degree questionnaires, whether 360-degree feedback matters, whether self–observer perceptual gaps matter, whether leaders' ratings can improve over time, and whether there are meaningful culture/gender/race issues with 360-degree feedback ratings. With respect to the first issue, researchers have reported that the construction of 360-degree feedback questionnaires is very important. Poorly conceived competency models and ill-designed questionnaire items can lead to spurious feedback results, thus depriving managers of the information they need to perform at a higher level.[133, 134, 135, 136, 137, 138, 139, 140] In terms of whether 360-degree feedback matters, a number of researchers have held that leaders who received 360-degree feedback had higher-performing work units than leaders who did not receive this type of feedback. These results indicate that 360-degree feedback ratings do matter.[141, 142, 143, 144, 145, 146, 147, 148, 149, 150, 151] But a study of 750 firms by Watson-Wyatt, a human resource consulting firm, reported that companies that used 360-degree feedback systems had a 10.6 percent decrease in shareholder value.[152] Although this research provides strong evidence that 360-degree feedback may not "work," it is important to note how these systems were being used in these firms. For the

FIGURE 7.5 Sources for 360-Degree Feedback

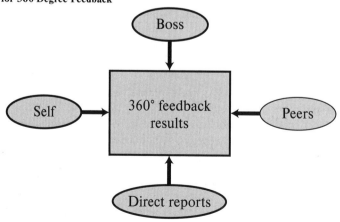

most part, Pfau and Kay examined firms using 360-degree feedback for performance appraisal, not development purposes. This distinction is important because most 360-degree feedback systems are not designed to make comparisons *between* people. Instead these systems are designed to tell leaders about their own relative strengths and development needs. But because 360-degree feedback tools are data based and provide good development feedback, many organizations have decided to modify the process for performance appraisal purposes. This can be a mistake: Many 360-degree feedback tools used in performance appraisals are often poorly constructed and result in such inflated ratings that the resulting feedback no longer differen-

FIGURE 7.6   Example of 360-Degree Feedback

Competency	Never 1	Seldom 2	Sometimes 3	Often 4	Always 5	Avg.
Thinking strategically						
Kim Converse						4.5
Manager						3.1
Others						4.8
All respondents						4.3
Personal drive						
Kim Converse						5.0
Manager						2.9
Others						4.8
All respondents						4.1
Planning and organizing						
Kim Converse						4.2
Manager						3.1
Others						4.6
All respondents						4.0
Inspiring aligned purpose						
Kim Converse						4.8
Manager						2.2
Others						4.4
All respondents						3.9

Inspiring Aligned Purpose

Successfully engages people in the mission, vision, values, and direction of the organization; fosters a high level of motivation.

Average Ratings for Each Item and Respondent Type

Items	Self	Manager	Others	All Respondents
1. Communicates a compelling vision of the future.	5.0	1.0	4.5	3.8
2. Provides a clear sense of purpose and direction for the team.	5.0	3.0	4.3	4.0
3. Sets challenging goals and expectations.	5.0	4.0	4.5	4.4
4. Fosters enthusiasm and buy-in for the direction of the team/organization.	5.0	1.0	4.8	4.0
5. Supports initiatives of upper management through words and actions.	4.0	2.0	4.0	3.2

Source: Adapted from K. Louiselle, G. J. Curphy, and S. Bridges, C3 360-Degree Feedback Report (Eagan, MN: Advantis Research and Consulting, 2003).

tiates between high, average, and low-level performers. The end result is a costly, time-intensive performance appraisal system that has little if any benefit to the individual or the boss and yields organizational results similar to those reported by Watson-Wyatt. The bottom line is that 360-degree feedback systems can add tremendous value, but only if they are well-conceived and used properly.[153, 154, 155, 156, 157, 158, 159, 160, 161, 162, 163]

> *In many cases the only person who is surprised by his or her 360-degree feedback results is the feedback recipient.*
>
> **Dianne Nilsen, leadership consultant**

As stated earlier, one advantage of 360-degree feedback is that it provides insight into self-perceptions and others' perceptions of leadership skills. But do self–observer gaps matter? Are leaders more effective if they have a high level of insight—that is, if they rate their strengths and weaknesses as a leader the same as others do? As depicted in **Figure 7.6**, some level of disagreement is to be expected because bosses, peers, and direct reports may have different expectations for a leader. Nevertheless, insight does not seem to matter for leadership effectiveness. Even leaders with large self–observer gaps were effective as long as they had high observer ratings. By contrast, the least effective leaders were those with high self and low others' ratings. The lesson here is the importance of managing public reputation—leadership is in the eyes of others. And the key to high observer ratings is to develop a broad set of leadership skills that will help groups to accomplish their goals.[164, 165, 166, 167, 168, 169] (See **Highlight 7.6**.)

How Should Millennials and Generation Z Leaders Manage Older Workers?

HIGHLIGHT 7.6

Many large industrial countries, such as China, Japan, Germany, and the United States, are experiencing an interesting demographic shift. Because people in these countries are living and working longer, a relatively large percentage of their workforces comprise people who are 50 to 65 years old. Many are also opting to work after they are eligible to retire. At the same time, birth rates in these countries have been declining and fewer young people are entering the workforce. Because these younger workers tend to be more technologically savvy than their older counterparts, many companies are offering under-30 applicants first-line supervisor or mid-level management positions even though they may have little previous management experience. The end result is that more and more Millennials and Generation Zers are managing employees who have 30 to 40 years of work experience. So what are the consequences associated with managing older workers, and what do younger managers need to do to engage and build teams that consist of older workers?

One thing Millennials and Generation Zers need to keep in mind is that there will be considerable resentment and negative reactions when older workers find out they are reporting to younger leaders. Moreover, research shows there is a strong relationship between older workers' reactions and performance and younger leaders' age differences. This means that if leaders and workers are only different in age by 2 to 4 years, then there will likely be minimal impact, but if that gap is 20 to 30 years, then this situation is likely to have a big impact on employee engagement and performance. In many ways, managing older workers has strong similarities to simply being an effective leader, but young leaders should make a point of demonstrating the following leadership behaviors:

Set an Example. Show up for work early, stay focused on people and getting things done while at work, treat people fairly, and leave late. Older workers appreciate leaders with a strong work ethic and get demoralized if they think their bosses are entitled or lazy.

Communicate Expectations. Clearly define what tasks need to be accomplished and how success will be measured. Solicit older workers' ideas on the best ways to get assigned tasks accomplished.

Ask for Inputs. Because older workers have considerable experience, they may have encountered similar problems in the past or know how best to get things done. Younger leaders taking advantage of this expertise are more likely to avoid making dumb, easily avoidable mistakes.

Be Confident. Younger leaders who appear intimidated and second-guess their decisions will have difficulties getting work done through older employees. Young leaders need to be open to inputs but be firm with their expectations and decisions.

Acknowledge Differences. Fifty-year-old employees have different needs, motivations, and worldviews than those in their 20s or 30s. Older workers may not want to play ping-pong during office hours or go out for beers after work.

Avoid Prejudgment. Younger leaders sometimes fall into the trap of thinking older workers are technophobes when in reality older workers are quite capable of learning new processes and systems.

Manage Mixed Teams. Younger leaders should look for opportunities that require younger and older subordinates to leverage their unique skills and experience in order to jointly solve problems or get tasks accomplished. Teams made up of generationally diverse team members often outperform those made up of similar generations.

Sources: "Elders Not Betters," *The Economist*, December 17, 2016, p. 59; P. Cappelli, "Engaging Your Older Workers," *Harvard Business Review*, November 2014, https://hbr.org/2014/11/engaging-your-older-workers; R. E. Silverman, "Young Boss May Make Older Workers Less Productive," *The Wall Street Journal*, December 20, 2016, www.wsj.com/articles/young-boss-may-make-older-workers-less-productive-1482246384; S. Tulman, "How Young Leaders Manage Older Employees," Business 2 Community, October 8, 2014, www.business2community.com/leadership/young-leaders-manage-older-employees-01029503#WvxkHR6cRr6ofVqk.97; F. J. Reh, "How to Manage Older Workers," *The Balance*, January 14, 2019, www.thebalance.com/how-to-manage-older-workers-2276082; and R. Jenkins, "Why Generational Diversity Is the Ultimate Competitive Advantage," *Inc.*, May 15, 2017, www.inc.com/ryan-jenkins/why-generational-diversity-is-the-ultimate-competitive-advantage.html.

Another line of research has looked at whether 360-degree feedback ratings improve over time. In other words, is it possible to change others' perceptions of a leader's skills? One would hope that this would be the case, given the relationship between others' ratings and leadership effectiveness. Walker and Smither reported that managers who shared their 360-degree feedback results with their followers and worked on an action plan to improve their ratings had a dramatic improvement in others' ratings over a five-year period.[170] Johnson and Johnson looked at 360-degree ratings over a two-year period and reported leadership productivity improvements of 9.5 percent for 515 managers in a manufacturing company.[171] A more recent article reviewed the findings from 24 different studies and concluded that 360-degree feedback ratings do change over time, but the amount of change tends to be small.[172] Other researchers aptly point out that 360-degree feedback alone is not a panacea to improve leadership skills. In addition to gaining insight from 360-degree feedback, leaders must also create a set of development goals and commit to a development plan if they want to see improvement in others' ratings (and, in turn, leadership effectiveness) over time.[173, 174, 175, 176, 177, 178, 179]

The last line of research has explored whether there are important cultural, racial, or gender issues with 360-degree feedback. In terms of cultural issues, some countries, such as Japan, do not believe peers or followers should give leaders feedback.[180, 181] Other countries, such as Saudi Arabia, tend more to avoid conflict and provide only positive feedback to leaders. The latter phenomenon also appears in the United States, where researchers working in small organizations or in rural communities often report similar findings. People seem more hesitant to give leaders constructive feedback if they have to deal with the consequences of this feedback both at and away from work. These findings further support the notion that 360-degree feedback is not a management panacea; societal or organizational culture plays a key role in the accuracy and utility of the 360-degree feedback process.[182, 183, 184, 185, 186, 187, 188, 189, 190]

> *Ask Americans how they stand compared with their fellow countrymen and in survey after survey, the vast majority rank themselves as "above average" in such areas as driving skills, sexual prowess, and general honesty."*
>
> **Chuck Shepherd,** *News of the Weird*

With respect to racial differences, a comprehensive study by Mount, Sytsma, Hazucha, and Holt looked at the pattern of responses from bosses, peers, and subordinates for over 20,000 managers from a variety of U.S. companies. In general, these researchers reported that Blacks tended to give higher ratings to other Blacks, irrespective of whether they were asked to provide peer, subordinate, or boss ratings. However, the overall size of this effect was small. White peers and subordinates generally gave about the same level of ratings to both Black and white peers and bosses. This was not the case for white bosses, however, who tended to give significantly higher ratings to whites who reported directly to them. These findings imply that Black leaders are likely to advance at a slower pace than their white counterparts because 80 to 90 percent of salary, bonus, and promotion decisions are made solely by bosses.[191, 192]

With respect to gender issues, research indicates that there are some slight gender differences. Female managers tend to get higher ratings on the majority of skills, yet their male counterparts are generally perceived as having higher advancement potential. There does not appear to be any same-sex bias in 360-degree feedback ratings, and female managers tend to be lower self-raters. Male managers tend to have less accurate self-insight and more blind spots when compared to their female counterparts. In summary, male and female 360-degree feedback ratings are similar, and any differences are of little practical significance.

One final 360-degree feedback finding has to do with the **contagion effect**. Research shows that emotions are contagious, which means that someone hanging out with a friend who is despondent, mad, or elated is much more likely to exhibit the same emotions. It turns out the contagion effect may also happen with good and bad leadership. Research on 360-degree feedback shows that those individuals who work for superiors receiving above-average ratings from others were more likely to receive above-average ratings themselves. One interpretation of this finding is that outstanding bosses attract and retain high-performing followers, and if these followers also happen to occupy leadership positions then they too are perceived to be effective leaders. The reverse also appears to be true, in that those leaders receiving below-average ratings were likely to have direct reports who also received below-average 360-degree feedback ratings from others. However, another interpretation of these findings is pervasive **rater bias**. It may be that some leaders work in functions, organizations, or cultures that tend to provide systematically higher or lower ratings that are unrelated to actual performance. Another explanation for these systematically higher or lower ratings may have to do with organizational performance. Raters may believe that great or poor organizational results are due to good or bad leadership, even though the results may be more a function of situational factors than leader behavior. Leaders may be doing all the right things, but substandard team or organizational results may affect 360-degree feedback ratings. More research needs to be done to determine whether winners beget winners or if perceived winners simply work in organizations that provide kinder and gentler ratings than deserved.[193]

What should a leadership practitioner take away from this 360-degree feedback research? First, given the popularity of the technique, it is likely that you will receive 360-degree feedback sometime in your career. Second, 360-degree feedback should be built around a competency model, which will describe the leadership behaviors needed to achieve organizational goals. Third, the organization may have different competency models to reflect the different leadership behaviors needed to succeed at different organizational levels. Fourth,

360-degree feedback may be one of the best sources of "how" feedback for leadership practitioners. Leaders tend to get plenty of "what" feedback—what progress they are making toward group goals, what level of customer service is being achieved, win–loss records, and so on; but they get little feedback on how they should act to get better results. Multirater instruments provide feedback on the kinds of things leaders need to do to build cohesive, goal-oriented teams and get better results through others. Fifth, effective leaders seem to have a broad set of well-developed leadership skills—they do not do just one or two things well and do everything else poorly. Instead they seem to possess a broad array of leadership strengths. Sixth, leaders need to create specific goals and development plans in order to improve leadership skills—360-degree feedback results give leaders ideas on what to improve but may not be enough in and of themselves to affect behavioral change. Seventh, leadership behavior can change over time, but it may take a year or two to acquire new skills and for the changes to be reflected in 360-degree feedback ratings. Finally, some cultural, racial, and gender issues are associated with 360-degree feedback, and practitioners should be aware of these issues before implementing any 360-degree feedback process.[194, 195, 196, 197] (See **Highlight 7.7.**)

Leadership Behavior: What We Know and What Remains to Be Answered

HIGHLIGHT 7.7

An important objective for leadership researchers has been to identify the behaviors that help or hinder a person's ability to engage followers, get results through others, or build cohesive, goal-oriented teams. The thousands of studies involving millions of leaders that have been conducted over the past 50 years show that the effective leadership behavior findings are fragmented and offer only a few general truths. About all we know at this point is that leaders who demonstrate more monitoring, problem-solving, planning, supporting, developing, empowering, facilitating, and networking behaviors are seen as more effective than those leaders who exhibit less of these behaviors. Because good marketing always trumps good science, many authors have used these findings as justification for writing books that advocate that the best leaders are those who adopt these five behaviors, seven habits, and more.

There are several reasons why the findings concerning leadership behaviors are so limited and the advice offered by the books advocating certain behaviors is wrong. First, leadership researchers tend to use different competency models and behavioral definitions, which makes it difficult to aggregate results. Second, situational and follower variables often dictate which leadership behaviors will be effective. Empowering someone to take the controls may not lead to good results if a person does not know how to fly and the plane is on fire. Third, the quality and timeliness of leadership behavior can have just as much impact as the frequency with which it is exhibited—just doing more coaching may not be as helpful as doing high-quality coaching at the right time. Fourth, leadership is a team sport, and getting groups of people to work effectively to solve problems or create action plans is much more complicated and requires a different set of behaviors than doing so on a one-on-one basis. Many leadership researchers and authors confuse the individual versus team distinction. Finally, many leadership researchers define leadership as those occupying positions of authority. For example, researchers may define leaders as all the store managers for a grocery chain. But what if the majority of the store managers were not very good at building teams or getting results through others? The results obtained may say more about the types of behaviors needed to get promoted than to get results through others or to build teams. As you will see in **Chapter 17**, 50 to 65 percent of the people in positions of authority are perceived to be incompetent, and if these individuals are included in a research study then they will obscure the results obtained. The upshot of all of this behavioral research is that we know more about what not to do than what to do to be effective leaders.

Sources: G. Yukl, "Effective Leadership Behavior: What We Know and What Questions Need More Attention,"

Academy of Management Perspectives 26, no. 4 (2012), pp. 66–85; G. J. Curphy, "Investing in the Wrong Vehicle: The Neglect of Team Leadership," in *Why Is the Leadership Development Industry Failing?* R. B. Kaiser (chair). Symposium conducted at the 28th Annual Conference for the Society of Industrial and Organizational Psychology, Houston, May 2013; R. B. Kaiser and G. J. Curphy, "Leadership Development: The Failure of an Industry and the Opportunity for Consulting Psychologists," *Consulting Psychology Journal: Practice and Theory* 65, no. 4 (2013), pp. 294–302; G. J. Curphy, "Leadership Master Class," Bratislava, Slovakia, March 31, 2017, and G. J. Curphy, D. Nilsen, and R. T. Hogan, *Ignition: A Guide to Building High Performing Teams* (Tulsa, OK: Hogan Press: 2019).

Summary

People in leadership positions exhibit a wide variety of behaviors, and researchers have explored whether there is a universal set of behaviors that differentiates effective from ineffective leaders or if there are situational or follower factors that influence the types of behavior needed to build teams or get results through others. To answer the first question, there does not appear to be a universal set of leadership behaviors that guarantees success across many or all situations. Although some types of task- and relationship-oriented leadership behaviors will likely improve the odds of success, the nature of the work to be performed, the situation, and the number and types of followers affect the specific kinds of task and relationship behaviors leaders need to demonstrate to be effective. **Chapter 14** describes a much more comprehensive list of the situational factors affecting leadership behavior, but some of the key situational factors reviewed in this chapter include the setting (community or organization) and organizational level. Competency models and 360-degree feedback can be used to describe how well someone is performing the behaviors needed to succeed in a particular position.

Leadership practitioners need to realize that they will ultimately be judged by the results they obtain and the behaviors they exhibit. Yet prior experience, values, and attributes play critical roles in how leaders go about engaging followers, building teams, and achieving results through others. For example, leaders who move into roles that involve solving complex business problems but lack relevant experience, analytic intelligence, and strong commercial values will struggle to be successful, and those with the opposite characteristics are much more likely to succeed. Having the right attributes, values, and experience does not guarantee that leaders will exhibit the right behaviors, but this improves the odds considerably.

This chapter offers some vital yet subtle suggestions on how to be effective as a leader. First, people moving into leadership roles need to understand the performance expectations for their positions. These expectations include not only the results to be achieved but also the behaviors that need to be exhibited. Organizational levels and competency models can help leaders determine the specific types of behaviors required to build teams and get results through others for the position in question. These frameworks also describe the behavioral changes leaders will need to make as they transition into new roles.

Second, understanding the behavioral requirements of various leadership positions and exhibiting needed behaviors can be two quite different things. That being the case, 360-degree feedback can give leaders insight into whether they need to do anything differently to engage followers, build stronger teams, or get better results through others. Although getting feedback from others can be an uncomfortable experience, this information is vital if people want to succeed as leaders. The 360-degree feedback process makes getting feedback from others more systematic and actionable, and as such it is an important tool in the development of leaders.

Third, getting feedback from others in and of itself may not result in behavioral change. For example, many people know they need to lose weight, yet they may not do anything about it. But if they build a plan that includes a modified diet and regular exercise and get regular feedback and encouragement from others, they are much more likely to lose weight. The same holds true for changing leadership behaviors. Building development plans and getting coaching from others will improve the odds of changing targeted behaviors or acquiring needed skills, so leaders who want to be more effective should have written development plans.

Key Terms

Leader Behavior Description
Questionnaire (LBDQ)

consideration

initiating structure

job-centered dimensions

goal emphasis

work facilitation

employee-centered dimensions

leader support

interaction facilitation

Leadership Grid

concern for people

concern for production

leadership behavior

leadership skill

executive presence

competency models

intrapersonal skills

interpersonal skills

leadership skills

business skills

portable skills

nonportable skills

hub-and-spoke model of
leadership

organizational level

Leadership Pipeline

on-boarding

community leadership

framing

building social capital

mobilization

360-degree, or multirater,
feedback

competency-based 360-degree
feedback questionnaires

leadership versatility approach

verbal 360-degree technique

contagion effect

rater bias

Questions

1. Could you create a competency model for college professors? For college students? If you used these competency models to create 360-degree feedback tools, who would be in the best position to give professors and students feedback?

2. What competencies would be needed by a U.S.-born leader being assigned to build power plants in China? What competencies would be needed by a Chinese-born leader being assigned to run a copper mine in Kenya?

3. Who learns more about being an effective leader—MBAs or restaurant managers? What do these two groups learn from their education and experience? Are these portable or nonportable skills?

4. The President of the United States, Donald Trump, developed a number of skills as a business leader and television celebrity. How did he leverage these skills during the coronavirus pandemic? What skills did he lack during the pandemic?

Activities

1. Identify two leadership positions and then determine the relative importance of the 16 competencies shown in **Figure 7.3**. You can do this by ranking each competency in order of importance, with the most important competency being assigned a 1, the second most important a 2, and so on. If you do this exercise with several partners ranking the same positions, does everyone give the 16 competencies about the same ranking? Why or why not?

2. Collect competency models from two organizations and assign them to the intrapersonal, interpersonal, leadership, and business categories described by Hogan and Warrenfelz. Do the competencies fit easily into the four categories? Which categories seem to be underrepresented or overrepresented by the competency models? Do these models say anything about building teams or achieving results?

3. Identify two leadership positions at your school or in organizations in your community and determine their organizational levels using the Leadership Pipeline.

4. Given the model of community leadership described earlier in this chapter, analyze an ongoing community change initiative. Has the leader framed the issue in a way that makes it easy for others to take action? Do the group members have strong bonds with other groups? Have they created a plan and mobilized a critical mass of people and resources to make the change become reality?

5. Given the model of community leadership described in this chapter, what would climate change advocates need to do to have a real impact on climate change?

Minicase

Paying Attention Pays Off for Andra Rush

Paying attention has been a key for Andra Rush. As a nursing school graduate, she was paying attention when other nurses complained about unfair treatment and decided she wanted to do something about it—so she enrolled in the University of Michigan's MBA program so she could do something about how employees were treated. As she completed her business courses and continued to work as a nurse, she was paying attention when a patient described his experience in the transport business. The business sounded intriguing, and so, with minimal experience and minimal resources, Rush took a risk and started her own trucking business. She scraped together the funds to buy three trucks by borrowing money from family and using her credit cards. She specialized in emergency shipping and accepted every job that came her way, even if it meant driving the trucks herself. She answered phones, balanced her books, and even repaired the trucks. She paid attention to her customers and made a point of exceeding their expectations regardless of the circumstances. When the terrorist attacks of September 11, 2001, shut down local bridges, Rush rented a barge to make sure a crucial shipment for DaimlerChrysler made it to its destination on time.

Rush continues to pay attention and credits her listening skills as a major reason for her success. Rush is distinct in the traditionally white male-dominated trucking industry—a woman and a minority (Rush is Native American) who credits her heritage and the "enormous strength" of her Mohawk grandmother for helping her prevail:

It is entirely possible that my Native spirit, communicated to me by my grandmother and my immediate family, have enabled me to overcome the isolation, historical prejudice, and business environment viewed as a barrier to Native- and woman-owned businesses. The willingness to listen, to understand first, and act directly and honestly with integrity is a lesson and code of conduct my elders have bequeathed to me. Being an entrepreneur has reinforced those lessons again and again.

Her Mohawk heritage is pervasive. Rush's company logo is a war staff with six feathers representing the Six Nations of the Iroquois: Mohawk, Onondaga, Oneida, Cayuga, Tuscarora, and Seneca. She believes in the power of a diverse workforce; as a result more than half of the 390 employees at Rush Trucking are women, and half are minorities.

Rush keeps close tabs on her company and its employees. Though the company has grown from its humble three-truck beginning to a fleet of 1,700 trucks, Rush still takes time to ride along with drivers. She has provided educational programs like "The Readers' Edge," a literacy program, to improve the skills and lives of her employees. Rush is actively involved in several organizations that work to improve the position of minorities—she's on the boards of directors of the Michigan Minority Business Development Council, the Minority Enterprise Development/Minority Business Development Agency, and the Minority Business Roundtable, and she has served as president of the Native American Business Alliance.

1. As we have discussed, competency models describe the behaviors and skills managers need to exhibit if an organization is to be successful. Consider the general competencies found in **Figure 7.3** and apply these to Andra Rush, providing examples of how these competencies apply.

2. How does the Leadership Pipeline apply to Andra Rush?

3. Andra Rush belongs to several volunteer organizations. Would her leadership style need to change as the president of the Native American Business Alliance versus the CEO of Rush Trucking? How would the community leadership model apply to Andra Rush?

N. Heintz, "Andra Rush, Rush Trucking," *Inc.*, April 1, 2004

Endnotes

1. G. J. Curphy, "Investing in the Wrong Vehicle: The Neglect of Team Leadership," in *Why Is the Leadership Development Industry Failing?* R. B. Kaiser (chair). Symposium conducted at the 28th Annual Conference for the Society of Industrial and Organizational Psychology, Houston, May 2013.

2. R. B. Kaiser, J. Lindberg McGinnis, and D. V. Overfield, "The How and What of Leadership," *Consulting Psychology Journal: Practice and Research* 64, no. 2 (2012), pp. 119–35.

3. G. J. Curphy, "Leadership Transitions and Teams," presentation given at the Hogan Assessment Systems International Users Conference, Istanbul, September 2003.

4. G. J. Curphy, "The Consequences of Managerial Incompetence," presentation given at the 3rd Hogan Assessment Systems International Users Conference, Prague, Czech Republic, September 2004.

5. G. J. Curphy, "Comments on the State of Leadership Prediction," in *Predicting Leadership: The Good, The Bad, the Indifferent, and the Unnecessary*, J. P. Campbell and M. J. Benson (chairs). Symposium conducted at the 22nd Annual Conference for the Society of Industrial and Organizational Psychology, New York, April 2007.

6. R. B. Kaiser and D. V. Overfield, "The Leadership Value Chain," *The Psychologist-Manager Journal* 13, no. 3 (2010), pp. 164–83.

7. D. S. Derue, J. D. Nahrgang, N. Wellman, and S. E. Humphrey, "Trait and Behavioral Theories of Leadership: An Integration and Meta-analytic Test of Their Relative Validity," *Personnel Psychology* 64, no. 1 (2011), pp. 7–52.

8. R. T. Hogan and G. J. Curphy, *Leadership Effectiveness and Managerial Incompetence*, unpublished manuscript, 2007.

9. R. Charan and G. Colvin, "Why CEOs Fail," *Fortune*, June 21, 1999, pp. 69–82.

10. M. Goldsmith and M. Reiter, *What Got You Here Won't Get You There* (New York: Hyperion, 2007).

11. Kaiser, Lindberg McGinnis, and Overfield, "The How and What of Leadership."

12. Kaiser and Overfield, "The Leadership Value Chain."

13. Derue et al., "Trait and Behavioral Theories of Leadership."

14. J. K. Hemphill, "The Leader and His Group," *Journal of Educational Research* 28 (1949): 225–29, 245–46.

15. J. K. Hemphill and A. E. Coons, "Development of the Leader Behavior Description Questionnaire," in *Leader Behavior: Its Description and Measurement*, eds. R. M. Stogdill and A. E. Coons (Columbus: Ohio State University, Bureau of Business Research, 1957).

16. E. A. Fleishman, "Twenty Years of Consideration and Structure," in *Current Developments in the Study of Leadership*, eds. E. A. Fleishman and J. G. Hunt (Carbondale: Southern Illinois University Press, 1973).

17. A. W. Halpin and B. J. Winer, "A Factorial Study of the Leader Behavior Descriptions," in *Leader Behavior: Its Descriptions and Measurement*, eds. R. M. Stogdill and A. E. Coons (Columbus: Ohio State University, Bureau of Business Research, 1957).

18. E. A. Fleishman, *Examiner's Manual for the Supervisory Behavior Description Questionnaire* (Washington, DC: Management Research Institute, 1972).

19. E. A. Fleishman, *Examiner's Manual for the Leadership Opinion Questionnaire*, rev. ed. (Chicago: Science Research Associates, 1989).

20. R. M. Stogdill, *Individual Behavior and Group Achievement* (New York: Oxford University Press, 1959).

21. R. Likert, *New Patterns of Management* (New York: McGraw-Hill, 1961).

22. D. G. Bowers and S. E. Seashore, "Predicting Organizational Effectiveness with a Four Factor Theory of Leadership," *Administrative Science Quarterly* 11 (1966), pp. 238–63.

23. Bowers and Seashore, "Predicting Organizational Effectiveness with a Four Factor Theory of Leadership."

24. B. M. Bass, *Bass and Stogdill's Handbook of Leadership*, 3rd ed. (New York: Free Press, 1990).

25. T. A. Judge, R. F. Piccolo, and R. Ilies, "The Forgotten Ones? The Validity of Consideration and Initiating Structure in Leadership Research," *Journal of Applied Psychology* 89, no. 1 (2004): 36–51.

26. R. Eisenberger, F. Stinglhamber, C. Vandenberghe, I. L. Sucharski, and L. Rhoades, "Perceived Supervisor Support: Contributions to Perceived Organizational Support and Employee Retention," *Journal of Applied Psychology* 87, no. 3 (2002), pp. 565–73.

27. Bass, *Bass and Stogdill's Handbook of Leadership*.

28. R. R. Blake and A. A. McCanse, *Leadership Dilemmas—Grid Solutions* (Houston, TX: Gulf, 1991).

29. R. R. Blake and J. S. Mouton, *The Managerial Grid* (Houston, TX: Gulf, 1964).

30. Blake and McCanse, *Leadership Dilemmas—Grid Solutions*.

31. E. Sinar, R. Wellins, M. Paese, A. Smith, and B. Watt, "High Resolution Leadership: A Synthesis of 15,000 Assessments into How Leaders Shape the Business Landscape," Development Dimensions International, www.ddiworld.com/hirezleadership.

32. C. Robie, K. Kanter, D. L. Nilsen, and J. Hazucha, *The Right Stuff: Understanding Cultural Differences in Leadership Performance* (Minneapolis, MN: Personnel Decisions International, 2001).

33. Judge, Piccolo, and Ilies, "The Forgotten Ones?"

34. M. Goff, *Critical Leadership Skills Valued by Every Organization* (Minneapolis, MN: Personnel Decisions International, 2001).

35. Judge, Piccolo, and Ilies, "The Forgotten Ones?"

36. Eisenberger et al., "Perceived Supervisor Support."

37. J. M. Schaubroeck, Y. Shen, and S. Chong, "A Dual-Stage Moderated Mediation Model Linking Authoritarian Leadership to Follower Outcomes," *Journal of Applied Psychology* 2, no. 2 (2017): 204–14.

38. Kaiser et al., "The How and What of Leadership."

39. S. Davis, J. Volker, R. C. Barnett, P. H. Batz, and P. Germann, *Leadership Matters: 13 Roles of High Performing Leaders* (Minneapolis, MN: MDA Leadership Consulting, 2006).

40. G. P. Hollenbeck, M. W. McCall, and R. F. Silzer, "Leadership Competency Models," *Leadership Quarterly* 17, no. 4 (2006), pp. 398–413.

41. L. Tischler, "IBM's Management Makeover," *Fast Company*, November 2004, pp. 112–16.

42. P. Lievens, J. I. Sanchez, and W. DeCorte, "Easing the Inferential Leap in Competency Modeling: The Effects of Task-Related Information and Subject Matter Expertise," *Personnel Psychology* 57, no. 4 (2004), pp. 881–904.

43. A. W. King, S. W. Fowler, and C. P. Zeithaml, "Managing Organizational Competencies for Competitive Advantage: The Middle-Management Edge," *Academy of Management Executive* 15, no. 2 (2001), pp. 95–106.

44. G. J. Curphy, *The Blandin Education Leadership Program* (Grand Rapids, MN: The Blandin Foundation, 2004).

45. G. J. Curphy, *Why Is the Leadership Development Industry Failing?* Presentation given at the Metro Industrial/Organizational Psychology Association, New York City, 2013.

46. G. J. Curphy and R. T. Hogan, "Managerial Incompetence: Is There a Dead Skunk on the Table?" working paper, 2004.

47. G. J. Curphy, "Is Your Leadership Development Process Broken? Using the Wrong Definitions of Leadership," Linked In, June 30, 2014, http://www.linkedin.com/pulse/20140630115952-36824143-is-your-leadership-development-process-broken-using-the-wrong-definitions-of-leadership.

48. G. J. Curphy, "The Fatal Flaw in Leadership Competency Models," Linked In, September 1, 2014, https://www.linkedin.com/pulse/20140901121513-36824143-the-fatal-flaw-in-leadership-competency-models.

49. K. Nei, K. Fuhrmeister, R. Fonseca, and L. Tecle, *Job Analytic Comparisons of Managerial and Leadership Competencies: Managerial vs. Leadership Critical Competencies* (Tulsa, OK: Hogan Assessment Systems, 2015).

50. S. Mautz. "Google Tried to Prove Managers Don't Matter. Instead, It Discovered 10 Traits of the Very Best Ones." https://www.inc.com/scott-mautz/google-tried-to-prove-managers-dont-matter-instead-they-discovered-10-traits-of-very-best-ones.html

51. Kaiser et al., "The How and What of Leadership."

52. Davis et al., *Leadership Matters.*

53. Hollenbeck et al., "Leadership Competency Models."

54. Lievens et al., "Easing the Inferential Leap in Competency Modeling."

55. D. Ulrich, J. Zenger, and N. Smallwood, *Results-Based Leadership* (Boston: Harvard Business School Press, 1999).

56. D. B. Peterson, "Making the Break from Middle Manager to a Seat at the Top," *The Wall Street Journal*, July 7, 1998.

57. Kaiser et al., "The How and What of Leadership."

58. Curphy, "The Consequences of Managerial Incompetence."

59. Curphy, "Comments on the State of Leadership Prediction."

60. Derue et al., "Trait and Behavioral Theories of Leadership."

61. Hollenbeck et al., "Leadership Competency Models."

62. Lievens et al., "Easing the Inferential Leap in Competency Modeling."

63. R. B. Kaiser and S. B. Craig, *Testing the Leadership Pipeline: Do the Behaviors Related to Managerial Effectiveness Change with Organizational Level?* Presentation given at the 1st Annual Leading Edge Consortium, St Louis, MO, 2008.

64. J. S. Shippmann, R. A. Ash, M. Battista, L. Carr, L. D. Eyde, B. Hesketh, J. Kehoe, K. Pearlman, E. P. Prien, and J. I. Sanchez, "The Practice of Competency Modeling," *Personnel Psychology* 53, no. 3 (2000), pp. 703–40.

65. R. T. Hogan and R. Warrenfelz, "Educating the Modern Manager," *Academy of Management Learning and Education* 2, no. 1 (2003), pp. 74–84.

66. A. H. Church, "Talent Management," *The Industrial-Organizational Psychologist* 44, no. 1 (2006), pp. 33–36.

67. Hogan and Warrenfelz, "Educating the Modern Manager."

68. D. Reimer, H. Feuerstein, S. Meighan, and S. Kelly, "It's Time for a Second Playbook: HR's Leadership Role in Transformation," Merryck & Co., www.merryck.com/wp-content/uploads/2017/07/It's-Time-for-a-Second-Playbook.pdf.

69. W. A. Gentry, L. S. Harris, B. A. Becker, and J. B. Leslie, "Managerial Skills: What Has Changed since the Late 1980s," *Leadership & Organizational Development Journal* 29, no. 2 (2008), pp. 167–81.

70. D. Ancona, T. W. Malone, W. J. Orlikowski, and P. M. Senge, "In Praise of the Incomplete Leader," *Harvard Business Review*, February 2007, pp. 92–103.

71. E. Cripe, "Are Competency Models Too Complex? *Workitect*, May 10, 2018, www.workitect.com/competency-models/competency-models-complex.

72. M. Roellig, "Cloud Leadership," *ACC Docket*, June 2019, pp. 24–25.

73. R. Charan, S. Drotter, and J. Noel, *The Leadership Pipeline: How to Build the Leadership-Powered Company* (San Francisco: Jossey-Bass, 2001).

74. R. B. Kaiser, S. B. Craig, D. V. Overfield, and P. Yarborough, "Differences in Managerial Jobs at the Bottom, Middle, and Top: A Review of Empirical Research," *The Psychologist-Manager Journal* 14, no. 2 (2011), pp. 76–91.

75. R. B. Kaiser and S. B. Craig, "Do the Behaviors Related to Managerial Effectiveness Really Change with Organizational Level? An Empirical Test," *The Psychologist-Manager Journal* 14, no. 2 (2011), pp. 92–119.

76. M. Porter and N. Nohria, "How CEOs Manage Time," *Harvard Business Review*, July–August 2018, pp. 42–59.

77. R. Hardin, *The Neglected Middle: Activating Middle Managers for Change*, unpublished manuscript, Rick Hardin & Associates, 2017.

78. R. Charan et al., *The Leadership Pipeline.*

79. A. Furnham, C. Humphries, and E. Leung Zheng, "Can Successful Sales People Become Successful Managers? Differences in Motives and Derailers across Two Jobs," *Consulting Psychology Journal: Practice and Theory* 68, no. 3 (2016), pp. 252–67.

80. R. T. Hogan, *Personality and the Fate of Organizations* (Mahwah, NJ: Lawrence Erlbaum Associates, 2007).

81. M. Watkins, *The First 90 Days: Critical Success Strategies for New Leaders at All Levels* (Boston, MA: Harvard Business School Press, 2003).

82. M. Roellig and G. J. Curphy, *How to Hit the Ground Running: A Guide to Successful On-Boarding* (North Oaks, MN: Curphy Leadership Solutions, 2012).

83. A. Kuzel, "Don't Promote Internally and Leave Employees Drowning," Chief Learning Officer, www.chieflearningofficer.com/2016/06/02/dont-promote-internally-and-leave-employees-drowning.

84. J. S. Lublin, "Going from Big Fish to Small Fish," *The Wall Street Journal*, May 30, 2019, p. B5.

85. G. J. Curphy, "Is Your Team Operating at the Right Level?" LinkedIn, August 28, 2018, www.linkedin.com/pulse/your-top-team-operating-right-level-gordon-gordy-curphy-phd.

86. G. J. Curphy, D. Nilsen, and R. T. Hogan, *Ignition: A Guide to Building High Performing Teams* (Tulsa, OK: Hogan Press, 2019).

87. J. Krile, G. J. Curphy, and D. Lund, *The Community Leadership Handbook: Framing Ideas, Building Relationships and Mobilizing Resources* (St. Paul, MN: Fieldstone Alliance, 2005).

88. B. C. Crosby and J. M. Bryson, "Integrative Leadership and the Creation and Maintenance of Cross-Sector Collaborations," *Leadership Quarterly* 21 (2010), pp. 211–30.

89. J. E. Bono, W. Shen, and M. Snyder, "Fostering Integrative Community Leadership," *Leadership Quarterly* 21 (2010), pp. 324–35.

90. N. M. Tichy and E. Cohen, *The Leadership Engine: How Winning Companies Build Leaders at Every Level* (New York: Harper Collins, 1997).

91. Curphy, "Investing in the Wrong Vehicle."

92. Kaiser et al., "The How and What of Leadership."

93. Derue et al., "Trait and Behavioral Theories of Leadership."

94. Hogan and Curphy, *Leadership Effectiveness and Managerial Incompetence.*

95. D. P. Campbell, G. J. Curphy, and T. Tuggle, *360-Degree Feedback Instruments: Beyond Theory.* Workshop presented at the 10th Annual Conference of the Society for Industrial and Organizational Psychology, Orlando, FL, May 1995.

96. G. J. Curphy, "Executive Integrity and 360-Degree Feedback," in *Assessing Executive Failure: The Underside of Performance*, R. T. Hogan (chair). Symposium presented at the 18th Annual Conference of the Society of Industrial and Organizational Psychology, Orlando, FL, 2003.

97. G. Toegel and J. A. Conger, "360-Degree Assessment: Time for Reinvention," *Academy of Management Learning and Education* 2, no. 3 (November 30, 2017), pp. 297–311.

98. R. B. Kaiser and S. B. Craig, "Building a Better Mousetrap: Item Characteristics Associated with Rating Discrepancies in 360-Degree Feedback," *Consulting Psychology Journal* 57, no. 4 (2005), pp. 235–45.

99. F. Morgeson, T. V. Mumsford, and M. A. Campion, "Coming Full Circle: Research and Practice to Address 27 Questions about 360-Degree Feedback Programs," *Consulting Psychology Journal* 57, no. 3 (2005), pp. 196–209.

100. J. W. Smither, M. London, and R. R. Reilly, "Does Performance Improve Following Multisource Feedback? A Theoretical Model, Meta-analysis, and Review of Empirical Findings," *Personnel Psychology* 58 (2005), pp. 33–66.

101. K. M. Nowack, "Leveraging Multirater Feedback to Facilitate Successful Behavioral Change," *Consulting Psychology Journal: Practice and Research* 61, no. 4 (2009), pp. 280–97.

102. J. E. Bono and A. E. Colbert, "Understanding Responses to Multi-Source Feedback: The Core of Self-Evaluations," *Personnel Psychology* 58 (2005), pp. 171–203.

103. D. W. Bracken, C. W. Timmreck, and A. H. Church, *The Handbook of Multisource Feedback* (San Francisco: Jossey-Bass, 2000).

104. K. Yong Kim, L. Atwater, P. C. Patel, and J. W. Smither, "Multisource Feedback, Human Capital, and the Financial Performance of Organizations," *Journal of Consulting Psychology* 101, no. 11 (2016), pp. 1569–84.

105. Campbell et al., *360-Degree Feedback Instruments.*

106. Curphy, "Investing in the Wrong Vehicle."

107. Curphy, "Comments on the State of Leadership Prediction."

108. Derue et al., "Trait and Behavioral Theories of Leadership."

109. Campbell et al., *360-Degree Feedback Instruments.*

110. Curphy, "Executive Integrity and 360-Degree Feedback."

111. Toegel and Conger, "360-Degree Assessment."

112. Kaiser and Craig, "Building a Better Mousetrap."

113. Morgeson et al., "Coming Full Circle."

114. Smither et al., "Does Performance Improve Following Multisource Feedback?"

115. Nowack, "Leveraging Multirater Feedback to Facilitate Successful Behavioral Change."

116. Bono and Colbert, "Understanding Responses to Multi-Source Feedback."

117. Bracken et al., *The Handbook of Multisource Feedback.*

118. P. W. B. Atkins and R. E. Wood, "Self-Versus Others' Ratings as Predictors of Assessment Center Ratings: Validation Evidence for 360-Degree Feedback Programs," *Personnel Psychology* 55 (2002), pp. 871–84.

119. K. M. Nowack and S. Mashihi, "Evidence-Based Answers to 15 Questions About Leveraging 360-Degree Feedback," *Consulting Psychologist Journal: Practice and Research* 64, no. 3 (2012), pp. 157–82.

120. Kaiser et al., "The How and What of Leadership."

121. Nowack and Mashihi, "Evidence-Based Answers to 15 Questions about Leveraging 360-Degree Feedback."

122. J. M. Jackman and M. H. Strober, "Fear of Feedback," *Harvard Business Review*, April 2003, pp. 101–8.

123. M. A. Peiperl, "Getting 360-Degree Feedback Right," *Harvard Business Review*, January 2001, pp. 142–48.

124. R. Hougaard and J. Carter, "Ego Is the Enemy of Good Leadership," *Harvard Business Review*, November 6, 2018, https://hbr.org/2018/11/ego-is-the-enemy-of-good-leadership.

125. Curphy, "Investing in the Wrong Vehicle."

126. Campbell et al., *360-Degree Feedback Instruments.*

127. Toegel and Conger, "360-Degree Assessment."

128. Kaiser and Craig, "Building a Better Mousetrap."

129. Nowack, "Leveraging Multirater Feedback to Facilitate Successful Behavioral Change."

130. Bracken et al., *The Handbook of Multisource Feedback.*

131. R. E. Kaplan and R. B. Kaiser, *Leadership Versatility Index* (Greensboro, NC: Kaplan DeVries, 2006).

132. R. E. Kaplan and R. B. Kaiser, "StopOverdoing Your Strengths," *Harvard Business Review*, February 2009, https://hbr.org/2009/02/stop-overdoing-your-strengths.

133. Curphy, "Investing in the Wrong Vehicle."

134. Curphy, "Comments on the State of Leadership Prediction."

135. Curphy and Hogan, "Managerial Incompetence."

136. Kaiser and Craig, "Building a Better Mousetrap."

137. Morgeson et al., "Coming Full Circle."

138. Jackman and Strober, "Fear of Feedback."

139. Peiperl, "Getting 360-Degree Feedback Right."

140. F. Sala, "Executive Blind Spots: Discrepancies between Self- and Other-Ratings," *Consulting Psychology Journal* 55, no. 4 (2003), pp. 222–29.

141. Curphy, "Investing in the Wrong Vehicle."

142. A. Kinicki, K. J. L. Jacobson, S. J. Peterson, and G. E. Prussia, "Development and Validation of the Performance Management Behavior Questionnaire," *Personnel Psychology* 66, no. 1 (2013), pp. 1–46.

143. D. Antonioni, "360-Degree Feedback for a Competitive Edge," *Industrial Management* 42 (2000), pp. 6–10.

144. F. Sala and S. A. Dwight, "Predicting Executive Performance with Multirater Surveys: Whom You Ask Makes a Difference," *Consulting Psychology Journal* 55, no. 3 (2003), pp. 166–72.

145. G. J. Curphy, "An Empirical Investigation of Bass' (1985) Theory of Transformational and Transactional Leadership," PhD dissertation, University of Minnesota, 1991.

146. G. J. Curphy, "The Effects of Transformational and Transactional Leadership on Organizational Climate, Attrition, and Performance," in *Impact of Leadership*, ed. K. E. Clark, M. B. Clark, and D. P. Campbell (Greensboro, NC: Center for Creative Leadership, 1992).

147. A. H. Church, "Managerial Self-Awareness in High-Performing Individuals in Organizations," *Journal of Applied Psychology* 82, no. 2 (1997), pp. 281–92.

148. A. H. Church, "Do Higher Performing Managers Actually Receive Better Ratings?" *Consulting Psychology Journal* 52, no. 2 (2000): 99–116.

149. J. Ghorpade, "Managing Six Paradoxes of 360-Degree Feedback," *Academy of Management Executive* 14, no. 1 (2000), pp. 140–50.

150. G. J. Greguras, C. Robie, D. J. Schleicher, and M. Goff III, "A Field Study of the Effects of Rating Purpose on the Quality of Multisource Ratings," *Personnel Psychology* 56, no. 1 (2003), pp. 1–22.

151. A. H. Church and J. Waclawski, "A Five-Phase Framework for Designing a Successful Multisource Feedback System," *Consulting Psychology Journal* 53, no. 2 (2001), pp. 82–95.

152. K. Pfau, "Does 360-Degree Feedback Negatively Affect Company Performance?" *HR Magazine*, June 2002, pp. 55–59.

153. G. Curphy, "Investing in the Wrong Vehicle."

154. D. P. Campbell, G. J. Curphy, and T. Tuggle, *360-Degree Feedback Instruments: Beyond Theory.* Workshop presented at the 10th Annual Conference of the Society for Industrial and Organizational Psychology, Orlando, FL, May 1995.

155. Kaiser and Craig, "Building a Better Mousetrap."

156. Morgeson et al., "Coming Full Circle."

157. K. M. Nowack, "Leveraging Multirater Feedback to Facilitate Successful Behavioral Change," *Consulting Psychology Journal: Practice and Research* 61, no. 4 (2009), pp. 280–97.

158. Bono and Colbert, "Understanding Responses to Multi-Source Feedback."

159. Bracken et al., *The Handbook of Multisource Feedback.*

160. Kinicki et al., "Development and Validation of the Performance Management Behavior Questionnaire."

161. Church and Waclawski, "A Five-Phase Framework for Designing a Successful Multisource Feedback System."

162. Pfau, "Does 360-Degree Feedback Negatively Affect Company Performance?"

163. G. J. Curphy, *Afterburner 360 Training Manual* (North Oaks, MN: Curphy Consulting Corporation, 2003).

164. Curphy, "Investing in the Wrong Vehicle."

165. G. J. Greguras and C. Robie, "A New Look at Within-Source Interrater Reliability of 360-Degree Feedback Ratings," *Journal of Applied Psychology* 83, no. 6 (1998), pp. 960–68.

166. M. K. Mount, T. A. Judge, S. E. Scullen, M. R. Sytsma, and S. A. Hezlett, "Trait, Rater, and Level Effects in 360-Degree Performance Ratings," *Personnel Psychology* 51, no. 3 (1998), pp. 557–77.

167. C. Ostroff, L. E. Atwater, and B. J. Feinberg, "Understanding Self-Other Agreement: A Look at Rater and Ratee Characteristics, Context, and Outcomes," *Personnel Psychology* 57, no. 2 (2004), pp. 333–76.

168. R. T. Hogan, *Personality and the Fate of Organizations* (Mahwah, NJ: Lawrence Erlbaum Associates, 2007).

169. M. Watkins, *The First 90 Days: Critical Success Strategies for New Leaders at All Levels* (Boston, MA: Harvard Business School Press, 2003).

170. A. Walker and J. W. Smither, "A Five-Year Study of Upward Feedback: What Managers Do with Their Results Matters," *Personnel Psychology* 52, no. 2 (1999), pp. 395–423.

171. K. Johnson and J. Johnson, *Economic Value of Performance Change after 360-Degree Feedback* (Minneapolis, MN: Personnel Decisions International, 2001).

172. Smither et al., "Does Performance Improve Following Multisource Feedback?"

173. Curphy, "Investing in the Wrong Vehicle."

174. Campbell et al., *360-Degree Feedback Instruments.*

175. A. Walker and J. W. Smither, "A Five-Year Study of Upward Feedback: What Managers Do with Their Results Matters," *Personnel Psychology* 52, no. 2 (1999), pp. 395–423.

176. Johnson and Johnson, *Economic Value of Performance Change after 360-Degree Feedback.*

177. C. F. Seifert and G. Yukl, "Effects of Repeated Multi-Source Feedback on the Influence Behavior and Effectiveness of Managers: A Field Experiment," *The Leadership Quarterly* 21, no. 5 (2010), pp. 856–66.

178. J. W. Smither, M. London, R. Flautt, Y. Vargas, and I. Kucine, "Can Working with an Executive Coach Improve Multisource Feedback Ratings over Time? A Quasi-Experimental Field Study," *Personnel Psychology* 56, no. 1 (2003), pp. 23–44.

179. W. W. Tornow and M. London, *Maximizing the Value of 360-Degree Feedback* (San Francisco: Jossey-Bass, 1998).

180. Tornow and London, *Maximizing the Value of 360-Degree Feedback.*

181. J. S. Chhokar, F. C. Brodbeck, and R. J. House, *Culture and Leadership across the World: The Globe Book of In-Depth Studies of 25 Societies* (Mahwah, NJ: Lawrence Erlbaum Associates, 2007).

182. Curphy, "Investing in the Wrong Vehicle."

183. Curphy, "The Consequences of Managerial Incompetence."

184. Curphy, *The Blandin Education Leadership Program.*

185. Curphy, *Why Is the Leadership Development Industry Failing?*

186. Campbell et al., *360-Degree Feedback Instruments.*

187. Toegel and Conger, "360-Degree Assessment."

188. Nowack and Mashihi, "Evidence-Based Answers to 15 Questions about Leveraging 360-Degree Feedback."

189. Pfau, "Does 360-Degree Feedback Negatively Affect Company Performance?"

190. Chhokar et al., *Culture and Leadership across the World.*

191. M. K. Mount, M. R. Sytsma, J. F. Hazucha, and K. E. Holt, "Rater–Ratee Effects in Development Performance Ratings of Managers," *Personnel Psychology* 50, no. 1 (1997), pp. 51–70.

192. H. J. Bernardin and R. W. Beatty, *Performance Appraisal: Assessing Human Behavior at Work* (Boston: Kent, 1984).

193. J. Zenger and J. Folkman, "The Trickle-Down Effects of Good (and Bad)Leadership," *Harvard Business Review*, January 2016, https://hbr.org/2016/01/the-trickle-down-effect-of-good-and-bad-leadership.

194. Nowack, "Leveraging Multirater Feedback to Facilitate Successful Behavioral Change."

195. A. H. Church and J. Waclawski, "A Five-Phase Framework for Designing a Successful Multisource Feedback System," *Consulting Psychology Journal* 53, no. 2 (2001), pp. 82–95.

196. Bernardin and Beatty, *Performance Appraisal.*

197. Personnel Decisions International, *PROFILOR® Certification Workshop Manual* (Minneapolis, MN: Author, 2007).

CHAPTER 8

Skills for Building Personal Credibility and Influencing Others

Introduction

In this second chapter dealing with leadership skills, our focus is on some of the most "basic" skills with which almost every leader should be equipped:

- Building Credibility
- Communication
- Listening
- Assertiveness
- Conducting Meetings
- Effective Stress Management
- Problem Solving
- Improving Creativity

Building Credibility

Interviews with thousands of followers as well as the results of over half a million 360-degree feedback reports indicate that credibility may be one of the most important components of leadership success and effectiveness.[1, 2] Employees working for leaders they thought were credible were willing to work longer hours, felt more sense of ownership in the company, felt more personally involved in work, and were less likely to leave the company over the next two years.[3] Given the difficulties companies are having finding and retaining talented leaders and workers and the role intellectual capital and bench strength play in organizational success, it would appear that credibility could have a strong bottom-line impact on many organizations. Credibility is a little like leadership in that many people have ideas about what credibility is, but there is little consensus on one "true" definition of credibility. This section will define what we believe credibility is, present the two components of credibility, and explore what leadership practitioners can do (and avoid doing) if they want to build their credibility.

> *Leaders know that while their position may give them authority, their behavior earns them respect. Leaders go first. They set an example and build commitment through simple, daily acts that create progress and momentum.*
>
> **Jim Kouzes and Barry Posner, leadership scholars**

The Two Components of Credibility

Credibility can be defined as the ability to engender trust in others. Leaders with high levels of credibility are seen as trustworthy; they have a strong sense of right and wrong, stand up and speak up for what they believe in, protect confidential information, encourage ethical discussions of business or work issues, and follow through with commitments. Sometimes dishonest leaders, personalized charismatic leaders, or power wielders can initially be seen by followers as credible, but their selfish and self-serving interests usually come to light over time. Credibility is made up of two components: expertise and trust. Followers will not trust leaders if they feel they do not know what they are talking about. Similarly, followers will not trust leaders if they feel confidential information will be leaked, if their leaders are unwilling to take stands on moral issues, or if their leaders do not follow through on their promises. Much about these two components of credibility has already been discussed in the **Chapter 3** sections "Building Technical Competence," "Building Effective Relationships with Superiors," and "Building Effective Relationships with Peers." What follows is a brief overview of these three skills as well as some additional considerations that can help leaders build their credibility.

Building Expertise

Expertise consists of technical competence as well as organizational and industry knowledge, so building expertise means increasing your knowledge and skills in these three areas. Building technical competence, described earlier in **Chapter 3**, concerns increasing the knowledge and repertoire of behaviors you can bring to bear to successfully complete a task. To build technical competence, leadership practitioners must determine how their jobs contribute to the overall mission of the company or organization, become an expert in those jobs through formal training or teaching others, and seek opportunities to broaden their technical expertise.

Nonetheless, building expertise takes more than just technical competence. Leaders also need to understand the company and the industry they are in. Many followers not only want leaders to coach them on their skills—they also look to their leaders to provide some context for organizational, industry, and market events. Building one's organizational or industry knowledge may be just as important as building technical competence. However, the ways in which leadership practitioners build these two knowledge bases are somewhat different from building technical competence. Building technical competence often takes more of a hands-on approach to development, but it is hard to do this when building organizational or industry knowledge. One way to build your organizational or industry knowledge is by regularly reading industry-related journals, annual reports, *The Wall Street Journal, Fortune, Inc.*, or various websites. Many leaders spend 5 to 10 hours a week building their industry and organizational knowledge using this approach. Getting a mentor or being coached by your boss is another way to build such knowledge. Other leadership practitioners have taken stretch assignments where they work on special projects with senior executives. Often these assignments allow them to work closely with executives, and through this contact they better understand the competitive landscape, the organization's history and business strategies, and organizational politics. The bottom line is that your learning is not over once you have obtained your degree. In many ways, it will have just started.

Finally, note that expertise is not the same thing as experience. It has been said that some leaders get one year's worth of experience out of five years' work, whereas others get five years' worth of experience from one year's work. The latter kind of leader presumably develops greater expertise for any given period of work than the former. Leaders who get the most from their experience regularly discuss what they have been learning with a partner, and they frequently update their development plans as a result of these discussions.

Building Trust

The second component of credibility is building trust, which can be broken down into clarifying and communicating your values, and building relationships with others. In many ways leadership is a moral exercise. For example, one key difference between charismatic and transformational leaders is that the latter base their vision on their own and their followers' values, whereas the former base their vision on their own possibly selfish needs. Having a strong values system is an important component both in the building blocks model of skills and in leadership success. Because of the importance of values and relationships in building trust, the remainder of this section explores these two topics in more depth.

Chapter 5 defined *values* as constructs representing generalized behaviors or states of affairs that are considered by the individual to be important. Provided that leaders make ethical decisions and abide by organizational rules, however, differences in values among leaders and followers may be difficult to discern. People do not come to work with their values marked on their foreheads, so others typically make inferences about leaders' values based on their day-to-day behaviors. Unfortunately, in many cases leaders' day-to-day behaviors are misaligned with their personal values; they are not living their work lives in a manner consistent with their values.

An example of a leader not living according to his values might be illustrative. An executive with an oil and gas firm was responsible for all drilling operations in western Canada. Because he felt the discovery of new oil and gas fields was the key to the company's long-term success, he worked up to 18 hours a day, pushed his followers to work similar hours, had little patience for and would publicly disparage any oil rig operators who were behind schedule, and almost fired a manager who gave one of his followers a week off to see the birth of his son back in the United States. As these behaviors continued over time, more and more of his followers either requested transfers or quit to join other companies. Because of these problems with turnover and morale, he was asked to participate in a formal coaching program. Not surprisingly, his 360-degree feedback showed that his boss, peers, and followers found him difficult to work with. These results indicated that he put a premium on getting ahead and economic rewards; yet when he was asked to name the things he felt were most important to him as a leader, his priorities were his family, his religion, getting along with others, and developing his followers (altruism). Obviously there was a huge gap between what he truly believed in and how he behaved. He felt the company expected him to hold people's feet to the fire and get results no matter what the cost, yet neither his boss nor his peers felt that this was the case. The executive had misconstrued the situation and was exhibiting behaviors that were misaligned with his values.

Although this case is somewhat extreme, it is not unusual to find leaders acting in ways that are misaligned with their personal values. One way to assess the degree to which leaders are living according to their personal values is by asking what they truly believe in and what they spend their time and money on. For example, you could write down the five things you believe most strongly in (your top five values) and then review your calendar, daytimer, checkbook, and credit card statements to determine where you spend your time and money. If the two lists are aligned, you are likely living according to your values. If not, you may be living according to how others think you should act. And if there is some discrepancy between the two lists, what should you do? Of course, some discrepancy is likely to occur because situational demands and constraints can influence how we behave. But large discrepancies between the lists may indicate that you are not living consistently with your values, and those you interact with may infer that you have a different set of values than those you believe in. A good first step in clarifying such a discrepancy is to craft a personal mission statement or a leadership credo that describes what you truly believe in as a leader.

Examples of different leadership credos for managers across corporate America can be found in **Highlight 8.1**. Several aspects of leadership credos are worth additional comment. First, leadership credos are personal and are closely linked with a leader's values—a credo should describe what the leader believes in and will or will not stand for. Second, it should describe an ideal state. A leader's behavior may never be perfectly aligned with his or her personal mission statement, but it should be a set of day-to-day behaviors that he or she will strive to achieve. Third, leadership credos should be motivating; leaders should be passionate and enthusiastic about the kind of leader they aspire to be. If the leader does not find his or her personal mission statement to be particularly inspiring, then it is hard to see how followers will be motivated by it. Much of the inspiration of a leadership credo stems from its being personal and values based. Fourth, personal mission statements should be made public. Leaders need to communicate their values to others, and a good way to do this is to display their leadership credos prominently in their offices. This not only lets others know what you as a leader think is important; it also is a form of public commitment to your leadership credo.

Sample Leadership Credos

HIGHLIGHT 8.1

As a leader, I . . .

. . . believe in the concept of whole persons and will seek to use the full range of talents and abilities of colleagues whenever possible.

. . . will seek to keep people fully informed.

. . . will more consistently express appreciation to others for a job well done.

. . . will take risks in challenging policies or protocol when they do not permit us to effectively serve our customers.

. . . will selectively choose battles to fight—rather than trying to fight all of the possible battles.

. . . will actively support those providing the most effective direction for our company.

. . . will seek to change the things I can in a positive direction and accept those things I have no chance or opportunity to change.

Source: *Impact Leadership* (Minneapolis, MN: Personnel Decisions International, 1995).

Another key way to build trust is to form strong relationships with others. There is apt to be a high level of mutual trust if leaders and followers share strong relationships; if these relationships are weak, the level of mutual trust is apt to be low. Techniques for building relationships with peers and superiors were described in **Chapter 3**. Perhaps the best way to build relationships with followers is to spend time listening to what they have to say. Because many leaders tend to be action oriented and are paid to solve (rather than listen to) problems, some leaders overlook the importance of spending time with followers. Yet leaders who take the time to build relationships with followers are much more likely to understand their followers' perspectives on organizational issues, intrinsic motivators, values, levels of competence for different tasks, and career aspirations. Leaders armed with this knowledge may be better able to influence and get work done through others. More about building relationships with followers can be found in **Chapter 12** under "Coaching."

Expertise × Trust

Leaders vary tremendously in their levels of both expertise and trust, and these differences have distinct implications for leaders wanting to improve their credibility. Consider leaders who are in the first quadrant of **Figure 8.1**. These individuals have a high level of trust and a high level of expertise; they would likely be seen by others as highly credible. Individuals in the second quadrant might include leaders who have spent little time with followers, who do not follow through with commitments, or who are new to the organization and have had little time to build relationships with coworkers. In all three cases, leaders wanting to improve their credibility should include building relationships with coworkers as key development objectives. Leaders in the third quadrant may be new college hires or people joining the company from an entirely different industry. It is unlikely that either type of leader would have the technical competence, organizational or industry knowledge, or time to build relationships with coworkers. These leaders may be in touch with their values and have a personal mission statement, but they will need to share their statement with others and act in a manner consistent with this statement to build their credibility. Other development objectives could include building expertise and strong relationships with others. Leaders in the fourth quadrant might include those promoted from among peers or transferring from another department within the company. Both sets of leaders may be in touch with their values, have a leadership credo, share strong relationships with coworkers, and have organizational and industry knowledge, but the former may need to develop leadership knowledge or skills and the latter technical competence if they wish to increase their credibility. Finally, note that leaders who do not strive to live up to their ideals or fail to follow through with their developmental commitments are likely to be seen as less trustworthy than those who do.

Communication

Bass[4] has defined *communication effectiveness* as the degree to which someone tells others something and ensures that they understand what was said. In a more general sense, effective communication involves the ability to transmit and receive information with a high probability that the intended message is passed from sender to receiver. Few skills are more vital to leadership. Studies show that good leaders communicate feelings and ideas, actively solicit new ideas from others, and effectively articulate arguments, advocate positions, and persuade others.[5, 6, 7] It seems likely the same can be said of good followers, though far less study has gone into that question. Moreover, the quality of a leader's communication is positively correlated with subordinate satisfaction[8] as well as with productivity and quality of services rendered.[9] Effective communication skills are also important because they give leaders and followers greater access to information relevant to important organizational decisions.[10]

A systems view of communication is depicted in **Figure 8.2**. Communication is best understood as a process beginning with an intention to exchange certain information with others. That intention eventually takes form in some particular expression, which may or may not adequately convey what was intended. The next stage is reception. Just as with a weak or garbled radio signal or malfunctioning antenna, what is received is not always what was sent. Reception is followed by interpretation. If a driver asks, "Do I turn here?" and a passenger answers, "Right," did the passenger mean *yes* or *turn right*? Finally, it is not enough merely to receive and interpret information; others' interpretations may or may not be consistent with what was intended at the outset. Therefore, it always helps to have a feedback loop to assess the overall effectiveness of any communication.

We also can use the scheme in **Figure 8.2** to think about the knowledge, behaviors, and criteria used to evaluate communication skills. According to this model, the knowledge component of communication skills concerns the intentions of the leader, knowing what medium is most effective, and knowing whether the message was heard and understood. The behavioral component of communication skills concerns the behaviors associated with communicating verbally and nonverbally. Feedback concerning whether the message was understood by the receiver constitutes the evaluative component of communication skills. An important aspect of feedback is that it is an outcome of the previous steps in the communication process. In reality, the effectiveness of the communication process depends on the successful integration of all the steps in the communication process. Effectiveness in just one step (such as speaking ability) is not enough. Successful communication needs to be judged in terms of the effective operation of the whole system.

The model also suggests a number of reasons why communication breakdowns might occur. For example, communication can break down because the purpose of the message was unclear, the leader's or follower's verbal and nonverbal behaviors were inconsistent, the message was not heard by the receiver, or someone may have misinterpreted the message. Most people see themselves as effective communicators, and senders and receivers of messages often seem disposed to believe communication breakdowns are the other person's fault. Communication breakdowns often lead to blaming someone else for the problem, or "finger pointing" (see **Figure 8.3**). One way to avoid the finger pointing associated with communication breakdowns is to think of communication as a process, not as a set of discrete individual acts (such as giving instructions to someone). By using the communication model, leadership practitioners can minimize the conflict typically associated with communication breakdowns.

FIGURE 8.1   The Credibility Matrix

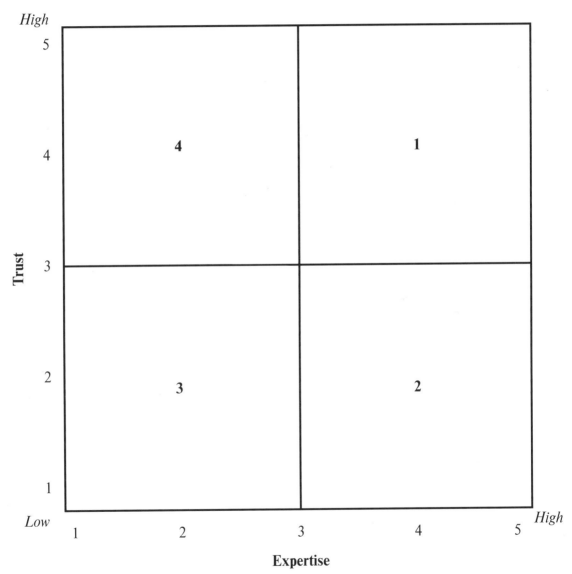

Source: G. J. Curphy, *Credibility: Building Your Reputation throughout the Organization* (Minneapolis, MN: Personnel Decisions International, 1997).

The model in **Figure 8.2** can give leadership practitioners many ideas about how to improve communication skills. They can do so by determining the purpose of their communication before speaking, choosing an appropriate context and medium for the message, sending clear signals, and actively ensuring that others understand the message. When this doesn't happen, communication breakdown can occur, as exemplified in **Figure 8.3**. The following is a more detailed discussion of some different ways in which leaders can improve their communication skills.

FIGURE 8.2   A Systems View of Communication

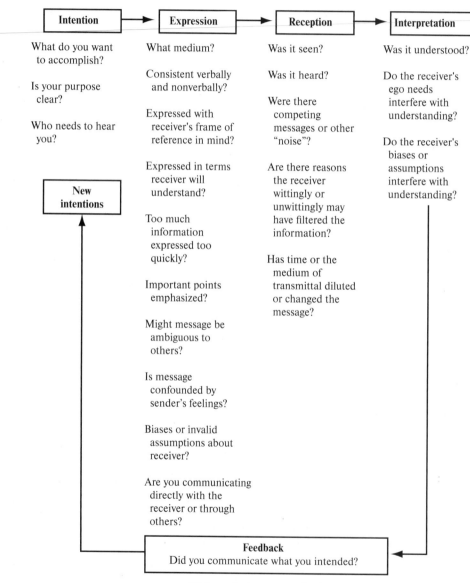

Know What Your Purpose Is

You will communicate more effectively with others if you are clear about what you intend to communicate. By knowing purpose, a leader or follower can better decide whether to communicate publicly or privately, orally or in writing, and so on. These decisions may seem trivial, but often the specific content of a message will be enhanced or diminished by how and where it is communicated.

Choose an Appropriate Context and Medium

There is a rule of thumb that says leaders should praise followers in public and punish them in private. It points out the importance of selecting physical and social settings that will enhance the effectiveness of any communication. If the leader has an office, for example, how much communication with subordinates should occur in her office and how much in the followers' workplace?

Sometimes, of course, an office is the best place to talk. Even that decision, however, is not all a leader needs to consider. The arrangement of office furniture can enhance or interfere with effective communication. Informal, personal communications are enhanced when two people sit at a 90-degree angle and are relatively close to each other; more formal communication is enhanced when the follower remains standing when the leader is sitting or if the leader communicates across his desk to followers.

Additionally, a leader's communications often take place in a whole organizational context involving broader existing practices, policies, and procedures. Leaders need to take care that their words and deeds do not inadvertently undercut or contradict such broader organizational communications, including their own bosses'. Organizational factors also help determine whether any particular communication is most appropriately expressed orally or in writing. Oral communication is the most immediate, the most personal, the most dynamic, and often the most effective; it is ideal when communication needs to be two-way or when the personalized aspect is especially important. At the other extreme, a more permanent modality is probably most appropriate when the leader needs a record of the communication or when something needs to be expressed in a particular way to different people, at different times, in different settings.

Send Clear Signals

Leaders and followers can enhance the clarity of their communications in several ways. First, it is helpful to be mindful of others' level of expertise, values, experiences, and expectations and how these characteristics affect their *frames of reference*. For example, the leader may brief followers on a new organizational policy, and they may come up with different interpretations of this policy based on their values and expectations. By being sensitive to followers' frames of reference and modifying messages accordingly, leaders can minimize communication breakdowns. Another way to clarify messages is to create a common frame of reference for followers before communicating a message. For example, consider the following passage:

FIGURE 8.3   Breakdowns in Communication Sometimes Lead to Finger Pointing

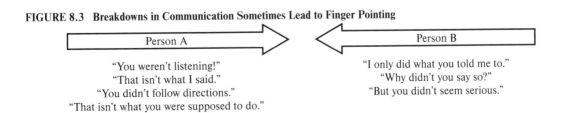

With hocked gems financing him, our hero bravely defied all scornful laughter that tried to prevent his scheme. "Your eyes deceive," he had said. "An egg, not a table, correctly typifies this unexplored planet." Now, three sisters sought sturdy proof.

Forging along, sometimes through calm vastness, yet more often over turbulent peaks and valleys, days became weeks as many doubters spread fearful rumors about the edge. At last, welcome winged creatures appeared signifying momentous success.[11]

Many people are slow to recognize that this passage is about Christopher Columbus. Once the correct frame of reference is known, however, the previously confusing elements become sensible. Followers more readily understand new or ambiguous material when leaders paint a common frame of reference prior to introducing new material.

Another way to send clear signals is to use familiar terms, jargon, and concepts. This can clarify and abbreviate messages when receivers are familiar with the terms. However, messages containing jargon can also confuse receivers unfamiliar with those terms. For example, a freshman cadet at the U.S. Air Force Academy might say to another, "I hope we get an ONP this weekend, because after three GRs, a PCE, and an SAMI, I'll need it." Because the second cadet understands this organizational jargon, he or she would have no difficulty understanding what was said. However, a person unfamiliar with the Air Force Academy would not have the slightest idea what this conversation meant. Leaders should make sure followers understand any jargon they use—especially if the followers are relatively inexperienced. (In case you were wondering, the cadet said, "I hope we get a pass to go downtown this weekend, because after three academic tests, a military test, and a room inspection, I'll need it.")

Two other ways to improve the clarity of messages are to use unambiguous, concrete terms and to send congruent verbal and nonverbal signals. For example, a leader who tells a follower, "Your monthly sales were down 22 percent last month" will more effectively communicate her concerns and cause less follower defensiveness than a leader who states, "Your performance has been poor." Thus the more specific the message, the less likely receivers will be confused about what it means. In addition, leaders will be more effective communicators if their nonverbal signals match the content of the message. Followers, like everyone, can get confused, and tend to believe nonverbal signals when leaders send mixed verbal and nonverbal messages.[12] Similarly, followers may send mixed messages to leaders; communication goes both ways.

One particularly destructive form of incongruent verbal and nonverbal signals is sarcasm. It is not the anger of the message per se but rather the implicit message conveyed by dishonest words that drives a wedge in the trust between leaders and followers. It is unwise for leaders to always share their transitory feelings with subordinates; but if a leader is going to share his or her feelings, it is important to do so in a congruent manner. Similarly, it can be just as unwise for followers to share transitory feelings with leaders; but if it's done, it's important for verbal and nonverbal behaviors to be congruent.

Actively Ensure That Others Understand the Message

Leaders and followers can ensure that others understand their messages by practicing two-way communication and by paying attention to others' emotional responses. Effective leaders and followers tend to actively engage in two-way communication (though this usually is more under the control of the leader than the follower). They can do so in many ways: by seeking feedback, by mingling in each other's work areas, and, in the case of leaders, by being sincere about having an open-door policy.[13]

Although such steps appear to be straightforward, leaders typically believe they utilize two-way communication more frequently than their followers perceive them to be using it.[14] Leaders can get clues about the clarity of their messages by paying attention to the nonverbal signals sent by their followers. When followers' verbal and nonverbal messages seem to be incongruent, it may be because the message sent to them was unclear. For example, followers may look confused when they verbally acknowledge that they understand a particular task. In this case, leaders may find it useful to address the mixed signals directly to clear up such confusion.

Listening

Our systems view of communication emphasized that effectiveness depends on both *transmitting* and *receiving* information. It may seem inconsistent, therefore, to distinguish the topic of listening from the more general topic of communication. Isn't listening part of communication? Of course; our separate treatment of listening is simply for emphasis. It seems to us that most discussions of communication emphasize the transmission side and neglect the receiving side. Good leaders and followers recognize the value of two-way communication. Listening to others is just as important as expressing oneself clearly to them. People in leadership roles are only as good as the information they have, and much of their information comes from watching and listening to what goes on around them.

At first it may seem strange to describe listening as a skill. Listening may seem like an automatic response to things being said, not something one practices to improve, like free throws. However, the best listeners are *active listeners*, not passive listeners.[15] In passive listening, someone may be speaking but the receiver is not focused on understanding the speaker. Instead the receiver may be thinking about the next thing he will say or how bored he is in listening to the speaker. In either case, the receiver is not paying attention to what the sender is saying. To get the fullest meaning out of what someone else says, we need to practice active listening. Individuals who are listening actively exhibit a certain pattern of nonverbal behaviors, do not disrupt the sender's message, try to put the sender's message into their own words, and scan the sender for various nonverbal signals. Knowing what nonverbal signals to send and correctly interpreting the sender's nonverbal signals are the knowledge component of listening skills. Nonverbal signals are the behavioral component, and how well we can paraphrase a sender's message makes up the evaluative component of listening skills.

In addition to helping us understand others better, active listening is a way to visibly demonstrate that we respect others. People, particularly those with high self-monitoring scores, can often sense when others are not truly paying attention to what they are saying. Followers will quickly decide it is not worth their time to give their leader information if they perceive they are not being listened to. Leaders may do the same. To avoid turning off others, leaders and followers can improve their active listening skills in a number of ways. Some of these tips include learning to model nonverbal signals associated with active listening, actively interpret the sender's message, be aware of the sender's nonverbal behaviors, and avoid becoming defensive. The following is a more detailed discussion of these four ways to improve active listening skills.

Demonstrate Nonverbally That You Are Listening

Make sure your nonverbal behaviors show that you have turned your attention entirely to the speaker. Many people mistakenly assume that listening is a one-way process. Although it seems plausible to think of information flowing only from the sender to the receiver, the essence of active listening is to see all communication, even listening, as a two-way process. Listeners show they are paying attention to the speaker with their own body movements. They put aside, both mentally and physically, other work they may have been engaged in. Individuals who are actively listening establish eye contact with the speaker, and they do not doodle, shoot rubber bands, or look away at other things. They show they are genuinely interested in what the speaker has to say.

Actively Interpret the Sender's Message

The essence of active listening is trying to understand what the sender means. It is not enough merely to be (even if you could) a perfect human tape recorder. We must look for the meaning behind someone else's words. In the first place, this means we need to keep our minds open to the sender's ideas. This, in turn, implies not interrupting the speaker and not planning what to say while the speaker is delivering the message. In addition, good listeners withhold judgment about the sender's ideas until they have heard the entire message. This way, they avoid sending the message that their minds are made up and avoid jumping to conclusions about what the sender is going to say. Another reason to avoid sending a closed-minded message is that it may lead others to *not* bring up things one needs to hear.

Another valuable way to actively interpret what the sender is saying is to *paraphrase* the sender's message. By putting the speaker's thoughts into their own words, leaders can better ensure that they fully understand what their followers are saying, and vice versa. The value of paraphrasing even a simple idea is apparent in the following dialogue:

Sarah: "Jim should never have become a teacher."
Fred: "You mean he doesnt like working with kids? Do you think hes too impatient?"
Sarah: "No, neither of those things. I just think his tastes are so expensive hes frustrated with a teachers salary."

In this example, Fred indicated what he thought Sarah meant, which prompted her to clarify her meaning. If he had merely said, "I know what you mean," Fred and Sarah mistakenly would have concluded they agreed when their ideas were far apart. Paraphrasing also actively communicates your interest in what the other person is saying. **Highlight 8.2** offers various "communication leads" that may help in paraphrasing others' messages to improve your listening skills.

Communication Leads for Paraphrasing and Ensuring Mutual Understanding

HIGHLIGHT 8.2

From your point of view . . .

It seems you . . .

As you see it . . .

You think . . .

What I hear you saying is . . .

Do you mean . . . ?

I'm not sure I understand what you mean; is it . . . ?

I get the impression . . .

You appear to be feeling . . .

Correct me if I'm wrong, but . . .

Attend to the Sender's Nonverbal Behavior

People should use all the tools at their disposal to understand what someone else is saying. This includes paraphrasing senders' messages and being astute at picking up on senders' nonverbal signals. Much of the social meaning in messages is conveyed nonverbally, and when verbal and nonverbal signals conflict, people often tend to trust the nonverbal signals. Thus no one can be an effective listener without paying attention to nonverbal signals. This requires listening to more than just the speaker's words themselves; it requires listening for feelings expressed via the speaker's loudness, tone of voice, and pace of speech as well as watching the speaker's facial expressions, posture, gestures, and so on. These behaviors convey a wealth of information that is immensely richer in meaning than the purely verbal content of a message, just as it is richer to watch actors in a stage play rather than merely read their script.[16] Although there may not be any simple codebook of nonverbal cues with which we can decipher what a sender feels, listeners should explore what a sender is trying to say whenever they sense mixed signals between the sender's verbal and nonverbal behaviors.

Avoid Becoming Defensive

Defensive behavior is most likely to occur when someone feels threatened.[17] Although it may seem natural to become defensive when criticized, defensiveness lessens a person's ability to constructively use information. Acting defensively may also decrease followers' subsequent willingness to pass additional unpleasant information on to the leader or other followers, or even the leader's willingness to give feedback to followers. Defensiveness on the part of the leader can also hurt the entire team or organization because it includes a tendency to place blame, categorize others as morally good or bad, and generally question others' motives. Such behaviors on a leader's part do not build a positive work or team climate.

Leaders can reduce their defensiveness when listening to complaints by trying to put themselves in the other person's shoes. Leaders have an advantage if they can empathize with how they and their policies are seen by others; they can better change their behaviors and policies if they know how others perceive them. Leaders need to avoid the temptation to explain how the other person is wrong and should instead just try to understand how he or she perceives things. A useful warning sign that a leader may be behaving defensively (or perhaps closed-mindedly) is if he enters a conversation by saying, "Yes, but. . . ."

Assertiveness

Assertive behavior and assertiveness skills are composed of behavioral, knowledge/judgment, and evaluative components. Individuals exhibiting assertive behavior (i.e., the behavioral component) are able to stand up for their own rights (or their group's rights) in a way that also recognizes the concurrent right of others to do the same (see **Highlight 8.3**). The knowledge/judgment component of assertiveness skills concerns knowing where and when not to behave assertively. People who are overly assertive may be perceived as aggressive and often may "win the battle but lose the war." Finally, the evaluative component comes into play when individuals are successful (or unsuccessful) in standing up for their own or their group's rights and continually working in an effective manner with others.

Assertiveness Questionnaire

HIGHLIGHT 8.3

Do you let someone know when you think he or she is being unfair to you?

Can you criticize someone else's ideas openly?

Are you able to speak up in a meeting?

Can you ask others for small favors or help?

Is it easy for you to compliment others?

Can you tell someone else you don't like what he or she is doing?

When you are complimented, do you really accept the compliment without inwardly discounting it in your own mind?

Can you look others in the eye when you talk to them?

If you could answer most of these questions affirmatively for most situations, then you probably behave assertively.

Source: Adapted from R. E. Alberti and M. L. Emmons, *Your Perfect Right* (San Luis Obispo, CA: Impact, 1974).

Perhaps the best way to understand assertiveness is to distinguish it from two other styles people have for dealing with conflict: acquiescence (nonassertiveness) and aggression.[18] *Acquiescence* is avoiding interpersonal conflict entirely either by giving up and giving in or by expressing our needs in an apologetic, self-effacing way. Acquiescence is *not* synonymous with politeness or helpfulness, though it is sometimes rationalized as such. People who are acquiescent, or nonassertive, back down easily when challenged. By not speaking up for themselves, they abdicate power to others and, in the process, get trampled on. Besides the practical outcome of not attaining our goals, an acquiescent style typically leads to many negative feelings such as guilt, resentment, and self-blame, as well as a low self-image.

Aggression, by contrast, is an effort to attain objectives by attacking or hurting others. Aggressive people trample on others, and their aggressiveness can take such direct forms as threats, verbal attacks, physical intimidation, emotional outbursts, explosiveness, bullying, and hostility—and such indirect forms as nagging, passive–aggressive uncooperativeness, guilt arousal, and other behaviors that undermine an adversary's autonomy. It is important to understand that aggressiveness is not just an emotionally strong form of assertiveness. Aggressiveness tends to be reactive, and it tends to spring from feelings of vulnerability and a lack of self-confidence. Aggressive people inwardly doubt their ability to resolve issues constructively through the give-and-take of direct confrontation between mutually respecting equals. Aggressiveness is a form of interpersonal manipulation in which we try to put ourselves in a "top dog" role and others in a "bottom dog" role.[19] Additionally, aggressive people have difficulty expressing positive feelings.

Assertiveness is different from both acquiescence and aggression; it is not merely a compromise between them or a midpoint on a continuum. Assertiveness involves direct and frank statements of our own goals and feelings, and a willingness to address the interests of others in the spirit of mutual problem solving and a belief that openness is preferable to secretiveness and hidden agendas. Assertiveness is the behavioral opposite of both acquiescence and aggression, as depicted in **Figure 8.4**. The qualitative differences between these three styles are like the differences between fleeing (acquiescence), fighting (aggression), and problem solving (assertiveness).

FIGURE 8.4   Relationships between Assertiveness, Acquiescence, and Aggression

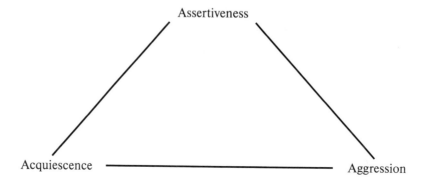

It may seem axiomatic that leaders need to behave assertively with subordinates. Sometimes, however, leaders also need to be assertive with their own bosses. Followers often need to be assertive with other followers and with their leaders. For example, mid-level supervisors need to communicate performance expectations clearly and directly to subordinates, and they need to be strong advocates for their subordinates' interests with senior supervisors. Likewise, leaders sometimes need to give their own superiors bad news, and it is best to do so directly rather than hesitantly and guardedly. Followers may sometimes need to be assertive with a peer whose poor work habits are adversely affecting the work group. In addition, leaders sometimes need to be assertive with representatives of other power-holding or special interest groups. For example, the leader of a community group seeking a new elementary school in a residential area may need to take an assertive stand with local school board officials.

Sometimes the hardest people to be assertive with are friends, family, and peers. Leaders who fail to be assertive with friends and peers run the risk of becoming victims of the Abilene paradox. The *Abilene paradox*[20] occurs when someone suggests that the group engage in a particular activity or course of action, and no one in the group really wants to do the activity (including the person who made the suggestion). However, because of the false belief that everyone else in the group wants to do the activity, no one behaves assertively and voices an honest opinion about it. Only after the activity is over does anyone voice an opinion (and it is usually negative). For example, someone in your group of friends may suggest that the group go to a particular movie on a Friday night. No one in the group really wants to go, yet because of the false belief that everyone else is interested, no one points out that the movie is not supposed to be good and the group should do something else instead. If group members' true opinions surface only *after* the movie, then the group has fallen victim to the Abilene paradox. We can avoid the Abilene paradox by being assertive when suggestions about group decisions and activities are first made.

Everyone can do several things to help themselves behave more assertively. These techniques include using "I" statements, speaking up for what we need, learning to say no, monitoring our inner dialogue, and being persistent. Next we discuss these assertiveness tips in more detail.

Use "I" Statements

Assertive people take responsibility for what they say. They are clear in their own minds and with others about what they believe and what they want. One of the easiest ways to do this is to use first-person pronouns when you speak. **Highlight 8.4** provides examples of how to be more assertive by using first-person pronouns.

Tips for Being Assertive

HIGHLIGHT 8.4

EXAMPLES OF GOOD AND BAD "I" STATEMENTS

Bad: Some people may not like having to maintain those new forms.

Good: I don't think these new forms are any good. I don't think they're worth the effort.

Bad: Maybe that candidate doesn't have all the qualifications we're looking for.

Good: I think his academic record looks fine, but we agreed to consider only candidates with at least five years' experience. I think we should keep looking.

TIPS FOR SPEAKING UP FOR WHAT YOU NEED

Do not apologize too much or justify yourself for needing help or assistance (e.g., "I just hate to ask you, and I normally wouldn't need to, but . . . ").

At the same time, giving a brief reason for your request often helps.

Be direct. Do not beat around the bush, hinting at what you need and hoping others get the message.

Do not play on someone's friendship.

Do not take a refusal personally.

TIPS FOR SAYING NO

Keep your reply short and polite. Avoid a long, rambling justification.

Do not invent excuses.

Do not go overboard in apologizing because you cannot do it.

Be up front about your limitations and about options you could support.

Ask for time to consider it if you need to.

Source: Adapted from K. Back and K. Back, *Assertiveness at Work* (New York: McGraw-Hill, 1982).

Speak Up for What You Need

No one has all of the skills, knowledge, time, or resources needed to do all the tasks assigned to their work group. Virtually everyone will need to ask superiors, peers, or subordinates for help at some time. Both effective leaders and effective followers ask for help from others when they need it. **Highlight 8.4** also provides guidelines for making requests for help.

Learn to Say No

No one can be all things to all people, but it takes assertiveness to say no to others. Leaders, for example, may need to say no to their own superiors at times to stand up for their subordinates' or organization's rights and to keep from spreading themselves too thin and detracting from other priorities. Additionally, people who cannot (that is, who *do not*) say no often build up a reservoir of negative emotions, such as those associated with the feeling of being taken advantage of. Tips for assertively refusing to do something also can be found in **Highlight 8.4**.

Monitor Your Inner Dialogue

Most of us talk to ourselves, though not out loud. Such self-talk is natural and common, though not everyone is aware of how much it occurs or how powerful an influence on behavior it can be. Assertive people have self-talk that is positive and affirming. Nonassertive people have self-talk that is negative, doubtful, and questioning. Learning to say no is a good example of the role self-talk plays in assertiveness. Suppose someone is asked to serve on a volunteer committee he simply does not have time for and that he wants to say no. To behave assertively, the person would need to talk to himself positively. He would need to ensure that he is not defeated by his own self-talk. It would hardly help the person's resolve, for example, to have an inner dialogue that says, "They'll think I'm selfish if I don't say yes," or "If they can make time for this committee, I should be able to make time for it, too." In learning to behave more assertively, therefore, it is necessary for leaders to become more aware of their own counterproductive self-talk, confront it, and change it.

Be Persistent

Assertive individuals stick to their guns without becoming irritated, angry, or loud. They persistently seek their objectives, even while facing another person's excuses or objections. Exchanging merchandise can provide a good occasion for assertive persistence. Suppose someone purchased a shirt at a department store, wore it once, and then noticed a seam was poorly sewn. A person acting assertively might have an exchange much like that found in **Highlight 8.5**. An assertive person is similarly persistent in standing up for her own or her group's rights.

Example Exchange between a Buyer and a Clerk

HIGHLIGHT 8.5

Buyer: "I bought this shirt last week, and its poorly made."

Clerk: "It looks like youve worn it. We dont exchange garments that already have been worn."

Buyer: "I understand that is your policy, but its not that I dont like the shirt. It is obviously defective. I didnt know it had these defects when I wore it."

Clerk: "Maybe this seam came loose because of the way you wore it."

Buyer: "I didnt do anything unusual. It is defective. I want it exchanged."

Clerk: "Im sorry, but you should have returned it earlier. We cant take it back now."

Buyer: "I understand your point, but I didnt get what I paid for. You need to return my money or give me a new shirt."

Clerk: "Its beyond my authority to do that. I dont make the policies. I just have to follow them."

Buyer: "I understand you dont think you have the authority to change the policy. But your boss does. Please tell her Id like to see her right now."

Conducting Meetings

Meetings are a fact of organizational life. It is difficult to imagine a leader who could (or should) avoid them, particularly when groups, committees, or teams have high levels of task or lateral interdependence. Well-planned and well-led meetings are a valuable mechanism for accomplishing diverse goals and are an important way of exchanging information and keeping open lines of communication within and between work groups or volunteer organizations.[21, 22] Although meetings have many advantages, they also cost time and money. The annual cost of meetings in the corporate sector alone may well be in the billions of dollars. Furthermore, unnecessary or inefficient meetings can be frustrating and are often a source of dissatisfaction for participants. Given the investment of time and energy meetings require, leaders have a responsibility to make them as productive as possible. Guth and Shaw[23] have provided seven helpful tips for running meetings, which are discussed in the following paragraphs.

Determine Whether It Is Necessary

Perhaps the most important step in conducting a meeting is to take the time to *determine whether a meeting is really necessary*. If you are evaluating whether to have a meeting, assess what it can accomplish. Call a meeting only if the potential benefits outweigh the costs. As part of this process, get the opinions of the other participants beforehand if that is possible. Moreover, if meetings are regularly scheduled, you should have significant business to conduct in each meeting. If not, these meetings should probably be scheduled less frequently.

List the Objectives

Once you have decided that a meeting is necessary, you should *list your objectives for the meeting and develop a plan for attaining them* in an orderly manner. Prioritize what you hope to accomplish at the meeting. It is often helpful to indicate approximately how much time will be spent on each agenda item. Finally, get the agenda and issues to be covered to the participants well in advance; also let them know who else will be attending.

Stick to the Agenda

Once the meeting gets started, it is important for leaders to *stick to the agenda*. It is easy for groups to get sidetracked by tangential issues or good-natured storytelling. Although you should try to keep a cooperative and comfortable climate in the meeting, it is better to err on the side of being organized and businesslike than being lax. If items were important enough to put on the agenda, they are important enough to attend to in the time allotted for the meeting.

Provide Pertinent Materials in Advance

Besides having an agenda, a meeting is often more effective if leaders also give the other participants *pertinent reports or support materials well in advance*. Passing out materials and waiting for people to read them at the meeting itself wastes valuable time. Most people will come prepared, having read relevant material beforehand, if you have given it to them, and almost everyone will resent making a meeting longer than necessary doing work that could and should have been done earlier. In a similar vein, prepare for any presentations you will make. If you did not provide reports before the meeting, it is often helpful to provide an outline of your presentation for others to take notes on. Finally, of course, be sure the information you distribute is accurate.

Make It Convenient

Another way to maximize the benefits of meetings is to *pick a time and place as convenient as possible for all participants*. Besides maximizing attendance, this will help keep key participants from being distracted with thoughts of other pressing issues. Similarly, choose a place that is suitable for the nature of the meeting. Be sure to consider whether you need such things as a table for the meeting (with seating around it for all participants); a whiteboard, an overhead projector, or similar audiovisual aids; coffee or other refreshments; and directions on how to find the meeting place. And start on time; waiting for stragglers is unfair to those who were punctual, and it sends the wrong signal about the seriousness of the meeting. Also plan and announce a time limit on the meeting beforehand, and stick to it.

Encourage Participation

Leaders have a responsibility to *encourage participation*; everyone at the meeting should have an opportunity to be heard and should feel some ownership in the meeting's outcome. In some cases you may need to solicit participation from quieter people at the meeting; these members often make valuable contributions to the group when given the chance. Furthermore, ensuring that the quieter members participate will also help you to avoid mistaking someone's quietness for implied consent or agreement. By the same token, you sometimes may need to curtail the participation of more outspoken participants. You can do this respectfully by merely indicating that the group has a good idea of their position and that it would be useful to hear from some others. You can also help encourage relevant participation by providing interim summaries of the group's discussion.

Keep a Record

During a meeting, the points of discussion and various decisions or actions taken may seem clear to you. However, do not trust your memory to preserve them all. *Take minutes for the record* so that you and others can reconstruct what the participants were thinking and why you did or did not take some action. Record decisions and actions to be taken, including *who* will be responsible for doing it and *when* it is supposed to be accomplished. Such records are also useful for preparing future meeting agendas.

By following the preceding simple steps, both leaders and followers are likely to get much more out of their meetings, as well as appear organized and effective.

Effective Stress Management

People use the term *stress* in different ways. Sometimes people use the term to describe particular sorts of events or environmental conditions. For example, fans might speculate that a football coach's heart attack was caused by the pressures of his profession. Other examples might include receiving a failing grade on a physics exam, or arriving noticeably late to an important meeting, or playing a sudden-death overtime in hockey. But people also use the term in a quite different way. Sometimes it refers to the *effects* of environments. The phrase "I'm feeling a lot of stress" might refer to various symptoms a person is experiencing, such as muscular tension or difficulty concentrating. Before we proceed further, therefore, it will be useful to agree on some conventions of terminology.

We will define *stress* as the process by which we perceive and respond to situations that challenge or threaten us. These responses usually include increased levels of emotional arousal and changes in physiological symptoms, such as increases in perspiration and heart rate, cholesterol level, or blood pressure. Stress often occurs in situations that are complex, demanding, or unclear. Stressors are specific characteristics in individuals, tasks, organizations, or the environment that pose some degree of threat or challenge to people (see **Highlight 8.6**). Although all the factors in **Highlight 8.6** probably have an adverse impact on people, the degree of stress associated with each of them depends on one's overall level of stress tolerance and previous experience with the stressor in question.[24] Similarly, it is important to realize that stress is in the eye of the beholder—what one person may see as challenging and potentially rewarding, another may see as threatening and distressful.[25, 26]

Stress Symptoms

HIGHLIGHT 8.6

Are you behaving unlike yourself?

Has your mood become negative, hostile, or depressed?

Do you have difficulty sleeping?

Are you defensive or touchy?

Are your relationships suffering?

Have you made more mistakes or bad decisions lately?

Have you lost interest in normally enjoyable activities?

Are you using alcohol or other drugs?

Do you seem to have little energy?

Do you worry a lot?

Are you nervous much of the time?

Have you been undereating or overeating?

Have you had an increase in headaches or back pains?

Who do you think typically experiences greater stress—leaders or followers? In one sense, the answer is the same as that for much psychological research: It depends. The role of leader certainly can be quite stressful. Leaders face a major stressful event at least once a month.[27] Followers' stress levels, by contrast, often depend on their leaders. Leaders can help followers cope with stress or, alternatively, can actually increase their followers' stress levels. Many leaders recognize when followers are under a lot of stress and will give them time off, try to reduce their workload, or take other actions to help followers cope. But about two out of three workers say their bosses play a bigger part in creating their stress than any other personal, organizational, or environmental factor.[28, 29] Others have reported that working for a tyrannical boss was the most frequently cited source of stress among workers. It is clear that leaders play a substantial role in how stressful their followers' work experience is, for good or ill.[30]

Stress can either facilitate or inhibit performance, depending on the situation. Too much stress can take a toll on individuals and organizations that includes decreased health and emotional well-being, reduced job performance, and decreased organizational effectiveness (see **Highlight 8.7** for an example of how too much stress impaired one person's performance).

Stress on a TV Game Show

HIGHLIGHT 8.7

The television game show *Wheel of Fortune* pits contestants against each other in trying to identify common sayings. By spinning a wheel, contestants determine varying dollar amounts to be added to their potential winnings.

This is similar to the game of Hangman, which you may have played as a child. It begins with spaces indicating the number of words in a saying and the number of letters in each word.

One player spins the wheel, which determines prize money, and then guesses a letter. If the letter appears somewhere in the saying, the player spins the wheel again, guesses another letter, and so on. The letters are "filled in" as they are correctly identified. A player may try to guess the saying after naming a correct letter.

If a player names a letter that does not appear in the saying, that prize money is not added to the contestant's potential winnings, and play moves on to another contestant.

One day a contestant was playing for over $50,000 to solve the following puzzle. Perhaps because of the stress of being on television and playing for so much money, the contestant could not accurately name a letter for one of the four remaining spaces. Most people, not experiencing such stress, easily solve the problem. Can you? For the answer, see the end of this box.

T H E   T H R I _ _
O F   _ I _ T O R Y
A N D   T H E
A G O N Y   O F
D E F E A T

Answer: The Thrill of Victory and the Agony of Defeat.

To understand the effects of stress, an analogy might be helpful. Kites need an optimal amount of wind to fly; they will not fly on windless days, and the string may break on a day that is too windy. You can think of stress as being like the wind on a kite: a certain level is optimal, neither too little nor too much. Another analogy is your car. Just as an automobile engine operates optimally within a certain range of revolutions per minute (RPMs), most people function best at certain levels of stress. Some stress or arousal is helpful in increasing motivation and performance, but too much stress can be counterproductive. For example, it is common and probably helpful to feel a little anxiety before giving a speech, but being too nervous can destroy one's effectiveness.

The optimal level of stress depends on a number of factors. One is the level of physical activity that the task demands. Another is the task's perceived difficulty. Performance often suffers when difficult tasks are performed under stressful situations. For example, think how one's performance might differ when first learning to drive a car with an instructor who is quiet and reserved rather than one who yells a lot. Chances are that performance will be much better with the first instructor than with the second.

Note that task difficulty is generally a function of experience; the more experience one has with a task, the less difficult it becomes. Thus the more driving experience one has, the easier the task becomes. Moreover, people not only cope with stress more readily when performing easier tasks—but they often need higher levels of stress to perform them optimally. One underlying purpose behind any type of practice (such as football, marching band, soccer, or drama) is to reduce task difficulty and help members or players perform at an even higher level under the stress of key performances and games.

Although stress can have positive effects, research has focused on the negative implications of too much stress on health and work. Stress has been linked to heart disease,[31, 32] immune system deficiencies,[33] and the growth rates of tumors.[34] And various studies have reported that work-related stress has caused a dramatic increase in drug and alcohol use in the workplace[35, 36] and that stress is positively related to absenteeism, intentions to quit, and turnover.[37] Stress can also affect the decision-making process. Although leaders need to act decisively in crises, they may not make good decisions under stress.[38, 39, 40] Some observers have suggested that people make poor decisions under stress because they revert to their intuition rather than thinking rationally about problems.[41, 42]

As we have noted, too much stress can take a toll on individuals and their organizations. Individuals can see their health, mental and emotional well-being, job performance, or interpersonal relationships suffer. For organizations, the toll includes decreased productivity and increased employee absenteeism, turnover, and medical costs. It stands to reason, then, that leaders in any activity should know something about stress. Leaders should understand the nature of stress because the leadership role itself can be stressful and because leaders' stress can impair the performance and well-being of followers. To prevent stress from becoming so excessive that it takes a toll in some important dimension of your own or your followers' lives, the following guidelines for effective stress management are provided.

Monitor Your Own and Your Followers' Stress Levels

One of the most important steps in managing stress is to *monitor your own and your followers' stress levels*. Although this seems straightforward, a paradoxical fact about stress is that it often takes a toll without one's conscious awareness. A person experiencing excessive stress might manifest various symptoms apparent to everyone but him or her. For that reason, it is useful to develop the habit of regularly attending to some of the warning signs that your stress level may be getting too high. Some warning signs of stress are listed in **Highlight 8.6**. If you answer yes to these questions, then your own or your followers' stress levels may be getting too high, and it would probably be a good idea to put some of the following stress management strategies into practice right away. Answering some of the questions affirmatively, however, does not necessarily mean your stress level is too high. There could, for example, be some other explanation.

Identify What Is Causing the Stress

Monitoring your stress will reduce the chances that it will build to an unhealthy level before you take action, but monitoring is not enough. Leaders also need to *identify what is causing the stress*. It may seem at first that the causes of stress always will be obvious, but that is not true. Sometimes the problems are clear enough even if the solutions are not (such as family finances or working in a job with a big workload and lots of deadlines). At other times, however, it may be difficult to identify the root problem. For example, a coach may attribute his anger to the losing record of his team, not recognizing that a bigger cause of his emotional distress may be the problems he is having at home with his teenage son. A worker may feel frustrated because her boss overloads her with work, not realizing that her own unassertiveness keeps her from expressing her feelings to her boss. Problem solving can be applied constructively to managing stress, but only if the problem is identified properly. Once the problem is identified, a plan for minimizing stress or the effects of the stressor can be developed.

One can be experiencing high levels of stress and not be aware of it, which further complicates identifying the cause of stress. If a leader is experiencing the stress of burnout, for example, it might be manifested by changes in the leader's interactions with subordinates such as encouraging them less frequently, asking for their opinions less frequently, and expressing confidence in them less frequently. Although subordinates may well notice the change, the leader herself may not.[43] In other words, the leader may be unaware that *she* is causing her workers' stress. That is another good reason to nurture relationships with at least a few other people who are willing to provide feedback to *you* (the leader) if they notice a change in your mood or behavior.

Practice a Healthy Lifestyle

Practicing a healthy lifestyle is one of the best ways to minimize stress. There are no substitutes for balanced nutrition, regular exercise, adequate sleep, abstention from tobacco products, and drinking only moderate amounts of (if any) alcohol as keys to a healthy life. A long-term study of the lifestyles of nearly 7,000 adults confirmed these as independent factors contributing to wellness and the absence of stress symptoms.[44] Insufficient sleep saps energy, interferes with alertness and judgment, increases irritability, and lowers resistance to illness. Exercise, besides being a valuable part of any long-term health strategy, is also an excellent way to reduce tension.

Learn How to Relax

Believe it or not, some people just do not know how to relax. Although physical exercise is a good relaxation technique, sometimes you will need to relax but not have an opportunity to get a workout. *Practicing other relaxation techniques* will come in handy when a situation prevents strenuous exercise. Also, of course, some people simply prefer alternative relaxation techniques to exercise. Deep-breathing techniques, progressive muscle relaxation, and thinking of calming words and images can be powerful on-the-spot calming techniques. They are applicable in stressful situations ranging from job interviews to sports. The effectiveness of these techniques is a matter of personal preference, and no single one is best for all purposes or all people.

Develop Supportive Relationships

Another powerful antidote to stress is *having a network of close and supportive relationships* with others.[45] People who have close ties to others through marriage, church membership, or other groups tend to be healthier than those with weaker social ties. Also, social supports of various kinds (such as the supportiveness of one's spouse, coworkers, or boss) can buffer the impact of job stress,[46, 47] and unit cohesion is believed to be a critical element of soldiers' ability to withstand the extreme physical and psychological stresses of combat.[48] Leaders can play a constructive role in developing mutual supportiveness and cohesiveness among subordinates, and their own open and frank communication with subordinates is especially important when a situation is ambiguous as well as stressful.

Keep Things in Perspective

As we noted earlier, the stressfulness of any event depends partly on how we interpret it, not just on the event itself. For example, a poor grade on an examination may be more stressful for one student than for another, just as a rebuke from a boss may be more stressful for one worker than for another. This is partly due, of course, to the fact that individuals invest themselves in activities to different degrees because they value different things. A problem in an area of heavy personal investment is more stressful than one in an area of little personal investment. It goes deeper than that, however. Managing stress effectively depends on *keeping things in perspective*. This is difficult for some people because they have a style of interpreting events that aggravates their felt stress.

Individuals who have relatively complex self-concepts, as measured by the number of different ways they describe or see themselves, are less susceptible to common stress-related complaints than are people with lesser degrees of self-complexity.[49] Take, for example, someone who has suffered a setback at work, such as having lost out to a colleague for a desired promotion. Someone low in self-complexity (such as a person whose self-concept is defined solely in terms of professional success) could be devastated by the event. Low self-complexity implies a lack of resilience to threats to one's ego. Consider, by contrast, someone with high self-complexity facing the same setback. The person could understandably feel disappointed and perhaps dejected about work, but if she were high in self-complexity, then the event's impact would be buffered by the existence of relatively uncontaminated areas of positive self-image. For example, she might base her feelings of professional success on more criteria than just getting (or not getting) a promotion. Other criteria, such as being highly respected by peers, may be even more important bases for her feelings of professional success. Furthermore, other dimensions of her life (like her leadership in a local political party or the support she provides to her family) may give her self-image a positive boost.

The A-B-C Model

Unfortunately, because there are no shortcuts to developing self-complexity, it is not really a viable stress management strategy. There are other cognitive approaches to stress management, however, that can produce more immediate results. These approaches have the common goal of changing a person's thoughts, or self-talk, about stressful events. One of the simplest of these to apply is called the *A-B-C model*.[50, 51]

To appreciate the usefulness of the A-B-C model, it is helpful to consider the chain of events that precedes feelings of stress. Sometimes people think of this as a two-step sequence. Something external happens (a stressful event), and then something internal follows (symptoms of stress). We can depict the sequence like this:

A. Triggering event (such as knocking your boss's coffee onto his lap).

B. Feelings and behaviors (anxiety, fear, embarrassment, perspiration).

In other words, many people think their feelings and behaviors result directly from external events. Such a view, however, leaves out the critical role played by our self-talk. The actual sequence looks like this:

A. Triggering event (knocking your boss's coffee onto his lap).

B. Your self-talk ("He must think I'm a real jerk.").

C. Feelings and behaviors (anxiety, fear, embarrassment, perspiration).

From this perspective you can see the causal role played by inner dialogue, or self-talk, in contributing to feelings of stress. Such inner dialogue can be rational or irrational, constructive or destructive—and which it will be is under the individual's control. People gain considerable freedom from stress when they realize that by changing their own self-talk they can control their emotional responses to events around them. Consider a different sequence for our scenario:

A. Triggering event (knocking your boss's coffee onto his lap).

B. Your thinking ("Darn it! But it was just an accident.").

C. Feelings and behavior (apologizing and helping clean up).

Thus a particular incident can be interpreted in several different ways, some likely to increase feelings of stress and distress, and others likely to maintain self-esteem and positive coping. You will become better at coping with stress as you practice listening to your inner dialogue and changing destructive self-talk to constructive self-talk. Even this is not a simple change to make, however. Changing self-talk is more difficult than you might think, especially in emotionalized situations. Because self-talk is covert, spontaneous, fleeting, and reflexive,[52] like any bad habit it can be difficult to change. Nevertheless, precisely because self-talk is just a habit, you can change it.

Finally, leaders need to recognize their role in their followers' stress levels. A leader in a stressful situation who is visibly manifesting some of the symptoms described in **Highlight 8.6** is not going to set much of an example for followers. On the contrary, because followers look to leaders for guidance and support, these behaviors and symptoms could become contagious and increase followers' stress levels. Leaders need to recognize the importance of role modeling in reducing (or increasing) followers' stress levels. Leaders also need to make sure their style of interacting with subordinates does not make the leaders "stress carriers."

Problem Solving

Success in life, and success in organizational settings depends upon solving problems. By its very definition, a problem means facing a situation for which you don't have an immediate solution. Fortunately, though, there are steps you can take to move you toward a constructive solution.

Identifying Problems or Opportunities for Improvement

The first step in solving a problem is to state it so that everyone involved in developing a solution has an informed and common appreciation and understanding of the task. This is a critical stage in problem solving and will take time and probably group discussion. It is dangerous to assume that everyone (or anyone) knows at the outset what the problem is. A hurried or premature definition of the problem (perhaps as a result of groupthink) may lead to considerable frustration and wasted effort. In counseling and advising, for example, a significant portion of the work with a client is devoted to clarifying the problem. A student may seek help at the school counseling center to improve his study skills because he is spending what seems to be plenty of time studying yet is still doing poorly on examinations. A little discussion, however, may reveal that he is having difficulty concentrating on schoolwork because of problems at home. If the counselor had moved immediately to develop the client's study skills, the real cause of his difficulties would have gone untreated, and the client might have become even more pessimistic about his abilities and the possibility that others could help him. Or consider a police chief who is concerned about the few volunteers willing to serve on a citizen's advisory committee to her department. There are many problems she might identify here, such as citizen apathy or poor publicity concerning the need and importance of the committee. The real problem, however, might be her own reputation for rarely listening to or heeding recommendations made by similar advisory committees in the past. If the chief were to take the time to explore and clarify the problem at the outset, she could discover this important fact and take steps to solve the real problem (her own behavior). If, by contrast, she pressed ahead aggressively, trusting her own appraisal of the problem, nothing likely would change.

The reason it helps to take time to define a problem carefully is that sometimes people mistake symptoms for causes. In the case of the student, his poor studying was a symptom of another cause (family difficulties), not the cause of his poor grades. In the case of the police chief, lack of citizen participation on the advisory committee was a symptom of a problem, not the problem itself. If a plan addresses a symptom rather than the causes of a problem, the desired results will not be attained. It also is important during this stage to avoid scapegoating or blaming individuals or groups for the problem, which may trigger defensiveness and reduce creative thinking. This is a stage where conflict resolution techniques and negotiating skills can be important. Finally, the statement of a problem should not imply that any particular solution is the correct one. The correct statement of the problem as just that—a problem—rather than as an implied solution is also the underlying assumption of the normative model described in **Highlight 8.8**.

Decision-Making and the Normative Model

HIGHLIGHT 8.8

Effective decision-making certainly aids in problem solving. But it also aids in building trust. It's hard to trust a leader who makes bad-quality decisions; it's equally hard to trust a leader who doesn't value the followers' inputs when the followers have the expertise. The Normative Decision Model can help leaders use the right amount of follower input while ensuring that the quality of the decision is maintained.

Obviously in some situations leaders can delegate decisions to followers or should ask followers for relevant information before making a decision. In other situations, such as emergencies or crises, leaders may need to make a decision with little, if any, input from subordinates. The level of input that followers have in the decision-making process varies substantially depending on the issue at hand, followers' level of technical expertise, or the presence or absence of a crisis. Although the level of participation changes due to various leader, follower, and situational factors, Vroom and Yetton maintained that leaders can often improve group performance by using an optimal amount of participation in the decision-making process. Thus, the normative decision model is directed solely at determining how much input subordinates should have in the decision-making process.

To determine which situational and follower factors affect the level of participation and group performance, Vroom and Yetton first investigated the decision-making processes leaders use in group settings. They discovered a continuum of decision-making processes ranging from completely autocratic (labeled "AI") to completely democratic, where all members of the group have equal participation (labeled "GII"). The complete range of decision processes are:

Autocratic Processes

- AI: The leader solves the problem or makes the decision by himself using the information available at the time.

- AII: The leader obtains any necessary information from followers, then decides on a solution to the problem herself. She may or may not tell followers the purpose of her questions or give information about the problem or decision she is working on. The input provided by them is clearly in response to her request for specific information. They do not play a role in the definition of the problem or in generating or evaluating alternative solutions.

Consultative Processes

- CI: The leader shares the problem with the relevant followers individually, getting their ideas and suggestions without bringing them together as a group. Then she makes a decision. This decision may or may not reflect the followers' influence.

- CII: The leader shares the problem with his followers in a group meeting. In this meeting, he obtains their ideas and suggestions. Then he makes the decision, which may or may not reflect the followers' influence.

Group Process

- GII: The leader shares the problem with his followers as a group. Together they generate and evaluate alternatives and attempt to reach agreement (consensus) on a solution. The leader's role is much like that of a chairperson, coordinating the discussion, keeping it focused on the problem, and making sure the critical issues are discussed. She can provide the group with information or ideas that she has, but she does not try to press them to adopt "her" solution. Moreover, leaders adopting this level of participation are willing to accept and implement any solution that has the support of the entire group.

Vroom and Yetton believed that there were two overarching criteria leaders should strive for: quality and acceptance. Leaders who make bad-quality decisions don't last long in their organizations. Leaders who make high-quality decisions but do not ensure sufficient acceptance by their followers may find that they have made a good decision, but it is never effectively implemented. (Followers have a lot more time to undermine the implementation of a decision they don't accept than leaders have to try and enforce it.)

The normative model is depicted in the form of a decision tree. Each node (A through G) has a question associated with it and the leader must answer either Yes or No. To use the decision tree, we start at the left by stating the problem and then proceed through the model from left to right. Every time a box is encountered, the question associated with that box must be answered with either a yes or a no response. Eventually, all paths lead to a set of decision processes that, if used, will lead to a decision that protects both quality and acceptance. The complete decision model is shown in this diagram.

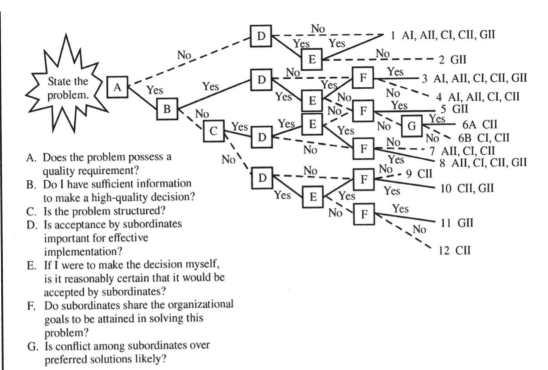

A. Does the problem possess a quality requirement?
B. Do I have sufficient information to make a high-quality decision?
C. Is the problem structured?
D. Is acceptance by subordinates important for effective implementation?
E. If I were to make the decision myself, is it reasonably certain that it would be accepted by subordinates?
F. Do subordinates share the organizational goals to be attained in solving this problem?
G. Is conflict among subordinates over preferred solutions likely?

Having reached a set of feasible alternatives that meet the desirable criteria for quality and acceptance among followers, the leader may then wish to consider additional criteria. One practical consideration is the amount of time available. If time is critical, the leader should select the alternative in the feasible set that is farthest to the *left*, again noting that the feasible set is arranged from AI through GII. It generally takes less time to make and implement autocratic decisions than it does to make consultative or group decisions. Nevertheless, the first step is to protect quality and acceptance (by using the model). Only *after* arriving at an appropriate set of outcomes should leaders consider time in the decision-making process. This tenet is sometimes neglected in the workplace by leaders who overemphasize time as a criterion. Obviously there are some situations where time is absolutely critical, as in life-or-death emergencies. Certainly no one would have expected U.S. Airways Captain Chesley "Sully" Sullenberger to pull out his Vroom–Yetton decision model after his Airbus A320 struck a flock of geese and he found himself plummeting toward the Hudson River in what had become a very large glider. But too often leaders ask for a decision to be made as if the situation were an emergency when, in reality, they (the leaders, not the situation) are creating the time pressure. Despite such behavior, it is difficult to imagine a leader who would knowingly prefer a fast decision that lacks both quality and acceptance among the implementers to one that is of high quality and acceptable to followers but that takes more time.

Source: Adapted from V. H. Vroom and P. W. Yetton, *Leadership and Decision Making* (Pittsburgh, PA: University of Pittsburgh Press, 1973).

As an application of these considerations, let us consider two pairs of problem statements that a teacher might present to his class as a first step in addressing what he considers to be an unsatisfactory situation. These samples of dialogue touch on many aspects of communication, listening, and feedback skills addressed earlier in this book. Here, however, our focus is on differences in defining problems. In each case, the second statement is the one more likely to lead to constructive problem solving.

A: I don't think you care enough about this course. No one is ever prepared. What do I have to do to get you to put in more time on your homework?

B: What things are interfering with your doing well in this course?

A: Your test grades are too low. Im going to cancel the field trip unless they improve. Do you have any questions?

B: I'm concerned about your test scores. They're lower than I expected them to be, and I'm not sure whats going on. What do you think the problem is?

Another aspect of this first stage of problem solving involves identifying those factors that, when corrected, are likely to have the greatest impact on improving an unsatisfactory situation. Because there are almost always more problems or opportunities for improvement than time or energy to devote to them all, it is crucial to identify those whose solutions offer the greatest potential payoff. A useful concept here is the *Pareto principle*, which states that about 80 percent of the problems in any system are the result of about 20 percent of the causes. In school, for example, most discipline problems are caused by a minority of the students. Of all the errors people make on income tax returns, just a few kinds of errors (like forgetting to sign) account for a disproportionately high percentage of returned forms. We would expect about 20 percent of the total mechanical problems in a city bus fleet to account for about 80 percent of the fleet's downtime. The Pareto principle can be used to focus problem-solving efforts on those causes that have the greatest overall impact.

Analyzing the Causes

Once a problem is identified, the next step is to analyze its causes. Analysis of a problem's causes should precede a search for its solutions. Two helpful tools for identifying the key elements affecting a problem situation are a cause-and-effect diagram (also called a "fishbone" diagram because of its shape or an Ishikawa diagram after the person who developed it) and force field analysis. Cause-and-effect diagrams use a graphic approach to depict systematically the root causes of a problem, the relationships between different causes, and potentially a prioritization of which causes are most important (see **Figure 8.5**).

Force field analysis (see **Figure 8.6**) also uses a graphic approach; it depicts the opposing forces that tend to perpetuate a present state of affairs. It is a way of depicting any stable situation in terms of dynamic balance, or equilibrium, between the forces that tend to press toward movement in one direction and other forces that tend to restrain movement in that direction. So long as the net sum of all the forces is zero, no movement occurs. When a change is desirable, force field analysis can be used to identify the best way to upset the balance between positive and negative forces so that a different equilibrium can be reached.

Developing Alternative Solutions

A procedure called *nominal group technique* (NGT) is a good way to generate ideas pertinent to a problem.[53] This procedure is similar to brainstorming (see **Highlight 8.9**) in that it is an idea-generating activity conducted in a group setting. With NGT, however, group members write down ideas on individual slips of paper, which are later transferred to a whiteboard or flipchart for the entire group to work with.

FIGURE 8.5 A Cause-and-Effect Diagram

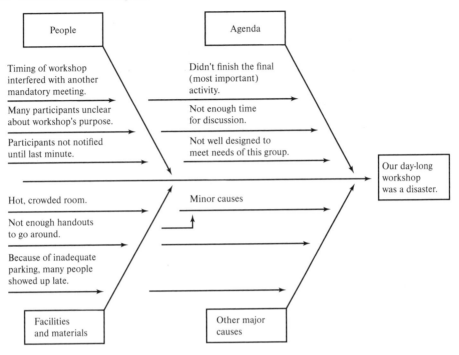

FIGURE 8.6   Force Field Analysis Example: Starting a Personal Exercise Program

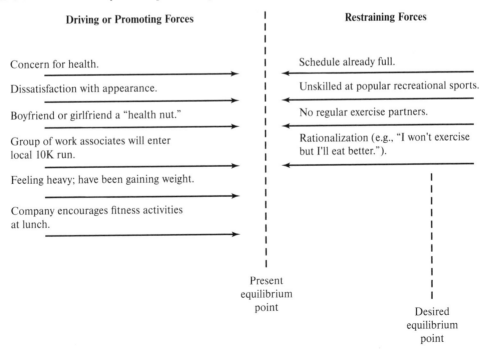

Steps for Enhancing Creativity through Brainstorming

HIGHLIGHT 8.9

Brainstorming is a technique designed to enhance the creative potential of any group trying to solve a problem. Leaders should use the following rules when conducting a brainstorming session:

1. Groups should consist of five to seven people; fewer than five can limit the number of ideas generated, but more than seven often can make the session unwieldy. It may be more important to carefully decide who should attend a session than how many people should attend.

2. Everybody should be given the chance to contribute. The first phase of brainstorming is idea generation, and members should be encouraged to spontaneously contribute ideas as soon as they get them. The objective in the first phase is quantity, not quality.

3. No criticism is allowed during the idea-generation phase. This helps to clearly separate the activities of imaginative thinking and idea production from idea evaluation.

4. Freewheeling and outlandish ideas should be encouraged. With some modification, these ideas may be eventually adopted.

5. "Piggybacking" off others' ideas should be encouraged. Combining ideas or extending others' ideas often results in better solutions.

6. The greater the quantity and variety of ideas, the better. The more ideas generated, the greater the probability a good solution will be found.

7. Ideas should be recorded—ideally on a whiteboard or large sheet of paper so that members can review all the ideas generated.

8. After all the ideas have been generated, each idea should be evaluated in terms of pros and cons, costs and benefits, feasibility, and so on. Choosing the final solution often depends on the results of these analyses.

Source: A. F. Osborn, *Applied Imagination* (New York: Scribner's, 1963).

Selecting and Implementing the Best Solution

The first solution one thinks of is not necessarily the best solution, even if everyone involved finds it acceptable. It is better to select a solution on the basis of established criteria. These include questions such as the following: Have the advantages and disadvantages of all possible solutions been considered? Have all the possible solutions been evaluated in terms of their respective impacts on the whole organization, not just a particular team or department? Is the necessary information available to make a good decision among the alternatives?

Assessing the Impact of the Solution

We should not assume that the preceding steps will guarantee that the actions implemented will solve the problem. The solution's continuing impact must be assessed, preferably by measurable criteria of success that all parties involved can agree on.

Improving Creativity

Leaders can do several things to increase their own and their followers' creativity. Some of these facilitating factors have already been discussed and include assuring adequate levels of technical expertise, delaying and minimizing the evaluation or judgment of solutions, focusing on the intrinsic motivation of the task, removing unnecessary constraints on followers, and giving followers more latitude in making decisions. One popular technique for stimulating creative thinking in groups is called *brainstorming* (discussed in **Highlight 8.9**).

Seeing Things in New Ways

An additional thing leaders can do to enhance creativity is to *see things in new ways*, or to look at problems from as many perspectives as possible. This is easier said than done. It can be difficult to see novel uses for things we are very familiar with. Psychologists call this kind of mental block *functional fixedness*.[54] Creative thinking depends on overcoming the functional fixedness associated with the rigid and stereotyped perceptions we have of the things around us.

One way to see things differently is to think in terms of analogies. This is a practical extension of Cronbach's definition of creativity—making fresh observations, or seeing one thing as something else.[55] In this case, the active search for analogies is the essence of the problem-solving method. In fact, finding analogies is the foundation of a commercial creative problem-solving approach called Synectics.[56] An example of the use of analogies in a Synectics problem-solving group concerned designing a new roofing material that would adjust its color to the season, turning white in the summer to reflect heat and black in the winter to absorb heat. The group's first task was to find an analogy in nature, and it thought of fishes whose colors change to match their surroundings. The mechanism for such changes in fish is the movement of tiny compartments of pigments closer to or farther away from the skin's surface, thus changing its color. After some discussion, the group designed a black roof impregnated with tiny white plastic balls that would expand when it was hot, making the roof lighter, and contract when it was cold, making the roof darker.[57]

Another way to see things differently is to try putting an idea or problem into a picture rather than into words. Feelings or relationships that have eluded verbal description may come out in a drawing, bringing fresh insights to an issue.

Using Power Constructively

In addition to getting followers to see problems from as many perspectives as possible, a leader can also *use her power constructively to enhance creativity*. As noted earlier, groups may suppress creative thinking by being overly critical or by passing judgment during the idea-generation stage. This effect may be even more pronounced when strong authority relationships and status differences are present. Group members may be reluctant to take the risk of raising a "crazy" idea when superiors are present, especially if the leader is generally perceived as unreceptive to new ideas; or they may be reluctant to offer an idea if they believe others in the group will take potshots at it in front of the leader. Leaders who wish to create a favorable climate for creativity need to use their power to encourage the open expression of ideas and to suppress uncooperative or aggressive reactions (overt or covert) between group members. Further, leaders can encourage creativity by rewarding successes and by not punishing mistakes. Leaders can also delegate authority and responsibility, relax followers' constraints, and empower followers to take risks. By taking these steps, leaders can help followers build idiosyncratic credits, which will encourage them to take risks and to be more creative. Along these same lines, the entire climate of an organization can be either more or less conducive to creative thinking—differences that may be due to the use of power within the organization. In an insightful turn of the familiar adage "Power corrupts," Kanter has noted how powerlessness also corrupts.[58] She pointed out how managers who feel powerless in an organization may spend more energy guarding their territory than collaborating with others in productive action. The need to actively support followers' creativity may be especially important for leaders in bureaucratic organizations because such organizations tend to be so inflexible, formalized, and centralized as to make many people in them feel relatively powerless.

Forming Diverse Problem-Solving Groups

Leaders can enhance creativity by *forming diverse problem-solving groups*. Group members with similar experiences, values, and preferences will be less likely to create a wide variety of solutions and more apt to agree on a solution prematurely than more diverse groups. Thus selecting people for a group or committee with a variety of experiences, values, and preferences should increase the creativity of the group, although these differences may also increase the level of conflict within the group and make it more difficult for the leader to get consensus on a final solution. One technique for increasing diversity and creativity in problem-solving groups involves the use of the four preference dimensions of the Myers-Briggs Type Indicator (MBTI). Evidence to support this specific approach appears scanty,[59] but perhaps preferences assume significance only after certain other conditions for group creativity have been met. For example, diversity cannot make up for an absence of technical expertise. Although the MBTI dimensions may be useful in selecting diverse groups, this instrument should be used only after ensuring that all potential members have high levels of technical expertise. Choosing members based solely on MBTI preferences ignores the crucial role that technical expertise and intrinsic motivation play in creativity. Another aspect of the relationship between creativity and leadership is described in **Highlight 8.10**.

Managing Creativity

HIGHLIGHT 8.10

R. T. Hogan and J. Morrison have maintained that people who are seen as more creative tend to have several distinguishing personality characteristics. In general, creative people are open to information and experience, have high energy, can be personally assertive and even domineering, react emotionally to events, are impulsive, are more interested in music and art than in hunting and sports, and, finally, are very motivated to prove themselves (that is, they are concerned with personal adequacy). Thus creative people tend to be independent, willful, impractical, unconcerned with money, idealistic, and nonconforming. Given that these tendencies may not make them ideal followers, the interesting question raised by Hogan and Morrison is this: How does one lead or manage creative individuals? This question becomes even more interesting when considering the qualities of successful leaders or managers.

As discussed earlier, successful leaders tend to be intelligent, dominant, conscientious, stable, calm, goal oriented, outgoing, and somewhat conventional. Thus we might think that the personalities of creative followers and successful leaders might be the source of considerable conflict and make them natural enemies in organizational settings. Because many organizations depend on creativity to grow and prosper, being able to successfully lead creative individuals may be a crucial aspect of success for these organizations. Given that creative people already possess technical expertise, imaginative thinking skills, and intrinsic motivation, Hogan and Morrison suggested that leaders take the following steps to successfully lead creative followers:

1. *Set goals:* Because creative people value freedom and independence, this step will be best accomplished if leaders set a high level of participation in the goal-setting process. Leaders should ask followers what they can accomplish in a particular time frame.

2. *Provide adequate resources:* Followers will be much more creative if they have the proper equipment to work with because they can devote their time to resolving problems rather than spending time finding the equipment to get the job done.

3. *Reduce time pressures, but keep followers on track:* Try to set realistic milestones and goals, and make organizational rewards contingent on reaching these milestones. Moreover, leaders need to be well organized to acquire necessary resources and to keep the project on track.

4. *Consider nonmonetary as well as monetary rewards:* Creative people often gain satisfaction from resolving the problem at hand, not from monetary rewards. Thus feedback should be aimed at enhancing their feelings of personal adequacy. Monetary rewards perceived as controlling may decrease rather than increase motivation toward the task.

5. *Recognize that creativity is evolutionary, not revolutionary:* Although followers can create truly novel products (such as the Xerox machine), often the key to creativity is continuous product improvement. Making next year's product faster, lighter, cheaper, or more efficient requires minor modifications that can, over time, culminate in major revolutions. Thus it may be helpful if leaders think of creativity more in terms of small innovations than major breakthroughs.

Source: R. T. Hogan and J. Morrison, "Managing Creativity," in *Create & Be Free: Essays in Honor of Frank Barron,* ed. A. Montouri (Amsterdam: J. C. Gieben, 1993).

Endnotes

1. Personnel Decisions International, *PROFILOR® Certification Workshop Manual* (Minneapolis, MN: Author, 1992).

2. J. M. Kouzes and B. Z. Posner, *The Credibility Factor* (San Francisco: Jossey-Bass, 1996).

3. Kouzes and Posner, *The Credibility Factor.*

4. B. M. Bass, *Bass and Stogdill's Handbook of Leadership*, 3rd ed. (New York: Free Press, 1990).

5. W. G. Bennis and B. Nanus, *Leaders: The Strategies for Taking Charge* (New York: Harper & Row, 1985).

6. R. M. Kanter, *The Change Masters* (New York: Simon & Schuster, 1983).

7. M. R. Parks, "Interpersonal Communication and the Quest for Personal Competence," in *Handbook of Interpersonal Communication,* eds. M. L. Knapp and G. R. Miller (Beverly Hills, CA: Sage, 1985).

8. R. J. Klimoski and N. J. Hayes, "Leader Behavior and Subordinate Motivation," *Personnel Psychology* 33 (1980), pp. 543–55.

9. R. A. Snyder and J. H. Morris, "Organizational Communication and Performance," *Journal of Applied Psychology* 69 (1984), pp. 461–65.

10. B. Fiechtner and J. J. Krayer, "Variations in Dogmatism and Leader-Supplied Information: Determinants of Perceived Behavior in Task-Oriented Groups," *Group and Organizational Studies* 11 (1986), pp. 403–18.

11. A. Sanford and S. Garrod, *Understanding Written Language* (New York: John Wiley, 1981).

12. M. S. Remland, "Developing Leadership Skills in Nonverbal Communication: A Situation Perspective," *Journal of Business Communication* 18, no. 3 (1981), pp. 17–29.

13. F. Luthans and J. K. Larsen, "How Managers Really Communicate," *Human Relations* 39 (1986), pp. 161–78.

14. P. J. Sadler and G. H. Hofstede, "Leadership Styles: Preferences and Perceptions of Employees of an International Company in Different Countries," *Mens en Onderneming* 26 (1972), pp. 43–63.

15. B. L. Davis, L. W. Hellervik, and J. L. Sheard, *The Successful Manager's Handbook*, 3rd ed. (Minneapolis, MN: Personnel Decisions International, 1989).

16. S. P. Robbins, *Organizational Behavior: Concepts, Controversies, and Applications* (Englewood Cliffs, NJ: Prentice Hall, 1986).

17. J. R. Gibb, "Defensive Communication," *Journal of Communication* 13, no. 3 (1961), pp. 141–48.

18. R. E. Alberti and M. L. Emmons, *Your Perfect Right* (San Luis Obispo, CA: Impact, 1974).

19. E. L. Shostrom, *Man, the Manipulator* (New York: Bantam, 1967).

20. J. B. Harvey, "The Abilene Paradox: The Management of Agreement," *Organizational Dynamics* 3 (1974), pp. 63–80.

21. Bass, *Bass and Stogdill's Handbook of Leadership*, 3rd ed.

22. C. A. O'Reilly, "Supervisors and Peers as Informative Sources, Group Supportiveness, and Individual Decision-Making Performance," *Journal of Applied Psychology* 62 (1977), pp. 632–35.

23. C. K. Guth and S. S. Shaw, *How to Put on Dynamic Meetings* (Reston, VA: Shopsmith, 1980).

24. P. E. Benner, *Stress and Satisfaction on the Job* (New York: Praeger, 1984).

25. C. D. McCauley, "Stress and the Eye of the Beholder," *Issues & Observations* 7, no. 3 (1987), pp. 1–16.

26. B. M. Staw, "Organizational Behavior: A Review and Reformulation of the Field's Outcome Variables," *Annual Review of Psychology* 35 (1984), pp. 627–66.

27. J. M. Ivancevich, D. M. Schweiger, and J. W. Ragan, "Employee Stress, Health, and Attitudes: A Comparison of American, Indian, and Japanese Managers," paper presented at the Academy of Management Convention, Chicago, 1986.

28. R. T. Hogan and A. M. Morrison, "The Psychology of Managerial Incompetence," paper presented at a joint conference of the American Psychological Association–National Institute of Occupational Safety and Health, Washington, DC, October 1991.

29. F. Shipper and C. L. Wilson, "The Impact of Managerial Behaviors on Group Performance, Stress, and Commitment," in *Impact of Leadership*, eds. K. E. Clark, M. B. Clark, and D. P. Campbell (Greensboro, NC: Center for Creative Leadership, 1992).

30. J. McCormick and B. Powell, "Management for the 1990s," *Newsweek*, April 1988, pp. 47–48.

31. M. Friedman and D. Ulmer, *Treating Type A Behavior and Your Heart* (New York: Knopf, 1984).

32. M. H. Frisch, "The Emerging Role of the Internal Coach," *Consulting Psychology Journal* 53, no. 4 (2001), pp. 240–50.

33. O. F. Pomerleau and J. Rodin, "Behavioral Medicine and Health Psychology," in *Handbook of Psychotherapy and Behavior Change*, 3rd ed., eds. S. L. Garfield and A. E. Bergin (New York: John Wiley, 1986).

34. A. Justice, "Review of the Effects of Stress on Cancer in Laboratory Animals: Importance of Time of Stress Application and Type of Tumor," *Psychological Bulletin* 98 (1985), pp. 108–38.

35. J. C. Latack, "Coping with Job Stress: Measures and Future Decisions for Scale Development," *Journal of Applied Psychology* 71 (1986), pp. 377–85.

36. D. Quayle, "American Productivity: The Devastating Effect of Alcoholism and Drug Use," *American Psychologist* 38 (1983), pp. 454–58.

37. M. Jamal, "Job Stress and Job Performance Controversy: An Empirical Assessment," *Organizational Behavior and Human Performance* 33 (1984), pp. 1–21.

38. F. E. Fiedler, "The Effect and Meaning of Leadership Experience: A Review of Research and a Preliminary Model," in *Impact of Leadership*, eds. K. E. Clark, M. B. Clark, and D. P. Campbell (Greensboro, NC: Center for Creative Leadership, 1992).

39. F. W. Gibson, "A Taxonomy of Leader Abilities and Their Influence on Group Performance as a Function of Interpersonal Stress," in *Impact of Leadership*, eds. K. E. Clark, M. B. Clark, and D. P. Campbell (Greensboro, NC: Center for Creative Leadership, 1992).

40. M. Mulder, R. D. de Jong, L. Koppelar, and J. Verhage, "Power, Situation, and Leaders' Effectiveness: An Organizational Study," *Journal of Applied Psychology* 71 (1986), pp. 566–70.

41. D. Weschler, *Weschler Adult Intelligence Scale: Manual* (New York: Psychological Corporation, 1955).

42. D. Tjosvold, "Stress Dosage for Problem Solvers," *Working Smart*, August 1995, p. 5.

43. L. L. Ten Brummelhuis, J. Haar, and M. Roche, "Does Family Life Help to Be a Better Leader? A Closer Look at Crossover Processes from Leaders to Followers," *Personnel Psychology* 67 (2014), pp. 917–49.

44. J. Wiley and T. Comacho, "Life-Style and Future Health: Evidence from the Alameda County Study," *Preventive Medicine* 9 (1980), pp. 1–21.

45. L. Berkman and S. L. Syme, "Social Networks, Host Resistance, and Mortality: A Nine-Year Follow-up Study of Alameda County Residents," *American Journal of Epidemiology* 109 (1979), pp. 186–204.

46. R. C. Cummings, "Job Stress and the Buffering Effect of Supervisory Support," *Group and Organizational Studies* 15, no. 1 (1990), pp. 92–104.

47. S. Jayaratne, D. Himle, and W. A. Chess, "Dealing with Work Stress and Strain: Is the Perception of Support More Important Than Its Use?" *Journal of Applied Behavioral Science* 24, no. 2 (1988), pp. 34–45.

48. West Point Associates, the Department of Behavior Sciences and Leadership, United States Military Academy, *Leadership in Organizations* (Garden City Park, NY: Avery, 1988).

49. P. W. Linville, "Self-Complexity as a Cognitive Buffer Against Stress-Related Illness and Depression," *Journal of Personality and Social Psychology* 52, no. 4 (1987), pp. 663–76.

50. A. Ellis and R. Harper, *A New Guide to Rational Living* (Englewood Cliffs, NJ: Prentice Hall, 1975).

51. J. Steinmetz, J. Blankenship, L. Brown, D. Hall, and G. Miller, *Managing Stress before It Manages You* (Palo Alto, CA: Bull, 1980).

52. M. McKay, M. Davis, and P. Fanning, *Thoughts and Feelings: The Art of Cognitive Stress Intervention* (Richmond, CA: New Harbinger, 1981).

53. A. L. Delbecq, A. H. Van de Ven, and D. H. Gustafson, *Group Techniques for Program Planning: A Guide to Nominal and Delphi Processes* (Glenview, IL: Scott Foresman, 1975).

54. K. Duncker, "On Problem Solving," *Psychological Monographs* 58, no. 5 (1945).

55. L. J. Cronbach, *Essentials of Psychological Testing*, 4th ed. (San Francisco: Harper & Row, 1984).

56. W. J. J. Gordon, *Synectics* (New York: Harper & Row, 1961).

57. Gordon, *Synectics.*

58. Kanter, *The Change Masters.*

59. P. W. Thayer, "The Myers-Briggs Type Indicator and Enhancing Human Performance," report prepared for the Committee on Techniques for the Enhancement of Human Performance of the National Academy of Sciences, 1988.

Part 3

Focus on the Followers

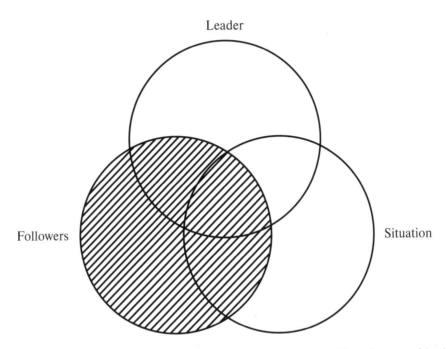

We began **Part 2** with the notion that the individual leader is the most critical element of leadership. We begin Part 3 by qualifying that sentiment. Although the importance of a good leader cannot be denied, followers play an equally important, if often overlooked, role in the success of any group or organization. There can be no leaders without followers, but most research to date has focused on leadership. Researchers have only recently given serious consideration to the topics of followers and followership.

This research has revealed several interesting questions and findings. First, virtually everyone is a follower at some point in his or her life. And perhaps more important, anyone occupying a position of authority plays a followership role at times: First-line supervisors report to mid-level managers, mid-level managers report to vice presidents, vice presidents report to CEOs, and CEOs report to boards of directors. Because the same people play both leadership and followership roles, it is hardly surprising that the values, bases of power, personality traits, mental abilities, and behaviors used to describe effective leaders can also be used to describe effective followers. Followers vary in all the same ways that leaders vary.

Better followership often begets better leadership.

Barbara Kellerman, Harvard University

Second, there are times when situational demands require that individuals in formal followership roles step into leadership roles. For example, a sergeant may take over a platoon when her lieutenant is wounded in battle, a volunteer may take over a community group when the leader moves away, a software engineer may be asked to lead a project because of unique programming skills, or team members can be asked to make decisions about team goals, work priorities, meeting schedules, and the like. That being the case, followers who are perceived to be the most effective are most likely to be asked to take the lead when opportunities arise, as peers usually see them as them informal leaders of their teams.[1] So understanding what constitutes effective followership and exhibiting those behaviors can help improve a person's promotion opportunities. Effective followership plays such an important role in the development of future leadership skills that freshman at all the U.S. service academies (the Air Force, Army, Navy, Coast Guard, and Merchant Marine academies) spend their first year in formal follower roles. Following the path set by the service academies, perhaps the most effective people in any organization are those who are equally adept at playing *both* leadership and followership roles. Many people make great leaders but ultimately fail because of their inability to follow orders or get along with peers. And other people are great at following orders but cause teams to fail because of their reluctance to step into leadership roles.

Third, it is important to remember the vital role followers play in societal change and organizational performance. The civil rights, Arab Spring, climate change, Brexit, and Hong Kong protests are good examples of what happens when angry followers decide to do something to change the status quo. And this is precisely why totalitarian societies, such as North Korea, Russia, Saudi Arabia, Turkmenistan, and Iran, tightly control the amount and type of information flowing through their countries. Organizational leaders should treat followers as important assets because they are the people creating the products, taking orders, serving customers, and collecting payments. Research has consistently shown that more engaged employees are happier, more productive, and more likely to stay with organizations than those who are disengaged.[2] Moreover, ethical followers can help leaders avoid making questionable decisions, and high-performing followers often motivate leaders to raise their own levels of performance.[3, 4] Wars are usually won by armies with the best soldiers, teams with the best athletes usually win the most games, and companies with the best employees usually outperform their competitors—so it is to a leader's benefit to choose and develop the best followers.[5, 6, 7, 8, 9, 10]

Fourth, although asking why anyone would want to be a leader is an interesting question, perhaps a more interesting question is asking why anyone would want to be a follower. Being a leader clearly has some advantages, but why would anyone freely choose to be a subordinate to someone else? Why would you be a follower? Evolutionary psychology hypothesizes that people follow because the benefits of doing so outweigh the costs of going it alone or fighting to become the leader of a group.[11] Thousands of years ago most people lived in small, nomadic groups, and these groups offered individuals more protection, resources for securing food, and mating opportunities than they would have had on their own. The groups with the best leaders and followers were more likely to survive, and those poorly led or consisting of bad followers were more likely to starve. Followers who were happy with the costs and benefits of membership stayed with the group; those who were not either left to join other groups or battled for the top spots. Evolutionary psychology also rightly points out that leaders and followers can often have different goals and agendas. In the workplace, leaders may be making decisions to maximize financial performance, whereas followers may be acting to improve job security. Therefore, leaders adopting an evolutionary psychology approach to followership must do all they can to align followers' goals with those of the organization and ensure that the benefits people accrue outweigh the costs of working for the leader; followers will either mutiny or leave if goals are misaligned or inequities are perceived.

However, social psychology tells us that something other than cost–benefit analyses may be happening when people choose to play followership roles. In some situations people seem too willing to abdicate responsibility and follow orders, even when it is morally offensive to do so. The famous Milgram experiments of the 1950s demonstrated that people would follow orders, even to the point of hurting others, if told to do so by someone they perceived to be in a position of authority. You would think the infamy of the Milgram research would subsequently inoculate people from following morally offensive or unethical orders, but a recent replication of the Milgram experiments showed that approximately 75 percent of both men and women will follow the orders of complete strangers who they believe occupy some position of authority.[12] Sadly, the genocides of Bosnia, Rwanda, Darfur, and Syria may be real examples of the Milgram effect. For leadership practitioners, this research shows that merely occupying positions of authority grants leaders a certain amount of influence over the actions of their followers. Leaders need to use this influence wisely.

Social psychology also tells us that identification with leaders and trust are two other reasons why people choose to follow. Much of the research in **Chapter 16** concerning charismatic and transformational leadership shows that a leader's personal magnetism can draw in followers and convince them to take action. This effect can be so strong as to cause followers to give their lives for a cause. The terrorist attacks of September 11, 2001; the Mumbai, Bali, and London Tube bombings; the attempted bombing of a Delta airlines flight in December 2009; and suicide bomber attacks in Iraq and Afghanistan are examples of the personal magnetism of Osama bin Laden and the Al-Qaeda cause. Although most people do not have the personal magnetism of an Osama bin Laden or a Martin Luther King, those who do need to decide whether they will use their personal magnetism for good or evil.

> *Instead of winning a war for talent, organizations appear to be waging a war on talent, repelling and alienating employees more successfully than harnessing their skills.*
>
> **Tomas Chamorro-Premuzic, Hogan Assessment Systems; Adam Yearsley, Red Bull.**

Trust is a common factor in these hypotheses of cost–benefit analysis, compliance with authority, or willing identification with leaders. It is unlikely that people will follow leaders they do not trust.[13] It can be hard to rebuild trust once it has been broken, and followers' reactions to lost trust typically include disengagement, leaving, or seeking revenge on their leaders. Trust in politicians in many countries is at an all time low, and this is causing high levels of resentment and a crisis in followership among citizens. Many acts of poor customer service, organizational delinquency, and workplace violence can be directly attributed to disgruntled followers,[14] and the economic downturn put considerable strain on trust between leaders and followers. Many leaders, particularly in the financial services industry, seemed happy to wreck the global economy and lay off thousands of employees while collecting multimillion-dollar compensation packages. Given the lack of trust between leaders and followers in many organizations these days, many talented individuals are exploring other job opportunities, opting for self-employment, starting their own companies, or working in small start-ups rather than taking jobs within larger organizations.[15] Because of the importance of trust in team and organizational performance, leaders need to do all they can to maintain strong, trusting relationships with followers.

The final question or finding of the followership research concerns follower frameworks. Over the past 40 years or so researchers such as Hollander,[16] Zaleznik,[17] Kelley,[18] Chaleff,[19] Kellerman,[20] Adair,[21] McCroskey and colleagues,[22] Potter and Rosenbach,[23] Curphy and Roellig,[24] Curphy and Hogan,[25] and Curphy, Nilsen, and Hogan[26] have developed various models for describing different types of followers. These models are intended to provide leaders with additional insight into what motivates followers and how to improve individual and team performance. The frameworks developed by these researchers usually describe three to six different followers types and have more similarities than differences; for illustration, a more detailed description of two of these models follows.

The Potter and Rosenbach Followership Model

Potter and Rosenbach[27] believe follower inputs are vital to team performance because followers are closest to the action and often have the best solutions to problems. Their model is based on two independent dimensions, which include follower performance levels and the strength of leader–follower relationships. The performance initiative dimension is concerned with the extent to which an individual follower can do his or her job, works effectively with other members of the team, embraces change, and views himself or herself as an important asset in team performance. Followers receiving higher scores on this dimension are competent, get along well with others, support leaders' change initiatives, and take care of themselves; those with lower scores do not have the skills needed to perform their jobs, do not get along with others, and actively resist change. The relationship initiative dimension is concerned with the degree to which followers act to improve their working relationships with their leaders. Followers receiving higher scores on this dimension are loyal and identify with their leaders' vision of the future but will raise objections and negotiate differences when need be; those with lower scores are disloyal, will not raise objections even when it would be beneficial to do so, and pursue their own agendas even when they are misaligned with those of their boss.

Because the performance and relationship initiatives are independent dimensions, they can be placed on vertical and horizontal axes and used to describe four different types of followers. As shown in the diagram, the different types of followers include subordinates, contributors, politicians, and partners. Subordinates are followers in the more traditional sense; they do what they are told, follow the rules, are low-to-medium performers, and do not have particularly good relationships with their leaders. These individuals often rise in more bureaucratic, hierarchical organizations because they tend to remain with organizations for long periods, stay out of trouble, and do not make waves.

Potter and Rosenbach Followership Model

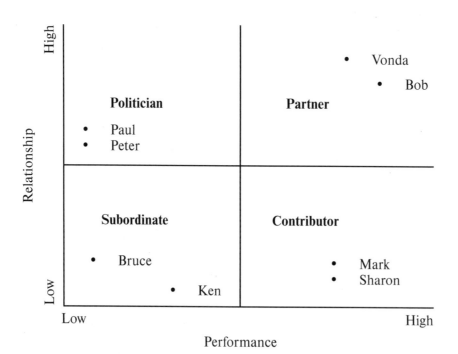

Contributors are different in that they are hard workers and often are motivated to be subject-matter experts in their organizations. Although these individuals can be great researchers, programmers, or accountants, they have no interest in interpersonal dynamics or building stronger relationships with their leaders. They rarely seek out their leaders' perspectives, generally wait for direction, and work best in jobs where they can be left alone to do their thing.

Politicians are an interesting group: These individuals put much more emphasis on getting along well with their boss than on getting things done. They are loyal and sensitive to interpersonal dynamics, and as such can give leaders good insights into other team members. There appear to be two types of politicians—some delight in playing the game and are good in positions that require lots of interaction with others. They often confuse activity with productivity, are administratively challenged, and are often found in sales or public relations because they are good at talking to people. The other type of politician tends to be manipulative, selfish, and have unhealthy needs to be the center of attention. These people play games, start rumors, get little done but take credit for others' work, and jockey to be seen as indispensable to their leaders. Leaders who fall under this type of politician's spell often have teams with poor morale and performance.

Partners are individuals who are committed to high performance and building good relationships with their leaders. Partners take the time to understand their leaders' perspectives and buy into their vision for the team. Because they are strongly motivated to make an impact, partners work closely with their leaders to identify issues and work out solutions. Unlike politicians, partners are much more likely to raise uncomfortable issues and hold leaders accountable for decisions.

Several aspects of the Potter and Rosenbach followership model are worthy of additional comment. First, the situation plays an important role in determining followership types. Some individuals may be partners in one software firm but subordinates in another firm or may move from contributor to subordinate when working for a new boss. Organizational culture, the demands of the position, available resources, other team members, and the leader all affect followership types. Second, although it is natural for leaders to think partners make the best followers, Potter and Rosenbach maintain that all four types of followers can play valuable roles in organizations. Nonetheless, if leaders want to surround themselves with partners, they need to create team climates that encourage effective followership. To do this, leaders must clearly spell out their performance and relationship expectations for followers. Leaders also need to role model partner behavior for their followers when given opportunities to do so, seek followers' input on issues and decisions, and do debriefings on projects to demonstrate effective followership and build trust. If leaders take all these actions and team members choose to remain subordinates, contributors, or politicians, then leaders may want to consider replacing these individuals with those who have the potential to become partners.

Third, the Potter and Rosenbach followership model is useful in that it helps leaders understand their own followership type, the different kinds of followers, what kind of followers they currently have, and what they can do to create effective followership. As depicted in the figure, leaders often find followership scatter plots helpful in determining how to best motivate and lead members of their teams.

However, this model has two potential drawbacks. First, the model puts much of the onus of effective followership on followers. It is up to followers to identify with their leaders, buy into their leaders' vision, raise objections, and perform at a high level. But it is difficult for followers to take these actions if their leaders have not articulated a compelling vision of the future, encouraged constructive feedback, or provided the resources needed for followers to perform at high levels. Here we see that leaders and followers play equally important roles in effective followership.

This leads us to the second drawback of the model. As we will discuss in more detail in **Chapter 17**, it may be that more than half the people occupying positions of authority are incompetent. That being the case, what happens to followership when the leader is dumb, unethical, or evil? The Potter and Rosenbach model states that the situation plays an important role in effective followership, but it may not take into account the role that ineffective leadership plays in followership. The next model, however, considers how managerial incompetence affects followership.

The Curphy and Roellig Followership Model

The Curphy and Roellig followership model[28] builds on some of the earlier followership research of Hollander,[29] Kelley,[30] Chaleff,[31] and Kellerman[32] and is similar to the Potter and Rosenbach model in that it also consists of two independent dimensions and four followership types. The two dimensions of the Curphy and Roellig model are critical thinking and engagement. Critical thinking is concerned with a follower's level of curiosity and ability to challenge the status quo, ask good questions, detect problems, and develop solutions. High scorers on critical thinking are continually asking why and identifying ways to improve productivity or efficiency, drive sales, reduce costs, and so forth; those with lower scores believe it is the role of management to identify and solve problems.

Curphy and Roellig Followership Model

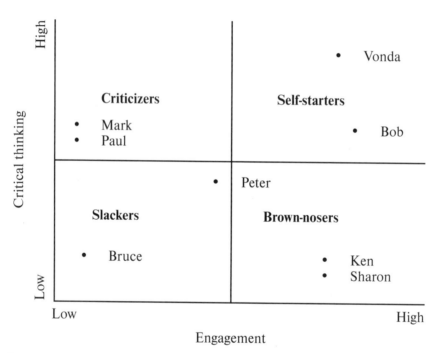

Engagement is concerned with the level of effort people put forth at work. High scorers like what they are doing, are optimistic and hardworking, put in long hours when needed, are enthusiastic about being part of the team, and are driven to achieve results; low scorers are lazy and disengaged and would rather be doing anything but the task at hand.

Like the Potter and Rosenbach followership model, the Curphy and Roellig model can be used to assess current followership types. Self-starters, such as Bob and Vonda in the figure, are individuals who are passionate about the team and will exert considerable effort to make it successful. They are also continually thinking of ways to improve team performance as they raise issues, develop solutions, and enthusiastically carry out change initiatives.[33, 34, 35] When encountering problems, self-starters are apt to resolve issues and then tell their leaders what they did rather than waiting to be told what to do. This followership type also helps to improve their leaders' performance because they will voice opinions prior to and provide constructive feedback after bad decisions.[36]

Self-starters are a significant component of high-performing teams and are by far the most effective follower-ship type. Leaders who want to have these followers should keep in mind the underlying psychological driver of this type and the behaviors they need to exhibit if they want to encourage self-starters. In terms of the underlying psychological driver, leaders need to understand that self-starters fundamentally lack patience. They do not suffer fools gladly and expect their leaders to promptly clear obstacles and acquire the resources needed to succeed. Leaders who consistently make bad decisions, dither, or fail to quickly secure needed resources or follow through on commitments are not apt to have self-starters on their teams. Because of their high expectations and impatience, in some ways self-starters may be the most difficult type to manage. Lead-ers need to bring their A game to the table if they want to encourage this follower type, and a key action is to articulate a clear vision and set of goals for their teams. Self-starters seek forgiveness rather than permis-sion, and if they do not know where the team is going, they may make decisions and take actions that are counterproductive. And self-starters whose decisions are overruled too many times are likely to disengage and become criticizers or slackers. In addition to making sure they understand the team's vision and goals, leaders also need to provide self-starters with needed resources, interesting and challenging work, plenty of latitude and regular performance feedback, recognition for strong performance, and promotion opportunities.[37] The bottom line is that self-starters can be highly rewarding but challenging team members, and leaders need to bring their best game to work if they want to successfully manage these followers.

Brown-nosers, such as Ken and Sharon in the figure, share the strong work ethic but lack the critical-thinking skills of self-starters. Brown-nosers are earnest, dutiful, conscientious, and loyal employees who will do what-ever their leaders ask them to do. They never point out problems, raise objections, or make any waves, and they do whatever they can to please their bosses. Brown-nosers constantly check in with their leaders and operate by seeking permission rather than forgiveness. It is not surprising that many leaders surround them-selves with brown-nosers—these individuals are sources of constant flattery and tell everyone how lucky they are to be working for such great bosses. They are also willing to take on many of the distasteful or unen-joyable tasks other followers are reluctant to do. It may also not be surprising that brown-nosers often go quite far in organizations, particularly those not having good performance metrics. Organizations lacking clear goals and measures of performance often make personnel decisions on the basis of politics, and brown-nosers work hard to have no enemies (they can never tell who their next boss will be) and as such play politics well.

Leaders and Yes Men

HIGHLIGHT PART 3.1

Although self-starters are the most effective fol-lowership type, there is research showing that the longer leaders remain in place, the more likely they will surround themselves with brown-nosers. This can easily be seen by examining the history of the top leaders surrounding U.S. President Donald Trump. Rex Tillerson, Larry McMaster, John Bolton, Jeff Sessions, James Comey, Jim Mattis, and John Kelly all spoke truth to power and told Donald Trump what he needed rather than what he wanted to hear. Their replacements, as well as the handful who remain in cabinet positions, have demonstrated unfailing loyalty and servility. Because of the power of the presidency, indentured servitude has extended to the Republican party, as U.S. congressmen and senators who were formerly critics of Trump have become his biggest cheer-leaders; those who spoke out have retired or were voted out of office. Many evangelical lead-ers have also seen the light, transforming into brown-nosing loyalists who conveniently overlook the fact that President Trump does not seem to do what Jesus Christ would do. It does not matter if someone has several extramarital affairs, separates families, puts kids in cages, taunts enemies and the disabled, and lies over 10,000 times while being in office—the ends justify the means and all will be forgiven.

So what should self-starters do if they find themselves working for leaders who want to surround themselves with brown-nosers? When bringing up uncomfortable truths, brown-nosers will gang up on self-starters and make excuses or counterarguments in support of their leaders. Sooner or later self-starters will be on the outs and perceived as criticizers. This could become a self-fulfilling prophecy, as the more their warnings and suggestions go unheeded, the more likely self-starters will become criticizers. The best remedy to prevent this from happening is to find another job, as effective leaders want nothing more than to surround themselves with self-starters.

Sources: J .Stoll, "Why CEOs Shouldn't Hang Around Too Long," *The Wall Street Journal*, Saturday–Sunday, October 6–7, 2018, p. B6; F. Bruni, "The Perverse Servility of Bill Barr," *The New York Times*, December 10, 2019, www.nytimes.com/2019/12/10/opinion/william-barr-trump.html; L. Kislik, "Managing an Employee Who Wants to Impress You All the Time," *Harvard Business Review*, September 13, 2019, https://hbr.org/2019/09/managing-an-employee-who-wants-to-impress-you-all-the-time; C. Joseph, "Congressional Retirement Tracker 2020: House Republicans Head for the Exits," *Vice News*, December 4, 2019, www.vice.com/en_us/article/j5yp37/republican-greg-walden-quits-congressional-retirement-tracker-for-2020; E. Dias and J. Peters, "Evangelical Leaders Close Ranks After Scathing Editorial," *The New York Times*, December 20, 2019, www.nytimes.com/2019/12/20/us/politics/christianity-today-trump-evangelicals.html; and J. Martin and M. Haberman, "Fear and Loyalty: How Donald Trump Took Over the Republican Party," *The New York Times*, December 22, 2019, www.nytimes.com/2019/12/21/us/politics/trump-impeachment-republicans.html.

Because brown-nosers will not bring up bad news, put everything in a positive light, never raise objections to bad decisions, and are reluctant to make decisions, teams and organizations consisting of high percentages of brown-nosers are highly dependent on their leaders to be successful. Leaders can do several things to convert brown-nosers into self-starters, however, and perhaps the first step is to understand that fear of failure is the underlying psychological issue driving brown-noser behavior. Often brown-nosers have all the experience and technical expertise needed to resolve issues, but they do not want to get caught making "dumb mistakes" and lack the self-confidence needed to raise objections or make decisions. Therefore, leaders wanting to convert brown-nosers need to focus their coaching efforts on boosting self-confidence rather than the technical expertise of these individuals. Whenever brown-nosers come forward with problems, leaders need to ask them how they think these problems should be resolved; putting the onus of problem resolution back on this type boosts both their critical-thinking skills and their self-confidence. Whenever practical, leaders need to support the solutions offered, provide reassurance, resist stepping in when solutions are not working out as planned, and periodically ask these individuals what they are learning by implementing their own solutions. Brown-nosers will have made the transition to self-starters when they openly point out both the advantages and disadvantages of various solutions to problems leaders are facing.

Bruce and Peter in the figure are slackers—they do not exert much effort toward work, believe they are entitled to a paycheck for just showing up, and that it is management's job to solve problems. Slackers are clever at avoiding work and are stealth employees: they often disappear for hours on end, make it a practice to look busy but get little done, have many excuses for not getting projects accomplished, and spend more time devising ways to avoid completing tasks then they would just getting them done. Slackers are content to spend entire days surfing the Internet, shopping online, chatting with coworkers, or taking breaks rather than being productive at work. Nonetheless, slackers want to stay off their boss's radar screens, so they often do just enough to stay out of trouble but never more than their peers.

Transforming slackers into self-starters can be challenging because leaders need to improve both the engagement and critical-thinking skills of these individuals. Many leaders mistakenly believe slackers have no motivation; but it turns out that slackers have plenty of motivation that is directed toward activity unrelated to work. This type of follower can spend countless hours on video games, riding motorcycles, fishing, side businesses, or other hobbies, and if you ask them about their hobbies, their passion shows. Slackers work to live rather than live to work and tend to see work as a means of paying for their other pursuits. Thus the underlying psychological driver for slackers is motivation for work; leaders need to find ways to get these individuals focused on and exerting considerably more effort toward job activities. One way to improve work motivation is to assign tasks that are more in line with these followers' hobbies. For example, assigning research projects to followers who enjoy surfing the Internet might be a way to improve work motivation. Improving job fit is another way to improve motivation for work. Many times followers lack motivation because they are in the wrong jobs, and assigning them to other positions within teams or organizations that are a better fit with the things they are interested in can improve both the engagement and critical-thinking skills of these individuals.

At the end of the day the work still has to get done, and many times the leader does not have the flexibility to assign preferred tasks or new jobs to these individuals (or would not want to reward them for substandard efforts). In this case leaders need to set unambiguous objectives and provide constant feedback on work performance, and then gradually increase performance standards and ask for more input on solutions to problems. Because slackers dislike attention, telling these individuals they have a choice of either performing at higher levels or becoming the focus of their leaders' undivided attention can help improve their work motivation and productivity. Leaders should have no doubt, however, that converting slackers to self-starters is difficult and time consuming. It may be easier to replace slackers with individuals who have the potential to become self-starters than to spend time on these conversion efforts.

The last of the four types, criticizers, are followers who are disengaged from work yet possess strong critical-thinking skills. But rather than directing their problem identification and resolution skills toward work-related issues, criticizers are instead motivated to find fault in anything their leaders or organizations do. Criticizers make it a point of telling coworkers what their leaders are doing wrong, how any change efforts are doomed to failure, how bad their organizations are compared to competitors, and how management shoots down any suggestions for improvement.[38] Criticizers are the most dangerous of the four types because they believe it is their personal mission to create converts. They are often the first to greet new employees and "tell them how things really work around here." And because misery loves company, they tend to hang out with other criticizers. Effectively managing teams and organizations with criticizers can be among the most difficult challenges leaders face.

Because they are motivated to create converts, criticizers are like an organizational cancer. And like many cancers, criticizers respond best to aggressive treatments. Leaders need to understand that the need for recognition is the key psychological driver underlying criticizer behavior. At one time criticizers were self-starters who got their recognition needs satisfied through their work accomplishments. But for some reason they were not awarded a promotion they felt they deserved, an organizational restructuring took away some of their prestige and authority, or they worked for a boss who felt threatened by their problem-solving skills. Criticizers act out because they crave recognition, and leaders can begin the reconversion to self-starters by finding opportunities to publicly recognize these individuals. As stated earlier, criticizers are good at pointing out how decisions or change initiatives are doomed to failure. When criticizers openly raise objections, leaders need to thank them for their inputs and then ask how they think these issues should be resolved. Most criticizers may initially resist offering solutions because they have drawers full of solutions that were ignored in the past and may be reluctant to share their problem-solving expertise in public. Leaders need to break through this resistance and may need to press criticizers for help. And once criticizers offer solutions that leaders can live with, leaders need to adopt these solutions and publicly thank criticizers for their efforts. Repeating this pattern of soliciting solutions, adopting suggestions, and publicly recognizing criticizers for their efforts will go a long way toward converting this group into self-starters. If leaders make repeated attempts to engage criticizers but they fail to respond, termination is a viable option for this type. For example, former U.S. president Barack Obama fired the commander of all U.S. and NATO forces in Afghanistan, Stanley McChrystal, when the general publicly criticized the administration in a *Rolling Stone* article.[39, 40] Because of criticizers' need to create similar-minded coworkers, leaders who do not aggressively deal with these individuals may eventually find themselves leading teams made up of nothing but criticizers. In these situations it may be the leaders who are asked to look for another job rather than the one or two criticizers they failed to deal with properly.

Sick of all the Bull—t

HIGHLIGHT PART 3.2

Criticizers are some of an organizations most disgruntled employees, and usually bad leadership is largely to blame for making this happen. Most of the time criticizers stay out of the limelight and voice their disappointment with leaders and organizations when meeting with like-minded colleagues, but once in a while they go public with their discontent. Jackson Racicot worked at an Edmonton Walmart for 18 months before he got so fed up with how he was being led that he turned in a resignation letter. But this was not before he got on the store's public address system, where he railed at the leadership at the store and how poorly Walmart treats employees across all of Canada. In his opening Racicot stated, "Attention all shoppers, associates, and management. I would like to say, to all of you today, that nobody should ever work here. Ever."

What would you do if you watched the video and were the district manager overseeing all the Walmart stores in Edmonton? How would you prevent criticizers from happening at your stores?

Source: K. Fida, "Sick of all the Bulls—t: Grande Prairie Teen's Video Quitting His Job at Walmart Goes Viral," *StarMetro Edmonton*, December 8, 2018, www.thestar.com/edmonton/2018/12/08/sick-of-all-the-bullshit-grand-prairie-teens-quitting-video-from-walmart-goes-viral.html.

Only the guy who isn't rowing has time to rock the boat.

Jean-Paul Sartre, French philosopher

Like the Potter and Rosenbach followership model, the Curphy and Roellig followership model has several aspects that are worth additional comment. First, the model can help leaders assess follower types and determine the best ways to motivate direct reports. Second, leaders need to understand that followership types are not static; they change depending on the situation. The following diagram depicts how a person's followership type changed as she switched jobs, inherited different bosses, was given different responsibilities, and so on. This particular individual started her professional career as a brown-noser, moved up to become a self-starter, spent some time as a criticizer, and is now a slacker. When asked why their followership type changed over time, most people say their immediate boss was the biggest factor in these changes. Thus leaders have a direct impact on effective followership—either by selecting direct reports with self-starter potential or developing direct reports into self-starters.

Curphy and Roellig Followership Journey Line

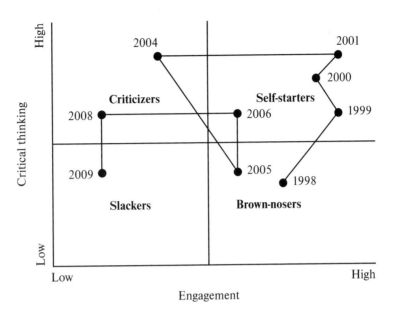

Third, it is not unusual for followers to start careers or new jobs as brown-nosers. New employees need time to learn the job before they feel comfortable making suggestions for improvement. The question for leaders is whether they take deliberate action to convert brown-nosers into self-starters. Fourth, organizations having decent selection processes are more likely to hire brown-nosers and self-starters than criticizers and slackers. Additional research has shown the longer people stay in organizations, the more likely they will be criticizers. Over time people learn how to develop critical-thinking skills about their functional expertise, and it is usually only a matter of time before these finely honed skills are trained on leaders, teams, and organizations.[41, 42] It only takes one bad apple to disrupt a team, so leaders need to aggressively deal with slackers and criticizers if they want to build high-performing teams. At the other extreme, teams and organizations populated with criticizers and slackers need to take a hard look at their leadership. The criticizer and slacker followership types may be ways that direct reports cope with clueless bosses.[43]

Fifth, because people in positions of authority also play followership roles, they need to realize how their own followership type affects how they lead others. For example, leaders who are self-starters are likely to set high expectations, reward others for taking initiative, and give top performers plenty of latitude and needed resources. Leaders who are brown-nosers will squelch objections and demand that direct reports check in constantly. They will also expect their employees to be loyal, do what they are told, and not make waves. Leaders who are slackers are laissez-faire leaders who are disengaged from work, are always unavailable and unresponsive to followers' requests, and lead teams that get little accomplished. Leaders who are criticizers will complain not only about their organizations but also about their employees. As such, these leaders tend to manage by exception and find fault in everything their followers do.

We started **Part 3** by stating that followers play an important role in team and organizational performance. We hope that some of the main research findings and questions about followership described in this section will prompt readers to give more thought to effective followership. The next four chapters will explore the topic of followers in considerably more detail. Individual followers differ in all the ways that individual leaders differ, but different things happen when groups of followers have to work together to get things done.

Leaders wanting to build winning teams need to be aware of the roles of employee motivation, engagement, and satisfaction and group dynamics play in team performance.

Followership and Confirmation Bias

HIGHLIGHT PART 3.3

An interesting aspect of followership concerns **confirmation bias**, which is the tendency for people to believe only information that confirms their beliefs. This bias was prevalent during the impeachment proceedings for Donald Trump in late 2019. Democrats believed Trump wanted Ukraine to investigate a political rival and withheld aid as leverage. They also asserted that Trump obstructed justice by blocking the testimony of key aides. Trump supporters believed that the impeachment hearings and trial was nothing more than a witch hunt to get Trump out of office before the 2020 election. The quid pro quo linking Ukraine aid and political favors did not happen, and the President was not obstructing justice but invoking executive privilege by blocking his staff from testifying. When presented with stories or data countering their beliefs, fervent followers on either side of the political aisle quickly dismissed this information as "alternative facts" and "fake news." The more counter-information was shared, the more readily it was dismissed and hardened peoples' positions.

This leads to an interesting notion about followership: Once followers come to the conclusion that their leader is effective, ineffective, or only out for himself or herself, it may be difficult for leaders to change these beliefs. Leaders who truly are effective and have followers who believe the same can do no wrong, as followers will readily overlook bad decisions or personal failings and acknowledge only the good things these leaders are accomplishing. The same is true for selfish or ineffective leaders; no matter

what he or she does to demonstrate effectiveness, it is likely to be attributed to luck or situational factors rather than personal choices. This gets back to the concept of reputation, described in **Chapter 6**, and the importance of establishing a good reputation when first moving into leadership roles. Effective leaders not only need to engage employees, build teams, and get things done; they also need to actively manage their image so that followers come to see that they are effective leaders. Those wanting to change followers' perceptions of their leadership effectiveness need to understand that it will take considerable time, effort, and focus to make this happen. A leader may be doing all the right things to change his or her reputation, but just one bad decision or action is all that is needed to confirm followers' beliefs that the leader is self-serving or ineffective.

Confirmation bias also comes into play with leaders' perceptions of followers. Self-starters and brown-nosers may be seen as doing no wrong despite evidence to the contrary, and followers perceived as criticizers or slackers may find it difficult to get their leaders to see them differently. In these situations it may be easier for followers to change their reputations by switching jobs or waiting until a new leader takes over the team.

Sources: K. Cherry, "How Confirmation Bias Works," *Very Well Mind*, February 19, 2020, www.verywell.com/what-is-a-confirmation-bias-2795024; S. Heshmat, "What Is Confirmation Bias?" *Psychology Today*, April 23, 2015, www.psychologytoday.com/blog/science-choice/201504/what-is-confirmation-bias; and M. Boot, "Impeachment Isn't Democrats vs. Republicans. It's Right vs. Wrong," *The Washington Post*, December 18, 2019, www.washingtonpost.com/opinions/2019/12/18/impeachment-isnt-democrats-vs-republicans-its-right-vs-wrong.

CHAPTER 9

Follower Motivation

Introduction

> *Polls estimate that if companies could get 3.7 percent more work out of each employee, the equivalent of 18 more minutes of work for each eight-hour shift, the gross domestic product in the U.S. would swell by $355 billion, twice the total GDP of Greece.*

The Gallup Organization

> *Hardly a competent workman can be found in a large establishment who does not devote a considerable amount of his time to studying just how slow he can work and still convince his employer that he is going at a good pace.*

Frederick W. Taylor, industrial engineer

Why do followers join some teams but not others? How do you get followers to exhibit enough of the critical behaviors needed for the team to succeed? And why are some leaders capable of getting followers to go above and beyond the call of duty? The ability to motivate others is a fundamental leadership skill and has strong connections to building cohesive, goal-oriented teams and getting results through others. The importance of follower motivation is suggested in findings that most people believe they could give as much as 15 percent or 20 percent more effort at work than they now do with no one, including their own bosses, recognizing any difference. Perhaps even more startling, these workers also believed they could give 15 percent or 20 percent *less* effort with no one noticing any difference. Moreover, variation in work output varies significantly across leaders and followers. The top 15 percent of workers in any particular job may produce 20 to 50 percent more output than the average worker, depending on the complexity of the job. Put another way, the best computer programmers or salesclerks might write up to 50 percent more programs or process 50 percent more customer orders.[1, 2, 3] Might better methods of motivating workers lead to higher productivity from *all* workers? Is motivating an individual follower different from motivating a group of followers? Are more motivated workers happier or more satisfied and engaged workers? Does money increase productivity and satisfaction, or can leaders do other things to increase the motivation and performance levels of their followers? For example, the U.S. Army has paid over $1 billion in annual retention bonuses.[4] Is this money well spent?

Creating highly motivated followers depends mostly on understanding others. Therefore, whereas motivation is an essential part of leadership, it is appropriate to include it in this part of the book, which focuses on followers. As an overview, this chapter addresses three key areas. First, we will examine the links among leadership, motivation, satisfaction, engagement, performance, and effectiveness—six closely related topics. Second, we will review some major theories and approaches to motivation, performance, and effectiveness. Third, and perhaps most important, we will discuss what leaders can do to enhance the motivation and performance of their followers and effectiveness of their teams if they implement these different techniques. Because of the depth and breadth of these follower-oriented topics, a more in-depth discussion of employee satisfaction and engagement can be found in **Chapter 10**, and **Chapter 11** reviews what we know about follower performance, effectiveness, and potential.

Defining Motivation, Satisfaction, Engagement, Performance, and Effectiveness

Motivation, satisfaction, engagement, performance, and effectiveness are clearly related. For example, Elon Musk spent only two days in the applied physics doctoral program at Stanford University before dropping out to pursue his entrepreneurial dreams. Musk could have stayed in the PhD program but was *motivated* to instead develop Internet, automotive, renewable energy, and space-oriented businesses. He was fully absorbed by and *engaged* in launching and growing these businesses and had to *perform* a number of behaviors related to obtaining funding, developing products, getting regulatory approvals, determining the right sales and business models, and the like. The *effectiveness* of these behaviors can be determined by reviewing the market share, number of cars sold, revenues, customer satisfaction, or other results associated with the companies he created—PayPal, Tesla, and SpaceX. We can also infer he was happier or more *satisfied* launching and running these businesses than he would have been obtaining his PhD.

Figure 9.1 provides an overview of the general relationships among leadership, motivation, satisfaction, engagement, performance, and effectiveness. As we can see, some leadership behaviors, such as building relationships or consideration (**Chapter 7**) result in more satisfied and engaged followers. These followers are less likely to leave the organization and more apt to help coworkers get things done (organizational citizenship behaviors), whereas unhappy and disengaged followers may not show up for work or could exhibit bad attitudes toward customers. Other leadership behaviors, such as setting goals, providing needed resources and feedback, and rewarding performance (initiating structure from **Chapter 7**) appear to increase follower engagement and performance levels. These leader behaviors let followers know what they need to do and how they need to change the frequency or delivery of the behaviors they are exhibiting toward customers and coworkers. Finally, team or unit effectiveness is the impact of these aggregated follower behaviors. Good examples here would be team win and loss records, monthly sales results for different Starbucks stores, or the election results for campaign teams.

As described in the opening to Part 3 and the introduction to this chapter, there is good research to support this causal chain.[5] Leadership behavior clearly has an impact on follower satisfaction and engagement levels, as effective leaders tend to engender loyalty and a strong work ethic, whereas disgruntled employees are the hallmark of ineffective leaders. Employee attitudes and behaviors have a direct impact on customer service, loyalty, and spending habits, and the aggregation of these customer results ultimately determine whether businesses survive or thrive. And individuals with higher performance and teams with higher effectiveness levels achieve more rewards, which further increase follower satisfaction, engagement, and performance.[6, 7] Thus, the leader's ability to motivate followers is vitally important to both the morale and effectiveness of the work group. However, the leader's use of motivational techniques is not the only factor affecting team effectiveness. Selecting the right people for the team, correctly using power and influence tactics, being seen as ethical and credible, possessing the right personality traits and high levels of intelligence, acquiring the necessary resources, and developing follower skills are other leadership factors affecting a group's ability to accomplish its goals. Finally, there is one other aspect of **Figure 9.1** that is worth noting: *Leaders rarely have a direct impact on customer satisfaction or unit or team effectiveness.* Just as athletic coaches are on the sidelines while their teams play games, organizational leaders typically are not doing the work of their employees. They are not writing code, making sales calls, dealing with customer inquiries, assembling equipment, and similar tasks—these behaviors are the primary responsibilities of their direct reports. Leaders may do some portion of these activities, but followers are the ones doing most of this work. Assembling the right team, keeping followers engaged, and ensuring everyone knows their roles and is exhibiting the right behaviors are critical for leaders who want to win (that is, be effective).

Most people probably think of motivation as dealing with choices about what we do and how much effort we put into doing it. Most researchers define **motivation** as anything that provides *direction, intensity,* and *persistence* to behavior.[8, 9, 10, 11] Thus, motivation comes into play whenever someone chooses an activity or task to engage in, puts forth a certain level of effort toward this activity, and persists with this effort for some time. Like personality traits, motivation is not directly observable; it must be inferred from behavior. We would infer that one person is highly motivated to do well in school if she spent a lot of time studying for exams. She could choose to spend her time and energy on socializing, intramurals, or volunteer work, but because she is spending time outlining readings and reviewing class notes, we say she is motivated to do well in school. At work, if one person regularly assembles twice as many iPads as any other person in his work group—assuming all have the same abilities, skills, and resources—then we likely would say this first person is more motivated than the others. We use the concept of motivation to explain differences we see among people in the energy and direction of their behavior. Thus the energy and effort J. J. Abrams expended directing *The Rise of Sky-*

FIGURE 9.1   Relationships among Leadership, Satisfaction, Engagement, Performance, and Effectiveness

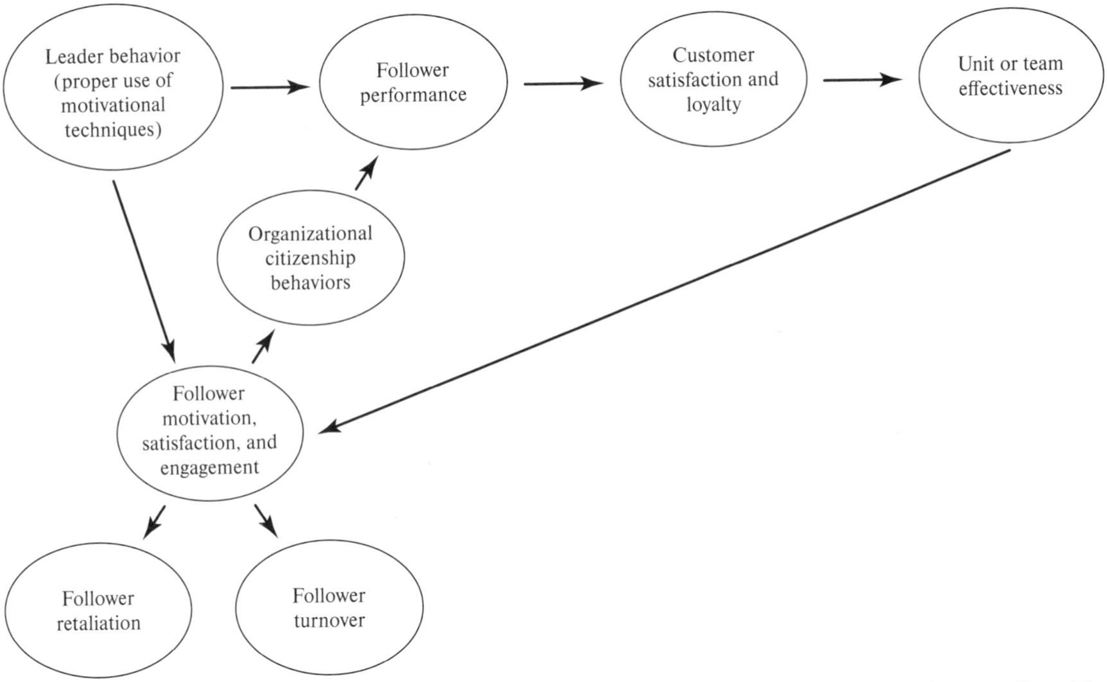

Sources: M. A. Huselid, "The Impact of Human Resource Management Practices on Turnover, Productivity, and Corporate Financial Performance," *Academy of Management Journal* 38, no. 4 (1995), pp. 635–72; T. Butorac, Recruitment and Retention: The Keys to Profitability at Carlson Companies, presentation given at Personnel Decisions International, Minneapolis, MN, June 11, 2001; D. J. Koys, "The Effects of Employee Satisfaction, Organizational Citizenship Behavior, and Turnover on Organizational Effectiveness: A Unit-Level, Longitudinal Study," *Personnel Psychology* 54, no. 1 (2001), pp. 101–14; J. Husserl, "Allied's Organizational Life Cycle," *Management Education & Development* 24, no. 3 (1998), p. 8; Sirota Consulting, Establishing the Linkages between Employee Attitudes, Customer Attitudes, and Bottom-Line Results (Chicago, IL: Author, 1998); D. S. Pugh, J. Dietz, J. W. Wiley, and S. M. Brooks, "Driving Service Effectiveness through Employee–Customer Linkages," *Academy of Management Executive* 16, no. 4 (2002), pp. 73–84; and B. Schneider, P. J. Hanges, D. B. Smith, and A. N. Salvaggio, "Which Comes First: Employee Attitudes or Organizational, Financial and Market Performance?" *Journal of Applied Psychology* 88, no. 5 (2003), pp. 836–51.

walker or the government of North Korea spends developing its missile and nuclear capabilities would be examples of the direction, intensity, and persistence components of motivation.

> *A company is always perfectly designed to produce what it is producing. If it has quality problems, cost problems, or productivity problems, then the behaviors associated with these outcomes are being reinforced. This is not conjecture. This is the cold, hard reality of human behavior.*
>
> **Anonymous**

Performance, by contrast, concerns behaviors directed toward the organization's mission or goals or the products and services resulting from those behaviors. At work or school we can choose to perform a wide variety of behaviors, but performance would include only those behaviors related to the production of goods or services or obtaining good grades. Performance differs from **effectiveness**, which generally involves making judgments about the adequacy of behavior with respect to certain criteria such as work group or organizational goals. In other words, is the leader's group, unit, or team achieving its overall goals, making an impact, or winning? Barry Jenkins spent several years creating the movie *Moonlight*. The behaviors he exhibited in getting the film made constitute performance; the revenues generated and Academy Awards won by the movie indicate his effectiveness as a movie director. However, performance and effectiveness are both affected by a variety of factors. Intelligence, skill, and the availability of key resources can affect a follower's behavior in accomplishing organizational goals (that is, performance) independently of that person's level of motivation. Likewise, market conditions, competitive products and services, government regulations, disruptive technology, bad press, and changing consumer preferences can affect team effectiveness. *Thus an adequate level of motivation may be a necessary but insufficient condition for performance and effectiveness.*

> *There is one virtue to the 35-hour workweek. It is one of the few French ideals that we don't need to worry about copyrighting. Nobody else wants it.*
>
> **Nicolas Sarkozy, French president, 2007-2012**

Job satisfaction is not how *hard* one works or how *well* one works, but rather how much one *likes* a specific kind of job or work activity. Job satisfaction deals with one's attitudes or feelings about the job itself, pay, promotion or educational opportunities, supervision, coworkers, workload, and so on.[12, 13, 14] Various polls over the past half-century have consistently shown that a majority of men and women report liking their jobs.[15, 16, 17, 18, 19] Research has also shown that people who are more satisfied with their jobs are more likely to engage in **organizational citizenship behaviors**—behaviors not directly related to one's job but helpful to others at work. Organizational citizenship behaviors create a more supportive workplace. Examples might include volunteering to help another employee with a task or project or filling in for another employee when asked. Happier workers tend to be more helpful workers.[20, 21, 22, 23, 24, 25, 26]

Over the past 15 years or so, employee **engagement** has replaced job satisfaction as the most important attitude in the workplace. Whereas job satisfaction is the extent to which people enjoy coming to work or are happy with their pay and benefits, employee engagement is the extent to which people are absorbed with, committed to, and enthusiastic about their assigned work tasks. Being happy about one's job is one thing; exerting the effort needed to perform these tasks and do them exceptionally well is another. Engagement has elements of job satisfaction and motivation, as unhappy and unmotivated employees are unlikely to do assigned work activities whereas satisfied and motivated employees allocate the time and exert the effort needed to complete assigned work activities. Seen in this light, employee engagement is a form of productivity, as highly engaged employees spend higher percentages of time performing work activities and disengaged employees will spend most of their time devising ways to avoid work.

Although people generally like the work they do, major events have caused changes in job satisfaction and engagement levels among employees in the United States. From roughly 2002 to 2007 the United States enjoyed strong economic growth, and companies rapidly expanded the products and services they provided. Because it took time to hire and train employees to meet increased demand, those already employed had to cope with larger workloads. This period also saw a tremendous amount of consolidation (companies buying one another) and reorganization (restructuring functions, processes, and personnel) to better meet increased demand. Change was an overarching theme from 2002 to 2007, and leaders and followers were continually devising new ways to deliver products and services to customers. This continuing cycle of consolidation, reorganization, and change made it difficult for employees to develop any loyalty for their organizations—they never knew if their work unit was going to be sold or merged with another work unit. This period, perhaps more than most, broke the implicit contract between employers and employees. Before 2002, many employees felt that if they worked hard they could spend their entire careers at a single company. But after all the acquisitions, downsizings, and restructurings, many employees developed more of a mercenary attitude toward employers. If they worked for a company that did not treat them well, had a bad boss, or did not get the pay or promotions they felt they deserved, they would find a position with another employer. And with the economy enjoying strong growth, there were plenty of opportunities for people to find other employment.

Although people were working longer hours and coping with more change than ever before, most people found 2002 to 2007 to be a cakewalk compared to what they experienced during the economic recession of 2007 to 2009. The global recession caused companies to freeze hiring and training programs and lay off record numbers of employees. The unemployment rate in the United States increased from 5 percent to over 10 percent, and many people went months or even years without finding meaningful work. Those lucky enough to remain employed wound up doing more than they did before with fewer resources and lower pay. Employees generally felt lucky to have a job and were not apt to complain (for fear of losing their jobs), but many were frustrated with their employers. This increased workload, sense of frustration, and employment uncertainty cut job satisfaction and employee engagement to record lows. With improvements in the global economy and technological advances over the past 10 years, employees are finding they have many more employment options than they had before. Some are opting to become self-employed contractors working from home in the gig economy, others have started their own companies or are working for small start-ups, and others are moving to organizations that provide more engaging work or better promotion possibilities. People are an organization's most important asset, as those with the most skilled and engaged employees are more likely to deliver the best results. Employees are likely to vote with their feet if treated poorly, and companies can ill-afford to lose their best and brightest people and are now bending over backward to retain their high performers. Beautiful corporate campuses, well-appointed offices, flexible work hours, the ability to work from home, wellness programs, corporate day care facilities, high-potential programs, and many other employee perks are all intended to help companies attract and retain the right people.[27, 28, 29, 30]

> *People who have jobs, rather than careers, worry about work–life balance because they are unable to have fun at work.*
>
> **Tomas Chamorro-Premuzic, consultant**

Today many leaders face the dual challenges of having to achieve increasingly difficult team goals while having fewer followers available to do the work. The best leaders and organizations understand that one way to meet these challenges is to recruit, develop, and retain top leadership and technical talent. Savvy companies that spend considerably more time and effort attracting, developing, and retaining the best people often report superior financial results.[31, 32, 33, 34, 35, 36, 37, 38, 39, 40, 41, 42] For example, many of the organizations appearing in *Fortune* magazine's "The 100 Best Companies to Work For" also do well when compared to the S&P 500 Index. *The best leaders may be those who can motivate workers to perform at a high level while maintaining an equally high level of employee engagement and job satisfaction.* See **Highlight 9.1** for a discussion of productivity and job satisfaction.

Motivation, Productivity, and Satisfaction across the Globe

HIGHLIGHT 9.1

The global recession of 2007–2009 caused U.S. and European businesses to downsize considerably, but since then many have been able to maintain customer satisfaction and revenue levels with fewer employees. In terms of the number of hours worked, the average U.S. employee works 137 hours per year more than the typical Japanese employee, 260 hours more per year compared to the average British employee, and 499 hours more than the average French employee. In other words, over a 40-year work career, U.S. employees will work the equivalent of 10 more years than the average French employee. The work ethic of the French has been mocked by outsiders for years and is seen as a significant barrier to the country's ability to compete in the global marketplace. U.S. companies are noted for having some of the highest productivity in the world, but might there also be a downside to these high productivity levels?

Research has shown that some of the risks associated with longer workweeks include job dissatisfaction, lower employee engagement, and distressed family and social relationships. Interestingly enough, there appears to be little relationship between work hours and physical health, and other research by Chamorro-Premuzic shows that workaholics have higher social status, high achievers live longer, and the 10 most workaholic nations produce most of the world's gross domestic product. Chamorro-Premuzic argues that many employees have become self-indulgent, pampered, and so enthralled with the pursuit of well-being that they have forgotten the value of hard work and achievement. He believes the pursuit of work–life balance is a myth perpetrated by positive psychologists and self-help gurus trying to make people feel good about their failures and inability to achieve things. People who put in long hours and hate their jobs are likely to suffer all the negative effects identified earlier. Those who are engaged, have fun at work, and view their current positions as part of a career path versus a job do not suffer these ill effects and end up being much more successful.

Do you think that workers today are not as motivated or achievement oriented as those in the past? Is there such a thing as work–life balance? Is working longer hours a good or bad thing?

Sources: J. M. Brett and L. K. Stroh, "Working 61 Plus Hours a Week: Why Do Managers Do It?" *Journal of Applied Psychology* 88, no. 1 (2003), pp. 67–78; "Schumpeter: Overstretched," *The Economist*, May 22, 2010, p. 72; "Schumpeter: The French Way of Work," *The Economist*, November 19, 2011, p. 71; H. Schachter, "Get Over It: There Is No Work–Life Balance, Just Work," *The Globe and Mail*, February 28, 2013; T. Chamorro-Premuzic, "Embrace Work-Life Imbalance," *Harvard Business Review*, February 12, 2013, https://hbr.org/2013/02/embrace-work-life-imbalan; and D. Ganster, C. Rosen, and G. Fisher, "Working Long Hours and Well-Being: What We Know, What We Not Know, and What We Need to Know," *Journal of Business Psychology* 33, no. 1 (2018), pp. 25–39.

Having now defined motivation, satisfaction, engagement, performance, and effectiveness, we can explore their relationships a bit further. We have already noted how motivation does not always ensure follower performance or team effectiveness. If followers lack the necessary skills or resources to accomplish a group task, then trying to motivate them more could be unproductive and even frustrating.[43, 44] For example, no high school basketball team is likely to defeat the Golden State Warriors, however motivated the players may be. The players on the high school team simply lack the abilities and skills of the Warriors players. Higher motivation will usually affect performance only if followers already have the abilities, skills, and resources to get the job done. Motivating others is an important part of leadership, but not all of it; pep talks and rewards are not always enough.

> *Always bear in mind that your resolution to succeed is more important than any other one thing.*

Abraham Lincoln, U.S. president, 1861-1865

The relationships between motivation, satisfaction, and engagement are more straightforward; in fact many theories of motivation are also theories of job satisfaction and employee engagement. The implicit link between satisfaction, engagement, and motivation is that satisfaction and engagement increase when people accomplish a task, particularly when the task requires a lot of effort. It might also seem logical that *performance* must be higher among more satisfied workers, but this is not always so.[45, 46, 47, 48, 49] Although satisfaction and performance are correlated, happy workers are not always the most productive ones; nor are unhappy or dissatisfied workers always the poorest performers. It is possible, for example, for poorly performing workers to be fairly satisfied with their jobs (maybe because they are paid well but do not have to work hard). It is also possible for dissatisfied workers to be relatively high performers (they may have a strong work ethic, have no other employment options, or be trying to improve the chances of getting out of their current job). Despite the intuitive appeal of believing that satisfied workers usually perform better, satisfaction has only an indirect effect on performance. It was precisely because the link between job satisfaction and performance was so tenuous that researchers began asking whether other employee attitudes were better predictors of job performance. Researchers then discovered that employee engagement, rather than job satisfaction, had strong relationships with job performance and team or unit effectiveness. Job satisfaction and employee engagement will be described in more detail in **Chapter 10**, and an example of a highly engaged, high-performing, and effective leader can be found in **Profiles in Leadership 9.1**. Nevertheless, having both satisfied *and* high-performing followers is a goal leaders should usually strive to achieve.

Ping Fu

PROFILES IN LEADERSHIP 9.1

Ping Fu is the Chinese-born cofounder and former CEO of Geomagic, a company that provides 3D imaging used in engineering, art, archeology, metrology, and biomechanical product design. Geomagic's technology is used in the creation of customized prosthetic limbs, and if you wore braces growing up, they may have been designed with the help of Geomagic technology.

Ping Fu's journey to becoming a corporate CEO is far from typical. She grew up in Shanghai in the home of two well-educated parents. At the age of eight she was listed as a "black" citizen—someone who had to atone for the greed and corruption committed by her parents and ancestors when Mao's cultural revolution swept the country. She spent the next years separated from her parents, working 14-hour days in a factory, foraging for scraps, and tending to her little sister between shifts. When the Cultural Revolution ended, she enrolled in school and eventually wrote her dissertation on China's one-child policy, where she found that the government's use of brutal enforcement techniques was causing shockingly high rates of infanticide. Her dissertation was leaked to the press, and its wide publication was a major embarrassment to the Chinese government. In 1984 China quietly deported Ping Fu to the United States.

Ping Fu learned English and computer programming while working as a babysitter, maid, and waitress. She eventually landed a job with the National Center for Supercomputing Applications (NCSA), where she worked on earthquake prediction modeling and 3D imaging. In 1997 she made a New Year's resolution to "create something of value" and left the NCSA to start up Geomagic. In early 2013 she sold the company to 3D Systems, a 3D printing company, for $55 million.

What theory or theories of motivation best explain Ping Fu's journey to CEO?

Sources: P. Fu, *Bend, Not Break* (New York: Penguin Group, 2012); "An Executive Memoir: The World Is 3D," *The Economist*, January 12, 2013, p. 72; and M. Kirkpatrick, "The Art of Resilience," *The Wall Street Journal*, January 9, 2013, p. A11.

Understanding and Influencing Follower Motivation

What do leaders do to motivate followers to accomplish group goals? Are all leaders and followers motivated the same way? Is there a universal theory of motivation? In other words, do Vladmir Putin, Ginni Rometty, Ben Carson, or Bill Belichick use the same or different techniques to motivate their followers? As described in **Highlight 9.2**, organizations spend billions on motivating employees; but do these interventions actually improve job satisfaction, retention, and performance? Research can answer these questions, and few topics of human behavior have been the subject of so much attention as that of motivation. So much has been written about motivation that a comprehensive review of the subject is beyond the scope of this book. We will, however, survey several major approaches to understanding follower motivation, as well as address the implications of these approaches for follower satisfaction and performance. These motivational theories and approaches give leaders a number of suggestions to get followers to engage in and persist with different behaviors. However, some motivational theories are particularly useful in certain situations but not as applicable in others. Just as a carpenter can build better wooden structures or furniture by having a larger set of tools, so can leaders solve a greater number of motivational problems among followers by becoming familiar with different motivational theories and approaches. People who have only hammers in their tool kits are likely to see every problem as a nail needing hammering, and it is not unusual for less effective leaders to call on a limited number of approaches to any motivational problem. *Leaders who know about different motivational theories are more likely to choose the right theory for a particular follower and situation, and often have higher-performing and more satisfied and engaged employees as a result.*

Organizations Spend Billions on Motivational Programs for Employees, and All They Get Are Burned Feet

HIGHLIGHT 9.2

Organizations are continually looking for quick fixes for their performance and effectiveness problems. The barriers to team or organizational performance often include a lack of resources and skills, unclear goals, poor performance or accountability standards, or incompe-

tent leadership. But rather than adopting methods to directly address these issues, many organizations instead have employees listen to motivational speakers or engage in whitewater rafting, bungee jumping, or firewalking events. The motivational speaking circuit includes former professional athletes, astronauts, fighter pilots, and military generals; successful and failed business leaders; politicians; psychologists; and consultants. Motivational speaking engagements can be lucrative—one of the authors worked with a speaker who gave one speech in Las Vegas at lunch and the same speech that evening in Minneapolis and made $150,000 for the day. The author also has worked with a group of ex–fighter pilots who do half-day "Business Is Combat" seminars for $30,000 to $75,000.

Companies think nothing of spending like this to motivate employees. For example, the software consulting firm EMC has spent $625,000 to have 5,000 employees walk over burning coals. But do expensive speakers and extreme activities actually improve organizational performance? Unfortunately, exhaustive research has shown virtually no link between motivational spending and company revenues, profitability, or market share. Perhaps the biggest problem is that employees may find it difficult to see the link between walking over a bed of hot coals or

participating in a Business Is Combat mission planning event and making another 20 sales calls every week. The problem is that these events do not address the root cause of many organizational woes but instead covertly shift the burden to "underperforming" employees. Other than bankrolling the motivation industry, these programs have another effect: Nine U.S. Air Force recruiters had to go to the emergency room after they received second- and third-degree burns on their feet after participating in one of these motivational programs.

Sources: D. Jones, "Firms Spend Billions to Fire Up Workers—With Little Luck," *USA Today*, May 10, 2001, pp. 1–2A; P. G. Chronis, "9 Burn Feet in National Guard Recruiters' Fire Walk," *Denver Post*, December 28, 1998, pp. 1A, 17A; G. J. Curphy and R. T. Hogan, "Managerial Incompetence: Is There a Dead Skunk on the Table?" working paper, 2004; and G. J. Curphy, M. J. Benson, A. Baldrica, and R. T. Hogan, *Managerial Incompetence*, unpublished manuscript, 2007.

The truth of the matter is that you always know the right thing to do. The hard part is doing it.

Norman Schwartzkopf, former U.S. Army general

Most performance problems can be attributed to unclear expectations, skill deficits, resource or equipment shortages, or a lack of motivation. Of these underlying causes, leaders seem to have the most difficulty in recognizing and rectifying motivation problems. An example might help to illustrate this point. A major airline was having serious problems with the customer service its flight attendants provided. Passenger complaints were on the rise, and airplane loading (the average number of people per flight) was decreasing. The perceived lack of customer service was beginning to cost the airline market share and revenues; to fix the problem it decided to have all 10,000 flight attendants go through a two-day customer service training program. Unfortunately, passenger complaints only got worse after the training. A thorough investigation of the underlying cause of the problem revealed that flight attendants knew what they were supposed to do, had all the skills necessary to perform the behaviors, and usually had the resources and equipment necessary to serve customers. The root cause was a lack of motivation to go the extra mile for customers. When asked what they found to be the most motivating aspect of being a flight attendant, most stated "time off." In other words, the flight attendants were most motivated when they were *not* at work. (Because of work schedules, flight attendants typically get two weeks off per month.) Given that a strong union represented the flight attendants, how would you go about solving this dilemma?

Your job is to figure out what you have to do in order to do what you want to do.

Jim Earley, consultant

As stated earlier, leaders can use many different theories and approaches to motivate followers. In this section we will discuss the key aspects of five popular and useful approaches to understanding motivation in work or leadership contexts. Some readers may wonder why these motivational approaches were included and others excluded, and sound arguments could be made for changing the motivational approaches described. Our intention is to provide a broad view of different motivational approaches and not be so comprehensive as to overwhelm readers. The five theories and approaches are listed in **Table 9.1**. For illustrative purposes, we will also discuss how leadership practitioners could apply these approaches to motivate two fictitious followers, Julie and Ling Ling. Julie is a 21-year-old ski lift operator in Banff, Alberta, Canada. Her primary job is to ensure that people get on and off her ski lift safely. She also does periodic equipment safety checks and maintains the lift lines and associated areas. Julie works from 8:30 a.m. to 5:00 p.m. five days a week, is paid a salary, and has a pass that allows her to ski for free whenever she is off work. Ling Ling is a 35-year-old real estate agent in Hong Kong. She works for an agency that locates and rents apartments for people on one-to three-year business assignments for various multinational companies. She works many evenings and weekends showing apartments, and she is paid a salary plus a commission for every apartment she rents. How the five approaches could be used to motivate Julie and Ling Ling will be discussed periodically throughout this section.

TABLE 9.1   **Five Motivational Approaches**

Theory or Approach	Major Themes of Characteristics
Motives or needs	Satisfy needs to change behavior
Achievement orientation	Possess certain personality traits
Goal setting	Set goals to change behavior
Operant approach	Change rewards and punishments to change behavior
Empowerment	Give people autonomy and latitude to increase their motivation for work

Motives: How Do Needs Affect Motivation?

One way to get followers to engage in and persist with the behaviors required to accomplish group goals is to appeal to their needs. **Needs** refer to internal states of tension or arousal, or uncomfortable states of deficiency that people are motivated to change. Hunger would be a good example of a need: People are motivated to eat when they get hungry. Other needs might include the need to live in a safe and secure place, to belong to a group with common interests or social ties, or to do interesting and challenging work. If these needs were not being met, people would choose to engage in and persist with certain behaviors until they were satisfied. According to this motivational approach, leadership practitioners can get followers to engage in and persist with certain behaviors by correctly identifying and fulfilling their needs.

Perhaps the most well-known needs theory is Maslow's hierarchy of needs.[50] Maslow posited that people were motivated by five basic needs, which include the need to survive physiologically, the need for security, the need for affiliation (that is, belongingness), the need for self-esteem, and the need for self-actualization. Although Maslow's theory provides some useful ideas on how to improve motivation, it has several limitations in that it does not make specific predictions on what an individual will do to satisfy a particular need.[51, 52] For example, someone driven to satisfy their need for affiliation may do so by joining a fitness club providing group spinning classes, volunteering at a homeless shelter, building a broader group of friends at work, or becoming more active on Facebook or LinkedIn. Moreover, for most (but not all) followers the needs for survival, security, and affiliation are largely satisfied, which means that leaders should focus more on helping followers satisfy their self-esteem and self-actualization needs if they want to boost motivation, performance, and effectiveness.

Drawing on the work of Maslow, Deci,[53] and Hackman and Oldham,[54] Daniel Pink described three fundamental needs that drive employees who create new products or services or perform complex, nonroutine work.[55] These needs include autonomy, mastery, and meaning. **Autonomy** is concerned primarily with making choices: Do followers have the freedom to work on things they find interesting, or are they given the latitude to get things done in ways that make sense to them? For example, some software companies allow workers to take one day off a month to work on any app or business problem they like. The only requirement is that after their day off, they show their work to their colleagues for suggestions and feedback. Other examples of autonomy in the workplace include flexible work hours, allowing employees to work at home or bring their pets to work, or letting sales representatives pick the customers they will pursue in an assigned geographic territory. Autonomy is a key factor in the gig economy, as the freedom to set one's own hours and be your own boss may be the primary motivator of Uber and Lyft drivers.[56]

> *Some players you pat their butts, other players you kick their butts, and some players you leave alone.*
>
> **Pete Rose, former professional baseball player**

Mastery is concerned with helping followers develop those skills that will enable them to perform at higher levels. This means that leaders need to set clear expectations for job performance, assess the capabilities of followers to meet these expectations, and then provide the support, coaching, and training needed to acquire and improve critical skills.[57] One critical aspect of mastery is providing followers with feedback on skill development or task progress.[58] The more followers can see that they are making progress, the more they will stay motivated to keep developing skills or do those activities associated with task accomplishment. **Meaning** is the notion of doing something that matters, having an impact, or being a part of something bigger than oneself.[59] Many knowledge workers want to work on things that make a difference, so one of the critical responsibilities of leaders is pointing out how the tasks and activities performed by followers help customers, the team, or the organization to be more successful. What may be inherently obvious to leaders may not be as clear to followers, so leaders wanting to capitalize on this motivational approach need to make the cause and effect or task–impact link explicit for followers.

There are some interesting aspects of autonomy, mastery, and meaning worth noting. First, Pink maintains that rewards and punishment work well for motivating employees doing routine, assembly-line work but do not help when it comes to performing complex tasks or creating new products. Although there is some research to back up this point, most professional athletes, movie stars, C-suite executives, mid-level leaders, and sales representatives do complex work yet have substantial percentages of their overall compensation tied to performance incentives. Would their work be of higher quantity or quality if these incentives were removed and they were just paid a higher base salary? Maybe, but maybe not. Many of those who work under pay-for-performance conditions like the fact that their compensation depends on their results and view bonuses as a way to determine their impact. Second, Pink believes followers need to be paid at market or better-than-market rates. Leaders need to get the money issue off the table for autonomy, mastery, and meaning to have an impact; otherwise, pay dissatisfaction will rule the day. Third, these concepts are very idiosyncratic; what may be interesting, impactful, developmental, or empowering to one follower may have just the opposite effect on another.[60] Fourth, although a lot has been written about how worker motivation differs by generational levels, it turns out that Gen Zers, Millennials/Gen Yers, Gen Xers, and Baby Boomers have a lot in common when it comes to autonomy, mastery, and meaning.[61]

Finally, leaders need to recognize that many jobs provide little autonomy or meaning and do not require a high level of mastery. Trying to motivate followers "in useless jobs that nobody wants to talk about" by appealing to their motives may be an exercise in futility.[62]

So what do leaders need to do if they want to use the drive approach to motivate followers to perform at higher levels? First, leaders will need to ensure that pay issues are not a source of dissatisfaction, for if followers feel they are being underpaid then any efforts to improve autonomy, mastery, or meaning will have little impact. Second, leaders need to have a clear understanding of how to minimize the rules governing followers' behavior, what followers specifically need to develop or improve in order to be better at their respective jobs, and what is personally meaningful to their followers. To motivate flight attendants, leaders would need to point out how their behaviors during the boarding process, while in flight, and when deplaning impact customer loyalty and can help the company achieve a number-one ranking in customer satisfaction. Causing concussions and knocking out the front teeth of paying customers while forcibly removing them from aircraft probably won't help flight attendants find meaning in their work.[63] Leaders would also need to help flight attendants develop those skills needed to be the best in the airlines, eliminate rules that prevented them from providing great customer service, and find ways to provide ongoing customer feedback. (See **Highlight 9.3**.)

Red Bull Gives You Wings

HIGHLIGHT 9.3

About 30 years ago, Austrian entrepreneur Dietrich Mateschitz was visiting Thailand on a business trip and happened to drink a local beverage called Krating Daeng to alleviate his jet lag. The beverage worked so well that Mateschitz went into partnership with the local producer, changed the flavor to better suit Western tastes, and started up a Red Bull production facility in Austria. Since then, Red Bull has grown to a $7+ billion business with over 10,000 employees scattered across the globe. The beverage business provides the bulk of these revenues, but the company also owns television channels, record labels, and a variety of professional sports teams, and sponsors approximately 700 extreme sport athletes, Red Bull Air Races, and Red Bull Crashed Ice and Cliff Diving events.

Unlike other companies, Red Bull has few rules and leaders are given considerable latitude to determine what they need to accomplish, how they will go about achieving their goals, the size of their budgets and staffs, how they will manage talent, and so on. They have been very successful with this approach, and much of this success can be attributed to a corporate culture built around four pillars or motivational drivers, which are meaning, mastery, freedom, and responsibility. Meaning has to do with making a difference in other peoples' lives or having an impact, and there are two aspects of meaning. Little "m" is about finding meaning in daily work; can employees see the connection between the activities they perform and their impact on team or organizational success? Big "M" refers to having a purposeful life and seeing how Red Bull can make a difference in their customers and consumers' lives. People can tolerate an incredible amount of stress and will exert high levels of effort when they can see that what they do matters, so an important job for Red Bull leaders is to help employees see the little "m" and big "M" in their work.

Mastery is about being competent or effective at whatever one does. This means understanding the range of skills required for the position, knowing which of these skills are strengths and which need to be improved, and then working to better all those required for the position. This includes not only making strengths even stronger but also engaging in additional training and practice to improve those skills that are not natural strengths. Freedom and responsibility have to do with self-governance, giving employees autonomy to complete work activities in a manner that makes sense to them, and being personally accountable for work outcomes. So employees have considerable latitude in how they get things done but will also be held responsible for the results. When freedom and responsibility are aligned with meaning and mastery, employees make better decisions on how to prioritize issues, how to best get work done, and what level of effort is needed to help teams and the broader organization be successful.

Mateschitz launched Red Bull with the four pillars of meaning, mastery, freedom, and responsibility and ensured these qualities continue to be the defining characteristics of the company's culture. Not surprisingly, Red Bull has very high levels of employee satisfaction and engagement and 30 years of phenomenal business results.

What would it be like to work at Red Bull? How would working at Red Bull be different from working for Amazon, Foxcomm, or AB InBev? Which company would you want to work for?

Sources: A. Yearsley, *Personal Communication*, April 3, 2017; and A. Yearsley and M. Hartgrove, *Personal Management Program 2 Participant Manual* (Fuschl am See, Austria: Red Bull, 2017).

Julie and Ling Ling's bosses would use similar approaches to motivate these two followers. Julie's boss would want to find out what is personally meaningful to Julie (that is, what she wants out of work). Her boss would also want to determine what behaviors she can already do and where she needs to improve to be an outstanding lift operator, and would also want to give her autonomy to run the lift any way she wants as long as it operates in a safe and efficient manner. Finally, Julie's boss would want to find ways to provide Julie with customer and operational feedback so that she could determine whether she was making progress toward her goals. Ling Ling's boss would want to make the connections between Ling Ling's job, customer satisfaction, and overall company results; help her develop the skills needed to be an outstanding real estate agent; give her regular feedback performance; and provide the autonomy to work whenever and wherever she wants and eliminate any rules or roadblocks that interfere with renting apartments.

Given that automation and outsourcing are eliminating many of the routine tasks performed by followers, focusing on autonomy, mastery, and meaning seems to make sense for those doing complex work or responsible for developing innovative products and services. But it may be some time before everyone becomes a knowledge worker, so leaders also need to use other motivational techniques to help those doing more routine work stay engaged and perform at high levels. The remainder of this section describes some of these other approaches.

The best job goes to the person who can get it done without passing the buck or coming back with excuses.

Napoleon Hill, author

Achievement Orientation: How Does Personality Affect Motivation?

Is it possible that some people are naturally more motivated or have "more fire in the belly" than others? Do some people automatically put forth a higher level of effort toward group goals simply because they are hardwired this way? Unlike Pink's theory, which claims that all people share some fundamental needs, this approach to motivation is simple: To improve group performance, leaders should select only followers who both possess the right skills and have a higher level of a personality trait called achievement orientation. (See **Highlight 9.4.**)

Are You Employable?

HIGHLIGHT 9.4

Employability can be defined as the ability to find a job, get hired, and keep a job, and it turns out that situational, follower, and leader factors all come into play when it comes staying gainfully employed. Clearly, situational factors affect employability. When the economy is booming jobs are plentiful, but they are few and far between during recessions. People can lose their jobs even when the economy is growing, as mergers, acquisitions, or bankruptcies can affect a person's employment status.

Leader biases also affect who gets hired or downsized. Favoritism influences hiring decisions, and office politics can play a bigger role in performance evaluations than objective performance results. Research has shown that performance review ratings for salespeople can be more highly correlated with completing paperwork and other administrative tasks than the dollar amounts sold. With many jobs lacking clear goals or more objective performance measures, leader bias may play a pervasive role in performance review ratings. Those who get along with others, do not make any enemies, and flatter their bosses may rise higher in organizations than those who produce results.

Follower characteristics also play a critical role in employability. Research shows that those who are smart, are creative, can solve problems, get things done, and are easy to get along with are much more likely to get hired and keep a job than those who are dumb, unimaginative, lazy, and difficult to be around. Adam Yearsley, the global head of talent management at Red Bull, has worked with a group of prominent psychologists to develop Wingfinder, an online assessment designed specifically to assess a person's employability. The assessment is free and can be accessed at www.wingfinder.com. Your Wingfinder results will tell you whether or not you are employable, but it is important to remember situational and leader factors also play critical roles in determining the number of jobs that need to be filled and who will fill them.

Sources: T. Chamorro-Premuzic, *The Talent Delusion* (London: Piatkus, 2017); A. Yearsley, "The Science behind Wingfinder," Red Bull Wingfinder, https://www.wingfinder.com/science; and A. Colquitt. "Performance Management: Current State, Future State," presentation given at the Minnesota Professional Psychology at Work meeting, Minneapolis, MN, September 18, 2018.

Atkinson has proposed that an individual's tendency to exert effort toward task accomplishment depends partly on the strength of his or her motivation to achieve success, or as Atkinson called it, **achievement orientation**.[64, 65] McClelland further developed Atkinson's ideas and said that individuals with a strong achievement orientation (or in McClelland's terms, a strong *need for achievement*) strive to accomplish socially acceptable endeavors and activities. These individuals also prefer tasks that provide immediate and ample feedback and are moderately difficult (that is, tasks that require a considerable amount of effort but are accomplishable). Additionally, individuals with a strong need to achieve feel satisfied when they successfully solve work problems or accomplish job tasks. Individuals with a relatively low need to achieve generally prefer easier tasks and do not feel satisfied by solving problems or accomplishing assigned tasks. McClelland maintained that differences in achievement orientation are a primary reason why people differ in the levels of effort they exert to accomplish assignments, objectives, or goals. Thus achievement orientation is a bit like "fire in the belly"; people with more achievement orientation are likely to set higher personal and work goals and are more likely to expend the effort needed to accomplish them. People with low levels of achievement motivation tend to set lower personal and work goals and are less likely to accomplish them.[66]

Achievement orientation is also a component of the Five Factor Model or OCEAN model of personality dimension of conscientiousness (see **Chapter 6**). Conscientiousness has been found to be positively related to performance across virtually all jobs as well as to predict success in school, in the military, in blue-collar and retail workers, and in management positions. All things being equal, people with higher levels of achievement orientation are likely to do better in school, pursue postgraduate degrees, get promoted more quickly, and get paid higher salaries and bonuses than their lower-scoring counterparts.[67, 68, 69, 70, 71, 72, 73, 74, 75, 76, 77, 78]

Given that individuals with higher achievement orientation scores set high personal goals and put in the time and effort necessary to achieve them, it is hardly surprising that achievement orientation is often a key success factor for people who advance to the highest levels of the organization. For example, achievement orientation appears to be a common success factor underlying the careers of Ping Fu, Mark Roellig, and James Mwangi (**Profiles in Leadership 9.1**, **9.2**, and **9.3**, respectively). Although achievement orientation is often associated with higher performance, high achievers can become demoralized when facing unclear or impossible tasks. Working with elite Army Ranger units, Britt found that these units almost always performed at high levels and were often successful. But when given unclear missions with few resources and impossible timelines, these same units could self-destruct quickly. In these situations the units felt they were being set up to fail, and fail they did. This phenomenon is clearly depicted in the movie *Black Hawk Down*, which tells the true story of Army Ranger units sent to Mogadishu, Somalia, to capture a Somalian warlord.[79] The important lesson here is that leaders need to give high achievers clear goals and the resources they need to succeed. (See **Highlights 9.4** through **9.6**.)

Mark Roellig

PROFILES IN LEADERSHIP 9.2

Mark Roellig recently retired as the chief technology and administrative officer of Mass Mutual Financial Group. But he took a highly unusual path to becoming the top IT leader of a *Fortune* 100 company. Growing up in Michigan, Roellig attended the University of Michigan to obtain an undergraduate degree in mathematics in three years. He went on to earn his law degree at George Washington University and an MBA from the University of Washington. Roellig started his professional career as an attorney practicing civil litigation at two law firms in Seattle before joining Pacific Northwestern Bell Telephone Company in 1983. He spent the next 17 years working in the law division of the company as it transformed from Pacific Northwestern Bell Telephone Company to US West to Qwest Communications. During this time, Roellig rapidly moved through the ranks and eventually became the executive vice president of public policy, human resources, and law for US West. In this role, he managed over 1,000 employees and an annual budget of $250 million.

After US West was acquired by Qwest Communications, Roellig spent some time as the general counsel at Storage Technology Corporation and Fisher Scientific International before becoming the executive vice president and general counsel at MassMutual. As in his previous general counsel roles, Roellig spent the next seven years systematically turning around and improving the performance of the law, public policy, and corporate services divisions. He did this by routinely soliciting survey and verbal feedback from internal customers; developing strategic plans for each division; setting clear individual, team, and division goals; using metrics to track performance; surrounding himself with top talent; building a high-performing leadership team; and creating a performance-based culture. Roellig obsesses over talent and spends a considerable amount of time hiring top people and putting them in various development programs and rotational assignments to help them develop needed skills. Over the years a number of his direct reports have gone on to be top leaders in other organizations.

In addition to surrounding himself with and developing the right people, Roellig also obsesses over customer satisfaction and performance. During his tenure, all three divisions saw steadily improving customer satisfaction and financial results while reporting the best employee engagement scores of the entire company. Because Roellig had such a good track record as a senior leader, he was asked in early 2017 to take over MassMutual's IT department. This 2,500-person department had recently failed to deliver a major companywide software conversion project and the CEO felt a leadership change was needed. This was a huge challenge for Roellig, as his professional background was in law rather than IT. As a lawyer he could accurately determine a company's legal needs, how to best structure a legal department to meet these needs, and quickly size up others' legal skills, and he knew where to find good talent. In this new job, Roellig did not have this experi-

ence to draw on to improve the IT department. He spent the next two years evaluating MassMutual's technology needs, satisfaction with IT services, functional and leadership capabilities of the IT department; creating an IT strategy; and selecting the IT leadership team.

What challenges do you think Mark Roellig faced in turning around a large IT department? What did he need to do to motivate and engage IT employees and get them to perform at high levels? How would you measure the effectiveness of the IT department at MassMutual? How would you use needs or achievement orientation to describe Roellig's career? Which motivational approaches best describe his leadership philosophy?

Sources: M. Roellig, *Summary of 2009 Law Division Activities*, presentation given to the MassMutual Audit Committee on April 13, 2010, in Springfield, MA; M. Roellig, *Personal Communication*, April 11, 2017; and T. Alexander, "Q&A with the EIC: How Mark Roellig Accelerated His Career with Technology," *ACC Docket*, March 23, 2017, www.accdocket.com/articles/mark-roellig-q-a-accelerate-your-career-technology.cfm.

Is Following Your Passion Good Career Advice?

HIGHLIGHT 9.5

Daniel Pink believes that meaning, mastery, and autonomy are critically important if knowledge workers are to perform at peak levels. But what should those performing complex, innovative work do when their leaders have not created work environments that satisfy these needs? In these situations, Pink believes employees should quit their current jobs and join organizations that better meet their needs. However, it turns out that following one's passion may not be as straightforward or satisfying as it first appears. First, simply moving from one organization to the next may not satisfy these needs. The new company may have a culture that is no better

at meeting these needs than the last one, and research shows that on average people hold seven different types of jobs over their careers. Most people have more than one passion, and these passions seem to shift over time. This implies that people's passions are fluid and constantly changing, so just moving to another organization may not meet these shifting needs. Second, interesting hobbies can become chores when people rely on them to make a living. People may really enjoy cooking or flying but often find being a line chef or a commercial airline pilot to be a burden. Third, a person may have a strong passion for and start a business around life coaching, fashion, or photography, but if they cannot convince others to buy their products or services then it will do them little good.

Instead of following one's passion, psychologist Dawn Graham suggests that people follow their **professional energy**. People should identify which aspects of work or projects they find energizing and then look for jobs or opportunities that have more of these activities. Some people may like solving customer problems, working under tight deadlines, or solving difficult problems. Others may like working with their hands, following checklists or established procedures,

or working in teams. The most engaged, highest performing, and most satisfied employees are likely to be those who spend most of their time doing those activities that give them professional energy, so it is incumbent on leaders to figure out what gives each of their followers professional energy and assign work activities accordingly.

Sources: D. Graham, "Why 'Follow Your Passion' Is Terrible Career Advice," http://drdawnoncareers.com/why-follow-your-passion-is-terrible-career-advice; and C. Gregoire, "Why 'Follow Your Passion' Is Bad Career Advice," *Huffington Post*, July 22, 2013, www.huffingtonpost.com/2013/07/22/sustainable-career_n_3618480.html.

Capacity is its own motivation.

David Campbell, Center for Creative Leadership

How could a leader apply this knowledge of achievement orientation to improve the performance of Julie, Ling Ling, and the flight attendants described earlier? Perhaps the first step would be to ensure that the hiring process selected individuals with higher levels of achievement orientation. Assuming they had higher scores, we would expect Ling Ling to work with her boss to set aggressive goals for renting apartments and then work as many nights and weekends as were needed to achieve them. We might also expect Ling Ling to obtain her MBA from Hong Kong University over the next few years. Julie could also be expected to set high personal and work goals, but she may find that her job limits her ability to pursue these goals. Unlike Ling Ling, who can control the number of nights and weekends she works, Julie has no control over the number of people who ride on her lift. The job itself may limit Julie's ability to fulfill her high level of achievement orientation. As a result, she may pursue other activities, such as becoming an expert skier, joining the ski patrol, doing ski racing, looking for additional responsibilities or opportunities for advancement, or finding another job where she has the opportunity to achieve and be rewarded for her efforts. Because Julie would set and work toward high personal goals, a good boss would work closely with her to find work-related ways to capitalize on her achievement orientation. Thus achievement orientation may be a dual-edged sword. Leadership practitioners may be able to hire a group of highly motivated followers, but they also need to set clear expectations, provide opportunities for followers to set and achieve work-related goals, and provide feedback on progress toward goals. Otherwise, followers may find different ways to fulfill their high levels of achievement orientation.

A good goal is like strenuous exercise—it makes you stretch.

Mary Kay Ashe, co-founder and former CEO of Mary Kay Cosmetics

Applying the achievement orientation approach to the flight attendant situation or to U.S. workers from 2002 to 2019 leads to some interesting thoughts. Perhaps the airline did not screen for conscientiousness when hiring flight attendants and does not have enough people with high scores to deliver good customer service. Or the company could have hired only people with high conscientiousness scores but not set any measurable goals, repeatedly ignored requests for better equipment, failed to back up staff when they were challenged by "bad" travelers, or not given any recognition for jobs well done. In this case the flight attendants could feel that they have been set up for failure. With respect to people working in the United States from 2002 to 2019, those with the highest levels of achievement orientation were most likely to be promoted during the economic boom and stay with their companies during the recession. However, because many companies went under or eliminated entire work units or functions, some achievement-oriented types found themselves out of jobs. Because work is so important to people with high levels of achievement orientation, these individuals found work elsewhere by becoming independent contractors, starting their own businesses, or joining start-ups where their higher motivational levels could have a greater impact.

Grit

HIGHLIGHT 9.6

One of the motivational concepts garnering a considerable amount of attention over the past five years is grit. **Grit** can be defined as a person's perseverance of effort and passion to achieve long-term goals. Those with high levels of grit have a high level of stamina and do whatever it takes to achieve an end result, be it graduating from college, becoming a CEO, or mastering a musical instrument. Those lacking grit are unwilling to put forth the energy or effort to achieve educational or career goals. University of Pennsylvania professor Angela Duckworth and her colleagues looked at the characteristics that predicted GPAs from Ivy League schools, success at the National Spelling Bee, and dropout rates from the United States Military Academy and concluded that grit was the single most important attribute shared by successful people.

Duckworth has created quite a following. Over 8 million people watched her TED talk before she even published her best-selling book. Organizations have adopted the grit mantra and send leaders and employees to grit workshops in order to boost performance. Grit has also captured the attention of educators; teachers now implement programs to improve student grit. On the face of it, it makes sense that those who work harder and longer would likely be more successful. However, is grit a novel concept, or is it a repackaging of what we already know?

Research shows that grit is mostly a relabeling of achievement orientation and the conscientious personality trait described in **Chapter 6**. Moreover, ascribing differences in school, sales, or career performance to grit says nothing about the situational or moral factors affecting students and employees. Student performance may suffer if they do not have enough to eat, worry about getting shot, or are assigned to substandard schools. Likewise, company revenues may be stellar if sales representatives are selling hot products or paying bribes, and luck and favoritism often play bigger roles in career advancement than grit. Moreover, grit's singular focus toward achieving long-term goals may limit experimentation and innovation. Given that grit has a strong personality component, it is likely that it is not amenable to the development interventions promoted in schools. Schools can throw considerable sums to improve student grit, but this is not likely to be money well spent.

Do you think that grit is anything more than achievement orientation? How would you use grit to motivate flight attendants, Julie, or Ling Ling?

Sources: A. Duckworth, *Grit: The Power of Passion and Perseverance* (New York: Scribner, 2016); D. Moreau., B. MacNamara, and D. Hambrick, "Overstating the Role of Environmental Factors in Success: A Cautionary Note," *Current Directions in Psychological Science* 28, no. 1 (2019), pp. 28–33; and D. Demby, "The Limits of 'Grit'," *The New Yorker*, June 21, 2016, www.newyorker.com/culture/culture-desk/the-limits-of-grit.

Goal Setting: How Do Clear Performance Targets Affect Motivation?

One of the most familiar and easiest formal systems of motivation to use with followers is **goal setting**. From the leader's perspective, this involves setting clear performance targets and then helping followers create systematic plans to achieve them. According to Locke and Latham, goals are the most powerful determinants of task behaviors. Goals direct attention, mobilize effort, help people develop strategies for achievement, and help people continue exerting effort until the goals are reached. This leads, in turn, to even higher goals.[80, 81, 82, 83, 84, 85]

> *Goal-setting theory has been rated #1 in importance among 73 management theories by organizational behavior scholars.*
>
> **Ed Locke, University of Maryland**

Locke and Latham reported that nearly 400 studies involving hundreds of tasks across 40,000 individuals, groups, and organizations in eight different countries have provided consistent support for several aspects of goal setting. First, this research showed goals that were both *specific* and *difficult* resulted in consistently higher effort and performance, when contrasted to "do your best" goals. Second, *goal commitment* is critical. Merely having goals is not enough. Although follower participation in setting goals is one way to increase commitment, goals set either by leaders unilaterally or through participation with followers can lead to necessary levels of commitment. Commitment to assigned goals was often as high as commitment to goals followers helped to set, provided the leader was perceived to have legitimate authority, expressed confidence in followers, and provided clear standards for performance. Third, followers exerted the greatest effort when goals were accompanied by *feedback*; followers getting goals or feedback alone generally exerted less effort. This need for feedback is precisely the same as noted earlier for mastery, in that followers are usually more motivated when they get regular updates on goal progress.

> *Well-defined goals help organizations avoid the "crisis du jour" mode of operating and give them permission to celebrate success.*
>
> **Bill Mease, consultant**

Several other aspects of goal setting are also worth noting. First, goals can be set for any aspect of performance, be it reducing costs, improving the quality of services and products, increasing voter registration, or winning a league championship. Nevertheless, leaders need to ensure that they do not set conflicting goals because followers can exert only so much effort over a given time.[86] Second, determining just how challenging to make goals creates a bit of a dilemma for leaders. Successfully completed goals give followers a sense of job satisfaction, and easy goals are more likely to be completed than difficult goals. However, easily attainable goals result in lower levels of effort (and performance) than do more difficult goals. Research suggests that leaders might motivate followers most effectively by setting moderately difficult goals, recognizing partial goal accomplishment, and making use of a continuous improvement philosophy by making goals incrementally more difficult.[87, 88, 89, 90, 91, 92]

A leader's implicit and explicit expectations about goal accomplishment can also affect the performance of followers and teams. Research by Dov Eden and his associates in Israel has provided consistent support for the Pygmalion and Golem effects.[93, 94] The **Pygmalion effect** occurs when leaders articulate high expectations for followers; in many cases these expectations alone will lead to higher-performing followers and teams. Unfortunately the **Golem effect** is also true—leaders who have little faith in their followers' ability to accomplish a goal are rarely disappointed. Thus a leader's expectations for a follower or team have a good chance of becoming a self-fulfilling prophecy (**Chapter 2**). These results indicate that leaders wanting to improve individual performance or team effectiveness should set high but achievable goals and express confidence and support that the followers can get the job done.[95, 96]

> *In the absence of clearly defined goals we become strangely loyal to performing daily trivia until we ultimately become enslaved by it.*

Robert Heinlein, author

How could leadership practitioners apply goal setting to Julie, Ling Ling, and the flight attendants to increase their motivation levels? Given the research findings just described, Julie's and Ling Ling's bosses should work with these two followers to set specific and moderately difficult goals, express confidence that they can achieve their goals, and provide regular feedback on goal progress. Julie and her boss could look at Julie's past performance or other lift operators' performance as a baseline, and then set specific and measurable goals for the number of hours worked, the number of people who fall off the lift during a shift, customer satisfaction survey ratings from skiers, the length of lift lines, or the number of complaints from customers. Similarly, Ling Ling and her boss could look at some real estate baseline measures and set goals for the number of apartments rented for the year, the total monetary value of these rentals, the time it takes to close a lease and complete the necessary paperwork, customer complaints, and sales expenses. Note that both Ling Ling's and Julie's bosses would need to take care that they do not set conflicting goals. For example, if Julie had a goal only for the number of people who fell off the lift, she might be likely to run the lift slowly, resulting in long lift lines and numerous customer complaints. In a similar vein, bosses need to ensure that individual goals do not conflict with team or organizational goals. Ling Ling's boss would need to make sure that Ling Ling's goals did not interfere with those of the other real estate agents in the firm. If Ling Ling's goals did not specify territorial limits, she might rent properties in other agents' territories, which might cause a high level of interoffice conflict. Both bosses should also take care to set measurable goals; that way they could give Julie and Ling Ling the feedback they need to stay on track. Goal setting could also help the airline company motivate flight attendants to provide better service to customers. Airline executives may believe customer satisfaction is critically important for keeping planes full, but they may not have set a specific goal for or devised a good way to measure customer satisfaction on individual flights. Customer service may improve only when the airline sets a clear customer satisfaction goal, makes feedback against the goal readily available, and holds flight attendants accountable for improved customer satisfaction results. For example, Delta Airlines has set specific goals for customer satisfaction and administers online surveys to random passengers after every flight in order to provide feedback about gate agent, pilot, and flight attendance performance.

> *If you can't measure it, then you can't manage it.*

Peter Drucker, leadership researcher

Although goal setting is a powerful motivational technique, there is a dark side to this approach in that *it may work too well*. Followers can get so focused on their goals that they are not willing to spend any time or effort on activities not aligned with goal accomplishment. This means they may not help customers or cooperate with coworkers if they have no goals pertaining to customer satisfaction or teamwork.[97] They may even go so far as to bend rules or break laws in order to achieve goals, as bankers at Wells Fargo did when they created over 2 million fake customer accounts in order to meet unrealistic sales goals.[98, 99, 100] Leaders sometimes get so focused on goals they end up winning the battle but lose the war. They may spend so much time and energy trying to achieve efficiency goals that they forget the purpose of their business is to attract and retain customers.[101, 102] The bottom line is that goal setting works, but leaders need to be very careful that followers' goals drive the right behaviors. Because goal setting is such a widely used and powerful motivational technique, more about this topic can be found in **Chapter 12**.

James Mwangi

PROFILES IN LEADERSHIP 9.3

One of the factors limiting economic growth in Africa is poor infrastructure. Much of Africa lacks the roads, train lines, electrical grids, and Internet access needed to move goods and services from place to place. One of these infrastructure limitations is banking. Many African nations operate on a cash basis and do not have the financial service systems needed to make deposits, transfer money, or take out loans.

In 1994 the Equity Building Society, a bank in rural Kenya that provided financial services to the poor, was on the verge of bankruptcy. Bad management, an economic downturn, and a number of bad loans had brought the bank to the brink of failure. The board of directors turned to James Mwangi for help, and he started the bank's transformation by converting loan owners to shareholders. This gave those holding loans an equity stake in the bank's future, and the number of bad loans eventually shrank to less than 1.5 percent of the total shillings loaned. Mwangi also changed the focus of the bank from providing home mortgages to issuing microloans to poor farmers and shopkeepers. Farmers could take out loans as small as 500 shillings (about $9.00) and use this money for seed, fertilizer, tools, and cell phones. Under Mwangi's leadership the Equity Building Society returned to solvency and expanded across Kenya. In 2000, the bank reported a net profit of 33.6 million shillings that had grown to over 12 billion shillings by the end of 2012. By 2014, the bank had expanded from Kenya into Uganda, South Sudan, Rwanda, and Tanzania and is now the largest banking conglomerate in Africa, serving over 12 million customers.

Do you think motives or needs, achievement orientation, grit, or goal setting best explain the success of the Equity Building Society?

Sources: "Kenya's Biggest Bank: The Cult of Equity," *The Economist*, December 8, 2012, p. 76; and C. Munda, "Equity Group Net Profit Falls on Rising Loan Defaults," *The Star*, March 15, 2017, www.the-star.co.ke/news/2017/03/15/equity-group-net-profit-falls-on-rising-loan-defaults_c1525498.

The Operant Approach: How Do Rewards and Punishment Affect Motivation?

One popular way to change the direction, intensity, or persistence of behavior is through rewards and punishments. It will help at the outset of this discussion of the **operant approach** to define several terms. A **reward** is any consequence that *increases* the likelihood that a particular behavior will be repeated. For example, if Julie gets a cash award for a suggestion to improve customer service at the ski resort, she will be more likely to forward additional suggestions. **Punishment** is the administration of an aversive stimulus or the withdrawal of something desirable, each of which *decreases* the likelihood that a particular behavior will be repeated.[103] Thus, if Ling Ling loses her bonus for not getting her paperwork in on time, she will be less likely to do so again in the future. Both rewards and punishments can be administered in a contingent or noncontingent manner. **Contingent** rewards or punishments are administered as *consequences of a particular behavior*. Examples might include giving Julie a medal immediately after she wins a skiing race or giving Ling Ling a bonus check for exceeding her sales quota. **Noncontingent** rewards and punishments are not associated with particular behaviors. Monthly paychecks might be examples if both Julie and Ling Ling receive the same amount of base pay every month whatever their actual effort or output. Finally, behaviors that are not rewarded may eventually be eliminated through the process of **extinction**.

You get what you reinforce, but you do not necessarily get what you pay for.

Fred Luthans, University of Nebraska, and Alexander Stajkovic, University of California, Irvine

There is ample evidence that, when implemented properly, the operant approach can be an effective way to improve follower motivation and performance.[104, 105, 106, 107, 108, 109, 110, 111, 112] Some of this research has also shown that rewards work better than punishments, particularly if administered in a contingent manner.[113, 114, 115, 116, 117, 118, 119] When comparing the relative impact of different types of rewards, Stajkovic and Luthans reported that incentive pay targeted at specific follower behaviors was the most effective, followed by social recognition and performance feedback, for improving follower performance in credit card processing centers.[120] Although some observers may argue otherwise, the research clearly shows that leaders who properly design and implement contingent reward systems do indeed increase follower productivity and performance. See **Highlights 9.7, 9.8,** and **9.9** for more information about incentive systems.

Professional Athlete and Executive Salary Demands

HIGHLIGHT 9.7

General managers are responsible for the overall performance of their professional sports teams. They help select players and coaches; negotiate media, player, coach, and stadium contracts; keep team morale at a high level; and take action to ensure the team wins the championship and makes money. One of the most difficult issues general managers deal with is negotiating contracts with players. Players look at their own pay and performance and compare them to those of other athletes in the league. If they feel their compensation is not consistent with that of other players, they usually ask to be traded or for a new contract to be negotiated. These comparisons have led to the $200 million–plus salaries now commanded by star players in basketball, football, and baseball. But what happens to team morale, the win–loss record, and financial performance when one or two players make substantially more money than the rest of the team? Research on professional baseball teams over an eight-year period indicated that teams with high pay dispersion levels (large gaps between the highest- and lowest-paid starting players) did less well financially and were less likely to win division championships. Researchers surmised that this drop in team performance was due to high levels of **pay**

dispersion, which eroded team performance and increased inequity for other players on the team. The trick for general managers seems to be to find enough financial rewards to induce higher levels of performance but not create inequity situations for the rest of the team.

The effects of pay inequity that are readily apparent with professional athletes' pay also hold true for top executives. Many boards of directors worry that if they do not pay their CEOs and top executives at least on par with those in other companies, they run the risk of executive turnover. But executives who negotiate large signing bonuses and big annual pay packages don't necessarily achieve better results than their lower-paid counterparts. Far too many executives tout the benefits of pay for performance but appear much more concerned with their own pay than their company's performance. For example, the compensation for the average U.S. worker rose at a 0.3 percent annual rate from 1980 to 2004, yet the average CEO's compensation grew at a rate of 8.5 percent annually. CEOs promised an average of 11.5 percent annual earnings growth over this period but actually only achieved 6 percent growth, which was slightly less than the annual percentage growth rate for the overall economy from 1980 to 2004. Despite the fact that the average CEO performed no better than the overall economy, in 1980 the average CEO made 42 times as much as the average worker, and by 2019 this had increased to 300 times the average worker's salary. The top executives in Japanese companies currently make 20 to 30 times more than the average employee, and there appears to be little relationship between CEO compensation and company performance. One has to wonder if companies with high pay dispersions achieve the same suboptimal results as do professional athletic teams with high pay dispersions. With workers putting in longer hours for less pay and the people on top getting fat paychecks and bonuses regardless of results, is it any wonder that workers are less satisfied and engaged?

Sources: M. Bloom, "The Performance Effects of Pay Dispersions on Individuals and Organizations," *Academy of Management Journal* 42, no. 1 (1999), pp. 25–40; J. Lublin, "Boards Tie CEO Pay More Tightly to Performance," *The Wall Street Journal*, February 21, 2006, pp. A1, A14; L. A. Bebchuk and J. M. Fried, "Pay without Performance: Overview of the Issues," *The Academy of Management Perspectives* 20, no. 1 (2006), pp. 5–24; J. Bogle, "Reflections on CEO Compensation," *The Academy of Management Perspectives* 22, no. 2 (2008), pp. 21–25; "Executive Pay: Neither Rigged or Fair," *The Economist*, June 25, 2016, pp. 15–20; "Cheques Need Balances," *The Economist*, June 25, 2016, pp. 12–13; "Schumpeter: Pay Dirt," *The Economist*, April 23, 2015, p. 60; J. S. Lublin, "Parsing the Pay and Performance of the Top CEOs," *The Wall Street Journal*, June 25, 2015, pp. B1, B4; R. L. Landis, "The 100 Most Overpaid CEOs: Are Fund Managers Asleep at the Wheel?" *As You Sow*, www.asyousow.org/reports/the-100-most-overpaid-ceos-2017-are-fund-managers-asleep-at-the-wheel; R. Umoh, "CEOs Make $15.6 Million on Average—Here's How Much Their Pay Has Increased Compared to Yours Over This Year," *CNBC*, January 22, 2018, www.cnbc.com/2018/01/22/heres-how-much-ceo-pay-has-increased-compared-to-yours-over-the-years.html; C. McGee, "Wall Street Chief's Pay Doesn't Sync with Returns," *The Wall Street Journal*, July 8, 2019, www.wsj.com/articles/wall-street-chiefs-pay-doesnt-sync-with-returns-11562580018; and P. Eaves, "It's Never Been Easier to Be a CEO, and the Pay Keeps Rising," *The New York Times*, May 24, 2019, www.nytimes.com/2019/05/24/business/highest-paid-ceos-2018.html.

The best way to demotivate and lose top performers is to reward mediocrity in an attempt to maintain the status quo.

Anonymous

How can a leader design and implement an operant system for improving followers' motivation and performance levels? Using operant principles properly to improve followers' motivation and performance requires several steps. First, *leadership practitioners need to clearly specify what behaviors are important*. This means that Julie's and Ling Ling's leaders will need to specify what they want them to do, how often they should do it, and the level of performance required. Second, *leadership practitioners need to determine if those behaviors are currently being punished, rewarded, or ignored*. Believe it or not, sometimes followers are actually rewarded for behaviors that leaders are trying to extinguish, and punished for behaviors that leaders want to increase. For example, Julie may get considerable positive attention from peers by talking back to her leader or for violating the ski resort dress code. Similarly, Ling Ling may be overly competitive and get promoted ahead of her peers (such as by renting apartments in her peers' territories), even when her boss extols the need for cooperation and teamwork. And leaders sometimes just ignore the behaviors they would like to see strengthened. An example here would be if Julie's boss consistently failed to provide rewards when Julie worked hard to achieve impressive safety and customer service ratings.

Third, *leadership practitioners need to find out what followers actually find rewarding and punishing*. Leaders should *not* make the mistake of assuming that all followers will find the same things to be rewarding or punishing. One follower's punishment may be another follower's reward. For example, Ling Ling may dislike public attention and actually exert less effort after being publicly recognized, yet some of her peers may find public attention rewarding. Fourth, *leadership practitioners need to be wary of creating perceptions of inequity when administering individually tailored rewards*. A peer may feel that she got the same results as Ling Ling, yet she received a smaller bonus check for the quarter. Leaders can minimize inequities by being clear and consistent with rewards and punishments. Fifth, *leadership practitioners should not limit themselves to administering organizationally sanctioned rewards and punishments*. Often leaders are limited in the amount of money they can give followers for good performance. However, research has shown that social recognition and performance feedback significantly improved productivity in followers, and these rewards do not cost any money.[121, 122, 123] Using ingenuity, leaders can often come up with an array of potential rewards and punishments that are effective and inexpensive and do not violate organizational norms or policies. Julie might find driving the Sno-Cat to be enjoyable, and her boss could use this reward to maintain or increase Julie's motivation levels for operating the ski lift. Finally, because the administration of noncontingent consequences has relatively little impact, *leadership practitioners need to hold followers accountable by administering rewards and punishments in a contingent manner whenever possible.* [124] **Highlight 9.8** provides examples of the unintended consequences of implementing an operant approach to boost organizational performance.

The Folly of Rewarding A While Hoping for B

HIGHLIGHT 9.8

Steven Kerr has written a compelling article detailing how many of the reward systems found in government, sports, universities, businesses, medicine, and politics often compel people to act in a manner contrary to that intended. For example, voters want politicians to provide the specifics of their programs or platform, yet politicians often get punished for doing so.

Some constituency is bound to be hurt or offended whenever the specifics of a program are revealed, which in turn will cost the politician votes. If a politician keeps overall goals vague, more voters are likely to agree with the politician and vote for him or her in the next election. Businesses, like universities and politicians, often use inappropriate reward systems. According to Kerr, the following are some of the more common management reward follies:

We hope for . . .	But we often reward . . .
Long-term growth	Quarterly earnings
Teamwork	Individual effort
Commitment to total quality	Shipping on schedule, even with defects
Reporting honest news	Reporting good news, whether it is true or not

Kerr states that managers who complain about unmotivated workers should consider the possibility that their current reward system is incongruent with the performance they desire. And nowhere is this lack of congruence between what companies want and what they reward more visible than with executive compensation. Boards often have to front millions of dollars to new CEOs to get them to join the company, and then often must provide stock options and other forms of compensation to retain these individuals even though they consistently fail to hit their numbers. Many corporations talk a good game when it comes to pay for performance, but their actions indicate they are more likely to reward tenure while hoping for improved performance.

Sources: S. Kerr, "On the Folly of Rewarding A, While Hoping for B," *Academy of Management Executive* 9, no. 1 (1995), pp. 7–14; S. Kerr, "Establishing Organizational Goals and Rewards," *Academy of Management Executive* 18, no. 4 (2004), pp. 122–23; S. D. Levitt and S. J. Dubner, *Freakonomics* (New York: HarperCollins Publishers, 2005); L. Bebchuck and J. Fried, *Pay without Performance* (Boston, MA: Harvard University Press, 2004); L. Bebchuck and J. Fried, "Pay without Performance: Overview of the Issues," *The Academy of Management Perspectives* 20, no. 1 (2006), pp. 5–24; P. Dvorak, "Limits on Executive Pay: Easy to Set, Hard to Keep," *The Wall Street Journal*, April 9, 2007, pp. B1, B5; and J. S. Lublin, "Boards Tie CEO Pay More Tightly to Performance," *The Wall Street Journal*, February 21, 2006, pp. A1, A4.

How am I supposed to feed my family on only $14 million a year?

Latrell Sprewell, former professional basketball player

The operant approach can also be used to improve customer service for flight attendants. Using the tenets described earlier, the airline would need to specify which customer satisfaction behaviors were important, determine if those behaviors were being reinforced or punished, determine what attendants found to be rewarding, and administer valued rewards whenever attendants demonstrated good customer service behaviors.

The operant approach continues to be a popular motivational technique in many companies today. Most organizations tout a pay-for-performance culture and pay bonuses or commissions for results obtained. This can be seen most clearly in sales positions, where salespeople are paid a percentage of the total dollars they sell. Needless to say, salespeople experienced a large drop in compensation when customers stopped buying products and services during the 2007–2009 recession, despite exhibiting all the behaviors needed to retain customers or get new business in the door. This example points out a shortcoming of the operant technique, which is that situational factors can overwhelm the effectiveness of a reward program. Sometimes people can get big bonuses or commissions without working hard because they are selling a hot product or the economy is experiencing a boom. Other times they may do all the right things but few people want to buy their products because of factors beyond their control (such as selling pickup trucks and large sports utility vehicles when gasoline is $4.00 per gallon).

Greed is another factor leaders need to keep in mind when implementing pay-for-performance programs. Performance bonuses can inadvertently induce followers to lie, cheat, break laws, and do other dumb things in order to achieve financial rewards. Incentives can induce companies to offer bribes to government officials to secure contracts, encourage salespeople to give kickbacks to customers for buying products and services, motivate administrators to lie about patient wait times at Veterans Administration hospitals, and induce car companies to insert bogus software to pass emissions control tests.[125, 126] Incentive systems clearly work when it comes to motivating follower behavior; leaders just need to ensure that they are inducing the right behaviors when it comes to pay for performance.

How Uber Motivates Drivers

HIGHLIGHT 9.9

Founded in 2009 by Garrett Camp and Travis Kalanick, Uber operates in nearly 800 cities across the globe and generates over $11 billion in annual revenues. Its phenomenal growth can be attributed to its ability to use technology, game theory, and psychology to disrupt the taxi industry. In terms of technology, Uber built an app that allowed drivers and passengers with smartphones to seamlessly connect with each other. Passengers simply have to identify where they want to be picked up, their final destination, and what level of service they would like.

The app then lets them know their estimated wait time, fare, and driver for the trip. Drivers are notified about trips and the names and location of their passengers.

Game theory comes into play by optimizing three sets of competing needs: those of passengers, drivers, and Uber. Passengers want short wait times, low fares, and pleasant rider experiences. Drivers want to maximize their revenues, which means they want fewer drivers (as this reduces competition and increases fares) and minimal amounts of idle time. Uber wants to dominate the markets where it plays, maximize passenger satisfaction and loyalty, maximize revenues, and minimize costs. To do this, drivers must have their own vehicles and pay for all insurance and maintenance, and Uber must have at least enough drivers to meet local demand and minimize driver turnover (and ideally have many more drivers than it needs, as a high supply of drivers will keep fares down). It also needs to handle the demand surges that occur when high numbers of passengers want rides at the same time, such as after sporting events or during rush hours.

Unlike most employers, Uber has no direct control over drivers, as they are self-employed business owners who can choose when, where, and how long they want to work. Uber uses a variety of psychological techniques to motivate driver behavior. For example, new drivers are guaranteed a minimum of $2,000/week if they drive at least 60 hours in a week. Drivers are also not told about passengers' final destinations until fares are accepted, which prevents drivers from accepting only more profitable fares. Drivers are given incentives to work longer hours, work peak hours in high-demand locations, and accept higher percentages of rides. For example, drivers earn $50 bonuses for providing 50 rides in a week and $500 for 120 rides a week; they also receive higher percentages of fares with higher acceptance rates; and are told how much money they are losing when working in nonpeak locations and hours versus how much money they could make by working high-demand hours. Uber also knows that most drivers have weekly revenue targets, so it lets drivers know how much progress they are making toward these targets, and how much they would likely earn toward their targets if they made the next trip. Uber also allows drivers and passengers to provide feedback on each other and gives out nonmonetary rewards, such as badges, for superior driver performance.

Despite all the psychological ploys, driver turnover is a big problem for Uber, as 50 percent of all drivers quit Uber in the first 12 months. How do meaning, mastery, autonomy, and goal setting come into play for Uber drivers? How does Uber capitalize on achievement orientation, and the operant approach to motivate drivers? What could Uber do to retain higher percentages of new drivers? What are the challenges for Uber leaders heading up operations in one of the 800 cities with Uber drivers?

Sources: A. Shontell, "All Hail the Uber Man! How Sharp-Elbowed Salesman Travis Kalanick Became Silicon Valley's Newest Star," *Business Insider*, January 11, 2014, www.businessinsider.com/uber-travis-kalanick-bio-2014-1; N. Scheiber, "How Uber Uses Psychological Tricks to Push Its Drivers' Buttons," *New York Times*, April 2, 2017, www.nytimes.com/interactive/2017/04/02/technology/uber-drivers-psychological-tricks.html; and C. Said, "Uber Incentives Aim to Lure Power Drivers," *San Francisco Chronicle*, March 26, 2016, www.sfchronicle.com/business/article/Uber-incentives-aim-to-lure-power-drivers-7089842.php.

Empowerment: How Does Decision-Making Latitude Affect Motivation?

Empowerment is the final approach to motivation that we discuss in this chapter. In general, people seem to fall into one of two camps with respect to empowerment. Some people believe empowerment is about delegation and accountability; it is a top-down process in which senior leaders articulate a vision and specific goals and hold followers responsible for achieving them. Others believe empowerment is more of a bottom-up approach that focuses on intelligent risk taking, growth, change, trust, and ownership; followers act as entrepreneurs and owners who question rules and make intelligent decisions. Leaders tolerate mistakes and encourage cooperative behavior in this approach to empowerment.[127, 128, 129, 130, 131] Needless to say, these two conceptualizations of empowerment have very different implications for leaders and followers. And it is precisely this conceptual confusion that has caused empowerment programs to fail in many organizations.[132] Because of the conceptual confusion surrounding empowerment, companies such as Motorola will not use this term to describe programs that push decision making to lower organizational levels. These companies would rather coin their own terms to describe these programs, thus avoiding the confusion surrounding empowerment.

Hemmed in by rules and treated as unimportant, people get even.

Rosabeth Moss Kanter, Harvard University

We define empowerment as having two key components. For leaders to truly empower employees, they must delegate leadership and decision making down to the lowest level possible. Employees are often the closest to the problem and have the most information, and as such can often make the best decisions. A classic example was the UPS employee who ordered an extra 737 aircraft to haul parcels that had been forgotten in the last-minute Christmas rush. This decision was clearly beyond the employee's level of authority, but UPS praised his initiative for seeing the problem and making the right decision. The second component of empowerment, and the one most often overlooked, is equipping followers with the resources, knowledge, and skills necessary to make good decisions. Often companies adopt an empowerment program and push decision making down to the employee level, but employees have no experience in creating business plans, submitting budgets, dealing with other departments within the company, or directly dealing with customers or vendors. Not surprisingly, ill-equipped employees can make poor, uninformed decisions, and managers in turn are likely to believe that empowerment was not all it was cracked up to be. The same happens with downsizing as employees are asked to take on additional responsibilities but are given little training or support. Such "forced" empowerment may lead to some short-term stock gains but tends to be disastrous in the long run. Thus empowerment has both delegation and developmental components; delegation without development is often perceived as abandonment, and development without delegation can often be perceived as micromanagement. Leaders wishing to empower followers must determine what followers are capable of doing, enhance and broaden these capabilities, and give followers commensurate increases in authority and accountability. In many ways the delegation and development components of empowerment are similar to the autonomy and mastery drives described earlier in this chapter.

The psychological components of empowerment can be examined at both macro and micro levels. Three macro psychological components underlie empowerment: motivation, learning, and stress. As a concept, empowerment has been around since at least the 1920s, and the vast majority of companies that have implemented empowerment programs have done so to increase employee motivation and, in turn, productivity. As a motivational technique, empowerment has a mixed record; often empowered workers are more productive than unempowered workers, but at times this may not be the case. When empowerment does not increase productivity, senior leaders may tend to see empowerment through rose-colored glasses. They hear about the benefits an empowerment program is having in another company but do not consider the time, effort, and changes needed to create a truly empowered workforce. Relatedly, many empowerment programs are poorly implemented—the program is announced with great fanfare, but little real guidance, training, or support is provided, and managers are quick to pull the plug on the program as soon as followers start making poor decisions. Adopting an effective empowerment program takes training, trust, and time, but companies most likely to implement an empowerment program (as a panacea for their poor financial situation) often lack these three attributes.[133, 134] Worker productivity in the United States and Europe are near all-time highs, but many companies are dealing with high levels of employee stress. Adding responsibilities to overfilled plates is likely to be counterproductive. As reported by Xie and Johns, some empowerment programs create positions that are just too big for a person to handle effectively, and job burnout is usually the result.[135]

Although the motivational benefits of empowerment are sometimes not realized, the learning and stress reduction benefits of empowerment are more clear-cut. Given that properly designed and implemented empowerment programs include a strong developmental component, a key benefit to these programs is that they help employees learn more about their jobs, company, and industry. These knowledge and skill gains increase the intellectual capital of the company and can be a competitive advantage in moving ahead. In addition to the learning benefits, well-designed empowerment programs can help reduce burnout. People can tolerate high levels of stress when they have a high level of control. Given that many employees are putting in longer hours than ever before and work demands are at an all-time high, empowerment can help followers gain some control over their lives and better cope with stress. Although an empowered worker may have the same high work demands as an unempowered worker, the empowered worker will have more choices in how and when to accomplish these demands and as such will suffer from less stress. Giving workers more control over their work demands can reduce turnover and in turn improve the company's bottom line. (See **Highlight 9.10**.)

Power and Empowerment

HIGHLIGHT 9.10

A famous Lord Acton quote is "Power corrupts," which essentially means that the more power one has the more likely one is to break laws, rules, and societal norms. Leadership researcher Rosabeth Moss Kanter has an interesting variation of this quote that relates to the concept of empowerment. According to Kanter, **powerlessness** also corrupts. In other words, if workers are given only a small amount of power, they will jealously guard whatever power they have. Employees with little power do not show their unhappiness by voicing their opinions but instead flex their muscles by demanding tribute before responding to requests. They rigidly adhere to the policies governing their position and ensure there are no exceptions to anyone following their rules. Customers are told to submit all required forms, get signed permissions from other entities, and follow bureaucratic procedures to the letter if they want anything done, and it will take requesters months to see tangible results. Because speed is an essential component of execution, powerlessness can paralyze companies needing to quickly build products, process orders, submit invoices, receive payments, service customers, or hire and train new employees.

An example of how powerlessness can impact a company's public reputation comes from the airline industry. Most airlines overbook flights, as a small percentage of passengers typically fail to show up for flights they have booked. They also have a set of rules for bumping paid passengers from overbooked flights. Some airlines bump passengers by flying status, others by ticket price or boarding order (that is, frequent fliers, those paying higher prices, and earlier boarders are less likely to get bumped). In April 2017 United Airlines had an overbooked situation and needed four volunteers to take another flight in order to accommodate a flight crew needing to go to another city. Gate agents and flight attendants offered passengers $800 in travel vouchers but got only two takers. The company then asked airport security to forcibly remove two other passengers, one of whom was a 69-year-old medical doctor who received a concussion, sinus damage, facial lacerations, and lost two teeth as a result of the rough treatment given by four airport police. The gate agents, flight attendants, and airport security were following United's bumping procedures, but videos of the incident went viral and the airline lost $770 million in stock value shortly thereafter. The CEO initially blamed the passenger for the problem but changed his tune a few days later when shareholder losses and customer reactions reached a crescendo.

What motivational approaches would best describe the gate agents, flight attendants, and members of the airport security detail? In what ways could United Airlines empower gate agents and flight attendants to deal with overbooked flights? How do motivation and the fundamental attribution error (**Chapter 2**) come into play with the CEO's announcements?

Sources: R. Moss Kanter, "Powerlessness Corrupts," *Harvard Business Review*, July–August 2010, p. 36; D. Victor and M. Stevens, "United Passenger Is Dragged from an Overbooked Flight," *The New York Times*, April 10, 2017, www.nytimes.com/2017/04/10/business/united-flight-passenger-dragged.html; R. Wile, "Here's How Much United Airlines Stock Tanked This Week," *Time*, April 14, 2017, http://time.com/money/4739880/united-airlines-fiasco-overbooked-passenger-dragged-stock-price-value; and

A. C. Ott, "Are Scorecards Killing Employee Engagement?" *Harvard Business Review*, July 12, 2011, https://hbr.org/2011/07/are-scorecards-and-metrics-kil.

There are also four micro components of empowerment. These components can be used to determine whether employees are empowered or unempowered, and include self-determination, meaning, competence, and influence.[136, 137, 138] Empowered employees have a sense of self-determination; they can make choices about what they do, how they do it, and when they need to get it done. Empowered employees also have a strong sense of meaning; they believe what they do is important to them and to the company's success. Empowered employees have a high level of competence: they know what they are doing and are confident they can get the job done. Finally, empowered employees have an impact on others and believe that they can influence their teams or work units and that coworkers and leaders will listen to their ideas. In summary, empowered employees have latitude to make decisions, are comfortable making these decisions, believe what they do is important, and are seen as influential members of their team. Unempowered employees may have little latitude to make decisions, may feel ill equipped and may not want to make decisions, and may have little impact on their work unit, even if they have good ideas. Most employees probably fall somewhere between the two extremes of the empowerment continuum, depicted in **Figure 9.2**.

Empowerment and the operant approach make an important point that is often overlooked by other theories of motivation: by changing the situation, leaders can enhance followers' motivation, performance, and satisfaction. Unfortunately many leaders naively assume it is easier to change an *individual* than it is to change the *situation*, but this is often not the case. The situation is not always fixed, and followers are not the only variable in the performance equation. Leaders can often see positive changes in followers' motivation levels by restructuring work processes and procedures, which in turn can increase their latitude to make decisions and add more meaning to work. Tying these changes to a well-designed and well-implemented reward system can further increase motivation. However, leaders are likely to encounter some resistance whenever they change the processes, procedures, and rewards for work, even if these changes are for the better. Doing things the old way is relatively easy—followers know the expectations for performance and usually have developed the skills needed to achieve results. Followers often find that doing things a new way can be frustrating because expectations may be unclear and they may not have the requisite skills. Leaders can help followers work through this initial resistance to new processes and procedures by showing support, providing training and coaching on new skills, and capitalizing on opportunities to reward progress. If the processes, procedures, and rewards are properly designed and administered, then in many cases followers will successfully work through their resistance and, over time, wonder how they ever got work done using the old systems. The successful transition to new work processes and procedures will rest squarely on the shoulders of leaders.

How could you use empowerment to improve the performance of Julie or Ling Ling or the customer service levels of flight attendants? What information would you need to gather, how would you implement the program, and what would be the potential pitfalls of your program? Some companies, like IBM and Hewlett-

FIGURE 9.2   The Empowerment Continuum

Empowered Employees   ←——————→   **Unempowered Employees**

- Self-determined.
- Sense of meaning.
- High competence.
- High influence.

- Other-determined.
- Not sure if what they do is important.
- Low competence.
- Low influence.

Packard, do not allow people to work from home as they feel that having employees work in an office boosts productivity and innovation.[139] Do you think not empowering employees to work from home is a good idea? What motivational approach would best describe employers' rationale for making this change? What motivational approach would best describe employees' resistance to working out of an office every day?

Summary

Some people believe it is virtually impossible to motivate anyone and that leaders can do little to influence people's decisions regarding the direction, intensity, and persistence of their behavior. Clearly followers bring a lot to the motivational equation, but we feel that a leader's actions can and do affect followers' motivation levels. If leaders did not affect followers' motivation levels, it would not matter whom one worked for—any results obtained would be solely due to followers' efforts. But as you will read in **Chapter 17**, whom one works for matters a lot.

We hope that after reading this chapter you will have a better understanding of how follower characteristics (needs and achievement orientation), leader actions (goal setting), and situational factors (contingent rewards and empowerment) affect how you and your followers are motivated (and demotivated). Moreover, you should be able to start recognizing situations in which some theories provide better insights about problems in motivation levels than others. For example, if you think about the reasons you might not be doing well in a particular class, you may see that you have not set specific goals for your grades or that the rewards for doing well are not clear. Or if you are working in a bureaucratic organization, you may see few consequences for either substandard or superior performance; thus there is little reason to exert extra effort. Perhaps the best strategy for leaders is to be flexible in the types of interventions they consider to affect follower motivation. That will require, of course, familiarity with the strengths and weaknesses of the different theories and approaches presented here.

Similarly, we need to consider how the five motivational approaches can be used with both individuals and teams. Much of this section focused on applying the five approaches to individuals, but the techniques can also be used to motivate teams of followers. For example, a leader must ensure followers share a common understanding of the team's purpose and goals; why does this team exist and what does it need to do to succeed? They should then hire team members with high levels of achievement orientation, clarify roles and responsibilities for everyone, and set high expectations for performance. Leaders should also empower their teams with the latitude needed to make timely decisions when accomplishing assigned tasks, and couple desired rewards with the achievement of team goals. Again, having a good understanding of the five motivational approaches will help leaders determine which ones will be most effective in getting teams to change behavior and exert extra energy and effort.

One of the most important tools for motivating followers has not been fully addressed in this chapter. As described in **Chapter 16**, charismatic or transformational leadership is often associated with extraordinarily high levels of follower motivation, yet none of the theories described in this chapter can adequately explain how these leaders get their followers to do more than they thought possible. Perhaps it is because the theories in this chapter take a rational or logical approach to motivation, yet transformational leadership uses emotion as the fuel to drive followers' heightened motivational levels. Just as our needs, thoughts, personality traits, and rewards can motivate us to do something different, so can our emotions drive us to engage in and persist with particular activities.

A good example here may be found in political campaigns. Do people volunteer to work for these campaigns because of some underlying need or personal goals, or because they feel they will be rewarded by helping out? Although these are potential reasons for some followers, the emotions generated by political campaigns, particularly when the two leading candidates represent different value systems, often seem to provide a better explanation for the large amount of time and effort people contribute. Leadership practitioners should not overlook the interplay between emotions and motivation, and the better able they are to address and capitalize on emotions when introducing change, the more successful they are likely to be.

A final point concerns the relationship between motivation, performance, and effectiveness. Many leadership practitioners equate the three, but as we pointed out earlier in this chapter, they are not the same concepts. Getting followers to put in more time, energy, and effort on certain behaviors will not help the team to be more successful if they are the wrong behaviors to begin with. Similarly, followers may not know how and when to exhibit behaviors associated with team effectiveness. Leadership practitioners must clearly identify the behaviors related to performance and effectiveness, coach and train their followers in how and when to exhibit these behaviors, and then use one or more of the theories described in this chapter to get followers to exhibit and persist with the behaviors associated with higher performance levels.

Key Terms

confirmation bias	autonomy	operant approach
motivation	mastery	reward
performance	meaning	punishment
effectiveness	achievement orientation	contingent
job satisfaction	professional energy	noncontingent
organizational citizenship	grit	extinction
behaviors	goal setting	pay dispersion
engagement	Pygmalion effect	empowerment
needs	Golem effect	powerlessness

Questions

1. Why do you think there are so many different theories or approaches to understanding motivation? Shouldn't it be possible to determine which one is best and just use it? Why or why not?

2. What theory of motivation best describes people's willingness to practice social distancing and remain in isolation during the lockdown phase of the coronavirus pandemic?

3. What is your own view of what motivates people to work hard and perform well?

4. Do you know of any cases in which reward systems are inconsistent with desired behavior? How are personal values related to rewards?

5. Some of the most well-known religious leaders in the United States preach the gospel yet live in multimillion dollar homes, drive expensive cars, and fly around the world in private jets. The money for these possessions comes from donations. What theory of motivation best explains this behavior on the part of these religious leaders? Their donors?

6. Elite performers, such as Olympians, U.S. Navy SEALs, or ultra-marathoners are said to have high levels of motivation. What theories of motivation best explain their willingness to endure the training needed to become a member of one of these elite units?

Activities

1. This chapter addressed how five motivation approaches could be used to improve the customer service levels of flight attendants. Divide the class into five groups, and assign each group one of the motivational approaches described in the chapter. Ask each group to design and implement a motivation program for 20 employees working in a local coffee shop. Each group should then give a 15-minute presentation on their findings. The presentation should include the approach the group used, how they would collect any needed additional data, program design, program implementation, potential barriers to the program, and how they would evaluate program effectiveness.

2. Ask someone to describe what their organization did to motivate employees during the coronavirus pandemic. Did the techniques work? Why or why not? What would they have done instead to keep employees motivated?

3. Split the class into three groups, and ask each group to discuss and report their findings for one of the following questions: What motivational approaches drive the behavior of the Hong Kong protesters? The transportation and government worker protests in France? The political rallies in Lebanon, Bolivia, Venezuela, and Sudan?

4. Conduct a large group discussion on China's extensive use of facial recognition and other electronic monitoring techniques in all its major cities. What effect does this have on the citizens of China? Are people more or less motivated or unaffected by working under these conditions? What are the advantages and disadvantages to living under these conditions?

5. Describe the motivational approaches you would use with a group of volunteers for a community, a group of employees in a for-profit business, or a platoon of soldiers.

6. Anthropologist David Graeber maintains that there are many "useless jobs that no one wants to talk about." Identify the most useless job on campus and determine what would need to happen to make it a more useful job.

Minicase

Initech versus the Coffee Bean

Consider Peter Gibbons, an employee of the fictional Initech Corporation from the movie *Office Space*. Peter has been asked to meet with efficiency experts (Bob and Bob) to discuss his work environment. One of the Bobs is curious about Peter's tendency toward underperformance and confronts him about his lack of attention to office policies and procedures. It seems Peter has been turning in his TPS reports late and without the company-mandated cover sheet:

Peter: You see, Bob, it's not that I'm lazy, it's that I just don't care.
Bob: Don't? Don't care?

Peter: It's a problem of motivation, all right? Now if I work my butt off and Initech ships a few extra units, I don't see another dime, so where's the motivation? And here's another thing, I have eight different bosses right now.

Bob: Eight?

Peter: Eight, Bob. So that means when I make a mistake, I have eight different people coming by to tell me about it. That's my only real motivation, not to be hassled, that and the fear of losing my job. But you know, Bob, that will only make someone work just hard enough not to get fired.

The environment at Initech is an all-too-familiar one for many office workers. It is an environment in which success is directly proportional to how busy you look, where questioning authority is taboo, and where meticulous attention to paperwork is the only way to get promoted.

Contrast Initech to the Coffee Bean—a chain of gourmet coffee shops. In an effort to boost employee morale and increase productivity, the management team at the Coffee Bean decided to pursue the FISH philosophy. FISH is a management training program that stresses fun in the workplace. It espouses four principles:

Play—"Work that is made fun gets done."

Make Their Day—"When you make someone's day through a small act of kindness or unforgettable engagement, you can turn even routine encounters into special memories."

Be There—"Being there is a great way to practice wholeheartedness and fight burnout."

Choose Your Attitude—"When you learn you have the power to choose your response to what life brings, you can look for the best and find opportunities you never imagined possible."

Stores in the Coffee Bean chain were encouraged to use these principles to make the stores a fun place for employees and customers. The stores have created theme days where employees dress up for themes (NFL day, basketball day, pajama day)—and then give discounts to customers who do the same. There are also trivia games in which customers who can answer trivia questions get discounts on their coffee purchases. Nancy Feilen, a Coffee Bean store manager, explains, "We tried to come up with something that would help strike up a conversation with guests and engage fun in the stores for team members and guests." In other stores, customers play Coffee Craps. Customers who roll a 7 or an 11 get a free drink. Some stores have used Fear Factor Fridays: If the store sells a certain number of drinks, one of the baristas will agree to some act—in one case, a barista ate a cricket.

The results? One store increased the average check by 12 percent in six months; turnover has decreased significantly—general managers typically left after 22 months with the chain but now stay an average of 31 months; and the turnover rate for hourly employees dropped to 69 percent from more than 200 percent over a three-year period.

So where would you rather work—Initech or Coffee Bean?

1. How would you gauge Peter Gibbons's achievement orientation? What are some of the needs not being met for Peter at Initech? What changes might improve Peter's motivation?

2. Would you judge the leaders at Initech as more likely to invoke the Pygmalion or the Golem effect? What about the environment at the Coffee Bean—Pygmalion or Golem effect?

3. Why has the Coffee Bean seen such a significant reduction in turnover?

Sources: "Office Space quotes," IMDB, www.imdb.com/title/tt0151804/quotes; "The FISH! Philosophy," *ChartHouse Learning*, www.fishphilosophy.com; and "'Go Fish': Coffee Company Takes a Cue from Seattle Seafood Market," *Nation's Restaurant News*, January 12, 2004, v38 i2 p. 16, www.swlearning.com/management/management_news/motivation_1004_001.html.

Endnotes

Part 3

1. K. Peters and A. Haslam, "Research: To Be a Good Leader, Start by Being a Good Follower," *Harvard Business Review*, August 6, 2018, https://hbr.org/2018/08/research-to-be-a-good-leader-start-by-being-a-good-follower.

2. G. Anders, "Management Leaders Turn Attention to Followers," *The Wall Street Journal*, January 24, 2007, p. B3.

3. S. Jones, "The Lost Art of Following," *Minneapolis Star Tribune*, October 7, 2007, pp. AA1–AA5.

4. E. Hollander, *Inclusive Leadership* (New York: Routledge/Taylor and Francis, 2008).

5. B. Shamir, "From Passive Recipients to Active Coproducers: Followers Role in the Leadership Process," in *Follower-Centered Perspectives on Leadership: A Tribute to the Memory of James R. Meindl*, eds. B. Shamir, R. Pillai, M. C. Bligh, and M. Uhl-Bien (Greenwich, CT: Inform. Age, 2007).

6. T. Chamorro-Premuzic and A. Yearsley, "The War for Talent Is Over, and Everyone Lost," *Fast Company*, March 25, 2017, www.fastcompany.com/3069078/the-war-for-talent-is-over-and-everyone-lost.

7. C. Hoption, "Learning and Developing Followership," *Journal of Leadership Education*, Summer 2014, pp. 129–37.

8. V. Van Brocklin, "Is 'Great Followership' the Real Secret to Great Leadership?" *Police One*, June 19, 2013, www.policeone.com/police-jobs-and-careers/articles/6283412-Is-great-followership-the-real-secret-to-great-leadership.

9. S. Shellenbarger, "Leader? No, Be a Follower'" *The Wall Street Journal*, September 30, 2015, pp. D1, D3.

10. G. J. Curphy and R. T. Hogan, *The Rocket Model: Practical Advice for Building High Performing Teams* (Tulsa, OK: Hogan Press, 2012).

11. M. Van Vugt, R. Hogan, and R. B. Kaiser, "Leadership, Followership, and Evolution: Some Lessons from the Past," *American Psychologist* 63, no. 3 (April 2008), pp. 182–96.

12. J. M. Burger, "Replicating Milgram: Would People Still Obey Today?" *American Psychologist* 64, no. 1 (2009), pp. 1–11.

13. Hollander, *Inclusive Leadership*.

14. P. Bordia, S. L. D. Restubog, and R. L. Tang, "When Employees Strike Back: Investigating Mediating Mechanisms between Psychological Contract Breach and Workplace Deviance," *Journal of Applied Psychology* 93, no. 5 (2008), pp. 1104–17.

15. Chamorro-Premuzic and Yearsley, "The War for Talent Is Over, and Everyone Lost."

16. Hollander, *Inclusive Leadership*.

17. A. Zaleznik, "The Dynamics of Subordinacy," *Harvard Business Review*, May–June 1965, pp. 119–131.

18. R. E. Kelley, *The Power of Followership: How to Create Leaders People Want to Follow, and Followers Who Led Themselves* (New York: Doubleday, 1982).

19. I. Chaleff, *The Courageous Follower*, 3rd ed. (San Francisco: Berrett-Koehler, 2009).

20. B. Kellerman, "What Every Leader Needs to Know about Followers," *Harvard Business Review*, December 2007, pp. 84–91.

21. R. Adair, "Developing Great Leaders, One Follower at a Time," in *The Art of Followership: How Great Followers Create Great Leaders and Organizations*, eds. R. E. Riggio, I. Chaleff, and J. Lipman-Blumen (San Francisco: Jossey-Bass, 2008), pp. 137–53.

22. J. C. McCroskey, V. P. Richmond, A. D. Johnson, and H. T. Smith, "Organizational Orientations Theory and Measurement: Development of Measures and Preliminary Investigations," *Communication Quarterly* 52 (2004), pp. 1–14.

23. E. H. Potter III and W. E. Rosenbach, "Followers as Partners: Ready When the Time Comes," in *Military Leadership*, 6th ed. (Boulder, CO: Westview Press, 2009).

24. G. J. Curphy and M. E. Roellig, *Followership*, unpublished manuscript (North Oaks, MN: Author, 2010).

25. Curphy and Hogan, *The Rocket Model*.

26. G. Curphy, D. Nilsen, and R. Hogan, *Ignition: A Guide to Building High Performing Teams* (Tulsa, OK: Hogan Press, 2019).

27. Potter and Rosenbach, "Followers as Partners."

28. Curphy and Roellig, *Followership*.

29. Hollander, *Inclusive Leadership*.

30. Kelley, *The Power of Followership*.

31. Chaleff, *The Courageous Follower*.

32. Kellerman, "What Every Leader Needs to Know about Followers."

33. U. K. Bindl, S. K. Parker, P. Totterdell, and G. Hagger-Johnson, "Fuel of the Self-Starter: How Mood Relates to Proactive Goal Regulation," *Journal of Applied Psychology* 97, no. 1 (2012), pp. 134–50.

34. G. Curphy, D. Nilsen, and R. Hogan, *Ignition: A Guide to Building High Performing Teams* (Tulsa, OK: Hogan Press, 2019).

35. G. J. Curphy and R. T. Hogan, *The Rocket Model: Practical Advice for Building High Performing Teams* (Tulsa, OK: Hogan Press, 2012).

36. E. R. Burris, "The Risks and Rewards of Speaking Up: Managerial Responses to Employee Voice," *Academy of Management Journal* 55, no. 4 (2012), pp. 851–75.

37. D. Mercer, *Follow to Lead: The 7 Principles of Being a Good Follower* (Mustang, OK: Tate Publishing, 2011).

38. E. Holm and J. S. Lublin, "Loose Lips Trip Up Good Hands Executive," *The Wall Street Journal*, August 1, 2011, pp. C1, C3.

39. M. Hastings, "The Runaway General," *Rolling Stone*, June 22, 2010, www.rollingstone.com/politics/news/the-runaway-general-20100622.

40. R. Sisk, "Gen. Stanley McChrystal to Meet with 'Angry' President Obama; Resignation Possible after 'Mistake'," *Daily News*, June 22, 2010, www.nydailynews.com/news/politics/gen-stanley-mcchrystal-meet-angry-president-obama-resignation-mistake-article-1.181477.

41. A. L. Blanchard, J. Welbourne, D. Gilmore, and A. Bullock, "Followership Styles and Employee Attachment to the Organization," *The Psychologist-Manager Journal* 12, no. 2 (2009), pp. 111–31.

42. D. Brooks, "The Follower Problem," *The New York Times*, June 11, 2012, www.nytimes.com/2012/06/12/opinion/brooks-the-follower-problem.html.

43. R. Sutton, "How a Few Bad Apples Ruin Everything," *The Wall Street Journal*, October 23, 2011, www.wsj.com/articles/SB10001424052970203499704576622550325233260.

Chapter 09

1. J. E. Hunter, F. L. Schmidt, and M. K. Judiesch, "Individual Differences in Output Variability as a Function of Job Complexity," *Journal of Applied Psychology* 74 (1990), pp. 28–42.

2. E. Matson and L. Prusak, "The Performance Variability Dilemma," *MIT Sloan Management Review* 45, no. 1 (2003), pp. 38–44.

3. B. Groysberg, *Chasing Stars: The Myth of Talent and the Portability of Performance* (Princeton, NJ: Princeton University Press, 2010).

4. Associated Press, "Democrats Hit Troop Extensions," *NBC News*, April 12, 2007, www.nbcnews.com/id/18072870/ns/politics/t/democrats-hit-troop-extensions-iraq.

5. R. T. Hogan, G. J. Curphy, R. B. Kaiser, and T. Chamorro-Premuzic, "Leadership in Organizations," in *The Sage Handbook of Industrial, Work, and Organizational Psychology. Volume 2: Organizational Psychology*, eds. N. Anderson, D. Ones, H. K. Sinangil, and C. Viswesvaran (London: Sage, 2017).

6. E. Holm and J. S. Lublin, "Loose Lips Trip Up Good Hands Executive," *The Wall Street Journal*, August 1, 2011, pp. C1, C3.

7. Blanchard, Welbourne, Gilmore, and Bullock, "Followership Styles and Employee Attachment to the Organization," *The Psychologist-Manager Journal*, 12(2), 111–131.

8. R. Kanfer, "Motivation Theory in Industrial and Organizational Psychology," in *Handbook of Industrial and Organizational Psychology*, vol. 1, eds. M. D. Dunnette and L. M. Hough (Palo Alto, CA: Consulting Psychologists Press, 1990), pp. 75–170.

9. E. A. Locke and G. P. Latham, "What Should We Do about Motivation Theory? Six Recommendations for the Twenty-First Century," *Academy of Management Review* 29, no. 3 (2004), pp. 388–403.

10. R. M. Steers, R. T. Mowday, and D. L. Shapiro, "The Future of Work Motivation Theory," *Academy of Management Review* 29, no. 3 (2004), pp. 379–87.

11. R. Kanfer, M. Frese, and R. E. Johnson, "Motivation Related to Work: A Century of Progress," *Journal of Applied Psychology*, 102, no. 3 (2017), pp. 338–55.

12. I. Smithey-Fulmer, B. Gerhart, and K. S. Scott, "Are the 100 Best Better? An Empirical Investigation of the Relationship between Being a 'Great Place to Work' and Firm Performance," *Personnel Psychology* 56, no. 4 (2003), pp. 965–93.

13. F. E. Saal and P. A. Knight, *Industrial Organizational Psychology: Science and Practice* (Belmont, CA: Brooks/Cole, 1988).

14. T. A. Judge, C. J. Thoresen, J. E. Bono, and G. K. Patton, "The Job Satisfaction–Job Performance Relationship: A Qualitative and Quantitative Review," *Psychological Bulletin* 127 (2001): 376–407.

15. D. P. Campbell and S. Hyne, *Manual for the Revised Campbell Organizational Survey* (Minneapolis, MN: National Computer Systems, 1995).

16. Health, Education, and Welfare Task Force, *Work in America* (Cambridge, MA: MIT Press, 1973).

17. R. Hoppock, *Job Satisfaction* (New York: Harper, 1935).

18. F. J. Smith, K. D. Scott, and C. L. Hulin, "Trends in Job-Related Attitudes in Managerial and Professional Employees," *Academy of Management Journal* 20 (1977), pp. 454–60.

19. G. L. Staines and R. P. Quinn, "American Workers Evaluate the Quality of Their Jobs," *Monthly Labor Review* 102, no. 1 (1979), pp. 3–12.

20. J. A. Colquitt, B. A. Scott, J. B. Rodell, D. M. Long, C. P. Zapata, D. E. Conlon, and M. J. Wesson, "Justice at the Millennium, a Decade Later: A Meta-Analytic Test of Social Exchange and Affect-Based Perspectives," *Journal of Applied Psychology* 98, no. 2 (2013), pp. 199–236.

21. R. Cropanzano, D. E. Rupp, and Z. S. Byrne, "The Relationship of Emotional Exhaustion to Work Attitudes, Job Performance, and Organizational Citizenship Behaviors," *Journal of Applied Psychology* 88, no. 1 (2003), pp. 160–69.

22. R. Ilies, B. A. Scott, and T. A. Judge, "The Interactive Effects of Personality Traits and Experienced States on the Intraindividual Patterns of Citizenship Behavior," *Academy of Management Journal* 49, no. 3 (2006), pp. 561–75.

23. B. R. Dineen, R. J. Lewicki, and E. C. Tomlinson, "Supervisory Guidance and Behavioral Integrity: Relationships with Employee Citizenship and Deviant Behavior," *Journal of Applied Psychology* 91, no. 3 (2006), pp. 622–35.

24. L. Y. Sun, S. Aryee, and K. S. Law, "High-Performance Human Resource Practices, Citizenship Behavior, and Organizational Performance: A Relational Perspective," *Academy of Management Journal* 50, no. 3 (2007), pp. 558–77.

25. J. Brockner, "Why It's So Hard to Be Fair," *Harvard Business Review*, March 2006, p. 122–30.

26. D. S. Whitman, D. L. Van Rooy, and C. Viswesvaran, "Satisfaction, Citizenship Behaviors, and Performance in Work Units: A Meta-Analysis of Collective Construct Relations," *Personnel Psychology* 63, no. 1 (2010), pp. 41–81.

27. Judge, Thoresen, Bono, and Patton, "The Job Satisfaction–Job Performance Relationship."

28. Campbell and Hyne, *Manual for the Revised Campbell Organizational Survey.*

29. Health, Education, and Welfare Task Force, *Work in America.*

30. Chamorro-Premuzic and Yearsley, "The War for Talent Is Over, and Every one Lost." Fast Company, March 15, 2017, https://www.fastcompany.com/3069078/the-war-for-talent-is-over-and-everyone-lost.

31. G. A. Gelade and M. Ivery, "The Impact of Human Resource Management and Work Climate on Organizational Performance," *Personnel Psychology* 56, no. 2 (2003), pp. 383–404.

32. Smithey-Fulmer, Gerhart, and Scott, "Are the 100 Best Better?"

33. "Schumpeter: Overstretched," *The Economist*, May 22, 2010, p. 72.

34. K. B. Paul and C. L. Johnson, "Engagement at 3 M: A Case Study," in *The Executive Guide to Integrated Talent Management*, eds. K. Oakes and P. Galahan (Alexandria, VA: ASTD Press, 2011), pp. 133–46.

35. D. Ulrich, "Integrated Talent Management," in *The Executive Guide to Integrated Talent Management*, ed. K. Oakes and P. Galahan (Alexandria, VA: ASTD Press, 2011), pp. 189–212.

36. R. Charan, S. Drotter, and J. Noel, *The Leadership Pipeline: How to Build the Leadership-Powered Company* (San Francisco: Jossey-Bass, 2001).

37. B. N. Pfau and S. A. Cohen, "Aligning Human Capital Practices and Employee Behavior with Shareholder Value," *Consulting Psychology Journal* 55, no. 3 (2003), pp. 169–78.

38. M. A. Huselid, R. W. Beatty, and B. E. Becker, "'A Players' or 'A Positions'? The Strategic Logic of Workforce Management," *Harvard Business Review*, December 2005, pp. 110–21.

39. G. J. Curphy and M. Roellig, "Followership," working paper, 2010.

40. R. T. Hogan, *Personality and the Fate of Organizations* (Mahwah, NJ: Lawrence Erlbaum Associates, 2007).

41. Chamorro-Premuzic and Yearsley, "The War for Talent Is Over, and Everyone Lost."

42. Groysberg, *Chasing Stars.*

43. J. P. Campbell, "The Cutting Edge of Leadership: An Overview," in *Leadership: The Cutting Edge*, ed. J. G. Hunt and L. L. Larson (Carbondale: Southern Illinois University Press, 1977).

44. J. P. Campbell, "Training Design for Performance Improvement," in *Productivity in Organizations: New Perspectives from Industrial and Organizational Psychology*, eds. J. P. Campbell, R. J. Campbell, and Associates (San Francisco: Jossey-Bass, 1988), pp. 177–216.

45. D. B. McFarlin, "Hard Day's Work: A Boon for Performance but a Bane for Satisfaction?" *Academy of Management Perspectives* 20, no. 4 (2006), pp. 115–16.

46. A. G. Walker, J. W. Smither, and D. A. Waldman, "A Longitudinal Examination of Concomitant Changes in Team Leadership and Customer Satisfaction," *Personnel Psychology* 61, no. 3 (2008), pp. 547–78.

47. Saal and Knight, *Industrial Organizational Psychology.*

48. M. T. Iaffaldano and P. M. Muchinsky, "Job Satisfaction and Job Performance: A Meta-analysis," *Psychological Bulletin* 97 (1985), pp. 251–73.

49. E. A. Locke and G. P. Latham, "Work Motivation and Satisfaction: Light at the End of the Tunnel," *Psychological Science* 1 (1990), pp. 240–46.

50. A. H. Maslow, *Motivation and Personality* (New York: Harper & Row, 1954).

51. Kanfer, "Motivation Theory in Industrial and Organizational Psychology."

52. E. I. Betz, "Two Tests of Maslow's Theory of Need Fulfillment," *Journal of Vocational Behavior* 24, (1984), pp. 204–20.

53. E. L. Deci, *The Psychology of Self-Determination* (Lexington, MA: Lexington Books, 1980).

54. J. R. Hackman and G. R. Oldham, *Work Redesign* (Reading, MA: Addison-Wesley, 1980).

55. D. H. Pink, *Drive: The Surprising Truth about What Motivates Us* (New York: Riverhead Books, 2009).

56. S. McFeely and R. Pendell, "What Workplace Leaders Can Learn from the Real Gig Economy," *Gallup*, August 16, 2018, www.gallup.com/workplace/240929/workplace-leaders-learn-real-gig-economy.aspx.

57. R. Quinn and A. Thakor, "Creating a Purpose Driven Organization," *Harvard Business Review*, July–August 2018, pp. 78–85.

58. T. M. Amabile, S. J. Kramer, E. Bonabeau, A. Bingham, R. E. Litan, J. Klein, and C. Ross, "What Really Motivates Workers?" *Harvard Business Review*, January–February 2010, pp. 44–45.

59. S. Murphy, *The Optimistic Workplace: Creating an Environment That Energizes Everyone* (Chicago: Amacom, 2015).

60. T. Chamorro-Premuzic, "What It Really Takes to Find Meaningful Work," *Fast Company*, June 2, 2015, www.fastcompany.com/3046825/what-it-really-takes-to-find-meaningful-work.

61. J. J. Deal, S. Stawiski, L. Graves, W. A. Gentry, T. J. Weber, and M. Ruderman, "Motivation at Work: Which Matters More, Generation or Managerial Level?" *Consulting Psychologist Journal: Practice and Research* 65, no. 1 (2013).

62. G. Graeber, *Bullshit Jobs* (New York: Simon & Schuster, 2019).

63. C. Domonoske, "Passenger Forcibly Removed from United Flight, Prompting Outcry," *NPR*, April 10, 2017, www.npr.org/sections/thetwo-way/2017/04/10/523275494/passenger-forcibly-removed-from-united-flight-prompting-outcry.

64. Kanfer, "Motivation Theory in Industrial and Organizational Psychology."

65. J. W. Atkinson, "Motivational Determinants of Risk Taking Behavior," *Psychological Review* 64 (1957), pp. 359–72.

66. D. C. McClelland, *Power: The Inner Experience* (New York: Irvington, 1975).

67. Hogan, *Personality and the Fate of Organizations.*

68. M. R. Barrick and M. K. Mount, "The Big Five Personality Dimensions and Job Performance: A Meta-analysis," *Personal Psychology* 44 (1991), pp. 1–26.

69. T. A. Judge and R. Ilies, "Relationship of Personality to Performance Motivation: A Meta-analytic Review," *Journal of Applied Psychology* 87, no. 4 (2002), pp. 797–807.

70. R. Hogan, T. Chamorro-Premuzic, and R. B. Kaiser, "Employability and Career Success: Bridging the Gap between Theory and Reality," *Industrial and Organizational Psychology: Perspectives on Science and Practice* 1, no. 6 (2013), pp. 3–16.

71. G. J. Curphy and K. D. Osten, *"Technical Manual for the Leadership Development Survey,"* Technical Report No. 93-14 (Colorado Springs, CO: U.S. Air Force Academy, 1993).

72. T. A. Judge and J. D. Kanmeyer-Mueller, "On the Value of Aiming High: The Causes and Consequences of Ambition," *Journal of Applied Psychology* 97, no. 4 (2012), pp. 758–75.

73. R. T. Hogan and J. Hogan, *Manual for the Hogan Personality Inventory* (Tulsa, OK: Hogan Assessment Systems, 1992).

74. D. L. Nilsen, *Using Self and Observers' Rating of Personality to Predict Leadership Performance,* unpublished doctoral dissertation, University of Minnesota, 1995.

75. S. A. Hewlett, "Executive Women and the Myth of Having It All," *Harvard Business Review,* April 2002, pp. 66–67.

76. G. J. Curphy, *Hogan Assessment Systems Certification Workshop Training Manuals* (Tulsa, OK: Hogan Assessment Systems, 2003).

77. R. Gregory, R. T. Hogan, and G. J. Curphy, "Risk-Taking in the Energy Industry," *Well Connected* 5, no. 6 (June 2003), pp. 5–7.

78. M. P. Wilmot and D. A. Ones, "A Century of Research on Conscientiousness at Work," *PNAS,* 2019, www.gwern.net/docs/conscientiousness/2019-wilmot.pdf.

79. T. W. Britt, "Black Hawk Down at Work," *Harvard Business Review,* January 2003, pp. 16–17.

80. E. A. Locke and G. P. Latham, "Building a Practically Useful Theory of Goal Setting and Task Motivation: A 35-Year Odyssey," *American Psychologist* 57, no. 9 (2002), pp. 705–18.

81. E. A. Locke, "Goal Setting Theory and Its Applications to the World of Business," *Academy of Management Executive* 18, no. 4 (2004), pp. 124–25.

82. G. P. Latham, "The Motivational Benefits of Goal Setting," *Academy of Management Executive* 18, no. 4 (2004), pp. 126–29.

83. E. A. Locke and G. P. Latham, "Has Goal Setting Gone Wild, or Have Its Attackers Abandoned Good Scholarship?" *Academy of Management Perspectives* 23, no. 1 (2009), pp. 17–23.

84. "Schumpeter: The Quantified Serf," *The Economist,* March 7, 2015, p. 70.

85. S. B. Sitkin, C. C. Miller, and K. E. See, "The Stretch Goal Paradox," *Harvard Business Review,* January–February 2017, pp. 93–99.

86. L. D. Ordonez, M. E. Schweitzer, A. D. Galinsky, and M. H. Bazerman, "Goals Gone Wild: The Systematic Side Effects of Overprescribing Goal Setting," *Academy of Management Perspectives* 23, no. 1 (2009), pp. 6–16.

87. S. Kerr and S. Landauer, "Using Stretch Goals to Promote Organizational Effectiveness and Personal Growth: General Electric and Goldman Sachs," *Academy of Management Executive* 18, no. 4 (2004), pp. 139–43.

88. Y. Fried and L. Haynes Slowik, "Enriching Goal-Setting Theory with Time: An Integrated Approach," *Academy of Management Review* 29, no. 3 (2004), pp. 404–22.

89. E. A. Locke, "Linking Goals to Monetary Incentives," *Academy of Management Executive* 18, no. 4 (2004), pp. 130–33.

90. S. B. Sitkin, K. E. See, C. C. Miller, M. W. Lawless, and A. M. Carton, "The Paradox of Stretch Goals: Organizations in Pursuit of the Seemingly Impossible," *Academy of Management Review* 36, no. 3 (2011), pp. 544–66.

91. M. Imai, *Kaizen: The Key to Japan's Competitive Success* (New York: Random House, 1986).

92. D. D. Van Fleet, T. O. Peterson, and E. W. Van Fleet, "Closing the Performance Feedback Gap with Expert Systems," *Academy of Management Executive* 19, no. 3 (2005), pp. 35–42.

93. O. B. Davidson and D. Eden, "Remedial Self-Fulfilling Prophecy: Two Field Experiments to Prevent Golem Effects among Disadvantaged Women," *Journal of Applied Psychology* 83, no. 3 (2000), pp. 386–98.

94. D. Eden, D. Geller, A. Gewirtz, R. Gordon-Terner, I. Inbar, M. Liberman, Y. Pass, I. Salomon-Segev, and M. Shalit, "Implanting Pygmalion Leadership Style through Workshop Training: Seven Field Experiments," *The Leadership Quarterly* 11, no. 2 (2000), pp. 171–210.

95. S. S. White and E. A. Locke, "Problems with the Pygmalion Effect and Some Proposed Solutions," *The Leadership Quarterly* 11, no. 3 (2000), pp. 389–416.

96. D. B. McNatt, "Ancient Pygmalion Joins Contemporary Management: A Meta-analysis of the Result," *Journal of Applied Psychology* 83, no. 2 (2000), pp. 314–21.

97. J. Warner, "Does Management by Objectives(MBO) Still Work as an Approach Today?" Ready to Manage, June 26, 2013, http://blog.readytomanage.com/does-management-by-objectives-mbo-still-work-as-an-approach-today.

98. C. Crimmins and K. Freifeld, "'Best Banker in America' Blamed for Wells Fargo Sales Scandal," *Reuters*, April 10, 2017, www.reuters.com/article/us-wells-fargo-accounts-idUSKBN17C18P.

99. B. Temkin, "Wells Fargo: A Lesson in Leadership & Culture Gone Awry," Experience Matters, September 21, 2016, https://experiencematters.blog/2016/09/21/wells-fargo-a-lesson-in-leadership-culture-gone-awry.

100. E. Glazer and C. Rexrode, "Wells Fargo CEO Defends Bank Culture, Lays Blame with Bad Employees," *The Wall Street Journal*, September 13, 2016, www.wsj.com/articles/wells-fargo-ceo-defends-bank-culture-lays-blame-with-bad-employees-1473784452.

101. M. Daly, "The Curse of Efficiency," *The Economist*, July 27, 2019, p. 55.

102. M. Harris and B. Tayler, "Don't Let Metrics Undermine Your Business," *Harvard Business Review*, September–October 2019, pp. 63–69.

103. R. D. Arvey and J. M. Ivancevich, "Punishment in Organizations: A Review, Propositions, and Research Suggestions," *Academy of Management Review* 5 (1980), pp. 123–32.

104. G. J. Curphy, "What We Really Know about Leadership (But Seem Unwilling to Implement)," presentation given at the Minnesota Professionals for Psychology Applied to Work, Minneapolis, MN, January 2004.

105. L. S. Anderson, *The Cream of the Corp* (Hastings, MN: Anderson Performance Improvement Company, 2003).

106. S. E. Markham, K. D. Scott, and G. H. McKee, "Recognizing Good Attendance: A Longitudinal Quasi-Experimental Field Study," *Personnel Psychology* 55, no. 3 (2002), pp. 639–60.

107. A. D. Stajkovic and F. Luthans, "Differential Effects of Incentive Motivators on Performance," *Academy of Management Journal* 44, no. 3 (2001), pp. 580–90.

108. F. Luthans and A. D. Stajkovic, "Reinforce for Performance: The Need to Go beyond Pay and Even Rewards," *Academy of Management Executive* 13, no. 2 (1999), pp. 49–57.

109. M. Bloom and G. T. Milkovich, "Relationships among Risk, Incentive Pay, and Organizational Performance," *Academy of Management Journal* 41, no. 3 (1998), pp. 283–97.

110. G. D. Jenkins, A. Mitra, N. Gupta, and J. D. Shaw, "Are Financial Incentives Related to Performance? A Meta-analytic Review of Empirical Research," *Journal of Applied Psychology* 83, no. 5 (1998), pp. 777–87.

111. J. L. Komacki, S. Zlotnick, and M. Jensen, "Development of an Operant-Based Taxonomy and Observational Index on Supervisory Behavior," *Journal of Applied Psychology* 71 (1986), pp. 260–69.

112. R. D. Pritchard, J. Hollenback, and P. J. DeLeo, "The Effects of Continuous and Partial Schedules of Reinforcement of Effort, Performance, and Satisfaction," *Organizational Behavior and Human Performance* 16 (1976), pp. 205–30.

113. Anderson, *The Cream of the Corp.*

114. Stajkovic and Luthans, "Differential Effects of Incentive Motivators on Performance."

115. Jenkins et al., "Are Financial Incentives Related to Performance?"

116. F. Luthans and R. Kreitner, *Organizational Behavior Modification and Beyond: An Operant and Social Learning Approach* (Glenview, IL: Scott Foresman, 1985).

117. P. M. Podsakoff and W. D. Todor, "Relationships between Leader Reward and Punishment Behavior and Group Process and Productivity," *Journal of Management* 11 (1985), pp. 55–73.

118. P. M. Podsakoff, W. D. Todor, and R. Skov, "Effects of Leader Contingent and Noncontingent Reward and Punishment Behaviors on Subordinate Performance and Satisfaction," *Academy of Management Journal* 25 (1982), pp. 810–25.

119. R. D. Arvey, G. A. Davis, and S. M. Nelson, "Use of Discipline in an Organization: A Field Study," *Journal of Applied Psychology* 69 (1984), pp. 448–60.

120. Stajkovic and Luthans, "Differential Effects of Incentive Motivators on Performance."

121. Markham, Scott, and McKee, "Recognizing Good Attendance."

122. Stajkovic and Luthans, "Differential Effects of Incentive Motivators on Performance."

123. S. Gregory, "The Most Common Type of Incompetent Leader," *Harvard Business Review*, March 30, 2018, https://hbr.org/2018/03/the-most-common-type-of-incompetent-leader.

124. R. Kaiser, "The Accountability Crisis," *Talent Quarterly*, The High Performance Issue, 2019, pp. 58–63.

125. C. Cancialosi, "The Dark Side of Bonus and Incentive Programs," *GothamCulture*, June 18, 2014, https://gothamculture.com/2014/06/18/forbes-dark-side-bonus-incentive-program.

126. R. Hotten, "Volkswagen: The Scandal Explained," *BBC*, December 10, 2015, www.bbc.com/news/business-34324772.

127. R. E. Quinn and G. M. Spreitzer, "The Road to Empowerment: Seven Questions Every Leader Should Consider," *Organizational Dynamics*, Autumn 1997, pp. 37–49.

128. S. H. Wagner, C. P. Parker, and N. D. Christiansen, "Employees That Think and Act Like Owners: Effects of Ownership Beliefs and Behaviors on Organizational Effectiveness," *Personnel Psychology* 56, no. 4 (2003), pp. 847–71.

129. A. Srivastava, K. M. Bartol, and E. A. Locke, "Empowering Leadership in Management Teams: Effects on Knowledge Sharing, Efficacy, and Performance," *Academy of Management Journal* 49, no. 6 (2006), pp. 1239–251.

130. S. E. Seibert, S. R. Silver, and W. A. Randolph, "Taking Empowerment to the Next Level: A Multiple-Level Model of Empowerment, Performance, and Satisfaction," *Academy of Management Journal* 47, no. 3 (2004), pp. 332–49.

131. M. Ahearne, J. Mathis, and A. Rapp, "To Empower or Not Empower Your Sales Force? An Empirical Examination of the Influence of Leadership Empowerment Behavior on Customer Satisfaction and Performance," *Journal of Applied Psychology* 90, no. 5 (2005), pp. 945–55.

132. Quinn and Spreitzer, "The Road to Empowerment."

133. J. Combs, Y. Liu, A. Hall, and D. Ketchen, "How Much Do High Performance Work Practices Matter? A Meta-analysis of Their Effects on Organizational Performance," *Personnel Psychology* 59 (2006), pp. 502–28.

134. L. R. Offermann, "Leading and Empowering Diverse Followers," in *The Balance of Leadership and Followership*, ed. E. P. Hollander and L. R. Offermann, Kellogg Leadership Studies Project (College Park: University of Maryland Press, 1997), pp. 31–46.

135. J. L. Xie and G. Johns, "Job Scope and Stress: Can Job Scope Be Too High?" *Academy of Management Journal* 38, no. 5 (1995), pp. 1288–1309.

136. Quinn and Spreitzer, "The Road to Empowerment."

137. Wagner et al., "Employees That Think and Act Like Owners."

138. G. M. Spreitzer, "Psychological Empowerment in the Workplace: Dimensions, Measurement, and Validation," *Academy of Management Journal* 38, no. 5 (1995), pp. 1442–65.

139. B. Kasanoff, "'Innovative' IBM Kills Working from Home," LinkedIn, March 26, 2017, www.linkedin.com/pulse/innovative-ibm-kills-working-from-home-bruce-kasanoff.

CHAPTER 10

Follower Satisfaction and Engagement

Introduction

Is it a leader's job to make followers happy? Are happy and satisfied followers better performers than those who are dissatisfied with their jobs? If leaders improve followers' attitudes toward work, should they see a commensurate increase in followers' performance? As described in **Chapter 9**, job satisfaction does not have a particularly strong relationship with job performance. Happy followers may be content with the situation and express little urgency to get anything done whereas dissatisfied workers sometimes produce superior results. Because the relationship between job satisfaction and job performance has been so tenuous, researchers started asking whether other follower attitudes might be better predictors of employee work behavior. Over the past 20 years, researchers have determined that employee engagement, a concept highly related to but different from job satisfaction and motivation, has stronger relationships with followers' performance levels and team or organizational effectiveness measures. Organizations seized upon these findings and routinely assess and implement approaches to improve employee engagement. Employee engagement has become a key metric for Human Resources and has grown to be a big business, with organizations spending over $700 million annually to improve engagement scores. Millions of employees around the globe are surveyed each year, and these results have yielded some interesting findings (see **Figure 10.1**).[1, 2, 3, 4,5]

Whereas employee satisfaction surveys typically ask followers about their attitudes toward a broad variety of factors, such as working conditions, stress levels, pay and benefits, job security, promotion opportunities, diversity, or top leadership, employee engagement is more focused on followers' attitudes toward the tasks and work activities they need to perform. Some people truly believe what they do is important and enjoy their work, whether they are designing marketing campaigns, operating power plants, writing computer code, or helping people obtain student loans. Others choose to work for the pay and benefits and find their jobs to be neither impactful nor enjoyable. Researchers have found that organizations with higher percentages of fully engaged employees tend to report better results than those with lower percentages of these followers, and employee engagement has now become the "holy grail" of employee attitudinal research.[6, 7, 8,9] Some consultants and organizations have come to believe that employee engagement is an end unto itself—getting followers to feel the work they do is interesting and important is the right thing to do. Although these altruistic notions are laudable, most organizations believe employee engagement is more a means to an end. Organizations exist to achieve results and are concerned primarily with effectiveness measures, such as market share, overall customer satisfaction levels, annual revenues, or followers' productivity levels. Top leaders see having highly engaged employees as a pathway to achieve superior results. [10, 11, 12, 13, 14,15]

> *Too many highly trained, committed professionals return again and again to the methodology that employee engagement programs are what "WE might do to make THEM feel invested in US." They are an HR brand-loyalty marketing program, really.*
>
> **Mark Kille, human resources consultant**

Understanding and Influencing Follower Satisfaction

This chapter begins with an overview of the follower satisfaction research. Although employee engagement has replaced satisfaction in many organizations, some organizations prefer to assess worker satisfaction rather than employee engagement. Moreover, much of what we know about employee engagement has its roots in the job satisfaction research, so reviewing these findings and their implications is important. The chapter then reviews how employee engagement is measured, what we know about this concept, and what leaders need to do to create highly engaged employees.

Although much of the attention has moved away from job satisfaction to employee engagement, there are several practical reasons why job satisfaction is still an important concept for leaders to think about. Research shows that turnover has soared from 1.7 million to over 3.5 million employees per month over the past 10 years and is now at a 17-year high. Research indicates that satisfied workers are more likely to continue working for an organization[16, 17, 18, 19, 20, 21, 22, 23,24,25,26,27,28] and more likely to engage in organizational citizenship behaviors that go beyond job descriptions and role requirements and help reduce the workload or stress of others in the organization. Dissatisfied workers are more likely to be adversarial in their relations with leadership (filing grievances, for example) and engage in diverse counterproductive behaviors.[29, 30, 31, 32, 33, 34, 35, 36, 37] Dissatisfaction is a key reason why people leave organizations, and many of the reasons people are satisfied or dissatisfied with work are within the leader's immediate control (see **Table 10.1**).[38, 39, 40, 41]

FIGURE 10.1   Relationships among Leadership, Satisfaction, Engagement, Performance, and Effectiveness

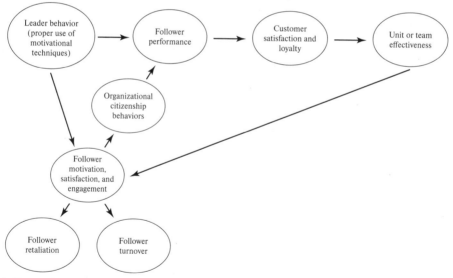

Sources: M. A. Huselid, "The Impact of Human Resource Management Practices on Turnover, Productivity, and Corporate Financial Performance," *Academy of Management Journal* 38, no. 4 (1995), pp. 635–72; T. Butorac, *Recruitment and Retention: The Keys to Profitability at Carlson Companies*, presentation given at Personnel Decisions International, Minneapolis, MN, June 11, 2001; D. J. Koys, "The Effects of Employee Satisfaction, Organizational Citizenship Behavior, and Turnover on Organizational Effectiveness: A Unit-Level, Longitudinal Study," *Personnel Psychology* 54, no. 1 (2001), pp. 101–14; J. Husserl, "Allied's Organizational Life Cycle," *Management Education & Development* 24, no. 3 (1998), p. 8; Sirota Consulting, *Establishing the Linkages between Employee Attitudes, Customer Attitudes, and Bottom-Line Results* (Chicago, IL: Author, 1998); D. S. Pugh, J. Dietz, J. W. Wiley, and S. M. Brooks, "Driving Service Effectiveness through Employee–Customer Linkages," *Academy of Management Executive* 16, no. 4 (2002), pp. 73–84; and B. Schneider, P. J. Hanges, D. B. Smith, and A. N. Salvaggio, "Which Comes First: Employee Attitudes or Organizational, Financial and Market Performance?" *Journal of Applied Psychology* 88, no. 5 (2003), pp. 836–51.

TABLE 10.1 Why People Leave or Stay with Organizations

Why Do People Leave Organizations?	Why Do People Stay with Organizations?
Limited recognition and praise	Promises of long-term employment
Compensation	Exciting work and challenge
Limited authority	Fair pay
Poor organizational culture	Encourages fun, collegial relationships
Repetitive work	Supportive management

Sources: SIGMA Assessment Systems, www.sigmaassessmentsystems.com; Pace Communication, *Hemispheres Magazine*, November 1994, p. 155; "Keeping Workers Happy," *USA Today*, February 10, 1998, p. 1; B. G. Graves, "Why People Quit Their Jobs," *Harvard Business Review*, September 2016, https://hbr.org/2016/09/why-people-quit-their-jobs; and B. Kaye and S. Jordan-Evans, *Love 'Em or Lose Em: Getting Good People to Stay*, 5th ed. (San Francisco: Berrett-Koehler, 2014).

Seventy to ninety percent of the decisions not to repeat purchases of anything are not about product or price. They are about dimensions of service.

Barry Gibbons, former CEO of Burger King

Although the total costs of dissatisfaction are difficult to measure, turnover can be a serious problem for leaders. The direct costs of replacing a first-line supervisor or an executive can range from $5,000 to $400,000 per hire, depending on recruiting, relocation, and training fees, and these costs do not include those associated with the productivity lost as a result of unfilled positions.[42] Another indirect cost is the loss of customers. A survey of major corporations showed that 49 percent switched to another vendor because of poor customer service.[43] Employees are probably not going to provide world-class service if they are unhappy with their job, boss, or company. The inability to retain employees, and in turn customers, directly affects revenues and makes investors think twice about buying stock in a company. Relatedly, Schellenbarger reported that 35 percent of investor decisions are driven by nonfinancial factors. Number 5 on a list of 39 factors investors weighed before buying stock was the company's ability to attract and retain talent. These findings imply that a company's stock price is driven not only by market share and profitability but also by service, retention, and bench strength considerations. Thus, employee satisfaction (or dissatisfaction) can have a major impact on the organization's bottom line.[44] (See **Highlight 10.1**.)

To be stupid, selfish, and have good health are the three requirements for happiness, although if stupidity is lacking, all is lost.

Gustave Flaubert, writer

The Grass Is Not Always Greener...

HIGHLIGHT 10.1

The promise of fabulous wealth, combined with the general dissatisfaction associated with working in large bureaucratic organizations, has prompted many people to take jobs with smaller start-up companies. Not only do jobs in these smaller firms maximize the concepts of meaning, mastery, and autonomy from **Chapter 9**, but members of start-ups that are acquired by larger companies often hit the jackpot. For example, Facebook paid $1 billion to acquire Instagram, a company with 13 full-time employees. It is uncertain how the proceeds of the sale were doled out, but needless to say some of these employees will never have to work another day in their lives. Over half of the world's billionaires made their fortunes starting and selling tech start-ups, and there are regular news articles about the latest tech darling being acquired by larger organizations. Despite all this publicity, there are many dangers associated with joining start-ups.

First, working for a start-up is not for the faint at heart. Start-ups demand brutal working hours, with 16-hour workdays, working weekends, and 24/7 availability the norm for most employees. Issues with work–life balance, relationships, and health are common complaints among start-up employees, and high burnout and turnover rates are the norm. Only 19 percent of start-up employees report being satisfied at work, and only 17 percent feel valued because of the lack of career progression and high job demands. Start-ups routinely administer lavish perks and stock options on employees to make up for these downsides. For example, Facebook will give $20,000 to any female employee who opts to have her eggs frozen. In reality these benefits are not awarded altruistically, but rather to keep costs under control and entice employees to keep working.

Most start-ups have trouble with cash flow, as it may be some time before they have a product to sell and any revenue coming in, but they have immediate costs associated with salaries, rent, equipment, and the like. To address this problem, start-ups seek funds from investors or venture capitalists and award stock grants to employees (for example, 10,000 shares in the company) rather than pay market-rate salaries or bonuses. To raise cash, employees are also sometimes asked to buy stock, usually at discounted rates. If the company was based on a faulty business model and fails to go public, then the stock becomes worthless and employees have spent one to five years of their lives being overworked and underpaid.

Even when companies are successfully acquired, there is no guarantee employees will be better for it. When start-ups are sold, primary owners and investors are the first paid; only then are the remaining proceeds divvied up among employees. Many times the money left over does not cover the wages or bonuses lost or stocks purchased while employees were working for the start-up. These gaps can be so extreme that some employees end up paying for the privilege of working for a start-up rather than being handsomely rewarded for taking big career risks.

Would you be happy working for a start-up? Why or why not?

Sources: V. Luckerson, "Here's Proof That Instagram Was One of the Smartest Acquisitions Ever," *Time*, April 19, 2016 http://time.com/4299297/instagram-facebook-revenue; "Schumpeter: The Other Side of Paradise," *The Economist*, January 16, 2016, p. 74; K. Benner, "When a Unicorn Start-Up Stumbles, Its Employees Get Hurt," *The New York Times*, December 27, 2015, www.nytimes.com/2015/12/27/technology/when-a-unicorn-start-up-stumbles-its-employees-get-hurt.html; R. Feintzeig, "Feeling Burned Out at Work? Join the Club," *The Wall Street Journal*, March 1, 2017, p. B6; and P. Cappelli, "Why Companies Are Paying Employees to Take Vacations," LinkedIn, www.linkedin.com/pulse/why-companies-paying-employees-take-vacations-peter-cappelli.

Employee turnover usually has an immediate impact on leadership practitioners. For example, shift managers, assistant managers, and managers in the retail, casual dining, fast-food, and coffee industries typically work in facilities reporting 100 to 200 percent annual turnover. In other words, every person in a store or restaurant is likely to be replaced during the course of a year, with some businesses needing to hire two replacements for everyone currently on staff. Imagine how much time these leaders spend recruiting, selecting, on-boarding, and training new hires; juggling schedules and filling in for workers to cover shifts; and dealing with disgruntled customers. High levels of turnover also make it difficult to get new staff members to perform at high levels and achieve restaurant or store customer service and financial results.

Although some level of **functional turnover** is healthy for an organization (some followers are retiring, did not fit into the organization, or were substandard performers), dysfunctional turnover is not. **Dysfunctional turnover** occurs when the "best and brightest" in an organization become dissatisfied and leave. Dysfunctional turnover is most likely to occur when the local economy is good and jobs are plentiful, as this gives high-performing followers other options for employment. Dysfunctional turnover also occurs when downsizing is a response to organizational decline (increased costs or decreased revenues, market share, or profitability). In these situations, dysfunctional turnover may have several devastating effects. First, those individuals in the best position to turn the company around are no longer there. Second, those who remain are even less capable of dealing with the additional workload associated with the downsizings. Compounding this problem is that training budgets also tend to be slashed during downsizings. Third, organizations that downsize have a difficult time recruiting people with the skills needed to turn the company around. Competent candidates avoid applying for jobs within the organization because of uncertain job security, and the less competent managers remaining with the company may decide not to hire anyone who could potentially replace them. Because leaders can play an important role in followers' satisfaction levels, and because followers' satisfaction levels can have a substantial impact on various organizational outcomes, it is worth examining this topic in greater detail (see **Highlight 10.2**).[45, 46, 47, 48, 49, 50]

The Misguided Pursuit of Happiness

HIGHLIGHT 10.2

Despite overwhelming research showing that job satisfaction does not have a particularly strong relationship with organization effectiveness, some consulting firms are pushing the idea that employee happiness can be a competitive advantage for companies wanting to achieve superior financial results. Some companies, such as Zappos or Google, now have executives with titles such as class president, chief happiness officer, or jolly good fellow, whose responsibilities are to bring empathy, support, and good cheer to employees. But it turns out that organizations would be far better off eliminating common worker annoyances, such as having to attend useless meetings, adhere to bureaucratic and often unnecessary rules, or work set office hours rather than going to an office party every Friday afternoon.

There are several other aspects of the pursuit of happiness that are problematic. Companies now demand that it is not enough for followers to simply complete assigned tasks; they now have to "whistle while they work" and project an image of happiness and contentment while work is being performed. Cleaning hotel rooms, working a cash register, or taking orders at a drive-through can be dreary enough work; it is even more difficult when followers have to smile and project a positive attitude while they are completing menial tasks. Research shows that followers are more likely to suffer burnout and leave organizations when they have to constantly project positive work attitudes.

Another problem with the pursuit of happiness is that it sets followers up for failure. Vincent Norman Peale, Joel Osteen, Tony Robbins, Rhonda Byrne, and other self-help gurus promote the idea that all one has to do is think happy thoughts and good things will happen. Unfortunately, just thinking that a number of lines of code are going to get written, homeless people are going to get fed, or packages are going to get delivered is not the same as actually doing the work, and there is little evidence to support the power of positive thinking. Moreover, the research shows that those who firmly believe that all they need to do is think positive thoughts to achieve results actually put in less effort to make it happen. These individuals also tend to be more disappointed when their ceaseless optimism fails to yield results.

Although the relationship between employee happiness and performance is tenuous at best, it may be helpful to fake happiness at work. On the one hand, nobody wants to work with someone who is constantly complaining, and happier people tend to get promoted over criticizers and whiners. Faking happiness may also be an important leadership quality, as followers would rather work for someone who is optimistic and resilient versus pessimistic and volatile. On the other hand, is it better to fake happiness or should leaders and followers be authentic and bring their true selves to work?

Should people be happy at work? Is it an organization's responsibility to ensure its employees are happy? Is it reasonable or intrusive for organizations to demand that employees project positive work attitudes? Should organizations use electronic monitoring to continually track employee happiness? If it were your company, what would be your expectations for employee attitudes at work?

Sources: "Schumpeter: Against Happiness," *The Economist*, September 24, 2015, p. 66; A. Alter, "The Powerlessness of Positive Thinking," *The New Yorker*, February 13, 2014, www.newyorker.com/business/currency/the-powerlessness-of-positive-thinking; J. Low, "Is Work Culture Overrated?" *The Low Down*, September 8, 2016, www.thelowdown-blog.com/2016/09/is-work-culture-overrated.html; T. Chamorro-Premuzic, "Is There a Case for Faking Happiness at Work?" *Forbes*, December 15, 2019, www.forbes.com/sites/tomaspremuzic/2019/12/15/is-there-a-case-for-faking-happiness-at-work; "Whistle While You Work," *The Economist*, November 2, 2019, p. 58; "The Spy Who Hired Me," *The Economist*, January 5, 2019, p. 46; W. Arruda, "How to Succeed by Being Your True Self at Work," *Forbes*, November 3, 2019, www.forbes.com/sites/williamarruda/2019/11/03/how-to-succeed-by-being-your-true-self-at-work; and C. White, B. Uttl, and M. Holder, "Meta-Analyses of Positive Psychology Interventions: The Effects Are Much Smaller Than Previously Reported," *PLOS ONE*, May 29, 2019, www.ncbi.nlm.nih.gov/pmc/articles/PMC6541265.

Global, Facet, and Life Satisfaction

There are different ways to look at a person's attitudes about work, but researchers usually collect these data using some type of job satisfaction survey.[51, 52, 53, 54, 55] Such surveys are usually sent to all employees, the responses are collected and tabulated, and the results are disseminated throughout the organization. **Table 10.2** presents examples of three different types of items typically found on a job satisfaction survey. Item 1 is a **global satisfaction** item, which assesses the overall degree to which employees are satisfied with their organization and their job. Items 2 through 7 are **facet satisfaction** items, which assess the degree to which employees are satisfied with different aspects of work, such as pay, benefits, promotion policies, working hours and conditions, and the like. People may be relatively satisfied overall but still dissatisfied with certain aspects of work. For example, from 2001 to 2011 job security was a primary factor driving employee satisfaction, and the economic downturn of 2007 to 2009 only heightened this concern. A study by the Society for Human Resource Management indicated that the opportunity to use skills and abilities, compensation, job security, communication, and relationships with immediate supervisors were the biggest drivers of overall job satisfaction.[56] A study of junior officers in the U.S. Army revealed that overall satisfaction had been in decline and a higher percentage of officers were choosing to leave the Army. The two primary reasons for this high level of dysfunctional turnover seemed to be dissatisfaction with immediate supervisors and top leadership. Many junior officers reported that they were tired of working for career-obsessed supervisors who had a strong tendency to micromanage and would just as soon throw them under a bus if it would advance their careers.[57, 58] This decline in global satisfaction is not limited to the U.S. Army: The same phenomenon has happened in many U.S. and European companies. Much of this decline can be attributed to higher follower expectations, greater follower access to information through technology, economic downturns, mergers and acquisitions, organizational downsizings, and incompetent bosses.

TABLE 10.2   **Typical Items on a Satisfaction Questionnaire**

1. Overall, I am satisfied with my job.

2. I feel the workload is about equal for everyone in the organization.

3. My supervisor handles conflict well.

4. My pay and benefits are comparable to those in other organizations.

5. There is a real future for people in this organization if they apply themselves.

6. Exceptional performance is rewarded in this organization.

7. We have a good health care plan in this organization.

8. In general, I am satisfied with my life and where it is going.

These items are often rated on a scale ranging from *strongly disagree* (1) to *strongly agree* (5).

> *Would life on a slave ship be much better if the galley master first asked the rowers to help write a mission statement? What employers need to come to terms with is the economic, cultural, and societal benefits of being loyal to their employees. If they don't, eventually their abuses will bite them on the ass.*
>
> **Daniel Levine, author**

Leadership practitioners should be aware of several other important findings regarding global and facet satisfaction. The first finding is that people generally tend to be happy with their vocation or occupation. They may not like the pay, benefits, or their boss, but they seem to be satisfied with what they do for a living. The second finding pertains to the **hierarchy effect**: In general, people with longer tenure or in higher positions tend to have higher global and facet satisfaction ratings than those newer to or lower in the organization.[59] Because people higher in the organization are happier at work, they may not understand or appreciate why people at lower levels are less satisfied. From below, leaders at the top can appear naive and out of touch. From above, the complaints about morale, pay, or resources are often perceived as whining. One of this book's authors once worked with a utilities company that had downsized and was suffering from all the ill effects associated with high levels of dysfunctional turnover. Unfortunately, the executive vice president responsible for attracting and retaining talent and making the company "an employer of choice" stated that he had no idea why employees were complaining and that things would be a lot better if they just quit whining. Because the executive did not understand or appreciate the sources of employee complaints, the programs to improve employee morale completely missed the mark, and the high levels of dysfunctional turnover continued. The hierarchy effect also implies that it will take a considerable amount of top leaders' focus and energy to increase the satisfaction levels of nonmanagement employees—lip service alone is never enough. See **Highlight 10.3** for examples of companies that do not seem to take employee satisfaction very seriously.

The Wall of Shame: The 10 Worst Companies to Work For in the United States

HIGHLIGHT 10.3

Most people want to work in companies where they feel valued, have good job security, and get paid a fair wage. Many organizations work hard to fulfill these needs and those that do are often seen as some of the best companies to work for in America. But other companies seem to treat employees as widgets in production lines and put little value on employee satisfaction or engagement. In the past it was hard to know how organizations treated their employees, but the advent of satisfaction and engagement surveys, the Internet, and social media has made this much easier. *Forbes* and *Inc.* magazines publish lists of top companies to work for based on employee surveys, and the *Indeed*, *Glassdoor*, and *TheJobCrowd* websites allow current and former employees to provide anonymous ratings and comments about employers. There appears to be ample interest in getting unvarnished views of employers, as *Glassdoor* has over 30 million members and *Indeed* gets over 250 million unique visitors a month.

Although the worst-companies-to-work-for list varies from year to year, it takes a considerable amount of time for a company to move from the bottom of the list. Put another way, the worst companies to work for have been that way for some time and will likely remain that way in the future. Although situational factors can affect employee ratings, more often than not top and middle management get all the credit for creating employee-unfriendly work environments. Some of the worst companies to work for in 2019 were as follows:

10. *Family Dollar Stores:* A regular on the top 10 list, this company, with 8,000+ stores across 46 states, boasts unqualified managers and poor work–life balance as the main reasons.

9. *Alorica:* It is difficult to create a company whose mission is "to create insanely great customer experiences" when staff are complaining about pay, work hours, overtime rates, and company culture.

8. *Speedway LLC:* Former employees are not happy with their stints at this gas station chain and only gave it a 2.6/5.0 average *Glassdoor* rating.

7. *CDK Global:* Even high-tech companies can be bad places to work. Former employees at this company cited poor pay and long work hours as reasons why they

left. Store closures, layoffs, and declining sales; long working hours; low pay; and out-of-touch management contributed to this ranking.

6. *US Security Associates:* Apparently walking around buildings, checking IDs, and monitoring security cameras is not particularly fulfilling; not getting paid well or having the support of top management does not help either.

5. *Genesis HealthCare:* One only hopes patients receive better care than employees. Inflexible upper management, low morale, and limited career opportunities are problems at this Pennsylvania-based health care provider.

4. *Frontier Communications:* Only 14 percent of *Glassdoor* reviews approved of the CEO's leadership; frequent and unnecessary changes and a poor working culture were hallmarks of this telecommunications provider.

3. *The Fresh Market:* Meager pay and poor work–life balance were common complaints among the former employees of this grocery chain.

2. *United Biosource:* Apparently fair pay, career stability, and a healthy work–life balance are not concerns at this pharmaceutical services support company.

1. *Union Pacific:* The worst company to work for in 2019, Union Pacific touts its "passion for performance, high ethical standards, and teamwork," yet *Glassdoor* reviews indicate it is falling well short in all three of these areas. Only 12 percent of former employees approved of how CEO Lance Fitz was running Union Pacific, and 78 percent would not recommend the company to a friend.

It appears that the worst companies to work for come from a broad spectrum of industries, but all share common themes. What theories of motivation or satisfaction would best explain the reasons that people choose to leave the worst companies to work for? What theories would best explain why people choose to remain with these companies? How would these compa-

nies stack up to the worst companies to work for in Western Europe or Asia?

Source: G. Parker, "The 20 Worst Companies to Work For in 2019," August 2019, *Money Inc.*, https://moneyinc.com/worst-companies-to-work-for/.

Compensation is another facet of job satisfaction that can have important implications for leadership practitioners. As you might expect, the hierarchy effect can be seen in pay: A survey of 3 million employees reported that 71 percent of senior management, 58 percent of middle management, and only 46 percent of nonmanagers rate their pay as "very good." Of nonmanagers, 33 percent rate their pay as "so-so" and 20 percent rate their pay as "very poor."[60] Given the wage gap between men and women, a disproportionate number of women can probably be found in these less satisfied groups. Many of these women may be the highest performers in their positions; therefore, this wage discrepancy, in combination with relatively small annual pay increases over the past few years, may contribute to disproportionately high levels of dysfunctional turnover among women.

> *Leaders are often the only people surprised by employee satisfaction results. In reality, employees have been talking about the issues identified in these surveys for quite some time.*
>
> **Dianne Nilsen, leadership consultant**

People who are happier with their jobs also tend to have higher life satisfaction ratings. **Life satisfaction** concerns one's attitudes about life in general, and Item 8 in **Table 10.2** is an example of a typical life satisfaction question. Because leaders are often some of the most influential people in their followers' lives, they should never underestimate the impact they have on their followers' overall well-being.

Job satisfaction surveys are used extensively in both public and private institutions. Organizations using these instruments typically administer them every one or two years to assess workers' attitudes about different aspects of work, changes in policies or work procedures, or other initiatives. Such survey results are most useful when they can be compared with those from some **reference group**. The organization's past results can be used as one kind of reference group—are people's ratings of pay, promotion, or overall satisfaction rising or falling over time? Job satisfaction ratings from similar organizations can be another reference group—are satisfaction ratings of leadership and working conditions higher or lower than those in similar organizations?

Figure 10.2 shows the facet and global satisfaction results for approximately 80 employees working at a medium-sized airport in the western United States. Employees completing the survey included the director of aviation and his supervisory staff ($n = 11$), the operations department ($n = 6$), the airfield maintenance department ($n = 15$), the communications department ($n = 6$), the airport facilities staff ($n = 12$), the administration department ($n = 10$), and the custodial staff ($n = 20$). The airport is owned by the city and has seen tremendous growth since the opening of its new terminal; in fact, less than two years later aircraft loads exceeded the capacity of the new terminal. Unfortunately, staffing had remained the same since the opening, and the resulting workload and stress were thought to be adversely affecting morale and job satisfaction. Because of these concerns, the director of aviation decided to use a job satisfaction survey to pinpoint problem areas and develop action plans to resolve them.

Scores above 50 on **Figure 10.2** are areas of satisfaction; scores below 50 are areas of dissatisfaction when compared to national norms. Here we see that airport employees are very satisfied with their benefits, are fairly satisfied with the work itself, but are dissatisfied with top leadership, ethics, supervision, feedback, promotion opportunities, and the like. All airport employees got to review these results, and each department discussed the factors underlying the survey results and developed and implemented action plans to address problem areas. Top leadership, in this case, the director of aviation, was seen as the biggest source of dissatisfaction by all departments. The director was a genuinely nice person and meant well, but he never articulated his vision for the airport, never explained how employees' actions were related to this mission, failed to set goals for each department, did not provide feedback, never clarified roles or areas of responsibilities for his staff, delegated action items to whomever he happened to see in the hall, often changed his mind about key decisions, and failed to keep his staff informed of airline tenant or city council decisions. When confronted with this information, the director placed the blame on the rapid growth of the airport and the lack of staffing support from the city (the fundamental attribution error from **Chapter 2**). The city manager then gave the director six months to substantially improve employee satisfaction levels. The director did not take the problem seriously; so, not surprisingly, the survey results six months later were no different for top leadership. The director was subsequently removed from his position because of his failure to improve the morale at the airport.

> *The question: If you had to describe your office environment as a type of television show, what would it be? The responses:* "Survivor," 38 percent; soap opera, 27 percent; medical emergency, 18 percent; courtroom drama, 10 percent; science fiction, 7 percent.

Andrea Nierenberg, New York University

It is not enough to merely administer surveys. Leaders must also be willing to take action on the basis of survey results or risk losing credibility and actually increasing job dissatisfaction. Upon receiving the results of these surveys, leaders with bad results may feel tempted not to share any results with their followers, but this is almost always a mistake. Although the results may not be flattering, the rumors are likely to be much worse than the results themselves. Followers will also be less willing to fill out subsequent satisfaction surveys if they see denial of the results and little change to the workplace. Furthermore, leaders feeling defensive about such results and who are tempted to hide them should remember that the bad results are likely to surprise no one but themselves; therefore, what's to hide? On a practical level, leaders should never assess employees' attitudes about work unless they are willing to share the results and take action.

FIGURE 10.2   Results of a Facet Satisfaction Survey

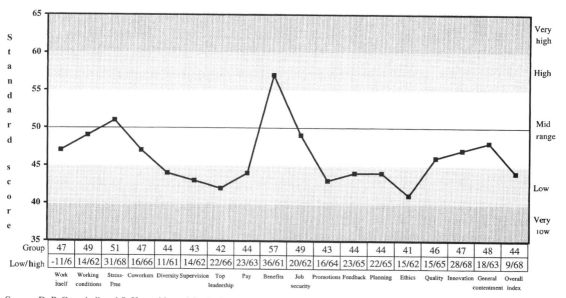

Source: D. P. Campbell and S. Hyne, *Manual for the Revised Campbell Organizational Survey* (Minneapolis, MN: National Computing Systems, 1995).

There are three actions leaders must take if they wish to improve scores on follower satisfaction surveys. First, they need to share the survey results with their followers. It is best if leaders do not interpret the survey results for followers, but instead have them work though the data and identify areas of improvement. Second, leaders need to be curious and open to feedback. Followers may identify performance expectations, meetings, decision-making, accountability, communication, or lack of resources as areas in need of improvement. These topics are often a reflection of how they are being led, and leaders need to avoid the temptation of rationalizing followers' recommendations. They should work closely with followers to find mutually agreed-upon solutions, as this will improve a leader's skills as well as follower satisfaction. Last, leaders and followers need to build action plans with periodic reviews to assess progress. Talk is cheap, actions are good, and progress reviews are even better at identifying leaders who are serious about follower satisfaction levels.

Two Theories of Job Satisfaction

As shown in **Table 10.3**, the five theories of motivation described in **Chapter 9** also provide insight into followers' levels of job satisfaction. For example, it would be difficult for followers to be satisfied about work if they did not think what they were doing was important, there were no clear goals or expectations about what they were supposed to do, rewards and punishments were administered at random, or they were being micromanaged. Two additional theories—organizational justice and Herzberg's two-factor theory—offer different explanations for job satisfaction.

TABLE 10.3   Seven Theories of Satisfaction

Theory or Approach	How Leaders Can Improve Job Satisfaction
Motives or needs	Helping ensure people's needs are satisfied
Achievement orientation	Securing needed resources, clearing obstacles, and allowing people to work on activities that matter to them
Goal setting	Setting high goals and helping people to accomplish them
Operant approach	Administering rewards
Empowerment	Giving people needed training and more decision-making authority
Organizational justice	Treating people fairly
Herzberg's two-factor theory	Giving people more meaningful work

Organizational Justice: Does Fairness Matter?

Organizational justice is based on the premise that people who are treated unfairly are less productive, less satisfied, and less committed to their organizations. Moreover, these individuals are likely to initiate collective action and engage in various counterproductive work behaviors.[61] According to Trevino, organizational justice is made up of three related components. **Interactional justice** reflects the degree to which people are given information about different reward procedures and are treated with dignity and respect. **Distributive justice** concerns followers' perceptions of whether the level of reward or punishment is commensurate with an individual's performance or infraction. Dissatisfaction occurs when followers believe someone has received too little or too much reward or punishment. Perceptions of **procedural justice** involve the process by which rewards or punishments are administered. If someone is to be punished, followers will be more satisfied if the person being punished has been given adequate warnings and has had the opportunity to explain his or her actions, and if the punishment has been administered in a timely and consistent manner.[62] Research has shown that these different components of organizational justice are related to satisfaction with the leader, pay, promotion, the job itself, organizational citizenship behaviors, and counterproductive work behaviors (in instances where perceived injustice was taking place).[63, 64, 65, 66, 67, 68, 69, 70, 71]

> *Fairness is what justice really is.*
>
> **Potter Stewart, U.S. Supreme Court justice**

So what should leaders do to improve follower satisfaction and reduce turnover using organizational justice theory? The underlying principle for organizational justice is fairness: What would the followers say about whether they were treated with dignity and respect, whether rewards were commensurate with performance, or whether rewards were administered fairly? Leaders who want to improve job satisfaction using this approach need to ensure that followers answer yes to these three questions; if not, leaders need to change the reward and punishment system if they want to improve job satisfaction using organizational justice theory. Brockner notes that fairness in the workplace makes intuitive sense but is woefully lacking in many organizations. Too many managers play favorites, avoid rather than directly deal with uncomfortable situations, or for legal reasons cannot reveal how certain issues were handled.[72] These instances of perceived unfairness are often the underlying causes of job dissatisfaction in many organizations.

The Happiest Occupations, States, and Countries

HIGHLIGHT 10.4

Polls show that job and life satisfaction vary considerably by occupation, state, and even the country in which one lives. And although the United States is the richest nation in the world, it ranked only 16th in life satisfaction. Life satisfaction surveys of 130,000+ people reveal the following (listed in order):

Happiest occupations: real estate agent, quality assurance engineer, senior sales representative, construction superintendent, senior applications developer, logistics manager, executive assistant, and assistant controller

Least happy occupations: associate attorney, customer service representative, clerk, registered nurse, teacher, marketing coordinator, pharmacy technician, and technical support manager

Happiest states: South Dakota, Vermont, Hawaii, Minnesota, and North Dakota

Least happy states: West Virginia, Louisiana, Arkansas, Mississippi, and Oklahoma

Happiest countries: Finland, Denmark, Norway, Iceland, and Netherlands

Least happy countries: South Sudan, Central Africa Republic, Afghanistan, Tanzania, and Rwanda

Sources: K. Gilcrest, "These Are the Happiest Countries in the World," CNBC, www.cnbc.com/2017/03/20/norway-ranked-worlds-happiest-country-as-the-us-gets-sadder.html; "The Happiest and Unhappiest Jobs," *Forbes*, www.forbes.com/pictures/efkk45ehffl/the-happiest-and-unhappiest-jobs; S. Ferro, "And the Most Miserable State in America Is...," *Mental Floss*, July 25, 2019, www.mentalfloss.com/article/552027/most-miserable-state-america; and M. Grothaus, "These Are the 10 Happiest and Unhappiest Countries in the World in 2019," *Fast Company*, March 21, 2019, www.fastcompany.com/90323247/these-are-the-10-happiest-and-unhappiest-countries-in-the-world-in-2019.

If you don't want people to have Mickey Mouse attitudes, then don't give them Mickey Mouse work.

Frederick Herzberg, researcher

Herzberg's Two-Factor Theory: Does Meaningful Work Make People Happy?

Herzberg developed the **two-factor theory** from a series of interviews he conducted with accountants and engineers. Specifically, he asked what satisfied them about their work and found that their answers usually could be sorted into five consistent categories. Furthermore, rather than assuming that what dissatisfied people was always just the opposite of what satisfied them, he also specifically asked what *dissatisfied* people about their jobs. Surprisingly, the list of satisfiers and dissatisfiers represented entirely different aspects of work.

Herzberg labeled the factors that led to *satisfaction* at work **motivators**, and he labeled the factors that led to *dissatisfaction* at work **hygiene factors**. The most common motivators and hygiene factors are listed in **Table 10.4**. According to the two-factor theory, efforts directed toward improving hygiene factors will not increase followers' motivation or satisfaction. No matter how much leaders improve working conditions, pay, or sick leave policies, for example, followers *will not* exert additional effort or persist longer at a task. For example, followers will probably be no more satisfied to do a dull and boring job if they are merely given pleasant office furniture. By contrast, followers may be asked to work in conditions so poor as to create dissatisfaction, which can distract them from constructive work.[73, 74, 75] (See **Highlights 10.4** and **10.5**.)

TABLE 10.4   **Motivators and Hygiene Factors of the Two-Factor Theory**

Hygiene Factors	Motivators
Supervision	Achievement
Working conditions	Recognition
Coworkers	The work itself
Pay	Responsibility
Policies/procedures	Advancement and growth
Job security	

Source: Adapted from F. Herzberg, *Work and the Nature of Man* (Cleveland, OH: World Publishing, 1966).

Role Ambiguity, Role Conflict, and Job Satisfaction

HIGHLIGHT 10.5

The seven theories of job satisfaction provide useful frameworks for understanding why people may or may not be happy at work. But two other key causes of job dissatisfaction do not fit neatly into one of these frameworks. The first has to do with **role ambiguity**, which occurs whenever leaders or followers are unclear about what they need to do and how they should do it. Many people come to work to succeed, but too many leaders set up followers for failure by not providing them with the direction, training, or resources they need to be successful. In these situations followers may exert a high level of effort, but they often are not working on the right things and as a result get little accomplished. This sense of frustration quickly turns to dissatisfaction and eventually causes people to look for someplace else to work. An example here is an executive vice president of human resources who left a position early in his career after he had been on the job for only two weeks. During those first two weeks he had never seen his boss, did not have a desk, and did not even have a phone. The irony was that he was working for a major Canadian phone company.

Role conflict occurs when leaders and followers are given incompatible goals to accomplish. For example, leaders may be told that their goals are to boost output while reducing head count. It will be difficult to achieve both goals unless the leader is given some new process, technology, or product that significantly increases worker productivity. When given seemingly incompatible goals, leaders often focus their efforts on accomplishing some goals to the exclusion of others. This may have been the case with BP's *Deepwater Horizon* oil rig disaster, where managers were told to drill for oil safely and in an environmentally friendly manner while reducing costs and boosting production. The managers on the rig seemed to focus on production and cost reduction goals, and the end result was the death of 11 workers and an unprecedented environmental disaster.

Although role conflict is a source of dissatisfaction, people need to realize that a key challenge for leaders is to successfully achieve seemingly incompatible goals. If the team has only a productivity goal, many leaders are likely to be successful in helping their team to accomplish this goal. If the team has productivity and profitability goals, fewer leaders are likely to be successful. And if the team has productivity, profitability, safety, quality, and customer satisfaction goals, an even smaller subset of leaders will be successful in all of these areas. The fact is that most teams and organizations have more than one goal, and effective leaders are able to get their teams to successfully accomplish all assigned goals. Hiring achievement-oriented team members, setting clear goals, regularly measuring and reporting on goal progress, clearing obstacles, obtaining needed resources, and providing contingent rewards will go a long way toward the successful accomplishment of multiple goals and improved employee satisfaction.

Sources: G. J. Curphy and R. Hogan, *The Rocket Model: Practical Advice for Building High Performing Teams* (Tulsa, OK: Hogan Press, 2012); "Building High Performing Teams," presentation given at the Minnesota Professionals for Psychology Applied to Work, Minneapolis, MN, February 2013; G. J. Curphy, *Applying the Rocket Model to Virtual Teams*, unpublished manuscript, 2013; G. J. Curphy and M. Roellig, *Followership*, unpublished manuscript, 2010; and G. Curphy, D. Nilsen, and R. Hogan, *Ignition: A Guide to Building High Performing Teams* (Tulsa, OK: Hogan Press, 2019).

Given limited resources on the leader's part, the key to increasing followers' satisfaction levels according to this two-factor theory is to just adequately satisfy the hygiene factors while maximizing the motivators for a particular job. It is important for working conditions to be adequate, but it is even more important (for enhancing motivation and satisfaction) to provide plenty of recognition, responsibility, and possibilities for advancement (see **Figure 10.3**). Although giving followers meaningful work and then recognizing them for their achievement seem straightforward enough, these techniques are underutilized by leaders.[76, 77, 78] In other words, Herzberg argues that leaders would be better off restructuring work to make it more meaningful and significant than giving out shirts with company logos or decreasing medical copays.

The two-factor theory offers leaders ideas about how to bolster followers' satisfaction, but it has received little empirical support beyond Herzberg's own results. Perhaps it is not an accurate explanation for job satisfaction despite its apparent grounding in data. We present it here partly because it has become such a well-known approach to work motivation and job satisfaction that this chapter would appear incomplete if we ignored it. One problem with two-factor theory, however, seems to lie in the original data on which it was based. Herzberg developed his theory after interviewing only accountants and engineers—two groups who are hardly representative of workers in other lines of work or activity. Furthermore, his subjects typically attributed job satisfaction to *their* skill or effort, yet blamed their dissatisfaction on circumstances beyond their control. This sounds suspiciously like the fundamental attribution error described in **Chapter 2**. Despite such limitations, the two-factor theory has provided useful insight into what followers find satisfying and dissatisfying about work as well as the factors driving employee engagement.

Understanding and Improving Employee Engagement

Organizations have nowhere to hide. They either have to adapt to the needs of the modern workforce, or they will find themselves struggling to attract and retain good employees and therefore customers.

Gallup, Inc.

As stated earlier in this chapter, employee engagement has been a hot topic over the past 20 years and organizations have spent billions doing surveys and implementing employee engagement improvement programs. But what is employee engagement? Is it different from employee motivation and satisfaction? How is it measured? Does it matter? And is there anything leaders can do to improve followers engagement levels? It can be difficult to answer these questions, as employee engagement can be a nebulous concept and many of the survey items used to measure job satisfaction are the same as those used to measure employee engagement. As a result, some aspects of job satisfaction are highly related to employee engagement. Moreover, organizations use different definitions of engagement when surveying employees and often report very different results.[79, 80] When all is said and done **employee engagement** pertains to followers' attitudes about the organization and their work activities. Are followers committed to their organizations? Do they find the work they do meaningful? Do they understand what they are expected to do? Do their opinions count? And does their job give them the opportunity to learn and do their best work? Fully engaged followers are believed to be more committed to team and organizational success, put forth more work-directed effort, and put in the hours necessary to complete assigned tasks; disengaged followers do not care about organizational success and are more interested in collecting paychecks than in completing work assignments.

As for job satisfaction, surveys are typically used to assess followers' engagement levels, and **Table 10.5** lists the items used in many employee engagement surveys. These surveys are typically administered every year or two to all employees in an organization and the results are analyzed to determine what percentage of people are actively engaged, engaged, disengaged, or actively disengaged. The use of common surveys has allowed organizations to benchmark themselves over time, against competitors, or against other organizations of similar size. Geographic regions, industry sector, economic conditions, leader effectiveness, job types, and engagement definitions all affect the percentage of followers falling into each of the four categories, and some interesting findings have been reported over the years. For example, only 13 percent of workers worldwide and 33 percent of American workers report being actively engaged at work; 16 percent report being actively disengaged at work. These morale and productivity killers wreak havoc on many teams and organizations. **Presen-**

FIGURE 10.3   Herzberg's Two-Factor Theory

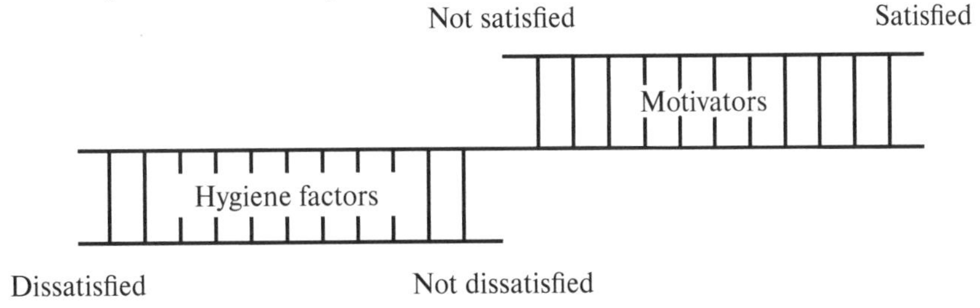

teeism (as opposed to absenteeism) is the notion of being at work while one's brain is not fully engaged; it is common in many organizations—some 51 percent of U.S. workers fit this description. Taken together, these results indicate leaders have a lot of work to do, as two-thirds of all U.S. workers are either not fully engaged or actively disengaged at work, and at any one time 51 percent are looking for other jobs.[81, 82]

TABLE 10.5   The Gallup Q^{12} Index

1. Do you know what is expected of you at work?
2. Do you have the materials and equipment to do your work?
3. At work, do you have the opportunity to do what you do best every day?
4. In the last seven days, have you received recognition or praise for doing good work?
5. Does your supervisor, or someone at work, seem to care about you as a person?
6. Is there someone at work who encourages your development?
7. At work, do your opinions seem to count?
8. Does the mission/purpose of your company make you feel your job is important?
9. Are your associates (fellow employees) committed to doing quality work?
10. Do you have a best friend at work?
11. In the last six months, has someone at work talked to you about your progress?
12. In the last year, have you had opportunities to learn and grow?

Source: Gallup Q^{12} Employee Engagement Survey, https://q12.gallup.com/public/en-us/Features.

At first blush, these employee engagement results are quite disappointing, as a majority of employees do not appear to be fully engaged at work. Yet, there is ample evidence showing that the way employee engagement is measured and reported needs to be taken into account. Some consulting firms only focus on those who report being highly engaged and market the fact that only a small minority of employees fit this category. Other firms combine the engaged and highly engaged categories and report that about two-thirds of employees are engaged. The employee engagement glass can be half-empty or half-full depending on which categories are used to report results. When the engaged and highly engaged categories are combined, employee engagement levels appear to be at an all-time high. This implies that leaders need to read the fine print whenever interpreting employee engagement results.[83, 84]

> *Employee Engagement Surveys are the business equivalent of giving prisoners in a penitentiary a survey to complete once a year and slide through the bars of their cells. The survey process cements an unequal power relationship.*
>
> **Liz Ryan, author**

One of the reasons employee engagement has become so popular over the years is the **engagement–shareholder value chain**, in which it is believed that higher employee engagement drives higher customer satisfaction, which in turn results in higher customer loyalty, sales, profitability, and share price. Explained another way, organizations with higher percentages of engaged and actively engaged followers should ultimately generate higher shareholder returns. Consulting firms that sell employee engagement surveys and improvement programs certainly believe this to be the case and offer statistical data to support the engagement–shareholder value chain, but the facts do not always line up with the marketing hype.[85, 86, 87] (See **Highlight 10.6** for an alternative view of employee engagement.)

There is a good reason why leaders should use some skepticism when reviewing the claim that engaged employees result in better organizational outcomes. Although positive relationships exist between employee engagement; job performance; and company revenues, profitability, and share price, the *causality* of these relationships has yet to be determined. It could be that higher customer satisfaction ratings, share prices, and profitability drive employee engagement rather than the other way around. In other words, does being on a winning team make followers more engaged and perform at higher levels, or are engaged followers a key factor driving team success? Consulting firms make money by pushing the idea that engagement drives performance and effectiveness, but strong arguments could be made that just the opposite is true.[88]

Several other cautions are in order when it comes to interpreting employee engagement survey results (as well as those from employee satisfaction surveys). First, in some organizations, these surveys have become somewhat of a Human Resources hammer. Leaders not achieving better-than-average results (and by definition, half will not) get "special attention" from the Human Resources department to fix their employee engagement "problem." Employees come to realize that the extra work to improve engagement gets in the way of doing the real work needed to achieve results, so employees game the survey by providing inflated results. One of the textbook authors saw this phenomenon in action when working with a top leadership team for a major medical device company. The company had lost market share and missed its financial targets for four years in a row, and leaders uniformly acknowledged that employee morale was low and functional turnover had become a major problem. Yet over the same four-year period, annual employee engagement results had steadily improved. Rather than patting themselves on the back for creating an engaged workforce, top leadership believed the results were spurious and created a task force to investigate what was really happening within the organization.

It is also important for leaders to realize that the results represent a snapshot in time, and situational factors can and do impact the percentages of engaged and fully engaged employees. New ownership, mergers, divestitures, macro-economic and political conditions, major change initiatives, business cycles, and organizational restructurings all affect employee engagement, so leaders need to ensure that action plans address factors they can control rather than situational or random events. Another problem is the frequency in which surveys are conducted can make tracking progress difficult—leaders and followers may have to wait another year or two before they can determine if actions taken had any impact. To address this issue, some organizations now ask subsamples of employees to rate their engagement on a monthly, weekly, or even daily basis. This approach provides leaders and followers with more frequent feedback, but situational factors and gamesmanship can just as easily affect these results.[89, 90]

Anonymity and reference groups can also be concerns with employee engagement surveys. Most surveys ask raters to provide demographic information, such as age, gender, ethnic group, education level, work unit, function, and the like. This information is necessary to accurately categorize the results—are females more engaged than males? Is the Human Resources staff less engaged than their counterparts in other functions? These results can be very helpful to leaders, but they can also be used to identify survey respondents. For example, a team developing software applications may have only one Hispanic female or one Indian male with a Master's degree. Survey respondents may inflate their ratings if they feel their results are not anonymous.[91] Reference or comparison groups can also be a problem. Should leaders compare their employee engagement results with those of similar teams elsewhere in the organization, overall organizational results, country or regional results, or global results? Arguments could be made for any of the comparisons, and leaders often have access to all of these analyses. But when all is said and done, the best comparisons may be those of the same team over time and against other similar teams across the organization. Leaders should pay attention to whether the employee engagement results of the team are getting better, staying the same, or getting worse over time and how they compare to other sales, finance, or IT teams within the organization.[92]

Two final issues leaders should be aware of when interpreting employee engagement or satisfaction survey results are the nature of the work performed and the personalities of those they lead. As described earlier in this chapter, some jobs are dull, repetitive, and boring, and no amount of cheerleading will make them any more engaging. At the end of the day, burgers still need to get flipped, floors mopped, and change provided, and there may be little leaders can do to improve the engagement of these employees. Compounding this problem is the fact that some followers may be hard wired to be disengaged. Research shows that personality traits have a major impact on engagement results; followers scoring lower on the personality traits of extraversion and conscientiousness and higher on neuroticism are less likely to be engaged than those having the opposite scores. This implies that one way to improve engagement scores is to hire followers who are by nature more outgoing, rule-abiding, hard-working, optimistic, resilient, and thick-skinned.[93, 94]

As described in the previous paragraphs, some caution should be used when interpreting employee engagement and satisfaction survey results. But what should leaders do once they have been provided the results and considered the potential factors affecting employee engagement? At one extreme, some organizations feel obligated to survey employees but not compelled to improve engagement scores. They do the surveys because other organizations are doing them, and this "keeping up with the Joneses" approach only serves to turn off employees who begin to believe that nothing will change because of the survey results. Other organizations erroneously believe perks cause employee engagement. It is true that flextime and being able to work from home can improve employee engagement but onsite massages, free beer, foosball tables, and great company cafeterias will never make up for 80-hour workweeks or mind-numbing work. The best approach is for leaders to share results with their followers and jointly identify the factors potentially affecting the results as well as areas of strength and improvement in the engagement scores. Leaders and followers should then build plans to improve employee engagement. Leaders then need to follow up to ensure that planned actions and periodic progress reviews take place.

Red Bull takes a different approach to employee engagement surveys that other organizations may want to consider adopting. Rather than sharing the results with leaders, the engagement survey results are shared directly with employees. Employees are asked to get together to review the results, build action plans, and share what they intend to do to improve engagement with their leaders.[95] This approach helps minimize the anonymity, reference group, and rating inflation problems noted earlier and increases the buy-in for those actions intended to improve employee engagement.

When all is said and done, perhaps the biggest obstacle to improving employee engagement is incompetent management. Some leaders have no idea how followers feel about work; others mistreat their followers and could not care less whether they are engaged. Other leaders simply do not know what followers want from work or how to make things better. If leaders believe that employee engagement is important to team or organizational effectiveness, they should take the results of engagement surveys seriously and work collaboratively with followers to devise and implement engagement improvement programs.[96, 97, 98, 99, 100, 101]

Some Problems with Employee Engagement

HIGHLIGHT 10.6

One issue leaders need to keep in mind is that engagement is not an end unto itself, but rather a means to an end. If leaders take the engagement–shareholder value chain seriously, then they want to create more engaged followers in order to help their teams and organizations be more effective, not to make workers happy. This perspective can set up unrealistic expectations for both leaders and followers. Followers may falsely believe that it is their right to be engaged and leaders can feel guilty if they do not have highly engaged followers. But there is only so much that leaders can do to make jobs engaging. Some aspects of every job are distasteful, and many jobs are tedious and boring. No amount of coddling or work redesign is going to make these work activities any more engaging.

Although disengaged and actively disengaged employees can make it difficult for leaders to build winning teams and achieve team goals, leaders also run the risk that highly engaged employees could burn out. Research has shown that some of the most engaged employees lack work–life balance, are often torn between competing demands, are continually sought out for opinions, and can feel so overwhelmed that they eventually leave organizations.

The last issue concerning employee engagement has to do with the fundamental attribution error described in **Chapter 2**. One interpretation of the items listed in **Table 10.5** is that leadership and other situational factors, rather than followers, are responsible for employee engagement. Yet followers ultimately determine whether they will be engaged or disengaged at work. In reality, leaders can only create environments that facilitate followers' engagement decisions. Followers in what many would consider to be interesting and impactful jobs can choose to be disengaged, and those working as cashiers, bank tellers, customer service representatives, or assembly-line workers can be highly engaged at work. Followers bear some responsibility for their own engagement.

Do you think engaged followers drive team and organizational success, or superior results drive follower engagement levels? Who do you think is responsible for employee engagement—leaders or followers? What would it be like to work with someone whose sole identity is with work?

Sources: R. Cross, R. Rebele, and A. Grant, "Collaboration Overload," *Harvard Business Review*, January–February 2016, pp. 74–79; M. M. Moon, "Overlooking the Role of the Job and Its Impact on Employee Engagement," LinkedIn, June 16, 2016, www.linkedin.com/pulse/overlooking-role-job-its-impact-employee-engagement-moon-phd; A. Levenson, "High Performance Work Design Trumps Employee Engagement," LinkedIn, April 6, 2017, www.linkedin.com/pulse/high-performance-work-design-trumps-employee-alec-levenson; R. Hogan and T. Chamorro-Premuzic, "Beyond the Hype: The Dark Side of Employee Engagement," Hogan Assessment Systems, 2015, www.hoganassessments.com/sites/default/files/uploads/Engagement%20Symposium.pdf; T. Chamorro-Premuzic, "The Dark Side of Employee Engagement," *Forbes*, May 20, 2014, www.forbes.com/sites/tomaspremuzic/2014/05/20/the-dark-side-of-employee-engagement; L. Garrad and T. Chamorro-Premuzic, "The Dark Side of High Employee Engagement," *Harvard Business Review*, August 2016, https://hbr.org/2016/08/the-dark-side-of-high-employee-engagement; W. Tincup, "The Long Con of Engagement," Fistful of Talent, http://fistfuloftalent.com/2012/08/the-long-con-of-engagement.html; G. J. Curphy. "Why Is Employee Engagement Stagnant?" The Rocket Model, February 22, 2016, www.therocketmodel.com/blog-articles/2016/2/22/why-is-employee-engagement-stagnant; A. Dizik, "The Problem with Very Engaged Employees," *The Wall Street Journal*, August 12, 2019, p. B7; T. Chamorro-Premuzic, "Bringing Your Whole Self to Work is a Bad Idea," *Fast Company*, December 23, 2019, www.fastcompany.com/90444640/bringing-your-whole-self-to-work-is-a-bad-idea; and J. Koretz, "What Happens When Your Career Becomes Your Whole Identity," *Harvard Business Review*, December 26, 2019, https://hbr.org/2019/12/what-happens-when-your-career-becomes-your-whole-identity.

Summary

This chapter has reviewed what we know about job satisfaction and employee engagement. Job satisfaction is the set of attitudes people have about work, their careers, and their lives. Although people are generally satisfied with their lives, they can have differing levels of satisfaction with benefits, pay, working conditions, or coworkers. Job satisfaction is also a leading indicator of employee turnover, as those who are unhappy are much more likely to look for another job and leave the organization. In the case of low-performing employees, this may be better for both the individual and the employer, but teams and organizations losing high percentages of their best and brightest may find it difficult to achieve long-term results.

The relationship between job satisfaction and performance has not been particularly strong over the past 60-plus years. Some workers are happy but get little done; some unhappy workers can be an organization's top performers. Because of the tenuous relationship between job satisfaction and performance, researchers began to explore whether other follower attitudes would be better predictors of job performance. Over the past 20 years they have found that employee engagement was more closely related to followers' performance levels and team and organizational effectiveness. Whereas job satisfaction tends to focus on overall happiness, employee engagement is concerned with followers' specific attitudes about the work they perform, the equipment they use, the impact of their work, recognition and rewards, and their immediate supervisors.

Survey results indicate that the percentage of employees who report being engaged or actively engaged is at an all-time high, and there is research showing more engaged employees provide better customer service, which, in turn, results in higher organizational revenues and profitability. Despite the intuitive appeal of the engagement–shareholder value chain, arguments can be made that better organizational results drive higher employee engagement scores rather than the other way around. Leaders also need to be aware that a number of factors, many of which are beyond their immediate control, affect employee engagement and satisfaction survey results. Local economic conditions, ill-conceived organizational policies, major change initiatives, anonymity concerns, demand effects, the nature of the work performed, follower expectations, and personality traits can and do impact employee engagement scores. However, the biggest reason for disengaged followers is incompetent bosses. Bad leaders can take the joy out of even the most interesting jobs, whereas great leaders can create environments where even seemingly boring jobs are important and engaging.

Key Terms

functional turnover	organizational justice	role ambiguity
dysfunctional turnover	interactional justice	role conflict
global satisfaction	distributive justice	employee engagement
facet satisfaction	procedural justice	presenteeism
hierarchy effect	two-factor theory	engagement–shareholder value chain
life satisfaction	motivators	
reference group	hygiene factors	

Questions

1. What do you find personally satisfying or dissatisfying at work or school? What happened to these satisfiers and dissatisfiers when you were going to school remotely during the coronavirus pandemic?

2. Do you think entrepreneurs are more satisfied and engaged than leaders working in medium- to large-sized organizations? Why or why not?

3. What is more important to the overall success of an organization—employee satisfaction or employee engagement? Why?

4. Say you were the principal of a small elementary school with 30 teachers. The results from the school district's annual employee engagement survey indicate that your staff are the least engaged across the entire district. What would you do to improve the engagement of your 30 teachers?

5. Restaurants, retail stores, and coffee shops have turnover rates that often exceed 100 percent a year. What would you do to reduce turnover among these workers?

Activities

1. Identify two companies you would like to work for and check out their *Indeed* or *Glassdoor* reviews. Would you still want to work for these companies? Why or why not? What might be the limitations of this information?

2. Gallup and Glint assess employee engagement very differently. Review the websites for these two organizations and identify the advantages and disadvantages of each approach. What kind of organizations would be best suited for each approach?

3. Uber and Lyft ask riders to rate their drivers after every ride. Do you believe that more engaged drivers get higher customer satisfaction ratings? How could you determine the factors underlying driver engagement scores? With Uber driver scores averaging 4.9/5.0, do you believe these scores accurately reflect riders' true satisfaction levels or do demand effects play some role in these results?

4. People often leave bosses, not organizations. Interview people who have 10 to 20 years of work experience and ask them to list the reasons they have left previous jobs. How many left because of bad bosses? How do the reasons for leaving relate to the concepts reviewed in this chapter?

5. Find someone who works in an organization that administers employee engagement surveys. How often are the surveys conducted, what are the factors affecting the survey results, who sees the results, and what did the organization do to improve employee engagement? How did the pandemic affect the results?

Minicase

The Case of the Troubled Casino

The Upper Midwest of the United States has lagged behind the economic recovery enjoyed by much of the rest of the nation. With an economy built largely on the steel, lumber, agriculture, and manufacturing industries, local businesses were hit by the triple challenges of declining commodity prices, globalization, and automation. Countries such as China and Canada offer cheaper steel or lumber, crop prices have been falling, and many manufacturing jobs either were replaced by robots or moved to China, Southeast Asia, or Mexico. Finding thriving businesses in this region can be difficult, and one of the few standouts has been in the gaming industry.

A small group of Native American tribal leaders opened the Brown Bear casino about 30 years ago. The facility was built on tribal land and as such is not subject to local, state, or federal taxes. Initially started as a relatively small stand-alone casino, the complex has grown to include 2,000 slot machines, 25 blackjack tables, a bingo hall for 600 players, a convention center, a 400+-room hotel, three restaurants, and a golf course. Over the years it has become a destination location for those wanting to play golf, see shows, enjoy good meals, and gamble without having to travel all the way to Las Vegas to make it happen.

The Brown Bear casino complex is now a $50 million business headed up by a general manager, who in turn oversees 11 different department heads, such as the chief financial officer, head of security, director of gaming operations, and so on. These 11 leaders manage the 1,200 employees working at the casino, hotel, convention center, and golf course. Although the casino enjoyed strong growth during its first 20 years of existence, it has not recovered fully from the economic recession of 2007 to 2009. Many of the good-paying jobs in the area disappeared, and as a result the local population has become considerably smaller and older. Compounding this problem is the fact that the gaming industry is facing increasing competition for customers' entertainment dollars. The chief marketing officer has implemented a number of campaigns to bring more and younger customers into the casino and increase their average spend per visit, but so far these efforts have yielded negligible results.

Although the casino is the largest employer in the area, staffing and employee engagement have been chronic problems. Many long-term employees appear to be completely checked out at work, biding their time until retirement, and they go out of their way to disparage those who put in an honest day's work. Despite paying a competitive wage and the relative scarcity of good-paying jobs the casino averages 30 percent annual turnover, with some positions reporting turnover rates over 100 percent. Turnover is not only taking a toll on the employees who remain (as they often have to pick up the slack for those who leave), but it also has an impact on the casino's customer satisfaction and financial results. Newer and less experienced staff do not know how to handle more complex customer issues, and it costs the casino $1,000 to $5,000 in recruiting fees for each new person hired. With 400 new staff being hired each year, these staffing fees are having a material impact on the company's bottom line.

The general manager has asked you to help reduce staff turnover, create a more engaged staff, improve the casino's customer satisfaction ratings, and ultimately have a positive impact on revenues and profitability.

1. How could you use the Curphy and Roellig Followership model described in the introduction to **Part 3** to assess employees at the casino?

2. How could you use the five approaches to motivation (**Chapter 9**), organizational justice, or the two-factor theory to reduce turnover and improve employee engagement?

3. What role do you think top, middle, and first-line management have on employee turnover? How would you assess the impact leadership has on employee engagement and turnover at the casino?

Endnotes

1. W. H. Macey and B. Schneider, "The Meaning of Employee Engagement," *Industrial and Organizational Psychology* 1 (2008), pp. 3–30.

2. Gallup, Inc., *The State of the American Workplace* (Washington, DC: Gallup, 2017).

3. R. Karsan and K. Kruse, *We: How to Increase Performance and Profits through Full Engagement* (Hoboken, NJ: Wiley, 2011).

4. I. Cioca, "Better Engagement Means Better Performance—or Does It?" *Science for Work*, September 26, 2019, https://scienceforwork.com/blog/employee-engagement-performance.

5. M. Hayes, F. Chumney, C. Wright, and M. Buckingham, *The Global Study of Engagement*, (Roseland, NJ: ADP Research Institute, 2018).

6. R. Hogan and T. Chamorro-Premuzic, "Beyond the Hype: The Dark Side of Employee Engagement," *Hogan Assessment Systems*, www.hoganassessments.com/sites/default/files/uploads/Engagement%20Symposium.pdf.

7. G. J. Curphy, "Why Is Employee Engagement Stagnant?" *The Rocket Model*, www.therocketmodel.com/blog-articles/2016/2/22/why-is-employee-engagement-stagnant.

8. Cioca, "Better Engagement Means Better Performance—or Does It?"

9. M. Effron, "The Myth of Low Engagement, and Why It Doesn't Matter Anyways," *The Talent Strategy Group*, October 25, 2018, www.talentstrategygroup.com/publications/the-myth-of-low-engagement.

10. T. Chamorro-Premuzic, "The Dark Side of Employee Engagement," *Forbes*, May 20, 2014, www.forbes.com/sites/tomaspremuzic/2014/05/20/the-dark-side-of-employee-engagement.

11. Curphy, "Why Is Employee Engagement Stagnant?"

12. L. Garrad and T. Chamorro-Premuzic, "The Dark Side of High Employee Engagement," *Harvard Business Review*, August 2016, https://hbr.org/2016/08/the-dark-side-of-high-employee-engagement.

13. W. Tincup, "The Long Con of Engagement," *Fistful of Talent*, August 10, 2012, http://fistfuloftalent.com/2012/08/the-long-con-of-engagement.html.

14. Cioca, "Better Engagement Means Better Performance—or Does It?"

15. Effron, "The Myth of Low Engagement, and Why It Doesn't Matter Anyways."

16. E. A. Locke and G. P. Latham, "What Should We Do about Motivation Theory? Six Recommendations for the Twenty-First Century," *Academy of Management Review* 29, no. 3 (2004), pp. 388–403.

17. J. C. McElroy, P. C. Morrow, and S. N. Rude, "Turnover and Organizational Performance: A Comparative Analysis of the Effects of Voluntary, Involuntary, and Reduction-in-Force Turnover," *Journal of Applied Psychology* 86, no. 6 (2001), pp. 1294–99.

18. J. A. Krug, "Why Do They Keep Leaving?" *Harvard Business Review*, February 2003, pp. 14–15.

19. A. Hewitt, *Trends in Global Employee Engagement* (Chicago: Author, 2011).

20. G. Curphy, "How You Lead Those You Perceive as Uncommitted? Start by Looking in the Mirror," *Journal of Character and Leadership Integration*, Winter 2011.

21. D. Rigby, "Look before You Lay Off," *Harvard Business Review*, April 2002, pp. 20–21.

22. D. S. Levine, *Disgruntled: The Darker Side of the World of Work* (New York: Berkley Boulevard Books, 1998).

23. "Workers Are Losing Their Chains," *The Economist*, September 22, 2018, p. 58.

24. A. Rubenstein, M. Eberly, T. Lee, and T Mitchell, "Surveying the Forest: A Meta-Analysis, Moderator Investigation, and Future-Oriented Discussion of the Antecedents of Voluntary Employee Turnover," *Personnel Psychology*, 71, (2018), pp. 23–65.

25. E. Sinar, "New Research Reveals How to Supercharge the Employee Experience," *Better Up*, www.betterup.com/en-us/blog/new-research-reveals-how-to-supercharge-the-employee-experience.

26. D. Nowak, "Here's the No. 1 Reason Why Employees Quit Their Jobs," *NBC News*, June 21, 2019, www.nbcnews.com/better/lifestyle/here-s-no-1-reason-why-employees-quit-their-jobs-ncna1020031.

27. K. Oakes, "Why Good Employees Leave," *Talent Quarterly*, Spring 2019, pp. 34–39.

28. D. Paquette, "Workers Are Ghosting Their Employers Like Bad Dates," *The Washington Post*, December 12,2018, www.washingtonpost.com/business/2018/12/12/workers-are-ghosting-their-employers-like-bad-dates.

29. B. E. Litzky, K. E. Eddleston, and D. L. Kidder, "The Good, The Bad, and the Misguided: How Managers Inadvertently Encourage Deviant Behaviors," *Academy of Management Perspectives* 20, no. 1 (2006), pp. 91–103.

30. D. W. Organ and K. Ryan, "A Meta-analytic Review of Attitudinal and Dispositional Predictors of Organizational Citizenship Behavior," *Personnel Psychology* 48 (1995), pp. 775–802.

31. L. A. Bettencourt, K. P. Gwinner, and M. L. Meuter, "A Comparison of Attitude, Personality, and Knowledge Predictors of Service-Oriented Organizational Citizenship Behaviors," *Journal of Applied Psychology* 86, no. 1 (2001), pp. 29–41.

32. R. C. Mayer and M. B. Gavin, "Trust in Management and Performance: Who Minds the Shop While Employees Watch the Boss?" *Academy of Management Journal* 48, no. 5 (2005), pp. 874–88.

33. B. J. Tepper, M. K. Duffy, C. A. Henle, and L. Schurer Lambert, "Procedural Injustice, Victim Precipitation, and Abusive Supervision," *Personnel Psychology* 59 (2006), pp. 101–23.

34. G. Strauss, "Workers Hone the Fine Art of Revenge: Acts of Violence, Harassment toward Boss on Rise in Corporate World," *Denver Post*, August 24, 1998, p. 6E.

35. A. E. Colbert, M. K. Mount, J. K. Harter, L. A. Witt, and M. R. Barrick, "Interactive Effects of Personality and Perceptions of the Work Situation on Workplace Deviance," *Journal of Applied Psychology* 89, no. 4 (2004), pp. 599–609.

36. B. Marcus and H. Schuler, "Antecedents of Counterproductive Behavior at Work: A General Perspective," *Journal of Applied Psychology* 89, no. 1 (2004), pp. 647–60.

37. R. P. Tett and J. P. Meyer, "Job Satisfaction, Organizational Commitment, Turnover Intention, and Turnover: Path Analyses Based on Meta-analytic Findings," *Personnel Psychology* 46 (1993), pp. 259–93.

38. Krug, "Why Do They Keep Leaving?"

39. Hewitt, *Trends in Global Employee Engagement.*

40. Curphy, "How You Lead Those You Perceive as Uncommitted?"

41. Tett and Meyer, "Job Satisfaction, Organizational Commitment, Turnover Intention, and Turnover."

42. G. J. Curphy, "In-Depth Assessments, 360-Degree Feedback, and Development: Key Research Results and Recommended Next Steps," presentation at the annual conference for HR managers at US West Communications, Denver, CO, January 1998.

43. T. Peters, *The Circle of Innovation: You Can't Shrink Your Way to Greatness* (New York: Random House, 1997).

44. S. Schellenbarger, "Investors Seem Attracted to Firms with Happy Employees," *The Wall Street Journal*, March 19, 1997, p. I2.

45. McElroy, Morrow, and Rude, "Turnover and Organizational Performance."

46. Krug, "Why Do They Keep Leaving?"

47. Rigby, "Look before You Lay Off."

48. A. G. Bedeian and A. A. Armenakis, "The Cesspool Syndrome: How Dreck Floats to the Top of Declining Organizations," *Academy of Management Executive* 12, no. 1 (1998), pp. 58–63.

49. P. W. Hom and A. J. Kinicki, "Towards a Greater Understanding of How Dissatisfaction Drives Employee Turnover," *Academy of Management Journal* 44, no. 5 (2001), pp. 975–87.

50. P. W. Hom, L. Roberson, and A. D. Ellis, "Challenging Conventional Wisdom about Who Quits: Revelations from Corporate America," *Journal of Applied Psychology* 93, no. 1 (2008), pp. 1–34.

51. Curphy, "How You Lead Those You Perceive as Uncommitted?"

52. Bedeian and Armenakis, "The Cesspool Syndrome."

53. Hom and Kinicki, "Towards a Greater Understanding of How Dissatisfaction Drives Employee Turnover."

54. D. P. Campbell, G. J. Curphy, and T. Tuggle, *360 Degree Feedback Instruments: Beyond Theory*, workshop presented at the 10th annual conference of the Society for Industrial and Organizational Psychology, Orlando, FL, May 1995.

55. P. Morrel-Samuels, "Getting the Truth into Workplace Surveys," *Harvard Business Review*, February 2002, pp. 111–20.

56. "Do You Know Which Employee Satisfaction Drivers to Watch?" *Talent Intelligence*, August 7, 2017, www.talentintelligence.com/blog/do-you-know-which-employee-satisfaction-drivers-to-watch.

57. Associated Press, "Military Pay Soars," April 11, 2007, http://military.com/daily-news.

58. "Reframing the Military's Junior Officer Retention Problem," *Task & Purpose*, November 17, 2015, https://taskandpurpose.com/leadership/reframing-the-militarys-junior-officer-retention-problem.

59. D. P. Campbell and S. Hyne, *Manual for the Revised Campbell Organizational Survey* (Minneapolis, MN: National Computer Systems, 1995).

60. C. Kleiman, "Survey: Job Satisfaction Can Be Costly to Employers," *Denver Post*, June 22, 1997, p. J-4.

61. B. H. Sheppard, R. J. Lewicki, and J. W. Minton, *Organizational Justice: The Search for Fairness in the Workplace* (New York: Lexington Books, 1972).

62. L. K. Trevino, "The Social Effects of Punishment in Organizations: A Justice Perspective," *Academy of Management Review* 17 (1992), pp. 647–76.

63. J. A. Colquitt, B. A. Scott, J. B. Rodell, D. M. Long, C. P. Zapata, D. E. Conlon, and M. J. Wesson, "Justice at the Millennium, a Decade Later: A Meta-Analytic Test of Social Exchange and Affect-Based Perspectives," *Journal of Applied Psychology* 98, no. 2 (2013), pp. 199–36.

64. P. A. Siegel, C. Post, J. Brockner, A. Y. Fishman, and C. Garden, "The Moderating Influence of Procedural Fairness on the Relationship between Work–Life Conflict and Organizational Commitment," *Journal of Applied Psychology* 90, no. 1 (2005), pp. 13–24.

65. J. A. Colquitt, "On the Dimensionality of Organizational Justice: A Construct Validation of a Measure," *Journal of Applied Psychology* 86, no. 2 (2001), pp. 386–400.

66. J. A. Colquitt, D. E. Conlon, M. J. Wesson, C. O. L. H. Porter, and K. Y. Ng, "Justice at the Millennium: A Meta-analytic Review of 25 Years of Organizational Justice Research," *Journal of Applied Psychology* 86, no. 2 (2001), pp. 425–45.

67. M. L. Ambrose and R. Cropanzano, "A Longitudinal Analysis of Organizational Fairness: An Examination of Reactions to Tenure and Promotion Decisions," *Journal of Applied Psychology* 88, no. 2 (2003), pp. 266–75.

68. B. J. Tepper and E. C. Taylor, "Relationships among Supervisors' and Subordinates' Procedural Justice Perceptions and Organizational Citizenship Behaviors," *Academy of Management Journal* 46, no. 1 (2003), pp. 97–105.

69. T. Simons and Q. Roberson, "Why Managers Should Care about Fairness: The Effects of Aggregate Justice Perceptions on Organizational Outcomes," *Journal of Applied Psychology* 88, no. 3 (2003), pp. 432–43.

70. E. C. Hollensbe, S. Khazanchi, and S. S. Masterson, "How Do I Assess If My Supervisor and Organization Are Fair: Identifying the Rules Underlying Entity-Based Justice Perceptions," *Academy of Management Journal* 51, no. 6 (2008), pp. 1099–116.

71. B. C. Holtz and C. M. Harold, "Fair Today, Fair Tomorrow? A Longitudinal Investigation of Overall Justice Perceptions," *Journal of Applied Psychology* 94, no. 5 (2009), pp. 1185–99.

72. J. Brockner, "Why It's So Hard to Be Fair," *Harvard Business Review*, March 2006, p. 122–30.

73. F. Herzberg, "The Motivation-Hygiene Concept and Problems of Manpower," *Personnel Administrator* 27 (1964), pp. 3–7.

74. F. Herzberg, *Work and the Nature of Man* (Cleveland, OH: World Publishing, 1966).

75. F. Herzberg, "One More Time: How Do You Motivate Employees?" *Harvard Business Review*, January 2003, pp. 87–96.

76. Herzberg, "One More Time."

77. K. B. Paul and C. L. Johnson, "Engagement at 3M: A Case Study," in *The Executive Guide to Integrated Talent Management*, ed. K. Oakes and P. Galahan (Alexandria, VA: ASTD Press, 2011), pp. 133–46.

78. G. J. Curphy and M. Roellig, "Followership," working paper, 2010.

79. Macey and Schneider, "The Meaning of Employee Engagement."

80. M. Effron, "The Myth of Low Engagement," The Talent Strategy Group, October 25, 2018, www.talentstrategygroup.com/publications/the-myth-of-low-engagement.

81. S. Simmerman, "Presenteeism: The Non-engagement of the Masses," LinkedIn, May 12, 2016, www.linkedin.com/pulse/presenteeism-non-engagement-masses-scott-simmerman-ph-d-.

82. Gallup, *The State of the American Workplace.*

83. Effron, "The Myth of Low Engagement."

84. M. Hayes et al., "The Global Study of Engagement."

85. Gallup, *The State of the American Workplace.*

86. R. Karsan and K. Kruse, *We: How to Increase Performance and Profits through Full Engagement* (Hoboken, NJ: Wiley, 2011).

87. D. MacPherson, K. Oehler, and C. Adair, *2017 Trends in Global Employee Engagement: Global Anxiety Erodes Employee Engagement Gains* (Lincolnshire, IL: A on Hewitt, 2017).

88. Cioca, "Better Engagement Means Better Performance—or Does It?"

89. S. Bridges, "Why Engagement Surveys Suck," *Bridges*, June 10,2019, https://sarahbridges.com/2019/06/why-engagement-surveys-suck.

90. "Making Frequent Feedback Work: Harnessing the Next-Generation of Employee Engagement Tools," *Korn Ferry*, 2018, https://focus.kornferry.com/wp-content/uploads/2015/02/Making-frequent-employee-feedback-work-Korn_Ferry.pdf.

91. D. Wilkie, "How Anonymous Is That Employee Satisfaction Survey?" *Society for Human Resource Management*, December 19, 2019, www.shrm.org/resourcesandtools/hr-topics/employee-relations/pages/how-anonymous-is-that-employee-satisfaction-survey.aspx.

92. Effron, "The Myth of Low Engagement."

93. T. Chamorro-Premuzic, L. Garrad, and D. Elzinga, "Is Employee Engagement Just a Reflection of Personality?" *Harvard Business Review*, November 28,2018, https://hbr.org/2018/11/is-employee-engagement-just-a-reflection-of-personality.

94. AON Hewitt Australia, "Wired for Engagement: Improved Engagement through Better Hiring," November 2017, www.aonhewitt.com.au/AON.Marketing/media/Australia/pdf/Resources/Reports%20and%20research/2017-Wired-for-Engagement.pdf.

95. A. Yearlsey, personal communication, April 3, 2017.

96. S. Walker, "One Fix for All That's Wrong: Better Managers," *The Wall Street Journal*, March 24, 2019, pp. B1–2.

97. Gallup, *The State of the American Workplace.*

98. M. Porter, "Employee Engagement Isn't Getting Any Better. Here's Why." December 15, 2015, https://blogs.perficient.com/2015/12/10/employee-engagement-isnt-getting-better-heres-why-2/.

99. M. Crowley, "Employee Engagement Isn't Getting Any Better and Gallup Shares the Surprising Reasons Why," *HR.com*, November 1, 2016, www.hr.com/en/magazines/ recognition_engagement_excellence_essentials/january_2016_recognition_engagement/ employee-engagement-isnt-getting-better-gallup-sha_ija0753e.html.

100. K. Grant, "Americans Hate Their Jobs and Even Perks Don't Help," *Today*, June 24, 2013, www.today.com/money/americans-hate-their-jobs-even-perks-dont-help-6C10423977.

101. R. Matuson, "The Gig Is Up! Stop Wasting Millions on Perks That Don't Work," LinkedIn, February 20, 2017, www.linkedin.com/pulse/gig-up-stop-wasting-billions-perks-dont-work-roberta-chinsky-matuson.

CHAPTER 11

Follower Performance, Effectiveness, and Potential

Introduction

> *It's true that hard work never killed anybody, but I figure, why take the chance?*

Ronald Reagan, former U.S. president

The previous two chapters described different ways to motivate and engage followers and keep them happy, which are essential leadership skills. Nor are they easy skills to master, as different situations require different motivational and engagement techniques. What motivates followers in certain situations may just as easily demotivate others, and as circumstances change, different followers can become engaged or disengaged. One hallmark of effective leadership is the ability to motivate and engage employees across a wide variety of situations.

Leadership is not a popularity contest, and it is important to keep in mind that motivating and engaging employees and creating self-starters are means to an end rather than final destinations. When all is said and done, *leaders exist to achieve results*. Groups of people are likely to get little done until someone sets a direction; clarifies goals and expectations; organizes and assigns work; motivates, engages, and develops employees; allocates resources wisely; monitors progress; and makes adjustments as needed in order to accomplish important team or organizational outcomes. This can be a formal or informal leader, but a team is likely to flail about and struggle to get anything done until somebody addresses these issues. Coaches get judged by their ability to win games, military leaders by their ability to win battles and wars, business leaders by their ability to achieve market share and financial results, and not-for-profit leaders by their ability to attract funding and deliver on their missions. People should be placed into positions of authority in order to improve the odds of a team winning or having an impact, and oftentimes this is even more challenging than engaging and motivating followers.

As seen in **Figure 11.1**, leader behavior and follower motivation, engagement, satisfaction, turnover, and organizational citizenship behaviors were covered in **Chapters 9** and **10**. This chapter focuses on Follower Performance and Unit and Team Effectiveness. **Performance** can be defined as what individual followers accomplish and the behaviors exhibited to achieve results. Do sales representatives achieve their monthly sales targets, and do they abide to company pricing guidelines or give large (and unauthorized) discounts to customers? Do baristas follow recommended drink preparation guidelines and achieve good customer service ratings?

Whereas performance focuses on followers' individual behaviors and accomplishments, **unit or team effectiveness** concerns collective results. When all the sales representatives' results are added together, did the sales team hit its monthly sales and profitability goals? Did the coffee shop hit its monthly revenue, profitability, number of customers, price per order, and customer satisfaction targets? How did the sales team do against other teams and was the coffee shop's performance better or worse than other coffee shops in the area? Leaders ultimately get judged on their results, and it is usually unit and team effectiveness measures that are used to make these evaluations. Like motivation and engagement, follower performance is another critical means to achieving superior team results.

> *Q: If women are better leaders why aren't more of them men?*
>
> *A: Because our standards are unfairly low when we evaluate men.*
>
> **Tomas Chamorro-Premuzic, Right Management**

Follower **potential** is the final topic we'll cover in this chapter, and it primarily centers around promotion determinations. Of 12 sales representatives on a sales team, who is best suited to be the next sales leader? Is the person with the best numbers capable of getting results through others and being the best sales leader? Or is someone with lower numbers but capable of inspiring others a better sales leader? What criteria would you use to determine which barista should be promoted to be the next shift supervisor? Elections are good examples of common potential decisions, as voters essentially make predictions about who would be the best president, prime minister, representative, mayor, or judge. Sometimes voters get it right, and other times their

FIGURE 11.1 Relationships among Leadership, Satisfaction, Engagement, Performance, and Effectiveness

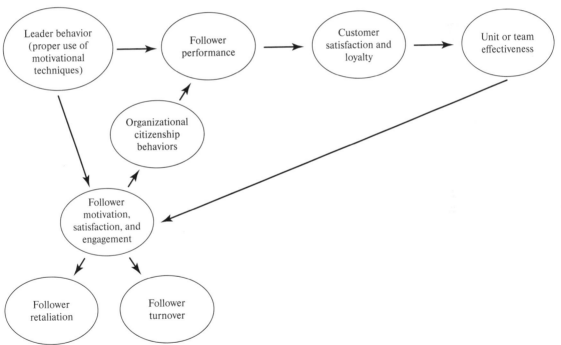

Sources: M. A. Huselid, "The Impact of Human Resource Management Practices on Turnover, Productivity, and Corporate Financial Performance," *Academy of Management Journal* 38, no. 4 (1995), pp. 635–72; T. Butorac, *Recruitment and Retention: The Keys to Profitability at Carlson Companies,* presentation given at Personnel Decisions International, Minneapolis, MN, June 11, 2001; D. J. Koys, "The Effects of Employee Satisfaction, Organizational Citizenship Behavior, and Turnover on Organizational Effectiveness: A Unit-Level, Longitudinal Study," *Personnel Psychology* 54, no. 1 (2001), pp. 101–14; J. Husserl, "Allied's Organizational Life Cycle," *Management Education & Development* 24, no. 3 (1998), p. 8; Sirota Consulting, *Establishing the Linkages between Employee Attitudes, Customer Attitudes, and Bottom-Line Results* (Chicago, IL: Author, 1998); D. S. Pugh, J. Dietz, J. W. Wiley, and S. M. Brooks, "Driving Service Effectiveness through Employee–Customer Linkages," *Academy of Management Executive* 16, no. 4 (2002), pp. 73–84; and B. Schneider, P. J. Hanges, D. B. Smith, and A. N. Salvaggio, "Which Comes First: Employee Attitudes or Organizational, Financial and Market Performance?" *Journal of Applied Psychology* 88, no. 5 (2003), pp. 836–51.

predictions turn out to be spectacularly wrong. Likewise, organizations make predictions about who should get promoted. They use a variety of techniques to make these determinations, some of which are less biased and more accurate than others. Leaders are responsible for their team's overall results and the performance of individual followers, and they are asked to provide recommendations on follower potential, so knowing these concepts is critically important.

Understanding and Managing Follower Performance

One of the greatest challenges leaders face is aligning talented and capable workers with the goals of the organization.

John Boudreau, University of Southern California

Follower performance falls into two major categories, and they are typically referred to as **the what and the how of performance**. The *what* pertains to task and goal accomplishment. What did the follower actually get done, what results did he or she obtain, or what projects did he or she complete? Sports examples of the *what* include batting averages, number of points or assists per game, or number of aces served. Business examples include the number of calls answered, monthly sales results, or the number of lines of code written. The *how* can be defined as those behaviors directed toward the accomplishment of team or organizational goals.[1] Examples might include the actions that caused an ice hockey player to take a penalty, how a sales representative answers customer calls, or a worker's actions when assembling cars during a shift. There are several aspects of follower performance that are worth noting. First, it is incumbent upon leaders to fully understand the team and organization goals, as these will dictate what followers need to get done and the type, intensity, and duration of follower behavior needed for goal accomplishment. Follower goals, task assignments, and behaviors should align with what the team needs to deliver and the rules under which it operates. Second and relatedly, leaders need to understand the context or situation in which these behaviors need to be exhibited: Are followers working on an assembly line, out of their homes, or in an office? What processes, procedures, and equipment will they be using? Do followers operate fairly independently, or do they rely on others for inputs, resources, and the like? What standards of behavior are required for goal success? How should performance and goal progress be measured (see **Profiles in Leadership 11.1**)?[2]

Mike Pompeo

PROFILES IN LEADERSHIP 11.1

Mike Pompeo grew up in southern California, and after graduating from high school, attended the United States Military Academy. He did quite well at West Point, graduating number one in his class, and then spent five years in the U.S. Army in Germany as a tank commander, executive officer, and maintenance officer. After his active duty stint, Pompeo attended Harvard Law School and then worked for a Washington, D.C. law firm for a few years. In 1998, he moved to Wichita, Kansas, where he and three fellow West Point graduates acquired several companies that manufactured parts for the aerospace industry. Pompeo and his partner stayed with Thayer Aerospace for eight years before selling the business in 2006. Shortly thereafter he was hired to be the president of Sentry International, an oil field equipment manufacturer that was a partner with Koch Industries.

In 2010, Pompeo ran for and convincingly won the 4th District congressional seat for Kansas.

He won the 2012, 2014, and 2016 elections by equally wide margins and was appointed to be the CIA Director shortly after U.S. President Donald Trump moved into office. He spent about a year running the CIA, where he was responsible for providing President Trump with daily intelligence briefings. As the CIA Director he also took direct command of the Counterintelligence Mission Center, got permission to make covert drone strikes without Pentagon involvement, and began negotiations with senior officials from North Korea. Pompeo moved into the Secretary of State role after President Trump fired Rex Tillerson in early 2018.

Tillerson had hollowed out the State Department during his short tenure as Secretary of State, and Pompeo inherited an organization with very low morale. With his public statements that directly contradicted the CIA on Mohammed bin Salman's direct involvement with the murder of Jamal Khashoggi, lying to Congress about civilian deaths in the war in Yemen, approving Turkey attacking the Kurds in Syria, publicly stating he had no knowledge of the infamous phone call between President Trump and President Zelensky of Ukraine on July 25, 2019 (even though he was on the call), the lack of support and outright deception regarding the reasons for the recall of Ambassador Marie Yovanovitch, and active participation in the shadow diplomacy being quarterbacked by Rudolph Giuliani in Ukraine,

chances are morale in the State Department has gone from bad to worse.

How would you evaluate the performance of Mike Pompeo as a West Point cadet, U.S. Army officer, Harvard Law School attendee, lawyer, business owner, U.S. Congressman, CIA Director, and Secretary of State? Would the criteria used to evaluate Pompeo's performance change as he changed roles? How so? Was Pompeo effective in these roles? How could you make this determination? Is loyalty or competence more important for these roles?

Sources: C. Tate, "Mike Pompeo: Just a Regular Guy among Trump Nominees Worth Millions, Billions," *McClatchy DC Report*, January 10, 2017, www.mcclatchydc.com/news/nation-world/national/national-security/article125710979.html; J. Gerstein, "Who Is Mike Pompeo?" *Politico*, January 12, 2017, www.politico.com/story/2017/01/who-is-mike-pompeo-233518; M. Hirsh and R. Grammer, "White House Digs Itself in Deeper on Khashoggi," *Foreign Policy*, December 4, 2018, https://foreignpolicy.com/2018/12/04/white-house-digs-itself-in-deeper-on-khashoggi-trump-refuses-to-address-murder-journalist-saudi-arabia-anger-congress-mohammed-bin-salman-complicit-war-in-yemen-humanitarian-disaster-gina-haspel; D. Larison, "Pompeo Lied to Congress about Yemen to Protect Arms Sales," *The American Conservative*, September 20, 2018, www.theamericanconservative.com/larison/pompeo-lied-to-congress-about-yemen-to-protect-arms-sales; and E. Wong and K. Vogel, "New Documents Reveal Details of Pompeo's Role in Ukraine Affairs," *The New York Times*, November 23, 2019, www.nytimes.com/2019/11/23/us/politics/pompeo-trump-ukraine-impeachment.html.

Third, followers can choose to spend their time engaging in different sorts of behavior at work; these behaviors may or may not be directed at goal accomplishment. Research shows that followers spend anywhere from one to three and a half hours on non-goal-oriented activities during the day, and the key for leaders is to get followers motivated to spend more of their time on work-related activities.[3] Fourth, motivation is not the only factor affecting follower performance. Followers' knowledge and experience, having the right hardware and software, and leveraging the right processes and procedures are just some of the many factors that affect followers' performance levels (see **Highlight 11.1**).

Factors Affecting Follower Performance

HIGHLIGHT 11.1

There are any number of factors that affect what followers accomplish and how they go about getting things done. Although leaders are quick to point fingers at followers when their results and behaviors fall short, perhaps the biggest follower performance inhibitor is the boss. Two of the bigger leader problems when it comes to substandard follower performance is absenteeism and time-wasting leadership.

Absenteeism leadership occurs when leaders are so busy traveling, attending meetings, or being otherwise preoccupied that they have little time for their followers and teams. They may be friendly and very complementary to their staffs, but in reality they have no idea what is happening and provide little helpful guidance or support to their followers. Because of their general cluelessness, they set goals and deadlines, assign projects, ignore requests, and make decisions that have little grounding in reality. Like the Pointy-Haired Boss in *Dilbert* cartoons, absenteeism leaders are silent organizational killers that followers immediately recognize but superiors often fail to detect.

Time-wasting leaders are also very prevalent in organizations. These are individuals who unintentionally assign work or set rules that are detrimental to a team's overall performance. Leaders tend to get more visibility by launching rather than completing projects, and as a result, some like to chase bright shiny objects and adopt the latest management fads. This causes followers to regularly shift gears and never reach closure on previously launched initiatives. Other time-wasting leader behaviors include presenteeism, executive magnification, and cookie licking. **Presenteeism** occurs when leaders insist that followers put in long hours at the office. An example of this comes from Jack Ma of AliBaba, who partly attributes the company's success to the 996 rule: All employees are expected to work from 9:00 a.m. to 9:00 p.m. six days a week. Research shows productivity drops precipitously after 50 hours a week, so chances are a large chunk of the 72 hours employees spend each week at AliBaba is unproductive. **Executive magnification** occurs when leaders engage in idle conversations that followers misinterpret as work mandates. Leaders may have a sidebar conversation about the color of an office they like, and before you know it, every office they visit is painted in the same color. The leader may have never intended this to happen but failed to appreciate the impact of their words on followers. **Cookie licking** occurs when leaders cannot let go of actions or decisions that should be delegated to their staffs. A CEO for a *Fortune* 50 company insisted on personally interviewing everyone being hired or promoted into a director-level position. With 500 new directors being appointed each year, the CEO caused incredible amounts of additional work for recruits, potential promotees, recruiters, HR staff, and hiring managers trying to accommodate the CEO's constantly changing schedule.

So what can followers do to successfully cope with absenteeism and time-wasting leaders? Putting in longer hours is probably not the solution, as spending more face time at work may be disengaging and not particularly productive. What may help is to first identify and prioritize those goals and actions that will have the greatest impact on team and organizational outcomes. Followers should then focus their efforts accordingly, jealously guard their time, and learn how to say no to additional work. This is a high-risk career strategy, however, as pursuing this path runs the risk of being seen as a bad organizational citizen or chronic underperformer if a follower fails to deliver. But those who do pull this off are likely to be more engaged and deliver on those tasks that really matter to a team.

Sources: S. Gregory, "The Most Common Type of Incompetent Leader," *Harvard Business Review*, March 30, 2018, https://hbr.org/2018/03/the-most-common-type-of-incompetent-leader; G. Curphy, "Clueless or Culpable," LinkedIn, June 1, 2015, www.linkedin.com/pulse/clueless-culpable-gordon-gordy-curphy-phd; R. Sutton, "How Bosses Often Waste Their Employees' Time," *The Wall Street Journal*, August 13, 2018, p. R2; "The Joy of Absence: Fighting the Curse of Presenteeism," *The Economist*, May 18, 2019, p. 55; and M. Hansen, "The Key to Success? Working Less," *The Wall Street Journal*, January 13–14, 2018, pp. C1–2.

Last, leaders need to be proficient at all three components of the **performance management cycle** when working with followers to accomplish group or organizational goals.[4, 5, 6, 7] As seen in **Figure 11.2**, the first component of this cycle is **planning**, which involves developing a thorough understanding of the team's or organization's goals, the role followers need to play in goal accomplishment, the context in which followers operate, what they need to get done, and the behaviors they need to exhibit for the team to be successful. The second component is **monitoring**, which includes tracking follower performance, sharing feedback on goal progress, providing needed resources and coaching, and the like. **Evaluating** makes up the third component in the cycle, and this entails providing some type of summary feedback on job performance to followers. Because the performance management cycle is so critical to being an effective leader, we will spend more time on each of the three components.

The Performance Management Cycle: Planning

Planning involves understanding how the team or organization defines success, understanding the context in which followers operate, determining what followers need to deliver and behave for the team to succeed, and then setting clear expectations for follower performance. To do this, leaders need to have a clear understanding of various roles played by their followers, the tasks to be accomplished, the tools to be used, the processes and procedures that need to be followed, and the interdependencies or contingencies among follower activities. By gaining a deep understanding of the work to be performed, leaders can design roles that take advantage of the needs, achievement orientation, goal setting, operant, and empowerment approaches to motivate and engage followers that were described earlier in Chapters 9 and 10.

One thing leaders need to determine when reviewing the work followers will be doing is whether all aspects of a job need to be performed equally well. An example might be the sweepers at Disneyland. Sweepers need to ensure their areas are free from litter, but their biggest contribution is to have positive and helpful interactions with customers. The same is true with salespeople; it is far more important for them to have a strong pipeline of potential business, have positive interactions with clients, write compelling proposals, and close business

FIGURE 11.2 The Performance Management Cycle

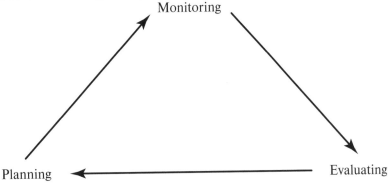

than it is to complete paperwork each week. This means that treating all aspects of a job as equally important usually leads to suboptimal team goal accomplishment, as followers will spend too much time exhibiting
behaviors that have little impact on team effectiveness. Leaders need to know which aspects of followers'
roles require high levels of performance and which ones only need to be done well enough.[8, 9] Unfortunately,
hiring managers and human resource professionals often make the mistake of wanting candidates who can
do every aspect of a position equally well, and as a result they miss out on hiring exceptional talent and take
too long to fill openings.[10]

> *If you set the bar low enough, there is no limit of what I can achieve for you.*
>
> **Jeff Baker, leadership trainer**

Setting clear, explicit, measurable, and agreed-upon goals for the what and how of follower performance is
extremely important. It will be very difficult for leaders to provide meaningful feedback, evaluate overall performance, and differentiate low from high performers if followers do not know what they need to deliver
and how they are supposed to behave.[11, 12] Another thing leaders need to do in planning is to make the
links between follower performance and team or organizational outcomes very explicit. Far too often leaders
assume these links are obvious and need no explanation, when more often than not followers may not understand why their behavior is important to team success.[13, 14] However, if the team has not defined winning
and has not developed a team scorecard, then it is difficult for leaders to make this link, provide feedback on
follower performance, or evaluate followers' contributions to team success.

The Performance Management Cycle: Monitoring

Monitoring consists of several leader behaviors, including observing followers' performance, providing feedback and coaching on followers' behaviors, securing needed resources, and regularly reviewing goal progress
with followers. Like planning, some of the work done by followers lends itself to monitoring better than others. It is usually more difficult to monitor knowledge work or activities that involve creativity or problem
solving than it is to monitor answering customer phone calls, assembling motorcycles, or building homes.
Followers may also be geographically dispersed, which can make monitoring difficult.[15]

Technological advances have allowed leaders to use **electronic performance monitoring** to a much greater
extent than ever before. Transponders attached to tractor-trailers allow trucking companies to monitor driver
performance 24 hours a day, companies are now tracking the e-mails of 27 million employees, Uber monitors customer and driver feedback immediately after rides, and calls to customer care centers are recorded
and routinely reviewed. Organizations like electronic performance monitoring as it is cheap, provides more
control, and helps take time-wasting behavior out of the workplace. But will these alternative forms of monitoring replace leaders when it comes to performance management? Probably not for some time, as customer
ratings are often inflated and not particularly accurate.[16] Someone also has to define what constitutes poor,
average, or superior performance and provide the coaching and support needed for followers to perform at
high levels. Moreover, there are big downsides to constantly being monitored. People do not like the intrusive
nature of electronic performance monitoring and being pushed to the limit at work. It also runs counter to
what we know about autonomy, empowerment, engagement, and creativity.[17, 18, 19, 20]

> *All animals are equal, but some animals are more equal than others.*
>
> **George Orwell, *Animal Farm***

Follower types and talent management practices also come into play with monitoring. Different follower
types were described in the introduction to **Part 3**, and self-starters, brown-nosers, slackers, and criticizers
each require different types of monitoring. For example, slackers and criticizers can cause considerable damage to team morale and organizational effectiveness if not monitored adequately. Some of these individuals

may falsify travel claims in order to steal from employers, steal customer identification information, or sabotage IT systems if disgruntled. Others completely check out of work. One manager for a Spanish water treatment company did not show up for work for six years, and the company found out only when he could not be located to be given his 20-year service award. And in a parting note to all employees, a German public-sector employee proudly stated he had done nothing productive in 14 years.[21, 22, 23]

> *Delegate the important stuff only to people who don't have time to help you. Idle people become even more useless if you give them mission-critical work to do.*
>
> **Robert Hogan and Tomas Chamorro-Premuzic, Hogan Assessment Systems**

At the other end of the performance spectrum, high performers can sometimes be overlooked or mistreated. Boris Groysberg has done considerable research looking at high flyers, those performing in the top 1 percent in the financial services industry. These individuals typically bring in 5–10 times the investments, management fees, or commercial loans of average bankers and are the people most likely to get poached by other companies. Groysberg found that, rather than letting these individuals do what they do best, which is to make their companies a lot of money, companies try to rein in these individuals by forcing them to do all aspects of their jobs equally well. High flyers do not react well to being micromanaged, and these high-maintenance prima donnas typically move on to other companies as a result. Groysberg's research also showed these individuals usually did not perform nearly as well in their new companies as they did previously. So high flyers may have great résumés and demand large salaries and signing bonuses to get hired away, but they are most likely to be average performers in their new jobs.[24, 25]

Talent hoarding can also be a problem for many organizations. Some followers are such high performers that leaders are loath to let them go or let others know about their exceptional performance. This tactic might optimize the team's effectiveness but is likely to suboptimize that of the organization, as the high-performing follower might make an even bigger contribution to organizational success if he or she were working on a different team. High-performing followers often become frustrated in these situations and leave companies in order to get promoted. Interestingly enough, poor-performing organizations were far more likely to engage in talent hoarding than high-performing firms, which only served to exacerbate their talent shortfalls.[26]

The monitoring phase of performance management is the most time-consuming. It may take leaders a few hours to determine what and how followers need to deliver, set follower goals and performance expectations, and help them see the links between their assignments and behaviors and important team outcomes. If performance feedback has been routinely documented, then it usually only takes a few hours to evaluate a follower's performance, write a performance review, and conduct an annual performance review session. Leaders should be spending considerably more time monitoring individual and team performance, providing ongoing feedback and coaching, clearing obstacles, lending support, adjusting individual goals, and shifting work to optimize team outcomes.

The Performance Management Cycle: Evaluating

> *Performance reviews are an expensive and complex way to make people unhappy.*
>
> **Kevin Murphy, Pennsylvania State University**

The last component in the performance management cycle is evaluating followers' performance, and in doing this organizations are trying to address three important issues. First, who are the organization's best and worst performers? Although immediate supervisors may have a fairly good handle on the performance of their direct reports, the higher one goes the less likely he or she will know the performance levels of everyone in their organization. Leaders with six team members will have a better idea about their high and low performers than leaders running 2,000-person operations spread out across the globe, yet both leaders need to know their followers' overall performance levels. Thus the **differentiation** of followers is a critical aspect of evaluating performance, and doing this well should systematically improve the quality of followers over time. Second, how should **performance consequences** be allocated to employees? Who should get rewarded for superior performance and who should be sent home? Should companies give everyone equal pay raises, only reward the top 20 percent, or routinely fire the bottom 10 percent? Most organizations consider themselves **meritocracies**, where those who get the best results are given the best rewards.[27, 28] Yet if overall performance cannot be judged fairly, then bonuses and promotions will be more a function of loyalty and office politics than of follower performance. Third, can followers get **personal growth** from summary judgments of performance? Do followers understand what they do well and not so well and what they need to do to improve? Do they care about their performance gaps? Given their overall performance, do they have more to gain by staying in their current roles, moving to other teams, or joining other organizations? In years past, most organizations focused on the differentiation and performance consequences aspects of performance evaluations. Personal growth has recently become a more important aspect of evaluation for some companies (see **Highlight 11.2**).[29, 30,31,32]

> *Only 21 percent of employees strongly agree their performance is managed in a way that motivates them to do outstanding work.*
>
> **Gallup, Inc.**

Are Meritocracies Fair?

HIGHLIGHT 11.2

Meritocracy is a social ideal that appeals to our sense of fairness. Most people believe that those who are more talented, work harder, and achieve better results deserve to get paid more than those who produce less. This notion is consistent with the concept of organizational justice described in **Chapter 10** and the pay for performance philosophy that underlies most performance management systems. But how well does this approach work in practice?

Research shows meritocracies work very well when job performance is pivotal to and can be directly linked to organizational outcomes, job performance is determined by individual rather than team efforts and is easily measured, the measures provide accurate information about job performance, there is a wide range of job performance, and only a few individuals turn out to be high performers. Sales positions usually meet these criteria, and pay for performance is an effective compensation strategy for

rewarding those individuals who make the greatest contributions to an organization's top line.

Other than sales, few positions in organizations meet the meritocracy criteria. Most of the people working in IT, operations, finance, customer service, human resources, legal, logistics, and purchasing rely on team members and other stakeholders to get things done. Their contributions are difficult to measure, and the connections between their accomplishments and organizational outcomes can be tenuous. This is equally true for senior executives. Organizations also prefer that everyone in finance, IT, operations, or legal perform at high levels and cannot determine if they have widely disparate levels of performance.

Despite the fact that the vast majority of jobs in organizations fail to meet the meritocracy criteria, most people get rewarded based on some kind of pay-for-performance management scheme. This causes all kinds of unintended consequences, as followers may work incredibly long (but unproductive) hours, hoard information, set others up for failure, become more self-ish and discriminatory, and be less self-critical under these conditions. They are also more likely to equate promotions and bonuses with talent and effort, when in reality connections, privilege, loyalty, favoritism, and luck turn out to be bigger factors in rewards and career advancement.

How much have your talents and efforts contributed to your success, and what role have your connections and luck played in your life?

Sources: D. Markovits, *The Meritocracy Trap* (New York: Penguin Press, 2019); C. Mark, "Meritocracy Doesn't Exist, and Believing It Does Is Bad for You," *Fast Company*, March 13, 2019, www.fastcompany.com/40510522/meritocracy-doesnt-exist-and-believing-it-does-is-bad-for-you; and A. Colquitt, "CEO Pay, Employee Pay, and Pay Inequality in Organizations: Meritocracy or Monkey Business?" February 25, 2019, www.alancolquitt.com/single-post/2019/02/25/CEO-Pay-Employee-Pay-and-Pay-Inequality-in-Organizations-Meritocracy-or-Monkey-Business.

Evaluation may well be the most controversial component of the performance management cycle. What we do know is that well over 90 percent of companies use some form of **performance appraisal**.[33, 34,35,36,37] Performance appraisals document a follower's overall performance over a defined time period, usually one year, but they can be done more frequently. The *what* and the *how* are the major components of most performance appraisal systems. The what evaluates the performance of followers against the goals outlined during the planning phase of the performance management cycle: How did the follower do against his sales goals, what was his overall customer satisfaction ratings, how many applications did he develop, or how many of his deliveries were successful? The how concerns evaluations of followers' work-related behaviors during the designated time period: Did she come in on time, get along with coworkers, help others, and willingly put in extra hours as needed? As seen in **Table 11.1**, most performance appraisal systems require leaders to rate the what and how of a follower's performance on a scale from 1 to 5, with 1 = fails to meet expectations, 3 = meets expectations, and 5 = greatly exceeds expectations. These two ratings are then combined to yield an overall performance rating for the time period. Leaders are also asked to provide documentation to justify these three performance appraisal ratings and write comments that summarize a follower's performance for the time period. In some organizations, followers are also asked to provide documentation; what, how, and overall performance ratings; and summary comments.

TABLE 11.1   Sales Representative Annual Performance Evaluation Ratings

Performance Component	Goal	Actual	Performance Rating (1–5)
Sales	$2,750,000	$2,900,000	4.0
Gross Margins	32%	29%	2.5
Customer Turnover	12%	12%	3.0
Net Promoter Score	62	50	2.0
Average What Rating			**2.9**
Weekly CRM Updates	Every Sunday	Late two weeks	2.5
Weekly Expense Reports	Every Sunday	Late five weeks	2.0
Discounting Products	Less than 5 percent of sales	11 percent of sales	2.0

Performance Component	Goal	Actual	Performance Rating (1–5)
Sales Call Rating	4.5 average over 12 months	4.2	2.5
Ride Along Rating	4.5 average over 12 months	4.3	2.5
Average How Rating			**2.3**
Overall Performance Rating			**2.6**

Several contentious issues surround the evaluation of followers' performance. First, as described in **Highlight 11.2**, some jobs are much more difficult to evaluate than others. This is particularly true for knowledge workers, who make up many positions in modern organizations.[38] Relatedly, it is very difficult for leaders to provide what, how, and overall performance ratings if followers' goals and expectations have not been clearly defined in the planning phase of the performance management cycle. As stated earlier, some organizations and functions can have difficulties setting measurable performance goals, and in the absence of these goals, leaders are likely to go with their gut judgments to evaluate overall performance. Needless to say, these judgments are likely to be biased and not reflect followers' actual performance levels. Second, leaders not understanding the job or its context can sometimes assign the wrong performance goals to followers. Followers may perform well against these goals but their performance may have little impact on team or organizational effectiveness.

Third, there is a sizable percentage of leaders who believe it is more important to be popular than fair. They would rather give all followers glowing ratings than have hard conversations with underperformers. This lack of differentiation is usually a recipe for mediocrity, as high performers leave to join teams where their talents are more appreciated and low performers believe they are the ones next in line for a promotion. Absentee leaders are apt to base their evaluations on loyalty rather than on actual performance, and time-wasting leaders confuse follower activity with productivity when it comes to evaluation ratings. It is worth noting that in all these situations, it is the leaders, not the followers, who are at fault for setting unclear or unimportant performance goals or not having an accurate assessment of actual follower contributions.[39]

Accuracy is not one of the top reasons why supervisors assign performance review ratings.

Alan Colquitt, Organizational Researcher

Fourth, many leaders and followers have negative reactions to the bureaucratic nature of performance appraisals. Most are governed by highly rule-bound processes and extensive forms that can take leaders and followers hours to complete—hours taken away from actual job performance. Deloitte noted that it took over 2 million hours to complete annual reviews for their 65,000 employees.[40] Doing performance appraisals can be burdensome, but it is entirely within a company's purview to change the bureaucratic nature of this process. Sometimes the misguided pursuit of fairness can overwhelm the need to be realistic when it comes to managing follower performance.

Perhaps the biggest controversy with performance appraisals has to do with numerical ratings. Performance ratings are certainly subject to bias and may not accurately identify followers' performance levels.[41, 42] Others believe subjectivity and bias to be so pervasive that performance appraisal ratings change little from year to year, with the favorites consistently getting higher ratings and outsiders being awarded lower ratings regardless of performance. Another problem is that it can lead to the "ranking and yanking" of followers, where ratings are used to weed out the bottom 10 percent of performers each year.[43]

There is good performance management research to counter these arguments. First, people are continually being rated. SAT scores, GPAs, FICO credit scores, Uber passenger scores, and the like are used to rate people, and those being rated do not seem to suffer as a result. Moreover, those companies that have moved away from providing performance review ratings still provide differentiated salary increases, bonuses, and promotions based on follower performance. In reality, these actions are simply alternative forms of ratings.[44, 45] Second, although ratings do suffer from subjectivity, nonrating reviews likely suffer from even more subjectivity. With a lack of numerical ratings there is no way to calibrate performance within or between teams, so merit increases are based on the whims of leaders. Third, research has shown that performance review ratings change considerably from year to year, and followers have only a 33 percent chance of being rated as a superior performer from one year to the next. This means that follower performance varies greatly across time, so using summary ratings to "rank and yank" employees is not a particularly good idea, as even the best employees can have off years if they are working on particularly difficult projects (see **Highlight 11.3**).[46]

Does Performance Management Work?

HIGHLIGHT 11.3

Organizations spend countless hours and billions of dollars setting follower goals, monitoring and developing their performance, conducting performance reviews, and making compensation decisions. An important question is whether any of these activities matter. Most organizations believe they do, as over 90 percent utilize some sort of goal setting, monitoring, evaluation, and pay-for-promotion system to align follower efforts and accomplishments with important organizational outcomes. Yet comprehensive research by Elaine Pulakos and her colleagues indicate that performance management systems are incredibly costly and have little if any impact on bottom-line results. If performance management systems are expensive and contribute little to an organization's annual revenues, profitability, or customer satisfaction scores, then why do them?

Despite all the problems with meritocracies, pay-for-performance, and performance management systems in general, there are still good reasons why organizations have some type of formal system. It may well be that Pulakos's findings are due more to the way performance management systems are run than flaws in the approach. No matter how well a performance management system is designed, it will never make up for clueless bosses. As you will read in **Chapter 17**, far too many organizations are riddled with incompetent leaders. Many performance management systems would also be improved if they were less bureaucratic, provided more frequent performance feedback, and shifted away from individual to more team-based evaluations and rewards. Performance management is here to stay, but there are things organizations can do to get more value out of these systems.

Sources: E. Pulakos, R. Mueller-Hanson, and S. Arad, "The Evolution of Performance Management: Searching for Value," *Annual Review of Organizational Psychology and Organizational Behavior* 6 (2019), pp. 249–71; D. Schleicher, H. Baumann, D. Sullivan, and J. Yim, "Evaluating the Effectiveness of Performance Management: A 30-Year Integrated Conceptual Review," *Journal of Applied Psychology* 104, no. 7 (2019), pp. 851–87; J. Bersin. "We Wasted Ten Years Talking about Performance Ratings. The Seven Things We've Learned," June 24, 2019, https://josh-bersin.com/2018/11/we-wasted-ten-years-talking-about-performance-ratings-the-seven-things-weve-learned; A. Colquitt, "Performance Management: Current State, Future State," presentation delivered to the Minnesota Professional Psychology at Work meeting, Minneapolis, MN, September 18, 2018; and A. Colquitt, "It's Differentiation Season (Redux)," January 21, 2019, www.alancolquitt.com/single-post/2019/01/21/Its-Differentiation-Season-Redux.

When all is said and done, organizations are looking for a process that systematically links follower behavior to team and organizational outcomes; provides followers with clear expectations about performance and ongoing feedback and coaching about their performance and goal progress; accurately differentiates between high- and low-performing followers; and can be used to provide followers with performance-based rewards in a fair and transparent manner. A well-designed performance management cycle can satisfy these needs. Moreover, the research is very clear that organizations whose leaders adopt a performance management mindset of setting clear performance expectations and goals, monitoring performance and providing feedback and coaching to improve performance, and periodically evaluating and reviewing results have much higher performance than firms that do not engage in these practices.[47, 48] Despite these findings, many leaders fall short when it comes to successfully implementing the three components of the performance management cycle with their followers. Sometimes it has to do with difficulties connecting follower performance with effectiveness, providing feedback and coaching on followers' performance, or providing performance reviews, but these activities are fundamental to good leadership. Doing performance management right is the hard work of leadership, and it will likely take up a large percentage of your time as you move into leadership roles (see **Highlight 11.4**).

The Dunning–Kruger Effect

HIGHLIGHT 11.4

Steve Jobs supposedly suffered from having an extreme "reality distortion field," where he only paid attention to information that conformed to his worldview and discounted, twisted, or ignored anything that ran counter to his beliefs. It turns out that everyone is biased and distorts reality in one way or another. What seems to vary is the degree to which this happens in individuals. A classic example of our reality distortion field comes into play when looking at identity (how we describe ourselves) versus reputation (how others describe us; see **Chapter 6** for more information). Some people have fairly accurate self-insight, whereas others are "leadership legends in their own minds who are charismatically challenged in the eyes of others."

A variation of the reality distortion field is the **Dunning–Kruger effect**, in which people systematically overestimate their own performance in areas where they lack competence and readily dismiss any information to the contrary. Moreover, those who *lack competence* have an unusually *high degree of confidence* that their estimates are correct. Students routinely overestimate their performance on tests, doctors and lawyers believe they are better than their performance would suggest, and you will never hear anyone admit they should not be behind the steering wheel, although by definition 50 percent of the people on the road are below-average drivers. This cognitive bias and false self-confidence make it virtually impossible for people to know the true extent of their inadequacies. It also makes it difficult for people to recognize the inadequacies of others. Research also shows that those who are competent tend to slightly underestimate their performance levels in areas where they have proven expertise.

Because no one is an expert at everything, everyone suffers from the Dunning–Kruger effect to some degree. It is most likely to occur when we need to make estimates about our performance in areas in which we have little expertise. It also comes into play with both followers and leaders in performance reviews. Followers often provide overinflated views of performance when submitting self-appraisals as part of their annual reviews and readily discount any information that runs contrary to their beliefs. Leaders may lack the expertise needed to accurately judge followers' performance and recognize the effort and contributions of direct reports. They may also be biased toward sorting followers into A (top performers), B (average performers), or C (bottom performers) based on an inaccurate understanding of the work performed and only consider information that confirms their judgments.

Can you think of any celebrities, reality TV stars, professional athletes, or politicians who suffer from the Dunning-Kruger effect? How would you rate U.S. President Donald Trump's reality distortion field?

Sources: W. Isaacson, *Steve Jobs* (New York: Simon & Schuster, 2011); G. J. Curphy and R. Kimball, *The Dark Side of Steve Jobs* (North Oaks, MN: Curphy Leadership Solutions, 2013); J. Kruger and D. Dunning, "Unskilled and Unaware of It: How Difficulties in Recognizing One's Own Incompetence Lead to Inflated Self-Assessments," *Journal of Personality and Social Psychology* 77, no. 6 (1999), pp. 1121–34; and D. Dunning, K. Johnson, J. Ehrlinger, and J. Kruger, "Why People Fail to Recognize Their Own Incompetence," *Current Directions in Psychological Science* 12, no. 3 (2003), pp. 83–87.

Understanding and Managing Unit and Team Effectiveness

Restaurants, salons and other concerns featured on reality TV shows such as Kitchen Nightmares—shows aimed at turning troubled businesses around—fail twice as often as the industry average.

Russell Sobel, Organizational Researcher

Whereas performance is concerned with individual followers' accomplishments and behavior, effectiveness is concerned with the collective outcomes or results of these behaviors. Again, effectiveness is usually the ultimate criterion by which leaders are judged: Did the team win? Did the company achieve its profitability or share price target? Did a higher percentage of students graduate from high school? In essence, effectiveness measures determine how teams or organizations define winning. Because effectiveness measures dictate what follower behaviors are needed by teams and organizations to win, it is incumbent upon leaders to clearly define or become familiar with these measures. Most teams and organizations define winning in multiple ways, as a casino might define success as achieving a certain market share, revenue, profitability, number of new customers, level of customer satisfaction, revenue per customer, and employee engagement and retention goals in a particular year.[49] **Table 11.2** provides an example of some of the effectiveness measures used to evaluate airline performance in the United States. Because of these results, Delta Airlines paid a $1.6 billion in bonuses to its 90,000 employees in 2020, which roughly translates into two months of pay. It has retained the number-one ranking since 2017, so they clearly are doing something right when it comes to motivating and engaging followers, managing their performance, and directing their efforts toward team and company effectiveness.[50, 51]

TABLE 11.2 Airline Rankings for 2019

Overall Ranking	On-Time Arrivals	Canceled Flights	Extreme Delays	Involuntary Bumping	Complaints
Delta	Delta	Delta	Alaska	Delta	Southwest
Alaska	Alaska	Allegiant	Southwest	United	Alaska
Southwest	Spirit	JetBlue	Delta	JetBlue	Delta
Allegiant	Southwest	Alaska	Allegiant	Spirit	JetBlue

Overall Ranking	On-Time Arrivals	Canceled Flights	Extreme Delays	Involuntary Bumping	Complaints
Spirit	Allegiant	Frontier	Spirit	Alaska	United
JetBlue	American	Spirit	American	Southwest	Allegiant
Frontier	United	United	United	Frontier	American
United	JetBlue	Southwest	Frontier	Allegiant	Frontier
American	Frontier	American	JetBlue	American	Spirit

Source: S. McCartney, "The Best and Worst U.S. Airlines of 2019," *The Wall Street Journal*, January 16, 2020, p. A9.

Like follower performance, there are several aspects of team or organization effectiveness measures that are worth noting. First, in some situations, leaders may need to define team goals. For example, a new software development team may not have a clear set of requirements or a timeline for releasing a new application. The better the leader can define the team's deliverables the better she will be able to manage the performance of her staff. In most cases, however, those setting organizational strategy, such as senior executives or a board of directors, determine team or organizational goals. Second, effectiveness measures all suffer from some degree of **criterion contamination**. Criterion contamination occurs when effectiveness measures are affected by factors unrelated to follower performance. For example, a casino's annual revenues are affected by the local economy, media reports, the arrival of new competitors, regulatory changes, and staff turnover, and some of these factors can have a greater impact on winning than follower performance. Leaders not only need to know how winning is defined, but they also need to know the various factors that affect goal accomplishment.

> *There is no such thing as an objective criterion.*
>
> **John Campbell, retired university professor**

Most teams and organizations have a set of goals or key performance indicators that they use to define winning, and progress against these goals is usually published in the form of a **team** or **balanced scorecard**.[52, 53, 54] (See **Highlight 11.5**.) For example, a scorecard for a sales team might consist of specific goals for the number of customer meetings, number of sales proposals written, percentage of sales proposals won, average deal size, total revenues, and profitability margins per month. Whereas a team scorecard defines how teams win, balanced scorecards usually define how the larger organization defines winning. Balanced scorecards will include organizational goals involving customers, marketing, sales, finance, operations, human resources, quality, safety, and the like to provide middle and more senior leaders with a comprehensive picture of organizational effectiveness. Thus, a balanced scorecard is usually made up of the most critical scorecard goals from the sales team, marketing team, operations team, and so on.

Balanced Scorecards

HIGHLIGHT 11.5

A practical method for implementing goal setting in organizations involves the creation of balanced scorecards. Kaplan and Norton argue that most of the measures typically used to assess organizational effectiveness are too limited in scope. For example, many organizations set goals and periodically review their financial results, but these indicators suffer from time lags (it may take a month or longer before the financial results of specific organizational activities are available) and say little about other key organizational effectiveness indicators, such as customer satisfaction, employee turnover, and operational results. To get around these problems, Kaplan and Norton advocate creating a set of goals and metrics for customers, employees, internal operations, and finance. Customer and employee goals and metrics make up leading indicators because problems with customer satisfaction and employee turnover often result in subpar operational and financial results.

Curphy has developed balanced scorecards for rural Minnesota hospitals and school districts. For example, hospitals begin this process with a comprehensive review of their market demographics, customer trends, financial performance, internal operations (pharmacy, surgical use, infection rates, radiology and lab use, and so on), and staffing and facility data. Key community and health care leaders then create a new five-year vision for the hospital and set strategic priorities in the customer, financial, internal operations, and workforce and facilities categories. These priorities are refined further to create clear, measurable goals with readily available metrics to track monthly progress. These balanced scorecard goals are used to drive specific department goals and track hospital effectiveness and have been very effective in helping all hospital employees understand how their efforts contribute to the hospital's overall results. In several cases, hospital effectiveness has improved dramatically as a result of these balanced scorecard efforts. A partial example of a typical balanced scorecard for one of these rural hospitals is as follows:

- **Customer:** Improve patient satisfaction ratings from 74 to 86 percent by January 1, 2022.

- **Customer:** Increase the number of live births from 12 to 20 per month by January 1, 2022.

- **Financial:** Reduce average accounts payable from 84 to 53 days by January 1, 2022.

- **Financial:** Increase operating margins from 2 to 6 percent by January 1, 2022.

- **Internal operations:** Increase orthopedic surgeries from 4 to 8 per day by March 1, 2022.

- **Internal operations:** Reduce patient infection rates from 1 to 0.5 percent by March 1, 2022.

- **Workforce:** Reduce days needed to hire nurses from 62 to 22 days by March 1, 2022.

- **Workforce:** Reduce employee turnover rates from 27 to 12 percent by March 1, 2022.

A monthly balanced scorecard report is included in all employee pay statements and is a key topic of discussion in hospital and department staff meetings. Staff members review goal progress and regularly devise strategies for achieving department and hospital goals. A nice aspect of the balanced scorecard is that it helps employees be proactive and gives them permission to win. In too many organizations, employees work hard but never see how their results contribute to team or organizational effectiveness. Adopting balanced scorecards is a way to get around these problems.

Sources: G. J. Curphy, *The Blandin Education Leadership Program* (Grand Rapids, MN: The Blandin Foundation, 2004); R. S. Kaplan and D. P. Norton, "The Balanced Scorecard: Measures That Drive Performance," *Harvard Business Review*, January–February 1992, pp. 71–79; R. S. Kaplan and D. P. Norton, *The Balanced Scorecard* (Boston, MA: Harvard Business School Press, 1996); R. S. Kaplan and D. P. Norton, *The Strategy Focused Organization* (Boston, MA: Harvard Business School Press, 2001); and G. Curphy and R Hogan, *The Rocket Model: Practical Advice for Building High Performing Teams* (Tulsa, OK: Hogan Press, 2012).

Team scorecards usually provide feedback on goal progress on a daily, weekly, or monthly basis, whereas balanced scorecards are usually generated on a monthly or quarterly basis. Both reflect the sum of the collective efforts of either team members or all the employees in an organization, with followers' performance being one of the many factors affecting goal progress. Leaders need to ensure followers understand how their performance contributes to team or organizational goal accomplishment and that it is much easier for some functions and organizations to define winning than others. It is usually easier for financial services, retail, food and beverage, energy, manufacturing, high-tech, health care, or communications industries to define winning than it is for government agencies, charitable or philanthropic organizations, nongovernmental organizations, the military during peacetime, or educational institutions. Likewise, marketing, sales, operations, supply chain, and finance have an easier time defining success than do the human resources, public relations, IT, or legal functions in organizations.[55, 56]

So what should leaders take away from the team and unit effectiveness discussion? First, effectiveness measures define how they will be ultimately evaluated as a leader. Coaches are judged by their win–loss records, business owners by their financial results, and the heads of homeless shelters by the number of people served. Second, multiple measures are often used to evaluate teams and units. Businesses not only get judged by their stock price, but also on their market share, revenues, profitability, employee engagement ratings, turnover rates, and customer satisfaction ratings. It is relatively easy to manage a single effectiveness measure; the hard part of leadership is simultaneously improving profitability, customer satisfaction, and employee engagement while reducing costs. Third, all the measures used to evaluate a team or unit's effectiveness are influenced by factors beyond a leader's control. Market and geopolitical conditions, competitors, suppliers, unfavorable press, and other factors often have a major impact on team results. Finally, leaders need to be clear about how their team is being evaluated, the factors affecting these measures, and the links between follower performance and team or unit effectiveness (see **Highlight 11.6**).

Force Multipliers or Team Killers?

HIGHLIGHT 11.6

Team and unit effectiveness is a function of individual follower performances, and leaders need to make sure that individual followers know what and how goals align with overall team outcomes. Followers may know what they need to deliver and the actions they need to take for the team to be successful, but what happens when there is a force multiplier or team killer in their midst?

A **force multiplier** is someone who makes the rest of the team better. These followers often possess a work ethic that sets a high bar for performance, willingly help others and go the extra mile, coach or train teammates, and make a team run smoother and be more effective. Stephen Curry, a player for the National Basketball Association's Golden State Warriors, is a good example of a force multiplier. He is not only an excellent shooter, but statistics show that when Curry is on the court, his teammates perform at higher levels than when he is sitting on the bench.

Unfortunately, followers can also be team killers. **Team killers** are individuals who inhibit rather than enhance overall team effectiveness. They may be criticizers or slackers as described at the beginning of Part 3, or they may just be individuals who are difficult to get along with; refuse to do their fair share of work; take shortcuts; and lie, cheat, steal, or engage in other types of unethical behavior. If left unchecked, these individuals can have a contagion effect on teams, as their actions and a corresponding lack of consequences may convince others to engage in the same behaviors. This implies that leaders not only need to define the what and how of individual follower performance, but they must also ensure the rules governing followers' collective behavior benefit rather than inhibit team effectiveness.

Sources: B. Cohen, "Curry Is Better Than You Think," *The Wall Street Journal*, May 30, 2019, p. A14; S. Dimmock and

W. Gerken, "How One Bad Employee Can Corrupt a Whole Team," *Harvard Business Review*, March 5, 2018, https://hbr.org/2018/03/research-how-one-bad-employee-can-corrupt-a-whole-team; and R. Hogan and J. Jacobsen,

"Find, Grow, and Retain Top Talent: A 5-Step Plan," *TalentQ*, November 18, 2019, www.talent-quarterly.com/single-article/find-grow-and-retain-top-talent-a-5-step-plan.

Understanding Follower Potential

As stated earlier in this chapter, two critically important responsibilities for leaders is to manage the performance of their individual followers and ensure their teams deliver targeted results. Another important duty is to identify followers with the potential to become future leaders and prepare them to assume roles with greater responsibility. This may turn out to be even more important than creating legions of high-performing followers, as most organizations report having serious shortfalls in leadership talent. Many do not have enough people with the leadership skills needed to develop new products, launch new services, start up new facilities, expand into new regions, or execute their business strategies. This problem is likely to worsen as Baby Boomers leave mid- and senior-level leadership positions for retirement.[57, 58, 59, 60, 61]

> *Out of every 100 men on the battlefield–10 shouldn't even be there, 80 are just targets, 9 are real fighters and we are lucky to have them for they the battle make. Ah but the One. One of them is a* Warrior. *He will bring the others back.*
>
> **Heraclitus, Greek philosopher**

Organizations have tried to solve this problem by hiring outside people into leadership positions. This approach has its own set of challenges, however. First, most people are poor judges of talent and only make good hiring decisions one-third to one-half of the time. In other words, most leaders would be better off flipping a coin rather than relying on their judgment when making hiring decisions.[62, 63, 64] Second, hiring people from the outside to fill leadership positions can be demoralizing for those in the company, as they may begin to feel that leaving the organization is the only way they can get promoted. Research shows organizations generally achieve better customer, financial, and employee engagement results when they promote from within, so the best way to tackle the leadership talent shortfall is to identify and develop followers who have the most potential to be effective leaders.[65] Leadership potential can be defined as a follower's capacity to advance one or more levels within the organization. In other words, what is the likelihood that a computer programmer would be a successful program manager, a sales manager has the potential to be a vice president of sales, or a regional president could be the future CEO of a *Fortune* 500 firm? Leadership potential is the likelihood candidates can successfully jump one or more levels in the Leadership Pipeline described in Chapter 7.

> *The war for talent is over, and everybody lost.*
>
> **Tomas Chamorro-Premuzic, Right Management**

Whereas potential is related to one's overall capacity for advancement (that is, does the follower have the "right stuff" to be a future leader), **readiness** is an evaluation of a follower's immediate promotability. Ready-now followers are those who need no additional training or experience to move into designated leader roles. Ready–12 months followers need another year of training and experience before they are ready to advance to the next level, and Ready–36 months need three more years of seasoning and training before being promoted. Followers can have high potential but low readiness for advancement. For example, a shift supervisor responsible for 20 servers at a large restaurant chain may be seen as having high potential to eventually become a district manager who oversees 10 different restaurants. But she may be rated as a Ready–36 month candidate for the district manager role, as she still needs training and experience as a bar manager, kitchen manager, assistant manager, restaurant manager, and in opening new restaurants before being promoted to oversee multiple restaurants. Although her district manager potential rating may not change, the shift supervisors' readiness ratings will likely change from Ready–36 months, Ready 12–months, and eventually to Ready-now as she gains more training and experience in these different roles.[66, 67] (See **Profiles in Leadership 11.2.**)

Mary Barra

PROFILES IN LEADERSHIP 11.2

Mary Barra is the current CEO and chairman of the board at General Motors (GM), an automobile manufacturer that generates over $150 billion in annual revenues and consists of 185,000 employees located in facilities across six continents. In the role since early 2014, Barra has been instrumental in helping GM design vehicles that customers want at a profitable price, such as Buicks, Corvettes, Camaros, Cadillacs, Cruzes, Impalas, Lincolns, Volts, Tahoes, and Yukons; school and shuttle buses; police cars; ambulances; and pick-up and dump trucks. When she first moved into the CEO role, Barra had to deal with a highly visible vehicle recall due to faulty ignition switches and shut down GM's Opel line of vehicles in Europe to focus on more profitable vehicles in China and North America. She managed both of these challenges quite successfully and turned her focus to launching a line of electric vehicles (the Chevy Bolt EV) a year before Tesla, incorporating technology and connectivity in all GM vehicles and leading the way in automated driverless vehicles.

Barra grew up in Michigan and her father was a long-time GM employee. She joined GM at the age of 18 as a co-op student, where she worked in the company while obtaining her undergraduate degree in electrical engineering at the General Motors Institute (which later became Kettering University). She quickly moved through various roles at GM and obtained an MBA from Stanford University while on a GM fellowship. Later in her career, Barra was the plant manager at a major automobile manufacturing facility,

held global vice president roles in manufacturing, human resources, purchasing, and supply chain, and was promoted to be the executive vice president of global product development, where she led teams developing the latest GM models and vehicles.

Barra has been instrumental in helping GM manufacture highly reliable, award-winning vehicles while returning to profitability (it had to take a multibillion-dollar government loan during the financial crisis in order to stay afloat). Because of her leadership, Barra was named by *Fortune* magazine as the Most Powerful Woman in Business in 2017 and *Forbes* magazine as the second Most Powerful Woman in Business in 2018. She was listed as the fifth Most Powerful Woman in the World in 2019 and was named as one of the 100 Most Influential People in the World by *Time* magazine. A member of both the Disney and General Dynamics boards, Barra ran into some trouble with U.S. President Trump when she announced GM would close five plants and lay off 14,000 employees at the end of 2019.

How would you rate Barra's potential and readiness to be GM's CEO when she was a plant manager? How would you evaluate her performance as a CEO and GM's effectiveness as a car company?

Sources: "A Look at Mary Barra, GM's First Female CEO," *The Wall Street Journal*, December 10, 2013, https://blogs.wsj.com/corporate-intelligence/2013/12/10/a-look-at-mary-barra-gms-first-female-ceo; J. Miller, "Mary Barra Is Running GM with a Tight Fist and an Urgent Mission," *Forbes*, May 2, 2017, www.forbes.com/sites/joannmuller/2017/05/02/mary-barra-is-running-gm-with-a-tight-fist-and-an-urgent-mission; "Mary Barra," *Fortune*, https://fortune.com/most-powerful-women/2019/mary-barra; General Motors, "Mary T. Barra," www.gm.com/company/leadership/corporate-officers/mary-barra.html; R.

Ferris, "GM to Halt Production at Several Plants, Cut More Than 14,000 Jobs," *CNBC*, November 26, 2018, www.cnbc.com/2018/11/26/gm-unallocating-several-plants-in-2019-to-take-3-billion-to-3point8-billion-charge-in-future-quarters.html; Fortune Editors, "These Are the Women CEOs Leading *Fortune* 500 Companies," *Fortune*, June 7, 2017, www.cnbc.com/2018/11/26/gm-unallocating-several-

plants-in-2019-to-take-3-billion-to-3point8-billion-charge-in-future-quarters.html; and *Forbes*, "The World's 100 Most Powerful Women," 2019, www.forbes.com/power-women/list/#tab:overall.

Succession planning is the process organizations use to make leadership potential and readiness decisions about followers. With small companies, succession planning is usually episodic and informal—someone in a leadership position retires or leaves to join another firm, which causes top management to make a replacement decision with an internal promotion or outside hire. More often than not, top managers "go with their gut" and rarely use data to make these as-needed promotion decisions. Larger organizations tend to use a more systematic process for collecting potential and readiness information about followers. As seen in **Figure 11.3**, **9-box matrices** are used to evaluate the performance and potential of followers, and this is usually done once per year. Leaders are asked to provide low-, moderate-, or high-performance and potential ratings for each of their direct reports, and these results are then used to indicate where followers currently stand in the 9-box matrix. For example, the names of high-performing/high-potential followers would be added to the top right box, those with moderate performance/low potential ratings would be added to the bottom middle box, and so on. Organizations then run **calibration meetings** to standardize ratings across leaders with similar groups of followers.

Potential—A guess about the future, which gets interpreted as a promise and then morphs into a defense of ego.

Adam Yearsley, Red Bull

FIGURE 11.3 9-Box Matrix

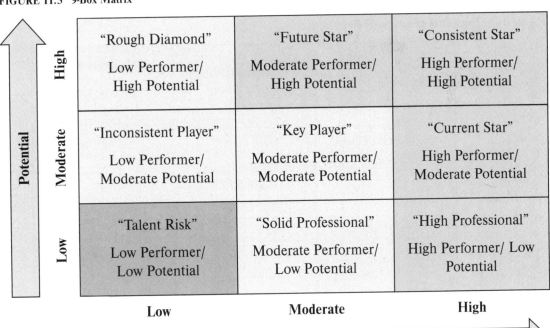

Using the scenario described earlier, the district manager would assign performance and potential ratings for her 10 restaurant managers. She would then provide the rationale for the 9-box matrix designation for each of her restaurant managers with her fellow district managers, district human resources managers, and the vice president in charge of the region during a calibration meeting. Using **Figure 11.4** as an example, she would explain why Joannie Cruz and Herb Johnson were high-performance/high-potential candidates and why she saw Kelvin Hobbes having a lot of potential but was not performing particularly well. In Kelvin's case, it could be that he is new to the restaurant manager role, the restaurant is undergoing a major renovation, or he is in the middle of turning around a chronically underperforming restaurant. Calibration meeting attendees would ask questions, offer feedback, recommend changes to followers' potential or performance ratings, and the like. This process would be repeated for every restaurant manager, which helps ensure performance and potential ratings are normalized across districts and tied to restaurant results (that is, low-performing districts will probably have more managers with low and moderate performance ratings than high-performing districts).

Some organizations also use **replacement tables** for key leadership positions. Companies first identify those leadership roles most critical to strategy execution and organizational effectiveness and then create tables that identify the candidates most likely to fill a particular role should the current occupant retire, take another job, be promoted, or get "hit by a bus." For example, a Bangalore start-up company might designate the vice president of software engineering as a critical leadership position. The vice president would create a replacement table that listed one to three people who could potentially replace her and their current readiness for the role (Ready–now, Ready–12 months, etc.). Replacement table results are reviewed by senior leaders on an annual basis, and many organizations are reporting that less than 50 percent of their critical leadership roles have Ready-now candidates, which is forcing them to look outside when these leaders need to be replaced.[68, 69, 70, 71, 72, 73] (See **Highlight 11.7.**)

FIGURE 11.4   Example of a Completed 9-Box Matrix

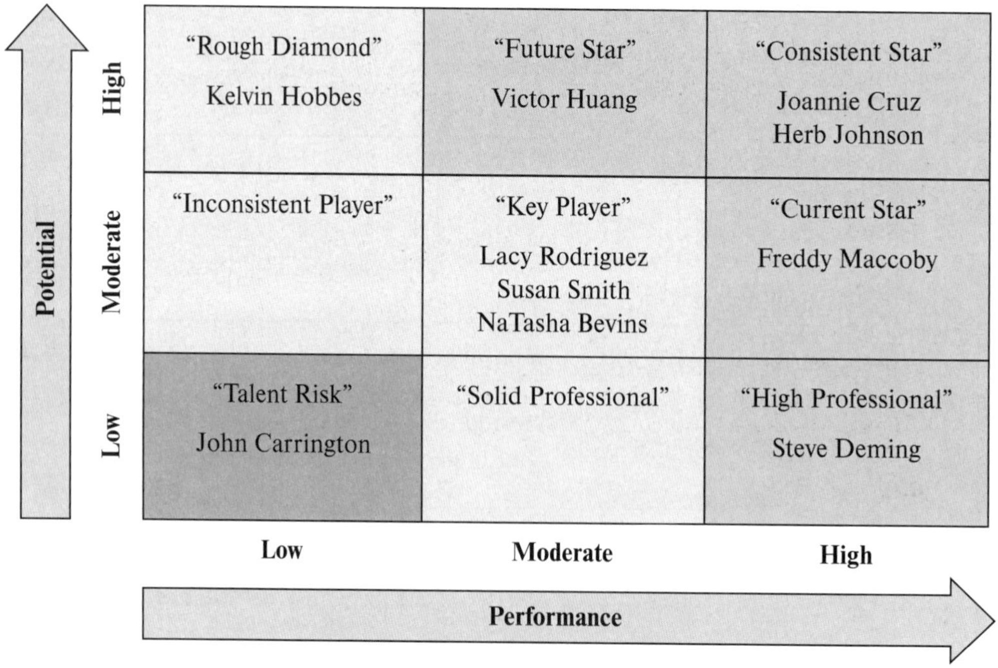

	Low	Moderate	High
High	"Rough Diamond" Kelvin Hobbes	"Future Star" Victor Huang	"Consistent Star" Joannie Cruz Herb Johnson
Moderate	"Inconsistent Player"	"Key Player" Lacy Rodriguez Susan Smith NaTasha Bevins	"Current Star" Freddy Maccoby
Low	"Talent Risk" John Carrington	"Solid Professional"	"High Professional" Steve Deming

Potential (vertical axis)

Performance (horizontal axis)

Succession Planning in Family Businesses

HIGHLIGHT 11.7

Many businesses across the globe are privately owned, and succession planning is a big problem for family-run companies. Research shows the likelihood of a family-owned business surviving into the second generation is only 30 percent. With the third generation, the survival rate decreases to 12 percent, and by the fourth generation, the survival rate of these businesses is only 3 percent. Many of the founders started these businesses as a way of providing for their children and subsequent generations, yet by the time the grandchildren are in a position to run the business the company has either gone bankrupt or been sold.

This lack of business continuity can be attributed mostly to poor succession planning. Like Tommy Callahan in the movie *Tommy Boy,* some members of subsequent generations feel entitled to collect dividends but have no interest in running family businesses. Others take positions in their family businesses but have no talent for leadership, and some with talent can have difficulties meeting the unrealistic expectations of the family members currently in charge. For example, 80 percent of the potential heirs of Chinese businesses expressed reluctance in taking over the business, primarily out of concern for meeting their fathers' expectations. Disagreements about governance, strategy, and ownership within and across generations can cause permanent ruptures in families.

Sometimes the lack of leadership talent can cause families to hire professional managers to run their businesses—Marriott, Hilton, Ford, and Lego are examples where there was not enough leadership talent within the families to run large, global companies. Those family businesses that do survive view succession planning as a long-term process, where family members often need to prove themselves by being successful in jobs outside the business, and then successfully run different parts of the business, before being allowed to take over. LVMH, Fox News, and Hancock Prospecting are examples of family-owned businesses taking a more deliberative approach to succession planning.

Perhaps nowhere is family succession planning more important than in the Middle East. The 5,000 family members in the House of Saud own much of Saudi Arabia's wealth; royal families also own the bulk of the wealth in Morocco, Jordan, Bahrain, and the United Arab Emirates. Getting succession planning right in these countries not only affects the family business, but it will also determine how these countries play on the world stage, how they view human rights, whether they will go to war, and so on.

How does family succession planning play out in the television series *Game of Thrones* or *Succession?* As an advocate for women's rights as well as the architect of the war in Yemen, the killing of journalist Jamal Khashoggi, and hacking of Jeff Bezos's personal phone, how has Mohammad bin Salman worked out as the Crown Prince (and de facto ruler) of Saudi Arabia? Do you know anyone whose family has its own business? If so, what is the business doing about succession planning?

Sources: A. Keyt, "The Difficult Succession Decision That Family Businesses Face," *The Wall Street Journal,* June 2, 2016, p. B1; "Schumpter: Succession Failure," *The Economist,* February 6, 2016, p. 61; "Schumpter: Reluctant Heirs," *The Economist,* December 5, 2015, p. 67; and C. Thorbecke, "UN Links Saudi Crown Prince to Hack of Jeff Bezos' Phone," *ABC,* January 22, 2019, https://abc-news.go.com/Business/officials-implicate-saudi-arabia-hacking-jeff-bezos-phone/story?id=68448839.

Organizations often use the results of 9-box matrices and replacement tables to identify people to send to **high-potential programs** to accelerate their ability to assume greater leadership responsibilities and plug the Ready-now gap for critical leadership positions. High-performance/high-potential types often get to attend customized leadership training programs, are sent back to school to obtain MBAs or other advanced degrees, are assigned executive coaches and mentors, work on high-visibility projects, are sent on ex-pat or other plum assignments, and are given exposure to the most senior leaders in an organization.[74, 75] Because these individuals are viewed as critical assets, many organizations differentially invest in their best and brightest people. For example, at one time Johnson & Johnson spent 75 percent of its corporate leadership development budget on the 10 percent of global leaders identified as high-potential candidates and the remainder on the 90 percent of leaders who did not make the short list (M. Benson, personal communication, March 2014). Organizations see high-performance/high-potential talent as special, as do those who achieve this designation.

And therein lies the rub. It only makes sense to differentially invest in high-performance/high-potential types if this talent is in roles that matter, the right candidates are included on the list, and candidates are evaluated and moved on and off high-performance/high-potential lists each year. With respect to the first point, not all jobs or functions are created equal. For some companies, such as General Motors or Tesla, marketing and engineering are critically important. In other companies, such as Pfizer or Boeing, research and development is pivotal to success, and others put a premium on consulting or sales. Yet in the spirit of inclusiveness many organizations make the mistake of treating all functions equally and identifying high-performance/high-potential types who will likely have little impact on company effectiveness measures. For example, high-performance/high-potential sales representatives and software engineers are likely to make big contributions to the effectiveness of Microsoft, Huawei, SAP, or Infosys but their counterparts in human resources or public affairs may not.[76, 77, 78] (See **Highlight 11.8**.)

Why Do So Many Incompetent Men Become Leaders?

HIGHLIGHT 11.8

Women make up 50 percent of the population in any country but only a minority serve on boards of directors or hold positions on top leadership teams. Tomas Chamorro-Premuzic believes leadership competence should be the sole criteria leaders should use when evaluating follower potential. According to Chamorro-Premuzic, the critical components of leadership competence include technical expertise, intelligence, people skills, and integrity. However, when it comes to picking people to fill leadership roles, style often trumps substance. Voters, recruiters, and organizational leaders often favor those individuals who come across as charismatic, confident, charming, politically astute, and self-focused. Whether they can engage and develop employees, build teams, and achieve superior results are not important considerations when it comes to evaluating potential. Most potential decisions are based on gut feeling, so decision makers favor those who appear leaderlike versus those who do not show up well but are effective leaders. Because the vast majority of leadership potential, performance, and readiness decisions are based solely on bosses' judgments (most of whom are men), rater bias plays a major role in why women fail to get promoted.

Systematically using data to make potential determinations would greatly reduce the impact of rater bias, broaden the pool of those being considered for promotion, and increase the percentages of women holding top positions in organizations. Although these data can be collected quite easily, so far many organizations have been resistant to go down this path. Whether this is organizational inertia, male decision makers falsely believing they are good judges of talent, not wanting to cede some control, or thinking the current system works fine as it got them into positions of authority, women will continue to be underrepresented in leadership positions as long as opinions are the key determinant of potential.

Sources: T. Chamorro-Premuzic, "If Women Are Better Leaders Why Aren't More of Them Leaders?" *Psychology Today*, April 13, 2019, www.psychologytoday.com/us/blog/mr-personality/201904/if-women-are-better-leaders-why-arent-more-them-leaders; T. Chamorro-Premuzic, *Why Do So Many Incompetent Men Become Leaders? (and How to Fix It)* (Boston, MA: Harvard Business Review Press, 2019); M. Symanski, "It's Time to Fix the Way the Army Selects Commanders," *Modern War Institute*, June 20, 2019, https://mwi.usma.edu/time-fix-way-army-selects-commanders; and D. Wallace, "The Uncanny Power of Incompetent Men," *Forge*, July 25, 2019, https://forge.medium.com/what-boris-johnsons-incompetence-can-teach-you-about-leadership-72a52e471e66.

Perhaps an even bigger problem with 9-box matrices and replacement tables is the process used to evaluate followers' potential, performance, and readiness levels. Research shows that the vast majority of decisions are based solely on management judgment and performance appraisal results, yet leaders are notoriously bad at judging talent and performance appraisal ratings can be biased and inaccurate. Biases and candidates' past performance color many of these ratings, and performance is not the same as potential. Being able to do one's current job well does not mean a person will succeed if promoted, as superior athletes often make lousy coaches and being an outstanding computer programmer or teacher is no guarantee that these individuals will be good directors of programming or high school principals. The end result is many of the candidates appearing on high-performance/high-potential lists are good individual contributors who know how to please their bosses but have questionable ability to be effective leaders.[79, 80, 81, 82, 83, 84, 85, 86]

One interesting aspect of potential, performance, and readiness is the role that data play in these evaluations. Most companies rely solely on a leader's judgment to evaluate followers, yet ample research shows that certain personality traits, intelligence (**Chapter 6**), 360-degree feedback ratings (**Chapter 7**), and team assessments are more accurate, less biased, and better predict candidates' effectiveness in new roles. Yet most companies use this information to provide candidates already on high-performance/high-potential lists with developmental feedback rather than using it as criteria for selection. As a result, only about one-third of promotion decisions based on these lists work out, as most high-performance/high-potential nominees are more a reflection of managers' biases and whims than true reflections of an organization's most capable talent.[87, 88, 89, 90, 91, 92, 93]

Table 11.3 describes three different methods organizations use when making determinations about potential. Boss ratings are by far the most prevalent approach, yet rater biases and inaccuracies often end up excluding those with the most leadership potential. Most bosses also have little familiarity with those nominated by other leaders, so few challenges about talent get raised during calibration meetings. A better approach is to include candidates' personality and intelligence results into calibration meeting discussions. Research shows that extraversion, conscientiousness, neuroticism, and intelligence are good predictors of leadership. In addition, dark side personality traits (described in Chapter 17) are among the best predictors of managerial derailment—those likely to fail in leadership positions. Adding these results to boss ratings make for interesting calibration meeting discussions, as bosses have to explain why their high potential ratings do not line up with candidates' personality or intelligence results.

TABLE 11.3   Methods for Determining Leadership Potential

Determining Leadership Potential	Pros	Cons
Traditional Approach:		
Boss Ratings	Widespread use	Bosses are not good judges of talent
	Bosses have complete control	Confidence is more important than competence
		Lack of standardization
		Lack of familiarity with candidates
		Politics
A Better Approach:		
Boss Ratings	Better predictors of leadership effectiveness and derailment	More expensive ($100–150 per candidate)
Personality Traits		Bosses discount data
Intelligence	More candidates added to pool	Bosses lose some control
	Fairer to employees	Cannot tell if candidates can build teams
	More insight into candidates	
The Best Approach:		
Boss Ratings	Best predictors of leadership effectiveness and derailment	Most expensive ($400–600 per candidate)
Personality Traits		Bosses discount data
Intelligence	More candidates added to pool	Bosses lose some control
Team Effectiveness	Fairer to employees	
	Can tell if candidates can build teams	
	More insight into candidates	

The best approach for identifying leadership potential includes boss ratings, personality and intelligence results, and candidates' **team effectiveness quotient (TQ)** scores. A key aspect of being an effective leader is the ability to build cohesive, goal-oriented teams, and TQ is a person's ability to build loyal followings and get a group of people working effectively together to achieve team goals. It turns out that some candidates are very good at building teams, and others are less adept. TQ scores are calculated using team members' ratings on a standardized measure of team dynamics and performance. By adding TQ to personality and intelligence results, decision makers will know the extent to which candidates are smart, resilient, ambitious, outgoing, decisive, hardworking, and can build teams. Leadership is a team sport, and most high-performance/high-potential candidates are being identified and groomed to lead teams that are of strategic importance to organizations. Knowing whether individuals have the ability to build teams before being moved into these roles can be very helpful.[94, 95, 96, 97, 98]

A final problem with high-performance/high-potential lists is their relative permanence. Candidates rarely come off these lists once nominated, yet there is ample research showing that job performance varies dramatically from one year to the next. For example, Cappelli's research showed that the odds of any person being rated as a high performer for two years in a row was only 33 percent.[99] This finding makes sense, as some candidates may be asked to do difficult assignments and their performance may suffer as a result. Nonetheless, confirmation bias (as described in the introduction to **Part 3**) can cause managers to see everything high-performance/high-potential candidates do in a positive light and ignore any data to the contrary. If measures of relevant experience, personality, and intelligence are used to identify potential, then these scores are unlikely to change much over time. But if the ability to build teams is added to potential calculations, then potential ratings are likely to change, as candidates who have been provided with the right feedback and training can learn how to build high-performing teams. If 360-degree feedback and *what* and *how* ratings are used to evaluate job performance, then candidates' low, moderate, and high ratings of performance are also likely to change from one year to the next.

So what are the implications of all of this for leaders? First, leaders need to understand that they may be called upon to evaluate followers' potential, performance, and readiness levels. Second, leaders should realize that how these concepts are defined varies considerably across organizations, so they need to know how their company is measuring potential, performance, and readiness. Third, they should also use data whenever possible when making these judgments. Performance and potential data can help reduce the impact of conscious and unconscious biases and expand the number of diverse and female candidates in talent pools. Fourth, if the same group of followers comes up on high-performance/high-potential lists every year, then there is likely some problem with how these lists are getting generated (see Profiles in Leadership 11.3).

Richard Branson

PROFILES IN LEADERSHIP 11.3

Richard Branson is the chairman of Virgin Industries, which owns such companies as Virgin Airlines, Virgin Records, Virgin Galactic, Virgin Fuels, Virgin Media, Virgin Comics, and Virgin Health Care. An entrepreneur since the age of 16, Branson had his first business success publishing *Student* magazine in 1966. From there he started Virgin Records, which at the time was an audio-record mail-order business. In 1972, he owned a chain of record stores, Virgin Records, and installed a recording studio. At the time the studio was used by a number of top bands, including Mike Oldfield, the Sex Pistols, and Culture Club.

In the 1980s, Branson ventured into the airline industry with the launch of Virgin Atlantic Airways. He expanded his airline holdings to include Virgin Express, a low-cost European carrier, and Virgin Blue, an Asia-Pacific carrier. In 2004, he partnered with Paul Allen and Burt Rutan to launch Virgin Galactic, a space tourism company. His Virgin Fuels business was launched to find more environmentally friendly fuels for automobiles and airplanes.

Having a long history of creating successful companies, selling them, and then using the proceeds to fund other business ventures, Branson sold Virgin Records to EMI for approximately $750 million and sold Virgin Mobile for $1.5 billion. Virgin Industries currently employs 50,000 people in 30 countries and generates $23 billion in annual revenues. With a personal net worth of over $4 billion, Branson has turned his attention to more humanitarian causes. Working with the likes of Nelson Mandela, Jimmy Carter, Desmond Tutu, and Bono, Branson is looking to develop peaceful resolutions to long-standing conflicts. He is an active promoter of using entrepreneurship to solve environmental problems.

What information or data would you use to identify successors for Richard Branson as the chairperson of Virgin Industries?

Sources: D. Freeman, "Virgin Galactic Founder Richard Branson Sets Date of First Trip Into Space," *NBC News*, February 9, 2019, www.nbcnews.com/mach/science/virgin-galactic-ceo-richard-branson-sets-date-first-trip-space-ncna969436; R. Branson, *Losing My Virginity: How I Survived, Had Fun, and Made a Fortune Doing Business My Way* (New York: Crown Business, 2011); K. Gilchrist, "How Richard Branson Started Virgin Atlantic with a Blackboard Selling $39 Flights," *CNBC*, December 29, 2019, www.cnbc.com/2019/12/30/richard-branson-started-virgin-atlantic-with-a-board-and-39-flights.html; and R. Branson, "Opinion: Richard Branson on Why Philanthropists Should Club Together," *Devex*, December 10, 2018, www.devex.com/news/opinion-richard-branson-on-why-philanthropists-should-club-together-93983.

Summary

It may well be that managing followers' performance and achieving team and organizational goals are the most critical responsibilities for leaders. Leaders get paid to achieve results, and this should be the primary reason that people are placed in positions of authority. Those promoted into leadership roles for reasons other than achieving results are destined to lead mediocre, underperforming teams. Put another way, athletic coaches, military commanders, and restaurant or retail store leaders should be picked for these roles because of their ability to motivate followers to exhibit the behaviors needed to achieve winning results. But this is often no easy task. Followers may not understand what they have to do or the degree to which they need to exhibit certain behaviors for the team to win; followers need to be monitored and given feedback and coaching to exhibit the right behaviors; and leaders need to be able to differentiate between high and low performers and administer rewards in a fair and transparent manner. Leaders who shirk these responsibilities to be popular or avoid negative Glassdoor reviews or employee engagement survey results usually end up managing teams that report lower levels of morale and effectiveness.

Leaders are sometimes asked to share their opinions about which followers deserve promotions. Potential pertains to a follower's overall capacity to assume more responsibility, move up one or more organizational levels, or become a leader. Potential is different from readiness, which relates to estimates of how much time it will take before followers would be able to handle the demands of a promotion. Some followers need little additional training or experience, whereas it may take another year or two before others would be effective in positions with greater responsibility. Leaders are often asked to provide potential, performance, and readiness ratings for replacement tables and 9-box matrices, two more formal techniques organizations use in succession planning.

Most organizations suffer from leadership bench strength issues and do not have enough of the right talent to fill key leadership roles. Outside hires can help fill these gaps, but more often than not, organizations are better off promoting from within. Most promotion decisions are based solely on the boss's recommendations, which tend to be riddled with biases and inaccuracies. This is one reason why diverse and female candidates are underrepresented in leadership positions. To address this problem, organizations need to systematically include personality, intelligence, and team-building ability into determinations of potential and succession planning discussions.

Key Terms

performance

unit or team effectiveness

potential

the what and the how of
performance

absenteeism leadership

time-wasting leaders

presenteeism

executive magnification

cookie licking

performance management cycle

planning

monitoring

evaluating

electronic performance
monitoring

talent hoarding

differentiation

performance consequences

meritocracies

personal growth

performance appraisal

Dunning–Kruger effect

criterion contamination

team scorecard

balanced scorecard

force multipliers

team killers

readiness

succession planning

9-box matrices

calibration meetings

replacement tables

high-potential programs

team effectiveness quotient (TQ)

Questions

1. CEOs make 312 times more than the average employee, and many of the organizations they lead have adopted a pay for performance philosophy. Do you think CEO positions fit well with the criteria associated with meritocracies? Do you think CEOs' compensation conforms to the pay for performance approach?

2. How do you think the coronavirus pandemic affected follower performance, unit effectiveness, and follower potential of warehouse workers at Amazon? Intensive care medical teams? Restaurant server teams? University professors?

3. Large Chinese cities make extensive use of facial recognition and other types of electronic monitoring, and enjoy low crime rates as a result. Do you think the price of being constantly monitored is worth the benefits?

4. What goals would you include in a balanced scorecard for a gasoline station? What would be some of the factors that could affect the station's ability to achieve these goals?

5. Did U.S. President Donald Trump and U.K. Prime Minister Boris Johnson get elected because of their leadership competence or because of their confidence and charisma? Defend your answer.

6. Who is the best person to get promoted? Someone who has been the team's top performer for the past two years? The most popular person on the team? Someone who is a solid performer, but also goes the extra mile to help others be successful? Defend your answer.

Activities

1. Divide the class into subteams, and ask each subteam to collect the average driver ratings for five Uber or Lyft drivers. What was the average of these scores? What was the subteam's average passenger scores? Do the scores accurately differentiate between good and bad drivers and passengers?

2. Find someone who had to work remotely for a company during the coronavirus pandemic. How did the company plan, monitor, and evaluate their performance?

3. Ask someone working in an organization to describe their performance management process. What is the purpose of the process? Do they like it? Why or why not? How does the process compare to the performance management cycle described in this chapter?

4. Suppose the owner of 12 fitness centers asked you to create a process for evaluating the effectiveness of each of his centers. Design a balanced scorecard for these facilities.

5. Talk to someone in human resources about how they do succession planning. What process do they use? What data are they using to measure performance and make potential decisions?

Minicase

Who Shall Rule?

Carlsson Systems Ltd. (CSL) is a $4 billion, 50-year-old manufacturer of headlights, taillights, and dashboards for trucks, vans, SUVs, and cars. Over the years, CSL formed strategic partnerships with car manufacturers around the globe and currently enjoys a 15 to 22 percent market share in these three major product lines. The company is made up of 22,000 employees, most of whom are working at 30 different parts manufacturing plants. All of the plants are located near major automotive production facilities in Europe, China, Japan, Korea, Mexico, Brazil, Canada, and the United States. The ideal contract for CSL is one in which it supplies all the headlights, taillights, and dashboards for a vehicle platform, such as the Chevrolet Impala or Toyota Tundra. However, most automotive manufacturers do not want to become overly dependent on single-source suppliers, so they often award dashboard contracts to one supplier or partial taillight contracts to another.

The company has performed at a much higher level than other automobile parts manufacturers and generated 10 to 13 percent margins for the past eight years (the industry average has hovered around 4 percent). Because of its financial success, CSL had the resources to invest in autonomous self-driving car research. CSL's Technology Division formed joint ventures with several major car companies and bought a number of small companies with hardware or software capabilities in this area. CSL's initial investments started quite small but now total over $400 million. The joint venture partners also invested heavily in this research, and together with this additional funding, CSL's Technology Division (90 percent of which is dedicated to self-driving cars) has become a $1 billion entity.

CSL's board of directors felt shareholders would see greater benefit if the Technology division was spun off into a separate company. The spin-off was overwhelmingly approved by shareholders, and the Board began the formal process of divesting the Technology division from CSL. It was going to take about a year to work through the regulatory approval processes with different countries around the globe, and during this time, the Board asked the 12 members of the Executive Leadership Team whether they wanted to stay with CSL or go to AutoDrive, the Technology division spin-off. The CEO and nine of the other Executive Leadership Team members opted to take positions at AutoDrive; only the general counsel and vice president of technology decided to stay with CSL.

This turn of events was a big surprise and an even bigger problem for CSL's Board. CSL was doing quite well, and its profitability fueled AutoDrive's ability to become a stand-alone company. But in nine short months,

CSL was facing the prospect of being rudderless, as it would not have a CEO, COO, CFO, CIO, CCO, CHRO, or the four presidents needed to run the Europe, Americas, China, or Asia-Pacific divisions. CSL had also not done a particularly good job with succession planning. The top leaders had put little effort in grooming successors, readiness tables included a large number of the same names, and many of those listed were taking positions with AutoDrive. The Board had no idea who had the potential to move into the top leadership roles or whether they had to hire from the outside to fill these positions.

Knowing that being a regional leader (such as the vice president of operations for China) to being a global leader (such as the COO) was a big leap for most people, the CSL Board asked you to provide recommendations on how it should evaluate internal candidates for CSL's Executive Leadership Team.

1. What education, background, and work history would you want ideal CEO candidates to have? What information would you need to determine their job performance and unit effectiveness over the past three years? What information would you need to determine their potential for the CEO position? What would cause you to recommend that the Board go outside of CSL for the next CEO?

2. What education, background, and work history would you want ideal CHRO candidates to have? What information would you need to determine their job performance and unit effectiveness over the past three years? What information would you need to determine their potential for the CHRO position? What would cause you to recommend that the Board go outside of CSL for the next CHRO?

3. One of the other positions that need to be filled is the president of the Asia-Pacific division. CSL APAC has eight plants located in Japan, Korea, India, Vietnam, Malaysia, and Indonesia. What education, background, and work history would you want ideal candidates for this position to have? What information would you need to determine their job performance and unit effectiveness over the past three years? What information would you need to determine their potential for the division president position? What would cause you to recommend that the Board go outside of CSL for the next division president?

Endnotes

1. J. P. Campbell, "Leadership, the Old, the New, and the Timeless: A Commentary" in *The Oxford Handbook of Leadership*, ed. M. G. Rumsey, (London: Oxford Press, 2013), pp. 401–22.

2. G. J. Curphy and R. T. Hogan, *The Rocket Model: Practical Advice for Building High Performing Teams* (Tulsa, OK: Hogan Press, 2012).

3. "Schumpeter: A Guide to Skiving," *The Economist*, October 25, 2014, p. 71.

4. J. Alumbaugh, "Develop a Performance Management Mindset," *Dairy Herd Management*, April 5, 2017, www.dairyherd.com/news/industry/develop-performance-management-mindset.

5. L. Goler, J. Gale, and A. Grant, "Don't Kill Performance Evaluations Yet," *Harvard Business Review*, November 2016, pp. 90–97.

6. M. Effron, "The Hard Truth about Effective Performance Management," The Talent Strategy Group, January 2013, http://talentstrategygroup1.com/wp-content/uploads/2013/01/The-Hard-Truth-about-Effective-Performance-Management.pdf.

7. D. Schleicher, H. Baumann, D. Sullivan, and J. Yim, "Evaluating the Effectiveness of Performance Management: A 30-Year Integrated Conceptual Review," *Journal of Applied Psychology* 104, no. 7 (2019), pp. 851–87.

8. J. Boudreau, "Is Meritocracy Overrated? Use with Caution," *Talent Quarterly, The Performance Issue* (New York: The Talent Strategy Group), pp. 26–31, www.talent-quarterly.com/the-performance-issue.

9. M. Hansen, "The Key to Success? Working Less," *The Wall Street Journal*, January 13–14, 2018, pp. C1–2.

10. G. J. Curphy, "Why Veterans Have a Hard Time Getting Hired," LinkedIn, May 23, 2016, www.linkedin.com/pulse/why-veterans-have-hard-time-getting-hired-gordon-gordy-curphy-phd.

11. M. Effron, "After the Storm: Five Years of Performance Management," The Talent Strategy Group, August 30, 2018, www.talentstrategygroup.com/publications/after-the-storm-five-years-of-performance-management.

12. Effron, "The Hard Truth about Effective Performance Management."

13. A. Yearsley and M. Hartgrove, *Personal anagement Program 2 Participant Manual* (Fuschl am See, Austria: Red Bull, 2017).

14. G. Curphy, D. Nilsen, and R. Hogan, *Ignition: A Guide to Building High Performing Teams* (Tulsa, OK: Hogan Press, 2019).

15. G. J. Curphy, *Applying the Rocket Model to Virtual Teams* (North Oaks, MN: Curphy Leadership Solutions, 2013).

16. "Barely Managing: User-Rating Systems Are Cut-Rate Substitutes for Skillful Managers," *The Economist*, June 30, 2018, p. 65.

17. D. P. Bhave, "The Invisible Eye? Electronic Performance Monitoring and Employee Job Performance," *Personnel Psychology* 27 (2014), pp. 605–34.

18. L. Kellaway, "Big Brother Management," *The Economist: The World in 2016*, p. 139.

19. "Schumpeter: Digital Taylorism: A Modern Version of 'Scientific Management' Threatens to Dehumanize the Workplace," *The Economist*, September 12, 2015, p. 63.

20. L. Webber, "At Kimberly-Clark, 'Dead Wood' Workers Have Nowhere to Hide," *The Wall Street Journal*, August 21, 2016, www.wsj.com/articles/focus-on-performance-shakes-up-stolid-kimberly-clark-1471798944.

21. "Schumpeter: The Enemy Within," *The Economist*, July 25, 2015, p. 53.

22. D. Uria, "Spanish Man Skipped Work for Six Years Unnoticed," UPI, February 12, 2016, www.upi.com/Odd_News/2016/02/12/Spanish-man-skipped-work-for-six-years-unnoticed/7751455305055.

23. "Schumpeter: A Guide to Skiving."

24. B. Groysberg, *Chasing Stars: The Myth of Talent and the Portability of Performance* (Princeton, NJ: Princeton University Press, 2010).

25. B. Groysberg, "The Emergence of Stars," presentation delivered at IESE, Barcelona, Spain, May 17, 2017.

26. J. S. Lublin, "The Danger of Being Too Good at Your Job," *The Wall Street Journal*, April 11, 2017, www.wsj.com/articles/the-danger-of-being-too-good-at-your-job-1491912000.

27. G. J. Curphy, "The Problem with Meritocracies," LinkedIn, August 26, 2016, www.linkedin.com/pulse/problem-meritocracies-gordon-gordy-curphy-phd.

28. Boudreau, "Is Meritocracy Overrated? Use with Caution."

29. Bersin, "We Wasted Ten Years Talking about Performance Ratings. The Seven Things We've Learned," June 24, 2019, https://joshbersin.com/2018/11/we-wasted-ten-years-talking-about-performance-ratings-the-seven-things-weve-learned.

30. A. Colquitt, "Remove the Shackles from Performance Management so It Can Serve Your Business," July 16, 2018, www.alancolquitt.com/single-post/2018/07/16/Remove-the-Shackles-from-Performance-Management-so-it-can-Serve-your-Business.

31. A. Colquitt, "Performance Management: Current State, Future State," presentation delivered to the Minnesota Professional Psychology at Work meeting, Minneapolis, MN, September 18, 2018.

32. C. Woolston, "Why Appraisals Are Pointless for Most People," *BBC*, May 2,2019, www.bbc.com/worklife/article/20190501-why-appraisals-are-pointless-for-most-people.

33. "Schumpeter: The Measure of Man," *The Economist*, February 20, 2016, p. 59.

34. E. Pulakos, R. Mueller-Hanson, and S. Arad, "The Evolution of Performance Management: Searching for Value," *Annual Review of Organizational Psychology and Organizational Behavior* 6 (2019), pp. 249–71.

35. Schleicher et al., "Evaluating the Effectiveness of Performance Management."

36. Bersin, "We Wasted Ten Years Talking about Performance Ratings."

37. Colquitt, "Performance Management."

38. Groysberg, "The Emergence of Stars."

39. Curphy and Hogan, *The Rocket Model.*

40. M. Effron, "We Love Ratings!" The Talent Strategy Group, April 26, 2015, www.talentstrategygroup.com/publications/performance-management/we-love-ratings.

41. R. Feintzeig, "The Trouble with Grading Employees," *The Wall Street Journal*, April 22, 2015, pp. B1, B7.

42. Goler et al., "Don't Kill Performance Evaluations Yet."

43. M. Effron, "The Worst Doctor at Harvard Medical School," The Talent Strategy Group, October 6, 2015, www.talentstrategygroup.com/publications/performance-management/the-worst-doctor-at-harvard-medical-school.

44. Effron, "We Love Ratings!"

45. T. Chamorro-Premuzic, "Why Ditching Appraisals Is a Stupid Idea," Hogan Assessments, November 24, 2015, http://info.hoganassessments.com/blog/why-ditching-appraisals-is-a-stupid-idea.

46. P. Cappelli, "Why Performance Reviews Are Now under Review," LinkedIn, June 24, 2016, www.linkedin.com/pulse/why-performance-reviews-now-under-review-peter-cappelli.

47. Webber, "At Kimberly-Clark, 'Dead Wood' Workers Have Nowhere to Hide."

48. N. Bloom and J. VanReenen, "Why Do Management Practices Differ across Firms and Countries?" *Journal of Economic Perspectives* 24, no. 1 (Winter 2010), pp. 203–24, www.aeaweb.org/articles?id=10.1257/jep.24.1.203.

49. Curphy, Nilsen, and Hogan, *Ignition.*

50. S. McCartney, "The Best and Worst U.S. Airlines of 2019," *The Wall Street Journal,* January 16, 2020, p. A9.

51. S. Stump, "Delta to Give Workers 2 Months' Extra Pay, a Total of $1.6 Billion in Bonuses," *Today*, January 21, 2020, www.today.com/news/delta-give-employees-1-6-billion-profit-sharing-bonuses-t172177.

52. Curphy and Hogan, *The Rocket Model.*

53. R. S. Kaplan and D. P. Norton, *Translating Strategy into Action: The Balanced Scorecard* (Boston: Harvard Business School Press, 1996).

54. Curphy, Nilsen, and Hogan, *Ignition.*

55. G. J. Curphy, *Rocket Model Certification Workshop* (North Oaks, MN: Curphy Leadership Solutions, 2017).

56. Curphy, Nilsen, and Hogan, *Ignition.*

57. T. Chamorro-Premuzic, *The Talent Delusion: Why Data, Not Intuition, Is the Key to Unlocking Human Potential* (London: Piatkus, 2017).

58. A. H. Church and C. T. Rotolo, "How Are Top Companies Assessing High-Potentials and Senior Executives? A Talent Benchmark Study," *Journal of Consulting Psychology: Practice and Research* 65, no. 3 (2013), pp. 199–223.

59. R. Kaiser and G. J. Curphy, "Leadership Development: The Failure of an Industry and the Opportunity for Consulting Psychologists," *Journal of Consulting Psychology: Practice and Research* 65, no. 4 (2013), pp. 294–302.

60. G. J. Curphy, R. Kaiser, and R. Hogan, *Why Is the Leadership Development Industry Failing? (and How to Fix It)* (North Oaks, MN: Curphy Leadership Solutions, 2015).

61. Hogan Assessment Systems, "Infographic: There's a Leadership Crisis Developing," February 15, 2017, www.hoganassessments.com/infographic-theres-leadership-crisis-developing.

62. Chamorro-Premuzic, *The Talent Delusion.*

63. Hogan Assessment Systems, "Potential Is Not Performance," January 18, 2017, www.hoganassessments.com/potential-is-not-performance.

64. Groysberg, *Chasing Stars.*

65. P. DeOrtentiis, C. Vam Iddekinge, R. Ployhart, and T. Heetderks, "Build or Buy? The Individual and Unit-Level Performance of Internally Versus Externally Selected Managers Over Time," *Journal of Applied Psychology* 108, no. 8 (2018), pp. 916–28.

66. Hogan Assessment Systems, "Potential Is Not Performance."

67. D. Logeland, "Who Can Lead?" *Twin Cities Business*, August, 2013, pp. 73–78.

68. Chamorro-Premuzic, *The Talent Delusion.*

69. Church and Rotolo, "How Are Top Companies Assessing High-Potentials and Senior Executives?"

70. Kaiser and Curphy, "Leadership Development."

71. Hogan Assessment Systems, *Infographic.*

72. A. H. Church, C. T. Rotolo, N. M. Ginther, and R. Levine, "How Are Top Companies Designing and Managing Their High Potential Programs? A Follow-Up Talent Management Benchmark Study," *Journal of Consulting Psychology: Practice and Research* 67, no. 1 (2015), pp. 17–47.

73. A. White, "Filling a Leaky Pipeline," Miles LeHane, May 13, 2015, www.mileslehane.com/blog/filling-a-leaky-pipeline-guest-blogger.

74. Kaiser and Curphy, "Leadership Development."

75. Church et al., "How Are Top Companies Designing and Managing Their High Potential Programs?"

76. Curphy et al., *Why Is the Leadership Development Industry Failing?*

77. B. Kaye and C. Johnson, "Are You Too Focused on High-Potentials?" *Talent Q, The New Thinking Issue*, 2018, pp. 19–21.

78. T. Chamorro-Premuzic, "Four Reasons Talented Employees Don't Reach Their Potential," *Harvard Business Review*, March 18, 2019, https://hbr.org/2019/03/4-reasons-talented-employees-dont-reach-their-potential.

79. Hogan Assessment Systems, "Potential Is Not Performance."

80. P. Cappelli, "Why Bosses Should Stop Thinking of 'A Players,' 'B Players' and 'C Players'," *The Wall Street Journal*, February 17, 2017, www.wsj.com/articles/why-bosses-should-stop-thinking-of-a-players-b-players-and-c-players-1487255326.

81. J. Zenger and P. Folkman, "Companies Are Bad at Identifying High-Potential Employees," *Harvard Business Review*, February 2017, https://hbr.org/2017/02/companies-are-bad-at-identifying-high-potential-employees.

82. G. J. Curphy, "Stupid High Potential Tricks," LinkedIn, September 8, 2015, www.linkedin.com/pulse/stupid-high-potential-tricks-gordon-gordy-curphy-phd.

83. G. J. Curphy, "Does High Potential Success Lead to Organizational Failure?" The Rocket Model, February 22, 2016, www.therocketmodel.com/blog-articles/2016/2/22/does-high-potential-success-lead-to-organizational-failure.

84. L. Finkelstein, D. Costanza, and G. Goodwin, "Do Your High Potentials Have Potential? The Impact of Individual Differences and Designation on Leader Success," *Personnel Psychology* 71, no. 1 (2018), pp. 3–22.

85. M. Effron, "Your Potential Model Is Wrong (or at Least Not Right)," The Talent Strategy Group, July 30, 2015, www.talentstrategygroup.com/publications/your-potential-model-is-wrong-or-at-least-not-right.

86. Zenger and Folkman, "Companies Are Bad at Identifying High-Potential Employees," *Harvard Business Review*, February 20, 2017, https://hbr.org/2017/02/companies-are-bad-at-identifying-high-potential-employees.

87. Church and Rotolo, "How Are Top Companies Assessing High-Potentials and Senior Executives?"

88. R. Silzer and A. H. Church, "The Pearls and Perils of Identifying Potential," *Industrial and Organizational Psychology* 2 (2009), pp. 377–422.

89. T. Chamorro-Premuzic, "What Science Tells Us about Leadership Potential," *Harvard Business Review*, September 2016, https://hbr.org/2016/09/what-science-tells-us-about-leadership-potential.

90. C. Boutelle, "Psychology of Leadership: A Cure for Collapsing Confidence in Leaders," SIOP, http://www.siop.org/article_view.aspx?article=1195.

91. K. Wilde, "Decision-Making in Talent Planning Requires Additional Attention in Today's Business Environment," *Talent Management Magazine*, March 2015.

92. A. Church and S. Ezama, "Six Truths about Using Personality Data for Talent Decisions," Talent Q, November 14, 2019, www.talent-quarterly.com/6-truths-about-personality-data.

93. MEffron, "Rethinking Potential: Should We Search for Hidden Gems, Shy-Po's and Repressed Performers?" The Talent Strategy Group, October 2, 2019, www.talentstrategygroup.com/publications/rethinking-potential-should-we-search-for-hidden-gems-shy-po-s-and-repressed-performers.

94. Curphy et al., *Ignition*.

95. G. Curphy and D. Nilsen, *The Team Assessment Survey* (North Oaks, MN: Curphy Leadership Solutions, 2019).

96. G. Curphy and D. Nilsen, *The Team Improvement Workshop Participant Manual* (North Oaks, MN: Curphy Leadership Solutions, 2020).

97. G. Curphy and D. Nilsen, "How Are You Choosing Your High Potentials?" presentation delivered to PsychPub, London, UK, March 4, 2020.

98. T. Chamorro-Premuzic, S. Adler, and R. Kaiser, "What Science Says about Identifying High Potential Employees," *Harvard Business Review*, October 3, 2017, https://hbr.org/2017/10/what-science-says-about-identifying-high-potential-employees.

99. Cappelli, "Why Performance Reviews Are Now under Review."

CHAPTER 12

Groups, Teams, and Their Leadership

Introduction

April 20, 2013; Loveland Pass, Colorado. The daily avalanche bulletin was straightforward and ominous: There was a serious risk of hard-slab avalanches on north-facing slopes, triggered near the tree line. Two days earlier, a snowboarder triggered the same type of large, fast-moving, destructive slide near the tree line on a north-facing slope near Vail Pass. And the six men reading these bulletins were hardly backcountry novices. They were among the most experienced members of a larger group of people gathered to raise money for the Colorado Avalanche Information Center. Their backgrounds were impressive from a technical perspective: a professional mountain guide and educator; an expert skier and avalanche safety advocate; an avid backcountry snowboarder; a snowboarder and geologic engineer; a professional snowboard sales representative; and an expert snowboarder and manager of a snowboard shop.

Yet after reading the bulletins and discussing them, the group packed their equipment, including avalanche safety gear, and proceeded to climb onto a known hard-slab north-facing slope at the tree line. At approximately 10:15 a.m., this group of men triggered a massive slide that was approximately two football fields wide and four football fields long in the Sheep Creek drainage area—an area known by all six of the men to be prone to the very kind of avalanche these experts had just discussed. All six were buried in the 60-mile-per-hour onslaught of heavy snow; only one survived.

How could six experts make such a tragic mistake? As we are learning, it had little to do with their individual expertise or equipment. As avalanche researcher Ian McCammon reports in his seminal study, it is more likely that they fell victim to group and social factors.[1] The snowboarders were members of a group and apparently knew more about the technical aspects of avalanches than they did about the powerful potential dangers of groups and teams.

Yet at the other extreme, groups and teams can deliver the most outstanding results imaginable, as has been demonstrated by the U.S. Navy SEALs. And in our increasingly complex world, groups and teams can accomplish feats impossible for lone individuals to achieve. Leaders in today's world must learn how to capture the best aspects of groups and teams while avoiding the pitfalls. Knowledge about groups and teams does not replace all you have learned thus far about individuals—it builds on that knowledge.

Certainly, leaders need to understand some things about themselves. Their skills, abilities, values, motives, and desires are important considerations in determining their leadership style and preferences. Leaders also need to understand, as much as possible, the same characteristics of their followers. But if you could know characteristics of both yourself and each of your followers, that would still not be enough. This is because groups and teams are different from the skills, abilities, values, and motives of those who compose them. Groups and teams have their own special characteristics.

Although much of the leadership literature today is about the individual who fills the leadership role, a survey of 35 texts about organizational behavior found that, in each one, the chapter about leadership is in the section on group behavior.[2] This should not be terribly surprising because groups (even as small as two people) are essential if leaders are to affect anything beyond their own behavior. What may be surprising is that the concept of groups is sometimes omitted entirely from books about leadership. The **group perspective** looks at how different group characteristics can affect relationships both with the leader and among the followers.

> *We are born for cooperation, as are the feet, the hands, the eyelids, and the upper and lower jaws.*
>
> **Marcus Aurelius, Roman emperor, 161-180**

With *teams* and *teamwork* being current buzzwords, it is worth clarifying the difference between groups and teams, although this difference is mostly one of degree. We will begin the chapter with that clarification. The larger distinction, as just noted, is between the characteristics of groups and the characteristics of individuals. We will spend the first half of the chapter discussing some factors that are unique to groups. Given the high interest in organizational teamwork, the latter portion of this chapter will present a model developed to help leaders design, diagnose, and leverage high-impact factors to create the conditions that foster team effectiveness. The chapter will conclude with a discussion of virtual teams, which are becoming ever more present, if not popular.

Individuals versus Groups versus Teams

As noted previously, there is a significant difference between individual work and group work. But what is the difference between group work and teamwork?

> *When it comes to anything that's social, whether it's your family, your school, your community, your business or your country, winning is a team sport.*
>
> **Bill Clinton, U.S. president, 1993-2001**

You will learn, in the next section of this chapter, that two identifying characteristics of groups are mutual interaction and reciprocal influence. Members of teams also have mutual interaction and reciprocal influence, but we generally distinguish teams from groups in four other ways. First, team members usually have a stronger sense of identification among themselves than group members do. Often both team members and outsiders can readily identify who is and who is not on the team (athletic uniforms are one obvious example); identifying members of a group may be more difficult. Second, teams have common goals or tasks; these may range from developing a new product to winning an athletic league championship. Group members, by contrast, may not have the same degree of consensus about goals that team members do. Group members may belong to the group for a variety of personal reasons, and these may clash with the group's stated objectives. (This phenomenon probably happens with teams, too, although perhaps not to the same extent.)

Third, task interdependence typically is greater with teams than with groups. For example, basketball players usually are unable to take a shot unless other team members set picks or pass the ball to them (see **Profiles in Leadership 12.1**). However, group members often can contribute to goal accomplishment by working independently; the successful completion of their assigned tasks may not be contingent on other group members. Of course task interdependence can vary greatly even across teams. Among athletic teams, for example, softball, football, soccer, and hockey teams have a high level of task interdependence, whereas swimming, cross-country, and track teams have substantially lower levels of task interdependence.

Phil Jackson

PROFILES IN LEADERSHIP 12.1

In **Part 2** of this book, which discussed individual leadership characteristics, it was fairly easy to come up with a leader who typified the particular aspect of leadership we were illustrating. This is not quite so easy for teams. If you consider Ginnett's definition of leadership ("The leader's job is to create the conditions for the team to be successful"), the real team leader might be behind the scenes or, in this case, not even on the court.

Phil Jackson is a basketball coach, but not just any coach. Jackson was the coach of champion Michael Jordan and ultimately of the championship-winning Chicago Bulls. Certainly basketball is a team sport; and as Michael Jordan and other Bulls found out, having arguably the best player in the sport does not necessarily translate into the best team in the game. In many of the years when Jordan won the individual scoring championship, the Bulls didn't win the championship. Jackson's job as head coach was to transform spectacular individual players into a spectacular team.

Perhaps the best way to get a sense of this challenge and the teamwork Jackson built to win the championship is to extract a few lines from his book *Sacred Hoops*:

> The most important part of the (coach's) job takes place on the practice floor, not during the game. After a certain point you have to trust the players to translate into action what

they've learned in practice. Using a comprehensive system of basketball makes it easier for me to detach myself in that way. Once the players have mastered the system, a powerful group intelligence emerges that is greater than the coach's ideas or those of any individual on the team. When a team reaches that state, the coach can step back and let the game itself "motivate" the players. You don't have to give them any "win one for the Gipper" pep talks, you just have to turn them loose and let them immerse themselves in the action. . . .

The sign of a great player was not how much *he* scored, but how much he lifted his teammate's performance. . . .

You can't beat a good defensive team with one man. It's got to be a team effort. . . .

It took a long time for Michael to realize he couldn't do it all by himself. Slowly, however, as the team began to master the nuances of the system, he learned that he could trust his teammates to come through in the clutch. It was the beginning of his transformation from a gifted solo artist into a selfless team player.
. . .

What appealed to me about the system was that it empowered everybody on the team by making them more involved in the offense, and demanded that they put their individual needs second to those of the group. This is the struggle every leader faces: how to get members of the team who are driven by the quest for individual glory to give themselves over wholeheartedly to the group effort.

Source: P. Jackson and H. Delehanty, *Sacred Hoops: Spiritual Lessons of a Hardwood Warrior* (New York: Hyperion, 1995).

Fourth, team members often have more differentiated and specialized roles than do group members. Group members often play a variety of roles within the group; however, team members often play a single, or primary, role on a team. Finally, bear in mind that the distinctions we have been highlighting probably reflect only matters of degree. We might consider teams to be highly specialized groups.

The Nature of Groups

Perhaps we should begin by defining what a **group** is. A group can be thought of as "two or more persons who are interacting with one another in such a manner that each person influences and is influenced by each other person."[3] Three aspects of this definition are particularly important to the study of leadership. First, this definition incorporates the concept of reciprocal influence between leaders and followers—an idea considerably different from the one-way influence implicit in the dictionary's definition of followers. Second, group members interact and influence each other. Thus, people waiting at a bus stop would not constitute a group because there generally is neither interaction nor influence between the various individuals. By contrast, eight people meeting to plan a school bond election would constitute a group because there probably would be a high level of mutual interaction among the attendees. Third, the definition does not constrain individuals to only one group. Almost everyone belongs to a number of different groups; an individual could be a member of various service, production, sports, religious, parent, and volunteer groups simultaneously.

Although people belong to many groups, just as they do to many organizations, groups and organizations are not the same thing (groups, of course, can exist within organizations). Organizations can be so large that most members do not know most of the other people in the organization. In such cases there is relatively little intermember interaction and reciprocal influence. Similarly, organizations typically are just too large and impersonal to have much effect on anyone's feelings, whereas groups are small and immediate enough to affect both feelings and self-image. People often tend to identify more with the groups they belong to than with the organizations they belong to; they are more psychologically invested in their groups. Also, certain important psychological needs (like social contact) are better satisfied by groups than by organizations.

Perhaps an example will clarify the distinction between groups and organizations. Consider a church so large that it may fairly be described as an organization—so large that multiple services must be offered on Sunday mornings, dozens of different study classes are offered each week, and there are numerous different choirs and musical ensembles. In such a large church, the members could hardly be said to interact with or influence each other except on an occasional basis. Such size often presents both advantages and disadvantages to the membership. On one hand, it makes possible a rich diversity of activities; on the other hand, its size can make the church itself (the overall organization) seem relatively impersonal. It may be difficult to identify with a large organization other than in name only ("I belong to First Presbyterian Church"). In such cases many people identify more with particular groups within the church than with the church itself; it may be easier to *feel* a part of some smaller group such as the high school choir or a weekly study group.

Although groups play a pervasive role in society, in general people spend little time thinking about the factors that affect group processes and intragroup relationships. Therefore, the rest of this section will describe some group characteristics that can affect both leaders and followers. Much of the research on groups goes well beyond the scope of this chapter (see Gibbard, Hartman, and Mann, 1974; Shaw, 1981; Hackman, 1990),[4, 5, 6] but six concepts are so basic to the group perspective that they deserve our attention. These six concepts are group size, stages of group development, roles, norms, cohesion, and communication. Five of them will be addressed in the following sections. The sixth, communication, permeates them all.

Group Size

The size of any group has implications for both leaders and followers. First, leader emergence is partly a function of group size. The greater number of people in a large versus a small group will affect the probability that any individual is likely to emerge as leader. Second, as groups become larger, **cliques** are more likely to develop.[7] Cliques are subgroups of individuals who often share the same goals, values, and expectations. Because cliques generally wield more influence than individual members, they are likely to exert considerable influence—positively or negatively—on the larger group. Leaders need to identify and deal with cliques within their groups; many intragroup conflicts are the results of cliques having different values, goals, and expectations.

Third, group size also can affect a leader's behavioral style. Leaders with a large **span of control** tend to be more directive, spend less time with individual subordinates, and use more impersonal approaches when influencing followers. Leaders with a small span of control tend to display more consideration and use more personal approaches when influencing followers.[8, 9, 10, 11] Fourth, group size also affects group effectiveness. Although some researchers have suggested the optimal number of workers for any task is between five and seven,[12, 13] it probably is wise to avoid such a simple generalization. The answer to the question of appropriate group size seems to be "just big enough to get the job done." Obviously the larger the group, the more likely it is that it will involve differentiated skills, values, perceptions, and abilities among its members. Also, more "people power" will certainly be available to do the work as group size increases.

> A committee is an animal with four back legs.
>
> **Jean le Carré, *Tinker Tailor Soldier Spy***

There are, however, limits to the benefits of size. Consider the question, "If it takes one person two minutes to dig a one-cubic-foot hole, how long will it take 20 people to dig the same size hole?" Actually, it probably will take the larger group considerably *longer,* especially if they all participate at the same time. Beyond the purely physical limitations of certain tasks, there may be decreasing returns (on a per-capita basis) as group size increases. This is true even when the efforts of all group members are combined on what is called an **additive task**. An additive task is one where the group's output simply involves the combination of individual outputs.[14] Such a case may be illustrated by the number of individuals needed to push a stalled truck from an intersection. One individual probably would not be enough—maybe not even two or three. At some point, though, as group size increases in this additive task, there will be enough combined force to move the truck. However, as the group size increases beyond that needed to move the truck, the individual contribution of each member will appear to decrease. Steiner[15] suggested this may be due to **process loss** resulting from factors such as some members not pushing in the right direction. Process losses can be thought of as the inefficiencies created by more and more people working together.

Group size can affect group effectiveness in a number of other ways. As group size increases, the diminishing returns of larger work groups may be due to **social loafing**,[16] which is the phenomenon of reduced effort by people when they are not individually accountable for their work. Experiments across different sorts of tasks have tended to demonstrate greater effort when every individual's work is monitored than when many individuals' outputs are anonymously pooled into a collective product. More recent evidence, however, suggests the process may be considerably more complicated than initially thought.[17] The performance decrement may be affected more by the level of task complexity or the reward structure (cooperative versus competitive) than by outcome attribution.

Sometimes working in the presence of others may actually increase effort or productivity through a phenomenon called **social facilitation**. Social facilitation was first documented in classic experiments at the Hawthorne plant of the Western Electric Company (see **Highlight 12.1**). However, social facilitation is not limited to research situations. It refers to any time people increase their level of work due to the presence of others. Typically this occurs when the presence of others increases individual accountability for work, in contrast to other occasions when being in a group reinforces individual anonymity and social loafing.[18]

Social Facilitation and the Hawthorne Effect

HIGHLIGHT 12.1

Social facilitation was first documented in experiments conducted at the Hawthorne plant of the Western Electric Company during the late 1920s and early 1930s. These classic studies were originally designed to evaluate the impact of different work environments. Among other things, researchers varied the levels of illumination in areas where workers were assembling electrical components and found that production increased when lighting was increased. When lighting was subsequently decreased, however, production again increased. Faced with these confusing data, the researchers turned their attention from physical aspects of the work environment to its social aspects. As it turns out, one reason workers' production increased was simply because someone else (in this case the researchers) had paid attention to them. The term *Hawthorne effect* is still used today to describe an artificial change in behavior due merely to the fact that a person or group is being studied.

Sources: E. Mayo, *The Human Problems of an Industrial Civilization* (New York: Macmillan, 1933); and R. M. Stogdill, "Group Productivity, Drive, and Cohesiveness," *Organizational Behavior and Human Performance* 8 (1972), pp. 26–43.

Developmental Stages of Groups

Just as children go through different stages of development, so do groups. Tuckman's[19] review of over 60 studies involving leaderless training, experimental, or therapeutic groups revealed that groups generally went through four distinct stages of development. The first stage, **forming**, was characterized by polite conversation, the gathering of superficial information about fellow members, and low trust. The group's rejection of emerging potential leaders with negative characteristics also took place during the forming stage. The second stage, **storming**, usually was marked by intragroup conflict, heightened emotional levels, and status differentiation as remaining contenders struggled to build alliances and fulfill the group's leadership role. The clear emergence of a leader and the development of group norms and cohesiveness were the key indicators of the **norming** stage of group development. Finally, groups reached the **performing** stage when group members played functional, interdependent roles that were focused on the performance of group tasks.

> *If you start yelling and becoming obtrusive and beboppin' around, you give the impression of insecurity, and that becomes infectious. It bleeds down into the actors, and they become nervous; then it bleeds down into the crew, and they become nervous, and you don't get much accomplished that way. You have to set a tone and just demand a certain amount of tranquility.*
>
> **Clint Eastwood, on being a film director**

The four stages of group development identified by Tuckman[20] are important for several reasons. First, people are in many more leaderless groups than they may realize. For example, many sports teams, committees, work groups, and clubs start out as leaderless teams. Team or club captains or committee spokespersons are likely to be the emergent leaders from their respective groups. On a larger scale, perhaps even many elected officials initially began their political careers as the emergent leaders of their cliques or groups, and were then able to convince the majority of the remaining members in their constituencies of their viability as candidates.

Another reason it is important to understand stages of group development is the potential relationships between leadership behaviors and group cohesiveness and productivity. Some experts have maintained that leaders need to focus on consideration or group maintenance behaviors during the norming stage to improve group cohesiveness, and on task behaviors during the performing stage to improve group productivity.[21, 22] They also have suggested that leaders who reverse these behaviors during the norming and performing stages tend to have less cohesive and less productive groups. Thus, being able to recognize stages of group development may enhance the likelihood that one will emerge as a leader as well as increase the cohesiveness and productivity of the group being led.

Tuckman's model is widely known if for no other reason than the fact that its components rhyme with each other; but it is not without criticism. Recall that the subjects for Tuckman's research were training, experimental, or therapy groups. None of these particularly represent teams forming to do work in an organizational context. For example, Ginnett observed many surgical teams and never once saw them engage in storming behaviors as they formed. You wouldn't want to be the patient if there was a formation argument between the surgeon, the anesthesiologist, and the scrub nurse about who was going to get to use the scalpel today.

Gersick[23] proposed a better model for teams in organizational settings. In studying **project teams**, she found that teams don't necessarily jump right in and get to work. Rather, they spend most of the first half of the team's life muddling through various ideas and strategies. Then, about midway into the project, the team seems to experience the equivalent of a midlife crisis where there is a flurry of activity and a reexamination of the strategy to see if it will allow them to complete their work. Gersick labeled this process **punctuated equilibrium**, which is obviously quite different from Tuckman's four-stage model.

Group Roles

Group roles are the sets of expected behaviors associated with particular jobs or positions. Most people have multiple roles stemming from the various groups with which they are associated. In addition, it is not uncommon for someone to occupy numerous roles within the same group as situations change. Ginnett[24] found that members of airline crews have varying roles over the course of a day. Although some behaviors were universally associated with certain roles, effective team members on these airline crews generally were more flexible in changing their behavior as other role demands changed. For example, whereas the captain of an airplane is responsible for its overall operation and decision-making during a flight, flight attendants often take over responsibility for planning and carrying out the crew's social activities in the evening (when the flight is over). One captain in the study, however, continued to make *all* the crew's decisions, including their evening social plans; he was inflexible with regard to the role of decision maker. Not coincidentally, he was seen as a less effective leader—even during the actual flights—than more flexible captains.

Some roles, like positions on athletic teams, have meaning only in relatively specific contexts. Generally speaking, for example, a person plays only a lineman's role during football games (admittedly, at many schools being an intercollegiate athlete is a role that extends to aspects of student life outside sports). Other roles are more general in nature, including certain common ones that play a part in making any group work—or not work—well. **Highlight 12.2** presents a vivid example of how powerful roles can be as determinants of behavior.

The Stanford Prison Experiment

HIGHLIGHT 12.2

A fascinating demonstration of the power of roles occurred when social psychologist Philip Zimbardo and his colleagues created a simulated prison environment at Stanford University. From a larger group of volunteers, two dozen male college students were randomly assigned to be either "prisoners" or "guards." The simulation was quite realistic, with actual cells constructed in the basement of one of the university buildings. The guards wore uniforms and carried nightsticks and whistles; their eyes were covered by sunglasses. The prisoners were "arrested" at their homes by police driving cars replete with blazing sirens. They were handcuffed, frisked, blindfolded, and brought to the "jail," where they were fingerprinted, given prisoner outfits, and assigned numbers by which they would henceforth be addressed.

It did not take long for the students' normal behavior to be overcome by the roles they were playing. The guards became more and more abusive with their power. They held prisoners accountable for strict adherence to arbitrary rules of prison life (which the guards themselves created) and seemed to enjoy punishing the prisoners for even minor infractions. They increasingly seemed to think of the prisoners—truly just other college students—as bad people. The emotional stress on the prisoners became profound, and just six days into the two-week schedule the experiment was halted. This unexpected outcome occurred because participants' roles had become their reality. They were not just students role-playing guards and prisoners; to a disconcerting degree they became guards and prisoners.

What should people conclude from the Stanford prison study? At an abstract level, the study dramatically points out how behavior is partly determined by social role. Additionally, it is clear how just being in the role of leader, especially to the extent that it is attended by tangible and symbolic manifestations of power, can affect how leaders think and act toward followers. Still another lesson people might draw involves remembering that the volunteers all had many different roles in life than those assigned to them in the study, though being a guard or a prisoner was certainly the salient one for this period. Whereas everyone has many roles, the salience of one or another often depends on the situation, and a person's behavior changes as his or her role changes in a group.

Source: P. Zimbardo, C. Haney, W. Banks, and D. Jaffe, "The Mind Is a Formidable Jailer: A Pirandellian Prison," *New York Times Magazine*, April 8, 1973, pp. 38–60.

In **Chapter 8,** leader behavior was characterized initially in terms of two broad functions. One deals with getting the task done (**task role**) and the other with supporting relationships within the work group (**relationship role**). Similarly, roles in groups can be categorized in terms of task and relationship functions (see **Highlight 12.3**). Many of the roles in **Highlight 12.3** are appropriate for followers, not just the official group leader; all of these different roles are part of the leadership process and all contribute to a group's overall effectiveness. Moreover, the distinction between task and relationship roles is somewhat arbitrary. It is sensible enough when looking at the short-term impact of any given behavior, but in another sense relationship roles are task roles. After all, task-oriented behavior may be adequate for accomplishing short-term objectives, but an appropriately cohesive and supportive group increases the potential for long-term effectiveness at future tasks as well as present tasks. Although the roles in **Highlight 12.3** generally contribute to a group's overall effectiveness, several types of problems can occur with group roles and can impede group performance. One type of role problem concerns the **dysfunctional roles**, listed in **Highlight 12.4**. The common denominator among these roles is how the person's behavior serves primarily selfish or egocentric purposes rather than group purposes.

Task and Relationship Roles in Groups

HIGHLIGHT 12.3

TASK ROLES

Initiating: Defining the problem, suggesting activities, assigning tasks

Information seeking: Asking questions, seeking relevant data or views

Information sharing: Providing data, offering opinions

Summarizing: Reviewing and integrating others' points, checking for common understanding and readiness for action

Evaluating: Assessing validity of assumptions, quality of information, reasonableness of recommendations

Guiding: Keeping group on track

RELATIONSHIP ROLES

Harmonizing: Resolving interpersonal conflicts, reducing tension

Encouraging: Supporting and praising others, showing appreciation for others' contributions, being warm and friendly

Gatekeeping: Assuring even participation by all group members, making sure that everyone has a chance to be heard and that no individual dominates

Source: Adapted from K. D. Benne and P. Sheats, "Functional Roles of Group Members," *Journal of Social Issues* 4 (1948), pp. 41–49.

Dysfunctional Roles

HIGHLIGHT 12.4

Dominating: Monopolizing group time, forcing views on others

Blocking: Stubbornly obstructing and impeding group work, persistent negativism

Attacking: Belittling others, creating a hostile or intimidating environment

Distracting: Engaging in irrelevant behaviors, distracting others' attention

Source: Adapted from K. D. Benne and P. Sheats, "Functional Roles of Group Members," *Journal of Social Issues* 4 (1948), pp. 41–49.

Another role problem is **role conflict**. Role conflict involves receiving contradictory messages about expected behavior and can in turn adversely affect a person's emotional well-being and performance.[25]

Role conflict can occur in several different ways. Perhaps most common is receiving inconsistent signals about expected behavior from the same person. When the same person sends mixed signals, it is called **intrasender role conflict** ("I need this report back in five minutes, and it had better be perfect"). **Intersender role conflict** occurs when someone receives inconsistent signals from several others about expected behavior. Still another kind of role conflict is based on inconsistencies between different roles a person may have. Professional and family demands, for example, often create role conflicts. **Interrole conflict** occurs when someone is unable to perform all of his roles as well as he would like. A final type occurs when role expectations violate a person's values. This is known as **person–role conflict**. An example of person–role conflict might occur if a store manager encourages a salesperson to mislead customers about the quality of the store's products when this behavior is inconsistent with the salesperson's values and beliefs.

A different sort of role problem is called **role ambiguity**. In role conflict, one receives clear messages about expectations, but the messages are not all congruent. With role ambiguity, the problem is lack of clarity about exactly what the expectations are.[26, 27] There may have been no role expectations established at all, or they may not have been clearly communicated. A person is experiencing role ambiguity if she wonders, "What am I supposed to be doing?" It is important for leaders to be able to minimize the degree to which dysfunctional roles, role conflict, and role ambiguity occur in their groups because these problems have been found to have a negative impact on organizational commitment, job involvement, absenteeism, and satisfaction with coworkers and supervisors.[28]

Group Norms

Norms are the informal rules groups adopt to regulate and regularize group members' behaviors. Although norms are only infrequently written down (see **Highlight 12.5**) or openly discussed, they nonetheless often have a powerful and consistent influence on behavior.[29] That is because most people are good at reading the social cues that inform them about existing norms. For example, most people easily discern the dress code in any work environment without needing written guidance. People also are apt to notice when a norm is violated, even though they may have been unable to articulate the norm before its violation was apparent. For example, most students have expectations (norms) about creating extra work for other students. Imagine the reaction if a student in some class complained that not enough reading was being assigned for each lesson or that the minimum length requirements for the term paper needed to be raised substantially.

Putting It in Writing

HIGHLIGHT 12.5

Sport humorist and author Rick Reilly noted that many of the behaviors that show up in sporting events are understood by virtually all participants (i.e., "norms") but are seldom if ever written down. Following are a few prime examples from a sampling of sports.

- HOCKEY:
  - The starting goalie is always the first player on the ice.
  - Never shoot the puck into the net after a whistle blows.

- BASKETBALL:
  - No NBA player attempting a layup in the fourth quarter of a tight game should go unfouled.
  - Scrubs stand during NBA timeouts.

- BASEBALL:
  - Hand the manager the ball when he comes to the mound to take you out.
  - Do not talk to or sit near a pitcher with a no-hitter going. And never bunt to break one up.

- GOLF:
  - Never walk on a player's putting line, including the two feet on the other side of the cup.
  - The caddie of the last player to putt plants the flag.

- FOOTBALL:
  - Never hit the quarterback during practice.
  - When a receiver drops a pass, go back to him on the next play.

Source: R. Reilly, *Sports Illustrated* vol. 104, no. 15 (2006), p. 76.

Norms do not govern all behaviors—just those a group feels are important. Norms are more likely to be seen as important and are more apt to be enforced if they (1) facilitate group survival; (2) simplify, or make more predictable, what behavior is expected of group members; (3) help the group avoid embarrassing interpersonal problems; or (4) express the central values of the group and clarify what is distinctive about the group's identity.[30]

The norms that group members value, such as those just listed, are essentially inward looking. They help the team take care of itself and avoid embarrassing situations caused by inappropriate member behaviors. Hackman[31] recommends that the leader has a responsibility to focus the team outwardly to enhance performance. Specifically, he suggests two core norms be created to enhance performance:

1. Group members should actively scan the environment for opportunities that would require a change in operating strategy to capitalize upon them.
2. The team should identify the few behaviors that team members must always do and those they should never do to conform to the organization's objectives.

By actively implementing these two norms, the team is forced to examine not only its organizational context but also the much larger industry and environmental shells in which it operates. One irony about norms is that an outsider to a group often is able to learn more about norms than an insider. An outsider, not necessarily subject to the norms herself, is more apt to notice them. In fact, the more "foreign" an observer is, the more likely it is the norms will be perceived. If a man is accustomed to wearing a tie to work, he is less likely to notice that men in another organization also wear ties to work, but is *more* likely to note that the men in a third organization typically wear sweaters or sweatshirts around the office.

Group Cohesion

Finding good players is easy. Getting them to play as a team is another story.

Casey Stengel, former MLB player and manager

Group cohesion is the glue that keeps a group together. It is the sum of the forces that attract members to a group, provide resistance to leaving it, and motivate them to be active in it. Highly cohesive groups interact with and influence each other more than less cohesive groups do. Furthermore, a highly cohesive group may have lower absenteeism and lower turnover than a less cohesive group, and low absenteeism and turnover often contribute to higher group performance; higher performance can, in turn, contribute to even higher cohesion, thus resulting in an increasingly positive spiral.

However, greater cohesiveness does not always lead to higher performance. A highly cohesive but unskilled team is still an unskilled team, and such teams will often lose to a less cohesive but more skilled one. Additionally, a highly cohesive group may sometimes develop goals that are contrary to the larger organization's goals. For example, members of a highly cohesive research team at a particular college committed themselves to working on a problem that seemed inherently interesting to them. Their nearly zealous commitment to the project, however, effectively kept them from asking, or even allowing others to ask, if the research aligned itself well with the college's stated objectives. Their narrow and basic research effort deviated significantly from the college's expressed commitment to emphasize applied research. As a result, the college lost some substantial outside financial support.

Other problems also can occur in highly cohesive groups. Researchers[32, 33] have found that some groups can become so cohesive they erect what amount to fences or boundaries between themselves and others. Such **overbounding** can block the use of outside resources that could make them more effective. Competitive product development teams can become so overbounded (often rationalized by security concerns or inordinate fears of "idea thieves") that they will not ask for help from willing and able staff within their own organizations.

One example of this problem was the failed mission to rescue U.S. embassy personnel held hostage in Iran during Jimmy Carter's presidency. The rescue itself was a complicated mission involving many different U.S. military forces. Some of these forces included sea-based helicopters. The helicopters and their crews were carried on regular naval vessels, though most sailors on the vessels knew nothing of the secret mission. Senior personnel were so concerned that some sailor might leak information, and thus compromise the mission's secrecy, that maintenance crews aboard the ships were not directed to perform increased levels of maintenance on the helicopters immediately before the critical mission. Even if a helicopter was scheduled for significant maintenance within the next 50 hours of flight time (which would be exceeded in the rescue mission), crews were not told to perform the maintenance. According to knowledgeable sources, this practice affected the performance of at least one of the failed helicopters, and thus the overall mission.

Janis[34] discovered still another disadvantage of highly cohesive groups. He found that people in a highly cohesive group often become more concerned with striving for unanimity than objectively appraising different courses of action. Janis labeled this phenomenon **groupthink** and believed it accounted for a number of historic fiascoes, including Pearl Harbor and the Bay of Pigs invasion. It may have played a role in the *Challenger* space shuttle disaster, and it also occurs in other cohesive groups ranging from business meetings to air crews, and from therapy groups to school boards.

What is groupthink? Cohesive groups tend to evolve strong informal norms to preserve friendly internal relations. Preserving a comfortable, harmonious group environment becomes a hidden agenda that tends to suppress dissent, conflict, and critical thinking. Unwise decisions may result when concurrence seeking among members overrides their willingness to express or tolerate deviant points of view and think critically. Janis[35] identified a number of symptoms of groupthink, which can be found in **Highlight 12.6**.

Symptoms of Groupthink

HIGHLIGHT 12.6

An illusion of invulnerability, which leads to unwarranted optimism and excessive risk taking by the group.

Unquestioned assumption of the group's morality and therefore an absence of reflection on the ethical consequences of group action.

Collective rationalization to discount negative information or warnings.

Stereotypes of the opposition as evil, weak, or stupid.

Self-censorship by group members from expressing ideas that deviate from the group consensus due to doubts about their validity or importance.

An illusion of unanimity such that greater consensus is perceived than really exists.

Direct pressure on dissenting members, which reinforces the norm that disagreement represents disloyalty to the group.

Mindguards who protect the group from adverse information.

Source: Adapted from I. L. Janis, *Groupthink*, 2nd ed. (Boston: Houghton Mifflin, 1982).

A policy-making or decision-making group displaying most of the symptoms in **Highlight 12.6** runs a big risk of being ineffective. It may do a poor job of clarifying objectives, searching for relevant information, evaluating alternatives, assessing risks, and anticipating the need for contingency plans. Janis[36] offered the following suggestions as ways of reducing groupthink and thus of improving the quality of a group's input to policies or decisions. First, leaders should encourage all group members to take on the role of critical evaluator. Everyone in the group needs to appreciate the importance of airing doubts and objections. This includes the leader's willingness to listen to criticisms of his or her own ideas. Second, leaders should create a climate of open inquiry through their own impartiality and objectivity. At the outset, leaders should refrain from stating personal preferences or expectations that may bias group discussion. Third, the risk of groupthink can be reduced if independent groups are established to make recommendations on the same issue. Fourth, at least one member of the group should be assigned the role of devil's advocate—an assignment that should rotate from meeting to meeting. Groupthink may have been one of the social factors that played a part in the avalanche tragedy described at the beginning of this chapter.

One final problem with highly cohesive groups may be what Shephard[37] has called **ollieism**. Ollieism, a variation of groupthink, occurs when illegal actions are taken by overly zealous and loyal subordinates who believe that what they are doing will please their leaders. It derives its name from the actions of Lieutenant Colonel Oliver North, who among other things admitted he lied to the U.S. Congress about his actions while working on the White House staff during the Iran–Contra affair. Shephard cited the slaying of Thomas À Becket by four of Henry II's knights and the Watergate break-in as other prime examples of ollieism. Ollieism differs from groupthink in that the subordinates' illegal actions usually occur without the explicit knowledge or consent of the leader. Nevertheless, Shephard pointed out that, although the examples cited of ollieism were not officially sanctioned, the responsibility for them still falls squarely on the leader. It is the leader's responsibility to create an ethical climate within the group, and leaders who create highly cohesive yet unethical groups must bear the responsibility for the group's actions.

After reading about the uncertain relationships between group cohesion and performance, and the problems with overbounding, groupthink, and ollieism, you might think cohesiveness should be avoided. Nothing, however, could be further from the truth. First, problems with overly cohesive groups occur relatively infrequently, and in general leaders will be better off thinking of ways to create and maintain highly cohesive teams than of not developing these teams out of concern for potential groupthink or overbounding situations. Second, perhaps the biggest argument for developing cohesive groups is to consider the alternative—groups with little or no cohesiveness. In the latter groups, followers would generally be dissatisfied with each other and the leader, commitment to accomplishing group and organizational goals may be reduced, intragroup communication may occur less frequently, and interdependent task performance may suffer.[38] Because of the problems associated with groups having low cohesiveness, leadership practitioners need to realize that developing functionally cohesive work groups is a goal for which they all should strive.

In summary, the group perspective provides a complementary level of analysis to the individual perspective presented earlier in this book. A follower's behavior may be due to his or her values, traits, or experience (the individual perspective), or this behavior may be due to the followers' roles, the group norms, the group's stage of development, or the group's level of cohesiveness (the group perspective). Thus, the group perspective can also provide both leaders and followers with a number of explanations for why individuals in groups behave in certain ways. Moreover, the six group characteristics just described can give leaders and followers ideas about factors that may be affecting their ability to influence other group members and how to improve their level of influence in the group.

Teams

With so much attention devoted to teams and teamwork in today's organizations, it is appropriate to spend a fair amount of time examining teams and the factors that impact their effectiveness. After considering some differential measures of team effectiveness, we will look at a comprehensive model of team leadership.

Effective Team Characteristics and Team Building

Teams definitely vary in their effectiveness. Virtually identical teams can be dramatically different in terms of success or failure (see **Highlight 12.7**). We must ask, therefore, what makes one team successful and another unsuccessful. Although this is an area only recently studied, exploratory work at the Center for Creative Leadership has tentatively identified several key characteristics for effective team performance (see **Highlight 12.8** for a historical perspective on teamwork from the Golden Age of Pirates).

Examples of Effective and Ineffective Teams

HIGHLIGHT 12.7

Most people can readily think of a number of examples of ineffective and effective teamwork. Consider the relative effectiveness of the teams depicted in the following two true stories:

Ineffective teamwork: After an airline flight crew failed to get a "nose gear down and locked" indicator light to come on while making a landing approach into Miami, all three crew members became involved in trying to change the burned-out indicator bulb in the cockpit. Nobody was flying the airplane, and none of them were monitoring the flight of the L-1011 as it descended into the Everglades and crashed.

Effective teamwork: The crew of a DC-10, having lost all capability to control the airplane through flight controls as a result of an engine explosion, realized they needed all the help they could get. Captain Al Haynes discovered that another experienced captain was traveling in the passenger cabin and invited him to come up to the cabin to help the regular crew out. Miraculously, their combined abilities enabled the crew—using techniques developed on the spot—to control the plane to within a few feet of the ground. Even though there were fatalities, over 180 people survived a nearly hopeless situation.

Teamwork from the Golden Age of Pirates

HIGHLIGHT 12.8

Thanks to Walt Disney Studios and their multiple versions of *Pirates of the Caribbean*, we all know about pirates and their life on the high seas. They were a ruthless band of ne'er-do-wells who, without a pirate captain that virtually kidnapped them from a bar, would probably have been otherwise completely unemployed. Once aboard ship, they and their 15 or so compatriots were harshly dealt with by an autocratic and dictatorial captain and his assistant. Violation of arbitrary rules would doom the poor sailor to walk the plank to a watery grave. When they did stumble upon a potential target of opportunity, they would try to outflank it and then, under a steady barrage of cannon fire, descend upon the other ship, usually sending it to the bottom of the ocean. The pirate crew, populated by men with severed arms and pegs for legs, would be forced to bury their treasure on some island and hope to recover it later.

There is one problem with our Walt Disney view of pirates—almost none of it is true, with the possible exception of the "ruthless" part. These big-screen images of pirates appear to be either a compilation of characters from novels such as Robert Louis Stevenson's *Treasure Island* or made up entirely from a screenwriter's imagination. Owing in large part to a magnificent traveling exhibit by the National Geographic Society, we now know a great deal more about what pirate life was really like. Combining these findings and artifacts with an authentic book on pirates, the exhibit has given us a very different picture and one that is surprisingly a lot closer to high-performance teamwork than you might expect.

Before we describe the real life of pirates during the Golden Age (approximately 1650–1730 in the Caribbean), it is important to understand that this is neither the sole period of piracy nor its sole geographic location. Pirates are known to have existed thousands of years ago, even before the emergence of the Egyptian civilization. Northern Europe had both Saxon and Viking pirates and the Islamic pirates of the Barbary Coast victimized the Mediterranean. There were pirates in the South China Sea in the 18th and 19th centuries. Even today, the Somali pirates are hunted by multinational flotillas. But here we are focusing our view on the Golden Age of Pirates and their exploits in the Caribbean and Atlantic coast of the United States.

Piracy in the Golden Age had an unusual birthplace. According to Captain Johnson, "privateers are the nursery for pirates." Privateers are private individuals or, in this case, ships, sanctioned and authorized by governments by a *letter of marque* to attack foreign shipping during wartime. Both the Spanish and the English governments had used them extensively to augment their navies. And so did the Americans. During the American Revolution, the Continental Navy had only 64 ships, but there were at least 700 privateers. In fact, these privateers brought such devastation on English commerce that the English merchants pressured King George to give up the fight in America. Even George Washington acknowledged that there would have been no victory in the American Revolution without privateers. This tradition was so prevalent that it is included in Article 1, Section 8, of the U.S. Constitution: "The Congress shall have Power to . . . grant Letters of Marque and Reprisal, and make Rules concerning Captures on Land and Water. . . ." But when the wars ended, piracy tended to replace privateering in the Caribbean.

If we now look at what we actually know about the pirates of the Golden Age, and use as our lens the upcoming perspective on organizational shells by Hackman and Ginnett for start-up of high-performance teams, we get an interesting highlight on teamwork.

Task

The task of pirates was indeed one that required a team. Rather than a random act of spontaneity, the overtaking of a target ship was a well-planned-out and orchestrated event. In fact, the pirate ship was uniquely selected for this capability. Ships like the *Whydah* were highly sought after by pirates. Until its capture by pirate leader Sam Bellamy, the *Whydah* had been a slaver. As we will see in the next section, on composition, this was critical to its mission as a pirate ship. For now, suffice it to say that the pirate team was most often not a band of 10 to 20 scraggly men but more likely an overwhelmingly large boarding party of up to 160 heavily armed troops. If at all possible, they never approached their target with cannons blazing in an attempt to sink their adversary. Their common task was to "liberate" the booty, not to sink it to the bottom of the sea. Because slave ships had to move their "human cargo" rapidly across the ocean, they were among the fastest vessels on the sea and thus were ideal for the pirate mission. A typical pirate attack involved overtaking the target vessel as rapidly as possible, and upon nearing it, raising the pirate flag to let the victims know they were about to be overwhelmed. In the highly coordinated boarding activity commanded by the pirate quartermaster (more about the quartermaster later), pirates were interested not only in the booty but also possibly in the ship and any able-bodied members of the captured crew who could augment their own resources. Crews attacked with speed, skill, and urgency, functioning as tight, cohesive units. Laziness, incompetence, disloyalty, and cowardice were never tolerated since those traits endangered everyone. The tactics were well known at the time: Surrender, and the life of the crew (minus the officers) would be spared. Any resistance at all would mean that the entire crew was murdered.

The reward structure associated with this task was interesting as well. The booty was divided among the pirates in a predetermined fashion. Although the captain and quartermaster received a larger portion than a working crew member, it was not disproportionate by today's executive compensation standards. A captain and a quartermaster might receive two to three times what the other members received. This will make more sense when we look at the authority dynamics.

Composition

As mentioned earlier, the pirate crew was large—in fact, too large to be considered a high-performance team today. A team of 160 now makes no sense. But that number really should be regarded as the pirate organization because the crew was subdivided into much smaller teams with specific tasks and objectives. Given that a pirate organization had up to 160 members, the slave ship was ideally suited to sustain them. Slave ships were perfect prizes for pirates: easy to maneuver, unusually fast, armed to the hilt—and provisioned with large galleys designed to feed the slave cargo and thus suitable for the large pirate crew.

Contrary to the movie version of pirate conscription, where it was often the government vessels that conscripted their crews, paying them little to nothing and generally abusing them, positions on a pirate vessel were much sought after. When word got around that a pirate captain was looking to fill or augment a crew, volunteers abounded. According to Captain Johnson, when a captain announced that his ship was "going on the account," every tavern, brothel, and alleyway buzzed with anticipation. One could not just volunteer and hope to be selected. A potential pirate crew member had to demonstrate competence at a particular required skill, be it carpenter, sail maker, rigger, cook, musician, or doctor. And all had to be fighters.

Finally, Hollywood versions are fond of characterizing pirates as a "motley crew." Crews included ordinary seamen, free Black men, political dissidents, escaped slaves, indentured servants, Africans freed from slave ships taken at sea, Native Americans, and runaway plantation workers, speaking many languages and hailing from many nations. Today, we might describe such a collection of team members not as "motley" but, in our more politically correct moments, as "appropriately diverse."

Norms

All groups have norms, but they are seldom written down. The pirates were better at this than many teams today. Not only did they write them down, but each potential crew member had to sign "The Articles" before they could become a member. It is also reported that members signed along the right and left margins, not at the bottom, signifying that no man was greater than the rules as a whole, but all agreed to them. One set of Articles has survived and is presented here:

Pirate Code of Conduct
Bartholomew Roberts Shipboard Articles 1721

- ARTICLE I - Every man shall have an equal vote in affairs of moment. He shall have an equal title to the fresh provisions or strong liquors at any time seized, and shall use them at pleasure unless a scarcity may make it necessary for the common good that a retrenchment may be voted.

- ARTICLE II - Every man shall be called fairly in turn by the list on board of prizes, because over and above their proper share, they are allowed a shift of clothes. But if they defraud the company to the value of even one dollar in plate, jewels, or money, they shall be marooned. If any man rob another he shall have his nose and ears slit, and be put ashore where he shall be sure to encounter hardships.

- ARTICLE III - None shall game for money either with dice or cards.

- ARTICLE IV - The lights and candles should be put out at eight at night, and if any of the crew desire to drink after that hour they shall sit upon the open deck without lights.

- ARTICLE V - Each man shall keep his piece, cutlass, and pistols at all times clean and ready for action.

- ARTICLE VI - No boy or woman to be allowed amongst them. If any man shall be found seducing any of the latter sex and carrying her to sea in disguise he shall suffer death.

- ARTICLE VII - He that shall desert the ship or his quarters in time of battle shall be punished by death or marooning.

- ARTICLE VIII - None shall strike another on board the ship, but every man's quarrel shall be ended on shore by sword or pistol in this manner. At the word of command from the quartermaster, each man being previously placed back to back, shall turn and fire immediately. If any man do not, the quartermaster shall knock the piece out of his hand. If both miss their aim they shall take to their cutlasses, and he that draweth first blood shall be declared the victor.

- ARTICLE IX - No man shall talk of breaking up their way of living till each has a share of 1,000. Every man who shall become a cripple or lose a limb in the service shall have 800 pieces of eight from the common stock and for lesser hurts proportionately.

- ARTICLE X - The captain and the quartermaster shall each receive two shares of a prize, the master gunner and boatswain, one and one half shares, all other officers one and one quarter, and private gentlemen of fortune one share each.

- ARTICLE XI - The musicians shall have rest on the Sabbath Day only by right. On all other days by favour only.

Three points stand out. First, nothing is mentioned about wayward pirates walking the plank; however, violating the rules (norms) was cause for literally being kicked off the team. Secondly, Article IX is clearly one of the earliest forms of disability compensation. If a pirate became disabled as a result of doing his job, he would receive up to 800 pieces of eight or roughly 10 years compensation. Finally, the crew was governed in a remarkably democratic style, which leads directly to our final factor in describing high-performance teams, the use of authority.

Authority

Authority on a pirate ship was drawn from the Articles. Not only were the decisions and rewards shared reasonably equally by all members of the crew, but the officers (the captain and the quartermaster) were elected positions. The captain dictated orders in battle and the quartermaster led the raiding parties, but many other on-board decisions were made by a majority vote, often by a show of hands. Captains were elected by a show of hands and could be removed by the same method. Incompetence by elected leaders was simply not tolerated. One crew went through a total of 13 captains in two months; infamous Captains Morgan, Kidd, and Blackbeard at one time or another were all voted out of office.[39] The quartermaster walked an even tighter line because he had to serve both the captain as his second in command and the crew, who had elected him. Thus the notion of the all-powerful captain and quartermaster who mercilessly inflicted pain on their crews is apparently far from the truth.

It appears that the men (and a few women) who were the pirates from the Golden Age of Piracy practiced many of the behaviors that we would expect of high-performance teams today. While condoning neither their objectives nor motives, perhaps it is most instructive to consider that high-performance teamwork is not something we have just invented in the 21st century. Apparently, teamwork has been around for quite some time—not out of fancy or the fad of the month—but out of necessity for accomplishing complex tasks.

Note: It is interesting that no one knows who Captain Charles Johnson actually was. Most seem to agree that this was a pseudonym, but the author's true identity remains a mystery. Some have argued that the true author was Daniel Defoe, more famous for his novel *Robinson Crusoe*.

"Elizabeth Era," http://www.elizabethan-era.org.uk/pirate-code-conduct.htm.

He that would be a leader must be a bridge.

Welsh proverb

The Center for Creative Leadership's research with teams indicated that successful and unsuccessful teams could be differentiated on the basis of eight key characteristics, the first six of which are concerned primarily with task accomplishment.[40] First, effective teams had a *clear mission* and *high performance standards*. Everyone on the team knew what the team was trying to achieve and how well he or she had to perform to achieve the team's mission. Second, leaders of successful teams often *took stock* of their equipment, training facilities and opportunities, and outside resources available to help the team. Leaders of effective teams spent a considerable amount of time *assessing the technical skills* of the team members. After taking stock of available resources and skills, good leaders would work to *secure resources and equipment* necessary for team effectiveness. Moreover, leaders of effective teams would spend a considerable amount of time *planning* and *organizing* to make optimal use of available resources, to select new members with needed technical skills, or to improve needed technical skills of existing members.

The last two characteristics of effective teams were concerned with the group maintenance or interpersonal aspects of teams. Hallam and Campbell's[41] research indicated that *high levels of communication* were often associated with effective teams. These authors believed this level of communication helped team members to stay focused on the mission and to take better advantage of the skills, knowledge, and resources available to the team. High levels of communication also helped to *minimize interpersonal conflicts* on the team, which often drained energy needed for team success and effectiveness. The characteristics of effective teams identified in this research provide leadership practitioners with a number of ideas about how they may be able to increase the effectiveness of their work units or teams.

Continuing research on teams suggest that one of the biggest differences both between groups and teams—as well as an important difference between average teams and high-performing teams—is the level of trust within and among the team members. This same research has found that trust building, which is probably one of the most critical aspect of high-performance teams, requires significant knowledge of each of the other individuals within the team. This knowledge comes from regular face-to-face interaction. The authors consulting work with high-performance teams has produced the same results. We have come to believe that what moves a "team" from individual or group work to high-performance teamwork is the development of trust.

A different avenue to group and team effectiveness has been to use a normative approach. One example of this technique is described in *Groups That Work (and Those That Don't)*.[42] Ginnett[43, 44] has developed an expanded model focusing specifically on team leadership, which we will examine in more detail later in this chapter. For now, our concern is with one of the three major leadership functions in Ginnett's model that focuses on team design. The model suggests four components of design of the team itself that help the team get off to a good start, whatever its task. This is important because it is not uncommon to find that a team's failure can be traced to its being set up inappropriately from the beginning. If a team is to work effectively, the following four variables need to be in place:

1. *Task:* Does the team know what its task is? Is the task reasonably unambiguous and consistent with the mission of the team? Does the team have a meaningful piece of work, sufficient autonomy to perform it, and access to knowledge of its results?

2. *Boundaries:* Is the collective membership of the team appropriate for the task to be performed? Are there too few or too many members? Do the members collectively have sufficient knowledge and skills to perform the work? In addition to task skills, does the team have sufficient maturity and interpersonal skills to be able to work together and resolve conflicts? Is there an appropriate amount of diversity on the team? That is, are members different enough that they have varied perspectives and experiences, and yet similar enough to be able to communicate and relate to one another?

3. *Norms:* Does the team share an appropriate set of norms for working as a team? Norms can be acquired by the team in three ways: (*a*) They can be imported from the organization existing outside the team, (*b*) they can be instituted and reinforced by the leader or leaders of the team, or (*c*) they can be developed by the team itself as the situation demands. If the team is to have a strategy that works over time, it must ensure that conflicting norms do not confuse team members. It also needs to regularly scan and review prevailing norms to ensure that they support overall objectives.

4. *Authority:* Has the leader established a climate where her authority can be used in a flexible rather than a rigid manner? Has she, at one end of the authority continuum, established sufficient competence to allow the group to comply when conditions demand (such as in emergencies)? Has she also established a climate such that any member of the team feels empowered to provide expert assistance when appropriate? Do team members feel comfortable in questioning the leader on decisions where there are no clear right answers? In short, have conditions been created where authority can shift to appropriately match the demands of the situation?

Many of these team design components may be imported from preexisting conditions in the organization within which the team is forming, from the industry in which the organization operates, or even from the environment in which the industry exists. To help team leaders consider these various levels, Hackman and Ginnett[45, 46] developed the concept of **organizational shells** (see **Figure 12.1**). Notice that the four critical factors for team design (task, boundary, norms, and authority) are necessary for the group to work effectively. In some cases, all the information about one of these critical factors may be input from the industry or organizational shell level. Here the leader need do little else but affirm that condition. In other cases, there may be too little (or even inappropriate) input from the organizational level to allow the team to work effectively. Here the leader needs to modify the factors for team design. Ideally this is done during the formation process—the final shell before the team actually begins work.

These ideas may require a new way of thinking about the relationship between a leader and followers. In many organizational settings, leaders are assigned. Sometimes, however, the people who create conditions for improved group effectiveness are not the designated leaders at all; they may emerge from the ranks of followers. This model has been used to differentiate between effective and ineffective "self-managing work groups"—teams where the followers and leaders were the same people. Moreover, because the model is prescriptive, it suggests what ineffective work groups can do to be successful. That same purpose underlies the following model as well.

> *The leaders who work most effectively, it seems to me, never say "I." And that's not because they have trained themselves not to say "I." They don't think "I." They think "we"; they think "team." They understand their job to be to make the team function. They accept responsibility and don't sidestep it, but "we" gets the credit. . . . This is what creates trust, what enables you to get the task done.*

> **Peter F. Drucker, management consultant**

Team Leadership Model

Because we have emphasized that leadership is a group or team function and have suggested that one measure of leadership effectiveness may be whether the team achieves its objectives, it is reasonable to examine a model specifically designed to help teams perform more effectively: the **Team Leadership Model (TLM)**[47, 48, 49] (shortened from earlier versions that called it the Team Effectiveness Leadership Model). Another way to think of this model is as a mechanism to first identify what a team needs to be effective, and then to point the leader either toward the roadblocks that are hindering the team or toward ways to make the team even more effective than it already is. This approach is similar to McGrath's[50] description of leadership, which suggested that the leader's main job is to determine the team's needs and then take care of them. This approach also

FIGURE 12.1   Organizational Shells

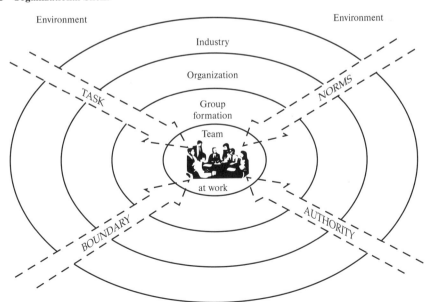

will require us to think about leadership not as a function of the leader and his or her characteristics but as a function of the team. As the title of the model suggests, team effectiveness is the underlying driver.

We have mentioned this model of group or team effectiveness briefly before, but now we will explore it in greater detail. The original model for examining the "engine of a group" was developed by Richard Hackman and has been the basis for much research on groups and teams over the last 30 years.[51] The model presented here includes major modifications by Ginnett and is an example of a leadership model that has been developed primarily using field research. While there have been controlled experimental studies validating portions of the model,[52] the principal development and validation have been completed using actual high-performance teams operating in their own situational contexts. Examples of the teams studied in this process include commercial and military air crews in actual line flying operations, surgical teams in operating suites, executive teams, product development and manufacturing teams, combat teams, fire department teams, and teams preparing the space shuttle for launch. A complete illustration of the model will be shown later. Because of its complexity, it is easier to understand by starting with a few simpler illustrations.

At the most basic level, this model (see **Figure 12.2**) resembles a systems theory approach with inputs at the base (individual, team, and organizational factors), processes or throughputs in the center (what the team does to convert inputs to outputs and what we can tell about the team by observing team members at work), and outputs at the top (how well the team did in accomplishing its objectives, ideally a high-performance team). It is often helpful to think of these components as parts of a metaphorical iceberg. While almost everyone can see the outputs of the team (the portion of the iceberg above the waterline), and some can see the processes, most of the inputs are in the organizational background (or underwater, in the iceberg metaphor). But anyone who has seen an iceberg recognizes that most of its mass is the part that is underwater—and this part supports the part that is visible. So it is with the leadership work in teams. Much of the leadership work is done in the background, and many of the components may be developed before the team is constituted. As we will see, the leader's job is to create the conditions for the team to be effective, and much of that work is done at the input level.

As helpful as the iceberg is as a metaphor, an iceberg is unwieldy and a little messy in a classroom. Therefore, the TLM will be presented from here on as a four-sided pyramid or, for those more geometrically gifted, a square pyramid. We will examine each of the major systems theory stages (input, process, output) as they apply to the TLM. However, we will proceed through the model in reverse order—looking at outputs first, then the process stage, and then inputs.

Outputs

What do we mean by outputs? Quite simply, **outputs** (see **Figure 12.3**) are the results of the team's work. For example, a football team scores 24 points. A production team produces 24 valves in a day. A tank crew hits 24 targets on an artillery range. Such raw data, however, are insufficient for assessing team effectiveness.

How do we know if a team's output is good? How do we know if a team is effective? Even though it was possible for the three teams just mentioned to measure some aspect of their work, these measurements are not helpful in determining their effectiveness, either in an absolute sense or in a relative sense. For comparison and research purposes, it is desirable to have some measures of team effectiveness that can be applied across teams and tasks. Hackman[53] argued that a group is effective if (1) the team's productive output (goods, services, decisions) meets the standards of quantity, quality, and timeliness of the people who use it; (2) the group process that occurs while the group is performing its task enhances the ability of the members to work as members of a team (either the one they were on or any new teams they may be assigned to in the future); and (3) the group experience enhances the growth and personal well-being of the individuals who compose the team.

Process

It should be obvious why leaders should be concerned with the outputs listed in the preceding section. After all, if a team does not "produce" (output), it cannot be considered effective. But what is process? And why should a leader care about it? There are several reasons why a leader might want to pay attention to the team's process—how the team goes about its work. Some teams may have such a limited number of products that the leader can ill afford to wait until the product is delivered to assess its acceptability to the client. For example, a team whose task is to build one (and only one) satellite to be launched into orbit will have no second chances. There may be no opportunity to correct any problem once the satellite is launched (or, as was the case with the flawed Hubble Space Telescope, correction can be made only at great expense). Therefore, it may be desirable for the leader of such a team to assess the team's work while it is working rather than after the satellite is launched. Other kinds of teams have such high standards for routine work that there simply are not enough critical indicators in the end product to determine effectiveness from outcome measures. As an example of this situation, a team operating a nuclear power plant is surrounded by so many technical backup systems that it may be difficult to determine team effectiveness by looking at "safe operation" as a measurement criterion. But we have evidence that not all teams in nuclear power plants operate equally well (Chernobyl and Three Mile Island are two examples). There is evidence that poor teamwork was a contribut-

FIGURE 12.2   An Iceberg Metaphor for Systems Theory Applied to Teams

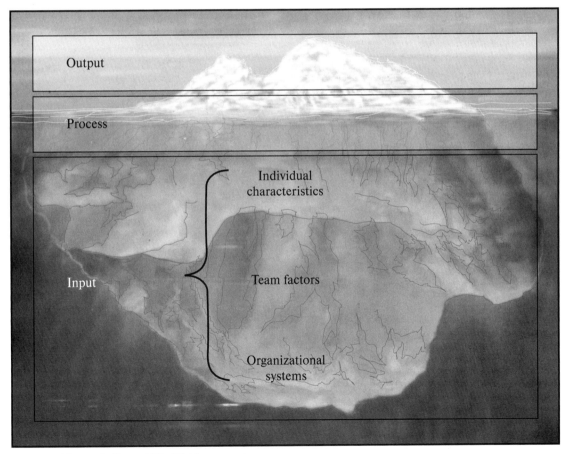

ing cause in the 2010 BP *Deepwater Horizon* accident in the Gulf of Mexico. It would seem helpful to be able to assess real teams "in process" rather than learn about team problems only after disastrous outcomes. Even leaders of noncritical teams might like to be able to routinely monitor their teams for evidence of effective or ineffective processes. So how teams go about their work can provide useful information to the leader.

Because process assessment is so important, let us focus for a moment on the block containing the four process measures of effectiveness in **Figure 12.4**. These four **process measures** of effectiveness provide criteria by which we can examine how teams work. If a team is to perform effectively, it must (1) work hard enough, (2) have sufficient knowledge and skills within the team to perform the task, (3) have an appropriate strategy to accomplish its work (or ways to approach the task at hand), and (4) have constructive and positive group dynamics among its members. The phrase *group dynamics* refers to interactions among team members, including aspects such as how they communicate with others, express feelings toward each other, and deal with conflict with each other, to name but a few characteristics. Assessing and improving group process is no trivial matter, as has been documented extensively in a comprehensive view of group process and its assessment by Wheelan.[54]

FIGURE 12.3   Basic TLM Outputs: Outcomes of High-Performance Teams

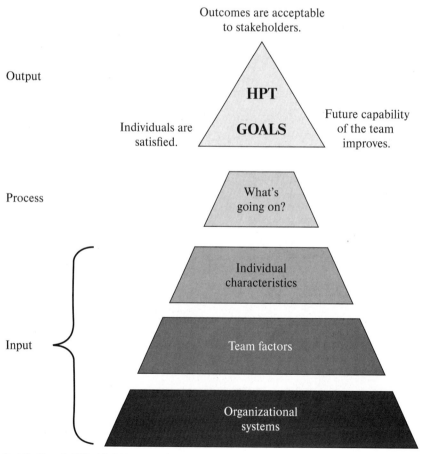

What should the leader do if she discovers a problem with one of these four process measures? Paradoxically, the answer is not to focus her attention on that process per se. While the four process measures are fairly good diagnostic measures for a team's ultimate effectiveness, they are unfortunately not particularly good leverage points for fixing the problem. An analogy from medicine would be a doctor who diagnoses the symptoms of an infection (a fever) but who then treats the symptoms rather than attacking the true underlying cause (a nail in the patient's foot). Similarly at the team level, rather than trying to correct a lack of effort being applied to the task at hand (perhaps a motivation problem), the team leader would be better advised to discover the underlying problem and fix that than to assume that a motivational speech to the team will do the job. This is not to imply that teams cannot benefit from process help. It merely suggests that the leader should ensure that there are no design problems (at the input level) that should be fixed first.

> *Individual commitment to a group effort—that is what makes a team work, a company work, a society work, a civilization work.*
>
> **Vince Lombardi, NFL Hall of Fame football coach**

Inputs

In a manufacturing plant, **inputs** are the raw materials that are processed into products for sale. Similarly in team situations, inputs are what is available for teams as they go about their work. However, an important difference between an industrial plant and a team is that for a plant, the inputs are physical resources. Often for team design, we are considering psychological factors. Levels of inputs range from the individual level to the environmental level. Some of these inputs provide little opportunity for the leader to have an influence—they are merely givens. Leaders are often put in charge of teams with little or no control over the environment, the industry, or even the organizational conditions. However, the leader can directly influence other inputs to create the conditions for effective teamwork.

FIGURE 12.4   TLM Process Variables: Diagnose the Team Using the Process Variables

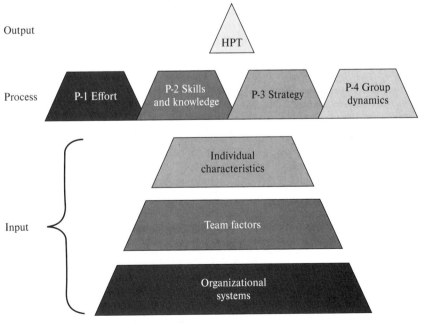

Figure 12.2 shows the multiple levels in the input stage of the model. Note that in addition to the four team variables earlier (task, composition, norms, and authority), there are input factors at the individual and organizational levels as well and that these levels both surround and affect the team design level.

Leadership Prescriptions of the Model

Creation

Following McGrath's[55] view of the leader's role (the leader's main job is to identify and help satisfy team needs), and Ginnett's definition that the leader's job is to create the conditions for the team to be successful, it is possible to use the TLM to identify constructive approaches for the leader to pursue. As described earlier in this chapter, what leaders do depends on where a team is in its development. Ideally we should build a team as we build a house or an automobile. We should start with a concept, create a design, engineer it to do what we want it to do, and then manufacture it to meet those specifications. The TLM provides the same linear flow for design of a team. The somewhat broader version of the TLM model is shown in **Figure 12.5**, and the leader should, as just noted, begin at the base with the dream, proceed through all the design variables, and then pay attention to the development needs of the team. In this way she can implement the three critical functions for team leadership: **dream, design**, and **development**.

Dream

> *If you want to build a ship, don't summon (call) people to buy wood, prepare tools, distribute jobs, and organize the work, (all necessary and important tasks); rather teach people the yearning for the wide, boundless ocean.*
>
> **Antoine de Saint-Exupery, French writer, poet and pioneering aviator**

FIGURE 12.5   Three Functions of TLM Leadership

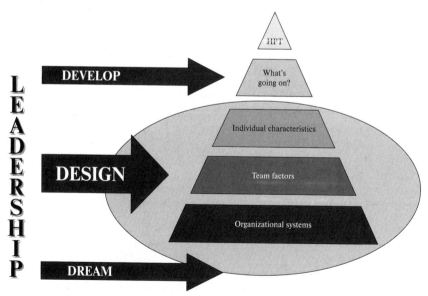

Obviously the team needs to have a clear vision. In their book *The Wisdom of Teams*,[56] Katzenbach and Smith suggested that this may be the most important single step in teamwork. If the team has a challenging and demanding goal, teamwork may be necessary to accomplish the task. In highly effective work teams, the leader ensures that the team has a clear vision of where they are going. The communication of a vision frequently involves metaphorical language so that team members actually "paint their own pictures" of where the team is headed.

Design

If you've ever watched a great coach, you might have marveled at his or her calm demeanor while the game is being played. Perhaps one of the biggest reasons for this composure is that coaches realize most of their work is done by the time the game starts. They have recruited the right players, they have trained and equipped them, they have designed a strategy for their opponents, and they have instilled in the team the appropriate attitudes and values. In short, they have already done the design work. The importance of the design function of leadership cannot be overstated. Whether in the start-up of a team or in the midstream assignment of leaders, designing the team is critical. Unfortunately this is also often the most frequently omitted step in the culture of many traditional organizations.

Managers have long been trained to detect deviations and correct them. But what if the deviations are not detectable until the output stage? At their best, managers often detect deviations at the process stage and attempt to fix them "right where they are seen." Far too often, little time or attention is focused at the organizational, team, and individual input levels. Senior-level leaders may resist changing the organizational systems for a number of reasons, including having a vested interest in maintaining the status quo (whatever it is, it has at least let them rise to their current position). And although individual team leaders may have little control over the organizational context and systems, they can always make an impact in their own team's design at both the individual and team levels.

Development

If the leader finds that the team has a clear sense of direction and vision, and the input variables at the individual, organizational, and team levels are contributing positively to team effectiveness (that is, the design portion of the leader's job has been taken care of), then she can turn her attention to the development level. Development is the ongoing work done with the team at the process level to continue to find ways to improve an already well-designed team. Given our individualistic culture, we have identified many teams in organizations that are apparently well designed and supported at the individual input level, but that have had no training or experience in the concept of teamwork. There are times when effective teamwork is based on very different concepts than effective individual work. For example, for a team to do well, the individuals composing the team must sometimes not maximize their individual effort. Referred to as *subsystem nonoptimization*, this concept is at first not intuitively obvious to many newly assigned team members. Nevertheless, consider the example of a high school football team that has an extremely fast running back and some good (but considerably slower) blocking linemen as members of the offense. Often team members are told they all need to do their absolute best if the team is going to do well. If our running back does his absolute best on a sweep around the end, he will run as fast as he can. By doing so, he will leave his blocking linemen behind. The team is not likely to gain much yardage on such a play, and the linemen and the running back, who have done their individual best, are apt to learn an important experiential lesson about teamwork. Most important, after several such disastrous plays, all the team members may be inclined to demonstrate poor team process (lower effort, poor strategy, poor use of knowledge, and poor group dynamics represented by intrateam strife). If we assume that all the input stage variables are satisfactorily in place, ongoing coaching may now be appropriate. The coach would get better results if he worked out a better coordination plan between the running back and the linemen. In this case, the fast running back needs to slow down (not perform maximally) to give the slower but excellent blockers a chance to do their work. After they have been given a chance to contribute to the play, the running back will have a much better chance to excel individually, and so will the team as a whole.

As straightforward as this seems, few leaders get the opportunity to build a team from the ground up. More often a leader is placed into a team that already exists; has most, if not all, of its members assigned; and is in a preexisting organizational context that might not be team friendly. Although this situation is more difficult, all is not lost. The TLM also provides a method for diagnosis and identification of key **leverage points** for on-the-fly change.

Diagnosis and Leverage Points

Let us assume that you, as a new leader, have been placed in charge of a poorly performing existing team. After a few days of observation, you have discovered that its members are just not working hard. They seem to be uninterested in the task, frequently wandering off or not even showing up for scheduled teamwork. By focusing on the process level of the TLM, we would diagnose this at the process level as a problem of effort. (The core or "engine" of the TLM is shown in **Figure 12.6**, which, as noted earlier, can be thought of as a four-sided pyramid.) Note that preceding the term *effort at the process level* is the label "P-1" and that all variables on this side of the pyramid have a "1" designation as well. Rather than just encouraging the team members to work harder (or threatening them), we should first look at the input level to see if there is some underlying problem. But you do not need to examine all 12 input variables (or, said another way, you do not need to spin the pyramid around to worry about each of the four faces). Because we have already diagnosed a P-1-level process problem, the TLM is designed to focus your attention on the key leverage points to target change for the specific problem identified in diagnosis. Each face of the pyramid shows the input variables at the individual, team, and organizational levels that most impact the process variable that we might diagnose. The factors on the "1" side of the pyramid are referred to as the leverage points for impacting P-1 effort. (See the "1" face of the pyramid in **Figure 12.6**.) The individual level (I-1) suggests that we look at the interests and motivations of the individual team members. These are referred to as **individual factors** in the model. If we have built a team to perform a mechanical assembly task, but the individuals assigned have little or no interest in mechanical work and instead prefer the performing arts, they may have little interest in contributing much effort to the team task. Here, using instruments such as the Campbell Interest and Skills Survey to select personnel may help our team's effort level from an individual perspective.[57]

It may seem tempting to move to the team-level inputs next, but remember that this model emphasizes how teams are influenced by both individual and organizational-level inputs. Therefore, we will look at the **organizational level** next. At the organizational level (O-1), the model suggests that we should examine the reward system that may be impacting the team. If the individuals have no incentive provided by the organization for putting forth effort, they might not be inclined to work hard. Similarly, the reward system may be structured to reward only individual performance. Such a reward structure would be inconsistent with designs for a team task, where interdependence and cooperation among members are often underlying premises. If a professional basketball organization rewards players based only on individual points scored, with no bonuses for team performance (games won or making the playoffs), you can expect little passing, setting picks for teammates, and so on.

Both the individual and organizational-level variables contribute to the team's ability to perform the task. But there can also be problems at the **team design** level. Here (T-1), a poorly designed task, is hypothesized to be unmotivating. If a job is meaningless, lacks sufficient autonomy, or provides no knowledge of results, we would not expect to see followers putting forth much effort.

In review, we just walked through an example of how to use the TLM model. We found key leverage points at various levels of the input stage that affect how the team works (team process). In the example cited, we diagnosed a process-level problem with effort (P-1), so we examined the 1-level variables at the individual, organizational, and team levels as the most likely location for finding input-stage problems. By the way, the concept of leverage point does not imply that only factors at the corresponding "numbers" should be considered. For example, a team's effort might be affected by an oppressive and authoritarian leader. As we will discuss next, this foundation-level variable can have a tremendous impact on the other variables. Indeed, so powerful is this component that we should examine the process measure of group dynamics (P-4) and its corresponding leverage points in more detail. Consider the following two examples:

Surgical team: A surgical team composed of highly experienced members is involved in a surgical procedure that each member has participated in numerous times before. During one portion of the procedure, the surgeon asks for a particular instrument. The scrub nurse looks across the table at the assistant with a questioning gaze and then hands the surgeon the instrument he requested. Recognizing that the instrument he has been handed (and asked for) is not correct for the current procedure, he throws it down on the table and curses at the scrub nurse. All members of the surgical team take a

FIGURE 12.6 Team Leadership Model

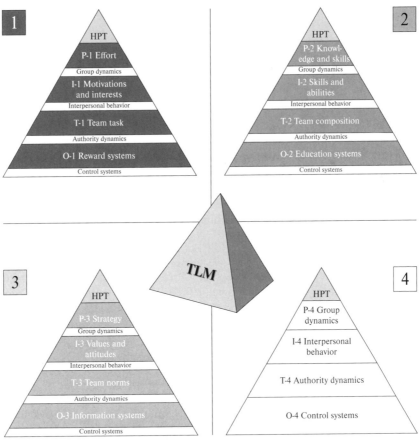

Source: R. C. Ginnett, *The Four Faces of the Pyramid of the Team Leadership Model.* Copyright 2005 Robert C. Ginnett, PhD. All rights reserved.

half-step back from the table and all casual conversation stops. No one offers any further voluntary assistance to the surgeon.

Commercial airline crew: A commercial airline crew is making a routine approach into an uncrowded airport on a clear day. The captain is flying and has declared a visual approach. His final approach to the runway is not good, which greatly complicates the plane's landing, and the landing is poor. After taxiing to the gate, the captain and his entire crew debrief (discuss) the poor approach, and the team members talk about what they could do individually and collectively to help the captain avoid or improve a poor approach in the future. The captain thanks the members for their help and encourages them to consider how they could implement their suggestions in other situations.

Obviously the group dynamics are very different in these two cases. In the first example, the surgeon's behavior, coupled with his status, created a condition inappropriate for effective teamwork. The airline captain in the second example, even though not performing the task well, created a team environment where the team was much more likely to perform well in the future. In both of these cases, we would have observed unusual (one negative and one positive) group dynamics while the team was at work. These are examples of the group dynamics at the P-4 level.

Again returning to the model for determining points of leverage, we would check the I-4 variable at the individual level to determine if the team members involved had adequate interpersonal skills to interact appropriately. At the organizational level, the O-4 variable would suggest we check organizational components to determine if any organizational control systems inhibit or overly structure the way in which the team can make decisions or control its own fate. Such factors may include organizational design or organizational structure limitations (such as functional hierarchies or "silos"), or it may be a rigid computerized control system that specifies every minute detail of the tasks not only for the team as a whole but for all the individuals composing the team. These excessive controls at the organizational level can inhibit effective teamwork. Finally, at the team design level, the T-4 variable would have us examine authority dynamics created between the leader and the followers. Authority dynamics describe the various ways the team members, including the leader, relate and respond to authority. It is at the team level that the followers have opportunities to relate directly with the team's authority figure, the team leader. The intricacies of how these various authority dynamics can play themselves out in a team's life are more complex than is warranted for this chapter; suffice it to say that authority relationships range from autocratic to laissez-faire. (For a more detailed explanation of this concept, see Ginnett.)[58] But even without further description, it should be no surprise that the varied group dynamics observed in the previous two examples were leveraged by the leaders' different uses of authority.

It would be simple if leaders could identify and specify in advance the ideal type of authority for themselves and their teams, and then work toward that objective. However, teams seldom can operate effectively under one fixed type of authority over time. The leader might prefer to use his or her favorite style, and the followers might also have an inherent preference for one type of authority or another; but if the team is to be effective, the authority dynamics they are operating with should complement the demands of the situation. Situations change over time, and so should the authority dynamics of the team. This idea is similar to a point made earlier in this book—that effective leaders tend to use all five sources of leader power.

In research on the behavior of leaders in forming their teams, Ginnett[59] found that highly effective leaders used a variety of authority dynamics in the first few minutes of a team's life. At one point in the first meeting of the team, the leader would behave directively, which enabled him to establish his competence and hence his legitimate authority. At another time, the same leader would actively seek participation from each member of the team. By modeling a range of authority behaviors in the early stages of team life, effective leaders laid the groundwork for continuing expectations of shifting authority as the situational demands changed.

Concluding Thoughts about the Team Leadership Model

Not all components of the TLM have been discussed here because of its complexity. For example, we have not discussed **material resources**. Even if a team is well designed, has superior organizational systems supporting its work, and has access to superior-quality ongoing development, without adequate physical resources it is not likely to do well on the output level. Also note that background shells (discussed earlier in this chapter) representing the industry and the environment have *not* been included in this simplified depiction of the TLM. Although the team leader may have little opportunity to influence these shells, they will certainly have an impact on the team.

Further, several feedback loops (not shown in the pyramid depictions of the TLM) provide information to various levels of the organization. Usually information is available to the organization as a whole (either formally or informally) about which teams are doing well and which are struggling. Whether leaders have access to this information is largely a function of whether they have created or stifled a safe climate. Feedback at the individual level can influence the perceived efficacy of the individual members of the team,[60, 61] and the overall potency of the team is affected even for tasks that the team has yet to attempt.[62]

> *The secret is to work less as individuals and more as a team. As a coach, I play not my eleven best, but my best eleven.*
>
> **Knute Rockne, famed Notre Dame football coach**

Finally, let us reinforce a limitation noted earlier. For ease of use and guidance, this model has been presented as if it were a machine (for example, if P-2 breaks, check I-2, O-2, and T-2). As with other models of leadership or other human systems, however, nothing is that simple. Obviously other variables affect teams and team effectiveness. There are also complex interactions between the variables described in this model. But we have considerable evidence that the model can be useful for understanding teams,[63] and, in light of the relationship between teams and leadership, we are now using it as an underlying framework in courses to help leaders more effectively lead their teams. While we have more than 20 years of experience using the TLM to help teams and team leaders, it is certainly not the only team model available. The "Rocket Model" will also be discussed in the next chapter.

It has been shown that leaders can influence team effectiveness by (1) ensuring that the team has a clear sense of purpose and performance expectations; (2) designing or redesigning input-stage variables at the individual, organizational, and team design levels; and (3) improving team performance through ongoing coaching at various stages, but particularly while the team is actually performing its task. These midcourse corrections should not only improve the team outcomes but also help to avoid many of the team-generated problems that can cause suboptimal team performance.[64] Whether the leader has the luxury of creation or is thrust into the leadership of an existing team, the TLM has been shown to be a useful tool in guiding leader behavior. It also is handy if you believe that a leader's job is to create the conditions for a team to be effective.

Let us integrate the variables from this model into our leader–follower–situation framework (see **Figure 12.7**). Clearly there are variables of importance in each of the three arenas. However, in this model leader characteristics play a lesser role because the leader's job is to work on what is not being provided for the team so that it can perform its task. The focus thus has shifted from the leader to the followers and to the situation.

Virtual Teams

Just as teams and teamwork have become essential to the accomplishment of work in organizations, so too is an understanding of teams that are not in a single location. With the movement toward the global marketplace and the resultant globalization of organizations, it is appropriate to briefly consider the difficulties and

FIGURE 12.7   Factors from the Team Leadership Model and the Interactional Framework

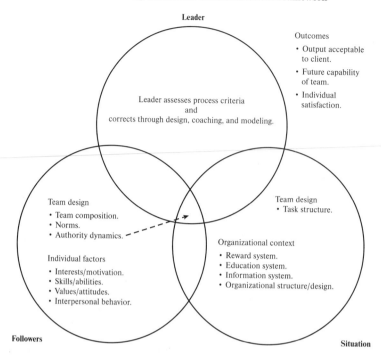

recommended solutions for leading **geographically dispersed teams (GDTs)**. There is considerable discussion about the labeling of such teams,[65] but for simplicity we will call them **virtual teams** here. And one word of caution: during the COVID-19 pandemic, many of us are experiencing *virtual meetings*, but these should not be confused with *virtual teams*. Just because it is virtual does not make it a team event. Meetings and teams are entirely different, whether they are virtual or not.

The marketplace for many firms is now the globe (see **Highlight 12.9**). Western corporations are recognizing that growth and development opportunities are often much greater in Russia and other nations of the former Soviet Union, China, Latin America, and Africa than they are in the markets of North America and Europe. But this realization brings new challenges for leading teams that are not only geographically dispersed but also often culturally different. Fortunately, information and communication technology offers some new opportunities, if not solutions, for these problems.[66] But is the mere opportunity to communicate electronically sufficient to ensure teamwork? Apparently not. (See **Highlight 12.10**.)

What Is the "Global Population" of Your Classroom?

HIGHLIGHT 12.9

The authors of this book attended a training session conducted by a major corporation intended for its newly appointed executives. One session

was devoted to demonstrating the need for a global perspective in today's environment. To illustrate the key point, the instructor divided the participants into unequal groups representing the geographic distribution of the world's population and had each group stand up in turn. As each group stood, she told them the proportion of the global population they represented. The proportions she used are provided here.

Australia and New Zealand	2%
North America	5%
Former Soviet Union	5%
Latin America	7%
Western/Eastern Europe	10%
Africa	12%
Asia	56%

You might try this in your classroom—it makes the point dramatically.

Leading Virtual Teams: 10 Principles

HIGHLIGHT 12.10

Terence Brake is the Director of Learning and Innovation for TMA World and specializes in globalization. He suggests the following guidance for leaders of virtual teams:

Virtual when used in relation to teamwork is an unfortunate term. It implies there is almost teamwork, but not quite. *Virtual* has associations with *nearly, close to,* and *bordering on.* As one wit said, "If you want virtual results, create a virtual team." Alternatively, it is a fortunate term if taken to imply that greater efforts are needed to achieve real teamwork in virtual teams. What principles can help you do this?

1. *Be proactive.* We often talk of virtual teams (VTs) as if they were all of a kind, but each one has its unique challenges. Some have a high level of cultural diversity. Others are more homogeneous. Some use one primary technology for collaboration, while others use a diverse mix. Some are short-lived, targeted on solving an immediate problem. Others are longer-term and strategic. Some cross time zones, and others none. By understanding the most likely challenges to occur, you can take proactive measures and increase team confidence. Confidence is a building block of virtual team performance.

2. *Focus on relationships before tasks.* Early on, team communications should have a significant "getting to know you" component. They should also demonstrate enthusiasm and optimism. Members need to feel valued for who they are, not just what they do. They need to feel engaged and connected. Trust is usually built early on virtual teams, or not at all. Some observers talk of the "virtual paradox"—virtual teams being highly dependent on trust, but not operating under conditions supportive of trust building. Trust is often built on perceived similarities,

but distance makes this process difficult. Chances for misunderstanding are also increased. Goodwill and engagement will solve most problems. Isolation and alienation create problems. Connect, and then collaborate.

3. *Seek clarity and focus early on.* Invest up-front time in clarifying the team's purpose and roles and responsibilities. There is enough uncertainty when working at a distance; it doesn't need to be added to by ambiguity and confusion. Clear purpose and accountabilities support cohesion. Translate purpose and overall accountabilities into specific objectives and tasks so that everyone knows what is expected, by whom, and by when. Virtual teams are highly susceptible to "focus drift" and fragmentation, so keep reminding the team of purpose, objectives, and so on.

4. *Create a sense of order and predictability.* In a world wanting us to embrace chaos, "order" and "predictability" might appear unfashionable. But they are critical to the success of virtual teams. Uncertainty creates anxiety, fear, and withdrawal. The result is a demotivated and unproductive team. Use common team tools, templates, and processes; have predetermined times for communicating together; check in with team members regularly without trying to micromanage; be accessible and an anchor point for the team. Shared expectations are psychological threads connecting separate minds.

5. *Be a cool-headed, objective problem solver.* Problems on virtual teams can appear larger than they actually

are; people feeling isolated can lose perspective. Small issues, quickly resolved when working face-to-face, often fester and spread paranoia and distrust. You should establish yourself as someone who is totally fair; you don't play favorites, and you don't overburden some at the expense of others. You also need to be pragmatic. When there is a problem, you keep calm, you engage the team in finding practical solutions, and you communicate often. Panic is a virus that breeds exceptionally well in silent, isolated spaces.

6. *Develop shared operating agreements.* To reduce threats of uncertainty and ambiguity, common methods and processes—operating agreements—need to be established quickly. These agreements provide the team with shared mental models for working together. Typically, operating agreements need to be created in areas such as planning, decision-making, communicating, and coordination. A team charter acts as a common reference point and can help orient new team members. Take time during team "meetings" to review how well the operating agreements are working.

7. *Give team members personal attention.* Just as you would on a face-to-face team, allocate time to "meet" with individuals. Find out how he or she is feeling about things. Give each person an opportunity to share personal successes, challenges, needs, and wants. It can be difficult to do this in team "meetings" where the emphasis is on shared tasks and problem solving. Empathize with that person who is on the road,

working at home, or in a remote office. Listening, caring, sympathizing, recognizing—they cost little, but benefit everyone.

8. *Respect the challenges of the virtual environment.* I once lived on a boat, and I soon learned to respect the power of nature—the winds, tides, swells, rain, ice, and drought. I had to pay very close attention to these elements or they could sink me, swamp me, or ground me. There is always the temptation to carry over habits from one environment (land, face-to-face teamwork) into another (river, working at a distance). We must recognize the differences and adapt. Listening, empathizing, communicating, coordinating, engaging, energizing, and enabling all need to be enhanced.

9. *Recognize the limits of available technologies.* Unless you really have to, don't try and do everything via a virtual team. Sometimes teams are working on projects so complex that no matter how much video- or teleconferencing time they have, it will not be enough. Sometimes it pays dividends to bring people together for a few days. Never assume that because you have been designated a "virtual" team, you must always work in that mode. Focus on cost/benefit over the life of the project. Technology is a tool, and all tools are good for some tasks and not others.

10. *Stay people-focused.* Distance can make faceless abstractions of us all. Never lose sight of the fact that your virtual team members are people, with all that that entails—needs for belonging, meaning, accomplishment, and recognition; feelings of frustration, anger, excitement, boredom, and alienation; political pressures and personal pressures. Think about those features of your physical workplace that enable teams to work well together, such as formal meeting rooms, informal spaces, and the coffee area, and see what you can do to humanize your virtual workplace—team pictures and bios, bulletin boards, chat areas.

Applying these virtual team leadership principles will help you avoid *almost* and *close to* teamwork. Virtual teamwork is only going to increase, so many of us need to reskill ourselves for leading at a distance.

Researchers at the Conference Board[67] have reported that five major areas must change for global teams to work. The five listed were senior management leadership; innovative use of communication technology; adoption of an organization design that enhances global operations; the prevalence of trust among team members; and the ability to capture the strengths of diverse cultures, languages, and people.

Even our editorial decision to call this section "virtual teams" might be an erroneous oversimplification. Hoch and Kozlowski[68] have noted that it is probably incorrect to categorize teams as either virtual or face-to-face. They believe "that this simple characterization glosses over a variety of nuanced dimensions that underlie a range of differences in the degree of *virtuality*." For an example of what might be considered a "micro geographically dispersed team," see **Figure 12.8**. This drawing illustrates the geographic distribution of a team performing da Vinci robotic-assisted surgery. Although the vast majority of the da Vinci surgical team resembles a more traditional surgical team (for example, anesthesiologist, physician assistant, scrub, and circulators), there are two notable differences. First is the addition of a robot that is actually touching the patient. Second, and most important for this discussion of geographic dispersion, note that the surgeon is the most geographically dispersed member of the entire team. He or she sits at a console 10 to 12 feet away from the patient and the rest of the team. Interestingly, the same guidelines that apply to effectively leading a globally dispersed team apply in the case as well. For example, technology (in this case, high-resolution monitors located in several places in the surgical suite) allow every member of the team to watch the surgery in better detail than was ever possible in traditional surgery. But this advance in technology is capitalized only if the leader makes it clear that anyone on the team may, and should, speak up if they see something important.

Armstrong and Cole[69] did in-depth studies of virtual teams and have reported three conclusions that should be considered by leaders of these teams. First, the distance between members of a virtual team is multidimensional. "Distance" includes not just geographic distance but also organizational distance (different group or department cultures), temporal distance (different time zones), and differences in national culture. Second, the impact of such distances on the performance of a distributed work group is not directly proportional to objective measures of distance. In fact, Armstrong and Cole suggested that a new measure of distance between group members that reflects the degree of group cohesion and identity—a measure of psychological distance between members—would predict group performance better than geographic distance. Finally, differences in the effects of distance on work groups are due at least partially to two intervening variables: (1) integrating practices *within* a virtual team, and (2) integrating practices *between* a virtual team and its larger host organization.

With increasing numbers of virtual teams, we are beginning to see evidence that these teams, when designed and constructed properly, might be even more effective than in-place teams. In a study of successful "far-flung teams,"[70] three rules emerged that enhanced the teams' performance. First, the leaders needed to select for diversity but then exploit that diversity for the team's benefit. Second, technology needed to simulate reality.

FIGURE 12.8   Robotic Surgery: A Micro Geographically Dispersed Team

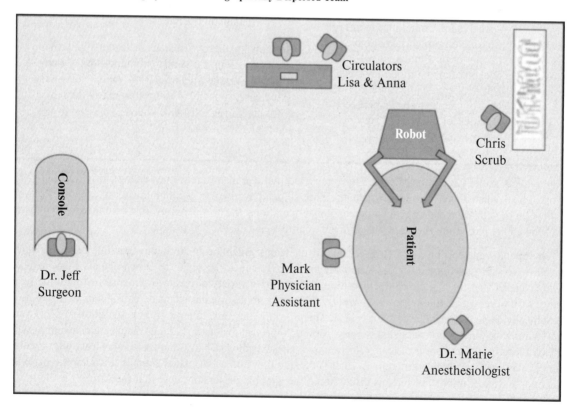

For example, e-mail was a poor way for a team to communicate because it either focused on one-on-one (as opposed to team-level) communications or drowned people in paperwork if everyone was copied. Surprisingly, the researchers didn't think much of videoconferencing. What seemed to work best was a specifically designed "virtual work space." This included not only a team Web space with a home page prominently displaying the team's mission but also pages for people, purpose, and a meeting center, among other features. Other teams have found wikis essential to keeping global teams up to date.[71] Third, leaders must be particularly diligent to hold virtual teams together. Face-to-face teams can confront forces that splinter the groups, but such forces can be accentuated in virtual teams. Leaders of successful virtual teams overcommunicated, pushed for the adoption of a common language, and merged work practices. One particularly successful tactic was to have team members work in ad hoc pairs for a week or two so that they would get to know each other better. This also seemed to discourage the formation of cliques. And, as described for the TLM earlier, the leaders spent a great deal of time working in the organizational background to ensure that team members were allotted sufficient time to work on the virtual project.

The implementation and use of virtual teams may well be outstripping the research on virtual teams. One of the biggest reasons for this may well be the shear difficulty of observing virtual or geographically dispersed teams. As researchers, we know that one of the characteristics that makes a team easier to observe is geographical proximity. In Ginnett's research on aircrews, once the cabin door was shut with the team inside, nobody left until we landed. Simultaneously observing a geographically dispersed team on five different continents does not offer researchers that same luxury. Nonetheless, research on virtual teams does continue. For example, as we have noted before, trust is a critical element of high-performance teams. Hacker and colleagues have reported similar findings for virtual teams.[72]

And just as virtual teams provide challenges to researchers, so too do they increase the difficulty of communicating and building trust for the team members and leaders. As a result, virtual teams appear to operate best with smaller numbers. Not unexpectedly, this is due to greater levels of difficulty in establishing the high levels of trust required for high performance in large teams.[73]

As a closing note on research in virtual teams, we have discovered that there may be useful research with application for leaders in virtual teams but that research may be spread among a wide variety of topics and even more diverse journals. For example, we have cited research previously in this chapter under the heading of "distributed leadership." But there can be similar findings in different journals under the heading of "shared leadership."[74] Similarly, topics possibly of use to leaders of virtual teams may be spread among such diverse fields as "distributed cognition" and "group mind." Nonetheless, it is safe to say that in a global marketplace, virtual teams are probably here to stay.

Finally, a number of frameworks under development can help leaders work with virtual teams, and these frameworks may provide specific useful factors. However, in our admittedly limited exposure to virtual teams in a pure research sense, a number of our clients have reported that the TLM has been quite useful in considering process problems and in suggesting appropriate leverage points for intervention. One thing is clear: Virtual teams require more leadership, not less.

On the Horizon

Two emerging themes from the literature are worth noting as we move forward in leading groups and teams. In December 2012, the Society of Industrial and Organizational Psychology devoted half its journal to **collective leadership** approaches. In their lead article,[75] the authors suggest an overview of five approaches to collective leadership: team leadership, network leadership, shared leadership, complexity leadership, and collective leadership. The authors of this article then present varying amounts of science and applications for the differing labels they have provided. Team leadership appears to be the most studied and applied whereas other categories are, at this time, purely theoretical with virtually no empirical research. Although the label *collective leadership* is relatively new, the concept is not. In the first edition of this textbook, published in 1990, we noted that leadership is fundamentally a group phenomenon, just as we have in this chapter. Whether or not this "collective leadership label catches on remains to be seen."

Another new concept seems more appealing. Labeled **clusters**, these are intact teams that are self-managed. Aron provides the following description of the cluster:

> Clusters are a radical alternative to our traditional notion of teams. They are formed outside a company context, but are hired and paid by companies as a unit, as a permanent part of the company. They manage, govern and develop themselves; define their own working practices and tools; and share out remuneration. Technology trends and tools like "the cloud," and collaboration suites, are evolving to make this more and more workable. The business or agency treats the cluster as an atomic unit of resource and it hires, fires and positions the cluster as a unit. Likewise, each cluster appears as such a unit in the business's organization chart. Clusters plug together like Lego bricks to achieve the business's goals.[76]

Source: D. Aron, "The Future of Talent is in Clusters," Harvard Business Review Blog Network, February 1, 2013.

This approach sounds very similar to the way the U.S. government employs the Navy SEALs. The SEALs are an intact team that trains together and manages themselves as a unit. When called upon, they are "hired" as a unit and perform as a unit. That business is considering such a concept makes sense because traditional methods of forming and developing a team within an organization, only to disband that team when the project is completed, inevitably results in value loss.

Summary

The group perspective showed that followers' behaviors can be the result of factors somewhat independent of the individual characteristics of followers. Group factors that can affect followers' behaviors include group size, stages of group development, roles, norms, and cohesion. Leadership practitioners should use these concepts to better understand followers' behaviors. Leaders should also use a team perspective for understanding follower behavior and group performance. Leadership practitioners need to bear in mind how a team's sense of identity, common goals or tasks, level of task interdependence, and differentiated roles affect functional and dysfunctional follower behavior. Additionally, because effective teams have several readily identifiable characteristics, leadership practitioners may want to use the suggestions provided by Hackman,[77] Ginnett,[78] or Hallam and Campbell[79] to develop more effective teams.

The Team Leadership Model posited that team effectiveness can best be understood in terms of inputs, processes, and outcomes. The input level consists of the individual characteristics of the followers; the design of the team itself; and various organizational systems that create the context in which the teams will operate. The process level concerns how teams behave while going about their tasks, and the output level concerns whether customers and clients are satisfied with the team's product, whether the team improves and develops as a performing unit, and whether followers are satisfied to be members of the team. By identifying certain process problems in teams, leaders can use the model to diagnose appropriate leverage points for action at the individual, team design, or organizational levels, or for ongoing development at the process level. Leaders concerned with teamwork in organizational settings have found this framework useful in helping them conceptualize factors affecting team effectiveness and identifying targets for change. Last, we mentioned the emerging concepts of collective leadership and clusters.

Key Terms

group perspective	relationship role	process measures
group	dysfunctional roles	inputs
cliques	role conflict	dream
span of control	intrasender role conflict	design
additive task	intersender role conflict	development
process loss	interrole conflict	leverage point
social loafing	person–role conflict	individual factors
social facilitation	role ambiguity	organizational level
forming	norms	team design
storming	group cohesion	material resources
norming	overbounding	geographically dispersed teams (GDTs)
performing	groupthink	virtual teams
project teams	ollieism	collective leadership
punctuated equilibrium	organizational shells	clusters
group roles	Team Leadership Model (TLM)	
task role	outputs	

Questions

1. How do the tenets of Ginnett's Team Leadership Model compare with the components of team performance described earlier?

2. Not all group norms are positive or constructive from the leader's perspective. If a group holds counterproductive norms, what should the leader do?

3. On the basis of what you know about global cultures, would people from the United States, Japan, or Chile be more comfortable with a group- or team-based approach to work?

Activity

NASA Exercise—Lost on the Moon

Your spaceship has crash-landed on the dark side of the moon and you are scheduled to rendezvous with the mother ship, which is 200 miles away on the lighted side of the moon. The crash has ruined the ship and destroyed all the equipment except for the 15 items listed here. Your crew's survival depends on reaching the mother ship, so you must choose the most critical items available to take on the 200-mile trip. Your task is to rank-order the 15 items in the order of their importance for your survival. Place a "1" beside the most important item, a "2" beside the second most important item, and so on, until you have ranked all 15 items.

_____ Box of matches

_____ Food concentrate

_____ 50 feet of nylon rope

_____ Parachute silk

_____ Solar-powered portable heating unit

_____ Two .45 caliber pistols

_____ One case of dehydrated milk

_____ Two 100-pound tanks of oxygen

_____ Stellar map

_____ Self-inflating life raft

_____ Magnetic compass

_____ Five gallons of water

_____ Signal flares

_____ First-aid kit with hypodermic syringes

_____ Solar-powered FM transmitter/receiver

Your instructor has the "NASA Expert" answers and the instructions for completing the exercise.

Minicase

Integrating Teams at Hernandez & Associates

Marco Hernandez is president of Hernandez & Associates Inc., a full-service advertising agency with clients across North America. The company provides a variety of marketing services to support its diverse group of clients. Whether called on to generate a strategic plan, create interactive websites, or put together a full-blown media campaign, the team at Hernandez & Associates prides itself on creative solutions to its clients' marketing challenges.

The firm was founded in 1990 with an emphasis in the real estate industry. It quickly expanded its client base to include health care, as well as food and consumer products. Like many small firms, the company grew quickly in the "high-flying" 1990s, but its administrative costs to obtain and serve businesses also skyrocketed. And, as with many businesses, the agency's business was greatly affected by the terrorist attacks of September 11, 2001, and the economic downturn that followed. Clients' shrinking budgets forced them to scale back their business with Hernandez & Associates, and staff cutbacks meant that clients needed more marketing support services as opposed to full-scale campaigns.

Hernandez & Associates now faced a challenge—to adapt its business to focus on what the clients were asking for. Specifically, clients, with their reduced staffs, were looking for help responding to their customers' requests and looking for ways to make the most of their limited marketing budgets. Its small, cohesive staff of 20 employees needed to make some fast changes.

As president of Hernandez & Associates, Marco Hernandez knew his team was up for the challenge. He had worked hard to create an environment to support a successful team—he recruited people who had solid agency experience, and he consistently communicated the firm's mission to his team. He made sure the team had all the resources it needed to succeed and continually took stock of these resources. He had built his team as he built his business and knew the group would respond to his leadership. But where to start? Getting the team to understand that growth depended on a shift in how it served its clients was not difficult—each of the employees of the small firm had enough contact with the clients that they knew client needs were changing. But making significant changes to the status quo at Hernandez & Associates would be difficult. Group roles had to change—creative folks had to think about how to increase a client's phone inquiries and website visits; account people needed a better understanding of the client's desire for more agency leadership. And everyone needed a better sense of the costs involved. The company as a whole required a more integrated approach to serving clients if they hoped to survive. Marco needed a plan.

1. Like many leaders, Marco has a team in place and does not have the luxury of building a new team to adapt to the changing business environment his firm now faces. Use the TLM to help Marco diagnose the problems faced by the firm and identify leverage points for change.

   a. Consider the major functions of the TLM—input, process, and output. Where do most of the firm's challenges fall?

   b. What are the team's goals for outputs?

2. Identify potential resources for Marco and his team in implementing a strategy to change the way they do business at Hernandez & Associates.

Endnotes

1. I. McCammon, "Evidence of Heuristic Traps in Recreational Avalanche Accidents," paper presented at the International Snow Science Workshop, Penticton, British Columbia, September 30–October 4, 2002.

2. R. C. Ginnett, "Effectiveness Begins Early: The Leadership Role in the Formation of Intra-Organizational Task Groups," unpublished manuscript, 1992.

3. G. S. Gibbard, J. J. Hartman, and D. Mann, *Analysis of Groups: Contribution to the Theory, Research, and Practice* (San Francisco: Jossey-Bass, 1974).

4. Gibbard et al., *Analysis of Groups.*

5. M. Shaw, *Group Dynamics: The Psychology of Small Group Dynamics*, 3rd ed. (New York: McGraw-Hill, 1981).

6. J. R. Hackman, *Groups That Work (and Those That Don't)* (San Francisco: Jossey-Bass, 1990).

7. G. A. Yukl, *Leadership in Organizations*, 1st ed. (Englewood Cliffs, NJ: Prentice Hall, 1981).

8. I. J. Badin, "Some Moderator Influences on Relationships between Consideration, Initiating Structure, and Organizational Criteria," *Journal of Applied Psychology* 59 (1974), pp. 380–82.

9. B. E. Goodstadt and D. Kipnis, "Situational Influences on the Use of Power," *Journal of Applied Psychology* 54 (1970), pp. 201–07.

10. D. Kipnis, S. M. Schmidt, and I. Wilkinson, "Intraorganizational Influence Tactics: Explorations in Getting One's Way," *Journal of Applied Psychology* 65 (1980), pp. 440–52.

11. J. G. Udell, "An Empirical Test of Hypotheses Relating to Span of Control," *Administrative Science Quarterly* 12 (1967), pp. 420–39.

12. B. M. Bass, *Leadership, Psychology, and Organizational Behavior* (New York: Harper, 1960).

13. B. P. Indik, "Organizational Size and Member Participation: Some Empirical Tests of Alternative Explanations," *Human Relations* 18 (1965), pp. 339–50.

14. I. D. Steiner, *Group Process and Productivity* (New York: Academic Press, 1972).

15. Steiner, *Group Process and Productivity.*

16. B. Latané, K. Williams, and S. Harkins, "Many Hands Make Light the Work: The Causes and Consequences of Social Loafing," *Journal of Personality and Social Psychology* 37, no. 6 (1979), 822–832.

17. D. B. Porter, M. Bird, and A. Wunder, "Competition, Cooperation, Satisfaction, and the Performance of Complex Tasks among Air Force Cadets," *Current Psychology Research and Reviews* 9, no. 4 (1991), pp. 347–54.

18. R. Zajonc, "Social Facilitation," *Science* 149 (1965), pp. 269–74.

19. B. W. Tuckman, "Developmental Sequence in Small Groups," *Psychological Bulletin* 63 (1965), pp. 384–99.

20. Tuckman, "Developmental Sequence in Small Groups."

21. Tuckman, "Developmental Sequence in Small Groups."

22. J. R. Terborg, C. H. Castore, and J. A. DeNinno, "A Longitudinal Field Investigation of the Impact of Group Composition on Group Performance and Cohesion," paper presented at the annual meeting of the Midwestern Psychological Association, Chicago, 1975.

23. C. J. G. Gersick, "Time and Transition in Work Teams: Toward a New Model of Group Development," *Academy of Management Journal* 31 (1988), pp. 9–41.

24. R. C. Ginnett, "Airline Cockpit Crew," in *Groups That Work (and Those That Don't)*, ed. J. Richard Hackman (San Francisco: Jossey-Bass, 1990).

25. M. Jamal, "Job Stress and Job Performance Controversy: An Empirical Assessment," *Organizational Behavior and Human Performance* 33 (1984), pp. 1–21.

26. R. J. House, R. S. Schuler, and E. Levanoni, "Role Conflict and Ambiguity Scales: Reality or Artifact?" *Journal of Applied Psychology* 68 (1983), pp. 334–37.

27. J. R. Rizzo, R. J. House, and S. I. Lirtzman, "Role Conflict and Ambiguity in Complex Organizations," *Administrative Science Quarterly* 15 (1970), pp. 150–63.

28. C. D. Fisher, and R. Gitleson, "A Meta-analysis of the Correlates of Role Conflict and Ambiguity," *Journal of Applied Psychology* 68 (1983), pp. 320–33.

29. J. R. Hackman, "Group Influences on Individuals," in *Handbook of Industrial and Organizational Psychology*, ed. M. D. Dunnette (Chicago: Rand McNally, 1976).

30. D. C. Feldman, "The Development and Enforcement of Group Norms," *Academy of Management Review*, January 1984, pp. 47–53.

31. J. R. Hackman, *Leading Teams—Setting the Stage for Great Performances* (Boston, MA: Harvard Business School Press, 2002).

32. C. P. Alderfer, "Group and Intergroup Relations," in *Improving Life at Work*, eds. J. R. Hackman and J. L. Suttle (Santa Monica, CA: Goodyear, 1977).

33. R. C. Ginnett, "The Formation Process of Airline Flight Crews," *Proceedings of the Fourth International Symposium on Aviation Psychology* (Columbus, OH, 1987).

34. I. L. Janis, *Groupthink*, 2nd ed. (Boston: Houghton Mifflin, 1982).

35. Janis, *Groupthink*, 2nd ed.

36. Janis, *Groupthink*, 2nd ed.

37. J. E. Shephard, "Thomas Becket, Ollie North, and You," *Military Review* 71, no. 5 (1991), pp. 20–33.

38. S. P. Robbins, *Organizational Behavior: Concepts, Controversies, and Applications* (Englewood Cliffs, NJ: Prentice Hall, 1986).

39. D. Pickering, *Pirates* (London: Harper Collins Publishers, 2006).

40. G. L. Hallam and D. P. Campbell, "Selecting Team Members? Start with a Theory of Team Effectiveness," paper presented at the Seventh Annual Meeting of the Society of Industrial/ Organizational Psychologists, Montreal, Canada, May 1992.

41. Hallam and Campbell, "Selecting Team Members? Start with a Theory of Team Effectiveness."

42. Hackman, *Groups That Work (and Those That Don't)*.

43. R. C. Ginnett, "Crews as Groups: Their Formation and Their Leadership," in *Crew Resource Management*, ed. B. Kanki, R. Hemreich, and J. Anca (San Diego, CA: Academic Press, 2010).

44. R. C. Ginnett, "Team Effectiveness Leadership Model: Identifying Leverage Points for Change," *Proceedings of the 1996 National Leadership Institute Conference* (College Park, MD: National Leadership Institute, 1996).

45. J. R. Hackman, "Group Level Issues in the Design and Training of Cockpit Crews," in *Proceedings of the NASA/MAC Workshop on Cockpit Resource Management*, eds. H. H. Orlady and H. C. Foushee (Moffett Field, CA: NASA Ames Research Center, 1986).

46. Ginnett, "Crews as Groups."

47. Ginnett, "Crews as Groups."

48. Ginnett, "Team Effectiveness Leadership Model."

49. R. C. Ginnett, "Team Effectiveness Leadership Model: Design and Diagnosis," *12th Annual International Conference on Work Teams* (Dallas, TX: 2001).

50. J. E. McGrath, *Leadership Behavior: Some Requirements for Leadership Training* (Washington, DC: Office of Career Development, U.S. Civil Service Commission, 1964).

51. Hackman, *Groups That Work (and Those That Don't)*.

52. K. W. Smith, E. Salas, and M. T. Brannick, "Leadership Style as a Predictor of Teamwork Behavior: Setting the Stage by Managing Team Climate," paper presented at the Ninth Annual Conference of the Society for Industrial and Organizational Psychology, Nashville, TN, 1994.

53. Hackman, *Groups That Work (and Those That Don't)*.

54. S. A. Wheelan, *Group Processes* (Needham Heights, MA: Allyn & Bacon, 1994).

55. McGrath, *Leadership Behavior*.

56. J. R. Katzenbach and B. K. Smith, *The Wisdom of Teams* (Boston: Harper Business, 1994).

57. D. P. Campbell, S. Hyne, and D. L. Nilsen, *Campbell Interests and Skill Survey Manual* (Minneapolis, MN: National Computer Systems, 1992).

58. Ginnett, "Crews as Groups."

59. Ginnett, "Crews as Groups."

60. A. Bandura, "Self-Efficacy: Toward a Unifying Theory of Behavioral Change," *Psychological Review* 84 (1977), pp. 191–215.

61. D. H. Lindsley, D. J. Brass, and J. B. Thomas, "Efficacy-Performance Spirals: A Multilevel Perspective," *Academy of Management Review* 20 (1995), pp. 645–78.

62. R. A. Guzzo, P. R. Yost, R. J. Campbell, and G. P. Shea, "Potency in Teams: Articulating a Construct," *British Journal of Social Psychology* 32 (1993), pp. 87–106.

63. Hackman, *Groups That Work (and Those That Don't)*.

64. I. D. Steiner, *Group Process and Productivity* (New York: Academic Press, 1972).

65. M. Kossler and S. Prestridge, "Geographically Dispersed Teams," *Issues and Observations* 16, nos. 2–3 (1996), pp. 9–11.

66. J. Lipnack and J. Stamps, *Virtual Teams: Reaching across Space, Time and Organizations with Technology* (New York: Wiley, 1997).

67. Conference Board, "Global Management Teams: A Perspective," *HR Executive Review* 4 (1996).

68. J. Hoch and S. Kozlowski, "Leading Virtual Teams: Hierarchical Leadership, Structural Supports and Shared Team Leadership," *Journal of Applied Psychology* 99, no. 3 (2014) pp. 390–403.

69. D. J. Armstrong and P. Cole, "Managing Distances and Differences in Geographically Distributed Work Groups," in *Distributed Work*, ed. P. Hinds and S. Kiesler, pp. 167–89 (Cambridge, MA: MIT Press, 2002).

70. A. Majchrzak, A Malhotra, J. Stamps, and J. Lipnack, "Can Absence Make a Team Grow Stronger?" *Harvard Business Review*, May 2004, pp. 131–37.

71. P. Dvorak, "How Teams Can Work Well Together from Far Apart," *The Wall Street Journal*, September 17, 2007, p. B-4.

72. J. V. Hacker, M. Johnson, C. Saunders, and A. L. Thayer, "Trust in Virtual Teams: A Multidisciplinary Review and Integration," *Australasian Journal of Information Systems* 23 (January 2019).

73. M. Hakanen and A. Soudunsaari, "Building Trust in High-Performing Teams," *Technology Innovation Management Review* 2, no. 6 (2012).

74. K. Fransen, E. Delvaux, B. Mesquita, and S. Van Puyenbroeck, "The Emergence of Shared Leadership in Newly Formed Teams with an Initial Structure of Vertical Leadership: A Longitudinal Analysis," *The Journal of Applied Behavioral Science* 54, no. 2 (2018), pp. 140–70.

75. F. J. Yammarino, E. Salas, A. Serban, K. Shirreffs, and M. Shuffler, "Collective Leadership Approaches: Putting the 'We' in Leadership Science and Practice," *Industrial and Organizational Psychology Perspectives on Science and Practice* 5, no. 4 (2012), pp. 382–402.

76. D. Aron, "The Future of Talent is in Clusters," *Harvard Business Review Blog Network*, February 1, 2013.

77. Hackman, *Groups That Work (and Those That Don't)*.

78. Ginnett, "Effectiveness Begins Early."

79. Hallam and Campbell, "Selecting Team Members? Start with a Theory of Team Effectiveness."

CHAPTER 13
Skills for Developing Others

Introduction

The skills chapter in **Part 2** addressed what might be considered relatively basic leadership skills such as listening and communication. In this chapter we will cover a number of additional leadership skills that are somewhat more advanced and that pertain particularly to the leader's relationship with followers. The skills addressed in this section include the following:

- Setting Goals
- Providing Constructive Feedback
- Team Building for Work Teams
- Building High-Performance Teams—The Rocket Model
- Delegating
- Coaching

Setting Goals

The Roman philosopher Seneca wrote, "When a man does not know what harbor he is making for, no wind is the right wind." Setting goals and developing plans of action to attain them are important for individuals and for groups. For example, the purpose or goal is often the predominant norm in any group. Once group goals are agreed on, they induce member compliance, act as a criterion for evaluating the leadership potential of group members, and become the criteria for evaluating group performance.[1]

Perhaps the most important step in accomplishing a personal or group goal is stating it right in the first place. The reason many people become frustrated with the outcomes of their New Year's resolutions is that their resolutions are so vague or unrealistic that they are unlikely to lead to demonstrable results. It is possible to keep New Year's resolutions, but we must set them intelligently. In a more general sense, some ways of writing goal statements increase the likelihood that we will successfully achieve the desired goals. Goals should be specific and observable, attainable and challenging, based on top-to-bottom commitment, and designed to provide feedback to personnel about their progress toward them. The following is a more detailed discussion of each of these points.

Goals Should Be Specific and Observable

As described in Chapter 10, research provides strong support for the idea that specific goals lead to higher levels of effort and performance than general goals. General goals do not work as well because they often do not provide enough information regarding which particular behaviors are to be changed or when a clear end state has been attained. This may be easiest to see with a personal example.

Assume that a student is not satisfied with her academic performance and wants to do something about it. She might set a general goal such as "I will do my best next year" or "I will do better in school next year." At first such a goal may seem fine; after all, as long as she is motivated to do well, what more would be needed? However, on further thought you can see that "do my best" or "do better" are so ambiguous as to be unhelpful in directing her behavior and ultimately assessing her success. General goals have relatively little impact on energizing and directing immediate behavior, and they make it difficult to assess, in the end, whether someone has attained them. A better goal statement for this student would be to attain a B average or to get no deficient grades this semester. Specific goals like these make it easier to chart progress. A more business-oriented example might be improving productivity at work. Specific goal statements in this case might include a 20 percent increase in the number of products produced by the work unit over the next three months or a 40 percent decrease in the number of products returned by quality control next year.

The idea of having specific goals is closely related to that of having observable goals. It should be clear to everyone when a goal has or has not been reached. It is easy to say your goal is to go on a diet, but a much better goal is "to lose 10 pounds by March." Similarly, it is easy to say a team should do better next season, but a better goal is to say the team will win more than half of next season's games. Note that specific, observable goals are also time limited. Without time limits for accomplishing goals, there would be little urgency associated with them. Neither would there be a finite point at which it is clear whether a person or group has accomplished the goals. For example, it is better to set a goal of improving the next quarter's sales figures than just improving sales.

Goals Should Be Attainable but Challenging

Some people seem to treat goals as a sort of loyalty oath they must pass, as if it would be a break with their ideals or reflect insufficient motivation if any but the loftiest goals were set. Yet to be useful, goals must be realistic. The struggling high school student who sets a goal of getting into Harvard may be unrealistic, but it may be realistic to set a goal of getting into the local state university. A civil rights activist may wish to eliminate prejudice completely, but a more attainable goal might be to eliminate racial discrimination in the local housing project over the next five years. A track team is not likely to win every race, but it may be realistic to aim to win the league championship.

The corollary to the preceding point is that goals should also be challenging. If goals merely needed to be attainable, then there would be nothing wrong with setting goals so easy that accomplishing them would be virtually guaranteed. As we have seen previously, setting easy goals does not result in high levels of performance; higher levels of performance come about when goals stretch and inspire people toward doing more than they thought they could. Goals need to be challenging but attainable to get the best out of ourselves.

Goals Require Commitment

There is nothing magical about having goals; having goals per se does not guarantee success. Unless supported by real human commitment, goal statements are mere words. Organizational goals are most likely to be achieved if there is commitment to them at both the top and the bottom of the organization. Top leadership needs to make clear that it is willing to put its money where its mouth is. When top leadership sets goals, it should provide the resources workers need to achieve the goals and then should reward those who do. Subordinates often become committed to goals simply by seeing the sincere and enthusiastic commitment of top leadership to them. Another way to build subordinate acceptance and commitment to goals is to have subordinates participate in setting the goals. Research on the effects of goal setting demonstrates that worker acceptance and satisfaction tend to increase when workers are allowed to participate in setting goals.[2, 3]

On the other hand, research is less conclusive about whether participation in goal setting actually increases performance or productivity. These mixed findings about participation and performance may be due to various qualities of the group and the leader. In terms of the group, groupthink may cause highly cohesive groups to commit to goals that are unrealistic and unachievable. Group members may not have realistically considered equipment or resource constraints or have the technical skills needed to successfully accomplish the goal. In addition, group members may not have any special enthusiasm for accomplishing a goal if the leader is perceived to have little expert power or is unsupportive, curt, or inept.[4, 5, 6] However, if leaders are perceived as competent and supportive, followers may have as much goal commitment as they would if they had participated in setting the goal. Thus participation in goal setting often leads to higher levels of commitment and performance if the leader is perceived to be incompetent, but it will not necessarily lead to greater commitment and performance than are achieved when a competent leader assigns a goal. Again, these findings lend credence to the importance of technical competence in leadership effectiveness.

Goals Require Feedback

One of the most effective ways to improve any kind of performance is to provide feedback about how closely a person's behavior matches some criterion, and research shows that performance is much higher when goals are accompanied by feedback than when either goals or feedback are used alone. Goals that are specific, observable, and time limited are conducive to ongoing assessment and performance-based feedback, and leaders and followers should strive to provide and seek regular feedback. Moreover, people should seek feedback from a variety of sources or provide feedback using a variety of criteria. Often, different sources and criteria can paint diverse pictures of goal progress, and people can get a better idea of the true level of their progress by examining the information provided and integrating it across the various sources and criteria.

Providing Constructive Feedback

Giving constructive feedback involves sharing information or perceptions with another about the nature, quality, or impact of that person's behavior. It can range from giving feedback pertaining specifically to a person's work (performance feedback) to impressions of how aspects of that person's interpersonal behavior may be pervasively affecting relationships with others. Our use of the term *feedback* here is somewhat different from its use in the systems view of communication (**Figure 8.2** in **Chapter 8**). In the communication model, the feedback loop begins with actively checking the receiver's interpretation of your own message and then initiating or modifying subsequent communications as necessary. A simple example of that meaning of feedback might be noting another person's quizzical expression when you try to explain a complicated point and realize you'd better say it differently. The skill of giving constructive feedback, however, inherently involves actively giving feedback to someone else.

Getting helpful feedback is essential to a subordinate's performance and development. Without feedback, a subordinate will not be able to tell whether she's doing a good job or whether her abrasiveness is turning people off and hurting her chances for promotion. And it's not just subordinates who need constructive feedback to learn and grow. Peers may seek feedback from peers, and leaders may seek feedback from subordinates. Besides fostering growth, effective supervisory feedback also plays a major role in building morale.

In many ways, the development of good feedback skills is an outgrowth of developing good communication, listening, and assertiveness skills. Giving good feedback depends on being clear about the purpose of the feedback and on choosing an appropriate context and medium for giving it. Giving good feedback also depends on sending the proper nonverbal signals and trying to detect emotional signals from whoever may be receiving the feedback. In addition, giving good feedback depends on being somewhat assertive in providing it, even when it may be critical of a person's performance or behavior. Although feedback skills are related to communication, listening, and assertiveness skills, they are not the same thing. Someone may have good communication, listening, and assertiveness skills but poor feedback skills. Perhaps this distinction can be made clearer by examining the knowledge, behavior, and evaluative components of feedback skills.

The knowledge component of feedback concerns knowing when, where, and what feedback is to be given. For example, knowing when, where, and how to give positive feedback may be very different from knowing when, where, and how to give negative feedback. The behavioral component of feedback concerns how feedback actually is delivered (as contrasted with knowing how it should be delivered). Good feedback is specific, descriptive, direct, and helpful; poor feedback is often too watered down to be useful to the recipient. Finally, one way to evaluate feedback is to examine whether recipients actually modify their behavior accordingly after receiving it. Of course this should not be the only way to evaluate feedback skills. Even when feedback is accurate in content and delivered skillfully, a recipient may fail to acknowledge it or do anything about it.

Although most leaders probably believe that feedback is an important skill, research has shown that leaders also believe they give more feedback than their subordinates think they do.[7] There are many reasons why leaders may be reluctant to give feedback. Leaders may be reluctant to give positive feedback because of time pressures, doubts about the efficacy of feedback, or lack of feedback skills.[8] Sometimes supervisors hesitate to use positive feedback because they believe subordinates may see it as politically manipulative, ingratiating, or insincere.[9] Leaders also may give positive feedback infrequently if they rarely leave their desks, if their personal standards are too high, or if they believe good performance is expected and should not be recognized at all.[10] Other reasons may explain the failure to give negative feedback,[11] such as fear of disrupting leader–follower relations[12] or fear of employee retaliation.[13]

Although there are a number of reasons why leaders are hesitant to provide both positive and negative feedback, leaders need to keep in mind that followers, committee members, or team members will perform at a higher level if they are given accurate and frequent feedback. It is difficult to imagine how work group or team performance could improve without feedback. Positive feedback is necessary to tell followers they should keep doing what they are doing well, and negative feedback is needed to give followers or team members ideas for how to change their behavior to improve their performance. Although accurate and frequent feedback is necessary, there are several other aspects of feedback that everyone can work on to improve their feedback skills, including making sure it's helpful, being direct, being specific, being descriptive, being timely and being flexible. **Highlight 13.1** gives examples of each of these different aspects of feedback, and the following is a more complete description of ways leaders can improve their feedback skills.

Tips for Improving Feedback Skills

HIGHLIGHT 13.1

BE HELPFUL

Do not: "I got better scores when I was going through this program than you just did."

Do: "This seems to be a difficult area for you. What can I do to help you master it better?"

BE DIRECT

Do not: "It's important that we all speak loud enough to be heard in meetings."

Do: "I had a difficult time hearing you in the meeting because you were speaking in such a soft voice."

BE SPECIFIC

Do not: "Since you came to work for us, your work has been good."

Do: "I really like the initiative and resourcefulness you showed in solving our scheduling problem."

BE DESCRIPTIVE

Do not: "I'm getting tired of your rudeness and disinterest when others are talking."

Do: "You weren't looking at anyone else when they were talking, which gave the impression you were bored. Is that how you were feeling?"

BE TIMELY

Do not: "Joe, I think I need to tell you about an impression you made on me in the staff meeting last month."

Do: "Joe, do you have a minute? I was confused by something you said in the meeting this morning."

BE FLEXIBLE

Do not (while a person is crying, or while he is turning red with clenched teeth in apparent anger): "There's another thing I want to tell you about your presentation yesterday . . . "

Do: When a person's rising defenses or emotionality gets in the way of really listening, deal with those feelings first, or wait until later to finish your feedback. Do not continue giving information.

Make It Helpful

The purpose of feedback is to provide others with information they can use to change their behavior. Being clear about the intent and purpose is important because giving feedback sometimes can become emotional for both the person giving it and the person receiving it. If the person giving feedback is in an emotional state (such as angry), she may say things that make her feel better temporarily but that only alienate the receiver. To be helpful, individuals need to be clear and unemotional when giving feedback, and they should give feedback only about behaviors actually under the other person's control.

People can improve the impact of the feedback they give when it is addressed to a specific individual. A common mistake in giving feedback is addressing it to "people at large" rather than to a specific individual. In this case, the individuals for whom the feedback was intended may not believe the feedback pertains to them. To maximize the impact of the feedback, people should try to provide it to specific individuals, not large groups.

Be Specific

Feedback is most helpful when it identifies particular behaviors that are positive or negative. One of the best illustrations of the value of specific feedback is in compositions or term papers written for school. If someone turned in a draft of a paper to the instructor for constructive comments and the instructor's comments about the paper were "Good start, but needs work in several areas," the writer would not know what to change or correct. More helpful feedback from the instructor would be specific comments like "This paragraph does not logically follow the preceding one" or "Cite an example here." The same is true of feedback in work situations. The more specifically leaders can point out which behaviors to change, the more clearly they let the other person know what to do.

Be Descriptive

In giving feedback, it is good to stick to the facts as much as possible, being sure to distinguish them from inferences or attributions. A behavior description reports actions that others can see, about which there can be little question or disagreement. Such descriptions must be distinguished from inferences about someone else's feelings, attitudes, character, motives, or traits. It is a behavior description, for example, to say that Sally stood up and walked out of a meeting while someone else was talking. It is an inference, though, to say she walked out because she was angry. However, sometimes it is helpful to describe both the behavior itself and the corresponding impressions when giving feedback. This is particularly true if the feedback giver believes that the other person does not realize how the behavior negatively affects others' impressions.

Another reason to make feedback descriptive is to distinguish it from evaluation. When a person gives feedback based mostly on inferences, he often conveys evaluations of the behavior as well. For example, saying "You were too shy" has a more negative connotation than saying "You had little to say." In the former case, the person's behavior was evaluated unfavorably and by apparently subjective criteria. Yet evaluation is often an intrinsic part of a supervisor's responsibilities, and good performance feedback may necessitate conveying evaluative information to a subordinate. In such cases, leaders are better off providing evaluative feedback when clear criteria for performance have been established. Filley and Pace have described criteria that can be used to provide evaluative feedback; some are listed in **Highlight 13.2**.[14]

Types of Criteria to Use for Evaluative Feedback

HIGHLIGHT 13.2

1. Compare behavior with others' measured performance. With this method, the subordinate's behavior is compared with that of her peers or coworkers; this is also called norm-referenced appraisal. For example, a subordinate may be told her counseling load is the lightest of all 10 counselors working at the center.

2. Compare behavior with an accepted standard. An example of this method would be a counselor being told her workload was substantially below the standard of

acceptable performance set at 30 cases per week. This is known as criterion-referenced appraisal.

3. Compare behavior with a previously set goal. With this method, the subordinate must participate in setting and agree with a goal. This is a form of criterion-referenced appraisal, with the subordinate's "ownership" and acceptance of the goal

before the fact critical to the feedback procedure.

4. Compare behavior with past performance.

Source: Adapted from A. C. Filley and L. A. Pace, "Making Judgments Descriptive," in *The 1976 Annual Handbook for Group Facilitators*, eds. J. E. Jones and J. W. Pfeiffer (La Jolla, CA: University Associates Press, 1976), pp. 128–31.

An issue related to impressions and evaluative feedback concerns the distinction between job-related (that is, performance) feedback and more personal or discretionary feedback. Although leaders have a right to expect followers to listen to their performance feedback, that is not necessarily true concerning feedback about other behaviors. Sharing perceptions of a person's behavior could be helpful to that person even when the behavior doesn't pertain specifically to his formal responsibilities; in such cases, however, it is the follower's choice whether to hear it or, if he hears it, whether to act on it.

Be Timely

Feedback usually is most effective when it is given soon after the behavior occurs. The context and relevant details of recent events or behaviors are more readily available to everyone involved, thus facilitating more descriptive and helpful feedback.

Be Flexible

Although feedback is best when it is timely, sometimes waiting is preferable to giving feedback at the earliest opportunity. In general, everyone should remember that the primary purpose of feedback is to be helpful. Feedback sessions should be scheduled with that in mind. For example, a subordinate's schedule may preclude conveniently giving him feedback right away, and it may not be appropriate to give him feedback when it will distract him from a more immediate and pressing task. Furthermore, it may not be constructive to give someone else feedback when the person receiving it is in an emotional state (whether about the behavior in question or other matters entirely). Moreover, it is important to be attentive to the other person's emotional responses while giving feedback and to be ready to adjust your own behavior accordingly.

A final important part of being flexible is to give feedback in manageable amounts. In giving feedback, you do not need to cover every single point at one time; doing so would only overload the other person with information. Instead, anyone who needs to give a lot of feedback to someone else may want to spread out the feedback sessions and focus on covering only one or two points in each session.

Give Positive as Well as Negative Feedback

Giving both positive and negative feedback is more helpful than giving only positive or negative feedback alone. Positive feedback tells the other person or the group only what they are doing right, and negative feedback tells the other person or group only what they are doing wrong. Providing both kinds of feedback is best.

Avoid Blame or Embarrassment

Because the purpose of feedback is to give useful information to other people to help them develop, talking to them in a way merely intended (or likely) to demean or make them feel bad is not helpful. Followers tend to be more likely to believe feedback if it comes from leaders who have had the opportunity to observe their behavior and are perceived to be credible, competent, and trustworthy.[15, 16, 17] Bass has pointed out that followers will continue to seek feedback even if their leaders are not competent or trustworthy—though they will not seek it from their leaders.[18] They will seek it from others they trust, such as peers or other superiors.

Team Building for Work Teams

Few activities have become more commonplace in organizations these days than "team-building workshops." One reason for this level of activity is the powerful shift that has occurred in the workplace from a focus primarily on individual work to team-centered work. Unfortunately, however, these activities do not always achieve their objectives. As noted earlier in this text, it doesn't make sense to hold teams responsible for work if nothing else in the organizational environment changes. Team-building interventions, at the team level, may help team members understand why they are having so much difficulty in achieving team objectives, and even suggest coping strategies for an intolerable situation. They are not, however, likely to remove root causes of problems. To better understand the importance of looking at teams this way, let's use an example of this kind of erroneous thinking from a different context.

Team-Building Interventions

Suppose you have decided that the next car you drive must have outstanding ride and handling characteristics. Some cars you test, such as some huge American-made automobiles, have outstanding ride characteristics, but you are not happy with their handling. They sway and "float" in tight slalom courses. Other cars you test have just the opposite characteristics. They are as tight and as stable as you could hope for in turns and stops, but their ride is so hard that your dental work is in jeopardy. But you do find one car that seems to meet your requirements: A Mercedes-Benz provides both a comfortable ride and tremendous road-handling characteristics in high-performance situations. There is, however, one small problem. The Mercedes costs a lot of money up front—more than you are willing to put into this project. So you arrive at an alternative solution. You find a used Yugo, a small car built in Yugoslavia and no longer imported into the United States, largely because of inferior quality. But it is cheap, and after purchasing it, you know you will have lots of money left over to beef up the suspension, steering, and braking systems to provide you with the Mercedes-Benz ride you really want.

Ludicrous! Obviously you are never going to get a Mercedes-Benz ride unless you are willing to put in considerable money and effort *up front* rather than doing little up front and putting all your money into repair work. But that is precisely what many organizations attempt to do with teams. They do not seem willing to create the conditions necessary for teamwork to occur naturally (a point we will discuss in the section "Team Building at the Top" in **Chapter 18**), but when the teams struggle in a hostile environment, as they invariably will, the leaders seem willing to pour tremendous amounts of money into team-building interventions to fix the problem. These types of team-building problems are those we would categorize as "top-down."

An equally vexing problem occurs when organizations are committed to teamwork and are willing to change structures and systems to support it, but are not committed to the "bottom-up" work that is required. This is best illustrated in the rationale for team training shown in **Figure 13.1**. In our work with organizations, we are frequently asked to help teams that are struggling. In **Figure 13.1** we would place these requests at the "TEAM" level, which is the third platform up from the bottom. We believe this type of intervention will work only if the team members have achieved a stable platform from which to work. In this case, that would include the two previous platforms in **Figure 13.1**. If the foundation is not well established, the solely team-based intervention often leads to intrateam competition or apathy and withdrawal.

As a basis for any work at the team level, individual team members must first be comfortable with themselves. They must be able to answer the questions "What do I bring to the team?" and "What do I need from the team?" Not answering these questions breeds inherent fear and mistrust. When these questions have been answered, team members are in a position to begin dealing at the interpersonal level, where they may now comfortably ask, "What do *you* bring to the team and what do *you* need from the team?" Not resolving these issues results in caution in dealing with other members, and interactions at the "polite façade" level rather than at the level of truth and understanding. If the first- and second-level platforms are in place, a true team-building intervention can be useful. (Incidentally, just because team members have not stabilized themselves at levels 1 and 2 does not mean an intervention cannot be conducted. Rather, it means a more extensive intervention will be required than a solely team-based effort.)

What Does a Team-Building Workshop Involve?

Hundreds, if not thousands, of team-building interventions are being conducted today. Many good sources, such as the *Team and Organization Development Sourcebook*, contain team-based activities focused on conflict resolution, problem solving, development of norms, trust building, or goal setting, to name a few.[19] Rather than trying to describe all these suggestions, however, we will describe a few recommendations that we have found useful and then share a few examples of interventions we have used.

FIGURE 13.1   A Rationale for Individual, Interpersonal, Team, and Organizational Training

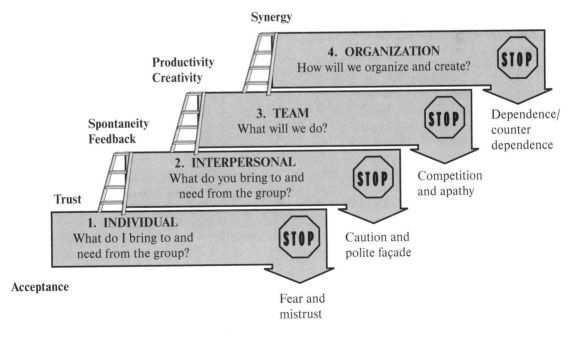

At the Center for Creative Leadership, staff are frequently asked to design custom team interventions for mid- to upper-level teams. Although we enter these design meetings with no agenda of activities, neither do we enter with a completely blank slate. We believe an intervention at the team level must meet three general requirements to be successful, and at least one activity must be included in the intervention pertaining to each of those three requirements.

The first requirement involves awareness raising. As we noted earlier in the text, not all cultures are equally prepared or nurtured in the concepts of teamwork. In fact, many of the lessons we think we have learned about teams are incorrect. So we need to dispel such myths and include a healthy dose of team-based research findings about how teams *really* work as a critical element of a workshop. Second, we need some diagnostic, instrument-based feedback so that team members can have a reasonably valid map of where they and their teammates now are located. Finally, each intervention must include a practice field, to use Senge's term.[20] Practice is necessary for athletic success, and it is necessary in organizations, too. It would be foolish to design a whole new series of plays for a hockey team to implement, talk about them in the locker room, but never actually practice any of them before expecting the team to implement them in a game. Similarly, if you are asking people to change their behaviors in the way they interact to improve teamwork, it is only fair to give them a practice field on which they can test their new behaviors in a reasonably risk-free, protected environment.

This is where experiential exercises can be useful, and here the quality of the team-building facilitator is important. Conducting a pencil-and-paper exercise in the classroom does not require the same facilitator skill set as that required to conduct, say, a team-rappelling exercise off the face of a cliff—few facilitators get those requirements wrong, and we have seldom discovered problems here. Where we have seen a significant breakdown in facilitator skills is in being able to link the exercise to the real world in which the team will be asked to perform. Facilitators must have not only a good sense of real-time team dynamics but also a sense of the business in which the team operates. They must help the participants make the links back to team dynamics that occur on the manufacturing floor or in the boardroom, and this seems to be the skill that distinguishes highly effective facilitators.

Examples of Interventions

Now let us provide a few examples of the range of interventions that can be included in team building. Ginnett conducted an intervention with three interdependent teams from a state youth psychiatric hospital. The teams included members of the administrative services, the professional staff, and the direct care providers. The members of each team were dedicated to their roles in providing high-quality service to the youths under their care, but the three groups experienced difficulty in working with each other. Extensive diagnosis of the groups revealed two underlying problems. First, each group had a different vision of what the hospital was or should be. Second, each group defined themselves as "care givers," thus making it difficult for them to ask others for help because, in their minds, asking for help tended to put them in the role of their patients. We conducted a series of workshops to arrive at a common vision for the hospital, but the second problem required considerably more work. Because the staff members needed to experientially understand that asking for help did not place them in an inherently inferior position, a "wilderness experience" was designed where the entire staff was asked to spend four days together in a primitive wilderness environment with difficult hiking, climbing, and mountaineering requirements. By the end of the experience, everyone had found an occasion to ask someone else for help. Even more important, everyone found that actually asking others for help—something they had previously resisted—moved the overall team much higher in its ability to perform. Considerable time was spent each evening linking the lessons of the day with the work in the hospital.[21]

In one of the more interesting programs we've conducted, a team of senior executives spent a week together at a ranch in Colorado. Each morning the team met for a series of awareness sessions and data feedback sessions. Afternoons were reserved by the chief operating officer for fun and relaxation, with the only requirement being that attendees participate as a team or subteams. As facilitators, we actively participated with the teams and related their team experiences each day to the lessons of the next morning, as well as to challenges facing the team in its normal work. In interventions like this we have learned that team building can be fun, and that the venues for it are almost limitless. Second, we have learned that being able to observe and process team activity in a real-time mode is essential for team-building facilitators. There is no substitute for firsthand observation as a basis for discerning group dynamics and noting the variety of revealing behaviors that emerge in unstructured team activities.

Building High-Performing Teams: The Rocket Model

As stated throughout this text, leadership is not an individual process. Rather, it involves influencing a group to pursue some type of overarching goal. From **Chapter 12** we know that teams vary in a number of important factors, such as group size, norms, development stages, and cohesion. We also know leaders need to take these factors into consideration when creating and leading teams. The Team Leadership Model introduced in **Chapter 12** provides a comprehensive description of team dynamics and what leaders must do if they want to create high-performing teams. What follows is a simpler model of team effectiveness that provides both prescriptive and diagnostic advice for building high-performing teams. The Rocket Model of Team Effectiveness is prescriptive in that it tells leaders what steps to take and when to take them when building new teams. The model can also be used as a diagnostic tool for understanding where existing teams are falling short and what leaders need to do to get them back on track.[22, 23, 24, 25, 26, 27, 28, 29, 30]

The Rocket Model is based on extensive research with thousands of teams in the health care, education, retail, manufacturing, service, software, telecommunications, energy, and financial service industries. The model has been used with executive teams at Red Bull, Groupon, Johnson & Johnson, Buffalo Wild Wings, Williams-Sonoma, Avanade, Toro, Home Depot, Dell, Waste Management, Polaris, Autoliv, and the Strategic Health Authority in the United Kingdom; mid-level management teams at Coca-Cola, Logitech, Symantec, 3M, AT&T, MassMutual, Cummins, Tellabs, Husky Energy, Faurecia, and a number of rural hospitals and school districts; and project teams at Pfizer, Medtronic, and Hewlett-Packard. The model seems to work equally well with different types of teams at different organizational levels in different industries. Leaders particularly like the Rocket Model because of its straightforward and practical approach to team building.

A diagram of the Rocket Model can be found in **Figure 13.2**. As shown, building a team can be analogous to building a rocket. Just as rockets operate in different environments (that is, low altitude, high altitude, or outer space), so must teams clearly define the context in which they operate. The booster stage is critical for getting a rocket off the ground; so, too, are the mission and talent stages critical next steps for a team. Once the mission and talent issues have been addressed, leaders need to work with team members to sort out team norms and buy-in, and so on. Research shows that the teams with the best results are usually those that report a high level of team functioning in all the Rocket Model components. Teams reporting a high level of functioning in only some of these components usually report mediocre results, and those with low functioning in all the components usually achieve few, if any, results. The following is a more in-depth description of the eight components of the Rocket Model.

Context: What Is the Situation?

A critical first step to building high-performing teams is gaining alignment on team context. Most teams either influence or are influenced by competitors, suppliers, customers, government regulators, market conditions, other internal teams, the larger organization, and more. All too often, team members have different assumptions about these constituencies, and as a result they may take well-intended but misguided actions that inadvertently destroy team morale and performance. This is particularly true when teams are made up of diverse members, are geographically dispersed, or experience considerable turnover. One noteworthy aspect of team context is the implicit nature of team member assumptions—team members rarely if ever articulate their assumptions about the situation. That being the case, an important step leaders need to take when building high-performing teams is to identify all the constituencies affecting the team (that is, customers, competitors, and the like) and then ask team members to share their assumptions about those constituencies. This sharing of information about the situation helps ensure everyone is on the same page about the challenges facing the team.

FIGURE 13.2   The Rocket Model

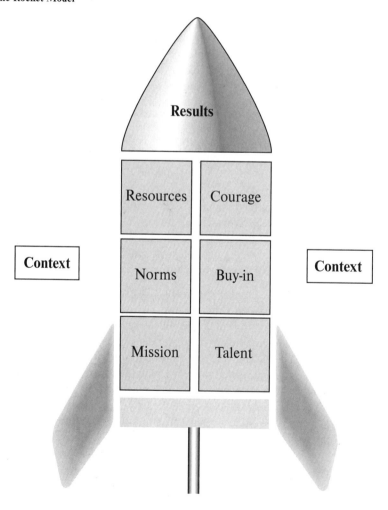

Assume you were a store manager at a new Starbucks coffee shop that was about to open and you wanted to use the Rocket Model to transform your two assistant store managers and 16 baristas into a high-performing team. One of the first things you would do is have everyone identify the constituencies affecting the team. These constituencies might include different customer segments, competing coffee shops, key suppliers, the local business environment, other Starbucks stores, the city health inspector, the district manager (your boss), and the larger Starbucks corporation. You and your staff would then need to agree on a set of assumptions for each constituency—will the other coffee shops lower prices or go out of business over the next year? Will corporate be launching new products or opening new stores in the city? Is the local community thriving or declining? After discussing and agreeing on the assumptions for each constituency, the team would then identify the greatest challenges facing the store over the next year.

Mission: What Are We Trying to Accomplish?

Once the situation has been clearly defined, the next thing a leader must do is to clarify the team's purpose, goals, and strategies. The mission component of the Rocket Model is concerned with setting a common direction for the team. In some cases the leader works closely with team members to sort out these issues; in other cases the leader makes these determinations; and in still other cases the organization may make these decisions. For this component of the model, who makes these decisions is not as important as ensuring that all the team members understand what the team is trying to accomplish and how they contribute to team success.

Several aspects of mission are worth noting. First, leaders need to realize that individual goals drive individual behavior and team goals drive team behavior. Therefore, if leaders want to encourage collaboration, they need to set team goals. Second, a common problem plaguing many teams is that they set vague or ill-defined team goals. Good team goals are specific, measurable, achievable, realistic, time-bound, and benchmarked. Benchmarking is a critical aspect of team goals, as far too many teams set only internal, continuous improvement-type goals (for example, sell X percent more coffee than last month). Continuous improvement goals are helpful, but high-performing teams also set goals that allow them to see how they stack up against the competition (for example, win–loss record or sales rankings against other stores in the area). Third, mission may be the most important component in the Rocket Model as it impacts all the other components. The mission of the team should determine the number and skills of people needed to achieve results (talent), the rules by which the team operates (norms), the equipment and budget needed (resources), and so forth. Because mission plays such a vital role in team building, leaders of underperforming teams often find it worthwhile to clarify the team's goals and benchmarks when striving to improve team performance.

Applying the Rocket Model to the Starbucks scenario, the store manager would work with the team to set goals for the upcoming year. These might include the specific revenue, profitability, cost, customer satisfaction, customer complaint, employee turnover, staff coverage, and health inspection rating goals the store needs to achieve each month or quarter. The team might also set revenue or customer satisfaction goals against the other Starbucks stores in the city, such as being in the top 5 out of 25 stores in customer satisfaction each month. The team leader would then build a team scorecard that included all the goals and tracked actual team performance on a monthly and quarterly basis.

Talent: Who Is on the Bus?

The talent component of the Rocket Model is about answering the six right questions: Does this team have the right number of people, with the right organizational structure, in the right roles, with the right skills, for the right reasons, and do team members get rewarded for effective teamwork? Teams with too many or too few people in ill-defined roles or with team members lacking the skills needed to achieve team goals often will report lower talent scores than teams having the right number of people with the right skills. Clarifying the reporting structure, defining roles and responsibilities, selecting the right kind of people, and continuously developing those skills needed to achieve team goals are the key leadership activities in this component of the Rocket Model. Professional athletic and elite military combat teams are very good at managing talent, as they ensure roles and responsibilities are clear, obsess over hiring decisions, and spend considerably more hours practicing than performing. The vast majority of private- and public-sector teams do just the opposite: They throw a group of available people together and expect them to produce. These latter teams do not think through who needs to be on the team, how they should be organized, spend little if any time developing needed skills, and never practice.

In the Starbucks example, talent would come into play when the store manager determined how many people would be needed to staff the store, defined the roles that need to be played in order to achieve the team goals, moved the two assistant store managers and 16 baristas into their respective roles, and clarified the what and the how for each team member during their shifts. The team leader would also want to provide ongoing training to his staff to make sure they were gaining the knowledge and skills needed to run shifts, make new drinks, serve customers, clean the equipment, open and close the shop, and complete other tasks.

Norms: What Are the Rules?

Once team members are in place and clearly understand the team's situation, goals, and roles, leaders need to address the norms component of the Rocket Model. Norms are the rules that govern how teams make decisions, conduct meetings, get work done, hold team members accountable for results, and share information. Several important aspects of norms are worth noting. First, the decisions the team makes, the way in which it makes decisions, how often and how long the team meets, and so forth should all be driven by the team's goals. Second, norms happen. If the team or team leader is not explicit about setting the rules that govern team behavior, they will simply evolve over time. And when they are not explicitly set, these rules may run counter to the team's goals. For example, one of the authors was working with a software development team that was responsible for delivering several new products over a six-month period. The time frame was aggressive, but one of the team norms that had evolved was that it was okay for team members to show up late to team meetings, if they even bothered to show up. However, the team meetings were important to the success of the team because they were the only time the team could discuss problems and coordinate its software development efforts. Team performance did not improve until a new norm was explicitly set for team meeting participation.

Third, there are many team norms. These norms might include where people sit in meetings, what time team members come in to work, what team members wear, the acronyms and terms they use, and so on. But of the domain of possible norms, those involving decision-making, communication, meetings, accountability, and self-adjustment seem to be the most important to team functioning. High-performing teams are explicit about what decisions the team makes and how it makes those decisions. These teams have also set rules about the confidentiality of team meetings, how and when information gets shared, and how difficult or controversial topics are raised in team meetings. High-performing teams also have explicit rules about behavior in team meetings and team member accountability. Finally, a hallmark of high-performing teams is routinely taking a step back and assessing team dynamics and performance. This is akin to sports teams watching game tapes, and for work teams, this means periodically reviewing what the team is doing well and how they could improve. In our Starbucks example, the store manager would work with the team to decide how often to meet and what to talk about during meetings, who gets to make the call on different store and customer issues, how information gets shared across shifts, how to handle staff tardiness, and other relevant issues.

Buy-In: Is Everyone Committed and Engaged?

Just because team members understand the team's goals, roles, and rules does not necessarily mean they will automatically be committed to them. Many times team members will nod their agreement to the team's goals and rules in team meetings, but then turn around and do something entirely different afterward. This is an example of a team that lacks buy-in. Teams with high levels of buy-in have team members who believe in what the team is trying to accomplish and enthusiastically put forth the effort needed to complete their assigned tasks and make the team successful.

There are three basic ways team leaders can build buy-in. One way to build buy-in is to develop a compelling team vision or purpose. Many times team members want to be part of something bigger than themselves, and serving on a team can be one venue for fulfilling this need. Whether or not team members will perceive the team to have a compelling vision will depend to a large extent on the degree to which the team's purpose and goals match up to their personal values. Charismatic or transformational leaders (**Chapter 16**) are particularly adept at creating visions aligned with followers' personal values. A second way to create buy-in is for the team leader to have a high level of credibility. Leaders with high levels of relevant expertise who share trusting relationships with team members often enjoy high levels of buy-in. Team members often question the judgment of team leaders who lack relevant expertise, and they question the agendas of team leaders they do not trust. And because people prefer to make choices as opposed to being told what to do, a third way to enhance team buy-in is to involve team members in the goal, role, and rule-setting process.

In our Starbucks example the store manager could articulate a compelling vision for the store; work on building strong relationships with all the employees; and involve the team in defining the context, setting team goals, clarifying role expectations, and the like. The store manager could determine whether buy-in was waxing or waning by observing whether team members were exhibiting the behaviors needed to achieve team goals and could provide coaching, remove obstacles, clarify work expectations, or implement different motivational interventions for those less committed to team success.

Resources: Do We Have Enough?

The resources component of the Rocket Model concerns the decision-making latitude and resources the team has to accomplish its goals. Teams reporting high levels of power have considerable decision-making authority and all the equipment, data, time, facilities, and funds needed to accomplish team goals. Teams with low resources often lack the necessary decision-making authority or budgets needed to get things done. One of the authors was working with a group of public school administrators who felt they had little power to make decisions affecting the school district. The district had had three superintendents over the previous four years, and as a result the school board had stepped in to take over the day-to-day operation of the schools.

To improve the resources component of the Rocket Model, team leaders will first need to determine if they have all the decision-making latitude and resources they need to accomplish team goals. If they do not have enough resources, they will need to lobby higher-ups to get what they need, devise ways to get team goals accomplished with limited resources, or revise team goals in light of the resource shortfalls. Most teams do not believe they have all the time, resources, or decision-making latitude they need to succeed, but more often than not they have enough of these things to successfully accomplish their goals. Good teams figure out ways to make do with what they have or devise ways to get what they need; dysfunctional teams spend their time and energy complaining about a perceived lack of resources rather than figuring out ways to achieve team goals. Along these lines, many poorly performing teams often make false assumptions or erect barriers that do not really exist. Team leaders need to challenge these assumptions and break barriers if they are to help the team succeed.

Because Starbucks coffee shops have a consistent look and feel, the store manager may not have a lot of latitude in determining the store location and layout, paint scheme, furniture, coffee-making equipment, supplies, refrigerators, cash registers, computers, software, uniforms, and so forth needed to achieve team goals. Any shortfalls of equipment or supplies could negatively impact team performance, however, so he or she would also need to secure new supplies, such as coffee, milk, pastries, or napkins as needed.

Courage: Is it Safe to Challenge Each Other?

Individual team members can understand what the team is trying to accomplish, be committed to achieving team objectives, and understand the rules by which the team gets work done, but they may not trust each other. Team trust happens when team members believe that everyone has the *ability* to accomplish assigned tasks, make decisions and take action for the benefit of the team (*benevolence*), and abide by the team's rules and follow through with commitments (*integrity*).[31] Problems in any one of these areas reduce team trust, so team leaders need to ensure that team members have the requisite skills, their actions are aligned with team goals, and they deliver on assigned tasks. Moderate levels of conflict are also a hallmark of high-performing teams. Team members can have strong disagreements over work assignments, team rules, underlying assumptions, sources of truth, data interpretation, problem identification, or solution recommendations, and a key team leader skill is getting these disagreements out in the open. High-performing teams do not eliminate conflict, but instead understand that some amount of tension can help figure out problems and generate creative solutions. The trick is to ensure that conflict does not become so intense that team members lose sight of the problem and begin attacking each other. One way leaders can improve courage is to work with team members to determine the rules for addressing team conflict. By contrast, some of the best techniques for destroying team courage are for leaders to either ignore interpersonal conflict or tell team members to "quit fighting and just get along."

Courage is one of the more easily observed components of the Rocket Model, as it is relatively easy to see if teams are experiencing too little or too much conflict. When it comes to team courage, many teams either suffer from artificial harmony or engage in outright feuding. Teams suffer from artificial harmony when team members refuse to raise controversial topics in team meetings yet complain about these issues to their teammates afterward. Something (usually fear of retaliation by the team leader or bad communication norms) prevents these issues from being raised and resolved, and as a result, team members disengage and team performance suffers. At the other extreme, some teams have members who are engaged in open feuding. When this occurs, team leaders often resort to sending the team to some sort of team-building program, such as an outdoor learning or high ropes course. In almost all these cases, these interventions have little if any long-term effect on team cohesiveness because the courage component of the Rocket Model is often a symptom of deeper team problems. More often than not, team members do not trust each other because of ability, benevolence, or integrity issues; unclear team goals and roles; ill-defined decision-making or accountability norms; uneven levels of commitment; resource shortfalls; and so forth. In other words, the reason team members experience interpersonal conflict often has to do with a problem in one or more of the other components of the Rocket Model. Successfully identifying and addressing these problem components will not only improve results but also help develop team courage. In our Starbucks example, the store manager should be on the lookout for areas of disagreement, identify their underlying cause, and get these issues quickly raised and resolved. These discussions should focus on the facts rather than on the personalities of those involved.

Results: Are We Winning?

The context through courage components of the Rocket Model describes the "how" of team building. In other words, these components tell team leaders what they specifically need to do to improve team mission, norms, and so forth. The results component of the Rocket Model describes the "what" of team building—what did the team actually accomplish? Like courage, results are a symptom or an outcome of the other components of the Rocket Model. High-performing teams get superior results because they have attended to the other seven components of the Rocket Model. Those teams achieving suboptimal results can improve their performance by focusing on problematic components of the Rocket Model. In our Starbucks example, if the store is failing to achieve its customer service or financial goals, then it could reexamine the goals, determine if it had any staffing shortfalls or talent gaps, review its rules to see if people were being held accountable for poor performance, acquire upgraded equipment, and so on.

One thing we know about successful military leaders and athletic coaches is that they obsess over winning. They are continually devising strategies and tactics to leverage their teams' strengths, minimize weaknesses, and defeat their opponents. Much of their time is spent teaching their teams how to win. Private- and public-sector leaders rarely teach their teams how to win. To do this, team leaders need to set well-defined team goals, create executable action plans with clear timelines and accountable parties to achieve these goals, and conduct periodic progress reviews to identify key learnings and revise strategies and plans as needed.

Implications of the Rocket Model

As stated at the beginning of this section, the Rocket Model is both prescriptive and diagnostic. When building a new team or determining where an existing team is falling short, leaders should always start with the context, mission, and talent components before moving to other parts of the model. Just as a rocket needs a large booster to get off the ground, teams need to have a common understanding of the situation, a set of well-defined team goals, and the right players to succeed. Along these lines, the Team Assessment Survey was designed to give teams feedback on where they stand with respect to the eight components of the Rocket Model.[32, 33] **Figures 13.3** and **13.4** show the assessment results for two business teams. **Figure 13.3** is a highly dysfunctional group of executives who led a multibillion-dollar division of a consumer products company. The division was struggling and a new division president had recently been appointed to turn things around. Scores on the Team Assessment Survey range from 0 to 100, with low scores being associated with dysfunctional teams, scores around 50 being on par with other teams across the globe, and scores above 75 associated with high-performing teams. The new division president has a lot of work to do to get this team performing, and she and the team should work through the context, mission, and talent components before working on the others. **Figure 13.4** shows the results for a C-suite team running 300 assisted living facilities across the United States. A detailed analysis of the report reveals the team has some strengths in resources and courage but needs to gain alignment on the challenges facing the team (context), create a team scorecard (mission), better clarify team member roles and responsibilities (talent), run more effective team meetings and incorporate better decision-making processes (norms), and spend more time reviewing results (results) in order to become high-performing.

Although everyone has been on groups and teams for most of their lives, most leaders and leaders-to-be do not know how to transform collections of individuals into high-performing teams. The Rocket Model was created to fill this gap. The model is very practical, can be applied to virtually any team, and is based on the premise that the best way to build teams is to identify and work on the issues that matter. The model is also predicated on the belief that a key leader role is to make the implicit explicit; this means leaders need to ensure everyone has the same understanding of team context, goals, roles, rules, and other details. Over 5,000 leaders have been trained on the Rocket Model and associated team improvement tools, and books such as *Ignition: Guide to Building High Performing Teams* and *The Rocket Model: Practical Advice for Building High Performing Teams* provide step-by-step instructions to leaders wanting to improve team functioning and performance.[34, 35]

FIGURE 13.3   Team Assessment Results for a Dysfunctional Construction Leadership Team

16	**Results: The team's track record.** Is the team delivering on its commitments? Does it accomplish important goals, meet stakeholders' expectations, and improve over time?
16	**Courage: The team's approach to managing conflict.** Do team members feel safe raising difficult issues and does conflict get managed effectively?
16	**Resources: The team's assets.** Does the team have the necessary physical and monetary resources, authority, and political support?
20	**Buy-In: The level of motivation among team members.** Are team members optimistic about the team's chances for winning and motivated to accomplish the team's goals?
4	**Norms: The team's formal and informal work processes.** Does the team use effective and efficient processes for running meeting, making decisions, and getting work done?
20	**Talent: The people who make up this team.** Does this team have the right number of people, are roles clear, and does it have the skills needed to succeed?
22	**Mission: The team's purpose and goals.** Why does the team exist? How does it define winning, and what are its strategies for accomplishing goals?
24	**Context: The situation in which the team operates.** Do team members agree about the team's political and economic realities, stakeholders, and challenges?

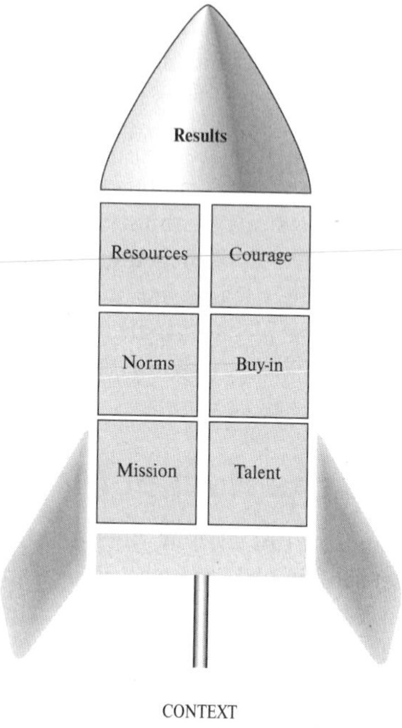

Delegating

Delegation is a relatively simple way for leaders to free themselves of time-consuming chores; give followers developmental opportunities; and increase the number of tasks accomplished by the work group, team, or committee. However, delegation is often an overlooked and underused management option.[36, 37] Delegation implies that someone has been empowered by a leader, boss, or coach to take responsibility for completing certain tasks or engaging in certain activities. Delegation gives the responsibility for decisions to those individuals most likely to be affected by or to implement the decision, and delegation is more concerned with autonomy, responsibility, and follower development than with participation. Research has shown that leaders who delegate authority more frequently often have higher-performing businesses,[38] but followers are not necessarily happier when their leaders frequently delegate tasks.[39] Bass[40] maintained that the latter findings were due to subordinates who felt they were not delegated the authority needed to accomplish delegated tasks, monitored too closely, or delegated only tasks leaders did not want to do. Nevertheless, Wilcox[41] showed that leaders who delegated skillfully had more satisfied followers than leaders who did not delegate well. Because leaders who delegate skillfully often have more satisfied and higher-performing work groups, teams, or committees, the following suggestions from Taylor[42] are provided to help leadership practitioners delegate more effectively and successfully. Taylor provided useful ideas about why delegating is important, common reasons for avoiding delegation, and principles of effective delegation.

FIGURE 13.4   Team Assessment Results for an Underperforming Assisted Living Leadership Team

40	**Results: The team's track record.** Is the team delivering on its commitments? Does it accomplish important goals, meet stakeholders' expectations, and improve over time?
66	**Courage: The team's approach to managing conflict.** Do team members feel safe raising difficult issues and does conflict get managed effectively?
68	**Resources: The team's assets.** Does the team have the necessary physical and monetary resources, authority, and political support?
46	**Buy-In: The level of motivation among team members.** Are team members optimistic about the team's chances for winning and motivated to accomplish the team's goals?
36	**Norms: The team's formal and informal work processes.** Does the team use effective and efficient processes for running meeting, making decisions, and getting work done?
40	**Talent: The people who make up this team.** Does this team have the right number of people, are roles clear, and does it have the skills needed to succeed?
6	**Mission: The team's purpose and goals.** Why does the team exist? How does it define winning, and what are its strategies for accomplishing goals?
32	**Context: The situation in which the team operates.** Do team members agree about the team's political and economic realities, stakeholders, and challenges?

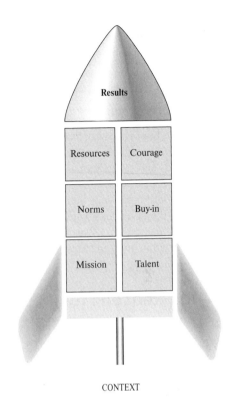

Why Delegating Is Important

Delegation Frees Time for Other Activities

The essence of leadership is achieving goals through others, not trying to accomplish them by oneself. Learning to think like a leader partly involves developing a frame of mind wherein you think in terms of the whole group's or organization's capabilities and not just your own. This requires a new frame of reference for many individuals, especially those whose past successes resulted primarily from personal achievement in interpersonally competitive situations. Still, leaders typically have so many different responsibilities that they invariably must delegate some of them to others.

It is not just the mere quantity of work that makes delegation necessary. There is a qualitative aspect, too. Because leaders determine what responsibilities will be delegated, the process is one by which leaders can ensure that their time is allocated most judiciously to meet group needs. The leader's time is a precious commodity that should be invested wisely in those activities that the leader is uniquely suited or situated to accomplish and that will provide the greatest long-term benefits to the group. What the leader *can* delegate, the leader *should* delegate.

Delegation Develops Followers

Developing subordinates is one of the most important responsibilities any leader has, and delegating significant tasks to them is one of the best ways to support their growth. It does so by providing opportunities for initiative, problem solving, innovation, administration, and decision-making. By providing practical experience in a controlled fashion, delegation allows subordinates the best training experience of all: learning by doing.

Delegation Strengthens the Organization

Delegation is an important way to develop individual subordinates, but doing so also strengthens the entire organization. For one thing, an organization that uses delegation skillfully will be a motivating one to work in. Delegation sends an organizational signal that subordinates are trusted and their development is important. Moreover, skillful delegation inherently tends to increase the significance and satisfaction levels of most jobs, thus making subordinates' jobs better. Delegation also can be seen as a way of developing the entire organization, not just the individuals within it. To the extent that a whole organization systematically develops its personnel using delegation, its overall experience level, capability, and vitality increase. Finally, delegation stimulates innovation and generates fresh ideas and new approaches throughout the whole organization.

Common Reasons for Avoiding Delegation

Delegation Takes Too Much Time

Delegation saves time for the leader in the long run, but it costs the leader time in the short run. It takes time to train a subordinate to perform any new task, so it often really does take less time for a leader to do the task herself than to put in the effort to train someone else to do it. When a task is a recurring or repetitive one, however, the long-term savings will make the additional effort in initial training worth it—both for the leader and for the subordinate.

Delegation Is Risky

It can feel threatening to delegate a significant responsibility to another person because doing so reduces our direct personal control over the work we will be judged by.[43] Delegation may be perceived as a career risk by staking our own reputation on the motivation, skill, and performance of others. It is the essence of leadership, though, that the leader will be evaluated in part by the success of the entire team. Furthermore, delegation need not and should not involve a complete loss of control by the leader over work delegated to others. The leader has a responsibility to set performance expectations, ensure that the task is understood and accepted, provide training, and regularly monitor the status of all delegated tasks and responsibilities.[44]

The Job Will Not Be Done as Well

Often the leader can do many specific tasks or jobs better than anyone else. That is not surprising—the leader is often the most experienced person in the group. This fact, however, can become an obstacle to delegation. The leader may rationalize not delegating a task to someone else because the follower lacks technical competence and the job would subsequently suffer.[45] However, this may be true only in the short term, and letting subordinates make a few mistakes is a necessary part of their development, just as it was for the leader at an earlier stage in her own development. Few things are likely to be so stifling to an organization as a leader's perfectionist fear of mistakes. When thinking about delegating tasks to others, leaders should remember what their own skill levels used to be, not what they are now. Leaders should assess subordinates' readiness to handle new responsibilities in terms of the former, not the latter.

The Task Is a Desirable One

A leader may resist delegating tasks that are a source of power or prestige. He may be willing to delegate relatively unimportant responsibilities but may balk at the prospect of delegating a significant one having high visibility.[46, 47] The greater the importance and visibility of the delegated task, though, the greater will be the potential developmental gains for the subordinate. Furthermore, actions always speak louder than words, and nothing conveys trust more genuinely than a leader's willingness to delegate major responsibilities to subordinates.

Others Are Already Too Busy

A leader may feel guilty about increasing a subordinate's already full workload. It is the leader's responsibility, though, to continually review the relative priority of all the tasks performed across the organization. Such a review might identify existing activities that could be eliminated, modified, or reassigned. A discussion with the subordinate about her workload and career goals would be a better basis for a decision than an arbitrary and unilateral determination by the leader that the subordinate cannot handle more work. The new responsibility could be something the subordinate wants and needs, and she might also have some helpful ideas about alternative ways to manage her present duties.

Principles of Effective Delegation

Decide What to Delegate

The first step leaders should take when deciding what to delegate is to identify all their present activities. This should include those functions regularly performed and decisions regularly made. Next leaders should estimate the actual time spent on these activities. This can be done fairly easily by developing and maintaining a temporary log. After collecting this information, leaders need to assess whether each activity justifies the time they are spending on it. In all likelihood, at least some of the most time-consuming recurring activities should be delegated to others. This process will probably also identify some activities that could be done more efficiently (by either the leader or someone else) and other activities that provide so little benefit they could be eliminated completely.

Decide Whom to Delegate To

There might be one individual whose talent and experience make her the logical best choice for any assignment. However, leaders must be careful not to overburden someone merely because that individual always happens to be the best worker. Additionally, leaders have a responsibility to balance developmental opportunities among all their followers. Leaders should look for ways to optimize, over a series of assignments, the growth of all subordinates by matching particular opportunities to their respective individual needs, skills, and goals.

Make the Assignment Clear and Specific

As with setting goals, leaders delegating an assignment must be sure the subordinate understands what the task involves and what is expected of him. Nevertheless, at times leaders provide too brief an explanation of the task to be delegated. A common communication error is overestimating our own clarity, and in the case of delegation this can happen when the leader already knows the ins and outs of the particular task. Some of the essential steps or potential pitfalls in an assignment that seem self-evident to the leader may not be as obvious to someone who has never done the assignment before. Leaders should welcome questions and provide a complete explanation of the task. The time leaders invest during this initial training will pay dividends later. When giving an assignment, leaders should ensure that they cover all the points listed in **Highlight 13.3**.

Points to Cover When Delegating a Task

HIGHLIGHT 13.3

How does the task relate to organizational goals?

When does the subordinate's responsibility for the task begin?

How has the task been accomplished in the past?

What problems were encountered with the task in the past?

What sources of help are available?

What unusual situations might arise in the future?

What are the limits of the subordinate's authority?

How will the leader monitor the task (such as by providing feedback)?

Finally, in covering these points, be sure to convey high confidence and expectations.

Assign an Objective, Not a Procedure

Indicate what is to be accomplished, not *how* the task is to be accomplished. End results are usually more important than the methods. It is helpful to demonstrate procedures that have worked before, but not to specify rigid methods to follow in the future. Leaders should not assume their ways always were and always will be best. Leaders need to be clear about the criteria by which success will be measured, but allowing subordinates to achieve it in their own ways will increase their satisfaction and encourage fresh ideas.

Allow Autonomy, but Monitor Performance

Effective delegation is neither micromanagement of everything the subordinate does nor laissez-faire indifference toward the subordinate's performance. Leaders need to give subordinates a degree of autonomy (as well as time, resources, and authority) in carrying out their new responsibilities, and this includes the freedom to make certain kinds of mistakes. An organizational climate in which mistakes are punished suppresses initiative and innovation. Furthermore, mistakes are important sources of development. Knowing this, one wise executive reassured a subordinate who expected to be fired for a gigantic mistake by saying, "Why should I fire you when I've just invested $100,000 in your development?"[48]

Once a task has been delegated, even though the subordinate's training and development are continuing, the leader should be cautious about providing too much unsolicited advice or engaging in "rescue" activities. An exception would be when a subordinate's mistake would put significant organizational assets at risk. By contrast, the leader needs to establish specific procedures for periodically reviewing the subordinate's performance of the delegated task. Leaders need to maintain good records of all the assignments they have delegated, including appropriate milestones and completion dates for each one.

Give Credit, Not Blame

Whenever leaders delegate, they must give subordinates *authority* along with responsibility. In the final analysis, however, leaders always remain fully responsible and accountable for any delegated task. If things should go wrong, the leaders should accept responsibility for failure fully and completely and never try to pass blame on to subordinates. By contrast, if things go well, as they usually will, leaders should give all the public credit to the subordinates. Also, when providing performance feedback privately to a subordinate, emphasize what went right rather than what went wrong. Leaders should not ignore errors in judgment or implementation, but they need not dwell on them, either. One helpful approach to performance feedback is called the "sandwich technique." With this technique, negative feedback is placed between two pieces of positive feedback. It affirms the subordinate's good work, puts the subordinate at least somewhat at ease, and keeps the ratio of positive and negative comments in balance. The idea of a sandwich, however, should not be taken too literally. There is nothing magical about two pieces of positive feedback for one piece of negative feedback. In fact, from the receiver's point of view the balance between positive and negative feedback may seem "about right" when the ratio is considerably higher than two to one.

Coaching

A key success factor in most organizations today is having leaders and followers with the right knowledge and skills. More and more, companies are looking at "bench strength" as a competitive advantage. There are essentially two ways to acquire bench strength: Employers can buy (that is, hire) the talent they need, or they can build their existing talent through development and coaching programs. Given that many employers face a labor shortage in certain critical positions, many are looking to build their own internal talent.[49] Much of this talent is being developed through informal coaching. As we noted in **Chapter 2**, most leaders engage in some form of informal coaching. But how good are they at coaching? The authors' conversations with a multitude of leaders indicate that almost every single one was unsure what to do as a coach. Some thought coaching involved directing their employees in how to do tasks. Others thought it involved counseling employees on personal problems. One stated that his only example of coaching came from his high school football coach, and he wouldn't wish that on anyone.

> *People who are coaches will be the norm. Other people won't get promoted.*
>
> **Jack Welch, former General Electric CEO**

Two thought leaders in this area are Peterson and Hicks,[50] who have described coaching as the "process of equipping people with the tools, knowledge, and opportunities they need to develop themselves and become more successful." According to Peterson and Hicks, good coaches orchestrate rather than dictate development. Good coaches help followers clarify career goals, identify and prioritize development needs, create and stick to development plans, and create environments that support learning and coaching. Coaching is really a blend of several different leadership skills. Being a good coach means having well-developed skills, determining where a follower is in the coaching process, and intervening as appropriate. The five steps of coaching give leaders both a good road map and a diagnostic model for improving the bench strength of their followers.

Peterson and Hicks pointed out that this model works particularly well for high performers—individuals who tend to benefit the most from, but are often overlooked by, leaders when coaching. We noted in **Chapter 9** that high performers produce 20 to 50 percent more than average employees,[51] so coaching can have a considerable impact on the bottom line if it is targeted at high performers. Further support for the idea that top performers may benefit the most from coaching comes from athletics. If you watch the Olympics, you have probably seen that many of the world's top athletes have at least one and sometimes two or three coaches. If these world-class athletes feel that coaching can enhance their performance, it is likely that good coaches can also enhance the performance of any organization's top employees. Although the five-step model described here also works with poorly performing employees, more appropriate interventions might also include diagnosing performance problems, goal setting, providing rewards and constructive feedback, and punishing these individuals, particularly if informal coaching is not achieving desired results.

Forging a Partnership

The first step in informal coaching involves establishing a relationship built on mutual trust and respect with a follower. If a follower does not trust or respect her leader, it is unlikely that she will pay much attention to his ideas for her development. There are several things leaders can do to forge a partnership with coachees. First, it will be much easier for leaders with high credibility to build strong partnerships with followers than this will be for leaders with low credibility. Therefore, leaders need to assess their credibility (see **Chapter 8**), and they may need to take appropriate developmental steps to improve their credibility before their coaching suggestions will have much impact. These developmental steps may include building technical and organizational knowledge as well as building strong relationships with the individuals they want to coach. Understanding the context in which the employee operates can be as important as the relationship the leader shares with the employee.

In **Chapter 8**, we noted that leaders also need to spend time listening to their coachees; they need to understand coachees' career aspirations, values, intrinsic motivators, view of the organization, and current work situation. Good coaches can put themselves in their coachees' shoes and can understand how coachees may view issues or opportunities differently than they do. While forging a partnership, leaders can also provide coachees with realistic career advice—sometimes coachees have unrealistic estimations of their skills and opportunities. For example, a new graduate from a top MBA program might want to be a partner at a consulting firm after two years with the company, but company policy may dictate that this decision will not be made until she has been with the firm for at least eight years. Her coach should inform her of this policy and then work with her to map out a series of shorter-term career objectives that will help her become a partner in eight years. If coaches do not know what drives their coachees' behaviors, then another step to forging a partnership is to start asking questions. This is an excellent opportunity for leaders to practice their listening skills so as to better understand their coachees' career aspirations and intrinsic motivators.

Inspiring Commitment: Conducting a GAPS Analysis

The second step in the coaching process is similar to the GAPS analysis and the gaps-of-the-GAPS analysis that were discussed in the "Development Planning" section in **Chapter 3**. The only difference is that these two analyses are now done from the coachee's perspective. **Figure 13.5** might help to clarify this difference in perspective. In the goals quadrant of the GAPS analysis the leader should write the coachee's career objectives, and in the perceptions quadrant the leader would write how the coachee's behavior affects others. It is possible that the leader may not be able to complete all of the quadrants of the GAPS for a coachee. If so, the leader will need to gather more information before going any further. This information gathering may include discussing career goals and abilities with the coachee, reviewing the coachee's 360-degree feedback results, asking peers about how the coachee comes across or impacts others, or asking human resources about the educational or experience standards relevant to the coachee's career goals. One way to gather additional information is to have both the leader and the coachee complete a GAPS analysis independently, and then get together and discuss areas of agreement and disagreement. This can help ensure that the best information is available for the GAPS analysis and also help to build the partnership between the leader and coachee. During this discussion the leader and coachee should also do a gaps-of-the-GAPS analysis to identify and prioritize development needs. Usually leaders will get more commitment to development needs if coachees feel they had an important role in determining these needs, and a gaps-of-the-GAPS discussion is a way to build buy-in. This discussion can also help ensure that development needs are aligned with career goals.

Growing Skills: Creating Development and Coaching Plans

Once the coachee's development needs are identified and prioritized, the third step in the coaching process involves coachees building development plans to overcome targeted needs. These plans are identical to those described in the "Development Planning" section in **Chapter 3**. Leaders generally do not build development plans for their coachees. Instead they may want to go over a sample (or their own) development plan and coach their coachees on the seven steps in building a plan. They can then either jointly build a plan or have the coachee individually build a plan for the leader to review. Giving coachees an important role in development planning should increase their level of commitment to the plan. Once a draft development plan is created, the leader and coach can use the development planning checklist in **Table 13.1** to review the plan.

In addition to the development plan, leaders must build a coaching plan that outlines the actions they will take to support their coachees' development. Some of these actions might include meeting with the coachees regularly to provide developmental feedback, identifying developmental resources or opportunities, or helping coachees reflect on what they have learned. As with development plans, leaders should share their coaching plans so that coachees know what kind of support they will be getting. This will also publicly commit the leaders to the coachees' development, which will make it more likely that they will follow through with the coaching plan.

Promoting Persistence: Helping Followers Stick to Their Plans

Having development and coaching plans in place is no guarantee that development will occur. Sometimes coachees build development plans with great enthusiasm but then take no further action. The fourth step in the coaching process is designed to help coachees "manage the mundane." An example of managing the mundane might be illustrative. One of the authors successfully completed a triathlon. The most difficult part of this accomplishment was not the event itself, but rather doing all the training needed to successfully complete the event. Similarly, the inability to stick to a diet or keep a New Year's resolution is primarily due to an inability to manage the mundane; people are initially committed to these goals but have a difficult time sticking to them. The same is true with development planning. Conducting a GAPS analysis and creating a development plan are relatively easy; sticking to the plan is more difficult. From the leader's perspective, a large part of coaching is helping followers stick to their development plans.

Several development planning steps are specifically designed to promote persistence. For example, ensuring alignment between career and development objectives, getting feedback from multiple sources on a regular basis, and reflecting with a partner can help keep coachees focused on their development. If the leader is a coachee's developmental partner, then reflection sessions can help followers persist with their development. If leaders are not designated as partners in the development plan, they should commit to meeting regularly with the coachees to discuss progress, what the leaders can do to support development, developmental opportunities, developmental feedback, and so forth.

FIGURE 13.5   A GAPS Analysis for an Employee

Goals: Where do you want to go?	**Abilities:** What can you do now?
Step 1: Career objectives: Career strategies:	*Step 2:* What strengths do you have for your career objectives? *Step 3:* What development needs will you have to overcome?
Standards: What does your boss or the organization expect?	**Perceptions:** How do others see you?
Step 5: Expectations:	*Step 4:* 360-degree and performance review results, and feedback from others: • *Boss* • *Peers* • *Direct reports*

Sources: D. B. Peterson and M. D. Hicks, *Leader as Coach* (Minneapolis, MN: Personnel Decisions International, 1996); and G. J. Curphy, *The Leadership Development Process Manual* (Minneapolis, MN: Personnel Decisions International, 1998).

Leaders can also help to promote persistence by capitalizing on coachable moments. Say a coachee was working on listening skills, and the leader and coach were in a staff meeting together. If the leader provides feedback to the coachee about her listening skills immediately after the staff meeting, the leader has capitalized on a coachable moment. To capitalize on a coachable moment, leaders must know the followers' developmental objectives, be in situations where they can observe followers practicing their objectives, and then provide immediate feedback on their observations. Few coaches capitalize on coachable moments, but they can go

TABLE 13.1   Development Plan Checklist

Objectives

- One-year career objective identified?
- No more than a total of two or three development goals?
- Areas in which the employee is motivated and committed to change and develop?

Criteria for Success

- Is the new behavior clearly described?
- Can the behavior be measured or observed?

Action Steps

- Specific, attainable, and measurable steps?
- Mostly on-the-job activities?
- Includes a variety of types of activities?
- Are activities divided into small, doable steps?

Seek Feedback and Support

- Involvement of a variety of others?
- Includes requests for management support?
- Are reassessment dates realistic?

Stretch Assignments

- Do the stretch assignments relate to the employee's career objectives?

Resources

- Uses a variety of books, seminars, and other resources?

Reflect with a Partner

- Includes periodic reviews of learning?

Source: G. J. Curphy, *The Leadership Development Process Manual* (Minneapolis, MN: Personnel Decisions International, 1998).

a long way toward promoting persistence in coachees. Note that capitalizing on coachable moments should take little time, often less than two minutes. In the example here, the leader could provide feedback to the coachee during their walk back to the office after the staff meeting.

Transferring Skills: Creating a Learning Environment

To build bench strength, leaders need to create a learning environment so that personal development becomes an ongoing process rather than a one-time event. As Tichy and Cohen[52] aptly point out, the most successful organizations are those that emphasize the learning and teaching process—they focus on continually creating leaders throughout the company. In reality, leaders have quite a bit of control over the learning environments they want to create for their followers, and they can use several interventions to ensure that development becomes an ongoing process. This represents the fifth step of the coaching process. Perhaps the most important intervention is for leaders to role-model development. In that regard, if leaders are not getting regular feedback from followers, they are probably not doing a good job of role-modeling development. By regularly soliciting feedback from followers, leaders are also likely to create a feedback-rich work environment. Once feedback becomes a group norm, people will be much more willing to help build team member skills, which in turn can have a catalytic effect on group performance. The leader will play a large role in this group norm because if the leader is feedback averse, feedback will be difficult to encourage among followers.

Leaders can also create learning environments by regularly reviewing their followers' development. Perhaps the easiest way to do this is by making leaders and followers development partners; then both parties can provide regular feedback and ongoing support. During these discussions, leaders and followers should review and update their development plans to capitalize on new development opportunities or acquire new skills. Leaders and followers can also review coaching plans to see what is and is not working and make the necessary adjustments.

> *Do what you can, where you are at, with what you have.*
>
> **Theodore Roosevelt, U.S. president, 1901-1909**

Concluding Comments

Perhaps one of the greatest misperceptions of coaching, and the primary reason leaders give for not coaching others, is that it takes a lot of time. In reality, nothing could be further from the truth. Leaders are working to build credibility, build relationships with followers, and understand followers' career aspirations and views of the world. Although these efforts take time, they are also activities leaders should be engaged in even if they are not coaching followers. Doing GAPS analyses, identifying and prioritizing development needs, helping followers create development plans, and creating coaching plans often take less than four hours. Although leaders will need to take these steps with all their followers, this time can be spread out over a four- to six-week period. The bottom line is that coaching really takes little additional time; it is more a function of changing how you spend time with followers so that you can maximize their development.

> *Inside every old company is a new company waiting to be born.*
>
> **Alvin Toffler, American writer and futurist**

Another note about the coaching model is that good coaches are equally versatile at all five steps of coaching. Some leaders are good at forging a partnership but then fail to carry development to the next level by conducting GAPS analyses or helping followers build development plans. Other leaders may help followers build development plans but do nothing to promote persistence or create a learning environment. Just as leaders need to develop their technical skills, so might they need to assess and develop coaching skills. It is important to remember that coaching is a dynamic process—good coaches assess where followers are in the coaching process and intervene appropriately. By regularly assessing where they are with followers, they may determine that the relationship with a particular follower is not as strong as they thought, and this lack of relationship is why followers are not sticking to their development plans. In this case a good coach would go back to forging a partnership with the follower and, once a trusting relationship had been created, go through another GAPS analysis, and so forth.

Finally, it is important to note that people can and do develop skills on their own. Nevertheless, leaders who commit to the five steps of informal coaching outlined here will both create learning organizations and help to raise development to a new level. Given the competitive advantage of companies that have a well-developed and capable workforce, in the future it will be hard to imagine leadership excellence without coaching. Good leaders are those who create successors, and coaching may be the best way to make this happen.

Endnotes

1. B. M. Bass, *Bass and Stogdill's Handbook of Leadership*, 3rd ed. (New York: Free Press, 1990).

2. M. Erez, P. C. Earley, and C. L. Hulin, "The Impact of Participation on Goal Acceptance and Performance: A Two-Step Model," *Academy of Management Journal* 28, no. 1 (1985), pp. 359–72.

3. E. A. Locke, G. P. Latham, and M. Erez, "Three-Way Interactive Presentation and Discussion," "A Unique Approach to Resolving Scientific Disputes," and "Designing Crucial Experiments," papers presented at the Society of Industrial and Organizational Psychology Convention, Atlanta, GA, 1987.

4. R. J. House, "Power in Organizations: A Social Psychological Perspective," unpublished manuscript, University of Toronto, 1984.

5. G. P. Latham and T. W. Lee, "Goal Setting," in *Generalizing from Laboratory to Field Settings*, ed. E. A. Locke (Lexington, MA: Lexington Books, 1986).

6. Locke et al., "Three-Way Interactive Presentation and Discussion," "A Unique Approach to Resolving Scientific Disputes," and "Designing Crucial Experiments."

7. M. M. Greller, "Evaluation of Feedback Sources as a Function of Role and Organizational Development," *Journal of Applied Psychology* 65 (1980), pp. 24–27.

8. J. L. Komacki, "Why We Don't Reinforce: The Issues," *Journal of Organizational Behavior Management* 4, nos. 3-4 (1982), pp. 97–100.

9. Bass, *Bass and Stogdill's Handbook of Leadership.*

10. S. Deep and L. Sussman, *Smart Moves* (Reading, MA: Addison-Wesley, 1990).

11. J. R. Larson Jr., "Supervisors' Performance Feedback to Subordinates: The Impact of Subordinate Performance Valence and Outcome Dependence," *Organizational Behavior and Human Decision Processes* 37 (1986), pp. 391–408.

12. E. L. Harrison, "Training Supervisors to Discipline Effectively," *Training and Development Journal* 36, no. 11 (1982), pp. 111–13.

13. C. K. Parsons, D. M. Herold, and M. L. Leatherwood, "Turnover during Initial Employment: A Longitudinal Study of the Role of Causal Attributions," *Journal of Applied Psychology* 70 (1985), pp. 337–41.

14. A. C. Filley and L. A. Pace, "Making Judgments Descriptive," in *The 1976 Annual Handbook for Group Facilitators*, eds. J. E. Jones and J. W. Pfeiffer (La Jolla, CA: University Associates Press, 1976).

15. R. W. Coye, "Subordinate Responses to Ineffective Leadership," *Dissertation Abstracts International* 43, no. 6A (1982), p. 2070.

16. P. L. Quaglieri and J. P. Carnazza, "Critical Inferences and the Multidimensionality of Feedback," *Canadian Journal of Behavioral Science* 17 (1985), pp. 284–93.

17. D. L. Stone, H. G. Gueutal, and B. MacIntosh, "The Effects of Feedback Sequence and Expertise of Rater of Perceived Feedback Accuracy," *Personal Psychology* 37 (1984), pp. 487–506.

18. Bass, *Bass and Stogdill's Handbook of Leadership.*

19. M. Silberman and P. Philips (eds.), *2005 ASTD Team & Organization Development Sourcebook* (Alexandria VA: ASTD Press, 2005).

20. P. M. Senge, *The Fifth Discipline: The Art and Practice of the Learning Organization* (New York: Doubleday/Currency, 1994).

21. R. C. Ginnett, "To the Wilderness and Beyond: The Application of a Model for Transformal Change," *Proceedings of the Ninth Psychology in the Department of Defense Symposium* (Colorado Springs, CO, 1984).

22. G. J. Curphy and R. T. Hogan, *The Rocket Model: Practical Advice for Building High Performing Teams* (Tulsa, OK: Hogan Press, 2012).

23. G. J. Curphy, *The Rocket Model*, pre-conference workshop delivered to the American Psychological Association Division 13 Midwinter Conference, Atlanta, GE, February 2013.

24. G. J. Curphy, "Applying the Rocket Model to Virtual Teams," unpublished manuscript, 2013.

25. G. J. Curphy, *Building High-Performing Teams Training Manual* (North Oaks, MN: Curphy Consulting Corporation, 2013.)

26. G. J. Curphy, D. Nilsen, and R. Hogan, *Ignition: A Guide to Building High Performing Teams* (Tulsa, OK: Hogan Press, 2019).

27. G. J. Curphy and D. Nilsen, *The Team Assessment Survey* (North Oaks, MN: Curphy Leadership Solutions, 2018).

28. G. J. Curphy, H. Lee, and D. Nilsen, *The Team Assessment Survey Technical Manual* (North Oaks, MN: Curphy Leadership Solutions, 2017).

29. G. J. Curphy and D. Nilsen, *Team Improvement Workshop Participant Manual* (North Oaks, MN: Curphy Leadership Solutions, 2020).

30. G. J. Curphy, "Curphy Leadership Solutions—The Rocket Model," January 2020, https://vimeo.com/384372065.

31. K. Basik, *The Team Trust Trifecta* (Charlotte, NC: Basik Insight, 2019).

32. Curphy and Nilsen, *The Team Assessment Survey.*

33. Curphy et al., *Team Assessment Survey Technical Manual.*

34. Curphy and Hogan, *The Rocket Model.*

35. Curphy et al., *Ignition.*

36. Curphy, *Team Assessment Survey II.*

37. C. R. Leana, "Power Relinquishment vs. Power Sharing: Theoretical Clarification and Empirical Comparison of Delegation and Participation," *Journal of Applied Psychology* 72 (1987), pp. 228–33.

38. D. Miller and J. M. Toulouse, "Strategy, Structure, CEO Personality and Performance in Small Firms," *American Journal of Small Business*, Winter 1986, pp. 47–62.

39. R. M. Stogdill and C. L. Shartle, *Methods in the Study of Administrative Performance* (Columbus, OH: Ohio State University, Bureau of Business Research, 1955).

40. Bass, *Bass and Stogdill's Handbook of Leadership.*

41. W. H. Wilcox, "Assistant Superintendents' Perceptions of the Effectiveness of the Superintendent, Job Satisfaction, and Satisfaction with the Superintendent's Supervisory Skills," PhD dissertation, University of Missouri, Columbia, 1982.

42. H. L. Taylor, *Delegate: The Key to Successful Management* (New York: Warner Books, 1989).

43. H. D. Dewhirst, V. Metts, and R. T. Ladd, "Exploring the Delegation Decision: Managerial Responses to Multiple Contingencies," paper presented at the Academy of Management Convention, New Orleans, LA, 1987.

44. Bass, *Bass and Stogdill's Handbook of Leadership.*

45. Dewhirst et al., "Exploring the Delegation Decision."

46. Bass, *Bass and Stogdill's Handbook of Leadership.*

47. Dewhirst et al., "Exploring the Delegation Decision."

48. M. W. McCall Jr., M. M. Lombardo, and A. M. Morrison, *The Lessons of Experience: How Successful Executives Develop on the Job* (Lexington, MA: Lexington Books, 1988).

49. N. M. Tichy and E. Cohen, *The Leadership Engine: How Winning Companies Build Leaders at Every Level* (New York: HarperCollins, 1997).

50. D. B. Peterson and M. D. Hicks, *Leader as Coach: Strategies for Coaching and Developing Others* (Minneapolis, MN: Personnel Decisions International, 1996), p. 14.

51. J. E. Hunter, F. L. Schmidt, and M. K. Judiesch, "Individual Differences in Output Variability as a Function of Job Complexity," *Journal of Applied Psychology* 74 (1990), pp. 28–42.

52. Tichy and Cohen, *The Leadership Engine.*

Part 4

Focus on the Situation

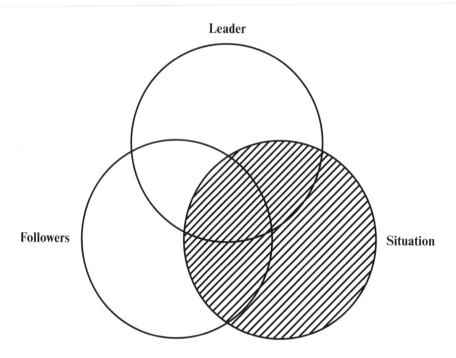

In previous chapters we noted that understanding leaders and followers is much more complicated than many people think. For example, we examined how leaders' personality characteristics, behaviors, and attitudes affect the leadership process. Similarly, followers' attitudes, experience, personality characteristics, and behaviors, as well as group norms and cohesiveness, also affect the leadership process. Despite the complexities of leaders and followers, however, perhaps no factor in the interactional framework is as complex as the situation. Not only do a variety of task, organizational, and environmental factors affect behavior, but the relative salience or strength of these factors varies dramatically across people. What one person perceives to be the key situational factor affecting his or her behavior may be relatively unimportant to another person.

Moreover, the relative importance of the situational factors also varies over time. Even during a single soccer game, for example, the situation changes constantly: The lead changes, the time remaining in the game changes, weather conditions change, injuries occur, and so on. Given the dynamic nature of situations, it may be a misnomer to speak of "the" situation in reference to leadership.

Because of the complex and dynamic nature of situations and the substantial role that perceptions play in the interpretation of situations, no one has been able to develop a comprehensive taxonomy describing all the situational variables affecting a person's behavior. In all likelihood, no one ever will. Nevertheless, considerable research about situational influences on leadership has been accomplished. Leadership researchers have examined how different task, organizational, and environmental factors affect both leaders' and followers' behavior, though most have examined only the effects of one or two situational variables on leaders' and followers' behavior. For example, a study might have examined the effects of task difficulty on subordinates' performance yet ignored how broader issues, such as organizational policy or structure, might also affect their performance. This is primarily due to the difficulty of studying the effects of organizational and environmental factors on behavior. As you might imagine, many of these factors, such as societal culture or technological change, do not easily lend themselves to realistic laboratory experiments in which conditions can be controlled and interactions analyzed. Nonetheless, it is virtually impossible to understand leadership without taking the situation into consideration. We examine various factors and theories pertaining especially to the situation in Part 4.

CHAPTER 14

The Situation

Introduction

April 16, 2007, was a dark day at Virginia Tech. On that day Cho Seung Hui went on a shooting rampage that killed 32 students and faculty and injured a host of others. There is no doubt that Cho was a villain, if not a deranged one, as he created a situation of terror in Norris Hall. But in that same awful situation, heroes were created. One was Zach Petkewicz.

Zach and his fellow classmates were in a classroom near the one where Cho initiated his massacre. They heard the initial gunshots through the walls and could hear them getting closer. At first everyone experienced fear and hid behind whatever they could find for protection. But it occurred to Zach that "there's nothing stopping him from coming in here. We were just sitting ducks." And that's when Zach and others took action.

Zach grabbed a table and shoved it against the door. Seeing his plan, other students joined him, pinning the table against the cinderblock walls around the door frame. They were just in time. Cho tried to get into their classroom next. Having tried the door handle and then brute force, Cho emptied a clip of ammunition through the door before giving up and moving on to another room.

Days after the assault, Zach Petkewicz was interviewed by Matt Lauer on NBC's *Today Show*. Lauer asked Zach if he could have predicted, before the shooting, how he would react. The young hero, whose first reaction had been fear, said that's not possible for anyone. "There's no way of telling what I would have done until you're put in that situation."

Zach was right about two things. First, as he said, it is difficult to predict anyone's behavior unless you take the situation into account. Second, we are coming to understand that the situation is one of the most powerful variables in the leadership equation. And that is the topic of this chapter. It is important to understand how the situation influences leaders and followers and, furthermore, that the situation is not just a "given" that leaders and followers must adapt to; sometimes, at least, leaders and followers can change the situation and thereby enhance the likelihood of desired outcomes. That's what Zach did: He changed the situation. Of course Zach reacted to a situation he was tragically confronted with, but leaders do not always need to be reactive. Leaders also can use their knowledge of how the situation affects leadership to proactively *change* the situation in order to enhance the likelihood of success. All too often, leaders and followers overlook how changing the situation can help them to change their behavior. This is called **situational engineering**.

> *When you've exhausted all possibilities, remember this: You haven't!*
>
> **Robert H. Schuller, minister and author**

Suppose, for example, that a leader received developmental feedback that she needed to spend more time interacting with subordinates. Even with the best intentions, such a goal can prove difficult to achieve, just as numerous New Year's resolutions fail. In both cases an important barrier to success is that people do not adequately address challenges posed by the situation in which they find themselves. After the holidays, many well-intentioned dieters don't lose weight because they fail to reduce the number of food cues around them. And a leader who may genuinely desire greater interaction with subordinates may nonetheless unwittingly subvert her own goal by continuing to define her tasks in the same way she always had. A better strategy could be to review her own tasks and then delegate some of them to subordinates. This would free up some of the leader's time and also create opportunities to interact with subordinates, for example, in mutually setting performance goals and meeting regularly to review their progress.[1]

> *Trying to change individual and/or corporate behavior without addressing the larger organizational context is bound to disappoint. Sooner or later bureaucratic structures will consume even the most determined of collaborative processes. As Woody Allen once said, "The lion and the lamb may lie down together, but the lamb won't get much sleep." What to do? Work on the lion as well as the lamb designing teamwork into the organization. . . . Although the Boston Celtics have won 16 championships, they have never had the league's leading scorer and never paid a player based on his individual statistics. The Celtics understand that virtually every aspect of basketball requires collaboration.*
>
> **Robert W. Keidel, leadership consultant**

Highlight 14.1 describes one of two horrific man-made disasters that occurred in 1986: the space shuttle *Challenger* accident. The other—the explosion of the nuclear power plant in Chernobyl—is presented in the Minicase at the end of this chapter. **Highlight 14.2** reflects on a different kind of situational factor representing a global challenge to leaders and followers literally everywhere, with no clear end in sight: the coronavirus pandemic.

Challenger: Man-Made Disaster I

HIGHLIGHT 14.1

January 28, 1986, was an unusually cold morning at the Kennedy Space Center with temperatures slowly rising to 36 degrees by 11:30 a.m. But that chill did not deter the spectators or millions of others watching on television around the world waiting to see the 25th Space Shuttle mission launch after a number of delays. This mission was special because, of the seven astronauts on board that morning, one was a teacher, Christa McAuliffe. Shortly after 11:38 a.m., the shuttle cleared the launch tower. Some reported seeing an unusual puff of smoke. As *Challenger* climbed into a cloudless blue sky, at about 46,000 feet, everyone realized something had gone terribly wrong. Then came the message over the loudspeaker:

"Flight controllers here looking very closely at the situation. Obviously a major malfunction.

We have no downlink. We have a report from the Flight Dynamics Officer that the vehicle has exploded."

As we later learned, the shuttle itself did not explode. Rather, as seen in the *Report of the Presidential Commission on the Space Shuttle Challenger Accident* (typically referred to as the Rogers Commission Report), the cause of the accident had been the "failure in the joint between the two lower segments of the Solid Rocket Motor." But to the general public, the cause of the accident became commonly known as the "O-ring" failure. The large rubber O-ring responsible for sealing the joint had failed and allowed a burn-through from the Solid Rocket Motor into the large main shuttle fuel tanks. So we know what caused the *Challenger* accident. Or do we?

Unfortunately, disasters and accidents seldom have a simple cause. This is because, whether they be airline crashes, Space Shuttle accidents, or nuclear power plant disasters (see the Mini-case at the end of this chapter), the people and the resources are embedded in more complex organizations, groups, teams, systems, and cultures. These and many other factors are what we are talking about when looking at the Situation.

Situational Variables Contributing to the *Challenger* Accident

Clearly, one of two conditions occurred with the decision making process surrounding the *Challenger* accident: either somebody made a poor decision to launch, or somebody failed to make a decision to NOT launch, or both. As we shall see, it was some muddied combination of poor decision making practices. But to understand the situation surrounding *Challenger*, it is helpful to briefly look back on the NASA decision process used during the historic Apollo missions to the moon.

The Apollo program was driven and directed by one man: Dr. Wernher Von Braun. As the father of both German rocketry and the early rocket program in the United States, everyone knew that Von Braun would make the critical decisions for Apollo. Here's one example. Thirty days prior to any scheduled Apollo launch, a meeting was held at the Marshall Space Flight Center in Huntsville, AL, where a representative from every mission critical contractor was required to attend. The meeting was chaired by Von Braun himself and the contractors were seated in hard metal chairs in a gymnasium. One-by-one, each contractor would have to stand up, face his peers, and guarantee that his component could "fly." And if he could not, then he had to face not only the pressure of his peers but the questioning of Von Braun to explain what they were doing to ensure success and how long their delay would hold up the schedule. The contractors referred to Von Braun's management style in the meetings as "management by embarrassment." This should not be seen as an endorsement of autocratic management, but rather as an example of ensur-

ing that the ultimate decision maker had direct access to those with the most valid information.

The situation had changed by the time the 25th Space Shuttle was to launch. NASA decision makers had labelled the Shuttle program as "safe." This was interpreted by many, both within and outside NASA administration, that launching a Shuttle was almost like running a commercial airline. Partly because of this ill-conceived confidence and partly because of cost concerns by congressional oversight committees, NASA had promised that the Shuttle program would be "commercially viable." (That is NASA-speak for "the Shuttle program would pay for itself.")

For a moment, let's step outside the NASA framework and take a more objective look at what is going on. As with most large endeavors in a capitalistic environment, there are usually three big driving criteria. For the Shuttle program, these were reliability/safety, cost, and schedule. During Apollo and early Shuttle days, reliability/safety was always the overriding winner. If they had to spend more money or push the launch schedule to later to ensure safety, that was okay. But by guaranteeing that the Shuttle would be commercially viable, NASA could no longer afford to ask for additional funding nor push the schedule out. The pressure was on to "make the launch date" and everyone (both NASA personnel and contractors) were aware of this driving force. Reliability/safety had lost its primary position in decision making.

Along with the move to make the Shuttle program more like a commercial airline came added bureaucracy and multiple layers of decision makers. Unlike Apollo where Von Braun himself was in the meetings where concerns were expressed, Shuttle had at least five layers of Go–No Go decision makers between the contractors and the ultimate launch directors. One of these contractors was Morton-Thiokol, the manufacturer of the solid rocket boosters.

The engineers at Morton-Thiokol had been examining the recovered solid rocket booster casings. (Besides the Shuttle itself, the only other component routinely recovered was the shell of the solid rockets.) In so doing, they noticed a troubling issue. On some of the launches, they were getting significant burn-through of the O-rings seated between major sections of the booster. But not on all launches.

After looking into the troubling problem, they believed they had discovered the cause. There was significant burn through on the O-rings any-time the ambient launch temperature was below 53 degrees Fahrenheit. In what may be as close to a smoking gun as we can find, a Morton-Thiokol engineer wrote a letter to the first level of decision makers at the Marshall Space Flight Center at Huntsville, AL, informing them of this finding and NOT recommending launch anytime the ambient temperature was below 53 degrees. But with pressure coming down from above to make the launch schedule, the letter was labeled "inconclusive" by the first level deci-sion team.

The night before the launch, the weather fore-cast called for freezing temperatures. Of equal, if not greater concern to the Morton-Thiokol team is that the ambient temperature at launch was predicted to be 36 degrees. That was enough for Morton-Thiokol engineer Roger

Boisjoly and his managers to make a call, again to the Marshall Space Flight Center on the evening of January 27. They "strongly recom-mended against the launch of the *Challenger* on the grounds that the O-rings had never been tested under freezing conditions."

William R. Lucas was the director of the Mar-shall Center and a clear "Go–No Go" decision maker. In his testimony before the Rogers Com-mission charged with investigating the accident, Lucas stated that while he had heard that Mor-ton-Thiokol had called the first level team with their concern, he was assured the next morning before launch that the concern had been resolved. Thus, no mention of the concern ever reached the final decision makers and the *Chal-lenger* launched. Seventy-three seconds later, all souls on board were lost, not because anyone had evil thoughts or desires towards them, but because the leadership did not appreciate the implications of the situation in which they were working and its impact on their decision mak-ing.

Sources: *Report of the Presidential Commission on the Space Shuttle Challenger Accident* (June 6, 1986); and P. K. Tomp-kins, *Organizational Communication Imperatives: Lessons of the Space Program* (Los Angeles, CA: Roxbury, 1992).

In a book designed to introduce students to the subject of leadership, a chapter about "the situation" poses some challenging obstacles and dilemmas. The breadth of the topic is daunting: It could include almost every-thing else in the world that has not been covered in the previous chapters! To the typical student who has not yet begun a professional career, pondering the magnitude of variables making up the situation is a formidable task. For one thing, the situation you find yourself in is often seen as completely beyond your control. How many times have you heard someone say, "Hey, I don't make the rules around here—I just follow them"? The subject is made more difficult by the fact that most students have limited organizational experience as a frame of reference. So why bother to introduce the material in this chapter? Because the situation we are in often explains far more about what is going on and what kinds of leadership behaviors will be best than any other single variable we have discussed so far.

In this chapter, we will try to sort out some of the complexity and magnitude of this admittedly large topic. First, we will review some of the research that has led us to consider these issues. Then, after examining a huge situational change that is now occurring, we will present a model to help us consider key situational variables. Finally, we will take a look forward through an interesting lens. Throughout the chapter, though, our objective will be primarily to increase awareness rather than to prescribe specific courses of leader action.

The way of the superior is threefold, but I am not equal to it. Virtuous, he is free from anxieties; wise, he is free from perplexities; bold, he is free from fear.

Confucius, Chinese philosopher

The appropriateness of a leader's behavior with a group of followers often makes sense only when you look at the situational context in which the behavior occurs. For example, severely disciplining a follower might seem a poor way to lead; but if the follower in question had just committed a safety violation endangering the lives of hundreds of people, then the leader's actions might be exactly right. In a similar fashion, the situation may be the primary reason personality traits, experience, or cognitive abilities are related less consistently to leadership effectiveness than to leadership emergence.[2, 3] Most leadership emergence studies have involved leaderless discussion groups, and for the most part the situation is quite similar across such studies. In studies of leadership effectiveness, however, the situation can and does vary dramatically. The personal attributes needed by an effective leader of a combat unit, chemical research and development division, community service organization, or fast-food restaurant may change considerably. Because the situations facing leaders of such groups may be so variable, it is hardly surprising that studies of leader characteristics have yielded inconsistent results when looking at leadership effectiveness across jobs or situations. Thus the importance of the situation in the leadership process should not be overlooked.

Historically, some leadership researchers emphasized the importance of the situation in the leadership process in response to the Great Man theory of leadership. These researchers maintained that the situation, not someone's traits or abilities, plays the most important role in determining who emerges as a leader.[4, 5, 6] As support for the situational viewpoint, these researchers noted that great leaders typically emerged during economic crises, social upheavals, or revolutions; great leaders were generally not associated with periods of relative calm or quiet. For example, Schneider[7] noted that the number of individuals identified as great military leaders in the British armed forces during any period depended on how many conflicts the country was engaged in—the higher the number of conflicts, the higher the number of great military leaders. Moreover, researchers advocating the situational viewpoint believed leaders were made, not born, and that prior leadership experience helped forge effective leaders.[8] These early situational theories of leadership tended to be popular in the United States because they fit more closely with American ideals of equality and meritocracy and ran counter to the genetic views of leadership that were popular among European researchers at the time.[9] (The fact that many of these European researchers had aristocratic backgrounds probably had something to do with the popularity of the Great Man theory in Europe.)

COVID-19: A World-Wide "Situation"

HIGHLIGHT 14.2

The coronavirus global pandemic struck just as this tenth edition of our textbook was in its final stages of preparation. We believe the magnitude of this "situation" demands mention in this text, yet at the present time there are no clear answers as to what the pandemic's lasting impact on our lives will be—or how leadership and followership will be affected, if at all. But even now we may at least speculate about certain sorts of lasting impact. For example, the public healthcare system likely will be strengthened to become nimbler and better fortified; laws may be changed to better protect workers, especially those whose occupations do not provide paid benefits; and perhaps scientists and other experts who caution about the dangers of climate change will find their advice better heeded.

Other changes too can be anticipated. Take education for example. Perhaps public education will move to a greater use of online teaching methods as the pandemic forced widespread school closings. And if greater online learning became the norm (which it might have anyway), imagine how educational leadership might evolve:

- What kinds of different challenges might principals and administrators face in managing the educational process?
- Would greater online requirements necessitate modified selection and performance evaluation criteria for teachers?
- How might such changes impact the attractiveness of the teaching profession?

And as we noted, that's just one example.

So as we are speculating about the lasting impact of the pandemic on life and leadership, let us invite you into the conversation... By the time you are reading this, the situation likely will have further changed—maybe with a "return to normalcy," but maybe not. So in your *present* circumstances reflect on these questions:

- Do you see any lasting impact of the pandemic on your life?
- What new or different challenges do you see leaders facing as a result of the pandemic?
- Do you see ways that follower expectations might be changing as a result of the pandemic, maybe in some sectors more than others?
- Have your own life aspirations and expectations changed as a result?

Source: M. Z. Barabak, "News Analysis: The Coronavirus Crisis Will Change America in Big Ways. History Says So," *Los Angeles Times*, April 6, 2020.

More recent leadership theories have explored how situational factors affect leaders' behaviors. In **role theory**, for example, a leader's behavior was said to depend on a leader's perceptions of several critical aspects of the situation: rules and regulations governing the job; role expectations of subordinates, peers, and superiors; the nature of the task; and feedback about subordinates' performance.[10] Role theory clarified how these situational demands and constraints could cause role conflict and role ambiguity.[11] Leaders may experience role conflict when subordinates and superiors have conflicting expectations about a leader's behavior or when company policies contradict how superiors expect tasks to be performed. A leader's ability to successfully resolve such conflicts may well determine leadership effectiveness.[12]

Another effort to incorporate situational variables into leadership theory was Hunt and Osborn's[13] **multiple-influence model**. Hunt and Osborn distinguished between microvariables (such as task characteristics) and macrovariables (such as the external environment) in the situation. Although most researchers looked at the effects tasks had on leader behaviors, Hunt and Osborn believed macrovariables have a pervasive influence on the ways leaders act. Both role theory and the multiple-influence model highlight a major problem in addressing situational factors, which was noted previously: that situations can vary in countless ways. Because situations can vary in so many ways, it is helpful for leaders to have an abstract scheme for conceptualizing situations. This would be a step in knowing how to identify what may be most salient or critical to pay attention to in any particular instance.

One of the most basic abstractions is **situational levels**. The idea behind situational levels may best be conveyed with an example. Suppose someone asked you, "How are things going at work?" You might respond by commenting on the specific tasks you perform ("It is still pretty tough. I am under the gun for getting next year's budget prepared, and I have never done that before."). Or you might respond by commenting on aspects of the overall organization ("It is really different. There are so many rules you have to follow. My old company was not like that at all"). Or you might comment on factors affecting the organization itself ("I've been really worried about keeping my job—you know how many cutbacks there have been in our whole industry recently."). Each response deals with the situation, but each refers to a different level of abstraction: the task level, the organizational level, and the environmental level. Each of these three levels provides a different perspective with which to examine the leadership process (see **Figure 14.1**).

These three levels certainly do not exhaust all the ways in which situations vary. Situations also differ in terms of physical variables like noise and temperature levels, workload demands, and the extent to which work groups interact with other groups. Organizations also have unique "corporate cultures," which define a context for leadership. And there are always even broader economic, social, legal, and technological aspects of situations within which the leadership process occurs. What, amid all this situational complexity, should leaders pay attention to?

The Task

How Tasks Vary, and What That Means for Leadership

The most fundamental level of the situation involves the tasks to be performed by individuals or teams within the organization. Several ways in which tasks vary are particularly relevant to leadership. Industrial and organizational psychologists spent much of the last half-century classifying and categorizing tasks to better understand how to enhance worker satisfaction and productivity. Some of this research has great relevance to leadership, particularly the concepts of task autonomy, feedback, structure, and interdependence.

Task autonomy is the degree to which a job provides an individual with some control over what he does and how he does it. Someone with considerable autonomy would have discretion in scheduling work and deciding the procedures used in accomplishing it. Autonomy often covaries with technical expertise: Workers with

FIGURE 14.1   An Expanded Leader–Follower–Situation Model

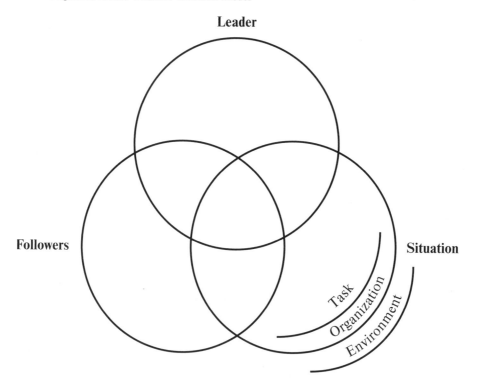

considerable expertise will be given more latitude, and those with few skills will be given more instruction and coaching when accomplishing tasks.[14, 15] Moreover, responsibility and job satisfaction often increase when autonomy increases.[16]

> *The brain is a wonderful organ; it begins working the moment you get up in the morning and does not stop until you get to the office.*
>
> **Robert Frost, American poet**

Another important way in which tasks vary is in terms of **task feedback**, which refers to the degree to which a person accomplishing a task receives information about performance *from performing the task itself.* In this context, feedback is received not from supervisors but rather from what is intrinsic to the work activity itself. Driving a car is one example of feedback intrinsic to a task. If you are a skilled driver on a road with a number of twists and turns, you get all the feedback you need about how well you are accomplishing the task merely by observing how the car responds to your inputs. This is feedback from the job itself as opposed to feedback from another person (who in this example would be a classic backseat driver). Extending this example to work or team settings, leaders sometimes may want to redesign tasks so that the tasks provide more intrinsic feedback. Although this does not absolve the leader from giving periodic performance feedback, it can free up some of the leader's time for other work-related activities. Additionally, leaders should understand that followers may eventually become dissatisfied if leaders provide high levels of feedback for tasks that already provide intrinsic feedback.[17, 18, 19]

> *If you want to give a man credit, put it in writing. If you want to give him hell, do it on the phone.*
>
> **Charles Beacham, corporate executive**

Perhaps the easiest way to explain **task structure** is by using an example demonstrating the difference between a structured task and an unstructured task. Assume the task to be accomplished is solving for x given the formula $3x + 2x = 15$. If that problem were given to a group of people who knew the fundamental rules of algebra, everyone would arrive at the same answer. In this example there is a known procedure for accomplishing the task; there are rules governing how one goes about it; and if people follow those rules, there is one result. These features characterize a *structured task.*

By contrast, if the task is to resolve a morale problem on a team, committee, or work group, there may be no clear-cut method for solving it. There are many different ways, perhaps none of which is obvious or necessarily best for approaching a solution. Different observers may not see the problem in the same way; they may even have different ideas of what morale is. Solving a morale problem, therefore, exemplifies an *unstructured task.*

People vary in their preferences for, or ability to handle, structured versus unstructured tasks. With the Myers-Briggs Type Indicator (MBTI), for example, perceivers are believed to prefer unstructured situations, whereas judgers prefer activities that are planned and organized.[20] Individuals with high tolerance for stress may handle ambiguous and unstructured tasks more easily than people with low tolerance for stress.[21] Aside from these differences, however, we might ask whether there are any general rules for how leaders should interact with followers as a function of task structure. One consideration here is that although it is *easier* for a leader or coach to give instruction in structured tasks, it is not necessarily the most helpful thing to do.

We can see this by returning to the algebra problem described earlier. If a student had never seen such an algebra problem before, it would be relatively easy to teach the student the rules needed to solve the problem. Once any student has learned the procedure, however, she can solve similar problems on her own. Extending this to other situations, once a subordinate knows or understands a task, a supervisor's continuing instruction (that is, initiating structure or directive behavior) may provide superfluous information and eventually become irritating.[22, 23] Subordinates *need* help when a task is unstructured, when they do not know what the desired outcome looks like, and when they do not know how to achieve it. Anything a supervisor or leader can do to increase subordinates' ability to perform unstructured tasks is likely to increase their performance and job satisfaction.[24] Paradoxically, though, unstructured tasks are by nature somewhat ill defined. Thus leaders often have more difficulty analyzing and providing direction in accomplishing such tasks. Nonetheless, reducing the degree of ambiguity inherent in an unstructured situation is a leadership behavior that followers usually appreciate.

Finally, **task interdependence** concerns the degree to which tasks require coordination and synchronization for work groups or teams to accomplish desired goals. Task interdependence differs from autonomy in that workers or team members may be able to accomplish their tasks in an autonomous fashion, but the products of their efforts must be coordinated for the group or team to succeed. Tasks with high levels of interdependence place a premium on leaders' organizing and planning, directing, and communication skills.[25] In one study, for example, coaches exhibiting high levels of initiating-structure behaviors had better-performing teams for sports requiring relatively interdependent effort, such as football, hockey, lacrosse, rugby, basketball, and volleyball; the same leader behaviors were unrelated to team performance for sports requiring relatively independent effort, such as swimming, track, cross country, golf, and baseball.[26] Thus the degree of task interdependence can dictate which leader behaviors will be effective in a particular situation.

Problems and Challenges

Astronaut Jim Lovell's words during the *Apollo 13* lunar mission, "Houston, we have a problem," launched a remarkable tale of effective teamwork and creative problem solving by NASA engineers working to save the lives of the imperiled crew when two oxygen tanks exploded en route to the moon. The problem they faced was urgent, critical, and novel: No one had ever confronted a problem like this before; no one had even anticipated it; and there were no established checklists, emergency procedures, or backup equipment that could be counted on to reach a viable solution. We might say, of course, that the engineers' task was to devise a solution, but we want to stress a distinction here between the connotation of *task* as it was examined in the preceding section and that of completely novel problems or challenges for which routine solutions do not exist. As we noted earlier, up to this point our treatment of tasks has derived largely from the perspective of industrial and organizational psychology wherein the task dimensions just described (and many others) represent ways to systematically and objectively describe relatively enduring aspects of routine work or jobs. Obviously the situation that the NASA engineers and astronauts faced was anything but routine.

Ronald Heifetz has been studying the leadership implications of problems and challenges like that for many years. He says that often we face problems or challenges for which the problem-solving resources already exist. In general, you can think of these resources as having two aspects: specialized methods and specialized expertise. There are many technical problems that we can solve by applying widely known though specialized methods for solution. A simple example might be determining the gas mileage your car gets on a cross-country trip. The rules are simple to follow, and they always work if you follow them correctly. At other times *we* may not know the answers, but it may be relatively easy to find the people who do. Maybe we can't fix the rattle coming from the car engine, but we believe the mechanic can do so. We may not know how to fix our ailment, but we believe the physician will know what to do. We may not know how to use a new software system, but we believe we can master it with assistance from an expert. Problems like these are what Heifetz calls **technical problems**. Even though they may be complex, there are expert solutions to them, and experts know how to solve them even if we don't.[27]

> *Rough waters are truer tests of leadership. In calm water every ship has a good captain.*
>
> **Swedish proverb**

But not all problems are like that. Some problems, by their nature, defy even expert solution. Some problems cannot be solved using currently existing resources and ways of thinking. In fact, it's the nature of such problems that *it can be quite difficult even reaching a common definition of what the problem really is*. Solving such problems requires that the systems facing them make fundamental changes of some kind. Heifetz calls these **adaptive problems**. Whereas technical problems can be solved without changing the nature of the social system within which they occur, *adaptive problems can be solved only by changing the system itself.*

At work, the most important issue in addressing technical problems is making sure they get to someone with the authority to manage the solution. According to Heifetz, however, most social problems turn out to be adaptive in nature. Almost by definition, then, significant organizational change is at least in part an adaptive challenge. Even a seemingly simpler leadership challenge at work, like getting someone else to take more seriously some constructive feedback, is actually an adaptive challenge rather than a technical one. But here is where the distinction between technical problems and adaptive problems can become blurred. Go back to our earlier example of seeing a physician for a medical problem—but let's assume it's your elderly parent rather than you who is the patient. Let's further assume that the physician correctly solves the technical problem and provides the correct technical solution—a particular medication that has a noticeable but tolerable side effect. Getting your parent to take the medicine if he doesn't want to turns this seemingly simple technical problem into a challenging adaptive one.

How do you know when a challenge is mostly a technical challenge or mostly an adaptive challenge? It's an adaptive challenge either wholly or mostly

- When people's hearts and minds need to change, and not just their standard or habitual behaviors.
- By a process of elimination—if every technical solution you can think of has failed to improve the situation, it is more likely to be an adaptive challenge.
- If there is continuing conflict among people struggling with the challenge.
- In a crisis, which may reflect an underlying or unrecognized adaptive problem.

> *Some problems are so complex that you have to be highly intelligent and well informed just to be undecided about them.*
>
> **Laurence J. Peter, management consultant**

Different leadership approaches are required to solve adaptive problems than are required to solve technical problems. That's because adaptive problems involve people's *values*, and finding solutions to problems that involve others' values requires the active engagement of *their* hearts and minds—not just the leader's. This is what Heifetz calls **adaptive leadership**. The importance of the difference between adaptive and technical problems will become clearer as we look later in the chapter at the organizational and environmental levels of the situation.

To summarize, **Table 14.1** shows the relationship between whether a problem or a challenge is mostly technical or adaptive in nature, the kind of work required to effectively address the challenge, and whom should be thought of as the "problem solver."[28]

TABLE 14.1   Adaptive and Technical Challenges

	What's the Work?	Who Does the Work?
Technical	Applying current know-how	Authorities
Adaptive	Discovering new ways	The people facing the challenge

The Organization

From the Industrial Age to the Information Age

All of us have grown up in the age of industry, but perhaps in its waning years. Starting just before the American Civil War and continuing through the last quarter of the 20th century, the industrial age supplanted the age of agriculture. During the industrial age, companies succeeded according to how well they could capture the benefits from "economies of scale and scope."[29] Technology mattered, but mostly to the extent that companies could increase the efficiencies of mass production. Now a new age is emerging, and in this information age many of the fundamental assumptions of the industrial age are becoming obsolete.

Kaplan and Norton[30] have described a new set of operating assumptions underlying the information age and contrasted them with their predecessors in the industrial age. They described changes in several ways that companies operate.

Cross Functions: Industrial age organizations gained competitive advantage through specialization of functional skills in areas like manufacturing, distribution, marketing, and technology. This specialization yielded substantial benefits but over time also led to enormous inefficiencies and slow response processes. The information age organization operates with integrated business processes that cut across traditional business functions.

Links to Customers and Suppliers: Industrial age companies worked with customers and suppliers via arm's-length transactions. Information technology enables today's organizations to integrate supply, production, and delivery processes and to realize enormous improvements in cost, quality, and response time.

Customer Segmentation: Industrial age companies prospered by offering low-cost but standardized products and services (remember Henry Ford's comment that his customers "can have whatever color they want as long as it is black"). Information age companies must learn to offer customized products and services to diverse customer segments.

Global Scale: Information age companies compete against the best companies throughout the entire world. In fact, the large investments required for new products and services may require customers worldwide to provide adequate returns on those costs.

Innovation: Product life cycles continue to shrink. Competitive advantage in one generation of a product's life is no guarantee of success for future generations of that product. Companies operating in an environment of rapid technological innovation must be masters at anticipating customers' future needs, innovating new products and services, and rapidly deploying new technologies into efficient delivery processes.

Knowledge Workers: Industrial companies created sharp distinctions between an intellectual elite on the one hand (especially managers and engineers) and a direct labor workforce on the other. The latter group performed tasks and processes under direct supervision of white-collar engineers and managers. This typically involved physical rather than mental capabilities. Now all employees must contribute value by what they know and by the information they can provide.

One needs only to reflect upon Kaplan and Norton's list of changing operating assumptions to recognize that the situation leaders find themselves in today is different from the situation of 20 years ago. What's more, it is probably changing at an ever-increasing rate. In a real sense, the pace of change today is like trying to navigate whitewater rapids; things are changing so rapidly that it can be difficult to get one's bearings. And the challenge of coping with the accelerating pace of change is due at least in part to inherent limitations human beings have in their information-processing capabilities, as is pointed out in **Highlight 14.3**. To understand how organizations cope with change, it will be helpful to look at two different facets of organizations: the formal organization and the informal organization, or organizational culture.

Accelerating Change I

HIGHLIGHT 14.3

One of the manifestations of having moved from the industrial age to the information age is the fact that, in many cases today, machines can make better decisions than humans. The primary basis for this was the exponential growth that has occurred in computer power. This acceleration in computing power was first postulated in 1965 by Gordon Moore, the cofounder of Intel. He proposed that computational processing power would double roughly every year, referred to as Moore's law, and his prediction has proven remarkably accurate over the last 50 years.

True as Moore's law may be, however, truly *grasping* the long-term implications of accelerating change like that is nearly impossible for humans. As a demonstration of our cognitive deficit there, let us propose a mental problem for you: Imagine that you have a very large piece of paper that is similar to printing paper; it is the same thickness as printing paper (about .004 inches thick), but its other dimensions are *much* larger. Now imagine folding that paper over in your mind, so that its thickness is now .008 inches thick (mathematically this is analogous to doubling computer power every year).

Then double it over again so that it becomes .016 inches thick, and so on, until you have doubled the thickness of that sheet of paper 40 times. After that 40th fold, how thick do you think your clump of paper would be? Would it be:

a) 7 inches thick

a) 70 inches thick

a) 700 inches thick

a) 7,000 inches thick

The answer is "none of the above" (don't you hate those kinds of questions!). The correct answer is that after 40 folds, the paper would be over 700,000 miles thick! And just as that result is incomprehensible to us, so we also find it nearly impossible to grasp how Moore's law makes computer intelligence unimaginably more powerful every year.

To learn more about how Moore's law is among one of the many items accelerating the pace of change today, you might look at Thomas Friedman's book *Thank You for Being Late—An Optimist's Guide to Thriving in the Age of Acceleration.*

Source: T. Friedman, *Thank You for Being Late* (New York: Picador, 2016).

The Formal Organization

The study of the **formal organization** is most associated with the disciplines of management, organizational behavior, and organizational theory. Nonetheless, many aspects of the formal organization have a profound impact on leadership, and so we will briefly review some of the most important of them.

> *A man may speak very well in the House of Commons, and fail very completely in the House of Lords. There are two distinct styles requisite.*
>
> **Benjamin Disraeli, former British prime minister**

Despite the dramatic changes in the way people work, the organizations in which they carry out that work have changed much less than might be expected.

The Economist, January 21, 2006

Level of authority concerns our hierarchical level in an organization. The types of behaviors most critical to leadership effectiveness can change substantially as we move up an organizational ladder. First-line supervisors, lower-level leaders, and coaches spend a considerable amount of time training followers, resolving work unit or team performance problems, scheduling practices or arranging work schedules, and implementing policies. Leaders at higher organizational levels have more autonomy and spend relatively more time setting policies, coordinating activities, and making staffing decisions.[31, 32] Moreover, leaders at higher organizational levels often perform a greater variety of activities and are more apt to use participation and delegation.[33, 34] A quite different aspect of how level of authority affects leadership is presented in **Highlight 14.4**.

The Glass Ceiling and the Wall

HIGHLIGHT 14.4

Although the past 25 years have been marked by increasing movement of women into leadership positions, women still occupy only a small percentage of the highest leadership positions. Researchers at the Center for Creative Leadership embarked on the Executive Woman Project to understand why.

They studied 76 women executives in 25 companies who had reached the general management level or the one just below it. The average woman executive in the sample was 41 and married. More than half had at least one child, and the vast majority were white.

The researchers expected to find evidence of a "glass ceiling," an invisible barrier that keeps women from progressing higher than a certain level in their organizations *because they are women*. One reason the women in this particular sample were interesting was precisely because they had apparently "broken" the glass ceiling, thus entering the top 1 percent of the workforce. These women had successfully confronted three different sorts of pressure throughout their careers, a greater challenge than their male counterparts faced. One pressure was that from the job itself, and this was no different for women than for men. A second level of pressure, however, involved being a female executive, with attendant stresses such as being particularly visible, excessively scrutinized, and a role model for other women. A third level of pressure involved the demands of coordinating personal and professional life. It is still most people's expectation that women will take the greater responsibility in a family for managing the household and raising children. And beyond the sheer size of such demands, the roles of women in these two spheres of life are often at odds (such as being businesslike and efficient, maybe even tough, at work yet intimate and nurturing at home).

Researchers identified the "lessons for success" of this group of women who had broken through the glass ceiling, and they also reported a somewhat unexpected finding. Breaking through the glass ceiling presented women executives with an even tougher obstacle. They "hit a wall" that kept them out of the very top positions. The researchers estimated that only a handful of the women executives in their sample would enter the topmost echelon, called senior management, and that none would become president of their corporation.

Sources: A. M. Morrison, R. P. White, and E. Van Velsor, *Breaking the Glass Ceiling* (Reading, MA: Addison-Wesley, 1987); and G. Morse, "Why We Misread Motives," *Harvard Business Review*, January 2003, p. 18.

Organizational structure refers to the way an organization's activities are coordinated and controlled, and it represents another level of the situation in which leaders and followers must operate. Organizational structure is a conceptual or procedural reality, however, not a physical or tangible one. Typically it is depicted in the form of a chart that clarifies formal authority relationships and patterns of communication within the organization. Most people take organizational structure for granted and fail to realize that structure is really just a tool for getting things done in organizations. Structure is not an end in itself, and different structures might exist for organizations performing similar work, each having unique advantages and disadvantages. There is nothing sacrosanct or permanent about any structure, and leaders may find that having a basic understanding of organizational structure is imperative. Leaders may wish to design a structure to enhance the likelihood of attaining a desired outcome, or they may wish to change a structure to meet future demands.

One important way in which organizational structures vary is in terms of their complexity. Concerning an organizational chart, **horizontal complexity** refers to the number of "boxes" at any particular organizational level. The greater the number of boxes at a given level, the greater the horizontal complexity. Typically greater horizontal complexity is associated with more specialization within subunits and an increased likelihood for communication breakdowns between subunits. **Vertical complexity** refers to the number of hierarchical levels appearing on an organizational chart. A vertically simple organization may have only two or three levels from the highest person to the lowest. A vertically complex organization, by contrast, may have 10 or more. Vertical complexity can affect leadership by impacting other factors such as authority dynamics and communication networks. **Spatial complexity** describes geographic dispersion. An organization that has all its people in one location is typically less spatially complex than an organization that is dispersed around the country or around the world. Obviously spatial complexity makes it more difficult for leaders to have face-to-face communication with subordinates in geographically separated locations, and to personally administer rewards or provide support and encouragement. Generally all three of these elements are partly a function of organizational size. Bigger organizations are more likely to have more specialized subunits (horizontal complexity) and a greater number of hierarchical levels (vertical complexity), and to have subunits that are geographically dispersed (spatial complexity).

Organizations also vary in their degree of **formalization**, or degree of standardization. Organizations having written job descriptions and standardized operating procedures for each position have a high degree of formalization. The degree of formalization in an organization tends to vary with its size, just as complexity generally increases with size.[35] Formalization also varies with the nature of work performed. Manufacturing organizations, for example, tend to have fairly formalized structures, whereas research and development organizations tend to be less formalized. After all, how could there be a detailed job description for developing a nonexistent product or making a scientific discovery?

The degree of formalization in an organization poses both advantages and disadvantages for leaders and followers. Whereas formalizing procedures clarifies methods of operating and interacting, it also may place demands and constraints on leaders and followers. Leaders may be constrained in the ways they communicate requests, order supplies, or reward or discipline subordinates.[36] If followers belong to a union, then union rules may dictate work hours, the amount of work accomplished per day, or who will be the first to be laid off.[37] Other aspects of the impact of formalization and other situational variables on leadership are presented in **Highlight 14.5**.

Is There Any Substitute for Leadership?

HIGHLIGHT 14.5

Are leaders always necessary? Or are certain kinds of leader behaviors, at least, sometimes unnecessary? Kerr and Jermier proposed that certain situational or follower characteristics may effectively neutralize or substitute for leaders' task or relationship behaviors. *Neutralizers* are characteristics that reduce or limit the effectiveness of a leader's behaviors. *Substitutes* are characteristics that make a leader's behaviors redundant or unnecessary.

Kerr and Jermier developed the idea of **substitutes for leadership** after comparing the correlations between leadership behaviors and follower performance and satisfaction with correlations between various situational factors and follower performance and satisfaction. Those subordinate, task, and organizational characteristics having higher correlations with follower performance and satisfaction than the two leadership behaviors were subsequently identified as substitutes or neutralizers. The following are a few examples of the situational factors Kerr and Jermier found to substitute for or neutralize leaders' task or relationship behaviors:

- A subordinate's ability and experience may substitute for task-oriented leader behavior. A subordinate's indifference toward rewards overall may neutralize a leader's task and relationship behavior.

- Tasks that are routine or structured may substitute for task-oriented leader behavior, as can tasks that provide intrinsic feedback or are intrinsically satisfying.

- High levels of formalization in organizations may substitute for task-oriented leader behavior, and unbending rules and procedures may even neutralize the leader's task behavior. A cohesive work group may provide a substitute for the leader's task and relationship behavior.

Source: S. Kerr and J. M. Jermier, "Substitutes for Leadership: Their Meaning and Measurement," *Organizational Behavior and Human Performance* 22 (1978), pp. 375–403.

Centralization refers to the diffusion of decision-making throughout an organization. An organization that allows decisions to be made by only one person is highly centralized. When decision-making is dispersed to the lowest levels in the organization, the organization is very decentralized. Advantages of decentralized organizations include increased participation in the decision process and, consequently, greater acceptance and ownership of decision outcomes. These are both desirable outcomes. There are also, however, advantages to centralization, such as uniform policies and procedures (which can increase feelings of equity) and clearer coordination procedures.[38] The task of balancing the degree of centralization necessary to achieve coordination and control, on the one hand, and gaining desirable participation and acceptance, on the other, is an ongoing challenge for the leader.

The Informal Organization: Organizational Culture

The word that sums up the **informal organization** better than any other is its *culture*. Although most people probably think of culture in terms of very large social groups, the concept also applies to organizations. **Organizational culture** has been defined as a system of shared backgrounds, norms, values, or beliefs among members of a group,[39] and **organizational climate** concerns members' subjective reactions to the organization.[40, 41] These two concepts are distinct in that organizational climate is partly a function of, or reaction to, organizational culture; our feelings or emotional reactions about an organization are probably affected by the degree to which we share the prevailing values, beliefs, and backgrounds of organizational members.[42, 43] If a person does not share the values or beliefs of the majority of members, then in all likelihood this person would have a fairly negative reaction about the organization overall. Thus organizational climate (and, indirectly, organizational culture) is related to how well organizational members get along with each other.[44, 45] Also note that organizational climate is narrower in scope but highly related to job satisfaction. Generally, organizational climate has more to do with nontask perceptions of work, such as feelings about coworkers or company policies, whereas job satisfaction usually also includes perceptions of workload and the nature of the tasks performed.

Just as there are many cultures across the world, there are a great number of different cultures across organizations. Members of military organizations typically have different norms, background experiences, values, and beliefs, for example, from those of the faculty at most colleges or universities. Similarly, the culture of an investment firm is different from the culture of a research and development firm, a freight hauling company, or a college rugby team. Cultural differences can even exist between different organizations within any of these sectors. The culture of the U.S. Air Force is different from the culture of the U.S. Marine Corps, and Yale University has a different culture than the University of Colorado even though they are both fine institutions of higher learning. Questions that suggest further ways in which organizational cultures may differ are listed in **Table 14.2**.

TABLE 14.2   **Some Questions That Define Organizational Culture**

- What can be talked about or not talked about?
- How do people wield power?
- How does a person get ahead or stay out of trouble?
- What are the unwritten rules of the game?
- What are the organization's morality and ethics?
- What stories are told about the organization?

Source: Adapted from R. H. Kilmann and M. J. Saxton, *Organizational Cultures: Their Assessment and Change* (San Francisco: Jossey-Bass, 1983).

One of the more fascinating aspects of organizational culture is that it often takes an outsider to recognize it; organizational culture becomes so second nature to many organizational members that they are unaware of how it affects their behaviors and perceptions.[46] Despite this transparency to organizational members, a fairly consistent set of dimensions can be used to differentiate between organizational cultures. For example, Kilmann and Saxton[47] stated that organizational cultures can be differentiated based on members' responses to questions like those found in **Table 14.2**. Another way to understand an organization's culture is in terms of myths and stories, symbols, rituals, and language.[48] A more detailed description of the four key factors identified by Schein can be found in **Highlight 14.6**.

Schein's Four Key Organizational Culture Factors

HIGHLIGHT 14.6

Myths and stories are the tales about the organization that are passed down over time and communicate a story of the organization's underlying values. Virtually any employee of Walmart can tell you stories about Sam Walton and his behavior—how he rode around in his pickup truck, how he greeted people in the stores, and how he tended to "just show up" at different times. The Center for Creative Leadership has stories about its founder, H. Smith Richardson, who as a young man creatively used the mail to sell products. Sometimes stories and myths are transferred between organizations even though the truth may not lie wholly in either one. A story is told at AT&T about one of its founders and how he trudged miles and miles through a blizzard to repair a faulty component so that a woman living by herself in a rural community could get phone service. Interestingly enough, this same story is told at MCI (now Verizon).

Symbols and artifacts are objects that can be seen and noticed and that describe various aspects of the culture. In almost any building, for example, symbols and artifacts provide information about the organization's culture. For example, an organization may believe in egalitarian principles, and that might be reflected in virtually everyone having the same size office. Or there can be indications of opulence, which convey a very different message. Even signs might act as symbols or artifacts of underlying cultural values. At one university that believed students should have first priority for facilities, an interesting sign showed up occasionally to reinforce this value. It was not a road sign, but a sign appearing on computer monitors. When the university's main computer was being overused, the computer was programmed to identify nonstudent users, note the overload, and issue a warning to nonstudent users to sign off. This was a clear artifact, or symbol, underlying the priority placed on students at that school.

Rituals are recurring events or activities that reflect important aspects of the underlying culture. An organization may have spectacular sales meetings for its top performers and spouses every two years. This ritual would be an indication of the value placed on high sales and meeting high quotas. Another kind of ritual is the retirement ceremony. Elaborate or modest retirement ceremonies may signal the importance an organization places on its people.

Language concerns the jargon, or idiosyncratic terms, of an organization and can serve several different purposes relevant to culture. First, the mere fact that some people know the language and some do not indicates who is in the culture and who is not. Second, language can also provide information about how people within a culture view others. Third, language can be used to help create a culture. A good example of the power of language in creating culture is in the words employees at Disneyland or Walt Disney World use in referring to themselves and park visitors. Employees—all employees, from the costumed Disney characters to popcorn vendors—are told to think of themselves as members of a cast, and never to be out of character. Everything happening at the park is part of the "show," and those who paid admission to enter the park are not mere tourists, but rather "the audience." Virtually everyone who visits the Disney parks is impressed with the consistently friendly behavior of its staff, a reflection of the power of words in creating culture. (Of course, a strict and strongly enforced policy concerning courtesy toward park guests also helps.)

Here is an example of how stories contribute to organizational culture. A consultant was asked to help a plant that had been having morale and production problems for years. After talking with several individuals at the plant, the consultant believed he had located the problem. It seems everyone he talked to told him about Sam, the plant manager. He was a giant of a man with a terrible temper. He had demolished unacceptable products with a sledgehammer, stood on the plant roof screaming at workers, and done countless other things sure to intimidate everyone around. The consultant decided he needed to talk to this plant manager. When he did so, however, he met an agreeable person named Paul. Sam, it seems, had been dead for nearly a decade, but his legacy lived on.[49]

Leaders must realize that they can play an active role in changing an organization's culture, not just be influenced by it.[50, 51, 52, 53] Leaders can change culture by attending to or ignoring particular issues, problems, or projects. They can modify culture through their reactions to crises, by rewarding new or different kinds of behavior, or by eliminating previous punishments or negative consequences for certain behaviors. Their general personnel policies send messages about the value of employees to the organization (such as cutting wages to avoid layoffs). They can use role modeling and self-sacrifice as a way to inspire or motivate others to work more vigorously or to interact with each other differently. Finally, leaders can also change culture by the criteria they use to select or dismiss followers. The payoff for such efforts is that having an optimal culture can enhance the likelihood an organization will be successful, as in studies that demonstrate how fostering an entrepreneurial culture can enhance organizational innovation.[54]

Changing an organization's culture, of course, takes time and effort, and sometimes it may be extremely difficult. This is especially true in very large organizations or those with strong cultures. New organizations, by contrast, do not have the traditions, stories or myths, or established rites to the same extent that older companies do, and it may be easier for leaders to change culture in these organizations.

Why would a leader *want* to change an organization's culture? It all should depend on whether the culture is having a positive or a negative impact on various desirable outcomes. We remember one organization with a very polite culture, an aspect that seemed positive at first. There were never any potentially destructive emotional outbursts in the organization, and there was an apparent concern for other individuals' feelings in all interactions. However, a darker side of that culture gradually became apparent. When it was appropriate to give feedback for performance appraisals or employee development, supervisors were hesitant to raise negative aspects of behavior; they interpreted doing so as not being polite. And so the organization continued to be puzzled by employee behavior that tended not to improve; the organization was a victim of its own culture.

At other times, organizational culture itself can be a victim of changes initially considered to be merely technical. A classic example of this pertains to the coal-mining industry in England. For hundreds of years coal was mined by teams of three people each. In England coal is layered in narrow seams, most only a few feet high. In the past the only practical means to get the coal out was to send the three-person teams of miners down into the mines to dig coal from the seam and then haul it to the surface on a tram. These mining teams had extremely high levels of group cohesiveness. A technological development called the long-wall method of coal extraction upset these close relationships, however. In the long-wall method, workers were arrayed all along an entire seam of coal rather than in distinct teams, and the method should have resulted in higher productivity among the miners. However, the breakdown of the work teams led to unexpected decreases in productivity, much higher levels of worker dissatisfaction, and even disruption of social life among the miners' families. Although the long-wall method was technically superior to the three-person mining team, the leaders of the coal-mining companies failed to consider the cultural consequences of this technological advancement.[55]

These examples help make the point that while organizational culture is a powerful aspect of the situation, it can also seem fairly elusive and unresponsive to simple executive orders to change. For those reasons and others, changing an organization's culture is usually both difficult and time consuming, typically taking years in large organizations. To put it differently, it is much easier to change formal aspects of the organization like its structure or policies than it is to change its culture. In our view, however, it is precisely those organizational change efforts that focus solely or primarily on the formal organization that tend to fail. Truly significant organizational change or transformation is unlikely to be successful without addressing organizational culture as well as the formal organization.

Furthermore, a change effort is more likely to be successful if it is based on an established theory of organizational culture, and not merely subjective preferences about what needs to change. Absent a guiding theory, misguided and superficial targets of change may be selected that miss the point and usually create problems rather than produce desired results. For example, efforts to create a more collaborative culture that target only surface behaviors such as "we'll dress and talk less formally" and "we'll spend more time in meetings together" invariably miss the point, waste energy, and breed cynicism.

You may not be surprised to learn that there are a number of theories of organizational culture. It will be sufficient for our purposes to examine just one of these theories to illustrate how culture theories systematically use abstract dimensions to depict the variety of ways in which living and working in one organization can feel so different from another. The theory we will focus on is Cameron and Quinn's **Competing Values Framework**.[56]

A Theory of Organizational Culture

The Competing Values Framework is depicted in **Figure 14.2**. It derives its name from the fact that the values depicted on opposite ends of each axis are inherently in tension with each other. They represent competing assumptions about the desired state of affairs in the organization. The core values at one end of each axis or continuum are opposed to the core values at the opposite end. Thus it is impossible for an organization to be both extremely flexible and extremely stable all the time. An organization's culture represents a balance or trade-off between these competing values that tends to work for that organization in its particular competitive environment.

Organizational cultures are not usually designed intentionally. That's one reason that people tend not to be consciously aware of their own organization's culture. In fact, it's usually only when an organization's culture is impeding organizational performance (typically in a changing competitive environment) that people become aware of any need for culture change. It's at just such times that it can be useful for people within an organization to consider something different. The Competing Values Framework was designed to help organizations be more deliberate in identifying a culture more likely to be successful given their respective situations, and in transitioning to it.

As you can see in **Figure 14.2**, the intersection of the competing values axes creates four quadrants describing four different combinations of values. The distinctive sets of values in these quadrants define four unique organizational cultures.

Organizations that emphasize stability and control, and also focus their attention inward (on how people within the organization interact with each other, on whether internal operating procedures are followed, and so forth), have a **hierarchy culture**. Organizations with a hierarchy culture tend to have formalized rules and procedures; they tend to be highly structured places to work. Following standard operating procedures (SOPs), is the rule of the day. The emphasis is on ensuring continuing efficiency, smooth functioning, and dependable operations. Examples of hierarchy cultures are government agencies, fast-food chains, and traditional large manufacturing companies.[57]

Organizations that, like hierarchy cultures, emphasize stability and control but focus their attention primarily on the external environment (outside the organization itself) are called **market cultures**. Their interest is more on interactions with external constituencies like customers and suppliers. Market cultures are competitive and results oriented, and the results that count most are typically financial measures of success such as profit. To ensure discipline in achieving these ends, there is great emphasis on achieving measurable goals and targets. Fundamentally, what characterizes market cultures is a pervasive emphasis on winning, often defined simply as beating the competition.[58]

Organizations that emphasize having a high degree of flexibility and discretion, and that also focus primarily inward rather than outward, are known as **clan cultures** because in many ways they can be thought of as an extended family. A strong sense of cohesiveness characterizes clan cultures along with shared values and a high degree of participativeness and consensus building. Clan cultures believe their path to success is rooted in teamwork, loyalty, and taking care of people within the organization, including their continuing development. In a real sense, clan cultures can be thought of as *relationship* cultures.[59]

Finally, organizations that emphasize having a high degree of flexibility and discretion, and that focus primarily on the environment outside the organization, are called **adhocracy cultures**. In many ways, adhocracy cultures represent an adaptation to the transition from the industrial age to the information age in that this form of organizational culture is most responsive to the turbulent and rapidly changing conditions of the present age. The name *adhocracy* has roots in the phrase *ad hoc*, which means temporary or specialized. Adhocracy cultures are by nature dynamic and changing so as to best foster creativity, entrepreneurship, and the ability to stay on the cutting edge. This requires a culture that emphasizes individual initiative and freedom.[60]

FIGURE 14.2 The Competing Values Framework

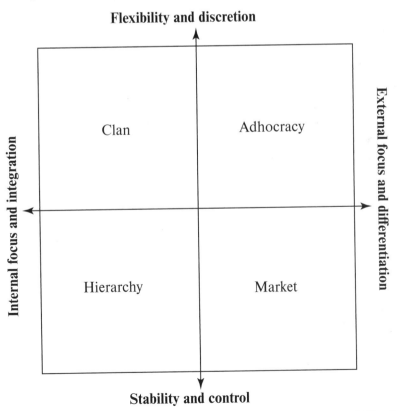

Source: K. S. Cameron and R. E. Quinn, *Diagnosing and Changing Organizational Culture* (Reading, MA: Addison-Wesley, 1999), p. 32.

In actuality, these four cultures represent idealized forms; no real organization probably exists whose culture can be completely described by just one quadrant. The complexities and necessities of organizational life and survival inevitably require that all cultures include elements from all four of the cultures (that is, all cultures put some value on all the competing values). What differentiates one culture from another, then, is the relative predominance of one culture type over the others. Nonetheless, it should be apparent that quite different approaches to leadership are called for based on which of these four distinctive cultures dominates any organization.

Leadership in hierarchy cultures, for example, emphasizes carefully managing information, monitoring detailed aspects of operations, and assuring operational dependability and reliability. In contrast, leadership in market cultures places a premium on aggressiveness, decisiveness, productivity (which is not the same as stability or continuity), and outperforming external competitors. Leadership in a clan culture focuses on process more than output, especially as it pertains to minimizing conflict and maximizing consensus. A premium is placed on leadership that is empathetic and caring and that builds trust. And leadership in adhocracy cultures requires vision, creativity, and future-oriented thinking.

One study on the role of culture in organizational performance uses these same four culture types, but rather than using them to distinguish *between* organizational cultures it instead suggests that, to be effective, organizations must have capabilities characteristic of all four of these organizational cultures. In other words, effective organizations probably pay attention to all four dimensions of culture.[61] That idea is elaborated further in **Table 14.3**.[62] But for significant organizational transformation to occur, efforts at changing culture—demanding as they undoubtedly would need to be—are not enough. Culture is just one element of an organization's comprehensive system, along with strategy, structure, leadership, and other high-performance work processes. For significant transformation to occur, these elements all need to be aligned, as evidenced in a recent comprehensive study of the Competing Values approach.[63]

TABLE 14.3   **Contributions to Organizational Effectiveness of Organizational Culture Emphases**

Culture Type	Primary Emphasis and Value
Clan	Creating trust, valuing affiliation and collaboration, promoting teamwork
Adhocracy	Building task involvement, creativity, and innovation; promoting autonomy and risk-taking
Market	Increasing productivity, valuing competitiveness and achievement, promoting profitability
Hierarchy	Clear rules and processes, efficiency and consistency, conformity and smooth functioning

An Afterthought on Organizational Issues for Students and Young Leaders

Let us conclude this section by adding an afterthought about what relevance organizational issues may have for students or others at the early stages of their careers, or at lower levels of leadership within their organizations. It is unlikely that such individuals will be asked soon to redesign their organization's structure or change its culture. As noted earlier, this chapter is not intended as a how-to manual for changing culture. But it has been our experience that younger colleagues sometimes develop biased impressions of leaders or have unrealistic expectations about decision-making in organizations, based on their lack of familiarity with, and appreciation of, the sorts of organizational dynamics discussed in this section. In other words, a primary reason for being familiar with such organizational variables is the context they provide for understanding the leadership process at your own level in the organization. Finally, we have worked with some senior leaders of huge organizations who have been with their companies for their entire careers. They have often been unable to identify *any* of the dimensions of their culture because they have never seen anything else. In these cases we were amazed by how junior managers were far better at describing the culture of the large organization. While these junior people may have had only five to eight years of total work experience, if that experience was obtained in several different organizations, they were much better prepared to describe the characteristics of their new large organization's culture than were the senior executives.

The Environment

The environmental level of the situation refers to factors outside the task or organization that still affect the leadership process. We will focus on two interrelated aspects of these extra-organizational aspects of the situation: (1) the ways in which leaders increasingly confront situations that are unexpected, unfamiliar, complex, and rapidly changing; and (2) the growing importance of leadership across different societal cultures.

Are Things Changing More Than They Used To?

One general aspect of the situation that affects leadership is the degree of change that's occurring. Leading in a relatively stable situation presents different challenges—generally simpler ones—than does leading in a dynamic situation. Many people think things *are* changing more than they used to, and at an increasing pace, but that's not so simple a question as it first might appear. For example, it may seem as though no age could possibly rival ours in terms of the transformative effect technology has had on our lives. But an interesting case can be made that technologies introduced to most Americans during the early to mid-20th century, such as indoor electric lighting, refrigerators, electric and natural gas ovens, and indoor plumbing, changed everyday life to a greater degree than new technologies of the past two decades.[64]

Nonetheless, although there's no argument that the generations growing up in the early part of the 20th century experienced profound transformations in life (television, the automobile, air travel, and atomic energy, to name a few), we believe that the nature of challenges facing leaders is changing as never before. Ronald Heifetz[65] argues that leaders not only are facing more crises than ever before but that a new mode of leadership is needed because we're in a *permanent* state of crisis. Thomas Friedman[66] provocatively titled his book *The World Is Flat* to convey how globalization and technology are radically changing how we live and work. And U.S. Army general David Petraeus used an oddly anachronistic painting in speaking with the troops he was soon to take command of in what was widely known as "the surge" in Iraq. The painting was *The Stampede*, painted by western artist Frederic Remington in 1908. It depicts a cowboy in the 1800s riding desperately to survive a stampeding herd of cattle panicked by a thunderstorm. As Thomas Ricks[67] tells the story in *The Gamble*, Petraeus used the painting to convey to his subordinates his notion of command. "I don't need to be hierarchical," he explained. "I want to flatten organizations. I'm comfortable with a slightly chaotic environment. I know that it's okay if some of you get out ahead of us. Some of the cattle will get out ahead and we will catch up with them. And some will fall behind and we will circle back and we won't leave them behind. . . . We're just trying to get the cattle to Cheyenne."

To appreciate the significance of what Petraeus was saying, contrast the language and images used here ("don't need to be hierarchical," "some of the cattle will get out") with the stereotypical notions of command and control in the military. Situational changes are being met with new approaches to leadership even within what is often regarded as the epitome of traditional top-down leadership.

We think Heifetz, Friedman, and Petraeus illuminate important ways in which the challenge of leadership is changing. It might be useful, therefore, to introduce a variation of **Figure 14.1**, which depicted the task, organizational, and environmental levels of the situation. In **Figure 14.3** we've added two vectors to the original diagram to highlight how two contrasting and multidimensional kinds of environments affect leadership. We don't intend the two vectors to imply there's a simple categorization of environments (either simple or complex); we use the representation in the figure to illustrate a range of possible environments. Nonetheless, change has become so fast and so pervasive that it impacts virtually every organization everywhere, and everyone in them. And appropriate to our times, an acronym has been given to this new state of affairs: **VUCA**. Coined by the Army War College, the term *VUCA* describes a world that is volatile, uncertain, complex, and ambiguous. **Highlight 14.7** raises an interesting question about how social media may be profoundly changing the environment in which organizations operate today.

FIGURE 14.3   Contrasting Different Environments in the Situational Level

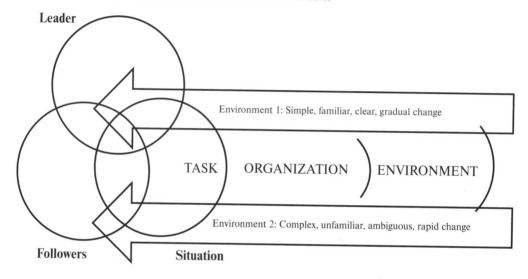

Shining a Light on Organizational Secrets

HIGHLIGHT 14.7

Virtually all organizations keep secrets—not only from people outside the organization but also from people within the organization. New technologies and norms, however, are making that more difficult. YouTube, Facebook, Twitter, and the like have created both pressure and opportunity for greater organizational transparency—whether organizations have wanted it or not. In this new environment, organizations may need to become more transparent or go extinct.

Extinction, of course, is a biological concept, and it may seem odd to use an evolutionary term to describe organizational adaptation to new realities. An article in *Scientific American*, however, makes an intriguing case that such adaptation may have Darwinian roots in the ways primitive life forms adapted eons ago to the presence of light. The authors base their ideas about the decreasing ability of organizations to keep secrets on the work of Oxford zoologist Andrew Parker.

Parker's hypothesis is that hundreds of millions of years ago, the atmosphere and chemistry of the shallow oceans began to change for the first time, allowing daylight to penetrate the seas. This new "lighted" environment presented myriad opportunities for evolutionary adaptation. Among other things, eyes began to evolve and it became an evolutionary advantage to be able to see (enabling life forms to detect dangers, find food, and the like).

What might that have to do with organizations today? "In earlier times, dictators could rule from behind high walls, relying on hierarchical organizations composed of functionaries with very limited knowledge of the organization of which they were a part and even less information about the state of the world, near and far." This was true in churches, which developed rituals and practices to keep the world at large at bay and members poorly informed (or even mis-

informed) about the nature of reality. And it was true in armies, too, which always have benefited from keeping capabilities and strategies secret from outsiders and insiders (a captured soldier with "too much" information, for example, creates a significant organizational vulnerability).

In today's environment of pervasive social media and investigative reporting, organizations will not be able to protect their secrets as they once did. As Joel Brenner, a former member of the U.S. National Security Agency said, "Very few things will be secret anymore, and those things which are secret won't stay secret very long." **Organizational transparency** is becoming the new reality.

Source: D. C. Dennett and D. Roy, "Our Transparent Future: No Secret Is Safe in the Digital Age. The Implications for Our Institutions Are Downright Darwinian," *Scientific American*, March 2015, pp. 64–69.

Another purpose of the vectors in **Figure 14.3** is to underscore how different levels of the situation interact. Thus relatively narrow and specific descriptions of job tasks tend to be most common and most appropriate in more formal and highly structured organizations having more hierarchical cultures. This set of situational levels is reasonably aligned to deal with what Heifetz called technical problems. Adaptive or wicked problems, by contrast, are more likely to be effectively addressed when tasks for individuals and teams are more fluid, in organizations that are less formal, less structured, and more agile and that have adhocracy-like cultures.

Of course we are not saying that once situational variables have been identified as corresponding more closely to the bottom vector, it's a simple matter for a leader to just "turn on" adaptive leadership. The whole point is that such leadership is inherently more than an individual leader or his behavior or skills. Certain kinds of established relationships with followers are vital, and distinctive skill sets on their parts are needed, as is a certain kind of organizational culture. Of course that is easier said than done. Maintaining relationships with followers continues to be critical, but the nature of "established relationships" has a different meaning and challenge when, for example, we are talking about relationships that exist primarily virtually. The Business Research Consortium has documented many ways the challenges of leadership are complicated when working virtually, including having the time needed to build team relationships, the prevalence of members multitasking during virtual team meetings, and the need to work across multiple time zones.[68]

> *I claim not to have controlled events, but confess plainly that events have controlled me.*

Abraham Lincoln, U.S. president, 1861–1865

In addition, Heifetz has described a thorny leadership challenge that can arise even after a challenge is recognized as an adaptive one. Followers generally want their leaders to be experts having all the answers (recall that, by definition, adaptive problems don't have expert solutions). He said, "When you attain a position of significant authority, people inevitably expect you to treat adaptive challenges as if they were technical—to provide for them a remedy that will restore equilibrium with the least amount of pain and in the shortest amount of time."[69] Furthermore, leaders themselves easily fall prey to the same expectation. People in positions of authority often take personal pride in being able to solve problems that others can't solve. When facing an adaptive challenge, it can be difficult for them to admit they've come to the limit of their expertise.[70]

To put it differently, leadership has never been easy and appears to be growing more difficult. A number of trends driving the changing nature of leadership are listed in **Highlight 14.8**. And a situational challenge that has always confronted leaders taking over new responsibilities is addressed in **Profiles in Leadership 14.1**.

Workplace Trends

HIGHLIGHT 14.8

In response to increasing competitiveness, uncertainty, globalization, and the pace of change, a number of leadership trends have been identified in how organizations can best face the future:

- Recognize that complex challenges are on the rise, and therefore that new approaches to leadership and leadership development will be required.

- Embrace innovation as a driver of future organizational success.

- Prepare for ever-greater levels of and need for virtual leadership, and that the skills it requires are different than those needed for face-to-face leadership.

- Collaboration across organizational boundaries (across teams, departments, units, regions, and so on) will be essential to organizational success.

- Because trust and respect will be vital, leaders will need to be more authentic in their roles than ever before.

- The next generation of leaders will place new kinds of leadership demands on their organizations.

- A crisis of talent in organizations is coming, and so organizations that have credible and established programs of talent development and succession planning will be at an advantage.

- Ensuring the health and fitness of all employees, leaders included, must become an organizational priority.

Source: A. Martin, *What's Next: The 2007 Changing Nature of Leadership Survey*, CCL Research White Paper (Greensboro, NC: Center for Creative Leadership). Center for Creative Leadership, CCL®, and its logo are registered trademarks owned by the Center for Creative Leadership. © 2007 Center for Creative Leadership. All rights reserved.

Mark Zuckerberg: Has Our Technology Outpaced Our Ability to Learn the Truth?

PROFILES IN LEADERSHIP 14.1

Mark Zuckerberg is facing intense criticism for not committing Facebook to do more to police and fact-check information disseminated over its platform. Critics say that "Facebook has too much power and that social media is warping democracy and undermining elections."With the 2020 presidential election looming, Facebook finds itself at the center of a controversy about whether it bears any responsibility for the accuracy of information it purveys.

The question has arisen because political advertising has changed dramatically in the digital era. Historically, political ads disseminated over traditional media have been subject to close public scrutiny and therefore tended to include few blatant falsehoods. But that has changed with digital media, particularly with what is called *microtargeting*. Microtargeting enables advertisers (e.g., political campaigns) to limit particular messages to quite narrow and specific groups of people, a practice that effectively eliminates the possibility that ideas can be debated in a public forum and exposed to the light of day. For example, microtargeting allows political advertisers to target ads to people who have shown interest in guns, immigration, or abortion based on what a Facebook user reads or comments on. Since the fall of 2019, Facebook has insisted that it will not fact-check political ads; but critics contend that practice gives politicians license to promulgate gross disinformation. It would, they say, inevitably contribute to a "tsunami of fake news." That would seem like no sound basis on which to hold a credible election. In response, a Facebook executive stated that the company "had a moral duty *not* to tip the scales against President Trump" in the election [italics added], likening the temptation to use Facebook's editorial powers to the corrupting influence of the ring in *The Lord of the Rings*.

Do you think that social media platforms should do more to control misinformation and disinformation disseminated in political ads they accept? Is it even feasible? Does Mark Zuckerberg have any responsibility for the potential political ramifications of the technology he (among others) unleashed?

Sources: B. Ortutay and M. Anderson, "Facebook Again Refuses to Ban Political Ads, even False Ones," *Associated Press*, January 9, 2020; and "Facebook: One Ring to Rule Them All?" *The Week*, January 17, 2020, p. 36.

Leading across Societal Cultures

A telling illustration of the role societal culture can play in leadership is provided by Malcolm Gladwell in his book *Outliers*. It concerns the role that culture played in a series of airline crashes, including that of Korean Air Flight 801 in 1997, which killed 228 of the 254 people on board. In fact, the loss rate (deaths per number of departing passengers) for Korean Air in the period from 1988 to 1998 was 17 times what it was for a representative American carrier. It may seem initially that the likely cause of such a difference would be deficiencies in the Korean pilots' technical flying expertise or knowledge, but that was not the case—nor is it usually the case. The kinds of errors that cause crashes are almost always errors of teamwork and communication rather than errors of flying skill. Careful analysis of those crashes reveals that a root cause was the Korean pilots' customary cultural deep respect for authority. The same factor also played a role in crashes of airliners piloted by crews of other nationalities sharing a similar respect for authority. Respect for authority in itself is neither a good nor a bad thing, but it can be a problem when it interferes with clear and direct communication about an emergency situation. That's just what was happening in these crashes. Strange as it may sound, the crews did not make the criticality of their situations crystal clear to air traffic controllers. Conversing with the controllers as equals, such as by correcting the controllers' understanding of the actual situations, would have seemed disrespectful from the crew's cultural perspective. (As a footnote, Korean Air has corrected its procedures and now has an exemplary safety record.)[71]

This is admittedly a dramatic illustration, and airline crashes are fortunately rare events. The point the story makes, however, applies to leaders of all sorts and in all places: Cultural differences—especially when they are not recognized and addressed—can create significant challenges to communication and teamwork. It's no surprise, then, that in recent years an increasing number of empirical studies have examined the challenges of leading across societal cultures. One value of such studies is that their findings can point out myths, mistaken assumptions, or invalid generalizations people have or make about leadership.

For example, a person regarded as an effective leader in one society may not be perceived as effective in another. That's what one study found in comparing evaluations by supervisors of the leadership effectiveness of female managers in Malaysia with those by supervisors of female managers in Australia. These findings appeared to be based not on an objective appraisal of the female managers' capability but rather on strongly held cultural beliefs about appropriate roles for women in society. There was a clear culturally based readiness by both male and female supervisors in Australia to value equality between the roles of men and women generally and in organizational roles specifically; this was not the case in Malaysia, where more gender-specific stereotypes were held. While these findings were not unexpected, they point out how research findings in Western cultures may not be transferable to developing cultures.[72]

Such findings have a practical importance beyond mere academic or scholarly interest. A survey of executives in the 500 largest corporations in the world showed that having competent global leaders was the most important contributor to business success (as discussed further in **Highlight 14.9**). What's more, 85 percent of those executives did not think their companies had sufficient numbers of competent global leaders.[73]

Global Leadership

HIGHLIGHT 14.9

There is no doubt about it: The world is getting smaller. Globalization has allowed goods and services to be manufactured, traded, and delivered in places no one thought possible just 10 or 20 years ago. World business leaders Jeffrey Immelt of General Electric, and Carlos Ghosn of Renault and Nissan Motors all believe these global trends are irreversible and gaining momentum. But what are the implications of globalization for leadership? It is clear that the ways in which leaders get results through others and build cohesive, goal-oriented teams will vary somewhat from one country to the next. For example, Malaysian leadership culture inhibits assertive, confrontational behavior and puts a premium on maintaining harmony. Effective leaders are expected to show compassion while demonstrating more of an autocratic than participatory leadership style. German leadership culture does not value compassion, and interpersonal relationships are straightforward and stern. Effective leaders in Germany generally value autonomy and participation but have a low team orientation.

So how does one lead in a global economy? Certainly appreciating what different cultures value and how things get done in different countries is an important first step. But do leaders need to do fundamentally different things to build teams or get results through others in India, Zimbabwe, or Estonia? Will leaders of the future need to speak multiple languages or actually live in other countries to be effective? The answers to these questions will depend to some extent on the global orientation of the organization. Some organizations, such as Waste Management or ServiceMaster, operate primarily in Canada and the United States and probably will not need to have leaders who have lived in other countries or speak multiple languages. Other organizations, such as 3M, Hewlett-Packard, Pfizer, BP, Levono, Nike, Toyota, or the British military have significant manufacturing, marketing, sales, or other operations in multiple countries. These organizations often use a global competency model to outline the expectations for leaders in all countries, and these models tend to vary more by company than by country (see **Figure 7.3** for an example of a competency model).

It seems likely that leaders who have spent time in other countries, have applied the action–observation–reflection model to maximize the lessons learned from their expatriot experiences, and can speak multiple languages would be better able to lead international organizations. But currently this is conjecture; more research is needed before we can definitively say whether international experience matters, how much and what kinds of experience are needed, what the key lessons to be learned from these experiences are, and how we should select and develop leaders to successfully lead international organizations. Unfortunately, even with considerable *time* spent in other cultures, some fail to note significant differences that in fact exist between them (for example, overgeneralizing that "all people are basically the same").

The good news here is that a group of 150 social scientists working on the GLOBE (Global Leadership and Organizational Behavior Effectiveness) project are actively seeking the answers to these questions and will soon be publishing their findings.

Sources: S. Green, F. Hassan, J. Immelt, M. Marks, and D. Meiland, "In Search of Global Leaders," *Harvard Business Review*, August 2003, pp. 38–45; J. C. Kennedy, "Leadership in Malaysia: Traditional Values, International Outlook," *The Academy of Management Executive* 16, no. 3 (2002), pp. 15–24; F. Brodbeck, M. Frese, M. Javidan, and F. G. Kroll, "Leadership Made in Germany: Low on Compassion, High in Performance," *The Academy of Management Executive* 16, no. 1 (2002), pp. 16–30; GLOBE program, http://mgmt3.ucalgary.ca/web/globe.nsf/index; B. Szkudlarek, J. Mcnett, L. Romani, and H. Lane, "The Past, Present and Future of Cross-Cultural Management Education: The Educators' Perspective," *Academy of Management Learning & Education* 12, no. 3 (2013), pp. 477–93; and M. E. Mendenhall, A. A. Arnardottir, G. R. Oddou, and L. A. Burke, "Developing Cross-Cultural Competencies in Management Education via Cognitive-Behavioral Therapy," *Academy of Management Learning & Education* 12, no. 3 (2013), pp. 436–51.

Without competent global leaders, misunderstandings and slights can occur when people from different cultures are working together. Here are two specific examples. First, consider the historic U.S. emphasis on individualism (the focus on *self*-confidence, *self*-control, *self*-concept, *self*-expression, or the way rugged individualists are heroically portrayed in film, television, and literature) and how it might impact work. Given an individualist perspective, certain management practices and expectations seem self-evident, such as the idea of individual accountability for work. When individual accountability is valued, for example, decision-making authority tends to be delegated to individual managers. What's more, those same managers may be inclined to take personal credit when the job is well done. A different norm, however, applies in industrialized Japan. Decision-making is often time consuming to ensure that everyone who will be affected by a decision has input on it beforehand. Another self-evident principle to the U.S. mind is that individual career progress is desirable and good. In some other cultures, however, managers resist competing with peers for rewards or promotions so as not to disturb the harmony of the group or appear self-interested.

Another example of potential conflict or misunderstanding can be seen in the case of orientation to authority—how people should handle power and authority relationships with others. The United States is a relatively young and mobile country, populated mostly by immigrants. Relative to other countries, there is little concern with family origin or class background. There is a belief that success should come through an individual's hard work and talent, not by birthright or class standing. This all leads to relative informality at work, even among individuals of strikingly different positions within a company. Subordinates expect their bosses to be accessible, even responsive in some ways to their subordinates. In some other cultures, however, higher status in a company confers nearly unchallengeable authority, and an expectation as well that most decisions will be referred *up* to them (as distinguished from delegated down to others).

What Is Societal Culture?

Before we look at more specific findings about leading across societal cultures, it will be useful first to clarify what the term *societal culture* means. **Societal culture** refers to those learned behaviors characterizing the total way of life of members within any given society. Cultures differ from one another just as individuals differ from one another. To outsiders, the most salient aspect of any culture typically involves behavior—the distinctive actions, mannerisms, and gestures characteristic of that culture. Americans visiting Thailand, for example, may find it curious and even bothersome to see male Thais hold hands with each other in public. They may react negatively to such behavior because it is atypical to them and laden with North American meaning ("It's okay for women to hold hands in public, but men shouldn't do that."). Salient as such behaviors are, however, they are just the tip of the iceberg. The mass of culture is not so readily visible, just as most of an iceberg lies beneath the water. Hidden from view are the beliefs, values, and myths that provide context to manifest behaviors.[74] A clear implication for business leaders in the global context, therefore, is the need to become aware and respectful of cultural differences and cultural perspectives. Barnum pointed out the importance of being able to look at one's own culture through the eyes of another:

> Consciously or unconsciously they will be using their own beliefs as the yardsticks for judging you, so know how to compare those yardsticks by ferreting out their values and noting where they differ the least and most from yours. For example, if their belief in fatalism outweighs your belief in accountability, there will be conflicts down the road. This is a severe problem in the Middle East, for instance, that affects management styles in companies and even the ability to market life insurance, which is frowned upon in communities where Muslim observances are strong.[75]

> *do believe in the spiritual nature of human beings. To some it's a strange or outdated idea, but I believe there is such a thing as a human spirit. There is a spiritual dimension to man which should be nurtured.*

Aung San Suu Kyi, Burmese politician

The GLOBE Study

GLOBE is an acronym for a research program called the Global Leadership and Organizational Behavior Effectiveness Research Program. It is the most comprehensive study of leadership and culture ever attempted, involving data collected from over 17,000 managers representing 950 companies in 62 countries.[76, 77]

Hofstede[78] was one of the pioneers in the study of beliefs and culture, and his seminal work provided some of the early roots of the GLOBE study. He identified five fundamental dimensions of cultural values and beliefs, and these, as well as dimensions drawn from the work of other researchers, became the nine dimensions of societal culture used in the GLOBE study. Because of the number of scales and complexity of findings, we'll look at representative findings from just two of those scales to convey the flavor of some of these cross-cultural findings. We'll look at the dimensions of future orientation and collectivism–individualism. Here's a brief definition of each of them:[79]

Future orientation: The degree to which individuals in organizations or societies engage in future-oriented behaviors like planning and investing in the future.

Collectivism: The degree to which individuals express pride, loyalty, and cohesiveness in their organizations, families, or similar small groups.

Table 14.4 presents some of the representative findings that differentiate cultures high or low on each of these dimensions. Cross-cultural differences on these and the other seven dimensions of culture used in GLOBE constitute a foundation for the GLOBE findings on differences in leadership across cultures.

TABLE 14.4   Representative Societal Differences on Two GLOBE Dimensions

Societies Higher on Collectivism Tend to	Societies Higher on Individualism Tend to
• Have a slower pace of life • Have lower heart attack rates • Assign less weight to love in marriage decisions • Have fewer interactions, but interactions tend to be longer and more intimate	• Have a faster pace of life • Have higher heart attack rates • Assign greater weight to love in marriage decisions • Have more social interactions, but interactions tend to be shorter and less intimate

Societies Higher on Future Orientation Tend to	Societies Lower on Future Orientation Tend to
• Achieve economic success • Have flexible and adaptive organizations and managers • Emphasize visionary leadership that is capable of seeing patterns in the face of chaos and uncertainty	• Have lower rates of economic success • Have inflexible and maladaptive organizations and managers • Emphasize leadership that focuses on repetition of reproducible and routine sequences

The heart of the conceptual model in the GLOBE research is what's called **implicit leadership theory**. This theory holds that individuals have implicit beliefs and assumptions about attributes and behaviors that distinguish leaders from followers, effective leaders from ineffective leaders, and moral from immoral leaders. The GLOBE model further posits that relatively distinctive implicit theories of leadership characterize different societal cultures from each other as well as organizational cultures within those societal cultures. GLOBE calls these **culturally endorsed implicit theories of leadership (CLT)**.

After detailed analysis of findings, GLOBE researchers identified six dimensions that were determined to be applicable across all global cultures for assessing CLT. Here are those six dimensions and a brief description of each:[80]

- **Charismatic/value-based leadership** reflects the ability to inspire, motivate, and expect high performance from others on the basis of firmly held core values.
- **Team-oriented leadership** emphasizes effective team building and implementation of a common purpose or goal among team members.
- **Participative leadership** reflects the degree to which managers involve others in making and implementing decisions.
- **Humane-oriented leadership** reflects supportive and considerate leadership as well as compassion and generosity.
- **Autonomous leadership** refers to independent and individualistic leadership.
- **Self-protective leadership** focuses on ensuring the safety and security of the individual or group member.

After analyzing the data from all the societies in the study, GLOBE researchers categorized them into 10 different societal clusters (such as Eastern Europe, Nordic Europe, Latin America, Southern Asia, and Anglo). Societies were included in a cluster based on criteria of relative similarity of values and beliefs *within* each cluster, and *differentiation* from other societal clusters. Again, it is beyond our purposes here to present a comprehensive description of all these societal clusters. It will suffice to look at just three of them so that you will have a general sense of the nature of the GLOBE findings. **Table 14.5** presents the relative rankings (high, medium, or low) for three different societal clusters on each of the six global CLT dimensions.[81]

TABLE 14.5   **Relative Rankings of Selected Societal Clusters on CLT Leadership Dimensions**

Societal Cluster	Charismatic/ Value-Based	Team-Oriented	Participative	Humane-Oriented	Self-Protective
Eastern Europe	Medium	Medium	Low	Medium	High
Anglo	High	Medium	High	High	Low
Middle East	Low	Low	Low	Medium	High

The considerable variation in views of what constitutes good leadership across different societal clusters evident in **Table 14.5** makes it clear that behaving effectively as a leader (and being perceived as effective) requires awareness of the cultural values and practices in the society within which one is working.

A final set of interesting findings coming out of GLOBE concerns the **universality of leadership attributes**. These findings both refine and temper the distinctiveness of societal CLTs exemplified in **Table 14.5**. They temper the impression we may get that different societies have completely different notions of what constitutes good and bad leadership by demonstrating that there is consensus across cultures on a number of desirable leadership attributes as well as consensus on what are considered to be universally negative leadership traits. But these findings also provide further insight into which attributes see much of the variability across cultures. GLOBE researchers identified 22 specific attributes and behaviors that are viewed universally across cultures as contributing to leadership effectiveness.[82] They are listed in **Table 14.6**. In addition, the project identified eight characteristics that are universally viewed as impediments to leader effectiveness (see **Table 14.7**). And GLOBE researchers identified 35 leader characteristics that are viewed as positive in some cultures but negative in others (some of these are listed in **Table 14.8**). This large set of culturally contingent characteristics apparently accounts for most of the variance across societal cultures.

TABLE 14.6   **Leader Attributes and Behaviors Universally Viewed as Positive**

Trustworthy	Positive	Intelligent
Just	Dynamic	Decisive
Honest	Motive arouser	Effective bargainer
Foresighted	Confidence builder	Win–win problem solver
Plans ahead	Motivational	Administratively skilled
Encouraging	Dependable	Communicative
Informed	Coordinator	Team builder
Excellence oriented		

Source: Adapted from House et al., "Cultural Influences on Leadership and Organizations: Project GLOBE," *Advances in Global Leadership*, vol. 1 (Stamford, CT: JAI Press, 1999), pp. 171–233.

TABLE 14.7   Leader Attributes and Behaviors Universally Viewed as Negative

Loner	Nonexplicit
Asocial	Egocentric
Noncooperative	Ruthless
Irritable	Dictatorial

Source: Adapted from House et al., "Cultural Influences on Leadership and Organizations: Project GLOBE," *Advances in Global Leadership*, vol. 1 (Stamford, CT: JAI Press, 1999), pp. 171–233.

TABLE 14.8   Examples of Leader Behaviors and Attributes That Are Culturally Contingent

Ambitious	Individualistic
Cautious	Logical
Compassionate	Orderly
Domineering	Sensitive
Formal	Sincere
Independent	Worldly

Source: Adapted from House et al., "Cultural Influences on Leadership and Organizations: Project GLOBE," *Advances in Global Leadership*, vol. 1 (Stamford, CT: JAI Press, 1999), pp. 171–233.

Summary

The situation may be the most complex factor in the leader–follower–situation framework. Moreover, situations vary not only in complexity but also in strength. Situational factors can play such a pervasive role that they can effectively minimize the effects of personality traits, intelligence, values, and preferences on leaders' and followers' behaviors, attitudes, and relationships. Given the dynamic nature of leadership situations, finding fairly consistent results is a highly encouraging accomplishment for leadership researchers.

As an organizing framework, this chapter introduced the concept of situational levels as a way to consider many situational factors. At the lowest level, leaders need to be aware of how various aspects of tasks can affect both their own and their followers' behaviors, and how they might change these factors to improve followers' satisfaction and performance. The organizational level includes both the formal organization and the informal organization. The formal organization involves the ways authority is distributed across various organizational levels and how organizational structure impacts the way activities in the organization are coordinated and controlled. The informal organization or the organizational culture can have a profound impact on the way both leaders and followers behave—and may be the least recognizable because it is the water in the bowl where all the fish are swimming. An increasingly important variable at the environmental level is societal culture, which involves learned behaviors that guide the distinctive mannerisms, ways of thinking, and values within particular societies.

Key Terms

situational engineering

role theory

multiple-influence model

situational levels

task autonomy

task feedback

task structure

task interdependence

technical problems

adaptive problems

adaptive leadership

formal organization

level of authority

organizational structure

horizontal complexity

vertical complexity

spatial complexity

formalization

substitutes for leadership

centralization

informal organization

organizational culture

organizational climate

myths and stories

symbols and artifacts

rituals

language

Competing Values Framework

hierarchy culture

market culture

clan culture

adhocracy culture

VUCA

organizational transparency

societal culture

GLOBE

future orientation

collectivism

implicit leadership theory

culturally endorsed implicit theories of leadership (CLT)

charismatic/values-based leadership

team-oriented leadership

participative leadership

humane-oriented leadership

autonomous leadership

self-protective leadership

universality of leadership attributes

Questions

1. The term *bureaucratic* has a pejorative connotation to most people. Can you think of any positive aspects of a bureaucracy?

2. During the coronavirus pandemic, to what extent did you observe people interpreting the situation differently? For example, people seeing it as a "true medical crisis" versus an "overblown problem" not meriting widespread restrictions on normal life? What conclusions do you draw from that about the challenge of getting large numbers of people aligned and committed to a demanding course of action?

3. What role do leaders play in creating a shared understanding of the situation a group, organization, or country faces? Is such a "shared understanding" even possible in a diverse society with countless and competing sources of information?

Activity

Your instructor has several exercises available that demonstrate the impact of situational factors on behavior. They are not described here because identifying the situational factors being manipulated in an exercise undercuts the purpose of that exercise.

Minicase

Chernobyl: Man-Made Disaster II

It may seem difficult to believe, but in 1986, *Challenger* was not the only man-made disaster to occur (see **Highlight 14.1**). But unlike the cold morning of the *Challenger* accident, April 25, 1986, brought a pleasantly warm day to the modern city of Pripyat in Ukraine. Pripyat had been built in close proximity to four large nuclear power reactors because that is where the workers, engineers, and support personnel would live.

During the day shift of April 25, a single remaining test to completely validate the RBMK Chernobyl Reactor 4 was scheduled. A highly trained and skilled crew comprised the day shift workers, and they were backed up by a specialist team of engineers brought in just for this final test. The test, which had been attempted several times before but never completed, was to assess a backup safety procedure. If external commercial power to the reactor cooling pumps was lost, could the winding-down turbines produce enough back-up power to maintain cooling water to the reactor core until the diesel generators could kick in—about 1 minute? To run this test, a number of standard safety systems would need to be shut down or bypassed, which the day shift accomplished.

Before they could run the actual test, another generating station in the Kiev power grid had to shut down. The Kiev controllers requested that the Chernobyl test be delayed. Both the day shift and the evening shift went home without completing the test, but also without restoring the safety systems. When the night shift came on, they had almost no time to prepare for a test that they did not expect to run. In fact, the operator responsible for running the reactor was a young engineer, Leonid Toptunov, who had worked independently as a "senior engineer" for only three months. Also present in the control room that evening was another unusual player. Anatoly Dyatlov, the deputy chief engineer for the entire Chernobyl Nuclear Power Plant, was there to supervise and direct the test. Dyatlov was not normally on the night shift, and his presence gave everyone else a sense of how important completion of this test was. Also, since Dyatlov outranked all other supervisory personnel present, his orders and instructions overrode any objections of other senior personnel present during the test and its preparation.

A little after 1:00 a.m. on the morning of April 26, the test began. As the reactor power was reduced, Toptunov, the very junior "senior engineer," was supposed to throw a switch changing the slowdown from Automatic to Manual. He missed that step, and shortly thereafter, the reactor dropped to an unsafe level of output. The RBMK reactors became unstable at low outputs, which is not a problem if the system is totally shut down. But since a certain level of power was needed to conduct the test, Dyatlov ordered the control rods be withdrawn to get the power back up. This started a complicated series of problems unique to RBMK-type reactors. Within seconds, the reactor was out of control. Due to the excessive buildup of heat within the reactor core, a steam explosion, followed by a likely hydrogen explosion, completely blew the top off the reactor, exposing the nuclear core and releasing radioactive material into the atmosphere.

Within the next three months, 28 of the 134 on-scene responders and staff died in addition to the two operation room staff who were killed immediately. Pripyat was completely evacuated and remains so today. A large exclusion zone was also established and evacuated. Radioactive particles from the core burn have been detected in widespread areas of Russia, Europe, Sweden, and beyond. Estimates of the long-term death rates from the Chernobyl release vary from 9,000 to 16,000 people.

Not unlike *Challenger* where an O-ring was identified as the direct cause of the accident, at Chernobyl, the failure of the least-experienced person in the control room to properly set a switch has been identified as the direct cause of the destruction of Reactor 4. And, if we were still focusing on the individual factors in leadership, as the earlier chapters of this book did, we might be done with our leadership search for causes.

Situational Variables Contributing to the Chernobyl Accident

To better understand the situational variables affecting the Chernobyl accident, we need to look back into the very culture surrounding not only nuclear reactors but the Soviet society in general.

The Soviet Union was a secretive society. And within that secretive society were various levels of secrets. Among the most secretive level was anything having to do with nuclear power. The Soviets were driven to produce nuclear weapons and warheads after Germany had invaded their land and killed thousands of their citizens during World War II. Now, the Cold War was on and everyone already knew that the United States had nuclear weapons as they had dropped two of them on Japan. However, the Soviets kept quiet. If the word "nuclear" appeared anywhere in the context of discussion, not only did the Soviets keep the secret from their adversaries but also from their own engineers and scientists.

The RBMK reactor that was the engineering culprit at Chernobyl was never originally intended to produce steam power for spinning turbines that would generate commercial electricity. The reactor's original purpose was to produce plutonium for nuclear weapons. This put everything about the RBMK reactor into the realm of the most secret of secrets.

Later, when commercial power from nuclear technology was growing worldwide, the Soviets took the knowledge from building the RBMK reactors and modified it to produce electricity. At the time of the Chernobyl buildup, there were already a number of RBMK electrical power stations in operation. As mentioned earlier, the RBMK reactor had a very strange and serious design flaw. As an RBMK reactor decreased its output, rather than settling down, it became more unstable. Did the Soviets at the highest levels in nuclear engineering know of this problem? Undoubtedly they did, because after the massive Chernobyl accident, investigations revealed that a similar situation had occurred previously at another RBMK reactor site that fortunately did not result in an explosion. Unfortunately, because of the secrecy around anything nuclear in the Soviet Union, other RBMK reactor operators were never told of this incident or potential problem.

The secrecy helps explain a major part of the problem. But there is another problem that does not have sufficient explanation. If the shutdown test was originally scheduled to occur on the day shift with the most senior and experienced operators as well as an augmented team of scientist and engineers observing, when the test had to be postponed, why were the safety measures not reinstated? And why was the test then pushed to the night shift with the most inexperienced operator and no augmenting specialist around?

To answer this question, we need to examine yet another situational variable that was operating in the background at Chernobyl. May Day, the Celebration of Spring and Labor, is an important day in the Soviet Union, and it was rumored that several important promotions would take place at the nuclear reactor site on that day. With May Day less than a week away, rumor had it that the overall Chernobyl plant director, Viktor Brukhanov, would be promoted and that Anatoly Dyatlov, the deputy chief engineer for operations (the unexpected senior man in the control room of Chernobyl 4 the night of the explosion) was in line to take Brukhanov's position. And it appeared that there was only one issue standing between these men and their promotions. Chernobyl Reactor 4 had never been officially certified because the very safety test that they were trying to accomplish on the night of the explosion had never been completed. With May Day approaching, Brukhanov and Dyatlov were determined to get the test done, even if it meant running it on the night shift with inexperienced personnel. And, as noted earlier, none of the men involved in Reactor 4's operation knew about the problems experienced by other RBMK reactors because of the veil of Soviet secrecy.

None of these factors can be explained at the individual level. But if we are to be effective leaders in complex environments, whether we are launching space shuttles or running faulty nuclear power plants, or even trying to understand the motives of senior school administrators, we simply cannot ignore situational variables. As leaders, even at lower levels in organizations, we may not be able to change these variables, but we cannot afford to discount them.

1. Do you think governmental deceptiveness and secrecy by any country played some part in the 2020 coronavirus pandemic getting so out of control?

2. Has this case study affected your attitudes about the degree of openness and transparency that should be required in organizations responsible for technologies that potentially place the public well-being at significant risk?

3. Do you think "politics" played a part in decisions and public pronouncements by officeholders at local, state, and/or federal levels in the 2020 coronavirus pandemic?

4. Has reading this case study of the Chernobyl nuclear disaster changed in any way your own attitudes about the safety of nuclear power?

Sources: T. INSAG-7, "The Chernobyl Accident: Updating of INSAG-1," A report by the International Nuclear Safety Advisory Group, International Atomic Energy Agency, Safety Series No. 75-INSAG-7, 1992, (ISBN: 9201046928); and A. Higginbotham, *Midnight in Chernobyl: The Untold Story of the World's Greatest Nuclear Disaster* (New York: Simon & Schuster, 2019).

Endnotes

1. T. J. Peters and R. H. Waterman, *In Search of Excellence* (New York: Harper & Row, 1982).

2. R. T. Hogan and J. Hogan, *Manual for the Hogan Personality Inventory* (Tulsa, OK: Hogan Assessment Systems, 1992).

3. G. Yukl, *Leadership in Organizations*, 2nd ed. (Englewood Cliffs, NJ: Prentice Hall, 1989).

4. A. J. Murphy, "A Study of the Leadership Process," *American Sociological Review* 6 (1941), pp. 674–87.

5. H. S. Person, "Leadership as a Response to Environment," *Educational Record Supplement*, no. 6 (1928), pp. 9–21.

6. G. Spiller, "The Dynamics of Greatness," *Sociological Review* 21 (1929), pp. 218–32.

7. J. Schneider, "The Cultural Situation as a Condition for the Condition of Fame," *American Sociology Review* 2 (1937), pp. 480–91.

8. Person, "Leadership as a Response to Environment."

9. B. M. Bass, *Bass and Stogdill's Handbook of Leadership*, 3rd ed. (New York: Free Press, 1990).

10. R. K. Merton, *Social Theory and Social Structure* (New York: Free Press, 1957).

11. J. Pfeffer and G. R. Salancik, "Determinants of Supervisory Behavior: A Role Set Analysis," *Human Relations* 28 (1975), pp. 139–54.

12. A. Tsui, "A Role Set Analysis of Managerial Reputation," *Organizational Behavior and Human Performance* 34 (1984), pp. 64–96.

13. J. G. Hunt and R. N. Osborn, "Toward a Macro-Oriented Model of Leadership: An Odyssey," in *Leadership: Beyond Establishment Views*, ed. J. G. Hunt, U. Sekaran, and C. A. Schriesheim (Carbondale: Southern Illinois University Press, 1982), pp. 196–221.

14. P. Hersey and K. H. Blanchard, *Management of Organizational Behavior: Utilizing Human Resources*, 3rd ed. (Englewood Cliffs, NJ: Prentice Hall, 1977).

15. P. Hersey and K. H. Blanchard, *Management of Organizational Behavior: Utilizing Human Resources*, 4th ed. (Englewood Cliffs, NJ: Prentice Hall, 1984).

16. J. R. Hackman and G. R. Oldham, *Work Redesign* (Reading, MA: Addison-Wesley, 1980).

17. R. J. House and G. Dressler, "The Path-Goal Theory of Leadership: Some Post Hoc and A Priori Tests," in *Contingency Approaches to Leadership*, eds. J. G. Hunt and L. L. Larson (Carbondale: Southern Illinois University Press, 1974).

18. J. P. Howell and P. W. Dorfman, "Substitute for Leadership: Test of a Construct," *Academy of Management Journal* 24 (1981), pp. 714–28.

19. S. Kerr and J. M. Jermier, "Substitutes for Leadership: Their Meaning and Measurement," *Organizational Behavior and Human Performance* 22 (1978), pp. 375–403.

20. I. B. Myers and B. H. McCaulley, *Manual: A Guide to the Development and Use of the Myers-Briggs Type Indicator* (Palo Alto, CA: Consulting Psychologists Press, 1985).

21. Bass, *Bass and Stogdill's Handbook of Leadership*.

22. J. D. Ford, "Department Context and Formal Structure as Constraints on Leader Behavior," *Academy of Management Journal* 24 (1981), pp. 274–88.

23. Yukl, *Leadership in Organizations*.

24. M. Siegall and L. L. Cummings, "Task Role Ambiguity, Satisfaction, and the Moderating Effect of Task Instruction Source," *Human Relations* 39 (1986), pp. 1017–32.

25. J. Galbraith, *Designing Complex Organizations* (Menlo Park, CA: Addison-Wesley, 1973).

26. L. Fry, W. Kerr, and C. Lee, "Effects of Different Leader Behaviors under Different Levels of Task Interdependence," *Human Relations* 39 (1986), pp. 1067–82.

27. R. A. Heifetz, *Leadership without Easy Answer* (Cambridge, MA: Belknap, 1998).

28. R. A. Heifetz and M. Linsky, *Leadership on the Line: Staying Alive through the Dangers of Leading* (Boston: Harvard Business School Press, 2002).

29. A. D. Chandler, *Scale and Scope: The Dynamics of Industrial Capitalism* (Cambridge: Harvard University Press, 1990).

30. R. S. Kaplan and D. P. Norton, *The Balanced Scorecard: Translating Strategy into Action* (Boston: Harvard Business School Press, 1996).

31. F. Luthans, S. A. Rosenkrantz, and H. W. Hennessey, "What Do Successful Managers Really Do? An Observational Study of Managerial Activities," *Journal of Applied Behavioral Science* 21 (1985), pp. 255–70.

32. R. C. Page and W. W. Tornow, "Managerial Job Analysis: Are We Any Further Along?" paper presented at a meeting of the Society of Industrial Organizational Psychology, Atlanta, GA, 1987.

33. G. Chitayat and I. Venezia, "Determinates of Management Styles in Business and Nonbusiness Organizations," *Journal of Applied Psychology* 69 (1984), pp. 437–47.

34. L. B. Kurke and H. E. Aldrich, "Mintzberg Was Right! A Replication and Extension of the Nature of Managerial Work," *Management Science* 29 (1983), pp. 975–84.

35. S. P. Robbins, *Organizational Behavior: Concepts, Controversies, and Applications* (Englewood Cliffs, NJ: Prentice Hall, 1986).

36. P. M. Podsakoff, "Determinants of a Supervisor's Use of Rewards and Punishments: A Literature Review and Suggestions for Future Research," *Organizational Behavior and Human Performance* 29 (1982), pp. 58–83.

37. T. H. Hammer and J. Turk, "Organizational Determinants of Leader Behavior and Authority," *Journal of Applied Psychology* 71 (1987), pp. 674–82.

38. Bass, *Bass and Stogdill's Handbook of Leadership*.

39. E. H. Schein, *Organizational Culture and Leadership: A Dynamic View* (San Francisco: Jossey-Bass, 1985).

40. Bass, *Bass and Stogdill's Handbook of Leadership.*

41. S. W. J. Kozlowski and M. L. Doherty, "Integration of Climate and Leadership: Examination of a Neglected Issue," *Journal of Applied Psychology* 74 (1989), pp. 546–53.

42. B. Schneider, P. J. Hanges, D. B. Smith, and A. N. Salvaggio, "Which Comes First: Employee Attitudes or Organizational Financial and Market Performance?" *Journal of Applied Psychology* 88, no. 5 (2003), pp. 836–51.

43. Schneider, "The Cultural Situation as a Condition for the Condition of Fame."

44. Bass, *Bass and Stogdill's Handbook of Leadership.*

45. Kozlowski and Doherty, "Integration of Climate and Leadership."

46. Bass, *Bass and Stogdill's Handbook of Leadership.*

47. R. H. Kilmann and M. J. Saxton, *Organizational Cultures: Their Assessment and Change* (San Francisco: Jossey-Bass, 1983).

48. Schein, *Organizational Culture and Leadership.*

49. B. Dumaine, "Creating a New Company Culture," *Fortune*, 1990, pp. 127–31.

50. B. M. Bass, *Leadership and Performance beyond Expectations* (New York: Free Press, 1985).

51. J. M. Kouzes and B. Z. Posner, *The Leadership Challenge: How to Get Extraordinary Things Done in Organizations* (San Francisco: Jossey-Bass, 1987).

52. Schein, *Organizational Culture and Leadership.*

53. N. M. Tichy and M. A. Devanna, *The Transformational Leader* (New York: Wiley, 1986).

54. G. Ahmetoglu, R. Akhtar, S. Tsivrikos, and T. Chamorro-Premuzic, "The Entrepreneurial Organization: The Effects of Organizational Culture on Innovation Output," *Consulting Psychology Journal and Research* 70 (2018), pp. 318–38.

55. F. E. Emery and E. L. Trist, "The Causal Texture of Organizational Environments," *Human Relations* 18 (1965), pp. 21–32.

56. C. S. Cameron and R. E. Quinn, *Diagnosing and Changing Organizational Culture* (Reading, MA: Addison-Wesley, 1999).

57. Cameron and Quinn, *Diagnosing and Changing Organizational Culture.*

58. Cameron and Quinn, *Diagnosing and Changing Organizational Culture.*

59. Cameron and Quinn, *Diagnosing and Changing Organizational Culture.*

60. Cameron and Quinn, *Diagnosing and Changing Organizational Culture.*

61. R. Hogan, R. B. Kaiser, and T. Chamorro-Premuzic, "An Evolutionary View of Organizational Culture," in *The Oxford Handbook of Organizational Climate and Culture*, eds. B. Schneider and K. M. Barbera (New York: Oxford University Press, 2014).

62. Hogan et al., "An Evolutionary View of Organizational Culture."

63. C. A. Hartnell, A. Y. Ou, A. J. Kinicki, D. Choi, and E. P. Karam, "A Meta-analytic Test of Organizational Culture's Association with Elements of an Organization's System and Its Predictive Validity on Organizational Outcomes," *Journal of Applied Psychology* 104 (2019), pp. 832–50.

64. M. Lind, "The Boring Age," *Time*, March 22, 2010, pp. 58–59.

65. R. Heifetz, A. Grashow, and M. Linsky, "Leadership in a (Permanent) Crisis," *Harvard Business Review*, July–August 2009, pp. 62–69.

66. T. Friedman, *The World Is Flat: A Brief History of the Twenty-First Century* (New York: Farrar, Straus and Giroux, 2005).

67. T. Ricks, *The Gamble* (New York: The Penguin Press, 2009).

68. D. Dennis, M. H. Overholt, and M. Vickers, "The New Dominance of Virtual Teams and Leaders," *Leadership Solutions 2014*, Business Research Consortium, pp. 1–27.

69. R. Heifetz, "An Interview with Ronald A. Heifetz: Interview by James Nelson," www.managementfirst.com/management_styles/interviews/heifetz.htm.

70. Heifetz, "An Interview with Ronald A. Heifetz."

71. M. Gladwell, *Outliers* (New York: Little, Brown and Company, 2005).

72. U. D. Jogulu and G. J. Wood, "A Cross-Cultural Study into Peer Evaluations of Women's Leadership Effectiveness," *Leadership & Organization Development Journal* 29, no. 7 (2008), pp. 606–16.

73. M. Javidan and R. J. House, "Cultural Acumen for the Global Manager: Lessons from Project GLOBE," *Organizational Dynamics* 29 (2001), pp. 289–305.

74. L. R. Kohls, *Survival Kit for Overseas Living* (Boston: Intercultural Press, 2001).

75. D. F. Barnum, "Effective Membership in the Global Business Community," in *New Traditions in Business*, ed. J. Renesch (San Francisco: Berrett-Koehler, 1992), p. 153.

76. R. House, P. Hanges, M. Javidan, P. Dorfman, and V. Gupta (eds.), *Culture, Leadership and Organizations: The GLOBE Study of 62 Societies* (Thousand Oaks, CA: Sage, 2004).

77. J. S. Chhokar, F. C. Brodbeck, and R. J. House (eds.), *Culture and Leadership around the World: The GLOBE Book of In-Depth Studies of 25 Societies* (Mahwah, NJ: Lawrence Erlbaum Associates, 2007).

78. G. Hofstede, *Cultural Consequences: Comparing Values, Behaviors, Institutions and Organizations across Nations*, 2nd ed. (Thousand Oaks, CA: Sage Publications, 2001).

79. Chhokar et al., "Introduction," in *Culture and Leadership around the World*, pp. 1–6.

80. P. W. Dorfman, P. J. Hanges, and F. C. Brodbeck, "Leadership and Cultural Variation: The Identification of Culturally Endorsed Leadership Profiles," in *Culture, Leadership and Organizations: The GLOBE Study of 62 Societies*, eds. R. House, P. Hanges, M. Javidan, P. Dorfman, and V. Gupta (Thousand Oaks, CA: Sage, 2004), pp. 669–719.

81. Dorfman et al., "Leadership and Cultural Variation."

82. R. J. House, P. Hanges, S. A. Ruiz-Quintanilla, P. W. Dorfman, S. A. Falkus and N. M. Ashkanasy, "Cultural Influences on Leadership and Organizations: Project GLOBE," *Advances in Global Leadership*, vol. 1 (JAI Press, 1999), pp. 171–233.

CHAPTER 15

Contingency Theories of Leadership

Introduction

If we were to provide an extremely short summary of the book to this point, we would say leadership is a process that involves aspects of the leader, the followers, and the situation. In **Part 1** we discussed the process aspects, while **Part 2** was devoted to the leader. **Part 3** focused on the followers, and in the previous chapter we discussed the situational components of leadership. You may have also noted that while we attempted to focus exclusively on the component of interest for each section, there were often overlapping areas in our leader–follower–situation (L-F-S) model. The overlap is genuine, and our attempts to segregate the concepts were done merely for simplicity.

It is also important to note that in adopting our L-F-S model, we deliberately followed a tradition in scientific theory development known as **parsimony**. A model that is parsimonious is one with the greatest explanatory power while using the fewest predictor variables as possible. We have chosen what we believe are the three most powerful predictor variables: the leader, the followers, and the situation.

But readers should recognize that the L-F-S model by no means encompasses all the potential variables or outcomes in understanding leadership. A study by Dinh and colleagues highlights this complexity. First, they report how much the leadership field has developed in recent decades. In their research, they identified a total of 66 different leadership theory domains. But even more important, they report that

> no unified theory of leadership currently exists. Leadership theory emphasizes many outcomes, from how leaders are perceived to how leaders affect unit performance; it involves actions of group members as well as those of formal leaders; it has been applied to levels that include events, individuals, dyads, groups, organizations, and political systems; it has focused on immediate and delayed effects; and it often incorporates contextual differences. Thus, it is not surprising that leadership involves 66 different theoretical domains and a wide variety of methodological approaches.[1]

But for this text, we will stick with just three: the leader, the followers, and the situation.

It is safe to say the world of leadership is a complex one. Even in our L-F-S model, multiple aspects come into play. Leadership is contingent on the interplay of all three aspects of our model, and these contingencies are the focus of this chapter.

> *It is a capital mistake to theorize before one has data.*
>
> **Sir Arthur Conan Doyle, author**

This chapter reviews four well-known contingency theories of leadership. The first, leader–member exchange (LMX) theory, focuses on the contingencies and interactions between the leader and the followers. The remaining three theories address certain aspects of the leader, the followers, and the situation. These theories also share several other similarities. First, because they are theories rather than someone's personal opinions, these models have been the focus of a considerable amount of empirical research over the years. Second, these theories implicitly assume that leaders are able to accurately diagnose or assess key aspects of the followers or the leadership situation. Third, with the exception of Fiedler's contingency model,[2, 3] leaders are assumed to be able to act in a flexible manner. In other words, leaders can and should change their behaviors as situational and follower characteristics change. Fourth, a correct match between situational and follower characteristics and leaders' behaviors is assumed to have a positive effect on group or organizational outcomes. Thus these theories maintain that leadership effectiveness is maximized when leaders correctly make their behaviors *contingent* on certain situational and follower characteristics. Because of these similarities, Chemers[4] argued that these contingency theories are more similar than different. He said they differ primarily in terms of the types of situational and follower characteristics upon which various leader behaviors should be contingent.

Leader–Member Exchange Theory

In **Chapter 1** we first noted a contingency when we mentioned the "in-group" and "out-group" interactions between leaders and followers. These relationships were originally described as vertical dyad linkages[5] but have developed over time into what is most often referred to today as **leader–member exchanges (LMXs)**. The main premise of these theories has remained unchanged, however. Fundamentally, LMX argues that leaders do not treat all followers as if they were a uniform group of equals. Rather, the leader forms specific and unique linkages with each subordinate, thus creating a series of dyadic relationships. In general, as just noted, the linkages tend to be differentiated into two major groups.

In the out-group, or low-quality exchange relationships, interpersonal interaction is largely restricted to fulfilling contractual obligations.[6] With other subordinates (the in-group), leaders form high-quality exchange relationships that go well beyond "just what the job requires." These high-quality relationships are indeed "exchanges" because both parties benefit. In exchange for higher levels of task performance[7] from subordinates, leaders may contribute empowerment,[8] sponsorship of subordinates in social networks,[9] and mentoring.[10]

There has been considerable evolution in LMX research and thinking over time. Early on, the focus was on stages of development as the process of the relationship developed. These stages typically were described as follows:

1. **Role-taking** happens early in a follower's work experience. Here the leader offers opportunities and evaluates the follower's performance and potential.

2. **Role-making** is the stage where a role is created based on a process of trust building. This is a fragile stage, and any perceived betrayals can lead to the follower being dropped from the developing in-group and assigned to the out-group.

3. **Routinization** occurs as the relationship becomes well established. It is at this stage that similarities (for the in-group) and differences (often accentuated for the out-group) become cemented.

Perhaps the biggest leap forward in LMX came 25 years after its introduction, in an article by Graen and Uhl-Bien.[11] In this publication, the authors expanded the descriptive portion of the model, which continued to focus on the dyadic processes between the leader and followers. However, the model also changed from merely describing the process to proposing a prescriptive process that would enhance organizational effectiveness. Most of us can identify with the descriptive components of LMX by thinking back to coaches or teachers from our past who had in-groups and out-groups. Now the model suggests behaviors that the leader should engage in to actively develop relationships (hence the prescriptive label) and build more in-group relations across the follower pool. This process of leadership is outlined in **Table 15.1**.

TABLE 15.1 The Cycle of Leadership Making

TIME →

Characteristic	Stranger	Acquaintance	Maturity
Relationship-building stage	Role-taking	Role-making	Role routinization
Reciprocity	Cash and carry	Mixed	In-kind
Time span of reciprocity	Immediate	Some delay	Indefinite
Leader–member	Low	Medium	High exchange
Incremental influence	None	Limited	Almost unlimited

Source: Adapted from G. B. Graen and M. Uhl-Bien, "Relationship-based Approach to Leadership: Development of Leader–Member Exchange (LMX) Theory over 25 Years: Applying a Multi-level Multi-domain Perspective," *Leadership Quarterly* 6 (1995), pp. 219–47.

The LMX leadership-making process moves from left to right in the table as indicated by the time arrow. Perhaps most important in the prescriptive notion of the model is the focus on the leader's responsibility to enhance overall organizational effectiveness by developing more in-groups and reducing the number of out-groups. In summary, the leadership-making process prescribes that the leader should work to develop special relationships with *all* followers; should offer each follower an opportunity for new roles, responsibilities, and challenges; should nurture high-quality exchanges with all followers; and should focus on ways to build trust and respect with all subordinates—resulting in the entire work group becoming an in-group rather than accentuating the differences between in-groups and out-groups.

Concluding Thoughts about the LMX Model

In its earlier form (the vertical dyad linkage model), LMX was one of the simplest of the contingency models. Looking at our leader–follower–situation model, it is easy to see that LMX, even today, is largely about the process of relationship building between the leader and the follower. The situation has barely crept in, and only if we consider the desire to increase organizational effectiveness by maximizing the number of in-groups the leader might develop. From an application perspective, perhaps the biggest limitation of LMX is that it does not describe the specific behaviors that lead to high-quality relationship exchanges between the leader and the follower. Nonetheless, LMX, as opposed to some of the subsequent contingency models, continues to generate research.[12, 13]

In fact, of all the contingency models presented here, we see more research articles related to LMX than to any of the other theories. The research addresses topics related to LMX including follower proactive personality,[14] the extent of the leader's social network,[15] the degree to which employees identify their supervisor with the organization,[16] employees' perceptions of both the procedural and distributive justice climate,[17] and the degree that followers perceive that the leaders treat all members fairly (not necessarily "equally") and that the leaders represent the group's values and norms.[18] On a broader level, LMX is being studied both across various countries[19] and with globally distributed teams.[20]

The Situational Leadership® Model

It seems fairly obvious that leaders do not interact with all followers in the same manner. For example, a leader may give general guidelines or goals to her highly competent and motivated followers but spend considerable time coaching, directing, and training her unskilled and unmotivated followers. Or leaders may provide relatively little praise and assurances to followers with high self-confidence but high amounts of support to followers with low self-confidence. Although leaders often have different interactional styles when dealing with individual followers, is there an optimum way for leaders to adjust their behavior with different followers and thereby increase their likelihood of success? And if there is, what factors should the leader base his behavior on—the follower's intelligence? Personality traits? Values? Preferences? Technical competence? A model called **Situational Leadership** offers answers to these two important leadership questions.

Leader Behaviors

The Situational Leadership model has evolved over time. Its essential elements first appeared in 1969,[21] with roots in the Ohio State studies, in which the two broad categories of leader behaviors, initiating structure and consideration, were initially identified (see **Chapter 7**). As Situational Leadership evolved, so did the labels (but not the content) for the two leadership behavior categories. Initiating structure changed to **task behaviors**, which were defined as the extent to which a leader spells out the responsibilities of an individual or group. Task behaviors include telling people what to do, how to do it, when to do it, and who is to do it. Similarly, consideration changed to **relationship behaviors**, or how much the leader engages in two-way communication. Relationship behaviors include listening, encouraging, facilitating, clarifying, explaining why a task is important, and giving support.

> *The real world is a messy place—yet, even a messy place can (should?) be attacked systematically.*
>
> **Alex Cornell, product designer at Facebook**

When the behavior of actual leaders was studied, there was little evidence to show these two categories of leader behavior were consistently related to leadership success; the relative effectiveness of these two behavior dimensions often depended on the situation. The Hersey and Blanchard Situational Leadership model explains why leadership effectiveness varies across these two behavior dimensions and situations. It arrays the two orthogonal dimensions as in the Ohio State studies and then divides each of them into high and low segments (see **Figure 15.1**). According to the model, depicting the two leadership dimensions this way is useful because certain combinations of task and relationship behaviors may be more effective in some situations than in others.

For example, in some situations high levels of task but low levels of relationship behaviors are effective; in other situations, just the opposite is true. So far, however, we have not considered the key follower or situational characteristics with which these combinations of task and relationship behaviors are most effective. Hersey says these four combinations of task and relationship behaviors would increase leadership effectiveness if they were made contingent on the readiness level of the individual follower to perform a given task.

Follower Readiness

In Situational Leadership, **follower readiness** refers to a follower's ability and willingness to accomplish a particular task. Readiness is not an assessment of an individual's personality, traits, values, age, and so on. It's not a personal characteristic, but rather how ready an individual is to perform a particular task. Any given follower could be low on readiness to perform one task but high on readiness to perform a different task. An experienced emergency room physician would be high in readiness on tasks like assessing a patient's medical status, but could be relatively low on readiness for facilitating an interdepartmental team meeting to solve an ambiguous and complex problem like developing hospital practices to encourage collaboration across departments.

FIGURE 15.1 The Situational Leadership Model

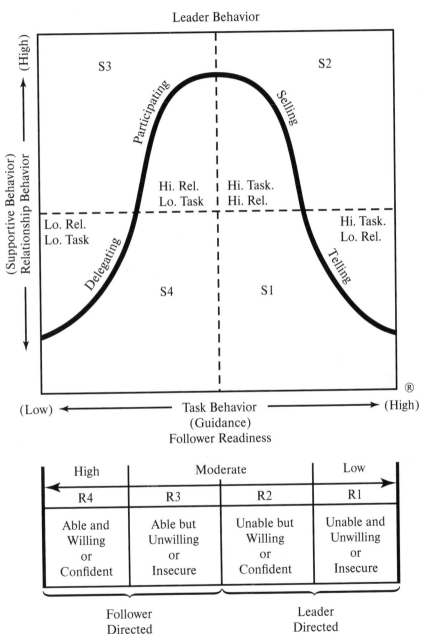

Source: P. Hersey, K. Blanchard, and D. Johnson, *Management of Organizational Behavior: Utilizing Human Resources*, 7th ed. (Englewood Cliffs, NJ: Prentice Hall, 1996), p. 200.

Prescriptions of the Model

Now that the key contingency factor, follower readiness, has been identified, let us move on to another aspect of the figure—combining follower readiness levels with the four combinations of leader behaviors described earlier. The horizontal bar in **Figure 15.1** depicts follower readiness as increasing from right to left (not in the direction we are used to seeing). There are four segments along this continuum, ranging from R1 (the lowest) to R4 (the highest). Along this continuum, however, the assessment of follower readiness can be fairly subjective. A follower who possesses high levels of readiness would clearly fall in the R4 category, just as a follower unable and unwilling (or too insecure) to perform a task would fall in R1.

To complete the model, a curved line is added that represents the leadership behavior that will most likely be effective given a particular level of follower readiness. To apply the model, leaders should first assess the readiness level (R1–R4) of the follower relative to the task to be accomplished. Next, a vertical line should be drawn from the center of the readiness level up to the point where it intersects with the curved line in **Figure 15.1**. The quadrant in which this intersection occurs represents the level of task and relationship behavior that has the best chance of producing successful outcomes. For example, imagine you are a fire chief and have under your command a search-and-rescue team. One of the team members is needed to rescue a backpacker who has fallen in the mountains, and you have selected a particular follower to accomplish the task. What leadership behavior should you exhibit? If this follower has both substantial training and experience in this type of rescue, you would assess his readiness level as R4. A vertical line from R4 would intersect the curved line in the quadrant where both low task and low relationship behaviors by the leader are most apt to be successful. As the leader, you should exhibit a low level of task and relationship behaviors and delegate this task to the follower. By contrast, you may have a brand-new member of the fire department who still has to learn the ins and outs of firefighting. Because this particular follower has low task readiness (R1), the model maintains that the leader should use a high level of task and a low level of relationship behaviors when initially dealing with this follower.

Hersey suggests one further step leaders may wish to consider. The model just described helps the leader select the most appropriate behavior given the current level of follower readiness. However, there may be cases when the leader would like to see followers increase their level of readiness for particular tasks by implementing a series of **developmental interventions** to help boost follower readiness levels. The process would begin by first assessing a follower's current level of readiness and then determining the leader behavior that best suits that follower in that task. Instead of using the behavior prescribed by the model, however, the leader would select the next higher leadership behavior. Another way of thinking about this would be for the leader to select the behavior pattern that would fit the follower if that follower were one level higher in readiness. This intervention is designed to help followers in their development, hence its name (see **Highlight 15.1**).

A Developmental Intervention Using the Situational Leadership Model

HIGHLIGHT 15.1

Dianne is a resident assistant in charge of a number of students in a university dorm. One particular sophomore, Michael, has volunteered to work on projects in the past but never seems to take the initiative to get started on his own. Michael seems to wait until Dianne gives him explicit direction, approval, and encouragement before he will get started. Michael can do a good job, but he seems to be unwilling to start without some convincing that it is all right, and unless Dianne makes explicit what steps are to be taken. Dianne has assessed Michael's readiness level as R2, but she would like to see him develop, both in task readiness and in psychological maturity. The behavior most likely to fit Michael's current readiness level is selling, or high task, high relationship. But Dianne has decided to implement a developmental intervention to help Michael raise his readiness level. Dianne can be most helpful in this intervention by moving up one level to participating, or low task, high relationship. By reducing the amount of task instructions and direction while encouraging Michael to lay out a plan on his own and supporting his steps in the right direction, Dianne is most apt to help Michael become an R3 follower. This does not mean the work will get done most efficiently, however. As we saw in the Vroom and Yetton model earlier, if part of the leader's job is development of followers, then time may be a reasonable and necessary trade-off for short-term efficiency.

Concluding Thoughts about the Situational Leadership Model

In **Figure 15.2** we can see how the factors in Situational Leadership fit within the L-F-S framework. In comparison to the Vroom and Yetton model, there are fewer factors to consider in each of the three elements. The only situational consideration is knowledge of the task, and the only follower factor is readiness. However, the theory goes well beyond decision-making, which was the sole domain of the normative decision model.

FIGURE 15.2   Factors from the Situational Leadership Model and the Interactional Framework

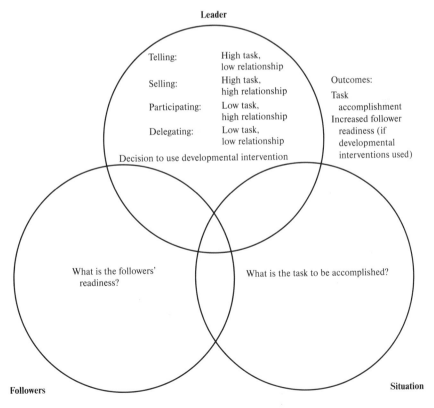

Situational Leadership is usually appealing to students and practitioners because of its common-sense approach as well as the ease of understanding it. Unfortunately there is little published research to support the predictions of Situational Leadership in the workplace.[22, 23] A great deal of research has been done within organizations that have implemented Situational Leadership, but most of those findings are not available for public dissemination.

In 2007, Blanchard modified the Situational Leadership prescriptions to specify more clearly the four definitions of follower developmental level and their four corresponding optimal styles of leadership.[24] Although this revision of the model, perhaps as a result of much criticism concerning the lack of prescriptive specificity, does create a more discrete typology of follower styles, research suggests that the original model is a better predictor of subordinate performance and attitudes than the revised version.[25]

Nevertheless, even with these shortcomings, Situational Leadership is a useful way to get leaders to think about how leadership effectiveness may depend somewhat on being flexible with different subordinates, not on acting the same way toward them all.

The Contingency Model

Although leaders may be able to change their behaviors toward individual subordinates, leaders also have dominant behavioral tendencies. Some leaders may be generally more supportive and relationship oriented, whereas others may be more concerned with task or goal accomplishment. The contingency model[26] recognizes that leaders have these general behavioral tendencies and specifies situations where certain leaders (or behavioral dispositions) may be more effective than others.

Fiedler's[27] **contingency model** of leadership is probably the earliest and most well-known contingency theory, and is often perceived by students to be almost the opposite of the Situational Leadership model. Compared to the contingency model, Situational Leadership emphasizes flexibility in leader behaviors, whereas the contingency model maintains that leaders are much more consistent (and consequently less flexible) in their behavior. The Situational Leadership model maintains that leaders who *correctly base their behaviors* on follower maturity will be more effective, whereas the contingency model suggests that leader effectiveness is determined primarily by *selecting the right kind of leader for a certain situation or changing the situation* to fit the particular leader's style. Another way to say this is that leadership effectiveness depends on both the leader's style and the favorableness of the leadership situation. Some leaders are better than others in some situations but less effective in other situations. To understand contingency theory, therefore, we need to look first at the critical characteristics of the leader and then at the critical aspects of the situation.

The Least Preferred Coworker Scale

To determine a leader's general style or tendency, Fiedler developed an instrument called the **least preferred coworker (LPC) scale**. The scale instructs a leader to think of the single individual with whom he has had the greatest difficulty working (that is, the least preferred co-worker) and then to describe that individual in terms of a series of bipolar adjectives (such as friendly–unfriendly, boring–interesting, and sincere–insincere). Those ratings are then converted into a numerical score.

In thinking about such a procedure, many people assume that the score is determined primarily by the characteristics of whatever particular individual the leader happened to identify as his least preferred coworker. In the context of contingency theory, however, the score is thought to *represent something about the leader, not the specific individual the leader evaluated.*

The current interpretation of these scores is that they identify a leader's *motivation hierarchy*.[28] Based on their LPC scores, leaders are categorized into two groups: **low-LPC leaders** and **high-LPC leaders**. In terms of their motivation hierarchy, low-LPC leaders are motivated primarily by the task, which means these leaders gain satisfaction primarily from task accomplishment. Thus their dominant behavioral tendencies are similar to the initiating structure behavior described in the Ohio State research or the task behavior of Situational Leadership. However, if tasks are being accomplished in an acceptable manner, low-LPC leaders will move to their secondary level of motivation, which is forming and maintaining relationships with followers. Thus low-LPC leaders will focus on improving their relationships with followers *after* they are assured that assigned tasks are being accomplished satisfactorily. If tasks are no longer being accomplished in an acceptable manner, however, low-LPC leaders will refocus their efforts on task accomplishment and persist with these efforts until task accomplishment is back on track.

In terms of motivation hierarchy, high-LPC leaders are motivated primarily by relationships, which means these leaders are satisfied primarily by establishing and maintaining close interpersonal relationships. Thus their dominant behavioral tendencies are similar to the consideration behaviors described in the Ohio State research or the relationship behaviors in Situational Leadership. If high-LPC leaders have established good relationships with their followers, they will move to their secondary level of motivation, which is task accomplishment. As soon as leader–follower relations are jeopardized, however, high-LPC leaders will cease working on tasks and refocus their efforts on improving relationships with followers.

You can think of the LPC scale as identifying two different sorts of leaders, with their respective motivational hierarchies depicted in **Figure 15.3**. Lower-level needs must be satisfied first. Low-LPC leaders will move "up" to satisfying relationship needs when they are assured the task is being accomplished satisfactorily. High-LPC leaders will move "up" to emphasizing task accomplishment when they have established good relationships with their followers.

Because all tests have some level of imprecision, Fiedler[29] suggested that the LPC scale cannot accurately identify the motivation hierarchy for individuals with intermediate scores. Research by Kennedy[30] suggested an alternative view. Kennedy has shown that individuals within the intermediate range of LPC scale scores may more easily or readily switch between being task- or relationship-oriented leaders than those individuals with more extreme scale scores. They may be equally satisfied by working on the task or establishing relationships with followers.

Situational Favorability

The other important variable in the contingency model is **situational favorability**, which is the amount of control the leader has over the followers. Presumably the more control a leader has over followers, the more favorable the situation is, at least from the leader's perspective. Fiedler included three subelements in situation favorability. These were leader–member relations, task structure, and position power.

Leader–member relations are the most powerful of the three subelements in determining overall situation favorability. They involve the extent to which relationships between the leader and followers are generally cooperative and friendly or antagonistic and difficult. Leaders who rate leader–member relations as high feel they have the support of their followers and can rely on their loyalty.

Task structure is second in potency in determining overall situation favorability. Here the leader objectively determines task structure by assessing whether there are detailed descriptions of work products, standard operating procedures, or objective indicators of how well the task is being accomplished. The more one can answer these questions affirmatively, the higher the structure of the task.

Position power is the weakest of the three elements of situational favorability. Leaders who have titles of authority or rank, the authority to administer rewards and punishments, and the legitimacy to conduct follower performance appraisals have greater position power than leaders who lack them.

The relative weights of these three components, taken together, can be used to create a continuum of situational favorability. When using the contingency model, leaders are first asked to rate items that measure the strength of leader-member relations, the degree of task structure, and their level of position power. These ratings are then weighted and combined to determine an overall level of situational favorability facing the leader.[31] Any particular situation's favorability can be plotted on a continuum that Fiedler divided into octants, representing distinctly different levels of situational favorability. The relative weighting scheme for the subelements and how they make up each of the eight octants are shown in **Figure 15.4**.

You can see that the octants of situational favorability range from 1 (highly favorable) to 8 (very unfavorable). The highest levels of situational favorability occur when leader-member relations are good, the task is structured, and position power is high. The lowest levels of situational favorability occur when there are high levels of leader-member conflict, the task is unstructured or unclear, and the leader does not have the power to reward or punish subordinates. Moreover, the relative weighting of the three subelements can easily be seen by their order of precedence in **Figure 15.4**, with leader-member relations appearing first, followed by task structure, and then position power. For example, because leader-member relations carry so much weight, it is impossible for leaders with good leader-member relations to have anything worse than moderate situational favorability, regardless of their task structure or position power. In other words, leaders with good leader-member relations will enjoy situational favorability no worse than octant 4; leaders with poor leader-member relations will face situational favorability no better than octant 5.

FIGURE 15.3   Motivational Hierarchies for Low- and High-LPC Leaders

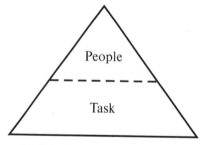

Low-LPC leader motivational hierarchy

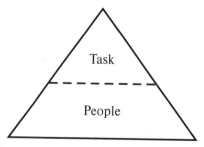

High-LPC leader motivational hierarchy

FIGURE 15.4   Contingency Model Octant Structure for Determining Situational Favorability

	High ⟵ Overall situation favorability ⟶ Low							
Leader–member relations	Good				Poor			
Task structure	Structured		Unstructured		Structured		Unstructured	
Position power	High	Low	High	Low	High	Low	High	Low
Octant	1	2	3	4	5	6	7	8

Prescriptions of the Model

Fiedler and his associates have conducted numerous studies to determine how different leaders (as described by their LPC scores) have performed in different situations (as described in terms of situational favorability). **Figure 15.5** describes which type of leader (high or low LPC) Fiedler found to be most effective, given different levels of situation favorability. The solid dark line represents the relative effectiveness of a low-LPC leader, and the dashed line represents the relative effectiveness of a high-LPC leader. It is obvious from the way the two lines cross and recross that there is some interaction between the leader's style and the overall situation favorability. If the situational favorability is moderate (octants 4, 5, 6, or 7), then those groups led by leaders concerned with establishing and maintaining relationships (high-LPC leaders) seem to do best. However, if the situation is either very unfavorable (octant 8) or highly favorable (octants 1, 2, or 3), then those groups led by the task-motivated (low-LPC) leaders seem to do best.

FIGURE 15.5   Leader Effectiveness Based on the Contingency between Leader LPC Score and Situation Favorability

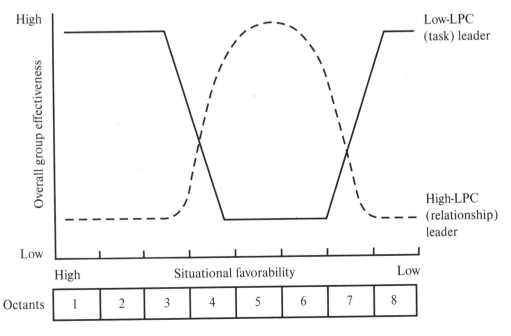

Fiedler suggested that leaders will try to satisfy their primary motivation when faced with unfavorable or moderately favorable situations. This means that low-LPC leaders will concentrate on the task and high-LPC leaders will concentrate on relationships when faced with these two levels of situational favorability. Nevertheless, leaders facing highly favorable situations know that their primary motivations will be satisfied and thus will move to their secondary motivational state. This means that *leaders will behave according to their secondary motivational state only when faced with highly favorable situations* (see **Highlight 15.2**).

High- and Low-LPC Leaders and the Contingency Model

HIGHLIGHT 15.2

Suppose we have two leaders, Tom Low (a low-LPC or task-motivated leader) and Brenda High (a high-LPC or relationship-motivated leader). In unfavorable situations, Tom will be motivated by his primary level and will thus exhibit task behaviors. In similar situations, Brenda will also be motivated by her primary level and as a result will exhibit relationship behaviors. Fiedler found that in unfavorable situations, task behavior will help the group to be more effective, so Tom's behavior would better match the requirements of the situation. Group effectiveness would not be aided by Brenda's relationship behavior in this situation.

In situations with moderate favorability, both Tom and Brenda are still motivated by their primary motivations, so their behaviors will remain the same. Because the situation has changed, however, group effectiveness no longer requires task behavior. Instead, the combination of situational variables leads to a condition in which a leader's relationship behaviors will make the greatest contribution to group effectiveness. Hence, Brenda will be the most effective leader in situations of moderate favorability.

In highly favorable situations, Fiedler's explanation gets more complex. When leaders find themselves in highly favorable situations, they no longer have to be concerned about satisfying their primary motivations. In highly favorable situations, leaders switch to satisfying their secondary motivations. Because Tom's secondary motivation is to establish and maintain relationships, in highly favorable situations he will exhibit relationship behaviors. Similarly, Brenda will also be motivated by her secondary motivation, so she would manifest task behaviors in highly favorable situations. Fiedler believed that leaders who manifested relationship behaviors in highly favorable situations helped groups to be more effective. In this case, Tom is giving the group what it needs to be more effective.

Several interesting implications of Fiedler's[32] model are worthy of additional comment. Because leaders develop their distinctive motivation hierarchies and dominant behavior tendencies through a lifetime of experiences, Fiedler believed these hierarchies and tendencies would be difficult to change through training. Fiedler maintained it was naive to believe that sending someone to a relatively brief leadership training program could substantially alter any leader's personality or typical way of acting in leadership situations; after all, such tendencies had been developed over many years of experience. Instead of trying to change the leader, Fiedler concluded, training would be more effective if it showed leaders how to recognize and change key situational characteristics to better fit their personal motivational hierarchies and behavioral tendencies. Thus, according to Fiedler, the content of leadership training should emphasize situational engineering rather than behavioral flexibility in leaders. Relatedly, organizations could become more effective if they matched the characteristics of the leader (in this case, LPC scores) with the demands of the situation (situational favorability) than if they tried to change the leader's behavior to fit the situation. These suggestions imply that high- or low-LPC leaders in mismatched situations should either change the situation or move to jobs that better match their motivational hierarchies and behavioral patterns.

Concluding Thoughts about the Contingency Model

Before reviewing the empirical evidence, perhaps we can attain a clearer understanding of the contingency model by examining it through the L-F-S framework. As shown in **Figure 15.6**, task structure is a function of the situation, and LPC scores are a function of the leader. Because position power is not a characteristic of the leader but of the situation the leader finds himself or herself in, it is included in the situational circle. Leader–member relations are a joint function of the leader and the followers; thus they belong in the overlapping intersection of the leader and follower circles.

As opposed to the dearth of evidence for Hersey and Blanchard's[33, 34] Situational Leadership model, Fiedler and his fellow researchers have provided considerable evidence that the predictions of the model are empirically valid, particularly in laboratory settings.[35, 36, 37, 38, 39] However, a review of the studies conducted in field settings yielded only mixed support for the model.[40] Moreover, researchers have criticized the model for the uncertainties surrounding the meaning of LPC scores,[41, 42, 43] the interpretation of situational favorability,[44, 45] and the relationships between LPC scores and situational favorability.[46, 47, 48] Despite such questions, however, the contingency model has stimulated considerable research and is the most validated of all leadership theories.

FIGURE 15.6   Factors from Fiedler's Contingency Theory and the Interactional Framework

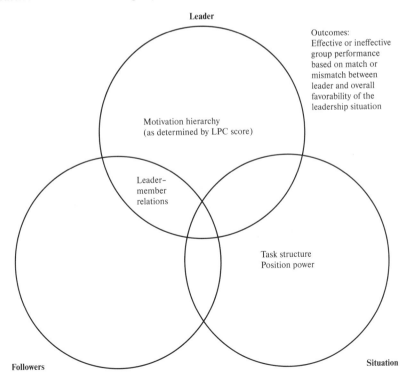

The Path–Goal Theory

Perhaps the most sophisticated (and comprehensive) of the five contingency models is path–goal theory. The underlying mechanism of **path–goal theory** deals with expectancy—a cognitive approach to understanding motivation in which people calculate effort-to-performance probabilities (If I study for 12 hours, what is the probability I will get an A on the final exam?), performance-to-outcome probabilities (If I get an A on the final, what is the probability of getting an A in the course?), and assigned valences or values of outcomes (How much do I value a higher GPA?). Theoretically, at least, people are assumed to make these calculations on a rational basis, and the theory can be used to predict what tasks people will put their energies into, given some finite number of options.

Path-goal theory uses the same basic assumptions as expectancy theory. At the most fundamental level, the effective leader will provide or ensure the availability of valued rewards for followers (the goal) and then help them find the best way of getting there (the path). Along the way, the effective leader will help the followers identify and remove roadblocks and avoid dead ends; the leader will also provide emotional support as needed. These task and relationship leadership actions essentially involve increasing followers' probability estimates for effort-to-performance and performance-to-reward expectancies. In other words, the leader's actions should strengthen followers' beliefs that if they exert a certain level of effort, they will be more likely to accomplish a task, and if they accomplish the task, they will be more likely to achieve some valued outcome.

Although uncomplicated in its basic concept, the model has added more variables and interactions over time. Evans[49] is credited with the first version of path–goal theory, but we will focus on a later version developed by House and Dressler.[50] Their conceptual scheme is ideally suited to the L-F-S framework because they described three classes of variables that include leader behaviors, followers, and the situation. We will examine each of these in turn.

Leader Behaviors

The four types of leader behavior in path–goal theory can be seen in **Table 15.2**. Like the Situational Leadership model, path-goal theory assumes that leaders not only may use varying styles with different subordinates but also may use differing styles with the same subordinates in different situations. Path-goal theory suggests that, depending on the followers and the situation, these different leader behaviors can increase followers' acceptance of the leader, enhance their level of satisfaction, and raise their expectations that effort will result in effective performance, which in turn will lead to valued rewards (see **Highlight 15.3**).

Shifting Behaviors at Caterpillar

HIGHLIGHT 15.3

James Despain was a leader with a very directive leadership style. He began his career at Caterpillar Inc. as a young man, sweeping the factory floor. He followed the lead of others of his generation—the 1950s were a time when leaders were the ultimate authority and words like *participative* and *consultative* were unheard of. Despain worked his way into supervisory positions and finally was named vice president of the track-type tractor division. Despain claims he "spent much of [his] career as a manager focusing on what employees were doing wrong." He focused on the tasks at hand and little else. But in the early 1990s Despain had to face some hard facts: His $1.2 billion division was losing millions of dollars per year, his management team was receiving hundreds of grievances from their employees, and morale at the Caterpillar plant was extremely low.

Despain and his leadership group identified the need for a strategic plan to transform the working culture. Key to the plan was determining a strategy for dealing with employee attitudes and behavior. Despain and his transformation team identified nine behaviors or "common values" that they wanted every employee to emulate every day—trust, mutual respect, customer satisfaction, a sense of urgency, teamwork, empowerment, risk taking, continuous improvement, and commitment. Employee evaluations were based on the manifestation of these behaviors. Above and beyond those behaviors, top executives and management were expected to lead by example and commit themselves to practice 100 positive leadership traits. Statements such as "I will know every one of my employees by name . . . will recognize their accomplishments with praise . . . will trust my employees to do

their work" became the new mantras for those in charge.

Through this process, Despain came to understand that "the most important thing for employees in the workplace is to achieve self-worth." The principal change he was striving to achieve was to make employees accountable for how their jobs got done; for workers, that meant stretching a little more every day to achieve their full potential. For managers, it meant shifting away from achieving traditional metrics and toward drawing desired behavior from workers. "And we found that the more we focused on behavior, the better the metrics got." The result: Despain's division cut its break-even point in half within five years of launching the transformation.

Source: J. Despain and J. Converse, ... *And Dignity for All: Unlocking Greatness through Values-based Leadership* (New York: Prentice Hall, 2003).

TABLE 15.2   The Four Leader Behaviors of Path–Goal Theory

Directive leadership. These leader behaviors are similar to the task behaviors from the Situational Leadership model. They include telling the followers what they are expected to do, how to do it, when it is to be done, and how their work fits in with the work of others. This behavior would also include setting schedules, establishing norms, and providing expectations that followers will adhere to established procedure and regulations.

Supportive leadership. Supportive leadership behaviors include having courteous and friendly interactions, expressing genuine concern for the followers' well-being and individual needs, and remaining open and approachable to followers. These behaviors, which are similar to the relationship behaviors in the Situational Leadership model, also are marked by attention to the competing demands of treating followers equally while recognizing status differentials between the leader and the followers.

Participative leadership. Participative leaders engage in the behaviors that mark the consultative and group behaviors described by Vroom and Yetton.[51] As such, they tend to share work problems with followers; solicit their suggestions, concerns, and recommendations; and weigh these inputs in the decision-making process.

Achievement-oriented leadership. Leaders exhibiting these behaviors would be seen as both demanding and supporting in interactions with their followers. First they would set challenging goals for group and follower behavior, continually seek ways to improve performance en route, and expect the followers to always perform at their highest levels. But they would support these behaviors by exhibiting a high degree of ongoing confidence that subordinates can put forth the necessary effort; will achieve the desired results; and, even further, will assume even more responsibility in the future.

The Followers

Path–goal theory contains two groups of follower variables. The first relates to the *satisfaction of followers*, and the second relates to the *followers' perception of their own abilities* relative to the task to be accomplished. In terms of followers' satisfaction, path–goal theory suggests that leader behaviors will be acceptable to followers to the degree that followers see the leader's behavior either as an immediate source of satisfaction or as directly instrumental in achieving future satisfaction. In other words, followers will actively support a leader as long as they view the leader's actions as a means for increasing their own levels of satisfaction. However, there is only so much a leader can do to increase followers' satisfaction levels because satisfaction also depends on characteristics of the followers themselves.

A frequently cited example of how followers' characteristics influence the impact of leader behaviors on followers' levels of satisfaction involves the trait of locus of control. People who believe they are "masters of their own ship" are said to have an internal locus of control; people who believe they are (relatively speaking) "pawns of fate" are said to have an external locus of control. Mitchell, Smyser, and Weed[52] found that follower satisfaction was not directly related to the degree of participative behaviors manifested by the leader; that is, followers with highly participative leaders were no more satisfied than followers with more autocratic leaders. However, when followers' locus-of-control scores were taken into account, a contingency relationship was discovered. As shown in **Figure 15.7**, internal-locus-of-control followers, who believed outcomes were a result of their own decisions, were much more satisfied with leaders who exhibited participative behaviors than they were with leaders who were directive. Conversely, external-locus-of-control followers were more satisfied with directive leader behaviors than they were with participative leader behaviors.

FIGURE 15.7   Interaction between Followers' Locus of Control Scores and Leader Behavior in Decision-Making

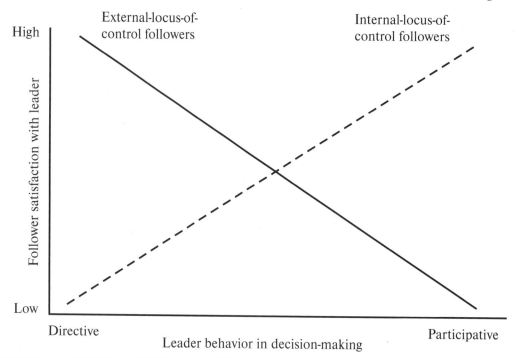

Source: Adapted from T. R. Mitchell, C. M. Smyser, and S. E. Weed, "Locus of Control: Supervision and Work Satisfaction," *Academy of Management Journal* 18 (1975), pp. 623–30.

Followers' perceptions of their own skills and abilities to perform particular tasks can also affect the impact of certain leader behaviors. Followers who believe they are perfectly capable of performing a task are not as apt to be motivated by, or as willing to accept, a directive leader as they would a leader who exhibits participative behaviors. Using the same rationale as for locus of control, we can predict the opposite relationship for followers who do not perceive that they have sufficient abilities to perform a task. Once again, the acceptability of the leader and the motivation to perform are in part determined by followers' characteristics. Thus path–goal theory suggests that both leader behaviors and follower characteristics are important in determining outcomes.

The Situation

Path–goal theory considers three situational factors that impact or moderate the effects of leader behavior on follower attitudes and behaviors. These include *the task, the formal authority system,* and *the primary work group.* Each of these three factors can influence the leadership situation in one of three ways. These three factors can serve as an independent motivational factor, as a constraint on the behavior of followers (which may be either positive or negative in outcome), or as a reward.

> *Although people object when a scientific analysis traces their behavior to external conditions and thus deprives them of credit and the chance to be admired, they seldom object when the same analysis absolves them of blame.*
>
> **B. F. Skinner, American psychologist**

However, these variables can often affect the impact of various leader behaviors. For example, if the task is structured and routine, the formal authority system has constrained followers' behaviors, and the work group has established clear norms for performance, then leaders would be serving a redundant purpose by manifesting directive or achievement-oriented behaviors. These prescriptions are similar to some of those noted in substitutes for leadership theory[53] because everything the follower needs to understand the effort-to-performance and performance-to-reward links is provided by the situation. Thus redundant leader behaviors might be interpreted by followers as either a complete lack of understanding or empathy by the leader, or an attempt by the leader to exert excessive control. Neither of these interpretations is likely to enhance the leader's acceptance by followers or increase their motivation.

Although we have already described how follower characteristics and situational characteristics can impact leader behaviors, path–goal theory also maintains that follower and situational variables can impact each other. In other words, situational variables, such as the task performed, can also impact the influence of followers' skills, abilities, or personality traits on followers' satisfaction. Although this seems to make perfect sense, we hope you are beginning to see how complicated path–goal theory can be when we start considering how situational variables, follower characteristics, and leader behaviors interact in the leadership process.

Prescriptions of the Theory

In general, path–goal theory maintains that leaders should first assess the situation and select a leadership behavior appropriate to situational demands. By manifesting the appropriate behaviors, leaders can increase followers' effort-to-performance expectancies, performance-to-reward expectancies, or valences of the outcomes. These increased expectancies and valences will improve subordinates' effort levels and the rewards attained, which in turn will increase subordinates' satisfaction and performance levels and the acceptance of their leaders.

Perhaps the easiest way to explain this complicated process is through an example. Suppose we have a set of followers who are in a newly created work unit and do not understand the requirements of their positions. In other words, the followers have a high level of role ambiguity. According to path–goal theory, leaders should exhibit a high degree of directive behaviors to reduce the role ambiguity of their followers. The effort-to-performance link will become clearer when leaders tell followers what to do and how to do it in ambiguous situations, which in turn will cause followers to exert higher effort levels. Because role ambiguity is assumed to be unpleasant, these directive leader behaviors and higher effort levels should eventually result in higher satisfaction levels among followers. **Figure 15.8** illustrates this process. Similarly, leaders may look at the leadership situation and note that followers' performance levels are not acceptable. The leader may also conclude that the current situation offers few, if any, incentives for increased performance. In this case the leader may use directive behaviors to increase the value of the rewards (or valence), which in turn will increase followers' effort levels and performance.

Concluding Thoughts about the Path–Goal Theory

Before getting into the research surrounding path–goal theory, you may wish to examine the theory using the L-F-S framework. As shown in **Figure 15.9**, the components of path–goal theory fit nicely into the L-F-S model. The four leader behaviors fit into the leader circle, the characteristics of the followers fit into the follower circle, and the task and the formal authority system fit into the situation circle. Of all the components of path–goal theory, the only "mismatch" with the L-F-S model deals with the primary work group. The norms, cohesiveness, size, and stage of development of groups are considered to be part of the follower function in the L-F-S model but are part of the situation function in path–goal theory. In that regard, we hasten to note we use the L-F-S framework primarily for heuristic purposes. Ultimately the concepts described in these five theories are sufficiently complex and ambiguous that there probably is no right answer in any single depiction.

FIGURE 15.8 Examples of Applying Path–Goal Theory

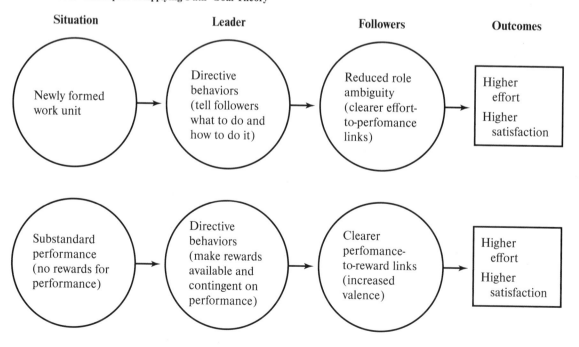

In terms of research, the path-goal theory has received only mixed support to date.[54, 55, 56, 57] Although many of these mixed findings may be due to the path-goal theory's exclusion of many of the variables found to impact the leadership process, it is also possible that a portion of these mixed findings may be due to problems with the theory. Yukl[58] maintained that most of these criticisms deal with the methodology used to study path-goal theory and the limitations of expectancy theory. Moreover, the path-goal theory assumes that the only way to increase performance is to increase followers' motivation levels. The theory ignores the roles leaders play in selecting talented followers, building their skill levels through training, and redesigning their work.[59]

> *To act is easy; to think is hard.*
>
> **Goethe, German writer**

Nonetheless, path-goal theory is useful for illustrating two points. First, as noted by Yukl,[60] "path-goal theory has already made a contribution to the study of leadership by providing a conceptual framework to guide researchers in identifying potentially relevant situational moderator variables." Path-goal theory also illustrates that, as models become more complicated, they may be more useful to researchers and less appealing to practitioners. Our experience is that pragmatically oriented students and in-place leaders want to take something from a model that is understandable and can be applied in their work situation right away. This does not mean they prefer simplicity to validity—they generally appreciate the complexity of the leadership process. But neither do they want a model that is so complex as to be indecipherable.

FIGURE 15.9   Factors from Path–Goal Theory and the Interactional Framework

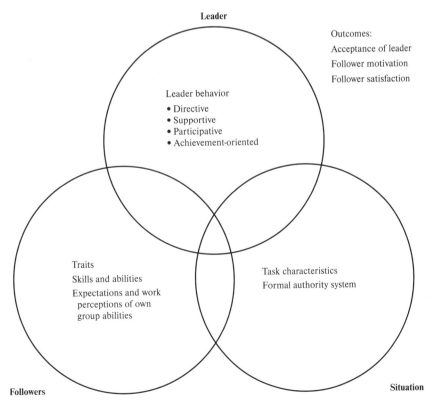

Summary

This chapter has provided an overview of four well-known contingency theories of leadership, which include leader–member exchange theory, the Situational Leadership model, the contingency model, and the path–goal theory. All four models are similar in that they specify that leaders should make their behaviors contingent on certain aspects of the followers or the situation to improve leadership effectiveness. In addition, all four theories implicitly assume that leaders can accurately assess key follower and situational factors. However, as the material in **Chapter 2** regarding perception shows, it is entirely possible that two leaders in the same situation may reach different conclusions about followers' levels of knowledge, the strength of leader–follower relationships, the degree of task structure, or the level of role ambiguity being experienced by followers. These differences in perception could lead these two leaders to reach different conclusions about the situation, which may in turn cause them to take different actions in response to the situation. Furthermore, these actions may be in accordance or in conflict with the prescriptions of any of these four theories. Also, the fact that leaders' perceptions may have caused them to act in a manner not prescribed by a particular model may be an underlying reason why these four theories have reported conflicting findings, particularly in field settings.

Another reason these theories have generally found mixed support in field settings is that they are all limited in scope. Recall our earlier comments about 66 different leadership domains. Many factors that affect leader and follower behaviors in work group, team, or volunteer committee settings are not present in laboratory studies but often play a substantial role in field studies. For example, none of the models take into account how levels of stress, organizational culture and climate, working conditions, technology, economic conditions, or types of organizational design affect the leadership process. Nevertheless, the four contingency theories have been the subject of considerable research; and even if only mixed support for the models has been found, this research has added to our knowledge about leadership and has given us a more sophisticated understanding of the leadership process.

Key Terms

parsimony

leader–member exchange (LMX)

role-taking

role-making

routinization

Situational Leadership

task behaviors

relationship behaviors

follower readiness

developmental interventions

contingency model

least preferred coworker (LPC) scale

low-LPC leaders

high-LPC leaders

situational favorability

path–goal theory

directive leadership

supportive leadership

participative leadership

achievement-oriented leadership

Questions

1. Given the description of the leadership situation facing the airplane crash survivors described in **Chapter 1**, how would leader–member exchange, the Situational Leadership model, the contingency model, and the path–goal theory prescribe that a leader should act?

2. Can leaders be flexible in how they interact with others? Do you believe leaders can change their behavior? Their personalities?

3. Think of a leadership situation with which you are familiar. Apply each of the theories in this chapter to the situation. Which theory best fits the interaction of the leader, followers, and situation in your example? Does any theory allow you to predict a likely or preferred outcome for a current challenge?

Minicase

Big Changes for a Small Hospital

As F. Nicholas Jacobs toured the Windber Medical Center facility, he was dismayed by the industrial pink-painted walls, the circa-1970 furniture, and the snow leaking through the windows of the conference room. Employees earned 30 percent less than their counterparts in the area, and turnover was steep. As Windber's newest president, Jacobs knew he was the facility's last hope—if he couldn't successfully turn around the aging facility, it would mean closing the doors forever.

Coming to Windber Medical Center in 1997, Jacobs was keenly aware that the hospital could be the next in a series of small hospitals that had fallen victim to a struggling economy. Determined to see that not happen, he began by making connections with the employees of the hospital and the community at large. Jacobs's first step was to interview the employees to find out firsthand what they wanted for the Windber community and the medical center. He also looked to members of local community groups like the local library, the Agency on Aging, and local politicians and asked these groups what they wanted from their local medical facility. When Jacobs realized that octogenarians made up a larger percentage of the population in Windber, Pennsylvania, than in all of Dade County, Florida, he made it a priority to provide more options to seniors for improving their health and quality of life. He set forth a vision of a medical center that was more of a community center—a center that would allow members of the community to exercise in a state-of-the-art facility while having access to professionals to answer health-related questions. Jacobs realized that keeping people in the community both physically and mentally healthy also meant keeping the hospital financially healthy. He made the center's new preventive care philosophy clear to the public: "Work out at our hospital so you can stay out of our hospital."

Jacobs's efforts have paid off—in an era when small hospitals are closing left and right, Windber Medical Center is thriving. Under Jacobs's leadership, Windber has established an affiliation with the Planetree treatment system, which integrates meditation, massage, music, and other holistic methods into traditional health care. Windber's wellness center, which offers fitness training, yoga, and acupuncture, among other treatments, opened in January 2000 and now generates over $500,000 annually. Gone are the pink walls and dated furniture—replaced with fountains, plants, and modern artwork. Jacobs recruited a former hotel manager to oversee food service. And despite the dismissal of about 32 employees (those used to a more traditional hospital setting had a tough time in the new environment), the staff has nearly doubled to 450 employees, and pay has improved. Windber has raised more than $50 million in public and private funding and has forged research partnerships with the Walter Reed Army Health System and the University of Pittsburgh, among others. The Windber Research Institute, Windber's heart disease reversal program, has treated about 250 patients.

1. Consider the factors from the Situational Leadership model outlined in **Figure 15.1**. Apply these factors to Jacobs and Windber.

2. How do you think Jacobs would score on the least preferred coworker (LPC) scale? Why?

3. Based on the success of Windber, in what range would you guess the overall situational favorability might fall for Jacobs on the continuum illustrated in **Figure 15.4**?

Source: A. Schlesinger, "Somerset County Hospital Is Epicenter of an Old Coal Company Town," *Post-Gazette*, January 13, 2004, www.post-gazette.com/pg/04013/260747.stm.

Endnotes

1. J. Dinh, R. Lord, W. Gardner, J. Meuser, R. Liden, and J. Hu, "Leadership Theory and Research in the New Millennium: Current Theoretical Trends and Changing Perspectives," *Leadership Quarterly* 25 (2014), pp. 36–62.

2. F. E. Fiedler, "Reflections by an Accidental Theorist," *Leadership Quarterly* 6, no. 4 (1995), pp. 453–61.

3. F. E. Fiedler, *A Theory of Leadership Effectiveness* (New York: McGraw-Hill, 1967).

4. M. M. Chemers, "The Social, Organizational, and Cultural Contest of Effective Leadership," in *Leadership: Multidisciplinary Perspectives*, ed. B. Kellerman (Englewood Cliffs, NJ: Prentice Hall, 1984).

5. G. Graen and J. F. Cashman, "A Role-Making Model of Leadership in Formal Organization: A Developmental Approach," in *Leadership Frontiers*, eds. J. G. Hunt and L. L. Larson (Kent, OH: Kent State University Press, 1976), pp. 143–65.

6. R. C. Linden and G. Graen, "Generalizability of the Vertical Dyad Linkage Model of Leadership," *Academy of Management Journal* 23 (1980), pp. 451–65.

7. S. J. Wayne, L. M. Shore, and R. C. Linden, "Perceived Organizational Support and Leader-Member Exchange: A Social Exchange Perspective," *Academy of Management Journal* 40 (1997), pp. 82–111.

8. G. Chen, B. L. Kirkman, R. Kanfer, D. Allen, and B. Rosen, "A Multilevel Study of Leadership Empowerment and Performance in Teams," *Journal of Applied Psychology* 92 (2007), pp. 331–46.

9. R. T. Sparrowe and R. C. Linden, "Two Routes to Influence: Integrating Leader-Member Exchange and Social Network Perspectives," *Administrative Science Quarterly* 50 (2005), pp. 505–35.

10. T. A. Scandura and C. A. Schriesheim, "Leader-Member Exchange and Supervisor Career Mentoring as Complementary Constructs in Leadership Research," *Academy of Management Journal* 37 (1994), pp. 1588–602.

11. G. B. Graen and M. Uhl-Bien, "Relationship-Based Approach to Leadership: Development of Leader-Member Exchange (LMX) Theory over 25 Years: Applying a Multi-Level Multi-Domain Perspective," *Leadership Quarterly* 6 (1995), pp. 219–47.

12. D. J. Henderson, R. C. Liden, B. C. Glibkowski, and A. Chaudhry, "LMX Differentiation: A Multilevel Review and Examination of Its Antecedents and Outcomes," *Leadership Quarterly* 20 (2009), pp. 517–34.

13. L. Atwater and A. Carmeli, "Leader-Member Exchange, Feelings of Energy, and Involvement in Creative Work," *Leadership Quarterly* 20 (2010), pp. 264–75.

14. Z. Zhang, M. Wang, and J. Shi, "Leader-Follower Congruence in Proactive Personality and Work Outcomes: The Mediating Role of Leader-Member Exchange," *Academy of Management Journal* 55, no. 1 (2009), pp. 111–30.

15. V. Venkataramani, S. Green, and D. Schleicher, "Well-Connected Leaders: The Impact of Leaders' Social Network Ties on LMX and Members' Work Attitudes," *Journal of Applied Psychology* 95, no. 6 (2010), pp. 1071–84.

16. R. Eisenberger, G. Karagonlar, F. Stinglhamber, P. Neves, T. Becker, M. G. Gonzalez-Morales, and M. Steiger-Mueller, "Leader-Member Exchange and Affective Organizational Commitment: The Contribution of Supervisor's Organizational Embodiment," *Journal of Applied Psychology* 95, no. 6 (2010), pp. 1085–103.

17. B. Erdogan and T. N. Bauer, "Differentiated Leader-Member Exchanges: The Buffering Role of Justice Climate," *Journal of Applied Psychology* 95, no. 6 (2010), pp. 1104–120.

18. D. DeCremer, M. van Dijke, and D. M. Mayer, "Cooperating When 'You' and 'I' Are Treated Fairly: The Moderating Role of Leaders Prototypicality," *Journal of Applied Psychology* 95, no. 6 (2010), pp. 1121–133.

19. T. Rockstuhl, J. H. Dulebohn, S. Ang, and L. M. Shore, "Leader-Member Exchange (LMX) and Culture: A Meta-Analysis of Correlates of LMX Across 23 Countries," *Journal of Applied Psychology* 97, no. 6 (2012), pp. 1097–130.

20. R. S. Gajendran and A. Joshi, "Innovation in Globally Distributed Teams: The Role of LMX, Communication Frequency, and Member Influence on Team Decisions," *Journal of Applied Psychology* 97, no. 6 (2012), pp. 1252–261.

21. P. Hersey and K. H. Blanchard, "Life Cycle Theory of Leadership," *Training and Development Journal* 23 (1969), pp. 26–34.

22. R. P. Vecchio, "Situational Leadership Theory: An Examination of a Prescriptive Theory," *Journal of Applied Psychology* 72 (1987), pp. 444–51.

23. G. Yukl and D. D. Van Fleet, "Theory and Research on Leadership in Organizations," in *Handbook of Industrial and Organizational Psychology,* eds. M. D. Dunnette and L. M. Hough (Mountain View, CA: Consulting Psychologists Press, 1992), pp. 147–97.

24. K. H. Blanchard, *Leading at a Higher Level* (Upper Saddle River, NJ: Prentice Hall, 2007).

25. G. Thompson and R. P. Vecchio, "Situational Leadership Theory: A Test of Three Versions," *Leadership Quarterly* 20 (2009), pp. 837–48.

26. Fiedler, "Reflections by an Accidental Theorist."

27. Fiedler, "Reflections by an Accidental Theorist."

28. F. E. Fiedler, "The Contingency Model and the Dynamics of the Leadership Process," in *Advances in Experimental Social Psychology*, ed. L. Berkowitz (New York: Academic Press, 1978).

29. Fiedler, "The Contingency Model and the Dynamics of the Leadership Process."

30. J. K. Kennedy, "Middle LPC Leaders and the Contingency Model of Leader Effectiveness," *Organizational Behavior and Human Performance* 30 (1982), pp. 1–14.

31. F. E. Fiedler and M. M. Chemers, *Improving Leadership Effectiveness: The Leader Match Concept*, 2nd ed. (New York: Wiley, 1982).

32. Fiedler, "Reflections by an Accidental Theorist."

33. Hersey and Blanchard, "Life Cycle Theory of Leadership."

34. P. Hersey and K. H. Blanchard, *Management of Organizational Behavior: Utilizing Human Resources*, 4th ed. (Englewood Cliffs, NJ: Prentice Hall, 1982).

35. Fiedler, "The Contingency Model and the Dynamics of the Leadership Process."

36. F. E. Fiedler, "Cognitive Resources and Leadership Performance," *Applied Psychology: An International Review* 44, no. 1 (1995), pp. 5–28.

37. Fiedler and Chemers, *Improving Leadership Effectiveness*.

38. L. H. Peters, D. D. Hartke, and J. T. Pohlmann, "Fiedler's Contingency Theory of Leadership: An Application of the Meta-analytic Procedures of Schmidt and Hunter," *Psychological Bulletin* 97 (1985), pp. 274–85.

39. M. J. Strube and J. E. Garcia, "A Meta-analytic Investigation of Fiedler's Contingency Model of Leadership Effectiveness," *Psychological Bulletin* 90 (1981), pp. 307–21.

40. Peters et al., "Fiedler's Contingency Theory of Leadership."

41. Kennedy, "Middle LPC Leaders and the Contingency Model of Leader Effectiveness."

42. R. W. Rice, "Construct Validity of the Least Preferred Co-Worker Score," *Psychological Bulletin* 85 (1978), pp. 1199–237.

43. C. A. Schriesheim and S. Kerr, "Theories and Measures of Leadership: A Critical Appraisal of Current and Future Directions," in *Leadership: The Cutting Edge*, eds. J. G. Hunt and L. L. Larson (Carbondale, IL: Southern Illinois University Press, 1977).

44. A. G. Jago and J. W. Ragan, "The Trouble with Leader Match Is That It Doesn't Match Fiedler's Contingency Model," *Journal of Applied Psychology* 71 (1986), pp. 555–59.

45. A. G. Jago and J. W. Ragan, "Some Assumptions Are More Troubling Than Others: Rejoinder to Chemers and Fiedler," *Journal of Applied Psychology* 71 (1986), pp. 564–65.

46. Jago and Ragan, "The Trouble with Leader Match Is That It Doesn't Match Fiedler's Contingency Model."

47. Jago and Ragan, "Some Assumptions Are More Troubling Than Others."

48. R. P. Vecchio, "Assessing the Validity of Fiedler's Contingency Model of Leadership Effectiveness: A Closer Look at Strube and Garcia," *Psychological Bulletin* 93 (1983), pp. 404–8.

49. M. G. Evans, "The Effects of Supervisory Behavior on the Path-Goal Relationship," *Organizational Behavior and Human Performance* 5 (1970), pp. 277–98.

50. R. J. House and G. Dressler, "The Path-Goal Theory of Leadership: Some Post Hoc and A Priori Tests," in *Contingency Approaches to Leadership*, eds. J. G. Hunt and L. L. Larson (Carbondale: Southern Illinois University Press, 1974).

51. R. H. G. Field, "A Test of the Vroom-Yetton Normative Model of Leadership," *Journal of Applied Psychology* 67 (1982), pp. 523–32.

52. T. R. Mitchell, C. M. Smyser, and S. E. Weed, "Locus of Control: Supervision and Work Satisfaction," *Academy of Management Journal* 18 (1975), pp. 623–30.

53. S. Kerr and J. M. Jermier, "Substitutes for Leadership: Their Meaning and Measurement," *Organizational Behavior and Human Performance* 22 (1978), pp. 375–403.

54. C. A. Schriesheim and A. S. DeNisi, "Task Dimensions as Moderators of the Effects of Instrumental Leadership: A Two Sample Replicated Test of Path–Goal Leadership Theory," *Journal of Applied Psychology* 66 (1981), pp. 589–97.

55. Schriesheim and Kerr, "Theories and Measures of Leadership."

56. Yukl, *Leadership in Organizations*.

57. C. A. Schriesheim, S. L. Castro, X. Zhou, and L. A. DeChurch, "An Investigation of Path–Goal and Transformational Leadership Theory Predictions at the Individual Level of Analysis," *Leadership Quarterly* 17 (2006), pp. 21–38.

58. Yukl, *Leadership in Organizations*.

59. Yukl and Van Fleet, "Theory and Research on Leadership in Organizations."

60. Yukl, *Leadership in Organizations*.

CHAPTER 16

Leadership and Change

Introduction

Organizations today face myriad potential challenges. To be successful they must cope effectively with the implications of new technology, globalization, changing social and political climates, new competitive threats, shifting economic conditions, industry consolidation, swings in consumer preferences, and new performance and legal standards. Think how technology enabled Mark Zuckerberg to create Facebook or the changes the U.S. military had to make as it shifted from stemming the tide of communism to fighting more regionalized conflicts. And consider how the events of September 11, 2001, the wars in Iraq and Afghanistan, the threats of global terrorism, the Arab Spring, the wars in Syria and Yemen, Brexit, the opioid crisis, disruptive technologies, globalization, trade wars, global warming, and the coronavirus pandemic have affected leaders in both the private and public sectors around the world. Leading change is perhaps the most difficult challenge facing any leader, yet this skill may be the best differentiator of leaders from managers and mediocre from exceptional leaders. The best leaders are those who recognize the situational and follower factors inhibiting or facilitating change, paint a compelling vision of the future, and formulate and execute a plan that moves their vision from a dream to reality.

> *There is nothing more difficult to take in hand, more perilous to conduct, or more uncertain of success, than to take the lead in the introduction of a new order of things.*
>
> **Niccolò Machiavelli, Italian Renaissance writer**

> *It is not necessary to change. Survival is not mandatory.*
>
> **W. Edwards Deming, quality expert**

The scope of any change initiative varies dramatically. Leaders can use goal setting, coaching, or performance management skills to effectively change the behaviors and skills of individual direct reports. But what would you need to do if you led a pharmaceutical company of 5,000 employees and you had just received FDA approval to introduce a revolutionary new drug into the marketplace? How would you get the research and development, marketing, sales, manufacturing, quality, shipping, customer service, accounting, and information technology departments to work together to ensure a profitable product launch? Or what would you do if you had to reduce company expenses by 40 percent for the next two years or deal with a recent acquisition of a competitor? **Table 16.1** identifies some of the common changes that take place in organizations, and it is obvious that changes of this magnitude involve more than coaching and managing the performance of individual followers.

TABLE 16.1   Common Types of Organizational Changes

Changes in organizational strategy
Geographic/international expansion
Mergers and acquisitions
Divestitures
Implementation of new IT systems
Automation and technology changes
Top leadership changes
Organizational restructurings
Culture changes
New policies, procedures, and processes
New product releases
New service offerings
Reporting and measurement system changes
Compensation, benefits, or retirement plan changes
Black swan events, such as the coronavirus pandemic

Source: J. Bohn, *Architects of Change* (Memphis, TN: CreateSpace, 2015).

Because this chapter builds on much of the content of the previous chapters, it is fitting that it appears toward the end of the text. To successfully lead larger-scale change initiatives, leaders need to attend to the situational and follower factors affecting their group or organization (**Chapters 9**, **10**, **11**, **12**, and **14**). They must also use their intelligence, problem-solving skills, creativity, and values to sort out what is important and formulate solutions to the challenges facing their group (**Chapters 5**, **6**, and **7**). But solutions in and of themselves are no guarantee for change. Leaders must use their power and influence, personality traits, coaching and planning skills, and knowledge of motivational techniques and group dynamics in order to drive change (**Chapters 3**, **4**, **8**, **9**, **10**, **12**, and **18**). Examples of what it takes to drive large-scale organizational change can be found in **Highlights 16.1** and **16.2**.

No Money, No Mission

HIGHLIGHT 16.1

Bethesda Lutheran Communities (BLC) is a 110-year-old Christian organization that provides services to the developmentally and intellectually disabled. These services include group and host homes, intermittent support, day programs, camps, vocational training, job placement, and transportation. The organization began with the opening of a single home in Watertown, Wisconsin, in 1904 and now consists of over 4,000 employees working in 325 facilities located across 13 states. BLC serves thousands of disabled individuals through government grants, philanthropy, and sales from 18 thrift stores.

Mike Thirtle has been the CEO of BLC since 2014. Prior to being named to fill the top position in the organization, Thirtle spent a year as executive vice president of strategy and chief information officer at BLC, and before that he spent almost 20 years in the U.S. Air Force and the Rand Corporation. A graduate of the U.S. Air Force Academy with a master's degree in economics, an MBA, and a PhD in policy analysis, Thirtle joined BLC because he was attracted to the faith-based mission of helping others less fortunate and to be in a role where he could have a major impact on the organization.

As executive vice president of strategy, Thirtle began to notice problems in BLC's financial situation. The organization was doing a tremendous job serving the disabled but was spending money at a much faster rate than it was bringing in. The previous CEO, COO, and CFO were vaguely aware of but did not seem to care about this problem. The financial system in place at the time made it difficult to track overall revenues versus expenses, BLC had a large rainy-day fund that could be used to cover revenue shortfalls, and the board of directors was much more interested in providing faith-based services than keeping abreast of how BLC was running as a business. The previous CEO also spent a lot of time and BLC funds on expensive junkets around the world and was more interested in enjoying the trappings of the office than in dealing with the day-to-day challenges of being a CEO. The previous CEO was let go in 2014 and Thirtle was asked to move into the top job.

Upon being named CEO, Thirtle began to upgrade the talent on his executive leadership team and do a deep dive on BLC's financial situation. He and his new CFO quickly realized that BLC would go bankrupt if it did not close over 100 money-losing facilities and let go of 1,300 employees within the next 12–18 months. BLC had never gone through an organizational restructuring before, and like Thirtle, many of its employees joined the company in order to serve the disabled. Moreover, thousands of developmentally disabled individuals were housed in the facilities targeted for closure, and Thirtle could not simply put those served out on the street. Thirtle and his executive leadership team had to assemble a plan that allowed BLC to systematically close facilities, track progress toward financial sustainability, place disabled individuals into new facilities, and communicate the rationale for these changes to parents and guardians, government officials, the board of directors, middle management, and line employees.

Under Thirtle's leadership, BLC has been able to staunch the flow of red ink and has now created a strategy on where the organization needs to be in the next 10 years. Thirtle believes that BLC can be an industry leader in helping the intellectually and developmentally disabled live independent lives and be fully integrated members of communities. His vision for making this happen is building homes that leverage technology that do just that, the first of which is scheduled to open in 2020.

What would you do if you were faced with a situation where the cost of doing business was far greater than the amount of revenues being generated, and many of those working for the organization were long-term employees who believed in the organization's mission? How easy or difficult would it be to drive these changes? What have been Thirtle's biggest challenges: turning around a nearly bankrupt organization or rallying the organization around his vision for the future?

Sources: G. J. Curphy, *Bethesda Lutheran Communities Executive Leadership Team Off-Site*, February 23–24 (North Oaks, MN: Curphy Leadership Solutions, 2017); G. J. Curphy, personal communication with Mike Thirtle, January 25, 2017; and G. J. Curphy, *Bethesda Lutheran Communities Business Committee Off-Site,* Chicago, IL, January 5–7, 2020.

There is no limit to what an organized group can do if it wants to.

George McLean, newspaper editor

Change in a Rural Community

HIGHLIGHT 16.2

Change does not just happen in organizations; it also occurs in communities. Whereas many suburbs are experiencing dramatic growth, most urban and rural communities are experiencing declines in population and business. Some rural communities are working hard to attract new businesses, such as ethanol plants and wind farms, and build new schools or new community centers; others are organizing to prevent Walmart or other large retailers from building stores in their communities. One of the real success stories of how a community transformed itself is Tupelo, Mississippi. Tupelo is famous for being the birthplace of Elvis Presley; in 1940 it also had the distinction of being the county seat of the poorest county in the poorest state in the country. But Lee County now has a medical center with over 6,000 employees, boasts 18 *Fortune* 500 manufacturing plants, and has added 1,000 new manufacturing jobs in each of the past 13 years. Tupelo now has a symphony, an art museum, a theater group, an 8,000-seat coliseum, and an outstanding recreational program. Its public schools have won national academic honors, and its athletic programs have won several state championships.

So how was Tupelo able to transform itself from a poor to a vibrant rural community? The town had no natural advantages, such as a harbor or natural resources, which would give it a competitive advantage. It also had no interstate highways, and the closest metropolitan centers were over 100 miles away. The key to Tupelo's success was the ability of the town's citizens to work together. More specifically, the citizens of Tupelo were able to (1) collaborate effectively in identifying the problems and needs of the community, (2) achieve a working consensus on goals and priorities, (3) agree on ways and means to implement goals and priorities, and (4) collaborate effectively on the agreed actions.

Tupelo's success started when local community members pooled resources to acquire a siring bull. The bull's offspring were used to start local ranches. Farmers shifted from planting cotton to growing crops needed to support the ranchers and local populace, and farming and ranching equipment distributors started up local operations. George McLean, the local newspaper publisher, kept the community focused on economic development and helped local entrepreneurs by subsidizing office and warehouse space. With various tax breaks and incentives from local bankers, furniture manufacturers started moving to town. A number of other businesses then sprang up to support the manufacturers, and community leaders made a concerted effort to expand and improve local health care and educational facilities to support the new workforce.

Despite the successes to date, Tupelo is facing even bigger challenges, as many of the local furniture manufacturers are being threatened by low-cost manufacturers in China. But if any community were to succeed in the face of challenge, it would likely be Tupelo. The community seems to have the leaders needed to help citizens fully understand these new challenges and what to do to meet them. What would you do to preserve jobs and attract new businesses if you were the mayor of Tupelo?

Source: V. L. Grisham Jr., *Tupelo: The Evolution of a Community* (Dayton, OH: Kettering Foundation Press, 1999).

As an overview, this chapter begins by revisiting the leadership versus management discussion from **Chapter 1**. We then describe a rational approach to organizational change and spell out what leaders can do if they want to be successful with their change efforts. This model also provides a good diagnostic framework for understanding why many change efforts fail. We include in this chapter a discussion of an alternative approach to change—charismatic and transformational leadership. The personal magnetism, heroic qualities, and spellbinding powers of these leaders can have unusually strong effects on followers, which often lead to dramatic organizational, political, or societal change. Unlike the rational approach to change, the charismatic and transformational leadership framework places considerable weight on followers' heightened emotional levels to drive organizational change. Much of the leadership research over the past 35 years has helped us better understand the situational, follower, and leader characteristics needed for charismatic or transformational leadership to occur. The chapter concludes with an overview of these factors and a review of the predominant theory in the field, Bass's theory of transformational and transactional leadership.[1]

The Rational Approach to Organizational Change

A number of authors have written about organizational change, including O'Toole,[2] Pritchett,[3] McNulty,[4] Heifetz and Linsky,[5] Moss Kanter,[6, 7] Krile, Curphy, and Lund,[8] Ostroff,[9] Rock and Schwartz,[10] Kotter,[11] Curphy,[12, 13] Burns,[14] Marcus and Weiler,[15] Bennis and Nanus,[16] Tichy and Devanna,[17] Bridges,[18] Collins and Porras,[19] Treacy and Wiersma,[20] Beer,[21, 22] Heifetz and Laurie,[23] and Collins.[24, 25] All these authors have unique perspectives on leadership and change, but they also share a number of common characteristics. Beer[26, 27] has offered a rational and straightforward approach to large-scale organizational change that addresses many of the issues raised by the other authors. Beer's model also provides a road map for leadership practitioners wanting to implement an organizational change initiative, as well as a diagnostic tool for understanding why change initiatives fail. According to Beer,

$$C = D \times M \times P > R$$

> *We've long believed that when the rate of change inside an institution becomes slower than the rate of change outside, the end is in sight. The only question is when.*

Jack Welch, former CEO of General Electric

The D in this formula represents followers' **dissatisfaction** with the current status quo. M symbolizes the **model** for change and includes the leader's vision of the future as well as the goals and systems that need to change to support the new vision. P represents **process**, which concerns developing and implementing a plan that articulates the who, what, when, where, and how of the change initiative. R stands for **resistance**; people resist change because they fear a loss of identity or social contacts, and good change plans address these sources of resistance. Finally the C corresponds to the **amount of change**. Notice that leaders can increase the amount of change by increasing the level of dissatisfaction, increasing the clarity of vision, developing a well-thought-out change plan, or decreasing the amount of resistance in followers. You should also note that the $D \times M \times P$ is a multiplicative function—increasing dissatisfaction but having no plan will result in little change. Likewise, if followers are content with the status quo, it may be difficult for leaders to get followers to change, no matter how compelling their vision or change plan may be. This model maintains that organizational change is a systematic process, and large-scale changes can take months if not years to implement.[28, 29, 30] Leadership practitioners who understand the model should be able to do a better job developing change initiatives and diagnosing where their initiatives may be getting stuck. Because change is an important component of leadership, we will go into more detail about each of the components of Beer's model.

> *The ultimate curse is to be a passenger on a large ship, to know that the ship is going to sink, to know precisely what to do to prevent it, and to realize that no one will listen.*

Myron Tribus, Massachusetts Institute of Technology

Dissatisfaction

Followers' level of satisfaction is an important ingredient in a leader's ability to drive change. Followers who are relatively content are not apt to change; malcontents are much more likely to do something to change the situation. Although employee satisfaction is an important outcome of leadership, leaders who want to change the status quo may need to take action to decrease employee satisfaction levels. Follower's emotions are the fuel for organizational change, and change often requires a considerable amount of fuel. The key for leadership practitioners is to increase dissatisfaction (D) to the point where followers are inclined to take action, but not so much that they decide to leave the organization. So what can leaders do to increase follower dissatisfaction levels? Probably the first step is to determine how satisfied followers are with the current situation. This information can be gleaned from employee satisfaction or engagement surveys, grievance records, turnover rates, Glassdoor or Yelp reviews, customer complaints, or conversations with followers. To increase dissatisfaction, leaders can talk about potential competitive, technology, or legal threats or employee concerns about the status quo. They can also capitalize on or even create some type of financial or political crisis, compare benchmarks against other organizations, or substantially increase performance standards. All of these actions can potentially heighten followers' emotional levels; however, leaders must ensure that these emotions are channeled toward the leader's vision for the organization (see **Highlight 16.3**).

Citizen Dissatisfaction and Guerrilla Warfare

HIGHLIGHT 16.3

Follower dissatisfaction should not be limited to organizations, as people can be just as unhappy with their government as they can be with their employers. The American Revolution, Gandhi's campaign to oust the British, Mao Zedong's and Fidel Castro's campaigns to convert China and Cuba to communist rule, the Arab Spring, the civil wars in Syria and Libya, and riots in Hong Kong are good examples of what can happen if those in charge let citizen dissatisfaction spin out of control. If the disenfranchised have no real outlet to vent their anger or change their government then they may resort to guerrilla warfare. Guerrilla warfare can be defined as a conflict with no front lines, no uniforms, no starting and ending points, that often targets civilians and can be quite deadly. It is the war of choice whenever someone wants to overthrow a government that has a formal army with superior firepower. But how long has guerrilla warfare been around? Does it work? What role is technology playing in guerrilla warfare?

It turns out that wars between uniformed armies, such as the American Civil War, World War II, or the first Gulf War are fairly rare; guerrilla warfare is much more prevalent. For example, the American Indians, the Vietcong, the African National Congress in South Africa, the Irish Republican Army, the FARC in Columbia, al-Qaeda in Iraq, the Taliban in Afghanistan, and the Syrian Free Army all adopted guerrilla warfare tactics. Guerrilla wars tend to be quite long, 7–10 years on average, and the likelihood of success is not particularly high. Guerrilla warriors won 25 percent of the time before 1945, and this percentage has only improved to 40 percent over the past 70 years. For some guerrilla warriors, such as the Irish Republican Army or the Hong Kong protesters, winning the war may not be as important as gaining valuable concessions from the opposition.

The key to winning or losing a guerrilla war is winning the hearts and minds of the populace. If noncombatants feel they are safer or better off with the opposition, they will support the guerrilla movement. Conversely, if civilians believe their government better serves these needs, then they will not support the movement. The use of car bombs, human shields, kidnapping, and assassinations is intended to show that the government cannot provide safety and security and win the hearts and minds of the greater population. Governments often play right into the hands of guerrilla warriors by adopting tactics that have little impact on the warriors but anger the greater population. The superior firepower strategy of "bombing people back to the Stone Age" and "shock and awe" used by the United States early in the Vietnam and second Iraq wars had minimal impact on enemy combatants but angered the local population. It was only when Generals Abrams and Petraeus introduced counterinsurgency tactics intended to win the hearts and minds of the local populace that the U.S. military started making progress in the Vietnam and Iraq wars.

Technology is playing a more important role in guerrilla warfare. Social media, YouTube videos, the Internet, and 24/7 news coverage all are now being used by both government and guerrilla forces to win popular support. Drones have made it possible for governments to kill guerrilla leaders with minimal civilian casualties.

Perhaps the next big front in guerrilla warfare will be cyberattacks. What will happen to the hearts and minds of citizens when their power and water are shut off or when financial systems are corrupted? What if these attacks originate from outside a country's borders? How do Kim Jong-un, Xi Jinging, Vladimir Putin, Nicolás Maduro, and Donald Trump use technology and the media to manage citizen dissatisfaction? What role is technology playing in the Syrian civil war? What tactics have the Hong Kong protesters used to foment opposition, and are these tactics working? Do guerrilla leaders use a rational or emotional approach to drive change?

Sources: S. Gorman and S. Hughes, "U.S. Steps Up Alarm Over Cyber Attacks," *The Wall Street Journal*, March 13, 2013, pp. A1 and A8; M. Boot, "The Guerrilla Myth," *The Wall Street Journal*, January 19–20, 2013, pp. C1–C2; M. Boot, *Invisible Armies: An Epic History of Guerrilla Warfare from Ancient Times to the Present* (New York: Liveright, 2013); T. E. Ricks, *Fiasco: The American Military Adventure in Iraq* (New York: Penguin, 2006); T. E. Ricks, *The Generals: American Military Command from World War II to Today* (New York: Penguin, 2012); and T. McLaughlin, "Hong Kong's Perfect Crisis," *The Atlantic*, January 29, 2020, www.theatlantic.com/international/archive/2020/01/hong-kong-protests-coronavirus-outbreak/605662.

Without a compelling vision, there is no way for people who lose the most to reconcile their losses.

Bill Mease, business consultant

Model

There are four key components to the model (*M*) variable in the change formula, and these include environmental scanning, a vision, the setting of new goals to support the vision, and needed system changes. As discussed earlier, organizations are bombarded constantly with economic, technological, competitive, legal, and social challenges. Good leaders continually scan the external environment to assess the seriousness of these threats. They are also adept at internal scanning; they understand where the organization is doing well and falling short. Thus keeping up to date on current events, spending time reviewing organizational reports, and taking time to listen to followers' concerns are some techniques leaders use to conduct external and internal scans.[31, 32, 33, 34, 35, 36, 37, 38, 39] This information in turn is used to formulate a vision for the change initiative. What would a new organization look like if it were to successfully counter the gravest external threats, take advantage of new market opportunities, and overcome organizational shortcomings? What would be the purpose of the new organization, and why would people want to work in it? A good vision statement should answer these questions. Fortunately, a vision statement does not have to be a solo effort on the part of the leader. Often leaders will either solicit followers for ideas or work with a team of followers to craft a vision statement.[40, 41, 42, 43, 44, 45, 46, 47] Both of these actions can help to increase followers' commitment to the new vision.

| *Without a clear vision and an explicit set of goals, all decisions are based on politics.*

Pete Ramstad, Toro

It is important to understand the difference between an organization's vision and goals. Just as ancient mariners used the stars to navigate, so should a vision provide guidance for an organization's actions. A vision helps an organization make choices about what it should and should not do, the kind of people it should hire and retain, the rules by which it should operate, and so on.[48, 49, 50, 51, 52] But just as the stars were not the final destination for the mariners, a vision is not the final destination for an organization. An organization's goals are the equivalent of the mariners' final destination, and they should spell out specifically what the organization is trying to accomplish and when they will get done.[53, 54, 55, 56, 57, 58, 59, 60] Depending on the organization, these goals might concern market share, profitability, revenue or customer growth, quality, the implementation of new customer service or information technology systems, the number of patents awarded, school test scores, fund-raising targets, or the reduction of crime rates. Thus an organization's goals can be externally or internally focused or both, depending on the results of the environmental scan and the vision of the organization. These goals essentially define what an organization needs to do to win, and those with no or ill-defined goals are much less likely to have change initiatives that succeed. **Highlight 16.4** provides an example of a vision statement and organizational goals for a waste-to-energy power company. (This company burns trash to create electricity.)

An Example of a Vision Statement and Organizational Goals

HIGHLIGHT 16.4

Vision Statement

To be the industry leader in waste-to-energy operating companies.

Selected Organizational Goals

Increase profitability growth from 5 to 8.5 percent.

Hold maintenance and repair spending to 2015 levels.

Maintain 92 percent boiler availability rate across all plants.

Reduce unscheduled boiler downtime by 29 percent.

Reduce accounting costs by 12 percent by centralizing the accounting function.

Achieve zero recordables and zero lost time safety incidents across all plants.

Implement a metals recovery system across all plants in order to boost recycle revenues by 26 percent.

Win five new waste-to-energy plant operating contracts in 2015.

Source: G. J. Curphy, *The Competitive Advantage Program for Wheelabrator Technologies Incorporated* (North Oaks, MN: Author, 2010).

After determining the organization's goals, the leader will need to determine which systems need to change for the organization to fulfill its vision and accomplish its goals. In other words, how do the marketing, sales, manufacturing, quality, human resource, shipping, accounting, or customer service systems need to change if the organization is to succeed? And does the current organizational structure or culture support or interfere with the new vision? Leaders wanting their organizational change initiatives to succeed will need to take a systems thinking approach after setting organizational goals.[61, 62, 63, 64, 65] **A systems thinking approach** asks leaders to think about the organization as a set of interlocking systems, and explains how changes in one system can have intended and unintended consequences for other parts of the organization. For example, if a company wanted to grow market share and revenue, it might change the compensation system to motivate salespeople to go after new customers. However, this approach could also cause a number of problems in the manufacturing, quality, shipping, accounting, and customer service departments. Leaders who anticipate these problems make all of the necessary systems changes to increase the odds of organizational success. Leaders may need to set goals and put action plans in place for each of these system changes. These actions can be contrasted to **siloed thinking**, in which leaders act to optimize their part of the organization at the expense of suboptimizing the organization's overall effectiveness.[66, 67, 68, 69] For example, the vice president of sales could change the sales compensation plan if she believed her sole concern was annual revenues. This belief could be reinforced if her compensation was based primarily on hitting certain revenue targets. If she were a siloed thinker, she would also believe that profitability, quality, or customer service were not her concerns. However, this mode of thinking could ultimately lead to her downfall: Quality and order fulfillment problems might cause customers to leave faster than new customers buy products.

> *Diplomacy without arms is like music without instruments.*
>
> **Frederick the Great, King of Prussia**

Figure 16.1 is a graphic depiction of a systems model for leadership practitioners. All the components of this model interact with and affect all the other components of the model. Therefore, leaders changing organizational vision or goals will need to think through the commensurate changes in the organization's structure, culture, systems, and leader and follower capabilities. Similarly, changes in the information or hiring systems can affect the organization's capabilities, culture, structure, or ability to meet its goals. One of the keys to successful organizational change is ensuring that all components in **Figure 16.1** are in alignment. A common mistake for many leaders is to change the organization's vision, structure, and systems and overlook the organization's culture and leader and follower capabilities. This makes sense in that it is relatively easy to create a new vision statement, organizational chart, or compensation plan. Leaders either discount the importance of organizational culture and capabilities, falsely believe they are easy to change, or believe they are a given because they are so difficult to change. It is possible to change the culture and capabilities of an organization, but it takes considerable time and focused effort. Unfortunately, about 70 percent of change initiatives fail, and the underlying cause for many of these failures is the leader's inability or unwillingness to address these culture and capabilities issues.[70, 71, 72, 73, 74, 75, 76, 77, 78, 79, 80, 81, 82]

> *Organizational change initiatives will only succeed when the changes are specified down to the individual employee level. Employees need to understand which old attitudes and behaviors are to be discarded and which new ones are to be acquired.*
>
> **Jerry Jellison, University of Southern California**

Process

At this point in the change process, the leader may have taken certain steps to increase follower dissatisfaction. She may also have worked with followers to craft a new vision statement, set new team or organizational goals, and determined what organizational systems, capabilities, or structures need to change. In many ways, the D and M components of the change model are the easiest for leadership practitioners to alter. The process (P) component of the change model is where the change initiative becomes tangible and actionable because it consists of the development and execution of the **change plan**.[83, 84, 85, 86, 87, 88] Good change plans outline the sequence of events, key deliverables, timelines, responsible parties, metrics, and feedback mechanisms needed to achieve the new organizational goals. They may also include the steps needed to increase dissatisfaction and deal with anticipated resistance, an outline of training and resource needs, and a comprehensive communication plan to keep all relevant parties informed. (See **Profiles in Leadership 16.1**.)

FIGURE 16.1   The Components of Organizational Alignment

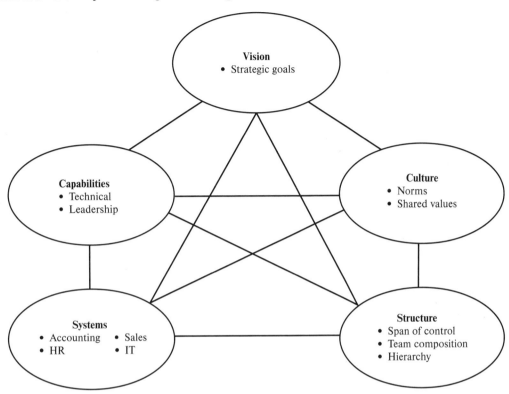

We live in evolutionary competition with microbes—bacteria and viruses. There is no guarantee we will survive.

Joshua Lederberg, Nobel Prize–winning molecular biologist

Dr. Anthony Fauci

PROFILES IN LEADERSHIP 16.1

Sometimes leaders are the source of change in their organizations, and at other times, situational factors can be so overwhelming that entire countries are forced to change. This is precisely what happened with the coronavirus pandemic of 2020, where an infection from a Wuhan, China, meat market spread across the globe in a few short months. Spearheading the U.S. response to the pandemic was Dr. Anthony

"Tony" Fauci, the head of the National Institute of Allergy and Infectious Diseases. Being a highly cited medical researcher, being awarded 30 honorary doctorate degrees, and having run the Institute for 36 years, Dr. Fauci's background and experience made him uniquely qualified to lead the U.S. national response during the COVID-19 crisis.

Growing up in Brooklyn, Dr. Fauci did his undergraduate at Holy Cross, where he was a premed and Greek classics major. He attended medical school at Columbia University, where he graduated first in his class. He joined the Public Health Service immediately afterward and spent his early years discovering cures for rare diseases. He was the point person for the country's response to the AIDs epidemic in the 1980s and played a key leadership role in getting retrovirus drugs distributed across the United States and Africa during the George W. Bush administration. These actions undoubtedly saved millions of lives. He was also in charge of the U.S. responses to the H1N1, SARS, MERS, Ebola, and Zika virus outbreaks, and because of his recommendations, the United States largely remained unaffected by these potential pandemics.

Although U.S. President Donald Trump likes to say there has never been anything like the coronavirus pandemic, in reality, pandemics have been around for at least 2,500 years. Dr. Fauci was an early advocate of handwashing, social distancing, limited travel, closing schools and businesses, and doing massive testing during the height of the pandemic. The U.S. economy largely came to a screeching halt as a result, and some news commentators, political leaders, and businesspeople strongly advocated against Fauci's recommendations. This group felt the damage to the U.S. economy far outweighed the cost of the lives lost from the coronavirus.

How would you rate U.S. President Donald Trump's ability to drive change during the coronavirus pandemic? What about Dr. Fauci's ability? Who had more impact on the country during the crisis?

Sources: M. Specter, "How Anthony Fauci Became America's Doctor," *The New Yorker*, April 20, 2020, www.newyorker.com/magazine/2020/04/20/how-anthony-fauci-became-americas-doctor; and D. Grady, "Not His First Pandemic: Dr. Anthony Fauci Sticks to the Facts," *The New York Times*, March 8, 2020, www.nytimes.com/2020/03/08/health/fauci-coronavirus.html.

Depending on the depth and breadth of change, change plans can be detailed and complicated. For example, the waste-to-energy company described earlier could no longer do what it had always done if it were to reach its goals outlined in **Highlight 16.4**. The company needed new behaviors, metrics, and feedback systems to achieve these goals. The company's change plan was quite extensive and consisted of an overall plan for the company as well as plant-specific goals and change plans. Each of these plans outlined the action steps, responsible parties, metrics, and due dates; progress against the plans was regularly reviewed in monthly plant business and operational reviews. The goals and change plans were constantly adjusted in these meetings to take into account unforeseen barriers, sooner-than-expected progress, and so on.

In terms of barriers to change, there is not a single rural community that wouldn't benefit from a few timely deaths.

Jim Krile, community researcher

Of course the plan itself is only a road map for change. Change will occur only when the action steps outlined in the plan are actually carried out. This is another area where leadership practitioners can run into trouble. One of the reasons why CEOs fail is an inability to execute, and this is also one of the reasons why first-line supervisors through executives derail.[89, 90, 91, 92] Perhaps the best way to get followers committed to a change plan is to have them create it. This way followers become early adopters and know what, why, when, where, who, and how things are to be done. Nevertheless, many times it is impossible for all the followers affected by the change to be involved with plan creation. In these cases follower commitment can be increased if the new expectations for behavior and performance are explicit, the personal benefits of the change initiative are made clear, and followers already have a strong and trusting relationship with their leader.[93, 94, 95] Even after taking all of these steps, leadership practitioners will still need to spend considerable time regularly reviewing progress and holding people accountable for their roles and responsibilities in the change plan. Followers face competing demands for time and effort, and a lack of follow-through will cause many followers to drop the change initiative off of their radar screens. Leaders should also anticipate shifts in followership types once the change plan is implemented. Self-starters may shift to become criticizers, brown-nosers to slackers, or slackers to criticizers. Leaders who address these shifts in types and inappropriate follower behaviors in a swift and consistent manner are more likely to succeed with their change initiatives (see **Profiles in Leadership 16.2**).

Muhammad Yunus

PROFILES IN LEADERSHIP 16.2

Muhammad Yunus was born as the third of nine children. He graduated 16th out of the 39,000 high school students who took national graduation exams in East Pakistan that year and attended Chittagong College to obtain bachelor's and master's degrees in economics. Yunus then worked in the Bureau of Economics and was a lecturer in Chittagong College before winning a Fulbright Scholarship. He used his scholarship to earn a PhD in economics at Vanderbilt University before returning to East Pakistan. East Pakistan had always been a poor country, but it became even poorer after suffering the Bangladesh Liberation War in the early 1970s. Upon his return to Bangladesh, Yunus began looking for effective ways to reduce the country's high poverty levels.

It was right after the war that Yunus lent a group of 42 women the equivalent of $27 to buy bamboo. The women had started up a small chair-building business, but their money lenders charged such high interest rates that all their profits were used up paying off their loans. The women essentially became indentured slaves, as the banks in Bangladesh were unwilling to lend money to anyone perceived to be a high credit risk. Yunus charged the women the equivalent of 4 percent on their loan and helped them break out of the cycle of poverty. This event was the beginning of Yunus's work in microlending, which refers to the practice of lending small amounts of money to poor entrepreneurs to help them start up and grow businesses. Yunus lent money to small groups he called "solidarity groups," designating them as people who were

more likely to repay loans and also help other members in time of need.

In 1983 Yunus opened Grameen Bank, a bank that specialized in providing group loans to poor entrepreneurs. Since then, the bank has expanded across multiple countries, has made over $7 billion in loans, and has seen a repayment rate of 96 to 97 percent. Yunus has probably done as much as anyone to improve the lives of the poor, and because of these efforts he has been listed as one of the top 12 greatest entrepreneurs of our time by *Money* magazine and as one of the 25 most influential business leaders in the past 25 years by Wharton Business School, and he received the Presidential Medal of Freedom in 2009 and the Nobel Peace prize in 2006. The Nobel Committee stated that "lasting peace cannot be achieved until large population groups break free of poverty ... and Yunus and Grameen Bank have shown that even the poorest of poor can work to bring about their own development."

Do you think Yunus used a rational or emotional approach to drive change in rural communities?

Sources: N. St. Anthony, "Small Loans, Big Results," *The Minneapolis-Star Tribune*, March 10, 2013, p. D3; J. W. Wellington, "With Bonsai People, a Closer Look at the Work of Muhammad Yunus," *Huffington Post*, September 21, 2011, http://huffingtonpost.com/john-wellington-ennis/bonsai-people_b_974972.html; "Muhammad Yunus Biography," The Nobel Prize, www.nobelprize.org/nobel_prizes/peace/laureates/2006/yunus-bio.html; and "'We Are All Entrepreneurs': Muhammad Yunus on Changing the World, One Microloan at a Time," *The Guardian*, March 29, 2017, www.theguardian.com/sustainable-business/2017/mar/29/we-are-all-entrepreneurs-muhammad-yunus-on-changing-the-world-one-microloan-at-a-time.

Resistance

Why would followership styles shift as a result of a change initiative? One reason is that it may take some time before the benefits of change are realized. Leaders, followers, and other stakeholders often assume that performance, productivity, or customer service will immediately improve upon the acquisition of new equipment, systems, behaviors, and so on. However, there is often a temporary drop in performance or productivity as followers learn new systems and skills. This difference between initial expectations and reality is called the **expectation–performance gap** and can be the source of considerable frustration (see **Figure 16.2**). If not managed properly, it can spark resistance (R), causing followers to revert back to old behaviors and systems to get things done. Leaders can help followers deal with their frustration by setting realistic expectations, demonstrating a high degree of patience, and ensuring that followers gain proficiency with the new systems and skills as quickly as possible. Good change plans address the expectation–performance gap by building in training and coaching programs to improve follower skill levels.[96, 97, 98]

> *Everybody resists change, particularly those who have to change the most.*
>
> **James O'Toole, Aspen Institute**

Another reason why followers might resist change is a fear of loss.[99, 100, 101, 102, 103, 104, 105, 106, 107, 108, 109, 110] Because of the change, followers are afraid of losing power, close relationships with others, valued rewards, and their sense of identity or, on the other hand, being seen as incompetent.[111] According to Beer,[112] the fear of loss is a predictable and legitimate response to any change initiative, and some of a leader's responses to these fears can be found in **Table 16.2**. Change initiatives are more likely to be adopted successfully if their change plans identify and address potential areas of resistance. People also seem to go through some predictable reactions when confronted with change. An example might help to clarify the typical stages

FIGURE 16.2   The Expectation–Performance Gap

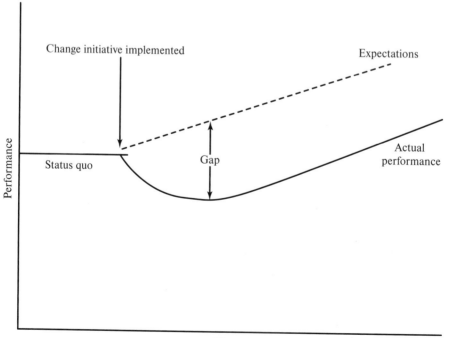

people go through when coping with change. Suppose you were working for a large company that needed to lay off 30 percent of the workforce due to a slowdown in the economy and declining profits. If you were one of the people asked to leave, your first reaction might be shock or surprise. You might not have been aware that market conditions were so poor or that you would be among those affected by the layoff. Next you would go through an anger stage. You might be angry that you had dedicated many long evenings and weekends to the company and now the company no longer wanted your services. After anger would come the rejection stage. In this stage you would start to question whether the company really knew what it was doing by letting you go and perhaps rationalize that they would probably be calling you back. In the final stage, acceptance, you would realize that the company might not ask you back, and you would start to explore other career options. These four reactions to change—shock, anger, rejection, and acceptance—make up what is known as the **SARA model**.[113] Most people go through these four stages whenever they get passed over for a promotion, receive negative feedback on a 360-degree report, get criticized by their boss, or the like.

Table 16.2   Common Losses with Change

Loss of	Possible Leader Actions
Power	Demonstrate empathy, good listening skills, and new ways to build power
Competence	Offer coaching, mentoring, training, peer coaching, job aids, and so forth
Relationships	Help employees build new relationships before change occurs or soon thereafter
Rewards	Design and implement a new reward system to support change initiative
Identity	Demonstrate empathy; emphasize value of new roles

Source: J. F. Krile, G. J. Curphy, and D. R. Lund, *The Community Leadership Handbook: Framing Ideas, Building Relationships, and Mobilizing Resources* (St Paul, MN: The Fieldstone Alliance, 2006).

Commitment is nice, but doses of compliance may be necessary.

Michael Beer, Harvard Business School

But what should a leadership practitioner do with the SARA model? Perhaps the first step is to simply recognize that change is going to stir emotions and people undergo four types of reactions when coping with change.[114] Second, leaders need to understand that individual followers can take more or less time to work through the four stages. Leaders can, however, accelerate the pace in which followers work though the four stages by maintaining an open door policy, demonstrating empathy, and listening to concerns. Third, it is important to note that people are not likely to take any positive action toward a change initiative until they reach the acceptance stage. This does not mean they are happy with the change—only that they accept the inevitability of the change. Fourth, leaders also need to understand that where people are in the SARA model often varies according to organization level. Usually the first people to realize that a change initiative needs to be implemented are the organization's top leaders. Like everyone else, they go through the four stages, but they are the first to do so. The next people to hear the news are middle managers, followed by first-line supervisors and individual contributors. These three groups also go through the emotional stages of the SARA model but do so at different times. These differences in emotional reactions by organizational level are depicted in **Figure 16.3**. What is interesting in **Figure 16.3** is that just when top executives have reached the acceptance stage, first-line supervisors and individual contributors are in the anger or rejection stages. By this time top leaders are ready to get on with the implementation of the change initiative and may not understand why the rest of the organization is still struggling. Because they are already at the acceptance stage, top leaders may fail to demonstrate empathy and listening skills, and this may be another reason for the depressed performance depicted in **Figure 16.2**.

Concluding Thoughts about the Rational Approach to Organizational Change

The situational, follower, and leader components of the rational approach to organizational change are shown in **Figure 16.4**. Although organizational vision, goals, and change plans are often a collaborative effort between the leader and followers, they are the primary responsibility of the leader. Leaders also need to think about the importance of critical mass for driving change.[115, 116, 117, 118, 119] They may be more successful by initially focusing their change efforts on early adopters and those on the fence rather than on those followers who are the most adamant about maintaining the status quo. Once a critical mass is reached, the adopters can exert peer pressure on followers who are reluctant to change.[120, 121, 122, 123] This approach also maintains that the leader needs both good leadership and good management skills if a change initiative is to succeed over the long term. Leadership skills are important for determining a new vision for the organization, increasing dissatisfaction, coaching followers on how to do things differently, and overcoming resistance. Management skills are important when setting new goals and creating, implementing, and reviewing progress on change plans. Both sets of skills not only are important components in organizational change but also may play a key role in determining whether a new company will succeed or fail. Because of their strong leadership skills, entrepreneurs are often good at starting up new organizations. Many of these individuals can get people excited about their vision for the new company. However, if entrepreneurs fail to possess or appreciate the importance of

FIGURE 16.3   Reactions to Change

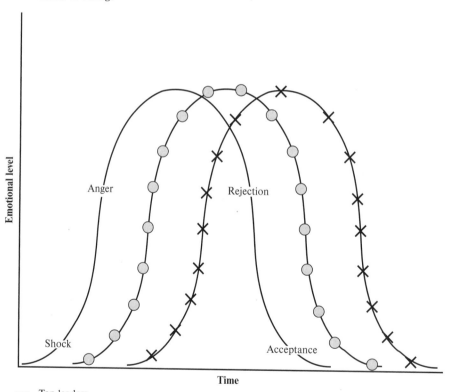

management skills, they may not create the systems, policies, and procedures necessary to keep track of shifting consumer preferences, revenues, customer satisfaction, quality, and costs. As a result, these individuals may not have the information they need to make good operational and financial decisions, and their companies eventually file for bankruptcy. But it is hard to see how planning and execution skills alone will result in the formation of a new company or drive organizational change. It is almost impossible to start up a new company—or for an organization to successfully change—if the person in charge does not have a compelling vision or fails to motivate others to do something different. Many of the other reasons why organizational change initiatives fail to have their roots in underdeveloped leadership or management skills.[124, 125]

Although both sets of skills are important, leadership practitioners should recognize that there is a natural tension between leadership and management skills. In many ways management skills help to maintain the status quo; they help to ensure consistency in behaviors and results. Leadership skills are often used to change the status quo; they help to change the purpose and processes by which an organization gets things done. Leaders who overuse or overemphasize either set of skills are likely to suboptimize team or organizational performance. Nonetheless, two leadership and management skills seem vitally important to driving change and are worth discussing in more detail. **Adaptive leadership** involves behaviors associated with being able to successfully flex and adjust to changing situations. Change, challenge, and adversity seem to be part of most organizations today, and the most effective leaders are those who readily adapt their leadership styles to

FIGURE 16.4   The Rational Approach to Organization Change and the Interactional Framework

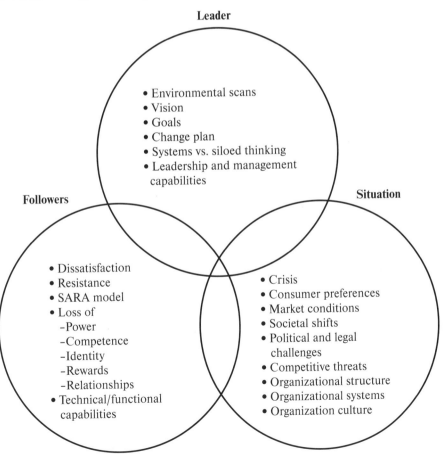

changing situational demands.[126, 127] And because of the constant bombardment of change, learning agility also seems to play a vital role in leadership effectiveness. **Learning agility** is the capability and willingness to learn from experience and apply these lessons to new situations.[128, 129, 130] The most effective leaders are those with high levels of learning agility and adaptability—not only do they know how to build teams and get results through others in changing situations but also they can flex and adjust their behavior as needed to adapt to situational demands. The first part of this chapter was designed to help leadership practitioners better understand when to use leadership and management skills in the change process, and education and experience can help leadership practitioners improve both sets of skills.

> *It takes an order of magnitude more effort to refute bullshit than create it.*
>
> **Alberto Brandolini, author**

Finally, it is worth noting that the rational approach gives leaders a systematic process for driving change and increasing understanding of why change initiatives succeed or fail in their respective organizations. Leadership practitioners can use the $C = D \times M \times P > R$ model as a road map for creating a new vision and goals, changing the products and services their organizations provide, or changing the IT, financial, operations, maintenance, or compensation systems used to support organizational goals. Likewise, leadership practitioners can also use this model to diagnose where their change initiatives have fallen short—perhaps followers were reasonably satisfied with the status quo or did not buy into the new vision and goals, critical systems changes were not adequately identified, or change plans were incomplete or improperly implemented. Given the explanatory power of the model, the rational approach to change gives leaders a useful heuristic for driving organizational and community change (see **Highlight 16.5**).

> *If you really want to understand something, then try to change it.*
>
> **Kurt Lewin, researcher**

#BlackLivesMatter

HIGHLIGHT 16.5

African Americans make up 12 percent of the general population but 50 percent of the prison population in the United States. Although more than a million African Americans are in prison, scant attention had been paid to these alarming statistics until the emergence of the Black Lives Matter movement. Alicia Garza, Patrisse Cullors, and Opal Tometi started Black Lives Matter after the 2012 acquittal of George Zimmerman, who at the time was accused of shooting unarmed teen Trayvon Martin. Initially started as a social media phenomenon, Black Lives Matter is now an international activist movement whose purpose is to draw attention to racial profiling and the unfair treatment of minorities by police and the criminal justice system and to eliminate racial inequality. The #BlackLivesMatter hashtag was created by Garza, Cullors, and Tometi in 2013, the term was designated the word of the year in 2014 by the American Dialect Society, the movement was on the short list of *Time* magazine's Person of the Year in 2015, and by 2016 the hashtag had been tweeted 30 million times.

Garza, Cullors, and Tometi not only brought heightened awareness to the plight of African Americans, but they also transformed this new focus into street action. Beginning with the protests in Ferguson, Missouri, after the police shooting of Michael Brown in 2013, thousands of street protests and demonstrations have erupted in communities, on college campuses, and during election campaign rallies across the

United States as well as in England, Australia, and Canada. The killing of George Floyd in Minneapolis, Minnesota on May 25, 2020 enabled the movement to organize major protests in the Twin Cities that spread out across the United States and rest of the world.

The 30 Black Lives Matter chapters are made up of volunteers. The movement has no formal hierarchy or structure, and chapters are asked to conform to a set of principles and goals but are not required to do so. There have been major political divisions associated with the movement, with Democrats generally supportive of Black Lives Matter and Republicans countering that "All Lives Matter" and that African Americans would be better served by focusing on intraracial crime statistics.

Has the Black Lives Matter movement resulted in any tangible gains for African Americas? How should it define winning, and what would it need to do to win? Did Alicia Garza, Patrisse Cullors, and Opal Tometi use a rational or emotional approach to drive change?

Sources: A. Garza, "A Herstory of the #BlackLivesMatter Movement," *The Feminist Wire*, October 7, 2014, http://www.thefeministwire.com/2014/10/blacklivesmatter-2; Black Lives Matter, www.blacklivesmatter.com; J. Cobb, "The Matter of Black Lives," *New Yorker*, March 14, 2016, http://www.newyorker.com/magazine/2016/03/14/where-is-black-lives-matter-headed; and A. Altman, "The Short List: Black Lives Matter," *Time*, 2015, http://time.com/time-person-of-the-year-2015-runner-up-black-lives-matter.

The Emotional Approach to Organizational Change: Charismatic and Transformational Leadership

Although the rational approach provides a straightforward model for organizational change, it seems that many large-scale political, societal, or organizational changes were not this formulaic. For example, it is doubtful that Jesus Christ, Muhammad, Joan of Arc, Vladimir Lenin, Adolf Hitler, Mahatma Gandhi, Mao Zedong, Martin Luther King Jr., the Ayatollah Khomeini, Nelson Mandela, Fidel Castro, Hugo Chávez, Osama bin Laden, or Donald Trump followed some change formula or plan, yet these individuals were able to fundamentally change their respective societies. Although these leaders differ in a number of important ways, one distinct characteristic they all share is charisma. Charismatic leaders are passionate, driven individuals who point out problems with the current situation and paint a compelling vision of a different future. Through this vision they can generate high levels of excitement among followers and build particularly strong emotional attachments with them. The combination of a compelling vision, heightened emotional levels, and strong personal attachments often compels followers to put forth greater effort to drive organizational or societal changes. The enthusiasm and passion generated by charismatic leaders seems to be a dual-edged sword, however. Some charismatic movements can result in positive and relatively peaceful organizational or societal changes; for example, Evo Morales has done a great deal to help the poor in Bolivia. On the downside, when this passion is used for selfish or personal gains, history mournfully suggests it can have an equally devastating effect on society. Examples here might include Zimbabwe President Robert Mugabe, Kim Jung-un of North Korea, or Nicolás Maduro in Venezuela.

> *The comment that best summarized the situation as I moved into the chancellor's role was when somebody told me that the Department of Education was there not to serve the kids, but to serve the employees.*
>
> **Joel Klein, former chancellor, New York City Department of Education**

What is it about charismatic leadership that causes followers to get so excited about future possibilities and change that they may willingly give up their lives for a cause? Even though many people conjure up images of charismatic individuals when thinking about leadership, the systematic investigation of charismatic leadership is relatively recent. The remainder of this chapter begins with a historical review of the research on charismatic leadership and the leader–follower–situation components of charismatic leadership. We will then review the most popular conceptualization of charisma: Bass's theory of transformational and transactional leadership.

> *An institution is the lengthened shadow of one man.*
>
> **Ralph Waldo Emerson, writer**

Charismatic Leadership: A Historical Review

Prior to the mid-1970s charismatic leadership was studied primarily by historians, political scientists, and sociologists. Of this early research, Max Weber arguably wrote the single most important work. Weber was a sociologist interested primarily in how authority and religious and economic forces affected societies over time. Weber maintained that societies could be categorized into one of three types of authority systems: traditional, legal–rational, and charismatic.[131]

In the **traditional authority system**, the traditions or unwritten laws of the society dictate who has authority and how this authority can be used. The transfer of authority in such systems is based on traditions such as passing power to the first-born son of a king after the king dies. Historical examples would include the monarchies of England from the 1400s to 1600s or the dynasties of China from 3000 B.C.E. to the 1700s. Traditional authority system are quite pervasive, and some higher visibility examples include Saudi Arabia, Kuwait, Jordan, North Korea, and Brunei.[132, 133] But these examples should not be limited to countries—many of the CEOs in privately held companies or publicly traded companies that are controlled by a majority shareholder are often the children or relatives of the previous CEO. Examples include Walmart, BMW, Samsung, Cargill, Amway, and Bechtel. Because most small businesses are family owned, examples of traditional authority systems occur whenever ownership is passed along to the next generation. Larger-scale organizational changes usually happen during or immediately after these transitions. An example might be the changes that have occurred in Saudi Arabia with the ascension of Crown Prince Mohammed bin Salman.

> *I do not believe in dynastic wealth. Why should people be given millions or billions of dollars just for being part of the lucky sperm club?*
>
> **Warren Buffett, investor**

In the **legal–rational authority system** a person possesses authority not because of tradition or birthright but because of the laws that govern the position occupied. For example, elected officials and most leaders in nonprofit or publicly traded companies are authorized to take certain actions because of the positions they occupy. The power is in the position itself rather than in the person who occupies the position. Thus Mike Pompeo can take certain actions not because of who he is or to whom he is related but because of his role as U.S. secretary of state.

Large-scale organizational changes usually occur after individuals are elected or appointed in legal–rational authority systems. U.S. President Donald Trump has led a number of highly visible policy and staff changes to the Environmental Protection Agency, Treasury and Commerce Departments, Department of Homeland Security, Department of Education, Department of Defense, State Department, and the Department of Justice. These changes have had a dramatic impact on other countries, organizations, and citizens. No doubt the next president will drive a different set of staffing and policy changes that he or she believes are in the best interest of the United States. Similar large-scale policy and staffing changes occur whenever officials are elected or appointed to key positions in other countries or when individuals are hired or promoted to be an organization's next CEO.

These two authority systems can be contrasted to the **charismatic authority system**, in which people derive authority because of their exemplary characteristics. Charismatic leaders are thought to possess superhuman qualities or powers of divine origin that set them apart from ordinary mortals. The locus of authority in this system rests with the individual possessing these unusual qualities; it is not derived from birthright or laws. According to Weber, charismatic leaders come from the margins of society and emerge as leaders in times of great social crisis. These leaders focus society both on the problems it faces and on the revolutionary solutions proposed by the leader. Thus charismatic authority systems are usually the result of a revolution against the traditional and legal–rational authority systems. Examples of these revolutions might be the overthrow of the Shah of Iran by the Ayatollah Khomeini, the ousting of the British in India by Mahatma Gandhi, the success of Martin Luther King Jr. in changing the civil rights laws in the United States, or the economic and social change movements led by Hugo Chávez in Venezuela. Charismatic authority systems often result in sudden, radical, and sometimes violent change, but tend to be much shorter lived than traditional or legal–rational authority systems. Charismatic leaders must project an image of success in order for followers to believe they possess superhuman qualities; any failures will cause followers to question the divine qualities of the leader and in turn erode the leader's authority.

A number of historians, political scientists, and sociologists have commented on various aspects of Weber's conceptualization of charismatic authority systems. Of all these comments, however, probably the biggest controversy surrounding Weber's theory concerns the locus of charismatic leadership. Is charisma primarily the result of the situation or social context facing the leader, the leader's extraordinary qualities, or the strong relationships between charismatic leaders and followers? A number of authors have argued that charismatic movements could not take place unless the society was in a crisis.[134, 135, 136] Along these lines, Friedland,[137] Gerth and Mills,[138] and Kanter[139] have argued that before a leader with extraordinary qualities would be perceived as charismatic, the social situation must be such that followers recognize the relevance of the leader's qualities. Others have argued that charismatic leadership is primarily a function of the leader's extraordinary qualities, not the situation. These qualities include having extraordinary powers of vision, the rhetorical skills to communicate this vision, a sense of mission, high self-confidence and intelligence, and high expectations for followers.[140, 141] Finally, several authors have argued that the litmus test for charismatic leadership does not depend on the leader's qualities or the presence of a crisis, but rather on followers' reactions to their leader. According to this argument, charisma is attributed only to those leaders who can develop particularly strong emotional attachments with followers.[142, 143, 144, 145, 146]

The debate surrounding charismatic leadership shifted dramatically with the publication of James MacGregor Burns's *Leadership*. Burns was a prominent political scientist who had spent a career studying leadership in the national political arena. He believed that leadership could take one of two forms. **Transactional leadership** occurred when leaders and followers were in some type of exchange relationship to get needs met. The exchange could be economic, political, or psychological, and examples might include exchanging money for work, votes for political favors, loyalty for consideration, and so forth. Transactional leadership is common but tends to be transitory in that there may be no enduring purpose to hold parties together once a transaction is made. Burns also noted that while this type of leadership could be quite effective, it did not result in organizational or societal change and instead tended to perpetuate and legitimize the status quo.[147] (See **Highlight 16.6.**)

Kleptocracies and Authority Systems

HIGHLIGHT 16.6

In the book *Guns, Germs, and Steel*, author Jared Diamond describes the historic, geographic, climatic, technologic, demographic, and economic factors that have caused human societies to emerge, thrive, or disappear. One phenomenon that appears across many groups as they grow to 100 or so people is the emergence of some form of government. Sometimes this government is based on the power of a family (traditional authority); other times it is more formalized (legal–rational authority); and at times it is based on a single leader (charismatic authority). Governments emerge because groups this size begin to recognize that they can solve common problems, such as finding food and shelter and defending against enemies by pooling resources rather than working as individuals. Thus members of the group give up certain liberties and resources but gain services they could ill afford on their own.

Some people perceive this exchange to be relatively fair; the services they receive seem to offset their costs in terms of taxes, food, and so on. But at other times these governments appear to be nothing more than *kleptocracies*—in which people pay large tributes to a small group of people at the top but get little in return. Kleptocracies can be found in traditional authority systems; what do British citizens get in return for paying taxes to support having a queen? Kleptocracies can also be found in legal–rational systems; the collapse of the financial services and automobile industries in 2007–2009 are examples of executives ripping off customers, employees, and shareholders. Charismatic leaders can also head up kleptocracies. At one time former Prime Minister Robert Mugabe was seen as a charismatic leader by many of his citizens, but with his $2 million birthday party, poverty rates at an all-time high, and inflation hovering at 8,000 percent per year, it seems that most citizens of Zimbabwe were not enjoying the same fruits of success.

Because charismatic leaders are more likely to emerge in a crisis, they may be more likely to appear when citizens believe their fees, taxes, goods, cattle, or people payments are misaligned with the benefits they are getting by keeping their government in place. This is precisely what happened when Mao, Lenin, and Castro led their communist revolutions in China, Russia, and Cuba. More recently, this same phenomenon has allowed charismatic leaders to be elected into the presidential suites in Venezuela and Ecuador. The Arab Spring was a revolt against the corrupt and unfair rule found in many Middle Eastern countries, and the (un)fairness of the tax versus service exchange is often used by politicians in the United States to get elected into office.

Any government where small groups of people enjoy a lion's share of the benefits is a kleptocracy. Given this definition, are Russia, Saudi Arabia, Brunei, the United Arab Emirates, Egypt, China, or the United States kleptocracies? What about large corporations, such as UnitedHealth Group, Comcast, BP, or InBev? Is your current government a kleptocracy? Why or why not? What information would you use to justify your answer?

Source: J. Diamond, *Guns, Germs, and Steel: The Fates of Human Societies* (New York: Norton, 1999).

The second form of leadership is **transformational leadership**, which changes the status quo by appealing to followers' values and their sense of higher purpose. Transformational leaders articulate the problems in the current system and have a compelling vision of what a new society or organization could be. This new vision of society is intimately linked to the values of both the leader and the followers; it represents an ideal that is congruent with their value systems. According to Burns, transformational leadership is ultimately a moral exercise in that it raises the standard of human conduct. This implies that the acid test for transformational leadership might be the answer to the question "Do the changes advocated by the leader advance or hinder the development of the organization or society?" Transformational leaders are also adept at **reframing** issues; they point out how the problems or issues facing followers can be resolved if they fulfill the leader's vision of the future. These leaders also teach followers how to become leaders in their own right and incite them to play active roles in the change movement (see **Profiles in Leadership 16.1**, **16.2**, **16.3**, **16.4**, and **16.5**).

The difference between a kleptocrat and a wise statesman, between a robber baron and a benefactor, is merely one of degree.

Jared Diamond, researcher

Nelson Mandela

PROFILES IN LEADERSHIP 16.3

South Africa was ruled by a white minority government for much of the past 200 years. Although Blacks made up over 75 percent of the populace, whites owned most of the property, ran most of the businesses, and controlled virtually all the country's resources. Moreover, Blacks did not have the right to vote and often worked under horrible conditions for little or no wages. Seeing the frustration of his people, Nelson Mandela spent 50 years working to overturn white minority rule. He started by organizing the African National Congress, a nonviolent organization that protested white rule through work stoppages, strikes, and riots. Several whites were killed in the early riots, and in 1960 the police killed or injured over 250 Blacks in Sharpeville. Unrest over the Sharpeville incident caused 95 percent of the Black workforce to go on strike for two weeks, and the country declared a state of emergency. Mandela then orchestrated acts of sabotage to further pressure the South African government to change. The organization targeted installations and took spe-

cial care to ensure that no lives were lost in the bombing campaign.

Mandela was arrested in 1962 and spent the next 27 years in prison. While in prison he continued to promote civil unrest and majority rule, and his cause eventually gained international recognition. He was offered but turned down a conditional release from prison in 1985. After enormous international and internal pressure, South African President F. W. de Klerk "unbanned" the ANC and unconditionally released Nelson Mandela from prison. Nonetheless South Africa remained in turmoil, and 4 million workers went on strike in 1992 to protest white rule. Because of this pressure, Mandela forced de Klerk to sign a document outlining multiparty elections. Mandela won the 1994 national election and was the country's first democratically elected leader.

Do you think Nelson Mandela is a charismatic leader? Why or why not?

Sources: M. Fatima, *Higher Than Hope: The Authorized Biography of Nelson Mandela* (New York: Harper & Row, 1990); and S. Clark, *Nelson Mandela Speaks: Forming a Democratic, Nonracist South Africa* (New York: Pathfinder Press, 1993).

All transformational leaders are charismatic, but not all charismatic leaders are transformational. Transformational leaders are charismatic because they can articulate a compelling vision of the future and form strong emotional attachments with followers. However, this vision and these relationships are aligned with followers' value systems and help them get their needs met. Charismatic leaders who are not transformational can convey a vision and form strong emotional bonds with followers, but they do so to get their own (that is, the leader's) needs met. Both charismatic and transformational leaders strive for organizational or societal change; the difference is whether the changes are for the benefit of the leader or the followers. Finally, transformational leaders are always controversial. Charismatic leadership almost inherently raises conflicts over values or definitions of the social good. Controversy also arises because the people with the most to lose in any existing system will put up the most resistance to a transformational change initiative. The emotional levels of those resisting the transformational leadership movement are often just as great as those who embrace it, and this may be the underlying cause for the violent ends to Martin Luther King Jr., John F. Kennedy, Mahatma Gandhi, Joan of Arc, and Jesus Christ. Burns stated that transformational leadership always involves conflict and change, and transformational leaders must be willing to embrace conflict, make enemies, exhibit a high level of self-sacrifice, and be thick-skinned and focused to perpetuate their cause (see **Profiles in Leadership 16.3**).[148, 149, 150, 151, 152, 153, 154]

Osama bin Laden

PROFILES IN LEADERSHIP 16.4

Osama bin Laden was a member of the prestigious bin Laden family in Saudi Arabia and the founder of Al-Qaeda. Bin Laden was born in Riyadh, Saudi Arabia, and was brought up as a devout Sunni Muslim. He attended the Al-Thager Model School in Jeddah, "the school of the elite," and was exposed to many teachings of the Muslim Brotherhood while growing up. He attended university after his secondary schooling, but it is uncertain what he majored in or whether he obtained a degree. At the age of 17, he married his first wife and reportedly had up to four wives and fathered anywhere between 12 and 24 children. In person he was said to be soft-spoken, charming, respectful, and polite. He appeared to live a life of discipline, simplicity, and self-sacrifice, preferring that his wealth be used to benefit Al-Qaeda rather than improve his personal lifestyle.

Bin Laden first engaged in militant activities in the late 1970s, when he moved to Pakistan to help the mujahideen fight a guerrilla war to oust the Soviet Union from Afghanistan. His family connections and wealth helped to fund many of the mujahideen's efforts over the next 10 years. Some of his money and arms may have come from the Central Intelligence Agency: The United States also wanted to get the Soviet Union out of Afghanistan.

After Iraq invaded Kuwait in 1990, bin Laden offered to protect Saudi Arabia with 12,000 armed men, but his offer was rebuffed by the Saudi royal family. Shortly thereafter, bin Laden publicly denounced the presence of coalition troops ("infidels") on Saudi soil and wanted all U.S. bases on the Arab peninsula to be closed. He eventually left Saudi Arabia to take up residence in Sudan, where he established a new base for mujahideen operations. The purpose of his African organization was to propagate Islamist philosophy and recruit new members to the cause. In 1996 bin Laden left Sudan and went to Afghanistan to set up a new base of operations, where he forged a close relationship with the leaders of the new Taliban government.

Bin Laden issued fatwas in 1996 and 1998 that stated that Muslims should kill civilians and military personnel from the United States and allied countries until they withdrew support for Israel and withdrew military forces from Islamic countries. It is believed he was either directly involved with or funded the 1992 bombing of the Gold Mihor Hotel in Aden, Yemen; the massacre of German tourists in Luxor, Egypt, in 1997; the 1998 bombings of two U.S. embassies in Africa; and the World Trade Center and Pentagon bombings on September 11, 2001. Bin Laden, Al-Qaeda, and its splinter movements were involved with the London subway bombing, the wars in Afghanistan and Iraq, and unrest in the Philippines, Thailand, Indonesia, and Somalia. Bin Laden was formulating a number of new terrorists attacks when he was killed by a U.S. Navy SEALs team during a raid in Abbottabad, Pakistan, in 2012.

It is clear that bin Laden had a following, and that following has grown into the tens of thousands over the past 20 years. These followers are very devoted; some are so committed that they volunteer to be suicide bombers. A much larger group may not play active roles in Al-Qaeda but are clearly sympathetic to its cause. But as strong as these followers' feelings were about bin Laden, others were just as intent to see him dead or behind bars.

Was Osama bin Laden a charismatic leader or a transformational leader? Would your answer to this question change if you were sympathetic to Al-Qaeda's cause? Do you think his death helped or hurt others' perceptions of bin Laden's charisma?

Sources: "Osama bin Laden," *The New York Times*, www.nytimes.com/topic/person/osama-bin-laden-19572011; and D. Johnson and B. Rowen, "Osama bin Laden Killed" *Infoplease*, February 28, 2017, www.infoplease.com/spot/osamabinladen.html.

Leadership researchers Gary Yukl, Jerry Hunt, and Jay Conger have all maintained that the publication of *Leadership* played a key role in renewing interest in the topic of leadership.[155, 156, 157] As a result, research over the past 35 years has explored cross-cultural, gender, succession, leader, follower, situational, and performance issues in charismatic or transformational leadership. From these efforts we now know that charismatic or transformational leadership is both common and rare. It is common because it can occur in almost every social stratum across every culture. For example, a high school student leader in France, a military cadet leader at the U.S. Naval Academy, a Kenyan community leader, an Indonesian hospital leader, or a Russian business executive could all be perceived as charismatic or transformational leaders. But it is also rare because most people in positions of authority are not perceived to be charismatic or transformational leaders. We also know that women such as Marine Le Pen, Oprah Winfrey, and Mary Barra tend to be perceived as more competent than their male counterparts and that transformational leadership results in higher group performance than transactional leadership.[158, 159, 160, 161, 162, 163, 164, 165, 166, 167, 168, 169, 170, 171, 172, 173, 174, 175, 176, 177] Although charismatic or transformational leadership often results in large-scale organizational change and higher organizational performance, there is little evidence that these changes remain permanent in organizational settings after the leader moves on.[178, 179] In addition, some researchers have found that charismatic or transformational leaders did not result in higher organizational performance, but they did earn higher paychecks for themselves.[180, 181, 182, 183, 184, 185] In other words, these leaders were good at garnering attention, hogging credit, and changing their respective organizations, but many of these changes did not result in higher organizational performance.

Charisma versus Humility

HIGHLIGHT 16.7

Some of the most common qualities associated with ideal leadership include visionary thinking, the ability to engage and inspire, motivating others, self-confidence, decisiveness, drive, approachability, and charm. These qualities can easily be seen in popular political leaders, business executives, and pastors running megachurches. Are the changes being promoted by these leaders for the good of the organizations they lead or their own personal benefit? The answer to this question might be surprising.

Research shows that the qualities described above are critically important to winning **within-group competitions**. In other words, what sort of characteristics does a person need to attract a large number of YouTube or Facebook followers and stand out from the crowd? Those who are perceived as visionary, inspirational, self-confident, and edgy are far more likely to get hired or promoted into leadership roles than their shyer, less colorful counterparts. Getting promoted is quite different from being effective, and leadership should ultimately be judged in terms of winning **between-group competitions**. Leadership should not be about who gets the most likes or who is named to be the team captain; it should be about a team's win and loss record and how it does in the playoffs. From a business perspective, leadership should be judged by how a company compares to its peers in customer satisfaction ratings, employee engagement scores, turnover rates, market share, stock price, or profitability. For nonprofits, the criteria should be how well the organization is fulfilling its mission compared to other organizations. How do schools compare on achievement exams or graduation rates, what are the patient error rates for hospitals, or how efficiently are funding dollars used to serve the homeless?

It turns out that **humility** is a much better predictor of leadership effectiveness (e.g., winning between group competitions) than charisma. Humble leaders are highly competent, good at engaging and developing staff, adept at building teams, and intensely focused on beating the competition. Humble leaders avoid the limelight, let their team or organizational accomplishments speak for themselves, and readily share credit. Most organizations want effective leaders in key roles, yet they often promote charismatic leaders over their more humble and competent counterparts. This difference between charisma and competence and winning the within–versus between–group competition may be a main reason why so few women are in top leadership positions. Whenever someone is advocating for a large-scale change, it is important to ask: Who benefits from the change and why is it being promoted? What do you think is more important: Winning the within- or between-group competition?

The coronavirus pandemic took a terrible toll on countries across the globe, but it also helped differentiate the real leaders from the posers. Dr. Tony Fauci, the head of the National Institute of Allergy and Infectious Diseases, as well as Mike DeWine (governor of Ohio), Jay Inslee (governor of Washington), Gavin Newsome (governor of California), and Gretchen Whitmer (governor of Michigan) were highly effectively leaders during the initial phases of the pandemic. Ron DeSantis (governor of Florida), Brian Kemp (governor of Georgia), and Greg Abbott (governor of Texas) dithered and delayed their lockdown decisions, and it cost their states greatly. Crises may be one of the best ways to differentiate humble, effective leaders from charismatic and incompetent wannabes.

Sources: K. Badura, E. Grijalva, D. Newman, T. Taiyi Yan, and G. Jeon, "Gender and Leadership Emergence: A Meta-Analysis and Exploratory Model," *Personnel Psychology*, 71, no. 3 (2018), pp. 335–68; B. Nevicka, A. Van Vianen, A. De Hoogh, and B. Voorn, "Narcissistic Leaders: An Asset or Liability? Leader Visibility, Follower Responses, and Group-Level Absenteeism," *Journal of Applied Psychology*, 103, no. 7 (2018), pp. 703–23; *The Economist*, "The Grinch That Sold Charisma," March 30, 2019, p. 67; S. Gregory, "Transformational Leadership: It's Not What You Think," *Hogan Assessments*, June 25, 2019, www.hoganassessments.com/transformational-leadership-its-not-what-you-think; R. Sherman, "Humility, Leadership, and Organizational Effectiveness," *Training Industry*, May 1, 2018, https://trainingindustry.com/articles/leadership/humility-leadership-and-organizational-effectiveness; N. Emler, "Charisma: Not a Recipe for Better Leadership," *Hogan Assessments*, April 23, 2018, www.hoganassessments.com/charisma-not-a-recipe-for-better-leadership; T. Chamorro-Premuzic, *Why Do So Many Incompetent Men Become Leaders? (and How to Fix It)* (Boston, MA: Harvard Business Review Press, 2019); and J. Vergauwe, B. Wille, J. Hofmans, R. Kaiser, and F. de Fruyt, "Too Much Charisma Can Make Leaders Look Less Effective," *Harvard Business Review*, September 26, 2017, https://hbr.org/2017/09/too-much-charisma-can-make-leaders-look-less-effective.

As a result of this research, we also have three newer theories of charismatic or transformational leadership. Conger and Kanungo[186] used a stage model to differentiate charismatic from noncharismatic leaders. Charismatic leaders begin by thoroughly assessing the current situation and pinpointing problems with the status quo. They then articulate a vision that represents a change from the status quo. This vision represents a challenge and is a motivating force for change for followers. The vision must be articulated in a way that increases dissatisfaction with the status quo and compels followers to take action. In the final stage, leaders build trust in their vision and goals by personal example, risk taking, and their total commitment to the vision. The theory developed by House and his colleagues[187, 188, 189] describes how charismatic leaders achieve higher performance by changing followers' self-concepts. Charismatic leaders are believed to motivate followers by changing their perceptions of work itself, offering an appealing vision of the future, developing a collective identity among followers, and increasing their confidence in getting the job done. Avolio and Bass's[190] theory of transformational and transactional leadership is essentially an extension of Burns's theory. Unlike Burns, who viewed transactional and transformational leadership as the extremes of a single continuum, Avolio and Bass viewed these two concepts as independent leadership dimensions. Thus leaders can be transformational and transactional, transactional but not transformational, and so on. Transformational leaders are believed to achieve stronger results because they heighten followers' awareness of goals and the means to achieve them, they convince followers to take action for the collective good of the group, and their vision of the future helps followers satisfy higher order needs. Because Avolio and Bass created a questionnaire to assess a leader's standing on transactional and transformational leadership, this theory is by far the most thoroughly researched and will be discussed in more detail later in this chapter.

What Are the Common Characteristics of Charismatic and Transformational Leadership?

Although there are some important differences in the theories offered by Conger and Kanungo, House, and Avolio and Bass, in reality they are far more similar than different. These researchers either do not differentiate charismatic from transformational leadership, or see charisma as a component of transformational leadership. Therefore, we will use these terms somewhat interchangeably in the next section, although we acknowledge the fundamental difference between these two types of leadership. A review of the common leader, follower, and situational factors from Burns and the three more recent theories can be found in **Figure 16.5**. Like the past debates surrounding charismatic leadership, modern researchers are divided on whether charismatic leadership is due to the leader's superhuman qualities, a special relationship between leaders and followers, the situation, or some combination of these factors. Irrespective of the locus of charismatic leadership, the research provides overwhelming support for the notion that transformational leaders are effective at large-scale societal or organizational change.

Leader Characteristics

Leadership researchers have spent considerably more time and effort trying to identify the unique characteristics of charismatic leaders than they have exploring follower or situational factors. This is partly because some researchers believe that it is possible to drive higher levels of organizational change or performance through the selection or training of charismatic leaders.[191, 192, 193, 194, 195, 196, 197, 198] Although some scholars have argued that the leader's personal qualities are the key to charismatic or transformational leadership, we do not believe the leader's qualities alone result in charismatic leadership.[199, 200] We do, however, acknowledge several common threads in the behavior and style of both charismatic and transformational leaders, and these include their vision and values, rhetorical skills, ability to build a particular kind of image in the hearts and minds of their followers, and personalized style of leadership.

Charismatic leaders are meaning makers. They pick and choose from the rough materials of reality and construct pictures of great possibilities. Their persuasion then is of the subtlest kind, for they interpret reality to offer us images of the future that are irresistible.

Jay Conger, University of Southern California

Never underestimate the power of purpose.

Price Pritchett, consultant

Vision

Both transformational and charismatic leaders are inherently future oriented. They involve helping a group move "from here to there." Charismatic leaders perceive fundamental discrepancies between the way things are and the way things can (or should) be. They recognize the shortcomings of the present order and offer an imaginative **vision** to overcome them. A charismatic leader's vision is not limited to grand social movements; leaders can develop a compelling vision for any organization and organizational level. This vision can have both a stimulating and a unifying effect on the efforts of followers, which can help drive greater organizational alignment and change and higher performance levels by followers (see **Figure 16.6**).[201, 202, 203] Paradoxically, the magic of a leader's vision is often that the more complicated the problem, the more people may be drawn to simplistic solutions.

FIGURE 16.5   Factors Pertaining to Charismatic Leadership and the Interactional Framework

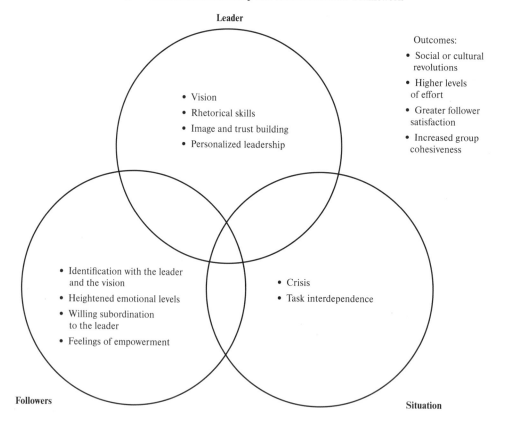

Leader

- Vision
- Rhetorical skills
- Image and trust building
- Personalized leadership

Outcomes:
- Social or cultural revolutions
- Higher levels of effort
- Greater follower satisfaction
- Increased group cohesiveness

- Identification with the leader and the vision
- Heightened emotional levels
- Willing subordination to the leader
- Feelings of empowerment

- Crisis
- Task interdependence

Followers

Situation

FIGURE 16.6   A Leader's Vision of the Future Can Align Efforts and Help Groups Accomplish More

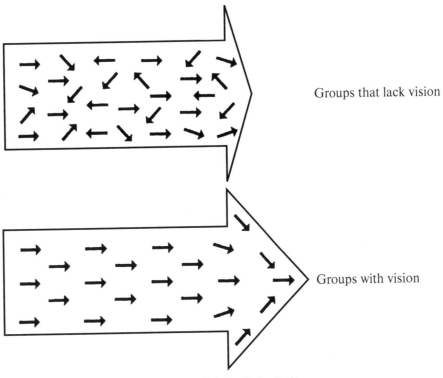

Groups that lack vision

Groups with vision

Source: Adapted from P. M. Senge, *The Fifth Discipline* (New York: Doubleday, 1990).

Facts tell, but stories sell.

Bob Whelan, NCS Pearson

Rhetorical Skills

In addition to *having* vision, charismatic leaders are gifted in *sharing* their vision. As discussed earlier, charismatic and transformational leaders have superb **rhetorical skills** that heighten followers' emotional levels and inspire them to embrace the vision. As it turns out, both the content of a transformational leader's speeches and the way they are delivered are vitally important.[204, 205, 206, 207, 208, 209, 210, 211, 212, 213] Charismatic leaders make extensive use of metaphors, analogies, and stories rather than abstract and colorless rational discourse to reframe issues and make their points. Often the delivery of the speech is even more important than the content itself—poor delivery can detract from compelling content. Adolf Hitler mastered his delivery techniques so well that his speeches can have hypnotic power even to people who do not understand German. Similarly, many people consider Martin Luther King Jr.'s "I Have a Dream" speech one of the most moving speeches they have ever heard. YouTube videos of Adolph Hitler, Martin Luther King Jr., Ronald Reagan, or Donald Trump's speeches show their masterful evocation of patriotic and cultural themes.

Setting an example is not the main means of influencing another; it is the only means.

Albert Einstein, physicist

Image and Trust Building

As demonstrated in **Profiles in Leadership 16.3** and **16.4**, transformational leaders build trust in their leadership and the attainability of their goals through an **image** of seemingly unshakable self-confidence, strength of moral conviction, personal example and self-sacrifice, and unconventional tactics or behavior.[214, 215, 216, 217, 218, 219, 220, 221] They are perceived to have unusual insight and ability and act in a manner consistent with their vision and values. Whereas transformational leaders **build trust** by showing commitment to followers' needs over self-interest, some charismatic leaders are so concerned with their image that they are not beyond taking credit for others' accomplishments or exaggerating their expertise[222] (see **Highlight 16.8**).

The Trouble with Superheroes

HIGHLIGHT 16.8

All publicly traded companies have boards of directors, whose primary responsibility is to increase shareholder value. People buy stock in companies such as Amazon or Apple, and their boards ensure top management makes the best use of this money to improve business performance. One of the most important decisions boards can make when it comes to improving shareholder value is succession planning. The board of directors make CEO hiring, compensation, and firing decisions and have a major say in who fills the other C-suite positions. Oftentimes changes in economic conditions, consumer preferences, competitive threats, suppliers, or regulatory policy cause business results to suffer, and when this occurs boards are likely to look for new CEOs who are perceived to be charismatic. There are some interesting research findings regarding CEO succession planning and organizational change that are worth discussing further.

One interesting finding is that CEOs account for only 5 percent of a company's performance. A company's revenue may increase from $1 billion to $2 billion dollars or its stock price may rise from $50 to $60, but the CEO has little direct impact on these improvements. CEOs will take full credit but economic conditions, globalization, technology, new products, or failed competitors often play more pervasive roles in com-

pany performance. CEOs also will claim that they are critical to motivating and inspiring employees, but research shows immediate supervisors have much greater impact on employee engagement. As such, it may be that immediate supervisors and middle managers play bigger roles in company performance than CEOs. A third research finding is that there is a negative correlation between outside CEO pay and company performance. The more boards pay to hire an outside superstar CEO, the more a company's performance is apt to decline. Other research shows there is very little relationship between CEO compensation, a CEO's ability to build teams, and company performance. CEOs may talk a good game when it comes to driving change and improving the organization, but the facts show that many are better at managing their careers than leading change.

Despite these findings, boards are hiring CEOs from the outside more than ever before. Since the 1970s the percentage of outsiders being hired as CEOs increased from 15 percent to over 33 percent and is even higher in the high-tech industry. Boards can get around the problems associated with hiring outside CEOs by adopting robust **succession planning processes**. Good succession plans identify the key knowledge, skills, and behaviors needed to be successful in top leadership positions; rigorously evaluate internal talent against these criteria; systematically develop those with the most potential to fill these positions; and conduct regular talent reviews. Companies that do this well, such as Medronic, PepsiCo, IBM, General Mills, Delta Airlines, Microsoft, and Proctor & Gamble, have several potential internal candidates who could step into the CEO or CFO role. These organizations do such a good job developing leadership talent that potential successors often get hired away by other companies. Despite the findings that internal candidates tend to make the best CEOs, most companies do not have strong succession planning processes, which is why boards go to the outside to hire "charismatic" or "transformational" CEOs.

Was your university president promoted from within, or did he or she come from another school? If the president did come from another school, then what does this say about your college's succession planning process? What message does this send to other leaders in your school about what it takes to get promoted? Do

you believe charisma or competence played a bigger role in this hiring/promotion decision?

Sources: "Schrumpeter: The Trouble with Superheros," *The Economist*, October 1, 2011, p. 74; "Schrumpeter: The Tussle for Talent," *The Economist*, January 8, 2011, p. 68; "In Praise of David Brent: Middle Managers Are Not as Useless as People Think," *The Economist*, August 27, 2011, p. 56; T. Hutzschenreuter, I. Kleindiest, and C. Greger, "How New Leaders Affect Strategic Change Following a Succession Event: A Critical Review of the Literature," *The Leadership Quarterly* 23, no. 5 (2012), pp. 729–55; PDI Ninth House, *Getting Succession Right: Six Essential Elements of Effective Succession Plans* (Minneapolis, MN: Author, 2011); B. Groysberg, L. K. Kelly, and B. MacDonald, "The New Path to the C-Suite," *Harvard Business Review*, March 2011, pp. 60–69; J. Collins, *Good to Great* (New York: Harper Business, 2001); T. Chamorro-Premuzic, "Charisma Has Its Downsides," *Management Today*, February 1, 2016, www.managementtoday.co.uk/charismatic-leadership-its-downsides/article/1380513; and M. Mayo, "If Humble People Make the Best Leaders, Why Do We Fall for Charismatic Narcissists?" *Harvard Business Review*, April 2017, https://hbr.org/2017/04/if-humble-people-make-the-best-leaders-why-do-we-fall-for-charismatic-narcissists.

Never tell people how to do things. Tell them what to do, and they will surprise you with their ingenuity.

George S. Patton, U.S. Army general

Personalized Leadership

One of the most important aspects of charismatic and transformational leadership is the personal nature of the leader's power. These leaders share strong, personal bonds with followers, even when the leader occupies a formal organizational role. It is this **personalized leadership** style that seems to be responsible for the feelings of empowerment notable among followers of charismatic or transformational leaders. Charismatic leaders seem more adept at picking up social cues and tend to be emotionally expressive, especially through such nonverbal channels as their eye contact, posture, movement, gestures, tone of voice, and facial expressions. Transformational leaders also empower followers by giving them tasks that lead to heightened self-confidence and creating environments of heightened expectations and positive emotions.[223, 224, 225, 226, 227, 228, 229, 230, 231, 232, 233, 234]

Follower Characteristics

If charismatic leadership were defined solely by a leader's characteristics, it would be relatively easy to identify individuals with good vision, rhetorical, and impression management skills and place them in leadership positions. Over time we would expect that a high percentage of followers would embrace and act on these leaders' visions. However, a number of leaders appear to possess these attributes yet are not seen as charismatic. They may be good, competent leaders, but they seem unable to evoke strong feelings in followers or to get followers to do more than they thought possible. In reality, charisma is probably more a function of the followers' reactions to a leader than of the leader's personal characteristics. If followers do not accept the leader's vision or become emotionally attached to the leader, then the leader simply will not be perceived to be either charismatic or transformational. Thus **charisma** is in the eyes and heart of the beholder; it is a particularly strong emotional reaction to, identification with, and belief in some leaders by some followers. Note that this definition is value-free—leaders seen as charismatic may or may not share the same values as their followers or meet Burns's criteria for transformational leadership. A recent example of followers' divergent reactions can be seen with Donald Trump as the President of the United States. Some followers, particularly those in the Republican party, perceive Donald Trump as a very charismatic leader. Most Democrats think he is only out for himself and will end up destroying the United States, yet he is clearly the same person. Both parties had just the opposite reactions to the previous U.S. President, Barack Obama. Many of the more popular conceptualizations of charisma and charismatic leadership today also define charisma in terms of followers' reactions to the leader.[235, 236, 237, 238, 239, 240, 241] Defining charisma as a reaction that followers have toward leaders makes it reasonable to turn our attention to the four unique characteristics of these reactions.

> *Being attacked by Rush Limbaugh is like being gummed by a newt. It doesn't actually hurt but it leaves you with slimy stuff on your ankle.*
>
> **Molly Ivins, writer**

Identification with the Leader and the Vision

Two of the effects associated with charismatic leadership include a strong affection for the leader and a similarity of follower beliefs with those of the leader. These effects describe a sort of bonding or **identification with the leader** personally and a parallel psychological investment to a goal or activity (a "cause") bigger than oneself. Followers bond with a leader because they may be intensely dissatisfied with the status quo and see the implementation of the vision as a solution to their problems. Being like the leader, or approved by the leader, also becomes an important part of followers' self-worth.[242, 243, 244, 245, 246, 247, 248]

Heightened Emotional Levels

Charismatic leaders are able to stir followers' feelings, and this **heightened emotional level** results in increased levels of effort and performance.[249, 250, 251, 252, 253, 254, 255, 256, 257, 258] Emotions are often the fuel driving large-scale initiatives for change, and charismatic leaders will often do all they can to maintain them, including getting followers to think about their dissatisfaction with the status quo or making impassioned appeals directly to followers. But charismatic leaders need to keep in mind that some people will become alienated with the vision and movement and can have emotions just as intense as those of the followers of the vision. This polarizing effect of charismatic leaders may be one reason why they tend to have violent deaths: those alienated by a charismatic leader are almost as likely to act on their emotions as followers within the movement.[259]

Willing Subordination to the Leader

Whereas the preceding factor dealt with followers' emotional and psychological closeness to the leader, **willing subordination to the leader** involves their deference to his or her authority.[260] Charismatic leaders often seem imbued with superhuman qualities. As a result, followers often naturally and willingly submit to the leader's apparent authority and superiority. Followers seem to suspend their critical thinking skills; they have few doubts about the intentions or skills of the leader, the correctness of the vision or change initiative, or the actions they need to take in order to achieve the vision. This can readily be seen in members of the Republican Party, as only a handful of Senate or House members dare to publicly speak out about President Donald Trump's behavior, no matter how egregious it may be.

We're not worthy; we're not worthy!

Wayne and Garth, "Wayne's World"

Feelings of Empowerment

Followers of charismatic leaders are moved to expect more of themselves, and they work harder to achieve these higher goals. Charismatic leaders set high expectations while expressing confidence in their abilities and providing ongoing encouragement and support. Somewhat paradoxically, followers feel stronger and more powerful at the same time they willingly subordinate themselves to the charismatic leader. These **feelings of empowerment**, when combined with heightened emotional levels and a leader's vision of the future, often result in increases in organizational, group, or team performance or significant social change.[261, 262, 263, 264, 265] (See **Table 16.3** for typical reactions to change requests.)

Table 16.3   Followers' Responses to Change

> **Malicious compliance:** This occurs when followers either ignore or actively sabotage change requests.
>
> **Compliance:** This takes place when followers do no more than abide by the policies and procedures surrounding change requests.
>
> **Cooperation:** Followers willingly engage in those activities needed to make the change request become reality.
>
> **Commitment:** Followers embrace change requests as their own and often go the extra mile to make sure work gets done. Charismatic and transformational leaders are adept at getting followers committed to their vision of the future.

Source: B. Yager (Boise, ID: The Bryan Yager Group, 2003).

President Donald Trump

PROFILES IN LEADERSHIP 16.5

No doubt the 45th U.S. president is one of the more controversial leaders on the world stage. So far in his tenure, he has done the following:

- Maintained he would have won the popular vote had it not been for 3 to 5 million illegal immigrants fraudulently voting for Hillary Clinton
- Claimed that the crowd at his inauguration was bigger than those for Barack Obama
- Banned citizens from several Middle Eastern, African, and Asian countries from traveling to the United States
- Encouraged Congress to remove health care coverage from millions of citizens
- Appointed a climate denier to head up the Environmental Protection Agency and someone who had never been an educator nor attended public schools to head up the Department of Education
- Managed to alienate traditional allies (Mexico, Canada, Germany, and France) while embracing traditional enemies (Russia and North Korea)
- Opted out of the Paris Climate Accord
- Shared highly classified intelligence with the Russians

- Switched positions on China being a currency manipulator
- Failed to release his tax statements
- Called James Comey, then the head of the FBI, a "showboater" before letting him go
- Maintained that Russia's involvement in the U.S. presidential election was "fake news" and that media bias prevented the real news from getting out to the public
- Equated neo-Nazis, members of the KKK, and believers of white supremacy with counter demonstrators
- Threatened to shut down the government if the U.S. Congress failed to allocate money for building a border wall with Mexico
- Made military and foreign aid contingent on investigating a political rival

Although Trump's approval ratings have been consistently lower than many other U.S. presidents, these actions appear to have little to no impact on those who voted for Trump in the 2016 election. This may be due to Trump's supporters seeing him as a charismatic or transformational leader. In viewing the leader, follower, and situational characteristics associated with this type of leadership though his supporters' eyes, it is easy to see why this is the case:

Leader Factors

- *Vision:* Both during and after the presidential campaign, Trump promoted "America First" and has renegotiated trade deals, imposed tariffs on China, sought to bring manufacturing jobs back to the United States, and has deported "job stealing" illegal immigrants back to Latin America.
- *Rhetorical skills:* Trump, an adept speaker, is very good at telling audiences what they want to hear, whether he is speaking about building a wall between the United States and Mexico, deploring the mainstream media, or protecting gun rights.

- *Image and trust building:* Honed over the years as the spokesperson for the Trump brand and a TV celebrity on *The Apprentice*, Trump focuses on projecting an image of success. He readily blames others and throws staff members under the bus in order maintain this image.
- *Personalized leadership:* Trump builds strong bonds with his followers, particularly during campaign rallies. Unemployed coal miners and manufacturing laborers believe Trump feels their pain and that he would do the right thing to bring jobs back to America.

Follower Factors

- *Identification with the leader and the vision:* Trump supporters believe there is no such thing as climate change, that the wall and deporting illegal immigrants is necessary to protect American jobs, that the middle class has been ignored by both political parties, and that America First will help restore to the United States what they perceive as its lost greatness.
- *Heightened emotional levels:* There were huge differences in both the size of and magnitude of emotions displayed at the political rallies staged by the Trump and rival campaigns. Trump wins hands-down.
- *Willing subordination to the leader:* Trump followers do not think critically about many of the president's proclamations. Mexico will not pay for a wall it does not want, and what would it really take to deport 11 million illegal immigrants, many of whom are contributing to the economy and have children who were born in the United States?
- *Feelings of empowerment:* After the election, supporters in states like Texas quickly sought to promote new laws related to guns, voting access, abortion, and LGBTQ rights that aligned with Trump's positions on these topics.

Situational Factors

- *Crises:* Although unemployment was low, crime rates were declining, and the stock market at record highs, Trump maintained America was in a crisis. He maintained that poorly negotiated trade deals were robbing America of good jobs, crime was at an all-time high, and inner cities were war zones.

- *Social networks:* With over 20 million Twitter followers, Trump has capitalized on and leveraged social media much better than any of his Democratic challengers and continues to use Twitter to make personal pleas and disparage opponents.

As long as Trump is able to maintain the image of success, his supporters are unlikely to change their opinions. One reason for Trump's aggressive attacks on the media is that the media may be the only ones able to challenge his image. By labeling the media as purveyors of "fake news" or "alternative facts," Trump is inoculating his followers against those stories that run counter to his success narrative.

What has Donald Trump done to reframe issues? Do you think Trump is a charismatic, humble, or transformational leader? Is Trump out for himself or the American people? What do you think people from outside the United States think of Donald Trump?

Sources: B. Stelter, "Donald Trump's Milestone: 20 Million Followers," *CNN*, January 16, 2017, http://money.cnn.com/2017/01/16/media/donald-trump-twitter-20-million-followers; and Z. Kanno-Youngs, "Trump Administration Adds Six Countries to Travel Ban," *The New York Times*, January 31, 2020, www.nytimes.com/2020/01/31/us/politics/trump-travel-ban.html.

Situational Characteristics

Many researchers believe that situational factors also play an important role in determining whether a leader will be perceived as charismatic. Perhaps individuals possessing the qualities of charismatic leaders are perceived as charismatic only when confronting certain types of situations. Because the situation may play an important role in the attribution of charisma, it will be useful to review some of the situational factors believed to affect charismatic leadership.

> *Celebrity is obscurity biding its time.*
>
> **Carrie Fisher, actress**

Crises

Perhaps the most important situational factor associated with charismatic leadership is the presence or absence of a **crisis**. Followers who are content with the status quo are relatively unlikely to perceive a need for a charismatic leader or be willing to devote great effort to fundamentally change an organization or society. By contrast, a crisis often creates "charisma hungry" followers who are looking for a leader to alleviate or resolve their crisis. Leaders are given considerably more latitude and autonomy and may temporarily (or sometimes permanently) suspend accepted rules, policies, and procedures to pull the organization out of the crisis. Some leaders may even create or manufacture crises to increase followers' acceptance of their vision, the range of actions they can take, and followers' level of effort. Although a crisis situation does not necessarily make every leader look charismatic, such a situation may set the stage for particular kinds of leader behaviors to be effective.[266, 267, 268, 269, 270, 271, 272, 273, 274]

> *Rules are good servants, but not always good masters.*
>
> **Russell Page, master landscaper**

Social Networks

Social networks can also affect the attribution of charisma. Attributions of charisma will spread more quickly in organizations having well-established social networks, where everybody tends to know everyone else. And more often than not charismatic leaders have bigger social networks and play a more central role in their networks than leaders seen as less charismatic.[275, 276] (See **Highlight 16.9.**)

Media and Charisma

HIGHLIGHT 16.9

Although social networking is critically important, much of the research on charismatic and transformational leadership took place before the advent of social media and 7 × 24-hour news coverage. It appears as if traditional media outlets as well as social media platforms such as Twitter, Facebook, LinkedIn, WeChat, Instagram, Weibo, YouTube, and Vimeo can be leveraged to boost a person's image in the eyes of followers as well as to mobilize resources to drive societal change. For example, Vladimir Putin does regular photo shoots fishing and riding horses while bare chested, playing hockey, doing archeological dives, flying airplanes, and the like, all in the spirit of enhancing his image as a leader of the Russian people. Donald Trump uses Twitter to promote his message of America First, and social media was used to organize the Arab Spring, Black Lives Matter, Hong Kong, and Iranian protests. Media is so powerful that the Publicity Department of the Central Committee in China spends nearly $10 million a year promoting Chinese policies in foreign media outlets. On the other hand, omnipresent smartphones can also shatter a leader's image, as happened when the video of Travis Kalanick, then Uber CEO, arguing with an Uber driver went viral. Thus, media (both traditional and social) represent a dual-edged sword; they can be leveraged to make average people seem charismatic and mobilize unorganized resources toward a cause, but they can also bring down those with carefully crafted images of success.

Traditional and social media are so powerful that some countries carefully control the messages that get disseminated to the public from these outlets. China, Russia, Saudi Arabia, North Korea, Kazakhstan, Venezuela, Belarus, and other nations routinely monitor and sensor Internet traffic and carefully orchestrate news broadcasts to maintain their autocratic and kleptocratic systems. The control of the media in these countries makes it very difficult for those not in power to challenge authority, raise environmental or land confiscation issues, publish information on voting irregularities, or mobilize protests for social justice. The United States, Canada, Germany, and other countries enjoy freedom of the press, which helps keep private-sector as well as local, state, and federal government leaders in check.

How does Donald Trump use traditional and social media to bolster his image? How is the media used to challenge or counter his images of success? What role do you think "fake news" or "alternative facts" played in the 2020 presidential election?

Sources: "Propaganda: Who Draws the Party Line?" *The Economist*, June 25, 2016, pp. 36–37; A. Ostrovsky, *The Invention of Russia: From Gorbachev's Freedom to Putin's War* (New York: Viking, 2015); and "Uber CEO Kalanick Argues with Driver over Falling Fares," YouTube, www.youtube.com/watch?v=gTEDYCkNqns.

Other Situational Characteristics

Two other situational characteristics may help or hinder the emergence of a charismatic leader. One of these is restructuring or organizational downsizing. Many people believe that these processes destroy the implicit contract between employer and employee and leave many employees disillusioned with corporate life. Because charismatic or transformational leadership is intensely relational in nature, destroying the implicit contract between leaders and followers greatly diminishes the odds of charismatic leadership emergence. But of all the situational variables affecting charismatic leadership, perhaps the most important and overlooked variable is **time**. Charismatic or transformational leadership does not happen overnight. It takes time for leaders to develop and articulate their vision, heighten followers' emotional levels, build trusting relationships with followers, and direct and empower followers to fulfill the vision. A crisis may compress the amount of time needed for charismatic leadership to emerge, whereas relatively stable situations lengthen this period.

Concluding Thoughts about the Characteristics of Charismatic and Transformational Leadership

Several final points about the characteristics of charismatic leadership need to be made. First, although we defined charisma as a quality attributed to certain leaders based on the relationships they share with followers, charismatic leadership is most fully understood when we also consider how leaders and situational factors affect this attribution process. The special relationships charismatic leaders share with followers do not happen by accident; rather, they are often the result of interaction between the leader's qualities, the degree to which a leader's vision fulfills followers' needs, and the presence of certain situational factors. Second, it seems unlikely that all the characteristics of charismatic leadership need to be present before charisma is attributed to a leader. The bottom line for charisma seems to be the relationships certain leaders share with followers, and there may be a variety of ways in which these relationships can develop. This also implies that charisma may be more of a continuum than an all-or-nothing phenomenon. Some leaders may be able to form particularly strong bonds with a majority, others with a few—and still others may not get along well with any followers. Third, it seems that charismatic leadership can happen anywhere—schools, churches, communities, businesses, government organizations, and nations—and does not happen only on the world stage.

Fourth, given that there are a number of ways to develop strong emotional attachments with followers, one important question is whether it is possible to attribute charisma to an individual based solely on his or her position or celebrity status. Some individuals in positions of high public visibility and esteem (film stars, musicians, athletes, television evangelists, or politicians) can develop (even cultivate) charismatic images among their fans and admirers. In these cases it is helpful to recognize that charismatic leadership is a two-way street. Not only do followers develop strong emotional bonds with leaders, but leaders also develop strong emotional bonds with followers and are concerned with follower development.[277, 278, 279] It is difficult to see how the one-way communication channels of radio and television can foster these two-way relationships or enhance follower growth. Thus, although we sometimes view certain individuals as charismatic based on media manipulation and hype, this is not transformational leadership.

So what can leadership practitioners take from this research if they want to use an emotional approach to drive organizational change? They will probably be more successful at driving organizational change if they capitalize on or create a crisis. They also need to be close enough to their followers to determine their sources of discontent and ensure that their vision provides a solution to followers' problems and paints a compelling picture of the future. Leaders must passionately articulate their vision of the future; it is difficult to imagine followers being motivated toward a vision that is unclear or presented by a leader who does not seem to really care about it. Leadership practitioners also need to understand that they alone cannot make the vision a reality; they need their followers' help and support to create organizational or societal changes. Along these lines, they will need to be a role model and coach followers on what they should (and should not) be doing, provide feedback and encouragement, and persuade followers to take on more responsibilities as their skills and self-confidence grow. Finally, leadership practitioners using this approach to organizational change also need to be thick-skinned, resilient, and patient (see **Highlight 16.10**). They will need to cope with the polarization effects of charismatic leadership and understand that it takes time for the effects of this type of leadership to yield results. However, the rewards appear to be well worth the efforts. There appears to be overwhelming evidence that charismatic or transformational leaders are more effective than their noncharismatic counterparts, whether they be presidents of the United States,[280] CEOs,[281, 282, 283] military cadets and officers,[284, 285, 286, 287] college professors,[288] or first-line supervisors and middle-level managers in a variety of public- and private-sector companies.[289, 290, 291, 292, 293, 294, 295, 296, 297]

Good to Great: An Alternative Framework to the Rational and Emotional Approaches to Organizational Change

HIGHLIGHT 16.10

An alternative conceptualization of organizational change comes from the book *Good to Great.* Jim Collins and his research team reviewed the financial performance of 1,435 companies that appeared on the *Fortune* 500 list from 1965 to 1995. From this list, 11 companies made the leap from being a good to a truly great company—a company that yielded financial returns much higher than those for the overall stock market or industry competitors for at least 15 consecutive years. For example, a dollar invested in these 11 companies in 1965 would have yielded $471 in January 2000, whereas the same dollar invested in the stock market would have returned $56. Collins's research indicates that these 11 companies all followed the same six rules:

1. *Level 5 leadership:* The *Good to Great* companies were led not by high-profile celebrity leaders but rather by humble, self-effacing, and reserved individuals who also possessed an incredibly strong drive to succeed.

2. *First who, then what:* Before developing a future vision or goals, these leaders first

made sure they had the right people with the right skills in the right jobs. Leadership talent management was a key focus of these top companies.

3. *Confront the brutal facts (yet never lose faith):* These leaders met reality head-on—they did not sugarcoat organizational challenges or difficulties. But they also had an unshakable faith in their organizations' ability to meet these challenges.

4. *The hedgehog concept:* These companies all focused on being the best in the world at what they did, were deeply passionate about their business, and identified one or two key financial or operational metrics to guide their decision-making and day-to-day activities.

5. *A culture of discipline:* Companies that had disciplined people did not need hierarchies, bureaucracies, or excessive controls because the people in the field knew what they needed to do and made sure it happened.

6. *Technology accelerators:* All these companies selectively used technology as a

means for enhancing business operations, but they were not necessarily leaders in technical innovation.

There were several other surprising findings in Collins's research. First, none of these top-performing companies was led by transformational or charismatic leaders. Second, because these top companies were constantly undergoing small but noticeable changes, they did not need to launch major change initiatives or organizational restructuring programs. Third, companies need to abide by all six of these rules to go from good to great; three or four of the six rules were not enough for companies to make the leap to becoming top performers.

How do you think a *Good to Great* leader would perform in a crisis? What would he or she do differently than a charismatic leader? What roles do humility and competence play in *Good to Great* companies versus those led by charismatic leaders?

Sources: J. Collins, *Good to Great* (New York: Harper-Collins, 2001); and J. Collins, "Level 5 Leadership: The Triumph of Humility and Fierce Resolve," *HBR on Point* (Boston, MA: Harvard Business School Press, 2004).

Bass's Theory of Transformational and Transactional Leadership

Much of what we know about the leader, follower, and situational characteristics associated with charismatic or transformational leaders comes from research on Bass's **theory of transformational and transactional leadership**.[298, 299, 300] Bass believed that transformational leaders possessed those leader characteristics described earlier and used subordinates' perceptions or reactions to determine whether a leader was transformational. Thus transformational leaders possess good vision, rhetorical, and impression management skills and use them to develop strong emotional bonds with followers. Transformational leaders are believed to be more successful at driving organizational change because of followers' heightened emotional levels and their willingness to work toward the accomplishment of the leader's vision. In contrast, transactional leaders do not possess these leader characteristics, nor are they able to develop strong emotional bonds with followers or inspire followers to do more than followers thought they could. Instead transactional leaders were believed to motivate followers by setting goals and promising rewards for desired performance.[301, 302, 303, 304, 305, 306] Avolio and Bass[307, 308] maintained that transactional leadership could have positive effects on follower satisfaction and performance levels, but they also stated that these behaviors were often underutilized because of time constraints, a lack of leader skills, and a disbelief among leaders that rewards could boost performance. Bass[309] also maintained that transactional leadership only perpetuates the status quo; a leader's use of rewards does not result in the long-term changes associated with transformational leadership.

Like the initiating structure and consideration behaviors described in **Chapter 7**, Bass hypothesized that transformational and transactional leadership comprised two independent leadership dimensions. Thus individuals could be high transformational but low transactional leaders, low transformational and low transactional leaders, and so on. Bass developed a questionnaire, known as the **Multifactor Leadership Questionnaire (MLQ)**, to assess the extent to which leaders exhibited transformational or transactional leadership and the extent to which followers were satisfied with their leader and believed their leader was effective. The MLQ is a 360-degree feedback instrument that assesses five transformational and three transactional factors and a nonleadership factor.[310, 311, 312, 313, 314, 315] The transformational leadership factors assess the degree to which the leader instills pride in others, displays power and confidence, makes personal sacrifices or champions new possibilities, considers the ethical or moral consequences of decisions, articulates a compelling vision of the future, sets challenging standards, treats followers as individuals, and helps followers understand the problems they face. The three transactional leadership factors assess the extent to which leaders set goals, make rewards contingent on performance, obtain necessary resources, provide rewards when performance goals have been met, monitor followers' performance levels, and intervene when problems occur. The MLQ also assesses another factor called laissez-faire leadership, which assesses the extent to which leaders avoid responsibilities, fail to make decisions, are absent when needed, or fail to follow up on requests.

Research Results of Transformational and Transactional Leadership

To date, over 350 studies have used the MLQ to investigate transformational and transactional leadership across a wide variety of situations. These results indicated that transformational leadership can be observed in all countries, institutions, and organizational levels, but it was more prevalent in public institutions and at lower organizational levels.[316, 317, 318, 319, 320] In other words, there seemed to be more transformational leaders in the lower levels of the military or other public-sector organizations than anywhere else. Second, there is overwhelming evidence that transformational leadership is a significantly better predictor of organizational effectiveness than transactional or laissez-faire leadership. Transformational leaders, whether they are U.S. presidents, CEOs, school administrators, or plant managers, seem to be more effective than transactional leaders at driving organizational change and getting results. Avolio and Bass[321] also believed that transformational leadership augments performance above and beyond what is associated with transactional leadership. Third, as expected, laissez-faire leadership was negatively correlated with effectiveness.

Given that the MLQ can reliably identify transformational leaders and that these leaders can drive higher levels of organizational change and effectiveness than their transactional counterparts, it seems reasonable to ask whether it is possible to train or select charismatic leaders. Fortunately researchers have looked at the effects of transformational leadership training on the performance of military, public-sector, and private-industry leaders in the United States, Canada, and Israel. Usually these training programs consisted of several one- to five-day training sessions in which participants learned about the theory of transformational and transactional leadership; received MLQ feedback on the extent to which they exhibit transformational, transactional, and laissez-faire leadership; and then went through a series of skill-building exercises and activities to improve their leadership effectiveness. This research provided strong evidence that it is possible for leaders to systematically develop their transformational and transactional leadership skills.[322, 323, 324, 325, 326, 327, 328, 329]

An alternative to training leaders to be more transformational is to select leaders with the propensity to be transformational or charismatic in the first place. Several researchers have looked at the importance of childhood experiences, leadership traits, and even genetics in transformational leadership. Zacharatos, Barling, and Kelloway[330] reported that adolescents who were rated by coaches and peers to be more transformational were also more likely to have parents who were transformational leaders. There is also evidence that certain OCEAN leadership traits (**Chapter 6**) can be reliably used to identify transformational leaders.[331, 332, 333, 334, 335, 336, 337, 338] Some of the most compelling evidence comes from Nilsen, who looked at the relationships between OCEAN personality traits and 125 CEOs. As shown in **Table 16.4**, not only are the OCEAN personality dimensions strongly correlated with certain components of transformational leadership, but the pattern of high and low correlations seems to make sense.[339] Given that certain leadership traits are related to transformational leadership, and that leadership traits have a genetic component, it is not surprising that some researchers also believe that some aspect of transformational leadership is heritable.[340]

Table 16.4   Correlations between Five Factor Model Dimensions and Charismatic Leadership Characteristics for 125 Corporate CEOs and Presidents

Personality Dimension	Transformational Leadership Characteristics			
	Visionary Thinking	Empowering Others	Inspiring Trust	High-Impact Delivery
Extraversion	.32	.33	.16	.47
Conscientiousness	−.08	−.01	.06	−.04
Agreeableness	.02	.52	.48	.35
Neuroticism	−.03	.29	.38	.22
Openness to experience	.47	.30	.14	.40

Source: D. Nilsen, "Using Self and Observers' Ratings for Personality to Predict Leadership Performance," unpublished doctoral dissertation, University of Minnesota, Minneapolis, 1995.

Despite this evidence that it may be possible to select and train transformational leaders, the fact remains that charisma ultimately exists in the eye of the beholder. Thus there can be no guarantee that leaders who have the right stuff and are schooled in the appropriate techniques will be seen as charismatic by followers. As discussed earlier, follower and situational variables play a key role in determining whether leaders are perceived as transformational and drive organizational change. Certain leaders may get higher transformational leadership scores as a result of a training program; but do they actually heighten followers' emotional levels, get followers to exert extra effort, and as a result achieve greater organizational change or performance after the program? Given what we know about individual differences and leadership skills training, it seems likely that a leader's personality will also play a major role in determining whether he or she will benefit from such training.

Several other important comments about the theory of transformational and transactional leadership are worth noting. First, and perhaps most important, this theory has generated a considerable amount of interest among leadership researchers. This research has helped leadership practitioners better understand the leader, follower, and situational components of charismatic or transformational leadership, whether transformational leaders are born or made, and so forth. Nevertheless, this approach to leadership may be more a reflection of socially desirable leadership behaviors than the full range of skills needed by leaders. For example, it seems likely that business leaders wanting to drive organizational change need to have a good understanding of the industry, business operations, market trends, finance, strategy, and technical or functional knowledge; they also need to effectively cope with stress, negotiate contracts with vendors, demonstrate good planning skills, and develop and monitor key metrics; and because large-scale change is never a solo effort, they need to be able to build high-performing senior leadership teams. Yet none of these attributes and skills are measured directly by the MLQ. This leads us to another point, which is that a primary problem with this theory is that there is only one way to be an effective leader, and that is by demonstrating transformational leadership skills. The contingency theories of leadership no longer matter, and situational or follower factors have little impact on leadership effectiveness. In all likelihood, leaders probably need to do more than just exhibit transformational leadership skills if they wish to achieve greater organizational change and performance.

Summary

This chapter reviewed two major approaches to organizational change. Although independent lines of research were used to develop the rational and emotional approaches to change, in reality these approaches have several important similarities. With the rational approach, leaders increase follower dissatisfaction by pointing out problems with the status quo, systematically identifying areas of needed change, developing a vision of the future, and developing and implementing a change plan. In the emotional approach, leaders develop and articulate a vision of the future, heighten the emotions of followers, and empower followers to act on their vision. Charismatic leaders are also more likely to emerge during times of uncertainty or crisis, and may actually manufacture a crisis to improve the odds that followers will become committed to their vision of the future. The rational approach puts more emphasis on analytic, planning, and management skills, whereas the emotional approach puts more emphasis on leadership skills, leader–follower relationships, and the presence of a crisis to drive organizational change. This chapter also described the steps leadership practitioners must take if they wish to drive organizational change. There is ample evidence to suggest that either the rational or the emotional approach can result in organizational change, but the effectiveness of the change may depend on which approach leadership practitioners are most comfortable with and the skill with which they can carry it out. Research also shows that charisma is very helpful in attracting attention and getting promoted, but competence and humility are more helpful to engaging and developing employees, building teams, achieving results that are better than the competition, and driving long-term changes that benefit the broader organization.

Key Terms

$C = D \times M \times P > R$

dissatisfaction

model

process

resistance

amount of change

systems thinking approach

siloed thinking

change plan

expectation–performance gap

SARA model

adaptive leadership

learning agility

traditional authority system

legal–rational authority system

charismatic authority system

transactional leadership

transformational leadership

reframing

within-group competition

between-group competition

humility

vision

rhetorical skills

image

build trust

succession planning process

personalized leadership

charisma

identification with the leader

heightened emotional level

willing subordination to the leader

feelings of empowerment

crisis

social networks

time

theory of transformational and transactional leadership

Multifactor Leadership Questionnaire (MLQ)

Questions

1. Kendall Jenner, Kim Kardashian, and Kylie Jenner respectively have 143.5, 122, and 121 million Twitter, Facebook, and Instagram followers. Who benefits from having all these followers? Are these individuals charismatic or effective leaders? What data would you need to gather to answer this question?

2. Are Vladimir Putin and Donald Trump humble, charismatic, or transformational leaders? Would your answers differ if you were a Russian citizen or a member of the Republican or Democratic parties in the United States?

3. Research shows that women are seen as more competent and transformational leaders, yet they hold relatively few top leadership positions compared to men. Why do you think this is the case? What, if anything, could you do to change this situation?

4. Which do you think was the most effective strategy during the coronavirus pandemic—the rational or emotional approach to organizational change?

5. Can leaders lack intelligence (as described in **Chapter 6**) and still be seen as charismatic?

6. How do humble, charismatic, and transformational leadership relate to the four followership types described in **Part 3** of this book? How might followership types change while implementing a major organizational change?

7. Suppose you wanted to build a new student union at your school. What would you need to do to make this happen if you used a rational versus an emotional approach to organizational change?

Activities

1. Work with a small group of classmates or coworkers to identify something that needs to change at your school or at work. Use the rational approach to change ($C = D \times M \times P > R$) to develop a plan for your change initiative.

2. Ask a mid-level leader or executive to describe the types of changes they needed to make during the coronavirus pandemic. Did this leader use more of a rational or an emotional approach to organizational change? What were employees' reactions, and was the change initiative successful? Why or why not?

3. Research the extent to which a local politician or business leader uses social media to bolster his or her image of success. How do they use social media to deal with mistakes or failures?

4. Take the "Do You Have Enough Humility to Lead?" quiz at *Bloomberg Businessweek*: www.bloomberg.com/news/articles/2020-01-24/do-you-have-enough-humility-to-lead. What do the results say about you and your classmates?

Minicase

Keeping Up with Bill Gates

Bill Gates inherited intelligence, ambition, and a competitive spirit from his father, a successful Seattle attorney. After graduating from a private prep school in Seattle, he enrolled in Harvard but dropped out to pursue his passion—computer programming. Paul Allen, a friend from prep school, presented Gates with the idea of writing a version of the BASIC computer language for the Altair 8800, one of the first personal computers on the market. Driven by his competitive nature, Gates decided he wanted to be the first to develop a language to make the personal computer accessible for the general public. He and Allen established the Microsoft Corporation in 1975. Gates's passion and skill were programming—he would work night and day to meet the extremely aggressive deadlines he set for himself and his company. Eventually Gates had to bring in other programmers; he focused on recent college graduates. "We decided that we wanted them to come with clear minds, not polluted by some other approach, to learn the way that we liked to develop software, and to put the kind of energy into it that we thought was key."

In the early days of Microsoft, Gates was in charge of product planning and programming while Allen was in charge of the business side. He motivated his programmers with the claim that whatever deadline was looming, no matter how tight, he could beat it personally if he had to. What eventually developed at Microsoft was a culture in which Gates was king. Everyone working under Gates was made to feel they were lesser programmers who couldn't compete with his skill or drive, so they competed with each other. They worked long hours and tried their best to mirror Gates—his drive, his ambition, his skill. This internal competition motivated the programmers and made Microsoft one of the most successful companies in the computer industry, and one of the most profitable. The corporation has created a tremendous amount of wealth—many of its employees have become millionaires while working at Microsoft, including, of course, Bill Gates. Over the past 20 years Gates has been one of the richest people in the world and had an estimated net worth of $87 billion in 2017.

Having done extremely well in the business world, Gates shifted his attention in 2008 when he retired from Microsoft in order to focus on the Bill and Melinda Gates Foundation. This foundation was created in partnership with Warren Buffett and its purpose is to alleviate extreme poverty, eradicate disease, and improve health care across the globe. Using business practices to improve philanthropic outcomes, the foundation has an endowment of over $35 billion and Gates has been very successful at getting others to donate to their cause. The foundation funds programs to control infectious diseases, such as malaria, HIV/AIDs, and tuberculosis; improve sanitation, nutrition, and family planning; prevent slavery and sex trafficking; help with agricultural development; and provide financial services, such as microlending, to the poor. These programs are making a tangible difference in tackling some of the world's biggest problems.

1. Would you classify Bill Gates as a humble, charismatic, or transformational leader? Do you think his leadership classification has changed over time? Why?

2. Does the Bill and Melinda Gates Foundation use a rational or an emotional approach to drive societal change?

Sources: Microsoft, www.microsoft.com; "Bill Gates v Steve Jobs," *BBC News*, November 24, 2003, http://news.bbc.co.uk/1/hi/programmes/worlds_most_powerful/3284811.stm; J. Mirick, "Bill Gates: Before Microsoft," http://ei.cs.vt.edu/~history/Gates.Mirick.html; L. Grossman, "The 2005 Time 100: Bill Gates," *Time*, April 18, 2005, http://content.time.com/time/specials/packages/article/0,28804,1972656_1972717_1974038,00.html; "Bill Gates Net Worth," *Celebrity Net Worth*, www.celebritynetworth.com/richest-businessmen/richest-billionaires/bill-gates-net-worth; "Foundation Fact Sheet," Bill & Melinda Gates Foundation, www.gatesfoundation.org/Who-We-Are/General-Information/Foundation-Factsheet; and "Annual Report, 2015," Bill & Melinda Gates Foundation, www.gatesfoundation.org/Who-We-Are/Resources-and-Media/Annual-Reports/Annual-Report-2015.

Endnotes

1. B. M. Bass, *Leadership and Performance beyond Expectations* (New York: Free Press, 1985).

2. J. O'Toole, *Leading Change* (San Francisco: Jossey-Bass, 1995).

3. P. Pritchett, *Firing Up Commitment during Organizational Change* (Dallas, TX: Pritchett and Associates, 2001).

4. E. McNulty, "Welcome Aboard (But Don't Change a Thing)," *Harvard Business Review*, October 2002, pp. 32–41.

5. R. A. Heifetz and M. Linsky, "A Survival Guide for Leaders," *Harvard Business Review*, June 2002, pp. 65–75.

6. R. Moss Kanter, "Leadership and the Psychology of Turnarounds," *Harvard Business Review*, June 2003, pp. 58–64.

7. R. Moss Kanter, *The Change Masters* (New York: Simon & Schuster, 1983).

8. J. Krile, G. J. Curphy, and D. Lund, *The Community Leadership Handbook: Framing Ideas, Building Relationships and Mobilizing Resources* (St. Paul, MN: Fieldstone Alliance, 2005).

9. F. Ostroff, "Change Management in Government," *Harvard Business Review*, May 2006, pp. 141–53.

10. D. Rock and J. Schwartz, "The Neuroscience of Leadership: Why Organizational Change Hurts," *Strategy 1 Business* 43 (2006) pp. 71–79.

11. J. Kotter, "Leading Change: Why Transformation Change Efforts Fail," *Harvard Business Review*, January 2007, pp. 96–103.

12. G. J. Curphy, *The Competitive Advantage Program for Wheelabrator Technologies Incorporated* (North Oaks, MN: Author, 2006).

13. G. J. Curphy, *Leadership, Teams, and Change Program for the New York City Leadership Academy* (North Oaks, MN: Author, 2005).

14. J. M. Burns, *Leadership* (New York: Harper & Row, 1978).

15. R. Marcus and R. Weiler, *Aligning Organizations: The Foundation of Performance* (Camden, ME: Brimstone Consulting Group, 2010).

16. W. G. Bennis and B. Nanus, *Leaders: The Strategies for Taking Charge* (New York: Harper & Row, 1985).

17. N. M. Tichy and M. A. Devanna, *The Transformational Leader* (New York: John Wiley, 1986).

18. W. Bridges, *Managing Transitions: Making the Most of Change* (Reading, MA: Addison-Wesley, 1991).

19. J. C. Collins and J. I. Porras, *Built to Last: Successful Habits of Visionary Companies* (Reading, MA: Perseus Books, 1997).

20. M. Treacy and F. Wiersma, *The Discipline of Market Leaders* (Reading, MA: Perseus Books, 1997).

21. M. Beer, *Leading Change*, Reprint No. 9-488-037 (Boston: Harvard Business School Publishing Division, 1988).

22. M. Beer, "Developing Organizational Fitness: Towards a Theory and Practice of Organizational Alignment," paper presented at the 14th Annual Conference of the Society of Industrial and Organizational Psychology, Atlanta, GA, 1999.

23. R. A. Heifetz and D. L. Laurie, "The Work of Leadership," *Harvard Business Review*, December 2001, pp. 131–40.

24. J. Collins, *Good to Great* (New York: HarperCollins, 2001).

25. J. Collins, *How the Mighty Fall* (New York: HarperCollins, 2009).

26. Beer, *Leading Change.*

27. Beer, "Developing Organizational Fitness."

28. Marcus and Weiler, *Aligning Organizations.*

29. Beer, *Leading Change.*

30. Beer, "Developing Organizational Fitness."

31. O'Toole, *Leading Change.*

32. Krile, Curphy, and Lund, *The Community Leadership Handbook.*

33. Kotter, "Leading Change."

34. Curphy, *The Competitive Advantage Program for Wheelabrator Technologies Incorporated.*

35. Marcus and Weiler, *Aligning Organizations.*

36. Beer, "Developing Organizational Fitness."

37. N. M. Tichy and N. Cardwell, *The Cycle of Leadership: How Great Companies Teach Their Leaders to Win* (New York: Harper Business, 2002).

38. G. J. Curphy and D. L.Nilsen, *Faurecia Clean Mobility Leadership Development Program* (North Oaks, MN: Curphy Leadership Solutions, 2016).

39. G. J. Curphy, *Bethesda Lutheran Communities Leadership Team Off-Sites*, March 23–24 (North Oaks, MN: Curphy Leadership Solutions, 2017).

40. Krile, Curphy, and Lund, *The Community Leadership Handbook.*

41. Marcus and Weiler, *Aligning Organizations.*

42. Bennis and Nanus, *Leaders.*

43. Tichy and Devanna, *The Transformational Leader.*

44. G. J. Curphy, *The Blandin Education Leadership Program* (Grand Rapids, MN: The Blandin Foundation, 2003).

45. G. J. Curphy and R. T. Hogan, *The Rocket Model: Practical Advice for Building High Performing Teams* (Tulsa, OK: Hogan Press, 2012).

46. G. J. Curphy, *Team Performance Improvement Workshop* (NorthOaks, MN: Curphy Leadership Solutions, 2017).

47. G. J. Curphy, D. Nilsen, and R. Hogan, *Ignition: A Guide to Building High Performing Teams* (Tulsa, OK: Hogan Press, 2019).

48. Rock and Schwartz, "The Neuroscience of Leadership."

49. Treacy and Wiersma, *The Discipline of Market Leaders.*

50. Curphy, *The Blandin Education Leadership Program.*

51. Curphy and Hogan, *The Rocket Model.*

52. G. J. Curphy, *Applying the Rocket Model to Virtual Teams* (North Oaks, MN: Author, 2013).

53. O'Toole, *Leading Change.*

54. Krile, Curphy, and Lund, *The Community Leadership Handbook.*

55. Collins and Porras, *Built to Last.*

56. Tichy and Cardwell, *The Cycle of Leadership.*

57. Curphy, *The Blandin Education Leadership Program.*

58. Curphy and Hogan, *The Rocket Model.*

59. Curphy, *Team Performance Improvement Workshop.*

60. Curphy, *Applying the Rocket Model to Virtual Teams.*

61. Marcus and Weiler, *Aligning Organizations.*

62. Tichy and Cardwell, *The Cycle of Leadership.*

63. Curphy, *The Blandin Education Leadership Program.*

64. P. M. Senge, *The Fifth Discipline: The Art and Practice of the Learning Organization* (New York: Doubleday/Currency, 1994).

65. S. Heidari-Robinson, "Making Government Re-Orgs Work," *Harvard Business Review*, March 30, 2107, https://hbr.org/2017/03/making-government-reorgs-work.

66. Marcus and Weiler, *Aligning Organizations.*

67. Tichy and Cardwell, *The Cycle of Leadership.*

68. Curphy, *The Blandin Education Leadership Program.*

69. Senge, *The Fifth Discipline: The Art and Practice of the Learning Organization.*

70. Heifetz and Linsky, "A Survival Guide for Leaders."

71. Moss Kanter, "Leadership and the Psychology of Turnarounds."

72. Moss Kanter, *The Change Masters.*

73. Krile, Curphy, and Lund, *The Community Leadership Handbook.*

74. Kotter, "Leading Change: Why Transformation Change Efforts Fail."

75. Beer, "Developing Organizational Fitness."

76. Heifetz and Laurie, "The Work of Leadership."

77. Curphy, *The Blandin Education Leadership Program.*

78. G. J. Curphy, *Strategy, Strategy Execution, and Change: The Culture Card Sort Exercise* (North Oaks, MN: Author, 2013).

79. M. L. Marks and P. H. Mirvis, "Making Mergers and Acquisitions Work," *Academy of Management Executive* 15, no. 2 (2001), pp. 80–94.

80. P. Pritchett and R. Pound, *Smart Moves: A Crash Course on Merger Integration Management* (Pritchett and Associates, 2001).

81. C. M. Ruvolo and R. C. Bullis, "Essentials of Cultural Change: Lessons Learned the Hard Way," *Consulting Psychology Journal* 55, no. 3 (2003), pp. 155–68.

82. Q. N. Huy, "In Praise of Middle Managers," *Harvard Business Review*, September 2001, pp. 72–81.

83. Krile, Curphy, and Lund, *The Community Leadership Handbook.*

84. Curphy, *The Competitive Advantage Program for Wheelabrator Technologies Incorporated.*

85. Curphy, *The Blandin Education Leadership Program.*

86. Pritchett and Pound, *Smart Moves.*

87. L. Bossidy and R. Charan, *Execution: The Discipline of Getting Things Done* (New York: Crown Business Publishing, 2002).

88. G. J. Curphy, *Buffalo Wild Wings Senior Leader Program* (NorthOaks, MN: Curphy Leadership Solutions, 2016).

89. Bossidy and Charan, *Execution.*

90. G. J. Curphy, A. Baldrica, and R. T. Hogan, *Managerial Incompetence*, unpublished manuscript, 2009.

91. R. Charan and G. Colvin, "Why CEOs Fail," *Fortune*, June 21, 1999, pp. 69–82.

92. L. Hirschhorn, "Campaigning for Change," *Harvard Business Review*, July 2002, pp. 98–106.

93. Krile, Curphy, and Lund, *The Community Leadership Handbook*.

94. Marcus and Weiler, *Aligning Organizations*.

95. Curphy and Hogan, *The Rocket Model*.

96. Curphy, *The Blandin Education Leadership Program*.

97. Curphy and Hogan, *The Rocket Model*.

98. Hirschhorn, "Campaigning for Change."

99. Hirschhorn, "Campaigning for Change."

100. McNulty, "Welcome Aboard (But Don't Change a Thing)."

101. Heifetz and Linsky, "A Survival Guide for Leaders."

102. Krile, Curphy, and Lund, *The Community Leadership Handbook*.

103. Ostroff, "Change Management in Government."

104. Rock and Schwartz, "The Neuroscience of Leadership."

105. Beer, *Leading Change*.

106. Heifetz and Laurie, "The Work of Leadership."

107. Curphy, *The Blandin Education Leadership Program*.

108. Pritchett and Pound, *Smart Moves*.

109. Ruvolo and Bullis, "Essentials of Cultural Change."

110. S. Oreg and Y. Berson, "Leadership and Employees' Reactions to Change: The Role of Leaders' Personal Attributes and Transformational Leadership Style," *Personnel Psychology* 64, no. 1 (2011), pp. 627–60.

111. S. Shellenbarger, "The Trouble with Office Luddites," *The Wall Street Journal*, June 11, 2019, p. A13.

112. Beer, *Leading Change*.

113. E. Kübler-Ross, *Living with Death and Dying* (New York: Macmillan, 1981).

114. S. Heidari-Robinson and S. Heywood, "Re-Orgs Are Emotional," *Harvard Business Review*, November 3, 2016, https://hbr.org/podcast/2016/11/re-orgs-are-emotional.

115. Krile, Curphy, and Lund, *The Community Leadership Handbook*.

116. Marcus and Weiler, *Aligning Organizations*.

117. Curphy, *The Blandin Education Leadership Program*.

118. Curphy and Hogan, *The Rocket Model*.

119. Huy, "In Praise of Middle Managers."

120. Krile, Curphy, and Lund, *The Community Leadership Handbook*.

121. Beer, "Developing Organizational Fitness."

122. Curphy, *The Blandin Education Leadership Program*.

123. Curphy and Hogan, *The Rocket Model*.

124. Kotter, "Leading Change."

125. Curphy, Baldrica, and Hogan, *Managerial Incompetence*.

126. R. B. Kaiser, "Introduction to the Special Issue on Developing Flexible and Adaptable Leaders for an Age of Uncertainty," *Consulting Psychology Journal: Practice and Research* 62, no. 2 (2010), pp. 77–80.

127. G. A. Yukl and R. Mahsud, "Why Flexible and Adaptable Leadership Is Essential," *Consulting Psychology Journal: Practice and Research* 62, no. 2 (2010), pp. 81–93.

128. K. De Muese, G. Dai, and G. S. Hallenbeck, "Learning Agility: A Construct Whose Time Has Come," *Consulting Psychology Journal: Practice and Research* 62, no. 2 (2010), pp. 119–30.

129. J. Bersin, "Predictions for 2017: Everything Is Becoming Digital," www.bersin.com/Practice/Detail.aspx?docid=20454.

130. K. Ferry, "Developing Learning Agility," www.kornferry.com/developing-learning-agility

131. M. Weber, *The Theory of Social and Economic Organization*, ed. Talcott Parsons, trans. A. M. Henderson and T. Parsons (New York: Free Press, 1964).

132. "Sovereign Immunity," *The Economist*, April 27, 2019, pp. 52–54.

133. C. Bradatan, "Democracy Is for the Gods," *The New York Times*, July 5, 2019, www.nytimes.com/2019/07/05/opinion/why-democracies-fail.html.

134. P. M. Blau, "Critical Remarks on Weber's Theory of Authority," *American Political Science Review* 57, no. 2 (1963), pp. 305–15.

135. E. Chinoy, *Society* (New York: Random House, 1961).

136. H. Wolpe, "A Critical Analysis of Some Aspects of Charisma," *Sociological Review* 16 (1968), pp. 305–18.

137. W. H. Friedland, "For a Sociological Concept of Charisma," *Social Forces*, no. 1 (1964), pp. 18–26.

138. H. H. Gerth and C. W. Mills, *Max Weber: Essays in Sociology* (New York: Oxford University Press, 1946).

139. R. M. Kanter, *Commitment and Community* (Cambridge: Harvard University Press, 1972).

140. R. C. Tucker, "The Theory of Charismatic Leadership," *Daedalus* 97 (1968), pp. 731–56.

141. T. E. Dow, "The Theory of Charisma," *Sociological Quarterly* 10 (1969), pp. 306–18.

142. B. R. Clark, "The Organizational Saga in Higher Education," *Administrative Science Quarterly* 17 (1972), pp. 178–84.

143. G. Deveraux, "Charismatic Leadership and Crisis," in *Psychoanalysis and the Social Sciences*, eds. W. Muensterberger and S. Axelrod (New York: International University Press, 1955).

144. J. V. Downton, *Rebel Leadership: Commitment and Charisma in the Revolutionary Process* (New York: Free Press, 1973).

145. J. T. Marcus, "Transcendence and Charisma," *Western Political Quarterly* 16 (1961), pp. 236–41.

146. E. Shils, "Charisma, Order, and Status," *American Sociological Review* 30 (1965), pp. 199–213.

147. Burns, *Leadership*.

148. N. Turner, J. Barling, O. Eptiropaki, V. Butcher, and C. Milner, "Transformational Leadership and Moral Reasoning," *Journal of Applied Psychology* 87, no. 2 (2002), pp. 304–11.

149. T. L. Price, "The Ethics of Authentic Transformational Leadership," *Leadership Quarterly* 14, no. 1 (2003), pp. 67–82.

150. J. Gooty, S. Connelly, J. Griffith, and A. Gupta, "Leadership, Affect, and Emotions: A State of the Science Review," *Leadership Quarterly* 21, no. 6 (2010), pp. 979–1004.

151. J. E. Bono and R. Ilies, "Charisma, Positive Emotions, and Mood Contagion," *Leadership Quarterly* 17 (2006), pp. 317–34.

152. S. Parameshwar, "Inventing Higher Purpose through Suffering: The Transformation of the Transformational Leader," *Leadership Quarterly* 17 (2006), pp. 454–74.

153. M. Greer, "The Science of Savoir Faire," *Monitor on Psychology*, January 2005, pp. 28–30.

154. J. M. Strange and M. D. Mumford, "The Origins of Vision: Effects of Reflection, Models, and Analysis," *Leadership Quarterly* 16 (2005) pp. 121–48.

155. G. Yukl, "An Evaluation of Conceptual Weaknesses in Transformational and Charismatic Leadership Theories," *Leadership Quarterly* 10, no. 2 (1999), pp. 285–306.

156. J. G. Hunt, "Transformational/Charismatic Leadership's Transformation of the Field: An Historical Essay," *Leadership Quarterly* 10, no. 2 (1999), pp. 129–44.

157. J. A. Conger and J. G. Hunt, "Charismatic and Transformational Leadership: Taking Stock of the Present and Future," *Leadership Quarterly* 10, no. 2 (1999), pp. 121–28.

158. E. E. Duehr and J. E. Bono, "Personality and Transformational Leadership: Differential Prediction for Male and Female Leaders," in *Predicting Leadership: The Good, The Bad, the Different, and the Unnecessary*, J. P. Campbell and M. J. Benson (chairs), annual meeting of Society of Industrial and Organizational Psychology, New York, April 2007.

159. B. M. Bass, "Two Decades of Research and Development in Transformational Leadership," *European Journal of Work and Organizational Psychology* 8, no. 1 (1999), pp. 9–32.

160. D. N. Den Hartog, R. J. House, P. J. Hanges, S. A. Ruiz-Quintanilla, P. W. Dorfman, and associates, "Culture Specific and Cross-Culturally Generalizable Implicit Leadership Theories: Are Attributes of Charismatic/Transformational Leadership Universally Endorsed?" *Leadership Quarterly* 10, no. 2 (1999), pp. 219–56.

161. A. H. Eagly and L. L. Carli, "The Female Leadership Advantage: An Evaluation of the Evidence," *Leadership Quarterly* 14 (2003), pp. 807–34.

162. J. B. Rosener, "Ways Women Lead," *Harvard Business Review* 68 (1990), pp. 119–25.

163. V. U. Druskat, "Gender and Leadership Style: Transformational and Transactional Leadership in the Roman Catholic Church," *Leadership Quarterly* 5, no. 1 (1994), pp. 99–120.

164. B. M. Bass and F. J. Yammarino, *Long-term Forecasting of Transformational Leadership and Its Effects among Naval Officers: Some Preliminary Findings*, Technical Report No. ONR-TR-2 (Arlington, VA: Office of Naval Research, 1988).

165. S. M. Ross and L. R. Offermann, "Transformational Leaders: Measurement of Personality Attributes and Work Group Performance," paper presented at the Sixth Annual Society of Industrial and Organizational Psychologists Convention, St. Louis, MO, April 1991.

166. B. J. Avolio and B. M. Bass, *Developing a Full Range of Leadership Potential: Cases on Transactional and Transformational Leadership* (Binghamton: State University of New York at Binghamton, 2000).

167. B. M. Bass, "Thoughts and Plans," in *Cutting Edge: Leadership 2000*, eds. B. Kellerman and L. R. Matusak (Carbondale, IL: Southern Illinois University Press, 2000), pp. 5–9.

168. G. J. Curphy, "An Empirical Investigation of Bass' (1985) Theory of Transformational and Transactional Leadership," PhD dissertation, University of Minnesota, 1991.

169. D. A. Waldman, G. G. Ramirez, R. J. House, and P. Puranam, "Does Leadership Matter? CEO Leadership Attributes and Profitability under Conditions of Perceived Environmental Uncertainty," *Academy of Management Journal* 44, no. 1 (2001), pp. 134–43.

170. T. Dvir, D. Eden, B. J. Avolio, and B. Shamir, "Impact of Transformational Leadership on Follower Development and Performance: A Field Experiment," *Academy of Management Journal* 45, no. 4 (2002), pp. 735–44.

171. J. E. Bono, "Transformational Leadership: What We Know and Why You Should Care!" Presentation delivered to the Minnesota Professionals for Psychology Applied to Work, Minneapolis, MN, September 2002.

172. B. M. Bass, B. J. Avolio, D. I. Jung, and Y. Berson, "Predicting Unit Performance by Assessing Transformational and Transactional Leadership," *Journal of Applied Psychology* 88, no. 2 (2003), pp. 207–18.

173. D. A. Waldman, M. Javidan, and P. Varella, "Charismatic Leadership at the Strategic Level: A New Application of Upper Echelons Theory," *Leadership Quarterly* 15, no. 3 (2004), pp. 355–80.

174. T. A. Judge and R. F. Piccolo, "Transformational and Transactional Leadership: A Meta-analytic Test of Their Relative Validity," *Journal of Applied Psychology* 89, no. 5 (2004), pp. 755–68.

175. R. T. Keller, "Transformational Leadership, Initiating Structure, and Substitutes for Leadership: A Longitudinal Study of Research and Development Project Team Performance," *Journal of Applied Psychology* 91, no. 1 (2006), pp. 202–10.

176. J. L. Whittington, V. L. Goodwin, and B. Murray, "Transformational Leadership, Goal Difficulty, and Job Design: Independent and Interactive Effects on Employee Outcomes," *Leadership Quarterly* 15, no. 5 (2004), pp. 593–606.

177. L. A. Nemanich and R. T. Keller, "Transformational Leadership in an Acquisition: A Field Study of Employees," *Leadership Quarterly* 18, no. 1 (2007), pp. 49–68.

178. J. A. Conger, "Charismatic and Transformational Leadership in Organizations: An Insider's Perspective on These Developing Streams of Research," *Leadership Quarterly* 10, no. 2 (1999), pp. 145–80.

179. B. Tranter, "Leadership and Change in the Tasmanian Environmental Movement," *Leadership Quarterly* 20, no. 5 (2009), pp. 708–24.

180. Conger, "Charismatic and Transformational Leadership in Organizations."

181. R. Khurana, "The Curse of the Superstar CEO," *Harvard Business Review*, September 2002, pp. 60–67.

182. H. L. Tosi, V. F. Misangyi, A. Fanelli, D. A. Waldman, and F. J. Yammarino, "CEO Charisma, Compensation, and Firm Performance," *Leadership Quarterly* 15, no. 3 (2004), pp. 405–20.

183. B. R. Agle, N. J. Nagarajan, J. A. Sonnenfeld, and D. Srinivasan, "Does CEO Charisma Matter? An Empirical Analysis of the Relationships among Organizational Performance, Environmental Uncertainty, and Top Management Team Perceptions of Charisma," *Academy of Management Journal* 49, no. 1 (2006), pp. 161–74.

184. T. Chamorro-Premuzic, "Charisma Has Its Downsides," *Management Today*, February 1, 2016, www.managementtoday.co.uk/charismatic-leadership-its-downsides/article/1380513.

185. M. Mayo, "If Humble People Make the Best Leaders, Why Do We Fall for Charismatic Narcissists?" *Harvard Business Review*, April 2017, https://hbr.org/2017/04/ if-humble-people-make-the-best-leaders-why-do-we-fall-for-charismatic-narcissists.

186. J. A. Conger and R. N. Kanungo, *Charismatic Leadership in Organizations* (Thousand Oaks, CA: Sage, 1998).

187. R. J. House, "A 1976 Theory of Charismatic Leadership," in *Leadership: The Cutting Edge*, eds. J. G. Hunt and L. L. Larson (Carbondale, IL: Southern Illinois University Press, 1977).

188. R. J. House and B. Shamir, "Toward an Integration of Transformational, Charismatic, and Visionary Theories," in *Leadership Theory and Research Perspective and Directions*, eds. M. Chemers and R. Ayman (Orlando, FL: Academic Press, 1993), pp. 577–94.

189. B. Shamir, R. J. House, and M. B. Arthur, "The Motivation Effects of Charismatic Leadership: A Self-Concept Based Theory," *Organizational Science* 4 (1993), pp. 577–94.

190. B. J. Avolio and B. M. Bass, "Transformational Leadership, Charisma, and Beyond," in *Emerging Leadership Vistas*, eds. J. G. Hunt, B. R. Baliga, and C. A. Schriesheim (Lexington, MA: D. C. Heath, 1988).

191. Greer, "The Science of Savoir Faire."

192. Bass, "Two Decades of Research and Development in Transformational Leadership."

193. Ross and Offermann, "Transformational Leaders."

194. Avolio and Bass, *Developing a Full Range of Leadership Potential.*

195. Bono, "Transformational Leadership."

196. Bass et al., "Predicting Unit Performance by Assessing Transformational and Transactional Leadership."

197. A. J. Towler, "Effects of Charismatic Influence Training on Attitudes, Behavior, and Performance," *Personnel Psychology* 56, no. 2, pp. 363–82.

198. R. Hooijberg and J. Choi, "From Selling Peanuts and Beer in Yankee Stadium to Creating a Theory of Transformational Leadership: An Interview with Bernie Bass," *Leadership Quarterly* 11, no. 2 (2000), pp. 291–300.

199. K. M. Boal and J. M. Bryson, "Charismatic Leadership: A Phenomenal and Structural Approach," in *Emerging Leadership Vistas*, eds. J. G. Hunt, B. R. Baliga, H. P. Dachler, and C. A. Schriesheim (Lexington, MA: Heath Company, 1988).

200. M. Kets de Vries, *The Leadership Mystique: A User's Guide for the Human Enterprise* (London: Financial Times/Prentice Hall, 2001).

201. J. M. Strange and M. D. Mumford, "The Origins of Vision: Charismatic versus Ideological Leadership," *Leadership Quarterly* 13, no. 4 (2002), pp. 343–78.

202. J. S. Mio, R. E. Riggio, S. Levin, and R. Reese, "Presidential Leadership and Charisma: The Effects of Metaphor," *Leadership Quarterly* 16 (2005), pp. 287–94.

203. L. J. Naidoo and R. G. Lord, "Speech Imagery and Perceptions of Charisma: The Mediating Role of Positive Affect," *Leadership Quarterly* 19, no. 3 (2008), pp. 283–96.

204. Mio et al., "Presidential Leadership and Charisma."

205. Naidoo and Lord, "Speech Imagery and Perceptions of Charisma."

206. R. McKee, "Storytelling That Moves People: A Conversation with Screenwriting Coach Robert McKee," *Harvard Business Review,* June 2003, pp. 51–57.

207. C. J. Palus, D. M. Horth, A. M. Selvin, and M. L. Pulley, "Exploration for Development: Developing Leaders by Making Shared Sense of Complex Challenges," *Consulting Psychology Journal* 55, no. 1 (2003), pp. 26–40.

208. Y. Berson, B. Shamir, B. J. Avolio, and M. Popper, "The Relationship between Vision Strength, Leadership Style, and Context," *Leadership Quarterly* 12, no. 1 (2001), pp. 53–74.

209. B. Shamir, M. B. Arthur, and R. J. House, "The Rhetoric of Charismatic Leadership: A Theoretical Extension, a Case Study, and Implications for Research," *Leadership Quarterly* 5 (1994), pp. 25–42.

210. A. R. Willner, *The Spellbinders: Charismatic Political Leadership* (New Haven, CT: Yale University Press, 1984).

211. V. Seyranian and M. C. Bligh, "Presidential Charismatic Leadership: Exploring the Rhetoric of Social Change," *Leadership Quarterly* 19, no. 1 (2008), pp. 54–76.

212. K. B. Boal and P. L. Schultz, "Storytelling, Time, and Evolution: The Role of Strategic Leadership in Complex Adaptive Systems," *Leadership Quarterly* 18, no. 3 (2007), pp. 411–28.

213. W. Liu, R. Zhu, and Y. Yang, "I Warn You Because I Like You: Voice Behavior, Employee Identifications, and Transformational Leadership," *Leadership Quarterly* 21, no. 1 (2010), pp. 189–202.

214. Parameshwar, "Inventing Higher Purpose through Suffering."

215. House, "A 1976 Theory of Charismatic Leadership."

216. J. A. Conger, *The Charismatic Leader* (San Francisco: Jossey-Bass, 1989).

217. B. M. Bass and B. J. Avolio, eds., *Increasing Organizational Effectiveness through Transformational Leadership* (Thousand Oaks, CA: Sage, 1994).

218. B. M. Bass, "Does the Transactional–Transformational Leadership Paradigm Transcend Organizational and National Boundaries?" *American Psychologist* 52, no. 3 (1997), pp. 130–39.

219. B. M. Bass and P. Steidlmeier, "Ethics, Character, and Authentic Transformational Leadership Behavior," *Leadership Quarterly* 10, no. 2 (1999), pp. 181–218.

220. J. J. Sosik, B. J. Avolio, and D. I. Jun, "Beneath the Mask: Examining the Relationship of Self-Presentation and Impression Management to Charismatic Leadership," *Leadership Quarterly* 13, no. 3 (2002), pp. 217–42.

221. R. Pillai, E. A. Williams, K. B. Lowe, and D. I. Jung, "Personality, Transformational Leadership, Trust, and the 2000 Presidential Vote," *Leadership Quarterly* 14, no. 2 (2003), pp. 161–92.

222. Conger, *The Charismatic Leader.*

223. Bass, *Leadership and Performance beyond Expectations.*

224. Gooty et al., "Leadership, Affect, and Emotions."

225. Bono and Ilies, "Charisma, Positive Emotions, and Mood Contagion."

226. Greer, "The Science of Savoir Faire."

227. Avolio and Bass, *Developing a Full Range of Leadership Potential.*

228. Conger, "Charismatic and Transformational Leadership in Organizations."

229. Bass and Avolio, eds., *Increasing Organizational Effectiveness through Transformational Leadership.*

230. Sosik, Avolio, and Jun, "Beneath the Mask."

231. B. M. Bass, *Bass and Stogdill's Handbook of Leadership*, 3rd ed. (New York: Free Press, 1990).

232. J. E. Bono and T. A. Judge, "Self-Concordance at Work: Toward Understanding the Motivational Effects of Transformational Leaders," *Academy of Management Journal* 46, no. 5 (2003), pp. 554–71.

233. G. J. Curphy, *Hogan Assessment Systems Certification Workshop Training Manuals* (Tulsa, OK: Hogan Assessment Systems, 2003).

234. J. Antonakis and R. J. House, "On Instrumental Leadership: Beyond Transactions and Transformations," presentation delivered at the UNL Gallup Leadership Summit, June 2004, Lincoln, Nebraska.

235. Bass, *Leadership and Performance beyond Expectations.*

236. Avolio and Bass, *Developing a Full Range of Leadership Potential.*

237. Conger and Kanungo, *Charismatic Leadership in Organizations.*

238. Willner, *The Spellbinders.*

239. J. M. Howell and P. Frost, "A Laboratory Study of Charismatic Leadership," *Organizational Behavior and Human Decision Processes* 43 (1988), pp. 243–69.

240. J. M. Howell and B. Shamir, "The Role of Followers in the Charismatic Leadership Process: Relationships and Their Consequences," *Academy of Management Review* 30, no. 1 (2005), pp. 96–112.

241. M. E. Brown and L. K. Trevino, "Leader–Follower Values Congruence: Are Socialized Charismatic Leaders Better Able to Achieve It?" *Journal of Applied Psychology* 94, no. 2 (2009), pp. 478–90.

242. M. G. Ehrhart and K. J. Klein, "Predicting Followers' Preferences for Charismatic Leadership: The Influence of Follower Values and Personality," *Leadership Quarterly* 12, no. 2 (2001), pp. 153–80.

243. R. G. Lord and D. J. Brown, "Leadership, Values, and Subordinate Self-Concepts," *Leadership Quarterly* 12, no. 2 (2001), pp. 133–52.

244. R. Kark, B. Shamir, and G. Chen, "The Two Faces of Transformational Leadership: Empowerment and Dependency," *Journal of Applied Psychology* 88, no. 2 (2003), pp. 246–55.

245. O. Epitopaki and R. Martin, "The Moderating Role of Individual Differences in the Relation between Transformational/Transactional Leadership Perceptions and Organizational Identification," *Leadership Quarterly* 16 (2005), pp. 569–89.

246. S. M. Campbell, A. J. Ward, J. A. Sonnenfeld, and B. R. Agle, "Relational Ties That Bind: Leader–Follower Relationship Dimensions and Charismatic Attribution," *Leadership Quarterly* 19, no. 5 (2008), pp. 556–68.

247. B. M. Galvin, P. Balkundi, and D. D. Waldman, "Spreading the Word: The Role of Surrogates in Charismatic Leadership Processes," *Academy of Management Review* 35, no. 3 (2010), pp. 477–94.

248. F. O. Walumbwa, B. J. Avolio, and W. Zhu, "How Transformational Leadership Weaves Its Influence on Individual Job Performance: The Role of Identification and Efficacy Beliefs," *Personnel Psychology* 61, no. 4 (2008), pp. 793–826.

249. Gooty et al., "Leadership, Affect, and Emotions."

250. Bono and Ilies, "Charisma, Positive Emotions, and Mood Contagion."

251. Greer, "The Science of Savoir Faire."

252. Bono and Judge, "Self-Concordance at Work."

253. Campbell et al., "Relational Ties That Bind."

254. S. Fox and Y. Amichai-Hamburger, "The Power of Emotional Appeals in Promoting Organizational Change Programs," *The Academy of Management Executive* 15, no. 4 (2001), pp. 84–94.

255. J. E. Bono, H. Foldes, G. Vinson, and J. P. Muros, "Workplace Emotions: The Role of Supervision and Leadership," *Journal of Applied Psychology* 92, no. 5 (2007), pp. 1357–67.

256. A. Erez, V. F. Misangyi, D. E. Johnson, M. A. LePine, and K. C. Halverson, "Stirring the Hearts of Followers: Charismatic as the Transferral of Affect," *Journal of Applied Psychology* 93, no. 3 (2008), pp. 602–16.

257. S. K. Johnson, "I Second That Emotion: Effects of Emotional Contagion and Affect at Work on Leader and Follower Outcomes," *Leadership Quarterly* 19, no. 1 (2008), pp. 1–19.

258. G. A. Van Kleef, H. van den Gerg, and M. W. Heerdink, "The Persuasive Power of Emotions: Effects of Emotional Expressionson Attitude Formation and Change," *Journal of Applied Psychology* 100, no. 4 (2015), pp. 1124–42.

259. R. J. House, J. Woycke, and E. M. Fodor, "Charismatic and Noncharismatic Leaders: Differences in Behavior and Effectiveness," in *Charismatic Leadership: The Elusive Factor in Organizational Effectiveness*, eds. J. A. Conger and R. N. Kanungo (San Francisco: Jossey-Bass, 1988), pp. 98–121.

260. Kark et al., "The Two Faces of Transformational Leadership."

261. Dvir et al., "Impact of Transformational Leadership on Follower Development and Performance."

262. Bass and Avolio, eds., *Increasing Organizational Effectiveness through Transformational Leadership.*

263. Bono and Judge, "Self-Concordance at Work."

264. M. Popper and O. Mayseless, "Back to Basics: Applying a Parenting Perspective to Transformational Leadership," *Leadership Quarterly* 14, no. 1 (2003), pp. 41–66.

265. J. M. Beyer, "Training and Promoting Charisma to Change Organizations," *Leadership Quarterly* 10, no. 2 (1999), pp. 307–30.

266. Waldman et al., "Does Leadership Matter?"

267. Bono, "Transformational Leadership,"

268. Tosi et al., "CEO Charisma, Compensation, and Firm Performance."

269. Boal and Bryson, "Charismatic Leadership."

270. Kets de Vries, *The Leadership Mystique.*

271. Bass, *Bass and Stogdill's Handbook of Leadership*, 3rd ed.

272. J. G. Hunt, K. B. Boal, and G. E. Dodge, "The Effects of Visionary and Crisis-Responsive Charisma on Followers: An Experimental Examination of Two Kinds of Charismatic Leadership," *Leadership Quarterly* 10, no. 3 (1999), pp. 423–48.

273. B. S. Pawar and K. K. Eastman, "The Nature and Implications of Contextual Influences on Transformational Leadership: A Conceptual Examination," *Academy of Management Review* 22, no. 1 (1997), pp. 80–109.

274. I. Boga and N. Ensari, "The Role of Transformational Leadership and Organizational Change on Perceived Organizational Success," *The Psychologist-Manager Journal* 12, no. 4 (2009), pp. 235–51.

275. J. C. Pastor, J. R. Meindl, and M. C. Mayo, "A Network Effects Model of Charismatic Attributions," *The Academy of Management Journal* 45, no. 2 (2002), pp. 410–20.

276. J. E. Bono and M. H. Anderson, "The Advice and Influence Networks of Transformational Leaders," *Journal of Applied Psychology* 90, no. 6, pp. 1301–14.

277. Burns, *Leadership.*

278. Dvir et al., "Impact of Transformational Leadership on Follower Development and Performance."

279. Popper and Mayseless, "Back to Basics."

280. R. J. Deluga, "American Presidential Proactivity, Charismatic Leadership and Rated Performance," *Leadership Quarterly* 9, no. 2 (1998), pp. 265–92.

281. Waldman et al., "Does Leadership Matter?"

282. Waldman et al., "Charismatic Leadership at the Strategic Level."

283. A. Fanelli and V. F. Misangyi, "Bringing Out Charisma: CEO Charisma and External Stakeholders," *Academy of Management Review* 31, no. 4 (2006), pp. 1049–61.

284. Bass, "Thoughts and Plans."

285. Curphy, "An Empirical Investigation of Bass' (1985) Theory of Transformational and Transactional Leadership."

286. G. J. Curphy, "The Effects of Transformational and Transactional Leadership on Organizational Climate, Attrition, and Performance," in *Impact of Leadership*, eds. K. E. Clark, M. B. Clark, and D. P. Campbell (Greensboro, NC: Center for Creative Leadership, 1992).

287. J. Adams, H. T. Prince, D. Instone, and R. W. Rice, "West Point: Critical Incidents of Leadership," *Armed Forces and Society* 10 (1984), pp. 597–611.

288. A. S. Labak, "The Study of Charismatic College Teachers," *Dissertation Abstracts International* 34 (1973), p. 1258B.

289. Avolio and Bass, *Developing a Full Range of Leadership Potential.*

290. Bono, "Transformational Leadership."

291. Judge and Piccolo, "Transformational and Transactional Leadership."

292. Keller, "Transformational Leadership, Initiating Structure, and Substitutes for Leadership."

293. Whittington et al., "Transformational Leadership, Goal Difficulty, and Job Design."

294. Nemanich and Keller, "Transformational Leadership in an Acquisition."

295. Bono and Judge, "Self-Concordance at Work."

296. S. J. Shin and J. Zhou, "Transformational Leadership, Conservation, and Creativity: Evidence from Korea," *Academy of Management Journal* 46, no. 6, pp. 703–14.

297. A. H. B. De Hoogh, D. N. Den Hartog, P. L. Koopman, H. Thierry, P. T. Van den Berg, J. G. Van der Weide, and C. P. M. Wilderom, "Leader Motives, Charismatic Leadership, and Subordinates' Work Attitude in the Profit and Voluntary Sector," *Leadership Quarterly* 16 (2005), pp. 17–38.

298. Bass, *Leadership and Performance beyond Expectations.*

299. Bass, "Does the Transactional-Transformational Leadership Paradigm Transcend Organizational and National Boundaries?"

300. Bass, *Bass and Stogdill's Handbook of Leadership*, 3rd ed.

301. Bass, *Leadership and Performance beyond Expectations.*

302. Avolio and Bass, "Transformational Leadership, Charisma, and Beyond."

303. Bass and Avolio, eds., *Increasing Organizational Effectiveness through Transformational Leadership.*

304. Bass, "Does the Transactional-Transformational Leadership Paradigm Transcend Organizational and National Boundaries?"

305. Sosik et al., "Beneath the Mask."

306. Antonakis and House, "On Instrumental Leadership."

307. Avolio and Bass, *Developing a Full Range of Leadership Potential.*

308. Avolio and Bass, "Transformational Leadership, Charisma, and Beyond."

309. Bass, "Does the Transactional-Transformational Leadership Paradigm Transcend Organizational and National Boundaries?"

310. Bass, "Does the Transactional-Transformational Leadership Paradigm Transcend Organizational and National Boundaries?"

311. A. E. Rafferty and M. A. Griffen, "Dimensions of Transformational Leadership: Conceptual and Empirical Extensions," *Leadership Quarterly* 15, no. 3 (2004), pp. 329–54.

312. J. Antonakis, B. J. Avolio, and N. Sivasubramainiam, "Context and Leadership: An Examination of the Nine Factor Full Range Leadership Theory Using the Multifactor Leadership Questionnaire," *Leadership Quarterly* 15, no. 2 (2003), pp. 261–95.

313. B. M. Bass and B. J. Avolio, *The Multifactor Leadership Questionnaire Report* (Palo Alto, CA: Mind Garden, 1996).

314. J. Rowold and K. Heinitz, "Transformational and Charismatic Leadership: Assessing the Convergent, Divergent, and Criterion Validity of the MLQ and CKS," *Leadership Quarterly* 18, no. 1 (2007), pp. 121–33.

315. R. F. Piccolo, J. E. Bono, T. A. Judge, E. E. Duehr, and J. P. Muros, "Which Leader Behaviors Matter Most: Comparing Dimensions of the LBDQ and MLQ," paper presented in J. P. Campbell and M. J. Benson (chairs), *Predicting Leadership: The Good, The Bad, the Different, and the Unnecessary*, Annual Meeting of Society of Industrial and Organizational Psychology, New York, April 2007.

316. Bass, "Two Decades of Research and Development in Transformational Leadership."

317. Avolio and Bass, *Developing a Full Range of Leadership Potential.*

318. Bass, "Thoughts and Plans."

319. Bono, "Transformational Leadership."

320. Sosik et al., "Beneath the Mask."

321. Avolio and Bass, *Developing a Full Range of Leadership Potential.*

322. Bass, "Two Decades of Research and Development in Transformational Leadership."

323. Avolio and Bass, *Developing a Full Range of Leadership Potential.*

324. Bono, "Transformational Leadership."

325. Bass, Avolio, Jung, and Berson, "Predicting Unit Performance by Assessing Transformational and Transactional Leadership."

326. Towler, "Effects of Charismatic Influence Training on Attitudes, Behavior, and Performance."

327. Bass and Avolio, *The Multifactor Leadership Questionnaire Report.*

328. M. Frese, S. Beimel, and S. Schoenborn, "Action Training for Charismatic Leadership: Two Evaluations of Studies of a Commercial Training Module on Inspirational Communication of a Vision," *Personnel Psychology* 56, no. 3 (2003), pp. 671-97.

329. J. Barling, C. Loughlin, and E. K. Kelloway, "Development and Test of a Model Linking Safety-Specific Transformational Leadership and Occupational Safety," *Journal of Applied Psychology* 87, no. 3 (2002), pp. 488-96.

330. A. Zacharatos, J. Barling, and E. K. Kelloway, "Development and Effects of Transformational Leadership in Adolescents," *Leadership Quarterly* 11, no. 2 (2000), pp. 211-26.

331. Ross and Offermann, "Transformational Leaders."

332. Antonakis and House, "On Instrumental Leadership."

333. House et al., "Charismatic and Noncharismatic Leaders."

334. T. A. Judge and J. E. Bono, "Five-Factor Model of Personality and Transformational Leadership," *Journal of Applied Psychology* 85, no. 5 (2000), pp. 751-65.

335. R. T. Hogan, G. J. Curphy, and J. Hogan, "What Do We Know about Personality: Leadership and Effectiveness?" *American Psychologist* 49 (1994), pp. 493-504.

336. G. J. Curphy, "New Directions in Personality," in *Personality and Organizational Behavior*, R. T. Hogan (chair). Symposium presented at the 104th Annual Meeting of the American Psychological Association, Toronto, Canada, 1996.

337. D. L. Nilsen, "Using Self and Observers' Rating of Personality to Predict Leadership Performance," unpublished doctoral dissertation, University of Minnesota, Minneapolis, 1995.

338. R. J. House, W. D. Spangler, and J. Woycke, "Personality and Charisma in the U.S. Presidency: A Psychological Theory of Leadership Effectiveness," *Administrative Science Quarterly* 36 (1991), pp. 364-96.

339. Nilsen, "Using Self and Observers' Rating of Personality to Predict Leadership Performance."

340. Hooijberg and Choi, "From Selling Peanuts and Beer in Yankee Stadium to Creating a Theory of Transformational Leadership."

CHAPTER 17

The Dark Side of Leadership

Introduction

Back in May 2005, one of the authors of this book was on a flight from Columbus, Ohio, to Minneapolis, Minnesota. Northwest Airlines Flight 1495 had a heavy passenger load and a crew of two pilots and three flight attendants. The two-hour flight seemed routine, but upon landing the author noticed the runway was lined with ambulances and fire trucks. The plane taxied off the runway and stopped some distance short of the gate. After waiting five minutes, one of the pilots got on the intercom and announced, "The plane has experienced a systems malfunction." The pilots and flight attendants did not say anything more, and about five minutes later the DC-9 began moving again.

The DC-9 had been traveling about 10 seconds when suddenly a loud boom filled the cabin and the plane came to an abrupt stop. Passengers were thrown violently forward in their seats, but luckily everyone was still wearing their seatbelts. The author and other passengers had assumed the plane was taxiing to its gate, but a look out the window showed that the DC-9 had collided with another aircraft. Apparently the pilots of the DC-9 had left the engines running and the plane had experienced a hydraulics failure, which caused it to lose all steering and braking capabilities. The DC-9 collided with a Northwest Airlines A-319 that was being pushed back from its gate, and the wing of the A-319 peeled back the first 10 feet of the roof of the DC-9 during the collision.

After the plane had stopped, the lead flight attendant unbuckled her seat belt and started running up and down the aisle yelling, "Assume the crash position! Assume the crash position!" The passengers were wondering how putting our heads between our knees was going to help when the plane had already come to a stop, but we dutifully complied with the flight attendant's request. After two to three minutes of running up and down the aisle and barking orders, the lead flight attendant hyperventilated and collapsed in a heap behind the first-class bulkhead. The two remaining flight attendants then got out of their seats to check on the lead flight attendant.

Most of the passengers started easing out of the crash position and began looking to the other flight attendants for guidance on what to do, but none was forthcoming. The author then got up and went to the cockpit door because he could tell that the wing of the A-319 had come in through the cockpit, and he was concerned about the pilots. He asked the pilots whether they needed any help, and one of them meekly replied that they needed medical attention. The author tried to open the door, but the door reinforcements added after 9/11 made it impossible to get in.

As the author was tugging on the cockpit door handle, he could overhear the two flight attendants discussing whether they should deplane the aircraft. One attendant asked, "Should we keep them on or get them off?" The other attendant replied, "I don't know, what do you think?" This conversation continued for three to four minutes, with the lead flight attendant still whispering in the background, "Assume the crash position.

Assume the crash position." During this time, one of the flight attendants came up to the cockpit door and asked the pilots what to do, but there was no response. She then went back to attend to the lead flight attendant.

At this time, the author noticed that jet fuel from the wing of the A-319 had leaked into the cockpit of the DC-9 and had seeped into the first-class cabin. He realized that his shoes and pants were covered in jet fuel and an errant spark would light up two planes full of people. He then turned and yelled at the flight attendants, "I am standing in jet fuel. Get everyone off the plane. NOW!" The two coherent flight attendants got up and proceeded to hustle everyone off the plane using the DC-9's rear exit. Being in the front of the cabin at the cockpit door, the author was the last in line to get off the plane. You can imagine how happy he was to see passengers at the rear of the aircraft taking the time to open the overhead bins and retrieve their luggage while he was standing in jet fuel. The flight attendants did not intervene more than giving some mild reminders to passengers to just exit the aircraft and leave the luggage behind.

All the passengers from both aircraft escaped with only a few minor injuries. The flight attendants were okay; the two DC-9 pilots needed some medical attention but were released the next day. But this incident provides several vivid examples of failures in leadership. The pilots failed to warn the passengers of the impending collision and did not use the thrust reversers to stop the plane. The lead flight attendant's instructions to assume the crash position after the plane was at a complete stop and then collapsing later did not instill confidence. The other two flight attendants needed to step into a leadership role and take over the situation but were unable to make a decision or tell passengers what to do. Northwest Airlines failed by having standard operating procedures (SOPs) that instructed pilots to leave the engines running in the event of an aircraft hydraulics failure. Instead, the SOP should have instructed pilots to shut down the engines and have the plane towed to a gate. The airline also failed when the author called in several times offering to describe the incident in order to improve training and was ignored. Later he learned that the airline formally rewarded the two pilots and three flight attendants for their outstanding actions during the emergency.

Although the telling of this story may appear a bit self-serving, in our minds leadership is the most important topic in the world today. Leadership determines whether countries are democracies or dictatorships or are at peace or war, whether businesses are good investments or kleptocracies, whether teams win or lose, whether health care and education reforms fail or succeed, and whether rural communities thrive or merely survive. Leadership plays a role in determining where you live, what schools you get into, what laws and rules you must obey, what occupations you enter, whether you have a successful career, and how your children are raised. It plays such a pervasive part in our lives that it is easy to overlook its impact on our day-to-day behaviors. Because of the profound ways in which leadership affects us all, it would be nice if the people in positions of authority were actually good at it. But research shows that most people are woefully inadequate when it comes to influencing an organized group toward accomplishing its goals. The purpose of this chapter is to describe the most common reasons why people fail in leadership positions and the steps we can take to improve our odds of success.

It is fitting that this chapter appears at the end of the book because it draws on much of the leader, follower, and situation material described in earlier chapters. Up until now the two things we know for certain are that there is no universally accepted definition of leadership and there are many different ways to lead. These two issues are big reasons why this book looks at leadership from so many perspectives, as the research on what it takes to be an effective leader simply does not cohere. Although there are disagreements among scientists and practitioners on what it takes to be a good leader, there is a high level of agreement on what constitutes bad leadership. Here the research is very consistent and aligns with many of our practical experiences, and the purpose of this chapter is to review the research pertaining to and some practical steps for avoiding destructive leadership, managerial incompetence, and managerial derailment. **Destructive leadership** is associated with individuals who are effective at engaging followers, building teams, and getting results through others, but who obtain results that are morally or ethically challenged or that undermine organizational or community success (see **Highlight 17.1**). An example here might be Adolf Hitler. Hitler was clearly able to rally an entire country around a common cause and conquered a number of countries, yet the end result was a continent in ruins and the death of over 20 million people. Unlike destructive leadership, **managerial incompetence** concerns a person's *inability* to engage followers, build teams, or get results through others. It turns out that a majority of people in positions of authority can have difficulties in one, two, or all three of these areas. **Managerial derailment** describes the common *reasons* why people in positions of authority have difficulty engaging followers, building teams, or getting results through others. Knowing the 10 root causes of managerial derailment and what to do to avoid these pitfalls can help you be more effective as a leader.

> *If you put on a blindfold and threw a dart at a map of the world, then there is a 70 percent chance that whatever country the dart lands on is run by some form of dictatorship.*
>
> **RT Hogan, Hogan Assessment Systems**

Who Shall Rule?

HIGHLIGHT 17.1

Destructive leadership can be defined as the ability to engage followers and build teams whose results do not serve the common good. Destructive leadership is prevalent in both dictatorships and democracies, but the checks and balances of the latter keep the destructive tendencies of elected leaders in check. Both dictators and those elected play the same game, which is to get into power, stay in power, and control resources. Autocrats are better at playing this game, as they tend to stay in power much longer than their democratically elected counterparts. Dictators only need to reward a small band of loyal followers who can manipulate the media, suppress the opposition, and control the populace, whereas democratically elected leaders can lose their jobs if they neglect their voters.

The destructive leadership tendencies of democratically led countries are readily evident whenever one political party controls all of the key institutions. Venezuela, Russia, and Turkey are all democracies, yet the Maduro, Putin, and Erdogan governments have changed the political, legal, criminal justice, media, and economic institutions in order to maintain power and control funds. These governments are associated with the high levels of political favoritism, corruption, crime, and media manipulation often found in dictatorships.

It is important to realize that the vast majority of countries around the world are dictatorships or autocracies. The spoils of the many are enjoyed by a few in China, North Korea, Azerbaijan, Uzbekistan, Iran, Saudi Arabia, Syria, Zimbabwe, Sudan, South Sudan, and many other countries. Some of these countries maintain the façade of democracy, but those in charge determine whether there will be elections, the slate of opposition candidates, how they can campaign, and the percentage of votes the incumbent will receive.

What are the worst countries when it comes to destructive leadership? What do those in power do to remain in power? Who benefits from these activities? Who suffers as a result? What has the Trump administration done to mainstream media, the courts, the EPA, NATO, and long-standing trade agreements to remain in power? Are these actions signs of "America First" or of destructive leadership?

Sources: M. Moynihan, "It's Good to Be Boss," *The Wall Street Journal*, September 24–25, 2011, p. C10; B. Bueno de Mesquita and A. Smith, *The Dictator's Handbook: Why Bad Behavior Is Almost Always Good Politics* (New York: PubliAffairs, 2011); R. Hogan, *How to Define Destructive Leadership* (Tulsa, OK: Hogan Assessment Systems, 2012); and "Conquering Chaos: Fixing Fragile Nations," *The Economist*, January 7, 2017, pp. 46–48.

Destructive Leadership

One way to evaluate leadership effectiveness is to look at a person's ability to engage and develop followers, build teams, and get results through others. Effective leaders are those who can meet all three criteria, whereas ineffective leaders have trouble engaging staff, building teams, or getting results. As described in **Chapter 16**, James MacGregor Burns has maintained that truly effective leaders need to meet an additional criterion, which is to raise the standard of human conduct and improve the lives of everyone they touch.[1] In other words, effective leaders must make the organizations or societies they belong to better places to work or live. Given these three criteria, we can see that there is a subset of leaders who are good at painting a compelling picture of the future and getting followers to drive the organizational or societal changes needed to make their vision become reality, yet the end result may be morally or ethically reprehensible or work against the common good. Some of these leaders are among the most infamous in history and include Alexander the Great, Genghis Khan, Attila the Hun, Ivan the Terrible, Vlad the Impaler, Napoleon Bonaparte, Adolf Hitler, Joseph Stalin, Mao Zedong, Pol Pot, Idi Amin, Saddam Hussein, Kim Jong-Un, Robert Mugabe, Fidel Castro, and Osama bin Laden. No one could argue about whether these individuals had a major impact on their countries and societies, but their collective influence killed hundreds of millions of innocent people. And such leaders who are still alive are interested only in enriching themselves and staying in power and often lead incredibly repressed societies or followers who are bent on delivering death and destruction (see **Profiles in Leadership 17.1** and **17.2.**)

Nicolás Maduro

PROFILES IN LEADERSHIP 17.1

Nicolás Maduro grew up in Caracas, Venezuela, and was working as a bus driver when he helped to found the Fifth Republic movement, an activist group dedicated to social justice and wealth redistribution. He was introduced to Hugo Chávez in the early 1990s, was elected to the National Assembly in 2000, and became speaker in 2005. He was asked to become the foreign minister of Venezuela by Chávez in 2006, a role he held until being named the vice president of the country in 2012. He became president of Venezuela with the death of Chávez in 2013 and has ruled by decree ever since.

Despite having proven oil reserves greater than Saudi Arabia, government mismanagement has caused Venezuela to endure soaring poverty and crime rates; regular food, medicine, and power shortages; unprecedented levels of child malnutrition and starvation; shortening life expectan-

cies; annual inflation rates of more than 2,000 percent; and ever-growing street protests. Although it controls the National Assembly, the opposition has been hamstrung by a series of rulings by Venezuela's Supreme Court and election authorities, both of which are filled by Chávez and Maduro cronies. Maduro has also shut down all independent press outlets and controls the army, which with the national police and armed bands of local supporters keep the local populace in check. Although four out of five Venezuelans feel Maduro is not doing a good job and would likely vote him out of office, it is uncertain if an election will happen any time soon. Maduro worked with the Supreme Court to reformulate the National Assembly with unelected supporters so that the constitution is changed to allow him to become president for life.

Because the economic and political prospects in Venezuela have become so dire, citizens are leaving the country at an unprecedented rate.

What would you do if you were a citizen of Venezuela? What role can or should other governments play to alleviate the situation in Venezuela?

Sources: "Hugo Chavez's Rotten Legacy," *The Economist*, March 9, 2013, p. 10; R. Carroll, *Comandante: Hugo Chavez's Venezuela* (New York: Penguin Press, 2013); "Now for the Reckoning," *The Economist*, March 9, 2013, pp. 23–26; CNN Library, "Nicolás Maduro Fast Facts," www.cnn.com/2013/04/26/world/americas/nicolas-maduro-fast-facts; S. G. Caracas, "Why Is Nicolás Maduro Still in Power?" *The Economist*, May 11, 2017, www.economist.com/blogs/economist-explains/2017/05/economist-explains-9; "Venezuela: President Maduro Granted Power to Govern by Decree," BBC News, March 16, 2015, www.bbc.com/news/world-latin-america-31899510; and J. Rothwell, H. Alexander, and A. Schaverien, "Venezuela Protests: 200,000 March Against Maduro as Riots and Looting Spread across the Country," *Telegraph*, May 21, 2017, www.telegraph.co.uk/news/2017/05/21/venezuela-protests-200000-march-against-president-maduro-riots.

David Koresh: Destructive Religious Leader

PROFILES IN LEADERSHIP 17.2

In April 1993, approximately 85 people died at a religious compound outside of Waco, Texas. Many of them died in the fire that consumed the compound, but a single bullet to the head had killed others. Twenty-five of the deceased were children. How did this happen? The story of David Koresh is a classic example of what can go wrong when bad leaders take charge.

By all accounts, David Koresh (born as Vernon Wayne Howell) had a miserable childhood. His mother was only 14 when David was born and went through two divorces before she was 20. David was abused by his uncle while growing up, and his mother decided to attend the local Seventh Day Adventist church when he turned nine. Apparently David loved church and religion and was spellbound during sermons. He memorized large portions of scripture and could effortlessly recite endless passages. However, in his later teen years, Koresh began to question why the church believed in modern-day prophets yet claimed that none had walked the earth for a long time. He also began to question the biblical interpretations of elders and eventually left the Seventh Day Adventists to join the Branch Davidians. The Branch Davidians believed not only in modern-day prophets but also in Armageddon. At the age of 24, Koresh took over the Branch Davidians by having intimate relations with their 67-year-old leader. He also secretly married a 14-year-old member of the sect and was subsequently kicked out of the church. He and many of the Branch Davidians left to start their own chapter outside Waco, Texas.

While starting his own church, Koresh became increasingly temperamental and violent. He made fellow members watch violent war movies and listen to his rock sessions, and he put them through long fasts and strange diets. At first, Koresh abided by his own rules, but eventually he claimed that God had told him it was all right for him, and only him, to violate these rules. Koresh took a number of wives, all of whom were under age 15. He eventually told the males that all the females in the church were to become his wives and their marriages were no longer valid. This bizarre behavior continued until agents from the Alcohol, Tobacco, and Firearms Bureau came to the compound to investigate allegations of firearms violations and child abuse in early 1993. Rather than allowing the agents to investigate, Koresh burned down the compound, killed many of his followers, and committed suicide.

Source: K. R. Samples, E. M. deCastro, R. Abanes, and R. J. Lyle, *Prophets of the Apocalypse: David Koresh and the Other American Messiahs* (Grand Rapids, MI: Baker Books, 1994).

Destructive leadership is not limited to government or political leaders—it occurs in virtually all other settings. The recession of 2007–2009 can be partially attributed to a number of destructive leaders in the financial services industry. Many greedy bank and insurance executives did a good job of building teams and generating profits, but the profits were gained by cooking the books, selling financial products that were doomed to fail, or funding subprime mortgages that owners could ill afford. The problem was so widespread in the financial services industry that it almost caused the collapse of the entire global economy. Wells Fargo's reputation has been negatively impacted as a result of overly zealous sales policies, and leaders at companies like Insys Therapeutics and Purdue Pharma are considered to be responsible for the large-scale opioid addition and overdose deaths of 400,000 U.S. citizens.[2, 3, 4, 5]

> *I was in the 1991 Gulf War, and I had less stress in the 1991 Gulf War than working for Wells Fargo.*
>
> **Former Wells Fargo employee**

Similarly, the massacres at My Lai, Serbia, Bosnia, Croatia, Rwanda, Darfur, and Syria show that destructive leadership also occurs in military settings. In the spirit of seeking revenge or ethnic cleansing, military commanders will rally the troops to kill everyone in particular villages and towns—even those who are not military combatants. Religious leaders can also exhibit destructive leadership. Jim Jones and David Koresh are two examples of highly charismatic religious leaders who developed cultlike followings and led their adherents to kill themselves (see **Profiles in Leadership 17.2**). And destructive leadership can occur at a variety of levels in organizations. Sometimes first-line supervisors, mid-level managers, and executives who disagree with company policies and strategies will motivate their followers to pursue courses of action that are not aligned with organizational interests. These actions and their subsequent results often lead to poor customer service, duplicative efforts, high levels of team conflict, and ultimately suboptimal financial performance. Although these leaders and followers may believe they are doing the right thing, their actions harm their organizations.[6, 7, 8, 9, 10, 11] (See **Profiles in Leadership 17.3**.)

Carrie Tolstedt: Whatever It Takes

PROFILES IN LEADERSHIP 17.3

At one time, Wells Fargo was the darling of the banking industry. Through a series of savvy mergers and acquisitions, the bank moved from a small regional player to one of the largest banks in the United States. It also was a huge proponent of cross-selling. Because banks make fees on different customer products, such as checking and savings accounts, credit and debit cards, personal loans, and home mortgages, Wells Fargo implemented a scheme to sell customers as many products as possible. It did not matter if the customers needed the products, employees just needed to sell them the products they did not already have. Bankers and tellers looked up accounts to see which products they should cross-sell when customers stopped by to make deposits or inquire about car loans.

The chief architect behind the cross-selling program was Carrie Tolstedt. The daughter of a banker and a 27-year Wells Fargo veteran, Tolstedt moved quickly through the ranks to become the head of Commercial banking. All the bank offices and branches reported to Tolstedt, and under her watch, tellers, bankers, and branches had very specific cross-selling goals and results were tracked up to four times a day. Sales goals were impossible to meet, and employees were routinely harassed, intimidated, and humiliated into breaking the law in order to meet quotas. Those who complained were threatened with being transferred to branches where someone had been killed or told to walk laps around the block in the hot sun. For a number of years, employees were far more likely to get fired for missing sales quotas than for doing anything illegal. Complainers were summarily fired and often blacklisted, which prevented them from ever working at other financial services companies.

To achieve their goals, employees opened over 2.1 million fake checking, credit card, and debit card accounts, some of which negatively impacted customers' credit scores and caused them to pay unwanted fees or lose homes and cars. Problems with the cross-selling program first started to crop up as early as 2004, but Tolstedt and other executives ignored the signals and passed off any illegal activities to a few "bad apples." When problems started becoming public, Tolstedt told the Board that 230 employees had engaged in illegal activities, when the real number was well over 5,000.

Since the Wells Fargo scam first came to light, shareholder returns at Citigroup, JP Morgan Chase, and Citigroup have improved about 100 percent, yet have only grown 6 percent at Wells Fargo. The bank also had to pay millions of dollars in fines and saw its reputation in ruins. The government and bank have clawed back a large chunk of Tolstedt's $125 million retirement package, but to this day, she argues that she did nothing wrong.

Would you classify Tolstedt as an effective leader or as a destructive one? Why?

Sources: R. Ensign and B. Eisen, "Wells Fargo Ex-CEO Banned for Life," *The Wall Street Journal*, January 24, 2020, pp. A1–2; J. Wieczer, "How Wells Fargo's Carrie Tolstedt Went from Fortune Most Powerful Woman to Villain," *Fortune*, April 10, 2017, https://fortune.com/2017/04/10/wells-fargo-carrie-tolstedt-clawback-net-worth-fortune-mpw; B. Levin, "6 Ways Wells Fargo Made Its Employees' Lives a Living Hell," *Vanity Fair*, April 10, 2017, www.vanityfair.com/news/2017/04/wells-fargo-john-stumpf-carrie-tolstedt; W. Frost, "Wells Fargo Report Gives Inside Look at the Culture that Crushed the Bank's Reputation," *CNBC*, April 10, 2017, www.cnbc.com/2017/04/10/wells-fargo-report-shows-culture-that-crushed-banks-reputation.html; and M. Hiltzik, "That Wells Fargo Accounts Scandal Was Even Worse Than You Can Imagine," *Los Angeles Times*, January 27, 2020, www.latimes.com/business/story/2020-01-27/wells-fargo-scandal.

> *Endangering human life for profit should be a crime.*
>
> **Suzy Kassem, author**

Barbara Kellerman correctly points out that the United States has an overly optimistic outlook on leadership. Most of the leadership books written for U.S. consumption have an overly positive tone and generally maintain that leadership is relatively easy to learn.[12] Similarly, many leadership training programs delivered in the United States are built on the erroneous assumption that leaders are inherently good and effective; destructive or incompetent leadership is the exception rather than the rule.[13, 14, 15] Yet Jared Diamond's book *Guns, Germs, and Steel: The Fates of Human Societies* shows that most societies from the earliest times to today have been kleptocracies.[16] Some are legitimized kleptocracies, where kings, queens, and elected officials dictate laws or write rules to increase their power or personal wealth. Dictators who emerge after violent overthrows of previous governments seem to benefit greatly from their change in status but rarely if ever improve the lot of commoners (see **Profiles in Leadership 17.1**). Thus, destructive leadership occurs when people in positions of authority use their team-building skills to achieve greedy, selfish, or immoral results. And as history mournfully suggests, evil, corrupt, greedy, and selfish leaders will likely be around for a long time.

> *167,000,000 people died of unnatural causes in the 20th century. Invading armies killed 30,000,000 people; the remainder were killed by their own governments. Leadership matters.*
>
> **Robert Hogan, American psychologist**

A final note about destructive leadership is worth discussing further: What may be considered destructive versus good leadership may be in the eye of the beholder. Although most people believe Kim Jong-Un and Alexander Lukashenko are egomaniacal despots, those loyal to these two individuals may see them as great leaders. And in reality those who are loyal to destructive leaders generally are rewarded for their efforts.

Sometimes this reward comes in the form of a bullet (Joseph Stalin, Mao Zedong, and Idi Amin did not hesitate to kill loyal followers whom they perceived as rivals), but more often than not loyal followers are richly rewarded with titles, wealth, and power. The same perspective could be applied to Osama bin Laden. Most people from Western cultures saw Osama bin Laden as a threat, but his followers saw his vision as a path to heaven. This concept of good versus destructive leadership could also be applied to U.S. President Donald Trump. Many Republicans elected Trump as a repudiation of Barack Obama's policies and to return the United States back to what they perceived as its lost greatness, whereas members of the Democratic Party think the country is heading in the wrong direction now and is destined to fail under Trump's leadership. Sometimes political, religious, or business leaders advocate what many people believe are the wrong things, but these turn out to be the right things over time. Lee Iacocca's push for a government bailout of Chrysler, Martin Luther King Jr.'s vision for civil rights, and Bill Clinton's intervention in the Yugoslavian civil war are all examples of leaders accused of doing bad things at the time but who in retrospect improved the organizations and societies they led. Thus, what constitutes destructive leadership might not be quite so clear-cut as we might think (see **Profiles in Leadership 17.3**).

Managerial Incompetence

For every person who's a manager and wants to know how to manage people, there are 10 people who are being managed and would like to figure out how to make it stop.

Scott Adams, creator of "Dilbert"

Whereas destructive leadership is associated with individuals who engage followers and build teams to achieve corrupt, selfish, or evil ends, incompetent management is associated with individuals who cannot engage followers, build teams, or get results through others. In other words, incompetent managers have difficulties building loyal followings or getting anything done. Research shows that there may be more incompetent than competent managers; the **base rate of managerial incompetence** may be 50 to 75 percent.[17, 18, 19, 20, 21, 22, 23] You might think the base rate of managerial incompetence could not be this high—too many countries, businesses, government and other nonprofit organizations, or volunteer organizations would simply fail if riddled with such a high percentage of incompetent leaders. But consider the following facts:

- Most countries are run by some form of dictatorship. Most ordinary citizens in Saudi Arabia, Syria, Belarus, Bahrain, Sudan, Jordan, Chad, Iran, Turkmenistan, China, and Russia do not have much say over who is in charge, what laws are made, and so on. Although the leaders of these countries have a following among a minority of people, the majority has little input into who leads them and often realizes few benefits.

- Many leaders of democratic countries are perceived as being unable to build teams or get results. U.S. president George W. Bush saw his approval ratings drop from 85 to 30 percent over his eight-year term, and Barack Obama experienced a 25-point approval rating drop during his first 18 months in office. With only a 43 percent approval rating, Donald Trump's ratings have been among the lowest for any U.S. president, and the U.S. Congress has less than a 15 percent approval rating among likely voters.[24, 25, 26, 27, 28]

- CEO departures averaged 114 per month in 2019. Some departures were due to retirements or taking jobs with other companies, but many were the result of unacceptable behavior and poor performance. High visibility examples include John Schnatter from Papa Johns, Adam Neumann from WeWork, Harvey Weinstein from the Weinstein Company, and leaders of Nike, Barnes & Noble, Texas Instruments, Amnesty International, and Boeing. If these trends continue, then approximately 50 percent of CEOs will be replaced every three years.[29, 30, 31, 32, 33, 34]

- In employee satisfaction surveys, more than 75 percent of all respondents indicate that the most stressful part of their job is their immediate boss.[35, 36] This finding holds true across countries and industries.

- Two-thirds of all U.S. workers are either not fully engaged or actively disengaged at work, and at any one time 51 percent are looking for other jobs.[37]

- Sixty percent of the participants in a high-performing division of a *Fortune* 100 company indicated that that their organization was successful despite their leaders. Thirty-five percent of the participants in a broader research study of high-performing companies said the same thing. Clueless bosses in high-performing companies attribute success to their own efforts, but it may be highly engaged employees working in high-performing teams that make the difference between winning and losing.[38]

- A study published in *Harvard Business Review* reported that only 30 percent of businesses had "healthy and respectful" work climates. A majority of organizations had dysfunctional and unhealthy work climates.[39, 40]

- At any one time the 800,000 employees of the U.S. Postal Service have filed 150,000 grievances against their supervisors.[41]

- Research shows that 50 to 90 percent of all new businesses fail within five years. This finding seems consistent across all business types and countries. Most of the failures can be attributed to managerial incompetence.[42, 43, 44, 45]

- BP, the energy company responsible for the Gulf of Mexico environmental disaster in 2010, has been cited 760 times and paid fines of $373 million for safety and environmental violations since 2005. The root causes of most major industrial accidents and incidents, such as the Bhopal, India, chemical spill, the Exxon Valdez disaster, the Texas City refinery explosion, or the wildfires of California and Australia can be traced back to poor management oversight or management cost-cutting initiatives.[46, 47, 48, 49]

- Research shows that 67 percent of all IT projects fail to deliver promised functionality, are not delivered on time, or do not stay within budgeted costs. This IT project failure rate has not improved much over the past 10 years, and U.S. businesses are now spending over $55 billion annually on poorly scoped or executed IT projects.[50]

- Over 70 percent of all mergers and acquisitions fail to yield projected improvements in profitability and synergies. Examples might include HP's acquisition of Autonomy or the Sears merger with Kmart.[51]

- A majority of large-scale organizational change initiatives fail to achieve their intended results.[52]

- Toxic, destructive, or abusive supervision is prevalent in both the public and private sectors. A U.S. Army study indicated that only 27 percent of officers could accurately identify ineffective leaders and 25 percent of the officer corps were either abusive to others or careerists out only for themselves. Another study indicated that over 60 percent of workers reported to an abusive or destructive leader sometime during their career.[53, 54, 55, 56]

- The U.S. Navy had four major boat incidents in the Pacific in 2017, including three collisions with other boats and a guided ship cruiser running aground in Tokyo Bay. Despite pleading for assistance from the captain, the U.S. Navy failed to adequately manage the coronavirus outbreak on the aircraft carrier the USS Teddy Roosevelt in March–April of 2020.

- In 2012, three Italian researchers were awarded the Ig Nobel Prize for demonstrating mathematically that organizations would become more efficient if they promoted people randomly. If the base rate of managerial incompetence ranges between 50 and 75 percent, then random promotions would be the best alternative.[57]

Seventy-five percent of employees would take a pay cut if it meant getting their boss replaced.

Robert Hogan, American psychologist

As unflattering as these statistics are, these examples may seem out of the realm of most readers. So let's make the concept of managerial incompetence a little more personal. One easy way to determine the level of incompetence among people in positions of authority is to do the **Dr. Gordy test**.[58, 59, 60, 61] To use this test, begin by counting the total number of people you have been led by or worked for in the past. This total should include past bosses, athletic coaches, team captains, choir directors, camp directors, and so on. In other words, it should include anyone with whom you played a formal followership role. Once you have arrived at a total, count the number of people in this group for whom you would willingly play, sing, or work again. In other words, how many of these people would you play a followership role for again if given a choice? Now calculate the percentage of competent leaders in the total group of leaders. When health care, education, business, military, and community leaders are asked the same question, most need only the digits on a single hand to count the number of leaders for whom they would willingly work again. The percentage of competent leaders people would willingly work for again varies dramatically across individuals, but the percentage seems to hover between 25 and 40 percent.[62, 63, 64, 65, 66] This means that most people would not work for a majority of leaders they have been exposed to.

Most of those taking the Dr. Gordy test do not view it as a popularity contest. Those who pass the test are often described as tough but fair leaders who inspired their followers and pushed their teams to achieve more than anyone thought possible. A critical follow-on question to the Dr. Gordy test is whether readers would make their followers' short lists. In other words, would you be in the 25 to 40 percent of leaders who pass the Dr. Gordy test or be with the majority of leaders who fail the exam? Most people fail the test, which implies that being an effective leader is no easy task. Like the Seth MacFarlane movie *A Million Ways to Die in the West*, there are a million ways for leaders to fail. The common reasons why leaders are unable to engage employees, build teams, or achieve results that beat the competition are described in more detail later in this chapter. Knowing what people do that causes them to be perceived as incompetent managers can help readers avoid making the same mistakes. (See **Highlights 17.2** and **17.3**.)

Incompetence in Government: Your Tax Dollars Hard at Work

HIGHLIGHT 17.2

Anyone keeping up with local, national, or global affairs will regularly see stories about managerial incompetence. This and **Highlight 17.3** provide examples of just a few incidents of managerial incompetence in the public and private sectors.

- *Military Officers Gone Wild:* Over the past ten years, a number of senior officers in the U.S. military have been relieved of command or demoted due to sexual harassment, extramarital affairs, using counterfeit chips at a casino, bribery, staying in $750/night hotel rooms with their spouses, drinking on the job, firing five aides in less than six months, or exhibiting a "management by blowtorch" leadership philosophy toward their staffs.

- *I Only Smoke Crack When I Am in a Drunken Stupor:* In a quote that instilled nothing but confidence in the intelligence of politicians, Rob Ford, the former mayor of Toronto, used this excuse when he finally admitted to using controlled substances while holding an elected position.

- *A Two-Year-Old Boy Trapped in a Man's Body:* Kevin Rudd, a former prime minister of Australia, suffered from the disease of always having to be the smartest man in the room and prone to wanting everything—NOW. When others did not recognize his brilliance or jump immediately to satisfy his needs, he would complain loudly while storming out of meetings.

- *PBS Comes to Washington:* Former U.S. representative Aaron Schock had his office in Washington, D.C., decorated like a set from *Downton Abbey* and appeared bare chested on the cover of *Men's Health.* He resigned shortly after an investigative journalist reported that Schock had also falsely claimed expenses for private air charters, professional football tickets, and over 90,000 miles of travel in his car.

- *A Far from Tranquil National Park:* Eighteen staff members at Yosemite National Park felt compelled to formally complain about rampant bullying, belittling, gender bias, favoritism, and repeated questioning of expertise by the park's senior leaders. The toxic work environment created by these leaders significantly eroded staff morale and performance.

- *The Avenging Attorney General:* Kathleen Kane was an up-and-coming star in the Democratic Party when she became the attorney general of Pennsylvania. Ruling by intimidation and constantly on the lookout for any perceived slights, she received a four-year jail sentence for obstruction of justice and perjury for leaking sealed grand jury records in an attempt to discredit a critic.

- *The Satanic Maintenance Man:* A maintenance manager for a public school district ruled by intimidation, pitted staff against each other, sexually harassed his female employees, and terrorized enemies by vandalizing and planting bombs at their homes. Despite two decades of this dysfunctional behavior, school superintendents kept him in the role as he got things done and saved the school district money.

- *A Totally Corrupt System:* As of mid-2019, 430 top politicians had been charged or convicted in the Operation Car Wash investigation in Brazil. Petrobras, the national oil and gas company, awarded contracts worth multiple billions of reals to construction companies that then funneled kickbacks to the Workers' Party and key elected officials.

- *The In Denial President:* U.S. President Donald Trump ignored the exhortations of leading health care professionals and key staff about the coronavirus pandemic for at least two months in early 2020. This delay, along with the lack of a coordinated plan, personal protection equipment, ventilators, COVID-19 treatment facilities, and continued dismissal of data and expert advice led to the unnecessary deaths of tens of thousands of U.S. citizens.

Have you recently read anything about managerial incompetence in the public sector?

Sources: C. Whitlock, "Pentagon Investigations Point to Military System That Promotes Abusive Leaders," *Washington Post*, January 28, 2014, https://www.washington-post.com/world/national-security/pentagon-investigations-point-to-military-system-that-promotes-abusive-leaders/2014/01/28/3e1be1f0-8799-11e3-916e-e01534b1e132_story.html; C. Whitlock, "Military Brass, Behaving Badly: Files Detail a Spate of Misconduct Dogging Armed Forces," *Washington Post*, January 26, 2014, https://www.washingtonpost.com/world/national-security/military-brass-behaving-badly-files-detail-a-spate-of-misconduct-dogging-armed-forces/2014/01/26/4d06c770-843d-11e3-bbe5-6a2a3141e3a9_story.html; D. Zwerdling, "Army Takes on Its Own Toxic Leaders," *NPR*, January 6, 2014, http://www.npr.org/2014/01/06/259422776/army-takes-on-its-own-toxic-leaders; E. Church and J. Friesen, "I Embarrassed Everyone in This City'" *The Globe and Mail*, November 6, 2013, pp. A1, A6–A8; P. Williams, "'Grandiose Narcissist', The Secret Diagnosis That Helped Bring Down Kevin Rudd," *Sydney Morning Herald*, September 9, 2013, http://www.smh.com.au/federal-politics/federal-election-2013/grandiose-narcissist-the-secret-diagnosis-that-helped-bring-down-kevin-rudd-20130909-2tfum.html; C. Cillizza, "Worst Week in Washington: Rep. Aaron Schock," *Washington Post Weekly*, March 22, 2015, p. 3; "Aaron Schock: At Play in Peoria," *The Economist*, March 21, 2015, p. 24; M. Doyle, "Yosemite Blasted Over 'Horrific' Working Conditions," *Star Tribune*, September 23, 2016, p. A7; J.

Hurdle and R. Perez-Pena, "Kathleen Kane, Former Pennsylvania Attorney General, Is Sentenced to Prison," *The New York Times*, October 25, 2016, https://www.nytimes.com/2016/10/25/us/kathleen-kane-former-pennsylvania-attorney-general-is-sentenced-to-prison.html; "Steven Raucci: Schenectady's Satanic Maintenance Man," Rumors on the Internet, November 23, 2010, https://rumorsontheinternets.org/2010/11/23/steven-raucci-schenectadys-satanic-maintenance-man; "Brazil Corruption Probe: Key Words and Names," *BBC*, July 12, 2017, http://www.bbc.com/news/world-latin-america-39576896; and C. Long, "Brazil's Car Wash Investigation Faces New Pressures," Foreign Policy, June 17, 2019, https://foreignpolicy.com/2019/06/17/brazils-car-wash-investigation-faces-new-pressures.

People don't leave companies, they leave bad bosses.

Beverly Kaye, CEO

Incompetence in the Private Sector: Greed, Sleaze, and Whacko Thinking

HIGHLIGHT 17.3

Managerial incompetence is not the exclusive purview of government; the private sector has more than enough "charismatically challenged" leaders to keep up with their nonprofit counterparts. Here are but a few examples:

- *Doing Anything to Get to the Top:* Travis Kalanick, the former CEO of Uber, was in charge when the company was accused of implementing software to defeat inspectors, stealing trade secrets on autonomous cars, engaging in deceptive trade practices in France, and continuing to track iPhone locations even after customers deleted the Uber app. Carrie Tolsedt, the former "most powerful banker in the United States," led a sales force that created over 2 million false customer accounts in order to hit unrealistic sales targets at Wells Fargo. Rebekkah Brooks, the editor of the top-selling United Kingdom newspaper, the *News of the World*, managed to get her publication shut down when a series of stories broke about the paper bribing police, entrapping celebrities, and using private investigators to illegally tap the phones of celebrities, sports stars, politicians, and the royal family to get material for stories.

- *Making Money Is Not the One Thing; It Is the Only Thing:* Research shows the more money people make, the more they feel a sense of entitlement and the meaner they get toward others. Don Blankenship and Stewart Parnell are two former CEOs who put financial results over worker and customer safety and were sentenced to time in prison as a result. Martin Shkreli, the former CEO of Turing Pharmaceuticals, hiked the price of a 62-year-old drug to fight parasitic infections in pregnant mothers, unborn children, and cancer and AIDS patients from $13.50 to $750 a tablet, saying the price hike would stimulate other drug companies to invent cheaper alternatives. The "Pharma Bro" is currently in jail for defrauding investors.

- *I Am Not a Crook:* Bernie Ebbers, the former CEO of WorldCom, cooked the books at one of the world's largest telecommunications companies; and Bernie Madoff, the former head of Bernard L. Madoff Investment Securities, ran a $65 billion Ponzi scheme. Both will likely spend the rest of their lives in jail.

- *Cheating Your Way to Sustainability:* Martin Winterkorn was the CEO at Volkswagen when news broke that the company had installed illegal software to defeat engine emissions tests. Volkswagen had to recall almost 500,000 vehicles and pay $14.7 billion in fines in the United States alone. Fiat Chrysler has been accused of doing the same in the United States.

- *Sleeping Your Way to the Top:* Roger Ailes was the brainchild behind Fox News and Bill O'Reilly the host of the number one watched cable show in the United States. Both were accused of pressuring up-and-coming female celebrities to sleep with them if they wanted to get promoted. Fox News paid over $30 million to keep these accusations quiet, and Ailes and O'Reilly were fired when news of the payments became public.

- *What Were They Thinking?* Management guru Peter Drucker once said, "Culture eats strategy for lunch." This may be true, but flawed business strategies doom companies much faster than bad cultures. Ron Johnson, a former Apple executive, was hired by JC Penney to be its CEO. Johnson tried to fashion JC Penney department stores after Apple retail stores, with disastrous results. Likewise, a succession of faulty strategic decisions by the CEOs at one-time industry leaders Borders and BlackBerry drove these companies into obscurity.

Have you recently read anything about managerial incompetence in the private sector?

Sources: F. Kalman, "What Uber's CEO Can Teach Us About Leadership," Talent Economy, March 9, 2017, http://www.talenteconomy.io/2017/03/09/what-ubers-ceo-leadership; B. Carlson, "Travis Kalanick Is Uber's Biggest Asset, and Now Its Biggest Liability," *Business Insider,* February 26, 2017, http://www.businessinsider.com/travis-kalanick-biggest-uber-asset-and-biggest-liability-2017-2; S. Andrews, "Untangling Rebekah Brooks," *Vanity Fair,* January 9, 2012, http://www.vanityfair.com/news/business/2012/02/rebekah-brooks-201202; E. Glazer, "Carrie Tolstedt: In the Eye of the Wells Fargo Storm," *The Wall Street Journal,* September 19, 2016, https://www.wsj.com/articles/carrie-tolstedt-in-the-eye-of-the-wells-fargo-storm-1474326652; J. Goodell, "The Dark Lord of Coal Country," *Rolling Stone,* November 29, 2010, http://www.rollingstone.com/politics/news/the-dark-lord-of-coal-country-20101129; M. Basu, "Salmonella: Peanut Exec Gets Groundbreaking Sentence," *CNN,* September 21, 2015, http://www.cnn.com/2015/09/21/us/salmonella-peanut-exec-sentenced; S. Berinato, "Executive Compensation: The More Leaders Make, the Meaner They Get," *Harvard Business Review,* June 29, 2010, https://hbr.org/2010/06/executive-compensation-the-mor; E. W. Dolan, "Study Finds Wealth Gives Rise to a Sense of Entitlement and Narcissistic Behaviors," Raw Story, August 25, 2013, http://www.rawstory.com/2013/08/study-finds-wealth-gives-rise-to-a-sense-of-entitlement-and-narcissistic-behaviors; C. Isadore and D. Goldman, "Volkswagen Agrees to Record $14.7 Billion Settlement over Emissions Cheating," *CNN,* June 28, 2016, http://money.cnn.com/2016/06/28/news/companies/volkswagen-fine; J. Ewing, "Fiat Chrysler to Modify 100,000 Vehicles After Accusations of Emissions Cheating," *The New York Times,* May 19, 2017, https://www.nytimes.com/2017/05/19/business/energy-environment/fiat-chrysler-diesel-emissions.html; F. Pallota, "Nine Months of Sexual Harassment Scandals Take Down Two Fox News Icons," *CNN,* http://money.cnn.com/2017/04/20/media/fox-news-sex-harassment/index.html; N. Raymond, "Martin Shkreli, Who Raised Drug Prices from $13.50 to $750, Arrested for Securities Fraud Probe," *Scientific American,* December 17, 2015, https://www.scientificamerican.com/article/martin-shkreli-who-raised-drug-prices-from-13-50-to-750-arrested-in-securities-fraud-probe; and B. Tuttle, "The 5 Big Mistakes That Led to Ron Johnson's Ouster at JC Penney," *Time,* April 9, 2013, http://business.time.com/2013/04/09/the-5-big-mistakes-that-led-to-ron-johnsons-ouster-at-jc-penney.

Companies get into trouble when they believe their own b.s. So do leaders.

Gordy Curphy, author

If the base rate of managerial incompetence is 50 to 75 percent, we might wonder how organizations can succeed with such a high percentage of ineffective people in positions of authority. Although managerial incompetence can be found in any organization, many businesses still make money, the U.S. military is capable of waging wars, children continue to get educated, and most people receive high-quality health care when they need it. The good news is that organizations may not actually need every person in a position of authority to be a **competent manager**. The keys to success may be for organizations to ensure that they have a higher percentage of competent managers than their competitors and that these individuals are in pivotal leadership roles. Research shows that organizations with higher percentages of competent managers occupying critical positions are more successful than those with fewer competent managers who are not well placed.[67, 68, 69, 70] The purpose of this chapter and book is to increase the odds of you becoming a competent manager and securing positions where you can have an impact on the success of your organization.

Managerial Derailment

So far we have described the concepts of destructive leadership and managerial incompetence. Destructive leadership is associated with individuals who have good team-building skills but achieve results that are morally reprehensible or undermine organizational success. Competent managers make up only a minority of people in positions of authority and are those who can engage followers, build teams, and achieve results that improve organizations, societies, or countries. Of course, if it were easy to be a competent manager, many more people would be in this category. Given that most people in positions of authority are either destructive or incompetent leaders, there must be many ways in which people can fail as leaders. The purpose of this section is to describe the most common reasons why people fail in leading others. (See **Highlight 17.4**.)

The Moronization of Management

HIGHLIGHT 17.4

Carl Icahn is a multibillionaire who made his fortune buying up companies that were poorly managed, straightening out their operations and finances, and then reselling them for a profit. Senior managers dislike Icahn because they often lose their jobs when he buys their companies; but many would argue that if they were doing their jobs, the company performance would be so good that Icahn would not see an opportunity to buy the company and flip it to make a profit. Icahn has a theory about U.S. businesses: Many senior executives are the "guys you knew in college, the fraternity president—not too bright, back slapping, but a survivor, politically astute, a nice guy." According to Icahn, to be a chief executive, people need to know how not to tread on anyone's toes on the way up. Eventually a person becomes the number two in the company and needs to be just a little worse than number one in order to survive. When the number two gets promoted to be the CEO, he in turn promotes someone a little less capable than him as the second-in-command. "It is survival of the unfittest—eventually we are all going to be run by morons." Icahn calls this phenomenon of repeatedly promoting people slightly less capable than the incumbent leader the **moronization of management**.

U.S. President Trump's cabinet has seen historical levels of employee turnover. Loyalty, rather than competence, seems to play a critical role in securing and maintaining a role in the Trump administration. How does this high level of turnover relate to the moronization of management?

Sources: Adapted from *The Economist*, February 11, 2006, p. 42; and G. J. Curphy, "The Moronization of Management," LinkedIn, January 5, 2015, www.linkedin.com/pulse/moronization-management-gordon-gordy-curphy-phd.

Over the past 40 years a considerable amount of research has been done on managerial derailment, and it is worthwhile to describe the lessons of these efforts because they apply to virtually anyone in a position of authority. Initial research on managerial derailment—whereby individuals who at one time were on the fast track only to have their careers derailed—was conducted in the early 1980s by researchers at the Center for Creative Leadership. The researchers went to the human resource departments in a number of *Fortune* 100 companies seeking lists of their **high-potential managers**. McCall and Lombardo[71] defined *high potentials* as individuals who had been identified as eventually becoming either the CEO/president or one of his or her direct reports sometime in the future. They waited for three years and then returned to these organizations to ask what had happened to the people on the lists. They discovered that roughly a quarter of the high potentials had been promoted to one of the top two levels in the organization, and an equal percentage had not yet been promoted but would be as soon as a position became available. Another 25 percent had left the companies; some had quit to form their own companies, and others were given better offers somewhere else. Finally, about a quarter of the people on the list were no longer being considered for promotion. Most of these individuals were let go or demoted to less influential and visible positions. This last group of individuals represented cases of managerial derailment.

Several other researchers have investigated the managerial derailment phenomenon.[72, 73, 74, 75, 76, 77, 78, 79, 80, 81, 82, 83, 84, 85, 86] This additional research used much larger samples (one researcher examined over 3,000 derailed managers), European and cross-generational samples, and more sophisticated assessment tools (such as 360-degree feedback instruments). Moreover, a substantially higher percentage of women and minorities were represented in this later research; the initial high-potential list was dominated by white males. As Van Veslor and Leslie[87] point out, this research focused on identifying factors that helped derailment candidates initially get identified as high potentials as well as factors contributing to their ultimate professional demise. Although these studies varied in many ways, there are many consistent findings across them. Both successful and derailed candidates were smart, ambitious, and willing to do whatever it took to get the job done, and they had considerable technical expertise. In other words, all of the high-potential candidates had impressive track records in their organizations.

> *Behind every great man is a woman rolling her eyes.*
>
> **Jim Carrey, actor**

> *When a doctor makes a poor diagnosis, the patient dies and they don't have to deal with it anymore. When lawyers fail to present a good case, their clients go to jail and they don't have to deal with it anymore. But when a hiring manager makes a mistake, they have to say "Good morning" to it every day.*
>
> **Pete Ramstad, former CHRO**

The derailed candidates, however, exhibited one or more behavioral patterns not evident in the high potentials who succeeded. Five key derailment themes run through the research results listed in **Table 17.1** and are described in more detail here. Note that the derailment themes included in the table have been consistently reported by researchers in both the United States and Europe. One derailment pattern identified in **Table 17.1** is a **failure to meet business objectives**. Although both successful and derailed managers experienced business downturns, the two groups handled setbacks quite differently. Successful managers took personal responsibility for their mistakes and sought ways to solve the problem. Derailed managers tended to engage in finger-pointing and blamed others for the downturn. *But as long as things were going well*, it was difficult to differentiate these two groups on this factor. Some of these managers were also untrustworthy. They blatantly lied about business results, cooked the books, or failed to keep promises, commitments, or deadlines. Others failed because they were not particularly smart or did not have an in-depth understanding of the business and as a result exercised poor judgment.

Table 17.1   Common Themes in Derailment Research

Skill Domain *Definition*	Benz (1985a)	McCall and Lombardo (1983)	Research Study	Morrison, White, and Van Velsor (1987)	McCauley and Lombardo (1990)	Lombardo and Eichinger (2006)	Rasch, Shen, Davies, and Bono (2008)
Business							
Ability to plan, organize, monitor, and use resources	Lacked business skill.	Specific business problems.		Performance problems.	Difficulty in molding a staff.	Poor administrative skills.	Poor task performance.
	Unable to deal with complexity.	Unable to think strategically.		Not strategic.	Difficulty in making strategic transition.	Lack of strategic thinking.	Poor planning, organization, and/or communication.
	Reactive and tactical.	Unable to staff effectively.		Restricted business experience.	Strategic differences with management.	Difficulty making tough choices.	
Leadership							
Ability to influence, build, and maintain a team; role modeling	Unable to delegate.	Overmanaging—failing to delegate.		Can't manage subordinates.		Failure to build a team.	Failure to nurture and manage talent.
	Unable to build a team.						Avoiding conflict and people problems.

Skill Domain *Definition*	Research Study					
	Benz (1985a)	McCall and Lombardo (1983)	Morrison, White, and Van Velsor (1987)	McCauley and Lombardo (1990)	Lombardo and Eichinger (2006)	Rasch, Shen, Davies, and Bono (2008)
Interpersonal						
Social skill, empathy, and maintaining relationships	Unable to maintain relationships with a network.	Insensitivity (abrasive, intimidating, bully).	Poor relationships.	Problems with interpersonal relationships.	Poor political skills. No interpersonal savvy.	Failure to consider human needs.
		Cold, aloof, arrogant.			Unable to deal with conflict.	
Intrapersonal						
Self-awareness and self-control, emotional maturity; integrity	Lets emotions cloud judgment.	Unable to adapt to a boss with a different style.	Unable to adapt to boss.	Too dependent on an advocate.	Questionable integrity.	Procrastination and time delays.
	Slow to learn.	Too dependent on an advocate.	Too ambitious.	Lack of follow-through.	Low self-awareness.	Poor emotional control.
	An "overriding personality defect."	Too ambitious.				Rumor-mongering and inappropriate use of information.
		Betrayal of trust.				

Source: J. Hogan, R. T. Hogan, and R. Kaiser, "Managerial Derailment," in *APA Handbook of Industrial and Organizational Psychology*, vol. 3, ed. S. Zedeck (Washington, DC: American Psychological Association, 2011). pp. 555–76.

Although the research cited in **Table 17.1** focused on failed high-potential candidates, the inability to achieve business results is not limited to this audience. Many people in positions of authority may not be high-potential candidates but are nonetheless unable to achieve business or organizational results. As described earlier, some are popular but confuse activity with productivity; others want their teams to get just enough done to stay off their boss's radar screens. Some may be motivated to achieve results but consistently make bad decisions or alienate team members by exhibiting behaviors that interfere with team cohesiveness, such as being unable to make decisions, micromanaging team members, or taking credit for others' work. One hallmark of effective leadership is the ability to get results across a variety of situations; those who cannot get anything noteworthy accomplished are destined to fail the Dr. Gordy test.

The second derailment pattern identified by Hogan, Hogan, and Kaiser was an **inability to build and lead a team**.[88] Some high-potential candidates derailed because they simply did not know how to build teams. Others failed by hiring staff members that were just like themselves, which only magnified their own strengths and weaknesses. Some wanted to stay in the limelight and hired staff less capable than they were. Still others micromanaged their staffs and wanted their followers to "check their brains at the door" before coming to work, even when they lacked relevant subject matter expertise. People in positions of authority who spend too much time doing activities that should be done by direct reports can also have difficulty building teams because they disempower all the managers who work for them. Because these leaders are making the decisions that their followers would normally make, followers become disengaged with work and team performance suffers.[89, 90, 91, 92, 93, 94, 95, 96, 97]

> *You would be talking with my boss, and suddenly she would snap. She'd lock eyes with you, and her voice would drop very low. It turns out that she learned this technique in an obedience class with her dog, and she found it to be an effective "tool" in managing people.*
>
> **Anonymous, jobs.aol.com**

Like the failure to meet business objectives, the inability to build or lead teams is a common reason why many people in positions of authority are seen as incompetent managers. Two underlying reasons for the inability to build teams are a lack of team-building know-how and dark-side personality traits. Many people can easily describe the best and worst teams they have ever been on, but when asked what they need to do to build high-performing teams, they are surprisingly inarticulate. In other words, most people in positions of authority understand the importance of teamwork but have no clue how to make it happen.[98, 99, 100] This lack of team-building know-how is one reason why some people are seen as incompetent managers, but another key reason is the presence of dark-side personality traits. These attributes will be described in more detail later in this chapter.

A third derailment pattern has to do with an **inability to build relationships** with coworkers. The derailed managers exhibiting this pattern of behavior were insensitive to the needs and plights of their followers and coworkers, and they were often overly competitive, demanding, and domineering. They embraced the "my way or the highway" school of management, and many were incapable of engaging employees. Many were extremely arrogant and truly believed no one in their organizations was as good as they were, and they let their coworkers know this every time they could. Some of these derailed managers also did whatever they felt necessary to get the job done, even if it meant stepping on a few toes. Unfortunately this is not a recommended technique for winning friends and influencing people. It is wise to remember the old adage that you should be careful whom you step on going up a ladder because you may meet them again on your way down. Many of these managers left a trail of bruised people who were waiting for the right opportunity to bring these leaders down.

The inability to get along with others is a fairly common derailment pattern among high potentials and anyone else in positions of authority. An example is a female vice president of marketing and sales for a software development company who was fired from her $200,000-a-year job for exhibiting many of the behaviors just listed. She was very bright, had an excellent technical background (she was an engineer), had already been the CEO of several smaller organizations, and worked long hours. Although she also had a strong leaderlike personality, she would quickly identify and capitalize on others' faults, constantly comment on their incompetence, talk down to people, run over her peers when she needed resources or support, promote infighting among her peers and subordinates, and expect to be pampered. Interestingly, she had no idea she was having such a debilitating effect on those she worked with until she received some 360-degree feedback. Had she received this feedback sooner, she might have been able to stop her career from derailing.

> *Half the CEOs in the world are below average.*
>
> **David Campbell, Center for Creative Leadership**

The inability to build relationships is not limited to taskmasters; other types of leaders can also have difficulties getting along with others. But rather than exhibiting a "my way or the highway" attitude, some fail to build relationships with followers because they regularly exhibit emotional outbursts and temper tantrums, falsely believe that followers are out to get them, fail to provide followers with needed resources or support, or burn out team members with constantly shifting priorities. These irritating, counterproductive behavioral tendencies are manifestations of dark-side personality traits, which will be described in more detail later in this chapter.

Charan and Colvin, Dotlich and Cairo, Hogan, Kaiser, Chamorro-Premuzic, and Curphy have all stated that people problems are also one of the primary reasons why CEOs fail.[101, 102, 103, 104, 105, 106, 107] However, unlike derailed first-line supervisors or mid-level managers, most CEOs get along with others in the company. The problem with some CEOs is that they get along with some of their direct reports too well and do not take timely action to address problem performers. More specifically, some CEOs fail because they place loyal subordinates into jobs they are incapable of handling, falsely believe they can help poorly performing subordinates to change ineffective behavior, do not want to offend Wall Street or the board by letting popular (but ineffective) executives go, or do not feel comfortable hiring outsiders to fill key executive positions.[108, 109]

Another derailment profile has to do with a leader's **inability to adapt** to new bosses, businesses, cultures, or structures. As pointed out earlier in this chapter, business situations require different leadership behaviors and skills, and some derailed managers could not adapt or adjust their styles to changing bosses, followers, and situations. They persisted in acting the same way when it was no longer appropriate to new circumstances. For example, a first-line supervisor for an electronics firm that built video poker machines was having a difficult time transitioning from his old job as a missile guidance repairman in the U.S. Air Force. He thought he should lead his subordinates the way he led others in the military: His staff should be willing to work long hours and over the weekends without being told to do so and to travel for extended periods with short notice. Their thoughts or opinions about ways to improve work processes did not matter to him, and he expected everyone to maintain cool and professional attitudes at work. After half of his staff quit as a direct result of his supervision, he was demoted and replaced by one of his subordinates.

> *Our investigation revealed that Katrina was a national failure, an abdication of the most solemn obligation to provide for the common welfare. At every level—individual, corporate, philanthropic, and governmental—we failed to meet the challenge that was Katrina. In this cautionary tale, all the little pigs built houses of straw.*
>
> **Congressional Report on the Government's Response to Hurricane Katrina**

The inability to adapt is not just a first-line supervisor or mid-level manager phenomenon, as newly hired senior leaders have sometimes tried to transform their organizations into those they had worked for in the past. Robert McNamara tried to turn the Department of Defense into Ford, John Sculley tried to turn Apple into Pepsi, Bob Nardelli tried to convert Home Depot into General Electric, Léo Apotheker tried to transform H-P into SAP, Ron Johnson tried to reshape JC Penney's into Apple stores, and Dave Calhoun is attempting to transform Boeing after the twin 737 MAX disasters. Given the success McNamara, Sculley, Nardelli, Apotheker, and Johnson had with their change initiatives, the future does not bode well for Calhoun.

In the past, organizations could afford to take their time in identifying and developing leadership talent. And as described earlier in this book, many of the best organizations today have strong programs for systematically developing leadership bench strength. However, organizations today are under increasing pressure to find good leaders quickly, and they are increasingly asking their own high-potential but inexperienced leadership talent to fill these key roles. Although these new leaders are bright and motivated, they often have narrow technical backgrounds and lack the leadership breadth and depth necessary for the new positions. The unfortunate result is that many of these leaders leave their organizations because of **inadequate preparation for promotion**. For example, a relatively young woman attorney was promoted to be the vice president of human resources in a large telecommunications firm. Although she was bright and ambitious, her previous management experience involved leading a team of six attorneys, whereas her promotion put her in charge of 300 human resources professionals. It soon became apparent that she lacked the skills and knowledge needed to manage a large, geographically dispersed human resources organization. Although she tried hard to succeed, she kept acting as a front-line supervisor instead of a functional leader and failed to earn the respect of her staff. After six months she was given a generous separation package and asked to leave the company.

Managerial derailment appears at about the same level of frequency in male and female managers.[110] Most who derail manifest several of these themes; the presence of only one of these behavioral patterns is usually not enough for derailment. The only exception to this rule is a failure to meet business objectives. Managers who do not follow through with commitments, break promises, lie, are unethical, and do not get results do not stay on the high-potential list for long. Although this research focused on derailment patterns for high-potential candidates, it seems likely that these five reasons for failure are universal. It would be difficult to perceive someone as a competent manager if he or she could not obtain business results or had difficulties adapting to new situations, building teams, or getting along with others. A bigger concern is why these managerial derailment patterns appear to be fairly obvious, yet so many people fail as leaders. In other words, if you asked a group of people why people in positions of authority fail, it is likely that you would hear the five reasons described in this section. Because these derailment factors are more or less public knowledge, it seems that simply being aware of the reasons why people fail in leadership positions does not seem to be enough to prevent it from happening. If we assume that most people move into managerial positions with positive intent and generally know the pitfalls to avoid in order to succeed, yet are still perceived to be incompetent managers, then there must be something else going on. We believe that managerial incompetence and derailment have some underlying root causes, and knowing what they are and what to do to minimize their impact will improve the odds of being perceived as a competent manager. Many of these root causes are variations of concepts presented earlier in this book.

The Ten Root Causes of Managerial Incompetence and Derailment

The research on managerial derailment provides a good starting point for investigating the underlying reasons why most people in positions of authority are perceived to be incompetent. Clearly a failure to achieve business objectives, an inability to build a team, or an inability to adapt to changing conditions will make leaders fail. But what causes people to fail to achieve business results or get along with others? Are these management failures due to character flaws on the part of the leader, pervasive situational factors, problematic followers, or some combination of all three factors? As shown in **Figure 17.1**, leader, follower, and situational

FIGURE 17.1   Why Leaders Fail

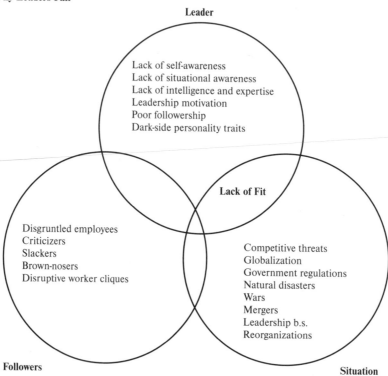

factors all play roles in managerial derailment. Sometimes leaders are put in situations where it is virtually impossible to build teams or achieve results; at other times a leader's own shortcomings cause managerial incompetence and derailment (see **Profiles in Leadership 17.4**). Looking over **Figure 17.1**, we might think it is next to impossible to be a competent manager because there are so many ways in which people in positions of authority can fail. For example, the global economy could take a significant downturn, hurricanes or terrorist events could disrupt supply chains, key followers could retire or be hired away by competitors, organizations could downsize or be acquired by other companies, new competitors could develop disruptive technologies and dominate the market, workers could go on strike, or the new CEO could be a taskmaster. The good news is that we can mitigate managerial derailment by understanding the 10 root causes, assessing the extent to which they are affecting our ability to build teams and get results through others, and then adopting some of the suggestions found in this section to minimize their effects.

Elizabeth Holmes and Theranos

PROFILES IN LEADERSHIP 17.4

Elizabeth Holmes was an undergraduate at Stanford University when she launched Thera-

nos in 2003. Holmes's idea was to revolutionize health care by replacing a wide range of blood tests done in a laboratory with a cheap and accurate alternative, one that would require only a single finger prick for blood. Despite having no formal education or experience in health care, medical engineering, or business, Holmes convinced a group of investors to fund her business. She used the initial proceeds to hire engineers and scientists to build a medical device to perform the blood tests.

By 2007 Theranos was valued at $197 million and Holmes began pitching her device to drug companies as a cheap and easy way to determine whether new drugs were working as intended, were safe, and were of the right dosage. By 2010 the Edison version of her blood testing device was announced and another round of investor funding resulted in the company being valued at over $1 billion. Holmes then started pitching the device to drug retailers in the United States, such as Walgreens and Safeway, as a way for these companies to capture the revenues for blood tests previously conducted in clinics and hospitals. Walgreens became an early adopter of the Edison device and planned on rolling them out on a national basis.

By 2014 Theranos was valued at $9 billion and Holmes's personal net worth was estimated to be $4.5 billion. However, around this time problems with the Edison device started coming to light. It turned out the device was woefully inaccurate, and 240 of the blood tests done by Edison failed to meet accepted scientific standards. As a result, thousands of patients were given false information about their health over an entire two-year period. In pitches to investors and large potential customers, Theranos cherry-picked test data to exclude any trial that showed inaccurate results and substituted the results from tests done using traditional lab equipment for those done with Edison. Holmes also made fraudulent claims about test accuracy in marketing materials and sales presentation, and she knew about the test accuracy issues for over 10 years. As a result of these problems, the SEC conducted an investigation. Theranos was banned from doing any medical testing for a two-year period, Holmes's net worth dropped from $4.5 billion to $0, and she is under indictment for wire fraud.

What is the relationship between integrity and entrepreneurism? Do you believe entrepreneurs always should be truthful, or do they sometimes need to stretch the truth to be successful?

Sources: "Theranos: Blood Sports," *The Economist*, April 23, 2016, p. 55; J. Carreyrou, "Theranos Growing Pains," *The Wall Street Journal*, December 25, 2015, pp. A1, A10; C. Weaver and J. Carreyrou, "Theranos Retreats from Blood Tests," *The Wall Street Journal*, March 24, 2017, pp. B1–B2; S. Westgard, "And Another Thing about Theranos...," LinkedIn, June 17, 2016, www.linkedin.com/pulse/another-thing-theranos-sten-westgard-1; J. Carreyrou, *Bad Blood: Secrets and Lies at a Silicon Valley Startup* (New York: Alfred A. Knopf, 2018); *The Inventor: Out for Blood in Silicon Valley*, HBO, 2019; and A. Hartmans and P. Leskin, "The Rise and Fall of Elizabeth Holmes, Who Started Theranos When She Was 19 and Became the World's Youngest Female Billionaire But Will Now Face a Trial over 'Massive Fraud'," *Business Insider*, February 11, 2020, www.businessinsider.com/theranos-founder-ceo-elizabeth-holmes-life-story-bio-2018-4.

Savvy managers figure out how to get things done, no matter what obstacles they face.

Mark Roellig, retired General Counsel

Figure 17.1 is not meant to be a comprehensive list of root causes—there are many reasons why people fail when in positions of power. However, the 10 root causes include the more common reasons why many people fail the Dr. Gordy test described earlier in this chapter. As an overview, certain situational and follower factors can make it difficult to engage followers, build teams, and get results. An example might include a commercial airline crew trying to deliver a planeload of international passengers to an airport that suddenly closes down due to a terrorist threat. The captain may have done a good job of getting the crew to work as a cohesive team to provide great passenger service but will not be able to achieve her on-time arrival goal because of the airport closure. Although situational and follower factors can sometimes play key roles, leader factors are much more likely to cause managerial incompetence and derailment. Some leaders cannot see how they impact others, some consistently exercise poor judgment, others do not value building teams or getting results, and others are such poor followers that they are fired from their leadership positions. Bad organizational practices also contribute to managerial incompetence, as many times companies have flawed understandings about effective leadership and end up hiring, developing, and promoting the wrong people for positions of authority.

1 and 2—Stuff Happens: Situational and Follower Factors in Managerial Derailment

The story in **Highlight 17.5** concerns a scenario in which situational factors interfered with a person's ability to build teams and get results through others. Although most leaders will not encounter events like the Fukushima nuclear reactor disaster, most had to deal with the coronavirus pandemic. Some leaders who had co-located followers prior to the pandemic had to learn how to manage a remotely located workforce. Others had to lay off all of their followers because their businesses were closed down, and some had to hire more employees to keep up with the increased demands for health care, personal protection equipment, ventilators, and food. It seems somewhat obvious, but situational and follower factors significantly affect a person's ability to engage followers, build teams, and get results.[111, 112, 113, 114] Situational and follower factors make up the first two root causes of managerial incompetence and include the following events:

- Pandemics, natural disasters, and wars.
- New competitive threats, globalization, disruptive technology, changing customer preferences, unreliable suppliers, new governments or government regulations, trade wars, or unfavorable media coverage.
- Mergers, acquisitions, divestitures, bankruptcies, new strategies, reorganizations, major change initiatives, incidents of workplace violence, or environmental disasters.
- New bosses, peers, or owners.
- Disengaged or disgruntled employees; disruptive worker cliques; and strikes or dysfunctional turnover.
- New jobs, responsibilities, or projects.

The Fukushima Daiichi Nuclear Power Plant Disaster

HIGHLIGHT 17.5

On March 11, 2011, a magnitude 9.0 earthquake occurred off the northeast corner of Japan. This was the most powerful earthquake to ever hit Japan and caused a tsunami whose waves were estimated to be over 140 feet tall. The waves hit the island of Honshu with little warning and completely destroyed 130,000 buildings and damaged almost 1 million others. Approximately 20,000 people were either confirmed dead or missing and over 4 million homes lost power. This event has been called the biggest natural disaster in modern history.

The Fukushima Daiichi nuclear power plant consists of six nuclear reactors near the Honshu coast. Although constructed to withstand natural disasters, the March 2011 earthquake and tsunami knocked the plant off the electrical grid and destroyed the backup generators for four reactors. With no power to run the water pumps needed to keep the reactors cool, hydrogen gas began building up to dangerous levels in some of the containment buildings. Being highly combustible, it was imperative that the plant operator, Tokyo Electric Power Company (TEPCO), cool the reactors using any means possible before a hydrogen gas explosion breached the containment walls and spread radioactivity across the region.

The plant was in major chaos after the tsunami: The power was out, all the buildings and equipment were damaged, and communication systems were down. Those on the ground made do with whatever they had to prevent a major nuclear disaster. One key decision was whether to use seawater to cool the reactors. The reactors normally used freshwater as a coolant because seawater would permanently destroy a multibillion-dollar reactor. Those at the plant were not empowered to make this decision and those leading TEPCO dithered in making the call. As a result, the hydrogen gas in three of the reactors blew up and caused major radiation leaks that contaminated a 20-mile radius. Not only did TEPCO take too long to make the decision, but the company also withheld information about the extent of the damage, including how much radiation had been released, who was affected, and what was being done to repair the damage.

The Japanese government's response to this natural disaster was also far from stellar. It took 10 days before Japan released oil from its strategic reserves to generate the power needed for the affected areas. Trucks carrying medical supplies, food, and water were prevented from using the northern expressway because they were not designated as emergency vehicles, even though the route had no other traffic at the time.

How did the situation affect the Fukushima Daiichi nuclear power plant manager and supervisors from building teams or getting results? How does the situation highlight managerial incompetence in TEPCO and the Japanese government?

Sources: "A Crisis of Leadership Too," *The Economist*, March 26, 2011, p. 14; N. Shirouzu, P. Dvorak, Y. Hayashi, and A. Morse, "Bid to 'Protect Assets' Slowed Reactor Fight," *The Wall Street Journal*, March 19–20, 2011, pp. A1, A8; M. Obe, "Fukushima Plant Hit by Power Outage," *The Wall Street Journal*, March 20, 2013, p. A10; and News Services, "Japan Upgrades Severity of Crisis," *StarTribune*, March 19, 2011, pp. A1, A11.

Sometimes things happen in life that are not part of the plan. When that happens, don't give up on your dreams, just find another way to reach them.

Ritu Ghatourey, Indian author

Figuring out how to engage staffs, build teams, and get things done despite potentially disruptive situational and follower factors is part of any leadership role, but at times these external factors can be so overwhelming that there may be little a person can do to be an effective leader. What is interesting is how leaders react when facing hopeless challenges. Competent managers take time to reflect on the situation, determine what they need to do differently, and then ensure that their decisions are executed. Competent managers often succeed where others fail because they investigate all the alternatives and then make the changes needed to maintain team cohesiveness and performance. Interestingly, one of these alternatives may include changing jobs or leaving the organization if the leader feels that others are better able to help the team cope with these challenges. Leaders may also believe that switching teams is a better option than remaining in the role and risk being seen as ineffective.

Incompetent managers facing hopeless situations tend to act quite differently: They are likely to keep doing what they have always done but expect to achieve different results. For example, when faced with challenging followers or situations, they may focus more closely on goals, metrics, and bottom-line results and spend even less time with the people on their teams. They might also increase their team-building and relationship-building behaviors and try to keep teammates happy rather than making them more productive. They could even become less likely to make decisions, take stands, lay out courses of action, or push team members to perform. Most incompetent managers try to leverage their strengths rather than change, which erodes their ability to build teams and get results.

> *The definition of neurotic management is to continue to do the same things but expect different results.*
>
> **Tom Peters, writer**

Three additional points about these overwhelming situational and follower factors are worth noting. Although many situational and follower factors are beyond a manager's control, the manager can control his or her reactions to these events. A manager can step back, reflect on the new situation, and determine what he or she needs to do differently; or the manager can continue to leverage his or her strengths and expect a different outcome. Reflection may be the key success factor when facing difficult situations, but too often people in positions of authority overreact, withhold information, and rush to judgment rather than explaining difficult facts and soliciting team members for ideas.

A second point concerns the concepts of episodic versus chronic incompetence. **Episodic managerial incompetence** occurs when people in positions of authority face extremely tough situational or follower events that temporarily interfere with their ability to build teams and get results. However, once they have reflected on and taken action to cope with the event, they quickly regain their ability to successfully build teams and get results. **Chronic managerial incompetence** occurs when taxing situational or follower events permanently disrupt a person's ability to build teams or get results. All competent managers experience occasional episodic managerial incompetence; the trick is to limit the frequency and duration of these occurrences. But given their preferred ways of dealing with challenging events, many in positions of authority seem to exemplify chronic managerial incompetence.

Finally, situational factors can also mask managerial incompetence. A leader may be heading up a company that has just released a highly desirable app or service and is making money despite bad management. When all is going smoothly, most people assume competent managers run organizations; it may take some kind of emergency or crisis before an organization's chronic managerial incompetence comes to light. To a large extent nobody thought about the leadership capabilities of FEMA, TEPCO, BP, and PG&E until the Hurricane Katrina, Fukushima, Gulf oil spill disasters, and California wildfires respectively. The high percentages of managerial incompetence in these companies became obvious only after these crises went public. Situational factors, social media, and the press can help to shine a bright light on the high levels of managerial incompetence existing in many organizations.

3—The Lack of Organizational Fit: Stranger in a Strange Land

The previous section described the role that situational and follower factors play in managerial competence and incompetence. Organizational culture also plays an important role in this matter. **Chapter 14** defined organizational culture as a system of shared backgrounds, norms, values, or beliefs among members of a group. All organizations have cultures, but the content and strength of the beliefs underlying these cultures can vary dramatically. For example, the shared beliefs, norms, and values of the U.S. Marine Corps are quite different from those of PETA or Greenpeace.

Organizational culture is not one of those pervasive situational factors that doom managers to fail, but a person's fit with an organization's culture can cause him or her to be seen as incompetent. **Organizational fit** can be defined as the degree of agreement between personal and organizational values and beliefs.[115, 116, 117, 118] If a person does not share the values or beliefs of the majority of members, then in all likelihood this person will be a poor fit with the organization, the third root cause of managerial incompetence and derailment. Many times people who do not fit with an organization's culture wield diminishing levels of influence, which interferes with their ability to engage followers, build teams, and get results. **Highlight 17.6** describes a classic example of how the lack of organizational fit can cause someone to be perceived as an incompetent manager. In many ways Ann was precisely what the organization needed to turn things around. She had all the knowledge and skills necessary to succeed, but the senior staff felt their other responsibilities were more important than fund-raising. Thus Ann recognized that she was in a no-win situation and left the organization.

Organizational Fit and Managerial Derailment

HIGHLIGHT 17.6

Ann had spent the past 30 years as a sales executive in the insurance industry. Savvy, sophisticated, and successful, over the years Ann had developed deep expertise in marketing, sales, contracting, invoicing, budgeting, and compensation. She also had over 20 years of sales leadership experience and had consistently built cohesive teams that exceeded their sales quotas. After a successful career of selling insurance, Ann was looking for a new challenge, and a local nonprofit organization needed an executive to head up its fund-raising function. The nonprofit had been around for over 50 years, employed more than 300 people, and specialized in helping developmentally disabled adults live more independent lives. To achieve this mission, the nonprofit provided lodging, skills training, transportation, and other services to its constituents. Ann was hired because the organization was running out of money—revenues were shrinking, expenses were rising rapidly, and donors were scaling back on their contributions. The main donor base was also growing old, and many major contributors were literally dying off.

Attracted to the mission and by the challenge of doing something new, Ann joined the organization and was told by the president to do whatever was needed to secure the existing funding base and find new sources of revenue. Ann started this effort by reviewing the donor database and soon discovered that the organization had done nothing more than send form thank-you letters to the major donors over the past five years. The organization had not visited or invited the donors to any functions or solicited funding from any new donors. She developed a strategic marketing plan that called for the senior staff to engage in a number of outreach activities with new and existing donors.

Ann was surprised by the organization's reaction to her strategic marketing plan. The president felt it was beneath her to engage in fund-raising activities and did not want the organization to be seen as having anything to do with fund solicitation. The president emphatically stated that the mission of the organization was to serve the developmentally disabled, not raise money. The rest of the senior staff wholeheartedly agreed with the president. Ann responded that the organization's costs were exceeding its revenues, and if the senior staff did not want to help generate more funding, then the alternative was to cut expenses. She reminded the staff that she had been told to do whatever was needed to raise cash, and now that her plan was put forward, it appeared that this was not really the case. The president said that money was not their concern and it was up to Ann, and Ann alone, to make things happen. Because of the organization's lack of urgency and genuine distaste for fund-raising, Ann felt like a fish out of water. The things she cared about were of no interest to the senior leadership team, even though her plan would allow the organization to continue its mission. Because of this lack of fit, Ann left the organization less than a year later, and the organization laid off staff members to reduce expenses.

Source: G. J. Curphy, A. Baldrica, and R. T. Hogan, *Managerial Incompetence*, unpublished manuscript, 2009.

No one is more hated than he who speaks the truth.

Plato

Organizations often realize that continuing to do things the same way will eventually result in failure, and one approach to fostering new ways of thinking is to hire people from the outside with different work experiences. New hires may have good ideas to remedy a situation, but whether they and their ideas are accepted will depend to a large extent on an organization's culture. The farther these ideas stray from the organization's prevailing values and beliefs, the more likely they are to be dismissed. Managers hired from the outside suffer the same fate as transplanted organs—those who are seen as a good fit are accepted, and those who are not are rejected. What is interesting about this phenomenon is that outsiders often possess exactly the knowledge and skills an organization needs to succeed, but the solutions proposed are so antithetical to its culture that people begin to question the intelligence of these outside hires.[119, 120, 121]

The organizational fit phenomenon occurs not only when outsiders are brought in; it also happens when companies promote people to be the next CEOs or acquire other organizations. New CEOs often take steps to mold the organization's culture around their own personal values and beliefs, and some managers may no longer fit into the new culture. Likewise, managers from an acquired company can have considerable difficulty fitting into the other organization's culture. Because of this lack of fit, leaders from the "old" culture or from acquired companies can be perceived as incompetent even though they may have all the skills needed to build teams and get results through others. Acquiring organizations often act on these perceptions and limit the influences and resources provided to these managers, essentially setting them up for failure. As described earlier in this book, many mergers and organizational changes fail, and this is often due to cultural fit issues.[122, 123, 124, 125]

What can leaders do to avoid being seen as organizational culture misfits? Perhaps the best thing to do is to minimize the risk of it happening at all. The first step in this process is for leaders to understand their own values, beliefs, and attitudes toward work. Some people go to work to make money, others are motivated by job security, and still others are driven to help others or make a difference. There are no right or wrong answers here, but it is important that people understand what they want out of a job. Once people clearly see what they want from work, the second step in the process is to determine the extent to which the cultures of potential employers are aligned with these beliefs. Determining an organization's culture may not be straightforward, however, because the underlying beliefs, norms, stories, and values are often unwritten. One way to determine an organization's culture is through informational interviews, in which employees are asked how things really get done, how employees treat each other, what is valued or punished, what the unwritten rules are, and so on. This information should help leaders determine the extent to which their personal values and beliefs are aligned with those of various employers. We realize there are times when people need to take jobs for the money and benefits, but they also need to realize that their level of satisfaction and ability to build teams and get results will be affected by the degree of fit between their personal values and the organization's culture. Those who do not fit run the risk of being seen as incompetent and may find that working elsewhere can help them be seen as competent managers.

4 and 5—More Clues for the Clueless: Lack of Situational and Self-Awareness

Most aircraft accidents are the result of pilot errors, and a lack of situational awareness is the leading cause of pilot errors.[126] **Situational awareness**, the fourth root cause, refers to a pilot's ability to be cognizant of and accurately assess risks before, during, and after a flight.[127] In other words, pilots with good situational awareness know what their aircraft is doing, the weather, the positions of other aircraft in the area, the relationship of their aircraft to the ground, and the like. Like pilots, people in positions of authority must also have a high degree of situational awareness if they want to be seen as competent managers. This means competent managers must accurately read the situational and follower factors affecting their teams and remain vigilant for changes. Competent managers not only have high levels of situational awareness—they also have high levels of **self-awareness**. As described in **Chapter 2**, individuals who are keenly aware of their own strengths and shortcomings often find ways to either manage or staff around their personal knowledge and skill gaps. In contrast, incompetent managers can have major situational and self-awareness blind spots, and these are the fourth and fifth root causes of managerial incompetence (see **Highlight 17.7**). They either are unaware of or discount the impact of key situational or follower events or overestimate their ability to build teams and get results.[128]

Situational and Self-Awareness and Managerial Incompetence

HIGHLIGHT 17.7

Dick was the chief of police in a medium-sized midwestern town. Because of a series of easily avoidable but high-profile blunders, the local newspaper and television stations were regularly running stories about department foul-ups. The city council began pressuring Dick to clean up the department's image, and he felt the best way to rectify the situation was to send a memo to the entire department. In the past Dick had relied on his executive assistant to write all his correspondence, but she was on vacation and he felt the memo could not wait until her return. He wrote the following memo and posted it at the department's main entrance:

Date: August 20, 2004

From: Dick Thompson, Chief of Police

Subject: Profesionalism

To: All Police Department Personal

It has come to my atention that the deparment lack profesionalism. I have seen several officers with dirty uniforms and untucked shirts and some of you need haircuts. We need to do a better job with our police reports—some have typological errors are not profesional. We need better in court too. Officers who can not meet

these standards will be unpromotionable. if you have any questions see you Captain.

Less than a day later the posted memo looked like this:

Date: August 20, 2004

From: Dick Thompson, Chief of Police
Spelling

Subject: (Profesionalism)

Spelling

To: All Police Department (Personal)

Spelling

It has come to my (atention) that the deparment lack
Spelling
(profesionalism.) I have seen several officers with

dirty uniforms and untucked shirts, and some of
also
you need ^haircuts. We need to do a better job with
typographical
our police reports—some have (typological) errors
Spelling   *to be*
are not (profesional.) We need ^better in court too.

Officers who can not meet these standards will be
Spelling   *I*
(unpromotionable) ^If you have any questions see
r   *Is this a word?*
you ^Captain.

Unfortunately for Dick, this memo was just the tip of the iceberg—he had a long history of misjudging events and making bad policy decisions, and as a result, department morale was in the dumps. The city council finally came to its senses and asked the chief to leave. However, Dick was hired as the chief of police in another midwestern town, thus perpetuating incompetent management. It turns out that this is actually fairly common, as many small towns and countries struggle to hire new police chiefs and fail to do proper due diligence on applicants.

What would you do to prevent an incompetent leader from being hired to be the next police chief for your town? What data would you gather and who would you talk to?

Sources: G. J. Curphy, A. Baldrica, and R. T. Hogan, *Managerial Incompetence*, unpublished manuscript, 2009; and J. Pilcher, A. Hegarty, E. Litke, and M. Nichols, "Fired for a Felony, Again for Perjury. Meet the New Police Chief," *USA Today*, October 14, 2019, www.usatoday.com/in-depth/news/investigations/2019/04/24/police-officers-police-chiefs-sheriffs-misconduct-criminal-records-database/2214279002.

Research shows that in many cases incompetence is bliss, at least for the person demonstrating incompetence. Researchers Dunning and Kruger[129] conducted a series of experiments that asked people to rate the funniness of 65 jokes. They then asked eight professional comedians to do the same and compared the differences between the experts' and test subjects' ratings. They found that some participants could not predict what others would find funny, yet they described themselves as excellent judges of humor. Similarly, Nilsen[130] reported that managers who consistently overrated their performance on 360-degree feedback instruments tended to overrate their performance on everything they did. Not only did these individuals believe they were good leaders, they also believed they were excellent drivers, mothers and fathers, athletes, dancers, judges of character, and so on, and they tended to overlook evidence that pointed to the contrary.

There appear to be two reasons why some leaders lack situational and self-awareness. First, some incompetent managers are self-deluding, and the most incompetent managers may be those who are the most self-deluding.[131] These managers suffer from having a highly active **reality distortion field**, where they only take in information that is aligned with their self-perceptions and discount any evidence to the contrary.[132, 133] Second, some incompetent managers lack situational and self-awareness because they fail to heed direct report feedback. Incompetent leaders may spend considerably more time paying attention to and developing relationships with those who control their fate (that is, superiors) than with team members. They are also in a position where they can and often do ignore any feedback from their staff, even when this information would help them build teams and get results through others. And by regularly shooting the messenger, incompetent leaders dampen any additional feedback that would make them more effective and push self-starters over to the dark side of followership.

> *If you lack self-awareness, you can't change. Why should you? As far as you're concerned you're doing everything right.*
>
> **Jim Whitt, motivational speaker**

So what can people in positions of authority do to eliminate a lack of situational and self-awareness as two underlying causes of managerial derailment and incompetence? Given the research findings, it is imperative that people wanting to be competent managers get regular feedback on their performance, ideally in the form of 360-degree feedback. It is also imperative that people in positions of authority regularly ask team members for ideas on improving team performance and find ways to stay abreast of important situational and follower events. By building teams of self-starters, competent managers encourage team members to share ideas and solutions for improving team morale and performance, even if this means telling leaders what they personally need to do differently in order to be more effective.

6—Lack of Intelligence and Expertise: Real Men of Genius

The sixth root cause of managerial derailment concerns judgment. People are put into positions of authority to make decisions. Each of these decisions is essentially a problem-solving exercise, and the history and success of any organization are the cumulative sum of these problem-solving exercises. Organizations that do a better job of identifying the right problems to solve and developing effective solutions to these problems are often more successful than those that solve the wrong problems or develop ineffective solutions. Management consultant Peter Drucker has said that most businesses get into trouble because senior managers exercise bad judgment.[134] Business leaders are supposed to direct resources toward activities that increase profitability, but they often decide to spend time and money completing projects that do not matter.

> *General Tommy Franks was strategically illiterate and refused to think seriously about what would happen after his forces attacked. . . . Franks fundamentally misconceived his war, leading to the deaths of thousands of Americans and an untold number of Iraqis.*
>
> **Thomas E. Ricks, journalist**

As described in **Chapter 6**, intelligence can be defined as the ability to think clearly. Some significant components of thinking clearly involve learning new information quickly, making good assumptions and inferences, seeing connections between seemingly unrelated issues, accurately prioritizing issues, generating potential solutions, understanding the implications of various decision options, and being quick on one's feet. Although research has shown that people in positions of authority are generally brighter than others, the intelligence of managers varies greatly.[135, 136]

Because a manager's intelligence is directly related to his or her ability to make decisions, intelligence also affects managers' ability to build cohesive teams and get results.[137, 138, 139, 140, 141] Smart managers tend to do a better job of recognizing problems, prioritizing issues, assigning team member roles, developing work processes, allocating workloads, hiring staff, and resolving problems, whereas less intelligent managers do more poorly on these issues. In other words, being smart improves the odds of being a competent manager; being less intelligent improves the odds of being perceived as incompetent.

But intelligence alone does not equal good judgment. A shortfall in critical knowledge also decreases a person's ability to solve problems and make decisions and increases the odds of managerial incompetence. **Subject matter expertise** can be defined as the relevant knowledge or experience a person can leverage to solve a problem. People with high expertise have a lot of relevant knowledge and experience, whereas those with low expertise are unfamiliar with the task or problem at hand. For example, a marketing executive with 10 years of experience living overseas will have a lot more knowledge of how to effectively drive sales in Europe than will someone new to marketing who has never lived in another country. People with a lot of relevant expertise know what is to be done, how to get things done, and the interconnections between different processes and activities. They know which levers to pull to obtain a particular outcome and understand how decisions can affect activities three or four steps later in a procedure. Managers with relevant expertise have "street smarts"; they can use their knowledge of the what, how, and interconnections to help their teams set the right goals, adopt efficient work processes, and get superior results.

All positions of authority require some level of technical expertise. For example, manufacturing managers need to understand the ins and outs of the manufacturing process, suppliers, maintenance and operations procedures, safety, process control methods, budgets, and related interconnections. People run the risk of being seen as incompetent managers any time they move into jobs that are unrelated to their technical or functional expertise (see **Highlight 17.8**). Like intelligence, however, technical expertise is no guarantee that a person will be a competent manager. Too many people are promoted into positions of authority because of their technical expertise but fail as managers. Often the best programmers or accountants do a great job writing programs or reconciling the books but have difficulty getting teams of people to write great software or conduct effective audits.[142] Even so, having relevant expertise increases the odds of being a competent manager, and lacking this expertise increases the likelihood of being perceived as incompetent.

Relevant Expertise and Managerial Derailment

HIGHLIGHT 17.8

Debbie was a general manager at a management consulting firm. Debbie's job was to ensure her office met its revenue, profitability, and productivity numbers each year. Her track record against these three criteria was less than stellar, as she had consistently missed her targets since taking over as the office leader. But she managed to convince the firm's senior leaders that the office's financial woes were primarily a function of the local economy and everyone in her office was working really hard. In reality, Debbie ran the office like a social club and was continually buying lunch for the office staff, setting up Friday night socials, and praising office staff for their performance (even though the office was not hitting its financial goals). Eventually everyone in the office came to believe that they were special and corporate would never understand the unique challenges they faced. Debbie often bragged that she had little financial savvy and even less interest in the performance of the office and truly believed her job was to improve staff morale.

One of Debbie's multibillion-dollar clients asked for help in hiring a new executive vice president of human resources. The previous head of human resources had been let go because he had been unable to resolve some major staffing, compensation, and HRIS issues that were hurting the company's bottom line. Debbie's firm specialized in the assessment of executive talent, and she led the effort to evaluate the top three candidates for the executive vice president position. Debbie determined that all three candidates had significant shortcomings and suggested that the client considers her as a candidate. Desperate to fill the position, the client decided to hire Debbie on the spot. Had the client followed the process used to evaluate the other candidates, it would have discovered that Debbie lacked any corporate, senior executive,

board of director, compensation, or HRIS experience; was likely to run human resources like a social club; and would foster a we–they mentality between her department and the rest of the company.

Although she was offered executive coaching from a former head of human resources to help her transition into her new role, Debbie felt she already knew what she needed to know and did not capitalize on this resource. Less than a month after starting, she made the first of what would be a series of fatal errors. Debbie looked somewhat frumpy and disheveled at her first board of directors meeting, and her presentation painted the CEO and several business unit leaders in an unflattering light. When the board raised questions about the costs and benefits of the strategic initiatives in her presentation, she stated that the company needed to do these things and costs were irrelevant. Board members were left scratching their heads and hoped that Debbie's performance would improve at subsequent meetings. The CEO then asked Debbie to provide more detailed cost and return-on-investment estimates for her strategic initiatives at the next senior staff meeting. When pressed for details, it became apparent that Debbie had no idea how much these initiatives would cost and whether any benefits would drop to the bottom line.

Over the next few months, several major HRIS problems occurred, and the new compensation system devised by Debbie caused unprecedented levels of turnover among sales staff. To counter these problems, Debbie added about 20 percent more staff and quickly began overspending her budget. The CFO kept reminding Debbie about the company's financial woes, but she countered that her people were the hardest working in the company and it would be some time before all their efforts paid off. As she had before, Debbie instituted regular lunches and happy hours and started pitting her staff against the rest of the organization. This went on for another six months before she was called into the CEO's office and let go. She got a nice six-figure severance package for her efforts, but it was clear that Debbie's lack of relevant

expertise was one reason she was eventually dismissed.

Source: G. J. Curphy, A. Baldrica, and R. T. Hogan, *Managerial Incompetence*, unpublished manuscript, 2009.

Whereas subject matter expertise pertains to the knowledge and skills associated with a particular functional area or process, such as accounting or contracting, **team-building know-how** can be defined as the degree to which a leader knows the steps and processes needed to build high-performing teams.[143, 144, 145, 146, 147, 148, 149, 150] As described earlier in this textbook, most people spend their careers working in groups but lack a fundamental understanding of what it takes to build cohesive, goal-oriented teams. Chances are good that most of these teams were led by those who were more dysfunctional than effective. These experiences lead to a lack of team-building know-how, which contributes to the high base rate of managerial incompetence. Although most people readily acknowledge the importance of teamwork, most managers have no idea how to make teamwork happen.

Talent wins games, but teamwork and intelligence win championships.

Michael Jordan

What can leaders do to make up for a lack of intelligence, relevant subject matter expertise, or team-building know-how? Technology and staffing can make up for shortfalls in intelligence and subject matter expertise. Some companies, such as McDonald's, Target, UPS, and Best Buy, have sophisticated systems that give managers real-time information about revenues, costs, inventory turns, and the like to help them make better store staffing and stocking decisions. Generally speaking, the better the systems, the lower the intelligence needed to operate the systems. What is fascinating is that people with managerial aspirations and lower intelligence often gravitate to organizations with good systems. In other words, it is not unusual to find less intelligent but competent managers in organizations having good systems. These managers have learned how to leverage technology to make good judgments, which in turn helps them build teams and get results. Another way people with less intelligence and subject matter expertise can improve the odds of becoming competent managers is to surround themselves with smart, experienced people. People in positions of authority can leverage the intelligence and experience of their staffs to identify and prioritize problems and develop solutions that help their teams succeed. A third way to improve the odds of becoming a competent manager is through hard work. There are many ways to succeed in any particular job, and people can sometimes compensate for their lower intelligence and expertise by putting in extra effort and working longer hours. Modeling a strong work ethic can also have a contagious effect on team members, which in turn can build team cohesiveness and drive team success. Attending training programs can also help leaders build relevant expertise and understand how to build high-performing teams. Along these lines, the Rocket Model described earlier in this textbook gives managers a practical framework for understanding the critical components of and actions needed to improve team functioning and performance.[151, 152]

7—Poor Followership: Fire Me, Please

Chapter 1 introduced the concept of followership and how anyone in a position of authority has to play both leader and follower roles. **Part 3** of this textbook provided a more detailed explanation of followership and introduced the Curphy and Roellig Followership Model. As a reminder, this model states that followers vary on two dimensions, which are critical thinking and engagement. Self-starters are followers who seek forgiveness rather than permission, offer solutions, and make things happen. Brown-nosers work hard but are loyal sycophants who never challenge their bosses; slackers do all they can to get out of work; and criticizers believe their purpose in life is to point out all the things their bosses and organizations are doing wrong. As described in **Highlight 17.9**, Joseph Lacher appeared to be someone who spent much of his career as a self-starter but became a criticizer after spending 20 months running Allstate's home and auto insurance business units. Although he was able to build a loyal staff, his ability to get results was severely limited once his criticisms became public. Angering one's boss through **poor followership**, the seventh root cause of managerial incompetence and derailment, is not a particularly effective career advancement strategy, and Lacher paid the price for his insubordination.

> *Managerial failure may be due more to having undesirable qualities than lacking desirable ones.*
>
> **R.T. Hogan, Hogan Assessment System**

Want to Lose Your $3,200,000 Job? Call Your Boss a F—g A—e!

HIGHLIGHT 17.9

Joseph Lacher graduated from the University of Notre Dame with a degree in aerospace engineering before joining the insurance industry in the early 1990s. He spent the first 18 years of his career working at Travelers Insurance, where he was quickly promoted to director, vice president, senior vice president, executive vice president, chief financial officer, and chief executive officer at different divisions in Travelers. Because of his rapid career progression, Lacher was hired by Allstate, the largest publicly traded insurance company in the United States. As the president of Allstate Protection Company and executive vice president of Allstate Insurance Company, Lacher was responsible for generating 80 percent of the company's $30+ billion in annual revenues.

Thomas Wilson, the CEO of Allstate, felt the property and automobile insurance businesses at Allstate were lagging behind its competitors and brought in Lacher to turn things around. Lacher introduced a number of initiatives to improve his businesses but became increasingly frustrated with the magnitude and speed of the changes he was allowed to make. After 20 months as the head of property and automobile insurance, there were few improvements to revenues and margins, and the CEO was becoming dissatisfied with Lacher's performance.

Allstate hosted an annual sales conference in 2011 that included more than 2,000 employees and agents. Lacher, one of the speakers at the conference, described initiatives to reduce the sales force and change compensation plans, initiatives that many in the audience did not like. Later that evening Lacher was at the bar speaking with some of the conference attendees who were disgruntled with his initiatives and said Tom Wilson was a "f—g a—e" if he didn't take responsibility for the home and automobile insurance business results. His comments permeated the conference the next day; eight weeks later Lacher resigned from his position. Apparently "you're not in good hands with Allstate" if you call your boss a "f—g a—e."

Was Joseph Lacher a competent manager, taskmaster, figurehead, or cheerleader at Travelers or Allstate Insurance? What kind of follower was Lacher when he worked in these two organizations? What information would you need to make these determinations?

Sources: E. Holm and J. S. Lublin, "Loose Lips Trip Up Good Hands," *The Wall Street Journal*, August 1, 2011, pp. C1, C3; and M. Duell, "Meet the Insurance Executive Who Lost $3m Job after Calling His Boss a 'F*****g A*****e' in Bar," *Daily Mail*, August 2, 2011, www.dailymail.co.uk/news/article-2021391/meet-insurance-executive-lost-3m-job-calling-boss-f—g-e-bar.html.

Highlight 17.9 illustrates how people in positions of authority who are criticizers often become incompetent managers. People in positions of authority who are brown-nosers and slackers are also likely to be seen as incompetent managers. With their eagerness to do whatever their superiors tell them to do and their inability to make independent decisions, brown-nosers are likely to be seen as incompetent managers. Slackers are so disconnected from the workplace that they are unlikely to build teams or get results, and criticizers are usually no fun to be around. Thus followership not only affects how one leads, it also determines whether one is seen as a competent or incompetent manager.[153]

> *A leader's job is to create committed followers. Bad leaders destroy their followers' sense of commitment.*
>
> **Dean Smith, college basketball coach**

So what can leaders do to avoid being seen as incompetent managers due to their followership types? The first thing they need to do is to realize that everything done at work (or even outside of work) counts. Day-to-day actions, work activities, Facebook and LinkedIn entries, tweets, blogs, and e-mail all affect their perceived followership types. It may not be enough to just build cohesive teams and get results—competent managers also need to build good relationships with peers and superiors if they want to get resources and decision-making latitude. Second, leaders need to honestly assess their follower type. If they are criticizers, brown-nosers, or slackers, they need to figure out why they are these less-effective follower types and what they need to do to become self-starters. As described in **Part 3**, a person's immediate boss is the leading cause of dysfunctional follower types. A leader may be working for a boss who is incompetent, in which case finding another boss may be a viable option. (See **Highlight 17.10.**)

Do Personnel Policies Promote Managerial (In)competence?

HIGHLIGHT 17.10

Ninety-three percent of the 250 West Point graduates surveyed in 2010 indicate that the best and brightest leaders leave the service early rather pursue full military careers. The number-one reason why good leaders leave the U.S. Army is not frequent deployments (which ranks fifth), but frustration with the personnel system. Only 7 percent think the military personnel system does a good job retaining strong leaders, and 65 percent feel the system creates a less-competent officer corps. The Army's loss is the private sector's gain, however, as having a military background improves the odds of becoming a corporate CEO three times more than any other life experience.

So what is it about the military personnel system that officers find so frustrating, and how does this system differ from those in the private sector? The U.S. military has a state-of-the-art personnel system from the 1960s: All job assignments are centrally planned; people with the same training are seen as functionally equivalent; officers must remain with the organization until their commitments are fulfilled; they must spend a certain time in grade before they are eligible for promotion; there are few meaningful metrics to measure results or team-building capabilities; innovation, risk taking, and failure are often career limiting; and everyone gets the same performance review ratings. All semblance of entrepreneurship and meritocracy are driven out of the system, and those who do stay in and get promoted in the military tend to be loyal, dutiful, and eager to please micromanagers who keep their bosses happy and get along with everyone.

This is quite different from many private-sector companies, where managers must recruit, hire, and live with their staffing decisions; employees tend to be treated as individuals; people can choose to leave employers if they are unhappy; there are better results and team-building metrics to judge performance; risk taking and innovation are rewarded; and promotions and compensation are more likely to be awarded on merit, rather than time in grade.

At one time the military personnel system was very similar to what is found in the private sector. When George Marshall was appointed the chief of staff of the Army and Army Air Corps in 1939, he believed that the 190,000 troops under his command were not even a "third-rate military power." Over the next two years he eliminated more than 600 senior officers he felt were deadwood, and when World War II began, the generals serving below him had three to four months to lead troops in combat. Marshall rewarded innovation, risk taking, adaptability, and actual results. Dwight D. Eisenhower was a lieutenant colonel in 1939 and rose to become a five-star general under the Marshall system. As much as Marshall rewarded good performance, he made equally quick decisions about those who were not successful. Marshall's system of reward and replacement fell by the wayside

during the Korean War, however, as only a handful of military generals have since been removed from office by the military. Whereas corporate CEOs have a life expectancy of only three to four years, few generals are ever replaced for poor performance or incompetence.

Are the top military leaders in the United States that much better than their private-sector counterparts, or is something else going on? What information would you need to gather if you wanted to make comparisons between military generals and corporate CEOs in their abilities to achieve results and build teams? Why do you think that most retired generals move into civilian jobs that are much narrower in scope and responsibility than their military responsibilities?

Sources: A. Roberts, "A Few Good Leaders of Men," *The Wall Street Journal*, October 29, 2012, p. A19; T. E. Ricks, *Fiasco: The American Military Adventure in Iraq* (New York: Penguin Press, 2006); T. E. Ricks, *The Generals: American Military Command from World War II to Today* (New York: Penguin Press, 2012); S. Jayson, "Bad Bosses Can Be Bad for Your Health," *USA Today*, August 5, 2012, www.usatoday.com/news/health/story/2012-08-05/apa-mean-bosses/56813062/1; C. Brooks, "Employees Reveal Why They Hate Their Bosses," *Yahoo*, February 14, 2012, http://news.yahoo.com/employees-reveal-why-hate-bosses-160226490.html; and T. Kane, "Why Our Best Officers Are Leaving" *The Atlantic*, January 2011, www.theatlantic.com/magazine/print/2011/01/why-our-best-officers-are-leaving/8346.

8—Dark-Side Personality Traits: Personality as a Method of Birth Control

Dark-side personality traits are the eighth root cause of managerial incompetence and involves irritating, counterproductive behavioral tendencies that interfere with a leader's ability to build cohesive teams and cause followers to exert less effort toward goal accomplishment.[154, 155, 156, 157, 158, 159, 160, 161, 162, 163, 164, 165, 166, 167] A listing of 11 common dark-side traits can be found in **Table 17.2**. Any of these 11 tendencies, if exhibited regularly, will decrease the leader's ability to get results through others. And if you consider some of the worst bosses you have worked for, chances are these individuals possessed some of these 11 dark-side personality traits.

Table 17.2   Dark-Side Personality Traits

Excitable	Leaders with these tendencies have difficulties building teams because of their dramatic mood swings, emotional outbursts, and inability to persist on projects.
Skeptical	Leaders with this dark-side trait have an unhealthy mistrust of others, are constantly questioning the motives and challenging the integrity of their followers, and are vigilant for signs of disloyalty.
Cautious	Because these leaders are so fearful of making "dumb" mistakes, they alienate their staffs by not making decisions or taking action on issues.
Reserved	During times of stress these leaders become extremely withdrawn and are uncommunicative, difficult to find, and unconcerned about the welfare of their staffs.
Leisurely	These passive–aggressive leaders will exert effort only in the pursuit of their own agendas and will procrastinate on or not follow through with requests that are not in line with their agendas.
Bold	Because of their narcissistic tendencies, these leaders often get quite a bit done. But their feelings of entitlement, inability to share credit for success, tendency to blame their mistakes on others, and inability to learn from experience often result in trails of bruised followers.
Mischievous	These leaders tend to be quite charming but take pleasure in seeing if they can get away with breaking commitments, rules, policies, and laws. When caught, they also believe they can talk their way out of any problem.
Colorful	Leaders with this tendency believe they are "hot" and have an unhealthy need to be the center of attention. They are so preoccupied with being noticed that they are unable to share credit, maintain focus, or get much done.
Imaginative	Followers question the judgment of leaders with this tendency because these leaders think in eccentric ways, often change their minds, and make strange or odd decisions.
Diligent	Because of their perfectionist tendencies, these leaders frustrate and disempower their staffs through micromanagement, poor prioritization, and an inability to delegate.
Dutiful	These leaders deal with stress by showing ingratiating behavior to superiors. They lack spines, are unwilling to refuse unrealistic requests, won't stand up for their staffs, and burn them out as a result.

Source: Hogan Assessment Systems, *The Hogan Development Survey* (Tulsa, OK: 2002).

It is probably not an exaggeration to state that if individuals with significant narcissistic characteristics were stripped from the ranks of public figures, the ranks would be perilously thinned.

Jerrold M. Post, political psychologist

Several aspects of dark-side personality traits are worth noting. First, everyone has at least one dark-side personality trait. **Figure 17.2** shows a graphic output from a typical dark-side personality assessment inventory, which shows that this individual has strong leisurely and diligent tendencies and moderate cautious and dutiful tendencies (scores above the 90th percentile indicate a high risk and within the 70th to 89th percentiles indicate a moderate risk of dark-side tendencies). The results in **Figure 17.2** indicate that when in a crisis this leader will slow down the decision-making process, not follow through on commitments, tend to micromanage others, and not stand up for his or her followers and get them the resources they need. Second, dark-side traits usually emerge during crises or periods of high stress and are coping mechanisms for dealing with stress. People act differently when under stress, and the behaviors associated with dark-side traits help leaders deal with stress more effectively. The problem is that although these coping behaviors positively affect leaders' ability to deal with stress, these same behaviors negatively affect followers' motivation and performance. Although yelling and temper tantrums might help leaders blow off steam (excitable), such behavior makes followers feel like they are walking on eggshells and wonder if they are going to be the next target of their leader's tirades.

> *There are two ways to measure a leader's dark side. Either have them take a dark-side personality trait assessment or get their followers into a bar, buy them a couple of drinks, and have them share how their boss is pissing them off.*
>
> **Gordy Curphy, author**

Third, dark-side traits have a bigger influence on performance for people in leadership versus followership roles. Individual contributors might have leisurely or cautious tendencies, but because they do not have to get work done through others these tendencies have less impact on their work units than if these same individuals were first-line supervisors or business unit leaders. These individual contributors may not be fun to work with, but their counterproductive tendencies will not be as debilitating as they would be if these people were leading teams. Fourth, dark-side traits are usually apparent only when leaders are not attending to their public image. In other words, people will not see the behaviors associated with dark-side traits when leaders are concerned with how they are coming across to others. These tendencies are much more likely to appear under times of stress, when leaders are multitasking or focusing on task accomplishment, during crises, or when leaders feel comfortable enough around others to "let their guard down."[168, 169, 170, 171, 172] And given

FIGURE 17.2 Leadership Challenge Profile

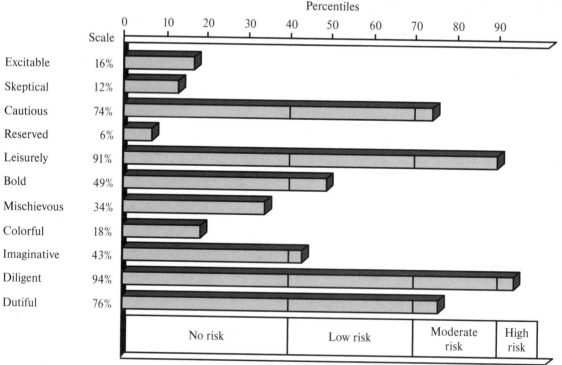

Source: Adapted from Hogan Assessment Systems.

the high levels of stress, challenge, and complexity associated with most leadership positions, the conditions are ripe for the appearance of dark-side traits.

Fifth, many dark-side traits covary with social skills and are difficult to detect in interviews or assessment centers or with bright-side personality inventories.[173, 174, 175, 176, 177] In other words, people who possess bold, mischievous, colorful, and imaginative dark-side traits often do well in interviews and get hired as a result. Only after these individuals have been on the job for some time do their dark-side tendencies begin to emerge. Sixth, the 11 dark-side personality traits are related to extreme FFM or OCEAN scores. For example, being diligent is often associated with extremely high conscientious scores, and being excitable is associated with extremely low neuroticism scores. However, just because a person has an extremely high or low OCEAN dimension score does not necessarily mean that he or she also possesses the corresponding dark-side personality trait. Seventh, the behaviors associated with dark-side personality traits can occur at any leadership level, and many times organizations tolerate these behaviors because a leader is smart or experienced or possesses unique skills (see **Profiles in Leadership 17.1**, **17.2**, **17.3**, and **17.4**). Along these lines, people with bold tendencies are particularly adept at moving up in organizations. Nothing ever got launched without a healthy dose of narcissism, and leaders with bold tendencies are quick to volunteer for new assignments, take on seemingly impossible challenges, and consistently underestimate the amount of time, money, and effort it will take to get a job accomplished. In some cases these leaders pull off the seemingly impossible and get promoted because of their accomplishments. But when things go badly (which they often do), these same leaders are quick to blame the situation or others for their failures and as a result never learn from their mistakes.[178, 179, 180, 181, 182, 183] (See **Highlight 17.11**.)

Digital Narcissism

HIGHLIGHT 17.11

Narcissism can be defined as a grandiose sense of self-importance, feelings of being extraordinarily talented and entitled, supreme self-confidence, taking big risks, wanting to be the center of attention, self-absorption, and seeing interpersonal relationships as way to exploit others and is closely related to the bold dark-side personality trait depicted in **Table 17.2** and **Figure 17.2**. Research shows that narcissism covaries with being seen as leader-like and self-ratings of leadership effectiveness. Other research has found that too much or too little narcissism negatively affects others' perceptions of leadership effectiveness. In other words, narcissists are often seen as being leaders, but whether or not they are actually any good at it is an entirely different thing. Having some self-confidence and being able to draw attention to oneself when needed can help leaders build

teams and get things done through others, but too much or too little self-confidence makes it difficult to build teams that achieve results.

Are the Internet, social media platforms, and smartphones causing people to become more narcissistic? A study of 37,000 U.S. college students showed that rates of narcissism have increased faster than those for obesity since the 1980s. Showing off has never been easier or more celebrated, and we now live in a world where people are constantly broadcasting their lives, celebrating themselves, and endlessly looking to gain status or approval. The pressure to keep up can cause people to set unrealistic goals, but many are unwilling to put in the time and effort needed to achieve the fame they so desperately desire.

Because narcissists are seen as leader-like, they often rise to the top of organizations, but power and narcissism are usually not a good combination. Narcissistic CEOs are more likely to make foolish acquisitions and risky business decisions, break rules, lie, cheat, control and manipulate others, ignore feedback, and expect others to cater to their whims and fawn over them. Overconfident self-deceivers are adept at deceiving others, at least for a while, but eventually they wear out their welcome when the downside of their narcissism comes to light. Men are more narcissistic than women, and the appearance of being leader-like may be more important than actual leadership effectiveness when organizations make promotion decisions.

Is U.S. President Donald Trump a narcissist? Why or why not? How about Jacinda Ardern, Kanye West, Serena Williams, or Satya Nadella? Are men more narcissistic than women? What information would you use to make these decisions?

Sources: E. Grijalva, P. D. Harms, D. A. Newman, B. H. Gaddis, and R. C. Fraley, "Narcissism and Leadership: A Meta-analytic Review of Linear and Nonlinear Relationships," *Personnel Psychology* 68, no. 1 (2015), pp. 1–48; C. J. Resick, D. S. Whitman, S. M. Weingarden, and N. J. Hiller, "The Bright-Side and Dark-Side of CEO Personality: Examining Core Evaluations, Narcissism, Transformational Leadership, and Strategic Influence," *Journal of Applied Psychology* 94, no. 6 (2009), pp. 1365–84; Hogan Assessment Systems, *Digital Narcissism*, www.hoganassessments.com/thought-leadership/digital-narcissism; "Schumpeter: Going Off the Rails," *The Economist*, November 30, 2013, p. 67; "Schumpeter: The Trump in Every Leader," *The Economist*, September 5, 2015, p. 63; J. Pfeffer, "Everything We Bash Donald Trump for Is Actually What We Seek in Leaders," *Deadalus Trust*, www.daedalustrust.com/everything-we-bash-donald-trump-for-is-actually-what-we-seek-in-leaders-2015; T. Chamorro-Premuzic, "Is Over-Confidence Poisoning Your Business?" *HRM*, December 4, 2015, www.hrmonline.com.au/section/featured/is-over-confidence-poisoning-business, S. Lamba and V. Nityananda, "Self-Deceived Individuals Are Better at Deceiving Others," *PLoS One*, August 24, 2014, http://journals.plos.org/plosone/article?id=10.1371/journal.pone.0104562; T. Chamorro-Premuzic, *Why Do So Many Men Become Incompetent Leaders? (and How to Fix It)* (Boston, MA: Harvard Business School Press, 2019); and E. Sadler-Smith, G. Robinson, V. Akstinaite, and T. Wray, "Hubristic Leadership: Understanding the Hazard and Mitigating the Risk," *Organizational Dynamics* 48, no. 2 (2019), pp. 8–18.

The final point to be made about dark-side tendencies is that they are probably the leading cause of managerial incompetence. Dark-side traits are prevalent (everybody has at least one), they are virtually impossible to detect using the most common selection techniques (interviews and résumés), and they tend to emerge during periods of stress (workloads, workplace stress, and burnout are at all-time highs these days). Competent managers are those who have gained insight into their dark-side traits and have found ways to negate their debilitating effects on followers.

> *The world is not full of assholes. But, they are strategically placed so that you'll come across one every day.*
>
> **Anonymous**

If virtually everyone has dark-side personality tendencies, what can individuals and organizations do about them? First and foremost, leaders and leaders-to-be need to identify their dark-side personality traits. This can be done by asking trusted others about how they act under pressure or what behaviors interfere with their ability to build teams, or by completing a dark-side personality assessment. Once these counterproductive tendencies are identified, leaders need to understand the situations or conditions in which these tendencies are likely to appear. Again, dark-side traits are most likely to appear under stress and heavy workloads, so finding ways to better manage stress and workloads will help reduce the impact of these dark-side tendencies. Just being aware of our dark-side tendencies and understanding the circumstances in which they appear will go a long way toward controlling the manifestation of counterproductive leadership behaviors. Exercise and other stress-reduction techniques, and having trusted followers who can tell leaders when they are exhibiting dark-side traits, can also help control these tendencies. Finally, having lower scores on the OCEAN dimension of neuroticism also helps with some of these dimensions because these leaders seem to be better able to cope with stress than those with high scores. (See **Highlight 17.12.**)

How the Mighty Fall

HIGHLIGHT 17.12

Chapter 16 included a highlight about Jim Collins's book *Good to Great*, which describes an alternative approach to organizational change. Collins and his research team investigated the performance of 1,400 publicly traded companies and determined that the top performers shared some common attributes. Several years later Collins and his team reexamined this database to determine if there were any common themes among once highly successful companies that subsequently failed. Some of these formerly high-flying companies included Zenith, Rubbermaid, Bear Sterns, Lehman Brothers, Circuit City, Ames Department Stores, and AIG. Collins believes companies that stumble go through the following five-stage process:

- *Stage 1–hubris born of success:* Great businesses become insulated by success, and leaders with strong business results often become arrogant, adopt an entitlement mentality, and lose sight of what made their companies successful. They often get away with poor business and staffing decisions because their companies have such strong balance sheets.

- *Stage 2–undisciplined pursuit of more:* Because of the arrogance in stage 1, top leaders focus on growth, acclaim, and whatever those in charge deem as "success" and pursue ideas that are unrelated to the core business. Organizations that cannot fill all their key positions with internal talent because of their growth initiatives are probably in stage 2 decline.

- *Stage 3–denial of risk and peril:* As the warning signs from stage 2 begin to emerge, companies place the blame for their lack of success on external factors rather than on their own risky decisions to expand. In this stage vigorous, fact-based discussions disappear, and top leaders explain away or discount negative information.

- *Stage 4–grasping for salvation:* As the warning signs translate to actual business results and companies begin to drown in red ink, they often grasp at anything that will save them. This salvation sometimes comes from outside charismatic leaders, bold but untested strategies, hoped-for blockbuster products, or game-changing acquisitions. The initial results from these activities may appear positive but are often short-lived.

- *Stage 5–capitulation to irrelevance or death:* Accumulated setbacks and the continuous erosion of financial performance causes top leaders to lose hope and sell out; and the longer companies remain in stage 4, the more likely they will be declared bankrupt or be acquired by their competitors.

Collins believes most companies go through some of these stages, but the successful ones recognize when they are in stages 1 or 2 and then take steps to avoid moving into stages 3 or 4. The farther companies slide down the five-stage process, the harder it is for them to turn things around.

Although Collins does not write about managerial incompetence or derailment in his book, what role do you think these concepts play in his five-stage process? Where do the root causes of managerial incompetence and derailment come into play in this five-stage process?

Source: J. Collins, *How the Mighty Fall* (New York: Harper-Collins, 2009).

9—Leadership Motivation: Get Promoted or Be Effective?

The ninth factor contributing to managerial incompetence and derailment has to do with motivation, and there are two aspects of **leadership motivation** worth noting. Some people in positions of authority are smart, have plenty of relevant expertise, do not have dark-side personality traits, and are excellent followers but have absolutely no desire to lead. Many of these individuals were self-starting followers—they solved problems, sought permission rather than forgiveness, were fully engaged, worked hard, completed assignments, never complained, and were fun to be around. Because of their strong work ethic and ability to get things done, these individuals are often awarded promotions for the contributions they make to their teams and organizations. It is not unusual for the best coders, sales representatives, customer service representatives, or teachers to be promoted into supervisory roles, and this notion fits in well with meritocracies, where the best performers are given the greatest rewards. But the decision to promote a team's best performers can have three unintended consequences. First, the team has lost its best players, as sales managers usually do not manage customer accounts and project managers no longer code. Second, the person being promoted may have outstanding individual contributor skills but questionable leadership skills. Writing code and sales contracts is very different from managing those building apps and closing deals with customers. Third, the person being promoted may have no desire to lead. He or she may take a promotion out of gratitude or to not make waves but may in reality prefer being an individual contributor rather than a leader. Those who lack the motivation to lead will likely make lousy leaders.[184] Organizations can avoid making this mistake by asking high performers about their motivation to lead before conferring promotions. If the motivation to lead is lacking, then organizations can still reward their high performers by giving them interesting work assignments, letting them work from home, giving them public recognition or bonuses, and the like.

A second and more insidious problem with leadership motivation concerns the underlying reasons for wanting to move into positions of authority. Thirty years ago Fred Luthans and his associates recorded the day-to-day activities performed by a large group of managers in a financial services firm and noted that most people fell into two leadership types. **Successful leaders** spent most of their day networking, staying on top of office politics, flattering superiors, doing whatever their bosses wanted, demonstrating unflagging loyalty, not making any waves, and self-promoting. They were essentially absenteeism leaders who only wanted to hear good news and spent relatively little time managing their people, teams, and business results.[185, 186, 187] The number-one motivator for these ambitious types was getting promoted, and the researchers reported that successful leaders moved through the ranks relatively quickly and made up the largest group in the study.

Effective leaders made up the second group of managers in this study, and the underlying motivation for these individuals was to beat the competition. In this case the competition was not the people in the offices next door, but rather the other sales teams, manufacturing plants, software development teams, or military units in their respective fields. Effective leaders spent most of their time engaging and developing followers, securing needed resources, clearing obstacles, building high-performing teams, fostering innovative ways to win, and driving results. They spent relatively little time managing their bosses or performing the strategic sucking-up behaviors associated with successful leaders. Luthans reported that effective leaders made up a minority of those observed, and only 10 percent of the managers in their sample exhibited the behaviors associated with both successful and effective leaders.[188, 189, 190, 191]

Most organizations want effective leaders to be in positions of authority, but more often than not, successful leaders are the ones tapped to fill these roles. This is particularly the case when organizations and functions lack accurate performance metrics and human judgment rules the day in promotion decisions. Many government agencies; the military; nongovernmental and charitable organizations; and the IT, legal, human resources, finance, public affairs, and corporate communications functions lack good performance metrics and as a result are often riddled with those who flatter their bosses and make no enemies but get little accomplished. When who you know and organizational politics play bigger factors in promotability than job performance, rest assured that these organizations and functions will be populated with high percentages of successful leaders. These leaders tend to surround themselves with other successful leaders, which leads to the moronization of management phenomenon described in **Highlight 17.4**. It is only when a crisis occurs, such as the coronavirus pandemic, that organizations can clearly differentiate between successful and effective leaders.

So what does leadership motivation mean for leaders and leaders-to-be? First, those wanting to become leaders need to be clear on their reasons for moving into positions of authority. If they are doing so out of a sense of obligation rather than a desire to be a leader, then they should think seriously about not taking a promotion, as those uninterested in doing what is needed to be an effective leader could eventually become disengaged and derail. Second, if people are pursuing promotions for their own selfish reasons and have no interest in using their positions to help their teams or organizations get better results, then they need to identify the organization's key power brokers and do all they can to network and please their bosses, as flattery rather than performance will be their route to the top. Those motivated to be effective leaders need to be ruthless judges of talent to ensure the right people are on the team; in addition, they need to engage and support their followers, help followers see the links between their individual activities and team success, get their followers working as a team, and relentlessly pursue results. People always have a choice when it comes to getting promoted, but their choices will have a profound impact on the people and teams they lead. Choose well.[192, 193, 194, 195]

10—Leadership B.S.: Myths That Perpetuate Managerial Incompetence

The final factor contributing to high rates of managerial incompetence and derailment concerns the misunderstandings organizations have about leadership. Because there is no commonly accepted definition of leadership, organizations often fall for the latest fads or marketing campaigns surrounding different leadership concepts and fail to think critically about the research or practical implications of these approaches. Although adopted with the right intentions, organizations promoting certain leadership concepts can unwittingly contribute to their managerial incompetence problems. Some of these more popular but misconstrued concepts include leader humility, authenticity, integrity, and servant leadership.

Jim Collins identified **humility** as a critical leadership attribute in his book *Good to Great*,[196] and it certainly helps leaders engage employees, build teams, and get results through others. Yet as we noted in the previous two sections, humble leaders often get left behind by their narcissistic, self-promoting counterparts, particularly in organizations and functions lacking robust, data-based performance management systems. Being humble is nice, but effective leaders wanting to get promoted need to master the art of self-promotion or run the risk of being passed over.[197] Likewise, **authenticity** is often touted as a critical component of effective leadership, and authentic leaders are believed to possess a high degree of insight into their strengths, limitations, and emotions; align their words and actions; and develop honest, transparent relationships with followers.[198] On the surface, authentic leadership makes sense, but dig a bit deeper and cracks begin to appear in the concept. First, according to this definition, Osama bin Laden and Adolf Hitler were authentic leaders. People can be true to their values and develop open relationships with their staffs and still be responsible for the deaths of millions of people. An argument could be made that these two leaders were not ethical, but they were highly ethical to their followers. Who gets to decide what is and is not ethical? Second, followers may not want their leaders to be authentic. Leaders, like everyone else, have thoughts and impulses followers do not want them to act upon, and one of the reasons organizations have policies and societies have laws is to keep leaders' more basic impulses in check. Ideally followers want leaders who can adjust their behavior to situational and follower demands and keep their egos under control.[199, 200, 201, 202]

Integrity and **servant leadership** can also lead to managerial incompetence. Followers certainly want leaders who tell the truth and whom they can trust, but research shows that 40 percent of people lie in any 24-hour period and 80 percent of dating profiles contain false information. Moreover, leaders often rationalize their lying (it is for the good of the team or organization) and followers often cannot immediately tell when they are being lied to. As a result, leaders break commitments all the time and followers end up trusting the wrong people. As a philosophy, servant leadership makes sense: If leaders take care of their followers, then followers will take care of customers and teams will achieve winning results. The problem is that in any situation, three competing interests are at play: those of the leader, the followers, and the organization. With CEO pay currently hovering around 300 times that of the average U.S. worker, it is easy to tell where many leaders' primary interests lie. Talking a good game about servant leadership is one thing; receiving huge bonuses, having a choice parking spot, sitting in a killer office, and flying on a corporate jet tells an entirely different story (see Highlight 17.13).[203, 204]

What Would Jesus Do?

HIGHLIGHT 17.13

Religious leaders often preach the importance of servant leadership to their followers. They believe they were placed on this earth to preach the good word, do good acts, and serve the ministry. But religious leaders who preach the prosperity gospel have somewhat of a different take. These leaders believe good things come to people who believe in the Lord, and the harder followers believe, the more they will prosper in terms of personal health, wealth, and happiness. The best way to show your faith in the Lord is by making financial contributions to the church. The bigger the donations, the more Jesus will take care of your material, financial, and spiritual needs. Two interesting questions about the prosperity gospel are: (1) is this really what Jesus would do; and (2) who truly benefits from this philosophy? Theologians can argue about the answers to the former, but here are some interesting facts about the latter:

- **Kenneth Copeland:** He has three private jets and recently asked his congregants to donate $20 million for a Gulfstream V. He uses his planes as a sanctuary to talk directly to God, as "commercial flights are tubes full of doped-up people and demons." He also preaches that if people love Jesus

hard enough, they will never suffer from PTSD or other mental illnesses.

- **Jesse Duplantis:** Not to be outdone, Jesse Duplantis claimed that God asked him to buy a Dassault 7X by name (God is apparently really into airplanes). His congregants were asked to pony up $54 million for the plane, which they did. The Dassault was added to his fleet of three other private jets. In justifying the purchase, Duplantis said, "I really believe that if Jesus was physically on the earth today, he wouldn't be riding a donkey."

- **Creflo Dollar:** Another adherent to the prosperity doctrine, Dollar launched Project 650 (Gulfstream's fanciest airplane) in 2015. All his 200,000 followers had to do was donate $300 each, and that is what they did.

Who benefits when religious leaders live in mansions; own multiple homes, yachts, and private aircraft; and drive around in six-figure cars? We can't tell how congregants benefit from the prosperity gospel, but pastors certainly do. Is the prosperity gospel a good example of servant leadership? Why or why not?

Sources: E. Ross, "6 Famously Awful Televangelists Who Are Somehow Still Around," *Cracked*, June 3, 2018, www.cracked.com/blog/6-famously-awful-televangelists-who-are-somehow-still-around; A. Willingham, "This Tele-vangelist Is Asking His Followers to Buy Him a $54 Million Private Jet," *CNN*, May 30, 2018, www.cnn.com/2018/05/30/us/jesse-duplantis-plane-falcon-7x-prosperity-gospel-trnd/index.html; and C. Kuruvilla, "Televangelist Kenneth Copeland Defends His Private Jets: 'I'm A Very Wealthy Man'," *Huffington Post*, June 5, 2019, www.huffpost.com/entry/kenneth-copeland-jet-inside-edition_n_5cf822fee4b0e63eda94de4f.

There is certainly nothing wrong with wanting our leaders to be humble, authentic, truthful, and service oriented. Things go awry when organizations promote these concepts, followers expect to see them in their leaders, and those getting promoted turn out to be ambitious, greedy, self-promoting politicians who would throw followers under a bus if it would help them get promoted. This disconnect between how things ought to be versus what really happens in organizations is likely a major contributor to employee disengagement and turnover. So what can organizations do to better align their own and employees' expectations about who should occupy positions of authority and who actually does so? First and foremost, organizations need to get more comfortable using data, rather than only human judgment, to make hiring, high-potential selection, performance, and promotion decisions. Time and again, data and statistical analysis has been proven to make better people decisions than human judgment, but senior leaders are reluctant to give up the notion that they are not good at picking winners. Second, organizations need to adopt better systems for evaluating and developing leadership talent. The billions of dollars spent on leadership development every year are largely wasted on the wrong people, content, and methodologies; better selection and performance management systems would also reduce managerial derailment and incompetence.[205]

Summary

As stated at the beginning of this chapter, leadership is arguably the most important concept in the world today. Who is in charge determines whom you can marry, where you work, how your kids will be educated, and whether you can travel freely or express your opinions. Although many people in Western societies take these freedoms (and to some extent leadership) for granted, most people in the world today do not enjoy these privileges. Most people live under some form of dictatorship and have little say in what they do, whom they interact with, or who is in charge. Although the people in charge of dictatorships may find leadership to be relatively easy, those in positions of authority in more democratically oriented countries often find leadership to be a tremendously complex task. To succeed in these roles, leaders need to engage and develop employees, build teams, and achieve results, but accomplishing these three ends is challenging. There are many ways for people in positions of authority to fail, and unfortunately most people are not particularly effective leaders.

This chapter began with a discussion of destructive leadership. Destructive leaders are those who can build teams but achieve results that are morally reprehensible or undermine organizational success. The current heads of North Korea, Belarus, South Sudan, Syria, and Turkmenistan could be considered destructive leaders in that they have built loyal teams of followers but have done little to improve the lives of the vast majority of their citizens. Destructive leadership is not restricted to the world stage: Many community and nonprofit leaders, first-line supervisors, mid-level managers, and executives who can build teams also get results that are misaligned with the needs of a majority of their constituents or their parent organizations. And exactly what constitutes good or destructive leadership may not be straightforward—perspectives matter, and initiatives initially deemed destructive might prove to be good in the long run.

Managerial incompetence describes people in positions of authority who have difficulties engaging followers, building teams, or getting results through others. Research shows that most people in positions of authority are perceived as incompetent by many of their followers. Managerial derailment is closely related to managerial incompetence and pertains to the reasons why competent managers can be seen as ineffective. Some of the reasons why high-potential leaders become ineffective managers are because of their unpreparedness for promotion or their inability to build teams, achieve business objectives, get along with others, or adapt to new situations. Although the managerial derailment research has been conducted on people who were once seen as high-potential candidates, it seems likely that these reasons for failure can apply to anyone in a position of authority.

The fact that most people know why leaders fail shows that simply knowing the common reasons for derailment is not enough to prevent it from happening. Something else must be occurring to cause a majority of persons in positions of authority to be seen as incompetent. Some not-so-obvious root causes for managerial incompetence and derailment include overwhelming situational and follower factors; a lack of organizational fit; limited situational and self-awareness; a shortage of intelligence and relevant expertise; poor followership; dark-side personality traits; problems with leadership motivation; and common misunderstandings about leadership. Unfortunately, any one of these factors can cause people in positions of authority to fail, and many times a combination of these underlying causes may be at fault. The good news is that leaders and leaders-to-be can take steps to mitigate the impact of these factors on their ability to build teams and get results.

Key Terms

destructive leadership

managerial incompetence

managerial derailment

base rate of managerial incompetence

Dr. Gordy test

competent manager

moronization of management

high-potential managers

failure to meet business objectives

inability to build and lead a team

inability to build relationships

inability to adapt

inadequate preparation for promotion

episodic managerial incompetence

chronic managerial incompetence

organizational fit

situational awareness

self-awareness

reality distortion field

subject matter expertise

team-building know-how

poor followership

dark-side personality traits

narcissism

leadership motivation

successful leaders

effective leaders

humility

authenticity

integrity

servant leadership

Questions

1. The base rate of managerial incompetence is estimated to be 50 to 75 percent. This means that a majority of people in positions of authority have difficulties getting a group of people to work effectively together or to get results. What do you think about this percentage of incompetent managers? For example, is it too high or low, and why?

2. Think about the ineffective leaders you have worked or played for. What dark-side traits did these leaders possess that caused them to be ineffective?

3. Do you know anyone who has been dismissed from a leadership position? What did the person do? Use the leader–follower–situation model and the 10 root causes of derailment to explain what happened.

4. What role would downsizing play in an organization's overall level of subject matter expertise?

5. How would you rate the situational awareness, self-awareness, reality distortion field, and relevant expertise of U.S. President Donald Trump during the coronavirus pandemic?

6. Is Xi Jinping, the president of China, a destructive, incompetent, successful, or effective leader? What data could you use to make this evaluation? Would your evaluation of Xi Jinping change if you lived in rural China, Tibet, or Hong Kong; were a member of the Communist Party; or owned a large business in China?

Activities

1. Count how many leaders for whom you have worked, played, or performed in the past. This number should include any position in which you were in a followership role. Once you have a total, count how many of these leaders for whom you would willingly work, play, or perform again. Then calculate the ratio of effective managers to total managers. What was the overall average and range of ratios for your group or class? What were the common characteristics of those who designated as the best and worst leaders for your group or class? What do these ratios say about how well organizations select and develop their leaders?

2. Get into small groups and discuss whether the following people were successful, effective, incompetent, or destructive leaders. Provide the rationale and facts to support your positions.

    • Daniel Ortega
    • Cristina Kirchner
    • Marilyn Hewson
    • Christine Lagarde
    • Jared Kushner
    • Joel Olsteen
    • Marine Le Pen
    • Abdel Fattah el-Sisi
    • Bernie Sanders
    • Ali Khamenei

3. Investigate and prepare short presentations about the underlying causes of derailment or incompetence for the following people:

    • Dennis Muilenburg
    • Abby Lee Miller
    • Jeffrey Immelt
    • Deborah Dugan
    • Travis Kalanick

- Adam Neumann
- Park Geun-hye
- Roger Ailes
- Jacob Zuma
- Bashar al-Assad
- Theresa May

Minicase

You Can't Make Stuff Like This Up

Steve once worked as a regional sales director for a large health insurance company called Blue Star Health. Blue Star Health was once quite successful but had become complacent over the past five years. Competitors gained market share using aggressive marketing and sales tactics, and Blue Star was selling antiquated products and using inefficient processes for settling claims. With falling revenues and margins, Blue Star became an acquisition target and was bought by Anthum, a *Fortune* 100 company. At the conclusion of the deal Anthum brought in an injection of cash, a reputation for operational excellence, and a new vice president of sales, Jim Blaylock. The CEO of Anthum described Jim as bright, experienced, successful, and "more energetic than the Energizer Bunny." Jim had joined the corporation immediately after college; because of his "potential" the company sent him to law school and rapidly promoted him into increasingly responsible positions. Senior management had tremendous confidence in Jim's leadership abilities and appointed him as the vice president of sales in Blue Star Health, even though he had no previous sales experience.

Steve was initially impressed with Jim's freshness and energy; he was constantly touting "midwestern values" and the "work ethic of the Midwest." However, the sales management team soon became disenchanted with his views: Steve and his sales team were working 70 to 80 hours a week and becoming exhausted and frazzled. Moreover, Jim's interactions with internal and external clients were lessons in poor human relations. He seemed to seek confrontations, and as time passed, his behavior became steadily more extreme. Jim harangued people, ignored appointments and made no excuses for missing them, made promises he never kept, called sales directors at 6:00 a.m. with insignificant questions, and abused brokers. Those who questioned Jim's leadership were summarily dismissed.

One day Jim asked Steve to arrange a meeting with a broker at 9:00 p.m. The broker was from a large benefit house and was older, and the meeting time was late. However, he was a longtime personal friend of Steve's and as a courtesy agreed to the meeting. Jim did not show up for the appointment and would not answer Steve's calls to his cell phone. After an hour, Steve and the broker went home. When Steve asked Jim why he missed the appointment, he said he was drinking with a friend and did not think the meeting with the broker was important. Jim refused to apologize to the broker and was surprised when business with the broker's organization came to an end.

Jim loved working on high-visibility projects and landed an opportunity to convert the membership of another acquired company to Anthum. This was an important project for Anthum, and shortly thereafter Jim set up an elaborate "war room" in which all sales planning and action would take place. He asked Steve to lead the conversion project, repeatedly announcing that the acquisition was to garner new contracts and to bring quality employees into the organization. At this point Steve had over 70 direct reports in five different locations across the state and some aggressive sales targets. It would be impossible for Steve to hit his revenue numbers and run the conversion project. But Jim cut Steve no slack, and the computer system intended to convert the contracts did not work. Jim spent no time with any of the newly acquired sales team members, and as a result they showed no interest in working for Anthum. Yet Jim made grandiose statements about the quality of the sales force at the acquired company, which implied the current sales employees were unsatisfactory and fostered a sense of mistrust in both sales organizations.

Because of Jim's shoddy treatment, the long hours, and poor sales and invoicing processes, the morale of the sales team began to plummet. Tantrums and tears occurred frequently, and Steve spent a lot of time smoothing ruffled feathers and telling team members that things would get better over time. But there was only so much Steve could do, and as team members began to quit, Jim blamed Steve for the decline in department morale. As the situation continued to deteriorate, Steve requested that Jim meet with the remaining staff to talk about their frustrations with Anthum. Jim opted to set up an all-employee breakfast at a local restaurant to address their concerns.

The night before the meeting a major snowstorm hit the city, and the streets were covered with a foot of snow. Some employees had to drive 40 miles to attend the meeting, but everyone made it to the restaurant. The only person missing was Jim, and Steve started calling him 10 minutes before the meeting start time to check on his status. Jim did not answer, so Steve began to call and leave messages every five minutes. Jim finally answered his phone 30 minutes after the meeting start time and told Steve that the reason he was not at the meeting was that he decided to go skiing and people would have to meet with him another day. He also asked Steve to quit bugging him by leaving messages every five minutes. Steve could do little to put a positive spin on this message, and the employees left the restaurant bitter and hurt. Of the 60 people who showed up for the meeting, only one was still with Anthum six months later. Jim never acknowledged his behavior and was "shocked" at the turnover in the sales group. Despite the turnover and declining sales revenues, Jim was still considered the company's darling, and it was commonly believed that the CEO tacitly condoned his behavior.

1. Was Jim Blaylock a destructive, incompetent, successful, or effective leader? What data would you use to make this determination?

2. If Jim was an incompetent manager, what do you think were the underlying root causes of his incompetence?

3. Why do you think Jim was seen as a high-potential candidate? Why did the CEO still think he was a high performer?

4. What would you do if you were Jim's boss and heard about the information described here?

5. What would you do if you were Steve?

Source: G. J. Curphy, A. Baldrica, and R. T. Hogan, *Managerial Incompetence*, unpublished manuscript, 2009.

Endnotes

1. J. M. Burns, *Leadership* (New York: Harper & Row, 1978).

2. W. Frost, "Wells Fargo Report Gives Inside Look at Culture that Crushed the Bank's Reputation," *CNBC*, April 10, 2017, www.cnbc.com/2017/04/10/wells-fargo-report-shows-culture-that-crushed-banks-reputation.html.

3. C. Dwyer, "Sacklers Withdrew Nearly $11 Billion from Purdue as Opioid Crisis Mounted," *NPR*, December 17,2019, www.npr.org/2019/12/17/788783876/sacklers-withdrew-nearly-11-billion-from-purdue-as-opioid-crisis-mounted.

4. J. Walker and J. Kamp, "Founder of Opioid Maker Gets Jail Time," *The Wall Street Journal*, January 24, 2020, pp. B1–2.

5. L. Strickler, "Purdue Pharma Offers $10–12 Billion to Settle Claims," *NBC News*, August 27, 2019, www.nbcnews.com/news/us-news/purdue-pharma-offers-10-12-billion-settle-opioid-claims-n1046526.

6. S. Einarsen, M. Schanke Aasland, and A. Skogstad, "Destructive Leadership Behavior: A Definition and Conceptual Model," *Leadership Quarterly* 18 (2007), pp. 207–16.

7. A. Padilla, R. T. Hogan, and R. B. Kaiser, "The Toxic Triangle: Destructive Leaders, Susceptible Followers, and Conducive Environments," *Leadership Quarterly* 18 (2007), pp. 176–94.

8. J. Schaubroeck, F. O. Walumbwa, D. C. Ganster, and S. Kepes, "Destructive Leadership Traits and the Neutralizing Influence of an 'Enriched' Job," *Leadership Quarterly* 18 (2007), pp. 235–51.

9. J. B. Shaw, A. Erickson, and M. Harvey, "A Method for Measuring Destructive Leadership and Identifying Destructive Leaders in Organizations," *Leadership Quarterly* 22 (2011), pp. 575–90.

10. M. Schanke Aasland, A. Skogstad, G. Notelaers, M. Birkeland Nielsen, and S. Einarsen, "The Prevalence of Destructive Leadership Behaviour," *British Journal of Management* 21 (2010), pp. 438–52.

11. W. Hirsch, "Ignoring Bad Leadership May Be Risky Business—Here's Why," *Science for Work*, May 7, 2018, https://scienceforwork.com/blog/bad-leadership.

12. B. Kellerman, "Bad Leadership: What It Is, How It Happens, Why It Matters," *Leadership for the Common Good* (Boston, MA: Harvard Business School Press, 2004).

13. G. J. Curphy, "Investing in the Wrong Vehicle: The Neglect of Team Leadership," in *Why Is the Leadership Development Industry Failing?* R. B. Kaiser (chair). Symposium conducted at the 28th Annual Conference for the Society of Industrial and Organizational Psychology, Houston, April 2013.

14. R. Kaiser and G. J. Curphy, "Leadership Development: The Failure of an Industry and the Opportunity for Consulting Psychologists," *Journal of Consulting Psychology: Practice and Research*, 65, no. 4 (2013), pp. 294–302.

15. G. J. Curphy, R. Kaiser, and R. Hogan, *Why Is the Leadership Development Industry Failing? (and How to Fix It)* (North Oaks, MN: Curphy Leadership Solutions, 2015).

16. J. Diamond, *Guns, Germs, and Steel: The Fates of Human Societies* (New York: Norton, 1999).

17. Kellerman, "Bad Leadership."

18. Curphy, "Investing in the Wrong Vehicle."

19. Diamond, *Guns, Germs, and Steel.*

20. M. M. Smith, "The Leadership Disconnect," O.C. Tanner, http://blog.octanner.com/leadership/the-leadership-disconnect.

21. B. Schyns and J. Schilling, "How Bad Are the Effects of Bad Leaders? A Meta-Analysis of Destructive Leadership and Its Outcomes," *Leadership Quarterly* 24 (2013), pp. 138–58.

22. G. J. Curphy, A. Baldrica, and R. T. Hogan, *Managerial Incompetence*, unpublished manuscript, 2009.

23. R. T. Hogan, *Personality and the Fate of Organizations* (Mahwah, NJ: Lawrence Erlbaum Associates, 2007).

24. T. Marcin, "Donald Trump's Latest Approval Ratings Plunged, Republicans Flee the President Amid Russia Controversies," *Newsweek*, May 20, 2017, www.newsweek.com/donald-trump-approval-rating-plunged-republicans-flee-president-amid-russia-612979.

25. Kaiser and Curphy, "Leadership Development."

26. R. B. Kaiser, "The Disconnect between Development and the Evolutionary Laws of Leadership," in *Why Is the Leadership Development Industry Failing?* R. B. Kaiser, (chair). Symposium conducted at the 28th Annual Conference for the Society of Industrial and Organizational Psychology, Houston, April 2013.

27. G. J. Curphy, R. Kaiser, and R. T. Hogan, *Why Is the Leadership Development Industry Failing? (And How to Fix It).* (North Oaks, MN: Curphy Consulting Corporation, 2014).

28. "How Unpopular Is Donald Trump?" Five Thirty Eight, https://projects.fivethirtyeight.com/trump-approval-ratings, accessed February 3, 2020.

29. "CharityBegins at Work," *The Economist*, June 8, 2019, p. 60.

30. "Horrible Bosses," *The Economist*, July 28, 2019, p.49.

31. J. Stoll, "The Rise of the Outsider CEO," *The Wall Street Journal*, December 14–15, 2019, p. B2.

32. A. Tangel, A. Sider, and A. Pasztor, "Boeing's CEO Struggles to Contain 737 MAXCrisis," *The Wall Street Journal*, December 23, 2019, pp. A1 and 10.

33. A. Tangel and D. Cameron, "Boeing Outs CEO Amid Crisis," *The Wall Street Journal*, December 24, 2019, pp. A1 and 7.

34. P. Leskin, "The Career Rise and Fall of Adam Neumann, the ControversialWeWork Cofounder," *Business Insider*, April 2, 2020, www.businessinsider.com/wework-ceo-adam-neumann-bio-life-career-2019-8.

35. Hogan, *Personality and the Fate of Organizations.*

36. Kaiser, "The Disconnect between Development and the Evolutionary Laws of Leadership."

37. Gallup, *The State of the American Workplace* (Washington, DC: Gallup, 2017).

38. A. Ovans, "Morning Advantage: How Bosses Do Harm," *The Conference Board*, October 11, 2012, www.conference-board.org/blog/postdetail.cfm?post=1125.

39. G. L. Neilson, B. A. Pasternack, and K. E. Van Nuys, "The Passive-Aggressive Organization," *Harvard Business Review*, October 2005, pp. 82–95.

40. M. Bardes Mawritz, D. M. Mayer, J. M. Hoobler, S. J. Wayne, and S. V. Marinova, "A Trickle-Down Model of Abusive Supervision," *Personnel Psychology* 62 (2012), pp. 325–57.

41. Hogan, *Personality and the Fate of Organizations.*

42. K. E. Klein, "What's Behind High Small-Biz Failure Rates," *Frontier Advice and Columns*, September 30, 1999, www.businessweek.com/smallbiz/news/coladvice/ask/sa990930.htm.

43. C. Denbow, "Small Business Failure," http://www.elib.org/articles/292/small-business.

44. C. Tushabomwe-Kazooba, "Causes of Small Business Failure in Uganda: A Case Study from Bushenyi and Mbarara," *African Studies Quarterly* 8, no. 4 (2006), pp. 1–12.

45. S. Ward, "Part 4: Avoiding Business Failure," *Small Business: Canada*, 1997, http://sbinfrocanada. about.com/cs/startup/a/startownbiz.

46. G. J. Curphy, *Why Is the Leadership Development Industry Failing? (And How to Fix It)*, presentation given to Metro, New York City, October 2013.

47. C. Johnson, *Visualizing the Relationship between Human Error and Organizational Failure*, 1998, www.dcs.gla.ac.uk/~johnson/papers/fault_trees/organizational_error.

48. K. Blunt and R. Gold, "PG&E Regulators Failed to Stop Crisis," *The Wall Street Journal*, December 9, 2019, pp. A1 and 12.

49. S. Newey, "Australia Is Burning—But Why Are the Bushfires So Bad and Is Climate Change to Blame?" *The Telegraph*, January 15, 2020, www.telegraph.co.uk/global-health/climate-and-people/australia-burning-bushfires-bad.

50. "Latest Standish Group CHAOS Report Shows Project Success Rates Have Improved by 50%," *BusinessWire*, March 25, 2003, www.businesswire.com/news/home/20030325005636/en/Latest-Standish-Group-CHAOS-Report-Shows-Project.

51. J. A. Warden and L. A. Russell, *Winning in Fast Time* (Montgomery, AL: Venturist Publishing, 2002).

52. J. P. Kotter, *Leading Change* (Boston: Harvard Business School Press, 1996).

53. Aasland et al., "The Prevalence of Destructive Leadership Behaviour."

54. Mawritz et al., "A Trickle-Down Model of Abusive Supervision."

55. J. P. Steele. *Antecedents and Consequences of Toxic Leadership in the U.S. Army: A Two Year Review and Recommended Solutions* (Technical Report 2011-3) (Ft. Leavenworth, KS: Center for Army Leadership, 2011).

56. L. Cranshaw, "Coaching Abrasive Leaders: Using Action Research to Reduce Suffering and Increase Productivity in Organizations," *The International Journal of Coaching in Organizations* 29, no. 8 (2010), pp. 59–77.

57. M. Abrahams, "Random Promotion May Be Best, Research Suggests," *The Guardian*, November 1, 2010, www.guardian.co.uk/education/2010/nov/01/random-promotion-research.

58. Curphy, "Investing in the Wrong Vehicle."

59. Curphy et al., *Managerial Incompetence.*

60. G. J. Curphy, *Team Consulting Workshop* (North Oaks, MN: Curphy Leadership Solutions, 2017).

61. G. J. Curphy, "Organizational Realpolitik and Leadership-Part I," LinkedIn, January 1, 2016, www.linkedin.com/pulse/organizational-realpolitik-leadership-i-gordon-gordy-curphy-phd.

62. Curphy, "Investing in the Wrong Vehicle."

63. M. M. Smith, "The Leadership Disconnect," http://blog.octanner.com/leadership/the-leadership-disconnect.

64. Curphy et al., *Managerial Incompetence.*

65. Hogan, *Personality and the Fate of Organizations.*

66. Kaiser, "The Disconnect between Development and the Evolutionary Laws of Leadership."

67. M. A. Huselid, R. W. Beatty, and B. E. Becker, "'A Players' or 'A Positions'? The Strategic Logic of Workforce Management," *Harvard Business Review*, December 2005, pp. 110–21.

68. J. W. Boudreau and P. M. Ramstad, "Talentship and the New Paradigm for Human Resource Management: From Professional Practices to Strategic Talent Decision Science," *Human Resource Planning* 28, no. 2 (2005), pp. 17–26.

69. J. Dowdy, S. Dorgan, T. Rippen, J. Van Reenen, and N. Bloom, *Management Matters* (London: McKinsey & Company, 2005).

70. G. J. Curphy, "The Seven Challenges for Team Leaders," *LinkedIn*, December 21, 2016, www.linkedin.com/pulse/six-challenges-team-leaders-gordon-gordy-curphy-phd.

71. M. W. McCall Jr. and M. M. Lombardo, "Off the Track: Why and How Successful Executives Get Derailed," Technical Report No. 21 (Greensboro, NC: Center for Creative Leadership, 1983).

72. D. L. Dotlich and P. E. Cairo, *Why CEOs Fail: The 11 Behaviors That Can Derail Your Climb to the Top and How to Manage Them* (New York: Wiley, 2001).

73. J. F. Hazucha, *PDI Indicator: Competence, Potential, and Jeopardy. What Gets Managers Ahead May Not Keep Them out of Trouble* (Minneapolis, MN: Personnel Decisions, September 1992).

74. M. M. Lombardo, M. N. Ruderman, and C. D. McCauley, "Explorations of Success and Derailment in Upper-Level Management Positions," paper presented at meeting of the Academy of Management, New York, 1987.

75. J. C. Hogan, R. T. Hogan, and R. B. Kaiser, "Managerial Derailment," in *APA Handbook of Industrial and Organizational Psychology*, Vol. 3, ed. S. Zedeck (Washington, DC: American Psychological Association, 2011), pp. 555–76.

76. E. Van Velsor and J. B. Leslie, "Why Executives Derail: Perspectives across Time and Cultures," *Academy of Management Executive* 9, no. 4 (1995), pp. 62–71.

77. H. J. Foldes and D. S. Ones, "Wrongdoing among Senior Managers: Critical Incidents and their Co-Occurrence," in *Predicting Leadership: The Good, The Bad, the Indifferent, and the Unnecessary*, J. P. Campbell and M. J. Benson (chairs). Symposium conducted at the 22nd Annual Conference for the Society of Industrial and Organizational Psychology, New York, April 2007.

78. M. J. Benson and J. P. Campbell, "Derailing and Dark Side Personality: Incremental Prediction of Leadership (In) Effectiveness," in *Predicting Leadership: The Good, The Bad, the Indifferent, and the Unnecessary*, J. P. Campbell and M. J. Benson (chairs). Symposium conducted at the 22nd Annual Conference for the Society of Industrial and Organizational Psychology, New York, April 2007.

79. V. J. Bentz, "Research Findings from Personality Assessment of Executives," in *Personality Assessment in Organizations*, eds. J. H. Bernadin and D. A. Bownas (New York: Praeger, 1985), pp. 82–144.

80. A. M. Morrison, R. P. White, and E. Van Velsor, *Breaking the Glass Ceiling* (Reading, MA: Addison-Wesley, 1987).

81. R. Rasch, W. Shen, S. E. Davies, and J. Bono, *The Development of a Taxonomy of Ineffective Leadership Behaviors*, paper presented at the 23rd Annual Conference of the Society for Industrial and Organizational Psychology, San Francisco, CA, 2008.

82. G. J. Curphy, "The Dark Side of Leadership," presentation given to the Vistage Group, Minneapolis, February 2013.

83. J. Martin and W. A. Gentry, "Derailment Signs across Generations," *The Psychologist-Manager Journal* 14 (2011), pp. 177–95.

84. J. Zenger and J. Folkman, "Are You Sure You're Not a Bad Boss?" *Harvard Business Review*, August 16, 2012, https://hbr.org/2012/08/are-you-sure-youre-not-a-bad-b.

85. R. Charan, S. Drotter, and J. Noel, *The Leadership Pipeline: How to Build the Leadership-Powered Company* (San Francisco: Jossey-Bass, 2001).

86. R. Charan and G. Colvin, "Why CEOs Fail," *Fortune*, June 21, 1999, pp. 69–82.

87. Van Velsor and Leslie, "Why Executives Derail."

88. Hogan et al., "Managerial Derailment."

89. G. J . Curphy, "Why Do Teams Fail?" LinkedIn, April 8, 2017, www.linkedin.com/pulse/why-do-teams-fail-gordon-gordy-curphy-phd.

90. G. J. Curphy, "The Rocket Model: Practical Advice for Building High Performing Teams," *Team Coaching Zone*, www.teamcoachingzone.com/gordoncurphy_phd.

91. Curphy, "Investing in the Wrong Vehicle."

92. Curphy et al., *Managerial Incompetence.*

93. Hogan, *Personality and the Fate of Organizations.*

94. Charan et al., *The Leadership Pipeline.*

95. G. J. Curphy and R. Hogan, *The Rocket Model: Practical Advice for Building High Performing Teams* (Tulsa, OK: Hogan Press, 2012).

96. G. Curphy, D. Nilsen, and R. Hogan, *Ignition: A Guide to Building High Performing Teams* (Tulsa, OK: Hogan Press, 2019).

97. G. Curphy, "Is Your Team Operating at the Right Level?" Linked In, August 28, 2018, www.linkedin.com/pulse/your-top-team-operating-right-level-gordon-gordy-curphy-phd.

98. Curphy and Hogan, *The Rocket Model: Practical Advice for Building High Performing Teams.*

99. Curphy, *Team Consulting Workshop.*

100. G. J. Curphy, *Leadership Master Class presentation*, Bratislava, Slovakia, March 31, 2017.

101. Curphy, "Investing in the Wrong Vehicle."

102. Curphy et al., *Managerial Incompetence.*

103. Hogan, *Personality and the Fate of Organizations.*

104. Dotlich and Cairo, *Why CEOs Fail: The 11 Behaviors That Can Derail Your Climb to the Top and How to Manage Them.*

105. Charan et al., *The Leadership Pipeline.*

106. Curphy and Hogan, *The Rocket Model.*

107. G. J. Curphy, "Why Leaders Fail," presentation given to NYLife, Dallas, May 2012.

108. Curphy et al., *Ignition.*

109. G. Curphy and D. Nilsen, "Your Top Talent Is Destroying Your Teams," *Talent Quarterly*, Summer 2018, pp. 36–40.

110. J. Bono, P. Braddy, Y. Liu, E. Gilbert, J. Fleenor, L. Quast, and B. Center, "Dropped on the Way to the Top: Gender and Managerial Derailment," *Personnel Psychology* 70, no. 4 (2017), pp. 729–68.

111. Curphy et al., *Managerial Incompetence.*

112. Curphy, "The Dark Side of Leadership."

113. Curphy and Hogan, *The Rocket Model.*

114. Curphy, "Why Leaders Fail."

115. Hogan, *Personality and the Fate of Organizations.*

116. Curphy, "The Dark Side of Leadership."

117. Curphy, "Why Leaders Fail."

118. J. Hogan and R. T. Hogan, *Motives, Values and Preferences Inventory Manual* (Tulsa, OK: Hogan Assessment Systems, 1996).

119. G. J. Curphy, "The Fastest Way to Lower Your IQ," LinkedIn, April 5, 2015, https://www.linkedin.com/pulse/fastest-way-lower-your-iq-gordon-gordy-curphy-phd.

120. Curphy and Nilsen, "Your Top Talent Is Destroying Your Teams."

121. Curphy et al., *Ignition*.

122. Curphy et al., *Managerial Incompetence*.

123. Hogan, *Personality and the Fate of Organizations*.

124. Warden and Russell, *Winning in Fast Time*.

125. Kotter, *Leading Change*.

126. P. A. Craig, *Controlling Pilot Error: Situational Awareness* (New York, NY: McGraw-Hill, 2001).

127. Craig, *Controlling Pilot Error*.

128. P. D. Harms, S. M. Spain, and S. T. Hannah, "Leader Development and the Dark Side of Personality," *Leadership Quarterly* 22 (2011), pp. 495–509.

129. J. Kruger and D. Dunning, "Unskilled and Unaware of It: How Difficulties in Recognizing One's Own Incompetence Lead to Inflated Self-Assessments," *Journal of Personality and Social Psychology* 77, no. 6 (1999), pp. 1121–34.

130. D. L. Nilsen, *Using Self and Observers' Ratings of Personality to Predict Leadership Performance*, unpublished doctoral dissertation, University of Minnesota, 1995.

131. R. I. Sutton, "Some Bosses Live in a Fool's Paradise," *Harvard Business Review*, June 3, 2010, http://blogs.hbr.org/cs/2010/06/some_bosses_live_in_a_fools_pa.html.

132. W. Isaakson, *Steve Jobs* (New York: Simon & Schuster, 2011).

133. G. J. Curphy, "Everyone's a Star in Their Own Movie, and That's a Problem," LinkedIn, December 14, 2014, www.linkedin.com/pulse/everyones-star-own-movie-thats-curphy%2C-phd.

134. P. F. Drucker, "The Theory of the Business," *Harvard Business Review*, September/October 1994.

135. R. T. Hogan and J. Hogan, *The Hogan Business Reasoning Inventory* (Tulsa, OK: Hogan Assessment Systems, 2007).

136. R. T. Hogan, *Intelligence and Good Judgment* (Tulsa, OK: Hogan Assessment Systems, 2008).

137. Curphy et al., *Managerial Incompetence*.

138. Hogan, *Personality and the Fate of Organizations*.

139. Curphy and Hogan, *The Rocket Model*.

140. Hogan, *Intelligence and Good Judgment*.

141. G. J. Curphy and R. T. Hogan, *A Guide to Building High Performing Teams* (North Oaks, MN: Curphy Consulting Corporation, 2010).

142. K. Shue, "Why Is My Boss Incompetent?" *Yale Insights*, April 20, 2018, https://insights.som.yale.edu/insights/why-is-my-boss-incompetent.

143. Curphy, "Investing in the Wrong Vehicle."

144. Curphy and Hogan, *The Rocket Model*.

145. Curphy and Hogan, *A Guide to Building High Performing Teams*.

146. Curphy, *Team Consulting Workshop*.

147. Curphy, "The Seven Challenges for Team Leaders."

148. Curphy, "Why Do Teams Fail?"

149. G. Curphy and D. Nilsen, *The Team Assessment Survey* (North Oaks, MN: Curphy Leadership Solutions, 2018).

150. Curphy et al., *Ignition*.

151. Curphy and Nilsen, *The Team Assessment Survey*.

152. Curphy et al., *Ignition: A Guide to Building High Performing Teams*.

153. G. J. Curphy and R. M. Roellig, *Followership* (North Oaks, MN: Curphy Consulting Corporation, 2010).

154. Curphy et al., *Managerial Incompetence*.

155. Hogan, *Personality and the Fate of Organizations*.

156. Dotlich and Cairo, *Why CEOs Fail*.

157. Hogan et al., "Managerial Derailment."

158. Benson and Campbell, "Derailing and Dark Side Personality."

159. Curphy, "Why Leaders Fail."

160. M. J. Benson and J. P. Campbell, "To Be, or Not to Be, Linear: An Expanded Representation of Personality and Its Relationship to Leadership Performance," *International Journal of Selection and Assessment* 15 (2007), pp. 232–49.

161. G. J. Curphy and R. T. Hogan, *Managerial Incompetence: Is There a Dead Skunk on the Table?* working paper, 2004.

162. G. J. Curphy and R. T. Hogan, *What We Really Know about Leadership (but Seem Unwilling to Implement)*, working paper, 2004.

163. R. T. Hogan and J. C. Hogan, "Assessing Leadership from the Dark Side," *International Journal of Selection and Assessment* 9, no. 1–2 (2001), pp. 40–51.

164. S. J. Peterson, B. M. Galvin, and D. Lange, "CEO Servant Leadership: Exploring Executive Characteristics and Firm Performance," *Personnel Psychology* 65 (2012), pp. 565–96.

165. S. B. Silverman, R. E. Johnson, N. McConnell, and A. Carr, "Arrogance: A Formula for Leadership Failure," *The Industrial-Organizational Psychologist* 50, no. 1 (2012), pp. 21–29.

166. R. T. Hogan, "Reflections on the Dark Side", *Talent Quarterly*, www.talent-quarterly.com/reflections-on-the-dark-side-tq-2016-issue8.

167. R. Kaiser, "Dealing with the Dark Side," *Talent Quarterly*, https://www.talent-quarterly.com/reflections-on-the-dark-side-tq-2016-issue8.

168. Curphy et al., *Managerial Incompetence*.

169. Hogan, *Personality and the Fate of Organizations*.

170. Hogan et al., "Managerial Derailment."

171. Curphy, "Why Leaders Fail."

172. Silverman et al., "Arrogance."

173. Curphy et al., *Managerial Incompetence*.

174. Hogan, *Personality and the Fate of Organizations*.

175. Hogan et al., "Managerial Derailment."

176. Curphy, "Why Leaders Fail."

177. Silverman et al., "Arrogance."

178. Curphy et al., *Managerial Incompetence*.

179. Hogan, *Personality and the Fate of Organizations*.

180. Hogan et al., "Managerial Derailment."

181. Curphy, "Why Leaders Fail."

182. Hogan and Hogan, "Assessing Leadership from the Dark Side."

183. T. Williams, "Can Too Much Charisma Make a Leader Ineffective?" *The Economist*, https://execed.economist.com/blog/industry-trends/can-too-much-charisma-make-leader-ineffective.

184. Shue, "Why Is My Boss Incompetent?"

185. S. Gregory, "The Most Common Type of Incompetent Leader," *Harvard Business Review*, March 30, 2018, https://hbr.org/2018/03/the-most-common-type-of-incompetent-leader.

186. D. King, "What's Worse Than a Tyrannical Leader? One Who Isn't There," *Hogan Assessments*, July 20,2018, www.hoganassessments.com/whats-worse-than-a-tyrannical-leader-one-who-isnt-there.

187. T. Gryta, J. Lublin, and D. Benoit, "'Success Theater' Masked the Rot at GE," *The Wall Street Journal*, February 22, 2018, pp. A1 and 8.

188. F. Luthans, S. A. Rosenkrantz, and H. W. Hennessey, "What Do Successful Managers Really Do? An Observational Study of Managerial Activities," *Journal of Applied Behavioral Science* 21 (1985), pp. 255–70.

189. G. J. Curphy, "Key Differences between Successful and Effective Leaders," LinkedIn, March 14, 2014, https://www.linkedin.com/pulse/20140314142437-36824143-key-differences-between-successful-and-effective-leaders.

190. G. J. Curphy, "Stupid High-Potential Tricks," LinkedIn, September 8, 2015, https://www.linkedin.com/pulse/stupid-high-potential-tricks-gordon-gordy-curphy-phd.

191. J. Hu, B. Erdogan, K. Jiang, T. Bauer, and S. Liu, "Leader Humility and Team Creativity: The Role of Team Information Sharing, Psychological Safety, and Power Distance," *Journal of Applied Psychology* 103, no. 3 (2018), pp. 313–23.

192. Curphy, *Team Consulting Workshop*.

193. Curphy, *Leadership Master Class presentation*.

194. J. Pfeffer, *Power: Why Some People Have It—and Others Don't* (New York: HarperCollins, 2010).

195. J. Pfeffer, *Leadership b.s.: Fixing Workplaces and Careers One Truth at a Time* (New York: Harper Business, 2015).

196. J. Collins, *Good to Great* (New York: HarperCollins, 2001).

197. Pfeffer, *Leadership b.s.*

198. B. George, "The Truth about Authentic Leaders," *Working Knowledge*, July 6, 2016, http://hbswk.hbs.edu/item/the-truth-about-authentic-leaders.

199. G. J. Curphy, "Everyone's a Star in Their Own Movie, and That's a Problem," Linked In, December 14, 2014, www.linkedin.com/pulse/everyones-star-own-movie-thats-curphy%2C-phd.

200. G. J. Curphy, "The Misguided Romance of Authentic Leadership," LinkedIn, August 11, 2014, www.linkedin.com/pulse/20140811130045-36824143-the-misguided-romance-of-authentic-leadership.

201. G. J. Curphy, "Organizational Realpolitik and Leadership Development—Part I," LinkedIn, January 1, 2016, www.linkedin.com/pulse/organizational-realpolitik-leadership-i-gordon-gordy-curphy-phd.

202. Pfeffer, *Leadership b.s.*

203. Pfeffer, *Leadership b.s.*

204. G. J. Curphy, "Organizational Realpolitik and Leadership Development—Part II," LinkedIn, January 11, 2016, www.linkedin.com/pulse/organizational-realpolitik-leadership-ii-gordon-gordy-curphy-phd.

205. Curphy, *Leadership Master Class presentation*.

CHAPTER 18

Skills for Optimizing Leadership as Situations Change

Introduction

In this final chapter we offer some ideas about skills appropriate to the last element of the interactional framework. These skills include relatively advanced leadership skills useful in various specific situational challenges:

- Creating a Compelling Vision
- Managing Conflict
- Negotiation
- Diagnosing Performance Problems in Individuals, Groups, and Organizations
- Team Building at the Top

Creating a Compelling Vision

Suppose you are running the computer department at an electronics store. Overall the store has been having a good year: Sales of cell phones, HDTVs and in-home theater equipment, and digital cameras have all been strong. But computer sales are lagging, and the store manager is exerting considerable pressure on you to increase sales. Your 11 sales associates are all relatively new to sales, and many do not have strong computer backgrounds. Your assistant department manager recently moved to the in-home theater department, and you have been screening candidates for this opening on your team. After failing to be impressed with the first four candidates interviewed, you notice that the next candidate, Colleen, has just moved to town and has a strong background in electronics sales. During the interview you become even more convinced that Colleen would be an ideal assistant department manager. Toward the end of the interview you ask Colleen if she has any questions about the position, and she states that she is considering several job offers and is asking all her prospective employers the same question, which is "Why should I work for you?"

What would you say if someone asked you this question? Would you be able to close the sale and make a strong case for getting someone to join your team? Believe it or not, many leaders cannot provide a compelling description of how they add value; as a result they have difficulty getting anyone excited to become part of their groups. And these struggles are not limited to new leaders—many seasoned leaders either do not have or cannot effectively articulate a clear and dynamic leadership vision. Yet many followers want to know where their team or group is going, how it intends to get there, and what they need to do to win. A leader's vision can answer these questions, explain why change is necessary, and keep team members motivated and focused. Because a leader's vision can have a pervasive effect on followers and teams, it is worth describing a process for building a compelling leadership vision.[1, 2]

Before discussing the four components of leadership vision, it is worth noting that most people don't get particularly excited about a leader's vision by sitting through lengthy PowerPoint presentations or formal speeches. People tend to get more involved when leaders use stories, analogies, and personal experiences to paint compelling pictures of the future. As such, a leader's vision should be a personal statement that should help listeners answer the following questions:

- Where is the team going, and how will it get there?
- How does the team win, and how does it contribute to the broader organization's success?
- How does the speaker define leadership?
- What gets the speaker excited about being a leader?
- What are the speaker's key values? In other words, what are the leader's expectations for team members, and what will she or he not tolerate as a leader?

If you are currently in a leadership position, ask yourself how your direct reports would answer these questions. Would each of them answer all five questions the same way, or would their answers differ? Alternatively, how would you answer these questions for your boss? If followers do not provide the same answers for these questions, leaders may need to create or better articulate their leadership vision. As shown in **Figure 18.1**, a leadership vision consists of four related components.

FIGURE 18.1 The Four Components of a Leadership Vision

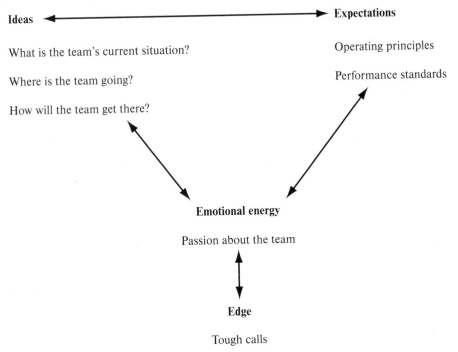

Ideas

What is the team's current situation?

Where is the team going?

How will the team get there?

Expectations

Operating principles

Performance standards

Emotional energy

Passion about the team

Edge

Tough calls

Stories, analogies, and metaphors

Ideas: The Future Picture

The idea component of a leader's vision begins with an honest assessment of the current situation facing the team.[3] Leaders need to clearly identify what the team is doing well, what it is not doing well, how it is performing compared to the competition, and what challenges it faces. Leaders should not pull any punches when assessing team performance because downplaying or overlooking team shortcomings will likely result in mediocrity. Once a leader has accurately assessed a team's strengths, weaknesses, and potential, he or she needs to clearly define where the team needs to be over the next 12–36 months. This future picture needs to describe the team's upcoming goals; the reputation it needs to have within the organization, among competitors, and with customers; and what strategies the team will pursue to achieve these outcomes. Ideas should also describe what changes the team must make to accomplish its major goals, explain why these changes are necessary, and give listeners hope for the future.[4]

Although leaders can complete the ideas component by themselves, they will often get considerably more commitment by working with their teams to assess the situation, set future team goals, and identify the changes needed for success. Whether the idea component is a solo or team effort, leaders will have successfully articulated their future pictures when everyone on their teams shares the same understanding of the situation and what they need to do to win.

Expectations: Values and Performance Standards

A leader's vision also needs to clearly describe her or his expectations for team member behavior. More specifically, what behaviors do leaders want team members to exhibit, and just as important, what behaviors will they not tolerate from team members? A leader's expectations for team members are highly related to his or her values. For example, if a leader believes winning is an important value, then he or she needs to say something about the levels of performance and commitment needed by team members. Or if leaders believe collaboration is an important value, they need to define how team members are supposed to work together. Because values and operating principles play such an important role in defining team member expectations, leaders should spend time identifying the team's core values and the positive and negative behaviors associated with these values. To improve understanding and buy-in, leaders can work with team members to jointly define a team's core values.

One important leadership role is to ensure that a team's core values are aligned with its future picture. For example, if the team has some aggressive performance goals, then its core values should include something about the performance and commitment expectations for individual team members. Team goals represent *what* a team must do to succeed; core values and operating principles represent *how* team members should behave if the team is to win. In addition, leaders should strive to implement a fairly limited (five to eight) set of core values. Team members often have difficulty recalling more than a half dozen core values, so the operating principles should be limited to only those values that are most directly related to team goals.

Leaders not only need to be role models for these core values—they also need to hold team members accountable for behaving in accordance with these operating principles. Nothing will erode a leader's credibility or team morale more quickly than leaders or team members not being held accountable for exhibiting behaviors that are misaligned with a team's operating principles. Leaders will have successfully conveyed their operating principles when everyone on the team understands and is behaving in accordance with the team's core values.

Emotional Energy: The Power and the Passion

The last two components of leadership vision, emotional energy and edge, are concerned more with delivery than content. Emotional energy is the level of enthusiasm leaders use to convey the future vision and the team's operating principles. Nothing kills follower enthusiasm and motivation for a leader's vision more quickly than a dull, monotone delivery. If leaders are not excited about where the team is going and how it will get there, it will be difficult to get others to join the effort. However, leaders who are excited about where their teams are going still need to make sure this enthusiasm is clear in the delivery of their vision. Emotional appeals make for compelling messages, and leaders should use a range of emotions when describing the future picture and operating principles. Leaders will have effectively mastered the emotional energy component when team members see that they are excited about where the team is going and about being in a leadership role.

Edge: Stories, Analogies, and Metaphors

Perhaps the most difficult component to master when it comes to creating a leadership vision is edge. Edge pertains to lessons of leadership learned through personal experience that are related to the team's future picture and core values. Edge includes personal stories and examples that can help color a team's future picture. For example, edge might include stories about teams that leaders have been on or have led in the past through similar situations. Edge would also include stories that illustrate why some of the team's core values are so important—examples of how team members did or did not act in accordance with a particular value and what happened as a result. Edge can also include slogans, analogies, and metaphors to help clarify and simplify where the team is going or what it stands for. In general, the more personal the examples and the simpler the stories, the more likely leaders will leave an impression on team members.

Leaders should not spend too much time worrying about edge until the team's future picture and core values are clearly defined. However, once these issues are clearly understood, leaders need to reflect on how their personal experiences can help team members understand where the team is going and why certain behaviors are important. They should also spend time brainstorming analogies, metaphors, and slogans that can distill team goals and behaviors into simple but memorable messages. As was described for the future picture and core values, these analogies and slogans do not have to be solo efforts; leaders can solicit team members' help in creating slogans that convey simple but compelling messages about the future direction for their teams.

Although ideas, expectations, emotional energy, and edge make up the four components of a leader's vision, several other leadership vision issues are worth noting. First, the delivery of a leader's vision improves with practice. The four components can help leaders define what they need to say and how they need to say it, but leaders should practice the delivery of their vision a number of times before going live with team members. Ideally they should use video recordings of some of these practice deliveries to ensure that key messages are being conveyed, the personal stories being used make sense and are easy to follow, and excitement and emotion are evident. Second, leaders need to remember that the most compelling presentations of leadership visions are relatively short and make sparing use of PowerPoint slides. Many of the best presentations of leadership visions are less than 10 minutes long and consist of no more than three to four slides. Third, leaders need to continually tie team events back to their vision and core values. Reminding team members how delegated tasks relate to the team's vision, tying team member feedback to core values, and explaining how staff and strategy changes relate to team goals and operating principles are all effective ways to keep team members focused and motivated toward a leader's vision. And fourth, having a clear and compelling leadership vision should go a long way in answering the question posed at the beginning of this section, which was "Why should I work for you?"

Managing Conflict

We read or hear in the daily news about various types of negotiations. Nations often negotiate with each other over land or fishing rights, trade agreements, or diplomatic relations. Land developers often negotiate with city councils for variances of local zoning laws for their projects. Businesses often spend considerable time negotiating employee salaries and fringe benefits with labor unions. In a similar fashion, negotiations every day cover matters ranging from high school athletic schedules to where a new office copying machine will be located. In one sense, all these negotiations, big or small, are similar. In every case, representatives from different groups meet to resolve some sort of conflict. Conflict is an inevitable fact of life and an inevitable fact of leadership. Researchers have found that first-line supervisors and mid-level managers can spend more than 25 percent of their time dealing with conflict,[5] and resolving conflict has been found to be an important factor in leadership effectiveness.[6] In fact, successfully resolving conflicts is so important that it is a central theme in some of the literature about organizations.[7, 8, 9] Moreover, successfully resolving conflicts will become an increasingly important skill as leadership and management practice moves away from authoritarian directives and toward cooperative approaches emphasizing rational persuasion, collaboration, compromise, and solutions of mutual gain.

What Is Conflict?

Conflict occurs when opposing parties have interests or goals that appear to be incompatible.[10] There are a variety of sources of conflict in team, committee, work group, and organizational settings. For example, conflict can occur when group or team members (1) have strong differences in values, beliefs, or goals; (2) have high levels of task or lateral interdependence; (3) are competing for scarce resources or rewards; (4) are under high levels of stress; or (5) face uncertain or incompatible demands—that is, role ambiguity and role conflict.[11] Conflict can also occur when leaders act in a manner inconsistent with the vision and goals they have articulated for the organization.[12] Of these factors contributing to the level of conflict within or between groups, teams, or committees, probably the most important source of conflict is the lack of communication between parties.[13] Because many conflicts are the result of misunderstandings and communication breakdowns, leaders can minimize the level of conflict within and between groups by improving their communication and listening skills, as well as by spending time networking with others.[14]

Before we review specific negotiation tips and conflict resolution strategies, it is necessary to describe several aspects of conflict that can have an impact on the resolution process. First, the size of an issue (bigger issues are more difficult to resolve), the extent to which parties define the problem egocentrically (how much they have personally invested in the problem), and the existence of hidden agendas (unstated but important concerns or objectives) can all affect the conflict resolution process. Second, seeing a conflict situation in win–lose or either–or terms restricts the perceived possible outcomes to either total satisfaction or total frustration. A similar but less extreme variant is to see a situation in zero-sum terms. A zero-sum situation is one in which intermediate degrees of satisfaction are possible, but increases in one party's satisfaction inherently decrease the other party's satisfaction, and vice versa. Still another variant can occur when parties perceive a conflict as unresolvable. In such cases neither party gains at the expense of the other, but each continues to perceive the other as an obstacle to satisfaction.[15]

Is Conflict Always Bad?

So far we have described conflict as an inherently negative aspect of any group, team, committee, or organization. This certainly was the prevailing view of conflict among researchers during the 1930s and 1940s, and it probably also represents the way many people are raised today (that is, most people have a strong value of minimizing or avoiding conflict). However, researchers studying group effectiveness today have come to a different conclusion. Some level of conflict may help bolster innovation and performance. Conflict that enhances group productivity is viewed as useful, and conflict that hinders group performance is viewed as counterproductive.[16] Various possible positive and negative effects of conflict are listed in **Highlight 18.1**.

Possible Effects of Conflict

HIGHLIGHT 18.1

Possible Positive Effects of Conflict	Possible Negative Effects of Conflict
Increased effort	Reduced productivity
Feelings get aired	Decreased communication
Better understanding of others	Negative feelings
Impetus for change	Stress
Better decision-making	Poorer decision-making
Key issues surface	Decreased cooperation
Critical thinking stimulated	Political backstabbing

Along these lines, researchers have found that conflict can cause a radical change in political power,[17, 18] as well as dramatic changes in organizational structure and design, group cohesiveness, and group or organizational effectiveness.[19, 20] Nevertheless, it is important to realize that this current conceptualization of conflict is still somewhat limited in scope. For example, increasing the level of conflict within a group or team may enhance immediate performance but may also have a disastrous effect on organizational climate and turnover. Leaders may be evaluated in terms of many criteria, however, only one of which is group performance. Thus leaders should probably use criteria such as turnover and absenteeism rates and followers' satisfaction or organizational climate ratings in addition to measures of group performance when trying to determine whether conflict is good or bad. Leaders are cautioned against using group performance alone because this may not reveal the overall effects of conflict on the group or team.

Conflict Resolution Strategies

In addition to spending time understanding and clarifying positions, separating people from the problem, and focusing on interests, leaders can use five strategies or approaches to resolve conflicts. Perhaps the best way to differentiate among these five strategies is to think of conflict resolution in terms of two independent dimensions: cooperativeness versus uncooperativeness and assertiveness versus unassertiveness (see **Figure 18.2**). Parties in conflict vary in their commitment to satisfy the other's concerns, but they also vary in the extent to which they assertively stand up for their own concerns.[21] Thus conflict resolution can be understood in terms of how cooperative or uncooperative the parties are and how assertive or unassertive they are.

Using this two-dimension scheme, Thomas[22] described five general approaches to managing conflict:

1. *Competition* reflects a desire to achieve one's own ends at the expense of someone else. This is domination, also known as a win–lose orientation.

2. *Accommodation* reflects a mirror image of competition—entirely giving in to someone else's concerns without making any effort to achieve one's own ends. This is a tactic of appeasement.

3. *Sharing* is an approach that represents a compromise between domination and appeasement. Both parties give up something, yet both parties get something. Both parties are moderately, but incompletely, satisfied.

4. *Collaboration* reflects an effort to fully satisfy both parties. This is a problem-solving approach that requires the integration of each party's concerns.

5. *Avoidance* involves indifference to the concerns of both parties. It reflects a withdrawal from or neglect of any party's interests.

FIGURE 18.2   Five Conflict-Handling Orientations, Plotted According to the Parties' Desire to Satisfy Own and Other's Concerns

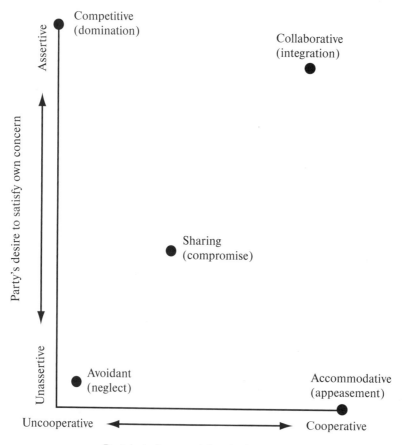

Source: Adapted from Kenneth W. Thomas and Ralph H. Kilmann, *The Thomas-Kilmann Conflict Mode Instrument* (Mountain View, CA: CPP, Inc., 1974, 2002).

Does one of these approaches seem clearly better than the others to you? Each of them does, at least, reflect certain culturally valued modes of behavior.[23] For example, the esteem many people hold for athletic, business, and military heroes reflects our cultural valuation of competition. Valuation of a pragmatic approach to settling problems is reflected in the compromising approach. Cultural values of unselfishness, kindness, and generosity are reflected in accommodation, and even avoidance has roots in philosophies that emphasize caution, diplomacy, and turning away from worldly concerns. These cultural roots to each of the approaches to managing conflict suggest that no single one is likely to be right all the time. There probably are circumstances when each of the modes of conflict resolution can be appropriate. Rather than seeking a single best approach to managing conflict, it may be wisest to appreciate the relative advantages and disadvantages of all the approaches, as well as the circumstances when each may be most appropriate. A summary of experienced leaders' recommendations for when to use each strategy is presented in **Highlight 18.2**.

Situations in Which to Use the Five Approaches to Conflict Management

HIGHLIGHT 18.2

COMPETING

1. When quick, decisive action is vital—such as emergencies.

2. On important issues where unpopular actions need implementing—cost cutting, enforcing unpopular rules, discipline.

3. On issues vital to company welfare when you know you're right.

4. Against people who take advantage of noncompetitive behavior.

COLLABORATING

1. To find an integrative solution when both sets of concerns are too important to be compromised.

2. When your objective is to learn.

3. To merge insights from people with different perspectives.

4. To gain commitment by incorporating concerns into a consensus.

5. To work through feelings that have interfered with a relationship.

COMPROMISING

1. When goals are important, but not worth the effort or potential disruption of more assertive modes.

2. When opponents with equal power are committed to mutually exclusive goals.

3. To achieve temporary settlements of complex issues.

4. To arrive at expedient solutions under time pressure.

5. As a backup when collaboration or competition is unsuccessful.

AVOIDING

1. When an issue is trivial or more important issues are pressing.

2. When you perceive no chance of satisfying your concerns.

3. When potential disruption outweighs the benefits of resolution.

4. To let people cool down and regain perspective.

5. When gathering information supersedes immediate decisions.

6. When others can resolve the conflict more effectively.

7. When issues seem tangential to or symptomatic of other issues.

ACCOMMODATING

1. When you find you are wrong—to allow a better position to be heard, to learn, and to show your reasonableness.

2. When issues are more important to others than yourself—to satisfy others and maintain cooperation.

3. To build social credits for later issues.

4. To minimize loss when you are outmatched and losing.

5. When harmony and stability are especially important.

6. To allow subordinates to develop by learning from mistakes.

Source: K. W. Thomas, "Toward Multidimensional Values in Teaching: The Example of Conflict Management," *Academy of Management Review* 2, no. 3 (1977), pp. 484–90. Copyright © 1977 Academy of Management, via Copyright Clearance Center.

Finally, winning a negotiation at your counterpart's expense is likely to be only a short-term gain. Leaders should attempt to work out a resolution by looking at long-term rather than short-term goals, and they should try to build a working relationship that will endure and be mutually trusting and beneficial beyond the present negotiation. Along these lines, leaders should always seek win–win outcomes that try to satisfy both sides' needs and continuing interests. It often takes creative problem solving to find new options that provide gains for both sides. Realistically, however, not all situations may be conducive to seeking win–win outcomes (see **Highlight 18.3**).

How to Swim with Sharks

HIGHLIGHT 18.3

It is dangerous to swim with sharks, but not all sharks are found in the water. Some people may behave like sharks, and a best-selling book for executives took its title from that theme. However, an article appeared in the journal *Perspectives in Biology and Medicine* over three decades ago claiming to be a translated version of an essay written in France more than a century earlier for sponge divers. The essay notes that while no one wants to swim with sharks, it is an occupational hazard for certain people. For those who must swim with sharks, it can be essential to follow certain rules. See if you think the following rules for interacting with the sharks of the sea serve as useful analogies for interacting with the sharks of everyday life:

Rule 1: Assume any unidentified fish is a shark. Just because a fish may be acting in a docile manner does not mean it is not a shark. The real test is how it will act when blood is in the water.

Rule 2: Don't bleed. Bleeding will prompt even more aggressive behavior and the involvement of even more sharks. Of course, it is not easy to keep from bleeding when injured. Those who cannot do so are advised not to swim with sharks at all.

Rule 3: Confront aggression quickly. Sharks usually give warning before attacking a swimmer. Swimmers should watch for indications an attack is imminent and take prompt counteraction. A blow to the nose is often appropriate because it shows you understand the shark's intentions and will respond in kind. It is particularly dangerous to behave in an ingratiating manner toward sharks. People who once held this erroneous view often can be identified by a missing limb.

Rule 4: Get out of the water if anyone starts bleeding. Previously docile sharks may begin attacking if blood is in the water. Their behavior can become so irrational, even including attacking themselves, that it is safest to remove yourself entirely from the situation.

Rule 5: Create dissension among the attackers. Sharks are self-centered and rarely act in an organized fashion with other sharks. This significantly reduces the risk of swimming with sharks. Every now and then, however, sharks may launch a coordinated attack. The best strategy then is to create internal dissension among them because they already are quite prone to it; often sharks will fight among themselves over trivial or minor things. By the time their internal conflict is settled, sharks often have forgotten about their organized attack.

Rule 6: Never divert a shark attack toward another swimmer. Please observe this final item of swimming etiquette.

Source: V. Cousteau, "How to Swim with Sharks: A Primer," *Perspectives in Biology and Medicine,* Summer 1973, pp. 525–28. Copyright © 1973 University of Chicago Press. Reprinted with permission of The Johns Hopkins University Press.

Negotiation

Negotiation is an approach that may help resolve some conflicts. The following negotiating tips, from Fisher and Ury,[24] include taking the time to prepare for a negotiating session; keeping the people and problems separate; and focusing on interests rather than on positions.

Prepare for the Negotiation

To successfully resolve conflicts, leaders may need to spend considerable time preparing for a negotiating session. Leaders should anticipate each side's key concerns and issues, attitudes, possible negotiating strategies, and goals.

Separate the People from the Problem

Fisher and Ury[25] also advised negotiators to separate the people from the problem. Because all negotiations involve substantive issues and relationships between negotiators, it is easy for these parts to become entangled. When that happens, parties may inadvertently treat the people and the problem as though they were the same. For example, a group of teachers angry that their salaries have not been raised for the fourth year in a row may direct their personal bitterness toward the school board president. However, reactions such as these are usually a mistake because the decision may be out of the other party's hands, and personally attacking the other party often makes the conflict even more difficult to resolve.

Leaders can do several things to separate the people from the problem. First, leaders should not let their fears color their perceptions of each side's intentions. It is easy to attribute negative qualities to others when we feel threatened. Similarly, it does no good to blame the other side for our own problems.[26] Even if this is justified, it is still usually counterproductive. Another thing leaders can do to separate the people from the problem is to communicate clearly. Earlier in this text we suggested techniques for active listening. Those guidelines are especially helpful in negotiating and resolving conflicts.

Focus on Interests, Not Positions

Another of Fisher and Ury's[27] main points is to focus on interests, not positions. Focusing on interests depends on understanding the difference between interests and positions. Here is one example. Say Raoul has had the same reserved seats to the local symphony every season for several years, but he was just notified that he will no longer get his usual tickets. Feeling irate, he goes to the ticket office to complain. One approach he could take would be to demand the same seats he has always had; this would be his *position*. A different approach would be to find alternative seats that are just as satisfactory as his old seats were; this would be his *interest*. In negotiating, it is much more constructive to satisfy interests than to fight over positions. Furthermore, it is important to focus both on your counterpart's interests (not position) and on your own interests (not position).

Diagnosing Performance Problems in Individuals, Groups, and Organizations

In many ways leaders will be only as effective as the followers and teams they lead. Along these lines, one of the more difficult issues leaders must deal with is managing individuals or teams that are not performing up to expectations. What makes this issue even more difficult is that although the lack of performance may be obvious, the reasons for it may not. Leaders who correctly determine why a follower or team is exhibiting suboptimal performance are much more likely to implement an appropriate intervention to fix the problem. Unfortunately, many leaders do not have a model or framework for diagnosing performance problems at work, and as a result many do a poor job of dealing with problem performers. The model in **Figure 18.3** gives leaders a pragmatic framework for understanding why a follower or team may not be performing up to expectations and what the leader can do to improve the situation. This model maintains that performance is a function of expectations, capabilities, opportunities, and motivation and integrates concepts discussed in more detail earlier in this book.

FIGURE 18.3   A Model of Performance

Performance $= f$ (Expectations $\times$ Capabilities $\times$ Opportunities $\times$ Motivation)

The model is also a modification of earlier models developed by various experts.[28, 29, 30] Because it is a multiplicative rather than a compensatory model, a deficit in any component should result in a substantial decrement in performance that cannot be easily made up by increasing the other components. An example might help illuminate this point. Recently one of the authors was asked to help the manager of a nuclear power plant fix several safety and operational issues affecting the plant. Apparently many plant personnel did not feel they had to comply with governmental regulations regarding the proper use of safety equipment. An investigation into the problem revealed that the expectations for compliance were clear, everyone had been trained in the proper use of safety equipment, and the equipment was readily available. However, many personnel felt the equipment and procedures were a nuisance and unnecessary. The plant manager's initial attempt to rectify this problem was to run all plant personnel through a three-day nuclear safety training program. Much to the manager's surprise, the training program actually appeared to decrease safety compliance. This was due to the fact that the underlying issue was not expectations, capabilities, or opportunities but rather motivation. Even 30 days of training would not have helped motivation, which was the underlying barrier to performance. Because there were few if any positive or negative consequences for the staff's use or neglect of the equipment, the problem did not improve until the manager implemented a system of rewards and punishments for safety compliance. A more thorough explanation of the components of the model and what leaders can do to improve performance follows.

Expectations

Performance problems often occur because individuals or groups do not understand what they are supposed to do. In many instances talented, skilled groups accomplish the wrong objective because of miscommunication or sit idly while waiting for instructions that never arrive. It is the leader's responsibility to ensure that followers understand their roles, goals, performance standards, and the key metrics for determining success. More information about goal setting and clarifying team goals and roles can be found in the "Setting Goals" and "Building High-Performance Teams" sections of **Chapter 13**.

Capabilities

Just because followers understand what they are supposed to do does not necessarily mean they can do it. Sometimes followers and teams lack the capabilities needed to achieve a goal or perform above expectations. Abilities and skills are the two components that make up capabilities. Ability is really another name for raw talent, and includes such individual variables as athleticism, intelligence, creativity, and personality traits. As such, abilities are characteristics that are relatively difficult to change with training. Because abilities are relatively insensitive to training interventions, sending people who lack the required abilities to more training or motivating them to work harder will have relatively little impact on performance. Instead the best remedy for this situation is to select individuals with the abilities needed for performance.

Although followers may have the raw talent needed to perform a task, they still may lack the skills needed to perform at a high level. Such is the case with many athletic teams or musical groups at the beginning of the season or when a work group gets new equipment or responsibility for tasks it has no previous experience with. As discussed in **Chapter 7** on leadership behavior, skills consist of a well-defined body of knowledge and a set of related behaviors. Unlike abilities, skills are amenable to training, and leaders with high levels of relevant expertise may coach others in the development of skills, see that they are obtained in other ways on the job, or send their followers to training programs to improve their skill levels.

Opportunities

Performance can also be limited when followers lack the resources needed to get the job done. At other times followers may lack the opportunity to demonstrate acquired skills. Such is the case when passengers are hungry but flight attendants have no meals to pass out during the flight. In this situation the flight attendants could have high levels of customer service goals, capabilities, and motivation but will still not be able to satisfy customer needs. Leaders must ensure that followers and teams have the needed equipment, financial resources, and opportunities to exhibit their skills if they want to eliminate this constraint on performance.

Motivation

Many performance problems can be attributed to a lack of motivation. The critical issue here is whether followers or groups choose to perform or exhibit the level of effort necessary to accomplish a task. If this does not occur, the leader should first try to learn why people are unmotivated. Sometimes the task may involve risks the leader is not aware of. At other times individuals or groups may run out of steam to perform the task, or there may be few consequences for superior or unsatisfactory performance. Leaders have several options to resolve motivation problems in followers and teams. First, they can select followers who have higher levels of achievement or intrinsic motivation for the task. Second, they can set clear goals or do a better job of providing performance feedback. Third, they can reallocate work across the team or redesign the tasks to improve skill variety, task significance, and task identity. Fourth, they can restructure rewards and punishments so that they are more closely linked to performance levels. See **Chapter 9** for more information about motivating followers.

Concluding Comments on the Diagnostic Model

In summary, this model provides an integrative framework for many of the topics affecting performance previously reviewed in this text. It reviews some of the factors that affect performance and suggests ideas for rectifying performance problems. However, this model addresses only follower, group, and organizational performance. Leaders need to remember that there are other desirable outcomes, too, such as organizational climate and job satisfaction, and that actions to increase performance (especially just in the short term) may adversely impact these other desirable outcomes.

Team Building at the Top

In certain ways, executive teams are similar to any other teams. For example, just about any group of senior executives that has faced a dire crisis and survived will note that teamwork was essential for its survival. In a nutshell, then, *when teamwork is critical*, all the lessons of the **Chapter 13** section "Building High-Performance Teams" apply. More specifically, to really benefit from a team-building intervention, individual members must be comfortable with their own strengths and weaknesses and the strengths and weaknesses of their peers. But this raises a question: If all this is true, why do we include a separate section about team building for top teams? Because two important differences between most teams and "teams at the top" should be addressed.

Executive Teams Are Different

As opposed to other kinds of work teams, not all the work at the executive level requires all (or even any) of the team to be present. An example might help. In our research on teams we studied the air crews that fly the B-1 bomber. These are four-person teams comprising an aircraft commander, a copilot, an offensive systems officer, and a defensive systems officer. While each has individual responsibilities, in every bombing run we observed, it was essential that the team work together to accomplish the mission. They had all the components of a true team (complex and common goal, differentiated skills, interdependence), and no individual acting alone could have achieved success. But this is not always the case for executive teams.

As Katzenbach[31] has observed, many top leadership challenges do not require teamwork at all. Furthermore, many top leadership challenges that do constitute real team opportunities do not require or warrant full involvement by everyone who is officially on the team. In fact, an official "team at the top" rarely functions as a collective whole involving all the formal members. Thus the real trick for executive teams is to be able to apply both the technical individual skills that probably got the individuals to the team and the skills required for high-performance teamwork when a team situation presents itself.

Applying Individual Skills and Team Skills

There are two critical requirements if this is to work. First, leaders must have the diagnostic skills to discern whether a challenge involves an individual situation or a team situation. Then leaders must "stay the course" when a team situation is present. This means, for example, when pressure for results intensifies, not slipping back into the traditional modes of assigning work to an individual (such as one member of that top team), but rather allowing the team to complete the work *as a team*. Again, Katzenbach stated this clearly:

> Some leadership groups, of course, err in the opposite way, by attempting to forge a team around performance opportunities that do not call for a team approach. In fact, the increasing emphasis that team proponents place on "team-based organizations" creates real frustrations as top leadership groups try to rationalize good executive leadership instincts into time-consuming team building that has no performance purpose. Catalyzing real team performances at the top does not mean replacing executive leadership with executive teams; it means being rigorous about the distinction between opportunities that require single-leader efforts and those that require team efforts—and applying the discipline that fits.[32]

To summarize this point, executives do not always need to perform as a team to be effective. But when they do need to perform as a team, the same lessons of team building discussed earlier can help enhance their team performance.

The second difference with executive teams is that they have an opportunity to enhance teamwork throughout their organization that few others have. It is our experience that *only the executive team can change organizational systems*. Recall that in **Chapter 12** we described the "Team Leadership Model" and mentioned four systems issues critical to team performance. These systems were all located at the organizational level and consisted of reward systems, education systems, information systems, and control systems. The impact of these systems can be so pervasive across the entire organization that a small change in a system can have monumental impact in the organization. In a sense, then, the executive team has the power to do widespread team building in a manner different from we have discussed to this point. For example, consider the impact of changing a compensation system from an individual-based bonus plan to a team-based bonus plan.

Tripwire Lessons

Finally, our experience in working with executives has taught us that leaders at this level have important lessons to learn about team building at the top. Richard Hackman,[33] in preparing the huge editorial task of having many people produce one coherent book (by his own admission, not necessarily the best of team tasks), assembled the various authors at a conference center. As one of the contributors, one of this text's authors (RCG) recalls the frustrating task of attempting to put together a simple checklist of steps to ensure that a team developed properly. As this arduous process dragged on and tempers flared, it became obvious that "Teamwork for Dummies" was never going to emerge. But something else did emerge. It became clear that *some behaviors leaders engaged in could virtually guarantee failure for their teams*. While not the intent, this experience yielded a worthwhile set of lessons. A condensed version of those lessons, labeled "trip wires" by Hackman, concludes our discussion of team building at the top.

Trip Wire 1: Call the Performing Unit a Team but Really Manage Members as Individuals

One way to set up work is to assign specific responsibilities to specific individuals and then choreograph individuals' activities so that their products coalesce into a team product. A contrasting strategy is to assign a team responsibility and accountability for an entire piece of work and let members decide among themselves how they will proceed to accomplish the work. Although either of these strategies can be effective, a choice must be made between them. A mixed model, in which people are told they are a team but are treated as individual performers with their own specific jobs to do, sends mixed signals to members, is likely to confuse everyone, and in the long run is probably untenable.

To reap the benefits of teamwork, a leader must actually build a team. Calling a set of people a team or exhorting them to work together is insufficient. Instead explicit action must be taken to establish the team's boundaries, to define the task as one for which members are collectively responsible and accountable, and to give members the authority to manage both their internal processes and the team's relations with external entities such as clients and coworkers. Once this is done, management behavior and organizational systems gradually can be changed as necessary to support teamwork.

Trip Wire 2: Create an Inappropriate Authority Balance

The exercise of authority creates anxiety, especially when a leader must balance between assigning a team authority for some parts of the work and withholding it for other parts. Because both managers and team members tend to be uncomfortable in such situations, they may collude to clarify them. Sometimes the result is the assignment of virtually all authority to the team—which can result in anarchy or a team that heads off in an inappropriate direction. At other times managers retain virtually all authority, dictating work procedures in detail to team members and, in the process, losing many of the advantages that can accrue from teamwork. In both cases the anxieties that accompany a mixed model are reduced, but at significant cost to team effectiveness.

Achieving a good balance of managerial and team authority is difficult. Moreover, merely deciding how much authority will be assigned to the group and how much will be retained by management is insufficient. Equally important are the domains of authority that are assigned and retained. Our findings suggest that managers should be unapologetic and insistent about exercising their authority over *direction*—the end states the team is to pursue—and over *outer-limit constraints on team behavior*—the things the team must always do or never do. At the same time managers should assign to the team full authority for the means by which it accomplishes its work—and then do whatever they can to ensure that team members understand and accept their responsibility and accountability for deciding how they will execute the work.

Few managerial behaviors are more consequential for the long-term existence of teams than those that address the partitioning of authority between managers and teams. It takes skill to accomplish this well, and this skill has emotional and behavioral as well as cognitive components. Just knowing the rules for partitioning authority is insufficient; leaders also need practice in applying those rules in situations where anxieties, including their own, are likely to be high. Especially challenging for managers are the early stages in the life of a team (when managers often are tempted to give away too much authority) and times when the going gets rough (when the temptation is to take authority back too soon). The management of authority relations with task-performing teams is much like walking on a balance beam, and our evidence suggests that it takes a good measure of knowledge, skill, and perseverance to keep from falling off.

Trip Wire 3: Assemble a Large Group of People, Tell Them in General Terms What Needs to Be Accomplished, and Let Them "Work Out the Details"

Traditionally, individually focused designs for work are plagued by constraining structures that have built up over the years to monitor and control employee behavior. When groups perform work, such structures tend to be viewed as unnecessary bureaucratic impediments to team functioning. Thus, just as managers sometimes (and mistakenly) attempt to empower teams by relinquishing all authority to them, so do some attempt to get rid of the dysfunctional features of existing organizational structures simply by taking down all the structures they can. Apparently the hope is that removing structures will release teams and enable members to work together creatively and effectively.

Managers who hold this view often wind up providing teams with less structure than they actually need. Tasks are defined only in vague, general terms. Group composition is unclear or fluid. The limits of the team's authority are kept deliberately fuzzy. The unstated assumption is that there is some magic in the group interaction process and that, by working together, members will evolve any structures the team needs.

This is a false hope; there is no such magic. Indeed, our findings suggest the opposite: Groups that have appropriate structures tend to develop healthy internal processes, whereas groups with insufficient or inappropriate structures tend to have process problems. Worse, coaching and process consultation are unlikely to resolve these problems precisely because they are rooted in the team structure. For members to learn how to interact well within a flawed or underspecified structure is to swim upstream against a strong current.

Trip Wire 4: Specify Challenging Team Objectives, but Skimp on Organizational Supports

Even if a work team has a clear, engaging direction and an enabling structure, its performance can go sour—or at least can fall below the group's potential—if the team is not well supported. Teams in high-commitment organizations fall victim to this trip wire when given "stretch" objectives but not the wherewithal to accomplish them; high initial enthusiasm soon changes into disillusionment.

It is no small undertaking to provide these supports to teams, especially in organizations designed to support work by individuals. Corporate compensation policy, for example, may make no provision for team bonuses and indeed may explicitly prohibit them. Human resource departments may be primed to identify individuals' training needs and provide first-rate courses to fill those needs, but training in team skills may be unavailable. Existing performance appraisal systems, which may be state-of-the-art for measuring individual contributions, are likely to be inappropriate for assessing and rewarding work done by teams. Information systems and control systems may give managers the data they need to monitor and control work processes, but they may be neither available nor appropriate for use by work teams. Finally, the material resources required for the work may have been prespecified by those who originally designed it, and there may be no procedure in place for a team to secure the special configuration of resources it needs to execute the particular performance strategy it has developed.

Aligning existing organizational systems with the needs of teams often requires managers to exercise power and influence upward and laterally in the organization. An organization set up to provide teams with full support for their work is noticeably different from one whose systems and policies are intended to support and control individual work, and many managers may find the prospect of changing to a group-oriented organization both unsettling and perhaps even vaguely revolutionary.

It is hard to provide good organizational support for task-performing teams, but generally it is worth the trouble. The potential of a well-directed, well-structured, well-supported team is tremendous. Moreover, stumbling over the organizational support trip wire is perhaps the saddest of all team failures. When a group is both excited about its work and all set up to execute it superbly, it is especially shattering to fail merely because the organizational supports required cannot be obtained. This is like being all dressed up and ready to go to the wedding only to have the car break down en route.

Trip Wire 5: Assume That Members Already Have All the Competence They Need to Work Well as a Team

Once a team is launched and operating under its own steam, managers sometimes assume their work is done. As we have seen, there are indeed some good reasons for giving a team ample room to go about its business in its own way; inappropriate or poorly timed managerial interventions have impaired the work of more than one group in our research. However, a strictly hands-off managerial stance also can limit a team's effectiveness, particularly when members are not already skilled and experienced in teamwork.

Endnotes

1. N. N. Tichy and N. Cardwell, *The Cycle of Leadership: How Great Companies Teach Their Leaders to Win* (New York: Harper Business, 2002).

2. G. J. Curphy, *The Role of the Supervisor Program for Andersen Corporation* (North Oaks, MN: Author, 2005).

3. J. Collins, *Good to Great* (New York: HarperCollins, 2001).

4. J. Krile, G. J. Curphy, and D. Lund, *The Community Leadership Handbook: Framing Ideas, Building Relationships, and Mobilizing Resources* (St. Paul, MN: Fieldstone Alliance, 2005).

5. K. W. Thomas and W. H. Schmidt, "A Survey of Managerial Interests with Respect to Conflict," *Academy of Management Journal* 19 (1976), pp. 315–18.

6. J. J. Morse and F. R. Wagner, "Measuring the Process of Managerial Effectiveness," *Academy of Management Journal* 21 (1978), pp. 23–35.

7. L. D. Brown, *Managing Conflict at Organizational Interfaces* (Reading, MA: Addison-Wesley, 1983).

8. W. G. Ouchi, *How American Business Can Meet the Japanese Challenge* (Reading, MA: Addison-Wesley, 1981).

9. T. J. Peters and R. H. Waterman, *In Search of Excellence* (New York: Harper & Row, 1982).

10. S. P. Robbins, *Organizational Behavior: Concepts, Controversies, and Applications* (Englewood Cliffs, NJ: Prentice Hall, 1986).

11. G. Yukl, *Leadership in Organizations*, 2nd ed. (Englewood Cliffs, NJ: Prentice Hall, 1989).

12. M. F. R. Kets de Vries and D. Miller, "Managers Can Drive Their Subordinates Mad," in *The Irrational Executive: Psychoanalytic Explorations in Management*, ed. M. F. R. Kets de Vries (New York: International Universities Press, 1984).

13. Thomas and Schmidt, "A Survey of Managerial Interests with Respect to Conflict."

14. Yukl, *Leadership in Organizations*.

15. K. W. Thomas, "Conflict and Conflict Management," in *Handbook of Industrial and Organizational Psychology*, ed. M. D. Dunnette (Chicago: Rand McNally, 1976).

16. Robbins, *Organizational Behavior*.

17. B. M. Bass, *Leadership and Performance beyond Expectations* (New York: Free Press, 1985).

18. A. R. Willner, *The Spellbinders: Charismatic Political Leadership* (New Haven, CT: Yale University Press, 1984).

19. N. C. Roberts and R. T. Bradley, "Limits of Charisma," in *Charismatic Leadership: The Elusive Factor in Organizational Effectiveness*, eds. J. A. Conger and R. N. Kanungo (San Francisco: Jossey-Bass, 1988), pp. 253–75.

20. R. M. Kanter, *The Change Masters* (New York: Simon & Schuster, 1983).

21. Thomas, "Conflict and Conflict Management."

22. Thomas, "Conflict and Conflict Management."

23. K. W. Thomas, "Toward Multidimensional Values in Teaching: The Example of Conflict Management," *Academy of Management Review* 2, no. 3 (1977), pp. 484–90.

24. R. Fisher and W. Ury, *Getting to Yes* (Boston: Houghton Mifflin, 1981).

25. Fisher and Ury, *Getting to Yes.*

26. R. R. Blake, H. A. Shepard, and J. S. Mouton, *Managing Intergroup Conflict in Industry* (Houston, TX: Gulf, 1964).

27. Fisher and Ury, *Getting to Yes.*

28. J. P. Campbell, "The Cutting Edge of Leadership: An Overview," in *Leadership: The Cutting Edge*, eds. J. G. Hunt and L. L. Larson (Carbondale, IL: Southern Illinois University Press, 1977).

29. J. P. Campbell, R. A. McCloy, S. H. Oppler, and C. E. Sager, "A Theory of Performance," in *Frontiers in Industrial/Organizational Psychology and Personnel Selection*, eds. N. Schmitt and W. C. Borman (San Francisco: Jossey-Bass, 1993), pp. 35–70.

30. J. W. Boudreau and P. Ramstad, *Beyond HR: The New Science of Human Capital* (Boston, MA: Harvard Business School Press, 2007).

31. J. R. Katzenbach, *Teams at the Top* (Boston: Harvard Business School Press, 1998).

32. Katzenbach, *Teams at the Top.*

33. J. R. Hackman, *Groups That Work (and Those That Don't)* (San Francisco: Jossey-Bass, 1990).

Name Index

Note: Page numbers followed by n indicate endnotes

H

S

T

Subject Index

A

A-B-C model, 287, 288

Abilene paradox, 279

Abilities, in GAPS analysis, 93, 94

Ability model, emotional intelligence, 184–185

Absenteeism leadership, 386

Abu Ghraib prison, 113

Acceptable behavior, bands of, 29

Acceptance, of change, 569

Accommodation, in conflict management, 674

Accountability, 338

Achievement-oriented leadership, 325–329, 545

Acquiescence, 278

Acquired leadership, 13, 14

Action
  in action-observation-reflection model, 42–43
  perception and, 48

Action learning, 62, 63
  basic philosophy of, 62
  effectiveness of, 62, 63
  training programs *versus,* 62

Action-observation-reflection (A-O-R) model, 42–43, 92
  action in, 42, 43
  observation in, 43
  perception in, 44–48
  reflection in, 43

Action steps, in development plan, 95

Active followers, 19

Active listening, 275, 276

Actor/observer difference, 48

Adaptive leadership, 501, 515, 571

Adaptive problems, 501, 515

Additive task, 420

Adhocracy cultures, 511, 512

Advantageous comparison, 147

Adventure-based approaches, to leader development, 61, 62

AERs. *See* After event reviews (AERs)

Affectivity
  and job satisfaction, 391, 394
  negative, 392

Afghanistan
  terrorism in, 302, 303, 556
  war in, 556, 578

African Americans, 572

African National Congress, 577

After event reviews (AERs), 52

Agenda, meeting, 282

Aggression, 278

Agreeableness, 175

AIG, 651

Airlines
  commercial crew, 444
  culture and crashes by, 517
  failures in leadership, 613
  systems malfunction, 612
  team model for crew, 422

Alibaba, 386

Alienated followers, 19

Alive! (Read), 3

Allstate Insurance Company, 644

Allstate Protection Company, 644

Al-Qaeda, 303, 561, 578

Amazon, 191, 325, 584

America First, 590

American Revolutionary War, 20

Ames Department Stores, 651

A Million Ways to Die in the West, 621

Amount of change, 560

Amway, 574

Analogies
  creativity and, 295
  and vision, 671

Analytic intelligence, 193

Andes survival scenario, 2, 4

Anger, change and, 569

A-O-R. *See* Action-observation-reflection (A-O-R) model

Apollo 13 mission, 500

Appearance, power and, 105, 106